Moss, Fletcher and Isaacs on the EU Regulation on Insolvency Proceedings

Moss, Fletcher and Isaacs on the EU Regulation on Insolvency Proceedings

Fourth Edition

Edited by

STUART ISAACS KC
TOM SMITH KC
CHRISTOPH PAULUS

Great Clarendon Street, Oxford, OX2 6DP,
United Kingdom

Oxford University Press is a department of the University of Oxford.
It furthers the University's objective of excellence in research, scholarship,
and education by publishing worldwide. Oxford is a registered trade mark of
Oxford University Press in the UK and in certain other countries

© The several contributors 2023

The moral rights of the authors have been asserted

First Edition published in 2002
Fourth Edition published in 2023

All rights reserved. No part of this publication may be reproduced, stored in
a retrieval system, or transmitted, in any form or by any means, without the
prior permission in writing of Oxford University Press, or as expressly permitted
by law, by licence or under terms agreed with the appropriate reprographics
rights organization. Enquiries concerning reproduction outside the scope of the
above should be sent to the Rights Department, Oxford University Press, at the
address above

You must not circulate this work in any other form
and you must impose this same condition on any acquirer

Public sector information reproduced under Open Government Licence v3.0
(http://www.nationalarchives.gov.uk/doc/open-government-licence/open-government-licence.htm)

Published in the United States of America by Oxford University Press
198 Madison Avenue, New York, NY 10016, United States of America

British Library Cataloguing in Publication Data
Data available
Library of Congress Control Number: 2023932664

ISBN 978-0-19-285523-7

DOI: 10.1093/law/9780192855237.001.0001

Printed and bound by
CPI Group (UK) Ltd, Croydon, CR0 4YY

Links to third party websites are provided by Oxford in good faith and
for information only. Oxford disclaims any responsibility for the materials
contained in any third party website referenced in this work.

Foreword

Much has transpired since the last revision of *The EU Regulation on Insolvency Proceedings* (3rd edn), in 2016. Over the past six years, insolvency laws have changed enormously within Europe: in 2016, the European Union substantially revised and recast its Regulation on Insolvency Proceedings; earlier EU reports, recommendations, and directives on the harmonization of EU member states' insolvency laws (finally) resulted, in 2019, in the EU Directive 'on preventive restructuring frameworks, on discharge of debt and disqualifications, and on measures to increase the efficiency of procedures concerning restructuring, insolvency and discharge of debt'; in reaction to this Restructuring Directive (as well as earlier instruments), a number of EU member states have revised (or are making steady progress toward revision of) their insolvency laws to make them more 'reorganization friendly', more efficient, more likely to result in the discharge of onerous debt obligations.

More than simply law reform, these EU initiatives have sought to create a new 'rescue culture' within Europe. This rescue culture, originating in US and UK law reform from the 1980s, prefers reorganization and restructuring over liquidation of financially distressed debtors; it favors pragmatism over formalism in seeking to maximize payments to the creditors of insolvent or near-insolvent debtors. Rather than rely on ancient principles of Roman law, which would dictate that a contractual agreement must be kept, modern rescue culture argues that contractual agreements should be renegotiated. This quest for financial rescue is described as 'cultural' in that it often is initiated from the 'bottom up'—from debtors, creditors, and insolvency practitioners and other professionals seeking efficiency through loss minimization.

And yet legal culture changes slowly, if at all, in reaction to dictates for law reform. Acculturation may be particularly slow where law reform initiatives press for change to ancient precepts, such as the principle of *pacta sunt servanda*. Other factors may stymie broad-based cultural movement. For example, European efforts to promote a rescue culture have occurred in the context of epochal shifts in the legal-political-economy—Brexit and the pandemic are only two such events. This background of populism, lockdown, inexpensive government-sponsored financing, disruption of global supply chains, and wartime threats of commodity shortages has complicated movement toward a culture favoring rehabilitation and restructuring.

In short, this has been a tumultuous six years for insolvency practitioners in Europe—for all of us, really.

After a storm, it is only reasonable to stop and examine the continued working order of our surroundings. In the wake of a financial crisis, for example, banking regulators may apply stress tests to assess the resilience of surviving financial institutions.

Understanding whether a rescue culture exists in Europe and how it developed is critical to assessing whether actors and institutions possess the resilience to continue these practices notwithstanding current events. Assessment of the resilience of insolvency law reforms, and of the effectiveness law reform initiatives to shift toward a rescue culture, present greater challenges than financial regulators' stress tests, however. Because assessments of law and culture are likely to rely more on qualitative than quantitative measurements, stress testing in this context is more nuanced and conclusive results more complicated. As applied to insolvency law reform efforts, moreover, these assessments confront practical realities: building shelter during a storm is likely to be less successful than building in advance; unfortunately, the push within Europe for a corporate rescue culture has mostly followed financial crises rather than preceding them.

Despite these challenges, it remains important to understand the acculturation of restructuring and rescue practices in Europe—not just 'how' but also 'whether' companies, insolvency practitioners and other professionals, as well as courts have internalized the policy imperative to rehabilitate rather than liquidate debtors in financial distress.

The task is not a simple one, of course. There are numerous perspectives to consider: law reform initiatives that are negotiated and produced within multiple EU entities; periodic study of past initiatives required by review clauses in the Insolvency Proceeding Regulation and Restructuring Directive; interpretation of these European laws by the courts of the 26 relevant member states and the EUCJ; transactional and litigation work by insolvency practitioners throughout Europe; academic writing on this EU law and practice; the broader global context in which a rescue culture develops through the work of Third Parties in Third Countries and before non-EU international organizations (such as UNCITRAL, the World Bank, and IMF).

This list may appear impossibly complicated but there is an important shortcut: *The EU Regulation on Insolvency Proceedings* (4th edn). This Treatise should be viewed as playing an important role in checking in on the continued effectiveness of the Insolvency Proceedings Regulation—both its continued effectiveness as law and as an inspiration for evolution toward a rescue culture.

First and foremost, this Treatise provides an up-to-date review of the EU Insolvency Proceeding Regulation. Its analysis, helpfully, addresses both historical background, up-to-the-minute revisions, and some prognosis for what to expect in the future. Coupled with analysis of the articles of this IP Regulation, this Treatise digs into EUCJ case law. Footnotes reference related EU directives, and legislation and case law from various member states. Importantly, the authors of this Treatise include practitioners and academics. The original treatise writers haled from the UK at a time when the UK was a member of the EU; despite Brexit and the untimely death of two of these authors, the Treatise retains analysis of UK law governing cross-border recognition of insolvency proceedings, including that applicable during the transition from EU membership, and, thus, benefits from longstanding experience in rescue culture. In addition, with this 4th edition, a new editor has been included from the Continent (Prof Dr Christoph G Paulus) and several continental academics and practitioners have joined to help with the revision of various chapters (Prof Dr Stephan Madaus, Tomáš Richter, Prof Dr Rolef de Weijs, Lilian Welling-Steffens, Georgina Peters, Felicity Toube QC, Jennifer Marshall, Prof Francisco Garcimartin, and Prof Gerard McCormack).

I close the Foreword to the 4th edition of this Treatise with the same query raised by the author of the Foreword to the 3rd edition: 'We all may be curious to see in which direction the new Insolvency Proceeding Regulation and the present book will push us: more towards compliance with the time-honored principle of *pacta sunt servanda* or more towards a new understanding of kind of floating contract obligations. It is to be assumed that this book will play a rather decisive part in the struggle.'

Susan Block-Lieb
Fordham University School of Law
July 2022

Preface to the Third Edition

Much has happened in the specialised realm of the EU Regulation on Insolvency Proceedings since the last edition of this work was committed to the press in the early months of 2009. Judicial decisions, both by the Court of Justice of the European Union itself and also by national courts, have been delivered with accelerating frequency, greatly adding to the corpus of jurisprudence relating to the Regulation's meaning and scope. Looming in the background was the prescribed date—1 June 2012—by which the Commission was required to deliver a report on the application of the Regulation, accompanied by any proposals for its reform that were considered to be needed. The prospect that substantial revisions to the original Regulation might be enacted at some point after June 2012 inevitably affected our plans for the timing of this third edition, and also the approach to be adopted. To serve our readers' needs to optimum effect, it was necessary to await the conclusion of the revision process so as to be able to produce a commentary that would provide an up to date account of the original Regulation—to serve during the transitional period during which it would remain applicable—together with a discrete treatment and analysis of the recast Regulation to which users of the work would increasingly need to refer in anticipation of the date when it would replace the text originally adopted in May 2000.

As so often in the history of the EU, target dates and deadlines experienced the phenomenon of elasticity, so that it was not until 20 May 2015 that the agreed, final text of the Recast Regulation, numbered as 2015/848, was formally adopted by the EU Parliament and Council acting in concert under the organisation's current constitutional procedure. In accordance with the 2-year 'grace' period prescribed by Article 92, the Recast Regulation will not commence to apply until 26 June 2017, leaving the original Regulation 1346/2000 to continue to apply to insolvency proceedings opened before that date. Accordingly, we have structured this edition to provide updated commentary on the Regulation as currently in force, complemented by detailed analysis of the provisions of the Recast Regulation indicating the important changes which will enter into effect in a few months' time.

Although the new edition has inevitably expanded by comparison to its predecessor, the overall structure of the book remains essentially unchanged. Chapters 1 to 7 provide the reader with thematic accounts of specific topics bearing upon the Regulation and its impact. The individual authors of these chapters, who are identified in the Contents Summary, remain unchanged with one exception: Professor Matthias Haentjens has assumed responsibility for Chapter 7, which has been completely re-written, and retitled, in the light of major changes to the law governing the insolvency of financial institutions under parallel legislative provisions enacted by the EU. In Chapter 8, which now contains article-by-article commentary to both the original Regulation and to the 2015 Recast, two additional experts—Professors Miguel Virgós and Francisco Garcimartín—have joined the group who provide additional comments to the text written by the two principal authors of the chapter. It is hoped that readers will find these indications of divergent opinions thought-provoking and also illuminating.

We also owe a special debt to several further colleagues at South Square, in addition to named authors of chapters, whose substantial contributions have been essential in enabling us to meet publishing deadlines, namely William Willson, Adam Al-Attar, Robert Amey, Andrew Shaw and Ryan Perkins. Their contributions have been acknowledged at the start of chapters 5 and 8.

For reasons indicated above, this edition has been produced during a period of uncertainty regarding the probable timing of the central event concerning the future shape and content of the EU Regulation. Even as late as May 2015 there was a genuine possibility that many months of inter-institutional negotiation between the EU Commission, Parliament and Council might be frustrated due to a malign combination of internal and external political events. Consequently, considerable demands were placed on all contributors to this book who were unable to finalize their material until the outcome of the revision process was known. We are most grateful to them for their patience and professionalism in completing their contributions in accordance with a timetable that had to be revised several times in response to the unpredictable course of developments within the EU. Our thanks are also due to the editorial and production teams of Oxford University Press, whose own working schedules had to endure the knock-on effects from the shifting fortunes of Euro-politics.

Gabriel Moss QC
Ian Fletcher LLD, QC (Hon.)
Stuart Isaacs QC
1 February 2016

Preface to the Second Edition

When the first edition of this work appeared in 2002, there was very little case law to cite and the contributors to the book had the difficult task of interpreting the Regulation with the assistance of the Virgos-Schmit Report and the Recitals, together with a limited volume of writings and talks on the subject. Since the first edition, there have been a number of significant cases, not only in the national courts, but also two reported decisions of the European Court of Justice, some further references to the ECJ and, too late to discuss in the text, which refers in detail to the Advocate General's Opinion, the ECJ's decision in the *Frick Teppichboden* case on 12 February 2009. There has also been much further writing and speaking in relation to the Regulation and the case law. The volume of material is now such that it would be impractical to include references to all of it, even if the contributors' linguistic abilities enabled them to do so. The EU has expanded and the Regulation now applies to 26 Member States with 21 language versions.

In order to keep the size of this volume within manageable proportions, and to maintain it as an attempt concisely to state the legal position as we saw it, we have focussed on what we believe to be the main cases and articles available in English or in translation into English, although a number of references to foreign language sources are also included. Not all the case law which touches on the Regulation is of real significance in interpreting it and therefore we have exercised a degree of selection even amongst the material available in English or translation into English. Likewise, in the case of articles and books, we have had to be selective and to focus on what we considered to be the most significant material.

Since the first edition, there have come into force the Directives dealing with credit institutions and insurance undertakings and these have been dealt with in a companion volume published by Oxford University Press in 2006: Moss & Wessels, *EU Banking and Insurance Insolvency*. Unfortunately, no such similar directive has appeared in respect of other types of proceedings excluded by Article 1(2) of the Regulation, namely 'investment undertakings which provide services involving the holding of funds or securities for third parties' and 'collective investment undertakings'. The unfortunate gap left in the case of 'investment undertakings' is illustrated by the recent case of *LBIE*, the principal Lehman Brothers company in the UK, which was an 'investment undertaking' and therefore excluded from the Regulation, but not included in any Directive.

The second edition retains the pattern followed by the first edition of having a series of narrative chapters giving an account of the principal features of the Regulation and a larger chapter providing an article by article commentary on the Regulation as a whole.

Chapter 1 by Professor Fletcher sets out the history of the Regulation and precursors and brings it up-to-date by reference to the Member States, now numbering 26, which are parties to the Regulation.

Chapter 2 by Stuart Isaacs QC and Richard Brent on the mode of interpretation of the Regulation as a community legal instrument is updated.

In Chapter 3, Professor Fletcher sets out the scope and jurisdiction of the Regulation. In Chapter 4 he sets out the choice of law rules. In each case, account is taken of developments in case-law since the first edition.

Chapter 5 by Gabriel Moss QC, Daniel Bayfield, and Georgina Peters deals with recognition and enforcement, not only under the Regulation, but under the three other bases available in England for recognizing or assisting foreign proceedings and foreign insolvency practitioners. The changes in statute and case law are taken into account.

In Chapter 6, Stuart Isaacs QC, Felicity Toube, Nick Segal, and Jennifer Marshall deal with the effect of the Regulation on cross border security and *quasi* security, updating these subjects in the light of further case-law and analysis.

Chapter 7 by David Marks QC deals with the regulation of financial services and markets in the EU in the light of the implementation of the Directives dealing with the reorganization and winding up of credit institutions and insurance undertakings. Although the types of proceedings dealt with here are outside the scope of the Regulation, knowledge of these areas is important for understanding the operation of the Regulation and its relationship to credit institution, insurance undertaking and other regulated activity insolvencies.

Chapter 8 by Gabriel Moss QC and Tom Smith, with the assistance of additional commentary by Professor Michael Bogdan, Justice Timo Esko, Professor Ian Fletcher QC, Stuart Isaacs QC, Professor Alberto Piergrossi, Professor Bob Wessels, and Alex Wood deals with the Regulation on an article by article basis, adding references to the significant case law developments.

Appendix 1 contains the updated text of the Regulation, as amended by reason of the accession of new Member States and changes in the insolvency proceedings in various States. Appendix 2 contains the Virgos-Schmit Report, an essential source of reference in the interpretation of the Regulation. We have been able to include some references to material towards the end of 2008, although in essence the text tries to state the law as at October 2008.

There are two judgments of particular interest which have come too late to be included in the book.

In *Nortel Networks SA* [2009] EWHC 206 (Ch) the English High Court, which had opened main proceedings in respect of a number of EU registered companies in the Nortel group, authorized the sending of Letters of Request to local EU courts asking them to ensure that the administrators were given notice of any application to open secondary proceedings. The judgment refers with approval to the view in the *Stojevic* case in Austria to the effect that Article 31(2) implies a duty on courts as well as liquidators to co-operate with each other. The judgment cites the decision of the Versailles Court of Appeal in the *Rover* case to the effect that even where there is jurisdiction to open secondary proceedings, these should not be opened unless they serve a useful purpose. The judgment also refers to the ruling in the Austrian *Collins & Aikman* decision to the effect that a stay under Article 33 is only a stay of the process of liquidation and not the secondary proceeding itself. The three cases cited are dealt with in the book.

The ECJ decision in *Christopher Seagon, in his capacity as liquidator in respect of the assets of Frick Teppichboden Supermärkte GmbH v Deko Marty Belgium NV*, (Case C-339/07) upheld the Advocate General's Opinion, which is dealt with in the book, in concise terms, holding that the courts of a Member State which opens main proceedings have jurisdiction to try a claim to avoid a transaction brought against a defendant in another Member State.

The first edition enjoyed widespread sales throughout the UK and Europe and has the distinction of being cited by the Advocate General's Opinions in the first two cases on the Regulation in which the ECJ has given judgments, namely *Eurofood* and *Staubitz-Schreiber*. It has also been cited widely in the English case law.

We are very grateful to all our contributors who made the second edition possible. We are also grateful for the continued support and assistance (and patience) of Oxford University Press, including their energetic and able marketing department. We are grateful also to a number of others knowledgeable in this field who have contributed ideas and suggestions, which appear in various places in Chapter 8. We also express our thanks to the organizers of conferences which have facilitated the discussion and debate relating to the Regulation, such as INSOL Europe and the European Academy of Law. We are always happy to receive suggestions relating to the book and any significant case law or articles which any of our readers feel we have overlooked or should take into account in any future edition.

One of the great problems of the subject is that no central registry of cross-frontier EU insolvency proceedings has been set up. This not only leads to situations where purportedly main proceedings can be opened in ignorance of each other in two different Member States, as in the *Stojevic* case, but also makes research and interpretation difficult and uncertain. It is to be hoped that the EU with its vast resources can remedy this situation. Meanwhile, we are happy to both receive and share news of significant case law developments with our readers. The text of this second edition shows the benefits of some of that sharing of information and we hope it will continue into the future.

We should finally mention the unfortunate impression that may have been given at the start of the case law that English courts were unjustifiably ready to find that the 'centre of main interests' of companies registered in other Member States were located in the UK. This misimpression appears to have been rectified by showing that the English courts look at the relevant criteria set out in the Regulation and the case law and make a proper judgment on the evidence available to them without any preference for the English jurisdiction. The fairness of the English procedure has been underlined by cases such as *Stojevic*, in which the opening of bankruptcy proceedings was set aside several years after the opening, on evidence being presented to the English court that there had been no jurisdiction in the UK, and the *Hans Brochier* case where the English court accepted at the prompting of the English administrators themselves that the opening of main administration proceedings in England had been unjustified because COMI had not effectively been moved from Germany.

We would hope that this type of result will reinforce the mutual respect and trust that is necessary for the working of the Regulation.

In practice, mutual trust and co-operation can best be developed by frequent cordial encounters both at conferences and by visits to each other's jurisdictions. Once judges, practitioners and lawyers have met, it is to be hoped that they will be more ready to trust each other and to co-operate in the way envisaged by the Regulation, in the interests of creditors and the public.

Gabriel Moss QC
Ian Fletcher LLD, QC (Hon)
Stuart Isaacs QC
South Square
Gray's Inn
London
WC1R 5HP
England
17 February 2009

Preface to the Fourth Edition

It is some six years since the publication of the previous edition of this work in 2016. At that time, although the Recast EU Regulation on Insolvency Proceedings (Regulation (EU) 2015/848) had been formally adopted on 20 May 2015, it had yet to apply. Following the expiry of the two-year grace period prescribed by Article 92, the Recast Regulation has now applied since 26 June 2017. This edition provides commentary on the Recast Regulation and how it has been applied since then. At the same time, the original Regulation (Regulation (EC) 1346/2000) remains relevant to consider, both as part of the history and development of the Recast Regulation and because the original Regulation has remained applicable to insolvency proceedings opened prior to 26 June 2017.

Perhaps the most seismic development so far as this edition is concerned has been the (to many, regrettable and unnecessary) departure of the United Kingdom from the European Union on 31 January 2020. That resulted in a need for us to re-think the focus and emphasis of the work. No longer does the Recast Regulation apply in the UK, although the tests from the Recast Regulation as a basis for opening UK insolvency proceedings are retained, despite the fact that the logic of Brexit suggested that the Recast Regulation should altogether cease to have any application or relevance as far as the UK is concerned. The ongoing potential application of the Recast Regulation in the UK is now the subject of an entirely new Chapter 9—but is addressed repeatedly also in other Chapters. Although the UK has now left the EU, we believe that an understanding and appreciation of the EU insolvency regime will remain important to many practitioners in the UK.

Apart from the new Chapter 9, the overall structure of the work remains unchanged. As with the previous edition, Chapters 1 to 7 give thematic consideration to specific topics. Chapter 1 (on the drafting of the original Regulation and its precursors) is materially unaltered from the original text by the late Professor Ian Fletcher. Chapter 8 retains a commentary on the original Regulation and the Recast Regulation updated to take account of developments since the last edition. For the purposes of this edition, we have retained the approach of dealing with the original Regulation as well as the Recast Regulation given that much of the case law continue to deal with the former.

Related to Brexit, we welcome a number of distinguished new contributors from the EU, both academics and practitioners, to reflect the fact that the Recast Regulation no longer applies in the UK. Professor Dr Stephan Madaus now contributes to Chapter 2. Tomáš Richter has assumed responsibility for Chapter 3 (Scope and Jurisdiction) and Professor Dr Rolef de Weijs and Lilian Welling-Steffens have assumed responsibility for Chapter 4 (Choice of Law Rules). Professor Francisco Garciamartin now contributes to Chapter 6 (Cross-Border Security and Quasi-Security) and Professor Gerard McCormack to Chapter 9. Professor Dr Christoph Paulus, who wrote the Foreword to the previous edition, has become a co-editor and a contributor to Chapter 8. Professor Dr Matthias Haentjens has remained responsible for Chapter 7 (Financial Institutions). We also express our appreciation to Professor Susan Block-Lieb for having generously agreed to write the Foreword to this edition.

The six or so years since the last edition have brought with them a considerable amount of new Directives and Regulations from Brussels as well as an increasing number of decisions from the CJEU. Where relevant, we have tried to incorporate these into the new text. There is no reason to think that the trend of increasing legislation and case law will not continue: we doubt whether insolvency law is about to lose its importance in the pan-European trade environment.

Last but not least, this preface would be incomplete without an acknowledgement of the very great contributions made in the development of insolvency law in general and to this work in particular by the late Professor Ian Fletcher, who passed away in 2018, and Gabriel Moss QC, who passed away less than one year later. This work was conceived by Gabriel and both he and Ian were co-editors of the previous editions. Their untimely deaths have deprived this edition of their scholarship, intellect, and erudition, which have been sorely missed.

Finally, we wish to express our gratitude to the other contributors to this edition, who have had to take on the burden of not only updating but in some instances also substantially revising their previous text and working with the new contributors; and to the editorial and production teams at Oxford University Press whose enduring patience in dealing with a motley collection of diverse lawyers and with ourselves has never failed to impress us.

The law is as stated on 30 November 2022.

Stuart Isaacs KC
Christoph G Paulus
Tom Smith KC
1 September 2022

Contents—Summary

Table of Cases	xix
Table of European Legislation and International Conventions	xxix
Table of Statutes	xxxix
Table of Statutory Instruments	xli
List of Contributors	xliii
List of Abbreviations	xlvii

1. Historical Overview: The Drafting of the Insolvency Proceedings Regulation and its Precursors — 1
   Prof Ian F Fletcher LLD QC (Hon)

2. The Insolvency Proceedings Regulation as an EU Legal Instrument — 16
   Stuart Isaacs KC and Prof Dr Stephan Madaus

3. Scope and Jurisdiction — 37
   Tomáš Richter

4. Choice of Law Rules — 63
   Prof Dr Rolef de Weijs and Lilian Welling-Steffens

5. Recognition and Enforcement — 95
   Georgina Peters

6. Cross-Border Security and Quasi-Security — 152
   Felicity Toube KC, Jennifer Marshall, and Prof Francisco Garcimartin

7. Financial Institutions — 198
   Prof Dr Matthias Haentjens

8. Commentary on the Original Insolvency Proceedings Regulation and the Recast Insolvency Proceedings Regulation — 262
   Prof Christoph Paulus and Tom Smith KC
   Incorporating additional commentary from previous editions provided by Prof Michael Bogdan; Justice Timo Esko; Prof Ian Fletcher LLD QC (Hon); Prof Francisco Garcimartin; Stuart Isaacs KC; Prof Alberto Piergrossi; Prof Miguel Virgos; Prof Bob Wessels; and Alex Wood.

9. The Ongoing Potential Application of the RR in the UK — 487
   Stuart Isaacs KC and Prof Gerard McCormack

Appendix 1	501
Appendix 2	531
Appendix 3	595
Index	651

Table of Cases

19 Entertainment Ltd, Re [2017] BCC 347 .... 5.83, 5.86

A, Proceedings brought by (Case C-523/07) ECLI:EU:C:2009:225; [2009] ECR I-2805 .... 8.562
Adams v Cape Industries plc [1990] Ch 433 .... 5.31
Administrativen sad Sofia-grad-Bulgaria-BT v Balgarska Narodna Banka
 (Case C-501/18) ECLI:EU:C:2021:249 .... 7.53
Agrokor DD, Re 591 BR 163; [2018] Bus LR 64 (Bankr SDNY 2018) 5.83, 5.86, 5.95, 9.27
Aim Underwriting Agencies (Ireland) Ltd, Re [2004] EWHC 2114 (Ch) 8.98
Akkurate Ltd, Re [2021] Ch 73 .... 5.176
Alderson v Temple (1768) 4 Burr 2235 .... 5.52
Alfred Shaw & Co Ltd, Re (1897) 8 QLJ 93 .... 5.58
Alitalia Linee Aeree Italiane SpA, Re [2011] 1 BCLC 606 .... 5.206, 8.395
Alivon v Furnival [1902] 2 KB 312 .... 5.15
Amtsgericht [AG] [District Court] Frankfurt, 24 January 2005, ZinsO (2005) 715 .... 8.302
Apcoa Parking Holdings GmbH, Re [2015] BCC 142 .... 5.56
Appell v Essent Netwerk BV (District Court of Hertogenbosch, 31 October 2005), ... 8.194
Apperley Investments Ltd & others v Monsoon Accessorize Ltd
 [2020] IEHC 523 .... 5.130, 5.167, 8.20, 8.300, 8.374, 8.521
Arena Corporation Ltd, The, Re [2003] EWHC 3032 (Ch); [2004] BPIR 375;
 [2004] EWCA Civ 371 .... 2.21, 8.05, 8.302
Aria Inc v Credit Agricole Corporate and Investment Bank
 [2014] EWHC 872 (Comm) 5.184, 8.323
Arm Asset Backed Securities SA, In the matter of [2014] EWHC 1097 (Ch), ... 2.23
Ashurst v Pollard [2001] Ch 595 (CA 5.180
Astora Women's Health LLC, Re [2022] EWHC 2412 (Ch) 5.83
Atlas Shipping A/S, In re 404 BR 726, (April 27 2009, SDNY) 9.27

Bakhshiyeva v Sberbank of Russia [2018] EWCA Civ 2802, [2019] 1 BCLC 1
 (sub nom Re OJSC International Bank of Azerbaijan) 9.24, 9.27, 9.29
Bamberski v Krombach (Case C-7/98) [2000] ECR I-1935; [2001] QB 709 .... 5.146
Banco de Portugal, Fundo de Resolução, Novo Banco SA, Sucursal en España v VR
 (Case C-504/19) ECLI:EU:C:2021:335 .... 7.99
Bank Handlowy w Warszawie SA v Christianpol sp z.o.o. (Case C-116/11)
 ECLI: EU:C 2012:739; [2013] Bus LR 956 .... 2.25, 2.26, 2.31, 3.03, 3.48, 5.130,
 5.167, 5.212, 5.221, 5.228, 8.04, 8.07, 8.177, 8.209, 8.381, 8.384, 8.515, 8.518, 8.644
Bank of Baroda v Maniar [2019] EWHC 2463 (Comm) 9.32
Bank of Credit and Commerce International SA, Re (No 10) [1997] Ch 213 .... 4.31
Banque Indosuez v Ferromet [1993] BCLC 112 .... 5.43
Baustahlgewebe GmbH v Commission (Case C-185/95 P) [1998] ECR I-8417 .... 5.146
BCCI (No 10), Re [1997] Ch 213 .... 5.60–5.62, 5.68, 5.71, 5.81
Bear Stearns High-Grade Structured Credit Strategies Master Fund, In re 389 BR 325
 (SDNY 2008) (US District Court of New York, 22 May 2008) 8.107
BenQ Mobile Holding BV [2008] BCC 489 .... 8.32, 8.56, 8.68, 8.74
Bernard L Madoff Investment Securities LL, Re [2010] BCC 328 .... 5.101, 5.210
Betcorp Ltd, Re 400 BR 266 (Bankr D Nev 2009) 5.86
Borovsky, Re [1902] 2 KB 312 .... 5.15
BRAC Rent-a-Car International Inc, Re [2003] BCC 248 .... 2.11, 2.23, 2.26–2.28, 8.96
Budeszentralamt v Heis [2020] 1 BCLC 649 .... 5.31

Burgo Group SpA v Illochroma SA and another (Case C-327/13)
    [2014] ECLI:EU:C:2014:2158; [2015] 1 WLR 1046; [2015] BCC 33 .... 2.12, 2.37, 3.41, 3.44,
        3.59, 5.130, 5.132, 5.167, 5.221, 8.41, 8.53, 8.60, 8.176, 8.216, 8.384, 8.392
Bussone v Italian Ministry for Agriculture (Case 31/78) [1978] ECR 2429..................... 2.12
Byers v Yacht Bull Corporation [2010] EWHC 133 (Ch); [2010] BCC 368;
    [2010] 2 BCLC 169; [2010] I L Pr 24; [2010] BPIR 535 .... 2.23, 5.176, 5.179, 8.09

Cambridge Gas Transport Corporation v Official Committee of Unsecured Creditors
    (of Navigator Holdings Plc) [2006] UKPC 26, [2007] 1 AC 508..................... 9.36, 9.37
Cambridge Gas Transport Corporation v Official Committee of Unsecured Creditors
    of Navigator Holdings plc [2007] 1 AC 508 (PC) 5.07, 5.13, 5.26, 5.27, 5.35, 5.36, 5.51
Cargill v Commission (Case 299/88) [1990] ECR I-1303 .... 2.07
CeDe Group AB v KAN sp z oo, in liquidation (Case C-198/18)
    ECLI:EU:C:2019:1001 .... 2.23, 3.11, 3.14, 4.17, 4.61, 5.179, 8.198, 8.234
Celestini v Saar-Sektkellerei Faber (Case C-105/94) [1997] ECR I-2971 .... 2.20
Centaur Litigation SPC v Terrill [2015] EWHC 3420 (Ch)............................... 9.35
Chen Yung Ngai Kenneth v Li Shu Chun [2021] 7 WLUK 158............................. 5.81
Chesterfield United Inc [2012] BCC 786, Re.. 5.101
China Agrotech Holdings Ltd, Re (2017) 2 CILR 526 .... 5.34
Ci4net.com Inc, Re [2004] EWHC 1941, [2005] BCC 277 .... 8.98, 8.119
CILFIT Srl v Ministry of Health (Case 283/81) [1982] ECR 3415 .... 2.06, 2.24, 2.36, 2.38
Cirio Finance Luxembourg SA, Tribunal of Rome, 26 November 2004, 2004 Foro it. 1567 ...... 8.106
Codere Finance (UK) Ltd, Re [2015] EWHC 3778 (Ch) 5.49
Collins & Aikman [2007] 1 BCLC 182, [2006] BCC 861 (HC) 8.179, 8.206, 8.649, 8.704, 8.738–8.740
Collins & Aikman [Landesgericht] [LG] [Regional Court] Leoben, 1 December 2005,
    17 p 56/05 m, NZI 2006, vol 11, 663.................................... 8.419
Collins & Aikman [Oberlandesgericht] [OLG] [higher regional court of appeal]
    Graz, 20 October 2005, 3 R 149/05, NZI 2006 vol 11, p 660 .... 8.402, 8.412
Collins & Aikman Corporation Group, Re [2006] BCC 606............................... 2.28
Collins & Aikman Europe SA, Re [2006] BCC 861 .... 5.221
Collins & Aikman Europe SA, Re [2007] 1 BCLC 182, [2006] BCC 861 .... 8.413
Collins & Aikman, Re [2006] BCC 606 .... 8.98, 8.103
Comité d'entreprise de Nortel Networks SA and others v Cosme Rogeau
    (Case C-649/13) ECLI:EU:C:2015:384 .... 3.53, 3.59, 4.60, 5.165, 5.170,
        5.210, 8.36, 8.378, 8.386, 8.387, 8.539
Commercial Bank of South Australia, Re (1886) 33 Ch D 174 .... 5.58
Commission v Council (Case C-300/89) [1991] ECR I-2867 .... 2.28
Commission v Greece (Case C-185/96) [1998] ECR I-6601.............................. 2.13
Commission v Greece (Case C-306/98) [1991] ECR I-5863.............................. 2.29
Commission v Jégo-Quéré et Cie (Case C-263/02P) [2004] ECR I-3425 .... 2.07
Condor Insurance Co Ltd, Re (2010) 601 F 3d 319................................. 9.25, 9.27
Condor Insurance Ltd, Re 601 F 3d 319.. 5.105
Connock and Boyden v Fantozzi [2011] EWHC 15 (Ch) 2.26
Consiglio di Stato (Cons. Stato) (Council of State) 6th Session, 25 January 2007,
    267/2006, (2007) 21 Diritto del commercio internazionale 513.................... 8.21, 8.130
Consorzio del Prosciutto di Parma v Asda Stores Ltd [2001] UKHL 7 .... 2.17
Cosco Bulk Carrier Co Ltd v Armada Shipping SA [2011] EWHC 216 (Ch) 5.95, 5.98
Costa v ENEL (Case 6/64) [1964] ECR 585....................................... 2.01
Coursier v Fortis Bank SA (Case C-267/97) [1999] ECR I-2543 .... 8.162
Crisscross Telecommunications Group, Re (20 May 2003)............................... 8.103
Cross Construction Sussex Ltd v Tseliki [2006] BPIR 888............................... 8.111
Customs and Excise Commissioners v Samex [1983] 3 CMLR 194......................... 2.24

Dahl v Kortleben [Bundesgerichtshof] [BGH] [German Federal Court of Justice],
    3 February 2011, V ZB 54/10.. 6.75
Daisytek-ISA Ltd, Re [2004] BPIR 30.. 8.97, 8.103, 8.106

Dallhold Estates (UK) Pty Ltd, Re [1992] BCLC 621 ....6.100
Dalnyaya Step LLC (No 2), Re [2019] BCC 1; [2019] BCC 23..................... 5.83, 5.92, 5.94
Damovo Group SA, Re (25 April 2007) 8.98
Dawson International Trading Ltd v SARL Regimentals, 13 September 2007 ....8.206
De Bloos SPRL v Bouyer SA (Case 14/76) [1976] ECR 149.................................8.50
Debtor, Re a, ex p Viscount of the Royal Court of Jersey [1981] Ch 384 ....5.12
Debtor, Re a (No 784 of 1991) [1992] Ch 554 ....8.120
Deep Black Drilling LLP, Re [2020] BCC 486 ....5.83
Derev [2021] Bus LR 685, Re..5.99
Deutsche Lufthansa (Case C-109/09) ECLI: EU:C:2011:129 ....8.384
Drax Holdings Ltd, Re [2004] 1 WLR 1049..5.56

Edgeworth Capital Luxembourg Sarl v Maud [2015] EWHC 3464 (Comm) 9.32
Eichler (No 2), Re [2011] BPIR 1293 .... 8.111, 8.116, 8.142
Elektrim v Vivendi [2008] EWHC 2155 (Comm), [2008] Lloyd's Rep 636,
    aff'd (CA) sub nom Syska v Vivendi Universal SA [2009] EWCA Civ 677,
    [2010] BCC 348 .... 8.201, 8.284, 8.292, 8.294, 8.295, 8.604, 8.606, 8.608
Emerald Pasture Designated Activity Co v Cassini SAS [2021] IL Pr 35........... 5.170, 5.175, 5.181
Emesa Sugar (Free Zone) NV v Aruba (Case C-17/98) [2000] ECR I-665 ....2.31
ENEFI Energiahatékonysági Nyrt v Direcția Generală Regională a Finanțelor Publice
    Brașov (DGRFP) (Case C-212/15) ECLI:EU:C:2016:427, Opinion of AG Bobek 9.32
ENEFI Energiahatékonysági Nyrt v Direcția Generală Regională a Finanțelor
    Publice Brașov (DGRFP) (Case C-212/15) ECLI:EU:C:2016:841 .... 4.09, 4.57, 6.22, 8.189,
                                                                          8.203, 8.206, 8.210, 8.442
Energotech Sarl, Re (Tribunal de Grande Instance) (TG) (High Court) Lure,
    29 March 2006...8.98, 8.103
Energy Group Overseas BV and Energy Group Holdings BV, Re (20 November 2003)
    (No judgment given) 8.98
England v Smith [2000] 2 BCLC 21 (CA) 5.79
English, Scottish and Australian Chartered Bank, Re [1893] 3 Ch 385......................5.58
Entertainment Limited, Re [2016] EWHC 1545 (Ch) 6.106, 6.108
Eridania v Minister of Agriculture and Forestry (Case 230/78) [1979] ECR 2749 ....2.12
ERSTE Bank Hungary Nyrt v Magyar Állam and others (Case C-527/10)
    [2012] ECLI:EU:C:2012:417; [2012] ILPr 38 .... 2.15, 2.20, 2.26, 4.23, 6.73, 8.221, 8.305
Erste Group Bank AG (London) v JSC (VMZ Red October) [2015] 1 CLC 706 (CA)............5.31
Eurodis Electron Plc, Re [2012] BCC 57 ....8.302, 8.710
Eurofood IFSC Ltd, Re [2004] BCC 383 .... 8.31, 8.129, 8.130
Eurofood IFSC Ltd, Re [2004] BCC 383 (Irish High Court)...........................1.24, 8.30
Eurofood IFSC Ltd, Re (Case C-341/04) ECLI:EU:C:2006:281; [2005] BCC 1021;
    [2006] ECR I-3813; [2006] BCC 397, CJEU (Grand Chamber) 1.24, 2.20, 2.23, 2.25,
                                    2.26, 2.28, 2.31, 3.26, 5.128, 5.130, 5.142, 5.144, 5.167, 5.231,
                                    8.04, 8.31, 8.68, 8.70, 8.75, 8.77, 8.79, 8.84, 8.90–8.92, 8.95,
                                    8.98, 8.103, 8.106, 8.126, 8.367, 8.368, 8.369, 8.371, 8.437
Eurofood IFSC Ltd, Tribunal of Parma, 20 February 2004, 2004 Foro it. 1567.................8.106
Eurotunnel Finance Ltd, Re [Tribunal de Commerce] [Commercial Court] Paris,
    2 August 2006 .... 8.98, 8.100, 8.103

Federal Bank of Australia Ltd, Re (1893) 62 LJ Ch 561 ....5.58
Felixstowe Dock v US Lines [1989] QB 360...5.44
Feniks sp z oo v Azteca Products & Services SL (Case C-337/17) ECLI:EU:C:2018:805;
    [2019] IL Pr 1 ....5.178, 8.161
Firswood Ltd v Petra Bank [1996] CLC 608 (CA) 5.42
Flightlease (Ireland) Ltd, Re [2005] IEHC 275 ....6.22, 8.292
Fondazione Enasarco v Lehman Brothers Finance SA [2009] 1 WLR 2168 ....5.182, 5.210
Fondazione Enasarco v Lehman Brothers Finance SA [2014] EWHC 34 (Ch) 5.170
Fondazione Enasarco v Lehman Brothers Finance SA and another [2014] EWHC 34 (Ch).......2.23

Foto-Frost v Hauptzollamt Lübeck Ost (Case 314/85) [1987] ECR 4199 ....2.30
France v Klempka [2006] BCC 841 (Cour de Cassation)................................2.10
Fratelli Variola SpA v Administration des finances italiennes (Case 34/73)
   [1973] ECR 981.. 2.10, 2.13
FSA v Dobb White & Co [2003] EWHC 3146 (Ch) 3.18, 7.19, 8.04, 8.09
F-Tex SIA v Lietuvis-Anglijos UAB 'Jadecloud-Vilma' (Case C-213/10)
   ECLI:EU:C:2012:215; [2013] Bus LR 232 .... 2.23, 4.60, 5.179, 8.148, 8.153, 8.581

Galapagos Bidco Sarl v DE [2022] IL Pr 17 .... 5.128, 5.130, 5.167
Galbraith v Galbraith [1910] AC 508 ....5.51
Gasser, Erich GmbH v MISAT srl (Case C-116/02) [2003] ECR I-14693; [2005] QB 1 .....8.129, 8.766
Gategroup Guarantee Ltd, Re [2021] BCC 549 .... 5.56, 5.164, 8.02
German Graphics Graphische Maschinen GmbH v Alice van der Schee
   (Case C-292/08) [2009] ECR I-8421; [2010] ILPr 1. ..... 2.23, 4.16, 4.37, 5.179, 8.152, 8.189, 8.241
Gibbs v La Société Industrielle et Commerciale des Métaux
   (1890) 25 QBD 399... 5.106, 5.107, 5.139, 9.27, 9.29
Global Distressed Alpha Fund v PT Bakrie Investindo [2011] EWHC 256 (Comm),
   [2011] 1 WLR 2038 ....9.28
Goldman Sachs International v Novo Banco SA [2018] UKSC 34, [2018] 1 WLR 3683 ....9.27
Gourdain, Henri v Franz Nadler (Case 133/78) [1979] ECR 733; 3 CMLR 180 ....2.23, 3.56,
                 3.58, 3.59, 4.60, 5.164, 5.173, 5.176, 5.177, 5.180, 5.181, 8.149, 8.162, 8.354
Graphische Maschinen GmbH v Van der Schee (Case C-292/08)
   [2009] ECR I-8421, [2010] ILPr 1..8.360
Grupo Torras SA v Sheikh Fahad Mohammad Al-Sabah [1995] 1 Lloyd's Rep 374.............8.162
Guardians of New Zealand Superannuation Fund et al v Novo Banco
   [2016] EWCA Civ 1092... 7.53, 7.60

H (Liquidator of GT GmbH) v HK (Case C-295/13) ECLI:EU:C:2014:2410;
   [2015] OJ C 46/9....................2.23, 4.11, 4.60, 5.176, 5.178, 8.155, 8.162, 8.165, 8.354
Hagen v Fratelli D&G Moretti [1980] 3 CMLR 253 ....2.35
Hamilton v Russell (1803) 1 Cranch 309 ....5.52
Handelsveem BV v Hill (Hoge Raad) (HR) (Supreme Court of the Netherlands)
   [2011] BPIR 1024... 5.176, 8.325, 8.615
Hans Brochier [Amtsgericht] [AG] [District Court] Nürnberg, ZIP 2/2007 81................8.372
Hans Brochier Holdings Ltd v Exner [2006] EWHC 2594 (Ch); [2007] BCC 127...... 8.121, 8.144, 8.373
Hauptzollamt Bremen v Kohn (Case 74/69) [1970] ECR 451 ....2.12
Hauptzollamt Hamburg v Bollmann (Case 40/69) [1970] ECR 69.........................2.12
Hayward (Deceased), Re [1997] Ch 45 ....5.180, 8.149
Heinrich [2009] (Case C-345/06) ECR I-1659 ....2.06
Hellas Telecommunications, In re II 535 BR 543 (Bkrtcy SDNY 2015)) 5.105, 9.27
Henwood v Barlow Clowes International Ltd [2008] EWCA Civ 577, [2008] All ER (D) 330 ....8.145
Heritable Bank plc v Landsbanki Islands hf [2013] 1 WLR 725 ....5.138
Hettlage-Austria, Re [Amtsgericht] [AG] [District Court] München, 4 May 2004 ....8.98
Hibernian Merchants Ltd, Re [1958] Ch 76..5.58
HIH Casualty and General Insurance Ltd, Re [2008] 1 WLR 852 .... 5.60, 5.61, 5.65, 5.67,
                                                                 5.68, 5.70, 5.72, 5.80, 5.81
HIH Casualty and General Insurance Ltd, Re [2008] UKHL 21, [2008] 1 WLR 852 ....9.36
HM Bulmer Ltd v J Bollinger SA [1974] Ch 401 ....2.39
HMRC v APS Samex [1983] 1 All ER 1042 ....2.39
Hong Kong Airlines Ltd, Re [2022] EWHC 3210 (Ch) 5.56
HP Bulmer v Bollinger [1974] Ch 401 ....2.01
Hughes v Hannover Rucksversicherungs AG [1997] BCC 921.............................9.34
Hughes v Hannover Ruckversicherungs AG [1996] 1 BCLC 497.........................8.463
Hughes v Hannover Ruckversicherungs AG [1996] 1 BCLC 497 (CA).....................5.79

Industria de Alimentos Nilza SA, Re [2021] BCC 383 .... 5.83, 5.101
ING Bank NV v Banco Santander SA [2020] EWHC 3561 (Comm)........5.170, 5.175, 5.176, 5.183

Interedil Srl, in liquidation v Fallimento Interedil Srl and Intesa Gestione
 Crediti SpA (Case C-396/09) [2011] ECR I-9915, [2012] BCC 851 .... 2.25, 2.33, 2.37, 3.26,
  3.40, 8.30, 8.40, 8.42, 8.43, 8.92, 8.94, 8.95, 8.103, 8.122, 8.132, 8.136, 8.552, 8.553
Investin Quay House Ltd, Re [2021] EWHC 2371 (Ch)....................................9.03
Irish Bank Resolution Corporation Ltd v Kaupthing Bank hf, EFTA Court,
 (Case E-18/11) 28 September 2012 ....7.58
Irish Bank Resolution Corporation Ltd v Quinn [2012] BCC 608...........................8.552
ISA Daisytek SAS, Re [2006] BCC 841, Cour de Cassation..................................8.98

Joint Administrators of Heritable Bank plc v Winding up Board of Landsbanki
 Islands HF [2013] UKSC 13, [2013] 1 WLR 725....................................9.27
Jules Dethier Equipement SA v Dassy (Case C-319/94) [1998] ECR I-1061....................2.40

Kireeva v Bedzhamov [2021] EWHC 2281 (Ch); Court of Appeal
 ([2021] EWCA Civ 35 (Ch); [2022] EWHC 2676 (Ch), ...5.11, 5.12, 5.14, 5.34, 5.114, 6.94
Kirtruna S L (Case C-313/07) [2008] ECR I-7907 ....2.26
Koninklijke Scholten Honig v Commission (Case 101/76) [1977] ECR 797.....................2.07
Kornhaas, Simona v Thomas Dithmar as liquidator of Kornhaas Montage und
 Diensteleistung Ltd (Case C-594/14), ECLI:EU:C:2015:806 .... 4.60, 8.214, 9.32
Kotnik and others v Državni zbor Republike Slovenije (Case C-526/14) 7.53, 7.60
Krombach v Bamberski (Case C-7/98) [2000] ECR I-1935...............................8.368
Kwok, Re [2023] EWHC 74 (Ch) 5.83

Larsen, Atlas Bulk Shipping A/S v Navios International Inc [2011] EWHC (Ch) 878...........6.106
Larsy v INASTI (Case C-118/00) [2001] ECR I-5063 ....2.16
Latam Finance Ltd, Re Grand Court of the Cayman Islands (Kawaley J), 29 July 2020..........5.210
LBI hf v Kepler Capital Markets SA and Frédéric Giraux (Case C-85/12)
 ECLI:EU:C:2013:697 .... 7.56, 8.203, 8.280, 8.283, 8.284
LBI hf v Merrill Lynch International Ltd, EFTA Court (Case E 28/13) 6.31, 6.32, 7.97,
  8.261, 8.262, 8.267
LBIE, Re [2010] EWHC 2914 (Ch)..8.535
Leigh Estates (UK) Ltd, Re [1994] BCC 292 ....8.04
Lemma Europe Insurance Co Ltd, Re [2016] EWCA Civ 484........................... 5.97, 5.98
Lennox Holdings plc, Re [2009] BCC 155 .... 2.31, 8.98
Lennox Holdings Plc, Re [2009] BCC 155..8.98
Leonmobili et Leone (Case C-353/15) ECLI:EU:C:2016:374 ....8.92
Lewis v Hyde [1997] BCC 976...5.52
LG Patra, Beschl.v.2.5.2007-316/06, ZIP 2007, 1875 (LS) 8.76
Li Shu Chung, Re [2021] 11 WLUK 462 ....5.94
Lutz, Hermann v Elke Bäuerle (Case C-557/13) ECLI:EU:C:2015:227; [2015] BCC 413;
 [2015] ILPr 21................................4.25, 4.28, 4.49, 4.50, 5.199, 6.13, 6.31, 6.36,
  6.51, 6.76, 6.81, 8.225, 8.262, 8.264, 8.265

Macaulay v Guaranty Trust Co of New York (1927) 44 TLR 99 ....5.15
Magyar Telecom BV, Re [2014] BCC 448...5.164
Marann Brooks CSV Ltd, Re [2003] BPIR 1159 (Ch D)............................. 2.23, 8.04
Mazur Media Ltd v Mazur Media GmbH [2004] 1 WLR 2966;
 [2005] 1 BCLC 305.. 6.22, 7.158, 8.215, 8.288, 8.292
McGrath v Riddell (sub nom Re HIH Casualty and General Insurance Ltd)
 [2007] 1 All ER 177 (CA)..5.76
Mederco (Cardiff) Ltd [2021] EWHC 386 (Ch), Re....................................5.120
Meeker v Wilson (1813) 1 Gall 419...5.52
Meilicke v ADV/ORGA FA Meyer AG (Case C-83/91) [1992] ECR I-4971 ....2.40
Mejnertsen, Finn v Betina Mandal Barsoe (Case C-148/08) ECLI:EU:C:2009:1
 (Order) (Withdrawn)..2.21, 5.115, 8.05, 8.302
Melars Group Ltd, Re [2021] BCC 835..8.30
Merdeco (Cardiff) Ltd, Re [2021] EWHC 386 (Ch) 9.03

Metzeler, In re 78 BR 674, 677 (Bkrtcy SDNY 1987) 9.27
MF Global UK Ltd (In Special Administration), Re [2015] EWHC 2319 ....5.175, 8.162
MG Probud Gdynia Sp Zoo v Hauptzollamt Saarbrucken (Case C-444/07)
    [2010] ECR I-417, [2010] BCC 453 .... 2.23, 2.26, 5.129, 5.144, 6.22, 8.205, 8.361, 8.364
MG Rover Belux SA/NV [2007] BCC 446..5.221
MG Rover Belux SA/NV, Re [2007] BCC 446..8.413
MG Rover España SA, Re [2006] BCC 599 ....5.221, 8.413
MG Rover, Re [2005] EWHC 874 (Ch) 8.103
MH and NI v OJ and Novo Banco SA (Case C-253/19) ECLI:EU:C:2020:585 ...... 3.25, 8.110, 8.563
Ministero delle Finanze v IN.CO. GE.'90 Srl (Joined Cases Case C-10 to 22/97)
    [1998] ECR I-6307 ....2.06
Mitchell, ex p Cunningham, Re (1884) 13 QBD 418 ....8.142
MPOTEC GmbH, Re Tribunal de Commerce (Commercial Court) Nanterre
    [2006] BCC 681 .... 8.98, 8.99, 8.103

National Bank of Greece and Athens SA v Metliss [1985] AC 509 ....5.106, 9.27
Netherlands and Van der Wal v Commission of the European Communities
    (Joined Cases C-174/98 P and C-189/98 P) [2000] ECR I-1; [2002] 1 C.M.L.R. 16.........5.146
Neu v Secrétaire d'Etat à l'Agriculture et à la Viticulture (Joined Cases C-90 and
    C-91/90) [1991] ECR I-3167..2.20
New Cap Reinsurance Corpn Ltd v Grant ('New Cap Re') [2013] 1 AC 236 (SC),..... 5.29, 5.31, 5.79
New Zealand Loan and Mercantile Agency Company v Morrison [1898] AC 349 ....9.27
Newham v Khatun [2005] 1 QB 37...8.57
Nickel & Goeldner Spedition GmbH v 'Kintra' UAB (Case C-157/13)
    ECLI:EU:C:2014:2145; [2015] QB 96............................... 2.23, 4.60, 5.170, 5.179,
                                                                     8.148, 8.154, 8.162, 8.354, 8.581
Nike v Sportland Oy (Case C-310/14) [2015] ECLI:EU:2015:690 .....4.50, 6.31, 6.32, 8.261, 8.267, 8.268
NK v Paribas Fortis NV (Case C-535/17) ECLI:EU:C:2019:96; [2019] IL Pr 10...........4.18, 4.60,
                                                                     4.61, 5.175, 5.179, 8.581
NMC Healthcare Limited (in administration), Re [2021] EWHC 1806 (Ch);
    [2022] BCC 171 .... 5.83, 5.97, 6.108
Nortel Group (Global Settlement), Re [2017] Bus LR 590................................5.212
Nortel Networks SA, Re [2009] EWHC 206 (Ch); [2009] BCC 343..............5.212, 8.179, 8.398,
                                                                     8.402, 8.649, 8.650, 8.684, 8.738–8.740
Nortel Networks SA, Re [2009] EWHC 1482 (Ch), [2010] BCC 21..........................8.595
Nortel Networks UK Ltd, Re [2015] EWHC (Ch) 2506; [2015] BCC 490....................5.212
North Australian Territory Co Ltd v Goldsborough, Mort & Co Ltd (1889) 61 LT 716...........5.58

Oberlandesgericht [OLG] [higher regional court of appeal] 20 October 2005, 3 R 149/05,
    NZI (Neue Zeitschrift fur Insolvenz und Sanierung) 2006, vol 11, 660..................5.221
Oberster Gerichtshof [OGH] [Austrian Supreme Court] 24 January 2006, 10 Ob 80/05w.......8.287
Oberster Gerichtshof [OGH] [Austrian Supreme Court]
    23 February 2006 9 Ob 135/04z..8.287, 8.291
O'Donnell and another v Governor and Company of the Bank of Ireland
    [2012] EWHC 3749 (Ch)... 2.27, 2.28, 8.142
Office Metro Ltd, Trillium (Nelson) Properties Ltd v Office Metro Ltd [2011] EWHC 1191,
    [2012] BCC 829 (Ch).. 2.28, 2.30, 8.48, 8.56, 8.57
Official Receiver v Eichler [2007] BPIR 1636 (HC) 8.111, 8.118
OGX Petróleo E Gás SA, Re [2016] Bus LR 121 .... 5.92, 5.94, 5.98
OJSC Ank Yugraneft, Re [2010] BCC 475 ....5.56
OJSC International Bank of Azerbaijan, Re [2018] Bus LR 1270 ....5.71, 5.102, 5.106, 6.106
Olympic Airlines SA Pensions & Life Assurance Scheme v Olympic Airlines SA
    [2015] 1 BCLC 589; [2015] 1 WLR 2399 (SC).......................... 8.171, 8.542, 8.543
Oriental Bank Corp, Re ex p Guillemain (1885) 28 Ch D 634..............................5.151
Owusu v Jackson [2005] QB 801...8.163

Pacific Andes Resources Development Ltd, Re [2016] SGHC 210 ....9.27
Paget Approbois SAS/Depeyre entreprises SARL,Alpha Insurance A/S
    (Case C-724/20) ECLI:EU:C:2022:9 ....7.158
Pan Ocean Co Ltd v Fibria Celulose S/A [[2014] EWHC 2124 (Ch),
    [2014] Bus LR 1041 ....5.102, 5.104, 5.107, 9.24–9.26
Pan Oceanic Maritime Ltd, Re [2010] EWHC 1734 (Ch) 5.97, 6.108, 9.22
Parfums Christian Dior SA v Evora BV (Case C-337/95) [1997] ECR I-6013 ....2.38
Parmalat Slovakia, Re (Municipal Court of Fejer/Székesfehérvár, 14 June 2004)................8.98
Pattni v Ali [2007] 2 AC 85 (PC)..5.23
Perpetual Trustee Co Ltd v BNY Corporate Trustee Services Ltd [2009] EWHC 1912 (Ch) 5.54
Phoenix Kapitaldienst GmbH, Re [2013] Ch 61..5.36
Picard v Primeo Fund [2013] (1) CILR 16; on appeal, [2014] (1) CILR 379 ....5.36
PIN Group SA [Amtsgericht] [AG] [District Court] Köln, 19 February (73 IE 1-08) 8.117
PJSC Bank Finance and Credit, Re [2021] BPIR 1228 ....5.83, 5.92
Plaumann (Case C-25/62) [1963] ECR I-211 ....2.07
Polmos Lancut SA, Polish Supreme Court, C III CZP 115/09, 20 January 2010..........8.393, 8.665
Polymer Vision R&D Ltd v Van Dooren [2011] EWHC 2951 (Comm)............. 2.23, 2.28, 5.182
PricewaterhouseCoopers v Saad Investments Company Limited [2014] 1 WLR 4482 (PC) 5.47
Private Equity Insurance Group v Swedbank (Case C-156/15) ECLI:EU:C:2016:851............7.38
Procureur-generaal bij het hof van beroep te Antwerpen v Zaza Retail BV
    (Case C-112/10) ECLI:EU:C:2011:743; [2011] ECR I-11525 ....2.26, 3.44, 8.188, 8.571
Public Prosecutor v Segard (as Administrator for Rover France SAS) (Cour d'appel)
    (Court of Appeal) Versailles, 15 December 2005....................8.180, 8.367, 8.369, 8.372

Queensland Mercantile Agency Co Ltd, Re (1888) 58 LT 878................................5.58

R (AB) v Secretary of State for the Home Department [2013] EWHC (Admin) 2.20
R Jung GmbH v SIFA SA [2006] BCC 678..8.459
R v Customs and Excise Commissioners, ex p Emu Tabac Sarl [1997] EuLR 153 ....2.24
R v Henn and Darby [1981] 1 AC 850 ....2.26
R v Stock Exchange ex p Else Limited [1993] QB 534 ....2.39
Radziejewsksi v Kronofogdemyndigheten i Stockholm (Case C-461/11) ECLI:EU:C:2012:704 .... 3.03
Rastelli Davide e C. Snc v Hidoux (Case C-191/10) [2011] ECR I-13209,
    [2013] 1 BCLC 329..8.101, 8.102, 8.557, 8.740
Rawlinson & Hunter Trustees SA v Kaupthing Bank HF [2012] BCC 441 ....8.293
Regeling v Bestuur van de Bedrijfsvereininging voor de Metaalnijverheid (Case C-125/97)
    [1998] ECR I-4493 ....2.26
Renault SA v Maxicar SpA (Case C-38/98) [2000] ECR I-2973 ....8.368
Rodenstock GmbH, Re [2011] Bus LR 1245 .... 5.56, 5.164, 5.170
Rodenstock GmbH, Re [2011] Bus LR 1245,...5.56
Rozhkov v Markus [2019] EWHC 1519 (Ch) 5.101
Rubin v Eurofinance SA [2012] UKSC 46, [2013] 1 AC 236 .... 5.07, 5.12, 5.24, 5.25,
            5.27–5.29, 5.71, 5.78, 5.86, 5.102, 5.103, 5.107, 5.166, 6.95, 9.37–9.40
Ryall v Rolle (1749) 1 Atkyns 165 ....5.52

Salvage Association, Re The [2003] EWHC 1028; [2003] BCC 504 (Ch) 2.11, 2.26, 2.28,
                                                                                8.20, 8.60, 8.521
Samsun Logix Corporation v DEF [2009] BPIR 1502 ....5.97, 6.108
Sanko Steamship Ltd, Re [2015] EWHC 1031 (Ch)..................................5.86, 5.94
SAS Frontrange Solutions France v Van der Schee as liquidator of WOCL BV
    Court of Appeal Paris..8.285
Schmid, Ralph v Lilly Hertel (Case C-328/12) ECLI:EU:C:2014:6; [2014] 1 WLR 633;
    [2014] BCC 25 ....3.21, 3.55, 4.03, 4.11, 4.34, 4.55, 4.60, 5.177, 8.15, 8.60, 8.165, 8.551
Schotte v Parfums Rothschild (Case 218/86) [1987] ECR 4905 ....8.50

SCI Senior Home v Gemeinde Wedemark, Hannoversche Volksbank eG,
(Case C-195/15) ECLI:EU:C:2016:804 .... 4.28, 6.53, 6.74, 8.224
SCT Industri AB v Alpenblume AB (Case C-111/08) [2009] ECR I-5655;
[2010] Bus LR 559 ....2.23, 5.177, 8.151, 8.361
Seagon, Christopher v Deko Marty Belgium NV (Frick Teppichboden) (Case C-339/07)
ECLI:EU:C:2009:83; [2009] ECR I-767; [2009] 1 WLR 2168 .... 2.23, 3.21, 3.55, 4.58,
4.60, 5.164, 5.177, 8.02, 8.115, 8.150, 8.162, 8.329, 8.354, 8.579
Secretary of State for the Home Department v ME and others (21 December 2011).............2.20
Secretary of State for Trade and Industry v Frid [2004] 2 AC 506............................4.31
Sedgwick Collins & Co v Rossia Insurance Co of Petrograd (Employers' Liability Assurance
Corporation garnishees) [1926] 1 KB 1 ....5.58
Shierson v Vlieland-Boddy [2005] EWCA Civ 974; [2005] 1 WLR 3966;
[2006] 2 BCLC 9, CA 2.23, 2.28, 8.29, 8.51, 8.119, 8.120, 8.131, 8.132
Shiloh Spinners Ltd v Harding [1973] AC 691 ....5.53
Shu Chung, Re [2022] BPIR 507..5.83
Singularis Holdings Ltd v PwC (Privy Council) [2014] UKPC 36; [2015] 1 AC 1675;
[2015] 2 WLR 971 (PC)................................5.07, 5.08, 5.14, 5.34, 5.36, 5.37, 5.39,
5.45, 5.46, 5.51–5.53, 5.59, 5.71, 9.37
Skarb Pánstwa Rzeczpospolitej Polskiej— Generalny Dyrektor Dróg Krajowych i
Autostrad v Stephan Riel (Case C-47/18) ECLI:EU:C:2019:754; [2019] ILPr 35 ....2.23, 3.59,
5.204, 8.148, 8.159, 8.454, 8.581
Skjevesland v Geveran Trading Co Ltd [2003] BCC 391, aff'd [2003] BCC 391 (Ch D) 8.109
Smile Telecoms Holdings Ltd, Re [2022] EWHC 740 (Ch)...................................5.56
Sobieski Sp Zo O (Tribunal de Commerce) (Commercial Court) Beaune, 16 July 2008) 8.103
Société d'Importation Edouard Leclerc Siplec v TFI Publicité SA (Case C-412/93)
[1995] ECR I-179 ....2.27
Sofiyski rayonen sad—Bulgaria Bulstrad Vienna Insurance Group AD v Olympic Insurance
Company Ltd (Case C-427/19) ECLI:EU:C:2020:914..................................7.125
Somafer SA v Saar-Ferngas AG (Case 33/78) [1978] ECR 2183 ....8.50
Southern Equities Corporation; England v Smith, Re [2000] 2 BCLC 21, CA 8.463
Sovereign Marine and General Insurance Co Ltd, Re [2007] 1 BCLC 228 ....5.56
Stanford International Bank Ltd, Re [2010] EWCA Civ 137; [2011] Ch 33........2.28, 5.86, 5.91, 9.20
Staubitz-Schreiber, Susanne (Case C-1/04) ECLI:EU:C:2006:39; [2006] ECR I-701;
[2006] BCC 639 .... 2.26, 3.25, 8.02, 8.04, 8.30, 8.115, 8.131, 8.135, 8.171
Stein v Blake [1996] AC 243, HL..4.31
Stichting Shell Pensioenfonds v Krys [2015] AC 616 (SC) 5.31
Stocznia Gdanska v Latreefers [2001] BCC 174 (CA) 5.56, 5.57
Stojevic, Re [2007] BPIR 141 (HC)...................................2.27, 2.28, 8.91, 8.109, 8.111
Stojevic, Re [Obergerichthof] [OGH] [Austrian Supreme Court] 8 Ob 135/04t,
17 March 2005...8.33, 8.370
Stojevic, Re [Oberlandesgericht] [OLG] [Higher Regional Court] Wien, 28 R 225/04w,
9 November 2004 .... 5.212, 8.43, 8.55, 8.57, 8.111, 8.366, 8.370, 8.402, 8.621, 8.684
Sturgeon Central Asia Balanced Fund Ltd, Re [2019] BCC 950 .... 5.83, 5.86, 5.94
Suidair International Airways Ltd, Re [1951] Ch 165..5.58
SwissAir Schweizerische Luftverkehr-Aktiengesellschaft, Re [2010] BCC 667 .... 5.72, 5.108
Syska v Vivendi Universal SA [2009] EWCA Civ 677, [2010] BCC 348,
[2010] 1 BCLC 467..2.27, 2.28, 4.58, 4.67, 8.293, 8.295

Tambrook Jersey Ltd, Re [2013] EWCA Civ 576; [2014] Ch 252 (CA) 5.77, 6.100
Tarragó da Silveira, Virgílio v Massa Insolvente da Espírito Santo Financial Group SA
(Case C-250/17) [2018] ECLI:EU:C:2018:398 .... 4.57, 6.22, 8.285
Television Trade Rentals Ltd, Re [2002] BCC 807 ....5.76
Telia AB v Hillcourt (Docklands) Ltd [2002] EWHC 2377 (Ch), [2003] BCC 856 .... 8.50, 8.52
Tendance Edition Ltd v L'URSSAF, Cour d'appel [CA] [regional court of appeal] Paris,
20 May 2008 ....8.135
Theophile, Re [1950] AC 186, HL..8.120
Transfield ER Cape Limited, Re [2010] EWHC 2851, recognition of BVI liquidation...........6.108

Trinity Mirror plc v Customs and Excise Commissioners [2001] EWCA Civ 65 . . . . .2.37
Trustees of the Olympic Airlines SA Pension & Life Insurance Scheme v
   Olympic Airlines SA [2013] EWCA Civ 643. . . . . 2.26, 2.28, 2.37, 5.91

Trustees of the Olympic Airlines SA Pension & Life Assurance Scheme v
   Olympic Airlines SA [2015] UKSC 27; [2015] 1 WLR 2399 . . . . 2.24, 8.01, 8.04, 8.39, 8.42,
                                                                                          8.46, 8.57, 8.169, 8.546, 8.547
Tünkers France und Tünkers Maschinenbau GmbH v Expert France
   (Case-641/16) ECLI:EU:C:2017:847; [2018] IL Pr 7 . . . . 4.60, 5.175, 5.179, 8.156, 8.582
TXU Europe German Finance BV, Re [2005] BCC 90; [2005] BPIR 209. . . . . 2.26, 8.98, 8.146

UB v VA, Tiger SCI, WZ, and Banque patrimoine et immobilier SA (Case C-493/18)
   ECLI:EU:C:2019:1046 . . . . 2.23, 3.57, 8.160, 8.582
UBS AG v OminiHolding AG [2001] 1 WLR 916, [2000] BCC 593. . . . . .8.149
UBS AG New York v Fairfield Centry Ltd [2019] UKPC 20; [2019] BCC 966 . . . . 5.105, 9.27, 9.34
Ultra Motorhomes International Ltd, Re [2006] BCC 57 . . . . 8.149, 8.462
Usines Coopératives de Déshydratation du Vexin v EC Commission (Case 244/88)
   ECLI:EU:C:1989:588; [1989] ECR I-3811. . . . . .2.07

Valach, Peter and others v Waldviertler Sparkasse Bank AG and others (Case C-649/16)
   ECLI:EU:C:2017:986 . . . . 3.25, 3.56, 3.59, 4.60, 5.175, 5.177, 8.156, 8.582
Van Buggenhout (Ch)ristian and another v Banque Internationale à Luxmbourg SA
   (Case C-251/12) [2013] ECLI:EU:C:2013:566 . . . . 2.24, 2.26
Van Buggenhout v Banque Internationale à Luxembourg SA (Case C-251/12) [2014] ILPr 28 . . . . 8.352
Van Gend en Loos v Nederlandse Adminsitratie der Belastingen (Case 26/62) [1963] ECR 1 . . . . .2.17
Vaneetveld v SA Le Foyer (Case C-316/93) [1994] ECR I-763 . . . . .2.40
VEBIC (Case C-439/08) [2010] ECR I-12471. . . . . .2.40
Vennink v Fortis Bank (Dutch Supreme Court, 9 January 2004) 8.109
Verwaltungsgericht Regensburg v 17.06.2014 -RO 4 E 14.898 [2014] EIRCR(A) 439. . . . . .6.77
Videology Ltd, Re [2018] EWHC 2186; [2019] BCC 195 (Ch) 5.83, 5.97, 5.109, 6.105,
                                                                                          6.108, 8.39, 8.95, 8.107, 9.20
Vinyls Italia SpA v Mediterranea di Navigazione SpA (Case C.54/16)
   ECLI:EU:C:2017:433 . . . . 4.50, 4.51, 6.31–6.33, 8.261, 8.263, 8.266
Vitro SAB de CV, 701 F 3d 1031 (5th Cir 2012). 5.103
Vizcaya Partners Ltd v Picard [2016] Bus LR 413. . . . . .5.29
Vocalion (Foreign) Ltd [1932] 2 Ch 196 . . . . .5.58
Von Colson and Kamann v Land Nordrhein Westfahlen (Case 14/83) [1984] ECR 1891. . . . . . . .2.15

Westwood Shipping Lines Inc v Universal [2012] EWHC 1394 (Comm). .8.76
Wiemer & Trachte GmbH v Zhan Oved Tadzher (Case C-296/17)
   ECLI:EU:C:2018:902 . . . . .3.55, 8.148, 8.158, 8.582
Wiener SI GmbH v Hauptzollamt Emmerich (Case C-338/95) [1997] ECR I-6495 . . . . .2.24
Wilcoxon, Ex p (1883) 23 Ch D 69 . . . . .5.52
Worsley v De Mattos (1758) 1 Bun 467 . . . . .5.52

Yacht Service BE v K Verhaegen, Gerechtshof (Hof) (Court of Appeal)'s-Hertogenbosch
   (The Hague) [2016] ECLI:NL:GHSHE:2016:3600. . . . . .6.55

Zerbone v Amministrazione delle Finanze (Case 94/77) [1978] ECR 99 .2.11
ZM, as liquidator of Oeltrans Befrachtungsgesellschaft mbH v E A Frerichs (Case C-73/20)
   ECLI:EU:C:2021:315 (judgment) (not yet published). 4.50, 8.273
Zuckerfabrik Watenstedt GmbHv Council (Case 6/68) [1968] ECR409. .2.07

Table of European Legislation and International Conventions

TREATIES & INTERNATIONAL CONVENTIONS

1957 Treaty of Rome................1.01, 1.12
   Art 61..............................2.33
   Art 61(c) 2.02–2.05, 2.20
   Art 67..............................2.33
   Art 67(1) 2.02–2.05, 2.20
   Art 68..................... 2.05, 2.32, 2.33
   Art 220.................... 1.01, 1.05, 1.10
   Art 230...........................2.03
1968 Convention on Jurisdiction and the Enforcement of Judgments in Civil and Commercial Matters (Brussels Convention) 1.10, 2.22, 2.23, 3.56, 4.43, 8.50, 8.775
   Art 1(2) 8.02
   Art 5(5) 8.50
   Art 27............................ 8.362
   Arts 31–51 .... 8.356
   Arts 38–58....................... 8.356
   Art 34(2) 8.356
1973 European Patent Convention....... 8.254
1975 Community Patent Convention..................4.48, 8.254
   Art 41 .... 8.254
1980 Convention on the Law Applicable to Contractual Obligations (Rome Convention) 4.33, 8.230
   Art 6............................. 8.247
   Art 7............................. 8.247
   Art 15.............................4.04
1989 Luxembourg Agreement 4.48
   Art 41............................4.48
1990 Istanbul Convention
   Art 2........................... 5.149
1992 Treaty of Maastricht 1.02, 1.05
1995 Convention on Insolvency Proceedings........ 1.05, 1.07, 1.19–1.23, 4.03, 6.43, 6.75
1997 Treaty of Amsterdam 2.32
Model Law on Cross-Border Insolvency (UNCITRAL)............ 5.02, 5.06, 5.41, 5.82–5.114, 6.103, 6.147, 8.107, 8.402, 8.563, 9.04, 9.15, 9.17–9.32
2001 Treaty of Nice.....................2.42

2005 Treaty and Act of Accession
   Art 56..............................1.25
2009 Treaty on European Union
   Art 1..............................9.18
   Art 4(3) 2.15
Treaty on the Functioning of the European Union (TFEU)
   Art 5..............................2.04
   Arts 49 ff 3.39
   Art 49............................2.37
   Art 51............................2.29
   Art 81................... 2.02–2.04, 2.20
   Art 81(2) 2.04, 2.05
   Art 256...........................2.42
   Art 263...........................2.07
   Art 267...........................2.40
   Art 294................2.02, 2.05, 2.20, 2.28
2019 Agreement on the withdrawal of the United Kingdom of Great Britain and Northern Ireland from the European Union and the European Atomic Energy Community (UK-EU Withdrawal Agreement) 9.01
   Art 67(3)(c) 5.117, 9.02
2020 Trade and Co-operation Agreement ... 9.01

REGULATIONS

1994 Regulation 40/94 Community Trademark [1994] OJ L 11/1 ... 4.48 , 8.254
   Art 21........................... 8.254
Regulation 2100/94 Plant Variety Rights [1994] OJ L 227/1 .... 4.48, 4.59–4.68, 8.254
   Art 25............................4.48
2000 Regulation 1346/2000 (OR) [2000] OJ L 160/1 ....1.01, 1.19–1.23, 1.28, 4.01, 4.28, 6.01, 6.60, 6.107, 7.18
   Recital (4) 8.322, 8.350
   Recital (9) 7.25
   Recital (13) 2.27, 8.88–8.93, 8.118
   Recital (16),....................8.66, 8.439
   Recital (25) 8.258
   Recital (22) 8.376
   Recital (24) 8.286
   Recital (25) 8.220
   Recital (27) 8.244

Recital (30) 8.349	Art 15 .... 4.58, 4.67, 8.245, 8.270–8.287,
Recital (36) 5.230	8.591, 8.609–8.613
Art 1 .... 8.01–8.15	Art 16 .... 2.21, 8.68, 8.69, 8.82, 8.131,
(1) 3.05, 3.06, 8.04, 8.07,	8.288–8.298, 8.616
8.74, 8.613(2) 8.09	(1) 8.126
Art 2 .... 8.16–8.59, 8.308	Arts 16–18 .... 8.27, 8.351
(b) 8.04	Art 17 .... 8.200, 8.271, 8.299–8.307,
(d) 8.17, 8.291	8.353, 8.617
(f) 8.294, 9.03	(2) 8.425
(g) 6.67	Art 18 .... 8.308–8.323
(h) 2.37, 8.64, 8.334	(3) 8.621
Art 3 .... 2.14, 2.18, 2.21, 3.21, 4.60,	Art 19 .... 8.324, 8.389, 8.623
8.04, 8.60–8.187, 8.193	Art 20 .... 4.16, 8.325–8.330, 8.624
(1) 2.14, 2.27, 3.21, 4.61, 5.229, 8.19,	(2) 8.404
8.232, 8.301, 8.334, 8.344, 8.376, 8.381	Art 21 .... 8.331–8.339, 8.348, 8.628
(2) 8.37, 8.189, 8.213, 8.221, 8.295,	(1) 8.139
8.302–8.306, 8.311–8.313,	Art 22 .... 8.340–8.345
8.321–8.323, 8.334, 8.344,	Art 24 .... 8.347–8.350, 8.643
8.373, 8.382, 8.384, 8.425, 8.427	(2) 8.643
(3) 3.49, 8.373	Art 25 .... 4.60, 5.163, 6.76, 8.79,
(4)(a) 3.44	8.319, 8.351–8.361, 8.621
Art 4 .... 3.13, 4.62, 8.187–8.212, 8.243,	(1) 3.21, 8.356, 8.385, 8.645
8.287, 8.375, 8.590, 8.658	(3) 5.163
(1) 4.61, 8.213, 8.215, 8.255, 8.271	Art 26 .... 8.78, 8.125, 8.126, 8.131, 8.290,
(2) 8.60, 8.271, 8.382	8.318, 8.362–8.372, 8.443, 8.649
(d) 3.12, 8.228, 8.234	Art 27 .... 3.49, 8.375–8.386, 8.390, 8.650
(e) 8.16, 8.164, 8.240	Art 28 .... 8.387, 8.653
(f) 8.272, 8.274, 8.277,	Art 29 .... 5.231, 8.80, 8.313,
8.286, 8.287, 8.591	8.388–8.392, 8.439, 8.670
(g) 8.269	Art 30 .... 8.393, 8.685
(h) 8.403, 8.445	Arts 31–35 .... 8.185, 8.374, 8.719
(m) 8.223, 8.226, 8.239,	Art 31 .... 8.394–8.40, 8.691
8.255, 8.256, 8.593	Art 32 .... 8.403–8.411
Arts 5–7 .... 8.255	(1) 8.442
Arts 5–15 .... 4.63, 7.70, 8.164,	Art 33 .... 8.412–8.420, 8.669
8.211, 8.301, 8.353	Art 34
Art 5 .... 4.63, 6.36, 6.52, 6.53, 6.74,	(1) 8.713
6.81, 8.211, 8.213–8.226, 8.239, 8.242,	(2) 8.307, 8.714
8.253, 8.311, 8.327, 8.593, 8.619, 8.624	Art 35 .... 8.428–8.429, 8.718
(1) 4.34, 6.74	Art 36 .... 8.185, 8.430–8.433, 8.719
(4) 8.255	Art 37 .... 2.11, 2.29, 5.232, 8.186,
Art 6 .... 3.12, 4.34, 4.63, 7.01, 8.211,	8.434–8.437, 8.721
8.227–8.235, 8.239, 8.269, 8.594	Art 38 .... 5.231–5.232, 8.66, 8.80,
Art 7 .... 4.63, 7.77, 8.211, 8.236–8.239,	8.438–8.441, 8.725
8.327, 8.595, 8.619, 8.624	Art 39 .... 8.406, 8.442–8.446, 8.726
Arts 8–15 .... 8.278	Art 40 .... 8.447–8.449
Art 8 .... 4.63, 6.18, 8.240–8.242,	(1) 8.459, 8.729
8.250, 8.596, 8.600	(2) 8.729
Art 9 .... 2.23, 7.01, 8.235, 8.243–8.244, 8.250	Art 41 .... 8.450–8.454, 8.736, 8.741
Art 10 .... 8.245–8.247, 8.250	Art 42 .... 8.455–8.459
Art 11 .... 4.65, 8.248–8.253,	(2) 8.738, 8.740
8.269, 8.602, 8.603	Art 43 .... 8.460–8.463
Art 12 .... 4.65, 8.254	(3)(b) 8.464
Art 13 .... 4.66, 6.81, 6.179, 8.225, 8.226,	Art 44 .... 8.464–8.465, 8.810
8.255–8.267, 8.592, 8.606	Art 45 ..... 1.25, 3.04, 3.07, 3.28, 8.466–8.468
Art 14 .... 4.34, 4.66, 8.268–8.269, 8.608	Art 46 .... 1.26, 8.469–8.471, 8.816

TABLE OF EUROPEAN LEGISLATION AND INTERNATIONAL CONVENTIONS   xxxi

Art 47............................ 8.460
   Annex A................1.28, 6.107, 8.18,
                       8.70, 8.72, 8.427
   Annex B.........1.28, 6.107, 8.172, 8.427
   Annex C..............1.28, 5.231–5.232,
                       8.70, 8.72, 8.161
2001 Regulation 44/2001 [2002] OJ
   L 12/1 (Brussels I)........2.22, 3.09, 3.56,
           3.58, 3.59, 4.43, 8.128, 8.188,
           8.230, 8.282, 8.357, 8.775
   Art 1(2)(b)................ 3.09, 8.150–8.159
   Art 27............................ 8.128
   Art 34(1) 8.362
   Arts 27–30........................ 8.128
   Arts 29–31..........................3.28
   Art 45(2) 8.356
   Art 68(2) 8.356
Regulation 1206/2001 [2001] OJ L 174
   (Taking of Evidence Regulation) 2.22
2003 Regulation 2201/2003 [2003] OJ
   L 338/1 (Brussels II).................2.22
2005 Regulation 603/2005 [2005] OJ
   L 100/1......................1.24, 8.467
2006 Regulation 694/2006 [2006]
   OJ L 121/1 ....1.24
Regulation 1791/2006 [2006] OJ L 363/1....1.25
2007 Regulation 681/2007 [2007]
   OJ L 159/1 ....1.24
Regulation 864/2007 [2007] OJ
   L 199/40 (Rome II)............. 4.14, 4.18
2008 Regulation 593/2008 [2008] OJ
   L 177/6 (Rome I)..... 4.09, 4.10, 4.13, 4.15,
          4.17, 4.33, 6.33, 6.140, 8.230, 8.267
   Recital (44) 4.33
   Recital (45) 4.33
   Recital (46) 4.33
   Art 2...............................4.33
   Art 3..................... 4.34, 4.40, 4.43
      (1)...............................4.34
      (2)...............................4.34
   Art 4(1)(c).........................4.40
   Art 8................... 4.43, 7.143, 8.247
   Art 9.......................4.43, 8.247
   Art 12..............................4.14
   Art 17..............................4.33
   Art 20..............................4.04
   Art 24..............................4.33
   Art 28..............................4.33
Regulation 788/2008 [2008] OJ L 213/1.....1.24
2010 Regulation 210/2010 [2010] OJ L 65/1.....1.24
Regulation 1095/2010 [2010] OJ
   L 331/84 (AIFMD)
   Art 4(1)(a).........................7.28
2011 Regulation 182/2011 [2011] OJ
   L 55/13......................... 8.815
Regulation 583/2011 [2011] OJ L 160/52 .... 1.24

2012 Regulation 648/2012 [2012] OJ
   L 201/1 (CRR, EMIR) 7.22, 7.36, 7.273
   Art 2(1) 7.08, 7.272
   Art 4...............................7.43
      (1)(1) 7.42, 7.169
      (1)(2) 7.169
      (1)(17) 7.13, 7.44, 7.173
      (1)(29) 7.178
      (1)(41) 7.178
      (1)(43) 7.13, 7.48
      (1)(44) 7.13, 7.48
Regulation 1215/2012 [2012] OJ L 351
   (recast Brussels, Brussels I *bis*) 2.22–2.23,
            4.37, 4.60, 5.28, 5.168–5.183,
            8.188, 8.230, 8.355, 8.775
   Art 1(2)(b)........................ 5.171
   Art 4...............................5.34
   Arts 20–23.........................4.43
   Arts 39–44...................5.168, 8.643
   Art 45............................ 8.362
   Arts 47–57...................5.168, 8.643
Regulation 1257/2012 [2012] OJ L 361/1 .... 8.604
Regulation 1260/2012 [2012] OJ
   L 361/89......................... 8.604
CJEU's Rules of Procedure [2012] OJ L 265.... 2.42
   Art 9..............................2.29
   Art 99..............................2.38
   Art 100............................2.40
   Art 105............................2.42
2013 Regulation 575/2013 [2013]
   OJ L 176/1 .... 7.24, 8.503
   Art 4(1) 3.17, 3.18, 7.169
2014 Regulation 655/2014 [2014] OJ
   L 189/59 (European Account
   Preservation Order Regulation)
   Art 4 .... 3.32, 8.526, 8.577–8.581
      (4)...............................6.60
Regulation 663/2014 [2014] OJ L 179/4.....1.24
Regulation 806/2014 [2014] OJ L 225/1
   (Single Resolution Mechanism
   Regulation - SRMR)........... 7.07–7.09,
                7.16, 7.47, 7.274
   Art 2........................7.165, 7.172
   Art 3(1)
      (15)............................ 7.170
      (21)............................ 7.171
      (33)............................ 7.210
   Art 7(2) 7.170, 7.178
   Art 10(1) 7.179
      (10) and (11) 7.179
   Art 10a........................... 7.180
   Arts 12–12k...................... 7.210
   Art 15(1) 7.194, 7.236
   Art 18
      (4)............................. 7.191
      (5)............................. 7.192

Art 20	Recitals (37)–(50) 4.12
(1) 7.197	Recital (39) 4.24
(5)(g) 7.197	Recital (40) 5.140
Art 22(1) 7.222	Recital (41) 3.49
Art 22	Recital (48) 5.204, 5.207, 5.209
(2) 7.174, 7.200	Recital (49) 5.204, 5.208
(4) 7.200	Recital (50) 5.208
(5) 7.203, 7.205	Recital (62) 3.66
Art 23 .... 7.196	Recital (63) 5.148
Art 24 .... 7.201	Recital (65) 3.28, 3.29, 5.125
Art 25 .... 7.204	Recital (66) 3.54, 4.12, 5.135
Art 26 .... 7.208	Recital (68) 4.21, 4.24, 4.27, 5.191,
Art 27	6.13, 6.38, 6.68, 6.74
(1) 7.211	Recital (71) 4.42
(2) 7.211	Recital (72) 4.43, 4.45
(3) 7.210, 7.212	Recital (88) 3.19, 4.52, 9.07
(5) 7.213	Art 1 .... 3.03, 3.17, 4.60, 6.14,
(16) 7.218	8.472–8.504, 8.521
Arts 38–41 .... 7.271	(1) 3.03, 3.05, 3.06, 3.07, 3.48,
Arts 67–79 .... 7.268	3.53, 4.26, 5.164, 8.514, 8.526
Art 85 .... 7.248	(a) 3.05, 3.08
Art 86 .... 7.248	(b) 3.05, 3.08, 3.53
2015 Regulation 2015/848 [2015] OJ	(c) 3.05, 3.06, 3.34
L 141/19 (RR) 1.28, 2.01, 3.01, 4.01–4.68,	(2) 3.18, 3.30, 5.01, 6.03, 7.02, 7.19
5.01–5.05, 6.01, 6.87, 7.47,	(c) 7.25
8.472–8.623, 9.04–9.32	Art 1(1) (Retained RR). 5.119
Retained RR. 2.30, 5.118–5.120,	Art 1A (Retained RR). 5.119
6.89–6.91, 9.02, 9.07–9.13	Art 1B (Retained RR) 5.119
(See also individual articles as listed below)	Art 2 .... 5.115, 8.505–8.554, 8.570
Recital (5) 3.29, 3.33, 3.34, 3.35	(1) 3.06, 8.480
Recital (6) 5.173	(3) 5.115
Recital (7) 3.09, 3.10, 8.588	(4) 8.475
Recital (9) .. 3.03, 8.475, 8.502, 8.516, 8.521	(5) 5.115, 5.148, 8.491
Recital (10) .. 3.06, 3.48, 8.489, 8.493, 8.514	(6) 5.115, 8.494
Recital (11) 3.34, 3.35, 8.496	(7) 5.115, 6.70
Recital (12) 3.07, 8.476	(8) 5.127, 6.39, 6.70, 6.153
Recital (13) 3.07, 8.478	(9) 3.52, 4.21, 4.24, 4.28, 4.63,
Recital (14) 3.06, 8.481–8.483,	6.57, 6.66–6.68, 6.141
8.508, 8.509	(i) 6.173
Recital (15) 3.07, 8.484, 8.523	(10) 2.37, 3.41, 5.132
Recital (16) 8.486	(11) 3.47, 5.115
Recital (17) 8.501	(12) 5.115, 5.148
Recital (19) 8.504	(13) 3.66, 5.115
Recital (20) 8.525	(14) 5.115
Recital (21) 8.524	Art 2(8) (Retained RR). 9.03
Recital (22) 5.191	Art 2(10) (Retained RR) 9.10, 9.20
Recital (23) 3.20, 3.24	Art 3 .... 3.25, 3.58, 4.60, 8.500,
Recital (24) 3.41	8.554–8.576, 8.580
Recital (25) 3.19, 3.42, 6.13, 6.15	(1) 3.06, 3.24, 3.25, 3.33, 3.35, 3.37,
Recitals (27)–(33) 3.26	3.53, 4.12, 4.48, 4.61, 5.115,
Recital (27) 7.34	5.130, 5.157, 6.36, 6.65, 8.551
Recital (29) 3.33, 8.551	(2) 3.42, 3.44, 3.51, 3.53, 4.12, 4.48,
Recital (30) 3.33, 3.35	5.115, 5.130, 5.140, 5.157
Recital (31) 3.33	(3) 4.12, 5.115
Recital (34) 3.29	(4) 3.44, 4.12, 3.45, 4.48, 5.115
Recital (35) 5.174, 8.587	Art 3 (Retained RR) 9.10

Art 4 . . . . 3.32, 8.526, 8.577–8.581	(1) 4.36, 4.37, 4.39, 5.193
(1) 3.11	(2) 4.37–4.39, 5.195
(4) 6.60	(3) 4.06, 4.39
Art 5 . . . . 3.29, 3.32, 5.130, 5.154,	Art 11 . . . . 4.03, 4.06, 4.40–4.42,
5.167, 8.526, 8.582–8.585	4.63, 8.596–8.597
(1) 3.47	(1) 4.40, 4.63
Art 6 . . . . 3.09, 3.21, 3.55, 4.60–4.61, 4.68,	(2) 4.41, 4.63
5.172, 5.173, 5.176, 6.82,	Art 12 . . . . 2.23, 4.42, 4.64, 7.32,
8.526, 8.586–8.589	7.34, 8.598–8.599
(1) 3.55–3.58, 9.02	(1) 4.42, 7.02
(2) 3.55, 3.57, 8.515	(2) 4.42, 7.01
(3) 3.57	Art 13 . . . . .4.03, 4.43–4.45, 8.600–8.601
Arts 7–18 . . . . 3.53, 4.02, 4.28	(1) 4.43, 4.45, 4.64, 7.81
Art 7 . . . . 3.30, 3.32, 3.37–3.39,	(2) 4.64
4.02, 4.05–4.20, 4.59, 4.62, 4.68, 5.140,	Art 14 . . . . .4.46–4.47, 4.65, 8.602
6.16, 6.31, 6.38, 6.39, 6.119, 8.590–8.592	Art 15 . . . . 4.48, 4.65, 8.603–8.605
(1) 3.11, 4.05, 4.12, 4.45, 4.61, 6.03	Art 16 . . . . 2.18, 4.06, 4.11, 4.35, 4.49–4.52,
(2) 3.54, 4.05–4.06, 4.50, 6.03, 6.34–6.41	4.66, 6.30–6.33, 6.80–6.81,
(a) 3.17, 3.18, 4.08	6.178–6.179, 8.592, 8.606–8.607
(b) 4.08, 4.16, 4.23, 6.18	Art 17 . . . . . . 4.34, 4.53–4.55, 4.58, 4.66, 8.608
(c) 4.62	Art 18 . . . . 4.06, 4.56–4.58, 4.67, 6.22,
(d) 3.12, 3.54, 4.09, 4.32,	8.591, 8.609–8.615
4.35, 6.19, 6.186	(3) 5.184
(e) 3.54, 4.10, 4.40	Art 19 . . . . 2.21, 5.124–5.132, 5.142, 5.164,
(f) 3.54, 4.57, 6.22	6.03, 6.36, 6.119, 8.530, 8.557, 8.616
(g) 4.09, 6.23–6.24	(1) 5.126, 5.141
(h) 4.09, 6.23–6.24	(2) 5.132
(i) 4.09, 6.25–6.28	Art 20 . . . . . . .5.133–5.142, 6.119, 8.557, 8.617
(k) 3.54	(1) 5.135–5.135, 5.140, 5.187, 6.119
(l) 6.25–6.27	(2) 5.141
(m) 3.34, 3.54, 4.06, 4.11, 4.25,	Art 21 . . . . 5.184–5.195, 8.618–8.622
4.35, 4.49–4.50, 4.62, 6.29–6.33,	(1) 5.184, 5.186, 5.187, 5.188
6.80, 6.81, 8.593	(3) 5.188
Art 7 (Retained RR) 9.30–9.32	Art 22 . . . . .5.149–5.150, 8.623
(2) 9.30	(2) 5.149
Arts 8 to 18 . . . . .3.11, 4.02–4.03,	Art 23 . . . . 4.27, 5.196–5.201, 8.624
4.19–4.59, 4.63, 7.70	(2) 5.200
Art 8 . . . . 2.18, 4.06, 4.20–4.30, 4.39,	Arts 24–27 . . . . 5.152
4.42, 4.49, 4.63, 5.186, 5.188, 5.191,	Arts 24–29 . . . . .5.151–5.162
5.193, 5.199, 6.10, 6.22, 6.27, 6.28,	Art 24 . . . . 3.07, 8.625–8.631
6.35–6.56, 6.67, 6.68–6.83, 6.91,	(1) 5.01, 5.152
6.111–6.125, 6.139, 6.148, 6.153,	(2) 3.07, 5.153
6.156–6.158, 6.165–6.178, 8.593	(j) 5.154
(1) 4.03, 4.22, 4.25–4.27, 4.29,	(3) 5.153
4.34, 4.39, 4.49, 6.52	(4) 5.154
(2) 4,28, 6.43, 6.50	(5) 5.155
(b) 6.48	Arts 25–27 . . . . 5.156
(3) 4.28, 6.43	Art 25 . . . . 3.07, 5.01, 8.632–8.633
(4) 4.06, 4.25, 6.81	Art 26 . . . . 8.634
Art 9 . . . . . 3.12, 4.03, 4.06, 4.09, 4.31–4.35, 4.42,	Art 27 . . . . 2.11, 5.153, 8.635–8.636
4.63, 6.19–6.21, 6.184–6.187, 7.80, 8.594	Art 28 . . . . 5.160, 8.515, 8.637–8.640
(1) 4.33, 4.35, 7.02	(1) 5.157
(2) 4.06	(2) 5.158
Art 9 (Retained RR) 6.90	Art 29 . . . . 5.160, 8.515, 8.641
Art 10 . . . . 4.06, 4.24, 4.36–4.39, 4.63, 4.64,	(1) 5.159–5.160
5.186, 5.188, 5.191, 5.193, 5.199, 7.77, 8.595	(2) 5.160

Art 30	5.160, 8.642
Art 31	8.643
Art 32	2.18, 5.163–5.183, 6.165–6.170, 8.500, 8.643–8.648
(1)	3.62, 3.64, 3.65, 5.164–5.168, 5.170, 5.173, 5.175
(2)	5.169, 5.170
Art 33	3.36, 5.142–5.148, 5.163, 5.167, 8.649
Art 34	3.48, 3.51, 8.650–8.652
Art 35	3.54, 3.55, 4.12, 8.653
Art 36	3.38, 3.39, 3.47, 3.64, 8.654–8.669
(2)	3.38
(8)	3.64
(9)	3.64
Art 37	5.190, 5.194, 8.670–8.673
(1)(a)	5.189
Art 38	3.47, 5.190, 5.194, 8.500, 8.515, 8.674–8.682
(1)	3.46
(2)	3.47
(3)	3.47, 3.65
Art 39	3.47, 8.683–8.684
Art 40	8.685
Arts 41–43	5.202–5.216
Arts 41–51	3.49
Art 41	5.202, 5.215, 8.686–8.690
(1)	5.202
(2)	5.205
(c)	5.206
(3)	5.211
Art 42	5.212, 5.215, 8.691–8.701
(1)	5.212–5.213
(2)	5.214
(3)	5.212, 5.214
Art 43	5.215, 8.702–8.708
Art 44	8.709
Art 45	3.16, 5.217–5.219, 8.710
(1)	3.50, 5.217
(b)	5.166
(2)	5.217
(3)	5.218
Art 46	5.166, 5.206, 5.220–5.222, 8.711
(1)	5.220
(2)	5.222
Arts 47–49	5.223–5.226
Art 47	8.712–8.715
(1)	5.223
(2)	5.224, 6.163
Art 48	5.225, 8.716–8.717
(1)	5.225
(2)	5.225
Art 49	8.718
Art 50	8.719
Art 51	2.11, 5.227–5.228, 8.720–8.724
(1)	5.227
Art 52	5.229–5.232, 8.725
Arts 53–55	3.53, 4.09, 6.24
Art 53	3.16, 6.24, 7.72, 8.726–8.728
Art 54	5.154, 6.24, 8.729–8.735
(1)	5.162
Art 55	6.24, 7.72, 8.736–8.745
Art 55(6)	5.155
Arts 56–77	5.216
Art 56	8.754–8.758
Art 57	8.128, 8.759–8.762
Art 58	8.763–8.764
Art 59	8.765
Art 60	8.766–8.770
Art 61	3.66, 8.771–8.772
(1)	3.67
Art 62	3.68, 8.773–8.775
Art 63	8.776–8.778
Art 64	8.779–8.780
Art 65	8.781–8.782
Art 66	8.783–8.784
(1)	3.69
Art 67	8.785
Art 68	8.786–8.790
Art 69	8.791–8.792
Art 70	8.793–8.794
Art 71	8.795
Art 72	8.796–8.799
Art 73	8.800
Art 74	8.801
Art 75	8.802–8.803
Art 76	8.515, 8.804
Art 77	8.805–8.806
Arts 78 to 83	8.807
Art 84	8.808–8.809
(1)	5.01, 7.01
(2)	8.460
Art 85	8.810–8.811
Art 86	8.812
Art 87	2.18, 8.813
Art 88	2.18, 8.814
Art 89	8.815
Art 90	2.18, 3.28, 8.816–8.820
Art 91	8.821–8.822
Art 92	3.02, 5.01, 8.823–8.825
Annex A	1.28, 3.03, 3.04, 3.07, 3.08, 3.10, 3.22, 4.26, 5.164, 6.14, 6.28, 6.107, 6.138
Annex B	1.28, 3.04, 5.115, 5.149
Annex C	1.28
Annex D	1.28
2021 Regulation 2021/23 [2021] OJ L 22/1 (Central Counterparties Regulation – CCPRRR)	7.08, 7.18, 7.30, 7.35–7.37, 7.272–7.281
Recital (4)	7.36, 7.273
Recital (10)	7.274
Title IV	7.275

Title VI	7.281
Title VII	7.281
Art 2(16)	7.37
Arts 9–14	7.275
Arts 15–17	7.275
Art 18 (1a) and (1b)	7.275
Art 18m	7.275
Art 20	7.276
Art 22(1)	7.277
Art 27(1)	7.278
Art 28(3d)	7.278
Art 29(1)	7.278
Art 30(1)	7.278
Arts 32–39	7.279
Arts 40 and 41	7.279
Arts 48–59	7.280
Arts 60–69	7.280
Art 70	7.280
Art 74(1)	7.280
Arts 76–80	7.281
Art 76(1)	7.281

DIRECTIVES

1973 Directive 73/239 [1973] OJ L 228	7.21
Art 6	8.114
1977 Directive 77/780 [1977] OJ L 322/30	8.09
1979 Directive 79/267 [1979] OJ L 63/1	7.21
Art 6	7.107, 8.11
1985 Directive 85/611 [1985] OJ L 375/3	8.09
1988 Directive 88/361 [1988] OJ L 178/5	7.18
1989 Directive 89/104 [1989] OJ L 207/44	4.48
Directive 89/391/EEC	4.45
Art 16(1)	4.45
1992 Directive 92/96 [1992] OJ L 360	7.21
1993 Directive 93/22 [1993] OJ L 14/127	8.09
1995 Directive 95/26 [1995] OJ L 168/7	8.09
1997 Directive 97/9 [1997] OJ L 84/22	7.189
1998 Directive 98/26 [1998] OJ L 166/45 (Settlement Finality Directive)	4.42, 7.09, 7.16, 7.30–7.36, 7.87, 8.244
Recital (7)	4.42
Art 3(1)	7.33
Art 7	7.33
Art 8	4.42
Art 9	
(1)	7.34, 7.38
(2)	7.86–7.88, 8.543
2000 Directive 2000/28 [2000] OJ L 275 (Banking Directive)	
Art 6(2)	7.44
Directive 2000/78/EC	4.45
2001 Directive 2001/17 [2001] OJ L 110/28 (Insurance Directive)	2.23, 7.04, 8.10
Recital (2)	7.04, 8.11
Recital (3)	7.05
Recital 21	7.137
Art 2	7.45, 7.113, 7.116, 7.129
Directive 2001/24 [2001] OJ L 125/15 (Credit Institutions Directive or Winding-up Directive)	3.17, 5.138, 7.04, 7.19, 7.18, 7.20, 7.25, 7.41–7.100, 8.13, 8.503
Recital (1)	7.05
Recital (2)	7.05
Recital (3)	7.47
Recital (6)	7.05
Recital (16)	7.60
Recital (23)	7.81
Recital (24)	7.81
Art 1	7.23, 7.41
(1)	7.44
(2)	7.44
(3)	7.25
(4)	7.43
Art 2	7.23, 7.41, 7.48, 7.50, 7.57
(b)	5.138
(2)	7.45
Arts 3–8	7.66
Art 3	7.53, 7.59–7.60, 7.63
Art 4	7.61
Art 6	7.62, 7.63
Art 7	
(2)	7.64
Art 8	7.65
(2)	7.65
Art 9	7.66
Art 10	7.75, 7.67, 7.124
(2)	7.69
(c)	7.80
(g)	7.72
Art 13	7.66, 7.71
Art 14	7.63
(1)	7.68
Art 16	7.72
(1)	7.72
(2)	7.72
Art 17(1)	7.63
Art 20–33	7.74
Art 20	7.74, 7.81, 7.84
(b)	7.82
(c)	7.81, 7.83
Art 21	7.74–7.76, 7.84
(1)	7.77
Art 22	7.74, 7.148
(1)	7.78–7.80
(2)	7.78–7.79
(3)	7.79
Art 23	7.74, 7.80
Arts 24–27	7.74, 7.81, 7.85, 7.88
Art 24	7.85–7.86, 7.152
Art 25	7.89, 7.93, 7.152

Art 26 . . . . 7.91–7.93, 7.152	Art 269(4) 7.116
Art 27 . . . . 7.94, 7.153	Arts 269–272 . . . . 7.116
Art 28 . . . . .7.95	Art 270 . . . . 7.117, 7.118, 7.123
Art 29 . . . . .7.96	Art 271 . . . . .7.119, 7.135
Art 30 . . . . .7.97	(2) 7.136
(1) 6.32, 7.97	Art 272 . . . . 7.120
Art 31 . . . . .7.98	Art 273 . . . . 7.123
Art 32 . . . . .7.99	(3) 7.121
Art 34 . . . . 7.100	(4) 7.122
2002 Directive 2002/47 [2002] OJ L 168	Arts 273–284 . . . . 7.121
(Financial Collateral Directive) 6.172,	Art 274 . . . . 7.124
6.174, 7.09, 7.16, 7.30, 7.38–7.40	(2) 7.126, 7.138
Art 7 . . . . .7.39	Art 275 . . . . 7.130
Art 8 . . . . .7.39	(1) 7.132
Art 9 . . . . 8.543	(b) 7.133
(1) 7.86–7.88	(2) 7.128
(2) 6.59, 7.93	(3) 7.131
Directive 2002/83 . . . . 7.21, 7.101	Art 277 . . . . 7.132
Directive 2002/87 [2002] OJ L 035 . . . . .7.24	Art 279 . . . . 7.134
Directive 2002/92 [2002] OJ L 009 . . . . .7.25	Art 280 . . . . 7.135
2004 Directive 2004/39 [2004] OJ	Art 281 . . . . 7.136
L 145/1 (Markets in Financial	Art 282 . . . . .7.137, 7.138
Instruments Directive, MiFID)	Art 283 . . . . .7.139, 7.141
Art 4(1)(1) 7.169	Art 285 . . . . .7.143–7.145
Annex I(A)(1)–(5) 7.169	Arts 285–292 . . . . 7.125
Annex I(B)(1) 7.169	Art 286(1) 7.147
2005 Directive 2005/68 [2005] OJ L 327 . . 7.108	Art 287 . . . . 7.148
2006 Directive 2006/48 [2006] OJ L 177 (CRD	(2) 7.149
IV) 7.23	Art 288 . . . . 7.150
Art 4 . . . . .7.44	Art 289 . . . . .7.151, 7.153
2007 Directive 2007/44 [2007] OJ L 177 . . . . 7.108	Art 290 . . . . .7.148, 7.154
2009 Directive 2009/65 [2009] OJ	Art 291 . . . . .7.156, 7.157
L 302 (UCITS IV) 7.26	Art 292 . . . . 7.158
Art 1(2) 7.27, 8.512	Arts 293–295 . . . . 7.159
Art 5 . . . . 8.513	Art 294 . . . . 7.160
Art 5(1) 8.512	Art 295 . . . . 7.161
Directive 2009/104 . . . . .4.45	Art 296 . . . . .7.162, 7.163
Directive 2009/138 [2009] OJ L 335	(1) 7.113
(Solvency II) 7.20, 7.22, 7.50, 7.51	Annex 1, Pt A 7.22
Recital (117) 7.106	2011 Directive 2011/61 [2011] OJ L 174
Art 2	(AIFM Directive) 7.25
(1) 7.22	Art 4(1)(a) 8.513
(2) 7.22, 7.102	2013 Directive 2013/34 [2013] OJ L 182 . . . . 8.751
(3) 7.22	Recital (31) 8.751
Art 13	2013 Directive 2013/36 [2013] OJ
(1) 7.22	L 176/338 (CRD IV) 7.24
(22) 7.151	Art 28(2) 7.169
Art 14 . . . . .7.22	2014 Directive 2014/49 [2014] OJ
Arts 64–69 . . . . 7.161	L 173/149 . . . . 7.06, 7.15, 7.189
Art 212(1) 7.170	Directive 2014/59 [2014] OJ L 173
Art 267 . . . . .7.101, 7.102	(Bank Recovery and Resolution
Art 268 . . . . 7.113	Directive BRRD) 7.07–7.09,
(b) 7.102	7.13, 7.16–7.18, 7.20, 7.42, 7.46, 7.47, 7.52,
(c) 7.116	7.53, 7.59, 7.80, 7.90, 7.274–7.281, 8.503
(g) 7.136	Recitals (8)–(10) 7.52
Art 269 . . . . 7.116	Recital (8) 7.264

Recital (50)	7.203, 7.205	(1)	7.190, 7.277
Recital (67)	7.209	(4)	7.190
Recital (81)	7.222	(5)	7.192
Recital (92)	7.243	Art 32a(1)	7.193
Recital (103)	7.264	Art 33	7.255
Art 1(1)	7.170, 7.172	(4)	7.190
(b)	.7.43	Art 34(1)	7.194
(c)	7.172	(1)(g)	7.236
(d)	7.172	Art 35	7.174, 7.195
(e)	7.173	(3)	7.196
Art 1(2) and (3)	7.169	(7)	7.196
Art 2	7.43, 7.171, 7.173, 7.174	(8)	7.195
(1)		Art 36	7.198
(1)	7.174	(1)	7.197, 7.198
(4)	7.170	(13)	7.198
(5)	7.171	Art 37	
(20)	7.175	(2)	7.174, 7.199
(37)	7.178	(3)	7.174, 7.200
(44)	7.178	(5)	7.200, 7.208
(50)	7.178	(6)	7.205
(57)	7.210	(9)	7.174
(71)	7.210	Art 38	
(26)	7.249	(1)	7.201
(84)	7.249	(3)	7.203
(85)	7.249	(4)	7.203
(87)	7.249	(6)	7.205
(89)	7.249	Art 39	7.202
Art 3	7.176	Art 40	
Art 4(1)	7.177	(1)	7.204, 7.205
Art 5(1)	7.177	(2)	7.204
Art 6	7.269	(7)	7.205
Art 7(1)	7.178	(9)	7.204
Art 12(1)	7.178	(10)	7.204
Art 15(1)	7.179	Art 41	
Art 16(1)	7.179	(1)	7.204
Art 16a	7.180	(2)	7.204, 7.206
Art 17	7.181	(3)	7.206
Art 17		(5)–(8)	7.206
(4)	7.179	Art 42	
(5)	7.174, 7.181	(1)	7.208
(a)	7.182	(2)(a)	7.208
Art 18	7.181	(3)	7.208
Art 19(2)	7.182	(5)	7.208
Art 27		Art 43	
(1)	7.183, 7.184	(2)	7.211
(3)	7.183	(3)	7.211
Art 28	7.185	Art 44	
Art 29	7.185	(2)	7.210, 7.212
Art 30		(3)	7.210, 7.213
(1)	7.187	Arts 45-45m	7.210
(2)	7.189	Art 47	7.217
(3)	7.187	Art 48	7.215
Art 31		(2)	7.216
(2)	7.52, 7.189	Art 49	7.214
(3)	7.189	Art 52	7.218
Art 32	7.255	Art 55	7.219–7.220

Arts 56–58 . . . . 7.221
Art 56(3) 7.221
Art 59 . . . . 7.199
   (4) 7.222
Art 60 . . . . 7.199, 7.215
Arts 63–72 . . . . 7.175
Art 63
   (1) 7.223
   (2) 7.235
   (4) 7.235
Art 64(1) 7.223
Art 66 . . . . 7.224
Art 67 . . . . 7.224
Art 68 . . . . 7.90, 7.93, 7.225
   (1) 7.226
   (3) 7.226
   (4) 7.226
Art 69 . . . . 7.229
   (1) 7.232
   (2) 7.232
Art 70 . . . . 7.229, 7.233
Art 71 . . . . 7.90, 7.93, 7.229, 7.234
Art 73 . . . . 7.236
Art 74(1) 7.237
Art 75 . . . . 7.237
Arts 76–80 . . . . 7.238, 7.239
Art 76 . . . . 7.239
   (1) 7.238, 7.239
   (3) 7.239
Art 77 . . . . 7.240
   (2) 7.240
Art 78 . . . . 7.240
   (2) 7.240
Art 79 . . . . 7.240
   (2) 7.240
Art 80(2) 7.241, 7.242
Art 81 . . . . 7.242
Art 83 . . . . 7.242
Art 84 . . . . 7.242
Art 85 . . . . 7.248
   (1) 7.243
   (2) 7.244
   (3) 7.244, 7.248
   (4) 7.245, 7.246
   (6) 7.248
Art 86 . . . . 7.247, 7.248
Art 88 . . . . 7.250
   (1)(f) 7.167
   (2) 7.251
   (3) 7.252
   (4) 7.251
(5) 7.252
  Art 89
   (1) 7.250
   (2) 7.250
   (4) 7.250

Art 90
   (1) 7.254
   (2) 7.254
Art 91 . . . . 7.256, 7.267
   (2)–(5) 7.215
Art 92 . . . . 7.267
   (1)–(4) 7.256
Art 93
   (1) 7.258
   (4) 7.258
Art 94 . . . . 7.259
   (2) 7.259
   (3) 7.259
Art 95 . . . . 7.260
Art 96 . . . . 7.261
Art 97 . . . . 7.262
Art 98 . . . . 7.263
Art 99 . . . . 7.264
Art 100 . . . . 7.265
Art 101(1) 7.266
Art 103 . . . . 7.266
Art 104 . . . . 7.266
Art 105 . . . . 7.267
Art 106 . . . . 7.267
Art 107 . . . . 7.267
Art 108 . . . . 7.15, 7.215, 7.269
Art 109 . . . . 7.267
Arts 110–114 . . . . 7.270
Art 117 . . . . .7.25
Art 118 . . . . 7.220
Directive 2014/65 [2014] OJ L 173
  (MiFID II) 7.25, 7.169
  Art 4
   (1) 7.43
   (21) 7.94, 7.151
  Annex I 7.42
2019 Directive 2019/1023 [2019] OJ
  L 172/18 (Restructuring and
  Insolvency Directive) 3.07
  Art 2(2) 3.08, 4.26
Directive 2019/879 [2019] OJ L 150/1
  (BRRD II) 7.07, 7.193

Table of Statutes

UK ACTS OF PARLIAMENT

1920 Administration of Justice Act..........6.92
1933 Foreign Judgments (Reciprocal
    Enforcement) Act 1933..........5.30, 6.92
1972 European Communities Act (c 68)....6.88
    s 2..........2.01
        (2)..........2.12
    s 3..........2.01
        (1)..........2.30
1977 Patents Act (c 37)..........8.254
1981 Senior Courts Act
    s 37(1)
1985 Companies Act (c 6)
    s 396..........8.253
    s 425..........8.352, 8.360
1986 Insolvency Act (c 45)..........2.11, 5.53, 5.97,
        5.111, 5.112, 5.120, 8.18
    Pt III..........3.04
    s 72A(3) and (4)..........2.04
    s 117
        (1)..........2.14
        (7)..........9.16
    s 122(1)(g)..........5.86
    s 127..........4.53
    s 130(2)..........4.28, 8.279
    s 143(1)..........5.60
    s 183..........4.28
    s 184..........4.28
    s 221..........8.146, 9.11
        (4)..........8.146
    s 225..........9.11
    s 234..........5.19, 5.20
    s 236..........5.176
    s 238..........5.51, 5.176
    s 239..........5.51, 5.176
    s 247(2)..........8.28
    s 248(b)(i)..........8.453
    s 265..........8.145
        (4) and (5)..........9.13
    s 304..........5.20
    s 304(3)..........5.19
    s 346..........4.28
    s 347..........4.28
    s 388..........3.17
        (4)..........5.17
    s 423..........5.51
    s 426..........5.02, 5.06, 5.41, 5.66, 5.70,
        5.73–5.82, 5.92, 6.92, 6.99–6.102,
        6.131, 8.464, 8.811, 9.04, 9.33–9.35
        (1)..........5.78

        (2)..........5.78
        (4)..........5.77–5.79, 9.41
        (5)..........5.75–5.76, 9.41
        (11)..........5.74
    s 436..........2.11
        (1)..........5.60
    s 436A..........2.11, 5.140
    Sch B1..........5.77
    para 43..........6.104, 6.106, 6.108–6.109, 6.132
    para 49(3)..........5.164, 8.22, 8.23, 8.518
    para 111(1A)..........5.119, 6.134
1989 Companies Act (c 40) Pt VII..........4.42
2000 Financial Services and Markets
    Act (c 8)..........4.42
Insolvency Act (c 39)
    s 14..........5.82
2002 Enterprise Act (c 40)..........8.171
2006 Companies Act (c 46)..........5.119, 8.352
    Pt 26..........5.86, 5.164, 8.352, 8.360,
        8.426, 8.487, 8.519
    Pt 26A..........5.164
2018 European Union (Withdrawal) Act....6.87
2020 European Union (Withdrawal
    Agreement) Act 2020..........6.87, 9.01

BELGIUM

Code of Private International Law, Art 43

BERMUDA

Companies Act 1981, s 195..........5.46

CAYMAN ISLANDS

Companies Law, s 103..........5.46

ITALY

Bankruptcy Act (Royal Decree No 267
    of 1942), Art 1(1)..........4.08
Civil Code, Art 2083..........4.08

NETHERLANDS

Bankruptcy Act
    Art 35..........4.28
    Art 53..........8.231
Civil Code
    Art 6:127..........8.231
    Art 10:127(1)..........4.21

SPAIN

Insolvency Act
  (recast)
    Art 723 .6.83–6.84, 6.86,
                                    6.114, 6.133
    Art 742 . . . . .6.86
    Art 754 . . . . .6.83

UNITED STATES OF AMERICA

Bankruptcy Code (COMI) 5.88
  Ch 7 . . . . 6.146, 6.151–6.152
  Ch 11 . . . . 5.103, 6.106–6.107,
                          6.146, 6.151–6.152, 8.519
  Ch 15 . . . . 6.147, 6.150–6.151, 9.27
  s 304 . . . . .6.151, 9.27

Table of Statutory Instruments

1986 Co-operation of Insolvency
 Courts (Designation of Relevant
 Countries and Territories) Order
 SI 1986/2123 .... 5.73, 9.33
Insolvency Rules (SI 1986/1925)........... 2.12
    r................................. 8.116
    r................................. 8.116
    r............................ 8.29, 8.517
    r............................. 7.64, 8.408
    r............................... 8.8, 8.408
    r.............................. 11.1, 8.408
    r.................................. 13.13
    (8)..................................8.85
    (9).................................. 8.164
    (10)................................. 8.185
    (11).................................8.16
    (14).................... 8.07, 8.185, 8.430
Co-operation of Insolvency Courts
 (Designation of Relevant Countries
 and Territories) Order
 (SI 1986/2123)................ 5.73, 8.465
1991 Financial Markets and Insolvency
 Regulations (SI 1991/880)............4.42
1994 Reciprocal Enforcement of
 Judgments (Australia) Order 1994
 (SI 1994/1901)......................5.30
1996 Co-operation of Insolvency Courts
 (Designation of Relevant Countries)
 Order (SI 1996/253)........... 8.465, 9.33
1998 Civil Procedure Rules (SI 1998/3132)
    Pt 68 ....2.41
    PD 68 ....2.41
Co-operation of Insolvency Courts
 (Designation of Relevant Countries
 Order (SI 1998/2766).......... 8.465, 9.33
1999 Financial Markets and Insolvency
 (Settlement Finality) Regulations
 (SI 1999/2979).......................4.42
2002 Insolvency Act 1986 (Amendment)
 Regulations (SI 2002/1037)...........2.11
Insolvency Act 1986 (Amendment) (No.2)
 Regulations (SI 2002/1240)
    reg 6 ....2.14
    reg 7 ....2.14
    reg 9 ....2.14
    reg 10 ....2.14
    reg 14 ....2.14
Insolvency (Amendment) Rules
 (SI 2002/1307).......................8.37
    r 4(3)..............................2.14

r 9 ....3.04
r 10(7)............................ 8.430
2003 Financial Collateral Arrangements
 (No.2) Regulations (SI 2003/3226)
 (FCA Regulations) 6.101–6.102, 6.109
    Pt 3 .... 6.101
    reg 15A 6.101, 6.109
2004 Insurers (Reorganisation and
 Winding Up) Regulations
 (SI 2004/353)................... 2.23, 8.10
Credit Institutions (Reorganisation and
 Winding Up) Regulations
 (SI 2004/1045)................. 8.13, 9.09
2005 Insolvency Act 1986 (Amendment)
 Regulations (SI 2005/879)............2.11
Cross-Border Insolvency Regulations
 (SI 2006/1030) (CBIR).... 6.92, 6.103–6.109,
                    6.131, 9.04, 9.15, 9.17–9.32
    Regs 1–8...........................5.83
    Reg 3(2) 5.06, 5.85
    Art 1(4) 5.98
    Art 2
        (a)...............................5.85
        (c)...............................9.20
        (e)...............................5.90
        (h)...............................5.90
        (g)...............................5.89
        (j) 5.86, 5.93
        (j) 5.93
        (k)...............................5.98
    Art 6 ....5.94
    Art 7 .... 5.88, 7.67
    Art 8 ....5.95
    Art 11 .... 5.111
    Art 12............................ 5.111
    Art 15
        (1)...............................5.92
        (2)–(4) 5.92
        (2)(a)–(c).......................5.93
        (3)...............................5.92
    Art 16............................ 5.92
        (1)...............................5.93
        (2A)..............................5.89
        (3)...............................5.89
    Art 17.............................5.94
        (1)(c) 5.92
        (2)...............................5.87
        (4)...............................5.94
    Art 19 .... 5.99, 9.19
    Art 20 ....9.19

(1) 5.96, 6.104, 6.106	rr 21.1–21.3 5.228
(2) 5.97, 9.22	r 21 . . . . 6.158
(3) 5.98, 6.104	rr 21.6–21.17 5.203
(4) 9.21	r 21.6 . . . . 5.154
(5) 5.97	r 21.6(2) 5.154
(6) 5.98, 9.26	r 21.8 . . . . 5.217
Art 21 . . . . 5.99–5.107,	r 21.16 . . . . 5.158
6.103–6.105, 9.22–9.29	2019 Credit Institutions and Insurance
(1)	Undertakings Reorganisation and
(a)–(g) 6.104	Winding Up (Amendment) (EU Exit)
(a) 5.107	Regulations (SI 2019/38) 5.138, 9.16
(b) 5.107	Insolvency (Amendment) (EU Exit)
(g) 5.102–5.105, 6.104, 6.108, 6.132	Regulations (SI 2019/146) (Insolvency
(2) 5.108–5.110	Exit Regulations) 6.89, 9.02, 9.07, 9.16
Art 22(2) 5.99	reg 1(3) 5.89, 5.140, 5.228
Art 23 . . . . 5.112	Sch 1, Pt 1 . . . . 5.122
Art 24 . . . . 5.112	paras 2 *et seq* 5.119
Arts 25–27 . . . . 5.113	para 2 . . . . 5.119
Art 27 . . . . 5.113	para 2(3) 5.119
Arts 28–32 . . . . 5.113	para 16 . . . . 5.140
Art 32 . . . . 5.114, 9.19	para 44(b)(ii) 5.119
Schs 1–5 . . . . .5.83	para 46 . . . . 5.228
Sch 1 . . . . 5.83, 9.20, 9.21	para 47(b) 5.115
Art 1(2) 5.41	paras 104–106 . . . . 5.228
Art 7 . . . . .5.06	para 106 . . . . 5.154, 5.158,
Art 21 . . . . 5.19, 2007	5.203, 5.216, 5.217
Cross-Border Insolvency Regulations	para 112 . . . . .5.89
(Northern Ireland) (SRI 2007/115) 5.83	para 113 . . . . .5.89
2016 Insolvency (England and Wales)	para 117 . . . . .5.89
Rules (2016/1024) (2016 Rules) 5.120	Civil Jurisdiction and Judgments
Pt 21 . . . . 5.203	(Amendment) (EU Exit)
r 1.2 . . . . 5.115, 5.119, 5.120	Regulations (SI 2019/479)
r 1.2(2) 5.203	reg 89 . . . . 5.117
r 1.7 . . . . .9.11	Insolvency (Amendment) (EU Exit)
r 2.14(2A) 9.11	(No. 2) Regulations
r 2.31 . . . . .9.11	(SI 2019/1459) 5.118, 9.02
rr 2.11–2.15 5.216	2020 Insolvency (Amendment) (EU Exit)
r 3.3(2)(h) 9.11	Regulations (SI 2020/ 647) 5.118, 9.02
r 7.51(n) 9.11	Civil, Criminal and Family Justice
r 8.3(q) 9.11	(Amendment) (EU Exit)
r 10.49(2)(f) 9.11	Regulations (SI 2020/1493)
r 14.25 . . . . 5.64, 6.190	reg 5 . . . . 5.117

List of Contributors

Felicity Toube KC specializes in domestic and cross-border insolvency and restructuring, commercial litigation, and company law. Felicity is regularly instructed in cases in the Cayman Islands, the BVI, Bermuda, and the ADGM. She acts as an expert (in the laws of England and other common law jurisdictions) in international proceedings (including in the USA). Felicity has acted on all the recent major corporate insolvencies, including: *Gategroup, NMC, Adler, Greensill, Pizza Express, Smile Telecoms, Codere, Swissport, Carluccios, Debenhams, Matalan, Saad, Madoff, Peak Hotels, Lehman, Stanford, Nortel*, and *MF Global*. She is a mediator (ADR Group), an arbitrator (CiArb), and Co-Chair of the INSOL ADR Colloquium. Felicity's publications include: Moss, Fletcher & Isaacs on the EU Regulation, Toube on 'International Asset Tracing in Insolvency' (OUP), and Halsbury's Laws on *Corporate Insolvency*. Felicity is a Vice President of III, and Chair of the Appeal Panel for ICAS. She also teaches on the BCL course at Oxford University and is currently undertaking a part-time DPhil in Law at Oxford University, focussing on issues of cross-border insolvency.

Jennifer Marshall is a partner in the global restructuring group of Allen & Overy LLP. She specializes in a wide range of work in commercial, banking, restructuring and insolvency law focussing, in particular, on cases with a cross-border angle. She advised a large number of counterparties of Lehman Brothers and the Icelandic banks following the failure of those entities. In particular, she advised one of the parties in the Lehman Brothers International (Europe) client money directions application (which went to the Supreme Court) and one of the parties in the Lehman Waterfall Application. She is currently advising the lenders and the receivers in relation to the OW Bunker group which involves insolvency proceedings in a large number of different jurisdictions across the world. Most recently Jennifer acted for Virgin Atlantic Airlines on the first use in the UK of the restructuring plan. Jennifer is the chairman of the Insolvency Subcommittee of the City of London Law Society and a former President of the Insolvency Lawyers Association. She is a member of the Banking Liaison Panel, a working group established by HM to consider bank and investment firm failure. Jennifer joined A&O in 1995, and has been a partner since 2006.

Francisco Garcimartín is Professor of Law at the Universidad Autónoma de Madrid. His main fields of expertise are focused on International transactions, cross-border insolvency, international litigation as well as cross-border company law. He has represented the Spanish government as national expert in different international organizations, such as UNIDROIT, UNCITRAL, The Hague Conference, or the Counsel of the European Union. He is a member of the EU Commission's Expert Groups on insolvency, company restructuring, assignment of claims and securities. He is also a member of the Expert Group appointed by the Justice Ministry to implement the EU Directive on restructuring frameworks and second chance in Spain. He is a lawyer at Linklaters Madrid.

Georgina Peters MA (Cantab) (Christ's College) was called to the English Bar in 2005 (Lincoln's Inn) and practises at South Square Chambers, London. She specializes in insolvency/restructuring, banking and finance litigation and company law. Georgina is experienced in complex and high-value restructuring cases, typically with international elements bordering multiple jurisdictions. In the past year, these have included cases concerning both English and US Chapter 11 proceedings (*Hertz, Valaris, Diamond Offshore Drilling*) and BVI proceedings (*Vidatel*). She has also appeared in two recent, high-profile restructuring trials concerning companies with operations in EU and non-EU jurisdictions (*Virgin Active, Caffè Nero*). From 2004 to 2006, Georgina worked as a referendaire at the CJEU, drafting complex legal documents in French, and at JeantetAssocies, Paris, a leading French commercial law firm.

Gerard McCormack is a Professor of International Business Law at the University of Leeds in the UK and a Barrister of Kings Inns Dublin. He has also held visiting appointments in Singapore, Canada, and Europe. He has researched and published extensively particularly in the areas of insolvency and secured credit law and carried out consultancy work on behalf of the European Commission. He is the author or co-author of a number of consultancy reports and legal opinions.

Ian Fletcher LLD KC (Hon) was Emeritus Professor of International Commercial Law and Senior Research Associate at University College London. Previously, he was Professor of Commercial Law at Queen Mary, University of London and Director of the Centre for Commercial Law Studies from 1994 to 2000. A graduate of Cambridge University, he undertook postgraduate studies at Tulane University, USA. He was called to the Bar by Lincoln's Inn in 1971, of which he was elected a Bencher in 2003, and was an Academic Member of South Square Chambers, Gray's Inn. He authored numerous books and articles including *The Law of Insolvency* (1990; 4th edition 2009); and *Insolvency in Private International Law* (OUP, 1999; 2nd edition 2005; Supplement to Second Edition 2007). He was a member of the American Law Institute, the Insolvency Lawyers' Association, INSOL International, and the International Insolvency Institute, and is an International Fellow of the American College of Bankruptcy. He was the editor-in-chief of the INSOL *International Insolvency Review* since 1992, and a specialist editor of *Palmer's Company Law* since 1987.

Lilian Welling-Steffens graduated from the University of Amsterdam in Dutch and Public International Law in 1992. Obtained her PhD in Private International Law (assignment of rights and obligations) from the University of Leiden in 1997. Worked as a lawyer for Loyens & Loeff from 1997 (then still Loeff Claeys Verbeke) through to 2005 in the Banking & Finance practice, focussing on structured finance. Worked as an associate professor in the Private Law Department of the University of Amsterdam from 2004 through to 2007 focussing on private international law and insolvency law. Lived and worked in Malawi from 2007 through to July 2015, as associate professor at the Catholic University of Malawi and the University of Malawi and ran her own legal consultancy from 2011 through to July 2015. Worked as a lawyer in the Banking & Finance group of Loyens & Loeff from September 2015 through to February 2020, when she joined Greenberg Traurig, LLP (Amsterdam) as Of Counsel, setting up the Finance & Restructuring Group and where she is responsible for the professional education and knowledge development within the firm in the Netherlands, focussing on insolvency law, private international law and property law. From 2015 through to 2021 she was an affiliated lecturer with the Department of Private International Law at the University of Leiden and from 2015 through to present she is an affiliated lecturer at the University of Amsterdam for Insolvency Law and Private International Law.

Matthias Haentjens is a full professor of civil law at Leiden Law School and of counsel at De Brauw Blackstone Westbroek. He obtained a Masters degree in Greek and Latin, and his PhD in law at the University of Amsterdam. He was a visiting scholar at Université de Paris II (Panthéon-Assas), Harvard Law School, New York University School of Law, and Ghent University. Professor Haentjens has been a member of the Expert Group on Securities and Claims at the European Commission, of the UNIDROIT Working Group on Bank Insolvency, and a Secretary to the Academic Board of the European Banking Institute.

Rolef de Weijs is Professor of National and International Insolvency Law at University of Amsterdam (Netherlands), visiting Professor at Riga Graduate School of Law (Latvia) and counsel at law firm Houthoff, Amsterdam. He obtained his master degree in Law and in Philosophy at the University in Groningen and an LLM degree from Harvard 2001. He is the chair of the Netherlands Association of Comparative and International Insolvency Law (NACIIL).

Prof Dr **Stephan Madaus** has held his chair at the Martin Luther University Halle-Wittenberg since April 2014, where he was the head of the Law School from 2016 to 2018. He is a Founding Member of the Conference of European Restructuring and Insolvency Law (CERIL) and has been appointed to the European Commission's Expert Group on Restructuring and Insolvency. He was co-chairing the Academic Committee of the International Insolvency Institute from 2018 to 2021. His research interests are in dealing with debt burdens and consequently focus on insolvency and restructuring law, with a special focus on the comparative analysis of relevant regulatory approaches in jurisdictions worldwide as well as in the soft law of international organizations.

Prof em Dr **Christoph G Paulus** was at the Humboldt-Universität zu Berlin/Germany from 1994 to 2019—holding a chair for Civil Law, Civil Procedure Law, Insolvency Law, and ancient Roman Law. He has worked several times as a consultant of both the IMF and the World Bank in Washington DC. Moreover, from 2006 through to 2011, he served as an adviser of the German delegation on the UNCITRAL insolvency law sessions. He has lectured worldwide and has held guest professorships at various universities; additionally, he is member of various international institutions such as the American College of Bankruptcy or the International Insolvency Institute (of which he has been a Vice-President until summer 2017). Since his retirement in spring 2019 he is Associate Member of South Square, London, and since 1 September 2019 Of Counsel with White & Case, Berlin. Currently he is member of the European expert group advising the Commission on its harmonization efforts in insolvency law.

Stuart Isaacs KC returned to private practice at the Bar in 2020, after several years as a disputes partner in a major US law firm in London. He practises at Wilberforce Chambers in the fields of commercial law, international arbitration and corporate and insolvency law. He also maintains his own practice in Singapore, where he was the first KC to be authorized to practise foreign law. His practice covers the range of Commercial Court and contentious Chancery work and he has been involved in many reported commercial and EU law cases, having argued over 20 cases in the CJEU. He regularly acts as an arbitrator and is an accredited mediator and has rights of audience in the UAE and the Singapore International Commercial Court and several Caribbean jurisdictions. He is a Deputy Judge of the High Court. He was educated at Downing College, Cambridge and the Université Libre de Bruxelles.

Tom Smith KC is a King's Counsel, practising at South Square in London. Tom specializes in commercial litigation and arbitration, banking and finance, corporate insolvency and restructuring, and company law including investment funds (hedge funds and private equity). He also practices in the fields of civil fraud and asset recovery, professional negligence and trusts. He has also been involved in many of the major restructuring and insolvency cases in recent years, including significant Supreme Court and Privy Council decisions in the fields of banking, insolvency and restructuring and investment funds. He frequently appears as an advocate both in England and in other jurisdictions including the Cayman Islands, the British Virgin Islands, Dubai, Bermuda, Trinidad and Tobago, and Gibraltar. In addition to the present work, he is also an editor of Company Voluntary Arrangements (OUP) and a contributor to Company Directors (OUP) and Cross-Border Insolvency (Bloomsbury). He practises in the areas of restructuring and insolvency, banking and finance, commercial litigation and civil fraud.

Tomáš Richter graduated from Charles University Law School Prague in 1994, received his LLM from the Central European University in Budapest in 1996, and PhD (2002) from the Masaryk University Law School in Brno. Between 2011 and 2014 he held the *Chair in Cross-Border Corporate Insolvency Law* at the Radboud University Nijmegen Law School. In 2018 he completed habilitation proceedings at the Prague School of Economics. He qualified as Czech advocate in 1998. He practices in Prague with secondments to London (1999) and Frankfurt (2002/2003). He currently serves as the Chair of *INSOL Europe's Academic Forum* and member of the Board of Directors of the International Insolvency Institute. He also serves on the group of private experts with whom the EU Commission consults legislative proposals in the field of insolvency and restructuring.

List of Abbreviations

AC	Appeal Cases (law reports of cases in the House of Lords, UK Supreme Court, and UK Privy Council)
AIF	alternative investment fund
AIFMD	Alternative Investment Fund Managers Directive
BCC	British Company Cases
BCLC	Butterworths Company Law Cases
BPIR	Bankruptcy and Personal Insolvency Reports
BRRD	Bank Recovery and Resolution Directive
CA	Court of Appeal
CCP	Central counterparty
CCPRRR	Regulation (EU) 2021/23 of the European Parliament and of the Council of 16 December 2020 on a framework for the recovery and resolution of central counterparties and amending Regulations
Ch or Ch D	Chancery Division of the High Court of Justice of England and Wales
CJEU	Court of Justice of the European Union
COMI	centre of main interests
Comm	Commercial Court – part of the Queen's Bench Division of the High Court of Justice of England and Wales
CVA	company voluntary arrangement
EBA	European Banking Authority
ECJ	European Court of Justice
EEA	European Economic Area
EU	European Union
EWCA	Court of Appeal of England and Wales
EWHC	High Court of England and Wales
HL	UK House of Lords (now the UK Supreme Court)
ICLQ	International and Comparative Law Quarterly
ILPr	International Litigation Procedure
JBL	Journal of Business Law
JOL	joint official liquidator
LIFFE	London International Financial Futures and Options Exchange
MiFID	Markets in Financial Instruments Directive
NYULR	New York University Law Review
OR	European Union: Council Regulation (EC) 1346/2000 of 29 May 2000 on Insolvency Proceedings (original Insolvency Regulation)
QBD	Queen's Bench Division of the High Court of Justice of England and Wales
RH	Rättsfall från hovrätterna (reports of decisions of Swedish courts of appeal)
ROT	reservation of title
RR	European Union: Regulation (EU) 2015/848 of the European Parliament and of the Council of 20 May 2015 on insolvency proceedings (recast) (recast Insolvency Regulation)

SRM	Single Resolution Mechanism
SRMR	Single Resolution Mechanism Regulation
TFEU	Treaty on the Functioning of the European Union
TIPS	Target Instant Payment Settlement
UCITS	undertakings for collective investment in transferable securities
UKPC	UK Privy Council
UKSC	UK Supreme Court
UNCITRAL	United Nations Commission on International Trade Law
WLR	Weekly Law Reports

1

HISTORICAL OVERVIEW

THE DRAFTING OF THE INSOLVENCY PROCEEDINGS REGULATION AND ITS PRECURSORS

A.	Preliminary	1.01		Insolvency Proceedings Regulation	
B.	History of the Convention Project: Evolution of the Text	1.03		('OR') 2000	1.19
				From Convention to Regulation	1.22
C.	The Phase I Draft Convention (1960–1980): Principal Features	1.08	E.	The OR in Force (31 May 2002)	1.24
				Post-2002 developments	1.24
D.	Phase II: The Convention on Insolvency Proceedings (1995) and its Relationship to the Original		F.	Revision of the OR (2012–2015)	1.26
			G.	The Recast Insolvency Proceedings Regulation 2015 ('RR')	1.28

A. Preliminary

This chapter provides a brief account of the protracted process which resulted in the adoption of the original Council Regulation (EC) 1346/2000.[1] That project had begun as a proposal to conclude a Convention among the EEC Member States to regulate the conduct of insolvency proceedings as between themselves. The need for such arrangements was foreseen at the time of drafting the Foundation Treaty of the EEC and was indeed covered by the terms of a specific provision of that Treaty.[2] Successive attempts to implement that provision, pursued first by the Commission and later by the Council, ultimately ended in failure although at various times it had seemed possible that agreement could be achieved among the states then participating.   **1.01**

The last hope of bringing the project to a successful conclusion appeared to have been extinguished when, in May 1996, a finalized Convention that had been signed by 14 of the 15 members of what had by that time become the EU, failed to come into effect due to the withholding of the signature of the United Kingdom. This had the unfortunate consequence of causing the text, negotiated by and apparently acceptable to all 15 states, to lapse. However,   **1.02**

---

[1] Council Regulation (EC) 1346/2000 of 29 May 2000 on insolvency proceedings [2000] OJ L160/1.
[2] Treaty establishing the European Economic Community, signed in Rome on 25 March 1957, commonly known as the (first) Treaty of Rome. Article 220(4) of that Treaty committed the Member States to negotiating a series of conventions for the benefit of their nationals, including one to secure 'the simplification of formalities governing the reciprocal recognition and enforcement of judgments of courts or tribunals and of arbitral awards'. The logical and legal bases for standardizing the intra-Community treatment of insolvency matters are more fully explored in IF Fletcher, *Conflict of Laws and European Community Law* (1982) chs 1, 2, and 6, esp at 187–90.

in a final demonstration of collective resolve the Council of Ministers, under the consecutive presidencies of Germany and Finland, revived the project in the form of a Regulation, thereby transforming it into a directly applicable legislative act under Community law. In its final iteration, the text was adopted as a Regulation of the EC Council on 29 May 2000. Having been adopted in that form the Regulation automatically entered into force on the appointed day—31 May 2002—in all the 14 Member States which were then participating in the legislative programme promulgated under the provisions of the EC Treaty (Denmark being for this purpose a non-participating state by virtue of its permanent exemption, under the terms of the Maastricht Treaty, from the effects of legislation adopted under Part IV of the European Community (EC) Treaty in its amended form). Subsequent increases in the membership of the European Union have raised the total number of Member States to 27 at the present time (following the United Kingdom's exit from the EU). The augmentations took place, first, in May 2004 (when 10 states simultaneously acceded to membership), second in January 2007 (when the accessions of Bulgaria and Romania took effect), and most recently in July 2013 (with the accession of Croatia). These developments brought about the situation where the OR was applicable in 26 states, with the position of Denmark continuing unchanged in this respect.

The principal phases of the evolution of the EC insolvency project are set out below.

B. History of the Convention Project: Evolution of the Text

1.03 Over the period from 1960 to 1996 the Insolvency Convention project featured on the agenda of the institutions of the EC/EU, particularly the Commission and the Council. During those years, work advanced in various stages of irregular duration, interspersed by periods of almost total quiescence. As the work progressed, the evolving text bore a succession of different titles, as reflected in the following, abbreviated account. The most intense periods of activity may be broadly divided into two principal phases, of which the first can be subdivided into two parts. The first part of Phase I occurred in the years prior to February 1970, when a group of experts drawn from the original six Member States,[3] convened by the European Commission, produced a text published as the Preliminary Draft Convention.[4] Following the accession of the first three additional Member States from 1 January 1973,[5] work was resumed on the basis of the 1970 text, with a view to its being adopted by all nine members. During this second part of Phase I, numerous modifications were made to

---

[3] The original six members of the European Communities (including the Coal and Steel and Atomic Energy Communities, as well as the Economic Community) were Belgium, France, (West) Germany, Italy, Luxembourg, and the Netherlands.

[4] E Comm Doc 3.327/1/XIV/70–F, dated 16 February 1970. An explanatory report, known as the Noel-Lemontey Report, was published as E Comm Doc 16.775/XIV/70–F. English versions of both texts were later published under the same documentary reference numbers, but substituting the suffix-letter 'E' in place of 'F'. The English version of the text of the Preliminary Draft Convention was published as Appendix 10 to the Report of the Bankruptcy Convention Advisory Committee, in August 1976 (Cmnd 6602). The chairman of the Advisory Committee was Kenneth Cork. He, subsequently, as Sir Kenneth Cork, was chairman of the Insolvency Law Review Committee whose report, generally known as the Cork Report, was published in June 1982 (Cmnd 8558). To avoid confusion, the report of the Advisory Committee is sometimes referred to as the Cork Report No 1.

[5] Denmark, the Republic of Ireland, and the United Kingdom together joined the European Communities as of 1 January 1973. Norway, which had also negotiated terms of accession, resiled from taking up membership following a negative outcome of its national referendum held for that purpose.

the original text, partly as a reflection of the general thrust of critical comments published after 1970, and partly in response to particular concerns of the new participants in the negotiations. The essential features of the Preliminary Draft were nevertheless largely carried through into the Draft Convention submitted to the Council in April 1980 for further study and potential adoption.[6] However, sustained resistance on the part of several Member States resulted in the discreet abandonment of further attempts to promote the adoption of the 1980 Draft, although no formal announcement was made of this. Several years of inactivity and uncertainty ensued.

The initiative which resulted in a relaunching of the project was taken by the Council of Ministers which, in May 1989 with the Community's membership already enlarged to 12 and soon destined to grow to 15,[7] established a new working party on the Bankruptcy Convention under the chairmanship of Dr Manfred Balz. Phase II was pursued with much vigour, and was also characterized by a greater openness in that the emerging versions of the text were given a considerable measure of publicity and exposure to informed comment, in marked contrast to the prevailing taste for secrecy which had attended most of the developments during Phase I. One source of inspiration for those engaged upon the task of shaping the Phase II text was the recently concluded Istanbul Convention produced under the auspices of the Council of Europe, and opened for signature on 5 June 1990.[8] In addition to adapting some innovations of the Istanbul text, the working party resurrected certain features of the Phase I concept, while expunging or modifying others in the interests of achieving a more workable, and politically acceptable, Convention in terms of the existing realities among a community of 15 states whose domestic laws exhibited, then as now, numerous differences in matters concerning credit, security, and insolvency.

1.04

During the course of the working party's cycle of activity, the EC officially transformed itself into the EU following the ratification of the Treaty of Maastricht, and a further impetus was imparted to such unifying projects as the Convention on Insolvency Proceedings. At a meeting of the EU Council of Ministers on 25 September 1995 the finalized text of the Convention was tabled for approval and, if possible, immediate adoption. The more cautious—and, in an EU context, somewhat novel—course was taken of an 'initialing' of the text by all 15 Member States, thereby precluding any further negotiation or textual amendment. It was agreed that after a brief interval to allow governments to study this final version the Convention would be opened for signature for a limited period of six months, within

1.05

---

[6] E Comm Doc III/D/72/80. The text of the Draft EEC Convention on Bankruptcy, Winding-up, Arrangements, Compositions, and Similar Proceedings was published in EC Bull Supp 2/82, together with a report by J Lemontey. The text was also published by the Department of Trade in April 1980 and is reproduced as Appendix C in Fletcher (n 2 above). See also [1981] OJ L391/23, for the Commission Opinion on its suitability for adoption.

[7] Greece became the tenth member of the EC in January 1981; Spain and Portugal joined in January 1986. A further three accessions took place in January 1993, when Austria, Finland, and Sweden became members of what had, by that time, become known as the EU, in consequence of the coming into force of the Treaty on European Union (the Maastricht Treaty) of 7 February 1992: [1992] OJ C224/1.

[8] European Convention on Certain International Aspects of Bankruptcy, ETS No 136. This Convention is discussed in IF Fletcher, *Insolvency in Private International Law* (2nd edn, 2005), ch 6. The text of the Istanbul Convention is reproduced in ibid, app III. Having failed to attract the necessary minimum of three ratifications, the Convention has never entered into force.

which it would have to be signed by all the 15 states, as required by Article 220 of the Treaty of Rome, or otherwise lapse.[9]

1.06 This arrangement was carried into effect at a further meeting in Madrid on 23 November 1995, on which date 12 Member States signed the Convention.[10] Within the following months, two of the remaining three Member States—Ireland and the Netherlands—added their signatures. During that period, an approved and revised version of the Explanatory Report to the Convention was put into circulation, thereby overcoming one of the technical obstacles to acceptance of the text of the Convention that had been raised by some members of the Council at the session in September.[11] The state of uncertainty as to whether the UK would become a signatory before the expiry of the six-month time limit on 23 May 1996 was maintained by the terms of a Report of the House of Lords Select Committee on the European Communities dated 26 March 1996.[12] The Committee's concluding opinion and recommendation, while acknowledging the generally favourable views of many of those whose evidence it had received, nevertheless advocated a cautious approach, and the need for further study and consideration, before a final decision should be taken by the Government.[13] This proved to be ominous, and when the deadline for completion of signatures passed on 23 May, the signature of the UK remained outstanding for reasons which only subsequently became fully apparent.[14]

1.07 For some time, as already stated, the EU Insolvency Convention languished in an uncertain limbo. When, in 1999, the project was revived in the form of a Regulation the substantive provisions of the Convention's text were incorporated with only a handful of alterations,

---

[9] Insolvency Convention (1995), Art 49(2), (3) (see also section D below). Community Conventions under Art 220 ECT (as originally numbered) are negotiated by all existing members of the Community (now the EU) as at the time of their adoption, and require the ratification of all members in order to enter into force. Indeed, the Convention of 29 February 1968 on the Mutual Recognition of Companies has never entered into force, for want of the necessary complement of ratifications. Once a Convention is in force, a requirement is imposed upon states which subsequently join the Community/Union to negotiate their accession to it as soon as practicable, as one of the terms of membership. Article 50 of the Insolvency Convention (1995) confirmed this requirement.

[10] The 12 states which signed the EU Convention on the day it was opened for signature (23 November 1995) were: Austria, Belgium, Denmark, Finland, France, Germany, Greece, Italy, Luxembourg, Portugal, Spain, and Sweden. The text of the Convention as opened for signature is reproduced in IF Fletcher, *Insolvency in Private International Law* (1st edn, 1999) app II. See also (1996) 35 International Legal Materials 1223.

[11] The Report on the Convention on Insolvency Proceedings, prepared by Professor M Virgos and Mr E Schmit (hereafter in this book referred to as the 'Virgos-Schmit Report' and reproduced at app 2), was circulated as EU Council Doc 6500/96, DRS 8 (CFC), bearing the date 3 May 1996. It was not officially published, and remains unapproved by the Council, with the consequence that it is technically not of the status of *travaux préparatoires*, either in relation to the Convention itself or to those provisions of Regulation 1346/2000 which are directly derived from the Convention. It is nevertheless a valuable aid to understanding the intended meaning of those provisions. An earlier, English version of the Virgos-Schmit Report, bearing the reference coding 11900/1/95 REV 1, was published as Annexe B to a Consultative Document, *EC Convention on Insolvency Proceedings*, published in February 1996 by the Insolvency Service of the Department of Trade and Industry. The latter version should be regarded as having been superseded by the revised text of 3 May 1996. Many invaluable insights into the Convention's intended effects can be found in M Balz, 'The European Union Convention on Insolvency Proceedings' (1996) 70 American Bankruptcy LJ 485.

[12] *7th Report: Convention on Insolvency Proceedings* (HL Paper (1995–96) 59). The chairman of the Select Committee was Lord Hoffmann.

[13] ibid paras 35–42. The minutes of oral and written evidence supplied to the Select Committee are annexed to the Report, separately paginated (1–52).

[14] Although the pretext for non-signature by the UK in May 1996 was the disagreement between the UK and its EC partners over the agricultural crisis caused by the BSE epidemic, it subsequently transpired that the UK Government had concluded that the Convention's failure to make clear and unambiguous provision for its application to the colony of Gibraltar was an insurmountable obstacle to UK acceptance of the text. Regulation 1346/2000, as an Act of the EC Council, applies to Gibraltar under usual principles of Community law.

other than essential drafting adjustments. For this reason, the evolution of the provisions during the successive phases of the Convention project—but especially during Phase II—is of more than merely historic interest. Indeed, in the absence of any official guide to the interpretation of the Regulation as finally enacted, the process by which the text of the Convention arrived at its concluded state in the autumn of 1995 merits careful study.

C. The Phase I Draft Convention (1960–1980): Principal Features

It might be supposed that, in the light of its subsequent abandonment, the Draft Convention that evolved over the years from 1960 to 1980 is primarily of historic interest. Nevertheless, it is as well that some account of its principal features, and also the reasons for its ultimate failure, should be recorded, partly to provide a better understanding of what was to transpire in Phase II of the project but also in the hope that the same errors will not be repeated in the course of some future project of this kind. A detailed analysis of the text will not be undertaken, however.[15]   **1.08**

The destiny of this first phase was effectively shaped by the circumstances under which the project began its life, during the early years of existence of the EEC itself. This was a period of rapid advance along the path towards European integration, with a Community of manageable size (consisting of the six founding members) being guided by a Commission whose zeal for the task entrusted to it was, for the first and perhaps only time in its history, matched by a generally favourable political climate across the Community.   **1.09**

The committee of experts originally formed in July 1960 to undertake the task of fulfilling the obligations imposed by Article 220 of the Treaty of Rome,[16] took an early decision to regard insolvency and related matters as a special subject requiring separate treatment.   **1.10**

---

[15] For detailed discussion of the Preliminary Draft Convention of 1970, see: J Noel and J Lemontey, 'Aperçus sur le projet de convention européenne relative à la faillite, aux concordats et aux procédures analogues' (1968) 4 Revue Trimestrielle de Droit Européen 703; A Hirsch, 'Vers l'universalité de la faillite au sein du marché commun?' (1970) Cahiers de Droit Européen 50; L Ganshof, 'L'élaboration d'un droit européen de la faillite dans le cadre de la CEE' (1971) Cahiers de Droit Européen 146; M Hunter, 'Draft Bankruptcy Convention of the European Economic Community' (1972) 21 ICLQ 682, and 'Draft EEC Bankruptcy Convention—A Further Examination' (1976) 25 ICLQ 310; KH Nadelmann, 'Common Market Bankruptcy Draft Convention—Foreign Assets and Related Problems' in *Conflict of Laws, International and Interstate* (1972) 340, and in (1970) Riv Dir Int Priv e Proc 501; the same author, 'Rehabilitating International Bankruptcy: Lessons Taught by Herstatt and Company' (1977) 52 NYULR 1, 27–32; K Lipstein, *The Law of the European Economic Community* (1974) 284; WC Hillman, 'An American Lawyer Looks at the Common Market Bankruptcy Convention' (1974) 48 American Bankruptcy LJ 369; J Lemontey, 'Perspectives d'unification du droit dans le projet de convention CEE relative à la faillite' (1975) Revue Trimestrielle de Droit Européen 172; J Noel, 'Lignes directrices du projet de convention CEE relative à la faillite' (1975) Revue Trimestrielle de Droit Européen 159; J Farrar, 'EEC Draft Convention on Bankruptcy and Winding Up' [1977] JBL 320; IF Fletcher, 'The Proposed Community Convention on Bankruptcy and Related Matters' in K Lipstein (ed), *Harmonisation of Private International Law by the EEC* (1978) 119 (also published in (1977) 2 EL Rev 15). From the UK perspective, the Report of the Bankruptcy Convention Advisory Committee (n 4 above) is of enduring value: see esp the 'Note of Reservations' by AE Anton at 105–28. For critical assessments of the 1980 version of the Draft Convention, see J Thieme, 'Der Entwurf eines Konkursübereinkommens der EG-Staaten von 1980' (1981) 45 Rabels Z 459; KH Nadelmann, 'A Reflection on Bankruptcy Jurisdiction: News from the European Economic Market, the United States and Canada' (1982) 27 McGill LJ 541; the same author, 'Bankruptcy Jurisdiction: News from the Common Market and a Reflection for Home Consumption' (1982) 56 American Bankruptcy LJ 65; IF Fletcher, *Conflict of Laws and European Community Law* (1982) ch 6 at 187–249; D Lasok and P Stone, *Conflict of Laws in the European Community* (1987) ch 10 at 397–413.

[16] See n 2 above.

Thereafter, work continued towards the preparation of what was to become the Brussels Convention of 27 September 1968 on Jurisdiction and the Enforcement of Judgments in Civil and Commercial Matters, of which Article 1(2) expressly declares that the Convention shall not apply to: 'bankruptcy, proceedings relating to the winding-up of insolvent companies or other legal persons, judicial arrangements, compositions and analogous proceedings'. A parallel group of experts drawn from the six Member States was therefore convened by the Commission to develop a Bankruptcy Convention which, it was envisaged, would complement the Brussels Convention and thereby accomplish the task of 'simplification of formalities governing the reciprocal recognition and enforcement of judgments' mentioned in the fourth indent of Article 220.

1.11 Although it was accepted that the ultimate shape and content of the Bankruptcy Convention would be determined by the special characteristics of its subject-matter, the fundamental approach followed by the expert negotiators closely matched that of the main, and faster-moving, project relating to civil and commercial judgments. In particular, the innovative approach embodied in the Brussels Convention of superimposing a unitary set of rules of direct jurisdiction in place of the variety of nationally evolved rules previously applied by the individual Member States in relation to matters governed by the Convention, was emulated in the terms of both of the Phase I versions of the Bankruptcy Draft as published in 1970 and in 1980 respectively.[17] Thus, the EEC Convention was conceived as a 'double', or 'direct' Convention, a radical advance upon anything previously attempted in the history of multilateral treaties in the field of bankruptcy.

1.12 Advocates of the use of a 'direct' type of Convention could legitimately emphasize its suitability for use within a community of states pursuing an integrationist programme whose aims included the creation of an internal market based upon the so-called 'four freedoms', namely the free circulation of persons, services, goods, and capital. To attain this goal, it was necessary to address the problem of distortion caused to the commercial and economic environment of the Community by differences in the Member States' legislative and administrative provisions. In this context, both the Brussels Convention and the proposed Bankruptcy Convention could be viewed as having an important role to play in terms of providing for the free circulation of judgments in a way that complements the freedoms expressly established by the Treaty of Rome. By imposing uniform codes of rules for the exercise of jurisdiction in international cases, the Conventions would enable the recognition and enforcement of judgments and orders to become virtually automatic processes, with minimal scope allowed for parties to challenge or resist at the enforcement stage. The Member States, and the courts and officials operating within them, would be obliged to give 'full faith and credit' to the legal determinations of equivalent institutions belonging to sister states.[18]

1.13 By opting for this more audacious and dirigiste model for the Bankruptcy Convention, the negotiators simultaneously assumed a more exacting responsibility in the matter of the technical quality of the Convention's design. Under a 'direct' Convention, all interested parties are compelled to rely almost totally on the integrity of the legal process at the point

---

[17] See 1970 Draft (n 4 above) Title II (Arts 3–17); 1980 Draft (n 6 above) Title II (Arts 3–16).
[18] The rationale behind the programme of legal harmonization of the EEC/EU, including the 'full faith and credit' concept in relation to civil and commercial judgments, is explored in Fletcher (n 2 above) in chs 1, 2, and 4. The application of these arguments to the area of bankruptcy is addressed in ibid, ch 6 at 187–94.

where jurisdiction is first exercised: there is only a limited possibility to rectify any misapplication or misuse of the Convention's provisions, and the expense of doing so can be considerable. Not only must the rules for allocation of jurisdiction be intrinsically sound and sensible, but also they must be well drafted so that their meaning and effects are as clear and unambiguous as possible, in the interests of enabling parties to understand their legal position and arrange their affairs with adequate certainty.

Unfortunately, the jurisdictional provisions of both of the principal Phase I texts failed to match these exacting, but vital, requirements. What was proposed was a three-tier hierarchy of jurisdictional criteria linking the debtor to the territory of the state in which proceedings could be opened. The first rank was accorded to the contracting state in which the debtor's 'centre of administration' (*centre des affaires*) is situated, the courts of that state being declared to have 'exclusive jurisdiction to declare the debtor bankrupt'.[19] The second rank was intended to apply to situations where the debtor's centre of administration is not located in any of the contracting states. In that event, the courts of any contracting state in which the debtor has an establishment are awarded jurisdiction to declare the debtor bankrupt.[20] Third, where neither the centre of administration nor any establishment is situated in a contracting state, an 'open season' is effectively declared by authorizing the courts of any contracting state whose law so permits to declare the debtor bankrupt. However, whereas the 1970 Draft would have allowed such bankruptcies to enjoy the full advantages of recognition and enforcement throughout the Community, the 1980 text was modified so as to exclude such bankruptcies from falling within the scope of the Convention.[21]

1.14

Even in this modified form, however, the proposed jurisdictional scheme was fraught with perils and uncertainties. Thus, as regards the primary criterion based upon the location of the debtor's 'centre of administration', there was scope for divergent approaches to be adopted by the courts of different states when applying the concept to the facts of actual cases. Although each version of the Draft supplied a definition of the expression as meaning 'the place where the debtor usually administers his main interests', this merely raises a whole series of further questions.[22] Similarly, with the secondary tier of jurisdictional competence,

1.15

---

[19] See Art 3(1) of both the 1970 and 1980 versions of the Draft (the wording is identical).
[20] See Art 4(1) of both the 1970 and 1980 versions (the wording is again identical).
[21] See Art 5 in the respective versions of 1970 and 1980. It may be observed that the earlier text was apparently intended to duplicate the effect of Art 4 of the Brussels Convention of 27 September 1968 (in force from 1 February 1973). The Convention of 1968 was superseded, except as regards Denmark, as from 1 May 2004 by Council Regulation (EC) 44/2001—the Brussels Regulation. That Regulation in turn was superseded and repealed by Regulation (EU) 2015/2012 of 12 December 2012, OJ L351/1, 20 December 2012, which became applicable from 10 January 2015. In both the Brussels Convention and the successive versions of the Brussels Regulation, Art 4 controversially allows the courts of contracting (or Member) states to deploy their full repertoire of domestic rules of jurisdiction—including those of an exorbitant nature—against those defendants in civil or commercial proceedings who happen not to be domiciled in any of the contracting/Member states. Judgments in such cases are nevertheless accorded the benefit of full faith and credit throughout the EC/EU territorial area. For trenchant criticism of this aspect of the original Brussels Convention see eg KH Nadelmann, 'Jurisdictionally Improper Fora in Treaties on Recognition of Judgments: The Common Market Draft' (1967) 67 Columbia L 995; 'The Outer World and the Common Market Experts' Draft of a Convention on Recognition of Judgments' (1967–68) 5 CML Rev 409; and 'The Common Market Judgments Convention and a Hague Conference Recommendation: What Steps Next?' (1968) 82 Harvard L Rev 1282; P Hay, 'The Common Market Preliminary Draft Convention on the Recognition and Enforcement of Judgments: Some Considerations of Policy and Interpretation' (1968) 16 AJCL 149, esp at 160–2.
[22] See Art 3(2) of the 1970 Draft; cf Art 3(2) and (3) of the 1980 Draft. Although both versions embody a rebuttable presumption, in the case of firms, companies, and legal persons, that the registered office is the place

based upon the presence of an establishment, the Draft failed to meet the requirement that it should embody sensible principles, and above all that it should respect the need for certainty. The 1970 Draft did not contain any definition of 'establishment', while the 1980 text merely offered the inadequate pronouncement that 'an establishment exists in a place where an activity of the debtor comprising a series of transactions is carried on by him or on his behalf'.[23] Given that this could result in the courts of several contracting states having concurrent jurisdiction, the sensitive issue of priority demands a carefully designed rule to promote the fairest and most efficient solution, rather than one which rewards pre-emptive tactics on a 'winner takes all' basis. Sadly, the Phase I Drafts promised no such outcome. Instead of a qualitative test to determine the most appropriate forum, purely mechanical rules were proposed which would have awarded Community-wide supremacy to the proceedings which were chronologically the first to open.[24] Worse yet—and surely the height of absurdity as a rule for adoption by a Community of supposedly sophisticated states—was the 'tie-breaking' provision for cases where proceedings were commenced on the same day in different courts having co-ordinate jurisdiction: it was solemnly proposed that precedence should be determined by the alphabetical order of the place names of the courts concerned![25]

1.16 The shortcomings of the jurisdictional rules of the Phase I Drafts were compounded by the unsuccessful attempt to simulate the embodiment of the twin principles of unity and universality of bankruptcy, and to misrepresent the degree to which they had genuinely been absorbed into the substance of the provisions to which the contracting states would be committing themselves.[26] If the proclamations within the texts themselves were taken at face value, proceedings opened according to the primary or secondary rules of jurisdiction would constitute the sole proceedings permitted to take place throughout the contracting states, and would have automatic effect in relation to the debtor's property anywhere within those states. By virtue of the choice of law rules within the Draft Convention, whose effect is generally to require the application of the law of the state in which proceedings are opened (the *lex concursus*) for most purposes associated with the proceedings and the administration and distribution of the estate,[27] it ought to follow that the rights of all creditors—secured or unsecured; preferential or non-preferential—would be determined by the provisions of the *lex concursus*. In reality, the negotiators arranged matters somewhat differently, so that the rights of

---

where the debtor's main interests are usually administered, the manner of rebutting this presumption, and the degree of proof needed, are left uncertain. Given the scope for different views regarding what amount to a debtor's 'main' interests, the potential instability of this basis of jurisdiction was disturbing. See also the various approaches offered by Arts 6 and 7 of the 1970 and 1980 Drafts respectively for cases where there has been a transfer of the centre of administration.

[23] See Art 4(2) of the 1980 Draft.
[24] See Arts 15(2) and 52(1) of the 1970 Draft; Arts 13(2) and 58(1) of the 1980 Draft.
[25] See Art 52(2) of the 1970 Draft; Art 58(2) of the 1980 Draft.
[26] See Art 2 (both Drafts), which bears the heading: *Unity of the Bankruptcy*, and Art 33 of the 1970 Draft and Art 34 of the 1980 Draft, both headed *Universality of the Bankruptcy*. For discussion of the two principles of unity and universality, see Fletcher (n 8 above) ch 1 esp at paras 1.11–1.13.
[27] See Arts 17, 18, 19, 20–22, 28, 30, and 32 of the 1970 Draft; Arts 15, 17, 18, 20–22, 29, 31, and 33 of the 1980 Draft.

secured and preferential creditors belonging to any of the contracting states could continue to be governed by the law of the *situs* of any secured property, and by the local law of the state under which a creditor's preferential status, and its relative ranking, was generated.[28] The negotiators had discovered at an early stage of their deliberations that the existing domestic laws of the original six Member States of the EEC differed from one another so fundamentally in such matters as their treatment of security, and the rights of preferential creditors, that it was impractical to attempt an alignment and harmonization of substantive laws for the foreseeable future.[29] However, the very same reasons which made it politically unacceptable for the Member States to abandon deeply embedded national traditions towards the treatment of these issues, made it equally unthinkable for any of them to accept the subordination of the rights and expectations of its own, local creditors to the regime of the *lex concursus*, where this happened to be that of some other state.

1.17 The theoretically elegant precepts of the scheme based upon unity and universality therefore yielded to the political imperatives of the shared desire on the part of the participating states to defend local practices in matters of the preferential treatment of certain types of claim in the process of distribution in an insolvency. This was achieved by means of an inelegant, and cumbersome, arrangement whereby the existence and ranking of preferential rights would be determined by the law of each contracting state under which a creditor was eligible to invoke such personal advantage, but only with respect to such assets as were actually situated in that state on the day when the bankruptcy opened.[30] This would have entailed the creation of a series of sub-estates, for accounting purposes, formed from each pool of assets realized in each of the states concerned. The sheer complexity of the exercise was truly horrifying, and would have resulted in much wasteful expenditure of administrative resources.

1.18 Even less palatable, however, was the cynical proposal for the manner of dealing with any assets recovered in non-contracting states, and with the claims of creditors from outside the frontiers of the European Community. Here, and here alone, the full rigours of the principles of unity and universality were to be applied, so that assets recovered from third states were to be amalgamated with those located in the *forum concursus* itself, and were likewise to be distributed in accordance with the rules contained in the *lex concursus*. It is surely distasteful, and also embarrassing, to have to acknowledge that such blatantly discriminatory treatment was considered by the authors of the successive versions of the Phase I Draft Convention to be an acceptable approach to the regulation of international insolvency, and was intended to be collectively embraced by an alliance of powerful, but not omnipotent, economically advanced states. Yet such was indeed the case, as the documentary evidence reveals. Fortunately, in the years after 1980, the tide of opposition to this fatally flawed, meretricious, and unworkable Draft gradually grew stronger, and it was consigned to oblivion.

---

[28] See Section VI of each of the two Drafts: Arts 40–46 of the 1970 Draft; Arts 43–52 of the 1980 Draft.
[29] See a comparative survey by Professor M Sauveplanne, published in October 1963 as EEC Commission Doc 8838/IV/63–E.
[30] See Arts 40–46 of the 1970 Draft; Arts 42–52 of the 1980 Draft.

D. Phase II: The Convention on Insolvency Proceedings (1995) and its Relationship to the Original Insolvency Proceedings Regulation ('OR') 2000

1.19 As mentioned in section B above, the committee of experts convened by the Council in 1989 to relaunch the project for a Bankruptcy Convention[31] adopted an eclectic approach in going about its task. Drawing together the more satisfactory elements from the two models closest to hand—the Phase I Draft EC Convention and the Istanbul Convention which was opened for signature on 5 June 1990—the committee sought to combine these with fresh elements of its own devising. It also appears to have been guided by a strong instinct to provide a workable set of rules that respond to issues actually encountered in practice, rather than to pursue some impossible and almost abstract theory about the way in which to legislate for the problems of international insolvency. The finished text produced by the Balz committee is one which, while by no means devoid of imperfections, has many positive virtues which under normal circumstances would have ensured its implementation by all members of the EU. Fortunately, despite the unfortunate further setback experienced between 1995 and 1999,[32] the product of the committee's labour was retrieved from limbo and the Convention's substantive provisions were implanted into the text of Regulation 1346/2000. Those provisions will be examined in detail in the subsequent chapters of this work. This account of the history of the project will conclude with a summary of the structure and main features of the Convention as agreed and initialled by all the Member States in November 1995, followed by a brief chronicle of events subsequent to the entry into force of the Regulation itself.

1.20 The finalized text of the Convention consisted of a total of 55 Articles, arranged into 6 chapters of varying length, together with 3 Annexes. It was self-evidently the product of an assessment on the part of the committee that there were minimal prospects in the foreseeable future of achieving any fundamental harmonization of the domestic laws of the 15 EU Member States in relation to credit, security, or insolvency matters. That being the case, the most important requirement in the context of the EU internal market was to establish clear rules to determine in which states insolvency proceedings are capable of being commenced, and what choice of law rules are to be applied in those proceedings in relation to the crucial issues typically to be encountered in a cross-border case. In that way, parties can arrange their affairs, and structure their business transactions, on the basis of reasonably dependable predictions concerning the substantive law by which their rights will be governed. The Convention therefore adopted the same strategic approach as the Phase I models, in that it was a 'direct' or 'double' Convention whose effect was to impose a uniform set of jurisdictional rules which must be applied in all the contracting states in cases falling within the ambit of its provisions.[33]

---

[31] Throughout this section the expression 'the Convention' denotes the European Union Convention on Insolvency Proceedings, opened for signature in Madrid on 23 November 1995 and signed by 14 of the 15 Member States (the exception being the United Kingdom) between that date and 23 May 1996, when the period permitted for signature expired (see paras 1.02 and 1.05–1.06 above).

[32] See paras 1.02 and 1.04–1.07 above.

[33] See Art 3 of the Convention, further discussed at paras 3.09 et seq below. This contrasts with the Istanbul Convention (n 8 above), which is an 'indirect' Convention containing rules for recognition and enforcement only.

D. PHASE II: CONVENTION ON INSOLVENCY PROCEEDINGS

Having laid the ground rules for jurisdiction and choice of law,[34] the Convention addressed the practical concerns of the office-holder who is responsible for administering the insolvency proceedings (referred to throughout as 'the liquidator'),[35] by provisions for recognition of the proceedings and for enabling the exercise of the liquidator's powers in other contracting states.[36] The concerns of creditors involved in a multi-jurisdictional insolvency were also taken into account in various ways, including simplification of the procedure for proving their claims.[37] The special facility under Chapter III to enable secondary proceedings to be opened, with effects restricted to the territory of a single contracting state, offered important advantages for certain types of creditors.[38] Lastly, to ensure that the Convention received a unified interpretation from the outset, provision was made in Chapter V for the ECJ to have jurisdiction to deliver interpretative rulings concerning the Convention and its various Annexes.[39]

1.21

From Convention to Regulation

In the transformation from Convention to Regulation, Chapters I to IV inclusive, comprising Articles 1 to 42, were directly transposed (with only two specific, albeit significant, exceptions),[40] but with drafting adaptations throughout the text to reflect the altered nature of the legal instrument itself.[41] As an EC legislative act, the OR did not need to contain any express provisions relating to its interpretation by the ECJ and therefore the whole of Chapter V of the Convention was discarded. The concluding chapter of the text, 'Transitional and Final Provisions' (numbered as Chapter VI in the Convention and there comprising Articles 47 to 55) reappears as Chapter V of the OR (comprising Articles 43 to 47). Several of the former provisions were only relevant to an instrument in the form of a Convention, and were accordingly omitted from Chapter V of the OR. The three Annexes, labelled as A, B, and C, were retained intact in the OR, save for the omission of references to Denmark and its legal institutions, and with some rephrasing of the listings of national procedures, reflecting developments during the interval between 1995 and 2000.[42]

1.22

---

[34] Choice of law rules are contained in Arts 4–15 inclusive, and are discussed in ch 4 below.
[35] Art 2(b) of the Convention.
[36] See Ch II of the Convention (Arts 16–26 inclusive).
[37] Ch IV of the Convention (Arts 39–42 inclusive).
[38] See Arts 27–38 inclusive.
[39] See Arts 43–46 inclusive.
[40] Art 5 was amended by inserting additional wording to indicate that the expression 'rights in rem' includes security effected in relation to 'both specific assets and collections of indefinite assets as a whole which change from time to time'. This amendment, proposed by the UK, was intended to ensure that the provisions in Art 5 are applicable to floating charges and to such security devices as fixed charges granted over receivables. The wording of Art 42 was amended at the request of Belgium, to accommodate the fact that the state has two official languages. The amendment makes it clear that a creditor is only required to provide a translation of his claim into one of the official languages of such a state.
[41] In addition to the replacement of references to 'this Convention' with 'this Regulation', references to 'the contracting states' (etc) throughout the text are replaced with references to 'the Member States' (etc).
[42] In the case of Austria, in comparison to the Convention, one procedure was eliminated from the entry in Annexe A, relating to insolvency proceedings referred to in Art 2(a) of the OR. In the cases of Belgium, the Netherlands, and Sweden, an additional procedure was included in each state's listing in Annexe A of the OR. In the case of the UK, the entry in Annexe A of the OR no longer makes express mention of the administration of the insolvent estate of a deceased person in England and Wales or in Northern Ireland (or its Scottish equivalent—Administration by a Judicial Factor), but the omission was apparently effected on the basis that such proceedings are included within the references to 'Bankruptcy' (England and Wales, Northern Ireland) and 'Sequestration' (Scotland). On the other hand, the UK entry in Annexe A of the OR expressly refers to 'Winding up ... subject to

1.23 There is one conspicuous contrast between the Convention and the OR which requires special comment. This concerns the elaborate series of numbered 'Recitals' (33 in all) which are placed at the beginning of the text of the OR. By contrast, the substantive Articles of the Convention of 1995 were preceded by a short Preamble, containing four unnumbered and somewhat routine paragraphs declaring the motivation and purposes which were to have supplied the basis for the Convention. The purpose of the extended sequence of Recitals to the OR is to furnish assistance in its interpretation by national courts, and by the ECJ. Having apparently determined that it was contrary to settled practice to generate an officially sanctioned 'Explanatory Report' to a Community Act in the form of a Regulation, the EC Council perceived that it was nevertheless desirable to furnish some aids to construction and application of its substantive provisions. This was achieved by extracting a number of propositions from the Virgos-Schmit Report[43] and placing them alongside freshly composed material, so as to provide explanatory statements about certain aspects of the OR and its underlying objectives. This has resulted in a somewhat uneven and selective set of guiding statements, which can be employed in the familiar process of 'purposive' interpretation of Community legal instruments.[44] Numerous issues will doubtless arise in practice for which the Recitals offer no clear guidance, thus leaving the Court to formulate its solution in accordance with what it perceives to be the most constructive way of attaining the overall goals mentioned in the Recitals.

E. The OR in Force (31 May 2002)

Post-2002 developments

1.24 Since the OR entered into force on 31 May 2002 there have been several developments necessitating amendments to the original text. Some of these amendments have been effected on the initiative of one or more of the participating Member States in order to ensure that the provisions of the OR are aligned with the current provisions and terminology utilized in the insolvency laws of the Member States concerned. Internal revisions to domestic insolvency procedures may necessitate amendments to the entries listed in Annexes A, B, or C of the OR under the name of that state. Such amendments can be made using the procedure specifically established by Article 45 for amending the Annexes by qualified majority vote of the Council. That procedure was used for the first time on 12 April 2005.[45] Further

---

the supervision of the court', which is a procedure still available under the law of Gibraltar, although it was abolished within the UK by the legislative reforms of 1985–86.

[43] See n 11 above.
[44] Issues of interpretation of the Regulation are discussed in ch 2 below.
[45] Council Regulation (EC) 603/2005 [2005] OJ L100/1 effective from 21 April 2005. Among the amendments made were changes to the entries for the UK in Annexes A and B (where the words 'including appointments made by filing prescribed documents with the court' were inserted in the references to administration, so as to reflect the amendments to the administration procedure made by the Enterprise Act 2002), and also to Annex C (where the office of provisional liquidator was added to the list of office holders fulfilling the definition of 'liquidator' for the purposes of Art 2(b)). The latter addition appears to have been prompted by the example of the proceedings before the Irish courts, and ultimately the ECJ, during 2004 in *Re Eurofood IFSC Ltd* [2004] BCC 383 (Irish High Court), in which the significance of the inclusion of the office of provisional liquidator in the equivalent entry for Ireland in Annex C became strongly apparent. This point was also a material factor in the subsequent ruling by the ECJ in its judgment dated 2 May 2006 in which the expression 'decision to open insolvency proceedings' for the purposes of Art 16(1) of the OR was construed as including a decision involving 'divestment of the debtor and the appointment

instances of use of the amending procedure under Article 45 occurred on 27 April 2006,[46] on 13 June 2007,[47] 24 July 2008,[48] 25 February 2010,[49] 9 June 2011,[50] and 5 June 2014.[51] On each occasion since 2006 the convenient practice has been adopted of replacing the entire texts of all three Annexes so as to provide a consolidated version of the text of each one, as in force from the date on which the amending Regulation took effect. As future amendments may be made to the Annexes using the same procedure, care should be taken to consult the most recent version of the text.

Separately from the above amendments made using the in-built procedure of Article 45, the OR underwent additional amendments in consequence of the successive enlargements to the membership of the EU that took effect in 2004, 2007, and 2013 respectively.[52] In each instance, under the terms of the relevant Treaty and Act of Accession the newly joining Member States became fully subject to all existing provisions of Community legislation (the so-called *acquis communautaire*), including the OR. Accordingly, special provisions were made in or pursuant to the Acts of Accession in each instance to amend the OR so that Annexes A, B, and C would include references to the relevant types of insolvency and winding-up proceedings, and also to the relevant types of office-holders under those proceedings, for each new Member State as of the date of entry.[53] The amending provisions also imported additional paragraphs into Article 44(1) of the OR to incorporate references to existing conventions to which any of the new Member States was a party, and whose effects were replaced by those of the OR in respect of proceedings opened after its entry into force for the state in question.

1.25

F. Revision of the OR (2012–2015)

The need for a systematic review and revision of the Regulation was foreseen by its Article 46, which imposes a duty on the Commission to initiate a process whereby reports on

1.26

---

of a liquidator referred to in Annex C to the Regulation': Case C-341/04 *Re Eurofood IFSC Ltd* [2006] ECR I-3813, at para 54 of the judgment.

[46] Council Regulation (EC) 694/2006 [2006] OJ L121/1 effective from 7 May 2006.
[47] Council Regulation (EC) 681/2007 [2007] OJ L159/1 effective from 21 June 2007.
[48] Council Regulation (EC) 788/2008 [2008] OJ L213/1 effective from 9 August 2008.
[49] Implementing Regulation of the Council (EU) 210/2010 [2010] OJ L65/1 effective from 2 April 2010.
[50] Council Implementing Regulation (EU) 583/2011 [2011] OJ L160/52 effective from 8 July 2011.
[51] Council Implementing Regulation (EU) 663/2014, [2014] OJ L179/4 effective from 9 July 2014. This text has been incorporated into the text of the OR as reproduced in app 1.
[52] See para 1.02 above.
[53] (a) The following ten states joined the EU with effect from 1 May 2004: Cyprus; Czech Republic; Estonia; Hungary; Latvia; Lithuania; Malta; Poland; Slovakia; and Slovenia. In the Treaty and Act of Accession signed in Athens on 16 April 2003, amendments to Regulation 1346/2000 are made by s 18A of Annex 2 to the Act of Accession, under the heading 'Cooperation in the fields of justice and home affairs': [2003] OJ L236/711–13. (b) Bulgaria and Romania joined the EU with effect from 1 January 2007. In the Treaty and Act of Accession signed in Luxembourg on 25 April 2005 provision was made in Art 56 of the Act of Accession for the amendment of a large number of elements of EC legislation, including the OR, by means of further Regulations. This was accomplished through Council Regulation (EC) 1791/2006 [2006] OJ L363/1, Annex 11A ('Judicial Cooperation in Civil and Commercial Matters'). Amendments were made to Art 44(1) of the OR, and to Annexes A, B, and C thereto, with effect from 1 January 2007 (Art 2). (c) Croatia joined the EU with effect from 1 July 2013: Treaty and Act of Accession of the Republic of Croatia, Brussels 7 November 2011, Art 3(3). Consequential amendments to Annexes A, B, and C of the OR were made by Council Regulation (EU) 517/2013 of 13 May 2013, Art 1(1)(k) together with Section 13.A.1 of the Annex thereto.

the application of the OR are to be presented to the European Parliament, Council, and Economic and Social Committee, 'accompanied if need be by a proposal for adaptation of the Regulation'. The first such report was required to be presented 'no later than 1 June 2012, and every five years thereafter'. In preparation for the drawing up of the first report, preliminary consultations and specially commissioned studies were commenced by the Commission in 2011. These were given added impetus by an initiative of the European Parliament resulting in the publication in June 2011 of a Report on insolvency proceedings in the context of EU company law together with recommendations to the Commission.[54] On 12 December 2012 the Commission unveiled its formal response to the duty imposed under Article 46 by publishing a proposal for a Regulation amending the OR,[55] to which the Parliament responded on 20 December 2013 with a Report containing numerous proposed amendments to the Commission's earlier text.[56] The Parliament voted on 5 February 2014 to adopt its own Legal Affairs Committee's proposed amendments to the Commission's proposals.[57] A process of inter-institutional negotiations then ensued, involving the Parliament, the Council, and the Commission, resulting in a declaration by the Council following its meeting on 5 and 6 June 2014 that agreement had been reached on a 'general approach on the proposal for a regulation amending the existing Council Regulation (1346/2000) on insolvency proceedings'.[58]

1.27 An important milestone was attained on 4 December 2014, when the Council of Justice Ministers adopted a political agreement on the renewed text of the OR as agreed with the European Parliament.[59] In preparation for the formal adoption of the Regulation a further series of steps took place. First, translations into all the Member States' official languages had to be made, with only technical/linguistic changes to be permitted (ie no changes of substance). The Council then formally adopted this text on 12 March 2015 as its 'first reading position' with a view to its being adopted in turn by the European Parliament (both at committee and plenary level).[60] The process was taken forward at meetings of the Parliament's

---

[54] European Parliament, Committee on Legal Affairs, Report with Recommendations to the Commission on Insolvency Proceedings in the Context of EU Company Law ('the Lehne Report'), with Motion for a Resolution of the Parliament (6 June 2011, 2011/2006 INI, PE467.008v02-00). In the motion the Parliament confirms 'that the recommendations respect the principle of subsidiarity and the fundamental rights of citizens'. For all related documents, see <http://www.europarl.europa.eu/sides/getDoc.do?type=REPORT&reference=A7-2011-0355&format=XML&language=EN> (accessed 17 December 2015). See also the Report published by INSOL Europe in May 2012, *Revision of the European Insolvency Regulation, Proposals by INSOL Europe* (Drafting Committee Chairman, Robert van Galen).

[55] European Commission, Proposal for a Regulation of the European Parliament and of the Council amending Council Regulation (EC) No 1346/2000 on Insolvency Proceedings, Strasbourg 12 December 2012, COM(2012) 744 final, 2012/0360 (COD).

[56] Report by the European Parliament's Committee of Legal Affairs on the Commission's Proposal for a Regulation amending Council Regulation 1346/2000, reference PE 519.449v02-00; RR\1014200EN.doc, An earlier, Draft Report, was published on 11 September 2013: PE 519.445v01-00.

[57] Legislative resolution adopted by the Parliament as text P7_TA(2014) 0093. See the Europa website at <http://www.europarl.europa.eu/sides/getDoc.do?pubRef=-//EP//TEXT+TA+P7-TA-2014-0093+0+DOC+XML+V0//EN&language=EN> (accessed 17 December 2015).

[58] Press release of the Council of the EU (Provisional Version) 10578/14 (OR.en), PRESSE 328; PRCO 31, on the 3319th Council Meeting—Justice and Home Affairs, Luxembourg, 5 and 6 June 2014, p 3.

[59] The document which formed the basis of the Council's decision at its meeting on 4 December 2014 bears the date Brussels, 20 November 2014, and the reference information Interinstitutional File: 2012/0360/COD; 15414/14, ADD 1; JUSTCIV 285, EJUSTICE 109, CODEC 2225. The document can be viewed at <http://register.consilium.europa.eu/doc/srv?l=EN&f=ST%2015414%202014%20ADD%201> (accessed 17 December 2015).

[60] The text of the recast Insolvency Regulation as approved by the Council at first reading on 12 March 2015 is published in the EU Official Journal, C series as Position (EU) No 7/2015 of the Council, OJ C141/1, 28 April 2015.

Legal Affairs Committee, and subsequently at a plenary session of the Parliament itself, on 7 and 20 May 2015 respectively.[61] Both meetings endorsed a proposal that the 'first reading position' of the Council should be adopted, thereby obviating the need for the Council to undertake a second reading and enabling the process of adoption of the revised Regulation to be concluded by the formal act of signing by the respective Presidents of the Parliament and of the Council, which duly took place on the same day, namely 20 May 2015. The recast Regulation was subsequently published in the Official Journal 'L' series on 5 June 2015 as Regulation (EU) 2015/848 and, in accordance with Article 92, entered into force 20 days afterwards on 26 June 2015.[62] However, it was provided in Article 92 that the RR would only enter into *application* 24 months after its entry into force. Thus the RR only began to apply to insolvency proceedings opened after 26 June 2017.[63] On that date, the OR was repealed in its entirety and ceased to have effect. In the meanwhile, it continued in force and was applicable to insolvency proceedings which fell within its scope and which had been opened before 26 June 2017.[64]

G. The Recast Insolvency Proceedings Regulation 2015 ('RR')

The RR represents an evolutionary development, based on the foundations of the OR which it fully replaced with effect from 26 June 2017. While the core principles on which the OR was based have been maintained, the opportunity was taken to adjust and refine their application, and important additional content added. The net effect is to lengthen the text by a considerable amount: the RR comprises 89 initial Recitals (in place of the original 33) and 92 Articles (in place of the original 47). The three Annexes, A, B, and C, which completed the OR have been reduced to two—now lettered as A and B—but this reduction is compensated for by the inclusion of two new Annexes, lettered as C and D, which provide useful information. Annex C lists the official citations of the OR and all successive amendments to it, all of which were repealed as from the effective date of the RR. Annex D supplies a correlation table to enable comparisons to be made with provisions of the OR, where these are recycled in the RR, as well as indicating those provisions which are completely new. While the provisions of the OR continued to apply to cases commenced prior to 26 June 2015, the provisions of the RR which became applicable automatically on and after that date had to begin to be taken into account in anticipating the potential consequences of an insolvency capable of occurring at a time when the RR became applicable. Where there is no relevant distinction to be made between the OR and RR, this book refers to both as 'the Insolvency Proceedings Regulation'.

1.28

---

[61] European Parliament legislative resolution of 20 May 2015 on the Council position at first reading with a view to the adoption of a regulation of the European Parliament and of the Council on insolvency proceedings (recast) (16636/5/2014—C8-0090/2015—2012/0360 (COD)) (Ordinary legislative procedure: second reading), viewable on the Europa website at <http://www.europarl.europa.eu/sides/getDoc.do?pubRef=-//EP//TEXT+TA+P8-TA-2015-0203+0+DOC+XML+V0//EN&language=EN> (accessed 17 December 2015).
[62] Regulation (EU) 2015/848 of the European Parliament and of the Council of 20 May 2015 on Insolvency Proceedings (recast), OJ L141/19, 5 June 2015, viewable at: <http://eur-lex.europa.eu/legal-content/EN/TXT/?uri=uriserv:OJ.L_.2015.141.01.0019.01.ENG> (accessed 17 December 2015).
[63] Art 84(1) of the RR.
[64] Arts 84(2) and 91 of the RR.

2

THE INSOLVENCY PROCEEDINGS REGULATION AS AN EU LEGAL INSTRUMENT

A. Introduction	2.01	
B. Legal Attributes	2.06	
'Direct applicability'	2.10	
'Direct effect'	2.17	
C. Meaning	2.19	
Interpretation and the European Union legal order	2.20	
Interpretation and the multilingual legal order	2.24	
D. Solving Interpretative Issues and Questions of Validity: The Court of Justice of the European Union	2.30	
Jurisdiction	2.32	
Criteria for references	2.34	
Procedure	2.41	

A. Introduction

2.01 The Insolvency Proceedings Regulation is a European Union legal instrument. More particularly, it is a form of EU subordinate legislation made under the Treaty on the Functioning of the European Union ('TFEU').[1] As such, its meaning and effects in national law are matters of EU law. This is because of the doctrine of the supremacy of EU law over national law.[2] In particular, in ascribing meaning, or giving effect, to an EU legal instrument, a Member State court must do so in accordance with the principles laid down by the CJEU.[3] The doctrine of supremacy also applied in UK courts[4] until the UK left the European Union at 11pm GMT on 31 January 2020 and ceased to be a Member State.[5] Since 1 January 2021, UK courts are no longer bound to the doctrine of the supremacy of EU law over national law. However, the interpretation of EU law in general and the Insolvency Proceedings Regulation in particular by the CJEU remains relevant as potential guidance for the UK courts. Accordingly,

---

[1] Following the coming into force of the Lisbon Treaty on 1 December 2009, the EC Treaty was amended, re-ordered, re-numbered, and re-named the Treaty on the Functioning of the European Union. The EU also replaced the European Community. There are three principal forms of legislation: Regulations, Directives, and Decisions. See Art 288 TFEU. In addition, the EU's institutions are able to adopt recommendations and opinions.

[2] See, generally, as a matter of EU law, Case 6/64 *Costa v ENEL* [1964] ECR 585.

[3] Since the coming into force of the Lisbon Treaty and the re-naming of the Court of First Instance as the General Court, the Court of Justice of the European Union is now referred to as 'CJEU', and the acronym ECJ often (but not always) used as a collective term for the CJEU, the General Court, and the Civil Service Tribunal.

[4] See s 3 of the European Communities Act 1972 and *HP Bulmer v Bollinger* [1974] Ch 401, 425 per Lord Denning MR.

[5] See further para 9.01 below.

the purpose of this chapter is to set out the particular legal attributes which the Insolvency Proceedings Regulation has as an EU measure and to describe the way in which it is to be understood as a matter of EU law. It also sets out the legal mechanisms established by the EU whereby solutions to questions of validity and interpretation may be obtained.

The OR itself was adopted under what were then Articles 61(c) and 67(1) of the ECT,[6] on the initiatives of Germany and Finland. Articles 61(c) and 67(1) themselves formed part of Title IV of what was then the EC Treaty.[7] This Title was concerned with the progressive establishment of 'an area of freedom, security and justice'. On 20 May 2015, the European Parliament and Council adopted the Insolvency Proceedings Regulation, this time under Article 81 TFEU (ex Article 65 EC) and in accordance with the ordinary legislative procedure laid down by Article 294 TFEU.[8] The term 'recast' is an EU legislative term of art: it refers to the adoption of a new legal act which incorporates in a single text both the substantive amendments made to an earlier act and the unchanged provisions of that act, which is repealed.[9]

2.02

That the OR was adopted under Articles 61(c) and 67(1), and their subsequent amendment and repeal by the Treaty of Lisbon, is not merely of background interest. It both governs the legal effect and affects the meaning and interpretation of the OR. This is also true, *mutatis mutandis*, of the RR and Article 81 TFEU.

2.03

The TFEU provisions, on the basis of which the Insolvency Proceedings Regulation was adopted, govern its legal effect in a number of ways. First, they provide the legal basis for its adoption by the EU. In the absence of a proper legal basis as provided by the Treaty, the measure would have been invalid. This is because the EU does not have any general competence to legislate, but only particular competences as provided by the governing treaties.[10] Second, by a combination of Article 69 EC[11] and Article 2 of the Protocol on the position of the UK and Ireland (Protocol 21) annexed to the ECT (and now to the TFEU), measures adopted under Article 61(c) EC (and now Article 81 TFEU) did not apply to the United Kingdom or Ireland unless these Member States, in accordance with Articles 3 and 4 of the Protocol, either notify the President of the Council that they wish to participate in its adoption or that they wish to accept the measure. The Insolvency Proceedings Regulation was binding on the UK by reason of the fact that the UK notified its intention to take part in its adoption.[12] Third, neither Article 61(c) nor Article 67(1) EC (nor Article 81 TFEU)

2.04

---

[6] See the preamble to the OR. However, the Lisbon Treaty substituted a new Art 67 for ex Art 61 EC and repealed ex Art 67 EC, creating a new Title IV with the heading 'Area of Freedom, Security and Justice'. New Title IV includes a new Chapter 3, concerning 'Judicial Cooperation in Civil Matters' and it was under this chapter that the Insolvency Proceedings Regulation was adopted.
[7] As explained above, old Title IV has now been abolished.
[8] This was on the initiative of the Commission in the ordinary way.
[9] This is further set out and explained in an inter-institutional agreement between the European Parliament, the Council, and the Commission dated 28 November 2001 and published in [2002] OJ C77 of 28 March 2002.
[10] Title I of Part 1 of the TFEU (Arts 2 to 6) now sets out the categories and areas of competence of the EU. This conferral of powers is generally known as 'the principle of the attribution of powers'.
[11] Now repealed by the Treaty of Lisbon.
[12] Recital (32) OR; see now Recital (87) RR. Ireland gave a similar notification. The Insolvency Proceedings Regulation does not, however, apply to Denmark by reason of Arts 1 and 2 of the Protocol on the position of Denmark as annexed to the EC Treaty, now TFEU. See Recital (33) OR (Recital (88) RR). Furthermore, the Insolvency Proceedings Regulation never applied to the Channel Islands or the Isle of Man, because those territories were the subject of special arrangements negotiated at the time of UK accession to the European Communities in 1972, whereby only a limited range of EC laws and policies apply to them (Act of Accession, 22 January 1972 (Cmnd 4862-I), Protocol No 3; TFEU, Art 355(5)(c)). Conversely, the Insolvency Proceedings

prescribed the form that measures adopted pursuant to them had to take. Accordingly, by Article 5 EC (Article 5 TFEU), the Community (and the EU) had to satisfy itself that in adopting the Insolvency Proceedings Regulation it was acting both consistently with the principle of subsidiarity and proportionately.[13] If it had not, in theory the Insolvency Proceedings Regulation was capable of being challenged as being in breach of the EC Treaty (now TFEU) and general principles of Community law.[14] Finally, Article 67(1) EC (Article 81(2) TFEU) prescribed the legislative process that had to be followed for the measure's valid adoption.

2.05 The Treaty Articles affect the Insolvency Proceedings Regulation's meaning and interpretation in three principal ways. The first is that they provide the purposive framework within which it is to be interpreted. This is significant because, as further described below,[15] in accordance with the usual rules of EU law construction, it is to be construed purposively. Moreover, this purpose is to be established, in part, by reference to the Community aims as set out in the TFEU and which the Insolvency Proceedings Regulation is intended to further. Second, in prescribing the legislative process for its adoption, Articles 81(2) and 294 TFEU not only set out the procedures which had to be observed to ensure the measure's valid adoption by the Community but also established the preparatory measures (or *travaux préparatoires*) which preceded it. This is important because, as also further described below, regard may legitimately be had to these measures as aids to its interpretation. Third, in the case of the OR, Title IV of the EC Treaty, and in particular Article 68 EC, originally prescribed the role that the ECJ was empowered to play in the interpretation of measures adopted under that Title, which include the Insolvency Proceedings Regulation. That role, as set out below, has now been expanded following the repeal of Article 68 EC by the Treaty of Lisbon and those restrictions therefore no longer apply either to the OR or to the RR.

B. Legal Attributes

2.06 A Regulation is a creature of the governing treaties of the EU. As such, its attributes are governed by the TFEU, and in particular by Article 288 TFEU. This provides that Regulations shall:

(1) have 'general application';
(2) be 'binding in their entirety'; and
(3) be 'directly applicable in all Member States'.

Regulation did apply to Gibraltar, which was included within the scope of the TFEU by virtue of Art 355(3) as one of the 'European territories for whose external relations a Member State' (in this instance, the UK) 'is responsible'.

[13] See Recital (5) OR as to why it is compatible with the principle of subsidiarity: its objectives 'cannot be achieved to a sufficient degree at national level'; see to similar effect Recital (86) RR; and see Recital (8) of both the OR and the RR as to why a Regulation, as opposed to any other form of Community instrument, is required: 'In order to achieve the aim of improving the efficiency and effectiveness of insolvency proceedings having cross-border effects, it is necessary, and appropriate, that the provisions ... should be contained in a [Community/Union] law measure which is binding and directly applicable in Member States.'
[14] The basis on which legislative acts may be challenged in direct actions before the ECJ is set out in Art 263 TFEU.
[15] See section on 'Meaning' at paras 2.19 et seq below.

Other Treaty Articles impose additional requirements. Article 296 TFEU requires Regulations to state the reasons on which they are based[16] and to refer to any proposals, initiatives, recommendations, requests, or opinions which were required to be obtained in accordance with the Treaty.[17] Article 297(1) TFEU provides that Regulations of the Council, such as the Insolvency Proceedings Regulation, are to be published in the *Official Journal*[18] and, more importantly, shall enter into force on the date specified in them.[19] Each official language version[20] of a Regulation is equally authentic.[21] Regulations—like all other Community legislative measures—are presumed to be valid unless and until declared invalid by the CJEU.[22]

Having 'general application' means that a Regulation 'applies to objectively determined situations and produces its legal effects to categories of persons envisaged in the abstract'.[23] A Regulation will be of general application notwithstanding that it will have different practical effects for the various persons to whom it applies.[24] The importance of this attribute is that it distinguishes a Regulation from other EU measures and, in particular, from Decisions, and it does so by the application of a substantive test and not by a test simply of form. The significance of this distinction in turn is that by Article 263 TFEU a 'natural or legal person', as opposed to a Community institution or Member State, may only challenge a Regulation in a direct action by alleging either that it is addressed to that person, that is, it is a Decision or that it is of 'direct and individual concern' to that person.[25] In relation to the Insolvency Proceedings Regulation, there can be no doubt that it is what it purports to be,

2.07

---

[16] These are the reasons set out in the Recitals (or preambles) to the Insolvency Proceedings Regulation.

[17] Art 67(1) EC provided that the Council was to act, *inter alia*, on the initiative of a Member State, and after consulting the European Parliament. Accordingly, the preamble to the OR refers to the initiative of Germany and Finland (published in [1999] OJ C221/8) and the opinion of the European Parliament. Additionally, the OR refers to the opinion of the Economic and Social Committee which was consulted at the request of the Council. The opinion was adopted on 26 January 2000 and is published in [2000] OJ C75/1. By contrast, the RR refers to the Commission's report on the application of the OR (Recital 1), the Commission's proposal, the transmission of the draft legislation to the national parliaments, the opinion of the Economic and Social Committee (published in [2013] OJ C271/55), the positions of the European Parliament (of 5 February 2014 and 20 May 2015), and the position of the Council at first reading (of 12 March 2015).

[18] The OR is published in [2000] OJ L160/1 and the RR in [2015] OJ L141/19.

[19] Art 47 OR provides that it was to enter into force on 21 May 2002 and Art 92 RR that it is to enter into force on the twentieth day following its publication. Arts 84 and 92 set out the (later) date for the application of its various Articles and deal with transitional arrangements.

[20] There are 24 official and working languages after the Irish language gained full official and working status on 1 January 2022: Bulgarian, Croatian, Czech, Danish, Dutch, English, Estonian, Finnish, French, German, Greek, Hungarian, Irish, Italian, Latvian, Lithuanian, Maltese, Polish, Portuguese, Romanian, Slovak, Slovenian, Spanish, and Swedish. There are 27 Member States.

[21] Case 283/81 *CILFIT Srl v Ministry of Health* [1982] ECR 3415, para 18.

[22] This is subject to the possible exception that a Regulation may be declared 'non-existent', but it remains open to doubt whether legislative (as opposed to administrative) acts of the Community are capable of being declared 'non-existent': see the Opinion of AG Ruiz-Jarabo in Joined Cases C-10 to 22/97 *Ministero delle Finanze v IN.CO. GE.'90 Srl* [1998] ECR I-6307, 6316. AG Sharpston in Case C-345/06 *Heinrich* [2009] ECR I-1659 suggested that a Commission Regulation should be declared non-existent due to its failure to be published in the *Official Journal*, but the CJEU declined to follow this and instead declared that the offending Annex to the Regulation (which had not been published) was of no binding force insofar as it imposed obligations on individuals (judgment of 10 March 2009).

[23] See eg Case C-244/88 *Usines Coopératives de Déshydratation du Vexin v EC Commission* [1989] ECR I-3811 and Case C-299/88 *Cargill v EC Commission* [1990] ECR I-1303.

[24] Case 6/68 *Zuckerfabrik Watenstedt GmbH v Council* [1968] ECR 409; Case 101/76 *Koninklijke Scholten Honig v EC Commission* [1977] ECR 797.

[25] ie distinguishes him or her individually in the same way as an addressee of a Decision: Case C-25/62 *Plaumann* [1963] ECR I-211; see also Case C-263/02P *EC Commission v Jégo-Quéré et Cie* [2004] ECR I-3425.

namely a measure of general application. As a consequence, it is immune to a direct challenge under Article 263 TFEU brought by individuals.[26]

2.08 'Binding in their entirety' means no more than that the provisions of a Regulation are to apply in identical terms throughout the EU. That is to say, the Insolvency Proceedings Regulation, like every other Regulation, is meant to be an instrument of uniformity. It is intended to be an instrument of a *single* EU legal order. However, in practice, the extent to which this aim is achieved will vary according to the way in which the interpretation and application of the Insolvency Proceedings Regulation may vary from Member State to Member State.[27] Nonetheless, the fact that the Insolvency Proceedings Regulation is intended to be an instrument of uniformity, as further discussed below, affects the way in which it should be interpreted in any one Member State.

2.09 'Directly applicable' means that a Regulation takes effect in the domestic legal system of any particular Member State automatically, when it comes into force, without the need for that Member State to transpose it into national legislation.[28] From this attribute flow a number of important legal consequences.

'Direct applicability'

2.10 The first is that Member States are under an obligation *not* to introduce national measures intended to give effect to the Regulation,[29] unless implementing measures are required as discussed below. If they did so, they would impose an obstruction between the Regulation and those subject to it. Such national measures would contradict the Regulation's 'direct applicability' and its simultaneous and uniform application in the EU legal order. Thus everyone must look to the same legal instrument, that is the Regulation, in whatever Member State they are domiciled as their source of legal rights.[30]

2.11 Implementing measures may be required in two circumstances. Sometimes a Regulation may expressly require that Member States take steps to implement it. This, however, was not the case with regard to the OR,[31] whereas the RR does expressly contemplate that the conditions for access to information to insolvency registers, which it requires to be established, may vary in the manner contemplated by Article 27. Member States may also adopt detailed

---

[26] It may nonetheless be the subject of an 'indirect' challenge brought by individuals in national proceedings through the instrumentality of Art 267 TFEU. This is discussed further at paras 2.23–2.39 below.
[27] The European e-Justice Portal was established in order to facilitate access to information about any commencement of insolvency cases in the national registers of national cases on the Insolvency Proceedings Regulation.
[28] Cf the requirement that a Directive be implemented by national measures in the Member States' legal systems.
[29] Case 34/73 *Fratelli Variola SpA v Administration des finances italiennes* [1973] ECR 981, esp paras 9–11.
[30] For an example of the direct applicability of the OR, see *Klempka v ISA Daisytek SA* [2003] BCC 984, 990H, where the Court of Appeal of Versailles held that, because Art 17 of the Regulation provides that the judgment opening proceedings produces its effects 'without further formality', the fact that French law requires a judgment opening insolvency proceedings to be published at the relevant Corporate Registry was irrelevant when considering the legal effect of the prior judgment of an English court opening main insolvency proceedings. The Versailles Court of Appeal's judgment was subsequently upheld by the Cour de Cassation: *French Republic v Klempka* [2006] BCC 841.
[31] But note that the Insolvency Proceedings Regulation does expressly provide that certain matters in connection with its operation are to be reserved to the Member States. See eg Art 4.2 which provides that the conditions for the opening of insolvency proceedings (as defined by Art 2(a) of the Insolvency Proceedings Regulation) are to be determined by 'the law of the State of the opening of proceedings'.

rules for the application of a Regulation where this is necessary to give full effect to it in their domestic legal systems.[32] For example, in the case of the OR while still in force in the UK, the Insolvency Act 1986 and the Insolvency Rules 1986 were amended[33] so as to give full effect to the rules that the Insolvency Proceedings Regulation laid down with regard to the allocation of jurisdiction and the enforcement of judgments. In particular, amendments were introduced to modify the definition of 'property' in section 436 of the 1986 Act;[34] to give effect to the extensive role that the Regulation gives to liquidators of other Member States, and in particular their right under Article 37 (now Article 51 RR) to apply to convert (in the context of the UK) administration and voluntary arrangements into winding-up proceedings;[35] to provide for a procedure (as required by the jurisdictional rules of the Regulation)[36] for liquidators to apply to the court for 'confirmation' of a creditors' voluntary winding-up;[37] and to make clear that administration orders could be made in relation to overseas registered and unregistered companies over which an English court has jurisdiction by virtue of Article 3 of the Regulation.[38]

Amendments to the Insolvency Act 1986 and the Insolvency Rules 1986 had themselves to comply with the provisions of the Insolvency Proceedings Regulation[39] as well as complying with general principles of EU law.[40] In particular, they could not alter the scope of the Insolvency Proceedings Regulation[41] or add to its provisions,[42] and they had to comply

2.12

---

[32] Case 94/77 *Zerbone v Amministrazione delle Finanze* [1978] ECR 99, para 27.
[33] See, with regard to the 1986 Act, the Insolvency Act 1986 (Amendment) Regulations 2002, SI 2002/1037; the Insolvency Act 1986 (Amendment) (No 2) Regulations 2002, SI 2002/1240; the Insolvency Act 1986 (Amendment) Regulations 2005, SI 2005/879; and, with regard to the 1986 Rules, the Insolvency (Amendment) Rules 2002, SI 2002/1307.
[34] This is because Art 3(2) of the Insolvency Proceedings Regulation limits the effects of proceedings commenced in a Member State on the basis of an establishment in that state to 'the assets of the debtor situated in the territory of the latter Member State'. Those assets are defined by Art 2(g) (now Art 2(9)). Accordingly, the Insolvency Act 1986 was amended by the insertion of a new s 436A so that references in that Act to 'property' (as defined in s 436) were deemed to be references to property which, where Art 3 of the Regulation applied, was property that might be dealt with in such proceedings. See reg 18 of the Insolvency Act 1986 (Amendment) (No 2) Regulations 2002, SI 2002/1240.
[35] See eg r 4 of the Insolvency (Amendment) Rules 2002, SI 2002/1307 in relation to company voluntary arrangements, r 5 in relation to administration, and r 7 in relation to individual voluntary arrangements.
[36] Art 2(a) (now Art 2(4)) and Annex A.
[37] Under existing legislation, 'confirmation by the court' was not a step required in relation to a creditors' voluntary winding-up, although it is a requirement for the application of the Insolvency Proceedings Regulation. Provision for it was made by r 9 of the Insolvency (Amendment) Rules 2002, SI 2002/1307.
[38] See *Re BRAC Rent-A-Car International Inc* [2003] BCC 248; *Re The Salvage Association* [2003] BCC 504. See s 1(4) Insolvency Act 1986 as amended by the Insolvency Act 1986 (Amendment) Regulations 2005 following (and in effect modifying) Blackburne J's judgment in *Re The Salvage Association*.
[39] Case 94/77 *Zerbone v Amministrazione delle Finanze* [1978] ECR 99, para 27. As a matter of English law, these amendments to implement the OR were introduced under powers granted (by way of amendment to the 1986 Act) by the Insolvency Act 1986 (Amendment) Regulations 2002, SI 2002/1037, which instrument was itself adopted under s 2(2), European Communities Act 1972, so as to enable the UK Government to comply with its obligations at the time under the ECT (now the TFEU).
[40] See Case C-327/13 *Burgo Group SpA v Illachroma SA and another* [2015] BCC 33 (CJEU, 4 September 2014), where the CJEU criticized Belgian rules on the opening of secondary proceedings following the opening of main proceedings insofar as they limited the persons entitled to request such proceedings to creditors resident or with a registered office in Belgium on the basis that such a restriction was inconsistent with the EU general principle of non-discrimination. The CJEU also noted that the exercise of discretion by a national court, when deciding to open secondary proceedings, although governed by the national law of the Member State of the court, must be exercised consistently with the objectives underlying secondary proceedings, the objectives underlying the main proceedings, and consistently with the principle of sincere co-operation as well as with general principles of EU law.
[41] Case 40/69 *Hauptzollamt Hamburg v Bollmann* [1970] ECR 69, para 5.
[42] Case 74/69 *Hauptzollamt Bremen v Kohn* [1970] ECR 451, para 1.

with the aim and objectives of the Regulation.[43] Further, as a matter of EU law, the amendments to domestic legislation adopted to give effect to EU law that is to the 1986 Act and the 1986 Rules were capable of review by the English courts so as to ensure their compatibility with the Insolvency Proceedings Regulation.[44] To the extent that the amendments did not comply with the Insolvency Proceedings Regulation, they were also *ultra vires* under English law.[45]

2.13 The doctrine of 'direct applicability' also entails a prohibition on Member States introducing new law which has the effect of modifying the legal effects of a Regulation.[46] In addition, in relation to pre-existing national law, it obliges Member States to repeal it. This is so even if it has become obsolete and the Member State in fact acts in a way that is compatible with EU law.[47] This is so as not to infringe the principle of legal certainty, and create what might otherwise be a potentially ambiguous legal situation.

2.14 By way of example, there was a potential conflict between section 117(1) of the Insolvency Act 1986 and the OR. This was because section 117(1) granted the English High Court jurisdiction to wind up *any* company registered in England and Wales. By contrast, by Article 3(1) OR, only the courts of the Member State within whose territory is situated 'the centre of the debtor's main interests' have jurisdiction.[48] Although there is a presumption that the registered office of a company is the centre of a company's main interests, it is capable of being rebutted. Accordingly, although section 117(1) of the Insolvency Act was permissive only and not mandatory, it was arguable that in the interests of legal certainty it required amendment to reflect the provisions of the OR. It was therefore amended by the addition of a new subsection (7), which provides that it is subject to Article 3 of the Insolvency Proceedings Regulation.[49] Other jurisdictional provisions of the Insolvency Act 1986 were similarly amended.[50]

2.15 Member States are not only under the negative obligation to ensure that the domestic legal order does not contain legislation that contradicts the Insolvency Proceedings Regulation. They are also, as a matter of EU law, under a positive obligation to ensure that the Regulation will be applied in practice. This obligation now derives from Article 4(3) of the TFEU which requires Member States to 'take any appropriate measure, general or particular' to ensure the fulfilment of obligations arising both under the treaties and resulting from the acts of the institutions of the EU. The significance of this obligation from the point of view of the Insolvency Proceedings Regulation is that it falls not simply on national governments, but

---

[43] Case 31/78 *Bussone v Italian Ministry for Agriculture* [1978] ECR 2429, para 36. For an example of where implementing measures have not complied with the aims and objectives of the OR, see the CJEU's criticism of Belgian rules regarding the opening of secondary proceedings following the opening of main proceedings in Case C-327/13 *Burgo Group SpA v Illochroma SA and another* [2015] BCC 33 (CJEU, 4 September 2014), referred to at n 40 above.

[44] Case 230/78 *Eridania v Minister of Agriculture and Forestry* [1979] ECR 2749, para 34.

[45] For the current position in the UK, see para 9.02 below.

[46] Case 34/73 *Fratelli Variola SpA v Administration des finances italiennes* [1973] ECR 981, paras 14–15.

[47] Case C-185/96 *EC Commission v Greece* [1998] ECR I-6601, para 32.

[48] This is subject to the exception that in addition the courts of Member States in which the debtor has an 'establishment' also have jurisdiction to open insolvency proceedings. See Art 3(2). Art 3(1) RR is in similar terms.

[49] Reg 6 of the Insolvency Act 1986 (Amendment) (No 2) Regulations 2002, SI 2002/1240.

[50] See eg regs 7, 9, 10, and 14 of the Insolvency Act 1986 (Amendment) (No 2) Regulations 2002. The Insolvency Rules were amended to ensure that the issue of whether there is jurisdiction under the Regulation is considered at the opening of proceedings. See eg r 4(3) of the Insolvency (Amendment) Rules 2002 in relation to company voluntary arrangements.

on all organs of the state. These include the courts[51] as well as administrative and government authorities.

Moreover, where a Member State fails to apply the Insolvency Proceedings Regulation, thereby causing loss and damage to an individual, in certain circumstances the individual is entitled, as a matter of EU law, to reparation for the loss and damage under the conditions laid down by the CJEU for Member State liability.[52]

'Direct effect'

The obligations which the doctrine of 'direct applicability' create, however, have to be distinguished from the doctrine of 'direct effect'. By saying that a particular EU provision has 'direct effect' is meant that it is intended to create rights for individuals which must be protected by the national courts.[53] That is to say individuals may rely on the provision in national courts so as to enforce the right that it is intended to create both as against the state and as against other individuals.[54] Although the CJEU has not expressly ruled on the question whether it is proper to draw a distinction between 'direct applicability' and 'direct effect' in the context of Regulations, and indeed it sometimes uses the words interchangeably, the better view is that such a distinction should be made.[55] Certainly the English courts recognized such a distinction. Thus, Lord Hoffmann had said that the fact that a Regulation 'is directly applicable does not necessarily mean that it creates rights and duties enforceable in the courts. It may, like some domestic statutes, create public duties without creating private law rights'.[56]

Certain provisions of the Insolvency Proceedings Regulation are clearly not intended to have 'direct effect' in the sense of creating rights for individuals. These include the provisions in the RR empowering the Commission to adopt implementing acts establishing the interconnection of insolvency registers or to amend standard forms,[57] and requiring the Commission to report on its application.[58] These are either procedural obligations or powers that are

---

[51] The origin of this doctrine is Case 14/83 *Von Colson and Kamann v Land Nordrhein Westfalen* [1984] ECR 1891, para 26, which concerned the implementation of a Directive. For its application in the context of the OR, see Case C-527/10 *ERSTE Bank Hungary Nyrt v Magyar Allam and others* [2012] ECLI:EU:C:2012:417, para 36, where the CJEU held that from 1 May 2004 (in accordance with the Accession Treaty) Hungarian courts are required in accordance with Art 16(1) to recognize any judgment opening insolvency proceedings handed down by a court of a Member State, without any further formality, including in respect of proceedings opened before 1 May 2004 (in the particular case, in Austria).
[52] Case C-118/00 *Larsy v INASTI* [2001] ECR I-5063, para 34. Note that the principle of Member State liability in damages was initially established by reference to the failure of Member States to implement Directives (on which there is an extensive case law). However, it is now recognized as a remedy generally for breach of a Member State's obligations under EU law, including those arising under Regulations.
[53] Case 26/62 *Van Gend en Loos v Nederlandse Administratie der Belastingen* [1963] ECR 1.
[54] The provision has both so-called 'horizontal' and 'vertical' direct effect. By contrast, provisions of Directives that have 'direct effect' have only 'vertical direct effect', ie they can only be relied on as against the state, and *not* as against other individuals.
[55] See eg the discussion in S Weatherill and P Beaumont, *EU Law* (3rd edn, 1999) 398–99.
[56] *Consorzio del Prosciutto di Parma v Asda Stores Ltd* [2001] UKHL 7, para 21. But note that he went on to say 'One would normally assume, however, that unless the Regulation contemplated that it would have to be fleshed out by domestic or Community legislation, it was intended to be effective to create rights or duties or both and not be what Lord Simonds once called a "pious aspiration".
[57] Arts 87 and 88.
[58] Art 90.

expressly limited to specific persons. But many of the substantive provisions, such as Article 3, which determines which Member States' courts are to have jurisdiction over insolvency proceedings, are likely to have direct effect. This is so notwithstanding that the meaning of certain key concepts, such as the 'centre of main interests' and 'establishment', which determine jurisdiction in accordance with the provisions of that Article, is unclear. There are in fact many expressions in the Regulation of which the meaning is unclear.[59] Such expressions are, however, capable of a single EU meaning which may, in the fullness of time, with the assistance of the jurisprudence of the CJEU, become clear. Similar comments equally apply to other provisions of the Insolvency Proceedings Regulation, for example Article 32 RR, which governs the recognition and enforceability of judgments, and refers to such potentially unclear concepts as judgments that are 'closely linked' with insolvency proceedings.

C. Meaning

2.19 The principles of interpretation that apply as a matter of EU law, when establishing the meaning of the Insolvency Proceedings Regulation, reflect its essential characteristics as a piece of EU subordinate legislation. These are that it is a piece of legislation that has to operate within a multilingual community, and that it has to apply uniformly because that community, despite comprising many different Member States, is but a single legal order. Further, as a piece of subordinate legislation, the Insolvency Proceedings Regulation has to respect and reflect the position that it occupies in the EU's legal hierarchy. These considerations underlie the particular interpretative techniques that have developed in EU law. As further explained below, they differ from the ordinary principles of English statutory interpretation, which themselves traditionally reflect a different legal order. In particular, English principles reflect a legal order which is predominantly monolingual,[60] and where the legislation is the product not of a bargaining process between Member States and the EU's institutions,[61] but the product of a single sovereign legislative assembly.

Interpretation and the European Union legal order

2.20 As a piece of subordinate legislation, the Insolvency Proceedings Regulation must be interpreted consistently with superior EU law rules that govern it. In particular, it must be interpreted consistently with the scheme laid down by the Treaty Articles under which it was adopted[62] and general principles of EU law.[63] 'General principles of EU law' mean those

---

[59] The expressions 'right in rem' in Art 8; the 'assets' of a debtor, which appears throughout the Regulation; 'act detrimental to all the creditors' and 'any means ... in the relevant case' in Art 16. There are many other examples.
[60] But note that this is changing. Subordinate legislation adopted by the Welsh Assembly has to be in both English and Welsh.
[61] The EU does not have a single legislature, but a number of legislative processes that apply in accordance with the provisions of the TFEU.
[62] These were Arts 61(c) and 67(1) EC in the case of the OR and Arts 81 and 294 TFEU in the case of the RR (see para 2.02 above). See eg Case 105/94 *Celestini v Saar-Sektkellerei Faber* [1997] ECR I-2971, para 32 citing in support Joined Cases C-90 and C-91/90 *Neu v Secrétaire d'Etat à l'Agriculture et à la Viticulture* [1991] ECR I-3167, para 12.
[63] See eg Case 105/94 *Celestini v Saar-Sektkellerei Faber* [1997] ECR I-2971, para 32 citing in support Joined Cases C-90 and C-91/90 *Neu v Secrétaire d'Etat à l'Agriculture et à la Viticulture* [1991] ECR I-3167, para 12. For

principles of law which have been recognized as such by the CJEU.⁶⁴ These include: the
principle of equal treatment or non-discrimination; respect for fundamental rights;⁶⁵ the
principle of legal certainty; and the principle of proportionality. This means that where a
provision of the Regulation is capable of more than one interpretation, in so far as possible an interpretation should be adopted which renders it compatible with these superior
sources of EU law.

2.21 By way of example, Article 3 of the Regulation provides that 'The courts of the Member State
within the territory of which the centre of a debtor's main interests is situated shall have
jurisdiction to open insolvency proceedings.' The term 'Member State' in the Regulation
is not defined. In *Re The Arena Corporation Ltd*,⁶⁶ Arena contended that the centre of its
main interests was Denmark, that Denmark was a Member State and therefore prima facie
insolvency proceedings should be commenced in Denmark and not in England. Lawrence
Collins J rejected the argument that Article 3 was applicable. Having regard to the Treaty
Articles under which the Regulation was adopted, the Protocol on the position of Denmark,
Denmark's decision not to opt in to the Regulation and Recital (33)⁶⁷ of the Regulation, he
had no doubt that 'the expression "Member State" in Article 3 was to be interpreted as excluding Denmark'.⁶⁸

2.22 The Insolvency Proceedings Regulation is also one of a number of measures designed to
create 'a European judicial area in civil matters, where citizens have a common sense of
justice throughout the Union and where justice is seen as facilitating the day-to-day life
of people'.⁶⁹ Other existing measures include the recast Council Regulation on jurisdiction and enforcement of judgments in civil and commercial matters ('Brussels I *bis*');⁷⁰ the
Council Regulation on jurisdiction and enforcement of judgments in matrimonial matters
(which also covers rights of access to children);⁷¹ and the Taking of Evidence Regulation.⁷²
The significance of this is that when interpreting the Insolvency Proceedings Regulation its

---

examples of where general principles of EU law were relied upon when construing an Article of the OR, see Case
C-341/04 *Eurofood IFSC Ltd* [2006] ECR I-3813, paras 65–67 (Art 26); Case C-527/10 *ERSTE Bank Hungary Nyrt
v Magyar Allam and others* [2012] ECLI:EU:C:2012:417 paras 39–42 (Art 5(1)).

⁶⁴ On general principles of EU law, see in particular T Tridimas, *The General Principles of EC Law* (3rd edn, Nov 2013).
⁶⁵ Since the coming into force of the Treaty of Lisbon, the EU has had its own Charter of Fundamental Rights, which has the same status as the EU treaties. However, the UK (together with Poland) negotiated Protocol 30 to the TFEU, as a result of which the rights set out in the Charter were not justiciable in English courts. (But for a different, and controversial, view see the CJEU's judgment in *Secretary of State for the Home Department v ME and others* (21 December 2011), para 120 and Mostyn J's observations on that judgment in *R (AB) v Secretary of State for the Home Department* [2013] EWHC (Admin), paras 13–14). The Protocol also provides that the Charter does not extend the ability of the CJEU to find that the UK's laws, regulations, administrative provisions, or practices are inconsistent with the fundamental rights, freedoms, and principles re-affirmed by the Charter.
⁶⁶ [2004] BPIR 377 (Lawrence Collins J).
⁶⁷ Now Recital (88) of the RR.
⁶⁸ [2004] BPIR 377, 385. The question whether Denmark is to be considered a Member State for the purpose of Art 16 OR (Art 19 RR) was the subject of a reference to the ECJ: Case C-148/08 *Mejnertsen v Barsoe*, but the case was closed and removed from the Register before its determination.
⁶⁹ See the Commission's Explanatory Memorandum attached to its Proposal for a Council Regulation establishing a general framework for Community activities to facilitate the implementation of a European judicial area in civil matters (COM/2001/0221 final) [2001] OJ C213/271.
⁷⁰ Regulation 1215/2012 of 12 December 2012 [2012] OJ L351, to which express reference is made in Recital (7) RR, replaced the original Brussels Regulation of 22 December 2000 [2001] OJ L12, which had replaced the 1968 Brussels Convention with effect from 1 March 2002.
⁷¹ Council Regulation (EC) 2201/2003 as amended, known as Brussels II.
⁷² Council Regulation (EC) 1206/2001.

role as an instrument in a wider EU legal order has to be considered. In other words, it has to be interpreted not only consistently with superior EU law, but also consistently with, and not in isolation from, the EU measures that are intended to complement it.

2.23 Of these, the most important is Brussels I *bis*.[73] This is because, historically, the Brussels Convention that preceded it was originally intended as a Convention concerning civil jurisdiction and judgments in non-insolvency matters that would be adopted in parallel with an insolvency Convention.[74] As a result, the Brussels Convention and Brussels I *bis* do not apply to 'bankruptcy, proceedings relating to the winding-up of insolvent companies or other legal persons, judicial arrangements, compositions and analogous proceedings'.[75] The test to be applied for determining whether the action falls within the Insolvency Proceedings Regulation is whether (i) the right or obligation relied upon 'finds its source in the common rules of civil or commercial law [in which case Brussels I *bis* applies] or derogates from them [in which case the Insolvency Proceedings Regulation applies]'[76] and (ii) the action is brought 'in the context of' insolvency proceedings.[77] The Insolvency Proceedings Regulation also makes express reference to other complementary EU regimes by reference to which the scope of its application ought to be determined. In particular, insolvency proceedings relating to financial institutions have their own regimes established by a series of Directives which, unlike the Insolvency Proceedings Regulation, are not directly applicable, but require to be implemented in the individual legal orders of the Member States. Thus the

---

[73] For an example of where reference to Brussels I and its predecessor, the Brussels Convention, was relied upon to assist in the interpretation of the Regulation, see *Re BRAC Rent-A-Car International Inc* [2003] BCC 248, 253B–D (Lloyd J). Indeed, the CJEU has also held that the Brussels I case law on the public policy exception to the recognition of foreign judgments may be transposed to the public policy exception provided by Art 26 OR: Case C-341/04 *Eurofood IFSC Ltd* [2006] ECR I-3813, para 64; Case C-444/07 *MG Probud Gdynia* [2010] ECR I-417, para 34. The CA further suggested (but did not decide) that (i) Brussels Convention case law on the meaning of the time when a court is first seised of a matter might be applied where determining 'the time of the opening of [insolvency] proceedings' for the purpose of the Regulation; and (ii) the burden of proof applicable to demonstrating the jurisdiction requirements of the Brussels and Lugano Conventions might also be applicable to the Regulation: see *Shierson v Vlieland-Boddy* [2005] EWCA Civ 974, paras 71–72 (Longmore LJ).

[74] It is because the Brussels Convention was always intended to have its complement in an insolvency regulation that the starting point for any consideration of the scope of the Insolvency Proceedings Regulation is the ECJ's determination in Case C-133/78 *Gourdain v Nadler* [1979] ECR 733 of the scope of the bankruptcy and winding-up exclusion in the Brussels Convention.

[75] Art 1(2)(b) of Brussels I *bis*. For an example of judicial reliance on the complementary purposes of Brussels I *bis* and the Insolvency Proceedings Regulation, see *Re Marann Brooks CSV Ltd* (Ch D, 4 December 2002) (Patten J); *Polymer Vision R&D Ltd v Van Dooren* [2011] EWHC 2951 (Comm) (Beatson J), esp at para 62; and for authoritative judicial discussions of the division of functions between Brussels I/Ibis and the Insolvency Proceedings Regulation, and the application of the 'dual criterion' that has to be fulfilled before actions fall within the scope of the Insolvency Proceedings Regulation (ie they must 'derive directly from insolvency proceedings and are closely connected with them' according to Art 6(1) RR), see: Case C-339/07 *Seagon* [2009] ECR I-767; Case C-111/08 *SCT Industri v Alpenblume AB* [2009] ECRI-5655; Case C-292/08 *German Graphics Graphische Maschinen GmbH v Alice van der Schee* [2009] ECRI-0842; Case C-213/10 *F-Tex SIA v Lietuvos-Anglijos UAB 'Jadecloud-Vilma'* [ECLI:EU:C:2012:215]; Case C-157/13 *Nickel & Goeldner Spedition GmbH v 'Kintra' USAB* [ECLI:EU:C:2014:2145]; Case C-47/18 *Riel* [ECLI:EU:C:2019:754]; Case C-198/18 *CeDe Group* [ECLI:EU:C:2019:1001]; Case C-493/18 *Tiger* [ECLI:EU:C:2019:1046]. For an English discussion, see *Byers and others v Yacht Bull Corporation* [2010] EWHC 133 (Ch) (Sir Andrew Morritt C) and more recently *Fondazione Enasarco v Lehman Brothers Finance SA and another* [2014] EWHC 34 (Ch) (David Richards J).

[76] Art 6(1) RR. The provision adopted CJEU case law; see eg Case C-295/13 *H v HK* (CJEU, 4 December 2014). Note that in this case, in contrast with the earlier judgment in Case C-157/13 *Nickel & Goeldner Spedition GmbH v 'Kintra' USAB* (CJEU, 4 September 2014), the rule of law relied on did not derive directly from insolvency proceedings, with the result that it could be relied upon outside the context of insolvency proceedings (ie it was not a rule of law 'specific to insolvency proceedings' (as in the case of *Nickel & Goeldner Spedition GmbH v 'Kintra' USAB*), although the rule of law did require the actual insolvency of the debtor).

[77] Case C-295/13 *H v HK* (CJEU, 4 December 2014). In this case, the CJEU considered that, if the same claim had been brought outside the context of insolvency proceedings, it 'may' have fallen within Brussels I *bis*.

Insolvency Proceedings Regulation does not apply[78] to insolvency proceedings concerning insurance undertakings,[79] credit institutions and investment firms.[80] Further, Article 12 provides that the rights and obligations of parties to a payment or settlement system should be governed solely by the law of the Member State that applies to that system. The purpose of this provision[81] is to preserve the particular insolvency regime that the EU has established by its Directive on settlement finality in payment and securities settlement systems.[82]

Interpretation and the multilingual legal order

As indicated above,[83] although the Insolvency Proceedings Regulation by reason of the doctrine of 'direct applicability' is to apply uniformly throughout the Member States, it applies through the medium of texts in 22 of the 23 official languages of the Community, each of which is authentic.[84] Strictly speaking, therefore, the English language version of the Insolvency Proceedings Regulation should not be considered in isolation from other language versions. This is in part because of the danger of mistranslation.[85] But more particularly it is to ensure, through comparing language versions, consistency of meaning.[86] In practice, it is neither proportionate nor feasible for national courts to consider all of the

2.24

---

[78] By Art 1(2).

[79] These are governed by Directive 2009/138/EC of the European Parliament and of the Council of 25 November 2009 on the taking-up and pursuit of the business of Insurance and Reinsurance (Solvency II) [2009] OJ L335/1, which replaced the Council Directive (EC) 2001/17 on the reorganisation and winding-up of insurance undertakings [2001] OJ L110/28.

[80] There are two relevant Directives. First the Council Directive (EC) 2001/24 on the reorganisation and winding-up of credit institutions [2001] OJ L125/15, implemented by the Credit Institutions (Reorganisation and Winding up) Regulations 2004, SI 2004/1045. See *In the matter of Arm Asset Backed Securities SA* [2014] EWHC 1097 (Ch), para 12 (Nugee J) for an example of where it was held that the interpretation of Art 10 of the Directive applied equally to Art 4(2) OR (Art 7(2) of the Recast Regulation). Second, the Directive (EU) 2014/59 of 15 May 2014 establishing a framework for the recovery and resolution of credit institutions and investment firms [2014] OJ L173/190.

[81] See Recital (71).

[82] European Parliament and Council Directive (EC) 98/26 on settlement finality in payment and securities settlement systems [1998] OJ L166/45 implemented in England and Wales by the Financial Markets and Insolvency (Settlement Finality) Regulations 1999. It is suggested, therefore, that terms such as 'payment or settlement systems' that are undefined in Art 12 should be interpreted consistently with the Directive.

[83] See para 2.09 above.

[84] Case 283/81 *CILFIT Srl v Ministry of Health* [1982] ECR 3415, para 18.

[85] Note in this context the correction to the Finnish version of the OR subsequently published in OJ [2001] L265/42 and the suggestion at para 8.45 of the 2nd edition of this work that the term 'goods' in Art 2(h) of the English language version of the OR is a mistranslation of the French '*biens*' and the German '*Vermögenswerten*', the better translation being 'assets'. The term 'assets' is now used in Art 2(10) of the RR. In *The Trustees of the Olympic Airlines SA Pension and Life Assurance Scheme v Olympic Airlines SA* [2015] UKSC 27, para 3, the UKSC stated that it was 'apparent from the equivalent term in the other language versions that ["goods"] means the same as "assets"'. Other possible mistranslations are indicated in the commentary.

[86] Eg it was suggested in the second edition of this work that the phrase 'all the creditors' in Art 4(2)(m) OR was better understood to mean 'the creditors as a whole' having regard to the German ('*Gesamtheit*') and French ('*ensemble*') versions. That interpretation has been adopted: see Art 7(2)(m) of the RR, which uses the phrase 'the general body of creditors'. Likewise, the phrase 'having an interest' in Art 34(2) OR, Art 47(2) RR is better understood as meaning 'interested', having regard to the French version ('*les créanciers intéressés*'): see the discussion at para 8.425 below. For an example of the approach of the CJEU (in that case, to the interpretation of Art 24(1) (now Art 31(1)), and the meaning of the phrase 'for the benefit of the debtor'), see Case C-251/12 *Christian Van Buggenhout and another v Banque Internationale à Luxembourg SA*, paras 28 and 29, where the Court considered the provision in its Spanish, French, Italian, Dutch, and Portuguese language versions and the relevant preamble in its German, English, and Swedish language versions, on a reference from a Belgian court. Other examples of where, having regard to other language versions, the better view is that the literal meaning of the English version should not be followed are provided in the commentary.

different language versions of the Insolvency Proceedings Regulation.[87] However, it is certainly appropriate, where key concepts are concerned,[88] that they are considered in alternative language versions as well as in the English version.[89] Where the difference between the language versions is crucial to the case, and the point is irresolvable on witness statement evidence, the question should arguably be referred to the CJEU for determination.[90]

2.25 However, even where there is consistency across language versions, the meaning of any particular provision of the Insolvency Proceedings Regulation is not necessarily its literal meaning. This is partly because the meaning of the literal term may vary from Member State to Member State. The consequence of applying a doctrine of 'literalism' in the EU context, unlike the UK statutory context, therefore may well promote divergence rather than uniformity, and so run counter to the legal effects that the measure is intended to produce. But it is also partly because EU law, intended to create a single *EU* legal order, requires an EU interpretation, provided that the provision in question does not make an express reference to the law of the Member States for the purpose of determining its meaning and scope.[91] Thus just as autonomous EU meanings have been given by the CJEU to many of the terms employed by the Brussels Convention on Civil Jurisdiction and Judgments (now Brussels I *bis*), so many of the terms employed in the Insolvency Proceedings Regulation, which is intended to complement this Convention,[92] will require autonomous EU meanings.[93]

2.26 These meanings should be established by adopting a 'purposive'[94] or 'teleological' method of construction.[95] Although this approach differs from ordinary English principles of

---

[87] Nor does the CJEU expect them to. See AG Jacobs's Opinion in Case C-338/95 *Wiener SI GmbH v Hauptzollamt Emmerich* [1997] ECR I-6495, para 65.
[88] See, eg in relation to the Insolvency Proceedings Regulation, the concept of a 'debtor's main interests' in Art 3(1), translated as '*le centre des intérêts principaux*' in the French version, and '*den Mittelpunkt seiner hauptsächlichen Interessen*' in the German version. Note, however, that the RR expands upon the meaning of this term by setting out presumptions in the case of individuals as well as companies and then providing examples in the recitals as to when those presumptions might be rebutted: see Recitals (28)–(31); see also Recitals (27) and (32).
[89] The Court of Appeal has set out how foreign language versions should be put before the court in English proceedings in *R v Customs and Excise Commissioners, ex p Emu Tabac Sarl* [1997] EuLR 153, 160.
[90] ibid. See also *Customs and Excise Commissioners v Samex* [1983] 3 CMLR 194, 210 per Bingham J. On references, see part D below.
[91] Case C-116/11 *Bank Handlowy w Warszawie SA v Christianpol sp z oo* [2012] ECLI:EU:C:2012:739 para 49 (a case concerning the interpretation of Art 4(2)(j) OR, Art 7(2)(j) RR). In the context of the Insolvency Proceedings Regulation, Member State autonomy is expressly preserved in relation to matters such as the law applicable to insolvency proceedings and their effects (save where the Regulation makes express provision): see Art 4(1) OR/Art 7(1) RR. But contrast this with Art 16(1) OR/Art 19(1) RR, where there is no express reference to national law; thus the CJEU held that the Art 16(1)/Art 19(1) concept of a 'judgment opening insolvency proceedings' must be interpreted as encompassing not only decisions that are formally described in national law as opening decisions but also 'a decision handed down following an application, based on the debtor's insolvency, seeking the opening of proceedings ... where that decision involves divestment of the debtor and the appointment of the liquidator': Case C-341/04 *Eurofood IFSC Ltd* [2006] ECR I-3813, para 54.
[92] See Recital (7) of the Insolvency Proceedings Regulation.
[93] The most obvious example of this is the concept of 'the centre of main interests' which the CJEU has held is to be given an 'autonomous meaning': Case C-341/04 *Eurofood IFSC Ltd* (ECJ, 2 May 2006), para 31. See also Case C-396/09 *Interedil Srl v Fallimento Interedil* [2011] ECR I-9915, para 43.
[94] *Re BRAC Rent-A-Car-International Inc* [2003] BCC 248, 254 (Lloyd J). For an example of the CJEU having regard to the 'purpose' of the Insolvency Proceedings Regulation as set out in its preambles with a view to determining the meaning of a particular provision, see Case C-1/04 *Staubitz-Schreiber* (ECJ, 17 January 2006), esp paras 24–28 and, more recently, Case C-328/12 *Schmid v Hertel* [2014] ECLI:EU:C:2014:6 (both cases concerning the meaning and scope of Art 3(1)).
[95] See the famous characterization by Lord Diplock in *R v Henn and Darby* [1981] 1 AC 850, 905 and for an example of its express adoption in the context of the Insolvency Proceedings Regulation, see *Connock and Boyden v Fantozzi* [2011] EWHC 15 (Ch) (Newey J), para 26.

statutory construction, where the legal meaning of an enactment usually corresponds to its grammatical meaning,[96] it would be wrong to characterize it as simply substituting 'inspiration' for methodology. Even 'a teleological interpretation is an interpretation *intra legem* rather than *extra legem* or *contra legem*'.[97] As a result, the interpretation has to be compatible with the wording of the Community law provision. Moreover, establishing the 'teleological' meaning of a Community law provision involves adopting a structured approach. It involves considering the nature of the provision in the Regulation (for example whether it is a derogation or forms part of the general scheme that the Regulation is intended to create).[98] This in turn will require considering the overall scheme and purpose of the Regulation of which it forms part,[99] and understanding it in the context of the system of Treaty provisions and other rules regarding the allocation of jurisdiction and recognition of judgments in civil matters of which it forms part.[100] In particular, in relation to this last matter, it involves having regard to the principle of 'mutual trust which has enabled a compulsory system of jurisdiction to be established'.[101]

---

[96] Bennion, Bailey, and Norbury, *Statutory Interpretation* (8th edn, 2020) section 10.8(1). But note (1) that this is not invariably the case: verbal ambiguity or evidence of a contrary legislative intention may lead to departures from the literal meaning of the words; and (2) the literal or grammatical meaning is accorded precedence on the fiction that it correctly conveys 'the legislative intention', ie the grammatical and legal meanings are the same.

[97] Case C-125/97 *Regeling v Bestuur van de Bedrijfsvereniging voor de Metaalnijverheid* [1998] ECR I-4493 per AG Cosmas at 4504; see also Case C-313/07 *Kirtruna S L* [2008] ECR I-7907, para 44.

[98] Eg Art 3(4) of the Insolvency Proceedings Regulation, which permits the opening of territorial insolvency proceedings prior to the opening of main insolvency proceedings in limited cases only, is to be interpreted restrictively, since one of the underlying purposes of the Regulation is the coordination of insolvency proceedings 'to satisfy the need for unity in the European Union' and 'such coordination cannot be ensured if main proceedings have not been opened': Case C-112/10 *Zaza Retail BV* [2011] ECR I-11525, para 22; Art 26 OR (now Art 33), which provides a 'public policy' exception to the general rule that insolvency proceedings opened in one Member State are to be recognized in another, should be construed narrowly since it operates by way of an exception to the general scheme of the Regulation, Case C-341/04 *Eurofood IFSC Ltd* [2006] ECR I-3813, para 64. By contrast the term 'court' eg as in Art 3(1), being the body to which jurisdiction is allocated by the Regulation, will be given a broad meaning (as it is in Recital (10) OR, Recital (20) RR), because it furthers the purpose or scheme of the Regulation, *Re The Salvage Association* [2003] BCC 504, 509 (Blackburne J), where the word 'court' in Art 3(1) of the Regulation was interpreted to encompass any body recognized as competent in a Member State to open insolvency proceedings, with the result that it was held that company voluntary arrangements were capable of falling within Art 3. See also *Re TXU Europe German Finance BV* [2005] BCC 90 (Registrar Baister): a creditors' voluntary winding-up of a foreign company may fall within Art 3(1) of the Regulation.

[99] Case C-116/11 *Bank Handlowy w Warszawie SA v Christianpol sp z oo* [2012] ECLI:EU:C:2012:739, para 67; as the 'wording' of Art 27(1) OR (Art 34 RR) was 'not entirely clear' (para 66), the CJEU considered it necessary to have regard to the Regulation's 'overall scheme' to determine whether the court of the Member State in which secondary proceedings had been opened was entitled to examine whether the debtor was insolvent, or was bound by the finding of the court of the Member State in which main insolvency proceedings had been opened. The CJEU concluded (para 74) that the examination of the debtor's insolvency by the court having jurisdiction to open main proceedings was binding, given divergent national definitions of insolvency and the absence of a defined concept of insolvency in the Insolvency Proceedings Regulation. See likewise the CA's reliance on 'the rationale of secondary proceedings' as supporting its interpretation of the meaning of 'establishment' as a condition for the opening of secondary proceedings in *Trustees of the Olympic Airlines SA Pension & Life Insurance Scheme v Olympic Airlines SA* [2013] EWCA Civ 643, para 31.

[100] For a 'model' example of such an approach, see the CJEU's consideration of Art 24(1) OR (Art 31(1) RR) in Case C-251/12 *Christian Van Buggenhout and another v Banque Internationale à Luxembourg SA* [2013] ECLI:EU:C:2013:566, where the Court, having set out general EU principles of interpretation (paras 26 and 27), then considered different language versions of the contested provision (paras 28 and 29), the aim of the provision, and finally the 'objectives pursued by the legislation of which it forms part' (paras 33–36).

[101] Case C-341/04 *Eurofood IFSC Ltd* [2006] ECR I-3813, para 40, a principle which the CJEU has emphasized a number of times as a rule to assist interpretation as embodied in Recital (22) OR, Recital (65) RR: Case C-444/07 *MG Probud Gdynia* [2010] ECR-I-417, paras 27 and 28; Case C-527/10 *ERSTE Bank Hungary Nyrt v Magyar Allam and others* [2012] ECLI:EU:C:2012:417, para 34.

2.27 The CJEU has recognized a number of 'aids' to establish the purpose underlying legislative provisions. Of these, the most important is the preamble or statement of reasons which, as indicated above, is a Treaty requirement.[102] For example, Recital (13) OR attempts to explain the meaning of the debtor's 'centre of main interests' in Article 3(1), an important concept that is not defined in that Article.[103] The recitals, however, do not have binding legal force. Where there is a conflict between the preamble and the text of the Regulation itself, the former must give way to the latter.[104]

2.28 In addition, regard may be had to the preparatory measures that preceded the adoption of the Regulation. These measures are not decisive, but only persuasive or confirmatory.[105] Within this category, greater weight is to be given to preparatory measures that are formally required by the legislative process and are referred to in the preamble to the measure. In the case of the OR, as indicated above, these were the initiative of Germany and Finland,[106] the opinion of the European Parliament[107] and the opinion of the Economic and Social Committee.[108] In the case of the RR, these are the proposal from the Commission,[109] the opinion of the European Economic and Social Committee,[110] the positions of the European Parliament and of the Council,[111] and the Commission's report of 12 December 2012 on the application of the OR.[112] Lesser weight (but some weight nonetheless, although this will vary to the extent that the document is publicly available) may be given to other preparatory measures. In the case of the Insolvency Proceedings Regulation, since it is intended to introduce by another means the November 1995 Convention on Insolvency Proceedings, which never came into force, it is legitimate also to have regard to that measure[113] and to the explanatory Virgos-Schmit Report that

---

[102] Art 296 TFEU (referred to in this chapter as the Recitals). See *Re BRAC Rent-A-Car-International Inc* [2003] BCC 248, 251C (Lloyd J): the recitals 'help to cast light on some of the substantive provisions'. See also the reliance on the recitals by Longmore LJ in *Syska v Vivendi Universal SA* [2009] EWCA Civ 677, para 17 when considering the 'rationale' (para 16) for the Art 15 (Art 18 RR) exception to the general rule that the law of the Member State within whose territory proceedings are opened is to determine the effects of opening the proceedings (Art 4/Art 7 RR).

[103] See now Recitals (27) to (31) of the RR. Old Recital (13) has now been deleted and superseded by the relevant case law as reflected in new sentences in Art 3(1). See likewise Recital (25) OR/Recital (68) RR, which sheds some light on the meaning of 'rights in rem' for the purpose of the Regulation (suggesting that the *lex situs* determines whether a particular right is a right in rem). In the case of the Insolvency Proceedings Regulation, a number of the recitals have in turn been derived from the Virgos-Schmit Report (on which see below), as a result of which a proper understanding of them requires that they be understood in the context of that report: see the remarks of Registrar Jacques in *Re Stojevic* [2007] BPIR 141, para 33 (in that case concerning Recital (13) OR, which he held had to be understood in the context of para 75 of the report) and *O'Donnell and another v Governor and Company of the Bank of Ireland* [2012] EWHC 3749 (Ch), paras 24–25 (Newey J) (also in relation to former Recital (13)).

[104] Case C-412/93 *Société d'Importation Edouard Leclerc Siplec v TFI Publicité SA* [1995] ECR I-179, paras 45–47.

[105] See the comments of AG Tesauro in Case C-300/89 *Commission v Council* [1991] ECR I-2867, 2895.

[106] [1999] OJ C221/8.

[107] It was delivered on 2 March 2000.

[108] [2000] OJ C75/1.

[109] COM(2012) 744 final of 12 December 2012.

[110] [2013] OJ C271/55.

[111] The European Parliament positions are dated 5 February 2014 and 20 May 2015 and that of the Council is dated 12 March 2015.

[112] [2000] OJ L160/1.

[113] The English version of the Convention is contained in a Consultative Document published in February 1996 by the Insolvency Service of the DTI. English courts also have regard, where the underlying concept is the same, to the UNCITRAL Model Law on Cross-Border Insolvency adopted by the General Assembly of the UN on 15 December 1997 and the case law of other countries which have implemented the UNICTRAL Model Law (eg the

accompanied it,[114] in particular as some of the statements contained in it found their way almost verbatim into the recitals to the Insolvency Proceedings Regulation.[115] In relation to the RR, some assistance may also be derived from the official documents generated by the Article 294 TFEU procedure for the adoption of legislation, and the exchanges between the European Parliament and the Council.

Finally, although declarations made by the Council cannot be relied on to modify the Regulation any more than any other EU measure,[116] such declarations, since they are now publicly available,[117] may arguably be taken into consideration where interpreting the Regulation. In this respect it is to be noted that when the OR was adopted, the Council minutes record that Portugal made a statement regarding the interpretation of Article 37 (now Article 51 RR, but in a significantly amended form).[118] This has since been published in the *Official Journal*,[119] and was indeed referred to in the footnotes to the published text of the OR.

2.29

US federal bankruptcy code which incorporated the UNCITRAL definition of 'establishment'): *Trustees of the Olympic Airlines SA Pension & Life Insurance Scheme v Olympic Airlines SA* [2013] EWCA Civ 643, paras 17, 23.

[114] This was the basis on which AG Jacobs had regard to the report as 'useful guidance': Case C-341/04 *Eurofood IFSC Ltd* [2006] ECR I-3813, para 2 (although the CJEU itself did not refer to it in that case). The report is by Professor Virgos and Mr Schmit. A bad translation was attached as Annex B to the Insolvency Service Consultation Document referred to above. A revised and improved version was produced by the EU Council (Doc 6500/96, DRS 8 (CFC) Brussels 3 May 1996) (see app 2). In the first few years of the Insolvency Proceedings Regulation there was some, but not universal, judicial scepticism about the use of the report. Thus, although Lloyd J had regard to the report in *Re BRAC Rent-A-Car-International Inc* [2003] BCC 248, 254D–G, he (properly) indicated that he was uncertain as to its status and therefore the weight to be placed on it. Blackburne J in *Re The Salvage Association* [2003] BCC 504, 509 likewise referred to the report as being of 'questionable status', although he was 'encouraged' by the report in adopting in that case a broad approach to questions of interpretation; by contrast Gabriel Moss QC, sitting as a Deputy High Court Judge in *Financial Services Authority v Dobb White & Co* [2003] EWHC 3146 (Ch), para 4 referred to it without hesitation. However, a judicial consensus emerged that the report could be relied on as an aid to interpretation: see most recently *Trustees of the Olympic Airlines SA Pension & Life Insurance Scheme v Olympic Airlines SA* [2013] EWCA Civ 643, para 20 where the CA expressly endorsed the view of Sir Andrew Morritt C in *In re Stanford International Bank Ltd* [2010] EWCA Civ 137, para 36 that the report is 'authoritative'. Thus, Lawrence Collins J cited the report without comment in *Re Collins & Aikman Corp Group* [2006] BCC 606, 610D, as did Beatson J *Polymer Vision R&D Ltd v Van Dooren* [2011] EWHC 2951 (Comm), para 49 and Mann J in *Re Office Metro Ltd* [2012] EWHC 1191 (Ch), paras 14–16. See also *Syksa v Vivendi Universal SA* [2009] EWCA Civ 677 where Longmore LJ noted (para 20) that the Virgos-Schmit Report had been intended to be the Official Report of the Bankruptcy Convention and considered that the fact that the Convention was never agreed and the Regulation was put in its place as not having 'detracted from the authority of that Report'. Likewise, Newey J relied on it in *O'Donnell and another v Governor and Company of the Bank of Ireland* [2012] EWHC 3749 (Ch); Newey J, more questionably, also cited a work co-authored by Professor Virgos on the Insolvency Proceedings Regulation, as did Longmore LJ in *Syksa v Vivendi Universal SA*, paras 22–23. However, the assistance to be derived from the report may vary from case to case and indeed from issue to issue: see the approach of the CA in *Shierson v Vlieland-Boddy* [2005] 1 WLR 3966, especially paras 47–50 (where the report was not particularly helpful on the question of the 'immutability' of a debtor's COMI) and 65–68 (where the court had particular regard to the 'guidance' provided by the report on the meaning of 'establishment' within Art 3(2) (Chadwick LJ)).

[115] See further the explanation at fn 23 to AG Jacobs' Opinion in Case C-341/04 *Eurofood IFSC Ltd* [2006] ECR I-3813. As to the consequence of this, see *Re Stojevic* [2007] BPIR 141 as discussed above at fn 104 on the need, where relevant, to understand the recitals in the context of the report.

[116] Case C-306/98 *EC Commission v Greece* [1991] ECR I-5863, para 8.

[117] Art 9 of the Council's Rules of Procedure.

[118] This was that 'Article 37... which mentions the possibility of converting territorial proceedings ... into winding-up proceedings, should be interpreted as meaning that such conversion does not exclude judicial appraisal of the state of the local proceedings (as in the case of Article 36) or of the application of interests of public policy as provided for in Article 26'.

[119] [2000] OJ C183/1.

D. Solving Interpretative Issues and Questions of Validity: The Court of Justice of the European Union

2.30 The CJEU is the apex court for the purpose of determining questions of the validity of the Insolvency Proceedings Regulation and of the interpretation of its provisions.[120] Its decisions are binding as a matter of EU law on the court which requested its opinion. Further, as a matter of English law, the generally accepted view is that the consequence of section 3(1) of the European Communities Act 1972 was to extend the doctrine of precedent to the decisions of the ECJ. As a result, English courts were bound to give effect when interpreting EU legislation such as the Insolvency Proceedings Regulation to decisions of the CJEU. In addition, as a matter of EU law, only the CJEU has jurisdiction to declare an EU measure (or particular provisions of such a measure) to be invalid.[121]

2.31 By contrast, the opinions of the Advocates General do not bind national courts. Nonetheless, English courts regarded their Opinions as being persuasive.[122] The extent to which they are persuasive will depend on the relationship between the Opinion and the judgment of the CJEU, that is if the Opinion is referred to in the judgment and the court expressly or impliedly adopts its reasoning,[123] it will be 'persuasive', but if the court rejects it or has not followed it, it will have little or no authority. The Advocate General's Opinion may also be useful where it provides guidance on matters that have not been discussed by the CJEU.[124] Additionally, the opinions of the Advocates General may be helpful sources of academic debate, relevant authorities, and legal argument, thereby indicating the legal framework for the CJEU's judgment, which might not otherwise be apparent, and, by providing its proper legal context, rendering the judgment more intelligible.[125]

---

[120] There have now been a series of references to the CJEU concerning the Insolvency Proceedings Regulation, the CJEU's first judgment being handed down in January 2006. It remains to be seen whether and, if so, to what extent, English courts may take guidance from the CJEU case-law when considering the RR, where it continues to apply in the UK, and the Retained Recast Regulation where it does not, see section A of Chapter 9 below. Although the decisions of the courts of other Member States were never formally binding on English courts, because the Insolvency Proceedings Regulation is an EU legal instrument, intended to have the same legal effects in all Member States, it was also appropriate for an English court to have regard to those decisions, in the interests of uniformity, where determining the meaning and effect of the Insolvency Proceedings Regulation. However, care needs to be taken when citing such cases: see the comments of Mann J in *Re Office Metro Ltd* [2012] EWHC 191 (Ch): '[Counsel] relies on the account of an Estonian case (it cannot be treated as a report) ... appearing in Insolvency Intelligence' (para 23); '[Counsel] also pointed to an English case ... of which no transcript is available' (para 24); 'The authorities [Counsel] relies on are neither clear nor strong' (para 26).

[121] Case 314/85 *Foto-Frost v Hauptzollamt Lübeck Ost* [1987] ECR 4199, paras 15–20.

[122] See the discussion at R Brent, *Directives: Rights and Remedies in English and Community Law* (2001) para 20.05.

[123] See Case C-116/11 *Bank Handlowy w Warszawie SA v Christianpol sp z oo* [2012] ECLI:EU:C:2012:739, paras 48, 66 for express references to the AG's Opinion in the CJEU's judgment.

[124] Eg the reliance placed by Lewison J on AG Jacob's Opinion in Case C-341/04 *Eurofood IFSC Ltd* [2006] ECR I-3813 in *Re Lennox Holdings plc* [2009] BCC 155, where the judge relied on the approval by the AG of the 'head office functions test' (sometimes referred to as the 'command and control' test) to displace the presumption that the company's COMI was the state where its registered office was located. He commented 'that the approach of the Advocate-General is a particularly helpful one'. Note, however, that the statement by C Ritter in 'A New Look at the Role and Impact of Advocates-General—Collectively and Individually' (2006) 12 Columbia European Law Review 751–74 that 'In cases where the ECJ did not rule on the substantive issues addressed in the AG's opinion ... [the AG's opinion] constitutes precedent *vis-à-vis* the CFI and *a-fortiori* the Commission' overstates the position. Although the opinion is 'the individual reasoned opinion ... of a Member of the Court of Justice' (Case C-17/98 *Emesa Sugar (Free Zone) NV v Aruba* [2000] ECR I-665, para 14), it forms part of the process of internal deliberation of the Court. Accordingly, it does not have the juridical status of a judgment and should not be relied on as such, even *faut de mieux*.

[125] See further on this C Ritter, 'A New Look at the Role and Impact of Advocates-General—Collectively and Individually' (2006) 12 Columbia European Law Review 751–74, section 3 'The role and influence of

Jurisdiction

Historically, the role that the ECJ was entitled to play in interpreting the Regulation or determining the validity of its provisions was somewhat different from the role that it ordinarily plays in relation to other EU secondary legislation. This was because, when the Insolvency Proceedings Regulation was adopted under Title IV of what was then the ECT, Member State cooperation in the field of 'freedom, security and justice' was not fully developed. In particular, under the reforms introduced by the Treaty of Amsterdam, Member States as well as the Commission were entitled to propose the adoption of legislation; the role of the European Parliament was limited to a right to be consulted and the co-decision procedure did not apply; and Article 68 EC limited the ECJ's jurisdiction to decide questions concerning the interpretation of the Insolvency Proceedings Regulation to the circumstance where national courts or tribunals 'against whose decisions there is no judicial remedy under national law' considered that a decision was 'necessary' to enable them to give judgment. The ECJ did not have any jurisdiction to accept references from inferior national courts.

2.32

However, the Treaty of Lisbon replaced Article 61 EC and repealed Articles 67 and 68 EC (being the Articles under which the OR was adopted). One consequence of this has been that the limitation on the right to refer a question to the CJEU disappeared.[126] As a consequence, pursuant to Article 267 TFEU, a court or tribunal against whose decision there is a judicial remedy 'may' refer a question concerning the Insolvency Proceedings Regulation to the CJEU, 'if it considers that a decision on the question is necessary to enable it to give judgment'; whereas a court or tribunal, against whose decision there is no judicial remedy under national law, 'must' make such a reference in these circumstances.

2.33

Criteria for references

There are therefore three considerations for a national court before it requests a ruling from the CJEU on the Insolvency Proceedings Regulation. They are whether: (i) the court or tribunal is a court or tribunal of last resort; (ii) the ruling is necessary for that body to give judgment; and (iii) if it is necessary, but the court or tribunal is not a court or tribunal of last resort, it should exercise its discretion to refer.[127]

2.34

As a matter of English law, courts of last resort included not only the UKSC but all courts and tribunals from which there was no possibility of appeal. For example, the CA was 'the ultimate court of appeal if leave to appeal to the House of Lords [now the UKSC] is not obtainable'.[128] This was equally true of all courts from which permission to appeal has been refused.

2.35

Advocates-General'. For an example of an English court's reliance on an Advocate-General's statement of general principle in relation to the Insolvency Proceedings Regulation, see *Polymer Vision R&D Ltd v Van Dooren* [2011] EWHC 2951 (Comm) (Beatson J), para 62.

[126] Case C-396/09 *Interedil Srl v Fallimento Interedil Srl* [2011] ECR I-9915, paras 18–19.
[127] There is extensive case law on when a referring body is a 'court or tribunal'. But in the context of references by English bodies applying the Insolvency Proceedings Regulation this is highly unlikely to be an issue.
[128] *Hagen v Fratelli D&G Moretti* [1980] 3 CMLR 253 per Buckley LJ at 255.

2.36 So far as the condition of 'necessity' is concerned, assuming that the issue is otherwise relevant to the matter to be determined, there are two circumstances in which a court or tribunal is relieved from making the request.[129] They are where the issue is nonetheless *acte clair*; and where the issue is substantially the same as a question previously raised before the CJEU.

2.37 *Acte clair* means that the correct application of EU law is so obvious as to leave no doubt as to the manner in which the question raised is to be resolved.[130] Strictly speaking, before a court can reach such a conclusion, it must be satisfied that the matter is 'equally obvious' to the courts of the other Member States and to the CJEU.[131] This is a high hurdle imposed in the interests of legal uniformity. But it is a hurdle that English courts approached pragmatically. For example, in considering whether an issue was *acte clair*, the CA took into account the existence of a body of case law from which it is possible to extrapolate applicable principles of law and the absence of conflicting decisions in other Member States.[132] In relation to the Insolvency Proceedings Regulation, some concepts (such as 'the centre of main interests' of a debtor) are novel to it and unlikely to be regarded as *acte clair*. But other concepts, which may be novel in the context of insolvency proceedings (such as the term 'establishment' in Article 3(2)) have behind them a body of Community law developed in other contexts.[133]

2.38 Strictly speaking, the fact that the same issue has previously been raised before the CJEU is not a bar to its being raised again.[134] This follows from the fact that the CJEU is not bound by its own earlier decisions. But the authoritative nature of a previous judgment may be such as to deprive the obligation of the national court to refer of any real purpose. Where the question raised is 'substantially the same as a question which has already been the subject of a preliminary ruling in a similar case'[135] there is thus no necessity to refer. It may, however, be a moot point in any given case whether the condition of 'substantial' identity is satisfied.

---

[129] The leading case is still Case 283/81 *Srl CILFIT v Ministry of Health* [1982] ECR 3415. But it has been suggested that the guidelines which this case lays down should be reconsidered and relaxed; and that in practice English courts tended to apply them less rigorously than they might so as not to overburden the CJEU with references.

[130] ibid para 16.

[131] ibid paras 16–17.

[132] See *Trinity Mirror plc v Customs and Excise Commissioners* [2001] EWCA Civ 65, paras 53–55.

[133] Eg in relation to the meaning of the term 'establishment', in addition to the definition set out at Art 2(10) RR, see the case law arising out of the right to establishment as provided by Art 49 TFEU, and in particular, in the context of the operation in the single market of EU 'passports', the distinction drawn between operating an 'establishment' in another Member State and the mere provision of cross-border services; and the case law arising out of Art 5(5) of the Brussels Convention, now Art 7(5) Brussels I bis. Case C-396/09 *Interedil Srl v Fallimento Interedil Srl* [2011] ECR I-9915, paras 60–64, however, has considered the meaning of this term specifically in the context of the Insolvency Proceedings Regulation; and the Court of Appeal in *Trustees of the Olympic Airlines SA Pension & Life Insurance Scheme v Olympic Airlines SA* [2013] EWCA Civ 646 has considered the meaning of 'establishment' more specifically yet in the context of opening 'secondary proceedings' within the meaning of the Insolvency Proceedings Regulation. See also now Case C-327/13 *Burgo Group SpA v Illochroma and another* [2014] ECLI:EU:C:2014:2158, [2015] BCC 33.

[134] Case 283/81 *Srl CILFIT v Ministry of Health* [1982] ECR 3415, para 15. However, Art 99 of the CJEU's Rules of Procedure (adopted 25 September 2012) provides that in this circumstance the Court may decide to rule by reasoned order. It may now also do this if the Court considers that the answer can be deduced from existing case law or where the answer to the question admits of no reasonable doubt. This provision was introduced as a means of speeding up the time taken to deal with preliminary references.

[135] Case C-337/95 *Parfums Christian Dior SA v Evora BV* [1997] ECR I-6013, para 29.

2.39 So far as concerns the exercise of a court's discretion (other than a court of last resort), the sort of factors that are relevant are whether the facts are established, such that it would enable a reference to be useful, and the questions to be referred are properly formulated; the time it may take to obtain a judgment; the expense of the reference; the importance of not overwhelming the CJEU with references; the need to be able to formulate the question clearly; the difficulty and importance of the point at issue; and the views of the parties.[136]

2.40 The CJEU may itself refuse to entertain a request. This may be for one of five principal reasons.

(a) On the ground that the order for reference is inadequate. The importance of the order for reference is that it is this document, and not the CJEU's file, that is circulated to the Member States and the EU's institutions to give them and the parties the opportunity to submit observations.[137] The criterion that the CJEU will apply to determine this issue is whether it is able to provide a useful answer to the issue referred on the basis of the information supplied.[138]

(b) Although it is up to the national court to determine whether the reference is necessary in order for it to give judgment, the CJEU nonetheless is entitled to refuse to consider it where the reference is 'manifestly irrelevant'. This, however, has happened only in rare cases.[139]

(c) The CJEU will decline jurisdiction where it is asked to give judgment on a hypothetical problem.[140] But again it will refuse a request on these grounds only in rare circumstances.

(d) In isolated cases, where there is evidence that the procedure is being abused (because, for example, the dispute between the parties in the national proceedings has been fabricated), it is entitled to decline jurisdiction.

(e) Where the national procedure has been terminated, or the claims settled, the CJEU must also refuse the request. This is because Article 267 TFEU grants it jurisdiction only in relation to a case that is 'pending' before a national court. However, this is subject to the important caveat that, if the withdrawal of the request for the preliminary ruling is made after the CJEU has given notice of the date of delivery of its judgment, the CJEU may nonetheless proceed to give judgment.[141] The purpose behind this reform is to prevent one party from settling the dispute at the last minute because it expects the preliminary ruling to be adverse to its interests, for example after hearing the Advocate General's Opinion.

---

[136] The classic statements remain: *HM Bulmer Ltd v J Bollinger SA* [1974] Ch 401 (Lord Denning MR); *HMRC v APS Samex* [1983] 1 All ER 1042 (Bingham J); *R v Stock Exchange ex p Else Limited* [1993] QB 534 (Sir Thomas Bingham MR).

[137] It should be noted that the reference is from the national court, and not from the parties to proceedings before that court.

[138] Case C-316/93 *Vaneetveld v SA Le Foyer* [1994] ECR I-763, 767 per AG Jacobs.

[139] Case C-319/94 *Jules Dethier Equipement SA v Dassy* [1998] ECR I-1061, para 20.

[140] Case C-83/91 *Meilicke v ADV/ORGA FA Meyer AG* [1992] ECR I-4971. See also Case C-439/08 *VEBIC* [2010] ECR I-12471, para 42.

[141] Art 100 of the CJEU's Rules of Procedure, adopted 25 September 2012.

Procedure

2.41 The CJEU has exclusive jurisdiction to decide requests for preliminary rulings.[142] The procedure is essentially non-contentious, reflecting the fact that it is the national court and not the parties to proceedings which makes the reference. There are no time limits for making a reference other than the national time limits applicable to the national proceedings. Nor are any specific requirements laid down by the CJEU as to the form of the reference, although (as indicated above) both the case law of the CJEU and Article 94 of its Rules of Procedure do lay down requirements as to its substantive content and its Recommendations (referred to above) also provide guidance on the form of reference. The CJEU also publishes 'Notes for the Guidance of Counsel'.[143]

2.42 The procedures of the CJEU are governed by its own Statute and its Rules of Procedure. In exceptional cases, it is now possible for a national court to request the CJEU to apply an accelerated or expedited procedure.[144] In addition, special provision is made for an 'urgent procedure' in relation to cases falling within Title 5 of Part Three of the TFEU (concerning 'Area of Freedom, Security and Justice'). The CJEU has indicated, however, that the expedited and urgent procedures are primarily intended for cases involving people in custody or likely to be deprived of their liberty, or for proceedings concerning parental authority or the custody of children.[145] In 2020 the average length of preliminary reference proceedings before the CJEU was 15.4 months.[146]

---

[142] Following the Treaty of Nice, Art 225 EC, now Art 256 TFEU, was amended to permit the General Court (formerly known as the Court of First Instance) to determine requests for preliminary rulings in specific areas to be laid down in the Court's Statute. None has been so far.

[143] There is no automatic oral hearing: it is necessary to submit reasoned requests for an oral hearing and, on a proposal from the Judge-Rapporteur and after hearing the Advocate General, the Court may decide not to hold a hearing: see Art 76 of the Rules of Procedure dated 25 September 2012.

[144] Art 105, Rules of Procedure of the CJEU dated 25 September 2012.

[145] They are rarely used: in 2013 the expedited procedure was not used at all and the urgent procedure only twice, whereas 699 new cases were brought before the CJEU in that year: Annual Report of the European Court of Justice, pp 9–10 (2013). In 2020, 556 cases included nine urgent procedures which lasted 3.9 months on average: Annual Report 2020 of the CJEU, pp 56–57.

[146] Annual Report of the CJEU, p 57 (2020). This was an improvement on earlier years: eg in 2003 the average length was 25.3 months (the longest annual average in the period 2000–07).

3

SCOPE AND JURISDICTION

A.	**Scope**	3.01		Jurisdiction to conduct territorial	
	Preliminary	3.01		insolvency proceedings	3.40
	Material scope of the RR	3.03		Grounds of jurisdiction	3.40
	Personal scope of the RR	3.15		Further conditions of opening territorial	
	Territorial scope of the RR	3.19		proceedings	3.43
B.	**International Jurisdiction**	3.23		The scope of territorial proceedings	3.49
	Jurisdiction to conduct main insolvency			Jurisdiction to conduct ancillary	
	proceedings	3.24		proceedings	3.55
	Grounds of jurisdiction	3.24		Jurisdiction to order protective and	
	Forum shopping	3.30		preservation measures	3.61
				Jurisdiction to conduct group	
				co-ordination proceedings	3.66

A. Scope

Preliminary

Since the previous edition of this book, the Insolvency Proceedings Regulation's scope—or, as it has also been called, its sphere of application[1]—has changed significantly. First, the entry into force of the RR in June 2017 substantially expanded the material scope of the Insolvency Proceedings Regulation by allowing more types of proceedings to be covered by it. Second, the exit of the UK from the EU in December 2020 without any substitute for the RR led to a shrinkage of the territory on which the RR applies. **3.01**

It has become customary[2] to think about the sphere of the Insolvency Proceedings Regulation's application in terms of the types of proceedings, the types of debtors, and the territories which it covers. This is how section A of this chapter will proceed as well.[3] **3.02**

---

[1] M Virgós, F Garcimartín, *The European Insolvency Regulation: Law and Practice* (Kluwer Law International 2004) p 21. (hereafter 'Virgos/Garcimartin').

[2] See Virgos/Garcimartin p 21 ff; R Bork, R Mangano, *European Cross-Border Insolvency Law* (Oxford University Press 2016) (hereafter 'Bork/Mangano').

[3] Of course, the Insolvency Proceedings Regulation also has its sphere of application in time, however, since all provisions of the RR have now entered into force (see Art 92 RR) this theme will not be dealt with in this chapter beyond this footnote.

Material scope of the RR

3.03 As regards the types of proceedings subject to it (a topic referred to as the 'material' or the 'substantive' scope), the RR first and foremost sealed the debate about the relationship between Article 1 and Annex A.[4] The last sentence of Article 1(1) now expressly provides that 'The proceedings referred to in this paragraph are listed in Annex A' and, to leave no doubt about this point whatsoever, Recital 9 provides that: 'This Regulation should apply to insolvency proceedings which meet the conditions set out in it, irrespective of whether the debtor is a natural person or a legal person, a trader or an individual. **Those insolvency proceedings are listed exhaustively in Annex A.** In respect of the national procedures contained in Annex A, this Regulation should apply without any further examination by the courts of another Member State as to whether the conditions set out in this Regulation are met. **National insolvency procedures not listed in Annex A should not be covered by this Regulation.**' (emphasis added).[5]

3.04 This legislative development not only created legal certainty in the application of the RR but it also confined any further debate about which particular national proceedings should or should not be covered by the Regulation to the political process. The fact that the RR did not take over Article 45 of the OR[6] also means that any amendments to Annex A are now the matter of standard legislative procedure in the EU,[7] as has indeed been the case with Regulation (EU) 2021/2260 of the European Parliament and of the Council of 15 December 2021 amending Regulation (EU) 2015/848 on insolvency proceedings to replace its Annexes A and B Regulation, which has amended Annex A of the RR with effect as of 16 January 2022. By definition, this also means that amendments to Annex A will be relatively few and far between with clear implications for Member States' ability to have newly fashioned types of proceedings added under the RR's scope.

3.05 Subject to the caveats made in paragraph 3.04, it is of course still important for private parties to know what sort of proceedings they may use, or be confronted with, within the RR's scope. A moment's comparison of Article 1(1) OR[8] with Article 1(1) RR reveals that a number of proceedings that would not have fallen within the material scope of the OR are liable to fall under the RR. Although still a marker of compliance with Article 1(1), divestment (full or partial) of the debtor is now but one of the possible criteria for eligibility (Article 1(1)(a) RR). The two others are control or supervision of the debtor's assets or

---

[4] See C-461/11 *Radziejewski v Kronofogdemyndigheten i Stockholm*, ECLI:EU:C:2012:704, paras 23 and 24; C-116/11 *Bank Handlowy w Warszawie SA, PPHU 'ADAX'/Ryszard Adamiak v Christianapol sp z oo*, ECLI:EU:C:2012:739, paras 31 to 35.

[5] Quite astonishingly to those familiar with the initial difficulties regarding this issue under the OR and unfamiliar with the 1970 draft Convention on Bankruptcy, Winding-up, Arrangements, Compositions, and Similar Proceedings, that draft already dealt with this point unequivocally by providing for the determinative nature of the list of procedures to be annexed to the Convention. See K van Zwieten in R Bork, K van Zwieten (eds), *Commentary on the European Insolvency Regulation* (Oxford University Press 2016) (hereafter 'Bork/van Zwieten') p 12, marg no 0.17.

[6] Article 45 OR provided that 'The Council, acting by qualified majority on the initiative of one of its members or on a proposal from the Commission, may amend the Annexes.'

[7] R Bork in Bork/Mangano p 58; K van Zwieten in Bork/van Zwieten pp 59 to 64, in particular marg no 1.03, 1.09, and 1.10.

[8] Article 1(1) OR provided that: 'This Regulation shall apply to collective insolvency proceedings which entail the partial or total divestment of a debtor and the appointment of a liquidator.'

affairs by the court (Article 1(1)(b) RR)⁹ and the availability of a temporary stay of individual enforcement in order to allow for negotiations between the debtor and its creditors, provided that suitable measures to protect the general body of creditors are in place and further provided that where the negotiations are not successful, the process converts into one that features at least one of the two former markers of compliance (Article 1(1)(c) RR).

Although Article 1(1) OR already insisted on collectivity as a marker of compliance, the RR took a more relaxed approach to the criterion, with Article 2(1) RR defining 'collective proceedings' as 'proceedings which include all or a significant part of a debtor's creditors, provided that, in the latter case, the proceedings do not affect the claims of creditors which are not involved in them' and Recital 14 explaining that '[....] Proceedings which involve only the financial creditors of a debtor should also be covered. [... and ...] the fact that some insolvency proceedings for natural persons exclude specific categories of claims, such as maintenance claims, from the possibility of a debt-discharge should not mean that such proceedings are not collective.' Having observed that, it is equally important to note that Recital 14 RR also harbours another important point regarding the marker of collectivity when it explains that '[...] Proceedings which do not include all the creditors of a debtor should be proceedings aimed at rescuing the debtor. Proceedings that lead to a definitive cessation of the debtor's activities or the liquidation of the debtor's assets should include all the debtor's creditors.' And, of course, that the operative provision of Article 1(1) RR provides, in its penultimate sentence, that 'Where the proceedings referred to in this paragraph may be commenced in situations where there is only a likelihood of insolvency, their purpose shall be to avoid the debtor's insolvency or the cessation of the debtor's business activities.' Taken together, these provisions show that the fact that the RR treats as eligible proceedings which are only partially collective does not mean that post-recast, the Insolvency Proceedings Regulation has done away with the common pool problem as a key definitional feature of insolvency proceedings.¹⁰ Rather, the RR has correctly recognized that, as the result of information asymmetries among various types of creditors, the common pool problem (and the ensuing 'race for the debtor's assets') may dawn on various pools of claimants at different stages of the gradual deterioration of the debtor's financial condition. This is amply evidenced by the countless 'standstill agreements' which are routinely entered into at early stages of financial distress among banks or other finance creditors involved in multi-lender financings of borrowers who have fallen on hard times. The fact that the debtor's impeding financial crisis is not yet transparent to all of its creditors does not make the emerging common pool problem any less severe, provided that those 'in the know' are owed sufficiently large amounts to destroy, *via* individual enforcement action, the going-concern value of debtor's assets or its cash-flow position. Being in essence a privately agreed 'temporary stay of individual enforcement actions', the standstill agreement does exactly what processes described under Article 1(1)(c) RR aim to do. And it also explains that by including partially collective proceedings and processes into the sphere of its application, the RR has done no more than what the restructuring market has been doing *via* private ordering since what now feels like time immemorial.

3.06

---

⁹ That control or supervision may occur *ex post*—Recital 10 RR provides in the last sentence that '[...] the term "control" should include situations where the court only intervenes on appeal by a creditor or other interested parties'. In this context, 'court' must be a court in the narrow sense—ie a judicial body, see Art 2(6)(ii) RR.
¹⁰ Cf H Eidenmüller, 'What are insolvency proceedings?' (2016) ECGI Working Paper No 335/2016.

3.07 In addition to being collective (in the above-mentioned, restricted sense of the term), the proceedings falling within the RR's scope must also be 'proceedings, including interim proceedings,[11] which are based on laws relating to insolvency and [which aim to achieve] rescue, adjustment of debt, reorganisation or liquidation' (Article 1(1) RR). It is submitted that this language is so broad as to be almost meaningless in practical terms. However, the next parameter is not: in order to be eligible, any such proceedings must be *public*. Recital 12 explains the publicity requirement in the following terms: 'This Regulation should apply to proceedings the opening of which is subject to publicity in order to allow creditors to become aware of the proceedings and to lodge their claims, thereby ensuring the collective nature of the proceedings, and in order to give creditors the opportunity to challenge the jurisdiction of the court which has opened the proceedings.' Recital 13 adds that: 'Accordingly, insolvency proceedings which are confidential should be excluded from the scope of this Regulation. While such proceedings may play an important role in some Member States, their confidential nature makes it impossible for a creditor or a court located in another Member State to know that such proceedings have been opened, thereby making it difficult to provide for the recognition of their effects throughout the Union.' Thus, while one may be duly skeptical about the usefulness of the other distinguishing features of eligible proceedings as rendered in the opening words of Article 1(1) RR, the marker of publicity, in connection with the provisions of Articles 24 and 25 on electronic insolvency registers and the information that must mandatorily be published therein (Article 24(2) RR), actually does constitute a very tangible definitional element for the purposes of delineating the material scope of the Regulation.[12]

3.08 One should therefore be able to summarize the Insolvency Proceedings Regulation's material scope such that, following the recast, the legislative process through which the contents of Annex A are determined should result in the RR only covering public proceedings displaying a meaningful element of collectivity, legislated for in national laws relating to insolvency, whereunder the debtor is subject to the constraints set out in Article 1(1)(a) or (b) or where creditors are temporarily subject to a stay pursuant to Article 1(1)(c) RR, aimed at supporting negotiations whose purpose it is to avoid the debtor's insolvency.[13]

3.09 Beyond the type of proceedings covered by the RR, questions relating to material scope traditionally address the boundaries between the spheres of application of the Regulation

---

[11] Recital 15 provides that 'This Regulation should also apply to proceedings that, under the law of some Member States, are opened and conducted for a certain period of time on an interim or provisional basis before a court issues an order confirming the continuation of the proceedings on a non-interim basis. Although labelled as "interim", such proceedings should meet all other requirements of this Regulation.'

[12] The publicity requirement also seems to work as one of the driving factors affecting the design of national implementations of Directive (EU) 2019/1023 of the European Parliament and of the Council of 20 June 2019 on preventive restructuring frameworks, on discharge of debt and disqualifications, and on measures to increase the efficiency of procedures concerning restructuring, insolvency and discharge of debt, and amending Directive (EU) 2017/1132 (Directive on restructuring and insolvency). There seems to be a trend towards optionality in national implementations whereunder the debtors may choose between 'local' preventive restructuring proceedings which are not necessarily subject to the publication requirements of Art 24 RR and thus not eligible under the RR, and 'public' or 'European' restructuring proceedings which are subject to the RR's publication requirements and thus benefit from its regime of EU-wide recognition and enforcement. See Annex A as amended by Regulation 2021/2260, featuring among others the *öffentliche Restrukturierungssache* for Germany, the *openbare akkoordprocedure buiten faillissement* for the Netherlands, or the *Europäische Restrukturierungsverfahren* for Austria.

[13] Elements (a), (b), and (c) may of course apply cumulatively or in combinations. Notably, defining the concepts of 'insolvency' and the 'likelihood of insolvency' remains within the exclusive power of the Member States—see Art 2(2) of the Directive on Restructuring and Insolvency.

and of Regulation 'Brussels I'.[14] These questions tend mostly to arise in relation to litigation ancillary to insolvency proceedings, given that Article 1(2)(b) of Brussels I limits the material scope of that regulation so as to exclude 'bankruptcy, proceedings relating to the winding-up of insolvent companies or other legal persons, judicial arrangements, compositions and analogous proceedings', and that Article 6 RR regulates jurisdiction to decide 'actions deriving directly from insolvency proceedings and closely linked with them'.[15] Recital 7 RR demands that *'The interpretation of this Regulation should as much as possible avoid regulatory loopholes between the two instruments* [i.e. the RR and Brussels I]*.'* There are now a number of CJEU cases listing various types of litigation commonly triggered by a debtor's general default or coming hand-in-hand with it and sorting those that fall under the RR from those that fall under Brussels I.[16]

3.10 Outside the context of ancillary litigation, the most excitement about what procedures are within or outside the material scope of the Insolvency Proceedings Regulation has traditionally been raised by the English scheme or arrangement,[17] a debate that is now moot as the result of Brexit. Still, it has left us a helpful reminder in Recital 7 RR that '[…] the mere fact that a national procedure is not listed in Annex A to this Regulation should not imply that it is covered by Regulation (EU) No 1215/2012.'

3.11 The inquiry into the material scope of the Insolvency Proceedings Regulation usually stops with the discussion of what insolvency proceedings, or ancillary actions, are or are not covered by it. However, there is now a further, more subtle issue of *which effects* of the proceedings covered by the RR fall within its scope and which perhaps do not. At first sight, such a question might seem odd since Article 7(1) RR expressly provides that 'Save as otherwise provided in this Regulation the law applicable to insolvency proceedings **and their effects** shall be that of the Member State within the territory of which such proceedings are opened' (emphasis added). From here, one would have thought that the RR quite naturally covers *all of the effects of insolvency proceedings falling within its material scope*, unless it expressly provides otherwise in its safe-harbour provisions (see Articles 8 to 18 RR). The CJEU thought otherwise when it decided the *CeDe Group* case.[18] The facts of that case were highly complicated and it just might be one of the cases where bad facts make bad law. Or, as an old proverb says, a case where an unclear question elicits an unclear answer.[19]

3.12 As follows from the judgment's recapitulation of the dispute in the main proceedings, the underlying situation which gave rise to the *CeDe Group* case involved a Polish insolvency practitioner[20] who sued the insolvent debtor's Swedish counterparty for performance of a contractual claim for payment of a sum of money allegedly owed to the Polish debtor. The Swedish counterparty raised a set-off counterclaim in defence against the suit. As such, the case should have a been a rather boring occasion for the application of Article 4(2)(d)

---

[14] Regulation (EU) No 1215/2012 of the European Parliament and of the Council of 12 December 2012 on jurisdiction and the recognition and enforcement of judgments in civil and commercial matters.
[15] See section B of this Chapter 3.
[16] For a recent review, see R van Galen, *An Introduction to European Insolvency Law* (Wolters Kluwer 2021) pp 21–22 (hereafter 'van Galen').
[17] Van Galen, pp 25 to 28.
[18] C-198/18 *CeDe Group AB v KAN sp z oo, in liquidation* ECLI:EU:C:2019:1001.
[19] In the Czech original, the proverb uses a less polite adjective.
[20] Referred to as 'liquidator' since the case had arisen and was decided under the Original Regulation.

OR (Article 7(2)(d) RR) and, potentially, the safe-harbour rule in Article 6 OR (Article 9 RR). Polish law, being the *lex fori concursus*, should have governed the conditions under which the Swedish counterparty could invoke set-off against the insolvent debtor's claim, and in case that *lex fori concursus* should have prevented the Swedish counterparty from effecting set-off, the Swedish counterparty could potentially have relied on the safe-harbour provision in Article 6 OR (Article 9 RR). This is exactly what the Insolvency Proceedings Regulation was made for.

3.13 Instead, the case made its way to the CJEU to which the Swedish Supreme Court posed several questions, the first being whether 'Article 4 of Regulation No 1346/2000 [must] be interpreted as meaning that it applies to an action which is brought before a Swedish court by the liquidator of a Polish company—which is the subject of insolvency proceedings in Poland—against a Swedish company for payment of goods delivered under an agreement into which the companies entered before that insolvency?' Posed this way, the question of course looks like a candidate for being found to lie outside the scope of the Insolvency Proceedings Regulation, because such action does not sound like a situation that would derive directly from insolvency proceedings or be closely linked to them. The problem plainly is, however, that it wasn't the action for performance under the pre-existing contract that brought the Insolvency Proceedings Regulation into play, but rather the set-off attempted by the insolvent debtor's counterparty, ie the 'mother of all insolvency law-related policy dilemmas'.[21]

3.14 Looking at the *CeDe Group* judgment, it seems obvious that the referring national court got tripped up by several complications, one stemming from the fact that Polish law apparently would not have restricted the set-off as such but the Polish insolvency practitioner still rejected it on some other grounds,[22] another being the fact that the Polish debtor's claim was subsequently assigned to a third party which, confusingly, also ended up insolvent.[23] But even allowing for all these distractions, it seems that the CJEU should still have known better than to hold, in effect, that a situation involving a dispute over a set-off attempted against a claim owed to a debtor subject to main insolvency proceedings conducted in a Member State is out of the scope of the Insolvency Proceedings Regulation. That is what the CJEU in essence did by holding that Article 4 OR, ie the key rule establishing the basis for the presumptively universal reign of *lex fori concursus* over the debtor's assets, debts, and other affairs, did not apply to the dispute. Accordingly, it is submitted that the *CeDe Group* case was decided incorrectly and that that judgment should not be followed. Had the *lex fori concursus* in question been one that bans or restricts insolvent set-off,[24] it would have (hopefully) been abundantly clear that the court's approach to the first question presented to it is simply untenable. If the Insolvency Proceedings Regulation is supposed to do what it is meant for, in particular support 'the proper functioning of the internal market [by making sure] that cross-border insolvency proceedings [...] operate efficiently and effectively' (Recital 3 RR), the courts should think much longer and much harder than the *CeDe*

---

[21] See P R Wood, *Principles of International Insolvency* (Sweet & Maxwell 2007) p 403.
[22] C-198/18 *CeDe Group AB v KAN sp z oo, in liquidation* ECLI:EU:C:2019:1001, para 12.
[23] *Ditto*, para 18.
[24] See B Hess, P Oberhammer, T Pfeiffer (eds), *European Insolvency Law. The Heidelberg-Luxembourg-Vienna Report of the Application of Regulation No. 1346/2000/ec on Insolvency Proceedings* (CH Beck Hart Nomos 2014) pp 200–202, marg no 766–78.

Group court had done before they start selectively denying the essential legal effects brought about by such insolvency proceedings and their *lex fori concursus*.

Personal scope of the RR

Subject to the exceptions discussed in paragraph 3.17 below, the question who may be a debtor in proceedings covered by the RR is for Member States to determine—Article 7(2)(a) RR clearly provides that 'The law of the State of the opening of proceedings shall determine [...] (a) the debtors against which insolvency proceedings may be brought on account of their capacity.'[25] **3.15**

Similarly, it is also for national law to determine—within the bounds of the non-discrimination principle of EU law[26]—who *needs to* participate in the proceedings in order to preserve his or her rights as a creditor.[27] Historically, the Insolvency Proceedings Regulation went to considerable lengths to make sure that Member States' public authorities could lodge their claims in insolvency proceedings in other Member States (see Recital 21 and Article 39 OR), and the RR still contains provisions to that effect in Recital 63 and Article 2(12) RR. Interestingly, by doing this, the RR also makes it clear that Member States may claim no sovereign immunity for their claims, whether these arise under private or public law, from the effects of insolvency proceedings conducted pursuant to the RR in other Member States. **3.16**

By way of exception to the rule in Article 7(2)(a) RR which leaves the personal scope to national law, the RR contains its own personal scope provision in Article 1(2) RR. Pursuant to that provision, the Regulation shall not apply to insolvency proceedings concerning insurance undertakings, credit institutions, investment firms and other firms, institutions and undertakings to the extent that they are covered by Directive 2001/24/EC, and to collective investment undertakings.[28] Commentaries on Article 1 tend to glide over this carve-out pointing to the special regulatory regimes to which these kinds of debtors are subject under harmonized national laws, including special procedures in the event of insolvency. While that is certainly true, it is also true that anyone interested, or even versed, in European cross-border insolvency law but not yet familiar with the EU insolvency regime applicable to these type of debtors will be in for a 'cultural shock' of sorts upon first delving into it. For whilst the cross-border insolvency regime applicable to all other debtors is defined by the uncertainties (and strategic shenanigans) inherent in the connecting factor of the 'centre of main interests', and whilst the process of resolving the debtor's general default may potentially be splintered among the jurisdictions, and governing laws, of several Member States as the result of the 'limited universality' of the jurisdictional regime applicable under the RR,[29] the European legislator will clearly have none of this with respect to the debtors carved-out from the Regulation's personal scope in Article 1(2) RR. Here, unity and universality reign supreme, and international jurisdiction is vested exclusively in the debtor's home Member **3.17**

---

[25] For a detailed taxonomy of debtors, see R Bork in Bork/Mangano, pp 42–54.
[26] R Bork, *Principles of Cross-Border Insolvency Law* (Intersentia 2017) p 63, marg no 2.62.
[27] The *right to* participate in insolvency proceedings anywhere within the EU Member States is anchored in Articles 45 and 53 RR.
[28] For details, see Chapter 7 below.
[29] See section B of this Chapter.

State[30] (which, for all intents and purposes, rather strongly resembles the connecting factor of incorporation, except that it is probably even more stable in time, and thus more difficult to manipulate strategically).[31] Whether this split between the 'home Member State / true unity and universality' approach for financial debtors on the one hand, and 'COMI / potential disunity and limited universality' for everyone else on the other hand can really be justified is an interesting question of policy (and politics). After all, a failure of a large, interconnected non-financial debtor may be systematically much more disruptive than the failure of a small-sized bank or another financial firm, and it is not immediately obvious why the EU citizens and businesses would be better off in a legal system in which the latter's insolvency should be resolved based on the 'home Member State / true unity and universality' approach, while the former's insolvency should be subject to the 'COMI / potential disunity and limited universality' approach.

3.18 Be that as it may, it is important to realize, in practical terms, that the 'home Member State / true unity and universality' approach applicable to debtors carved-out from the RR's scope can by definition only apply to debtors who are *actually properly authorized* to conduct the relevant regulated financial business. That approach can only ever function if there actually is the connecting factor of a home Member State, ie a Member State 'in which [the relevant debtor] has been granted authorization'[32] not if there is one—or quite possibly more (!)—Members States aggrieved by the fact that the debtor has been violating their financial regulation by conducting finance business in their territory without the requisite licence or other authorization. A debtor who conducts such business without the requisite authorization clearly cannot be subject to the 'home Member State / true unity and universality' approach, because it does not have a 'home Member State' in the legal sense of term. Therefore, as English case law has rightly recognized,[33] debtors who conduct the activities reserved to the businesses carved-out from the RR's scope by Article 1(2) RR without the requisite authorization fall under the RR's personal scope just as all other debtors do.[34]

Territorial scope of the RR

3.19 Interestingly, perhaps the most important rule regarding the territorial sphere of application of the RR is not to be found in the operative provisions but in a Recital, although its formulation is unmistakably one of an operative rule. Recital 25 RR reads: 'This Regulation applies only to proceedings in respect of a debtor whose centre of main interests is located in the Union.' Here, the term 'Union' must be read so as to exclude Denmark to which the Regulation does not apply.[35] The upshot of this rule is that with respect to debtors whose

---

[30] See eg Arts 3 and 9 of Directive 2001/24/EC of the European Parliament and of the Council of 4 April 2001 on the reorganization and winding up of credit institutions (consolidated text). 'Home Member State' is defined by cross-reference to Art 4(1)(43) of Regulation (EU) No 575/2013 of the European Parliament and the Council of 26 June 2013 on prudential requirements for credit institutions and investment firms and amending Regulation (EU) No 648/2012 as 'the Member State in which an institution has been granted authorization'.
[31] See eg W-G Ringe in Bork/van Zwieten, pp 138–39, and the sources cited therein.
[32] See again for example Art 4(1)(43) of Regulation (EU) 575/2013.
[33] See *FSA v Dobb White & Co* [2003] EWHC 3146 (Ch); R Bork in Bork/Mangano, pp 54–55, marg no 2.38, 2.39.
[34] Subject only to provisions of national law (Art 7(2)(a) RR).
[35] See Recital 88 RR. And now, of course, also the UK.

COMI is outside the EU (or in Denmark), ie in situations that could be thought of as potential 'inbound exterritoriality', national rules on cross-border insolvency proceedings apply instead of the RR.[36]

The question of 'outbound exterritoriality', ie whether the RR has the ambition to extend its effects outside of the EU, is not dealt with expressly in its operative provisions either. Recital 23 RR provides in its second sentence that 'Those [ie the main] proceedings have universal scope and are aimed at encompassing all the debtor's assets', however, that language is immediately preceded by Recital 22 which also deals with the 'universal scope' of the main proceedings, but which clearly limits that notion to effects within the territory of the EU. Also, in the very next sentence, Recital 23 proceeds to explain that those extraterritorial effects may be mitigated through the effects of the opening of secondary proceedings in other Member States—a context which would once again clearly seem to limit the debate in Recital 23 to intra-EU situations.

3.20

Nevertheless, from early on, it was proposed that the Insolvency Proceedings Regulation should indeed be interpreted as having world-wide effects, at least in the sense that the main proceedings encompass all of the debtor's assets, and affect all of the debtor's creditors, wherever located.[37] It has been submitted that the question of the Insolvency Proceedings Regulation's outbound extraterritoriality was settled in the CJEU *Schmid v Hertel* case.[38] Although time may prove this reading of *Schmid v Hertel* correct, the case was defined much more narrowly than that. The question at the heart of *Schmid v Hertel* was one of jurisdiction to conduct ancillary litigation (an avoidance action) involving an EU (German) debtor's insolvency practitioner in main insolvency proceedings as plaintiff, and a non-EU (Swiss) resident as defendant. It is true that the CJEU held that the German court had jurisdiction to hear the case and in the line of arguments leading to that holding, it said that the '[a]pplication of Article 3(1) of the [Original] Regulation cannot therefore, as a general rule, depend on the existence of a cross-border link involving another Member State'.[39] One must, however, bear in mind that the judgment was concerned with the OR, which did not include Article 6 RR that now grants express jurisdiction to EU courts to decide ancillary actions. In pre-recast law, that jurisdictional ground was judge-made law developed by the CJEU based on Article 3 and Article 25(1) OR.[40] Read in the context of the RR, the *Schmid v Hertel* decision can safely be relied on in order to interpret Article 6 RR such that it vests in EU courts the jurisdiction to hear avoidance actions against defendants residing outside the EU as well as inside. It can also be relied on to support the view that a cross-border element, whether involving EU Member States or other States, need not be established in order for the RR to apply within the EU.[41] But really not much more than that. In particular, the *Schmid v Hertel* judgment does not say anything that could be used to support

3.21

---

[36] R Bork in Bork/Mangano, p 71, marg no 2.76. For a radically different approach, see the 1970 draft Convention on Bankruptcy, Winding-up, Arrangements, Compositions, and Similar Proceedings, cited in K van Zwieten in Bork/van Zwieten, p 12, marg no 0.18.
[37] See the Virgos-Schmit Report p 15, para E(19)(a), p 51, para 73. See also Virgos/Garcimartin, p 54, marg no 72. However, Virgos/Garcimartin have also argued that the same conclusion does not hold for questions of conflicts of laws (*ditto*, pp 23–24), which seems to echo the position in Virgos/Schmit, p 30, para 44(b).
[38] C-328/12 *Ralph Schmid v Lilly Hertel* ECLI:EU:C:2014:6; R Bork in Bork/Mangano, p 69, marg no 2.72, p 74, marg no 2.81.
[39] C-328/12 *Ralph Schmid v Lilly Hertel* ECLI:EU:C:2014:6, para 29.
[40] C-339/07 *Christopher Seagon v Deko Marty Belgium NV* ECLI:EU:C:2009:83.
[41] *Ditto*, paras 24, 28.

the grand extraterritorial ambition (dating back to the Virgos-Schmit Report, but not reliably expressed in the Insolvency Proceedings Regulation) to include into its sphere of application all of the debtor's assets, whether located in or outside the EU. That question might still have to wait for its day in court. After all, the position adopted by the CJEU in *Schmid v Hertel* differs from that proposed in the Virgos-Schmit Report,[42] so it still remains to be seen whether, when the 'grand question of extraterritoriality' comes to be decided by the CJEU, the two positions will dovetail or not.

3.22 A final comment on the RR's territorial scope relates to the position of Ireland. Unlike Denmark, which has been exempt from the Insolvency Proceedings Regulation's sphere of application in the inbound as well as the outbound direction, Recital 3 of amending Regulation (EU) 2021/2260 seems to suggest that while Ireland's own insolvency proceedings remain in Annex A following the amendment thereof by that regulation,[43] Ireland will not be under an obligation to recognize proceedings added to the amended Annex A by other Member States.[44] This is a unique situation in which a Member State seems to have cherry-picked the RR's territorial scope, having its own proceedings recognized in the outbound direction, but not being obligated to recognize proceedings added in respect of other Member States (over and above the contents of Annex A as originally promulgated in the RR) in the inbound direction.

B. International Jurisdiction

3.23 The Insolvency Proceedings Regulation establishes Member States' international jurisdiction with respect to several types of proceedings, namely (a) main insolvency proceedings, (b) territorial insolvency proceedings, (c) ancillary proceedings, (d) proceedings concerning protective and preservation measures, and (e) group co-ordination proceedings. This section B will review these types of jurisdiction in that order.

Jurisdiction to conduct main insolvency proceedings

Grounds of jurisdiction

3.24 It is by now commonplace that only one set of main insolvency proceedings may be conducted over one and the same debtor within the EU.[45] In this sense, jurisdiction to open and conduct main insolvency proceedings (ie proceedings with a universal effect, at least within the EU[46]) is exclusive, and this exclusivity is enjoyed by the Member State in which the debtor's centre of main interests ('COMI') is situated (Article 3(1) first sentence RR).

---

[42] R Bork in Bork/Mangano, p 69, marg no 2.72.
[43] See the items under the heading ÉIRE/IRELAND in the amended Annex A.
[44] Recital 3 of Regulation (EU) 2021/2260 provides that 'In accordance with Articles 1 and 2 and Article 4a(1) of Protocol No 21 on the position of the United Kingdom and Ireland in respect of the area of freedom, security and justice, annexed to the Treaty on European Union and to the Treaty on the Functioning of the European Union, and without prejudice to Article 4 of that Protocol, *Ireland is not taking part in the adoption of this Regulation and is not bound by it or subject to its application*.' (emphasis added).
[45] K van Zwieten in Bork/van Zwieten, p 1, marg no 0.01; *Ditto*, W-G Ringe, p 177, marg no 3.211.
[46] See Recital 23 of the RR.

3.25 Alas, the COMI is a fact- and time-sensitive ground of jurisdiction, as follows from its definition given in Article 3(1) second sentence RR: 'The centre of main interests shall be the place where the debtor conducts the administration of its interests on a regular basis and which is ascertainable by third parties.' Working out which Member State is the one exclusively entitled to conduct the main insolvency proceedings may be all but straightforward in actual court practice. In order to alleviate the difficulties involved in establishing the relevant facts, Article 3 RR contains several presumptions as to the localization of the debtor's COMI, depending on whether the debtor in question is a company or another legal person, an individual exercising independent business or professional activities, or any other individual.[47] As regards the time-sensitivity of the COMI, it was held by the CJEU early on that the relevant time at which the factual circumstances determining the localization of the COMI are deemed 'locked' in one place for jurisdictional purposes is the time when the debtor lodges the request to open insolvency proceedings.[48] Second, in the very same provisions in which Article 3(1) RR establishes the factual presumptions as to the localization of COMI cited above, those presumptions are removed in case that the facts referred to for the purposes of the presumptions have changed in a 'suspect period' of three to six months prior to the filing of the insolvency petition.

3.26 Nevertheless, given the fact- and time-sensitivity of the COMI concept, uncertainties, disputes, and even jurisdictional conflicts are to an extent inevitable even in circumstances where the facts relevant to establishing jurisdiction have not been strategically manipulated but are 'merely' unclear.[49] These led among others to two seminal CJEU judgments, *Eurofood*[50] and *Interedil*.[51] Some of the holdings from those judgments have since been codified in the RR, in several formulations included in Recitals 27 to 33 and particularly in Article 4(1) RR, which expressly requires national courts seised of a request to open insolvency proceedings *ex officio* to examine whether they have jurisdiction pursuant to Article 3 RR and to include in the judgment opening insolvency proceedings, the grounds on which the jurisdiction of the court is based.

3.27 Having observed all that, one must still accept that, given the inherently fact- and time-sensitive nature of the concept of COMI, both honest mistakes and manipulative

---

[47] The presumptions are that the COMI is in the Member State of the debtor's registered office, the principal place of business, or habitual residence, respectively. See Art 3(1), paras 2, 3, and 4. In a recent case dealing with the last of those presumptions, the CJEU ruled that the first and fourth subparagraphs of Art 3(1) of Regulation 2015/848 must be interpreted as meaning that the presumption established in that provision for determining international jurisdiction for the purposes of opening insolvency proceedings, according to which the centre of the main interests of an individual not exercising an independent business or professional activity is his or her habitual residence, is not rebutted solely because the only immovable property of that person is located outside the Member State of habitual residence. C-253/19 *MH and NI v OJ and Novo Banco SA* ECLI:EU:C:2020:585.

[48] C-1/04 *Susanne Staubitz-Schreiber* ECLI:EU:C:2006:39. The case involved a debtor insolvency petition but one must assume that the result, being an application of the *perpetuatio fori* principle, would apply equally irrespective of whether the insolvency proceedings were commenced upon a petition filed by the debtor, a creditor, or another party (where national law gives other parties standing to file for the opening of insolvency proceedings). The CJEU confirmed the *Staubitz-Schreiber* approach in 2022 with respect to the RR in Case C-723/20 *Galapagos BidCo. Sàrl v DE, in its capacity as liquidator of Galapagos SA, Hauck Aufhäuser Fund Services SA, Prime Capital SA* ECLI:EU:C:2022:209.

[49] Cf the upsides of the 'home Member State/true unity and universality system' applicable to debtors carved-out from the RR's personal scope referred to in para 3.17.

[50] C-341/04 *Eurofood IFSC Ltd* ECLI:EU:C:2006:281.

[51] C-396/09 *Interedil Srl, in liquidation v Fallimento Interedil Srl and Intesa Gestione Crediti SpA.* ECLI:EU:C:2011:671.

misrepresentations of the facts relevant to establishing international jurisdiction are nevertheless likely to arise from time to time. If such circumstances result in a contest for jurisdiction among the courts of several Member States (referred to as 'positive conflict' of jurisdictions),[52] such conflicts must be resolved on the basis of what has been called 'the principle of priority'.[53] This principle is embodied in Recital 65 RR which provides *inter alia* that: 'The recognition of judgments delivered by the courts of the Member States should be based on the principle of mutual trust. To that end, grounds for non-recognition should be reduced to the minimum necessary. **This is also the basis on which any dispute should be resolved where the courts of two Member States both claim competence to open the main insolvency proceedings. The decision of the first court to open proceedings should be recognised in the other Member States without those Member States having the power to scrutinise that court's decision.**' (emphasis added).

3.28 A moment's consideration of Recital 65 should reveal that the 'principle of priority' as described above is a very different matter from the approach to international *lis pendens* adopted in the non-insolvency context, in particular in Articles 29 to 31 of Brussels I. Although a proposal was made early on to apply the court-first-seised approach in matters subject to the Insolvency Proceedings Regulation by analogy,[54] that approach has clearly not been adopted in practice. Races to the insolvency court room, and to the insolvency-order-first-issued, are therefore very much part of the reality of the cross-border insolvency system created in the EU by the Insolvency Proceedings Regulation. If anything, the 'principle of priority' as it is framed in Recital 65 RR is actually liable to stoke up those sorts of races rather than mitigate them.

3.29 The principle in Recital 65 RR that '[t]he decision of the first court to open proceedings should be recognised in the other Member States without those Member States having the power to scrutinise that court's decision' has its corollary in Article 5 RR (and Recital 34 RR) which provide for judicial review of the decision to open main insolvency proceedings on grounds of international jurisdictions at the instigation of the debtor or any creditor before the courts of the Member State, which has claimed jurisdiction by opening the main insolvency proceedings. Article 5 RR has been variously described as creating a 'free-standing and independent judicial remedy, which is available to all creditors and the debtor alongside any national remedies',[55] 'not only guarantee[ing] the option of judicial review but provid[ing] a remedy in itself'[56] or as 'not [being] an appeal [...] mean[ing] that there will be no room for any prohibition of fresh evidence which the national law referred to could provide for'.[57] Although one may have understanding, and even sympathy, for this sort of interpretation, that does not help resolve the immense practical difficulties triggered by it in any real-life procedural situation. It is notable that all of the interpretations referred to above immediately admit that the practical details of such remedy will have to in any case be provided by national procedural law.[58] One could accordingly just as well argue that what Article 5(1)

---

[52] R Mangano in Bork/Mangano, p 101, marg no 3.57.
[53] *Ditto*, pp 102–104.
[54] See Virgos/Garcimartin, p 52.
[55] W-G Ringe in Bork/van Zwieten, p 195, marg no 5.01.
[56] M Brinkmann in M Brinkmann (ed), *European Insolvency Regulation: Article-by-Article Commentary* (CH Beck Hart Nomos 2019) p 71, marg no 8 (hereafter 'Brinkmann (ed)').
[57] R Mangano in Bork/Mangano, p 101, marg no 3.56.
[58] W-G Ringe in Bork/van Zwieten, p 199, marg no 5.16; M Brinkmann in Brinkmann (ed), pp 71–72, marg no 8, 9; R Mangano in Bork/Mangano, p 101, marg no 3.55.

RR really does is that it requires that Member States fashion appropriate remedies in their national insolvency proceedings allowing the debtor and the creditors to challenge insolvency orders in main proceedings opened by their national courts on jurisdictional grounds. The end effect would be the same, but the road to it would seem a lot less precarious.

Forum shopping

What makes all these jurisdictional debates so charged is of course the potential for *forum shopping*, ie strategic selection of the jurisdiction in which to file for the main proceedings. That proposition is particularly problematic in the EU where, under Article 7 RR, the court selected determines (with narrowly defined exceptions) the governing insolvency law as well (hence *lex fori concursus*).[59] Changing the COMI after a debt has been incurred thus in effect amounts to unilaterally changing the loan or other financing agreement mid-stream, which may be especially toxic where the governing insolvency law connected with the new jurisdiction provides for a distributional outcome different from that which would obtain under the insolvency law of the original jurisdiction. Although these strategies would surely be considered and evaluated by private actors in any system that ties governing insolvency law to court jurisdiction, the factually malleable jurisdictional ground of the COMI makes such strategies much more feasible than more rigid (and more stable) grounds of jurisdiction.[60] **3.30**

Lenders active in the European corporate credit markets understood the risks related to the jurisdictional grounds of COMI very early on, as evidenced by borrowers' representations as to the Member State of its COMI at the time of entering into loan agreements and the related events of default triggered by a change of the COMI to another Member State while the loan is outstanding. These provisions have been a staple of European loan agreements for the past 20 years. **3.31**

Now, quite obviously, no one would have a reason to complain about *Pareto efficient* changes of COMI—ie such changes of the grounds of international insolvency jurisdiction (and, by operation of Article 7 RR, the applicable insolvency law) that would make none of the stakeholders affected by the debtor's general default worse off, and at least one of them (or better yet, at least one class of them) better off.[61] The perennial practical trouble is that establishing whether a proposed COMI shift (or, indeed, any other legal change) does or does not represent a *Pareto* improvement may of course be rather difficult in the procedural reality, such as in a jurisdictional determination under Article 4 or in the application of a remedy under Article 5 RR. Nevertheless, the Recitals are on several locations visibly concerned about 'fraudulent or abusive' forum shopping and, interpreted with the principle of *Pareto* efficient outcomes in mind, those provisions can be applied in order to support exactly such outcomes in jurisdictional disputes. **3.32**

---

[59] Obviously, the situation in the US is a lot less charged in this context because US bankruptcy law is federal and applies (or at least should apply) uniformly irrespective of the State or district in which the proceedings are conducted.

[60] Cf once again the 'home Member State/true unity and universality' approach applied by the EU to debtors carved-out from the RR's scope by its Art 1(2).

[61] See eg R Cooter, T Ulen, *Law & Economics, Fifth Edition (Pearson International Edition)* (Pearson Addison Wesley 2008) p 16.

3.33 The principal provision addressing the risks related to forum shopping is Recital 5 RR which provides that 'It is necessary for the proper functioning of the internal market to avoid incentives for parties to transfer assets or judicial proceedings from one Member State to another, **seeking to obtain a more favourable legal position to the detriment of the general body of creditors** (forum shopping)' (emphasis added). Transfers of assets or judicial proceedings motivated by such ulterior motives are further referred to in the preamble as 'fraudulent or abusive forum shopping' (Recitals 29 and 31 RR), and the marker of 'fraud or abuse' in this particular context seems to be expressed most poignantly in the test of whether 'it can be established that the principal reason for moving was to file for insolvency proceedings in the new jurisdiction and where such filing would materially impair the interests of creditors whose dealings with the debtor took place prior to the relocation' (Recital 30 RR, the last sentence). Recital 30 RR applies that test expressly to individuals not exercising an independent business or professional activity, and mentions it for the specific purpose of rebutting the presumption set out in the fourth paragraph of Article 3(1) RR, however, there seems to be no reason why this standard could not attain wider application, since it directly addresses the most toxic risk arising out of the RR's rules on jurisdiction and governing law, ie the risk that after having incurred debt, the borrower will strategically select a new forum whose governing insolvency law will result in an uncompensated redistribution of wealth between the various claimants against his or her assets. The last sentence of Recital 30 RR is clearly primarily concerned about involuntary redistributions of wealth from the creditors as a whole to the debtor. There may, however, be equally egregious attempts to use a COMI shift so as to achieve uncompensated redistribution of wealth among various classes of creditors, which is a risk that is always present if the new *lex fori* ranks creditors' claims differently from the *lex fori* against whose backdrop the financial structure was originally negotiated.

3.34 In addition to Recital 5, the concept of the 'general body of creditors' is used in Recital 11 and in Articles 1(1)(c) and 7(2)(m) RR. In all those instances, the concept seems to refer to the totality of the debtors' creditors in a somewhat abstract sense. Of course, if all the debt owed by the debtor only has one rank (there are only general, unsecured, unsubordinated creditors), this abstraction will fit reality quite well. In more complicated capital structures involving various seniorities of debt as well as equity, the abstraction will sooner or later run into its limits. However, this is where the concept of *Pareto* efficiency can help. Viewed through its lenses, a COMI shift will clearly not be 'fraudulent or abusive' if none of the various investor classes is made worse off as the result of the application of the new *lex fori*. If this is so, neither the debtor (in the corporate context its shareholders) nor any class of its creditors clearly will have 'obtain[ed] a more favourable legal position to the detriment of the general body of creditors' as *per* the test in Recital 5 RR nor, by definition, will the interests of creditors whose dealings with the debtor took place prior to the relocation have been materially impaired, as *per* the test in Recital 30 RR. The opposite will obviously also hold true.

3.35 So, *Pareto* efficiency may perhaps help interpret the forum shopping rules as to their substance, in particular distinguishing fraudulent or abusive forum shopping from unobjectionable moves of COMI. But the quest does not stop there. The next difficulty is that even where the court seised of an insolvency petition could work out whether, upon it accepting jurisdiction, the detrimental effects illustrated in Recitals 5 or 11 RR would obtain, the RR says nothing on account of what should happen next in terms of procedure. Recital 5 RR is on a preventive mission to avoid incentives to engage in fraudulent or abusive forum shopping, whilst Recital 30 RR is in the business of rebutting the presumptions of the localization of COMI established in Article 3(1) RR. No provision in the RR seems to legislate for situations in which the preventive mission failed and where, with or without the presumptions in Article 3(1) RR, under all of the definitions and tests in the RR and the relevant case law, the COMI has been successfully relocated. And where, upon the application of the new *lex fori*, the debtor or one or more classes of its investors now stand to obtain a more favorable legal position to the detriment of the general body of creditors (Recital 5 RR) or, alternatively, the principal reason for moving indeed was to file for insolvency proceedings in the new jurisdiction and the filing is now bound to materially impair the interests of creditors whose dealings with the debtor took place prior to the relocation (Recital 30 RR). Certainly, the RR does not allow the court seised of the insolvency petition to reject jurisdiction, and it is questionable whether national procedural law could lead to such an outcome, since the result of such rejection would be that the debtor would in effect end up without any forum to conduct main insolvency proceedings in the EU—hardly a palatable outcome, quite possibly amounting to *denegatio iustitiae*.

3.36 It seems that presently, the only remedy against a procedurally successfully completed, yet substantively fraudulent or abusive COMI shift, is the public policy defence under Article 33 RR. Yet it will be immediately obvious that this is a very crude remedy that may not succeed on merits, and also may or may not be useful in practice, depending on the forum in which, and the purposes for which, the denial of recognition could be applied for.

3.37 One should therefore close the debate observing that, as matters stand, the RR's malleable jurisdictional ground of COMI pursuant to Article 3(1) RR, combined with the effects of the rule on governing insolvency law pursuant to Article 7 RR, may create powerful incentives for strategic shifts of insolvency jurisdiction throughout the 27 Member States, and that the Insolvency Proceedings Regulation, even after having been recast, does not seem to provide countermeasures that would be proportionate to the risks created by it.

3.38 One way to limit these risks would obviously be to harmonize the substance of the Members States' insolvency laws, in particular their distributional schemes. Another, less ambitious way, might be to enact a safe-harbour from the effects of Article 7 RR where a COMI shift had taken place. Such a safe-harbour provision could perhaps mirror the rule on governing law established in Article 36(2) RR. Under Article 36 RR, it is possible to avoid the opening of territorial proceedings provided that the insolvency practitioner in the main proceedings gives an undertaking pursuant to Article 36 RR. As the result of such undertaking, the proceeds from the assets located in the Member State in which the territorial proceedings could otherwise be opened will be distributed pursuant to the distributional rules that would apply under that Member State's insolvency law, even as the rest of the distributions are governed by the *lex fori concursus* applicable in the main proceedings.

3.39 Granted, Article 36 RR suffers from a number of serious problems that mostly came about as the result of that provision being the result of tinkering in the European Parliament rather than of a proper legislative drafting process. However, unlike Article 36 RR, which would really have to be well thought through and drafted in order to work with tolerable degrees of risk to those involved, in particular the insolvency practitioner in the main proceedings and the creditors on both sides of the relevant border, a safe-harbour rule shielding creditors from fraudulent or abusive COMI shifts does not. In a sense, the cruder the rule would be, the better because the harder it would be for the planners of the fraudulent or abusive COMI shift to reliably 'price in' its costs. In essence, the safe-harbour rule would merely provide, by way of exception to Article 7 RR, that distributions to creditors whose claims had arisen prior to the relocation of the debtor's COMI will, upon a petition to the court in the main proceedings in which any such creditor shows that the application of the new *lex fori* would be materially detrimental to his or her claims, be governed by the distributional rules of the insolvency law of the Member State in which the COMI was at the time when the creditor's claim was constituted. A provision like this might have been hard to imagine under the OR. But in the world of the RR which already features the complicated Article 36, this would be nothing out of the ordinary. It would also not require a major intervention into the RR's grounds of jurisdiction based on the concept of the COMI,[62] and would no doubt be compliant with the freedom of establishment under Articles 49 ff TFEU.

Jurisdiction to conduct territorial insolvency proceedings

Grounds of jurisdiction

3.40 It is now also commonplace that, in addition to the COMI, the only other eligible ground of international insolvency jurisdiction under the RR is an 'establishment', defined in Article 2(10) RR as 'any place of operations where a debtor carries out or has carried out in the 3-month period prior to the request to open main insolvency proceedings a non-transitory economic activity with human means and assets'. In *Interedil*, the CJEU observed with respect to the definition (as it previously appeared in Article 2(h) OR) that '[t]he term "establishment" within the meaning of Article 3(2) of Regulation No 1346/2000 must be interpreted as requiring the presence of a structure consisting of a minimum level of organisation and a degree of stability necessary for the purpose of pursuing an economic activity. The presence alone of goods in isolation or bank accounts does not, in principle, meet that definition.'[63] The vantage point from which the presence of an establishment in a given Member State must be evaluated is, similarly as with the COMI, an objective one, ie that of third parties: 'Since, in accordance with Article 3(2) of the Regulation, the presence of an establishment in the territory of a Member State confers jurisdiction on the courts of that State to open secondary insolvency proceedings against the debtor, it must be concluded that, in order to ensure legal certainty and foreseeability concerning the determination of the courts with jurisdiction, the existence of an establishment must be determined, in the same way as the location of the centre of main interests, on the basis of objective factors which are ascertainable by third parties.'[64]

3.41 Some establishments grow organically over time while others may appear overnight. One example of the latter situation might be a foreign acquisition structured as an 'asset deal'. Another example would be a COMI shift effected with respect to an operating company

---

[62] Cf W-G Ringe in Bork/van Zwieten, pp 138–39.
[63] C-396/09 *Interedil Srl, in liquidation v Fallimento Interedil Srl and Intesa Gestione Crediti SpA* ECLI:EU:C:2011:671, ruling no 4.
[64] *Ditto*, para 63.

(rather than a holding or financing company or another special purpose vehicle). Such a shift will almost by definition result in an establishment being 'left behind' on the ground in the original jurisdiction, at least in the short run. Recital 24 RR now expressly recognizes as much in a codification of the CJEU judgment in *Burgo v Illochroma*.[65] The three-month look-back period added into the definition of the establishment in Article 2(10) RR appears to try to militate against potential efforts to 'wipe out the traces' left in the original jurisdiction upon a COMI shift.[66]

Unlike with the COMI, of which there can only ever be one, it is certainly possible for a debtor to have more than one establishment across the EU. Accordingly, the jurisdiction to open and conduct territorial insolvency proceedings is non-exclusive in the sense that territorial insolvency proceedings can, at least in theory, be opened and conducted in such number of Members States as there are debtor's establishments across the EU, provided, of course, that the debtor has its COMI in the EU as well.[67]

3.42

Further conditions of opening territorial proceedings

Contrary to the main proceedings, establishing grounds of jurisdiction might not, and in some cases will not, be a sufficient condition for the court seised to open territorial proceedings. The further conditions will depend on whether main proceedings have already been opened in the EU or not.

3.43

Where this is not the case, territorial proceedings (these will then be called 'territorial' in the narrower sense of the word used by the Regulation for this purpose, and will usually be referred to 'independent territorial proceedings'[68]) may only be opened in the Member State where the debtor has an establishment provided that further conditions set out in Article 3(4) RR are met. These are either (a) the circumstance that main proceedings cannot be opened in the Member State in which the debtor's COMI is situated 'because of the conditions laid down by the law of that Member State',[69] or (b) the fact that the opening is requested either by a creditor whose claim arises from or is in connection with the operation of an establishment,[70] or a public authority which, under the law of the Member State within the territory of which the establishment is situated, has the right to request the opening of insolvency proceedings.[71] Of course, in line with Recital 25 and the opening words of

3.44

---

[65] C-327/13 *Burgo Group SpA v Illochroma SA and Jérôme Theetten* ECLI:EU:C:2014:2158.
[66] W-G Ringe in Bork/van Zwieten, p 169.
[67] Article 3(2) RR starts with this proviso expressly, however, this already follows from the key rule in Recital 25 RR—if the debtor's COMI was not in the EU, the RR would not apply at all and any insolvency proceedings opened in any of the Member States would not fall within its territorial sphere of application.
[68] R Bork in Bork/Mangano, p 236, marg no 7.14.
[69] In Case C-112/10 *Procureur-generaal bij het hof van beroep te Antwerpen v Zaza Retail BV* ECLI:EU:C:2011:743, the CJEU held that '[t]he expression "conditions laid down" in Article 3(4)(a) of Council Regulation (EC) No 1346/2000 of 29 May 2000 on insolvency proceedings, which refers to conditions, which, under the law of the Member State where the debtor has the centre of its main interests, prevent the opening of main insolvency proceedings in that State, must be interpreted as not referring to conditions excluding particular persons from the category of persons empowered to request the opening of such proceedings.'
[70] This is the definition of a 'local creditor' as that term is defined in Art 2(11) EIR. In the *Zaza Retail* case, the CJEU ruled that '[t]he term "creditor" in Article 3(4)(b) of the Regulation, which is used to designate the persons empowered to request the opening of territorial insolvency proceedings, must be interpreted as not including an authority of a Member State whose task under the national law of that State is to act in the public interest, but which does not intervene as a creditor, or in the name or on behalf of those creditors.'
[71] On the other hand, in the *Burgo Group v Illochroma Case*, the CJEU ruled that '[t]he right to seek the opening of secondary proceedings cannot, however, be restricted to creditors who have their domicile or registered office

Article 3(2) RR, the court seised will also have to be satisfied that the debtor's COMI actually is in one of the EU's Member States (other than in Denmark).

3.45 Where main proceedings have already been opened over the same debtor elsewhere in the EU, the actual opening of territorial proceedings (which would then be referred to as 'secondary proceedings'[72]) will be subject to several hurdles.

3.46 First, under Article 38(1) RR, '[a] court seised of a request to open secondary insolvency proceedings shall immediately give notice to the insolvency practitioner or the debtor in possession in the main insolvency proceedings and give it an opportunity to be heard on the request'. It follows that until such notice has been served and a meaningful time period has elapsed thereafter, an insolvency order opening the secondary proceedings may not be handed down by the court seised even if the court has no doubt about it having jurisdiction on account of there being an establishment within the court's jurisdictional territory.

3.47 Further, that notice and the period that must by necessity follow it may result in further hurdles to the opening of the secondary proceedings. First, under Article 38(3) RR, the insolvency practitioner in the main proceedings or the debtor in possession may request a delay of the opening of the secondary proceedings of up to three months in order to allow for negotiations between the debtor and its creditors, provided that a temporary stay of individual enforcement has been granted in the main proceedings[73] and that the interests of local creditors are suitably protected.[74] Second, the insolvency practitioner in the main proceedings may avert the opening of secondary proceedings completely by giving an undertaking pursuant to Article 36 RR, provided that such undertaking is accepted in the procedure described in that provision and further provided that, if a request to open secondary proceedings has nevertheless been presented, the court seised is satisfied, pursuant to Article 38(2) RR, that the undertaking adequately protects the general interests of local creditors. Compliance by the court seised with the provisions of Article 38 is subject to judicial review in the Member State in which the secondary proceedings have been opened, or at least have been applied for, at the instigation of the insolvency practitioner in the main proceedings pursuant to Article 39 RR. Similarly as with respect to Article 5(1) RR, Article 39 legislates for this remedy in a manner so sparce that procedural details must necessarily be provided by national law, here the law of the Member State in which the secondary proceedings have been opened, or at least have been applied for (usually referred to as the *lex fori concursus secundarii*).[75]

---

within the Member State in whose territory the relevant establishment is situated, or to creditors whose claims arise from the operation of that establishment.' C-327/13 *Burgo Group SpA v Illochroma SA and Jérôme Theetten* ECLI:EU:C:2014:2158.

[72] This is what independent territorial proceedings will be called as well subsequent to the opening of main proceedings (see the last sentence of Art 3(4) RR).
[73] It has been rightly suggested that Art 38(3) RR must be interpreted broadly so that stays arising in the main proceedings by operation of law qualify just as well as court-ordered stays. See eg S Madaus in Brinkmann (ed), pp 328–29, marg no 19).
[74] Once again, it should be remembered that the test whether a creditor is 'local' does not depend on the place of the creditor's residence or other such criteria but on whether his or her claims against the debtor arose from or in connection with the operation of the establishment on which the jurisdiction of the court seised is based (Art 2(11) RR).
[75] S Madaus in Brinkmann (ed), pp 332–33.

Finally, it should be noted that the second sentence of Article 34 RR provides, in a (partial) **3.48** codification of CJEU's decision in the *Bank Handlowy v Christianapol* case[76] that '[w]here the main insolvency proceedings required that the debtor be insolvent, the debtor's insolvency shall not be re-examined in the Member State in which secondary insolvency proceedings may be opened'. What this means, in essence, is that the court seised of a request to open territorial proceedings may not apply an insolvency test that would otherwise be applicable under its own *lex fori concursus*, and must instead rely on, and recognize, the finding that the debtor is insolvent made by the court in the main proceedings pursuant to the insolvency test prescribed by the *lex fori consursus* applicable in those main proceedings.[77] However, given the material scope of the RR (see Article 1(1) RR), it is entirely possible that the main proceedings would have been opened without a determination as to the debtor's insolvency. If this were to be the case, the court seised of a request to open territorial proceedings would be able to apply the insolvency test under its *lex fori concursus secundarii*.[78]

The scope of territorial proceedings

Where territorial proceedings are admissible pursuant to the provisions reviewed above, **3.49** their material scope will be the same as that of the main proceedings.[79] The OR's insistence that the territorial proceedings must be winding-up proceedings[80] was dropped in the RR.[81] But even though the selection of proceedings available in the jurisdiction of the establishment is not limited any longer, the way those proceedings may be conducted is—see the provisions on co-ordination, co-operation, and other interactions between main and territorial proceedings in Chapter III (Articles 41 to 51) of the RR. All these are aimed at increasing, as far as possible, the probability that territorial proceedings will be conducted in a manner that is conducive towards preservation of value for the debtor's creditors (see Recital 40) rather than its dissipation (Recital 41). But it goes without saying that the risk that the opening of territorial proceedings will result in the latter outcome is ever present.

The personal scope of territorial proceedings will also be the same as that of the main proceedings, both as regards the definition of debtors and the delineation of creditors.[82] For the avoidance of doubt, it is worth repeating here that the creditors' right to participate in the territorial proceedings is in no way limited by reference to territorial circumstances—under Article 45(1) RR, all creditors may submit their claims to all insolvency proceedings conducted with respect to the debtor. **3.50**

Being 'territorial proceedings', it is literally by definition that their scope differs from **3.51** the main proceedings as regards the territorial sphere of their application. Article 34 RR

---

[76] C-116/11 *Bank Handlowy w Warszawie SA and PPHU 'ADAX'/Ryszard Adamiak v Christianapol sp z oo* ECLI:EU:C:2012:739, ruling no 3.
[77] S Madaus in Brikmann (ed), pp 274–75.
[78] Accordingly, one must therefore conclude that main proceedings opened based on the mere likelihood of insolvency (Recital 10, the penultimate sentence Art 1(1) RR) would not prevent the application of an insolvency test pursuant to the *lex fori concursus secundarii*, provided of course, that that *lex fori* prescribed the application of an insolvency test with respect to the particular type of proceedings applied for before the court seised.
[79] See paras 3.03–3.14 above.
[80] Cf Arts 3(3) and 27 OR.
[81] For some of the implications of this change, see T Richter, 'Parallel Reorganizations under the Recast European Insolvency Regulation—Selected EU Law Issues' (2018) 27(3) International Insolvency Review 340–73.
[82] See paras 3.15–3.18 above.

provides, in its last sentence, that '[t]he effects of secondary insolvency proceedings shall be restricted to the assets of the debtor situated within the territory of the Member State in which those proceedings have been opened'. Article 3(2) contains the same rule. The effect of this is that a separate insolvency estate is created in the territory of each Member States whose court opened the territorial proceedings.[83]

3.52 Rules on the localization of assets belonging to the territorial estate(s) are provided in Article 2(9) RR, and assets not listed there must be localized pursuant to the national conflicts of law rules as per the applicable *lex fori*.[84] It has been submitted that the relevant time at which localization of assets is to be decided is the date of the opening of the territorial proceedings, with subsequent movements of assets between Member States being irrelevant.[85] While that is probably correct, it must also obviously be the case that assets *newly acquired* by the debtor in the territory of the Member State in which the territorial proceedings are conducted also become subject to those territorial proceedings. This outcome is dictated, among others, by the requisite symmetry between, on the one hand, the presumable rule on the allocation of post-commencement claims among the various insolvency estates[86] and, on the other hand, the identity of the estate which gets to benefit from assets acquired in consideration of such post-insolvency claims having been incurred.

3.53 As should already be apparent from what has just been stated, to say that the effects of territorial insolvency proceedings shall be restricted to the assets of the debtor situated in the territory of the Member State in which those proceedings are conducted, as Article 3(2) RR does, is but a first approximation to the problem. The rule actually only states the most trivial part of the delineation exercise necessitated by any system of cross-border insolvency law based on limited universality and limited unity,[87] ie a system such as that established under the RR which allows for the parallel conduct of more than one set of insolvency proceedings over one and the same debtor. After all, as can be gleaned from a number of provisions of the RR, most particularly Articles 7 to 18 RR, but also, in a more succinct form, Article 1(1) RR, the remit of insolvency proceedings stretches far beyond the debtor's assets,[88] ie the left-hand side of its balance sheet. It includes above all the resolution of the debtor's strained capital structure, which means, in all cases other than that of a simple liquidation, renegotiating the amounts and other terms of its debt, ie the stuff of the right-hand side of the balance sheet. Yet, on that account, it has duly been noted that there simply is no meaningful relation between the location of a debtor's asset and the content of a debtor's obligations,[89]

---

[83] R Bork in Bork/Mangano, p 255, marg no 7.55.
[84] S Madaus in Brinkmann (ed), p 277, marg no 36.
[85] *Ditto*, marg no 35.
[86] See R Bork in Bork/Mangano, pp 257–58, marg no 7.61 who has proposed that post-commencement claims be allocated among the several estates based on which insolvency practitioner caused them to arise. This eminently sensible criterion gets blurred if the debtor remains in possession in more than one of the parallel proceedings. But the guiding principle and the outcome must still remain the same.
[87] R Bork in Bork/Mangano, p 231, marg no 7.05.
[88] For a testimony of how hard it can be delineate the assets, see CJEU Case C-649/13 *Comité d'entreprise de Nortel Networks SA and others v Cosme Rogeau liquidator of Nortel Networks SA* ECLI:EU:C:2015:384, in which the court essentially ducked the hard task of allocating jurisdiction among the competing national courts in the main and the territorial proceedings by holding that they both have jurisdiction to rule what assets belong to what estate (in legal terms, their jurisdiction is 'concurrent', see the first paragraph of the ruling), and that if they cannot agree, the quicker will win (in legal terms, 'the risk of concurrent judgments can be avoided by requiring any court before which a related action has been brought to recognise an earlier judgment delivered by another court with jurisdiction under Article 3(1) or, as the case may be, Article 3(2)', see para 45).
[89] G Ch Paulus, *Europäische Insolvenzordnung, Kommentar, 3. Auflage* (RIW 2010) p 308.

and similarly, that a territorial splitting of a legal essence of a claim is impossible.[90] It has therefore been submitted that proceedings under Article 3(2) RR are really only territorial with respect to assets but universal with respect to creditors.[91] And, as if that was not difficult enough, there are the debtor's 'affairs',[92] ie in particular the web of contractual and other relations which the balance sheet does not capture at all, or at best only partially, but which is the lifeblood of any business and the key to the resolution of its general default. All in all, a much better way of defining the scope of the territorial proceedings would be for the RR to provide that '[the m]ain proceedings do not produce effects with regard to **assets or legal relationships** that fall within the ambit of the (secondary) territorial proceedings'.[93]

What territorial proceedings actually do then in terms of their scope is that they create an 'enclave' in the otherwise universal effects of the main proceedings. Recital 66 RR imports as much when it states that 'the law of the Member State of the opening of proceedings should be applicable (lex concursus). **This rule on conflict of laws should be valid both for the main insolvency proceedings and for local proceedings**. The lex concursus determines all the effects of the insolvency proceedings, both procedural and substantive, on the persons and legal relations concerned. It governs all the conditions for the opening, conduct and closure of the insolvency proceedings.' (emphasis added). Equally, Article 35 RR provides that '[s]ave as otherwise provided for in this Regulation, the law applicable to secondary insolvency proceedings shall be that of the Member State within the territory of which the secondary insolvency proceedings are opened'. Upon a moment's inspection of the—non-exclusive—list of matters governed by the *lex concursus* in Article 7(2) RR, it becomes clear that in some respects, the borders of the 'enclave' can be defined with reasonable degrees of precision while in others, one may struggle to see how one and the same issue could be governed in parallel by two (or more) sets of insolvency laws.[94] The further away from the relatively straightforward issue of allocation of assets between the several estates, the more blurred the boundaries, and the bigger the legal uncertainties as regards the delineation of the main and the territorial estates. The social costs of these uncertainties must be counted among the costs of the system of limited universality and unity established by the Regulation. **3.54**

Jurisdiction to conduct ancillary proceedings

Recital 35 RR provides that '[t]he courts of the Member State within the territory of which insolvency proceedings have been opened should also have **jurisdiction for actions which derive directly from the insolvency proceedings and are closely linked with them**. Such actions should include avoidance actions against defendants in other Member States and **3.55**

---

[90] A Herrchen in K Pannen (ed), *European Insolvency Regulation* (De Gruyter Recht 2007) pp 497–98.
[91] W-G Ringe in Bork/van Zwieten, p 171, marg no 3.186. This seems unobjectionable with respect to pre-commencement creditors, ie those that must (usually) submit their claims into the insolvency proceedings *via* the claims submission process (see, at the EU level, Arts 53 to 55 RR). However, the position with respect to post-commencement creditors is different—see R Bork cited in note 98.
[92] As in the demand in Art 1(1)(b) RR that 'the assets *and affairs* of a debtor are subject to control or supervision by a court' (emphasis added).
[93] M Veder in Bork/van Zwieten, p 319, marg no 20.17 (emphasis added).
[94] The obviously difficult ones are in particular the issues named in Art 7(2)(d), (e), (f), (k), and (m) RR.

actions concerning obligations that arise in the course of the insolvency proceedings, such as advance payment for costs of the proceedings. […]' (emphasis added). This, together with the operative provision of Article 6(1) RR is essentially a codification of the CJEU's seminal judgment in *Seagon v Deko Marty*[95] which filled a legislative void in the OR.[96] As has already been observed above, under the interpretation given by the CJEU in the *Schmid v Hertel* case, this jurisdiction is extraterritorial in that it grants EU courts jurisdiction to hear related actions against non-EU defendants.[97] Questionable though it may seem,[98] this jurisdiction is also exclusive, at least as regards litigation between EU residents.[99]

3.56 Being a situation of general default, insolvency is bound to trigger litigation about all sorts of issues related to the debtor (or, in any case, a debtor who has assets or debts worth litigating over). Only some of that litigation will fall under the jurisdiction pursuant to Article 6(1) RR, namely 'actions which derive directly from the insolvency proceedings and are closely linked with them, such as avoidance actions'. This formula originates from CJEU case law pre-dating the Insolvency Proceedings Regulation, in particular the *Gourdain v Nadler* case.[100] Applying the formula to the OR, the CJEU repeatedly held that 'with regard to the first criterion, in order to determine whether an action derives directly from insolvency proceedings, the decisive factor applied by the Court to identify the area within which an action falls is not the procedural context of the action but its legal basis. According to that approach, it must be determined whether the right or obligation which forms the basis of the action has its source in the ordinary rules of civil and commercial law or in derogating rules specific to insolvency proceedings.'[101] In addition, it has rightly been suggested that 'if a claim exists regardless of proceedings, e.g. under company law, a sufficient dependence could be established by the fact that the claim is premised on the insolvency of the debtor and aims at protecting the collective interest of all creditors'.[102] And although it may not be immediately obvious how an action which derives directly from the insolvency proceedings could be not closely linked with them, one example is where the claim in question was assigned.[103] There is now a rather long line of CJEU cases sorting those actions which, being 'related enough' to the insolvency proceedings, fall under the Insolvency Proceedings Regulation from those which do not.[104] In line with the principle that the Insolvency

---

[95] C-339/07 *Christopher Seagon v Deko Marty Belgium NV* ECLI:EU:C:2009:83.
[96] Once again, it is remarkable that the 1970 draft Convention on Bankruptcy, Winding-up, Arrangements, Compositions, and Similar Proceedings already dealt with this point unequivocally by establishing court jurisdiction for related actions, including actions for the avoidance of antecedent transactions. See K van Zwieten in R Bork/van Zwieten, pp 12–13, marg no 0.18.
[97] The *Schmid v Hertel* case (C-328/12 ECLI:EU:C:2014:6) pre-dates the RR but there seems to be a consensus that it applies under it as well.
[98] Cf W-G Ringe in Bork/van Zwieten, p 211.
[99] C-296/17 *Wiemer & Trachte GmbH v Zhan Oved Tadzher* ECLI:EU:C:2018:902. That judgment was given under the OR, however, it dates from 2018, a year that not only follows the promulgation of the RR but also its entry into force. If anything, the new provision of Art 6 RR, in particular Art 6(2) has reinforced arguments for exclusivity. Luckily, the ruling in *Wiemer & Trachte* is expressly limited to situations in which the defendant is resident in another Member State and accordingly, the argument that the extraterritorial jurisdictional element originating from *Schmid v Hertel* is not exclusive is not precluded by it.
[100] C-133/78 *Henri Gourdain v Franz Nadler* ECLI:EU:C:1979:49, interpreting the scope of the Brussels Convention preceding Regulation Brussels I.
[101] See eg C-649/16 *Peter Valach and others v Waldviertler Sparkasse Bank AG and others* ECLI:EU:C:2017:986, para 29.
[102] S Madaus in Brinkmann (ed), p 80, marg no 20.
[103] *Ditto*, marg no 21.
[104] Van Galen, pp 21–22.

Proceedings Regulation and Brussels I should dovetail as much as possible (see Recital 7 RR), the CJEU has not yet found an action triggered by insolvency that would end in a 'no-man's-land' between to the two regulations.

The provision of Article 6(2) RR, establishing alternative jurisdiction based on the defendant's domicile for situations where an action under Article 6(1) RR is brought together with another action against the same defendant and where the actions are 'so closely connected that it is expedient to hear and determine them together to avoid the risk of irreconcilable judgments resulting from separate proceedings' (Article 6(3) RR) was most likely intended to help facilitate the efficient conduct of insolvency proceedings. Unfortunately, it also cemented the view that the jurisdiction under Article 6(1) RR is exclusive, which, depending on the circumstances of the case, may be quite unhelpful to the chances that the ancillary litigation will in the end effect really be successful from the estate's point of view.[105]

3.57

In addition to the need to sort the grounds of jurisdiction between that under the Regulation and Brussels I, there is potentially another area of jurisdictional competition in relation to ancillary litigation, that between main and territorial proceedings. Article 6(1) RR grants jurisdiction to 'the courts of the Member State within the territory of which insolvency proceedings have been opened in accordance with Article 3'. However, as follows from Article 3 RR, the debtor may be subject to two or potentially more sets of insolvency proceedings in the EU, depending on how many establishments it has got in the Member States. In this context, the *Gourdain* formula acquires an additional, territorial meaning. The words 'shall have jurisdiction for **any action which derives directly from the insolvency proceedings and is closely linked with them**, such as avoidance actions' in Article 6(1) RR, when read in order to allocate jurisdiction between the courts conducting the main and the territorial proceedings, may only mean that the courts of Member State(s) in which territorial proceedings are conducted only have jurisdiction under Article 6(1) RR insofar as the relevant ancillary action derives *directly from such territorial proceedings* and *is closely linked with them*. With respect to the archetypal avoidance actions mentioned expressly at the end of Article 6(1) RR, the courts conducting territorial proceedings will clearly have jurisdiction over avoidance actions concerning the assets belonging to the territorial estate,[106] in particular actions to avoid charges or other encumbrances created over such assets or transfers of such assets to the extent that the asset in question was still in the territory of the Member State in which the territorial proceedings are conducted at the day of the opening of such proceedings. However, avoidance actions which do not directly concern the assets of the territorial estate, in particular actions to avoid transactions that have given rise to a debt or that led to the extinguishment of a debt, will more likely than not fall within the ancillary jurisdiction of the courts of the Member State conducting the main insolvency proceedings. This is because, as has been mentioned above, there is usually no meaningful relation between the location of a debtor's asset (which determines the scope of the territorial

3.58

---

[105] For a desperate, and ultimately futile attempt by a national insolvency court to help the plaintiff escape from the exclusivity of jurisdiction under Art 6(1) RR, see Case C-493/18 *UB v VA, Tiger SCI, WZ, and Banque patrimoine et immobilier SA* ECLI:EU:C:2019:1046.

[106] See similarly, albeit with respect to the issue of the law governing such avoidance actions, Virgos/Garcimartin, pp 177–78, para 330(c).

insolvency jurisdiction pursuant to Article 3(2) RR) and the content (or indeed the extent) of a debtor's obligations.[107]

3.59 Outside the field of avoidance actions, its seems reasonably clear that when applied in the territorial sense, the *Gourdain* formula will vest jurisdiction in the courts conducting territorial insolvency proceedings over actions such as that in the *Valach* case, ie actions aiming to establish liability in connection with the exercise of decision-making powers in the territorial insolvency proceedings,[108] actions aiming to determine the existence of claims submitted into the territorial proceedings,[109] and actions aiming to determine whether assets belong to the territorial estate.[110] But this is much less likely to be so in the other cases where the CJEU had found in the past that court jurisdiction was based on the Insolvency Proceedings Regulation and not Brussels I.[111] In particular, an action such as the one decided in the foundational *Gourgain v Nadler* case, ie an action against *de facto* or *de iure* directors of the debtor company on the grounds of liability for deficiency of assets[112] seems unlikely to fall within the jurisdiction of the territorial courts. This is because director liability for pre-insolvency conduct *has no particularly close link to the territorial proceedings* (the second element of the *Gourdain* formula), even if the *lex fori concursus secundarii* provided substantive grounds for them (the first element of the *Gourdain* formula). Rather, such liability may (or indeed may not, depending on the attitudes and rules of each national law) attach to the fact that the debtor company ended up insolvent, and it is hard to see how this circumstance could be closely linked to any particular assets localized in any particular place, including the territory of the Member State conducting the territorial proceedings. Actions to establish this sort of liability therefore seem like an obvious candidate to fall exclusively within the universal ancillary jurisdiction of the courts of the Member State conducting the main proceedings. Except perhaps in a situation in which a successful COMI shift had resulted in an establishment being 'left behind' in the original Member State of incorporation,[113] in which case the *lex fori consursus secundarii* (including the corporate law rules under which the debtor company was presumably incorporated) *may actually have a lot closer link to* the question of director liability for pre-insolvency conduct (the second element of the *Gourdain* formula) *than the law governing the main proceedings*.

3.60 This last caveat immediately illustrates that whilst some of the instances where ancillary jurisdiction will have to be allocated between the main and the territorial proceedings may be reasonably clearcut, others will be really vexed. The social costs of the uncertainties and jurisdictional disputes resulting from the latter cases belong on the account of the system of limited universality and unity established by the Insolvency Proceedings Regulation.

---

[107] See para 3.53 above.
[108] See eg C-649/16 *Peter Valach and others v Waldviertler Sparkasse Bank AG and others* ECLI:EU:C:2017:986.
[109] C-47/18 *Skarb Pánstwa Rzeczpospolitej Polskiej—Generalny Dyrektor Dróg Krajowych i Autostrad v Stephan Riel* ECLI:EU:C:2019:754, para 38.
[110] However, as has been mentioned before, the territorial court's jurisdiction in this case will be non-exclusive, concurrent with the court in the main proceedings, with the first judgment to be issued taking precedence—see Case C-649/13 *Comité d'entreprise de Nortel Networks SA and others v Cosme Rogeau liquidator of Nortel Networks SA* ECLI:EU:C:2015:384.
[111] Van Galen, p 21.
[112] C-133/78 *Henri Gourdain v Franz Nadler* ECLI:EU:C:1979:49, para 5.
[113] See Case C-327/13 *Burgo Group SpA v Illochroma SA and Jérôme Theetten* ECLI:EU:C:2014:2158.

Jurisdiction to order protective and preservation measures

Once insolvency proceedings have been opened, the issuance of protective and preservation measures does not really require a separate ground of jurisdiction because such preservation and protective measures as the relevant court may issue pursuant to its own *lex fori concursus* will be subject to recognition and enforcement pursuant to the first subparagraph of Article 32(1) RR, just as all other decisions by that court which concern the course and closure of the insolvency proceedings.[114] Of course, given the limitations of the territorial scope of territorial insolvency proceedings, it will be the main insolvency proceedings whose preservation or protective measures will have the main importance in any cross-border insolvency situation. **3.61**

The third subparagraph of Article 32(1) RR extends the regime of recognition and enforcement under Article 32(1) RR to judgments relating to preservation measures taken after the request for the opening of insolvency proceedings or in connection with it. It has been observed that this rule protects the transnational effects of main proceedings applied for in a Member State.[115] In the context of this chapter, this rule also in essence creates a separate ground of jurisdiction to issue preservation and protective measures while a decision to open insolvency proceedings is still pending, **3.62**

It has been suggested that the fact that the RR does not also extend such jurisdiction to protective or preservation measures issued *prior to the filing* of a request for the opening of insolvency proceedings is a mistake and a lacuna.[116] Although that argument is in a way understandable, it can be countered by observing that, before a request for the opening of insolvency proceedings is even made, there is simply no ground on which the insolvency courts of any Member State could verify whether or not they are even likely to have jurisdiction under the RR. In such circumstances, it may be dubious whether the RR's material scope should really be extended this far. **3.63**

The RR actually does establish jurisdiction to order protective measures in a situation in which a request to open insolvency proceedings has (at least potentially) not even been made, however, the procedural context is different. Article 36(9) RR provides that '[l]ocal creditors may also apply to the courts of the Member State in which secondary insolvency proceedings could have been opened in order to require the court to take provisional or protective measures to ensure compliance by the insolvency practitioner with the terms of the undertaking'. This jurisdiction is established concurrently with that of the court in the main insolvency proceedings (see the preceding provision of Article 36(8) RR) and is specifically aimed at protecting local creditors (ie creditors whose claims arose from or in connection with the operation of an establishment in the Members State whose courts benefit from this grant of jurisdiction) in connection with an undertaking made by the insolvency practitioner in the main proceedings in order to pre-empt the opening of secondary proceedings in that other Member State. It should be obvious, then, that the circumstances in this sort of case differ substantially from those in which the alleged gap in Article 32(1) **3.64**

---

[114] P Oberhammer in Bork/van Zwieten, p 383, marg no 32.40.
[115] *Ditto*, marg no 32.39.
[116] Virgos/Garcimartin, p 208, para 391; R Bork in Bork/Mangano, p 178, marg no 5.28.

third subparagraph RR has been identified. The protective measures under Article 36(9) RR are meant to 'ensure compliance by the insolvency practitioner with the terms of the undertaking'. In a situation where an undertaking under Article 36 RR has been given, there will be very little doubt indeed that the debtor has an establishment in the territory of the Member State whose courts are vested with the jurisdiction pursuant to Article 36(9) RR. That situation will therefore suffer from none of the factual uncertainties that would permeate an extended general grant of jurisdiction to issue protective or preservation measures in the circumstances described in paragraph 3.63.

3.65 Finally, under Article 38(3) RR, the court seised of a request to open secondary insolvency proceedings may order 'protective measures to protect the interests of local creditors by requiring the insolvency practitioner or the debtor in possession not to remove or dispose of any assets which are located in the Member State where its establishment is located unless this is done in the ordinary course of business. The court may also order other measures to protect the interest of local creditors during a stay, unless this is incompatible with the national rules on civil procedure.' Similarly as under the third subparagraph of Article 32(1) RR, this is a grant of jurisdiction at the moment insolvency proceedings have not been opened, however, in circumstances where grounds of the jurisdiction should be apparent not only from the request to open secondary proceedings but also from the request to temporarily stay such opening, presented by the insolvency practitioner in the main proceedings or the debtor in possession.

Jurisdiction to conduct group co-ordination proceedings

3.66 Article 61 RR establishes jurisdiction to conduct group co-ordination proceedings. Pursuant to Recital 62 RR, such jurisdiction will only be established if insolvency proceedings relating to different members of the same group of companies[117] have been opened in more than one Member State.

3.67 Pursuant to Article 61(1) RR, jurisdiction to open and conduct the group co-ordination proceedings can be vested in 'any court having jurisdiction over the insolvency proceedings of a member of the group'. The choice not to limit this ground of jurisdiction only to particularly relevant members of the group, or to courts conducting main, rather than territorial proceedings has apparently been a deliberate one.[118]

3.68 In contrast to competitions for jurisdiction to open insolvency proceedings proper, Article 62 RR establishes jurisdiction priority of the court first seised.

3.69 Uniquely in the context of the whole RR, Article 66(1) RR allows for exclusive jurisdiction to conduct the group co-ordination proceedings to be established by an agreement. Such agreement must be reached among at least two-thirds of all insolvency practitioners appointed in insolvency proceedings of the members of the group.

---

[117] That term is defined in Art 2(13) RR.
[118] J Schmidt in Bork/van Zwieten, pp 619–20.

4
CHOICE OF LAW RULES

A. **The Recast Regulation ('RR')**	4.01	
Preliminary	4.01	
General principles	4.02	
Renvoi	4.04	
B. **The Basic Choice of Law Rule (Article 7 RR)**	4.05	
Lex Concursus	4.05	
Delineation of the scope of the RR and other fields of law	4.13	
Time limitation	4.14	
Binding nature of guarantees	4.15	
Ownership of an asset	4.16	
Action for performance of a contract	4.17	
A tort case against a third party	4.18	
C. **Exceptions to the Basic Choice of Law Rule (Articles 8–18 RR)**	4.19	
Exception I: Third parties' rights in rem (Article 8 RR)	4.20	
The situs of the property	4.24	
The time factor	4.25	
Meaning of 'rights in rem'	4.28	
Floating charge security, etc	4.29	
Exception II: Set-off (Article 9 RR)	4.31	
Exception III: Reservation of title (Article 10 RR)	4.36	
Exception IV: Contracts relating to immovable property (Article 11 RR)	4.40	
Exception V: Payment systems and financial markets (Article 12 RR)	4.42	
Exception VI: Contracts of employment (Article 13 RR)	4.43	
Exception VII: Rights subject to registration (Article 14 RR)	4.46	
Exception VIII: European patents with unitary effect and Community trade marks (Article 15 RR)	4.48	
Exception IX: Detrimental acts protected from avoidance (Article 16 RR)	4.49	
Exception X: Protection of third-party purchasers (Article 17 RR)	4.53	
Exception XI: Effects on pending lawsuits or arbitral proceedings (Article 18 RR)	4.56	
D. **Material Scope of Choice of Law Rules**	4.59	
Preliminary	4.59	
Actions deriving directly from insolvency proceedings and closely linked with them	4.60	
E. **Principal Amendments made in the Recast Regulation ('RR') in relation to the Original Regulation ('OR')**	4.62	
The Basic Choice of Law Rule (Article 4 OR now Article 7 RR): Lex concursus	4.62	
Exceptions to the Basic Choice of Law Rule (Articles 5-15 OR now Articles 8–18 RR)	4.63	
The impact of the newly introduced Article 6 RR on the applicable law	4.68	

A. The Recast Regulation ('RR')

Preliminary

Section A of this chapter provides an overview of the uniform rules of choice of law which are applicable to all proceedings governed by the EU Insolvency Regulation Recast ('RR'). The EU Insolvency Regulation Recast has replaced the original EC Insolvency Regulation ('OR') and is applicable to insolvency proceedings opened on or after 26 June 2017.[1] The

4.01

---

[1] The provisions of the OR are thus still applicable to insolvency proceedings opened prior to 26 June 2017 and to all actions commenced in relation to such insolvency proceeding.

choice of law rules are contained in Articles 7–18 RR and are substantially the same as their equivalents in the OR. Some provisions have been clarified rather than amended. The remainder of this section A will set out the general principles of the RR in relation to its choice of law provisions. Section B will discuss the general workings of the RR as to its choice of law provision in Article 7 and its system of the *lex concursus* (the law of the court that has opened insolvency proceedings) as the general rule. Section C will discuss the exceptions to this system, which are codified in Articles 8-18 RR. Section D will look at the material scope of the choice of law rules as a result of the introduction of a new provision in Article 6 RR and will analyse the more complicated relation between applicable law and competence as to topics not covered in Articles 7 and 8-18 RR. Commentary on the individual Articles is supplied in chapter 8 below. Section E provides a summary of the principal amendments that the RR has made to the OR.

General principles

4.02 Private international law answers three main questions: which court has competence to hear an international case; which law should the court apply to such case; and will its ruling be recognized and enforced in other jurisdictions. Outside of insolvency law in a European context of commercial law, questions as to competence are primarily covered by the Brussels I Regulation (recast) and questions as to applicable law are generally answered by the Rome I (contractual obligations) or Rome II Regulation (non-contractual obligations), whereas issues of property law are still mostly dealt with by national private international law rules. The practitioner will appreciate the simplicity of the overall structure of the RR. The RR, as did the OR, answers all three questions in respect of insolvency proceedings and actions arising out of such insolvency proceedings and which are closely linked to such insolvency proceedings. In that sense the RR can be seen as exceptional in the field of private international law. In addition, the basic structure is so that the court that has competence to open the insolvency proceedings will also apply its own insolvency law. This is based on Article 7 RR, which provides that the applicable law is the insolvency law of the Member State of the court of opening, commonly referred to as the *lex concursus*. There are exceptions to this basic rule in Articles 8-18 RR. Articles 7–18, thereby amount to a miniature code of uniform conflict of laws rules which are integral to the RR's operation. As will be seen, however, the choice of law rules in the RR are not all encompassing or do not constitute a choice of law rule in the strict sense of the term at all. This means that in several cases the provisions in Articles 8-18 RR necessarily lead back to choice of law rules in other EU Regulations or the national law of the Member States. Because the Member States' domestic insolvency laws remain unharmonized at present[2] it is essential that there should be clear, and uniform, rules to determine which state's law is to be applicable to issues which are typically encountered during the course of insolvency proceedings. This enables affected parties to calculate in advance the legal risks inherent in their relationship with a debtor whose circumstances bring it within the ambit of the RR in the event of insolvency. In most cases,

---

[2] In November 2020 the EU Commission launched its initiative to enhance the convergence of insolvency laws and adopt either a Recommendation or a Directive in the second quarter of 2022: 'The initiative aims to address major discrepancies in national substantive insolvency laws that were recognized as obstacles for the establishment of a well-functioning Capital Markets Union.' Documentation and feedback on the consultation held between 18 December 2020 and 26 March 2021 can be accessed on Insolvency laws: increasing convergence of national laws to encourage cross-border investment (europa.eu) (accessed 3 February 2022).

the rules contemplate a choice only between the laws of different Member States. In certain situations, however, the drafting of the relevant provision clearly allows for the possibility that the law of some third state may be applicable. Those instances are noted below in discussing the contents of Articles 8–18.

Apart from certain exceptions discussed below, the RR is so drafted as to confine the scope of the uniform choice of law rules to a choice between the laws of different Member States. Consequently, where the facts of a case raise the issue of the potential application of the law of a non-EU state, it is left for each Member State to resolve the conflict according to its own rules of private international law. In relation to the equivalent provisions embodied in the 1995 version of the Convention, the Virgos-Schmit Report emphasized in paragraph 44[3] that the choice of law provisions were deliberately limited to regulating the 'intra-Community effects' of insolvency proceedings: where non-Member States are concerned it is the responsibility of each Member State to define the appropriate conflict of laws rules, unless otherwise provided in the RR.[4] This is, unfortunately, a recipe for instability and uncertainty, particularly where the assets to which the alternating conflicts rules are to apply are mobile, and therefore capable of being subject to different rules according to their whereabouts at the relevant time. Variability of outcome will therefore remain a possibility for cases where the potentially applicable law is that of some third state, as the choice of law rules of different Member States could give rise to the application of different laws in cases with identical material facts. Variability may, however, also arise due to the fact that not all Articles 8–18 RR provide a uniform conflict of laws rule to determine the applicable law to the issue at hand. Such provisions either state that rights are not affected by the *lex concursus*, without determining the applicable law to such right (like Article 8(1) RR) or refer to the law applicable to the employment contract without providing a choice of law rule to determine such applicable law (see Article 13 RR). This also means that a court will have to apply its own private international law rules to determine the applicable law. It must then subsequently apply the rule from the RR if the applicable law is the law of a Member State (for instance in case of Article 13 RR). However, if the applicable law is found to be the law of a non-EU state, the court must then also apply its own private international law rules to determine whether to apply the same rule as set forth in the RR (for instance the rule set forth in Article 11 RR), unless the relevant provision of the RR is not limited to the applicability of the law of a Member State (for instance Article 9 RR). The crucial question will therefore be which Member State's courts have jurisdiction, according to the rules described in chapter 3 above. This is a factor to be borne in mind when calculating the effects of the RR's rules on such important matters as security rights, reservation of title agreements, interests in property which is subject to public registration, contracts of employment and contracts relating to immovable property, and on the rights and obligations of parties

4.03

---

[3] See also para 93 of the Virgos-Schmit Report, and also M Balz, 'The European Union Convention on Insolvency Proceedings' (1996) 70 American Bankruptcy LJ 485, 507. On the Virgos-Schmit Report to the former EC Convention project, and its status as an aid to interpretation of provisions contained in the Regulation on Insolvency Proceedings, see para 1.06 above, n 11 and text thereto.

[4] In several Articles of the RR reference is made to the laws of a State instead of to the laws of a Member State so that in some instances the RR does regulate the effects of insolvency proceedings vis-à-vis third countries (see below in paras 4.32 and 4.53). In the case *Schmid/Hertel* (14 January 2014, C-328/12) the Court of Justice ruled that an action falling within the scope of the RR may also be brought before the court that opened main proceedings against a person without the COMI in a Member State and thus extending the scope of the RR beyond the limits of the Member States.

operating in regulated financial markets.[5] The rules which are discussed below can also determine whether a creditor will have the benefit of set-off in the event of the insolvency of a counter-party to whom it is simultaneously indebted.[6]

Renvoi

4.04 An important general point about the choice of law provisions in the RR is that wherever they make reference to 'the law', this denotes the substantive, domestic law of the Member State concerned. The complexities—not to say inconsistencies—of the doctrine of *renvoi* are not intended to form part of the approach to be followed under the RR. In modern treaties which embody uniform conflicts rules it is quite often the case that a specific provision is included to the effect that references to the law of a state or country are not to be interpreted as including a reference to the choice of law rules which are in force there.[7] Indeed, to allow recourse to *renvoi* would defeat the very objective of seeking to harmonize choice of law rules by means of such an international agreement. The RR is intended to follow this approach, although no express provision to that effect was incorporated into the actual text.[8]

B. The Basic Choice of Law Rule (Article 7 RR)

Lex Concursus

4.05 Article 7 RR expresses the basic principle that the law of the Member State in which proceedings are opened according to the RR (referred to as 'the state of opening') is to be applied to those proceedings, and shall determine their effects, except in so far as the RR expressly provides to the contrary. The matters which are to be governed by the law of the state of opening (the *lex concursus*) are mentioned in a non-exhaustive list in Article 7(2), while the particular exceptions to the regime of the *lex concursus* are contained in Articles 8–18. The opening words of Article 7(2) supply a broad proposition stating that the law applicable to insolvency proceedings and their effects shall be that of the Member State within the territory of which such proceedings are opened.[9] Paragraph 2 of the Article further declares that the law of the state of the opening of proceedings shall determine the conditions for the opening of those proceedings, how they are to be conducted, and their closure. Under this formula, many matters of substance are determined by the law of the state of opening, as well as all matters of a procedural nature. The latter is in conformity with accepted principles

---

[5] See section C below.
[6] See sections B and C below, with reference to Arts 7(2)(d) and 9 respectively, and the further commentary to Art 9 in ch 8 below.
[7] See eg EC Convention on the Law Applicable to Contractual Obligations (the Rome Convention) of 19 June 1980, Art 15 (which has the heading 'Exclusion of *renvoi*'): 'The application of the law of any country specified by this Convention means the application of the rules of law in force in that country *other than its rules of private international law*' (emphasis added). The Rome Convention, which was in force among Member States during the period when the text of the OR was negotiated and enacted, was replaced in relation to all Member States except Denmark with effect from 17 December 2009 by Regulation (EC) 593/2008 of 17 June 2008 (the Rome I Regulation) [2008] OJ L177/6. Art 20 of that Regulation replicates verbatim the wording of Art 15 of the Rome Convention, save for the addition of the following words at the end of the sentence: '... unless provided otherwise in this Regulation.'
[8] See Virgos-Schmit Report (n 3 above), para 87.
[9] This proposition is qualified by the opening words of Art 7(1): 'Save as otherwise provided by this Regulation ....' See section C below.

of conflict of laws both in and outside of insolvency proceedings; ie that all matters of a procedural nature are governed by the law of the competent court hearing the case (the *lex fori*).

Further to this general proposition, thirteen particular matters are singled out for special mention in Article 7(2) as being for determination by the *lex concursus*, but the list is by no means exhaustive. These are: **4.06**

(a) against which debtors insolvency proceedings may be brought on account of their capacity;
(b) the assets which form part of the estate and the treatment of assets acquired by or devolving on the debtor after the opening of the insolvency proceedings;
(c) the respective powers of the debtor and the insolvency practitioner;
(d) the conditions under which set-offs may be invoked;[10]
(e) the effects of insolvency proceedings on current contracts to which the debtor is party;[11]
(f) the effects of the insolvency proceedings on proceedings brought by individual creditors, with the exception of lawsuits pending;[12]
(g) the claims which are to be lodged against the debtor's estate and the treatment of claims arising after the opening of insolvency proceedings;
(h) the rules governing the lodging, verification, and admission of claims;
(i) the rules governing the distribution of proceeds from the realization of assets, the ranking of claims, and the rights of creditors who have obtained partial satisfaction after the opening of insolvency proceedings by virtue of a right in rem or through a set-off;[13]
(j) the conditions for and the effects of closure of insolvency proceedings, in particular by composition;
(k) creditors' rights after the closure of insolvency proceedings;
(l) who is to bear the costs and expenses incurred in the insolvency proceedings; and
(m) the rules relating to the voidness, voidability, or unenforceability of legal acts detrimental to all the creditors.[14]

Although many of the matters referred to in paragraphs (a) to (m) above are largely self-explanatory, as they are classic issues of insolvency law, some comments are appropriate here. **4.07**

Paragraph (a) is particularly significant in view of the wide diversity between the insolvency laws of the 26 participating EU Member States concerning the types of debtors to which the different kinds of insolvency proceedings are applicable.[15] Variations also occur with regard **4.08**

---

[10] See however section C below, in relation to the effect of Art 9 (Exception II).
[11] See section C below, in relation to Art 11 (Exception IV).
[12] See section C below, in relation to Art 18 (Exception XI).
[13] See section C below, in relation to Arts 8 and 9 (Exceptions I and II).
[14] The provision in Art 7(2)(m) is given precedence over the special rules in favour of the application of some law other than the *lex concursus*, in Arts 8, 9, and 10: see Arts 8(4), 9(2), and 10(3). However, para (m) is expressly prevented from applying in cases which fall within Art 16 (acts detrimental to all the creditors): see section C below (Exception IX).
[15] Under the laws of Belgium, France, Greece, Italy, Luxembourg, Portugal, and Spain, respectively, insolvency proceedings cannot take place in relation to debtors who are not classified as traders (*commerçants*). In the case of Italy, by Art 1(1) of the Bankruptcy Act (Royal Decree No 267 of 1942) small-scale traders (*piccoli imprenditori*), as defined by Art 2083 of the Civil Code, are excluded from the operation of the insolvency law.

to the treatment of after-acquired property, the composition of the estate available for distribution among creditors, and the extent to which certain assets are exempt from forming part of it. These are among the issues which paragraph (b) brings under the control of the *lex concursus*.

4.09 The importance of paragraphs (g), (h), and (i) should also be noted, since they ensure that the law of the state of opening is determinative of each stage of the process of distribution of the estate, including the following matters: what debts are, and are not, provable;[16] the treatment of post-commencement claims against the estate; all aspects bearing upon proof and admission of claims, keeping in mind that there are also mandatory rules to be found in Arts 53–55 RR; the vital question of the ranking of claims for purposes of distribution; and also the treatment of partly secured creditors who wish to lodge proof for the balance of any claim which has been partly recouped through the enforcement of *in rem* security or the operation of set-off.[17] By virtue of paragraph (d) the basic approach to be followed in relation to set-off is also that of the state of opening, so that parties' expectations of how the doctrine of set-off will affect their position in the event of their debtor's insolvency are primarily determined by reference to the law of the state where insolvency proceedings can be opened, with however a possible escape for the counterparty under Art 9 RR.[18]

4.10 Paragraph (e) concerns several areas in relation to current contracts. The *lex concursus* may contain rules about the validity or applicability of so-called *ipso facto* clauses.[19] It may also grant the insolvency practitioner special termination rights with respect to certain contracts, regardless of the *lex causae* of the contract. However, questions as to the validity or the binding nature of a contract, any disputes arising out of a contract, or the counterparty's entitlement to damages remain exclusively governed by the *lex causae* of the contract determined in accordance with the provisions of the Rome I Regulation.

4.11 A much discussed topic is the choice of law rules as to transaction avoidance. The potential for avoidance of an insolvent debtor's pre-insolvency proceedings transactions, and likewise of any acts or dispositions of property carried out after the opening of proceedings, is one of the key aspects of the insolvency process. Moreover, the relevant rules are subject to crucial variations as between different jurisdictions. Hence the importance of Article 7(2)(m), which establishes the basic rule that the *lex concursus* shall be applied to determine the validity or otherwise of the debtor's legal acts detrimental to the general body of creditors. This provision is particularly far-reaching in its effect, because it is intended not merely to determine what procedural steps must be taken to bring about the invalidation or avoidance of such transactions, but also to displace any law which might otherwise have been applicable

---

[16] This is strictly limited to the provability of debts; ie which debts are eligible for a distribution from the bankrupt estate. If the insolvency practitioner wishes to challenge the existence of the debt, the law applicable to such debt in accordance with the general conflicts of laws rules of the court (under for instance the Rome I Regulation) continues to determine whether the debt validly exists. In Court of Justice 25 November 2021 C-25/20 (*Alpine Bau*), the Court of Justice ruled that the law of the proceedings in which the insolvency practitioner wishes to submit his claims determines the period within which the insolvency practitioner must lodge claims in that other proceedings.

[17] In Court of Justice 9 November 2016 C-212/15 (*ENEFI/DGRFP*), the court ruled that the effects of insolvency proceedings on creditors who had not participated in those proceedings must be assessed under the *lex concursus*.

[18] See, however, Art 9, discussed in section C below (Exception II).

[19] Clauses in contracts that provide that a party may terminate the contract or suspend the performance of its obligations merely because of the other party's insolvency. See also R van Galen, *An Introduction to European Insolvency Law* (2021) no 111.

to determine the validity of the transaction, had insolvency not supervened.[20] However, Article 16 superimposes a rule whose effect is to disapply Article 7(2)(m) in certain, due to Court of Justice case law quite stringent, circumstances, with the consequence that the avoidance rule of the *lex concursus* is displaced in favour of the rule of the *lex causae* of the transaction; ie the law of a Member State other than the state of the opening of insolvency proceedings. This important exception to the application of the *lex concursus*, and the quite limiting interpretation by the Court of Justice, is considered in section C below.[21]

The above account of the dominant role accorded to the *lex concursus* serves to emphasize the substantial benefits which accrue from the opening of proceedings within the scope of application of the RR. The basic choice of law rule that insolvency proceedings are governed by the *lex concursus*, applies both to main proceedings within Article 3(1) on the basis of Article 7(1) RR and to territorial proceedings (whether secondary or freestanding) within paragraphs 2–4 of Article 3 based on Article 35 RR.[22] This supplies one of the main reasons why parties may seek to avail themselves of any opportunity to bring about the commencement of secondary insolvency proceedings under the RR, since this will result in the application of the law of that Member State, instead of the law of the state in which the main proceedings have been opened, to the process of administering and distributing the assets located within the state in which the secondary proceedings take place.[23] **4.12**

Delineation of the scope of the RR and other fields of law

It must also be noted here that more general private law matters that may arise in the context of insolvency proceedings, but which do not derive directly from the insolvency proceedings and are not closely linked with them (see further below under Section D), are not governed by the *lex concursus* but by the law determined by the more general conflict of laws rules of the forum (such as those of the Rome I Regulation) as there is no reason to treat them differently in the context of an insolvency proceedings than outside such context. Examples of such issues are discussed below. **4.13**

Time limitation
One of such issues is for example whether a claim submitted by a creditor is barred by time limitation. This is not a typical insolvency issue and is thus not governed by the *lex concursus*. In some Member-States time limitations of a creditor's claim were treated as a **4.14**

---

[20] Virgos-Schmit Report (n 3 above) para 90. See also Balz (n 3 above) 511–12. Note the additional force bestowed on Art 7(2)(m) by the decision of the Court of Justice in Case C-328/12 *Schmid v Hertel* [2014] 1 WLR 633, [2014] BCC 25 (First Chamber, 14 January 2014) affirming that where insolvency proceedings are opened in Germany by virtue of the debtor's German COMI, transaction avoidance proceedings can be brought in that jurisdiction against parties whose place of residence is not within the territory of any Member State. See also the decision of the Court of Justice in Case C-295/13 (H qq/HK) in respect of a German provision regarding directors' liability in respect of which the Court of Justice not only ruled that such action commenced by the insolvency practitioner falls within the scope of the RR but also ruled that such action can be brought before the courts of the opening of the proceedings against a director whose place of residence is not within the territory of any Member State.

[21] See section C (Exception IX).

[22] See also Recital (66) to the RR. On the distinction between main and territorial (secondary) proceedings, and the criteria for opening them.

[23] On the relationship between main and secondary proceedings and the co-operation between the insolvency practitioners in the main and secondary proceedings see Recitals 37 through to 50 RR and see generally ch 3 section 3.40 et seq above and in detail ch 8, sections 8.373 et seq and 8.650 et seq below.

procedural issue and were thus held to be governed by the *lex fori* (the law of the competent court) whereas other jurisdictions treated it as a material issue which is governed by the *lex causae* of the legal relationship from which the claim has arisen. The Rome I Regulation (in Article 12) and the Rome II Regulation (in Article 15) explicitly determine that the *lex causae* is applicable to 'prescription and limitation of actions'. Under the national private international law rules of the UK, however, time limitation issues were always considered procedural but the UK was obliged to apply the *lex causae* as a result of the EU Regulations. As the UK will no longer apply the Rome I and Rome II Regulations, a UK court may now choose to revert to the UK rules on time limitation rather than the *lex causae* of the claim.[24]

Binding nature of guarantees

4.15 Whether the obligations under a guarantee, securing obligations of the insolvent debtor, are binding on the guarantor is solely governed by the law applicable to the guarantee in accordance with the provisions of the Rome I Regulation, as these are not obligations of the insolvent debtor.

Ownership of an asset

4.16 The question as to the ownership of a certain asset is left to the governing law of the asset in accordance with the private international law rules of the competent court.[25] Once it has been determined that the insolvent debtor is the rightful owner of the asset, the *lex concursus* determines whether such asset falls within the insolvent estate or is kept outside of the insolvency proceedings (Article 7(2)(b) RR).

Action for performance of a contract

4.17 An action brought by the insolvency practitioner of an insolvent company for the payment of goods delivered under a contract concluded before the insolvency proceedings were opened with a counterparty is governed by the *lex causae* of the contract in accordance with the provisions of the Rome I Regulation.[26]

A tort case against a third party

4.18 A tort case brought by the insolvency practitioner against a third party for a wrongful act committed prior to the insolvency proceedings is solely governed by the law applicable to the wrongful act in accordance with the provisions of the Rome II Regulation.[27]

C. Exceptions to the Basic Choice of Law Rule (Articles 8–18 RR)

4.19 As noted above, Article 7 RR opens with the significant words of exception: 'Save as otherwise provided in this Regulation'. The primary rule in favour of the application of the *lex*

---

[24] See M Bogdan and M Pertegás Sender, *Concise Introduction to EU Private International Law* (4th edn, 2019) p 141.
[25] Court of Justice 10 September 2009, Case C-292/08 (*German Graphics*).
[26] Court of Justice 21 November 2019 Case C-198/18 (*CeDe Group AB v KAN sp z oo in bankruptcy*).
[27] Court of Justice 6 February 2019 Case C-535/17 (*NK v BNP Paribas Fortis NV*).

concursus is therefore subject to displacement in favour of another law under specified circumstances. The provisions which establish the particular cases of exception are contained in Articles 8–18 RR. Some of these provisions are not conflict of laws rules in the true meaning of the term as they do not determine the applicable law to the particular issue that has been carved out from the applicability of the *lex concursus* but grant a form of immunity from the effects of the insolvency proceedings. Such provisions leave the determination of the applicable law on the carved-out matter or right to the general conflict of laws rules of the forum. Each of these exceptions to the general conflict of laws rule in Article 7 RR will be examined in turn.

Exception I: Third parties' rights in rem (Article 8 RR)

The first major exception to the *lex concursus* rule of Article 7 is provided by Article 8, whose purpose is to confirm the rights of parties to enter into transactions under which proprietary interests are created in favour of a creditor by way of security for the debt or obligation due from the debtor.[28] In practice, the essential purpose of such forms of security is that it enables the secured party to have direct recourse to the collateral in the event that the debtor does not pay or perform—and especially where this occurs by reason of the debtor's insolvency. It must be noted that for the purpose of Article 8 RR the laws of every concerned jurisdiction should fully accept and recognize a right *in rem* that has been validly created (and perfected) under its applicable law and as such is enforceable even in the event of the debtor's insolvency.

4.20

Article 8 does not provide the conflict of laws rules to determine the applicable law under which a right *in rem* in respect of certain assets must be created (and perfected), nor is there another EU or global private international law instrument including conflict of laws rules that determine the applicable law to security rights or other rights *in rem*. This means that each jurisdiction will continue to apply its national private international law rules to determine the applicable law to a security right and consequently determine whether such right has been validly created and will be recognized by such jurisdiction. A fairly generally applied conflict of laws rule in the area of security rights over real property or tangible assets is that the law of the location of the collateral is applicable.[29] In respect of other asset types some jurisdictions afford the asset a fictitious situs. For the purposes of Article 8, the RR does the same in Article 2(9).[30] The possibility which has to be confronted in a cross-border case is that the (fictitious) location of the collateral, either at the time of opening of proceedings or at some other material time, may be in a different state from that in which insolvency proceedings are opened. In that event, given the variations between national laws concerning real security and the impact of insolvency upon such arrangements, there is a very real prospect that different conclusions as to the secured creditor's rights may be

4.21

---

[28] For additional commentary on Art 8 and its effects, see ch 8 below. See also M Virgos and F Garcimartin, *The European Insolvency Regulation: Law and Practice* (2004) 91–108; B Wessels, *International Insolvency Law* (4th edn, 2017) paras 10639–60 and R van Galen, *An Introduction to European Insolvency Law* (2021) pp 65–72.

[29] See for instance Art 10:127(1) of the Dutch Civil Code; Art 87 of the Belgian Code of Private International Law; Art 43 of the German Einführungsgesetz zum Bürgerlichen Gesetzbuche.

[30] See the propositions embodied in Recital 68 to the RR.

reached under the *lex concursus*, the applicable law as to the valid creation and perfection of such real security and the *lex situs* at the time of enforcement. It is possible that these three are the same but just as possible that they are not. Such uncertainty could have serious repercussions for the stability and cost of transactions concluded in a transnational context. Also of concern to a secured creditor is the extent to which, even if the right *in rem* is recognized, its enforcement or realization may be inhibited in some way which may erode its economic value, for example through the application of a comprehensive stay and moratorium during the course of an insolvency or reorganization procedure.

4.22 Article 8 RR supplies a rule which significantly reinforces the position of the secured creditor whose collateral is situated, at the time of opening of proceedings, in a different Member State from that in which insolvency proceedings take place. To the extent that the *lex situs* upholds the rights of the secured creditor and allows him to enforce those rights over the collateral, for example through sale or foreclosure, in spite of the debtor's insolvency, such rights are to be respected even if this is contrary to the effects that would be produced according to the *lex concursus*.[31] It thus grants the secured creditor 'immunity' from the applicability of the *lex concursus*. Article 8(1) states:

> The opening of insolvency proceedings shall not affect the rights *in rem* of creditors or third parties in respect of tangible or intangible, moveable or immoveable assets, both specific assets and collections of indefinite assets as a whole which change from time to time, belonging to the debtor which are situated within the territory of another Member State at the time of the opening of proceedings.

4.23 It should be noted how widely the terms of this provision are drawn in relation to the types of assets to which it can have application. All types of property are capable of being affected, including such commercially important items as book debts and other accounts receivables, intellectual property rights, equity participations (most notably shares), and assets that are of a future character at the time the security interest is created but which have come into existence by the time insolvency proceedings are opened. However, an asset, and thus the immunity granted to the secured creditor in relation to that asset, is only within the ambit of this article if it is located within the territory of one of the Member States (other than the state of opening) at the time of opening. Where the *situs* of the asset at the relevant time is in some third (non-member) state,[32] Article 8 is not applicable and it is left to the *lex concursus* alone to determine to what extent, if at all, rights *in rem* over such assets can be respected or in some way taken into account.[33] Finally, Article 8 provides that only rights *in rem* on assets located in another Member State are made immune for the applicability of the *lex concursus* and not the assets themselves. The assets themselves are part of the insolvent estate, provided that the *lex concursus* identifies them as such.[34] This means that a secured

---

[31] See Recital 68 to the RR.
[32] In this context, the expression 'third state' must be taken to include Denmark and the United Kingdom as a result of BREXIT.
[33] Note the possibility that Art 8 may operate with retrospective effect in the case of insolvency proceedings commenced before the accession of a newly joining Member State, provided that the assets in question to which a right in rem is asserted were situated in that state at the time of its accession to the EU: Court of Justice 21 December 2012, C-527/10 (*ERSTE Bank Hungary Nyrt v Republic of Hungary*), <https://curia.europa.eu/juris/document/document.jsf?text=&docid=124745&pageIndex=0&doclang=EN&mode=req&dir=&occ=first&part=1> (accessed on 3 February 2022).
[34] See Article 7(2) under (b) RR.

creditor, after enforcing its rights and applying the proceeds to its claim must surrender any surplus to the insolvency estate.[35]

The situs of the property

There is an obvious need for certainty with regard to the method of identifying the location of an asset for the purposes of applying the rule in Article 8. Some assistance is provided by the new Article 2(9) RR, which defines the expression, 'the Member State in which assets are situated' in relation to eight kinds of assets and is thus more detailed and specific than the three particular kinds of property that were included in the OR. This, however, does not in itself constitute a major shift or amendment as to the location of such assets, but rather clarifies the position in relation to certain asset types. It must be emphasized that the indication of locality of the assets listed in Article 2(9) RR is included for the purposes of Article 8 and Article 10 (see below) RR and, in addition, to determine whether the asset falls within the main proceedings or within secondary proceedings where these have been opened. It does not intend to prescribe a conflict of laws rule in the area of property law in respect of such assets.[36] Article 2(9) provides as follows:

4.24

(i) registered shares in companies, other than financial instruments (see below under (ii)) are located in the Member State within the territory of which the company having issued the shares has its registered office;[37]

(ii) financial instruments, the title to which is evidenced by entries in a register or account maintained by or on behalf of an intermediary (so called book entry securities), have their *situs* in the Member State in which the register or account in which the entries are made is maintained;[38]

(iii) cash held in accounts with a credit institution is located in the Member State indicated in the account's IBAN, or, for cash held in accounts with a credit institution which does not have an IBAN, in the Member State in which the credit institution holding the account has its central administration or, where the account is held with a branch, agency, or other establishment, the Member State in which the branch, agency, or other establishment is located;[39]

---

[35] Virgos-Schmit Report (n 3 above), under para 99.

[36] See also Recitals 39 and 68 RR, the latter of which seems to suggest that the EU may have given an entry point for the development of EU conflict of laws rules regarding rights *in rem*. On the other hand the rules set forth in the proposal for a Regulation on the law applicable to third-party effects of the assignment of claims 2018/0044 (COD) (<https://eur-lex.europa.eu/legal-content/EN/TXT/PDF/?uri=CONSIL:ST_14544_2021_INIT&from=EN>) (accessed on 28 January 2022)—hereinafter the 'Assignment Regulation') chooses a different connecting factor in respect of claims than set forth in Art 2(9) RR.

[37] In some Member States this is also the connecting factor for the choice of law rule in relation to rights in rem over registered shares whereas other Member States refer to location of the shareholders' register or the law applicable to the issuing company, which may be the law of the registered seat or the real seat depending on the particular Member State.

[38] This connecting factor is also used in the Financial Collateral Directive (2002/47/EC) to determine the law applicable to rights in rem over book-entry securities where Art 9(1) of the Financial Collateral Directive provides: 'Any question with respect to any of the matters specified in para 2 arising in relation to book entry securities collateral shall be governed by the law of the country in which the relevant account is maintained' (underlining added).

[39] Under the Assignment Regulation the third-party effects of an assignment of, or the creation of a security right over, cash held in bank accounts is governed by the law governing the account holder's claim against the account bank. This may or may not be the same law as the law of the IBAN Member State.

(iv) property and rights, ownership of or entitlement to which is entered in a public register other than registered shares in a company has its situs in the Member State under the authority of which the register is kept;

(v) European patents are located in the Member State for which the European patent is granted;[40]

(vi) copyright and related rights are located in the Member State within the territory of which the owner of such rights has its habitual residence or registered office;

(vii) any other tangible property has its situs, somewhat prosaically, in the Member State within the territory of which the property is physically located; and

(viii) claims against third parties, other than those relating to cash held in accounts, have their situs in the Member State within the territory of which the debtor of the claims has the centre of its main interests, as determined in accordance with Article 3(1) RR.[41]

The fictitious situs of claims (other than bank account claims) for the purposes of Article 8 RR is a logical choice as it generally coincides where a right *in rem* over a claim or receivable is enforced and Article 8 RR applies in situations where a creditor wants to enforce its right *in rem* over such a claim or receivable. As rights *in rem* over claims and receivables are very often enforced through collection from the debtor of such a claim or receivable and applying the proceeds of such collection to the outstanding claim or receivable, the place of enforcement is the place where the debtor is located. In RR terms at the debtor's COMI.

The time factor

4.25 The relevant time at which the location of an asset is to be determined for a creditor to enjoy the advantage of Article 8, according to the terms of Article 8(1), is the opening of insolvency proceedings. This could give rise to difficulties if the asset is of a 'movable'[42] nature and its location has changed between the time at which the right *in rem* was created and the time when proceedings are opened. The rule could work to the disadvantage of the supposedly secured party if the asset happens to be located at the relevant time in a jurisdiction whose law does not recognize or afford protection to the security interest in question. Conversely, it would be a cause for concern as far as the authority of the insolvency practitioner or the interests of unsecured parties are concerned if it should transpire that the consequence of such a relocation is that the asset in question has been removed from the territory over which the *lex concursus* is applicable. Another possibility is that the rights of the secured creditor are less susceptible to avoidance than they would otherwise have been. This particular contingency is, however, countered by the provision in Article 8(4), which preserves the applicability of the actions for avoidance of antecedent transactions that form part of the *lex concursus*, as laid down in Article 7(2)(m).[43] Conversely, a creditor who takes security over an asset of

---

[40] Recital 39 RR provides that the RR must provide that European patents (and other European IP rights) should only be included in main insolvency proceedings.

[41] On the centre of main interests, see ch 3, section A above.

[42] This could refer to a movable tangible asset, but also to a receivable as the debtor's COMI could have changed.

[43] See the decision of the CJEU in Case C-557/13 *Lutz v Bäuerle*, 16 April 2015 [2015] BCC 413 (not yet reported but viewable at <http://curia.europa.eu/juris/celex.jsf?celex=62013CJ0557&lang1=en&type=TXT&ancre=>) in which the Court, while confirming that Art 8 enables the creditor to assert, even after the opening of insolvency proceedings, a right in rem established before the opening of those proceedings, noted that Art 8(4) preserves the possibility of avoidance proceedings being brought under the *lex concursus*, in which event the defence provided under Art 16 may become applicable (see para 4.49 below).

which the (fictitious) location can change over time on the basis that the law of its current *situs* recognizes the creditor's right *in rem* and confers satisfactory protection in the event of the debtor's insolvency, must consider the possibility that the asset may be moved to another Member State, or to some third state, and thereby become subject to a different legal regime at the relevant time, which may not recognize the creditor's right at all or may impose other restrictions on its enforcement in the event the asset has been moved to the Member State where insolvency proceedings have been opened. Article 8(1) is interpreted in such a way that the right *in rem* over an asset located in a Member State other than that of the opening of insolvency proceedings is made insolvency immune, not only from the *lex concursus* but also from the insolvency law provisions of the Member State of the asset's location. If possible, the terms of the transaction should be so designed as to minimize the consequent risks of such relocation. Any relocation of assets from the Member State where the proceedings have been opened to another Member State after such opening of proceedings does not lead to the application of Article 8(1) and thus the *lex concursus* still applies in respect of such asset.

It is generally held that one of the consequences of the applicability of Article 8(1) is for instance that an automatic stay under the *lex concursus* would not affect the right of the creditor to enforce its right *in rem*, or that the authority of an insolvency practitioner to demand that a creditor enforces its rights in respect of an asset within a certain period of time does not apply.[44] There is also a strong argument that the immunity granted by Article 8 RR cannot be undermined by a composition plan offered by the debtor which affects the rights of the secured creditor.[45] Restructuring proceedings aimed at saving the debtor from insolvency may now be brought within the ambit of the RR[46] and thus broadening its scope on types of proceedings compared to its predecessor OR. Member States may request the EU Commission to place such proceedings on Annex A to the RR, provided they qualify, so that these restructuring proceedings may benefit from the universal recognition granted by the RR in the EU Member States (other than Denmark). Article 8, however, could throw a big spanner in the wheel for such a restructuring plan to be successful.[47,48] It will be up to the Court of Justice to ultimately determine the scope of the immunity granted by Article 8, also in light of the EU's current policy to promote the restructuring of debt.[49] **4.26**

It should also be noted that the rule in Article 8(1) is so drafted as to confine its effects to cases where the subject-matter of the security is situated within the territory of another Member State at the time of opening of proceedings. Where assets are situated in a third state, the effect of the opening of insolvency proceedings upon the rights of the secured party is not determined by Article 8. In such cases, the law of the state of opening of proceedings, including its rules of private international law, will primarily determine the rights of any parties which are amenable to the jurisdiction of the *lex concursus*. However, according to **4.27**

---

[44] See B Wessels, *International Insolvency Law* (4th edn, 2017) para 10657.
[45] See also R van Galen, *An Introduction to European Insolvency Law* (2021) para 161.
[46] See Art 1(1) RR under c and the closing sentence.
[47] This interpretation of Art 8 would also undermine the EU's own efforts to move towards a more preventive restructuring environment as set forth in the Restructuring Directive (Directive (EU) 2019/1023 of the European Parliament and of the Council of 20 June 2019 on preventive restructuring frameworks, on discharge of debt and disqualifications, and on measures to increase the efficiency of procedures concerning restructuring, insolvency, and discharge of debt, and amending Directive (EU) 2017/1132.
[48] See, however, Chr Paulus, *Europäische Insolvenzverordnung* (2021) pp 278–80, who argues that Art 8 does not provide such extensive immunity.
[49] By, *inter alia*, its publication of the Restructuring Directive.

standard conflict of laws principles, the court will apply the private international rules of its own jurisdiction to determine the applicable law which governs the validity of the security interest as at the time of its creation,[50] whether such security right will be recognized and if recognized what the effect of insolvency proceedings on the rights of the secured party are. Conversely, the rights of any parties which are not so subject to the authority of the law of the state of opening will in practice be determined by the extent to which the law where the asset can be located or enforced is prepared to recognize and give effect to the foreign insolvency proceedings. If the rights of the secured creditor are held to prevail over the claims of the insolvency practitioner appointed in the foreign proceedings, the secured creditor may be able to retain the fruits of exercising the rights previously bargained for, unless it proves necessary to participate in the insolvency process in respect of any unsecured balance of claim. In such circumstances, the duty to account for the fruits of the enforcement of security will arise, in accordance with the principle of hotchpot.[51]

Meaning of 'rights in rem'

4.28 The OR did not supply an exhaustive definition of the expression 'rights in rem' and the RR still does not. Although, it is held that the question whether a certain right constitutes a right *in rem* is to be determined by the relevant Member State[52] and may therefore differ from one Member State to the other, Article 8(2) and (3) furnish some indication of the meaning to be attributed to the expression. Supplementary guidance, albeit of a persuasive character only, can be found in the Virgos-Schmit Report.[53] For a right to qualify as a right *in rem* within the meaning of Article 8(1) it must pass two tests: (i) it must qualify as a right *in rem* under its applicable law as determined by the private international law rules of the court of the relevant asset's *situs* (as determined by Article 2(9) RR) at the time of the opening of insolvency proceedings and (ii) it must meet the requirements of Article 8(2) or (3).[54] Article 8(2) is essentially concerned to describe the nature and content of rights which qualify as rights *in rem* within Article 8(1). It states that they shall, in particular, mean:

(a) the right to dispose of assets or have them disposed of and to obtain satisfaction from the proceeds of or income from those assets, in particular by virtue of a lien or a mortgage;
(b) the exclusive right to have a claim met, in particular a right guaranteed by a lien in respect of the claim or by assignment of the claim by way of a guarantee;
(c) the right to demand the assets from, and/or to require restitution by, anyone having possession or use of them contrary to the wishes of the party so entitled; and
(d) a right *in rem* to the beneficial use of assets.

---

[50] The applicable law is sometimes referred to generically as the *lex situs* and in respect of movable tangible property and real property the interpretation of *situs* is fairly universal. This is not the case for receivables, registered shares, IP, or book entry securities. Although the term *lex situs* is also used for these kinds of assets the outcome of the applicable law varies greatly between jurisdictions.

[51] See Art 23 RR, on which there is commentary in ch 8 below.

[52] Recital 68 RR; Virgos-Schmit Report, nos 43 and 100 and the Court of Justice in *Lutz/Bäuerte* C-557/13.

[53] See n 3 above, at nos 94–106 inclusive. For critical discussion of the treatment of secured creditors under the substantially identical provisions of the proposed EC Convention of 1995, see J Garrido, 'Some Reflections on the EU Bankruptcy Convention and its Implications for Secured Creditors' (1998) 7 International Insolvency Review 79. For a comprehensive study of security interests in the context of the Regulation, see M Veder, *Cross-Border Insolvency Proceedings and Security Rights* (2004) esp ch 4. See further in ch 6 below.

[54] Court of Justice 26 October 2016, C-195/15 (SCI/Wedemark).

The above list of attributes that are associated with various kinds of rights *in rem* is intended as a guide to the task of characterization, which, however, as mentioned remains to be determined by the governing law of the right *in rem* according to the private international law rules of the Member State where the assets are located. The RR just as the OR, following the policy adopted by the draftsmen of the former Convention text of 1995, has deliberately refrained from imposing its own definition of a right *in rem* which could result in rights having to be classified in a way which is in conflict with the approach followed by its *lex causae*; the law governing the particular right (which in respect of some classes of assets is the law of its original *situs*).[55] Nevertheless, a more *dirigiste* approach is taken by Article 8(3) in respect of rights which are recorded in a public register and enforceable against third parties, whereby a right *in rem* may be obtained. Such a right is to be considered a right *in rem* throughout all Member States, irrespective of any contrary conclusions to be derived from the provisions of national law.[56] The Virgos-Schmit Report to the Convention emphasized that the provisions of Article 8 only protect pre-existing rights which were created before the insolvency proceedings were opened.[57] Therefore, creditors who have not succeeded in creating and perfecting their right to be treated as secured under its governing law before the time of opening of insolvency proceedings in another Member State, are subject to the effects of the *lex concursus*, in accordance with the basic principle of Article 7 RR. This would be the case, for example, with creditors who have commenced such processes as distress or execution which are incomplete at the time of opening of insolvency.[58] Another example regards rights *in rem* over future assets. If an asset, over which a right *in rem* has been created in advance, is 'acquired' after the opening of insolvency proceedings, the question is whether the right *in rem* is to be considered to have been created prior to or after the opening of such insolvency proceedings. The answer to this question depends both on the law applicable to the asset and the *lex concursus*.

Floating charge security, etc
In the absence of an exhaustive definition of 'rights *in rem*', either for the specific purposes of Article 8 or more generally, it is necessary to establish whether certain types of security, such as the floating charge in Ireland or the pledge on commercial business in Luxembourg and Belgium,[59] fall within the ambit of this important exception to the regime of the *lex concursus*. Article 8(1) makes clear that they do as it refers to rights in rem in respect of 'both individual assets and collections of indefinite assets as a whole which change from time to time'.[60] Whether a right *in rem* is held to be valid and enforceable depends on the private international law rules of the Member State where it is to be enforced. These may be those of the *lex concursus* if the asset has its 'situs' in the Member State where insolvency proceedings have been opened, or of the law of another Member State if the assets are located there at the time of the opening of proceedings. This of course is the case for all rights

4.29

---

[55] Virgos-Schmit Report (n 3 above) para 100.
[56] ibid para 101.
[57] ibid paras 96, 103.
[58] See eg Insolvency Act 1986, ss 130(2), 183, 184, 346, and 347 and Art 35 of the Dutch Bankruptcy Act.
[59] The new Belgian act on security interests on movable assets, which entered into force on 1 January 2018, broadened the scope of this form of pledge.
[60] See also Virgos-Schmit Report (n 3 above), para 104, in relation to Art 5 Insolvency Convention which did not contain this reference.

in rem which have been created under one law and must be enforced under another due to the fact that these assets have moved from one jurisdiction to another.

4.30 One final observation may be made with respect to Article 8 and its effects. Although it can provide protection for the secured creditor against the direct disturbance of expectations founded upon the provisions of the *lex situs*, it does not immunize the creditor against the invocation of processes which may be available under the law of the *situs* itself in the event of the debtor's insolvency. In order to bring such remedies into operation, however, it would be necessary for the insolvency practitioner in the main proceedings, or some other qualified party, to procure the opening of secondary insolvency proceedings under the *lex situs*, and in this way provoke such consequences for the holder of the right *in rem* as may be available under the insolvency law of that state. Naturally, such secondary proceedings can only be commenced if the debtor has an establishment in that Member State.[61]

Exception II: Set-off (Article 9 RR)

4.31 The laws of the Member States diverge sharply over the operation of set-off in the event of a debtor's insolvency. In the United Kingdom and Ireland, set-off is treated as a mandatory process which must be applied, as a matter of public policy, in both individual and corporate insolvencies in which the necessary requirement of mutuality is present.[62] In the Netherlands the circumstances under which set-off can be invoked are broadened under its insolvency law and a multi-party set-off arrangement validly made prior to an insolvency of one of the parties is upheld. The ratio behind the Dutch rule is that if a creditor of the insolvent company is also its debtor, 'the creditor may consider the debt it owes the insolvent company as collateral for its claim against the insolvent company' and thus rely on set-off if certain requirements are met. As a consequence of treating set-off as a kind of security right of the counterparty of the insolvent debtor and viewing this as mandated by reasonableness, the scope of set-off in case of insolvency of the counterparty is actually broadened. In other civil law systems, on the other hand, the prevailing view is that insolvency set-off constitutes a violation of the principle of *pari passu* distribution, and that as a matter of public policy it must be confined to the most carefully limited circumstances, as where the cross-liabilities arise out of one and the same contract or obligation. Therefore, in a cross-border insolvency, the outcome for any creditor who is also a debtor to the estate can be drastically affected by the way in which the issue of applicable law is resolved, if the competing laws happen to represent the different schools of opinion with regard to set-off.[63] Particularly in major commercial operations where large sums of money are involved, the ability to predict the applicable law and to take its provisions on set-off fully into account is vitally important in the assessment of risk. Clear, and uniformly applicable, choice of law rules are therefore essential.

---

[61] Virgos-Schmit Report (n 3 above) para 98.

[62] See *Stein v Blake* [1996] AC 243, HL; *Secretary of State for Trade and Industry v Frid* [2004] 2 AC 506, HL. For authoritative accounts of the subject of set-off, see PR Wood, *English and International Set-Off* (1989); R Derham, *Set-Off* (4th edn, 2010).

[63] For a vivid illustration of this problem, see *Re Bank of Credit and Commerce International SA (No 10)* [1997] Ch 213. For comment on that case, see IF Fletcher [1997] Journal of Business Law 471–76; S Shandro (1998) 7 International Insolvency Review 63.

4.32 We have seen above that Article 7(2)(d) establishes a basic rule to the effect that it is for the *lex concursus* to determine the conditions under which set-offs may be invoked. Accordingly, any party to an international transaction who wishes to calculate the consequences of the other party's insolvency in the event that there are subsisting debts or liabilities in both directions must first determine which Member State is destined to become the forum for main insolvency proceedings, or for any secondary proceedings, involving the other party as the insolvent debtor. It is of course perfectly possible that the mutual dealings between the parties may have as their respective governing laws either the same country's law, or the laws of different countries, and that these may or may not happen to be Member States of the European Union. The possible variations are therefore very numerous. Under the primary rule of Article 7(2)(d), however, it is entirely a matter for the *lex concursus* to determine whether, in the course of applying its doctrine of set-off, any account will be taken of the fact (if such is the case) that either of the cross-obligations is governed by a foreign law under which a different approach is followed. Clearly, there are latent perils for the unwary, whose assumptions may be founded upon familiar rules of the law of the state in which their own business has been conducted, and of the law or laws by which their contractual relationships are designed to be governed.

4.33 Although the fate of any creditor who is simultaneously a debtor to the insolvent estate is primarily controlled by the set-off rule of the *lex concursus*, Article 9 establishes one, carefully limited, exception to this. If the result produced by application of the *lex concursus* is that set-off is not applicable to the cross-claims in question, the creditor may have recourse in the alternative to the exception supplied by Article 9(1), which provides that the creditor shall not be deprived of the right to demand the set-off of his claims against the claims of the debtor, 'where such a set-off is permitted by the law applicable to the insolvent debtor's claim'.[64] This somewhat ponderous phrase is intended to denote 'the law applicable to the claim where the insolvent debtor is the creditor in relation to the other party'.[65] To establish the law by which the relevant claim is governed (assuming it to be contractual), a common set of choice of law rules is supplied by the Rome I Regulation on the Law Applicable to Contractual Obligations, which is applicable in all Member States of the European Union, with the exception of Denmark.[66] The Rome I Regulation, as a legislative act of the EU, is confined in its application to those states which are members of the European Union and which participated in its adoption.[67] Like its predecessor the Rome Convention, the Rome

---

[64] For the question which law determines whether a creditor may invoke set-off the Rome I Regulation provides the same conflict of laws rule in Art 17.

[65] Virgos-Schmit Report (n 3 above) para 108. The rationale expressed in that paragraph is epitomized in Recital (26) to the Regulation. Some writers employ the expression 'the passive claim' to denote the insolvent debtor's claim against the proving creditor (ie the claim where the insolvent debtor is the creditor in relation to the other party), to be contrasted with the 'active' claim owed to that creditor by the estate (ie the claim in respect of which proof will be lodged in the insolvency).

[66] Regulation (EC) 593/2008 of the European Parliament and Council of 17 June 2008 on the law applicable to contractual obligations [2008] OJ L177/6 (see n 7 above). By Recital (46) to the Rome I Regulation it is declared that by virtue of its opt-out granted under the Maastricht Treaty on European Union, Denmark does not participate in the adoption of the Regulation and is not bound by it or subject to its application. By virtue of Art 24, the Rome Convention continues to apply to Denmark.

[67] Although at the time of adoption of the Rome I Regulation the United Kingdom exercised its own opt-out facility (as recorded in Recital (45)) a subsequent change of position by the United Kingdom came about following further negotiations. In July 2008 the Government formally notified the EU Commission that it would opt in to the Regulation and by Decision 2009/26/EC [2009] OJ L10/22 the Commission decided that the Rome I Regulation would apply to the United Kingdom. With BREXIT of course the Rome I Regulation will not be applied by the

I Regulation is based upon the principle that the governing law of any contract to which its provisions apply may be that of some third state, rather than being limited to the laws of the Member States themselves and with that it has a universal scope.[68] The Regulation applies to contracts concluded after 17 December 2009.[69]

4.34 Significantly, Article 9 RR omits any reference to 'the Member States', or their respective laws, in creating the exception in favour of the rule of set-off that is operated by 'the law applicable to the insolvent debtor's claim'. It therefore follows that in this instance the law of some third state could furnish the basis for allowing the creditor to have the benefit of set-off which would otherwise be excluded under the regime of the *lex concursus*.[70] With this possibility in mind therefore, where parties are in a position to choose the law by which their transactions are governed, they may well deem it expedient to ensure that a clear, express choice is made in favour of the law of a country whose rule concerning set-off is most suited to their requirements. Article 3 of the Rome I Regulation gives effect to such an act of choice, which can be made with respect to the whole or to a particular part of the contract.[71]

4.35 One notable feature of Article 9 OR is that it can only operate, if at all, in such a way as to allow a set-off to be invoked in circumstances where otherwise it would be excluded: it does not allow a creditor to be denied the benefit of a set-off which is already available under the *lex concursus* in accordance with the rule in Article 7(2)(d). Once again, it is to be observed that Article 9(2) preserves the application of Article 7(2)(m) in relation to cases benefiting from the exception created under Article 9(1). Consequently, the avoidance rules of the *lex concursus* continue to be applicable to any challenge to the validity or enforceability of any claim to which the doctrine of set-off may otherwise be applicable by virtue of Article 9(1), in which event the defence provided under Art 16 may become applicable (see below in para 4.49).

---

courts in the UK, but many of its rules have been incorporated into its domestic legislation. Ireland separately chose to take part in the adoption and application of the Regulation: Recital (44).

[68] Art 2 of the Rome I Regulation states: 'Any law specified by this Regulation shall be applied whether or not it is the law of a Member State'. Art 2 of the Rome Convention is identical in substance, save that the expressions 'Convention' and 'Contracting State' are used instead of 'Regulation' and 'Member State'.

[69] ibid, Art 28.

[70] This conclusion, based on the unrestricted terms in which Art 9 is drafted, is not universally accepted. Some commentators have sought to claim that an implied restriction must be read into the text to limit its scope of application to cases where the claim in question is governed by the law of an EU Member State. See eg Virgos-Schmit Report, para 93; M Virgos and F Garcimartin, *The European Insolvency Regulation: Law and Practice* (2004) 91 (§137) and 117 (§189); cf B Wessels, *International Insolvency Law* (2017) para [10665], where the various writers' views are surveyed, with the author affirming a personal position aligned with that stated in the present text. The Court of Justice also seems to confirm the view that Art 9 RR is not restricted to the application of the law of a Member State in *Schmid/Hertel* (16 January 2014 C-328/12) where in para 22 of its judgement it states: 'It is true that the application of a number of the Regulation's provisions requires the presence of connecting factors within the territory or the legal system of at least two Member States, as is the case with Article 5(1)' of the OR (Art 8(1) RR). To continue in para 23: 'However, other provisions of the Regulation, such as Article 6 [Article 9 RR] and 14 [Article 17 RR], do not contain restrictions of this kind.'

[71] Rome I Regulation, Art 3(1). Note also that Art 3(2) allows the parties to agree at any time to subject their contract to a law other than that which previously governed it, whether as a result of earlier choice or by reason of absence of choice as to governing law. There is a proviso to Art 3(2) whose effect is to prevent such subsequent changes of governing law from adversely affecting third parties (such as creditors generally), and it is also the case that any change of this nature would have to be effected prior to the opening of insolvency proceedings.

C. EXCEPTIONS TO BASIC CHOICE OF LAW RULE (ARTICLES 8–18 RR)

Exception III: Reservation of title (Article 10 RR)

The practice of including a reservation of title clause within a contract of sale, as a means of affording protection to an unpaid seller in the event of the buyer's insolvency, is treated in different ways under the laws of the Member States of the European Union.[72] To minimize the uncertainty associated with cross-border cases, special rules are needed. Article 10 RR provides two such rules, which introduce exceptions to the application of the *lex concursus* in relation to contracts to which the insolvent debtor is a party. As is the case with Article 8 RR, it does not provide conflict of laws rules to determine the governing law of a retention of title clause and the consequences thereof, but rather provides the buyer or the seller, as the case may be, with immunity from the application of the *lex concursus*. The rules in Article 10 deal, respectively, with the insolvency of the buyer or of the seller, and in each instance the relevant factor is the *situs* of the subject-matter of the contract of sale at the time of opening of insolvency proceedings. Article 10 applies where this is in a Member State other than the state of opening. Where Article 10(1) provides for a rule very similar to Article 8(1), Article 10(2) contains more of a material rule which displaces the effects of the application of the *lex concursus*.

4.36

Article 10(1) applies in a case where insolvency proceedings are opened against the purchaser of an asset for which the price has not been paid in full. It provides that the seller's rights based on a reservation of title ('ROT') clause shall not be affected by the opening of proceedings where the asset in question is at that time situated within the territory of a Member State other than the state of opening.[73] Therefore, any provisions within the *lex concursus* whereby the ROT clause is rendered ineffective as against the claims of the insolvency practitioner—for example due to lack of formal registration, or on other grounds—would not affect the seller's right to retake the asset provided that such a right is conferred by the law that governs the ROT clause and its consequences under the circumstances existing at the relevant time. Whether the ROT clause is valid and what the consequences of such an ROT clause are in relation to the asset is determined by its governing law. That governing law is not determined by Article 10(1) but arguably by the private international law rules of the court where the purchaser wants to exercise its rights in relation to the asset for which the ROT clause was made; the private international law rules of the *lex situs* at the time of the exercise. The rights protected by the ROT under its applicable law cannot be affected by the provisions of the *lex concursus* if the asset is located in a Member State other than the state of opening at the time such insolvency proceedings were opened. The terms of Article 10(1) are such that regardless of a change in location of the asset subsequent to the opening of proceedings, the provision of Article 10(1) continues to apply.[74] Considering the above, the exact way in which this provision will operate in practice is far from clear.

4.37

---

[72] On the inability of the EU Member States to agree on terms of harmonization of their treatment of reservation of title, see G McCormack, *Reservation of Title* (1990) 210–20.

[73] Cf the ruling of the Court of Justice in Case C-292/08 *German Graphics GmbH v van der Schee* [2009] ECR I-8421, where the asset covered by the ROT clause was situated, at the relevant time, in the Member State of the opening of insolvency proceedings concerning the purchaser of the asset. Consequently, Art 10(1) provided no protection to the unpaid seller. The Court of Justice did rule, however, that the question whether the ROT was valid and thus that the seller had retained ownership based on the ROT (the question as to who owned the asset) did not fall within the scope of the RR and must thus be litigated before a court that had jurisdiction based on the Brussel I Regulation (recast). The question how rights of the seller under a valid ROT are affected by the insolvency does fall within the scope of the RR.

[74] This is the view expressed in the Virgos-Schmit Report (n 3 above) para 113.

4.38 Article 10(2) is concerned with the position where it is the seller of an asset who, following its delivery, is the subject of insolvency proceedings. Where, due to the effects of an ROT clause, the seller retains ownership of the asset even after delivery, the consequence might be that the asset is regarded as part of the insolvent estate and thus liable to repossession by the insolvency practitioner, leaving the buyer to lodge proof for any damage incurred.[75] The provision in Article 10(2) alleviates the buyer's predicament by declaring that the opening of insolvency proceedings shall not constitute grounds for rescinding or terminating the sale, and shall not prevent the buyer from acquiring title, where at the time of opening the asset sold is situated within the territory of a Member State other than the *forum concursus*. This provision is not a choice of law rule but is a uniform rule of substantive law whose application is confined to specially defined circumstances.

4.39 Finally, Article 10(3) preserves the application of the avoidance rules of the *lex concursus* in cases falling within the ambit of either Article 10(1) or (2). The fact that in each of those paragraphs, reference is made to the *situs* of the asset as being within the territory of a Member State necessarily means that Article 10 has no application to cases where the asset is situated in some third state at the relevant time. See further on the *situs* Article 2(9) RR and the discussions above in 4.24.

Exception IV: Contracts relating to immovable property (Article 11 RR)

4.40 It is usually the case that an insolvency practitioner can choose whether to confirm or to terminate any executory contract to which the debtor is a party at the time of commencement of insolvency proceedings.[76] Article 7(2)(e) asserts the basic principle that the *lex concursus* determines the effects of insolvency upon current contracts to which the debtor is a party. However, Article 11(1) creates an exception to this rule for cases of contracts conferring the right to acquire or make use of immovable property which is situated within the territory of a Member State other than the state of opening. The Article provides that the effect of insolvency upon such contracts will be governed solely by the *lex situs*. The Virgos-Schmit Report explains at paragraph 118 that the reference to the exclusive application of the law of the *situs* includes the insolvency law of that state, so that parties to an international contract for the sale of land or the leasing of immovable property need to inform themselves about the relevant provisions of the insolvency law of the Member State in which the property is situated, in order to understand the consequences of the insolvency of the other party. This provision is not applicable to cases where the property is situated in some third state, and it is therefore left to the *lex concursus*, including the conflict rules of that system, to resolve the issue. Although, according to standard principles of conflict of laws it is generally the case that questions concerning rights *in rem* over, and succession to, immovable property are referred to the *lex situs*, this is not necessarily the applicable law to a contract of sale[77] or a lease agreement in respect of immovable property. The Rome I Regulation allows parties

---

[75] Such a claim would of course be subject to deduction of the price due from the buyer.
[76] For analysis of the problems of executory contracts (a neglected topic in the literature of insolvency under UK law), see the writings of authors commenting from the standpoint of American law: JL Westbrook, 'A Functional Analysis of Executory Contracts' (1989) 74 Minnesota L Rev 227; V Countryman, 'Executory Contracts in Bankruptcy' (Parts 1 and 2) (1973) 57 Minnesota L Rev 439, and (1974) 58 Minnesota L Rev 479.
[77] That a contract of sale also falls within the scope of Art 11 is also held by Chr Paulus in *Europäische Insolvenzverordnung* (2021) p 292 and R van Galen in *An Introduction to European Insolvency Law* (2021) para 123.

to choose the law applicable to a contract of sale or lease agreement in respect of immovable property[78] and the *lex situs* is only applicable in absence of a choice.[79] So even if parties to such a contract have chosen a law other than the law of the *situs* of the immovable property to which the contract relates, Article 11(1) RR forces them to take into account the provisions of the *lex situs* in the event of an insolvency of one of the parties.

The RR introduces a second subsection to the provision regarding contracts relating to immovable property. Article 11(2) provides that if the law of the Member State applicable to such contracts requires that such contract may only be terminated or modified with the approval of the court opening insolvency proceedings, the court that opened the main insolvency proceedings will have jurisdiction provided that no secondary proceedings have been opened in the Member State where the immovable property is located. If the latter is the case then the court that has opened the secondary proceedings will quite naturally have jurisdiction.

4.41

Exception V: Payment systems and financial markets (Article 12 RR)

An especially sensitive area, in view of its commercial and societal importance, is the effect of insolvency upon executory contracts between parties operating within an organized payment or settlement system, or a particular financial market. In the interest of sustaining confidence in the integrity of the arrangements to which the participants have originally assented upon joining the system or market in question, Article 12(1) imposes a special choice of law rule whereby the effects of insolvency proceedings on the rights and obligations of parties to a payment or settlement system or to a financial market will be governed solely by the law of the Member State applicable to that system or market.[80] This rule in favour of the exclusive application of the systemic law is reinforced by the provision in Article 12(2) whereby any action for voidness, voidability, or unenforceability of payments or transactions carried out under the system or market in question, and which may be detrimental to creditors generally, is nevertheless declared to be subject to the law applicable to the relevant payment system or financial market. The practice followed in Articles 8, 9, and 11 RR, of reserving the application of the avoidance rule of the *lex concursus* as referred to in Article 7(2)(m), is here relinquished in favour of the total prevalence of the law which is applicable to the payment system or market, thereby enabling parties to base their expectations purely upon a single set of rules without having to take into account the various national laws to which counter-parties may be personally subject, and by which the insolvency of any of them may happen to be governed. It must be emphasized, however, that the

4.42

---

[78] Article 3 Rome I Regulation.
[79] Article 4(1)(c) Rome I Regulation.
[80] See Recital (71) RR. Now that the United Kingdom is no longer a member of the EU, all such UK markets, whose rules contain provisions for closing out contracts and netting in the event of insolvency of a member, like the London International Financial Futures and Options Exchange (LIFFE); the International Stock Exchange of the United Kingdom and Republic of Ireland; the London Metal Exchange, and the London Commodity Exchange no longer fall within the scope of the RR and thus not within the scope of Art 12(1). Examples of such markets in the Member States are: Euronext (Amsterdam, Brussels, Paris, Dublin, and Lisbon) and the Frankfurt Stock Exchange. Examples of payment systems in the EU: TIPS (Target Instant Payment Settlement); Clearing Service Austria (Austria); CEC (Belgium); SICOI (Portugal). See ch 7 below. For the UK these are regulated in the Companies Act 1989, Part VII (*Financial Markets and Insolvency*), as amended by and under the Financial Services and Markets Act 2000, together with the Financial Markets and Insolvency Regulations 1991, SI 1991/880, as amended, and Council Directive (EC) 98/26 (the Settlement Finality Directive [1998] OJ L166/45) as transposed for UK purposes by SI 1999/2979 (the Financial Markets and Insolvency (Settlement Finality) Regulations 1999).

rules of Article 12 RR are only applicable in a situation where the system or market is operating under the law of one of the Member States and thus no longer to systems operating under the laws of the United Kingdom.[81] Moreover, there is a special proviso in Article 12(1) RR to the effect that it is without prejudice to the effect of Article 8 RR, which provides that rights *in rem* over assets located in a Member State other than the state of opening shall not be affected by the insolvency proceedings.[82]

Exception VI: Contracts of employment (Article 13 RR)

4.43 A further category of executory contracts for which special considerations arise is the employment relationship. Indeed, special rules are already operative under the Brussels I Regulation (recast)[83] and the Rome I Regulation[84] to regulate jurisdictional and choice of law aspects of contracts of employment. To protect the interests of employees, Article 13(1) RR stipulates that the effects of insolvency proceedings on employment contracts and relationships shall be governed solely by the law of the Member State applicable to the contract of employment, including its insolvency law.[85] To ascertain the applicable law, the courts of all Member States will apply the provisions of the Rome I Regulation, notably Articles 3, 8, and 9 thereof. Although a limited choice of law may be included in an employment contract based on these provisions, it can be held that, overall, the application of these provisions will lead to the law of the place where the employee habitually carries out his work. If this produces the conclusion that the contract is governed by the law of one of the Member States, the rule of Article 13(1) RR will apply. If the law of some third state is indicated, however, the effects of insolvency will be determined by the *lex concursus*, with reference as appropriate to any provisions of the private international law of that system.

4.44 The RR introduced a new subsection to Article 13 which provides that the courts of the Member State in which secondary insolvency proceedings may be opened shall retain jurisdiction to approve the termination or modification of employment contracts even if no such secondary proceedings have been opened. Secondary proceedings may be opened in a Member State where the debtor has an establishment. To avoid having to open secondary proceedings to grant the courts of that Member State jurisdiction to approve the termination of employment contracts of employees working for such establishment, this new subsection was introduced.[86]

---

[81] The conflict of laws rule under Art 12 RR corresponds with the conflict of laws rule included in Art 8 of the Settlement Finality Directive, which provides: 'In the event of insolvency proceedings being opened against a participant in a system, the rights and obligations arising from, or in connection with, the participation of that participant shall be determined by the law governing that system.' Although 'system' is limited to systems governed by laws of Member States, Recital (7) of the Directive allows Member States to apply the rules of the Directive, thus including Art 8, to so-called third-country systems including the UK. This means that the protection afforded under Art 12 RR may through the implementation of the Settlement Finality Directive in the national laws of the Member States also be granted to participants of UK payment systems and financial markets.

[82] See Exception I at paras 4.20–4.30 above.

[83] Regulation (EU) 2015/2012 of 12 December 2012, on Jurisdiction and the Recognition and Enforcement of Judgments in Civil and Commercial Matters (recast) OJ L351/1, 20 December 2012, which became applicable from 10 January 2015, Arts 20–23. The Regulation of 2012 replaced Council Regulation (EC) 44/2001, of 22 December 2000, [2001] OJ L12/1. The latter Regulation replaced, with effect from 1 March 2002, the Brussels Convention (originally concluded on 27 September 1968 and several times subsequently amended and expanded) with respect to 27 of the then 28 EU Member States (the exception being Denmark).

[84] Regulation (EC) 593/2008 of the European Parliament and Council of 17 June 2008 on the law applicable to contractual obligations [2008] OJ L177/6, n 7 and 67 above, Art 8.

[85] See Recital (72) RR and Virgos-Schmit Report, para 125.

[86] See also R van Galen, *An Introduction to European Insolvency Law* (2021), para 133.

It should also be emphasized that Article 13(1) is confined to the question of the effect of **4.45**
insolvency upon the contract of employment as such, including the issue as to whether the
contract is automatically terminated by the insolvency of either party to it, or whether the
insolvency practitioner has the option to affirm or rescind the contract, subject to specified terms. Article 13 does not purport to regulate other issues such as the ranking of employees' claims for unpaid wages or salaries, and the mode of treatment to be accorded to
these claims. Such questions remain subject to the *lex concursus*, in accordance with Article
7(2)(i).[87] It is also the case that in many states nowadays there is a statutory scheme under
which, in the event of their employer's insolvency, employees are guaranteed a measure of
payment out of a national fund, with the state then becoming subrogated to the employee
in respect of that portion of the latter's claim against the employer. Paragraph 128 of the
Virgos-Schmit Report asserts that such guaranteed payments, since they are maintained
under provisions of the national law of the Member State concerned, are subject to the law
of that state. Such protection of employees and the system of guaranteed payments are all
based on EU Directives[88] which should have been implemented in each Member State and
thus the protection afforded should be similar in all Member States.

Exception VII: Rights subject to registration (Article 14 RR)
National laws usually operate a system of public registration for many kinds of rights or **4.46**
interests over immovable property. Such registration forms an essential aspect of the safeguards for other parties who may have or acquire interests in the same property. Certain
kinds of movable property, including ships and aircraft, are likewise subject to public registration in the state in which they are principally kept, or from which they are operated. Such
registers play important roles in the protection of trade and the maintenance of certainty,
and also in ensuring compliance with health and safety regulations affecting the assets in
question. The casual location of such assets, which may be of very large value, should not be
the decisive criterion by which to determine the effects of insolvency proceedings upon the
rights of the debtor in relation to them. Both with immovable property and with movables
of this kind, there is the possibility of a conflict between the provisions of the law of the state
under whose authority the register is maintained and the provisions of the *lex concursus*.

Article 14 RR provides that, where the register is kept under the authority of a Member **4.47**
State, it is the law of that state, and not the *lex concursus*, which shall determine the effects
of insolvency proceedings on the rights of the debtor in immovable property, a ship, or an
aircraft subject to public registration. However, it should be noted that this choice of law
provision does not include the word 'solely', and that this omission is intended to enable
the *lex concursus* to continue to play a part in the process of determining the net effect of
insolvency upon the rights which are the subject of registration. In the words of paragraph
130 of the Virgos-Schmit Report, 'a sort of cumulative application of both laws is necessary'.
What appears to be envisaged is that there should be an interaction between the insolvency

---

[87] Recital (72) RR and Virgos-Schmit Report (n 3 above), para 128.
[88] See for instance: Council Directive 2000/78/EC of 27 November 2000 establishing a general framework for equal treatment in employment and occupation; Council Directive of 12 June 1989 on the introduction of measures to encourage improvements in the safety and health of workers at work (89/391/EEC); and Directive 2009/104/EC of the European Parliament and of the Council of 16 September 2009 concerning the minimum safety and health requirements for the use of work equipment by workers at work (second individual Directive within the meaning of Article 16(1) of Directive 89/391/EEC).

practitioner and the official by whom the relevant register is maintained, to arrange for appropriate entries to be made in the register that will reflect the fact that insolvency proceedings are taking place in a different Member State. It will remain a matter for the law of the state of registration to determine what effects this process shall have upon the rights of the debtor in the property concerned.

Exception VIII: European patents with unitary effect and Community trade marks (Article 15 RR)

4.48 In view of the fact that arrangements are already in force within the European Union to regulate patents, trademarks, and the rights of plant breeders throughout the whole territory of the Union,[89] it is appropriate that the RR should endeavour to complement the provisions already operating with regard to the treatment of such forms of intellectual property in cases of insolvency of those who own or have interests in the rights concerned. Each of the existing arrangements concluded under EU law contains a rule to the effect that a Community right arising thereunder may be included only in the first proceedings that are opened in a contracting state.[90] Under the provisions of the RR, however, it can sometimes happen that the 'first' proceedings to be opened are not main proceedings under Article 3(1), but are territorial proceedings within the meaning of Article 3(2) and (4).[91] This has necessitated a special rule, contained in Article 15 RR, whereby a European patent with unitary effect, a Community trademark or any similar right established by Union law may be included only in main insolvency proceedings which are opened under Article 3(1). This provision is operative only when the debtor has his centre of main interests in a Member State, for this is an essential condition to the opening of proceedings under Article 3(1). Where the debtor's centre of main interests is located outside the Union, the rules of the individual enactments relating to intellectual property are applicable without modification, with the consequence that the right in question is included in the insolvent estate of the first proceedings to be opened in a Member State.[92]

Exception IX: Detrimental acts protected from avoidance (Article 16 RR)

4.49 According to Article 7(2)(m) RR the law of the state of the opening of proceedings shall determine the rules relating to voidness, voidability, or unenforceability of legal acts detrimental to all the creditors. However, Article 16 RR supplies a rule which operates by way of exception to this general proposition, to the effect that Article 7(2)(m) shall not apply where the person who benefited from a legal act detrimental to all the creditors provides proof that:

(i) the act is subject to the law of a Member State other than that of the State of opening of proceedings; and

---

[89] Community Patent Convention [1975] OJ L17/1, as modified by the Luxembourg Agreement of 30 December 1989 [1989] OJ L401/10; Council Directive (EEC) 89/104 [1989] OJ L207/44; and Council Regulation (EC) 40/94 on the Community Trademark [1994] OJ L11/1; Council Regulation (EC) 2100/94 on Community Plant Variety Rights [1994] OJ L227/1.
[90] Luxembourg Agreement, Art 41; Trademark Regulation, Art 21; Regulation on Plant Variety Rights, Art 25 (all previous footnote).
[91] See ch 3, section A above.
[92] See Virgos-Schmit Report (n 3 above), paras 133, 134.

(ii) the law of that Member State does not allow any means of challenging that act in the relevant case.

Protection is thereby given to parties who have reasonably relied upon the validity of a transaction whose governing law happens to be that of a Member State, and which is unimpeachable under the concrete circumstances of the case according to both the insolvency law and the general law of that state.[93] It should be observed that if the governing law of the transaction is that of a non-EU Member State the exception under Article 16 does not apply, and that the avoidance rule of the *lex concursus* can then be applied irrespective of whether the transaction would be unavoidable under the general and insolvency laws of the other state. The supporting rationale of this article is the protection of a party's legitimate expectations formed with reference to the circumstances prevailing at the time of entering into a transaction which is subsequently threatened under the legal provisions of the state in which the counterparty is later the subject of insolvency proceedings. The Court of Justice has affirmed that the special protection afforded by Article 16 RR is not available in the case where the acts which are subject to reversal took place after the opening of insolvency proceedings.[94] Such extended application would go beyond what is necessary to protect legitimate expectations and the certainty of transactions in Member States other than that in which proceedings are opened. This is because, in the Court's reasoning, as from the opening of insolvency proceedings the creditors of the debtor concerned are able to predict the effects of the application of the *lex fori concursus* on the legal relations which they maintain with that debtor. However, in a case concerning the exercise of a right *in rem* to which the protective provision of Article 8(1) RR was applicable, the Court ruled that in order that the main purpose of Article 8 RR may be attained it is necessary for the creditor to be able to exercise rights validly established prior to the opening of insolvency proceedings even after the date of opening. Accordingly, it must be possible for the creditor to rely on the protective defence offered by Article 16 in a situation in which a payment, challenged by an insolvency administrator, of a sum of money attached before the opening of the insolvency proceedings was made only after the opening of those proceedings.[95]

4.50 A further notable effect of Article 7(2)(m) RR is that it has been designed to surmount one of the controversial aspects of the application of transaction avoidance rules in cases of conflict of laws, namely the possibility of cumulative application of the rules of more than one system in order to decide whether the transaction is valid. The rule supplied by paragraph (m) of Article 7(2) RR ensures that under most circumstances only a single avoidance rule—that of the *lex concursus*—is applicable. This greatly simplifies the task of the insolvency practitioner in seeking to bring about the avoidance of such transactions. However, in the special situation covered by Article 16 the other party to the transaction with the debtor is effectively allowed to ward off any attack based upon the avoidance rule of the *lex concursus*, by arguing that the legal act is valid and cannot be avoided under the law by which it is properly governed. The Court of Justice has not made it easy for the other party to invoke the protection of Article 16. To be successful in challenging the avoidance under the *lex concursus*, the other party must prove that the act cannot be challenged under the

---

[93] ibid paras 135–39.
[94] Court of Justice 16 April 2015 C-557/13 (Lutz v Bäuerle).
[95] Court of Justice 16 April 2015 C-557/13 (*Lutz v Bäuerle*) at paras 32–43.

lex causae or that the conditions which should be met under the *lex causae* in order for the challenge to be upheld have not been fulfilled.[96] In Nike/Sportland the Court of Justice ruled that these concern challenges both under the insolvency laws of the *lex causae* as well as under the general rules and principles of the *lex causae*.[97] Article 16 does allow a defence that is based on the assertion that a limitation period under the governing law has expired.[98] Also, for the purposes of Article 16, the applicable procedural requirements under the *lex causae* for setting aside the challenged act must be observed by the insolvency practitioner together with those under the *lex concursus*. This, however, does not mean that the other party can benefit from whatever procedural rules are more favourable to him under the *lex causae*.[99] Article 16 grants the other party a defence against the avoidance action under the *lex concursus*. If, however, the act is in any way avoidable under the *lex causae* and the defence thus fails, the avoidance action and all of its consequences are governed exclusively by the *lex concursus*.[100]

4.51 A lingering question is to what extent there are limitations to opportunistic choices of law, where parties only opt for a set of laws to benefit from relaxed rules on transactions avoidance. The question becomes especially pressing if the choice is made at a moment where insolvency is already imminent. In *Vinyls Italia/Mediterranea di Navigazione*,[101] the Court of Justice creates room to invoke the doctrine of abuse of Union law, thereby providing a framework for assessment. The mere fact that another law provides more protection against transaction avoidance will of course not be sufficient.

4.52 Finally, the other party can only invoke Article 16 if the law in question is that of another Member State which is participating in the RR. In this respect it should be remembered that Denmark, although a member of the EU, does not count as a 'Member State' for the purposes of the RR due to its having secured a permanent opt-out from this sector of EU legislation, as stated in Recital (88).[102] Therefore the benefit of Article 16 cannot be claimed in a case where the transaction in question is governed by Danish law. As a result of BREXIT the same is obviously true if the *lex causae* of the challenged act is English law. It remains now to be seen whether professional parties in Europe will opt for a different law to govern their contract in order to benefit from relaxed rules on transaction avoidance.

---

[96] Court of Justice 15 October 2015, C-310/14 (*Nike/Sportland*); Court of Justice 8 June 2017, C-54/16 (*Vinyls Italia/Mediterranea di Navigazione*); and Court of Justice 22 April 2021, C-73/20 (*ZM/Frerichs*).
[97] Court of Justice 15 October 2015, C-310/14.
[98] Court of Justice 16 April 2015 C-557/13 (*Lutz v Bäuerle*).
[99] Court of Justice 8 June 2017, C-54/16 (*Vinyls Italia/Mediterranea di Navigazione*).
[100] See also RJ van Galen, *An Introduction to European Insolvency Law* (2021) para 140; and Virgos and Garcimartín, *The European Insolvency Regulation: Law and Practice* (2004) 232.
[101] Court of Justice 8 June 2017, C-54/16 (*Vinyls Italia/Mediterranea di Navigazione*). See on the concept of abuse of Union law in the setting of insolvency law, H Eidenmüller, 'Abuse of Law in the context of European Insolvency Law', ECFR 2009/1 and RJ de Weijs and M Breeman, 'Comi-migration: Use or Abuse of Union Law' (2015) 11(4) European Company and Financial Law Review 495–530. See for the criteria of abuse of union law, CJEU in *Vinyls*: 'In that context, it is apparent from well-established case-law that a finding of abuse requires a combination of objective and subjective elements. First, with regard to the objective element, that finding requires that it must be apparent from a combination of objective circumstances that, despite formal observance of the conditions laid down by Community rules, the purpose of those rules has not been achieved. Second, such a finding requires a subjective element, namely that it must be apparent from a number of objective factors that the essential aim of the transactions concerned is to obtain an undue advantage. The prohibition of abuse is not relevant where the economic activity carried out may have some explanation other than the mere attainment of an advantage.'
[102] See para 1.02 above.

C. EXCEPTIONS TO BASIC CHOICE OF LAW RULE (ARTICLES 8–18 RR)

Exception X: Protection of third-party purchasers (Article 17 RR)

It is usually the case that under the provisions of national law the opening of insolvency proceedings causes the debtor to be deprived of the power to deal with or dispose of property to the detriment of the general body of creditors. According to the circumstances of the disposition, such transactions may be declared to be void under all circumstances, or in other instances may be subject to validation by the court at its discretion, or subject to defined conditions.[103]

4.53

However, where the property which is improperly disposed of by the debtor is subject to some form of public registration, a policy dilemma is caused by the possibility that the transaction with the third party may take place before the fact of the insolvency is placed upon the record. Such parties, consulting the record in its unamended state, may be prejudiced by their reliance upon the information thereby obtained. Consequently, in the interest of maintaining confidence in the integrity of the public register, the national law of the state in which the register is maintained may embody a rule to protect a party who has dealt in good faith and for valuable consideration, and in reliance upon the information carried on the face of the register at the time in question. In cases of international insolvency, where the state of opening of proceedings and the state where the register is maintained are separate from each other, the interval before the register can be amended may be even longer, thus allowing more time in which such transactions may take place. If the protection to be accorded to the third party is made to depend upon the *lex concursus*, that party may suffer injustice due to reliance that was originally and reasonably placed upon the rule contained in the *lex situs* (in the case of immovable property), or in the law of the state in which the register is maintained (in the case of ships or aircraft, or of securities whose existence is dependent upon registration). Article 17 RR accordingly creates a rule to protect third-party purchasers to whom the debtor, other than gratuitously, has disposed of any of these kinds of assets by an act concluded after the opening of insolvency proceedings. The validity of the act of disposal is governed by the *lex situs* in the case of an immovable asset, and in the case of registrable assets by the law of the state under whose authority the register is kept.

4.54

The drafting of Article 17 omits any reference to 'Member State' in its provision regarding the law to govern the validity of the acts to which it is applicable, and it would therefore appear that the provision can be applied to cases where the *situs* of the immovable property, or the place where the register is maintained, is located in some third state. Although the Virgos-Schmit Report, written with reference to the provisions of the corresponding Article of the 1995 version of the proposed Convention, appears to contradict the indications conveyed by the terms of the Article itself, by consistently referring to 'contracting state' in relation to the scope of its application,[104] the idea that the RR does not regulate the effects of insolvency proceedings vis-à-vis third countries[105] has not been confirmed by the Court of Justice. On the contrary, in *Schmid/Hertel*, it acknowledged that an action falling within the scope of the RR could also be brought before the court that opened the main proceedings against a person without residence or COMI in a Member State.[106] In light of the above it is

4.55

---

[103] Insolvency Act 1986, s 127.
[104] Virgos-Schmit Report (n 3 above), paras 140, 141.
[105] ibid para 11.
[106] Court of Justice 16 January 2014, C-328/12 (*Schmid/Hertel*), see also footnote 70.

generally held that the protection afforded by Article 17 also applies if the register is kept in a third state. Conversely, the scope of Article 17 is widened in another respect by a further statement in the Report that: 'An act of disposal must be understood to include not only transfers of ownership but also the constitution of a right *in rem* relating to such property.'[107]

Exception XI: Effects on pending lawsuits or arbitral proceedings (Article 18 RR)

4.56 The laws of the Member States of the European Union differ from one another with regard to the effect of insolvency proceedings on a pending lawsuit to which the debtor is a party. These differences concern not only the forcible interruption of proceedings by virtue of an automatic stay, but also the possible removal of litigation from the civil or commercial court which would normally have jurisdiction, into the exclusive control of the insolvency court, under the principle known as *vis attractiva concursus*. This principle is by no means universally, or even uniformly, applied, and there are likewise variations of approach to such matters as the possible lifting of the stay upon proceedings at the discretion of the insolvency court. Potentially, much confusion and uncertainty could result in a given case due to the presence of conflicting rules contained respectively in the *lex concursus* and in the law of the state in which the litigation is pending.

4.57 Article 18 imposes a uniform choice of law rule in favour of the sole application of the law of the forum in which the lawsuit is pending. The scope of this rule is likely to be of considerable practical importance, and hence the terms of the Article should be noted with some care. First, a distinction is to be made between the effects of insolvency on individual enforcement actions (such as distress, execution, attachment, and sequestration), as opposed to pending lawsuits. The former are governed by the law of the state of opening, as provided by Article 7(2)(f),[108] whereas only the latter are affected by Article 18.[109] The Article refers expressly to 'a pending lawsuit or pending arbitral proceedings concerning an asset or a right which forms part of a debtor's insolvency estate'. Accordingly, if the asset happens to be excluded from the effects of insolvency and is not considered part of the insolvency estate according to the *lex concursus*, it would be unaffected by Article 18.[110] It is also essential to the application of Article 18 that the lawsuit in question should be pending in another Member State: litigation in third states is not within the ambit of this provision. Where the rule applies, it is for the law of the state where litigation is pending (including the procedural law of that state) to determine whether or not the proceedings are to be suspended or whether they may continue subject to terms or conditions, including any procedural modifications which may be necessary in view of the fact that the debtor has been deprived of the powers of administration and disposal of his property, with the insolvency practitioner having been substituted in his place.[111]

4.58 As the provision was drafted under the OR (in Article 15) it was unclear whether arbitral proceedings would fall within its ambit as it only referred to a 'lawsuit pending'. That limited

---

[107] ibid para 141. See also RJ van Galen, *Introduction to European Insolvency Law* (2021), para 125.
[108] See Court of Justice 9 November 2016, C-212/15 (*ENEFI/DGRFP*).
[109] See Court of Justice 6 June 2018, C-250/17 (*Virgílio Tarragó da Silveira/Massa Insolvente da Espírito Santo Financial Group, SA*).
[110] For an account of the position under English law concerning property in the ownership of a bankrupt individual which does not vest in the trustee in bankruptcy, see IF Fletcher, *The Law of Insolvency* (5th edn, 2017, paras 8-055–8-085.
[111] See further the commentary to Art 18 in ch 8 below.

wording gave rise to a degree of uncertainty as to Article 15 OR's true scope of application. The expression 'a lawsuit pending' is undoubtedly applicable to a broad spectrum of matters and proceedings which may be conducted before a duly constituted court or tribunal. What was not clear was whether the expression 'lawsuit pending' also intended to apply to arbitration proceedings. The English Court of Appeal delivered a carefully reasoned judgment in which it concluded that 'lawsuit pending' in the context of Article 15 OR must be taken to include pending references to arbitration,[112] but as the Court of Justice had not ruled on this matter under the OR this remained uncertain. This uncertainty has now been clarified in Article 17 RR which explicitly refers to both a 'pending lawsuit' and 'pending arbitral proceedings'.

D. Material Scope of Choice of Law Rules

Preliminary

Although Article 7 and Articles 8–18 RR provide a miniature code of choice of law rules, they are not all encompassing. There are still actions and questions of great practical and societal importance, that are not addressed in these Articles and for which it is not clear whether they fall within the material scope of the RR. These mainly relate to directors' liability and possibly also to rights and responsibilities of shareholders. Under the OR it was unclear whether actions not specifically dealt with in the OR could fall within the competence of the court of opening. A question immediately and undeniably connected to the question of competence is that of applicable law. Case law of the Court of Justice under both the OR and the RR as to competence for an action not specifically dealt with in the RR, also sheds light on the question of choice of law in this respect. **4.59**

Actions deriving directly from insolvency proceedings and closely linked with them
Article 6 is a new provision in the RR and fills a void under the OR in conformity with case law of the Court of Justice. Article 6 is a codification of case law of the Court of Justice under the OR, which case law remains relevant for the interpretation of Article 6 RR.[113] Where Article 1 in combination with Article 3 of both the OR and the RR provides the general scope of both Regulations which makes them applicable to insolvency proceedings (as defined therein) and provides explicitly that the court of the COMI of the debtor has jurisdiction to open (main) insolvency proceedings, it was unclear under the OR whether the same court had jurisdiction to hear cases arising in connection with such insolvency proceedings. The Virgos-Schmit Report[114] indicates that the relationship between the Brussels I **4.60**

---

[112] *Syska v Vivendi Universal SA* [2009] EWCA Civ 677, [2010] BCC 348. See comments on the proceedings by Fletcher in (2009) 22 Insolvency Intelligence 60–62; 155–57. For an extensive review of the literature and national case law relating to Art 15 OR see B Wessels, *International Insolvency Law* (2017) paras 10710–13.

[113] See: Court of Justice 12 February 2009, C-339/07 (*Seagon qq/Deko Marty*); Court of Justice 19 April 2012, C-213/10 (*F-Tex*); Court of Justice 16 January 2014, C-328/12 (*Schmid/Hertel*); Court of Justice 4 September 2014, C-157/13 (*Nickel & Goeldner Spedition/Kintra*); Court of Justice 4 December 2014, C-295/13 (*H/HK*); Court of Justice 11 June 2015, C-649/13 (*Nortel*); Court of Justice 9 November 2017, C-641/16 (*Tünkers*); Court of Justice 20 December 2017, C-649/13 (*Valach/Waldviertel*); Court of Justice 6 February 2019, C-535/17 (*NK qq/BNP Paribas Fortis*).

[114] See para 77.

Regulation and the OR is determined by Article 25 OR. In Court of Justice 22 February 1979 C-133/78 (*Gourdain/Nadler*), the Court of Justice used exactly this criterium to determine the scope of Article 1 second paragraph of what is now the Brussel I Regulation (recast).[115] That provision determines that the Brussel I Regulation (recast) is not applicable to 'bankruptcy, proceedings relating to the winding-up of insolvent companies or other legal persons, judicial arrangements, compositions and analogous proceedings'. The Court of Justice referred to the nature of the claim as the delineation criterium to determine whether a claim falls within the scope of the Brussels I Regulation (recast). In accordance with that criterium the Court of Justice ruled that claims that arise directly from the insolvency proceeding and are closely connected thereto do not fall within the scope of the Brussels I Regulation (recast). The Virgos-Schmit Report[116] states that the logical interpretation of that case law is that such claims fall within the scope of the OR/RR. This logical interpretation has been confirmed in the Court of Justice's case law on the OR and RR, so that already under the OR the court that opened the insolvency proceedings also had jurisdiction over claims arising directly from, and are closely connected to, the insolvency proceedings.[117] Article 6 RR codifies the Court of Justice case law and explicitly provides that the courts that have opened the insolvency proceedings in accordance with Article 3 RR also have jurisdiction for any action which derives directly from those insolvency proceedings and which is closely linked to such proceedings.[118] It, furthermore, provides a specific example, namely avoidance actions.[119] The Court of Justice has on various occasions applied this criterium to determine whether an action falls within the scope of the RR or the Brussels I Regulation (recast). A discussion of this case law follows in Chapter 8 but is touched on in this chapter.

4.61 Although Article 6 RR only refers to jurisdiction for such actions, the provision also entails that in the event the action falls within the scope of the RR pursuant to Article 6, such action will also be governed by the *lex concursus* pursuant to Article 7(1) RR (see below). Article 6 RR thus establishes *Gleichlauf* (jurisdiction and applicable law coincide). That the principle of *Gleichlauf* applies has been confirmed by the Court of Justice implicitly in *Kornhaas/ Ditmar* and *NK qq/BNP Parisbas Fortis* and explicitly in *CeDe Group/KAN*.[120] In an earlier case (Court of Justice 4 December 2014 C-295/13 (*H qq/HK*) the Court of Justice had already ruled that an action for directors' liability on the basis of a provision in the German Companies Act, instigated by the appointed insolvency practitioner, constituted an action that arises directly from the insolvency proceedings and is closely connected thereto and thus that the German court, where insolvency proceedings had been opened, had jurisdiction to hear the case. In *Kornhaas/Ditmar* the same provision was the subject matter of the prejudicial questions put to the Court of Justice. This time, however, the question did

---

[115] At that time still the Brussels I Convention.
[116] See para 77.
[117] Court of Justice 19 April 2012, C-213/10 (*F-Tex*); Court of Justice 16 January 2014, C-328/12 (*Schmid/Hertel*); Court of Justice 4 September 2014, C-157/13 (*Nickel & Goeldner Spedition/Kintra*); Court of Justice 4 December 2014, C-295/13 (*H/HK*); Court of Justice 11 June 2015, C-649/13 (*Nortel*); Court of Justice 9 November 2017, C-641/16 (*Tünkers*); Court of Justice 20 December 2017, C-649/16 (*Valach/Waldviertel*); Court of Justice 6 February 2019, C-535/17 (*NK qq/BNP Paribas Fortis*).
[118] See also Recital 35 RR.
[119] This was also the action that was under scrutiny in *Gourdain/Nadler*.
[120] Respectively: Court of Justice 10 December 2015 C-594/14; Court of Justice 6 February 2019 C-535/17; Court of Justice 21 November 2019 C-198/18.

not concern jurisdiction but applicable law. The following question was put to the Court of Justice:

> If an insolvency practitioner brings an action before a German court against a director of an English company, in respect of whose assets in Germany insolvency proceedings have been opened pursuant to Article 3(1) OR, the purpose of the action being to seek reimbursement of payments which the director made before the opening of the insolvency proceedings but after the company had become insolvent, is that action governed by German insolvency law within the meaning of Article 4(1) OR?

The Court of Justice answered the question in the affirmative and ruled that such action falls within the scope of Article 4(1) OR (Article 7(1) RR) and is thus governed by German insolvency law, the *lex concursus* in this case.

E. Principal Amendments made in the Recast Regulation ('RR') in relation to the Original Regulation ('OR')

The Basic Choice of Law Rule (Article 4 OR now Article 7 RR): Lex concursus

4.62 The basic choice of law rule, titled 'Applicable law', now contained in Article 7 RR (discussed above at paras 4.05–4.10), has remained, in substance, identical to Article 4 OR. As set out above only a small number of drafting adjustments have been made, such as that in Article 7(2)(c) RR where the term 'insolvency practitioner' is substituted for 'liquidator'. A welcome correction has been made to the wording of the former Article 4(2)(m)—now numbered as Article 7(2)(m)—where the illogical reference to 'acts detrimental to all the creditors' has been replaced with the more appropriate phrase 'acts detrimental to the general body of creditors'.

Exceptions to the Basic Choice of Law Rule (Articles 5–15 OR now Articles 8–18 RR)

4.63 As has been made clear above no changes of substance have been made to the provisions 5, 6, or 7 OR which are now enacted as Article 8 RR (Third parties' rights in rem);[121] Article 9 RR (Set-off);[122] or Article 10 RR (Reservation of title).[123] Very relevant for Articles 8 and 10 (and also Article 11 RR in respect of immovable property) of course is the elaboration of the definition of the expression 'the Member State in which assets are situated' in Article 2(9) RR.[124] The text of Article 11(1) RR is identical to that of Article 8 OR, but an additional provision has been inserted as Article 11(2) to enable the court which opened the main

---

[121] Discussed at paras 4.20–4.30 above.
[122] See paras 4.31–4.35 above.
[123] See paras 4.36–4.39 above.
[124] See para 4.24 above.

proceedings to exercise jurisdiction to approve the termination or modification of such contracts subject to certain conditions.

4.64 No changes of substance have been made in Article 12 RR (Payment systems and financial markets),[125] and Article 13(1) RR (Contracts of employment) maintains the same wording as that employed in Article 10 OR.[126] However, an entirely new paragraph is added as Article 13(2) to enable the courts of the Member State in which secondary proceedings could be opened to retain jurisdiction to approve the termination or modification of those contracts of employment which are governed by the law of that state even if no insolvency proceedings have been opened in that Member State. This provides a safeguard for the interests of employees, for example in the event of recourse to a synthetic secondary proceeding as described in chapter 3.[127]

4.65 Article 14 RR (Effects on rights subject to registration) is unchanged from the provision of Article 11 OR.[128] Article 15 RR has merely been updated to reflect the changes in terminology brought about by the evolution of the European Union since Article 12 OR was drawn up in the year 2000 and now refers to 'European patent with unitary effect and a Community trade mark'.[129]

4.66 Both Article 16 RR (Detrimental acts) and Article 17 RR (Protection of third-party purchasers) are unchanged in substance by comparison with their counterparts in Articles 13 and 14 respectively of the OR.[130]

4.67 As discussed above a welcome clarification has been made in the enactment of Article 18 RR (Effects of insolvency proceedings on pending lawsuits or arbitral proceedings) by including a specific reference to arbitral proceedings.[131] This outcome is in line with the conclusion formed by the English Court of Appeal, applying a purposive approach to the interpretation of Article 15 OR.[132]

The impact of the newly introduced Article 6 RR on the applicable law

4.68 Article 6 RR codifies case law of the Court of Justice under the OR and provides that actions arising directly from the insolvency proceedings and which are closely connected thereto fall within the scope of the RR. Although Article 6 only refers to the fact that the court of opening will also have jurisdiction over such actions, the principle of *Gleichlauf* leads to the applicability of the *lex concursus* to such action in accordance with Article 7 RR.

---

[125] See para 4.42 above.
[126] See paras 4.43–4.45 above.
[127] See paras 3.21 and 3.32 above.
[128] See paras 4.46–4.47 above.
[129] See para 4.48 above.
[130] See paras 4.49–4.52, and 4.53–4.55 above respectively.
[131] See paras 4.56–4.58 above.
[132] *Syska v Vivendi Universal SA* [2009] EWCA Civ 677, [2010] BCC 348 (CA), para 4.58 above.

5
RECOGNITION AND ENFORCEMENT

A.	Introduction[1]	5.01		Public policy exception to	
B.	Recognition and Enforcement Outside			recognition: Article 33	5.142
	the Insolvency Proceedings Regulation	5.06		Proof of insolvency practitioner's	
	The common law	5.07		appointment: Article 22	5.149
	Recognizing the authority of a foreign			Publication and registration: Articles 24 to 29	5.151
	office-holder	5.12	D.	Recognition of Judgments under	
	Recognizing foreign orders against third			the Regulation	5.163
	parties	5.21		Recognition of judgments: Article 32	5.163
	Judicial assistance: general principles	5.32		Enforcement: interaction with the Recast	
	Judicial assistance: stay of proceedings			Judgments Regulation	5.168
	and related relief	5.40		Judgments outside the Regulation: the	
	Judicial assistance: obtaining information	5.45		'dovetailing' principle	5.169
	Judicial assistance: claw-back claims	5.50		CJEU case law	5.177
	Ancillary insolvency proceedings	5.55		English case law	5.180
	Section 426 of the Insolvency Act 1986	5.73	E.	Enforcement of the Rights and	
	UNCITRAL Model Law	5.82		Powers of Insolvency Practitioners	5.184
	Origins and enactment	5.82		Powers of the insolvency	
	Scope	5.86		practitioner: Article 21	5.184
	Foreign main proceeding and non-main			Equal treatment of creditors—	
	proceeding	5.89		'hotchpot': Article 23	5.196
	Conditions for recognition	5.92		Duty of co-operation: Articles 41 to 43	5.202
	Effects of recognition: automatic relief	5.96		Co-operation and communication	
	Effects of recognition: discretionary relief	5.99		between insolvency practitioners	5.202
	Rights of direct access and intervention	5.111		Co-operation and communication	
	Co-operation between courts and			between courts	5.212
	officeholders	5.113		Exercise of creditors' rights: Article 45	5.217
C.	Recognition under the Regulation	5.115		Staying the realization of assets in	
	Use of terms	5.115		secondary proceedings: Article 46	5.220
	Effect of Brexit: current application of the			Closure of insolvency proceedings:	
	Regulation in the UK	5.117		Articles 47 to 49	5.223
	General principle of recognition: Article 19	5.124		Conversion of secondary insolvency	
	Effects of recognition: Article 20	5.133		proceedings: Article 51	5.227
				Preservation measures: Article 52	5.229

A. Introduction

This chapter is concerned with the recognition and enforcement of insolvency proceedings both under and outside Insolvency Proceedings Regulation (EU) 2015/848 (Regulation).[2]   **5.01**

---

[1] The author of this chapter is Georgina Peters. In previous editions of this work, the late Gabriel Moss QC and Daniel Bayfield KC were co-authors, with the assistance of, variously, William Willson, Andrew Shaw, Robert Amey, and Ryan Perkins, all of South Square Chambers, London.
[2] Regulation (EU) 2015/848 of the European Parliament and of the Council of 20 May 2015 on insolvency proceedings (recast), OJ L141/19, 5 June 2015. The Regulation applies to insolvency proceedings opened in Member States on or after 26 June 2017: Art 84(1). It has had effect since that date (Art 92), save for (so far as concerns this

5.02 Section A deals with three sources of recognition and judicial assistance which are available outside the Insolvency Proceedings Regulation: English common law, section 426 of the Insolvency Act 1986 (the '1986 Act'), and the UNCITRAL Model Law. The Model Law is likely to bear increased importance in future years, in light of the departure of the United Kingdom ('UK') from the European Union ('EU')—'Brexit'.

5.03 Brexit has led to legislation bringing the application of the Insolvency Proceedings Regulation in the UK to an end. As explained in Section D, whilst UK domestic legislation has retained certain jurisdictional provisions of the Regulation (in a significantly narrowed form), the principal impact has been that those provisions which rely on reciprocity between EU Member States have been repealed. So insolvency proceedings commenced in the UK (on or after 11 pm on 31 December 2020, being the end of the withdrawal transition period) no longer enjoy automatic recognition in Member States. Likewise, insolvency proceedings opened in Member States will not be automatically recognized and enforced in the UK.

5.04 Sections C to E deal with those provisions of the Regulation that are relevant to recognition and enforcement of insolvency proceedings. The basic scheme of the Regulation is that if insolvency proceedings are properly opened in a Member State (having the relevant jurisdiction to do so), their conduct is governed by the law of that Member State and judgments of its courts concerning the course of the proceedings will be automatically recognized by other Member States, together with any judgments deriving directly from the proceedings and which are closely linked with them.

5.05 The provisions relevant to recognition and enforcement under the Regulation are rather lengthy and complex; since its aim is to ensure that comity is preserved in respect of the universal effect of the insolvency proceedings, as well as that of the rights and powers of insolvency practitioners appointed in them. Equally, the Regulation contains detailed provision for the duty of co-operation and co-ordination between office-holders and courts, in cases with international elements where multiple proceedings are opened (or might potentially be opened) in different Member States.

B. Recognition and Enforcement Outside the Insolvency Proceedings Regulation

5.06 Outside the Insolvency Proceedings Regulation, the law of recognition and judicial assistance derives from three main sources: the common law, section 426 of the 1986 Act, and the UNCITRAL Model Law, as implemented under the Cross-Border Insolvency Regulations 2006, SI 2006/1030 (the 'CBIR').[3] This chapter examines each source in turn. The common

---

chapter) Arts 24(1) and 25, which have applied from (respectively) 26 June 2018 and 26 June 2019 (concerning the establishment and interconnection of insolvency registers).

[3] Pre-Brexit, cases to which the Regulation had no application (and recourse to other sources of law might have been necessary) included those where: the debtor's proceedings were not included in Annex A; the debtor's COMI was situated in a third (non-EU) country; or the debtor was a type of entity falling within the Art 1(2) exclusions (eg credit institutions or insurers, to which specialist EU Directives apply: see G Moss and B Wessels, *EU Banking and Insurance Insolvency* (2nd edn, 2017)).

law is supplemented (rather than superseded) by the CBIR and section 426, and all three sources of law are concurrently applicable.[4]

The common law

The common law of recognition and assistance has been delineated by two major judgments at the highest appellate levels: *Rubin v Eurofinance SA*[5] (Supreme Court) and *Singularis Holdings Ltd v PwC* (Privy Council).[6] Between *Rubin* and *Singularis*, almost everything that Lord Hoffmann said in the Privy Council case of *Cambridge Gas Transport Corp v Official Committee of Unsecured Creditors of Navigator Holdings plc*,[7] which was previously the leading authority in this area, has been overruled.

5.07

Perhaps as a result, the practical importance of the common law in England has been significantly reduced in recent years. As Lord Sumption observed in *Singularis*,[8] the statutory power of the English court to wind up a foreign company, together with the judicial practice of permitting such liquidations to proceed on a basis ancillary to the principal liquidation, has arrested the development of the common law. The combined effect of *Rubin* and *Singularis* has been to narrow the prospects of successfully engaging common law judicial assistance. Post-Brexit, it remains to be seen whether there will be a resurgence of recourse to the common law.

5.08

It is sometimes said that the common law of recognition and judicial assistance is underwritten by the concept of universalism. The concept was explained by Lord Hoffmann in *Cambridge Gas*:[9]

5.09

> The English common law has traditionally taken the view that fairness between creditors requires that, ideally, bankruptcy proceedings should have universal application. There should be a single bankruptcy in which all creditors are entitled and required to prove. No one should have an advantage because he happens to live in a jurisdiction where more of the assets or fewer of the creditors are situated.

However, the principle of universalism is heavily qualified on pragmatic grounds. English law makes no real attempt to ensure that there is only one insolvency proceeding per debtor, and it is relatively straightforward to commence insolvency proceedings in England even if proceedings in the place of the debtor's domicile are already underway abroad.

5.10

The terminology of recognition and judicial assistance can be confusing, and is not used in a consistent manner throughout the cases (or the legislation).[10] For present purposes, it is

5.11

---

[4] CBIR, Sch 1, Art 7. CBIR, Reg 3(2) also provides for its provisions to prevail in the case of any conflict between the Model Law and 'British insolvency law' or Part 3 of the 1986 Act. 'British insolvency law' is defined in Sch 1, Art 2(a).
[5] [2013] 1 AC 236 (SC).
[6] [2015] 2 WLR 971 (PC).
[7] [2007] 1 AC 508 (PC).
[8] [15].
[9] [16]. For a description of the history of this theory in early insolvency law, see J Tribe and S Baister, 'Lord Bathurst's Gift: The Genesis of the Golden Thread' (2019) 32(1) Insolvency Intelligence 7.
[10] See N Segal, J Harris, and M Morrison, 'Assistance to foreign insolvency office-holders in the conflict of laws: is the common law fit for purpose?' (2017) 30(8) Insolvency Intelligence 117, in which the authors seek to rationalize the case law.

important to distinguish between recognition of: (i) a foreign office-holder's authority to act on behalf of the debtor; and (ii) an order made by a foreign court against third parties in the course of insolvency proceedings. The preconditions for (and consequences of) the first form of recognition are very different from those for the second form. Furthermore, there is a conceptual distinction between the principles that apply to recognition and those which apply to the question of what, if any, judicial assistance ought to be given by the English court to a foreign office-holder following recognition.[11] Each concept is considered below.

Recognizing the authority of a foreign office-holder

5.12 If an office-holder ('O') is appointed in foreign insolvency proceedings, the law of the relevant foreign state ('S') will ordinarily grant O extensive authority to act on behalf of the debtor ('D'). For example, O will often have authority under the law of S to deal with and dispose of D's worldwide assets, and authority to cause D to bring legal proceedings against third parties in D's own name. The English court will recognize O's authority to act on D's behalf (in accordance with the law of S), provided that D was domiciled in S at the time when insolvency proceedings commenced in S.[12] There are a number of standard bars to recognition at common law, such as fraud, public policy, and prejudice to local creditors.[13]

5.13 Traditionally, a corporation is deemed to be domiciled in the place of its incorporation. This test is ill-suited to the modern world, where corporations are frequently registered in offshore or 'letterbox' jurisdictions with which they have no real connection. In *Cambridge Gas*, Lord Hoffmann proposed a development of the common law, whereby a corporation would be deemed to be domiciled in the place of its centre of main interests ('COMI'), which would have brought the common law into harmony with the Regulation and CBIR. However, the Supreme Court in *Rubin* rejected Lord Hoffmann's suggestion in *Cambridge Gas*.[14] The place of incorporation thus retains its traditional connection with the concept of domicile.

5.14 Where an individual is subject to insolvency proceedings, many jurisdictions provide for the debtor's property (wherever situated) to vest in the office-holder (eg a trustee in bankruptcy). The English court will recognize that the debtor's movable property situated in England has vested in the office-holder, provided that the latter was appointed in the place of the debtor's domicile.[15] This doctrine does not apply to immovable property.[16] The domicile of an individual is determined by a more fact-sensitive test.[17]

---

[11] *Kireeva v Bedzhamov* [2021] EWHC 2281 (Ch), para 107, per Snowden J.
[12] *Rubin v Eurofinance SA* [2013] 1 AC 236 (SC), para 13; *Dicey, Morris & Collins on The Conflict of Laws* (15th edn, 2012 (as supplemented)) at 30R-100.
[13] See *Re a Debtor, ex p Viscount of the Royal Court of Jersey* [1981] Ch 384 at 402 (Goulding J); R Sheldon, *Cross-Border Insolvency* (4th edn, 2015), ch 11. These grounds were considered in the recognition context in *Kireeva v Bedzhamov* [2021] EWHC 2281 (Ch), per Snowden J, para 132 et seq; and before the Court of Appeal ([2021] EWCA Civ 35 (Ch)), paras 26–41 (reversing the judge's decision on the fraud ground and remitting the matter to the High Court, which—following a trial of the issues remitted by the Court of Appeal—upheld Snowden J's original decision to recognize the Russian bankruptcy: see [2022] EWHC 2676 (Ch), per Falk J, paras 8–10 and 100).
[14] [2013] 1 AC 236 (SC), paras 121–29.
[15] *Singularis Holdings Ltd v PwC* [2015] 2 WLR 971 (PC), para 12, and the authorities cited therein.
[16] ibid. The principle that there is no common law power to make an order vesting immovable property in a foreign trustee, or authorizing the trustee to sell the property for the benefit of the foreign insolvency, was recently upheld and applied by the Court of Appeal in *Kireeva v Bedzhamov* [2021] EWCA Civ 35, paras 37–67. The Court refused to 'equate' common law recognition and the jurisdiction under section 426 of the 1986 Act for this purpose: paras 94–97. The first instance judgment of Snowden J contains a detailed analysis of the relevant authorities: [2021] EWHC 2281 (Ch), paras 195–240.
[17] See R Sheldon, *Cross-Border Insolvency* (4th edn, 2015) at paras 8.13 et seq.

5.15 Upon recognition of the authority of a foreign office-holder, the office-holder will be permitted to sue in his or her own name before the English court.[18]

5.16 If the English court declines to recognize an office-holder's authority to act on the debtor's behalf, a number of consequences may follow. Where the debtor owns land or goods situated in England, the office-holder may be liable for trespass or conversion. The office-holder may be liable for procuring breaches of contract to which the debtor is a party. There may also be scope for criminal liability, depending on the facts.

5.17 Even if the English court recognizes the authority of a foreign office-holder to act on the debtor's behalf, the office-holder faces two potential problems. First, section 389 of the 1986 Act makes it a criminal offence to act as 'an insolvency practitioner'[19] without proper authorization. Few foreign insolvency practitioners will have such authorization. The criminal offence applies to acting not only in respect of English incorporated companies, but also foreign companies which the English court has jurisdiction to wind up.[20] It is thought that the English authorities in England do not regard a foreign office-holder appointed in foreign insolvency proceedings as coming within the criminal offence, although there remains an element of uncertainty for the foreign office-holder unless specific authority is sought from the English court to carry out the relevant acts, eg dealing with assets.

5.18 For example, the court can provide a degree of protection to a foreign office-holder by appointing him or her as a receiver of the debtor's property. Such an appointment derives from the statutory power conferred on the court in civil litigation.[21] A receiver is an officer of the English court, and interference with the receiver is a contempt of court.[22] The receiver must act according to the directions of the English court, and must accept its jurisdiction.

5.19 Secondly, section 234 of the 1986 Act provides English administrators, administrative receivers, liquidators, and provisional liquidators with special statutory protection in the event that such a person seizes or disposes of property which does not belong to the insolvent company. Section 304(3) accords a similar immunity to trustees in bankruptcy. The statutory protection does not extend to a seizure or disposal which results from the insolvency practitioner's own negligence. The protections do not apply to a foreign office-holder. It is possible, however, that they could be applied pursuant to the CBIR.[23]

5.20 Even if the English court has appointed the foreign office-holder as a receiver, sections 234 and 304 of the 1986 Act do not apply. However, the court has the power, upon the release or discharge of a receiver, to protect him or her from liability for acts done in the course of their duties (after investigating any known claims).[24]

---

[18] See *Alivon v Furnival* [1902] 2 KB 312; *Macaulay v Guaranty Trust Co of New York* (1927) 44 TLR 99; *Re Borovsky* [1902] 2 KB 312.
[19] As defined by the 1986 Act, section 388. In respect of a company, this means a liquidator, provisional liquidator, administrator, administrative receiver, monitor, or CVA nominee/supervisor (but would not extend to a court-appointed receiver).
[20] See s 388(4) of the 1986 Act. Where the CBIR apply, Art 8 provides an exemption.
[21] Senior Courts Act 1981, s 37(1).
[22] See G Lightman and G Moss, *The Law of Administrators and Receivers of Companies* (6th edn, 2017) ch 29.
[23] Eg by way of discretionary relief under Art 21, following recognition of a foreign main or non-main proceeding: see paras 5.100 et seq below.
[24] See G Lightman and G Moss, *The Law of Administrators and Receivers of Companies* (6th edn, 2017) ch 29, at para 29-030.

Recognizing foreign orders against third parties

5.21 It is common for judgments to be entered against third parties in the course of insolvency proceedings. In all developed jurisdictions, transactions effected by the debtor prior to the onset of insolvency are liable to be avoided in certain circumstances, and transferees may be ordered to restore money or other assets to the estate.

5.22 Therefore, it is necessary to identify the circumstances in which foreign judgments against third parties, delivered by a foreign court in the course of insolvency proceedings, can be recognized in England. The recognition of such judgments does not automatically follow from the recognition by the English court of the authority of the foreign office-holder. It is a matter of significant practical import, since the English assets of a defendant to a foreign action may become liable to enforcement measures (eg attachment and seizure) if a foreign judgment is recognized by the English court.

5.23 Outside the insolvency context, the recognition of foreign judgments is a substantial topic within private international law. Traditionally, English law distinguishes between two categories of judgments: judgments in rem and judgments in personam. A judgment in personam binds only the parties to the proceedings in which the judgment was made, whereas a judgment in rem is binding on all persons, whether parties or not.[25] In general, judgments in rem relate to the ownership of property (or the status of a person), whereas judgments in personam require specified persons to pay a sum of money or to perform an action.

5.24 Rule 43 of *Dicey, Morris & Collins on the Conflict of Laws*[26] ('*Dicey*') describes the circumstances in which a judgment in personam will be recognized at common law:

> A court of a foreign country outside the United Kingdom has jurisdiction to give a judgment *in personam* capable of enforcement or recognition as against the person against whom it was given in the following cases:
>
> First Case—If the person against whom the judgment was given was, at the time the proceedings were instituted, present in the foreign country.
>
> Second Case—If the person against whom the judgment was given was claimant, or counterclaimed, in the proceedings in the foreign court.
>
> Third Case—If the person against whom the judgment was given submitted to the jurisdiction of that court by voluntarily appearing in the proceedings.
>
> Fourth Case—If the person against whom the judgment was given had before the commencement of the proceedings agreed, in respect of the subject matter of the proceedings, to submit to the jurisdiction of that court or of the courts of that country.

5.25 By contrast, a judgment in rem will only be recognized at common law if the relevant property was situated in the jurisdiction where the judgment was made at the time of the proceedings: see Rule 47 of *Dicey*.[27]

5.26 In *Cambridge Gas*, Lord Hoffmann suggested that judgments delivered in the course of insolvency proceedings fall into a *sui generis* third category, being neither judgments in

---

[25] See *Pattni v Ali* [2007] 2 AC 85 (PC); *Dicey, Morris & Collins on the Conflict of Laws* (15th edn, 2012 (as supplemented)) ch 14.
[26] 15th edn, 2012 (as supplemented); see *Rubin v Eurofinance SA* [2013] 1 AC 236 (SC), para 108.
[27] See also *Rubin v Eurofinance SA* [2013] 1 AC 236 (SC), para 132.

personam nor judgments in rem.[28] Applying this analysis, Lord Hoffmann held that an order of the US Bankruptcy Court for the confiscation of shares belonging to a third party could be recognized in the Isle of Man, notwithstanding that the third party was not present in the US and had not submitted to the jurisdiction of the US Bankruptcy Court, and notwithstanding that the shares were situated outside the US. In short, the normal grounds for the recognition of a judgment in personam or in rem did not exist.

However, Lord Hoffmann's analysis was rejected by the Supreme Court in *Rubin*. Lord Collins, who gave the leading speech, held that judgments in insolvency proceedings must be either judgments in rem or judgments in personam, and that the ordinary principles of recognition under English private international law (embodied in Rules 43 and 47 of *Dicey*) apply equally within the insolvency context.[29] *Cambridge Gas* was held to be wrongly decided. There is no 'third category' of judgments, with special rules of recognition.

5.27

The facts of *Rubin* illustrate the impact of this analysis. An insolvent trust ('TCT') had entered into insolvency proceedings under Chapter 11 of the US Bankruptcy Code. A claw-back action was brought against the officers and promoters of TCT before the US Bankruptcy Court. The defendants were not present in the relevant US jurisdiction at any material time, did not submit to the jurisdiction of the US Bankruptcy Court and did not defend the proceedings. The US Bankruptcy Court entered judgment against the defendants. Lord Collins held that this constituted a judgment in personam. Applying Rule 43 of *Dicey*, recognition was impossible.

5.28

In the Supreme Court, the *Rubin* case was joined to the case of *New Cap Reinsurance Corpn Ltd v Grant* ('*New Cap Re*'), which raised similar issues. The company had entered into liquidation in Australia. A claw-back action was brought against a Lloyd's syndicate before the Supreme Court of New South Wales. That court entered judgment against the syndicate. The syndicate was not present in Australia at any material time, and did not defend the proceedings. However, it had previously participated in the liquidation by filing proofs of debt and participating in creditors' meetings. This proved to be crucial. Lord Collins held that such conduct constituted a submission to the jurisdiction of the Australian court, with the consequence that the judgment against the syndicate fell to be recognized in England.[30]

5.29

Technically, the judgment of the Australian court was required to be registered under the Foreign Judgments (Reciprocal Enforcement) Act 1933, rather than being recognized or enforced at common law. The 1933 Act applies to judgments given by the courts of various Commonwealth nations, including judgments in 'civil and commercial matters' given by the courts of Australia.[31] The grounds for registration under the 1933 Act are substantially the same as the grounds for recognition at common law.[32] Lord Collins held that judgments in claw-back proceedings constitute 'civil and commercial matters'.[33]

5.30

---

[28] [2007] 1 AC 508 (PC), paras 15–22.
[29] [2013] 1 AC 236 (SC), paras 115–32. An identical approach in the insolvency context was adopted by the Privy Council in *Vizcaya Partners Ltd v Picard* [2016] Bus LR 413.
[30] [2013] 1 AC 236 (SC), paras 158–67.
[31] See the Reciprocal Enforcement of Judgments (Australia) Order 1994, SI 1994/1901.
[32] See *Dicey*, Rule 54.
[33] [2013] 1 AC 236 (SC), para 175.

5.31 The principle that a foreign creditor submits to the jurisdiction of the court supervising a company's insolvency by proving in that insolvency, has been subsequently applied in further cases at appellate level.[34] In *New Cap Re*, Lord Collins reached this conclusion by applying the general rule that the relevant party must have 'taken some step which is only necessary or useful if' an objection to jurisdiction 'has been actually waived, or if the objection to jurisdiction has never been entertained at all'.[35] The practical consequence of *New Cap Re* is that a defendant (or potential defendant) to a foreign claw-back action must exercise caution before submitting a proof of debt in the foreign insolvency proceedings.[36]

Judicial assistance: general principles

5.32 Judicial assistance involves the grant of relief (beyond mere recognition) in support of foreign insolvency proceedings. It is only available at common law for insolvency proceedings in the place of the debtor's domicile, as explained above. Judicial assistance is sometimes sought by way of a formal letter of request from the foreign court conducting the insolvency proceedings.

5.33 At common law, the standard forms of judicial assistance in the insolvency context include: (i) an order for the stay of proceedings against the debtor; (ii) an order requiring a third party to provide relevant information to the foreign office-holder (whether by oral examination or document production); and (iii) an order for the remission of assets situated in England to the foreign office-holder, for distribution in the foreign insolvency proceedings. All three forms of judicial assistance are discussed below.

5.34 However, the categories of judicial assistance are not closed, and the common law may develop new forms of judicial assistance to meet new challenges.[37] Indeed, 'the courts have repeatedly recognised not just a right but a duty to assist in whatever way they properly can'.[38] This has been described as the principle of 'modified universalism',[39] which 'has not been discredited'.[40]

5.35 In *Cambridge Gas*, Lord Hoffmann sought to identify the permissible scope of judicial assistance. He said:[41]

---

[34] See *Stichting Shell Pensioenfonds v Krys* [2015] AC 616 (SC), per Lords Sumption and Toulson, at paras 27–32; *Erste Group Bank AG (London) v JSC (VMZ Red October)* [2015] 1 CLC 706 (CA), per Gloster LJ, at paras 63–73, describing the bank's participation in the Russian insolvency as 'full-blooded'.

[35] See [2013] 1 AC 236 (SC), paras 159–60, and the cases cited at para 160, including *Adams v Cape Industries plc* [1990] Ch 433, per Scott J (first instance).

[36] See also (in a slightly different context) *Bundeszentralamt v Heis* [2020] 1 BCLC 649, per Hildyard J, para 63, as to the further consequences of submission to the jurisdiction on this basis (application for stay of appeals against rejection of proof refused).

[37] *Singularis Holdings Ltd v PwC* [2015] 2 WLR 971 (PC), para 19. In the Cayman Islands decision *Re China Agrotech Holdings Ltd* (2017) 2 CILR 526, Segal J made an order permitting foreign liquidators to apply to promote a parallel scheme of arrangement in that jurisdiction. However, extending the categories of assistance will not be permitted where it conflicts with an existing principle of the law relating to common law judicial assistance: *Kireeva v Bedzhamov* [2021] EWHC 2281 (Ch), per Snowden J, paras 253–54 (no power to vest immovable property in foreign office-holder, upheld on this ground by the Court of Appeal: [2021] EWCA Civ 35).

[38] ibid, para 23.

[39] ibid, para 15 ('the principle of modified universalism, namely that the court has a common law power to assist foreign winding up proceedings so far as it properly can').

[40] ibid, para 19. For a case in which the principle of modified universalism was (unsuccessfully) relied on to circumvent the jurisdictional rule in the Recast Judgments Regulations, Art 4, see *WWRT Ltd v Tyshchenko* [2021] Bus LR 972, per Bacon J.

[41] [2007] 1 AC 508 (PC), para 22.

What are the limits of the assistance which the court can give? In cases in which there is statutory authority for providing assistance, the statute specifies what the court may do ... At common law, their Lordships think it is doubtful whether assistance could take the form of applying provisions of the foreign insolvency law which form no part of the domestic system. But the domestic court must at least be able to provide assistance by doing whatever it could have done in the case of a domestic insolvency. The purpose of recognition is to enable the foreign office holder or the creditors to avoid having to start parallel insolvency proceedings and to give them the remedies to which they would have been entitled if the equivalent proceedings had taken place in the domestic forum.

5.36 This has been described as the 'as if' basis for judicial assistance, whereby domestic insolvency law is applied 'by analogy'. In *Singularis*, the Privy Council unanimously rejected Lord Hoffmann's analysis. Lord Collins, with whom the entire court agreed, said that Lord Hoffmann had engaged in a 'plain usurpation of the legislative function'.[42] To that extent, *Singularis* represents the overruling of *Cambridge Gas*, as well as the overruling or disapproval of several subsequent decisions applying Lord Hoffmann's reasoning—including *Re Phoenix Kapitaldienst GmbH*[43] and the (then) first instance judgment in the Cayman Islands case *Picard v Primeo Fund*.[44]

5.37 When the court grants judicial assistance in support of foreign insolvency proceedings, it is not, according to the Privy Council in *Singularis*, applying domestic legislation 'by analogy'. Rather, the court is simply exercising its common law powers. As Lord Sumption said in *Singularis*:[45]

> First, there is a principle of the common law that the court has the power to recognise and grant assistance to foreign insolvency proceedings. Second, that power is primarily exercised through the existing powers of the court. Third, those powers can be extended or developed from existing powers through the traditional judicial law-making techniques of the common law. Fourth, the very limited application of legislation by analogy does not allow the judiciary to extend the scope of insolvency legislation to cases where it does not apply. Fifth, in consequence, those powers do not extend to the application, by analogy 'as if' the foreign insolvency were a domestic insolvency, of statutory powers which do not actually apply in the instant case.

5.38 Lord Sumption declined to provide a general account of the circumstances in which the common law should be extended to facilitate judicial assistance, or to identify the categories of the 'existing powers of the court' which would in principle afford judicial assistance. He said that the issue 'does not admit of a single, universal answer'.[46] He did, however, identify five basic constraints on the availability of judicial assistance:[47]

---

[42] [2015] 2 WLR 971 (PC), para 64.
[43] [2013] Ch 61.
[44] [2013] (1) CILR 16; on appeal, [2014] (1) CILR 379.
[45] [2015] 2 WLR 971 (PC), para 38. For a criticism of several aspects of the judgment in *Singularis*, see G Moss and I Fletcher, 'A Saad Affair' (2015) 28(4) Insolvency Intelligence 49–55. Their view was that in reality, cross-border judicial assistance can only work on an 'as if' basis.
[46] At para 19.
[47] At para 25.

(1) First, the court is not entitled to provide assistance in support of a voluntary liquidation, or any other proceedings which are not conducted by an officer of the court.[48]
(2) Secondly, judicial assistance cannot be used to enable a foreign office-holder to do something that he cannot do under the law by which he was appointed.
(3) Thirdly, judicial assistance is only available when it is necessary for the performance of the office-holder's functions.
(4) Fourthly, the exercise of judicial assistance must be consistent with the substantive law and public policy of the assisting court.
(5) Fifthly, where the office-holder seeks an order which requires actions to be taken by a third party, he must be prepared to pay the third party's reasonable costs of compliance.

5.39 The third and fourth propositions are unlikely to prove controversial. As noted, public policy, prejudice to local creditors and fraud are standard bars to recognition at common law. The second proposition was more controversial, and proved fatal to the appeal in *Singularis*. This is discussed further below (paragraphs 5.46 et seq).

Judicial assistance: stay of proceedings and related relief

5.40 Historically, one of the most common forms of judicial assistance involved imposing a stay of proceedings brought against the debtor in England (or related relief, such as discharging or refusing to grant an injunction affecting the debtor or his property). The importance of such relief has been greatly reduced by the provisions of the CBIR, which enable foreign office-holders to obtain a stay of English proceedings by making a straightforward application to the court (see paragraphs 5.96 et seq).

5.41 However, this form of common law judicial assistance remains significant in several offshore jurisdictions which have not enacted the UNCITRAL Model Law, and in all other cases where the CBIR or section 426 do not apply.[49]

5.42 Thus, in *Firswood Ltd v Petra Bank*,[50] a Jordanian bank had entered into liquidation. One of the bank's creditors assigned its claim to a party who had knowledge of the liquidation. The assignee attempted to sue the bank in England. The Court of Appeal refused to allow the action to proceed, thereby (in effect) giving judicial assistance to the liquidation in Jordan.

5.43 Likewise, in *Banque Indosuez v Ferromet*,[51] Hoffmann J held that he should do his utmost to co-operate with the US Bankruptcy Court and prevent any action which might disturb the orderly administration of the company in US Chapter 11 proceedings. An action had been brought in England for an injunction against property belonging to the company, over which a bank asserted rights of security. Such claims would have been impossible in the US, pursuant to the statutory stay created by the Chapter 11 proceedings. Hoffmann J thought it

---

[48] There is no obvious basis for this proposition. Lord Sumption said that a voluntary liquidation is 'essentially a private arrangement' (para 25), but this is incorrect: in all known jurisdictions, a voluntary liquidation brings into effect a statutory scheme which radically affects the rights of third parties (especially creditors), involving a high level of actual or potential judicial scrutiny and oversight.
[49] For example, where the debtor falls within one of the excepted categories in the CBIR, Sch 1, Art 1(2).
[50] [1996] CLC 608 (CA).
[51] [1993] BCLC 112.

right to co-operate with the US Bankruptcy Court by refusing to grant an injunction which would undermine the stay of creditors' remedies.

In *Felixstowe Dock v US Lines*,[52] a creditor in England had obtained an interim freezing order against the assets of a US corporation. The corporation went into Chapter 11 proceedings, and applied for the injunction to be discharged (so that the assets could be repatriated to the US and used in the restructuring). Hirst J dismissed the application. This case can be explained on the basis that Hirst J regarded the restructuring as being biased in favour of US creditors and discriminatory against local creditors.[53]

5.44

Judicial assistance: obtaining information
A common form of judicial assistance involves the foreign office-holder seeking an order to obtain information from a third party (eg by oral examination or document production). *Singularis* is the leading case on this form of judicial assistance.[54]

5.45

Singularis was an appeal brought by the company's Joint Official Liquidators ('JOLs'). A winding-up order had been made against the company in the Cayman Islands, its place of incorporation. The JOLs believed that PwC, the company's former auditors, had information which would assist in tracing its assets. To that end, the JOLs sought to obtain (*inter alia*) PwC's working papers. Under section 103 of the Cayman Islands Companies Law, the Grand Court of the Cayman Islands was empowered to compel the production of 'documents belonging to the company'. Section 103 did not assist the JOLs, who accepted that PwC's working papers did not belong to the company.[55] In an attempt to circumvent this difficulty, the JOLs sought judicial assistance in Bermuda, where the relevant PwC entity was registered.

5.46

If the company had been wound up in Bermuda, PwC could have been compelled to produce its working papers pursuant to section 195 of Bermuda's Companies Act 1981, which is more broadly drafted. However, no attempt was made to obtain a winding-up order in Bermuda, and the Privy Council held in a related appeal that the Supreme Court of Bermuda had no jurisdiction to make such an order.[56] Rather than seeking to engage section 195 directly, the JOLs argued that the Supreme Court of Bermuda had a common law power to order production.

5.47

By a bare majority,[57] the Privy Council held that there is 'a power at common law to assist a foreign court of insolvency jurisdiction by ordering the production of information in oral or documentary form which is necessary for the administration of a foreign winding up'.[58] As Lord Sumption observed, 'the recognition by a domestic court of the status of a foreign

5.48

---

[52] [1989] QB 360.
[53] Lord Hoffmann, 'Cross-Border Insolvency', the 1996 Denning Lecture. See also G Moss, 'Comparative Bankruptcy Cultures: Rescue or Liquidation? Comparison of Trends in National Law—England' (1997) 115 Brooklyn Journal of International Law 135–36.
[54] [2015] 2 WLR 971 (PC).
[55] Lord Sumption expressly doubted whether this concession was correctly made, at para 30.
[56] *PricewaterhouseCoopers v Saad Investments Company Limited* [2014] 1 WLR 4482 (PC).
[57] Lords Sumption, Collins, and Clarke comprised the majority. Lords Mance and Neuberger dissented on this point, the former in fairly strong terms: paras 130–48. Unusually, all five members of the Privy Council delivered an opinion.
[58] Per Lord Sumption, para 25. See also Lord Collins at para 33 and Lord Clarke at para 112.

liquidator would mean very little if it entitled him to take possession of the company's assets but left him with no effective means of identifying or locating them.'[59] However, he emphasized that the Board 'would not wish to encourage the promiscuous creation of other common law powers to compel the production of information,'[60] and stressed the limitations and constraints on judicial assistance.

5.49 For present purposes, the basic problem identified by Lord Sumption was that judicial assistance cannot enable a foreign office-holder to do something which he cannot do under the law by which he was appointed. Since the Grand Court of the Cayman Islands had no power to require third parties to provide documents to the JOLs which did not belong to the company itself, it would be improper to grant the assistance sought.[61] He agreed with the lower court's characterization of the application as 'forum-shopping'.[62]

Judicial assistance: claw-back claims

5.50 For a number of reasons, a foreign office-holder may wish to bring claw-back proceedings before the English court (rather than the court of the home state). The proposed defendant may be present in England, and unwilling to submit to the jurisdiction of foreign court, or may have assets situated in England available for execution. The claw-back provisions in the home jurisdiction may not be applicable, or may not be adequate to provide the desired relief.

5.51 It is considered that the English court can provide judicial assistance at common law to a foreign office-holder by permitting him or her to bring claw-back proceedings in England. The more difficult question is what is the substantive law that the English court should apply. It is clear, following *Singularis*, that the court cannot apply the English statutory claw-back provisions under sections 238, 239, and 423 of the 1986 Act 'as if' the foreign insolvency was an English law proceeding. Likewise, the English court cannot directly apply foreign law (ie the claw-back provisions under the foreign law by which the office-holder was appointed).[63]

5.52 As explained, following *Singularis*, the English court can only provide judicial assistance by exercising its 'existing powers' at common law. As to this, the English court has a longstanding common law power to avoid preferences and transactions defrauding creditors. As Bowen LJ said in *Ex p Wilcoxon* (1883) 23 Ch D 69, 74:

> Everybody knows that originally there was no express statutory enactment in regard to fraudulent preference. But from the time of Lord Mansfield down to 1869 the courts

---

[59] Per Lord Sumption, para 23.
[60] Per Lord Sumption, para 25.
[61] Per Lord Sumption, para 29. For a criticism of Lord Sumption's reasoning and analysis, see G Moss and I Fletcher, 'A Saad Affair' (2015) 28(4) Insolvency Intelligence 49–55: the insolvency laws of different (common law) jurisdictions are far from homogeneous. Applying Lord Sumption's reasoning, small differences between the insolvency laws of two jurisdictions (such as the length of a claw-back period or the permissible scope of a private examination) may lead to judicial assistance being denied.
[62] The use of the term 'forum shopping' can be problematic. In the modern English restructuring context, it has been recognized that adopting certain reorganization structures intended to benefit creditors generally, may constitute a form of 'good forum shopping': see, eg, *Re Codere Finance (UK) Ltd* [2015] EWHC 3778 (Ch), per Newey J.
[63] Even Lord Hoffmann in *Cambridge Gas* had rejected the idea of being able to apply foreign law: [2007] 1 AC 508 (PC), para 22. As Lord Loreburn said in *Galbraith v Galbraith* [1910] AC 508, 510, '[a] foreign [insolvency] law … has no operation in England, while the English law … applies only to cases of English bankruptcy, and therefore the [foreign] trustee may find himself (as in this case) falling between two stools'.

considered that certain transfers of property were frauds upon the bankruptcy law, though there was no statutory enactment upon the subject.[64]

In a purely domestic context, the court's inherent power to avoid preferences and transactions defrauding creditors is no longer relevant, and has been superseded by the 1986 Act. But in the context of common law judicial assistance (where the 1986 Act does not apply), it is arguable that the 1986 Act did not extinguish the court's inherent claw-back powers.[65] If this analysis is correct, then the English court may be able to provide judicial assistance to a foreign office-holder by avoiding preferences and transactions defrauding creditors at common law. However, this may in practice be of limited utility: applying *Singularis*, relief will still be refused where it is not available under the law of the home state. **5.53**

Likewise, it appears that the English court can give judicial assistance to a foreign office-holder by avoiding contracts that contravene the English common law anti-deprivation rule, even if insolvency proceedings have not commenced in England (again, so long as it does not afford relief which not available to the foreign office-holder in the home state).[66] **5.54**

Ancillary insolvency proceedings

The English courts have a long established jurisdiction to permit insolvency proceedings to be commenced, even though proceedings have already commenced in respect of the debtor in its place of domicile. The English proceedings are said to be 'ancillary' to the 'principal' proceedings abroad. **5.55**

Certain criteria must be satisfied at common law in order for ancillary insolvency proceedings to be commenced. Most importantly, there will, save in exceptional cases, have to be shown a sufficient connection between the foreign company and the English jurisdiction. This may be proved by the presence of assets or a business, or other points of connection with England.[67] The sufficiency of the connection might be demonstrated by the petition debt being governed by English law,[68] or certain of the company's debts being English law governed debts.[69] In **5.56**

---

[64] See also: (in relation to preferential transactions) *Lewis v Hyde* [1997] BCC 976, 980; *Worsley v De Mattos* (1758) 1 Bun 467; *Alderson v Temple* (1768) 4 Burr 2235; and (in relation to transactions defrauding creditors) *Ryall v Rolle* (1749) 1 Atkyns 165; *Hamilton v Russell* (1803) 1 Cranch 309; *Meeker v Wilson* (1813) 1 Gall 419.

[65] As Lord Wilberforce said in *Shiloh Spinners Ltd v Harding* [1973] AC 691, 723, 'where the courts have established a general principle of law or equity, and the legislature steps in with particular legislation in a particular area, it must, unless showing a contrary intention, be taken to have left cases outside that area where they were under the influence of the general law'.

[66] See, eg, *Perpetual Trustee Co Ltd v BNY Corporate Trustee Services Ltd* [2009] EWHC 1912 (Ch), paras 27–28 and 47–48.

[67] *Stocznia Gdanska v Latreefers* [2001] BCC 174 (CA). See also *Re Drax Holdings Ltd* [2004] 1 WLR 1049, para 26 in which Lawrence Collins J held that the criteria went to the discretion of the court, rather than to its jurisdiction; *Re Sovereign Marine and General Insurance Co Ltd* [2007] 1 BCLC 228; *Re OJSC Ank Yugraneft* [2010] BCC 475, per Christopher Clarke J, [20]; *Re Rodenstock GmbH* [2011] Bus LR 1245, per Briggs J, para 23; and *Re Apcoa Parking Holdings GmbH* [2015] BCC 142, per Hildyard J, para 212.

[68] *Stocznia Gdanska v Latreefers* [2001] BCC 174 (CA).

[69] Eg *Re Rodenstock GmbH* [2011] Bus LR 1245 (in respect of debts compromised under a scheme of arrangement). The 'sufficient connection' test is also routinely applied in modern restructuring cases to determine whether the English court has jurisdiction to sanction schemes of arrangement or restructuring plans under Parts 26 and 26A of the Companies Act 2006, where the scheme or plan company is incorporated abroad: see, for recent examples, *Re Smile Telecoms Holdings Ltd* [2022] EWHC 740 (Ch), per Lord Justice Snowden, at paras 60–61; and *Re Hong Kong Airlines Ltd* [2022] EWHC 3210 (Ch), per Sir Alastair Norris, paras 19–20.

modern cases, the fact that a company's COMI is situated in England will likely constitute a sufficient connection.[70]

5.57 For example, in *Stocznia Gdanska v Latreefers*[71] the underlying dispute was between a Polish shipyard and the Latvian state shipping company. The Latvian shipping company had used an 'off-the-shelf' Liberian company to enter into certain shipbuilding contracts, which defaulted. The Court of Appeal found there to be sufficient points of contact with the English jurisdiction to enable the English court to assume jurisdiction to wind up the company. The default arose under English law governed contracts and the Liberian company was controlled through London agents. The judgment debt upon which the insolvency proceedings were based had also been granted by the English court.

5.58 Where the English court declares English insolvency proceedings shall be 'ancillary' to principal proceedings abroad, no fixed or rigid course of conduct is set in motion.[72] However, in a classic ancillary winding-up, the essential function of the English liquidator is to collect assets belonging to the debtor which are situated in England (but not the assets situated abroad), and to remit those assets to the principal proceedings for *pari passu* distribution among the debtor's worldwide creditors.[73] The ancillary liquidator also collects claims against the debtor in England for remission to the main proceedings.

5.59 Subject to those exceptions, the full scope of domestic English insolvency law applies. As Lord Sumption put it in *Singularis*:[74]

> In these cases, the court is exercising the ordinary powers of the English court to control the winding-up of a company, which are wholly statutory. But the court was using them for a purpose which differed from that for which they were conferred, and on principles which departed from those applicable by law in the winding up of an English company. To that extent only, the English courts were exercising a common law power.

5.60 So although an English liquidator has a duty under the 1986 Act to get in assets belonging to the company 'wherever situated',[75] the concept of this being in effect modified by the directions of the English court to the liquidator is well-established.[76] The *situs* of the debtor's assets will be determined in accordance with the general rules of private international law.[77]

5.61 However, an English ancillary liquidator may not remit assets to the principal proceedings where such remission would be contrary to justice or on public policy grounds. The scope of

---

[70] Cf, in the restructuring context, *Re Smile Telecoms Holdings Ltd* [2022] EWHC 740 (Ch), per Lord Justice Snowden, at para 60; following *Re Gategroup Guarantee Ltd* [2021] BCC 549, per Zacaroli J, para 21.
[71] [2001] BCC 174 (CA).
[72] See R Sheldon, *Cross-Border Insolvency* (4th edn, 2015) at para 7.16.
[73] *Re Commercial Bank of South Australia* (1886) 33 Ch D 174; *Re Queensland Mercantile Agency Co Ltd* (1888) 58 LT 878; *North Australian Territory Co Ltd v Goldsborough, Mort & Co Ltd* (1889) 61 LT 716; *Re Federal Bank of Australia Ltd* (1893) 62 LJ Ch 561; *Re English, Scottish and Australian Chartered Bank* [1893] 3 Ch 385; *Re Alfred Shaw & Co Ltd* (1897) 8 QLJ 93; *Sedgwick Collins & Co v Rossia Insurance Co of Petrograd (Employers' Liability Assurance Corp garnishees)* [1926] 1 KB 1; *Re Vocalion (Foreign) Ltd* [1932] 2 Ch 196; *Re Hibernian Merchants Ltd* [1958] Ch 76; *Re Suidair International Airways Ltd* [1951] Ch 165.
[74] [2015] 2 WLR 971 (PC), para 10.
[75] 1986 Act, ss 143(1) and 436(1).
[76] *Re HIH Casualty and General Insurance Ltd* [2008] 1 WLR 852; *Re BCCI (No 10)* [1997] Ch 213.
[77] See *Dicey, Morris & Collins on The Conflict of Laws* (15th edn, 2012 (as supplemented)), ch 22 for a summary of the relevant rules.

this exception is somewhat unclear, and is illustrated by two important cases: *Re BCCI (No 10)*[78] and *Re HIH Casualty and General Insurance Ltd.*[79]

In *Re BCCI (No 10)*, the insolvent bank entered into liquidation in Luxembourg (where it was incorporated) and in England. There were significant differences between the law of set-off in England and in Luxembourg, which Sir Richard Scott VC explained at 252: **5.62**

> A creditor has a deposit of £1,000 and an outstanding loan of £200. He is a net creditor for £800 and, in England, would receive £320 if a 40% dividend were declared. In Luxembourg, the creditor would be entitled to a dividend of £400 but the £400 would be applied in discharging the £200 loan. So the creditor would receive only £200.

The English liquidators applied for directions as to whether the English assets should be remitted to Luxembourg for distribution in the principal liquidation. Sir Richard Scott VC directed the English liquidators to remit the English assets to the Luxembourg liquidators, but to retain sufficient funds to compensate creditors who would otherwise be disadvantaged by the Luxembourg set-off rules. In effect, the retained funds were designed to ensure that creditors who proved in the English liquidation received the same amount as they would have received if the English assets had not been remitted to Luxembourg. **5.63**

This result was justified on the basis that the ancillary nature of an English winding-up did not relieve the English court of its obligation to apply mandatory rules of English insolvency law (and, in particular, the set-off rules in rule 14.25 of the Insolvency (England and Wales) Rules 2016/1024 (the '2016 Rules')). Remitting the retained sums would have amounted to a *de facto* disapplication of rule 14.25. The essential principles were summarized by Sir Richard Scott VC at 246: **5.64**

> (1) Where a foreign company is in liquidation in its country of incorporation, a winding up order made in England will normally be regarded as giving rise to a winding up ancillary to that being conducted in the country of incorporation. (2) The winding up in England will be ancillary in the sense that it will not be within the power of the English liquidators to get in and realise all the assets of the company worldwide. They will necessarily have to concentrate on getting in and realising the English assets. (3) Since in order to achieve a *pari passu* distribution between all the company's creditors it will be necessary for there to be a pooling of the company's assets worldwide and for a dividend to be declared out of the assets comprised in that pool, the winding up in England will be ancillary in the sense, also, that it will be the liquidators in the principal liquidation who will be best placed to declare the dividend and to distribute the assets in the pool accordingly. (4) None the less, the ancillary character of an English winding up does not relieve an English court of the obligation to apply English law, including English insolvency law, to the resolution of any issue arising in the winding up which is brought before the court. It may be, of course, that English conflicts of law rules will lead to the application of some foreign law principle in order to resolve a particular issue.

In *Re HIH*, the House of Lords revisited the issue of remission. The issue was whether English ancillary liquidators should be directed to remit the English assets of an insolvent **5.65**

---

[78] [1997] Ch 213.
[79] [2008] 1 WLR 852 (HL).

insurance company to Australian principal liquidators, to be distributed in accordance with priorities applicable under Australian domestic law. The Australian priorities were radically different from the English law priorities applicable at the time the English proceedings were opened: in particular, the proceeds of reinsurance policies held by the company would be applied in discharge of its underlying liabilities which had been reinsured, rather than being distributed *pari passu* among the company's general creditors.

5.66 There were two possible grounds for remission. First, an Australian court had written a letter of request to the English court asking for the English assets to be remitted under section 426 of the 1986 Act. Secondly, the Australian liquidators argued that remission could be ordered by way of common law judicial assistance. The House of Lords unanimously agreed that the English assets should be remitted to Australia, but differed as to the legal basis for remission.

5.67 By a majority, the House of Lords held that all of the English assets should be remitted to Australia pursuant to section 426 of the 1986 Act, notwithstanding the substantial differences between the two systems of priorities.[80] This aspect of *HIH* is considered below. However, the House of Lords was divided on the question of whether the English assets could also be remitted to the Australian liquidation by way of common law judicial assistance. Lords Hoffmann and Walker held that the remission could and should be directed at common law; Lords Scott and Neuberger rejected this proposition; and Lord Phillips declined to express a view. In short, there was a '2.5 to 2.5' split.[81]

5.68 Lord Scott's reasoning in *HIH* on the issue of common law judicial assistance is similar to his reasoning in *BCCI (No 10)*. The radical differences between English and Australian law meant that remission would, in substance, involve the disapplication of the English statutory scheme. As a matter of basic constitutional theory, the English court has no power to override an Act of Parliament: therefore, remission could not be ordered at common law.[82] Lord Neuberger adopted a similar analysis.[83]

5.69 By contrast, Lord Hoffmann held that:[84]

> The whole doctrine of ancillary winding up is based upon the premise that in such cases the English court may 'disapply' parts of the statutory scheme by authorising the English liquidator to allow actions which he is obliged by statute to perform according to English law to be performed instead by the foreign liquidator according to the foreign law (including its rules of the conflict of laws). These may or may not be the same as English law.

5.70 On this footing, Lord Hoffmann held that the English court has a common law discretion (supplemental to its powers under section 426) to remit English assets in an ancillary

---

[80] Excluding Lord Hoffmann (who considered that section 426 was irrelevant to the issue of remission) and Lord Walker (who agreed with Lord Hoffmann).
[81] This phrase is derived from Lord Neuberger's speech to the Insolvency Lawyers Association on 16 November 2008, entitled 'Insolvency, Internationalism and Supreme Court Judgments'. For a fuller consideration of the judgment, see G Moss, '"Modified Universalism" And The Quest For The Golden Thread' (2008) 21 Insolvency Intelligence 145, and the conclusions reached at 146 and 151.
[82] [2008] 1 WLR 852 (HL), paras 59–61.
[83] ibid, para 75.
[84] ibid, para 19.

liquidation to the principal liquidation, to be distributed within a different system of priorities (which may be substantially different from the English insolvency waterfall). He observed that the principle of universalism:[85]

> ... requires that English courts should, so far as is consistent with justice and UK public policy, co-operate with the courts in the country of the principal liquidation to ensure that all the company's assets are distributed to its creditors under a single system of distribution.

In light of the decisions in *Singularis* and *Rubin*, it is questionable whether Lord Hoffmann's analysis based on the common law will be followed in the context of ancillary liquidations. It thus appears that *BCCI (No 10)* may still be an authoritative guide to the circumstances in which the court will remit assets in an ancillary liquidation by way of common law judicial assistance (as opposed to the use of statutory powers). The power of remittal at common law is now likely to be subject to the constraint that it cannot be used to undermine the statutory rights of English creditors to a *pari passu* distribution.[86]

5.71

Nevertheless, it has been confirmed that there is nothing in *HIH* which calls into question the long-established principle that the court has the power to order the remittal of assets to a foreign liquidation where the local law provides for a *pari passu* distribution.[87] So the mere fact that foreign priorities are not completely identical to English priorities should not be treated as an automatic bar to remission, provided (as noted above) that the *pari passu* principle is respected.

5.72

Section 426 of the Insolvency Act 1986

Section 426 creates a statutory obligation for English courts to assist insolvency proceedings from countries specified by delegated legislation where a request has been made for assistance by the relevant foreign court. The designated countries are, except for the Republic of Ireland and Hong Kong, all members of the Commonwealth.[88]

5.73

Section 426(4) of the 1986 Act provides that: 'The courts having jurisdiction in relation to insolvency law in any part of the United Kingdom shall assist the courts having the

5.74

---

[85] ibid, para 30. Lord Hoffmann explained the result in *BCCI (No 10)* on the basis that it had not been just for the Luxembourg rules of set-off to apply to claims which were governed by English law: para 17. He did not consider that Australian exceptions to the *pari passu* principle suffered from any such defect. Lord Hoffmann was influenced by recent amendments to the English statutory scheme for insolvent insurance companies (at para 32), which created exceptions to the *pari passu* principle (although those exceptions are rather different from the exceptions established by the Australian legislation, and were not yet in force at the time the *HIH* proceedings were commenced).
[86] As to this, see the first instance judgment of Hildyard J in *Re OJSC International Bank of Azerbaijan* [2018] Bus LR 1270, at para 142(4).
[87] *Re SwissAir Schweizerische Luftverkehr-Aktiengesellschaft* [2010] BCC 667, para 10.
[88] The Co-operation of Insolvency Courts (Designation of Relevant Countries and Territories) Order 1986, SI 1986/2123 designated (1) the Republic of Ireland, (2) the ten UK Overseas Territories (Anguilla, Bermuda, Cayman Islands, Falkland Islands, Gibraltar, Hong Kong, Montserrat, St Helena, Turks and Caicos Islands, and the Virgin Islands), and (3) six independent members of the Commonwealth (Australia, the Bahamas, Botswana, Canada, New Zealand, and Tuvalu). The Co-operation of Insolvency Courts (Designation of Relevant Countries) Order 1996, SI 1996/253 designated South Africa and Malaysia and the Co-operation of Insolvency Courts (Designation of Relevant Countries) Order 1998, SI 1998/2766 designated Brunei Darussalam, all three countries being independent members of the Commonwealth.

corresponding jurisdiction in ... any relevant country'. This extends to the Channel Islands and the Isle of Man: section 426(11).[89]

5.75 Section 426(5) describes the assistance which a UK court may give. A request from the court of a relevant country is 'authority for the court to which the request is made to apply, in relation to any matters specified in the request, *the insolvency law which is applicable by either court in relation to comparable matters falling within its jurisdiction*. In exercising its discretion under this subsection, a court shall have regard in particular to the rules of private international law' (emphasis added).

5.76 As can be seen, the scope of assistance available under section 426(5) is considerably broader than that available at common law. It permits the English court to apply English law (ie on the 'as if' basis) or foreign law, as it deems it appropriate (and without the qualifications imposed at common law), albeit that in determining which law to apply, the court is required to have regard to the rules of private international law.[90]

5.77 The English court has jurisdiction to grant relief under section 426(4) even if no insolvency proceedings have commenced in the requesting country.[91] Section 426(4) is to be given a broad interpretation: provided that the request relates to insolvency in some way, the section 426(4) jurisdiction is engaged. So the English court had jurisdiction to accede to a letter of request from the Royal Court of Jersey to appoint administrators over a Jersey-incorporated company (where no analogous procedure was available) under Schedule B1 to the 1986 Act.[92]

5.78 Although section 426(4) must be construed in a broad manner, it does not permit recognition of a foreign judgment.[93] Section 426(4) is not concerned with recognition or enforcement, but with judicial assistance (which is a different concept).[94] In this respect, it contrasts with section 426(1) and (2), which deals with the enforcement of orders from one part of the UK in another part of UK.

5.79 Since its enactment, a considerable body of authority has developed on the meaning and application of section 426. The Court of Appeal has held that giving assistance under section 426 is not mandatory, although the court should assist if it is properly able to do so.[95] In the first instance judgment in *New Cap Re*, Lewison J described the discretion as 'a limited one' (at [32]):[96]

---

[89] The Secretary of State has power to designate further countries as 'relevant': section 426(11). As noted in the preceding footnote, a number of further countries have been designated. It might have been expected that designation would be based on the availability of reciprocal judicial assistance, but no such check appears to have been carried out prior to designation.
[90] A cross-reference which has been criticized as unclear both by Lawrence Collins J in *Re Television Trade Rentals Ltd* [2002] BCC 807 and by Sir Andrew Morritt C in *McGrath v Riddell (sub nom Re HIH Casualty and General Insurance Ltd)* [2007] 1 All ER 177 (CA).
[91] *Re Tambrook Jersey Ltd* [2014] Ch 252 (CA).
[92] ibid.
[93] *Rubin v Eurofinance SA* [2013] 1 AC 236 (SC), para 152.
[94] ibid.
[95] *Hughes v Hannover Ruckversicherungs AG* [1996] 1 BCLC 497 (CA). See also *England v Smith* [2000] 2 BCLC 21 (CA)—the reasoning of which is not easy to reconcile with *Hughes*, although it affirms the non-mandatory nature of section 426. In *England v Smith*, the Court of Appeal viewed judicial comity as the starting point on a section 426 request (permitting examination under Australian insolvency law, which would not have been allowed in a domestic case). The Australian court having made the order for examination, Morritt LJ held that the English court should not perform that task again unless it was shown that the requesting court had been ignorant of some material fact or subsequent events undermined the justification for the order: at para 22 et seq.
[96] [2011] EWHC 677 (Ch).

Although section 426(4) is couched in mandatory terms, it is common ground that the court retains a discretion, but the discretion is a limited one. The discretion should be exercised in favour of assisting a foreign court unless it would be improper to do so. The scope of the discretion has been considered twice by the Court of Appeal in *Hughes v Hannover Re* [1997] 1 BCLC 497, and *England v Smith* [2000] BPIR 28. Morritt LJ gave the leading judgment in both cases. To the untutored eye, they exhibit different approaches; but the latter case must be taken as having explained the former. The latter case emphasises the mandatory terms in which section 426(4) is drawn; the important public policy of comity between nations; and the weight that must be given to the very fact that a foreign court has asked for assistance, all the more so if the foreign court has itself considered whether a request should be made.

5.80 As discussed above, one of the leading cases on section 426 is the House of Lords decision in *Re HIH Casualty and General Insurance Ltd*.[97] The majority held that the English assets should be remitted pursuant to section 426, notwithstanding the differences in the two systems of priorities: see paragraphs 5.65–5.72.

5.81 The courts have emphasized the fact sensitive nature of the discretion, which must be applied on a case by case basis.[98] It is, however, suggested that *HIH* is authority for the proposition that in a case to which section 426 applies, remission can and probably will be ordered of assets (net of costs and preferential claims) unless it is negatived by considerations of justice or public policy. The precise content of 'justice' in this context has not been fully worked out in the case law, but a different system of priorities will not necessarily make remission 'unjust' or contrary to English public policy.[99] By contrast, a material difference in the rules of set-off in relation to creditors whose debts are governed by English law may make such remission unjust, as in *BCCI (No 10)*.[100] Unfair discrimination, eg on the grounds of nationality or residence, may violate English public policy and prevent remission.

UNCITRAL Model Law

Origins and enactment

5.82 In May 1997 the United Nations Commission on International Trade Law, UNCITRAL, adopted a Model Law[101] on Cross-Border Insolvency.[102] Provision was included in the

---

[97] [2008] 1 WLR 852 (HL).
[98] See *Chen Yung Ngai Kenneth v Li Shu Chun* [2021] 7 WLUK 158 (unrep), at para 32 (Hong Kong trustees in bankruptcy authorized to take steps to determine and realise interests in immovable properties situated in England in accordance with English insolvency law).
[99] See Lord Scott, at para 62.
[100] [1997] Ch 213.
[101] The Model Law is considered in this chapter, particularly given that (post-Brexit) it is likely to assume increased significance as a tool for recognition and assistance in the UK. There have now been a significant number of English decisions under the Model Law (in addition to those of other enacting states), and an extensive analysis is outside the scope of this work. A number of English texts contain more detailed treatment of the Model Law. See, eg: G Lightman and G Moss, *The Law of Administrators and Receivers of Companies* (6th edn, 2017), ch 32; R Sheldon, *Cross-Border Insolvency* (4th edn, 2015), ch 3; P Wood, *Principles of International Insolvency* (3rd edn, 2019), ch 66.
[102] UNCITRAL 30th Session, 12–30 May 1997: Official Records of the General Assembly of the United Nations, 52nd Session, Supplement No 17 (A152/17), Part II, paras 12–225. The text of the Model Law as adopted is included in that document as Annex I (68–78).

Insolvency Act 2000 for the Model Law to be given effect in the United Kingdom by regulations made by statutory instrument.[103] The enabling provision allowed for implementation with or without modification and it further allowed for amendment of any provision of section 426 of the 1986 Act.

5.83 The Model Law was enacted in Great Britain,[104] on 4 April 2006, by the Cross-Border Insolvency Regulations 2006 ('the CBIR')[105] and in Northern Ireland, on 12 April 2007, by the Cross-Border Insolvency Regulations (Northern Ireland) 2007.[106] The CBIR are composed of six parts: (1) the enacting provisions themselves (Regulations 1–8); and (2) five Schedules. The text of the Model Law in the modified form in which it applies in Great Britain is contained in Schedule 1. Various procedural matters are dealt with in the remaining Schedules.

5.84 The policy was to adopt the Model Law in a form which tracked the UNCITRAL version as closely as possible, but there have been important changes (in particular, those concerning the rights of secured creditors: see paragraph 5.98).

5.85 The Model Law modified what is described as British insolvency law[107] and, in the case of any conflict between the Model Law and British insolvency law, the provisions of the CBIR are to prevail.[108]

Scope

5.86 The Model Law enables a 'foreign representative'[109] of a debtor to apply for recognition in the courts of an enacting state. Its scope is more modest than the Insolvency Proceedings Regulation, being limited to questions of 'recognition' of foreign proceedings[110] (in fact,

---

[103] Insolvency Act 2000, s 14.
[104] In this context, this means the jurisdictions of (i) England and Wales and (ii) Scotland.
[105] SI 2006/1030. There have now been countless applications under the CBIR. Most recently, see eg: *Re NMC Healthcare Ltd* [2022] BCC 171; *Re Li Shu Chung* [2022] BPIR 507; *Re PJSC Bank Finance and Credit* [2021] BPIR 1228; *Re Industria de Alimentos Nilza SA* [2021] BCC 383; *Re Deep Black Drilling LLP* [2020] BCC 486; *Re Sturgeon Central Asia Balanced Fund Ltd* [2019] BCC 950; *Re Dalnyaya Step LLC* [2019] BCC 1; [2019] BCC 23; *Re Videology* [2019] BCC 195; *Re Agrokor DD* [2018] Bus LR 64; *Re 19 Entertainment Ltd* [2017] BCC 347; *Re Astora Women's Health LLC* [2022] EWHC 2412 (Ch); *Re Kwok* [2023] EWHC 74 (Ch). For a selection of cases decided in and prior to 2015, see para 5.76, n 106, of the third edition of this work.
[106] Statutory Rules of Northern Ireland 2007/115.
[107] Defined in Art 2(a).
[108] Reg 3(2) of the CBIR.
[109] 'Foreign representative' is defined under Art 2(j) of the CBIR and Art 2(d) of the Model Law as 'a person or body, including one appointed on an interim basis, authorised in a foreign proceeding to administer the reorganization or the liquidation of the debtor's assets or affairs or to act as a representative of the foreign proceeding'. For a debtor in possession, this can include the debtor itself and each of its directors: *Re 19 Entertainment Ltd* [2017] BCC 347. In the restructuring context, the English court has approved dozens of schemes of arrangement under Part 26 of the Companies Act 2006, in which (typically) a director of the debtor has subsequently obtained recognition of the scheme under Chapter 15 of the US Bankruptcy Code.
[110] 'Foreign proceeding' is defined under Art 2(i) of the CBIR and Art 2(a) of the Model Law as 'a collective judicial or administrative proceeding in a foreign State, including an interim proceeding, pursuant to a law relating to insolvency in which proceeding the assets and affairs of the debtor are subject to control or supervision by a foreign court, for the purpose of reorganisation or liquidation'. For cases which have considered the proper interpretation and application of this term, see eg: *Re Stanford International Bank Ltd* [2011] Ch 33; *Rubin v Eurofinance SA* [2013] 1 AC 236 (SC), para 27; *Re Sanko Steamship Ltd* [2015] EWHC 1031 (Ch), para 28; *Re Sturgeon Central Asia Balanced Fund Ltd* [2019] BCC 950; [2020] BCC 389 (terminating the recognition). In *Stanford*, para 28 the Court of Appeal confirmed that the reference to 'interim proceeding' would extend to an English provisional liquidation. The Court also held that the appointment of a receiver by the US SEC did not constitute a 'foreign proceeding', not being designed to effect a reorganization or a liquidation of the company, and did not provide for the possibility of

mainly judicial assistance to them) and of the rights of the 'foreign representative' to obtain access to, and assistance from, courts of enacting states. However, the geographical impact of the Model Law is unrestricted. For example, it applies in Great Britain and Northern Ireland in respect of all foreign countries without any requirement of reciprocal recognition.[111] The philosophy is that the UK should set an example for other countries.

Unlike the Regulation, the Model Law and the CBIR do not embody any rules of jurisdiction or choice of law. On the other hand, 'recognition' of foreign proceedings under the Model Law and the CBIR is based on the criteria employed in the Regulation to differentiate between main proceedings and secondary, or territorial, proceedings. The CBIR utilize similar criteria to designate foreign insolvency proceedings as either 'foreign main' or 'foreign non-main' proceedings for the purposes of recognition and assistance, by reference to the existence (respectively) of the debtor's COMI or an 'establishment' (Article 17(2)).[112]

5.87

Importantly, however, the COMI and 'establishment' criteria are intended in the CBIR to be *additional* bases for giving judicial assistance beyond pre-existing bases for 'recognition'.[113] Unfortunately, in the United States enactment of the Model Law in Chapter 15 of the US Bankruptcy Code, the COMI and establishment criteria have so far been treated as exclusive bases for 'recognition'[114] and have restricted rather than enlarged the ability of the US courts to assist foreign insolvency and rescue proceedings.

5.88

Foreign main proceeding and non-main proceeding

A foreign main proceeding is a 'foreign proceeding taking place in the State where the debtor has the centre of its main interests' (Article 2(g) of the CBIR).[115] Whilst COMI is not defined in the CBIR, Article 16(2A) contains a presumptive rule that where the 'EU Insolvency Regulation' applies, COMI is to be determined in accordance with it.[116] Article 16(3) further entitles the court to presume that that the debtor's registered office, or habitual residence in the case of an individual, is presumed to be the COMI. The concept of

5.89

---

a *pari passu* distribution to creditors. In *Sturgeon*, Chief ICC Judge Briggs terminated the recognition order in respect of a just and equitable winding-up or a Bermuda company under the Bermudian equivalent of the 1986 Act, section 122(1)(g), observing (at para 117) that it would be contrary to the stated purpose and object of the Model Law to interpret foreign proceedings to include a solvent debtor, and more especially, to include actions which have the purpose of producing a return to members and not creditors. He held that the words 'for the purpose' in Art 2(i) should be read as meaning the purpose of insolvency (liquidation) or severe financial distress (reorganization). A broad approach has been adopted in the US to the meaning of 'foreign proceeding': see eg *Re Betcorp Ltd* 400 BR 266 (Bankr D Nev 2009). This approach seems unlikely to be followed in this jurisdiction; although see the *obiter* observations of the Deputy Judge to the contrary in *Re Agrokor DD* [2018] Bus LR 64, para 63.

[111] By the start of 2021, some 49 states had adopted the Model Law; however, as noted, a foreign representative is able to rely on and engage the CBIR irrespective of whether reciprocal arrangements have been enacted in the home state. In 2021, UNCITRAL produced an extensive 'Digest of Case Law on the UNCITRAL Model Law on Cross-Border Insolvency': <https://uncitral.un.org>. It reflects the case law of the enacting states and is therefore a valuable aid to interpretation of the Model Law—particularly in light of Article 8 of the Model Law, referred to below, which promotes uniformity in application of the Model Law. The revised 2013 Guide to Enactment and the 2009 Practice Guide on Cross-Border Cooperation are also valuable aids to interpretation.
[112] Which is in terms identical to those of Art 17(2) of the Model Law.
[113] And are treated in the same way under the Model Law. See Art 7 of the CBIR and of the Model Law and para 90 of the Guide to Enactment.
[114] Moss, 'Bitter Pill Delivered by Judge Sweet' (2008) 21 Insolvency Intelligence 118.
[115] Which is in terms identical to those of Art 2(b) of the Model Law.
[116] Art 16(2A) was introduced, post-Brexit, by the The Insolvency (Amendment) (EU Exit) Regulations 2019, SI 2019/146, reg 1(2), Sch, paras 112, 113, and 117.

COMI under the Model Law should be construed in substantially the same way as under the Insolvency Proceedings Regulation.[117] This does not, however, necessarily mean that all the provisions in the Insolvency Proceedings Regulation (and the CJEU jurisprudence interpreting them) can be 'read across' to the Model Law.

5.90 A foreign non-main proceeding is a 'foreign proceeding, other than a foreign main proceeding, taking place in a State where the debtor has an establishment' (Article 2(h) of the CBIR).[118] 'Establishment' is defined as 'any place of operations where the debtor carries out a non-transitory economic activity with human means and assets or services' (Article 2(e) of the CBIR).[119] This excludes the possibility that the mere presence of assets belonging to the debtor can be regarded as founding the exercise of insolvency jurisdiction capable of international recognition. Nor will a purely temporary or occasional place of operations provide a basis for the exercise of jurisdiction.

5.91 Following *Stanford*,[120] it is likely that the court will construe the term 'establishment' in substantially the same manner under the Insolvency Proceedings Regulation and the Model Law.[121] Of course, this also does not mean that all the provisions in the Insolvency Proceedings Regulation regarding establishments can be 'read across' to the Model Law. Furthermore, there are crucial differences between the current definition of 'establishment' in the Regulation and the definition of the same term in the Model Law: the definition in the Regulation now includes a 'look back' period of three months, which has no equivalent under the Model Law.

Conditions for recognition

5.92 By Article 15(1) of the CBIR,[122] a foreign representative may apply to the court of an enacting state for recognition of the foreign proceeding in which he has been appointed.[123] Recognition will be accorded where the grounds set out in Article 17(1) of the CBIR[124] can be shown to exist. In seeking recognition, the foreign representative is subject to a duty to

---

[117] *Re Stanford International Bank Ltd* [2011] Ch 33 (CA), para 54. There are now numerous decisions which have considered the application of the COMI under the CBIR, which is necessarily a fact sensitive exercise. For a careful consideration of the COMI test under the CBIR, particularly in relation to groups, see *Re Videology* [2019] BCC 195, para 19; in which case, Snowden J refused to find, in relation to an English registered company (with its registered office in England) which was a subsidiary of a US group, that the US Chapter 11 proceedings in relation to the US group were foreign main proceedings. He made clear that the COMI of companies within a *group* had to be separately assessed, and the English company had not displaced the presumption that its COMI was located in the place of its registered office in England (although the Chapter 11 proceedings were recognized as foreign non-main proceedings, the evidence supporting the finding of an 'establishment' in the US).
[118] Which is in terms identical to those of Art 2(c) of the Model Law.
[119] In largely similar terms to those of Art 2(f) of the Model Law, save that Art 2(e) of the CBIR replaces the term 'goods' with 'assets'. The definition clearly embraces both tangible and intangible assets.
[120] *Re Stanford International Bank Ltd* [2011] Ch 33 (CA).
[121] As to the concept of an establishment, see the leading Supreme Court case of *Trustees of the Olympic Airlines SA Pension & Life Assurance Scheme v Olympic Airlines SA* [2015] 1 WLR 2399.
[122] Which is in terms identical to those of Art 15(1) of the Model Law.
[123] See Arts 15(2)–(4) for the documentation to be provided in support of the application and Art 16 which sets out certain presumptions in this respect.
[124] Although the grounds are for the most part the same as those specified by Art 17(1) of the Model Law, Art 17(1)(c) of the CBIR imposes the additional requirement for recognition that Art 15(3) is satisfied. That provision differs from its counterpart in the Model Law, in its requirement that the application be accompanied by a statement identifying not simply all *foreign proceedings* in respect of the debtor that are known to the foreign representative, but also all proceedings under British insolvency law and s 426 requests known to the foreign representative.

make full and frank disclosure to the court, which extends to the consequences that recognition may have on third parties not before the court.[125]

5.93 When deciding whether the criteria as to a 'foreign proceeding' or 'foreign representative'[126] are met, Article 16(1) contains a presumptive rule entitling the court to rely on any decision or certificate commencing the proceeding or appointing the representative[127] which indicates this to be the case.

5.94 Even where the Article 17 conditions are satisfied, Article 6[128] allows recognition or assistance to be refused where it would be 'manifestly contrary' to the public policy of Great Britain.[129] Further, by Article 17(4) of the CBIR[130] recognition which has already been granted may be modified or terminated, in the event of changed circumstances or further information coming to the notice of the court which reveals that the grounds for granting recognition were in fact fully or partially lacking.[131] Although the Model Law provides no other basis on which recognition can be refused, in *Re OGX Petróleo E Gás SA*,[132] Snowden J considered that the court must also have residual discretion to refuse recognition where an abuse of process has occurred.

5.95 This is balanced by Article 8, an important provision which promotes international uniformity of application and the observance of good faith.[133] As with the Regulation, the underlying intention is to ensure that comity is achieved in the context of cross-border insolvency proceedings.

Effects of recognition: automatic relief

5.96 The more direct and automatic effects (including an automatic stay) are accorded in the case of foreign main proceedings, whereas relief and assistance is placed upon a discretionary basis in the case of foreign non-main proceedings. Article 20(1) of the CBIR[134] lists the effects of recognition of a foreign main proceeding which are automatic and do not depend on the exercise of judicial discretion. Specifically:

---

[125] *Re OGX Petróleo E Gás SA* [2016] Bus LR 121, per Snowden J; followed in *Re Dalnyaya Step LLC (No 2)* [2019] BCC 23; *Re PJSC Bank Finance and Credit* [2021] BPIR 1228, paras 2–4.
[126] As defined in Arts 2(i) and 2(j).
[127] Which is required to be provided in support of a recognition application: see Arts 15(2)(a)–(c).
[128] Art 6 of the Model Law institutes the same public policy exception.
[129] See *Re Dalnyaya Step LLC (No 2)* [2019] BCC 1 (recognition subsequently revoked in [2019] BCC 23, per Vos C), in which Rose J held that the Art 6 exception was engaged due to the difficulty of enforcing a costs order in Russia, and ordered the foreign representative to provide security for costs in an application under the 1986 Act, section 236. See, however, *Re Li Shu Chung* [2021] 11 WLUK 462 (unrep), para 30, in which Flaux C rejected the bankrupt's application for security for costs against the Hong Kong trustees, finding (on the facts at issue) that to do so 'would potentially give the green light to the disruption of the recognition process under the CBIR'.
[130] Art 17(4) of the Model Law accords the courts the same power. However, Art 17(4) of the CBIR extends yet further in also providing that in such a case, the court may, on the application of the foreign representative or a person affected by recognition or of its own motion, modify or terminate recognition either altogether or for a limited time, on such terms and conditions as the court thinks fit.
[131] As occurred in eg *Re Sturgeon Central Asia Balanced Fund Ltd* [2019] BCC 950; [2020] BCC 389; *Re Dalnyaya Step LLC (No 2)* [2019] BCC 1; [2019] BCC 23, per Vos C (lack of full and frank disclosure); *Re Sanko Steamship Co Ltd* [2015] EWHC 1031 (Ch) (recognition by English court of termination of Japanese proceedings).
[132] [2016] Bus LR 121, para 60.
[133] See, however, the recognition that decisions of foreign courts will not be helpful where they are 'based on different adaptions of the Model Law or ... do not accord with the preparatory materials (reports of working groups) that led to the CBIR': *Re Agrokor DD* [2018] Bus LR 64, para 36.
[134] Which is the same as Art 20(1) of the Model Law.

(a) a stay on the commencement or continuation of individual actions or proceedings concerning the debtor's assets, rights, obligations, or liabilities;
(b) a stay on execution against the debtor's assets; and
(c) a suspension of the debtor's right to transfer, encumber, or otherwise dispose of any assets.

5.97 Article 20(2) of the CBIR[135] delineates the extent of the automatic stay and suspension, which are to be the same in scope and effect as if the debtor had been subject to analogous proceedings under the 1986 Act and are to be subject to the same powers of the court and the same prohibitions, limitations, exceptions, and conditions as would apply under the law of Great Britain in such a case.[136] Article 20(5) provides that the stay does not affect the right to request or otherwise initiate the commencement of a proceeding under British insolvency law, or the right to file claims in such a proceeding.[137]

5.98 Of much significance are the additional provisions instituted by the CBIR, in particular Article 20(3), which provides that the automatic stay and suspension does not affect a number of specified rights. That includes the right to take steps to enforce security over the debtor's property or repossess goods in the debtor's possession under a hire purchase agreement,[138] or the right of a creditor to set off its claim against a claim of the debtor, if such rights would have been exercisable in the event of the debtor's bankruptcy, sequestration, or winding-up (as the case may be). The stay also does not affect any right exercisable under a financial market contract in connection with provisions of UK legislation excluded from the scope of the Model Law by Article 1(4). Finally, Article 20(6) allows an application to be made by the foreign representative or a person affected by the automatic stay and suspension for an order that it be modified or terminated, in whole or in part.[139] The court may grant the same relief of its own motion.

Effects of recognition: discretionary relief

5.99 Pre-recognition, temporary relief may be ordered under Article 19.[140] It provides for discretionary relief under the law of the enacting state from the time of the filing of the application for recognition, until its determination. A non-exhaustive list of examples of such relief is

---

[135] By Art 20(2) of the Model Law the enacting state may impose any exceptions to the automatic stay and suspension which are found elsewhere in its domestic insolvency law.
[136] Art 20(2) refers to the stay which occurs on the making of a winding-up order, rather than the moratorium which is applicable in administration under para 43 of Sch B1 to the 1986 Act: *Cosco Bulk Carrier Co Ltd v Armada Shipping SA* [2011] EWHC 216 (Ch), per Briggs J, para 45; *Re Lemma Europe Insurance Co Ltd* [2016] EWCA Civ 484, para 1. The court has a discretion, however, in an appropriate case, to make an order under Art 21(1)(g) which replicates the administration moratorium. Where the foreign proceeding is in the nature of a rescue or reorganization process (rather than a liquidation), then the moratorium is usually modified so that it reflects that which is applicable in an English administration: *Re Videology* [2019] BCC 195, per Snowden J, at para 19. See also, eg: *Samsun Logic Corp v DEF* [2009] BPIR 1502; *Re Pan Oceanic Maritime Ltd* [2010] EWHC 1734 (Ch); *Re NMC Healthcare Ltd* [2022] BCC 171.
[137] See the equivalent provisions at Art 20(3) and (4) of the Model Law.
[138] Defined under Art 2(k).
[139] See: *Cosco Bulk Carrier Co Ltd v Armada Shipping SA* [2011] EWHC 216 (Ch), per Briggs J, paras 47–48; *Re Lemma Europe Insurance Co Ltd* [2016] EWCA Civ 484; *OGX Petróleo E Gás SA* [2016] Bus LR 121. In *OGX*, Snowden J held that the fact that a creditor affected by the stay would not be subject to the foreign proceedings (because they were excluded from its scope), would constitute a reason to lift or modify the stay. Further, that this should be disclosed at the time that recognition is sought, with a view to the court modifying the stay from the outset.
[140] Which is identical to Art 19 of the Model Law.

provided under Article 19(a)–(c). By Article 22(2),[141] the court may also attach conditions to any relief granted under Article 19 or 21.[142]

5.100 Post-recognition, Article 21 of the CBIR[143] sets out the forms of relief which may be granted on recognition of a foreign proceeding, whether main or non-main. It confers a general discretionary power upon the court of the enacting state to grant 'any appropriate relief', including the forms of relief instanced at Article 21(1)(a)–(g). The effects set out in Article 20(1) are repeated. The relief specified at Article 21(1)(d)–(g) will thus be discretionary even in the case of a foreign main proceeding. Article 21(1)(d) enables the court on the application of the foreign representative to provide for the examination of witnesses, the taking of evidence, and the delivery of information concerning the debtor's assets.

5.101 So in *Re Bernard L Madoff Investment Securities LLC*,[144] the court concluded that the provision had both a jurisdictional and a discretionary component: the court had to be satisfied that the information sought concerned the debtor's assets, affairs, rights, and obligations, and that, having regard to all the circumstances of the case, the interests of the persons against whom the order was sought were sufficiently protected.

5.102 Article 21(1)(g) empowers the court to grant 'any appropriate relief' upon the recognition of a foreign proceeding. The scope (and limits) of Article 21(1)(g) has been considered at appellate level in two important cases: *Rubin v Eurofinance SA*[145] and *Re OJSC International Bank of Azerbaijan*;[146] as well as in the first instance decision *Pan Ocean Ltd v Fibria Celulose S/A*.[147]

5.103 In *Rubin*, discussed above (paragraphs 5.27 et seq), the Supreme Court held that Article 21 could not be invoked to enable the enforcement of a foreign transaction avoidance judgment, despite that judgment deriving directly from recognized foreign proceedings and being closely connected to them.[148] It considered it highly unlikely that the Model Law

---

[141] The same provision is contained in Art 22(2) of the Model Law, save that Art 22(2) of the CBIR extends further in providing that such conditions may include provision by the foreign representative of security or caution for the proper performance of his functions.

[142] See, however, *Re Derev* [2021] Bus LR 685, per Adam Johnson J, for a case in which interim relief, in the form of a worldwide freezing order, was not continued under Art 21.

[143] Which provides for the same relief as Art 21 of the Model Law.

[144] [2010] BCC 328. See also *Re Chesterfield United Inc* [2012] BCC 786 (orders for examination); *Rozhkov v Markus* [2019] EWHC 1519 (Ch) (solicitors ordered to provide information to protect debtor's assets); *Re Industria de Alimentos Nilza SA* [2021] BCC 383, per ICC Judge Burton (order for document production).

[145] [2013] 1 AC 236.

[146] [2018].

[147] [2014] Bus LR 1041.

[148] One important consequence of *Rubin* in the international restructuring context, is that whilst proceedings under Chapter 11 of the US Bankruptcy Code can be the subject of a recognition application under the CBIR, a US court order confirming a Chapter 11 reorganization plan could not be recognized and enforced by the English court under the CBIR. This would mean, eg, that any director or third party releases confirmed in the plan could not be recognized in the UK on this basis. There has been significant debate in other states about whether Art 21 provides the necessary authority for the recognition and enforcement of insolvency-related judgments. The debate has extended to the proper interpretation of Art 7. In *Vitro SAB de CV*, 701 F 3d 1031 (5th Cir 2012), the US Court of Appeals for the Fifth Circuit denied enforcement of a third-party release provision in a reorganization plan approved by the Mexican court, concluding that the language of Arts 7 and 21 of the Model Law prevented the enforcement of third-party leases (the decision being founded in part on the particular approach of local US law to non-consensual releases). Recognizing this uncertainty, and with the specific intention of introducing a harmonized procedure for recognition and enforcement, in 2018 UNCITRAL adopted a Model Law on Recognition and Enforcement of Insolvency-Related Judgments. To the author's current knowledge, it has not so far been implemented in any state.

intended to deal with the recognition of judgments by implication. Lord Collins[149] held, at [143]:

> It would be surprising if the Model Law was intended to deal with judgments in insolvency matters by implication. Articles 21, 25 and 27 are concerned with procedural matters. No doubt they should be given a purposive interpretation and should be widely construed in the light of the objects of the Model Law, but there is nothing to suggest that they apply to the recognition and enforcement of foreign judgments against third parties.

5.104 In *Pan Ocean*, Morgan J held that Article 21(1)(g) could not be applied to restrain the exercise of a contractual right to terminate an executory contract governed by English law, in circumstances where the counterparty was a debtor in Korean insolvency proceedings, the trigger for the termination right was the appointment of the Korean administrators, and Korean insolvency law arguably rendered such rights void or (at least) unenforceable. If granted, the injunction sought by the administrators would have given effect to Korean law in an English court.

5.105 In a lengthy judgment (citing numerous US authorities), Morgan J rejected the application. He held that Article 21(1)(g), despite its apparent breadth, does not authorize the court to grant relief which would not be available in a domestic English insolvency. The judge noted that the *travaux préparatoires* for the Model Law indicated that the relevant working group had considered making provision in Article 21(1)(g) for the grant of relief available under the foreign law, but ultimately decided against this.[150] The approach to interpretation favoured by the US Bankruptcy Court in *Re Condor Insurance Ltd*[151] and *Re Hellas Telecommunications II*,[152] based on a very different legislative history, was not followed.

5.106 Lastly, in *Re OJSC International Bank of Azerbaijan*, the Court of Appeal held that Article 21 could not be applied to stay enforcement action by creditors *after* foreign reorganization proceedings (recognized as main proceedings) had been closed, with a view to preventing (indefinitely) enforcement by creditors with English law-governed debts who had not submitted to the jurisdiction of the foreign court but who were, as a matter of the foreign (Azeri) law, bound by the reconstruction plan. The decision brought into play the '*Gibbs* rule', being the common law rule that a debt governed by English law could not be discharged by a foreign insolvency proceeding unless the creditor had submitted to it.[153] Seeking a stay of indeterminate duration would, in fact, bring about a result that would circumvent the *Gibbs* rule.

5.107 The argument that Article 21(1)(a) or (b) could be invoked to restrict enforcement, to assist those proceedings even after they had closed, was rejected. The Court held expressly that there was 'no warrant for treating the relevant article 21 powers as other than procedural in nature, with the main object of providing a temporary "breathing space" ... '.[154] Following *Pan Ocean* and *Rubin*, the Court held: first, that it would be 'wrong in principle to use the

---

[149] With whom Lord Walker and Lord Sumption agreed. Lord Clarke dissented, but not on this point.
[150] At para 87.
[151] 601 F 3d 319.
[152] 535 BR 543, 566–67. See also *UBS AG New York v Fairfield Centry Ltd* [2019] BCC 966 (PC), para 15.
[153] *Gibbs v Société Industrielle des Métaux* (1890) 25 QBD 399, approved by the House of Lords in *National Bank of Greece and Athens SA v Metliss* [1985] AC 509, 523.
[154] Paragraph 89.

powers in article 21(1)(a), (b) or any other provisions of the Model Law … so as to circumvent the English law rights of the English creditors under the *Gibbs* rule'; and secondly, that a stay could not properly be granted or prolonged beyond the end of the Azeri reconstruction plan.[155]

Article 21(2) is an equally significant provision. It allows the foreign representative to apply to the court of the enacting state for an order entrusting the distribution of assets located in that state to him or to another person designated by the court.[156] In deciding whether to grant such relief to a representative of a foreign non-main proceeding, Article 21(3) requires the court to be satisfied that the relief relates to assets that, under the law of Great Britain, should be administered in the foreign proceeding or concerns information required in it. It therefore provides an additional mechanism for the court to remit assets to a foreign office-holder, in addition to its powers at common law and under section 426 of the 1986 Act.

5.108

Article 21(3) was considered by Snowden J in *Re Videology Ltd*[157] (who described it as 'rather obscurely worded'). Having considered the explanation in the 2013 Guide to Enactment, paragraphs 193 and 194, he observed (at [105]) that in a case where there is a UK main proceeding and recognition is sought for a foreign non-main proceeding:

5.109

> it is important to ensure that the relief granted following recognition is limited to assets which the English court envisages should be dealt with in the foreign non-main proceedings. But where the English court has considered the alternatives and finds it advantageous and appropriate in the interests of creditors to permit all of the debtor's assets to be administered in foreign insolvency proceedings, then there is no reason to consider any further limitation on the relief granted.

It remains unclear whether the English court would (or could) use Article 21(2) to order the remission of assets to a jurisdiction with substantially different priorities than the priorities which prevail in England. However, the mere fact that foreign priorities are not identical to English priorities is not a bar to remittal, provided that the *pari passu* principle is respected.

5.110

Rights of direct access and intervention

Article 11 of the CBIR[158] confers on the foreign representative the right to apply to commence a proceeding under the 1986 Act as if he were an office-holder appointed under the Act, whether or not recognition has been granted.[159] For those purposes, the foreign representative may have been appointed in a foreign main proceeding or a foreign non-main proceeding (but must have been appointed in one or the other).[160] Article 12[161] allows the foreign representative to participate in a proceeding regarding the debtor under the local insolvency laws.

5.111

---

[155] Per Henderson LJ, paras 95 and 98.
[156] Remittal was ordered under Article 21(2) in *Re SwissAir Schweizerische Luftverkehr-Aktiengesellschaft* [2010] BCC 667 (in which the order was made both under the court's inherent power and under Art 21(2)).
[157] [2019] BCC 195.
[158] As permitted by Art 11 of the Model Law.
[159] The right of direct access to the court is accorded by Art 9 and is of much significance in promoting the timely and effective operation of cross-border insolvency proceedings.
[160] Art 11 of the Model Law refers simply to a foreign representative without requiring his appointment in foreign main or non-main proceedings.
[161] Entitlement to participate is provided for under Art 12 of the Model Law.

5.112 Under Article 23,[162] a foreign representative has standing to apply to obtain an order under the avoidance provisions contained in the 1986 Act. This right exists regardless of whether or not there are concurrent proceedings in this jurisdiction. Where there are, the foreign representative will first require the court's permission.[163] Under Article 24,[164] upon recognition of a foreign proceeding the foreign representative acquires standing to intervene in any proceedings in which the debtor is a party.

Co-operation between courts and office-holders

5.113 The CBIR also provide for co-operation between courts and office-holders. By virtue of Articles 25–27,[165] the courts of Great Britain may rely on provisions entitling them to co-operate with foreign courts and foreign representatives. A list of the forms of co-operation is set out under Article 27 and expressed in general terms. Articles 28–32[166] operate to co-ordinate concurrent proceedings, by directing the types of procedures to be followed in such cases.

5.114 Of further note is Article 32, which adopts the 'hotchpot' principle (as it is known in English domestic law) and applies it to concurrent proceedings. It is a rule that prevents a creditor from receiving distributions in respect of its claim in both a foreign proceeding and insolvency proceedings in this jurisdiction (relating to the same debtor), until such time as creditors of the same class have received payment in equal proportion.[167]

C. Recognition under the Regulation

Use of terms

5.115 The Regulation, Article 2 contains a number of definitions relevant to the concepts and provisions that deal with the system of recognition under the Regulation. In particular:[168]

---

[162] As permitted by Art 23 of the Model Law.
[163] See further Art 23(6) and also Art 23(2)–(4) and (7)–(9) of the CBIR, which contain provisions additional to those contained in Art 23 of the Model Law. Both the CBIR (para 5) and Model Law (para 2) provide that when the foreign proceeding is a foreign non-main proceeding, the court must be satisfied that the Art 23 application relates to assets that, under the law of Great Britain, should be administered in the foreign non-main proceeding.
[164] Standing to intervene is also given by Art 24 of the Model Law.
[165] Also Arts 25–27 of the Model Law in almost identical terms. Art 26(1) of the CBIR ensures that a British insolvency office-holder will co-operate with foreign courts or foreign representatives only to the extent consistent with his other duties under the law of Great Britain.
[166] Arts 28–32 of the Model Law are broadly the same. The CBIR have inserted an additional provision at Art 29(b)(iii), which states that when a concurrent proceeding under British insolvency law commences after the filing of the application for recognition of the foreign proceeding, any proceedings brought by the foreign representative by virtue of Art 23(1) before the proceeding in Great Britain commenced shall be reviewed by the court, which may give such directions as it thinks fit as to the continuance of those proceedings.
[167] For recent confirmation of this rule in the international insolvency context, see the first instance judgment of Snowden J in *Kireeva v Bedzhamov* [2021] EWHC 2281 (Ch), paras 97–98.
[168] The Insolvency (England and Wales) Rules 2016/1024 (the '2016 Rules'), rule 1.2 contains certain definitions which are relevant to (and derive from) the Regulation. The 2016 Rules were amended by the Insolvency (Amendment) (EU Exit) Regulations 2019, SI 2019/146, Sch 1(4), para 47(b), on the UK's exit from the EU on 31 December 2020. Rule 1.2, as amended, now contains definitions of 'Article 1.2 Undertaking', 'centre of main interests', 'COMI proceedings', 'establishment', and 'establishment proceedings'. 'Member State liquidator' is no longer defined in rule 1.2 of the 2016 Rules.

C. RECOGNITION UNDER THE REGULATION

- 'Insolvency practitioner' is defined by reference to the persons and bodies identified in Annex B to the Regulation, and as having the functions, including on an interim basis, which are expressly identified in Article 2(5), being to;[169]
    (i) verify and admit claims submitted in insolvency proceedings;
    (ii) represent the collective interests of the creditors;
    (iii) administer, either in full or in part, assets of which the debtor has been divested;
    (iv) liquidate the assets referred to in point (iii); or
    (v) supervise the administration of the debtor's affairs;
- 'Debtor in possession' is defined in Article 2(3) to mean:[170]

    a debtor in respect of which insolvency proceedings have been opened which do not necessarily involve the appointment of an insolvency practitioner or the complete transfer of the rights and duties to administer the debtor's assets to an insolvency practitioner and where, therefore, the debtor remains totally or at least partially in control of its assets and affairs;

- 'Judgment opening insolvency proceedings' is defined in Article 2(7) to include:
    (i) the decision of any court to open insolvency proceedings or to confirm the opening of such proceedings; and
    (ii) the decision of a court to appoint an insolvency practitioner;
- 'The time of the opening of proceedings' is defined in Article 2(8) to mean:

    the time at which the judgment opening insolvency proceedings becomes effective, regardless of whether the judgment is final or not;

- 'Court means not only a judicial body of a Member State but, as applicable under the Regulation,[171] also any other competent body empowered by national law to open insolvency proceedings, to confirm such opening or to take decisions in the course of such proceedings: Article 2(6);
- 'Territorial proceedings' mean proceedings opened pursuant to Article 3(2) and (4) *prior* to the opening of main proceedings under Article 3(1);
- 'Secondary proceedings' mean proceedings opened in accordance with Article 3(2) *after* the opening of main proceedings: see Article 3(3);
- 'Local creditor' is defined in Article 2(11) to mean:

    a creditor whose claims against a debtor arose from or in connection with the operation of an establishment situated in a Member State other than the Member State in which the debtor's centre of main interests is located;

- 'Foreign creditor' is defined in Article 2(12) to mean:

    a creditor which has its habitual residence, domicile, or registered office in a Member State other than the State of the opening of proceedings, including the tax authorities and social security authorities of Member States;

---

[169] The term 'insolvency practitioner' was used for the first time in the Regulation; under the Original Regulation, the relevant insolvency administrator was referred to as a 'liquidator'.
[170] 'Debtor in possession' was a new concept introduced by the Regulation (not featuring in the Original Regulation).
[171] Art 2(6)(i) identifies the provisions of the Regulation by reference to which a 'court' must mean only the judicial body of a Member State.

- 'Group of companies' is defined in Article 2(13) to mean:

    a parent undertaking and all its subsidiary undertakings;

- 'Parent undertaking' is defined in Article 2(14) to mean:

    an undertaking which controls, directly or indirectly, one or more subsidiary undertakings. An undertaking which prepares consolidated financial statements in accordance with Directive 2013/34/EU of the European Parliament and of the Council[172] shall be deemed to be a parent undertaking;

- References to 'Member States', the 'European Union', or 'EU' refer to all Member States except Denmark;[173]

- References to the 'UK' include Gibraltar but exclude the Channel Islands and the Isle of Man.

5.116 In this chapter, references to the 'Virgós-Schmit Report' are to the report by Professor Miguel Virgós and Etienne Schmit on the Bankruptcy Convention which did not ultimately come into force.[174]

Effect of Brexit: current application of the Regulation in the UK

5.117 The Regulation is no longer applicable in the UK in its pre-existing form: this took effect from 11 pm on 31 December 2020, being the end of the transition period following the UK's withdrawal from the EU.[175] Article 67(3)(c) of the UK-EU Withdrawal Agreement[176] provides that the Regulation will continue to apply in respect of main proceedings opened on or before that date.

5.118 The Insolvency (Amendment) (EU Exit) Regulations 2019[177] (the 'Exit Regulations'), which give effect to Article 67(3)(c), repeal the vast majority of the provisions of the Regulation. As a result, the Regulation **has** been retained in an amended (and significantly narrowed) form (the 'Retained Regulation'), which governs insolvency proceedings that commenced after 11 pm on 31 December 2020.

5.119 The Retained Regulation maintains a modified version of the jurisdictional tests for the opening of insolvency proceedings, which now sit alongside the UK's domestic provisions

---

[172] Directive 2013/34/EU of the European Parliament and of the Council of 26 June 2013 on the annual financial statements, consolidated financial statements and related reports of certain types of undertaking (OJ L182, 29 June 2013, p 19).

[173] See Recital 88 of the Regulation. However, on 9 April 2008, the Juzgado de lo Mercantil No 1 referred this question to the CJEU in Case C-148/08 *Finn Mejnertsen v Betina Mandal Barsoe* [2008] OJ C142/19–20. The reference was not, however, ultimately determined by the CJEU.

[174] Professor Miguel Virgós, of the Universidad Autonoma of Madrid and Etienne Schmit, Magistrate, Deputy Public Prosecutor, Luxembourg.

[175] By virtue of Regulation 89 of the Civil Jurisdiction and Judgments (Amendment) (EU Exit) Regulations 2019, SI 2019/479, as amended by Regulation 5 of the Civil, Criminal and Family Justice (Amendment) (EU Exit) Regulations 2020, SI 2020/1493.

[176] [2019] OJ C383/1.

[177] The Insolvency (Amendment) (EU Exit) Regulations 2019, SI 2019/146, as amended by the Insolvency (Amendment) (EU Exit) (No. 2) Regulations 2019, SI 2019/1459 and the Insolvency (Amendment) (EU Exit) Regulations 2020, SI 2020/647, which give effect to Art 67(3)(c) of the Withdrawal Agreement [2019] OJ C383/1.

on jurisdiction. The Exit Regulations, Schedule 1 (Part 1, paragraphs 2 et seq) have the effect of *extending* the pre-existing grounds for jurisdiction to open insolvency proceedings in the UK. In its retained form:

(1) Article 1(1) of the Retained Regulation, as amended by the Exit Regulations, Sch, Part 1, paragraph 2(3), now provides that the grounds for jurisdiction to open insolvency proceedings set out in paragraph 1B of the Retained Regulation are *in addition to* any grounds for jurisdiction to open such proceedings which apply under UK insolvency law; and

(2) Articles 1A and 1B of the Retained Regulation, as also amended by paragraph 2(3), have the effect of extending the jurisdiction to open insolvency proceedings to cases where the debtor's COMI is in the UK or a Member State and there is an establishment in the UK.[178]

5.120 Accordingly, jurisdiction to open insolvency proceedings in respect of a company that is not incorporated in England and Wales—if it is incorporated in an EEA state or (wherever it is incorporated) has its COMI in the UK or an EU Member State (other than Denmark)—has been expressly preserved by the 1986 Act and 2016 Rules.[179]

5.121 The Explanatory Memorandum to the Exit Regulations[180] makes clear at paragraph 7.4 (*Jurisdiction*) that:

The instrument retains the existing jurisdiction enjoyed in the UK under the EUIR, which will sit alongside the UK's pre-existing jurisdictional tests. If the debtor's centre of main interests is in the UK, if the debtor has an "establishment" in the UK, or if a test set out in existing domestic insolvency law is met, then the UK courts will have jurisdiction to open proceedings. This ensures that there is no narrowing of the UK courts' jurisdiction following the UK's exit from the EU.

5.122 The principal impact of the Exit Regulations, Sch 1, Part 1, is that those provisions which rely on reciprocity between EU Member States have been repealed. Insolvency proceedings commenced in the UK (on or after **11 pm on 31 December 2020**) therefore no longer enjoy automatic recognition in Member States. Likewise, **insolvency proceedings opened in EU Member States will not be automatically recognized and enforced in the UK.**

5.123 As will be explained in this chapter, given that the recognition and enforcement provisions in the Regulation relied heavily on reciprocal application between Member States,

---

[178] Eg, in the case of an English administration, para 111(1A) of Sch B1 to the 1986 Act now provides that a 'company' for purposes of Sch B1 includes (a) a company registered under the Companies Act 2006, (b) a company incorporated in a EEA state, or (c) a company not incorporated in an EEA state but with its COMI in an EU member state (other than Denmark) or in the UK: see Exit Regulations, Sch 1(2), para 44(b)(ii).

[179] The Retained Regulation continues to apply to insolvency proceedings commenced on or after the end of the transition period, but has no relevance to jurisdiction over an English company, for which jurisdiction to open insolvency proceedings applies *irrespective* of whether the company's COMI is in the UK. However, if the company's COMI is also within the UK ('COMI proceedings'), then the Retained Regulation would provide an *additional* basis for jurisdiction: see *Re Mederco (Cardiff) Ltd* [2021] EWHC 386 (Ch), para 58. 'COMI proceedings' are now defined by rule 1.2 of the 2016 Rules, as 'insolvency proceedings in England and Wales to which the EU Regulation applies where the centre of the debtor's main interests is in the United Kingdom'.

[180] <https://www.legislation.gov.uk/uksi/2019/146/memorandum/contents>

the UK Government expressed the view that it was not appropriate (or desirable) for the UK to continue the system unilaterally.[181] Absent such reciprocal application, it would have created an obligation for the UK to recognize incoming insolvency judgments from EU Member States, without any reciprocal recognition for UK insolvency proceedings in Member States.

General principle of recognition: Article 19

5.124 'Recognition of Insolvency Proceedings' is governed by Chapter II of the Regulation. Article 19 (*Principle*) is the core provision of the Regulation which provides a uniform rule for the immediate and automatic recognition of judgments opening insolvency proceedings in all EU Member States.

5.125 The concept of automatic recognition is explained by Recital (65) to the Regulation:

> This Regulation should provide for immediate recognition of judgments concerning the opening, conduct and closure of insolvency proceedings which fall within its scope, and of judgments handed down in direct connection with such insolvency proceedings. Automatic recognition should therefore mean that the effects attributed to the proceedings by the law of the Member State in which the proceedings were opened extend to all other Member States. The recognition of judgments delivered by the courts of the Member States should be based on the principle of mutual trust. To that end, grounds for non-recognition should be reduced to the minimum necessary. This is also the basis on which any dispute should be resolved where the courts of two Member States both claim competence to open the main insolvency proceedings. The decision of the first court to open proceedings should be recognised in the other Member States without those Member States having the power to scrutinise that court's decision.

5.126 Article 19(1) establishes the principle of immediate and automatic—throughout the EU—recognition of insolvency proceedings opened in accordance with the jurisdictional scheme of Article 3.[182] Article 19(1) provides that:

> Any judgment opening insolvency proceedings handed down by a court of a Member State which has jurisdiction pursuant to Article 3 *shall be recognised in all other Member States from the moment that it becomes effective in the State of the opening of proceedings*.
>
> The rule laid down in the first subparagraph shall also apply where, on account of a debtor's capacity, insolvency proceedings cannot be brought against that debtor in other Member States (emphasis added).

5.127 Recognition takes place from 'the time of the opening of proceedings'; being the time at which the judgment opening insolvency proceedings becomes effective, regardless of whether the judgment is final or not: Article 2(8). The time that the judgment becomes

---

[181] See the Explanatory Memorandum to the Exit Regulations, para 7, which explains that given that no reciprocal deal was concluded with the EU to replicate the system established by the Regulation, it was not appropriate to incorporate the existing Regulation into domestic law in its existing form.

[182] Jurisdiction is dealt with in ch 3 of this work (Scope and Jurisdiction).

effective is assessed by reference to the Member State in which the proceedings were opened.[183]

5.128 Thus, the Regulation affords immediate recognition of judgments concerning the opening, conduct, and closure of insolvency proceedings which fall within its remit. The general principle of recognition is based on the principle of mutual trust:

> It is indeed that mutual trust which has enabled not only the establishment of a compulsory system of jurisdiction which all the courts within the purview of the Regulation are required to respect, but also as a corollary the waiver by the Member States of the right to apply their internal rules on recognition and enforcement of judgments handed down in the context of insolvency proceedings.[184]

5.129 Recital 65 states, in consequence, that grounds for non-recognition should be reduced to the minimum necessary. This was confirmed by the CJEU in *MG Probud Gdynia sp z oo* decision.[185]

5.130 Courts in other Member States are not entitled to review the merits of the judgment opening main proceedings, even if a potential challenge is based on the misapplication of the Regulation.[186] In *Re Eurofood IFSC Ltd*,[187] the CJEU interpreted the predecessor to Article 19[188] as meaning that main proceedings had to be recognized by courts of other Member States without those courts being able to review the jurisdiction of the court of the opening state. A party wishing to challenge the court's determination of its jurisdiction was required to rely on the remedies provided in the laws of the Member State where the relevant proceedings were opened. Article 5 (*Judicial Review of the decision to open main insolvency proceedings*) now applies to any challenge, which makes specific provision for the debtor or any creditor to challenge the decision opening main proceedings on grounds of international jurisdiction: see further Chapter 3 of this work.

5.131 Article 19(2) provides that recognition of the proceedings opened pursuant to Article 3(1) (which are main proceedings) does not preclude the opening of proceedings by a court in another Member State pursuant to Article 3(2). The proceedings referred to in Article 3(2) are defined as 'secondary insolvency proceedings' (within the meaning of Chapter III of the Regulation).

5.132 Article 19(2) therefore confirms that the recognition of main proceedings does not preclude the subsequent opening of secondary proceedings in Member States, where the debtor has an establishment within the meaning of Article 2(10). It is possible that where main

---

[183] In the English law context, pre-Brexit, the judgment opening insolvency proceedings meant the making of a court order pursuant to which the debtor entered into the insolvency proceeding: eg, the making of a winding-up order, not the filing of the winding-up petition.
[184] See Case C-444/07 *MG Probud Gdynia sp z oo* [2010] BCC 453, para 28; C-341/04 *Re Eurofood IFSC Ltd* [2006] BCC 397, para 40; *Galapagos BidCo Sàrl v DE* [2022] IL Pr 17, para 35.
[185] [2010] BCC 453, paras 31–33.
[186] Case C-341/04 *Re Eurofood IFSC Ltd* [2006] BCC 397, para 38 et seq; C-116/11 *Bank Handlowy w Warszawie SA v Christianpol sp z oo* [2013] Bus LR 956, para 41; C-327/13 *Burgo Group SpA v Illochroma SA* [2015] 1 WLR 1046, paras 27–39; *Galapagos BidCo Sàrl v DE* [2022] IL Pr 17, para 35; see also the Irish case *Apperley Investments Ltd v Monsoon Accessorize Ltd* [2019] IEHC 523, paras 81–86.
[187] Case C-341/04 *Re Eurofood IFSC Ltd* [2006] BCC 397, para 38 et seq.
[188] Original Regulation, Art 16.

proceedings have been opened in a Member State other than that in which the debtor's registered office is situated, secondary proceedings may subsequently be requested in the Member State of the debtor's registered office.[189]

Effects of recognition: Article 20

5.133 Article 20 sets out the effects of the immediate and automatic recognition of the opening of insolvency proceedings. It distinguishes between the effects of recognition of main, territorial, and secondary proceedings.

5.134 Article 20(1) provides the basis for main proceedings having universal scope. It states that:

> the judgment opening insolvency proceedings as referred to in Article 3(1) shall, *with no further formalities,* produce the same effects in any other Member State as under the law of the State of the opening of proceedings, unless this Regulation provides otherwise and as long as no proceedings referred to in Article 3(2) are opened in that other Member State (emphasis added).

5.135 Recognition has its effects under Article 20(1) 'with no further formalities'. This means without any need to issue local proceedings to create such effects, or to comply with any local registration requirements (subject to the general provisions contained in Articles 24 to 29, addressed below). The 'effects' are not spelt out and depend on the law of the proceedings: the *lex concursus*.[190] Recital (66) makes clear that:

> The *lex concursus* determines all the *effects* of the insolvency proceedings, both procedural and substantive, on the persons and legal relations concerned. It governs all the conditions for the opening, conduct and closure of the insolvency proceedings (emphasis added).

5.136 As the Virgos-Schmit Report explains in paragraph 154 (see Appendix 2):

> From the time fixed by the law of the State of the opening, the judgment opening proceedings produces its effects with equal force in all [Member States]. The divestment of the debtor, the appointment of the liquidator, the prohibition on individual executions, the inclusion of the debtor's assets in the estate regardless of the State in which they are situated, the obligation to return what has been obtained by individual creditors after opening, etc, are all effects laid down by the law of the State of the opening which are simultaneously applicable in all [Member States].

5.137 For example, in the English law context, if (pre-Brexit) main proceedings had been opened in England by means of an administration order,[191] the mandatory statutory stay on execution by judgment creditors would have extended throughout the EU, subject to the exceptions set out in the Regulation.[192]

---

[189] C-327/13 *Burgo Group SpA v Illochroma SA* [2015] 1 WLR 1046, paras 27–39.
[190] As a matter of English law, such 'effects' would include, eg: the vesting of property in a trustee in bankruptcy, the replacement of the agency of directors of a company in liquidation with that of the liquidator, the statutory stay on creditors' remedies, etc.
[191] See further the commentary on Art 19 in ch 8 of this work.
[192] When considering analogous stay or moratorium provisions under other national laws, the qualification 'unless this Regulation provides otherwise' in Art 20(1), must include a reference to Art 18, which provides that

The limits of the (analogous) regime for recognition under the Credit Institutions Directive were considered by the UK Supreme Court in *Heritable Bank plc v Landsbanki Islands hf*.[193] The decision arose in the context of similar provisions contained in Directive 2001/24/EC,[194] which derive in significant part from the Insolvency Proceedings Regulation. The issue was the recognition and effect in Heritable's administration of any extinction of Heritable's claims as a matter of Icelandic insolvency law in Landsbanki's winding-up. The continued existence of those claims was critical to Heritable being able to rely on them as being available for set-off against Landsbanki's claims in its administration. This depended on the proper construction of the regime for recognition contained in Directive 2001/24/EC (and UK Regulations implementing the Directive).[195] Landsbanki, in effect, sought recognition in Heritable's Scottish law-governed administration of the discharge of Heritable's claims which had, as a matter of Icelandic law, occurred in Landsbanki's winding-up.

5.138

The Supreme Court rejected Landsbanki's contention that the Directive required the effects of Icelandic insolvency law on Heritable's claims lodged in (but subsequently withdrawn from) its winding-up to extend to Heritable's administration, holding that the claims subsisted for set-off purposes in Heritable's administration. The Court interpreted the recognition scheme of the Directive (as implemented) to mean that the discharge of a debt under the insolvency law of a Member State is effective only for the purpose of the creditor's right to a dividend in those proceedings, and does not have the effect of discharging it for all purposes.[196] The fact that Heritable was also subject to insolvency proceedings governed by the Directive was not critical to that conclusion (as Lord Hope made clear at [60]).

5.139

The recognition of main proceedings will be limited by the opening of secondary proceedings (if any) in accordance with Article 3(2). This is made clear by the final sentence of Article 20(1). It reflects the fact that main proceedings have universal effect and scope as regards the debtor's assets, wherever situated, whilst secondary proceedings protect local interests[197] and for this purpose the national law applies.[198] Thus, the effects of main

5.140

---

the effects of insolvency proceedings on a pending lawsuit or pending arbitral proceedings concerning an asset or right which forms part of a debtor's insolvency estate, shall be governed solely by the law of the Member State in which that lawsuit is pending or the arbitral tribunal has its seat: see further the commentary on Art 20 in ch 8 of this work.

[193] [2013] 1 WLR 725, para 44 et seq.

[194] Directive 2001/24/EC of 4 April 2001 on the reorganization and winding-up of credit institutions, OJ 2001 L125, p 15. The scope of application of the Regulation expressly excludes, *inter alia*, credit institutions (Art 1(2)(b)), dealt with separately under Directive 2001/24/EC. Directive 2001/24/EC differs from the Regulation in that it has effect throughout the European Economic Area (EEA), which includes Iceland. It also does not allow secondary proceedings.

[195] Directive 2001/24/EC was transposed into English law by the Credit Institutions (Reorganisation and Winding up) Regulations 2004, SI 2004/1045; post-Brexit, it exists in the form amended by the Credit Institutions and Insurance Undertakings Reorganisation and Winding Up (Amendment) (EU Exit) Regulations 2019, SI 2019/38.

[196] This conclusion was reached independently of the *Gibbs* rule, explained at para 5.106 above.

[197] However, Recital (40) points out that secondary proceedings can also assist in the administration of an 'estate' where it is too complex to administer as one unit, or where differences in the legal systems concerned are so great that difficulties arise from extending the effects deriving from the law of opening states to another state in which the assets are located.

[198] Art 7 (*Applicable law*); Art 3(2) (*International jurisdiction*). Notably, post-Brexit, section 436A of the 1986 Act—which contained a modified definition of 'property' to accommodate the restriction on what assets are covered by territorial and secondary proceedings under the Regulation—has been repealed by the Exit Regulations, reg 1(3), Sch, para 16.

proceedings do not extend to assets or legal relationships which are subject to the jurisdiction of the secondary proceedings. However, main proceedings may influence the conduct of secondary proceedings as a result of the co-ordination and subordination rules set out in the Regulation, to which secondary proceedings and, to a lesser extent, territorial proceedings opened prior to main proceedings, are subject (as to which see below).[199]

5.141 Territorial and secondary proceedings affect only the assets situated in the state opening those proceedings. It follows that their recognition pursuant to Article 19(1) does not lead to their effects being extended to property situated in other Member States. Their effects cannot be challenged in other Member States, but any restrictions on creditors' rights can only affect assets in another Member State if the relevant creditors consent: Article 20(2).

Public policy exception to recognition: Article 33

5.142 The recognition scheme under Articles 19 to 20 is based on a presumption that a judgment opening insolvency proceedings is valid. The only ground for opposing recognition is that the foreign judgment is contrary to the public policy of the recognizing state.[200]

5.143 Article 33 provides that a state may refuse to recognize insolvency proceedings where 'the effects of such recognition or enforcement would be *manifestly contrary to that State's public policy*, in particular its fundamental principles or the constitutional rights and liberties of the individual' (emphasis added). The Virgos-Schmit Report states in paragraph 206:

> Public policy operates as a general clause as regards recognition and enforcement, covering fundamental principles of both substance and procedure.
> Public policy may thus protect participants or persons concerned by the proceedings against failures to observe due process. Public policy does not involve a general control of the correctness of the procedure followed in another [Member] State, but rather of essential procedural guarantees such as the adequate opportunity to be heard and the rights of participation in the proceedings ...

5.144 Article 33 therefore sets a high threshold for non-recognition based on public policy grounds. The public policy exception was considered by the CJEU for the first time in *Re Eurofood IFSC Ltd*,[201] which effectively held that recourse to it will only be permitted in exceptional cases. The CJEU also confirmed that the case law relating to public policy under the Recast Judgments Regulation is transposable to the interpretation of (what is now) Article 33.[202]

5.145 Drawing on case law decided under the analogous public policy exception in the original precursor to the Recast Judgments Regulation,[203] the CJEU held that any perceived

---

[199] The final sentence of Recital (40) contemplates that the insolvency practitioner in main proceedings may request the opening of secondary proceedings 'where the efficient administration of the insolvency estate so requires'. The need for co-operation is emphasized in Recitals (48) and (49).
[200] Case C-341/04 *Re Eurofood IFSC Ltd* [2006] BCC 397, para 38 et seq.
[201] C-341/04 *Re Eurofood IFSC Ltd* [2006] BCC 397. See further the commentary on Art 33 in ch 8 of this work.
[202] At para 64; see also Case C-444/07 *MG Probud Gdynia sp z oo* [2010] BCC 453, para 34.
[203] The original 1968 Convention: Convention on Jurisdiction and the Enforcement of Judgments in Civil and Commercial Matters, signed in Brussels on 27 September 1968.

infringement of local public policy law would have to constitute 'a manifest breach of a rule of law regarded as essential in the legal order of the State in which enforcement is sought or of a right recognised as being fundamental within that legal order'. Further, in the procedural law context, the CJEU observed that it is a general principle of EU law that everyone is entitled to a fair legal process; which extends, in insolvency law, to the equality of arms principle.

The relevant conclusions were set out at [62] et seq: **5.146**

62. In the context of the Brussels Convention, the Court of Justice has held that, since it constitutes an obstacle to the achievement of one of the fundamental aims of that Convention, namely to facilitate the free movement of judgments, recourse to the public policy clause contained in Art. 27(1) of the Convention is reserved for exceptional cases (*Bamberski v Krombach* (Case C-7/98) [2000] E.C.R. I-1935; [2001] Q.B. 709, paras 19 and 21).

63. Considering itself competent to review the limits within which the courts of a Contracting State may have recourse to that concept for the purpose of refusing recognition to a judgment emanating from a court in another Contracting State, the Court of Justice had held, in the context of the Brussels Convention, that recourse to that clause can be envisaged only where recognition or enforcement of the judgment delivered in another Contracting State would be at variance to an unacceptable degree with the legal order of the State in which enforcement is sought inasmuch as it infringes a fundamental principle. The infringement would have to constitute a manifest breach of a rule of law regarded as essential in the legal order of the State in which enforcement is sought or of a right recognised as being fundamental within that legal order (*Bamberski v Krombach* (above), paras 23 and 37).

64. That case-law is transposable to the interpretation of Art. 26 of the regulation.

65. In the procedural area, the CJEU has expressly recognised the general principle of Community law that everyone is entitled to a fair legal process (*Baustahlgewebe GmbH v Commission of the European Communities* (Case C-185/95 P) [1998] E.C.R. I-8417, paras 20 and 21; *Netherlands and Van der Wal v Commission of the European Communities* (Joined Cases C-174/98 P and C-189/98 P) [2000] E.C.R. I-1; [2002] 1 C.M.L.R. 16, para.17; and *Bamberski v Krombach*, para.26). That principle is inspired by the fundamental rights which form an integral part of the general principles of Community law which the Court of Justice enforces, drawing inspiration from the constitutional traditions common to the Member States and from the guidelines supplied, in particular, by the European Convention for the Protection of Human Rights and Fundamental Freedoms, signed in Rome on November 4, 1950.[204]

66. Concerning more particularly the right to be notified of procedural documents and, more generally, the right to be heard, referred to in the referring court's fifth question, these rights occupy an eminent position in the organisation and conduct of a fair legal process. In the context of insolvency proceedings, the right of creditors or their representatives to participate

---

[204] The EU Charter of Fundamental Rights, which became binding on the EU with the entry into force of the Treaty of Lisbon in December 2009, is a modern codification consistent with the European Convention: see <http://ec.europa.eu/justice/fundamental-rights/charter/index_en.htm>.

in accordance with the equality of arms principle is of particular importance. Though the specific detailed rules concerning the right to be heard may vary according to the urgency for a ruling to be given, any restriction on the exercise of that right must be duly justified and surrounded by procedural guarantees ensuring that persons concerned by such proceedings actually have the opportunity to challenge the measures adopted in urgency.

> 67. In the light of those considerations, the answer to the fifth question must be that, on a proper interpretation of Art.26 of the Regulation, a Member State may refuse to recognise insolvency proceedings opened in another Member State where the decision to open the proceedings was taken in flagrant breach of the fundamental right to be heard, which a person concerned by such proceedings enjoys.

5.147 Significantly, the CJEU held further (at [68]) that the court faced with the decision whether to recognize the opening of proceedings must not apply the standard of its own procedural law to determine whether the proceedings were conducted appropriately, but may only examine whether a flagrant breach of the fundamental right to be heard occurred:

> 68. Should occasion arise, it will be for the referring court to establish whether, in the main proceedings, that has been the case with the conduct of the proceedings before the Tribunale civile e penale di Parma. In that respect, it should be observed that the latter court cannot confine itself to transposing its own conception of the requirement for an oral hearing and of how fundamental that requirement is in its legal order, but must assess, having regard to the whole of the circumstances, whether or not the provisional liquidator appointed by the High Court was given sufficient opportunity to be heard.

5.148 Public policy derives from national law, such that the concept does not necessarily have a uniform content throughout the EU (particularly in the substantive law context). One common public policy exception is the non-recognition by some jurisdictions of foreign tax laws. However, Article 2(12) of the Regulation expressly includes the tax and social security authorities of Member States within the definition of 'foreign creditor'; and Recital (63) refers expressly to the right of such authorities to lodge claims in each pending insolvency proceeding. It thus appears that the tax and social security claims of one Member State cannot be regarded as being within the Article 33 public policy exception in the courts of another state.

Proof of insolvency practitioner's appointment: Article 22

5.149 To facilitate a foreign insolvency practitioner (defined by Article 2(5) and identified in Annex B) to take timely and effective action in other Member States, Article 22 is aimed at ensuring that any local formal requirements to recognition under the local law are overridden. It establishes a simple means of providing proof of appointment, by a certified copy of the original decision appointing the insolvency practitioner, or by any other certificate issued by the court which has jurisdiction. The local jurisdiction can, however, require a translation of the relevant document into one or more of the local official languages.[205]

---

[205] Art 22, second paragraph; which goes on to make clear that no legalization or other similar formality is required. Art 22 derives from Art 2 of the 1990 Istanbul Convention. It was not thought necessary to establish a uniform model for the certificate attesting the appointment of the liquidator.

5.150 The practical importance of Article 22 is clear: it limits the costs that the insolvency practitioner will have to incur before acting outside the territory of the opening state and enables actions to be taken quickly and effectively in relation to assets situated in another Member State.

Publication and registration: Articles 24 to 29

5.151 An important element of a foreign insolvency practitioner's ability to rely on the automatic effects of the insolvency proceedings in other Member States, may be the existence of actual or constructive notice in such states of the proceedings or the appointment. For example, in English law the authority of agents to deal with third parties ceases from the date of the winding-up order, but it has been held that this only affects a third party abroad when he has notice of the court order.[206]

5.152 To this end, Articles 24 to 27 contain provisions for the establishment, interconnection, and accessing of insolvency registers. Article 24(1) imposes a mandatory obligation on Member States to establish and maintain in their territory one or several registers in which information concerning insolvency proceedings is published ('insolvency registers'). That information is required to be published as soon as possible after the opening of insolvency proceedings.

5.153 Article 24(2) requires such information to be made publicly available, subject to the conditions laid down in Article 27. It identifies a list of 'mandatory information' which is required to be included in the insolvency register; this includes, in particular, a statement whether the proceedings are main, territorial, or secondary proceedings. Member States are, however, expressly permitted to include other documents or additional information in their national insolvency registers, such as directors' disqualifications related to insolvency (Article 24(3)).

5.154 There is an exception to the publication requirements prescribed by Article 24(4), paragraph 1, in the case of individuals not exercising an independent business or professional activity, provided that known foreign creditors are informed, pursuant to Article 54 (and by reference to Article 24(2)(j)),[207] of the court before which and, where applicable, the time limit within which, a challenge of the decision opening insolvency proceedings is to be lodged in accordance with Article 5. If a Member State makes use of that exception, the insolvency proceedings cannot affect the claims of foreign creditors who have not received such information (Article 24(4), paragraph 2).

5.155 There is also a limitation imposed by Article 24(5) on the legal effects which information that is published in the insolvency registers may have: such information cannot have any legal effects other than those set out by the national law, as well as by Article 55(6) (time limit for lodging claims by foreign creditors).[208]

---

[206] *Re Oriental Bank Corp, ex p Guillemain* (1885) 28 Ch D 634.
[207] Pre-Brexit, the Member State liquidator's duty to inform creditors in other Member States under Art 54 was expressly preserved by the 2016 Rules, rule 21.6(2). Rule 21.6 has now been repealed by the Exit Regulations, Sch 1, para 106.
[208] Art 55(6) provides that the *lex concursus* is to determine the period in which creditors are required to lodge claims. However, it also expressly provides that foreign creditors are to be given not less than 30 days following the

5.156 Articles 25 to 27 make detailed provision for the establishment and interconnection of insolvency registers by the Commission under a decentralized system, and the conditions of access to the insolvency registers by Member States.

5.157 Article 28(1) is a key provision imposing a mandatory obligation on the insolvency practitioner or debtor in possession to request that notice of the judgment opening insolvency proceedings, and (where appropriate) the decision appointing the insolvency practitioner, be published in any other Member State where the debtor possesses an establishment. The publication is required to specify the insolvency practitioner appointed, and whether the jurisdiction rule applied is that under Article 3(1) or (2) (ie main or territorial proceedings).

5.158 Article 28(2) confers a power to request that such information is published in any other Member State where the insolvency practitioner or the debtor in possession deems it necessary in accordance with the publication procedures provided for in that Member State.[209]

5.159 Article 29(1) imposes a further mandatory obligation on an insolvency practitioner or debtor in possession to take all necessary measures to ensure registration of the opening of insolvency proceedings in other Member States in two situations: first, where it is required by the law of a Member State in which an establishment of the debtor is located and the establishment been entered into a public register; and secondly, where it is required by the law of a Member State in which immovable property belonging to a debtor is located. The specified registers are a land register, company register, or any other public register.

5.160 Article 29(2) then makes clear that registration in any other Member State (ie not falling within the circumstances identified in Article 29(1)) is permitted, provided that such registration is allowed by the state in which the register is kept.[210]

5.161 Neither publication nor registration is laid down as a condition precedent to recognition in the Regulation, and it is considered that neither should be regarded as such even when compulsory under the local law.

5.162 Article 54(1) also requires immediate individual notice to be given by the court of the Member State in which insolvency proceedings have been opened, or the insolvency practitioner appointed by that court, to inform immediately the known foreign creditors. Such individual notice is required to contain the information identified in Article 54(2). Again, compliance with this obligation is not stipulated to be a condition precedent to recognition under the Regulation.

---

publication of the opening of insolvency proceedings in the insolvency register; and further, that where a Member State relies on the Art 24(4) exception (cf individuals), the 30-day period runs from the time when a creditor is informed about the insolvency proceedings under Art 54.

[209] Prior to the UK's exit from the EU, the 2016 Rules, rule 21.16, required any notice published by a 'member State liquidator' under Art 28, in relation to insolvency proceedings concerning a company with an establishment situated in England and Wales, to be published in the Gazette. Rule 21.16 has now been repealed by the Exit Regulations, Sch 1, para 106.

[210] By Art 30, the costs of publication and registration under Arts 28 to 29 are to be regarded as costs and expenses incurred in the proceedings.

D. Recognition of Judgments under the Regulation

Recognition of judgments: Article 32

Article 32 deals with the recognition of judgments relating to the conduct and closure of insolvency proceedings and of judgments made in the framework of those proceedings. A significant body of authority concerning the predecessor to Article 32, being Article 25 of the Council Regulation (EC) 1346/2000 of 29 May 2000 on Insolvency Proceedings (the 'Original Regulation'), has considered its interpretation. Such decisions will continue to be relevant to the application of Article 32, since the provisions are materially identical.[211]

5.163

Article 32(1) covers three types of judgment, which are required to be automatically recognized in other Member States with no further formalities. These are:

5.164

(1) Judgments handed down by a court whose judgment concerning the opening of proceedings is recognized in accordance with Article 19, and which concern the course and closure of insolvency proceedings, as well as compositions[212] approved by that court;

(2) Judgments 'deriving directly from the insolvency proceedings and which are closely linked with them',[213] even if they were handed down by another court;[214]

(3) Judgments relating to preservation measures[215] taken after the request for the opening of insolvency proceedings or in connection with it. The judgment relating to preservation measures is effective from the moment a request for the

---

[211] There is one non-administrative change: Art 25(3) of the Original Regulation contained a saving for judgments which 'might result in a limitation of personal freedom or postal secrecy', which no longer appears in Art 32. The Virgós-Schmit Report, para 193 described the right of postal secrecy as 'an area which relates directly to fundamental rights'. Although there is an argument that the removal of Art 25(3) from the Regulation was deliberately intended to remove the postal secrecy exception, since the right of postal secrecy is enshrined as a fundamental right in the constitutions of many Member States, the better view is that circumstances which would have justified refusal of recognition under Art 25(3) will similarly justify refusal of recognition under the public policy exception in Art 33. Notably, the Art 25(3) saving was not moved to the preamble to the Regulation (as occurred in other instances where text in the main body of the Original Regulation was removed).

[212] Pre-Brexit, this would appear to have captured an English scheme of arrangement under Part 26 of the Companies Act 2006 proposed by an administrator under the 1986 Act, Sch B1, para 49(3), even though the same scheme sanctioned outside of formal insolvency proceedings would not have fallen within the scope of the Regulation: not being identified in Annex A, as recognized in *Re Rodenstock GmbH* [2011] Bus LR 1245, *Re Magyar Telecom BV* [2014] BCC 448, and a consistent line of subsequent English authority. By contrast, post-Brexit, if the Regulation had not ceased to have application (in its pre-existing form), then according to English first instance authority a restructuring plan under Part 26A of the 2006 Act would have satisfied the Article 1(1) (*Scope*) definition of insolvency proceedings: *Re Gategroup Guarantee Ltd* [2021] BCC 549, per Zacaroli J, paras 104–37. The broader effect of *Gategroup* (irrespective of Brexit), if upheld by future courts, is that Part 26A restructuring plans would be excluded from the scope of the Recast Judgments Regulation and (as was the issue in *Gategroup*) the Lugano Convention on Jurisdiction and Enforcement of Judgments in Civil and Commercial Matters 2007.

[213] A formulation closely tracking that adopted in C-133/78 *Gourdain v Nadler* [1979] ER 733, para 4, which decided that proceedings commenced in a court not specializing in bankruptcy can still be bankruptcy proceedings if they 'derive directly from the bankruptcy' and are 'closely connected' with the bankruptcy. For further consideration of this formulation, see paras 5.169–5.183 immediately below.

[214] Such a court can be in the same or even a different Member State as the court seized of the insolvency proceedings: C-339/07 *Seagon v Deko Marty Belgium NV* [2009] 1 WLR 2168, 2186 per Advocate General Ruiz-Jarabo Colomer, para 67.

[215] Such measures take their character from the nature of the right they serve to protect and therefore fall outside the scope of the Judgments Regulation: see the Virgós-Schmit Report, para 199; further, C-143/78 *De Cavel v De Cavel* [1979] ECR 1055, which was a case concerning the matrimonial property exclusion to the original 1968 Convention.

5.165 There are (at least) three important consequences of Article 32(1). First, it follows from the fact of automatic recognition that if the same issue is pending before courts in two different Member States, both of which would otherwise have jurisdiction, the first judgment in time ought to prevail, since the other court will be bound to recognize it.[217]

5.166 Secondly, the inclusion in Article 32(1) (second para) of judgments deriving directly from insolvency proceedings (the meaning and import of which is considered in paragraphs 5.169–5.183), has the significant consequence that it ought to be possible for such a judgment to be eligible for automatic recognition and enforcement in all Member States, even where the judgment has been given in default of appearance, provided that the defendant was served with the relevant document(s) instituting proceedings in sufficient time to enable the defendant to defend the proceedings.[218] If correct, it would lie in contrast to the position under English common law, as established by the Supreme Court decision in *Rubin v Eurofinance SA*,[219] considered in Section B above.

5.167 Thirdly, it follows from the limited grounds on which recognition can be refused, that a judgment falling within Article 32(1) cannot be reviewed as to its substance in a court of the Member State in which recognition or enforcement is sought. Matters of substance must be raised before the courts of the Member State in which proceedings are opened.[220] Moreover, the court of the recognizing state may not impugn the jurisdiction of the court of the opening state.[221] That challenge must also be taken in the state in which proceedings are opened (to which, as noted, Article 5 may have application). Recognition of judgments is, of course, subject to the public policy exception under Article 33 (see paragraphs 5.142–5.148).[222]

Enforcement: interaction with the Recast Judgments Regulation

5.168 As noted, recognition of the judgments identified in Article 32 is automatic. However, subsequent enforcement of such judgments is required to take place in accordance with Articles 39 to 44 and 47 to 57 of the Recast Judgments Regulation: Article 32(1) (first paragraph).

---

[216] Virgós-Schmit Report, para 198.
[217] C-649/13 *Comité d'entreprise de Nortel Networks SA and others v Rogeau* [2016] QB 109. Where there is a conflict of jurisdictions under the Regulation, the general rule is that it is the first judgment in time which prevails: see eg *Re X* [2014] ILPr 35 in the context of the opening of main proceedings.
[218] See Recast Judgments Regulation, Arts 45(1)(b) and 46.
[219] [2013] 1 AC 236 (SC); English private international law does not permit enforcement of a foreign judgment delivered in default of appearance in transaction avoidance proceedings, even where the judgment was delivered by the bankruptcy court whose jurisdictional competence would be recognized at common law.
[220] Virgós-Schmit Report, para 202(1).
[221] Virgós-Schmit Report, para 202(2); see Case C-341/04 *Re Eurofood IFSC Ltd* [2006] BCC 397, para 38 et seq; C-116/11 *Bank Handlowy w Warszawie SA v Christianpol sp z oo* [2013] Bus LR 956, [41]; C-327/13 *Burgo Group SpA v Illochroma SA* [2015] 1 WLR 1046, paras 27–39; *Galapagos BidCo Sàrl v DE* [2022] IL Pr 17, para 35; see also the Irish case *Apperley Investments Ltd v Monsoon Accessorize Ltd* [2019] IEHC 523, paras 81–86.
[222] See also the commentary on Art 33 in ch 8 of this work.

Judgments outside the Regulation: the 'dovetailing' principle

Furthermore, Article 32(2) provides that the recognition and enforcement of judgments not falling within paragraph 1 shall be governed by the Recast Judgments Regulation (to the extent it applies to the relevant judgment). **5.169**

Articles 32(1) (second paragraph) and 32(2) reflect a principle underpinning both instruments which is of long standing: the Regulation and the Recast Judgments Regulation[223] are intended to be mutually exclusive, but also to 'dovetail almost completely with each other … [t]o avoid, as far as possible, leaving lacunae between the scope of the two [regulations]'.[224] It means that there should be no gap between matters covered by both instruments. The dovetailing principle derives support from the *travaux préparatoires* for the Original Regulation, and has been endorsed by the CJEU: see eg *Nickel & Goeldner Spedition GmbH v 'Kintra' UAB*;[225] *Comité d'entreprise de Nortel Networks SA v Rogeau*.[226] At least in theory, it is intended to ensure that both instruments constitute a complete and comprehensive regime for all civil proceedings. **5.170**

The Recast Judgments Regulation applies in 'civil and commercial matters', and does not apply to 'bankruptcy, proceedings relating to the winding-up of insolvent companies or other legal persons, judicial arrangements, compositions and analogous proceedings': see Article 1(2)(b). As noted, it is well established that Article 1(2)(b) of the Recast Judgments Regulation should be construed so as to dovetail with the Regulation, leaving no gaps between the two instruments. On this approach, the carve-out in Article 1(2)(b) only applies to proceedings which fall within the Regulation. **5.171**

The 'dovetailing' principle is relevant to two elements of the Regulation: jurisdiction and recognition. First, it is relevant to the jurisdictional rule prescribed by Article 6, which accords jurisdiction to the courts of the opening Member State 'for any action which *derives directly from* the insolvency proceedings *and is closely linked* with them, such as avoidance actions' (emphasis added). Secondly, as noted, it is reflected in Article 32 which governs which judgments benefit from the principle of automatic recognition within the EU. **5.172**

The language of the '*Gourdain* test'[227] adopted in both Articles 6 and 32 is conjunctive. Article 32 thus requires both criteria of 'direct derivation' from *and* 'close link' with the insolvency proceedings to be satisfied. This formulation does not reprise the reference in Article 6 to an avoidance action as an example of a judgment which would benefit from the **5.173**

---

[223] As originally conceived, the principle related to the original 1968 Convention.
[224] Schlosser Report on the Convention of 9 October 1978 on the association of the Kingdom of Denmark, Ireland and the United Kingdom of Great Britain and Northern Ireland to that Convention and to the protocol on its interpretation by the Court of Justice [1979] OJ C59/91, para 53. Recognizing that this intention was expressed in the context of the failed Bankruptcy Convention, it was nevertheless expressly confirmed by Briggs J in *Re Rodenstock GmbH* [2011] Bus LR 1245, para 47 and David Richards J in *Fondazione Enasarco v Lehman Brothers Finance SA* [2014] EWHC 34 (Ch), para 28. More recently, it has been upheld by the English courts in *ING Bank NV v Banco Santander SA* [2020] EWHC 3561 (Comm), per Cockerill J, para 142 and *Emerald Pasture Designated Activity Co v Cassini SAS* [2021] IL Pr 35, per Zacaroli J, para 19—although, as explained below, its application in practice can be more complex.
[225] [2015] QB 96, para 21.
[226] [2015] BCC 490, para 26.
[227] As noted, the formulation tracks the category of judgments described by the CJEU in C-133/78 *Gourdain v Nadler* [1979] ER 733, para 4, which were held should be excluded from the scope of the 1968 Convention.

automatic recognition rule, but it is clear from Article 6 that the draftsman contemplated that, at least in principle, an action bearing the features which typically form part of avoidance actions in insolvency law should be treated as falling within Article 32(1).[228]

5.174 Beyond this, the Regulation does not attempt to identify the further categories of proceedings or judgments which might be characterized as deriving directly from insolvency proceedings. Some (limited) amplification of this category of proceedings (and it should follow, judgments granted in them) is contained in Recital (35):

> ... Such actions should include avoidance actions against defendants in other Member States and actions concerning *obligations that arise in the course of the insolvency proceedings*, such as advance payment for costs of the proceedings. In contrast, actions for the performance of the obligations under a contract concluded by the debtor prior to the opening of the proceedings do not derive directly from the proceedings. Where such an action is related to another action based on general civil and commercial law, the insolvency practitioner should be able to bring both actions in the courts of the defendant's domicile if he considers it more efficient to bring the action in that forum. This could, for example, be the case where the insolvency practitioner wishes to combine *an action for director's liability on the basis of insolvency law* with an action based on company law or general tort law (emphasis added).

5.175 The distinction between judgments falling within Article 32(1), and those granted in ordinary commercial proceedings which happen to arise in the course of an insolvency, is not always straightforward. In more recent cases, the courts have approached the matter by asking the following question: 'Does the basis of the action find its source in the common rules of civil and commercial law or in the rules specific to insolvency proceedings?'[229] Put differently, the decisive criterion is not the procedural context of which the action forms part, but its *legal basis*.[230]

5.176 The English court has recognized that the *Gourdain* test, as now embodied in Articles 6 and 32, can be difficult to apply.[231] In certain cases, it will be clear that the relief sought is only available as a result of applicable insolvency law, and not as part of the general law.[232] In other cases, the mere fact that proceedings are brought by the office-holder will not of itself be sufficient. The issue has generated a substantial volume of case law, both at CJEU level and before the national courts.

---

[228] This interpretation is supported by Recital (6), which—in introducing Art 32—refers to judgments in proceedings which fall under Art 6.
[229] Eg: *Tünkers France v Expert France* [2018] IL Pr 7, para 22; C-535/17 *NK v BNP Paribas Fortis NV* [2019] IL Pr 10, para 28; *Re MF Global* [2015] EWHC 2319 (Ch), per David Richards J, para 43; *Valach v Waldviertler Sparkasse Bank AG* [2018] IL Pr 9, para 29.
[230] *ING Bank NV v Banco Santander SA* [2020] EWHC 3561 (Comm), per Cockerill J, para 176; *Emerald Pasture Designated Activity Co v Cassini SAS* [2021] IL Pr 35, per Zacaroli J, paras 25 and 45.
[231] *ING Bank NV v Banco Santander SA* [2020] EWHC 3561 (Comm), per Cockerill J, para 152.
[232] Under English insolvency law, actions under sections 236, 238, or 239 of the 1986 Act in principle satisfy the *Gourdain* test: on section 236, see *Re Akkurate Ltd* [2021] Ch 73, per Vos C, [59]; on section 238, see *Byers v Yacht Bull Corp* [2010] 2 BCLC 169. Likewise, a claw-back action brought by a liquidator under section 423 will likely satisfy the test: C-295/13 *H (Liquidator of GT GmbH) v HK* [2015] OJ C46/9. An order under section 366 for an inquiry into a bankrupt's dealings and property has been held by the Supreme Court of the Netherlands to derive directly from bankruptcy law: *Handelsveem BV v Hill* [2011] BPIR 1024.

CJEU case law

There have been a number of cases in which the CJEU has found that the relief sought was based solely on the provisions of the applicable insolvency law.[233] Where proceedings related to the exercise by the office-holder of a power for the benefit of creditors, the extent of the powers demonstrated the necessary connection to the conduct of the insolvency proceedings.[234]

5.177

A claw-back action brought by an office-holder will likely fall within the Regulation, even though the relevant cause of action was capable of being asserted without formal insolvency proceedings being commenced.[235] However, where such an action is brought in circumstances where the (insolvent) debtor is not subject to insolvency proceedings, it will most likely fall outside the Regulation.[236]

5.178

Equally, there have been a number of cases in which the CJEU has found that an action brought by office-holders in the context of an insolvency proceeding did not bear a sufficient connection to the insolvency.[237] The fact that the claim was originally conferred on the office-holder by applicable insolvency law, will not necessarily mean that the exception applies following its assignment to a creditor.[238] Significant factors will be whether the assignee is able freely to decide in their own interest whether to pursue the claim (rather than the collective interest of creditors), and would be entitled to retain the proceeds.

5.179

English case law

Cases in which the English courts have considered the application of the *Gourdain* test have typically involved challenges to the jurisdiction of the English court. Examples of claims or applications brought by an office-holder which were held to arise under the general law and did not satisfy the *Gourdain* test, have been for a declaration as to the beneficial ownership of a yacht[239] and for an order for sale of a foreign property registered in the bankrupt's name.[240]

5.180

In the financial context, a claim for declarations as to the borrower's obligations under a facilities agreement, which related to the effects of a French *sauveguarde* proceeding, was

5.181

---

[233] Eg: C-133/78 *Gourdain v Nadler* [1979] ER 733; *Seagon v Deko Marty Belgium NV* [2009] 1 WLR 2168 (German liquidator's action to set aside transfer of money into the account of a Belgian company under German Insolvency Code); C-328/12 *Schmid v Hertel* [2014] 1 WLR 633 (avoidance action where defendant was in a third (non-EU) country); C-111/08 *SCT Industri v Alpenblume* [2010] Bus LR 559; C-649/16 *Valach v Waldviertler Sparkasse Bank AG* [2018] IL Pr 9 (tort action against creditors arising out of their conduct in voting on a restructuring plan).

[234] C-111/08 *SCT Industri v Alpenblume* [2010] Bus LR 559 (Swedish action to confirm alleged invalidity of share transfer in the proximity of insolvency).

[235] C-295/13 *H (Liquidator of GT GmbH) v HK* [2015] OJ C46/9 (liquidator's claim against company director for payments made after the onset of insolvency).

[236] Case C-337/17 *Feniks sp z oo v Azteca Products & Services SL* [2019] IL Pr 1.

[237] Eg: C-292/08 *German Graphics Graphische Maschinen GmbH v Schee* [2009] ECR I-8421(action based on reservation of title clause); C-157/13 *Nickel & Goeldner Spedition GmbH v 'Kintra' UAB* [2015] QB 96 (debt action); C-641/16 *Tünkers France v Expert France* [2018] IL Pr 7; C-535/17; *NK v BNP Paribas Fortis NV* [2019] IL Pr 10 (action against third party causing loss to general body of creditors); C-198/18 *CeDe Group AB v KAN sp z oo* [2020] 1 WLR 2871 (action for payment of goods).

[238] C-213/10 *F-Tex SIA v Lietuvos-Anglijos UAB 'Jadecloud-Vilma'* [2013] Bus LR 232.

[239] *Byers v Yacht Bull Corp* [2010] 2 BCLC 169.

[240] *Ashurst v Pollard* [2001] Ch 595 (CA), following the earlier decision in *Re Hayward* [1997] Ch 45 (concerning a similar fact pattern).

eld to exist independently of and prior to the *sauveguarde*—consequently not satisfying the *Gourdain* test.[241]

5.182 In other commercial cases which have been decided to contrary effect, it has been held that a claim relating to negotiations and a settlement between the claimants and the Dutch trustee, which was the direct consequence of the trustee's exercise of powers under Dutch insolvency law to conduct the insolvency proceedings, bore the necessary connection with the insolvency proceedings.[242] Similarly, proceedings challenging a Swiss liquidator's rejection of a claim were sufficiently connected to the Swiss liquidation, not least because the challenge could only arise under Swiss insolvency law and formed an integral part of the liquidation.[243]

5.183 In a more complex case, the bank's interest claims under various finance agreements entered into with a Spanish company in liquidation, were pursued against a (solvent) third party which had subsequently assumed the Spanish company's liabilities.[244] Cockerill J held (*obiter*) that the scope of the assumption of the respondent's liabilities, which formed the legal basis of the claim, depended upon the effect of Spanish insolvency law. Accordingly, she concluded that the claim derived directly from the Spanish liquidation.[245]

E. Enforcement of the Rights and Powers of Insolvency Practitioners

Powers of the insolvency practitioner: Article 21

5.184 Article 21(1) provides, subject to very important exceptions, that the insolvency practitioner appointed by a court which has jurisdiction under Article 3(1), may exercise 'all the powers conferred on it, by the law of the State of opening of proceedings, in another Member State'. The insolvency practitioner's substantive powers will be determined by the law of the state of the proceedings in respect of which he has been appointed. Likewise, his obligations are determined by the law of the same state. It is likely that the manner in which those powers may be exercised must be in accordance with the relevant local law.[246]

5.185 Thus, in the case of main proceedings opened in eg France, unless and to the extent one of the exceptions applies, the powers of the insolvency practitioner, as determined in accordance with applicable French law, will automatically be exercisable in all other Member States.

5.186 Article 21(1) specifically mentions the insolvency practitioner's power to remove the debtor's assets from the territory of the Member State in which they are situated, subject to

---

[241] *Emerald Pasture Designated Activity Co v Cassini SAS* [2021] IL Pr 35, per Zacaroli J, paras 45–52.
[242] *Polymer Vision R&D Ltd v Van Dooren* [2012] IL Pr 14, per Beatson J.
[243] *Fondazione Enasarco v Lehman Brothers Finance SA* [2009] 1 WLR 2168, per David Richards J.
[244] *ING Bank NV v Banco Santander SA* [2020] EWHC 3561 (Comm), per Cockerill J.
[245] Paragraphs 184–91.
[246] This follows from the language of Art 18(3) (considered below). It is also consistent with the approach adopted by the English High Court in *Aria Inc v Credit Agricole Corporate and Investment Bank* [2014] EWHC 872 (Comm), per Leggatt J, para 60, which applied English law to procedural matters in relation to Greek insolvency proceedings.

Article 8 (third parties' rights in rem) and Article 10 (reservation of title) (as to which, see below).

The main exceptions built into Article 21(1) are the existence of local proceedings or of any preservation measure (which would have contrary effect) further to a request for the opening of insolvency proceedings. In either case, the effect of the local proceedings or preservation measure would be to negate the exercise of the powers of the insolvency practitioner appointed in the main proceedings. The limitation based on the existence of local proceedings mirrors the restriction on the effects of recognition of the main proceedings in Article 20(1). **5.187**

In addition to the general exceptions to situations where the powers can be exercised, there are also important restrictions in those situations where the powers can be exercised: **5.188**

(1) Article 21(3) provides that the insolvency practitioner must comply with the law of the Member State within whose territory he intends to act, in particular with regard to procedures for the realization of assets. It also makes clear that the powers exercisable by the insolvency practitioner in other Member States there do not include 'coercive measures' (unless so ordered by a court of that Member State) or the right to rule on legal proceedings or disputes;[247]
(2) As noted, Article 21(1) expressly subjects the power to remove property in another Member State to Articles 8 and 10.

The restriction on the use of coercive measures pursuant to the law of the main proceedings means that the insolvency practitioner may himself wish to request the opening of secondary proceedings in order to make use of coercive measures under local law. He has the right to do so under Article 37(1)(a). **5.189**

Any party who, under the local law, has power to request the opening of insolvency proceedings, can also try to stop property being removed by the insolvency practitioner in the main proceedings by requesting the opening of secondary proceedings in the state in which the property is located: Articles 37 and 38. **5.190**

Article 8 preserves the position of rights in rem, ie proprietary rights.[248] It provides that the opening of insolvency proceedings shall not affect the rights in rem of creditors or third parties in relation to assets of the debtor situated in another Member State. Article 8(2) sets out particular examples of rights in rem which include, amongst others, liens and mortgages. The absence of a definition appears to be deliberate and designed to leave the question of what constitutes a right in rem to the law of the Member State where the assets in question are located. **5.191**

It should be noted, however, that rights in rem are not entirely immune from the effect of proceedings to which the Regulation relates. If, for example, the law of the Member State **5.192**

---

[247] See the commentary on Art 21(3) in ch 8 of this work.
[248] The effect of the Regulation on cross-border security rights (and in particular, Art 8) is dealt with in ch 6 of this work; this chapter contains only brief treatment of Arts 8 and 10, so far as relevant to Art 21. The importance of protecting creditors who have rights in rem in relation to the debtor's assets is expressly recognized in Recitals (22) and (68). The Regulation recognizes that such protection is crucial to banks and other lenders in the granting of credit.

where the assets are located imposes a stay on the enforcement of security following the commencement of a local insolvency proceeding, the office-holder in the main proceedings or any other person empowered to do so might request secondary insolvency proceedings to be opened in that Member State if the debtor has an establishment there. The secondary proceedings would be conducted according to local law and affect the rights of secured creditors with assets in that jurisdiction in the same way as in purely domestic proceedings.

5.193 Article 10 addresses reservation of title. Article 10(1) provides that the opening of insolvency proceedings against the purchaser of an asset shall not affect sellers' rights to that asset that are based on a reservation of title where, at the time of the opening of the insolvency proceedings, the asset is situated in a Member State other than the state of the opening of those proceedings. Accordingly, an effective reservation of title is also a limitation on the ability of the foreign office-holder to remove assets.

5.194 The Regulation does not provide any immunity from suit for the wrongful removal of or wrongful interference with property or contracts. So if a foreign office-holder appointed in main proceedings removes assets from another Member State which, unknown to him, are subject to third-party rights or reservation of title, the office-holder may still be personally liable and liability will not automatically be limited by reference to local statutory immunities. Accordingly, a foreign office-holder may run the risk of personal liability in other Member States.[249] If there is an establishment in the relevant Member State, it may be necessary or useful for the office-holder to commence or procure secondary proceedings in the state where relevant assets are situated (as above, pursuant to Articles 37 to 38).

5.195 Article 10(2) provides that the opening of insolvency proceedings against the seller of an asset, *after* its delivery, shall not constitute grounds for rescinding or terminating the sale and shall not prevent the purchaser from acquiring title where, at the time of the opening of insolvency proceedings, the asset sold is situated in a Member State other than the State of the opening of proceedings. The buyer will not, therefore, be prevented from acquiring title where, at the time of the opening of the proceedings, the purchased asset is located within the territory of a different Member State.

Equal treatment of creditors—'hotchpot': Article 23

5.196 The universal scope of main proceedings, being that main proceedings should produce similar effects within all of the Member States, has been considered above. Article 23 (*Return and imputation*) seeks to guarantee the equal treatment of all the creditors of a single debtor.

5.197 Article 23(1) provides that where a creditor, after the opening of main proceedings, by any means (though in particular, through enforcement) obtains total or partial satisfaction of its claim out of assets of the debtor situated in another Member State, the creditor shall return what it has obtained to the office-holder, subject to Articles 8 and 10.

---

[249] Were the matter to have arisen under English law (pre-Brexit), the risk may have been significant, since liability in tort (delict) for removal of or interference with movables is, under English law, strict and not dependent on proof of knowledge or negligence.

5.198 This rule of 'return'[250] has as its clear aim the furtherance of the *pari passu* principle: a creditor who, after the opening of proceedings, obtains total or partial satisfaction of its claim individually breaches the principle of collective satisfaction on which insolvency proceedings are based. The office-holder may demand either the return of the assets or the equivalent in money.

5.199 The rule of 'return' operates expressly subject to Articles 8 and 10.[251] That is because a creditor who obtains satisfaction of claims secured by rights in rem created before the opening of insolvency proceedings, is realizing its own proprietary interest and does not enrich itself to the detriment of the estate. It therefore cannot be said to be acting in breach of the principle of collective satisfaction. However, in *Lutz v Bäuerle* (Case C-557/13)[252] the CJEU held that the predecessor to Article 8, combined with (the predecessor to) Article 16, could protect a right in rem acquired after the opening of main insolvency proceedings if the time for challenging the creation of the right in rem under the law governing its creation had passed.

5.200 Article 23(2) further (and expressly) reinforces that principle by providing that:

> In order to ensure the equal treatment of creditors, a creditor which has, in the course of insolvency proceedings, obtained a dividend on its claim shall share in distributions made in other proceedings only where creditors of the same ranking or category have, in those other proceedings, obtained an equivalent dividend.

5.201 The Virgós-Schmit Report, paragraph 175 identifies four rules which apply to distribution:

(1) No creditor may obtain more than 100 per cent of its claim;
(2) The total original amount of the claim (100 per cent of its initial value) is to be taken into account where a dividend has already been paid (and not the remaining amount);
(3) A claim is not taken into account in the distribution until such time as the creditors with the same ranking have obtained an equal percentage of satisfaction in those proceedings as that obtained by its holder in the first proceedings;
(4) The ranking or category of each claim is determined for each of the proceedings by the law of the State of the opening of proceedings, in which distribution is to be effected; hence the ranking of the same claim lodged in two different proceedings may not be the same in both.

Duty of co-operation: Articles 41 to 43

Co-operation and communication between insolvency practitioners

5.202 Article 41 imposes on insolvency practitioners a duty to co-operate with one another. Where there are at the same time main and either territorial or secondary proceedings, co-operation and information between insolvency practitioners is vital to ensure efficient

---

[250] Art 23 is titled 'return and imputation'. As noted at para 5.114 above, English domestic law recognizes a similar rule known as 'hotchpot'.
[251] See paras 5.191–5.195 above for a brief discussion of Arts 8 and 10.
[252] [2015] BCC 413.

insolvency administration across the Member States, and to avoid conflict or wasteful duplication.

5.203 Article 41(1) states that[253]

> The insolvency practitioner in the main insolvency proceedings and the insolvency practitioner or practitioners in secondary insolvency proceedings concerning the same debtor shall cooperate with each other to the extent such cooperation is not incompatible with the rules applicable to the respective proceedings. Such cooperation may take any form, including the conclusion of agreements or protocols.

5.204 The rationale behind the duty to co-operate is clear, and is explained in Recitals (48) and (49). The purpose behind having main and secondary proceedings is the effective preservation and realization of the total assets of the debtor within the EU. That can only happen if the office-holders co-operate with each other and share information. The CJEU has recognized that the duty to co-operate and communicate in Article 41 also[254]

> … makes it possible to avoid the risk of irreconcilable judgments by laying down rules on information and cooperation in cases of parallel insolvency proceedings.

5.205 Article 41(2) expressly identifies three categories of co-operation which insolvency practitioners are required, where relevant, to pursue, namely to:

> (a) as soon as possible communicate to each other any information which may be relevant to the other proceedings, in particular any progress made in lodging and verifying claims and all measures aimed at rescuing or restructuring the debtor, or at terminating the proceedings, provided appropriate arrangements are made to protect confidential information;

> (b) explore the possibility of restructuring the debtor and, where such a possibility exists, coordinate the elaboration and implementation of a restructuring plan;

> (c) coordinate the administration of the realization or use of the debtor's assets and affairs; the insolvency practitioner in the secondary insolvency proceedings shall give the insolvency practitioner in the main insolvency proceedings an early opportunity to submit proposals on the realization or use of the assets in the secondary insolvency proceedings.

5.206 In this way, Article 41(2)(c) demonstrates the dominant role of main proceedings. It may enable the office-holder in main proceedings to prevent the office-holder in secondary proceedings from doing something which would be detrimental to that which the main office-holder is attempting to achieve.[255] To this end, and in appropriate circumstances, he may seek a stay of the secondary proceedings pursuant to Article 46 (as to which, see below).

---

[253] Pre-Brexit, the 2016 Rules, Part 21, expressly provided for the duty of co-operation between insolvency practitioners appointed in English proceedings and in proceedings in other Member States (defined, by former rule 1.2(2) of the 2016 Rules, as a 'member State liquidator'). Part 21, rules 21.6 to 21.17, have now been repealed by the Exit Regulations, Sch 1, para 106.

[254] C-47/18 *Skarb Państwa Rzeczpospolitej Polskiej—Generalny Dyrektor Dróg Krajowych i Autostrad v Riel, acting as liquidator of Alpine Bau GmbH* [2019] ILPr 35, para 45 (expressly endorsing the observations of the Commission).

[255] Precisely this scenario occurred in *Re Alitalia Linee Aeree Italiane SpA* [2011] 1 BCLC 606. The English court considered the extent to which the office-holder in main proceedings may influence the conduct of secondary proceedings, in the context of the predecessor to Art 41. The opening of extraordinary administration proceedings in Italy (main proceedings) were followed by winding-up proceedings (secondary proceedings) in England. In respect of monies held in a bank account in England, the English court rejected the Italian administrator's contention

E. ENFORCEMENT OF RIGHTS AND POWERS OF INSOLVENCY PRACTITIONERS

5.207 The primacy of main proceedings is reinforced in Recital (48), which goes on to amplify what the legislator intended by the opportunity for an office-holder in main proceedings to intervene in secondary proceedings:

> (48) .... In order to ensure the dominant role of the main proceedings, the insolvency practitioner in such proceedings should be given several possibilities for intervening in secondary insolvency proceedings which are pending at the same time. In particular, the insolvency practitioner should be able to propose a restructuring plan or composition or apply for a suspension of the realization of the assets in the secondary insolvency proceedings. ....

5.208 Furthermore, Recitals (49) and (50) expand on the form which such co-operation may take, and how it is to be documented:

> (49) In light of such cooperation, insolvency practitioners and courts should be able to enter into agreements and protocols for the purpose of facilitating cross-border cooperation of multiple insolvency proceedings in different Member States concerning the same debtor or members of the same group of companies, where this is compatible with the rules applicable to each of the proceedings. Such agreements and protocols may vary in form, in that they may be written or oral, and in scope, in that they may range from generic to specific, and may be entered into by different parties. Simple generic agreements may emphasise the need for close cooperation between the parties, without addressing specific issues, while more detailed, specific agreements may establish a framework of principles to govern multiple insolvency proceedings and may be approved by the courts involved, where the national law so requires. They may reflect an agreement between the parties to take, or to refrain from taking, certain steps or actions.

> (50) Similarly, the courts of different Member States may cooperate by coordinating the appointment of insolvency practitioners. In that context, they may appoint a single insolvency practitioner for several insolvency proceedings concerning the same debtor or for different members of a group of companies, provided that this is compatible with the rules applicable to each of the proceedings, in particular with any requirements concerning the qualification and licensing of the insolvency practitioner.

5.209 Co-operation between insolvency practitioners and courts will evidently need to be documented and tailored according to the particular circumstances of, and issues arising in, the relevant proceedings. The final sentence of Recital (48) suggests that insolvency practitioners and courts should take into account 'best practices' for co-operation in cross-border insolvency cases, referring generally to principles and guidelines adopted by European and international organizations, and 'in particular the relevant guidelines prepared by the United Nations Commission on International Trade Law (Uncitral)'.

5.210 A number of informal guidelines have been proposed, which include the European Communication and Cooperation Guidelines published by INSOL Europe in July 2007. The latter guidelines were expressly referred to in the co-ordination protocol adopted in the *Nortel* case, with the result that the guidelines were relevant to the interpretation of

---

that the duty of co-operation required the English liquidators to pay those monies to employees (holding ordinary unsecured claims) to carry into effect a sale arranged by the Italian administrator in the main proceedings. Such assets fell to be applied in accordance with the local (English) law, as the law applicable to the secondary proceedings.

the parties' obligations under the protocol.²⁵⁶ There are a number of other well-known instances in which office-holders or courts from different Member States have co-operated in relation to proceedings pending in multiple jurisdictions: eg the *Lehman Brothers* case, which involved 17 jurisdictions worldwide, and the *Bernard Madoff* case, which involved eight jurisdictions worldwide.²⁵⁷

5.211 By Article 41(3), the duty of co-operation is extended to main, secondary, or territorial proceedings in which the debtor remains in possession of its assets.

Co-operation and communication between courts

5.212 Article 42 expressly imposes, for the first time in the history of the Insolvency Proceedings Regulation, a duty of co-operation and communication between the courts of Member States. It is stated to be for the express purpose of facilitating the co-ordination of main, territorial, and secondary proceedings concerning the same debtor (Article 42(1)). This duty codifies case law decided under the Original Regulation, which held that such an obligation was to be implied.²⁵⁸ In particular, in the *Bank Handlowy* case, the CJEU—founding its approach on Article 4(3) of the Treaty on Economic Union—held that (at [67]):

> The principle of sincere cooperation laid down in article 4(3) EU requires the court having jurisdiction to open secondary proceedings, in applying [Arts 33 and 34 of Original Regulation], to have regard to the objectives of the main proceedings and to take account of the scheme of the Regulation, which ... aims to ensure efficient and effective cross-border insolvency proceedings through mandatory coordination of the main and secondary proceedings guaranteeing the priority of the main proceedings.

5.213 Article 42(1) provides that a court before which a request to open insolvency proceedings is pending, or which has opened such proceedings, shall co-operate with any other court in the same position. The duty exists to the extent that such co-operation is not incompatible with the rules applicable to each of the proceedings. For that purpose, the courts are expressly empowered, where appropriate, to appoint an independent person or body acting on its instructions, provided that it is not incompatible with the rules applicable in the relevant jurisdictions.

5.214 In complying with this duty of co-operation, Article 42(2) makes clear that the courts, or any appointed person or body acting on their behalf, may communicate directly with, or

---

²⁵⁶ C-649/13 *Comité d'entreprise de Nortel Networks SA and others v Rogeau* [2016] QB 109; see the Opinion of Advocate-General Mengozzi, para 26.

²⁵⁷ For the approach of the Cayman Islands courts to cross-border co-ordination and protocols, see the summary in *Re Latam Finance Ltd,* Grand Court of the Cayman Islands (Kawaley J), 29 July 2020, paras 28–32.

²⁵⁸ *Bank Handlowy w Warszawie SA v Christianpol sp z oo* [2013] Bus LR 956, para 67; *Re Nortel Networks SA* [2009] BCC 343; *Re Stojevic* (Higher Regional Court, Vienna, 9 November 2004) 28 R 225/04. In *Nortel*, administration orders were made for 19 EMEA group companies—for which the main purpose was to facilitate a co-ordinated scheme with the Canadian and US companies for restructuring Nortel's global operations. Many of the entities were incorporated or had establishments in other Member States. To pre-empt the possibility of multiple secondary proceedings, the English court made orders which expressly acknowledged the administrators' ability to make payments to local creditors which would depart from the UK statutory scheme of distribution. Ultimately: (i) secondary insolvency proceedings were opened in respect of NNSA in France (see [2015] EWHC (Ch) 2506, per Snowden J, para 43); (ii) CVAs were promulgated in respect of other EMEA companies, it being recognized that the English court did not, in fact, have the power to disapply the statutory scheme of distribution (ibid, para 38); and (iii) the English court approved a global settlement encompassing the vast majority of worldwide claims ([2017] Bus LR 590).

request information or assistance directly from, each other provided that such communication respects the procedural rights of parties to the proceedings and the confidentiality of information. Further, the courts may comply with this duty of co-operation 'by any means that the court considers appropriate': Article 42(3). Article 42(3) identifies the following (non-exhaustive) categories of co-operation:

(a) co-ordination in the appointment of the insolvency practitioners;
(b) communication of information by any means considered appropriate by the court;
(c) co-ordination of the administration and supervision of the debtor's assets and affairs;
(d) co-ordination of the conduct of hearings;
(e) co-ordination in the approval of protocols, where necessary.

5.215 Article 43 extends the duty of co-operation and communication prescribed by Articles 41 to 42, to the direct and individual relationships between insolvency practitioners and courts.

5.216 Chapter V, Articles 56 to 77, contain provisions dealing expressly with insolvency proceedings of members of a group of companies.[259] Detailed provision is made for the duty of co-operation, communication, and co-ordination between insolvency practitioners and courts in proceedings concerning members of a group of companies.[260] Those provisions are set out and commented on in Chapter 8 of this work.

Exercise of creditors' rights: Article 45

5.217 Article 45(1) provides that any creditor may lodge its claim in the main proceedings and in any secondary proceedings.[261] Article 45(2) provides that:

> The insolvency practitioners in the main and any secondary insolvency proceedings shall lodge in other proceedings claims which have already been lodged in the proceedings for which they were appointed, provided that the interests of creditors in the latter proceedings are served by doing so, subject to the right of creditors to oppose such lodgement or to withdraw the lodgement of their claims where the law applicable so provides.

5.218 Finally, Article 45(3) provides that the insolvency practitioner in the main or secondary proceedings shall be entitled to participate in other proceedings on the same basis as a creditor, in particular by attending creditors' meetings.

---

[259] So far as relevant, pre-Brexit, the 2016 Rules, rules 2.11–2.15 made provision to reflect certain powers of member State liquidators in relation to groups of companies, primarily relating to applications to open 'group co-ordination proceedings'. Rules 2.11 to 2.15 have now been repealed by the Exit Regulations, Sch 1(4), para 106.

[260] Such provision is particularly pertinent in light of the *Nortel* proceedings, addressed above. For groups or sub-groups such as the EMEA Nortel entities, the express co-ordination provisions in Chapter V could now be directly tailored to co-ordinate proceedings opened in multiple jurisdictions.

[261] Prior to the UK's exit from the EU, the effect of Art 45 was reflected in the 2016 Rules, rule 21.8, in terms which facilitated the participation by a member State liquidator in English insolvency proceedings, in the same manner as enjoyed by creditors exercising rights in English insolvency proceedings. Rule 21.8 has now been repealed by the Exit Regulations, Sch 1, para 106. Sch 1 also makes extensive provision revoking the numerous references under the 2016 Rules to the rights which could formerly be exercised by a member State liquidator in English proceedings (as a deemed creditor).

5.219 The aim of Article 45 is evidently to facilitate creditors in exercising their rights to claim against the debtor in other proceedings relating to that debtor, as well as to permit the relevant office-holder to reinforce their influence in other proceedings to achieve the satisfaction of creditors' claims.[262] It follows that any provision of local law in a state in which secondary proceedings have been opened, which purports to restrict the lodging of claims to 'local creditors', would not be permissible. In an analogous context (right to request the opening of secondary proceedings), the CJEU has upheld a general principle of non-discrimination as between creditors.[263]

Staying the realization of assets in secondary proceedings: Article 46

5.220 Article 46 further demonstrates the primacy of main proceedings. Article 46(1) entitles the insolvency practitioner in main proceedings to request the court which opened secondary proceedings to stay the process of realization of assets. The court is required to stay the process on receipt of such request, but may require the insolvency practitioner in the main proceedings to take any suitable measures to guarantee the interests of the creditors in the secondary proceedings, as well as of individual classes of creditors. The court is entitled to reject the request only if it is manifestly of no interest to the creditors in the main proceedings. The stay may only be ordered for a period of up to three months, but is renewable for further three-month periods.

5.221 The powers of the local court in considering a request for a stay are therefore limited. The court does, however, have the power to require the insolvency practitioner in the main proceedings to ensure that the interests of the creditors in the secondary proceedings are protected. It is conceivable that responsive measures might involve some form of mechanism to ensure that local creditors as a whole, and each class of local creditors, are better off than they would have been in a liquidation.[264] As noted above, the general duty of sincere co-operation between main and secondary insolvency practitioners, upheld by the CJEU in the *Bank Handlowy* decision, applies equally in relation to the interpretation of Article 46.[265]

5.222 The insolvency practitioner in the main proceedings is similarly entitled to request that the stay be terminated, as may a creditor and the insolvency practitioner in the secondary proceedings: Article 46(2). If the application is made by a creditor or office-holder appointed in secondary proceedings, the test to apply is whether such an order is justified, in particular, by the interests of creditors in the main proceedings or secondary proceedings. The court thus appears to have a discretion as to whether to terminate the stay.

---

[262] The Virgós-Schmit Report, paras 235–40 deals with creditors' rights in some detail, by reference to the Convention.

[263] *Burgo Group SpA v Illochroma SA* [2015] 1 WLR 1046, paras 49 and 64.

[264] The measures could be analogous to those used in a series of cases which have come before the English courts: *Re Collins & Aikman Europe SA* [2006] BCC 861; *Re MG Rover España SA* [2006] BCC 599; *Re MG Rover Belux SA/NV* [2007] BCC 446. Art 46 confirms a decision of the Austrian Court of Appeal in Graz in *Collins & Aikman*, in the context of the Original Regulation, which held that the stay only operated on the process of liquidating assets and not the secondary proceedings as a whole: Oberlandesgericht, 20 October 2005, 3 R 149/05, NZI (Neue Zeitschrift für Insolvenz und Sanierung) 2006, vol 11, 660.

[265] *Bank Handlowy w Warszawie SA v Christianpol sp z oo* [2013] Bus LR 956, para 67.

Closure of insolvency proceedings: Articles 47 to 49

5.223 The insolvency practitioner in main proceedings is granted a power by Article 47(1) to propose a restructuring plan, a composition or a comparable measure, to enable secondary proceedings to be closed without the debtor entering into liquidation. It operates where the law of the Member State in which secondary proceedings have been opened allows for the proceedings to be closed in this way, and must be conducted in accordance with the procedure of the relevant Member State. The CJEU has held that the date at which insolvency proceedings are closed is determined by the *lex concursus*.[266]

5.224 Article 47(2) makes clear that any such restructuring plan or composition can only operate as an adjustment or modification of creditors' rights in relation to assets falling within the scope of secondary proceedings, subject to the consent of affected creditors. It provides that any restriction on creditors' rights, such as a stay of payment or discharge of debt, shall have no effect in respect of assets of a debtor that are not covered by those proceedings, without the consent of all creditors having an interest.

5.225 Article 48 addresses the impact of the closure of insolvency proceedings. It provides that the closure of insolvency proceedings shall not prevent the continuation of other insolvency proceedings concerning the same debtor which are still open at that point in time: Article 48(1). Article 48(2) also makes clear that the dissolution of a legal person or company by reason of insolvency proceedings in the Member State of that person's or company's registered office, will not take effect until any other insolvency proceedings concerning the same debtor have been closed, or the insolvency practitioner(s) in such proceedings have given consent to the dissolution.[267]

5.226 Where the insolvency practitioner in secondary proceedings succeeds in meeting all of the creditors' claims allowed in those proceedings and holds surplus monies or other assets, he is obliged to transfer that surplus to the insolvency practitioner in the main proceedings.

Conversion of secondary insolvency proceedings: Article 51

5.227 The insolvency practitioner in the main proceedings is further empowered by Article 51(1) to request that any secondary proceedings be converted into another type of insolvency proceedings listed in Annex A to the Regulation, provided that: (i) the conditions for opening that type of proceeding under national law are fulfilled, and (ii) the proposed type of proceeding is the most appropriate as regards the interests of local creditors and coherence between the main and secondary insolvency proceedings.

5.228 This follows the guidelines given by the CJEU in the *Bank Handlowy* case.[268] When considering any such request, the court of the Member State in which the secondary proceedings

---

[266] ibid, para 52.
[267] Art 48 addresses the problems experienced in *Re Eurodis Electron Plc* [2012] BCC 57, in which the company was dissolved in its country of incorporation (Belgium) at a time when English administration proceedings (main proceedings) remained extant. The English High Court (per Mann J) concluded that it was impossible to continue the English proceedings.
[268] *Bank Handlowy w Warszawie SA v Christianpol sp z oo* [2013] Bus LR 956.

have been opened, is expressly empowered to seek information from the insolvency practitioners involved in both proceedings.[269]

Preservation measures: Article 52

5.229 In order to preserve the debtor's assets during the period between the request for the opening of an insolvency proceeding and the decision on that application, the Regulation envisages the appointment of a temporary administrator. Article 52 provides that where the court of a Member State which has jurisdiction to open main proceedings pursuant to Article 3(1), appoints a temporary administrator to ensure the preservation of the debtor's assets, the temporary administrator is empowered to request any measures to secure and preserve any of the debtor's assets situated in another Member State, provided for under the law of that state. That order operates between the date of the application requesting the opening of insolvency proceedings and the judgment opening them.

5.230 The rationale behind Article 52 is contained in Recital (36). It explains that, both prior to and after the commencement of insolvency proceedings, preservation measures are important 'to guarantee the effectiveness of the insolvency proceedings'. It also stresses the importance of the availability of such measures from the perspective of main proceedings (in respect of assets situated in the territory of other Member States), as well as for an insolvency practitioner temporarily appointed *prior to* the opening of the main proceedings. In such case, the office-holder 'should be able, in the Member States in which an establishment belonging to the debtor is to be found, to apply for the preservation measures which are possible under the law of those Member States'.

5.231 This reflects the decision of the CJEU in *Re Eurofood IFSC Ltd* (referring to the predecessor to Article 52):[270]

> 57. In that respect, it should be noted that Art.38 of the Regulation must be read in combination with Art.29, according to which the liquidator in the main proceedings is entitled to request the opening of secondary proceedings in another Member State. That Art.38 thus concerns the situation in which the competent court of a Member State has had main insolvency proceedings brought before it and has appointed a person or body to watch over the debtor's assets on a provisional basis, but has not yet ordered that that debtor be divested or appointed a liquidator referred to in Annex C to the Regulation. In that case, the person or body in question, though not empowered to initiate secondary insolvency proceedings in another Member State, may request that preservation measures be taken over the assets of the debtor situated in that Member State.

5.232 The CJEU went on to hold that Article 38 did not apply to a situation where the court had appointed a provisional liquidator (identified in Annex C) and had divested the debtor of

---

[269] The 2016 Rules, rules 21.1 to 21.3 contained express provision for the situation where a 'member State liquidator' appointed in main proceedings (outside the UK) applied to the English court under Art 51 for conversion of winding-up proceedings of one kind into winding-up proceedings of another kind, or conversion of an IVA into bankruptcy or *vice versa*. Post-Brexit, those rules have been repealed by the Exit Regulations, reg 1(3), Sch, paras 46, 104–106.

[270] Case C-341/04 *Re Eurofood IFSC Ltd* [2006] BCC 397, ECJ (Grand Chamber).

control of the business, since such appointment opened the proceeding and gave rise to the right to apply to open secondary proceedings in the other Member State (under the predecessor to Article 37). The decision illustrates the difficulties inherent in determining whether a specific measure ordered after a request to open insolvency proceedings—such as the appointment of a provisional liquidator—is only a preservation measure or in fact qualifies as a judgment opening insolvency proceedings.

6

CROSS-BORDER SECURITY AND QUASI-SECURITY

A.	Introduction	6.01
B.	EU Legal Framework	6.11
	The purposes of the RR	6.11
	Insolvency proceedings to which the RR applies	6.14
	Articles which are of particular relevance to secured creditors	6.16
	Article 7	6.16
	Article 7(2)(b): The assets which form part of the estate	6.18
	Article 7(2)(d): The conditions under which set-offs may be invoked	6.19
	Article 7(2)(f): Stay of enforcement proceedings	6.22
	Articles 7(2)(g) and (h): Proof of debt	6.23
	Articles 7(2)(i) and (l): Distribution of proceeds (questions of priority)	6.25
	Article 7(2)(j): The effects of closure of insolvency proceedings, in particular by composition	6.28
	Article 7(2)(m): Rules relating to the voidness, voidability, or unenforceability of legal acts detrimental to the general body of creditors	6.29
	Other matters not expressly covered by Article 7(2)	6.34
	Article 8	6.35
	What is a right in rem?	6.42
	Both specific assets and collections of indefinite assets	6.46
	The right to dispose of assets and to obtain satisfaction from the proceeds	6.48
	Other rights expressly set out in Article 8	6.50
	CJEU case law	6.51
	Where is a secured asset located?	6.56
	Registered shares	6.58
	Book-entry securities	6.59
	Bank accounts	6.60
	European patents	6.62
	Copyrights	6.63
	Tangible assets	6.64
	Claims	6.65
	What does the time of the opening of proceedings means?	6.69
	What does 'shall not affect' mean?	6.74
	Relationship between Article 8 and Article 16	6.80
	Assets located in the United Kingdom	6.82
	Effects of insolvency proceedings opened in the UK on rights in rem over assets located in the EU	6.85
C.	UK Legal Framework	6.87
	Status of the RR in the United Kingdom	6.87
	Recognition of EU insolvency proceedings (and the impact on secured assets located in the UK) outside of the RR	6.92
	Common law	6.94
	Section 426 Insolvency Act 1986	6.99
	Cross-Border Regulations	6.103
D.	Practical Examples	6.110
	Example 1 (Spanish borrower with establishment in Ireland, assets in the EU, local law security)	6.110
	Issues arising: summary	6.111
	Issues arising: commentary	6.115
	Example 2 (Spanish borrower with establishment in Ireland, assets in the EU, Spanish law security)	6.135
	Issues arising: summary	6.136
	Issues arising: commentary	6.137
	Example 3 (Spanish borrower with establishment outside the EU, security over claims governed by EU law and non-EU law)	6.144
	Issues arising: summary	6.145
	Issues arising: commentary	6.149
	Example 4 (Spanish borrower, assets in the EU, impact of a restructuring proceeding that purports to release secured indebtedness)	6.154
	Issues arising: summary	6.155
	Issues arising: commentary	6.157
	Example 5 (German borrower with establishment in Spain, assets in the EU, impact of restructuring proceeding in Spain)	6.159
	Issues arising: summary	6.160
	Issues arising: commentary	6.162
	Example 6 (Spanish borrower, assets in the EU, impact of restructuring proceeding on intercreditor agreement)	6.164
	Issues arising: summary	6.165
	Issues arising: commentary	6.168
	Example 7 (German borrower, security over bank account held through the Irish branch of a German bank)	6.171
	Issues arising: summary	6.172
	Issues arising: commentary	6.173
	Example 8 (Spanish borrower, security over shares in an EU subsidiary, claw-back claim)	6.175

Issues arising: summary	6.176	in respect of a bank account in	
Issues arising: commentary	6.177	England)	6.181
Example 9 (Luxembourg borrower with		Issues arising: summary	6.182
establishment in Ireland, set-off rights		Issues arising: commentary	6.186

A. Introduction

The first part of this chapter deals with the impact of insolvency proceedings recognized by the RR on the rights of secured creditors with assets in the EU, particularly the rights of such creditors to enforce their security and participate in the relevant insolvency proceedings. The second part of this chapter deals briefly with the impact of such insolvency proceedings on the rights of secured assets with assets in the UK following the UK's withdrawal from the European Union, although a detailed consideration of this topic is outside the scope of this publication. The third part of this chapter includes some practical examples intended to show how the legal principles may work in practice. **6.01**

The following sections refer to the RR as currently in force, ie Regulation (EU) 2015/848 of the European Parliament and of the Council on insolvency proceedings. This new version has replaced the previous regulation (OR), Regulation 1346/2000, as of 26 June 2017.

Throughout this chapter, there are references to the rights and position of banks and other financial entities as secured creditors. The RR does not address the position of banks as a separate class of creditor but the position of banks under EU law does impact on the rights of secured creditors as a whole. In any event, as the holders of security will often include financial lenders in the context of commercial lending arrangements, this chapter refers to, and considers the impact of the RR on those financial lenders which hold security or quasi-security. **6.02**

As the RR does not apply to the insolvency procedures which can be commenced in respect of banks and other credit institutions (Article 1(2)), this chapter does not address the regime which applies to bank insolvencies under EU law. This regime is addressed in chapter 7 below. **6.03**

Instead, the chapter addresses, in particular: **6.04**

(a) the cross-frontier security rights of financial lenders which hold security over the assets of companies or persons who enter into insolvency proceedings regulated by the RR; and
(b) the effect of those insolvency proceedings on the lender' security interests.

This chapter identifies those Articles of the RR which are particularly relevant to the position of a financial lender as a secured creditor, addresses the interpretation of those provisions (including the identification of difficult points of construction), and considers the practical aspects and the issues which are likely to face financial lenders seeking to enforce security following the RR coming into force. **6.05**

As set out below, the basic principle, as Article 7(1) makes clear, is that the law of the place where insolvency proceedings are opened (the inelegantly termed 'state of the opening of proceedings') governs each of the sub-paragraphs which are set out in Article 7(2). Although choice of law questions are generally dealt with in chapter 4 above, this chapter looks at Article 7(1) in the context of security and quasi-security. As the judgment opening main proceedings is to produce the same effects in any other Member State as under the state of the opening of proceedings unless the RR provides otherwise (Article 19), main proceedings **6.06** opened in one Member State could potentially affect the secured creditor's rights to enforce its security in another Member State subject to the exceptions discussed below.

6.07 At the end of this first part of the chapter, nine hypothetical factual examples are set out. Together, these examples explore, from a practical perspective, some of the ways in which the RR may impact on the rights of secured creditors (or creditors with quasi-security). In each case, there is a brief description of the facts, a summary (by way of a number of brief statements) of the key issues raised, and a commentary on those issues.

6.08 So far as the authors are aware, there are only a few cases which touch upon the impact of the RR on the rights of secured creditors, including two decisions of the Court of Justice of the European Union (CJEU). In the light of the limited case law available on this issue, the analysis in this chapter merely reflects the authors' views. In many cases, the lack of clarity as to the meaning of relevant provisions of the RR means that further questions of interpretation are likely to be referred by national courts to the CJEU for a preliminary ruling.

6.09 The focus of the practical examples tends to be primarily, although not solely, on EU insolvency or enforcement procedures and on rights in rem which would be recognized as a matter of Member States' law.

6.10 In general, a secured creditor will be concerned with whether it can enforce its security in a particular jurisdiction and about the effect which the opening of insolvency proceedings in respect of the borrower will have on the lender's rights as secured lender. These overriding concerns can be broken down into a number of key questions which are explored through the practical examples in the final section of this chapter. In particular, a secured creditor may have the following questions:

(a) What impact will the opening of main proceedings have on the enforcement of security over assets located: (i) in the jurisdiction where those proceedings are opened; and (ii) in other Member States and, in particular, what will be the effect of the statutory moratorium on the enforcement of security which arises in main proceedings? (See Examples 1 and 2)

(b) Will a security agreement governed by the law of one Member State be recognised as creating a valid right in rem in another Member State for the purposes of Article 8? (See Example 2)

(c) Where is a secured asset (including for example, claims, shares, or a bank account) located for the purposes of the RR, and which court will determine this issue? (See Examples 3, 7, and 8)

(d) What impact will the opening of secondary proceedings have on the enforcement of security over assets located: (i) in the jurisdiction where those proceedings are opened; and (ii) in other Member States? (See Examples 1 and 5)

(e) In the case of either main or secondary proceedings, what will the effect be if different rules apply regarding the priority of secured and unsecured claims under: (i) the insolvency law of the jurisdiction where the insolvency proceedings are opened; and (ii) the law applicable to the relevant right in rem? (See Example 1)

(f) Could main proceedings have the effect of discharging secured liabilities and, if so, what effect will this have on the enforcement of security over assets located: (i) in the jurisdiction where those proceedings have commenced; and (ii) in other Member States? (See Example 4)

(g) What impact will main or secondary proceedings have on an intercreditor agreement between the secured creditors, particularly where that agreement is governed by a different law from that of the Member State in which the insolvency proceedings are commenced? (See Example 6)

(h) How will the opening of main or secondary proceedings affect rights of set-off and which law will determine whether such a right exists? (See Example 9)

B. EU Legal Framework

The purposes of the RR

As the recitals demonstrate, the RR attempts to strike a balance between giving extra-territorial effect to the main proceedings and the need to preserve the predictability of secured transactions entered into in accordance with the laws of a particular Member State.[1]   6.11

In particular the recitals reveal that the purposes of the RR are: 6.12

(a) to enable cross-border insolvency proceedings to operate efficiently and effectively;
(b) to provide for co-ordination of the measures to be taken regarding an insolvent debtor's assets;
(c) to avoid forum shopping.[2]

Against this background, however, the 'interest of each State in protecting its market's trade, in the form of respect of rights in rem acquired over assets of the debtor located in that State under the law that is applicable before the opening of the insolvency proceedings' is acknowledged (paragraph 100 of the Virgos-Schmit Report).[3] The challenge for those drafting the Regulation was the divergence of views regarding the impact of insolvency proceedings on security, with some Member States being traditionally more pro-secured creditor than others. The compromise adopted in the RR is that, whereas under Article 7 the law of the state of opening generally applies to issues arising in the insolvency proceedings, by virtue of Article 8, that law shall not affect creditors' rights in rem in relation to assets located in a different Member State (discussed below). The RR thus acknowledges the importance of security rights for the granting of credit. As explained in recital 68 of the RR: 6.13

> There is a particular need for a special reference diverging from the law of the opening State in the case of rights in rem, since such rights are of considerable importance for the granting of credit. The basis, validity and extent of rights in rem should therefore normally be determined according to the *lex situs* and not be affected by the opening of insolvency proceedings. The proprietor of a right in rem should therefore be able to continue to assert its right to segregation or separate settlement of the collateral security.

---

[1] See Recitals (22), (67), and (68).

[2] Recitals (29) and (31) clarify that it is only the avoidance of fraudulent or abusive forum shopping (where the purpose is to obtain a more favourable legal position to the detriment of the general body of creditors) which is against the purpose of the Regulation, and not 'good' forum shopping.

[3] See paragraph 2.28 above and n 96 thereto regarding whether it is legitimate to have regard to the Report as an aid to interpretation of the Regulation and the problems with the translation of the Report.

The CJEU confirmed this justification in *Lutz v Bäuerle* citing Recital 68 (Recital 25 at that time):[4]

> the legislature intended to provide for a special reference diverging from the *lex fori concursus* in the case of rights in rem, since these rights are of considerable importance for the granting of credit. According to the same recital, the proprietor of a right in rem accrued before the opening of the insolvency proceedings should therefore be able to continue to assert, after that opening, his right to segregation or separate settlement of the collateral security.

Insolvency proceedings to which the RR applies

6.14 As stated elsewhere in this book, Annex A of the RR sets out those main proceedings to which the RR applies. In general terms, both liquidation and restructuring insolvency proceedings, as defined in Article 1, are covered by the RR but only insofar as they are included in Annex A.

6.15 Moreover, the RR only applies between Member States (excluding Denmark), ie to the effects in other Member States of insolvency proceedings opened in a Member State, against debtors whose centre of main interests is a Member State (see Recital 25). Conversely, it does not apply to the effects in third countries (eg the United Kingdom) of insolvency proceedings opened in a Member State, nor to the recognition of effects in the Member States of insolvency proceedings opened in third countries.

Articles which are of particular relevance to secured creditors

Article 7

6.16 The text of Article 7 is as follows (emphasis added):

> 1. Save as otherwise provided in this Regulation, the law applicable to insolvency proceedings and their effects shall be that of the Member State within the territory of which such proceedings are opened (the 'State of the opening of proceedings').
> 2. The law of the State of the opening of proceedings shall determine the conditions for the opening of those proceedings, their conduct and their closure. In particular, it shall determine the following:
>   (a) the debtors against which insolvency proceedings may be brought on account of their capacity;
>   (b) the assets which form part of the insolvency estate and the treatment of assets acquired by or devolving on the debtor after the opening of the insolvency proceedings;
>   (c) the respective powers of the debtor and the insolvency practitioner;
>   (d) the conditions under which set-offs may be invoked;
>   (e) the effects of insolvency proceedings on current contracts to which the debtor is party;
>   (f) the effects of the insolvency proceedings on proceedings brought by individual creditors, with the exception of pending lawsuits;

---

[4] C-557/13, *Hermann Lutz v Elke Bäuerle* [2015] ECLI:EU:C:2015:227, para 38.

(g) the claims which are to be lodged against the debtor's insolvency estate and the treatment of claims arising after the opening of insolvency proceedings;

(h) the rules governing the lodging, verification and admission of claims;

(i) the rules governing the distribution of proceeds from the realisation of assets, the ranking of claims and the rights of creditors who have obtained partial satisfaction after the opening of insolvency proceedings by virtue of a right in rem or through a set-off;

(j) the conditions for, and the effects of closure of, insolvency proceedings, in particular by composition;

(k) creditors' rights after the closure of insolvency proceedings;

(l) who is to bear the costs and expenses incurred in the insolvency proceedings;

(m) the rules relating to the voidness, voidability or unenforceability of legal acts detrimental to the general body of creditors.

6.17 A secured creditor will be interested, in particular, in those Articles which are emphasized in bold type in paragraph 6.16 above. Each of these Articles is discussed in further detail below.

Article 7(2)(b): The assets which form part of the estate

6.18 It is essential for a secured creditor to be able to maintain its security rights in an insolvency procedure which is governed by the RR. Subject to the discussion of Article 8 below, and assuming that the security right has been validly created and perfected under the applicable law (which is a necessary preliminary question), it will be the law of the Member State in which insolvency proceedings have been opened which will determine whether the secured assets:

(a) are excluded from the estate as a result of the creditor's security right; or
(b) form part of the estate, but nevertheless remain subject to the security right.

Article 7(2)(d): The conditions under which set-offs may be invoked

6.19 A right to set-off may well be relevant, for example, if a creditor wishes to net or combine accounts. Again, the validity of rights of set-off, or the extent to which set-offs are permitted, will be determined in the first instance by the law of the state of the opening of proceedings (subject to Article 9 discussed directly below). Whether such a set-off is permitted will depend upon the answers to two separate questions:

(a) is there a right of set-off under the applicable law; and
(b) is such a right of set-off valid after the commencement of insolvency proceedings?

6.20 However, by virtue of Article 9, the opening of insolvency proceedings will not affect the right to set-off, where set-off is permitted by the law applicable to the insolvent debtor's claim. This goes to the first of the two questions referred to above. Article 9 is likely to have little effect in some Member States in particular where there is the mandatory operation of wide insolvency set-off rules. However, Article 9 will be of great value to a creditor against whom the insolvent debtor has a cross-claim governed by the law of a Member State which allows set-off, if insolvency proceedings have been opened in another Member State whose laws do not allow it.

6.21 Article 9 raises some difficult questions of interpretation, some of which are considered in chapter 8 below. In particular, Article 9 raises the question of what law will be applicable to the insolvent debtor's claim and this is explored further in Example 9 below. For example, it may be that set-off would be permitted in insolvency proceedings in relation to the debtor in the Member State whose law is applicable to the insolvent debtor's claim, but a right of set-off is not available outside such insolvency proceedings. Article 9 does not make any reference to the fact that different set-off rules may apply before and after an insolvency of the debtor in a particular Member State and this issue is also explored further in Example 9.

Article 7(2)(f): Stay of enforcement proceedings

6.22 This Article addresses the question of the stay of proceedings brought by individual creditors. The RR distinguishes between the effects of insolvency on individual enforcement proceedings and those on lawsuits pending. Article 7(2)(f) only covers individual enforcement actions, including judicial or quasi-judicial proceedings, and preservation measures.[5] Thus, the effects of the insolvency proceedings on individual enforcement actions such as distress, executions, attachments, or sequestrations, are governed by the law of the state where insolvency proceedings are opened. Subject to the discussion of Article 8 below, the main insolvency proceedings can stay, if the action has already started, or prevent, if not yet started, any individual enforcement action brought by the creditors against the debtor's assets in other states. Conversely, the effects of the insolvency proceedings on other legal proceedings concerning the assets or rights of the estate, eg actions for a declaration of monetary obligations which merely determine the rights and obligations of the debtor, are governed by the law of the Member State where these proceedings are underway (Article 18).[6] In other words, the law of the forum where such lawsuit is pending will determine the effect on the proceedings before it of any main and secondary insolvency proceedings. This will not prevent an insolvency practitioner from seeking a stay of the proceedings in the relevant Member State, but the question of whether such stay will be granted will be a matter for the law of the Member State where the proceedings have been commenced.[7]

Articles 7(2)(g) and (h): Proof of debt

6.23 Under this Article, the law of the state of the opening of proceedings will govern the manner in which the proof of debt procedure is operated. The proof of debt procedure is, of course, relevant to the question of when a debt is admissible to proof, the manner in which it should be dealt with, the ability of a creditor to appeal such proof, and the ability of a creditor to make an application which attacks the proof of another. Of particular relevance to a creditor's security rights will be the question of the manner in which the creditor will be able to value the security and thereafter to prove for the unsecured portion of the debt. In

---

[5] See CJEU C-444/07, *MG Probud Gdynia sp z oo* [2010] ECLI:EU:C:2010:24, para 44; C-212/15 *ENEFI Energiahatékonysági Nyrt v Direcția Generală Regională a Finanțelor Publice Brașov* [2016] EU:C:2016:841, paras 32–33; C-250/17, *Virgílio Tarragó da Silveira v Massa Insolvente da Espírito Santo Financial Group SA* [2018] ECLI:EU:C:2018:398, paras 24–33; Virgós-Schmit Report, para 142; Miguel Virgós and Francisco Garcimartin, *The European Insolvency Regulation. Law and Practice* (Kluwer, 2004) 76–77; Andreas Piekenbrock, 'Article 7' in Moritz Brinkmann (ed), *European Insolvency Regulation* (Beck-Hart-Nomos, 2019) para 60.

[6] See *Mazur Media Ltd v Mazur Media GmbH* [2005] 1 BCLC 305 and *Re Flightlease (Ireland) Ltd* [2005] IEHC 275. In addition to decisions from a number of other Member States' courts, the Austrian Supreme Court has handed down a number of decisions on Art 18 (former Art 15). Divergences exist in the case law on a number of interpretation issues which arise in relation to Art 18 (former Art 15); such issues are beyond the scope of this chapter.

[7] See Francisco Garcimartin and Miguel Virgos 'Article 18' in Reinhard Bork and Kristin van Zwieten (eds), *Commentary on the European Insolvency Regulation* (2nd edn, OUP, 2022) para 18.09.

addition, the law of the state of the opening of proceedings will govern the issue of whether such security can be revalued at any time.

Chapter IV of the RR (Articles 53–55) sets out a number of uniform rules which relate to the provision of information for creditors and lodgement of their claims: 6.24

(a) Article 53 provides that any creditor who has his habitual residence, domicile, or registered office in a Member State other than the state of the opening of proceedings, including tax authorities and social insurance institutions, has the right to lodge claims in the insolvency proceedings in writing. It also makes it clear that representation by a lawyer or another legal professional shall not be mandatory for the sole purpose of lodging of claims.
(b) Article 54 provides for the duty of the court or the insolvency practitioner to inform known creditors in other Member States of various matters, including time limits for lodging of claims. This information is to be provided using a standard notice and in the official language or one of the official languages of the state of the opening of proceedings.
(c) Article 55 provides that any creditor in other Member States may lodge its claim using a standard form, which will indicate eg the nature of the claim, the date on which it arose, and its amount, as well as whether the creditor alleges preference, security in rem, or a reservation of title in respect of the claim, and what assets are covered by the guarantee which the creditor invokes. The standard claims form shall be accompanied by copies of any supporting documents. This information is to be provided in one of the official languages of the institutions of the Union. Moreover, the Regulation states that claims shall be lodged within the period stipulated by the law of the state of the opening of proceedings and in the case of a foreign creditor, that period shall not be less than 30 days following the publication of the opening of insolvency proceedings in the insolvency register of the state of the opening of proceedings.

Articles 7(2)(i) and (l): Distribution of proceeds (questions of priority)
The law of the state of the opening of proceedings will govern the question of when and how distributions of proceeds will take place. It will also govern the question of whether distributions can be made at all in certain insolvency proceedings. In addition, the governing law will determine the ranking and treatment of claims in the insolvency proceedings (including, for example, whether any claims are to be given preferential status in the insolvency proceedings).[8] Article 7(2)(i) also determines whether a secured creditor that has obtained partial satisfaction of its claim, either through the exercise of a right in rem or by way of set-off, may make a claim in the insolvency proceedings for the balance of its claim.   6.25

Questions regarding the ranking and treatment of claims may be very significant where there are insufficient monies to pay the creditors in full. Where a person or a company is insolvent, there will not be enough money to pay all of its liabilities, whether incurred pre-or   6.26

---

[8] The priority of secured claims *inter se* will be determined by other matters such as the date of registration of the security or any deed of priorities in accordance with the applicable law (see Example 6).

post-insolvency procedure. Under the law of many Member States, the insolvency practitioner is only entitled to pay monies out of the estate which fall within certain prescribed categories such as expenses of the insolvency proceeding; dividends to creditors in respect of provable debts; or return of any surplus to the shareholders of the company. All of these questions will be governed by the law of the state of the opening of proceedings.

6.27 In Member States where floating charges are legally recognized, certain categories of preferential claims have priority to the claims of a floating charge-holder but not to the claims of a fixed charge-holder. It is not clear whether these rules of priority fall within Article 7(2)(i). Although the priority given to preferential debts arises, generally, pursuant to the insolvency legislation, it is at least arguable that these rules relate to the priority of security (since they regulate the relationship between secured creditors and preferential creditors) and are not therefore an effect of the insolvency procedure. This is considered further in the context of Example 1 (in paragraph 6.110 below). Furthermore, difficult questions arise regarding the effect on Article 7(2)(i) of Article 8 (discussed below) if there are different rules regarding the ranking of secured claims under the law of the state of the opening of proceedings and the law of the Member State where the secured assets are located.

Article 7(2)(j): The effects of closure of insolvency proceedings, in particular by composition
6.28 Main proceedings may have the effect of varying or discharging creditor claims even in circumstances where a particular creditor has not consented to that variation or discharge. For example, collective arrangements (compositions) under the insolvency legislation are available under the Regulation as main proceedings if included in Annex A. If approved by the requisite majority of members and creditors, a collective arrangement (composition) will bind all unsecured creditors. Under the law of some Member States, these collective arrangements may also bind secured creditors, who vote collectively but as a separate class (one such example is the compromise plan in French safeguard proceedings which will be approved if the requisite majorities of creditors approve the plan; another such example is the Spanish restructuring plans).[9] The question of whether a discharge or variation of the creditor's secured debt through such a compromise would affect its rights in rem for the purposes of Article 8 is considered further below and is explored in Example 4.

Article 7(2)(m): Rules relating to the voidness, voidability, or unenforceability of legal acts detrimental to the general body of creditors
6.29 The law of the state of the opening of proceedings governs questions of void, voidable, or unenforceable legal acts detrimental to the general body of creditors such as transactions at undervalue or preferences. This may, of course, affect a secured creditor where, for example, a charge is to be granted at a date which is proximate to insolvency proceedings, particularly where no new monies are advanced by the creditor at the time the charge is granted.

6.30 By virtue of Article 16, Article 7(2)(m) does not apply where the person who benefited from an act detrimental to all the creditors provides proof that:

---

[9] Under the new Spanish Insolvency Act (recast) unsecured creditors may force a restructuring plan on secured creditors. However, and in addition to the general conditions and safeguards, Article 651 of the Insolvency Act establishes special provisions protecting secured creditors.

(a) the act is subject to the law of a Member State other than that of the State of the opening of proceedings; and

(b) the law of that Member State does not allow any means of challenging that act in the relevant case.

6.31 The CJEU has addressed some of the questions raised by this provision. Firstly, as an exception to the general principle (Article 7), the CJEU has held that it must be interpreted restrictively.[10] Secondly, the phrase 'by any means' indicates that the act must not be capable of being challenged using either the insolvency rules (ie the specific insolvency avoidance actions) or the general rules of the national law applicable to that act.[11] Thirdly, the phrase 'in the relevant case' implies that a concrete assessment of the specific act in question must be undertaken. The test is whether the requirements for a challenge to the impugned act under the *lex causae* are fulfilled (or not) in the specific case at hand, that is, 'its application is subject to the condition that, after taking into account of all the circumstances of the case, the act at issue cannot be challenged on the basis of the law governing the act'.[12] Fourthly, the defence under Article 16 covers both substantive and procedural provisions, and therefore also limitation periods or other time-bars under the *lex causae*.[13] For example, if the act was capable of being challenged according to the *lex causae* but the time for bringing that action has lapsed, there is no reason to consider the act challengeable any more, with the result that the defendant can successfully invoke the 'veto' provided by Article 16. The same conclusion is applicable if a procedural requirement established by the *lex causae* for the exercise of an avoidance action, for example a notice requirement, is not met in the case at hand.[14] The key factor is to assess what a foreign judge—the judge of the Member State whose law applies to the act—would have decided if insolvency proceedings had been opened in his or her Member State in a similar case, that is, whether the judge would have set aside the transaction or not. Thus, it is a sort of 'as if' rule: the act must be treated 'as if' insolvency proceedings had been opened in the Member State which governs such an act.

6.32 The burden of proof is the result of a combination of uniform rules and national law. The reference in Article 16 to the 'the person who benefited ... provid[ing] proof' implies that neither the court nor the insolvency practitioner can raise the application of Article 16 of their own motion. Rather, the onus is on the beneficiary to assert the application of Article 16 and to submit proof that under the law governing the impugned act there is no possibility, or no longer any possibility, to challenge that act, whether for substantive or procedural reasons, in the particular circumstances of the case at hand.[15] That is, the defendant must show that the *lex causae*, taken as a whole, does not enable that act to be challenged.[16] But Article 16 does not establish rules on more specific procedural aspects. According to the CJEU, elements such as (i) the ways in which the evidence is to be elicited, (ii) what

---

[10] C-310/14, *Nike v Sportland* [2015] ECLI:EU:2015:690, para 18.
[11] *Nike* (n 9) para 36.
[12] *Nike* (n 9) para 22; CJEU C-54/16 *Vinyls Italia SpA v Mediterranea di Navigazione Spa* [2017] ECLI:EU:C:2017:433, para 39; EFTA Court, E-28/13, *LBI hf v Merrill Lynch Int Ltd* [2014] para 75.
[13] See *Lutz* (n 4) para 49 ('the defence which it establishes also applies to limitation periods or other time-bars relating to actions to set aside transactions under the *lex causae*'); *LBI hf* (n 11) para 77.
[14] See *Lutz* (n 4) para 56.
[15] *Nike* (n 9) paras 25 and 39 (Article 16 places the burden on the defendant to prove both the facts from which the conclusion can be drawn that the act is unchallengeable and the absence of any evidence that would militate against the conclusion).
[16] *Nike* (n 9) para 39.

evidence is to be admissible before the appropriate national court, (iii) or the principles governing that court's assessment of the probative value of the evidence adduced before it, are therefore governed by the procedural rules of the *lex fori concursus*.[17] In a case applying a similar rule contained in Directive 2001/24/EC,[18] the EFTA Court also stated that the standard of proof is determined by the *lex fori concursus*.[19] This conclusion requires, however, a qualification. The principle of effectiveness prevents national rules from making it excessively difficult or impossible in practice to exercise the rights conferred by Article 16. In particular, that principle precludes, first, the application of national rules of procedure that would make reliance on Article 16 impossible or excessively difficult by providing for rules which are too onerous, especially in connection with proof of the negative, namely that certain circumstances did not exist. Secondly, that principle also precludes national rules of evidence that are not sufficiently rigorous, the application of which would, in fact, have the effect of shifting the burden of proof laid down in Article 16.[20] As a consequence of this, the CJEU has concluded that the national court before which an action to set aside an act is brought may rule that it is for the applicant to establish the existence of a provision of the *lex causae* on the basis of which that act can be challenged *only where* that court considers that the defendant has *first* proven, in accordance with the *lex fori*, that the act at issue cannot be challenged on the basis of the *lex causae*.[21] Additionally, the CJEU has also clarified that the form and the time-limit in which a person benefiting from an act that is detrimental to all the creditors must raise an objection under Article 16, and the question whether that article may also be applied by the competent court of its own motion, if necessary, after the time-limit allowed to the party concerned has expired, fall within the procedural law of the Member State on whose territory the dispute is pending. Naturally, this law must not be less favourable than the law governing similar domestic situations (principle of equivalence) and must not make it excessively difficult or impossible in practice to exercise the rights conferred by EU law (principle of effectiveness).[22]

6.33 The *lex causae*—the law governing the act being contested—is determined by the general conflict of laws rules of the forum. For example, if the challenged act is a contract, the law applicable will be determined by the Rome I Regulation. In this regard, the CJEU has concluded that Article 16 may be validly relied upon where the parties to a contract, who have their head offices in a single Member State on whose territory all the other elements relevant to the situation in question are located, have designated the law of another Member State as the law applicable to that contract, provided that those parties did not choose that law for abusive or fraudulent ends.[23]

Other matters not expressly covered by Article 7(2)

6.34 The list in Article 7(2) is not exhaustive and there may be other procedural and substantive effects of the main proceedings which are to be determined by the law of the State of the

---

[17] *Nike* (n 9) para 28; *Vinyls* (n 11) at 25.
[18] Art 30(1) of the Directive.
[19] *LBI hf* (n 11) para 78.
[20] *Nike* (n 9) para 29.
[21] ibid para 45.
[22] *Vinyls* (n 11) para 33.
[23] *Vinyls* (n 11) para 56.

opening of proceedings. For example, that law may determine what voting rights and other opportunities to participate in the proceedings are given to creditors.

Article 8

The text of Article 8, which almost exactly matches Article 5 of the OR, is as follows: **6.35**

1. The opening of insolvency proceedings shall not affect the rights *in rem* of creditors or third parties in respect of tangible or intangible, moveable or immoveable assets, both specific assets and collections of indefinite assets as a whole which change from time to time, belonging to the debtor which are situated within the territory of another Member State at the time of the opening of proceedings.
2. The rights referred to in paragraph 1 shall, in particular, mean:
   (a) the right to dispose of assets or have them disposed of and to obtain satisfaction from the proceeds of or income from those assets, in particular by virtue of a lien or a mortgage;
   (b) the exclusive right to have a claim met, in particular a right guaranteed by a lien in respect of the claim or by assignment of the claim by way of a guarantee;
   (c) the right to demand assets from, and/or to require restitution by, anyone having possession or use of them contrary to the wishes of the party so entitled;
   (d) a right *in rem* to the beneficial use of assets.
3. The right, recorded in a public register and enforceable against third parties, based on which a right *in rem* within the meaning of paragraph 1 may be obtained shall be considered to be a right *in rem*.
4. Paragraph 1 shall not preclude actions for voidness, voidability or unenforceability as referred to in point (m) of Article 7(2).

Article 8 is clearly relevant to secured creditors, in particular banks, funds, and bondholders. Rights in rem, including those security rights which will often be held by financial creditors, are not affected by the opening of insolvency proceedings provided that the rights in rem relate to assets situated outside the Member State in which proceedings are opened. As the CJEU put it in *Lutz v Bäuerle*, Article 8 seeks 'to enable the creditor to assert effectively, and even after the opening of insolvency proceedings, a right in rem established before the opening of those proceedings'.[24] The Virgos-Schmit Report notes that in order to understand the functioning of Article 8 (originally Article 5) account should be taken of the fact that main insolvency proceedings based on Article 3(1) have a universal scope and, under Article 19, the judgment opening the proceedings is to have the same effect throughout the whole European Union. All the assets of a debtor are subject to the main proceedings, irrespective of the state where they are situated, unless secondary proceedings are opened. Therefore some protection is required in relation to certain transactions completed in other Member States.[25]   **6.36**

Article 8 does not determine whether assets which are subject to rights in rem are to be excluded from or included in the insolvent estate in the main proceedings, but rather the RR   **6.37**

---

[24] (n 4) para 39.
[25] Paragraph 95.

allows a secured creditor to enforce those rights in rem over assets which, at the time of the opening of proceedings, are located in a Member State other than the Member State where the main proceedings have been opened. Therefore, although the law of the main proceedings stipulates that all assets are part of the estate, in fact the holder of the right in rem retains certain rights with respect to the assets over which the holder's debt is secured (subject to the matters discussed below).

6.38 As the Virgos-Schmit Report suggests, at paragraph 97, the fundamental policy behind Article 8 is to protect the trade in the Member State where the assets are situated, and legal certainty in relation to the rights over those assets. Rights in rem have a very important function with respect to credit and the mobilization of wealth. This policy is reflected in Recital 68: 'There is a particular need for a special reference diverging from the law of the opening State in the case of rights *in rem*, since such rights are of considerable importance for the granting of credit.' Rights in rem insulate their holders against the risk of insolvency of the debtor and the interference of third parties. They allow credit to be obtained under conditions which would not be possible without provisions which protect the provision of this credit by way of security. Rights in rem can only properly fulfil their function if they are not adversely affected by the opening of main proceedings in other Member States. In addition, Article 8 protects the holders of security rights against unilateral modifications of the insolvency regime. The *lex fori concursus* is determined by the location of the debtor's centre of main interests ('COMI'). This implies that the debtor, in principle, could unilaterally modify that law by moving its COMI from one Member State to another. These COMI-shifts can be used strategically or opportunistically. The exceptions to Article 7, including in particular Article 8, protect against these types of conduct.

6.39 Article 8 only applies to the rights in rem which are created before the opening of proceedings. This term is defined in Article 2(8) (see below paragraph 6.70). When various steps are necessary for the perfection of a right in rem according to the applicable law, all of the necessary acts must be completed prior to the opening of proceedings. If the rights in rem are created after the opening of proceedings, Article 7 applies. Note, however, that the application of this provision has a very restricted scope: within the limitations derived from the debtor's insolvency, eg with regard to its capacity, the validity and perfection of rights in rem created after the opening of proceedings continue governed by the general conflict of laws rules, typically the *lex rei sitae*.

6.40 Article 8 gives rise to difficulties of interpretation in a number of important respects including:

    (a) What is a right in rem and what law determines this?
    (b) Where is a secured asset located and what law determines this?
    (c) What does it mean to say that the insolvency proceedings shall not 'affect' the right in rem? In particular:
        (i) Is an insolvency practitioner entitled to discharge the security by paying the secured creditor a sum equal to the value of the secured asset?
        (ii) Does the protection given by Article 8 extend to the secured debt or merely the security interest over the relevant assets?
        (iii) What impact does Article 8 have on an intercreditor agreement between the secured creditors?

(d) As Article 8 requires the secured asset to be located in another Member State at the time of opening of the relevant insolvency proceedings, how is this expression to be interpreted?

(e) Article 8 does not protect a right in rem from any claw-back challenge under the law of the relevant insolvency proceedings but how does Article 8 relate to Article 16 in this regard?

6.41 Each of these questions is explored through the 9 factual examples in this chapter but is summarised briefly below.

What is a right in rem?

6.42 Article 8 raises the question of what 'rights in rem' are the subject of the protection given by this provision and what law is to determine whether a right is to be regarded as a right in rem for the purposes of Article 8. Does this expression include all types of security and quasi-security interest (such as retention of title clauses, flawed asset arrangements, finance leases, and sale and repurchase agreements)? What about powers of attorney which may be given to support or protect the security interest—do these form part of the right in rem? And what about rights in rem which may be recognized by one Member State but not others (such as the beneficial interest under a trust)?

6.43 The Regulation provides no definition of a right in rem. However, Article 8(2) contains a list of typical attributes of rights in rem, and Article 8(3) states that a right which is entered in a public register and is enforceable against third parties shall be considered to be a right in rem. The Virgos-Schmit Report states that the failure to provide a definition (at least in respect of the November 1995 Convention on Insolvency Proceedings) was deliberate, allowing the law of the state where the assets are located to determine the question of whether a right is a right in rem.[26] But, as confirmed by the CJEU, following the Virgos-Schmit Report, the Regulation implicitly imposed certain limits to national law (below paragraphs 6.51–6-55). As has been said, it is a two-stage approach: first, national law determines the attributes of a right and whether it is regarded as a right in rem, but, if so, the Regulation determines whether such a right fulfils the requirements set out in Article 8.[27]

6.44 Paragraphs 102–104 of the Virgos-Schmit Report provide some guidance in relation to what will constitute a right in rem. Those paragraphs are more explicit in their indication of the intended scope of the Article (at least in the form which that Article took when the Insolvency Proceedings Regulation was to be issued as a Convention). It appears that:

(a) a right in rem is not to be given an unreasonably wide interpretation. It should not include, for instance, rights simply reinforced by a right to claim preferential payment;

---

[26] See Virgos-Schmit Report, para 100.
[27] See Michael Dahl/Justus Kortleben, 'Article 8' in Moritz Brinkmann (n 5) paras 8–10. Also Virgós/Garcimartín (n 5) para 149 clarifying this reference to national law in the following terms. Article 8.2 contains a typological description of what is meant by a right *in rem* for the purposes of this provision. Its function is to operate as a limit to the characterization of a right as a right *in rem* under national law. Only those rights conferred by national laws that conform to that *typological characterisation* are protected by Article 8.1 of the RR; see also R Snowden, 'Article 8' in Bork/van Zwieten (n 7) para 8.25. This function of Article 8.2 has been confirmed by the CJEU, see *Lutz* (n 4) para 28 and *Senior* (n 32) para 23 (infra paras 6.51-6.54).

(b) a right in rem may not only be established with respect to floating charge assets but also rights which are characterised under national law as rights in rem over intangible assets or over other rights;

(c) Article 8 was drafted under the assumption that a right in rem has basically two characteristics:

- its direct and immediate relationship with the asset to which it relates, which remains linked until the debt has been satisfied (without depending upon the asset belonging to a person's estate, or on the relationship between the holder of the right in rem and another person);
- the absolute nature of the allocation of the right to the holder. In other words, the person who holds a right in rem can enforce it against anyone who interferes with his right without his consent. Such rights are typically protected by actions to recover the property which is subject to the right in rem. The right in rem survives a transfer of the asset to a third party (in other words, it can be claimed against a purchaser, unless that purchaser is acting bona fide).

6.45 The following provisions of Article 8 will also be helpful in determining whether particular rights in rem fall within Article 8.

Both specific assets and collections of indefinite assets

6.46 Article 8 clearly applies to both fixed charge assets ('specific assets') and floating charge assets ('collections of indefinite assets'). This means that a secured creditor with a floating charge which may not be recognized in the Member State where insolvency proceedings are opened will still be able to enforce that floating charge in another Member State where the floating charge is recognized, provided that the security is properly created and perfected according to the law of the *situs* of the secured assets in question. This is of particular importance as floating charges or equivalent security rights, which cover a pool of present and future assets, tangible and intangible, the composition of which changes from time to time (this is probably what the expression 'collections of indefinite assets' means), may exist in some European jurisdictions. Naturally, these types of security rights may only be enforced over specific assets, within the pool of assets described in the charge, when they 'crystallise'.[28]

6.47 It is not clear, however, whether the same analysis would apply in relation to, for example, the beneficial interests created by a constructive or remedial trust where such a trust is not recognized in the Member State where insolvency proceedings are opened.

The right to dispose of assets and to obtain satisfaction from the proceeds

6.48 In principle, under Article 8(2)(b), this includes the right to appoint a receiver to dispose of the assets. The Virgos-Schmit Report suggests that, for example, the owner of the right in rem may exercise the right to separate the security from the estate and, where necessary, to realize the asset individually to satisfy the claim in accordance with the *lex causae*.

---

[28] This raises the question of whether these 'floating' security rights may even crystallize after insolvency proceedings are opened and thus cover specific assets acquired by the debtor post-commencement, see on this issue Virgós/Garcimartín (n 5) para 157.

The priority of his right to collect on the proceeds should not be overruled by the *lex fori concursus*, ie the holder of the security may enforce his claim and his right to payment from the encumbered assets irrespective of the priorities of other creditors under the *lex fori concursus*. In addition, the insolvency practitioner, even if he is in possession of the asset, cannot take any decision in relation to that asset which might affect the right in rem created over it, without the consent of its holder.[29]

However, the *lex rei sitae* may give certain priorities to other creditors (eg a 'super-privilege' to employees or a right of retention to a depositary), which apply irrespective of the debtor's insolvency. These preferential rights should be respected since the intention of Article 8 is to ensure the secured creditors are not adversely affected by the opening of insolvency proceedings in another Member State but not to put them in a better position.[30] Likewise, the *lex rei sitae* also covers priorities between holders of concurring security rights, including between the beneficiaries of a floating charge, on the one hand, and a holder of a security right over a specific asset, on the other. **6.49**

Other rights expressly set out in Article 8
Article 8(2) provides a list of the types of rights which are normally considered by national laws to be rights in rem: **6.50**

(a) the right to dispose of assets or have them disposed of and to obtain satisfaction from the proceeds of or income from those assets, in particular by virtue of a lien or a mortgage;
(b) the exclusive right to have a claim met, in particular a right guaranteed by a lien in respect of the claim or by assignment of the claim by way of a guarantee;
(c) the right to demand assets from, and/or to require restitution by, anyone having possession or use of them contrary to the wishes of the party so entitled;
(d) a right *in rem* to the beneficial use of assets.

CJEU case law
In *Lutz v Bäuerle*, the CJEU has affirmed that an attachment may be categorized as a right in rem.[31] The facts of the case may be summarized as follows. ECZ GmbH was a German company whose registered office was, at the material time, in Tettnang (Germany). Its object was the sale of cars. ECZ GmbH has a subsidiary in Bregenz (Austria)—the debtor company in this case. Mr Lutz purchased a car from this company but, owing to the failure to deliver that car, he brought an action before the Bezirksgericht Bregenz (District Court, Bregenz) seeking reimbursement of the price which he had paid to that company. On 17 March 2008, that court issued an enforceable payment order against that company. On 13 April 2008, the debtor company filed an application before the Amtsgericht Ravensburg (District Court, Ravensburg, Germany) for insolvency proceedings to be opened. On 20 May 2008, after the Bezirksgericht Bregenz had granted leave to enforce its payment order of 17 March 2008, three bank accounts held by the debtor company at a bank established in Austria were attached. Finally, and after the Amtsgericht Ravensburg opened insolvency **6.51**

---
[29] Virgós-Schmit Report, para 95 in fine.
[30] Virgós/Garcimartín (n 5) para 154; Snowden (n 26) 8.29.
[31] (n 4).

proceedings against the debtor company on 4 August 2008, the bank holding the debtor company's bank accounts that had been attached paid Mr Lutz the sum of EUR 11,778.48. By a letter of 3 June 2009, the then liquidator informed Mr Lutz that he was challenging the enforcement which had been authorized by the Bezirksgericht Bregenz, and also the payment made by the bank.

6.52 Against this background, the CJEU concluded that the right resulting from the attachment of the bank accounts at issue in the main proceedings was in fact capable of constituting a 'right in rem' within the meaning of Article 8(1) (Article 5 in the former version of the Regulation), provided that, under the national law concerned (in the present case, Austrian law), that right was exclusive in relation to the other creditors of the debtor company, which is a matter for the referring court to ascertain.[32]

6.53 In *Senior Home v Gemeinde Wedemark,* the CJEU has concluded that Article 8 also covers rights in rem that arise by operation of law.[33] *Senior Home* was a real estate company under French law, that owned an immovable property located in Wedemark (Germany). By decision of 6 May 2013, it was put into court-supervised administration by the tribunal de grande instance de Mulhouse (Regional Court, Mulhouse, France). On 15 May 2013, the Wedemark local authority applied for the sale at a public auction of Senior's property to recover arrears of real property tax that remained outstanding. Under French law, the opening of the court-supervised administration procedure essentially precludes the compulsory sale at issue. However, in accordance with German law, debts due in respect of real property taxes are public charges on real property which are rights *in rem*, and the owner of the encumbered real property must accept enforcement of the instrument recording those debts against that property. The issue for the CJEU was whether this right of the tax authorities may be characterized as a right in rem for the purpose of Article 8 of the European Regulation (Article 5 in the former version).

6.54 The Court based its decision of the General Advocate Opinion, that in turn had followed the Virgos-Schmit Report.[34] The Court considered 'that the rights regarded as "*in rem*" by the national legislation at issue must satisfy certain criteria in order to fall within Article 8. In particular, those two characteristics mentioned above (supra para. 6.44(c)): a right in rem entails a right which directly and immediately encumbers an asset and, secondly, the holder of such a right can enforce it against the owner of the encumbered asset and third parties'.[35] The CJEU concluded that both requisites were met in this case, irrespective of whether the security was created by operation of law. According to the court, the limitation of this provision to rights in rem granted in the context of contractual transactions derives neither from its wording nor from the recitals of the RR. As a consequence of this characterization, the German local authorities' rights in rem were insulated from the opening of insolvency proceedings in France and they were, thus, entitled to continue with the compulsory sale of Senior's real property and collect on the proceeds.

---

[32] Lutz (n 4), para 28.
[33] C-195/15, *SCI Senior Home, in administration v Gemeinde Wedemark, Hannoversche Volksbank eG* [2016] ECLI:EU:C:2016:804, para 32.
[34] Paragraph 22.
[35] Paragraph 23.

Reference should also be made to a Dutch judgment that has concluded that Article 8 is not applicable to a right of retention.[36] **6.55**

Where is a secured asset located?

The protection given by Article 8 only applies where the encumbered asset is situated within the territory of a Member State other than the one in which the insolvency proceedings are commenced. Hence the location of a secured asset is crucial. **6.56**

Article 2(9) establishes eight uniform rules for the location of assets. **6.57**

Registered shares
Unless they are represented by book-entry, registered shares in companies are situated in the Member State within the territory of which the company having issued the shares has its registered office. Thus, for example, registered shares in a Dutch company are deemed to be located in The Netherlands and registered shares in a Luxembourg company are deemed to be located in Luxembourg. The location of the centre of the main interest of the company having issued the shares is not relevant for this purpose. **6.58**

Book-entry securities
Financial instruments, the title to which is evidenced by entries in a register or account maintained by or on behalf of an intermediary ('book entry securities'), are situated in the Member State in which the register or account in which the entries are made is maintained. This rule is taken from Article 9(2) of the Financial Collateral Directive.[37] **6.59**

Bank accounts
Cash held in accounts with a credit institution are situated in the Member State indicated in the account's IBAN, or, for cash held in accounts with a credit institution which does not have an IBAN, the Member State in which the credit institution holding the account has its central administration. However, where the account is held with a branch, agency or other establishment, the bank account is deemed to be located in the Member State in which that branch, agency, or other establishment is located. This rule, which is taken from Article 4(4) of the Regulation on the European Account Preservation Order, has clarified a controversial issue that arose under the OR.[38] **6.60**

Registered assets. Property and rights, ownership of, or entitlement to which is entered in a public register, are situated in the Member State under the authority of which the register is kept. **6.61**

---

[36] *Yacht Service BE v K Verhaegen* [2016] ECLI:NL:GHSHE:2016:3600, accessible at European Insolvency Regulation—INSOL Europe (insol-europe.org).
[37] Directive 2002/47/EC of the European Parliament and of the Council of 6 June 2002 on financial collateral arrangements.
[38] See para 6.56 in the first edition of this book.

European patents

6.62 European patents are situated in the Member State for which the European patent is granted.

Copyrights

6.63 Copyrights and related rights are situated in the Member State within the territory of which the owner of such rights has its habitual residence or registered office.

Tangible assets

6.64 Tangible assets are situated in the Member State within the territory of which the property is situated, unless they are covered by any of the rules mentioned above. In particular, if the ownership over a tangible asset is registered in a public register, eg a ship, the Member State under the authority of which the register is kept displaces the physical location as the relevant rule.

Claims

6.65 Claims, other than cash accounts (see above paragraph 6.60), are deemed to be situated in the Member State within the territory of which the third party required to meet the claims, ie the underlying debtor or *debitor debitoris*, has the centre of its main interests, as determined in accordance with Article 3(1).

6.66 Article 2(9) of the Regulation is intended to be exhaustive. The text also clarifies that, where an asset falls within more than one category, there should be no overlap between the various limbs of the definition: thus, to use the earlier example of a ship whose ownership was recorded in a public register, this provision makes it clear that the ship will be located in the Member State under whose authority the register is kept; or, in the case of registered shares represented by book-entries, the location of the securities account prevails over the registered office of the issuing company.

6.67 The location rules contained in Article 2(9) focuses on specific assets. This means that when the security right covers a pool or collection of assets, some of them may be located in the State of the opening of proceedings and some of them in other Member States.[39]

6.68 As recital 68 explains, the application of Article 8 presupposes that (i) the asset is located in a Member State different from that where insolvency proceedings are opened, and (ii) the security right has been created under that law as *lex situs*. However, this is not always the case. For example, when the encumbered asset is a claim, the Member State where this claim is located may be different from the law applicable to the security right. In accordance with, for example, Spanish general conflict of laws rules, the law applicable to the creation of security rights over a claim is the law governing this claim, which may not coincide with its location under Article 2(9). In this regard, scholars have defended a 'teleological reduction' of Article 8 when the claim is located in another Member State but the law applicable to the security rights over such a claim coincided with the *lex fori concursus*.[40]

---

[39] See, pointing out this problem, Snowden (n 26) at 8.41 (and concluding that 'It would take a purposeful decision to read Article 8 as applicable to the entire security irrespective of the deemed location of some of the charged assets under Article 2(g)')

[40] Virgos/Garcimartin (n 4) para 159.

What does the time of the opening of proceedings means?

6.69 This expression is relevant in two contexts. First it appears that only rights in rem that are in existence at the time of the opening of the relevant insolvency proceedings are protected by Article 8.[41] Secondly, Article 8 only applies in relation to assets which are located in another Member State at the time of opening of proceedings.

6.70 The time of the opening of proceedings is defined by Article 2(8) as 'the time at which the judgment opening proceedings becomes effective, whether it is a final judgment or not'. According to Article 2(7), the term 'judgment opening proceedings' includes 'the decision of any court to open insolvency proceedings or to confirm the opening of such proceedings and the decision of a court to appoint an insolvency practitioner'. The time of effectiveness of this decision is determined by the *lex concursus*.

6.71 It is unclear, however, what the position should be if (as a matter of the insolvency law of the Member State in which insolvency proceedings are commenced) there is a concept of 'relation-back' so that the relevant insolvency proceedings are deemed to commence on the date the petition or application is filed (rather than the date on which the order is made).

6.72 Furthermore, the Article does not address the question as to what happens if assets are moved from one state to another after proceedings have started. It appears from the wording of Article 8 that it is sufficient for the assets to be located in another Member State at the time of the opening of proceedings, even if the assets are subsequently moved, whether out of the European Union or to the Member State where proceedings have been opened.

6.73 The CJEU has clarified that Article 8 applies where: (a) insolvency proceedings have been opened in an existing Member State prior to the accession of a new Member State to the European Union; and (b) the assets which are subject to the right in rem are situated in the new Member State on the date it accedes to the European Union.[42]

What does 'shall not affect' mean?

6.74 Article 8 states that the opening of insolvency proceedings shall not affect the rights in rem of creditors or third parties. The Article therefore raises the question of the meaning of the words 'shall not affect'. No definition is provided by the Regulation, but it is to be expected that this expression will be construed in order to give effect to the purpose of the Article, namely to protect third-party rights in rem. Some indication of the intention of the Regulation in this regard is given by recital 68. This states that the basis, validity, and extent of a right in rem should normally be determined according to the *lex rei sitae* and should not be affected by the opening of insolvency proceedings. The Recital states that the proprietor of the right in rem should be able to continue to assert his right to segregation or separate settlement of the collateral security, 'as if' no insolvency proceedings had been opened.[43]

---

[41] Virgos-Schmit Report, para 96.
[42] C-527/10 *ERSTE Bank Hungary Nyrt v Magyar Allam, BCL Trading GmbH, ERSTE Befektetesi Zrt*, [2021] ECLI:EU:C:2012:417.
[43] Virgos/Garcimartin (n 5) at 164; Bob Wessels, *Volume X. International Insolvency Law, Part II. European Insolvency Regulation*, at 10635(iii); recently, Dahl/Kortleben (n 26) paras 25–26; Snowden (n 26) para 8.10 ('This

Article 8 does not entail a reference to the insolvency rules of the *lex rei sitae*, and therefore it is not a true insolvency conflict-of-laws rule but a 'negative substantive rule'.[44] That Recital also indicates that the insolvency practitioner in the main proceedings should be able to open secondary proceedings in the jurisdiction where the rights in rem arise if the debtor has an establishment there—such secondary proceedings may have an impact on the enforcement of security and this is discussed further in Example 1.

6.75 The mere vesting of title to the asset over which security exists in the insolvency practitioner in the main proceedings does not, at least according to the German Supreme Court,[45] affect the rights in rem of creditors. This conclusion seems likely to be followed in other Member States because the rights in rem are not affected; there has merely been a change in the person against whom they can be enforced. An illustration of the operation of this provision is the case where the insolvency practitioner of the main proceeding intends to carry out a sale of the business which includes assets located in other Member States. If these assets are encumbered by a security right, the insolvency practitioner in the foreign insolvency proceedings cannot prevent the holder of such a right from enforcing it and collecting in the proceeds, irrespective of the priorities of other creditors under the *lex fori concursus*, even if this enforcement were not possible under the insolvency rules of the Member State where main insolvency proceedings are opened and/or the insolvency rules of the Member State where the asset is located.[46] Naturally if after the enforcement there are any outstanding amounts in favour of the creditor, they will fall within the scope of the insolvency proceedings. Conversely, any excess over the secured obligation will form part of the insolvency estate.[47]

6.76 The CJEU seems to follow this interpretation. In *Lutz*,[48] and referring to paragraph 68 (then 25) of the Regulation, it stated that:

> 39. In order to achieve that objective, Article 5(1) of Regulation No 1346/2000 [Article 8(1) of Regulation No 2015/848] states that the opening of insolvency proceedings 'shall not affect' the rights in rem falling within the scope of that provision. Obviously, that rule seeks, inter alia, to enable the creditor to assert, effectively and even after the opening of insolvency proceedings, a right in rem established before the opening of those proceedings.

could have the effect that rights in rem over assets that are situated in a Member State other than that in which the debtor has its COMI or an establishment will end up being wholly insulated for the effect of the insolvency of the debtor[...]'). Naturally, the doctrine of 'fraudulent location of assets' might apply, see Virgos-Schmit para 105; also Dahl/Kortleben, ibid para 22, but without much indication about what this doctrine includes (see Snowden, n 26, at fn 12). Conversely, some scholars have sought to limit the scope of Article 8 by arguing that it is only the 'opening' of the proceedings what does not affect rights in rem, but no other decisions or orders made during those proceedings, as discussed by Wessels, at 10634 with further references.

[44] Advocate General M Spuznar in *Senior Home v Gemeinde Wedemark* (n 32) para 31: 'Article 5 of Regulation No 1346/2000 [Article 8 of Regulation 2015/848] is not a conflict-of-laws rule but a "negative" substantive rule, the purpose of which is to uphold rights in rem acquired before the opening of the insolvency proceedings,' references omitted).
[45] V ZB 54/10, German Federal Court of Justice (BGH), 3 February 2011; Dahl/Kortleben (n 26), para 26.
[46] See Snowden (n 26), paras 8.16–8.17, providing more examples, and 8.28. This overprotection has been criticized from a policy perspective but was accepted by the negotiators of the Convention of 1995 (see Virgos/Garcimartin n 5, para 164) and has not been amended by the Insolvency Regulation recast even if there have been some proposals to change the approach (see INSOL Revision of the European Insolvency Regulation, 2012, para 5.9).
[47] Virgos/Garcimartin (n 5) para 166; Snowden (n 26), 8.20.
[48] (n 4).

40. However, in order to enable a creditor to assert his right in rem effectively, that creditor must be able to exercise that right after the opening of the insolvency proceedings, in principle under the *lex causae*. The special feature of Article 5 of Regulation No 1346/2000 [Article 8 of Regulation 2015/848] is thus that it seeks to protect not only acts completed before the opening of the insolvability proceedings but also, and above all, acts taking place after the opening of those proceedings.

One important question is unanswered by the Regulation and is not addressed in the Virgos-Schmit Report.[49] Does the Article merely protect the right in rem in the strict sense (ie the security interest over the relevant assets) or does it also protect the underlying secured debt? In other words, does Article 8 prevent a composition plan or proceeding which would be effective under the state of the opening of main proceedings from amending or discharging the debtor's secured indebtedness and therefore protect the secured creditor's rights to enforce its security in respect of that indebtedness over assets located in another Member State? Although such a result would seem to be far from the intentions of the draftsman, it cannot be completely excluded.[50] This issue is explored further in Example 4.

6.77

A second question which arises from the use of the words 'shall not affect the rights in rem of creditors' is what effect (if any) Article 8 would have on the turnover trust provisions in an intercreditor agreement between the secured creditors *inter se*.[51] This is also explored through Example 6. This is likely to depend on whether (but for Article 8) the insolvency proceedings in question purport to affect the rights of the secured creditors as between themselves (rather than merely affecting the position as between the insolvent debtor and its creditors). It is at the very least possible that under the law of the Member State where main proceedings are opened a collective arrangement (if properly drafted) could affect the position between a creditor and a third party (such as another creditor).

6.78

Finally in this context, the question arises as to whether Article 8 would prevent an insolvency practitioner in the main proceedings from 'paying off' the secured creditor, thereby gaining control of the secured asset. The Virgos-Schmit Report makes it clear that, if the value of the security is greater than the value of the secured claim, the creditor will be obliged to surrender to the insolvent estate any surplus proceeds of sale[52] and this is unobjectionable. The Report also states that the insolvency practitioner has the power to decide on the immediate payment of the secured claim and thus to avoid any loss in value that certain assets could suffer if they were to be realised separately.[53] This is more problematic as it

6.79

---

[49] See app 2 below.
[50] The INSOL register records a summary of case in relation to a debt discharged under English law. The German court held that the debt discharge did not affect a mortgage on real estate in Germany entered into prior to the debt discharge even if the debt discharge was recognized in Germany, see Verwaltungsgericht Regensburg v 17.06.2014 – RO 4 E 14.898 [2014] EIRCR(A) 439, accessible at European Insolvency Regulation—INSOL Europe (insol-europe.org). It is also noted that one of the authors of the European Convention on Insolvency Proceedings, Professor Balz, considers that secured creditors may not be impaired by a plan: see M Balz, 'The European Convention on Insolvency Proceedings' (1996) 70 ABLJ 485, 509. The same conclusion is reached by other authors, see, for example, also interpreting Article 8 as protecting secured creditors from being impaired by a plan, Virgos/Garcimartin (n 5) paras 163–64; Snowden (n 26) paras 8.42–8.46. It is also worth noting, however, that from a policy perspective, such a conclusion is not fully consistent with the objectives of Directive (EU) 2019/1023 on restructuring and insolvency, which promotes the effectiveness of restructuring plans at an EU level.
[51] See also Snowden (n 26) paras 8.47–8.49.
[52] Para 99 (see app 2).
[53] ibid.

could be argued that such a right on the part of the insolvency practitioner affects the right in rem of the secured creditor, particularly in circumstances where the security is underwater. For example, if the secured debt is 100 but the secured asset (at the current time) is only worth 80, the secured creditor would be deprived of its chance to wait and see if the value of the secured asset might increase in the future if the insolvency practitioner in the main proceedings were able to discharge the security by paying the secured creditor 80.

Relationship between Article 8 and Article 16

6.80 Article 8(4) states that Article 8(1) shall not preclude actions for voidness, voidability, or unenforceability as referred to in Article 7(2)(m). The general rule is that such matters are determined by the law of the Member State in which the insolvency proceedings are commenced. However, this is subject to the defence in Article 16 where the act in question is subject to the law of another Member State and that law does not allow any means of challenging that act in the relevant case.

6.81 The relationship between Articles 8 and 16 was considered by the CJEU in *Lutz v Bäuerle*.[54] The CJEU held that while Article 16 (at that time, Article 13) is not, in principle, applicable to acts which take place after the opening of the insolvency proceedings, in certain circumstances that provision would be applicable if an act takes place after the opening of insolvency proceedings on the basis of rights established before the opening of the insolvency proceedings. The CJEU's decision related to a payment made post-insolvency in respect of a right in rem created pre-insolvency and was reached on the basis of the wording of Article 8 (then Article 5) of the Regulation. In principle, Article 8 provides protection for rights in rem of creditors or third parties in respect of property situated within the territory of another Member State at the time of the opening of the insolvency proceedings. Article 8(4) specifically provides that it shall not preclude actions for voidness, voidability, or unenforceability as referred to in Article 7(2)(m) of the Regulation. But this provision is in turn limited by Article 16. Therefore, even where a payment is made after the commencement of the insolvency proceedings, if the payment is made pursuant to a right in rem granted prior to the insolvency proceedings being commenced, Article 16 may still provide a defence to a challenge of the post-insolvency payment.

Assets located in the United Kingdom

6.82 The reference in Article 7 to the *lex fori concursus* includes its conflict-of-laws rules when the encumbered asset is located in a third country. Therefore, if the encumbered asset is located in the United Kingdom, in particular in England, the conflict-of-laws rules of the Member State where main insolvency proceedings are opened will determine whether the effects of those proceedings are governed by the *lex fori concursus*, by the *lex rei sitae* or whether a similar solution to Article 8 applies, and therefore those proceedings 'shall not affect' the security rights created over those assets.

[54] (n 4).

Spanish insolvency conflict-of-laws rules, for example, depart from the approach laid down by Article 8 of the Regulation and establish a reference to the insolvency provision of the *lex rei sitae*. Pursuant to Article 723 of the Spanish Insolvency Act (recast), '**The effects of insolvency proceedings on the rights in rem of a creditor or third party in respect of properties, goods or rights** of any kind whatsoever belonging to the debtor, including collections or assets as a whole which may change from time to time, and which are situated in the territory of another country at the time the insolvency proceedings are declared open, **shall be governed exclusively by the law of this country**' (emphasis added).[55]

6.83

The practical consequences of this approach are that the security right will be treated '*as if* the insolvency proceedings had been opened in England. Thus, from a Spanish law perspective: (i) English law governs the creation, validity and general effectiveness of the security interest; (ii) and English insolvency rules govern its insolvency treatment, in particular its ranking or enforceability. The word 'exclusively' in that provision is intentionally included to ensure the all-encompassing nature of the reference to the law of the State concerned. Thus, this reference may cover other aspects, such as the duration of the stay, the procedural obligations of the collateral taker, for example, the insinuation of its claim in the insolvency proceedings, and the consequences of non-compliance with those obligations on its collateral. Where the relevant foreign law provides for different insolvency proceedings, eg restructuring or liquidation, the principle of functional equivalence applies, ie the rules of the foreign insolvency proceedings that are equivalent to the Spanish insolvency proceedings should apply. Naturally, certain adaptations may be required. The consequences of these rules are further considered in Example 1.

6.84

Effects of insolvency proceedings opened in the UK on rights in rem over assets located in the EU

Likewise, the effects of insolvency proceedings opened in the United Kingdom, eg in England, on rights in rem over assets located in the EU are not governed by the RR, but by the private international law rules of each Member State. Thus, the law of each Member State will determine whether those proceedings may have any effect on those rights; and if so, whether these effects are determined by English law as *lex fori concursus* or by the insolvency rules of the corresponding Member State.

6.85

Under Spanish insolvency conflict of laws rules, for example, if the encumbered asset is located in Spain, the Spanish insolvency rules applies. This is the 'mirror effect' of Article 723 of the Spanish Insolvency Act. Thus, if main insolvency proceedings are opened in England, even if they are recognized in Spain in accordance with Article 742,[56] their effects will not be determined by English insolvency rules, but by Spanish insolvency rules.

6.86

---

[55] Note the new Spanish Insolvency Act (recast) has excluded the application of this conflict-of-laws rule in preventive restructuring proceedings. This means that Spanish provisions on restructuring plans, including the stay, also apply to rights in rem over assets located in a third country (see Art. 754).

[56] This provision lays down the general conditions for the recognition of foreign insolvency proceedings in Spain, which include, for example, that the debtor's COMI be located in the country where the insolvency proceedings are opened.

C. UK Legal Framework

Status of the RR in the United Kingdom

6.87 As is dealt with elsewhere in this publication,[57] the United Kingdom (UK) ceased to be a member of the European Union (EU) on 31 January 2020. However, under the European Union (Withdrawal) Act 2018, as amended by the European Union (Withdrawal Agreement) Act 2020, all EU law (direct and indirect) continued to apply in the UK and the EU as if the UK were a Member State until the end of the transition period, being 11:00 pm (GMT) on 31 December 2020.

6.88 Accordingly, with effect from 1 January 2021, among other things:

(a) the European Communities Act 1972, the legal basis for EU law having effect and supremacy in English law, was repealed such that EU law no longer applies in the UK;
(b) unless otherwise amended or repealed by a Brexit SI (defined below), EU law, as it stood at the end of the transition period, was converted into domestic law and laws that were made in the UK in order to implement EU obligations were preserved. This body of converted EU law and preserved domestic law is referred to in the UK Withdrawal Act (and in this chapter) as 'retained EU law'; and
(c) various pieces of secondary legislation in the form of statutory instruments (the **Brexit SIs**), made by government ministers to correct deficiencies in legislation that would otherwise no longer operate appropriately once the UK left the EU and to deal with areas of law where there was effectively no new reciprocal agreement between the EU and the UK, came into effect. One such piece of legislation was the RR, which clearly relies on reciprocity between the Member States.

6.89 As a consequence, on and from 1 January 2021, the RR ceased to have direct applicability in the UK. On 1 January 2021, the RR was retained into English law (the retained law being referred to in this chapter as the **Retained RR**) and simultaneously amended by the Insolvency (Amendment) (EU Exit) Regulations 2019 (as amended from time to time, the **Insolvency Exit Regulations**) to remove the majority of its provisions relating to jurisdiction, recognition of proceedings, and choice of law derogations.

6.90 The reason for revoking the choice of law derogations in the Retained RR was to avoid any preferential treatment of the EU compared to other countries (in circumstances where the EU did not reciprocate such preferential treatment). Accordingly, any choice of law derogations that only applied to the laws or territory of EU Member States have been removed in the Retained RR on the basis that the EU would not be required to respect English law in these circumstances. The authors note that, while this is the rationale that the UK Government expressed for the revocations, there are certain choice of law derogations in the Regulation that are agnostic as whether the applicable law is the law of an EU Member State. Despite this fact, these derogations have nonetheless been revoked in the Retained RR. Among such revoked derogations is the choice of law exception for set-off rights contained in Article 9 of the RR. The rationale for its removal from the Retained RR is unclear,

---

[57] Cf Chapter 9.

as it now appears to create asymmetry between the UK and EU. In particular, EU courts may still be required, pursuant to Article 9, to give effect to set-off rights under an English law contract where English law is the applicable law for the purposes of Article 9,[58] whereas in contrast the UK courts are no longer required to give effect to set-off rights under a contract governed by the law of an EU Member State where that law is the applicable law for Article 9 purposes. Whether the English courts will reach the same position as would the EU courts, by applying principles of private international law, remains to be seen.

For the purposes of this chapter, it is important to note that the Retained RR does not contain any equivalent of Article 8 of the Regulation. Pre-'Brexit', where secured assets were located in England, but insolvency proceedings falling within the Regulation were commenced in an EU Member State, Article 8 ensured that, although the English courts were required to recognize the EU insolvency proceedings under the Regulation, those insolvency proceedings would not affect the secured assets located in England for the reasons given in this chapter. Post-'Brexit', the Retained RR no longer contains this derogation. However, as the effect of the Retained RR was to remove the provisions regarding recognition of the effects of EU insolvency proceedings, the English courts are no longer required to recognize the effects of the EU insolvency proceedings under the Retained RR. Whether the English courts will recognize and give effect to such EU insolvency proceedings in a manner which would impact upon secured assets located in England will now be a matter of English conflict-of-law rules outside of the Regulation. These rules are considered below. **6.91**

Recognition of EU insolvency proceedings (and the impact on secured assets located in the UK) outside of the RR

Chapter 5 of this publication considers the recognition of insolvency proceedings (and the enforcement of the rights and powers of liquidators) outside of the RR and summarizes the main sources for the law of recognition and judicial assistance namely: **6.92**

(a) the common law;
(b) section 426 of the Insolvency Act 1986;
(c) the Cross-Border Insolvency Regulations 2006, SI 2006/1030 (the **Cross-Border Regulations**).[59]

This chapter therefore only considers, at a high level, how each of these sources of cross-border insolvency law may impact on the recognition of EU insolvency proceedings in the UK in circumstances where there are secured assets located in the UK. **6.93**

---

[58] Some legal scholars, however, understand Art 9 to apply only where the law governing the set-off is that of another Member State. The omission of this reference in the drafting of this provision is said by those commentators, including one of the authors of this chapter, to be unintentional and does not seem consistent with the rest of the choice of law rules established by the Regulation.

[59] In addition, there are various UK statutes such as the Administration of Justice Act 1920 and the Foreign Judgments (Reciprocal Enforcement) Act 1933 that would allow for the registration and enforcement of final monetary judgments from the superior courts of certain designated countries. In a European context, the Administration of Justice Act 1920 would apply to monetary judgments from Austria, Belgium, France, Germany, Italy, the Netherlands, Malta, and Cyprus whereas the only EEA Member State to fall within the scope of the Foreign Judgments (Reciprocal Enforcement) Act 1933 is Norway.

Common law

6.94 As referred to in paragraph [5.08], a distinction needs to be made between: (a) the recognition of a foreign office-holder's authority to act on behalf of the debtor; (b) the recognition of an order made by the foreign court against third parties in the course of insolvency proceedings; and (c) judicial assistance involving the grant of additional relief beyond mere recognition in support of foreign insolvency proceedings.[60] Although (a) could be relevant in relation to a liquidator's ability to take possession of secured assets in the UK, it is (b) and (c) that are more likely to have an impact on a secured creditor's ability to enforce its security over assets in the UK.

6.95 A court order from an EU Member State could purport to impact on a secured creditor's ability to enforce its security in the UK, including for example a court order in relation to a claw-back action or in respect of the validity of the security under the laws of the EU Member State. As referred to in paragraph [5.23], following the decision in *Rubin v Eurofinance SA*,[61] judgments in insolvency proceedings must either be:

(a) judgments in rem which will only be recognised at common law if the relevant property is situated in the jurisdiction where the judgment was made at the time thereof; hence there will be no recognition under the common law of a judgment in rem of the court of an EU Member State in relation to secured assets located in the UK; or

(b) judgments in personam which will be recognised at common law if (in broad terms) the defendant (in this case the secured creditor) is present in the EU Member State where the judgment was made or had submitted to the proceedings in that EU Member State (see paragraph [5.20]).[62]

6.96 A clawback order is likely to be treated as a judgment in personam for these purposes (and so subject to the rules discussed in paragraph [5.20]), whereas a court order in relation to the title of the debtor or the secured creditor to a particular secured asset may well be a judgment in rem, although that will depend on the precise terms of the order in question. If the judgment is a judgment in rem, it would be necessary for the liquidator to obtain a court order in the UK, as the place where the secured assets were located.

6.97 The forms of judicial assistance in insolvency proceedings that are available under the common law are discussed in paragraph [5.29]. This could include (a) an order staying the enforcement of security over assets in the UK;[63] and (b) an order for the remission of secured assets located in the UK to the foreign office-holder, for distribution in the foreign insolvency proceedings. However, any order for such relief under the common law is at the

---

[60] Although not in the context of secured assets, the Court of Appeal considered judicial assistance under the common law in *Kireeva (as bankruptcy trustee of Georgy Ivanovich Bedzhamov) v Bedzhamov* [2022] EWCA Civ 35. In refusing to grant assistance to the Russian trustee appointed under a Russian bankruptcy order in connection with real estate of the bankrupt located in London, Newey LJ (giving the lead judgment) held that such assistance could not extend to immovable assets in England. This decision may be relevant if a creditor has security over real property in the UK. The question of assistance has been remitted to the High Court, and a hearing is awaited.

[61] [2013] 1 AC 236.

[62] Note that a secured creditor may be deemed to have submitted to the EU insolvency proceedings by submitting a proof of debt in those proceedings; see para [5.25].

[63] As referred to in para 5.34, the importance of this form of relief has been greatly reduced by the provisions of the Cross-Border Regulations discussed below.

discretion of the court. In circumstances where the secured assets are located in the UK and there is valid security (as a matter of the relevant UK law) over such assets, it remains to be seen whether the court would grant such relief.

It therefore follows that in circumstances where there is an EU insolvency proceeding, the impact of the common law on a secured creditor's ability to enforce its security over assets in the UK will depend on the specific facts and the relief being sought from the relevant UK court. 6.98

Section 426 Insolvency Act 1986

As referred to in paragraph [5.65], section 426 of the Insolvency Act 1986 obliges the English court to assist insolvency proceedings from countries specified by delegated legislation where a request has been made for assistance by the relevant foreign court. The only European Member State that has been specified for these purposes is Ireland. Hence section 426 may be relevant where (for example) a borrower is subject to insolvency proceedings in Ireland and the Irish court makes a request for assistance to a court in the UK. It is possible that such assistance could impact on secured assets in the UK for the reasons given below. 6.99

The assistance that can be provided under section 426 is very broad and can include either the application of foreign law (ie the law of the requesting court) or the application of English law. For example, if a borrower were the subject of examinership in Ireland (which, as a matter of Irish law, gives rise to a stay on the enforcement of security), the Irish court could make a request, under section 426, to the English court requesting assistance in the form of recognition of that stay in respect of secured assets in England. Alternatively, the Irish court could request that the English court give assistance by making an administration order in respect of the borrower, pursuant to which there is a moratorium on the enforcement of security.[64] In such circumstances, the secured creditor would need to seek the leave of the English court to enforce its security.[65] 6.100

The position under section 426 would be different if the security in question were to constitute 'financial collateral' falling under the Financial Collateral Arrangements (No 2) Regulations 2003 (the **FCA Regulations**). Regulation 15A of the FCA Regulations provides that a court shall not, in pursuance of section 426 of the Insolvency Act 1986 or any other enactment or rule of law, recognize or give effect to (a) any order made by a foreign court exercising jurisdiction in relation to insolvency law or (b) any act of a person appointed in such foreign country to discharge any functions under insolvency law insofar as the making of the order or the doing of the act would be prohibited by Part 3 of the FCA Regulations in the case of an English court or a relevant office holder. 6.101

---

[64] See, for example, *Re Dallhold Estates (UK) Pty Ltd* [1992] BCLC 621; *Re Tambrook Jersey Ltd* [2013] EWCA Civ 576.
[65] Alternatively, if the secured creditor had notice of the section 426 hearing, it could argue that the assistance to be given by the English court should not prevent it from enforcing its security. Whether the English court will give leave to the secured creditor allowing it to enforce (or will modify the assistance given under section 426 in this respect) may well turn on the same balancing exercise as the English court undertakes when considering an application for leave to enforce security pursuant to para 43(2) of Schedule B1 to the Insolvency Act 1986.

6.102 This provision appears to be intended to ensure that an insolvency order made by a foreign court, or an act by a foreign insolvency office holder, cannot be enforced by a UK court if such an order or act could not be made by a UK court or office holder in similar circumstances. However, there may be issues in determining whether the order or act would or would not have been available to a UK court or office-holder in similar circumstances. This issue will involve considering whether the foreign insolvency law provisions in question are analogous to the English insolvency law provisions disapplied by the FCA Regulations. If the UK court concludes that they are analogous, no assistance may be granted pursuant to section 426 of the Insolvency Act 1986 (or pursuant to the relevant provisions for recognizing foreign insolvency judgments). There has not yet been any case that has considered Regulation 15A.

Cross-Border Regulations

6.103 The third form of recognition outside of the Regulation is recognition under the Cross-Border Regulations, which enacted into the laws of Great Britian the UNCITRAL Model Law on Cross-Border Insolvency (see paragraphs [5.82]–[5.114]). The Model Law enables a 'foreign representative' of a debtor to apply for recognition in the courts of an enacting state. The scope of the 'recognition' is more modest than under the RR, being limited to questions of 'recognition' of the foreign proceedings (in fact, mainly judicial assistance to them) and of the rights of the 'foreign representative' to obtain access to, and assistance from, the courts of enacting states.

6.104 In particular, the Cross-Border Regulations provide for two forms of assistance:

(a) In the case of a foreign 'main' proceeding (see [paragraph 5.89]), the automatic effect of recognition (under Article 20(1) of the Cross-Border Regulations) is a stay that is broadly equivalent to the stay that would arise in an English bankruptcy (in the case of an individual) or liquidation (in the case of a company). In other words, there is a stay on: the commencement or continuation of individual actions or proceedings concerning the debtor's assets, rights, obligations and liabilities; a stay on execution against the debtor's assets; and a suspension of the debtor's right to transfer, encumber or otherwise dispose of any assets. However, this does not include a stay on the enforcement of security or the exercise of self-help remedies such as certain forms of set-off. Article 20(3) of the Cross-Border Regulations expressly states that the automatic stay does not affect the right to take any steps to enforce security over the debtor's property or the right of a creditor to set-off its claim against a claim of the debtor, if such rights would have been exercisable in the event of the debtor's bankruptcy or winding up (as the case may be);

(b) In addition, however, (under Article 21 of the Cross-Border Regulations) the court has the power, on a discretionary basis, to grant 'any appropriate relief' including the forms of relief listed in Article 21(1)(a)–(g). This is the case in both 'main' and 'non-main' proceedings (see [paragraph 5.100]). Article 21(1)(g) gives the court the power to grant 'any additional relief that may be available to a British insolvency officeholder under the law of Great Britain, including any relief provided under paragraph 43 of Schedule B1 to the Insolvency Act 1986'. Paragraph 43 of Schedule B1 is the stay that arises in an English administration which does include a stay on the enforcement of security.

6.105 The case law on Article 21 (discussed below) reveals that the English courts will customarily grant relief in the form of the administration moratorium where the foreign main proceedings are in the nature of a restructuring or reorganization proceeding (comparable to an English administration) rather than being in the nature of a bankruptcy or liquidation proceeding (comparable to an English liquidation). The position is less clear in relation to foreign non-main proceedings.[66] However, it should be noted that none of the orders for discretionary relief in the form of the administration moratorium appear to have been opposed by secured creditors, so the position may be different if a secured creditor were to appear and to argue that the stay should not be granted.

6.106 The reasoning of the English courts for the position stated above is as follows:

(a) Where the foreign main proceeding is in the form of a liquidation or bankruptcy, the automatic stay arising under Article 20(1) will usually provide a sufficient moratorium, since the stay that is imposed under Article 20(1) 'is imposed in the same terms as if the debtor had entered into an analogous insolvency proceeding in England, namely a winding-up under the 1986 Act'.[67]

(b) However, as the automatic stay under Article 20(1) is primarily designed for foreign liquidations or bankruptcies, the limitations of such a stay may not be sufficiently wide to provide appropriate recognition for a foreign proceeding that is more akin to a restructuring or administration rather than to a liquidation. In particular, the lack of a moratorium on the enforcement of security may interfere with the goal of recognition of the foreign main proceeding, which is 'to have in the recognising state the same effect as if the insolvency proceeding had been opened in the recognising state'[68] and to put the debtor 'on a similar footing in England with regard to any action against it by creditors, such as it would be if proceedings were being conducted in the [state whose proceedings are recognised]'.[69] Mr Jeremy Cousins QC concluded in *Re Entertainment Limited*, a case where discretionary relief was requested after recognition of US Chapter 11 Proceedings as foreign main proceedings, that 'it is entirely consistent with the policy behind the adoption of the Model Law that ... relief [should be granted] of a kind which is similar to the moratorium relief provided in para. 43 of sch. B1 of the 1986 Act.'[70]

6.107 In light of the above, it will be important (as a starting point) to identify the nature of the foreign proceeding, and in particular whether it is more analogous to a winding-up or bankruptcy or to an administration or restructuring. Common features that the court emphasizes in this regard are the continuation or resumption of trading by the company,

---

[66] In *Re Videology Limited* [2018] EWHC 2186 (Ch), Snowden J took a more reticent approach to granting relief under Art 21 in the form of an administration moratorium where foreign non-main proceedings were involved; he requested additional evidence to ascertain if 'it would still be appropriate to grant relief under the Model Law preventing individual action by creditors or the commencement of insolvency proceedings in the UK' [para 24]. This may suggest that a higher standard applies for granting relief in the form of an administration moratorium in foreign non-main proceedings.
[67] Hildyard J in *Re OJSC International Bank of Azerbaijan* [2018] EWHC 59, para 97.
[68] Norris J in *Larsen, Atlas Bulk Shipping A/S v Navios International Inc* [2011] EWHC (Ch) 878, para 23.
[69] Mr Jeremy Cousins QC in *Re Entertainment Limited* [2016] EWHC 1545 (Ch), paras 10–11.
[70] ibid at para 20.

the similarity of the proceedings to US Chapter 11 or debtor in possession proceedings,[71] and the purpose of the proceedings to facilitate rehabilitation/reconstruction. In a European context, under the OR (Council Regulation (EC) No 1346/2000 of 29 May 2000 on Insolvency Proceedings), this would have been the difference between the proceedings listed in Annex B which were limited to winding-up proceedings and those listed in Annex A which included reorganization proceedings. However, there is no longer such a distinction in Annex A of the RR.

6.108 Attention is drawn to the following cases, each of which is an example of a case where discretionary relief under Article 21(1)(g) in the form of applying paragraph 43 of Schedule B1 to the Insolvency Act 1986 was granted: *Samsum Logix Corporation v DEF*;[72] *Re Pan Oceanic Maritime Limited*;[73] *Re Transfield ER Cape Limited*;[74] *Re Entertainment Limited*;[75] *Re Videology Limited*;[76] *Re NMC Healthcare Limited (in administration)*.[77]

6.109 Finally, it is worth noting again that the position may be different in relation to financial collateral falling under the FCA Regulations (see paragraph [6.101]). Under the Cross-Border Regulations,[78] no relief may be granted that would be prohibited under Part 3 of the FCA Regulations (*Modification of insolvency law*) in an English insolvency or would interfere with or be inconsistent with any rights of a collateral-taker under Part 4 of the FCA Regulations (*Right of use and appropriation*). This carve out follows from the fact that the moratorium under paragraph 43 of Schedule B1 to the Insolvency Act 1986 would not prevent the enforcement of financial collateral in the context of an English administration. It is therefore logical that any relief granted to a foreign proceeding would also not prevent any such enforcement. The same effect is achieved by Regulation 15A of the FCA Regulations (see paragraph [6.101–6.102]).

D. Practical Examples

Example 1 (Spanish borrower with establishment in Ireland, assets in the EU, local law security)

6.110 Borrower A has its centre of main interests in Spain and a branch office in Ireland. It has assets in both of these jurisdictions and also in Germany and in England although it has no branch offices there. The bank takes security over all the assets in Spain, Ireland, Germany, and England under the laws of these jurisdictions. The bank complies with all perfection

---

[71] See also: Snowden J in *Re Videology Limited*, para 83.
[72] [2009] EWHC 576, recognition of Korean proceedings.
[73] [2010] EWHC 1734, recognition of US Chapter 11 proceedings.
[74] [2010] EWHC 2851, recognition of BVI liquidation. Note the judgment in this case is very short and gives little insight as to why a moratorium under the terms of para 43 of Schedule B1 to the Insolvency Act 1986 was granted when the foreign proceedings would appear to be in the nature of liquidation proceedings. It does appear, however that the company was continuing to trade.
[75] [2016] EWHC 1545, recognition of US Chapter 11 proceedings.
[76] [2018] EWHC 2186, recognition of US Chapter 11 proceedings as foreign non-main proceedings.
[77] [2021] EWHC 1806 (Ch), recognition of administration under Abu Dhabi Global Market Insolvency Regulations 2015.
[78] Schedule 1, Art (1)(4).

requirements in all relevant jurisdictions. There are no grounds for challenging the security under Spanish, Irish, German, or English law. Borrower A becomes insolvent and the security becomes enforceable. What are the options for the bank in respect of the security over the assets in each jurisdiction and how would these options be affected if insolvency proceedings were opened in respect of A in a particular jurisdiction?

Issues arising: summary

Assets in Spain 6.111
- Main proceedings would need to be opened in Spain as the centre of main interests is there.
- If insolvency proceedings are opened, this will affect the bank's ability to enforce its security over assets in Spain and Article 8 will not be relevant in this context as the assets are located in the same Member State as the state where proceedings are opened.

Assets in Ireland 6.112
- If the branch in Ireland is sufficient for there to be an establishment there, territorial or secondary insolvency proceedings could be opened in Ireland.
- Following the changes that were made to the RR, such territorial or secondary proceedings could now include reorganization proceedings (ie examinership) that would impact upon the enforcement of security over assets in Ireland.
- If no territorial or secondary proceedings are commenced in Ireland, but an insolvency practitioner was appointed in Spain, Article 8 should allow the bank to enforce its security over assets in Ireland notwithstanding the moratorium on security enforcement which arises in a Spanish insolvency proceeding.
- Any surplus monies following the enforcement of the security in Ireland should be handed to the insolvency practitioner in the main proceedings.

Assets in Germany 6.113
- As there is no establishment in Germany, there can be no secondary proceedings there.
- Article 8 should allow the bank to enforce its security over assets in Germany in accordance with German law and procedure notwithstanding any moratorium which may arise in either the main or the secondary proceedings.

Assets in England 6.114
- The question of whether insolvency proceedings may be opened in England in respect of A is not determined by the RR, but by English law. For the reasons given in paragraph [6.134] below, it may be possible to have an English administration or liquidation of A following 'Brexit'.
- From a Spanish law perspective, Article 8 does not apply. Under Article 723 of the Insolvency Act, the bank will be allowed to enforce its security over assets in England in accordance with English law and procedure including any moratorium which may arise under English law.

Issues arising: commentary

Assets in Spain. As A's centre of main interests is in Spain, any main insolvency proceedings 6.115 which are opened under the RR would need to be opened in Spain. The types of proceedings which could be opened as main proceedings in Spain are insolvency proceedings (either compulsory or voluntary) or preventative restructuring proceedings, which qualify as insolvency proceedings under the RR.

6.116 **No main proceedings opened in Spain.** If no such proceedings have been opened at the time the security becomes enforceable, the bank will be able to take steps to enforce the security in accordance with Spanish substantive and procedural law.

6.117 **Insolvency or preventive restructuring proceedings are opened in Spain.** The opening of insolvency or preventive restructuring proceedings in Spain will prevent the bank from enforcing the collateral during the legal moratorium which arises under these proceedings and its security rights may be affected by a collective composition plan if a sufficient majority of secured creditors vote in favour. Article 8 is not relevant in relation to the security over the assets in Spain because those assets are situated in the Member State where insolvency proceedings are opened.

6.118 **Assets in Ireland: no territorial or secondary proceedings in Ireland.** If the moratorium which arises in the main proceedings in Spain does not prevent the enforcement of security in another Member State (a matter which is considered below), it will be necessary to open secondary proceedings in the Member State where the secured assets are located in order to take advantage of any stay which may arise in those secondary proceedings.

6.119 If main insolvency proceedings in respect of A are opened in Spain, and no secondary proceedings have been opened in Ireland, in principle, the moratorium on the enforcement of claims which arises in the Spanish proceedings should be recognized across the European Union and so affect the enforcement of claims in Ireland. Since, according to Spanish law, the moratorium has extra-territorial effect, this will be recognized across the European Union under Articles 19 and 20 of the Regulation. In particular, Article 20(1) provides that the judgment opening the main proceedings is to produce the same effects in any other Member State as under the law of the state of opening (unless the RR states otherwise). Therefore, a moratorium determined by the *lex fori concursus* falls within Article 7 and will extend its effects to other Member States. However, this extra-territorial effect will be subject to Article 8. This provision protects rights in rem and so should allow a secured creditor to enforce its security over assets located in another Member State notwithstanding any moratorium on security enforcement which arises in the state where proceedings are opened, even if that moratorium purports to have extra-territorial effect.

6.120 Applying this analysis to the facts of Example 1, as the assets in Ireland are situated within the territory of another Member State at the time of the opening of proceedings in Spain, and assuming the bank has effective security over those assets as a matter of Irish law, Article 8 should allow the bank to enforce its security in Ireland.

6.121 Article 8 refers to rights in rem in respect of specific assets or collections of indefinite assets as a whole which change from time to time, and so the rights in rem covered by Article 8 would include the bank's floating security over the assets in Ireland.

6.122 There is also a question as to whether the Spanish court may, acting in personam, restrain a Spanish creditor (or a foreign creditor who is subject to the jurisdiction of the Spanish court) from taking action to enforce security abroad. Although this in personam injunctions are not referred to specifically in Article 8, the ability to grant such an injunction would seem to be inconsistent with Article 8.

6.123 In conclusion, it seems unlikely that the moratorium which arises in Spanish insolvency or preventive restructuring proceedings would prevent the bank from enforcing its security over the assets in Ireland and, if A wished to prevent the enforcement of security over its assets in Ireland, it would be necessary for it to commence secondary proceedings in Ireland in order to take advantage of any stay which may arise as a matter of Irish law. This is considered further in paragraph [6.127] below.

6.124 Moreover, Article 8 states that the opening of insolvency proceedings is not to affect the rights in rem of creditors in respect of assets situated in another Member State and a right to have a claim met out of secured assets in priority to other unsecured creditors may be an incident of the right in rem. Therefore, it seems likely that Irish law, as the applicable law of the security, would determine the priority of payments as between the bank and any preferential creditors, irrespective of the Spanish insolvency rules on the distribution of proceeds from the realization of assets and the ranking of claims.

6.125 If the value of the secured assets in Ireland is greater than the value of the bank's secured liability, and the bank takes steps to enforce its security over the Irish assets, the bank will be obliged to surrender to the insolvency practitioner of the main proceedings any surplus proceeds of sale. This is because Article 8 states that the proceedings shall not affect rights in rem in respect of assets located in another Member State and does not state that the proceedings shall not affect *assets* located in another state.[79] This also means that the insolvency practitioner in the main proceedings could choose to pay the secured claim and thus avoid any loss in value that the secured assets might suffer if they were to be realized separately.

6.126 **Territorial or secondary proceedings in Ireland**. As A has an establishment in Ireland, territorial or secondary proceedings may be opened in Ireland. These proceedings would be conducted according to Irish law and will affect rights in rem in Ireland in exactly the same way as those proceedings would have affected rights in rem in Ireland if the proceedings had been purely domestic proceedings.

6.127 The effects on the secured creditor's rights will depend on the type of proceedings opened in Ireland. Under Irish law, a company examinership would give rise to a moratorium on the enforcement of security. Conversely, compulsory winding-up and creditors' voluntary winding-up (with confirmation of the court) would not affect the enforcement of security although they may impact on the priority of payments pursuant to that security. Given that, under the RR, secondary proceedings do not need to be limited to winding up proceedings, A (or its insolvency officeholder in the Spanish main proceedings) may want to consider commencing an Irish examinership in Ireland in order to give rise to a moratorium on the enforcement of secured assets in Ireland.

6.128 **Assets in Germany**. The main difference here is that, as there is no establishment in Germany, it will not be possible to open territorial or secondary proceedings in Germany to impact on the enforcement of security in that Member State.

---

[79] See the Virgos-Schmit Report, para 99 (app 2 below).

6.129 Article 8 should enable the bank to enforce its security notwithstanding any moratorium on enforcement which might arise as a consequence of the Spanish proceedings. However, the bank must enforce its security in accordance with German law and procedure. So, for example, under German law, where the security is over land, the security must be enforced by means of public auction and/or court administration (unless A agrees to another method of enforcement such as a private sale although that is rare in practice).

6.130 If the secured assets in Germany are worth more than the secured liability, any surplus proceeds of sale would need to be handed over to the insolvency practitioner in the main proceedings in Spain.

6.131 Assets in England: recognition of Spanish proceedings. The first question to consider is whether the Spanish insolvency or preventative restructuring proceedings (including the stay on security enforcement) would be recognized in England and/or whether judicial assistance would be given to such proceedings. As referred to in Part C of this chapter, the Retained RR does not require the English courts to recognize and give effect to the Spanish proceedings and instead the question of whether (and to what extent) the Spanish proceedings will be recognized in England will be determined by English private international law (and in particular the common law and the Cross-Border Regulations[80]).

6.132 For the reasons given in paragraphs [6.105]–[6.109] above, the English court may be prepared to grant discretionary relief under Article 21(1)(g) of the Cross-Border Regulations by granting the stay that would apply in an English administration under paragraph 43 of Schedule B1 to the Insolvency Act 1986 in circumstances where the Spanish proceedings are more akin to restructuring proceedings compared with winding up proceedings. Hence this relief might be available as long as the Spanish proceedings are preventative restructuring proceedings (as opposed to insolvency proceedings). Any such stay would prevent the enforcement of security over the assets in England unless the secured creditor got the permission of the court to enforce.

6.133 It is not clear, however, whether the English court would take into account (when deciding whether to grant such discretionary relief under the Cross-Border Regulations) that, from a Spanish choice of law perspective, under Article 723 of the Spanish Insolvency Act, the bank will be allowed to enforce its security over assets in England in accordance with English law and procedure including any moratorium which may arise under English law.[81]

6.134 Assets in England: impact of English insolvency proceedings. The second question is whether A (or the Spanish insolvency officeholder of A) could commence insolvency proceedings in England which may prevent the enforcement of the security over the assets in England. Post 'Brexit', it is no longer necessary for A to have its centre of main interests, or any establishment, in England for such insolvency proceedings to be commenced. A could be subject to a compulsory liquidation in England if it has 'sufficient connection' with England (and the presence of secured assets and an English law security agreement is likely to meet this test). However, such a liquidation does not give rise to a stay on the enforcement of security. Furthermore, A could be subject to an English administration on the

---

[80] Spain is not a relevant country for the purposes of section 426 of the Insolvency Act 1986.
[81] It could be that the stay under para 43 of Sch B1 to the Insolvency Act 1986 could be treated as a moratorium under English law for these purposes.

basis that it is incorporated in an EEA Member State,[82] although whether the English court would exercise its discretion to make such an order (or whether an administrator would accept an out of court appointment) may depend on the specific facts. An English administration would result in a stay on the enforcement of the security without the consent of the administrator or the leave of the court.

Example 2 (Spanish borrower with establishment in Ireland, assets in the EU, Spanish law security)

Borrower B has its centre of main interests in Spain and a branch office in Ireland. It has granted security over its assets in Spain, Ireland, and Germany under a Spanish law governed debenture but the lender has not taken local security in Ireland and Germany. B becomes insolvent. Would the bank be able to enforce its security over the assets in all three jurisdictions and what would be the impact of the opening of main or secondary proceedings? **6.135**

Issues arising: summary
As with Example 1, main proceedings can be commenced in Spain and secondary proceedings can be commenced in Ireland (if the Irish branch office gives rise to an establishment) but not in Germany. The issue here is whether the Spanish law governed debenture would be recognized as giving rise to a valid security interest over the assets in Ireland and Germany for the purposes of Article 8. It appears that issues relating to the creation, validity, and scope of the security as a right in rem will be determined by the applicable law under the usual conflict of laws rules regarding security interests. **6.136**

Issues arising: commentary
Assets in Spain. The analysis will be as set out in paragraphs [6.115]–[6.117] above. **6.137**

Assets in Ireland: no secondary or territorial proceedings in Ireland. As mentioned above, Spanish insolvency and preventive restructuring proceedings are included in Annex A of the Regulation and therefore they will automatically be recognized in other Member State. Only confidential proceedings are excluded. In such a case, Irish private international rules will determine whether the effects of the confidential proceedings, in particular the stay, are recognized in Ireland. **6.138**

The question of whether the security agreement governed by Spanish law would give rise to a right in rem over the assets in Ireland to which Article 8 would apply is a separate question. Article 8 does not define what a right in rem is for the purposes of the RR and it does not state which jurisdiction's law is to determine the matter. Moreover, the RR does not establish which law applies to the creation of security interests. It is possible (though perhaps unlikely) that the Spanish court (as the court of the Member State where the main proceedings are opened or whose law is expressed to govern the security agreement) and the Irish court (as the court of the Member State where the assets appear to be located or **6.139**

---

[82] Paragraph 111(1A) of Sch B1 to the Insolvency Act 1986.

where secondary proceedings could be commenced) could come to different conclusions regarding the applicable law governing the security interest.

6.140 Furthermore, a number of different laws could be relevant to the question of whether there is a valid right in rem. For example, the contractual aspects of the security (including such matters as whether an agreement exists at all, the formalities of the agreement, and its interpretation) will be governed by the Rome I Regulation. However, the validity of the security will also depend on whether it has been properly registered in the relevant jurisdiction, whether any perfection requirements (such as notifying a debtor of an assignment of receivables) have been complied with and whether title can pass by mere agreement or whether there needs to be physical delivery: these issues will generally (though not always) be determined by the *lex rei sitae* of the relevant asset and this will depend in turn on the nature of the asset in question.

6.141 In respect of tangible property where rights of ownership do not have to be registered in a public register, the RR provides that the property will be treated as being located in the Member State where it is physically located. Therefore, in the case of real or immovable property located in Ireland, Irish law (as the *lex rei sitae*) will determine the proprietary effects of the security (including such factors as the registration and perfection requirements). In the case of property and rights which are registered in a public register located in Ireland, Article 2(9) states that these assets will be located in Ireland as the Member State under the authority of which the register is kept. The RR states that, for the purposes of the RR, a 'claim' is located in the Member State where the third party required to meet the claim has its centre of main interests. Therefore, in the case of a contractual right, the home jurisdiction of the third-party debtor is likely to be relevant rather than the governing law of the contract. This question is further explored in Example 3. In the case of a bank account held with an Irish branch of an overseas bank, the bank account is deemed to be located in Ireland for the purposes of the RR.

6.142 **Territorial or secondary proceedings in Ireland.** As with Example 1, if territorial or secondary insolvency proceedings are commenced in Ireland and these proceedings (as a matter of Irish law) impose a stay on the enforcement of security, the enforcement of the security over the Irish assets will be affected by such a stay notwithstanding the fact that the security is expressed to be governed by Spanish law.

6.143 **Assets in Germany.** The analysis here will be the same as set out above in relation to the assets in Ireland—assuming that German law is the applicable law according to the normal pre-insolvency conflict of law rules, German law will determine whether the security agreement which is expressed to be governed by Spanish law is effective to create a security interest over the assets located in Germany. The key difference (as with Example 1) is that it will not be possible to have secondary proceedings in Germany which could have any effect on the enforcement of the security.

Example 3 (Spanish borrower with establishment outside the EU, security over claims governed by EU law and non-EU law)

6.144 Borrower C has its centre of main interest in Spain. It also has a branch in New York and a claim governed by New York law against a debtor whose centre of main interest is also in

New York. C has also a claim against an Italian debtor. This claim is governed by Spanish law. Prior to its insolvency, C had granted two security rights (pledges) over the two claims. The pledge over the New York law claim has been created and perfected under New York law ('the NY pledge'). The pledge over the Spanish law claim has been created and perfected under Spanish law ('the Spanish pledge').

Issues arising: summary

The Regulation is only binding on Member States. With regard to jurisdictions that are not Member States (which includes New York), each Member State will apply its own rules regarding matters such as the impact of insolvency proceedings commenced in that Member State on assets located in the other jurisdiction. **6.145**

Moreover, it may be possible for C or its creditors to file for relief under chapters 7 or 11 of the US Bankruptcy Code on the basis of the branch in New York. As a matter of US bankruptcy law, the moratorium on creditor action which arises as a consequence of the filing of a petition under the US Bankruptcy Code would have a worldwide effect but it will be a matter for the Spanish court to determine what effect the US bankruptcy proceedings have on the enforcement of security in Spain. **6.146**

Alternatively, the insolvency administrator in the Spanish insolvency proceedings may apply for recognition of those proceedings in the United States under chapter 15 of the US Bankruptcy Code (which implemented in the United States the UNCITRAL Model Law on insolvency proceedings). If such recognition is granted, there would be an automatic stay on the enforcement of the security over the assets in New York unless the US bankruptcy court ordered otherwise. **6.147**

The effect on the Spanish pledge is determined by the RR. The issue here is whether Article 8 would apply since the encumbered asset (as a 'claim') is deemed to be located in Italy, notwithstanding the fact that the Spanish pledge (and the claim) is governed by Spanish law. **6.148**

Issues arising: commentary

As with Example 1, main proceedings can be commenced in Spain. Since C does not have an establishment in Italy, no secondary proceedings can be commenced here. The opening of insolvency proceedings in the United States (US) is determined by US bankruptcy law, not by the RR. **6.149**

Assets in New York. From a Spanish conflict of laws perspective, the effects of the Spanish insolvency proceedings on the NY pledge are governed by either New York state law or US federal law as the case may be. In any event, as the RR is only binding on Member States (of which the United States is, of course, not one) the US bankruptcy court would not be required by the RR to recognize the insolvency proceedings opened in Spain. However, it may be possible for C to file a bankruptcy petition in the US or for the Spanish insolvency practitioner to apply for recognition of the Spanish insolvency proceedings under chapter 15 of the US Bankruptcy Code. It will then be a matter of US bankruptcy law as to what effect a full bankruptcy proceeding or an order recognizing the Spanish proceedings under chapter 15 would have on the enforcement of the security over the assets located in New York. **6.150**

6.151 Once main insolvency proceedings have been commenced in Spain, one option would be for the Spanish insolvency practitioner to apply for recognition of the Spanish insolvency proceedings as 'foreign main proceedings' under chapter 15 of the US Bankruptcy Code on the basis that C has its centre of main interests in Spain. Provided that the US bankruptcy court is satisfied that C does indeed have its centre of main interests in Spain, the court would be obliged to recognize the proceedings as foreign main proceedings with the consequence that there would be an automatic stay on the enforcement of security over the assets in New York unless the court ordered otherwise. Unlike the former provisions of section 304 of the Bankruptcy Code, the US bankruptcy court would not need to be satisfied that, as a matter of Spanish insolvency law, the stay on enforcement of security would extend to the assets in New York as chapter 15 expressly provides for a stay equivalent to that which would arise if bankruptcy proceedings were commenced under chapters 7 and 11 of the US Bankruptcy Code (see below) upon recognition of foreign main proceedings under chapter 15 of the US bankruptcy code.

6.152 Alternatively, C, or a creditor of C, may file a petition for bankruptcy proceedings under chapter 7 or 11 of the US Bankruptcy Code. The filing of a petition under chapter 7 or 11 of the US Bankruptcy Code creates and operates as an immediate continuing injunction against virtually all creditor actions against the debtor and so would prevent the enforcement of security in the United States (unless the secured creditor were to seek and obtain relief from the automatic stay).

6.153 **Assets in Italy.** With regard to the Spanish pledge, the RR does apply. In principle, the claim against the Italian debtor is deemed to be located in Italy, where it has its centre of main interests (see Article 2(9)(viii) of the RR). However, according to Spanish general conflict of laws rules, the validity and effectiveness of pledge over that claim is determined by the law governing the corresponding claim, ie Spanish law. The question whether Article 8 applies in this case is debatable. Even if the underlying claim is located in a Member State different from that where main insolvency proceedings are opened, some scholars understand that insofar as the *lex fori concursus* coincides with the law governing the security, Article 8 should not apply (supra paragraph [6.68]).

Example 4 (Spanish borrower, assets in the EU, impact of a restructuring proceeding that purports to release secured indebtedness)

6.154 Borrower D has its centre of main interests in Spain and assets in Spain and the Netherlands. There is no establishment in the Netherlands. The bank has entered into a Dutch law governed loan agreement and has taken security over the assets in the Netherlands pursuant to Dutch law. A preventive restructuring arrangement is proposed in respect of D in Spain which has the effect of discharging D's debts. What effect would the collective arrangement have on the bank's ability to enforce its security in the Netherlands?

Issues arising: summary

6.155 As D's centre of main interests is in Spain, a preventive restructuring arrangement can be implemented as main proceedings and the effects of this collective arrangement would be recognized by all Member States.

Under Spanish insolvency law, a preventive restructuring arrangement can affect the rights of a secured creditor to enforce its security if a qualified majority of secured creditors consents to the proposals. Thus, even if the bank does not consent to the arrangement, it may be affected if a majority vote in favour. In such a case, however, Article 8 protects its security right over the assets located in The Netherlands

6.156

Issues arising: commentary
In principle, as a matter of Spanish insolvency law, the discharge or variation of contractual rights which arises pursuant to a preventive restructuring arrangement is effective in relation to all the obligations of the debtor, no matter what the governing law of the debt in question is and regardless of the domicile of the creditor concerned. The discharge or variation can apply to financial secured creditors if a qualified majority of the secured creditors votes in favour of the arrangement. Hence, a Spanish preventive arrangement would be effective to discharge or vary any liabilities owed by D to the bank under the Dutch law governed loan agreement.

6.157

If, as a matter of the insolvency law of the relevant Member State, the main proceeding has the effect of discharging the obligations of the debtor in all jurisdictions, the question arises whether Article 8 would allow a secured creditor to enforce its security in another Member State notwithstanding the discharge of the secured liability pursuant to the main proceedings. The RR is not clear in this regard. Whilst Article 8 states that the opening of proceedings shall not 'affect' the rights in rem of creditors in respect of assets in another Member State, it could be argued that this does not prevent the discharge of the secured liability. However, without any underlying secured liability for the security to secure, the rights in rem would be worthless. Relevant legal scholars thus interpret Article 8 as a rule that also protects security rights in relation to a discharge of the secured obligation (see supra paragraph [6.77]).

6.158

Example 5 (German borrower with establishment in Spain, assets in the EU, impact of restructuring proceeding in Spain)

Borrower E has its centre of main interests in Germany and an establishment in Spain. The bank has security over assets in Italy (where there is no establishment) under a security document governed by Italian law. Is it possible to have a preventive restructuring arrangement in Spain and, if so, what effect will this have on the bank's ability to enforce its security in Italy?

6.159

Issues arising: summary
Main proceedings will need to be commenced in Germany but secondary proceedings can be commenced in Spain. Following the RR, these proceedings may be restructuring or liquidation proceedings.

6.160

However, since the secondary proceedings opened in Spain are territorial, they will not include the assets located in Italy. The bank's security right over these assets will thus not be affected by the Spanish proceedings.

6.161

Issues arising: commentary

6.162 As there is an establishment in Spain, it will be possible to open territorial or secondary proceedings in that jurisdiction. In principle, it is possible to carry out a preventive restructuring arrangement by way of secondary proceedings. Under the RR, these proceedings are not limited to liquidation proceedings.

6.163 Article 47(2) states that any restriction of creditors' rights arising from a composition or rescue will only apply to assets covered by the secondary proceedings and not to the debtor's other assets situated outside that Member State (unless creditors having an interest agree to the restriction of rights over assets in other Member States). Thus, this means that a bank with a loan agreement governed by Italian law would not be prevented from pursuing assets outside Spain, and in particular from enforcing its security rights over assets in Italy.

Example 6 (Spanish borrower, assets in the EU, impact of restructuring proceeding on intercreditor agreement)

6.164 Company F has its centre of main interests in Spain and assets (but not an establishment) in Ireland. F has granted security over its assets to both senior and junior lenders. The financing agreements are governed by Irish law and include an intercreditor agreement which provides that, if the junior lenders recover any monies at a time when amounts are still due to the senior lenders, the junior lenders will hold those recoveries on trust for the senior lenders (ie standard turnover trust wording). The facility agreements require the unanimous consent of the lenders to any reduction in the amount of the secured indebtedness. F is placed into preventive restructuring proceedings in Spain and the requisite majorities of creditors approve a plan whereby F's indebtedness under the facility agreements is reduced. Under the plan, it is proposed that the senior lenders will only receive 45 per cent of their indebtedness and the junior creditors will receive five per cent of their indebtedness. Notwithstanding the plan, can the senior lenders enforce their security over the assets in Ireland and would the junior lenders be required to turn over to the senior lenders any amounts they receive pursuant to the terms of the intercreditor agreement?

Issues arising: summary

6.165 Under Article 32 of the RR, a preventive restructuring arrangement approved by the Spanish court (as the court that commenced main insolvency proceedings in relation to F) must be recognized in all Member States. As with all main proceedings, the effects of the preventive procedure are subject to Article 8. The question therefore arises as to whether Article 8 would enable the senior creditors: (i) to enforce their security over the assets in Ireland notwithstanding the Spanish collective arrangement; and (ii) to enforce their rights pursuant to the intercreditor agreement.

6.166 For the reasons given in paragraph [6.77] above, it is not clear whether Article 8 merely protects the right in rem in the strict sense (ie the security interest over the relevant assets) or whether it also protects the underlying secured debt. Article 8 may be thought to enable a secured creditor to enforce its security over assets in another Member State notwithstanding a compromise of the secured indebtedness pursuant to the main proceedings.

The impact of the collective arrangement on any intercreditor arrangements between the junior and senior lenders will, in principle, depend upon Spanish insolvency law (and whether such an arrangement purports to affect the rights of creditors *inter se* as a matter of Spanish insolvency law). 6.167

Issues arising: commentary

The issues arising in relation to a compromise as part of main insolvency proceedings, and its impact on rights in rem over assets in another Member State, are discussed in paragraphs [6.77] and [6.157]–[6.158] above. Although such a compromise must be recognized in all Member States pursuant to Article 32 of the RR, the authors consider that such recognition must be subject to Article 8.[83] Although there is a question as to whether a distinction can be drawn between the right in rem itself and the underlying secured debt (and there is a further factual and legal question as to whether the right in rem itself has been compromised), assuming that there has been no compromise of the right in rem, it would seem to rob Article 8 of any purpose if the secured debt could be compromised to 45 per cent (or even 99.9 per cent) of its face value though a compromise in the main proceedings and the secured creditor could only enforce its security over assets in another Member State to the extent of the compromised debt.[84] Making these assumptions, the authors consider that Article 8 would enable the senior lenders to enforce their security over the assets in Ireland notwithstanding the compromise as part of the Spanish preventive restructuring proceedings. This is subject, of course, to any 'no action' clauses in the security or other finance documents which may prevent the lenders taking any enforcement action otherwise than through the security trustee. 6.168

If, contrary to the view expressed above, Article 8 does not enable the senior lenders to enforce their security over the assets in Ireland (or if the senior lenders choose not to do so or are prevented from doing so by any 'no action' clauses), the question arises as to whether, pursuant to the intercreditor agreement, the senior lenders could require the junior lenders to turn over to them any recoveries which the junior lenders may make pursuant to the Spanish main proceedings or whether the Spanish main proceedings could affect the terms of the intercreditor agreement in this regard. The first question which arises is whether, as a matter of Spanish law, the restructuring proceedings are capable of affecting the rights of creditors *inter se* or whether such proceedings can only affect the position as between F and its creditors. If the Spanish proceedings could have an impact on the position between creditors, the second question to ask is whether the senior lenders could rely on RR (including Article 8) to protect their rights under the intercreditor agreement. 6.169

In principle, as a matter of Spanish law, a Spanish restructuring plan may not seek to take effect so as to override the rights and priorities contained within an intercreditor agreement. Assuming, however, that such an override were possible, under Article 32, such effect 6.170

---

[83] The contrary view has been taken by Professor Wessels in his article 'The Secured Creditor in Cross Border Finance Transactions under the EU Insolvency Regulation' (2003) 18 Journal of International Banking Law and Regulation 135, 140.
[84] This is certainly the view of Philip Smart in 'Rights in Rem, Article 5 and the EC Insolvency Regulation: An English Perspective' (2006) 15 International Insolvency Review 17, 33.

would need to be recognized in Ireland. It is difficult to see how Article 8 could protect the rights of the senior lenders under the intercreditor agreement. Article 8 refers to rights in rem over assets of the insolvent debtor; as a matter of Irish law, the turnover trust created by the inter-creditor agreement would create a right in rem over assets of the junior lenders (ie any recoveries made by them pursuant to the Spanish collective arrangement) but would not create rights in rem over assets of F.

Example 7 (German borrower, security over bank account held through the Irish branch of a German bank)

6.171 Company G has its centre of main interests in Germany and no establishments in any other Member State. In April 2018, it granted security to bank J over a bank account held through the Irish branch of Deutsche Bank AG pursuant to an Irish law security agreement. In 2020, G became insolvent and was placed into self-management proceedings in Germany. Such proceedings give rise to a stay on the enforcement of security. Can J enforce its security over the bank account notwithstanding the German stay?

Issues arising: summary

6.172 In addition to issues and protections arising under Article 8 of the RR, J may also be able to rely on the Financial Collateral Directive (and the Irish law implementing such directive) in order to enforce its security notwithstanding the German moratorium.

Issues arising: commentary

6.173 In the current example, the application of Article 2(9)(iii) of the RR leads to the conclusion that the bank account is located in Ireland (as the place of the branch holding the account) rather than in Germany (as the place of Deutsche Bank AG's centre of main interests). On this analysis, the secured asset would be located in a Member State other than the one in which the main insolvency proceedings are commenced. Thus, in accordance with Article 8 of the RR, the security rights over the bank account will not be affected by the opening of main insolvency proceedings in Germany.

6.174 Leaving aside the issues that arise under the RR, J may also be able to rely on Council Directive (EC) 2002/47 of 6 June 2002 on financial collateral arrangements (the 'Financial Collateral Directive') in order to enforce its security over the bank account (which would constitute 'financial collateral' for these purposes). The application of the Financial Collateral Directive is beyond the scope of this book but, in brief, J's ability to rely on such legislation will depend upon how it has been implemented in Ireland.

Example 8 (Spanish borrower, security over shares in an EU subsidiary, claw-back claim)

6.175 Borrower H has its centre of main interest in Spain. Prior to its insolvency, H had granted a security rights (a pledge) over the registered shares of a subsidiary incorporated in Luxembourg. The pledge is governed by Luxembourg law. Insolvency proceedings are commenced in Spain, and the insolvency practitioner brings an action before the Spanish court to set aside the pledge in accordance with Spanish claw-back rules.

Issues arising: summary

Asset in Luxembourg. In principle, the registered shares are deemed to be located in Luxembourg and therefore Article 8 applies. However, this provision does not prejudice the application of the Spanish insolvency rules on transaction avoidance. If the pledge may be set aside under these rules, Article 16 still gives the secured creditor the possibility to invoke Luxembourg law if under this law the pledge cannot be challenged. 6.176

Issues arising: commentary

According to Article 2(9)(i) of the RR, registered shares in companies are deemed to be located in the Member State within the territory of which the company having issued the shares has its registered office. In this example, the shares are located in Luxembourg and thus, under Article 8, the opening of insolvency proceedings in Spain shall not affect the rights of the secured creditor over those shares. The secured creditor may enforce the pledge and collect on the proceeds irrespective of the Spanish insolvency proceedings. 6.177

However, Article 8 does not preclude the application of the Spanish rules on the voidness, voidability, or unenforceability of legal acts detrimental to the general body of creditors. If the pledge may be set aside under these rules, the secured creditor may still benefit from the application of Article 16. Thus, the security right will remain unaffected by the Spanish insolvency proceedings if Luxembourg law does not allow any means of challenging that act in the relevant case. 6.178

The Virgos-Schmit Report states that 'Article 16 [Article 13] acts as a veto against the invalidity of the act decreed by the law of the State of the opening' (ie in this case Spanish law) and that the aim of the Article is to uphold the legitimate expectations of creditors or third parties regarding the validity of the act under the normally applicable national law and to prevent interference from a different '*lex concursus*'.[85] 6.179

In order for the defence to be available, it would be necessary for the secured creditor to establish that: 6.180

(a) the security right was 'subject to' Luxembourg law and not Spanish law (ie the law of a Member State other than the state of the opening of the proceedings);
(b) Luxembourg law does not allow a challenge first by 'any means' and secondly 'in the relevant case'. The phrase 'any means' indicates that the act must not be capable of being challenged using either the insolvency rules (ie the specific insolvency avoidance actions) or the general rules of the national law applicable to that act. The phrase 'in the relevant case' implies that a concrete assessment of the specific act in question must be undertaken, based on the facts of the case. The meaning of these expressions has been further analysed above in paragraph [6.31].

---

[85] Virgos-Schmit Report, paras 135–39 (app 2 below).

Example 9 (Luxembourg borrower with establishment in Ireland, set-off rights in respect of a bank account in England)

6.181 The centre of main interests of borrower I is in Luxembourg and it has an establishment in Ireland. The bank has a claim against I under an English law governed unsecured loan agreement but also has an obligation to I in respect of a deposit account located in England and governed by English law terms and conditions. I becomes insolvent and the bank wants to be able to set-off against its obligation in respect of the deposit account the amounts owed to it by I under the loan agreement.

Issues arising: summary

6.182 Main proceedings in respect of I must be commenced in Luxembourg but secondary proceedings can be commenced in Ireland.

6.183 The conditions in which rights of set-off may be invoked in the main proceedings will be a matter of Luxembourg insolvency law.

6.184 However, Article 9 provides additional protection for certain rights of set-off which are not available in the main proceedings. Rights of set-off which are permitted by and arise in accordance with the law applicable to I's claim cannot be affected by the opening of insolvency proceedings. Article 9 does not expressly state that the applicable law needs to be the law of a Member State.[86] This leads to questions regarding the law applicable to I's claim.

6.185 If the set-off rights which are relied upon under Article 9 are only available in a liquidation of I in England, it may be necessary to commence liquidation proceedings in order to make use of those set-off rights, although this is not clear.

Issues arising: commentary

6.186 As the centre of main interests is in Luxembourg, main insolvency proceedings would be opened in this jurisdiction and Luxembourg law would determine the conditions under which rights of set-off could be invoked in the main proceedings.[87] However, this will not be attractive to the bank because rights of set-off are very limited under Luxembourg law. The bank will not wish to pay over to I the amount of the deposit and then claim for the full amount owing by I pursuant to the loan agreement.

6.187 Article 9 may provide an answer for the bank. This Article states that the opening of insolvency proceedings shall not affect the right of creditors to demand the set-off of their claims against the claims of the debtor where such a set-off is permitted by the law applicable to the insolvent debtor's claim. In the case of I's claim in respect of the deposit, it is likely that the applicable law will be English law as the governing law of the deposit agreement.[88] The position may be less clear in relation to a cross-claim which arises as a matter of tort; there may

---

[86] Although see para 6.90 above for the possibility that Art 9 should be read as only applicable to the law of a Member State.
[87] Art 7(2)(d).
[88] The nature and type of set-off seem to be irrelevant for the purposes of Art 9 which simply focuses on the cross-claim which forms the basis of the creditor's set-off and the law relating to it.

be an issue regarding which choice of law rules should decide the applicable law in a case involving a foreign element.

Depending on the terms of the deposit agreement, it may be that, as a matter of English law, the bank does not have a right of pre-insolvency set-off (for example because the bank has agreed to repay the amount of the deposit without set-off or counterclaim). However, in an English liquidation, the bank may well have a right of set-off under Rule 14.25 of the Insolvency (England and Wales) Rules 2016 (which is mandatory and overrides any contractual exclusions of set-off if the requisite conditions for set-off under Rule 14.25 are met). This raises the question whether the bank needs to commence a liquidation in England in respect of I in order to benefit from the safe-harbour provisions in Article 9. Article 9 is silent in this regard. **6.188**

On the facts of this particular example, it is assumed (for the reasons given above) that the insolvency set-off rules under English law would be wider than any contractual set-off rights. This is because the insolvency set-off rules under English law are very wide and are automatic and self-executing on the commencement of the insolvency. It is perhaps more likely to be the case in other jurisdictions that the insolvency set-off rules will be narrower than any contractual provisions. This gives rise to the question of whether Article 9 refers to the insolvency set-off rules of the applicable law, the contractual set-off rules, or the rules that would be available on the applicable facts (eg in this case the contractual rules if there is, in fact, no liquidation in England). One possibility is to consider (for the purposes of Article 9) the applicable law's set-off rules in the case of a hypothetical insolvency proceeding that is analogous to the main insolvency proceedings although this is not without its difficulties. **6.189**

In the current case, it would be possible to commence an English liquidation (to bring into play the insolvency set-off rules under Rule 14.25 of the Insolvency (England and Wales) Rules 2016 if there is a sufficient connection with England and it may be that the English governing law of the loan agreement and deposit agreement would be sufficient for these purposes. However, had the insolvent debtor's claim been governed by the law of a Member State (for example Ireland), it would be necessary for the debtor to have an establishment in that jurisdiction in order for the bank to commence secondary proceedings falling under the RR. **6.190**

7
FINANCIAL INSTITUTIONS

A. **General Framework**	7.01	
EU Framework for financial institution insolvencies	7.01	
Common principles	7.10	
B. **Financial Institutions Excluded from the RR**	7.19	
Insurance undertakings	7.20	
Credit institutions	7.23	
Investment firms	7.25	
Collective investment undertakings	7.26	
C. **Settlement Finality, Central Counterparties, and Financial Collateral**	7.30	
Settlement Finality Directive	7.30	
Central Counterparties Regulation	7.35	
Financial Collateral Directive	7.38	
D. **Winding-Up Directive**	7.41	
Winding-Up Directive: scope and definitions	7.41	
Winding-Up Directive: reorganization measures	7.59	
Winding-Up Directive: winding-up proceedings	7.66	
Winding-Up Directive: common provisions	7.73	
E. **Solvency II**	7.101	
Solvency II: scope	7.101	
Solvency II: selective commentary	7.106	
F. **Bank Recovery and Resolution Directive**	7.164	
Title I: scope and definitions	7.164	
Title II: preparation	7.176	
Title III: early intervention	7.183	
Title IV: resolution	7.188	
Title V: cross-border group resolution	7.249	
Title VI: relations with third countries	7.258	
Title VII: financing arrangements	7.264	
Title VIII: penalties	7.270	
G. **Central Counterparties Regulation**	7.272	

A. General Framework

EU Framework for financial institution insolvencies

7.01 Article 1(2)[1] of Regulation (EU) 2015/848 of the European Parliament and of the Council of 20 May 2015 on insolvency proceedings (recast) (the RR[2]) provides that:

This Regulation shall not apply to proceedings referred to in paragraph 1 that concern:

(a) insurance undertakings;
(b) credit institutions;
(c) investment firms and other firms, institutions and undertakings to the extent that they are covered by Directive 2001/24/EC; or
(d) collective investment undertakings.

---

[1] Great thanks are due to Martijn Gijsen for his research assistance.
[2] The RR is a recast of Council Regulation (EC) 1346/2000 of 29 May 2000 on insolvency proceedings, OJ L160 (OR). The RR will apply to insolvency proceedings (as defined in the RR) opened after 26 June 2017 (see Art 84(1) RR). Prior to that date, the OR will continue to apply.

7.02 Before turning to a consideration of the regimes which apply to each of the categories of entities set out in this Article 1(2) taking into account the effect of Articles 9(1) and 12(1) RR,[3] it is proposed to review the major legal and policy elements behind the need to segregate these aspects of the financial services markets designated by these Articles from the general ambit of the Insolvency Proceedings Regulation.[4]

7.03 For all of the categories of financial institutions listed above, EU regulation has been adopted so that they can and must make use of a single authorization granted by the home Member State's supervisory authority. This form of authorization has often been referred to as the European passport. In practical terms it means that the financial institution is allowed to operate cross-border (including through internet or by telephone) and through branches in other Member States without further authorization from the relevant host state or states.

7.04 The original regulation introducing the European passport for insurance undertakings and credit institutions, however, did not contain co-ordination rules in the event of credit institutions or insurance undertakings' reorganization or winding-up. Specifically, the second Recital of the Insurance Directive stated that insurance Directives providing for a single authorization system within a 'Community scope' for insurance undertakings did not contain co-ordination rules in the event of there being winding-up proceedings. Therefore, the European legislature introduced in 2001 both the Council Directive (EC) 2001/17 (Insurance Directive)[5] and the Council Directive (EC) 2001/24 on the reorganisation and winding up of credit institutions (the Credit Institutions Winding-Up Directive or Winding-up Directive).[6] The Winding-Up Directive had to be implemented by Member States by 5 May 2004 and has, most recently, been amended by the Bank Recovery and Resolution Directive (BRRD).[7] The Winding-Up Directive in effect grew out of the 2000 Banking Directive.[8] While the Winding-Up Directive is still in force (as amended over time), the Insurance Directive has been replaced by Title IV (Articles 267–296) of the Solvency II Directive since 1 January 2016.[9]

---

[3] For a fuller review of these provisions, see Chapter 8 below.

[4] Regulation (EU) 2015/848 of the European Parliament and of the Council of 20 May 2015 on insolvency proceedings, OJ L141. The subject matter of this chapter is covered extensively in a related publication, Moss, Wessels, Haentjens (eds), *EU Banking and Insurance Insolvency* (2nd edn, 2017).

[5] Directive 2001/17/EC of the European Parliament and of the Council of 19 March 2001 on the reorganisation and winding-up of insurance undertakings, OJ L110.

[6] Directive 2001/24/EC of the European Parliament and of the Council of 4 April 2001 on the reorganisation and winding up of credit institutions, OJ L125.

[7] Directive 2014/59/EU of the European Parliament and of the Council of 15 May 2014 establishing a framework for the recovery and resolution of credit institutions and investment firms and amending Council Directive 82/891/EEC, and Directives 2001/24/EC, 2002/47/EC, 2004/25/EC, 2005/56/EC, 2007/36/EC, 2011/35/EU, 2012/30/EU and 2013/36/EU, and Regulations (EU) No 1093/2010 and (EU) No 648/2012, of the European Parliament and of the Council, OJ L173.

[8] Council Regulation (EC) No 44/2001 of 22 December 2000 on jurisdiction and the recognition and enforcement of judgments in civil and commercial matters, OJ L12. In turn amended by Directive 2000/46/EC of the European Parliament and of the Council of 18 September 2000 on the taking up, pursuit of, and prudential supervision of the business of electronic money institutions, OJ L275. The Banking Directive has been recast in European Parliament and Directive 2006/48/EC of the European Parliament and of the Council of 14 June 2006 relating to the taking up and pursuit of the business of credit institutions, OJ L177. However, for the purposes of this chapter reference will continue to be made to the 2000 Directive and its terms.

[9] Directive 2009/138/EC of the European Parliament and of the Council of 25 November 2009 on the taking-up and pursuit of the business of Insurance and Reinsurance (Solvency II), OJ L335, as amended by Directive 2013/58/EU of the European Parliament and of the Council of 11 December 2013 amending Directive 2009/138/EC (Solvency II) as regards the date for its transposition and the date of its application, and the date of repeal of certain Directives (Solvency I), OJ L341.

7.05 Recitals (1) and (2) of the Winding-Up Directive expressly state that it is in the interests of the proper functioning of the internal market first that co-ordination rules be established at EU level in order to regulate reorganization measures or winding-up proceedings with regard to credit institutions and secondly, that any obstacles otherwise set up in the face of the freedom of establishment and of the provision of services within the EU be alleviated or removed, especially in the case of institutions holding or operating branches in other Member States. The Insurance Directive (and therefore, its successor Solvency II Title IV) takes a somewhat different approach in that Recital (3), while promoting the benefits of the establishment of co-ordination rules, militates against the need to engage in a 'winding-up situation'.[10]

7.06 As a consequence of the Global Financial Crisis of 2008, a European Banking Union has been established, which consists of three legs. First, a Single Supervisory Mechanism has been put in place, under which the European Central Bank acts as the single prudential supervisor responsible (directly or indirectly) for all credit institutions in the Eurozone and states that wish to accede.[11] This Single Supervisory Mechanism should contribute to the prevention of bank insolvencies. A harmonized bank insolvency regime for the EU forms the Banking Union's second leg and will be discussed more extensively below. Initially, the Commission proposed to create a common European deposit guarantee scheme as the third leg of the Banking Union, but until the moment of writing, this has proven too ambitious politically. A recast of the deposit guarantee scheme Directive, however, has been adopted on 16 April 2014,[12] whilst the Commission's latest attempt to further unify the EU's deposit guarantee schemes has been published on 24 November 2015 as the (draft) European Deposit Insurance Scheme Regulation.[13]

7.07 The EU harmonized bank insolvency regime, or Banking Union's second leg represented a major overhaul of the rules governing credit institutions and certain investment firms that experience financial difficulties. It provides for a comprehensive framework with an aim to 'provide authorities with a credible set of tools to intervene sufficiently early and quickly in an unsound or failing institution so as to ensure the continuity of the institution's critical financial and economic functions, while minimising the impact of an institution's failure on the economy and financial system'.[14] It consists of the BRRD and a Single Resolution Mechanism (SRM). While the BRRD applies to all EU Member States, its application in the Eurozone has been unified by means of the SRM. Under this mechanism, established by a Single Resolution Mechanism Regulation (SRMR),[15] 'a centralised power of resolution is

---

[10] Cf Recital (6) in the Winding-Up Directive which expressly states that it is 'necessary to establish mutual recognition by the Member States of the measures taken by each of them to restore to viability the credit institutions which it has authorised'.

[11] Council Regulation (EU) 1024/2013 of 15 October 2013 conferring specific tasks on the European Central Bank concerning policies relating to the prudential supervision of credit institutions, OJ L287/63. As of 1 October 2020, Bulgaria and Croatia have so acceded.

[12] Directive 2014/49/EU of the European Parliament and of the Council of 16 April 2014 on deposit guarantee schemes, OJ L173.

[13] Proposal for a Regulation of the European Parliament and of the Council amending Regulation (EU) 806/2014 in order to establish a European Deposit Insurance Scheme COM/2015/0586 final—2015/0270 (COD).

[14] Recital (5) BRRD.

[15] Regulation (EU) 806/2014 of the European Parliament and of the Council of 15 July 2014 establishing uniform rules and a uniform procedure for the resolution of credit institutions and certain investment firms in the

established and entrusted to the Single Resolution Board [...] and to the national resolution authorities'.[16] Since 2021, BRRD II[17] has added several material elements to BRRD, which will be further discussed below, in Part F.

To complement the framework for the recovery and resolution of credit institutions and certain categories of investment firms already in existence, the EU legislature has adopted in 2020 a Regulation for the recovery and resolution of central counterparties ('CCPs'),[18] ie the legal persons that interpose themselves 'between the counterparties to the contracts traded on one or more financial markets, becoming the buyer to every seller and the seller to every buyer'.[19] This CCP Regulation is largely based on the BRRD and SRMR, but intends to take into account the specificities of this category of financial institutions. Similarly, the EU Commission has published in September 2021 a proposal for a Directive on the recovery and resolution of insurance undertakings.[20] **7.08**

All these instruments introduce a harmonized or even unified, specialist regime for the management of financial institutions suffering from financial distress. This has diminished the relevance of the Winding-Up Directive, which is primarily a conflict of laws instrument that determines which national (insolvency) law to apply in a bank insolvency. However, experience since the adoption of BRRD and SRMR has shown that national (insolvency) laws remain of great importance, both within a resolution process, and outside of it. These national (insolvency) laws have not (yet) been harmonized, so that significant differences remain. More generally put, the EU legislature has not addressed financial institution insolvencies in a comprehensive manner but rather tailors instruments to specific institutions or to specific functions these institutions perform. For example, and in addition to the specialist resolution regimes referred to above, the EU has regulated financial institutions where they act as participants in market infrastructures and as counterparties in certain financial collateral transactions. This concerns the Settlement Finality Directive[21] and the Financial Collateral Directive[22] respectively. **7.09**

---

framework of a Single Resolution Mechanism and a Single Resolution Fund and amending Regulation (EU) No 1093/2010, OJ L225.

[16] Recital (11) SRMR.
[17] Directive (EU) 2019/879 of the European Parliament and of the Council of 20 May 2019 amending Directive 2014/59/EU as regards the loss-absorbing and recapitalization capacity of credit institutions and investment firms and Directive 98/26/EC, OJ L150.
[18] Regulation (EU) 2021/23 of the European Parliament and of the Council of 16 December 2020 on a framework for the recovery and resolution of central counterparties and amending Regulations (EU) No 1095/2010, (EU) No 648/2012, (EU) No 600/2014, (EU) No 806/2014 and (EU) 2015/2365 and Directives 2002/47/EC, 2004/25/EC, 2007/36/EC, 2014/59/EU, and (EU) 2017/1132, OJ L22.
[19] Article 2(1) of Regulation (EU) No 648/2012 of the European Parliament and of the Council of 4 July 2012 on OTC derivatives, central counterparties, and trade repositories (EMIR).
[20] Proposal for a Directive of the European Parliament and of the Council establishing a framework for the recovery and resolution of insurance and reinsurance undertakings and amending Directives 2002/47/EC, 2004/25/EC, 2009/138/EC, (EU) 2017/1132, and Regulations (EU) No 1094/2010 and (EU) No 648/2012, COM/2021/582 final. This Chapter will not discuss this proposed Directive in detail, as we focus on current law, and the proposal may be subject to change or not be adopted at all.
[21] Directive 98/26/EC of the European Parliament and of the Council of 19 May 1998 on settlement finality in payment and securities settlement systems, OJ L166.
[22] Directive 2002/47/EC of the European Parliament and of the Council of 6 June 2002 on financial collateral arrangements, OJ L168.

Common principles

7.10 This is not the place to discuss the finer aspects of the common principles that govern cross-border bank and insurance company insolvencies. Yet some words should be said about these principles, which, to a greater or lesser extent, may be relevant for any bank or insurance company insolvency in the EU spanning more than one jurisdiction.

7.11 First, the principle of unity means that only one state, namely that state in which the registered seat, head office, or centre of main interests is located, should determine the course of the insolvency of a bank or insurance company that has operations in multiple jurisdictions. In consequence, an overseas branch of a bank or insurance company would be subject to the latter's insolvency laws and regulations. The governing law is thus referred to as the *lex concursus*.

7.12 Second, the principle of universality means that the *lex concursus* will govern all the terms and effects of the insolvency and will do so beyond the territorial borders of the state where the insolvency proceedings have been opened. This principle is therefore to be contrasted with the principle of territoriality which has the opposite effect.

7.13 Third, the principle of single entity means that in practical terms, the insolvent entity be wound up as a single legal entity by its home state. The assets of a branch therefore are to be administered by the insolvency procedures instigated by that state's jurisdiction.[23] In general terms, Solvency II Title IV and the Winding-Up Directive adopt the universalist and single entity approach discussed just now. The BRRD, however, takes a more nuanced approach. See below, paragraph 7.47.

7.14 In addition to the common principles discussed above, there are at least three other elements of relevance in the context of (cross-border operating) financial institutions.

7.15 First, bank and insurance company insolvency law generally derogates from the *pari passu* or *paritas creditorum* principle, so that in the insolvency of these categories of firms, creditor hierarchy is different from general insolvency law. In bank insolvency law, for instance, depositors rank higher than other (senior) creditors. See, for instance, Article 108 BRRD and Directive 2014/49/EU of the European Parliament and of the Council of 16 April 2014 on deposit guarantee schemes.[24]

7.16 Second, specific categories of financial contracts are treated differently than in general insolvency laws. Below, in paragraph […], financial collateral arrangements and close-out netting will be more extensively discussed, the use of which is liberalized under the Settlement Finality and Financial Collateral Directives (but somewhat restricted again in the BRRD and SRMR).

---

[23] Art 4(1)(43) CRR (defined below) provides that the home state means 'the Member State in which an institution has been granted authorization', while Art 4(1)(44) of the same CRR provides that the host state is 'the Member State in which an institution has a branch or in which it provides services'. Art 4(1)(17) CRR defines a branch as 'a place of business which forms a legally dependent part of an institution and which carries out directly all or some of the transactions inherent in the business of institutions'.

[24] Directive 2014/49/EU of the European Parliament and of the Council of 16 April 2014 on deposit guarantee schemes, OJ L173.

7.17 Finally, and related to the 'common principles' discussed above, financial group companies are treated differently under international insolvency laws than under general insolvency law. The BRRD, for instance, has specific rules for the treatment of group companies as a whole. See below, paragraph 7.47 and paragraphs 7.256–7.261. This is different under general insolvency law, which is commonly characterized by an entity-by-entity approach.

7.18 In the following, we will first discuss, in some detail, the (definitions of the) entities that fall outside of the scope of the RR. This discussion will then be supplemented by an introduction into several instruments of EU law which purport to harmonize specific financial market activities and have specific relevance for insolvency law. Subsequently, a selective commentary of the Winding-Up Directive and Title IV of Solvency II will be given. This Chapter concludes with a selective commentary of the BRRD and the CCP Regulation. For a brief survey of the evolution of the earlier Directives in particular Council Directive (EC) 88/361[25] and Council Regulation (EC) 1346/2000,[26] see the corresponding chapter in the earlier editions of this work.[27]

B. Financial Institutions Excluded from the RR

7.19 Recital (9) RR requires that it apply to insolvency proceedings concerning national and legal persons,[28] whereas Article 1(2) specifically excludes four categories of financial institutions and related entities, namely:

(i) insurance undertakings;
(ii) credit institutions;
(iii) investment firms and other firms, institutions and undertakings to the extent that they are covered by Directive 2001/24/EC; and
(iv) collective investment undertakings.

Recital (19) RR stresses that these four categories are subject to special arrangements and notes that 'the national supervisory authorities have wide-ranging powers of intervention'. The four categories in question, however, are not further considered, let alone defined by the RR. One has to turn to other instruments of EU law for that purpose,[29] which we will now do.

Insurance undertakings

7.20 As already stated above, insurance undertakings are the subject of Solvency II and the proposal for a Directive on the recovery and resolution of insurance undertakings. Most

---

[25] Council Directive 88/361/EEC of 24 June 1988 for the implementation of Art 67 of the Treaty, OJ L178/5.
[26] Council Regulation (EC) No 1346/2000 of 29 May 2000 on insolvency proceedings, OJ L160.
[27] See, eg, pp 132–33 in the first edition, entitled 'Background: the treaty framework'.
[28] The insolvency proceedings to which the Insolvency Regulation applies are set out in Annex A.
[29] Note, however, *FSA v Dobb White & Co* [2004] BPIR 479 which stresses that insofar as an entity otherwise caught by the four categories but not otherwise subject to a discrete EU regime is concerned, the Insolvency Regulation will apply.

of the matters provided for by Solvency II and the proposed Directive are reflected in the Winding-Up Directive and BRRD, respectively, and vice versa.

7.21 An 'insurance undertaking' is any entity covered by the First Council Directive (EEC) 73/239, which dealt with direct insurance other than life insurance as well as by Council Directive (EEC) 79/267 (Direct Life Insurance Directive), which dealt with direct life assurance. Both of these Directives were supplemented by Council Directive (EEC) 92/96 as further supplemented (the so-called Third Life Assurance Directive), which was, in its turn, repealed and replaced by Directive 2002/83/EC of the European Parliament and of the Council of 5 November 2002 concerning life assurance.[30]

7.22 Solvency II now covers both direct life and non-life insurance undertakings, as well as reinsurance undertakings (see Article 2(1)). According to Article 13 point 1 of Solvency II, an insurance undertaking means 'a direct life or non-life insurance undertaking which has received authorisation in accordance with Article 14'. Article 14 directs the reader to Article 2(2) for non-life insurance (which directs, in part, to activities of the classes set out in Part A of Annex I), and to Article 2(3) for life insurance (which provision also contains a list of activities).

Credit institutions

7.23 Article 1 Winding-Up Directive refers to a precursor of the CRR and CRD IV for the definition of 'credit institution' (which definition has not been materially changed since), whilst Article 2 Winding-Up Directive points to CRR for the definition of 'branch' (Article 2).

7.24 Under Article 4(1)(1) of Regulation (EU) 575/2013 of the European Parliament and of the Council of 26 June 2013 on prudential requirements for credit institutions and investment firms and amending Regulation (EU) 648/2012 (CRR),[31] a 'credit institution' is 'an undertaking the business of which is to take deposits or other repayable funds from the public and to grant credits for its own account'. Article 2(5) of Directive 2013/36/EU of the European Parliament and of the Council of 26 June 2013 on access to the activity of credit institutions and the prudential supervision of credit institutions and investment firms, amending Directive 2002/87/EC and repealing Directives 2006/48/EC and 2006/49/EC (CRD IV)[32] excludes certain institutions, principally central banks of the Member States and other financial institutions such as friendly societies and post office giro institutions from this definition. Article 4(1)(17) CRR defines a 'branch' as meaning 'a place of business which forms a legally dependent part of an institution and which carries out directly all or some of the transactions inherent in the business of institutions'.

---

[30] Directive 2002/83/EC of the European Parliament and of the Council of 5 November 2002 concerning life assurance, OJ L345.
[31] Regulation (EU) No 575/2013 of the European Parliament and of the Council of 26 June 2013 on prudential requirements for credit institutions and investment firms and amending Regulation (EU) No 648/2012, repealed by Solvency II, OJ L176.
[32] Directive 2013/36/EU of the European Parliament and of the Council of 26 June 2013 on access to the activity of credit institutions and the prudential supervision of credit institutions and investment firms, amending Directive 2002/87/EC and repealing Directives 2006/48/EC and 2006/49/EC, as amended from time to time, OJ L176.

Investment firms

Article 1(2)(c) RR also excludes from its scope 'investment firms and other firms, institutions and undertakings to the extent that they are covered by the [Winding-Up Directive]'. The Winding-Up Directive, however, does not define, nor does it (directly) concern investment firms. It concerns credit institutions, which nonetheless may also function as investment firms or other categories of financial institutions. For the definition of 'investment firm', reference must be had to Article 4(1)(1) of MiFID II,[33] which says that an 'investment firm' 'means any legal person whose regular occupation or business is the provision of one or more investment services to third parties and/or the performance of one or more investment activities on a professional basis'. 'Investment services and activities' are then defined as 'any of the services and activities listed in Section A of Annex I [of MiFID II] relating to any of the instruments listed in Section C of Annex I [of MiFID II]'. In general terms, this will cover any enterprise which regularly carries out as a professional activity investment activities or investment services. This would include receiving or dealing with financial instruments such as securities, either on the undertaking's own behalf or on behalf of third parties, providing investment advice, and managing investment portfolios.

7.25

Collective investment undertakings

A 'collective investment undertaking' as such is not defined in EU legislation. Yet the EU legislator has adopted two instruments that cover the most important (sub)categories of collective investment undertakings, viz undertakings for collective investment in transferable securities (UCITS) and alternative investment funds (AIFs). UCITS are regulated by means of the UCITS IV Directive[34] and AIFs by means of the AIFMD Directive.[35]

7.26

Article 1(2) UCITS IV defines a UCITS as: 'an undertaking: (a) with the sole object of collective investment in transferable securities or in other liquid financial assets referred to in Article 50(1) of capital raised from the public and which operate on the principle of risk-spreading; and (b) with units which are, at the request of holders, repurchased or redeemed, directly or indirectly, out of those undertakings' assets.' In short: open-ended collective investment funds, or anybody whose sole aim is to deal with the collective investments of transferable securities from capital raised from the public and whose operations are subject to the principles of risk spreading and risk sharing and the shares or units of which are,

7.27

---

[33] Directive 2014/65/EU of the European Parliament and of the Council of 15 May 2014 on markets in financial instruments and amending Directive 2002/92/EC and Directive 2011/61/EU, OJ L173, as amended from time to time. Confusingly, Art 1(3) Winding-Up Directive, as added by Art 117 BRRD, refers to investment firms as defined in CRR, which redirects to Directive 2004/39/EC, the precursor of MiFID II.

[34] Directive 2009/65/EC of the European Parliament and of the Council of 13 July 2009 on the co-ordination of laws, regulations and administrative provisions relating to undertakings for collective investment in transferable securities (UCITS), as amended from time to time, OJ L302. The latest overhaul was effectuated through Directive (EU) 2019/2162 of the European Parliament and of the Council of 27 November 2019 on the issue of covered bonds and covered bond public supervision and amending Directives 2009/65/EC and 2014/59/EU, OJ L328.

[35] Directive 2011/61/EU of the European Parliament and of the Council of 8 June 2011 on Alternative Investment Fund Managers and amending Directives 2003/41/EC and 2009/65/EC and Regulations (EC) 1060/2009 and (EU) 1095/2010 (AIFMD), OJ L174.

on the bearer's request, bought or paid back directly or indirectly from the assets of those bodies.[36]

7.28 Pursuant to Article 4(1)(a) AIFMD, alternative investment funds are 'collective investment undertakings, including investment compartments thereof which raise capital from a number of investors, with a view to investing it in accordance with a defined investment policy for the benefit of those investors and do not require authorisation pursuant to [UCITS IV].'

7.29 For purposes of the Insolvency Regulation, both in its original and recast versions, most probably both UCITS and AIFs as just defined are excluded from its scope, but maybe also other collective investment undertakings not so defined.

C. Settlement Finality, Central Counterparties, and Financial Collateral

Settlement Finality Directive

7.30 As stated above, several EU instruments aim to harmonize specific financial market activities and have specific relevance for insolvency law. As a gross oversimplification, these instruments intend to address the systemic risk that may materialize as a result of certain financial market activities. These instruments and activities mainly concern the centralized clearing and settlement of financial transactions, and the provision of collateral in that context. More specifically, the following paragraphs will subsequently discuss the Settlement Finality Directive, the CCP Regulation, and the Financial Collateral Directive.

7.31 The Settlement Finality Directive[37] has as its objective the reduction of risk by providing principally for the finality of settlement of the transfers of funds and securities through payment and securities settlement systems. This is particularly relevant for cases where the insolvency of one party arises, as such insolvency may have systemic consequences if it would be allowed to affect the other participants in such payment and securities settlement systems.

7.32 Article 12 of the RR addresses 'payment systems and financial markets', without defining any of those terms. The Settlement Finality Directive defines a 'system' (which includes both payment and securities settlement systems, but not financial markets) as 'a formal arrangement: between three or more participants, […] with common rules and standardised arrangements for the clearing, whether or not through a central counterparty, or execution of transfer orders between the participants governed by the law of a Member State chosen by the participants; […], and designated, without prejudice to other more stringent conditions of general application laid down by national law, as a system and notified to the European Securities and Markets Authority by the Member State whose law is applicable, after that Member State is satisfied as to the adequacy of the rules of the system.'

---

[36] See the Virgos-Schmit Report 1996, para 60.
[37] The Council Directive (EC) 98/26 on settlement finality in payment and securities settlement systems, OJ L166.

7.33 Pursuant to Article 3(1) Settlement Finality Directive, the netting or setting-off of claims must be enforceable after the opening of insolvency proceedings of one of the participants in a system (as defined above), provided there has been a prior 'transfer order'. Also and importantly, Article 7 Settlement Finality Directive provides that insolvency proceedings cannot have retroactive effects on the rights and obligations of a participant arising from, or in connection with, its participation in a system before the moment of opening of such proceedings. In other words, the so-called 00-hours rule is disapplied for this specific instance.

7.34 Recital (27) and Article 12 RR expressly recognize that the specific provisions of the Settlement Finality Directive in general take precedence over the general rules in the RR. As a major derogation, Article 8 Settlement Finality Directive provides that the rights and obligations arising from, or in connection with, the participation of a participant in a settlement system is determined by the law governing that system, should insolvency proceedings be opened against that participant. In addition, the rights of a system operator or of a participant to collateral security provided to them in connection with a system, and the rights of central banks of the Member States or the European Central Bank to collateral security provided to them, are not to be affected by insolvency proceedings against the participant, the system operator, a counterparty to central banks of the Member States or the European Central Bank, or any third party which provided the collateral security, whilst such collateral security may be realized for the satisfaction of those rights (Article 9(1) Settlement Finality Directive).

Central Counterparties Regulation

7.35 As just discussed, the Settlement Finality Directive covers 'systems', ie both payment and securities settlement systems, and specifically addresses the situation where one or more participants to those systems fall insolvent. This directive therefore does not primarily address the situation in which the operator of a payment or securities settlement system suffers from financial distress. This is the topic of the CCP Regulation.

7.36 Since the Global Financial Crisis of 2008, it was recognized that a CCP insolvency would have systemic consequences, but also that CCPs should play a larger role in the clearing of, specifically, derivatives transactions.[38] Therefore, it was decided that significant categories of derivatives transactions should be required by law to be centrally cleared. In other words, for significant categories of derivatives transactions, a CCP must be interposed between the counterparties to those derivatives transactions, thus becoming the buyer to every seller and the seller to every buyer. In the EU, this central clearing requirement has been laid down in the EMIR, ie Regulation (EU) No 648/2012. It took almost 10 years for the adoption of the CCP Regulation, which now provides for rules of substantive insolvency law and which introduced a specialist resolution regime for CCPs.

---

[38] Recital (4) Regulation (EU) 2021/23 of the European Parliament and of the Council of 16 December 2020 on a framework for the recovery and resolution of central counterparties and amending Regulations (EU) No 1095/2010, (EU) No 648/2012, (EU) No 600/2014, (EU) No 806/2014 and (EU) 2015/2365 and Directives 2002/47/EC, 2004/25/EC, 2007/36/EC, 2014/59/EU and (EU) 2017/1132 (CCP Regulation), OJ L22/1.

7.37 The substantive content of the CCP Regulation will be summarized below, in Part G of this Chapter. Here, it suffices to say that pursuant to Article 2(16) CCP Regulation, a 'financial market infrastructure' can be a central counterparty or CCP, a central securities depository, a trade repository, and a 'system' as defined in the Settlement Finality Directive. The term financial market infrastructure therefore covers both CCPs and payment and securities settlement systems.

Financial Collateral Directive

7.38 It was already stated above that Article 9(1) Settlement Finality Directive addresses the effect of insolvency proceedings for the rights of a system operator or of a participant in a system to collateral that has been provided in connection with a system. The Financial Collateral Directive takes this a step further, and more generally provides rules for financial collateral transactions, ie for credit transactions where the collateral consists of cash, financial instruments or certain credit claims, not necessarily in connection with a payment or securities settlement system.[39]

7.39 Before the Global Financial Crisis of 2008, it was generally believed financial collateral transactions greatly contribute to the reduction of systemic risk. This view has been nuanced since, but in June 2002, the Financial Collateral Directive was adopted, and it sought to ensure that the operation of close-out netting provisions present in most financial collateral transactions would not be hindered by, in short, insolvency law prescriptions. See Article 7 Financial Collateral Directive. Also, under Article 8 Financial Collateral Directive, insolvency provisions are disapplied which declare invalid or void or reverse financial collateral arrangements. Equally disapplied are insolvency provisions which declare invalid or void the provision of financial collateral on the sole basis that the financial collateral arrangement has come into existence, or the financial collateral has been provided on the day of the commencement of winding-up proceedings or reorganization measures, or in a prescribed period prior to, and defined by reference to, the commencement of such proceedings or measures. Similarly, the provision of top-up or substitute collateral is thus safeguarded from insolvency provisions.

7.40 The scope of the so-called 'safe harbours' discussed above, has been limited to some extent in the context of the recently introduced, specialist bank resolution regime, as policy makers and legislators realized after the Global Financial Crisis of 2008 that these safe harbours could also have a procyclical effect, and thus could contribute to the realization of systemic risk, rather than decrease such risk, especially in the context of a bank insolvency.

---

[39] See, on financial collateral transactions extensively eg M Haentjens (ed), *Financial Collateral* (OUP, 2020). In *Private Equity Insurance Group/Swedbank,* the CJEU considered whether and in what circumstances cash deposited in an account constitutes 'financial collateral' as defined in the Collateral Directive. See CJEU 10 November 2016, C-156/15, ECLI:EU:C:2016:851 (*Private Equity Insurance Group/Swedbank*), C-156/15.

D. Winding-Up Directive

Winding-Up Directive: scope and definitions

Articles 1 and 2 of the Winding-Up Directive determine the scope of the Directive. Pursuant to Article 1 Winding-Up Directive, this Directive applies to credit institutions, and, since the enactment of the BRRD, also to certain categories of investment firms. **7.41**

As indicated above,[40] the definition of 'credit institution' has to be gleaned from Article 4(1)(1) CRR, namely 'an undertaking the business of which is to take deposits or other repayable funds from the public and to grant credits for its own account'. This means that if what purports to be a bank within a given national system does not satisfy this definition of a credit institution, the Directive will not apply. Should that entity be subject to a form of collective proceeding, the Insolvency Regulation will generally apply. **7.42**

For the definition of 'investment firm', reference must be had, as stated above, to Article 4(1)(1) MiFID II, which says that an 'investment firm' 'means any legal person whose regular occupation or business is the provision of one or more investment services to third parties and/or the performance of one or more investment activities on a professional basis'. 'Investment services and activities' are then defined as 'any of the services and activities listed in Section A of Annex I [of MiFID II] relating to any of the instruments listed in Section C of Annex I [of MiFID II]'. Article 1(4) Winding-Up Directive now states that in as far as resolution tools are applied and resolution powers are exercised to 'financial institutions, firms and parent undertakings' as covered by BRRD, the Winding-Up Directive also applies to the same. These institutions are further defined (via Article 2 BRRD) in Article 4 CRR. More notable for these purposes, financial institutions may be subsidiaries of, in short, a credit institution or investment firm, a (parent) financial holding company, or (parent) mixed holding company (Article 1(1)(b) BRRD). **7.43**

From Article 1(1) and 1(2), it follows that the Winding-Up Directive applies to banks and certain investment firms with at least one branch within a Member State other than the Member State in which it has its head office. A 'branch' is defined in Article 4(1)(17) CRR as meaning: 'a place of business which forms a legally dependent part of an institution and which carries out directly all or some of the transactions inherent in the business of institutions.'[41] **7.44**

In case a credit institution has its head office outside the EU, the provisions of the Winding-up Directive only apply if the credit institution has branches in at least two Member States. See Article 2(2). This is a so-called de minimis rule. **7.45**

The Winding-up Directive is silent on the question whether its rules also apply in the insolvency of a credit institution based in a third country, but with assets in the EU. Such a rule will especially be missed now that the United Kingdom has left the EU. In such a situation, **7.46**

---

[40] See above at para 7.23.
[41] This is on the basis that the reference to 'headquarters' can be taken to mean 'head office'; reference should be made to Art 6(2) of the 2000 Banking Directive which stipulates that each Member State shall require that 'any credit institution which is a legal person and which, under its national law, has a registered office shall have its head office in the same Member State as its registered office': now see Art 4 of Directive (EC) 2006/48.

the national rules on jurisdiction and conflict of laws will probably apply. It must be noted, however, that since the Financial Stability Board (FSB) has adopted its Key Attributes and these Key Attributes have now been implemented by a significant number of countries, the substantive rules regarding the resolution of credit institutions are harmonized. Moreover, the Key Attributes as well the BRRD contain a specific regime on how cross-border, extra-EU bank insolvencies must be handled by the relevant authorities.

7.47 Recital (3) makes it clear that the Winding-Up Directive takes a single entity approach but only as between a credit institution and its branches. As a matter of principle, no such approach is taken as between the institution and its subsidiaries. The latter are treated as legally self-standing entities and thus subject to the (insolvency) laws of the Member States in which they are incorporated or by which they are regulated. In general terms, EU law does not treat groups of companies as a single entity either for the purposes of general corporate law or with regard to insolvency law. The BRRD and SRMR, however, do treat group companies as a whole under certain circumstances, and require the relevant authorities to co-operate. Moreover, the BRRD contains specific rules for intragroup financing arrangements.[42] Also, the RR now contains provisions that resemble the rules of the BRRD and cater for the co-operation and communication where there are insolvency proceedings which relate to two or more members of a group of companies, as well as for 'group co-coordination proceedings'. This is not to say that the courts across the EU may not still agree or arrange to entrust a reorganization measure or winding-up proceedings to the same person or group of persons in respect of a group of interrelated entities.

7.48 Article 2 deals with some important definitions. Two of the most important ones are 'home Member State' and 'host Member State'. Both terms find their meanings in the CRR. A 'home Member State' means the Member State of origin, that is the state which grants authorization to the credit institution.[43] This will be the Member State where the credit institution is incorporated. That is the state in which a reorganization measure or winding-up proceeding in respect of a credit institution must be opened. A 'host Member State' is a Member State in which a credit institution has a branch or in which it provides services.[44] A 'branch' according to the CRR is a 'place of business which forms a legally dependent part of an institution and which carries out directly all or some of the transactions inherent in the business of institutions'. See also paragraphs 7.11–7.13 above.

7.49 For the organization of the Winding-Up Directive, of great importance are the definitions of 'reorganisation measures' and 'winding-up proceedings'.

7.50 The Directive defines 'reorganisation measures' in much the same terms as Solvency II.[45] In the context of reorganization measures, an 'administrator' is any person or body appointed by the administrative or judicial authorities whose task it is to administer such measures.[46] In contrast, a 'liquidator' means any person or body appointed by the administrative or judicial authorities 'whose task it is to administer winding-up proceedings'.[47]

---

[42] See below at paras 7.256–7.261.
[43] Art 4(1)(43) CRR.
[44] Art 4(1)(44) CRR.
[45] See below at para 7.103.
[46] Art 2, fifth definition.
[47] Art 2, eighth dash.

7.51 The Winding-Up Directive, similar to Solvency II, lists two elements which constitute 're-organisation measures': (i) the aim of the measures must be to preserve or restore the financial situation of a credit institution; and (ii) the effect of the measures is such that it must have a potential for affecting third parties' pre-existing rights, including measures involving the possibility of a suspension of payments, suspension of enforcement measures, or the reduction of claims.

7.52 Prior to the BRRD, the above definitions seemed to exclude formal regulatory intervention designed to stem or stop a bank's increasingly worsening financial position, which may not affect third parties' pre-existing rights.[48] Since the enactment of the BRRD, however, 're-organisation measures' also include 'the application of the resolution tools and the exercise of resolution powers' provided for in the BRRD, to be discussed below.[49] As a consequence of those tools and powers, third parties' pre-existing rights are not necessarily affected.[50]

7.53 Also, as a consequence of the enactment of the BRRD, the scope of the definition of 're-organisation measures' can be wide. For instance, the scope of the definition of 'reorganisation measures', and more specifically whether it includes certain actions taken by authorities in the context of a bank resolution, was a central issue in [2016] EWCA Civ 1092 (*Guardians of New Zealand Superannuation Fund et al v Novo Banco*), which was handed down on 4 November 2016. In *Kotnik and others v Državni zbor Republike Slovenije* (Case C-526/14), the CJEU decided that 'reorganisation measures' must be interpreted as meaning that (also) burden-sharing measures such as those provided for in points 40 to 46 of the Banking Communication fall within the scope of the concept of 'reorganisation measures'. The wide scope of the definition of 'reorganisation measures' may have far reaching consequences, especially in the light of Article 3 Winding-Up Directive (to be discussed below, paragraph 7.59. These far reaching consequences may require a resolution authorities to be cautious not to take measures that qualify as 'unjustified and disproportionate interference with the exercise of the right of ownership of depositors with that institution'.[51]

7.54 'Winding-up proceedings' are defined as meaning 'collective proceedings opened and monitored by the administrative or judicial authorities of a Member State with the aim of realising assets under the supervision of those authorities, including where the proceedings are terminated by a composition or other similar measure'.

7.55 Thus, this definition seems to consist of three constitutive elements. First, there must be a collective proceeding; secondly, such a proceeding must be opened and monitored by the administrative or judicial authorities of a Member State; and thirdly, they should be opened with the aim of realizing assets under the supervision of those authorities including where the proceedings are terminated by a composition or other similar means.

7.56 It is not always immediately apparent when a reorganization measure might be said to end and a winding-up proceeding begin. A line of demarcation might emerge on account of

---
[48] This view seems reinforced by Recitals (8)–(10) BRRD.
[49] At paras 7.184 et seq.
[50] Cf the 'resolution objectives' set out in Art 31(2) BRRD.
[51] The CJEU has held that under certain circumstances reorganization measures might constitute an unjustified and disproportionate interference with the exercise of the right of ownership of depositors with the credit institution. Whether this is the case, is up to the national courts to verify. See CJEU 25 March 2021, Case C-501/18 (*The Administrativen sad Sofia-grad – Bulgaria – BT v Balgarska Narodna Banka*): OJ C364, 8.10.2018, at paras 102–11.

the fact that the latter type of proceeding must, in the case of a credit institution, be opened and monitored by a Member State's administrative or judicial authority. Article 3 of the Winding-Up Directive, on the other hand, provides unequivocally that the 'administrative or judicial authorities of the home Member State must have sole power to decide upon and to implement the reorganisation measures' provided for in the law and practices in force in that Member State.[52]

7.57 As stated already above, Article 2 Winding-Up Directive defines an 'administrator' as a person or body appointed by the administrative or judicial authorities whose task it is to administer reorganization measures. In contrast, a 'liquidator' means any person or body appointed by the administrative or judicial authorities whose task it is to administer winding-up proceedings.

7.58 'Administrative or judicial authorities' are such administrative or judicial authorities of a Member State 'as are competent for the purposes of reorganisation measures or winding-up proceedings'. This will clearly cover a single centralized body in which all of these functions are vested, as well as a single body dealing with one or more aspects of the competencies under consideration. The way in which the competencies are divided will depend on the supervisory structure of the Member State involved.

Winding-Up Directive: reorganization measures

7.59 Article 3 emphasizes that the administrative or judicial authorities of the home Member State alone shall be empowered to decide on the implementation of one or more reorganization measures affecting credit institutions. The same Article makes it clear that once implemented such measures are to be fully effective throughout the EU without further formality. Thus, Article 3 codifies the general principles set out above,[53] in that it affirms not only the principle of unity but also the principles of universality and single entity with regard to the effect of reorganization measures.[54] Moreover, the same Article clothes the home Member State with exclusive jurisdiction exercised via its administrative or judicial authority to decide upon the implementation of one or more reorganization measures. This exclusiveness is nuanced by the introduction of resolution colleges under the BRRD.[55]

7.60 In *Guardians of New Zealand Superannuation Fund et al v Novo Banco* [2016] EWCA Civ 1092, as mentioned above, the scope of the definition of 'reorganisation measures' was a central issue. The scope of this definition is especially important from the perspective of Article 3 Winding-Up Directive, because this provision gives 'reorganisation measures' (as defined) such wide reach. This also became apparent in CJEU *Kotnik and others v Državni zbor Republike Slovenije* (Case C-526/14), where the Court reaffirmed in paragraph 105: '... the reorganisation measures taken by the administrative or judicial authorities of

---

[52] See Recital (6), first sentence, Winding-Up Directive. See, for example, CJEU Case C-85/12 *re LBI hf vs Kepler Capital Markets SA and Frédéric Giraux*, 24 October 2013, ECLI:EU:C:2013:697 for an extensive interpretation of Arts 3 and 9.
[53] At paras 7.11 and 7.12.
[54] See also Recital (16).
[55] See below at para 7.242.

the home Member State, that is, the Member State in which a credit institution has been authorised, must have, in all the other Member States, the effects which the law of the home Member State confers on them. . . .'

Article 4 requires the administrative or judicial authorities of the home Member State to inform, without delay, the competent authorities of the host Member State or States of their decision to adopt any reorganization measures 'including the practical effects which such measures may have, if possible before it is adopted or otherwise immediately thereafter'. There seems to be no restriction on the methods by which the information can be given. **7.61**

Article 6 imposes on the administrative or judicial authorities in a home Member State an obligation to publish notice of the implementation of any reorganization measures which have been implemented where they are 'likely to affect the rights of third parties in a host Member State'. An extract of the relevant decision must be published in the *Official Journal* of the EC and in two newspapers in each host Member State. The other precondition to the obligation to publish is that an appeal 'may be brought' in the home Member State against the decision ordering the measures. **7.62**

In addition to the overall requirement that due publication be made in accordance with Article 6, Article 7 imposes the obligation on the administrative or judicial authorities to inform 'known creditors' who have their domiciles, normal places of residence, or head offices in other Member States if: (i) the legislation of the home Member State requires lodgement of a claim with a view to its recognition; or (ii) provides for compulsory notification of the measure to creditors who have their domiciles, normal places of residence or head offices in that State. This information is to be given in accordance with the procedures laid down in Articles 14 and 17(1).[56] **7.63**

Article 7(2) confirms that where the home Member State's laws or rules provide for the creditors domiciled or resident in that state the right to lodge there claims there, non-home Member State creditors must enjoy the same rights. **7.64**

As stated above, in case a credit institution has its head office outside the EU, the provisions of the Winding-up Directive only apply if the credit institution has branches in at least two Member States. In such a case, Article 8 requires the administrative or judicial authorities of the host Member State that has decided to adopt reorganization measures, to inform, without delay, 'by any available means, the competent authorities of the other host Member States in which the institution has set up branches.' Moreover, pursuant to Article 8(2), the administrative or judicial authorities involved must 'endeavour to coordinate their actions.' **7.65**

Winding-Up Directive: winding-up proceedings

Much the same rules and principles as are found in Articles 3–8 inclusive with regard to reorganization measures apply equally to the opening of and publication relating to winding-up proceedings in Articles 9 and 13 respectively. **7.66**

---

[56] Which address the provision of information to known creditors as issues of the relevant languages respectively.

7.67 However, Article 10 contains a critical provision regarding the applicable law to winding-up proceedings. A credit institution is to be wound up 'in accordance with the laws, regulations and procedures applicable to its home Member State insofar as this Directive does not provide otherwise'. This is almost an identical provision to that set out in Article 7 of the RR save that in Article 10(1) reference is made to the 'laws', etc of the home Member State (*lex domus*), whilst in the context of the RR, the applicable law is that of the law of the state of the opening of proceedings (*lex concursus*). Under both regimes, the *lex domus* and *lex concursus* respectively have universal application within the European Union (subject to the specified exceptions).

7.68 Pursuant to Article 14(1), when winding-up proceedings are opened, the administrative or judicial authority of the home Member State or the liquidator shall without delay individually inform known creditors who have their domiciles, normal places of residence, or head offices in other Member States, except in cases where the legislation of the home state does not require lodgement of the claim with a view to its recognition. This provision of information is critical for the possibility to lodge claims under Article 16, to be discussed below. In that context, the EFTA Court has defined 'known creditor' as meaning:

> those who are already known by the credit institution to be creditors, those creditors who may be discovered by a reasonably diligent responsible winding up authority, such as by requesting information on the identity of creditors from a securities holding service, and those creditors who bring themselves to the attention of the credit institution at any stage prior to the final date imposed by national law for submission of claims to the responsible winding-up authority.[57]

Perhaps even more importantly, it held that:

> article 14 […] precludes a rule of national law which, following the publication of an invitation to lodge claims directed towards known creditors who have their domicile, permanent residence or head offices in other EEA States, allows for the cancellation of claims that have not been lodged even if these creditors have not been individually notified and the national legislation requires the lodgement of the claim with a view to its recognition.[58]

7.69 Article 10(2) then provides that the *lex domus* is to determine 'in particular' a non-exhaustive list of specific matters and questions such as the powers of the credit institution and of the liquidator, the claims and treatment of such claims, the rules governing distributions, and the question and incidence of costs and expenses. The list is similar to the list found in Article 7(2) RR.

7.70 However, there is no equivalent in this Directive to the provisions of Articles 8–18 RR (equivalent to Articles 5–15 OR) which list those subjects excluded from the *lex concursus*. For these topics, both the Winding-up Directive and Solvency II Title IV contain specific provisions that determine the applicable law (different from the *lex concursus*).

7.71 A word should be said at this point regarding Article 15, which provision reflects the terms of Article 31 RR. It is conceivable that some persons may be unaware of the opening of

---

[57] EFTA Court, Case E-18/11 *Irish Bank Resolution Corporation Ltd and Kaupthing Bank hf*, 28 September 2012, at [98].
[58] ibid at [99].

proceedings affecting a credit institution. In such circumstances they might act in good faith but they do so in the face of otherwise valid winding-up proceedings. Article 15 provides that where a person has honoured its obligation towards a credit institution, that person will be deemed to have discharged it, even though that credit institution is subject to winding-up proceedings opened in another Member State, and the obligation should have been honoured for the benefit of the liquidator in those proceedings. Notably, Article 15 requires as a condition that the credit institution in question is not a legal person. This condition (which is absent in Article 31 RR) must probably be understood so that it must concern the situation where a person honours an obligation to a branch office of the credit institution in a host Member State. Moreover, Article 15 contains two rebuttable presumptions. First, if the obligation is honoured *before* the publication provided for in Article 13 has been effected, the person honouring the obligation shall be presumed to have been <u>unaware</u> of the opening of insolvency proceedings. Second, if the obligation is honoured *after* the publication has been effected, the person honouring the obligation is presumed, again in the absence of proof to the contrary, to have been <u>aware</u> of the opening of proceedings.

Article 16 deals with the right to lodge claims. This Article reflects Articles 53 and 55 of the RR. Article 10(2)(g) provides that the law of the home Member State shall determine the rules governing the lodging, etc of claims. Article 16(1) and (2) address the cases of claims by creditors whose domiciles, normal places of residence or head offices are in Member States other than the home Member State. Article 16(2) provides that these creditors are to be treated in the same way and are to be accorded the same ranking as claims of an equivalent nature lodged by home Member State-based creditors. This may be considered a derogation from Article 10(2)(g). The notion of equal treatment in Article 16(2) has no corresponding provision in the Insolvency Regulation. **7.72**

Winding-Up Directive: common provisions

This Title IV concerns 'Provisions Common to Reorganisation Measures and Winding-up Proceedings'. The entirety of this Title is, in effect, a derogation from the application of the law of the home Member State (*lex domus*), similar to the exceptions to the application of the *lex concursus* contained in the RR. **7.73**

Title IV comprises Articles 20–33 inclusive. There Articles contain two types of exceptions to the application of the *lex domus*. The first concerns situations in which the *lex domus* is not to affect certain rights: the second represents cases where law other than the *lex domus* applies. The former group comprises Articles 21, 22, and 23: the latter, Articles 20, 24, 25, 26, and 27. **7.74**

Article 21 states that the adoption of reorganization measures or the opening of winding-up proceedings 'shall not affect the rights in re of creditors or third parties in respect of tangible or intangible, moveable or immoveable assets' which belong to the credit institutions which are situated within the territory of another Member State at the time of the adoption of the measures or the opening of the proceedings. Reference to 'rights in re' is no doubt the same as one made to 'rights in rem' and it can therefore be assumed that the legal position of third parties in this respect is in effect the same as that provided for by Article 8 RR. **7.75**

7.76 Thus, Article 21 excludes from the effects of the adoption of any reorganization measures or the opening of winding-up proceedings rights in rem of creditors or third parties regarding assets belonging to credit institutions which at those times are situated within the territory of another Member State. Article 21 does not have its own definition of a right in rem. It provides a non-exhaustive list of types of rights which most national laws would generally regard as rights in rem, including 'the right to dispose of assets or have them disposed of and to obtain satisfaction from the proceeds of or income from those assets, in particular by virtue of a lien or a mortgage' (ie security rights) and 'the right to demand the assets from, and/or to require restitution by, anyone having possession or use of them contrary to the wishes of the party so entitled'.

7.77 Article 22 deals with reservation of title. It therefore covers the same content as Article 10 of the RR. Article 22(1) addresses the case where a credit institution, which is subject to reorganization measures or winding-up proceedings, as a purchaser, is obliged to allow a seller to preserve their rights based on the reservation of title. In such a case and for the provision to apply, the asset must be located at the relevant time (ie when the measures are adopted or the proceedings opened) in a Member State other than the state in which the measures or proceedings take place.

7.78 Article 22(2) deals with the analogous case where the credit institution acts as the seller. In such a case, the provision effectively allows the sale and reservation of title to remain valid after the adoption of reorganization measures or opening of winding-up proceedings. If the purchaser makes payment, it will be allowed to acquire title of the asset(s) delivered. As in the case of Article 22(1), the asset must be located in a Member State other than the state of opening, at the time the measures are adopted or the proceedings opened.

7.79 In derogation of Articles 22(1) and (2), Article 22(3) provides that actions for voidness, voidability, or unenforceability can nevertheless be brought under the *lex domus* in respect of the legal acts which involve reservation of title.

7.80 Article 23 deals with set-off. It provides in Article 23(1) that the adoption of reorganization measures or the opening of winding-up proceedings shall not affect the right of a creditor to demand a set-off where set-off is permitted. This reflects the rule in Article 9 RR. Article 10(2)(c) of the Directive determines that it is for the laws, regulations, and procedures of the home Member State, that is the *lex domus*, to determine whether set-off is allowed. Article 23(1), however, says that this law may not affect the right of creditors of the credit institution to invoke set-off, provided such set-off is allowed under the law that applies to the claim that the creditor(s) in question wish to discharge through set-off. In other words, set-off must be allowed to the extent 'permitted' by the law applicable to the credit institution's claim,[59] and if this is the case, the *lex domus* cannot affect this right.

7.81 The second group of Articles in Title IV referred to above consists of Articles 20, and 24–27 inclusive. Article 20(a) deals with employment contracts and reflects a similar exemption put forward in Article RR. Recitals (23) and (24) of the Directive recognize that contracts of employment with credit institutions need to be protected. Article 20(a) therefore provides that 'employment contracts and relationships' shall be governed solely by the law of the

---

[59] On set-off rights under the BRRD, see below at para 7.150.

Member State applicable to that contract and relationship, which thus represents a derogation from the general applicability of the *lex domus*.

Article 20(b) applies an analogous rule with regard to contracts which confer 'the right to make use of or acquire' immovable property, that is the applicable law of the law of the Member State within the territory in which the immovable property is situated. **7.82**

Article 20(c) provides that rights subject to registration in respect of immovable property, ships, or aircraft are to be governed, as in the case of Article 20(b), 'solely' by the law of the Member State under the authority of which the relevant register is kept. **7.83**

This is a convenient point at which to observe that even as regards the subject-matter of Article 20, there may well be a considerable degree of overlap between the rules set out in Article 20 on the one hand and on the other, certain other Articles either within the same group of Articles or drawn from the earlier group of Articles already considered. So, for example, a right in rem may well have to be considered within the ambits of both Article 20(c) and Article 21. **7.84**

Articles 24–27 inclusive deal with the *lex rei sitae*, netting agreements, repurchase agreements, and regulated markets respectively. Article 24 deals with rights in 'instruments'. Instruments are defined by reference to the definition of 'financial instruments' of Article 4(1), point (50)(b) of Regulation (EU) No 575/2013 (CRR), which definition includes securities, derivatives, and cash instruments. More specifically, Article 24 concerns 'the enforcement of proprietary rights in instruments or other rights in such instruments the existence or transfer of which presupposes their recording in a register'. In such cases the law of the Member State where that register is held or located will apply. The applicable law could therefore quite easily be the law of a Member State other than the home Member State or even that of a host Member State. **7.85**

This Article 24 provision mimics Article 9(2) Settlement Finality Directive and Article 9(1) Financial Collateral Directive, and is a reflection of the so-called PRIMA or Place of the Relevant Intermediary Approach.[60] These Directives, however, all have a different scope, whilst the precise formulation of the PRIMA rule in those Directives also differs. The Settlement Finality Directive and the Winding-up Directive both specifically concern insolvency, whilst the Financial Collateral Directive concerns specific financial collateral arrangements (not necessarily in insolvency). **7.86**

More specifically, Article 9(1) Financial Collateral Directive provides: '[the applicable law is the] law of the country in which the relevant account is maintained.' This rule therefore has been considered a variation of PRIMA, in effect resulting in 'PRACA': the Place of the Relevant Account Approach. The rule is not entirely consistent with the rules found in the Winding-Up Directive (and Settlement Finality Directive), because these latter directives point to the place where the relevant register, account, or centralized deposit system is *located*, whilst the Financial Collateral Directive refers to the place where the 'relevant account is *maintained*'. This may indicate the place where the relevant intermediary is registered, since it is the intermediary that must be considered to maintain the account. **7.87**

---

[60] The following paragraphs are based on M Haentjens (ed), *Financial Collateral* (OUP 2020), paras 4.51 et seq.

7.88 However, the main criticism on all the EU versions of PRIMA or PRACA is that it remains unclear in which jurisdiction the relevant register or account, respectively, is actually located or maintained.[61] This connecting factor could point to the local branch of the custodian where the account is opened, to the head offices, a place of incorporation (*lex societas*) or the place where the account is technically, that is operationally, administered. In its Communication of 12 March 2018, the Commission addressed the different wordings of Articles 9(2) Settlement Finality Directive, 24 Winding-up Directive, and 9(1) Financial Collateral Directive.[62] First, the Commission stated that ultimately, it is for the CJEU to interpret European legislation, but that this matter has so far not been submitted to it.[63] Second, the Commission is of the view that 'located' of the Settlement Finality and Winding-up Directives means the same as 'maintained' of the Financial Collateral Directive, so that all Directives must be interpreted to refer to the law of the jurisdiction where the relevant securities account is maintained.[64]

7.89 Article 25, which deals with netting agreements, provides that such agreements 'shall be given solely by the law of the contract which governs such agreements'. This issue thus is to be determined under the *lex contractus* rather than under the *lex domus*. In other words, whether netting is allowed must be answered under the law of the netting arrangement, that is the law the parties choose to apply to their repurchase agreement, securities lending, or International Swaps and Derivatives Association (ISDA) Master Agreement. It is possible that this is the law of a state which is not part of the European Economic Area. By way of example, the extent to which the rights and obligations following a derivatives contract, including the collateral provided thereunder, are allowed to be set off against each other in order to calculate an aggregated balance must be determined under the law applicable to the relevant derivatives contact. This rule therefore amounts to a reference to the Rome I Regulation.

7.90 Since the enactment of the BRRD, Article 25 of the Winding-Up Directive is without prejudice to Articles 68 and 71 BRRD, which in essence say that the mere taking of a 'crisis prevention measure or a crisis management measure' (as defined under the BRRD) may not, in itself, lead to the termination of a contract (Article 68) and that resolution authorities have the power to temporarily suspend termination rights (Article 71). BRRD thus disapplies certain contractual termination grounds that might otherwise have remained immune as they were to be governed solely by the law of the contract which governs such agreements.

7.91 The Winding-up Directive also contains a specific conflict-of-laws rule for repurchase agreements. Remarkably, it does not do so for other types of standardized collateral transactions, nor for collateral transactions in general. Article 26 Winding-up Directive provides that repurchase agreements are to be governed 'solely by the law of the contract which governs such agreements'.

7.92 Similar to the specialist rule for netting arrangements discussed above, this Article 26 Winding-up Directive determines that repos are to be determined under the *lex contractus*

---

[61] T Keijser, *Transnational Securities Law* (OUP, 2014), 287.
[62] Communication on the applicable law to the proprietary effects of transactions in securities COM/2018/089 final.
[63] ibid, 5.
[64] ibid, 5–6.

rather than under the *lex domus*. However, the provision also states that it is to be applied 'without prejudice to Article 24', which provision has been discussed above and concerns 'the enforcement of proprietary rights in instruments' that are, in short, credited to accounts. This reference to Article 24 indicates that the scope of this Article 26 Winding-up Directive is limited to the contractual relationship between the parties to the repurchase agreement and does not extend to the relationship between the parties and the collateral assets. Consequently, it remains the law of the Member State where the insolvent credit institution has been licensed that governs the issue of how the collateral provider must lodge her claim for return of the securities with the liquidator, and it remains the applicable non-insolvency law that governs her claim for return of those securities. The latter law is, pursuant to Article 24 Winding-up Directive, to be determined 'by the law of the Member State where the register, account, or centralised deposit system in which those rights are recorded is held or located'.

Moreover, the treatment of proprietary rights regarding securities in repos have their own, specialist conflicts of law rule, viz Article 9(2) Collateral Directive. Also as regards repos, Articles 68 and 71 BRRD disapply certain contractual termination grounds that might otherwise have remained immune as they were to be governed solely by the law of the contract which governs such agreements. Also considering Article 25 Winding-up Directive on netting discussed above, the relevance of this Article 26 Winding-up Directive is therefore limited. **7.93**

Finally, Article 27 provides that transactions carried out in the context of a 'regulated market' shall be governed solely by the law of the contract which governs such transactions. A regulated market is 'defined' by reference to Article 4(1), point (21) of MiFID II, which says that a regulated market means 'a multilateral system operated and/or managed by a market operator, which brings together or facilitates the bringing together of multiple third-party buying and selling interests in financial instruments—in the system and in accordance with its non-discretionary rules—in a way that results in a contract, in respect of the financial instruments admitted to trading under its rules and/or systems, and which is authorised and functions regularly and in accordance with Title III of this Directive'. This conflict of laws rule is limited to the contractual aspects of these transactions, as the proprietary issues are to be determined under Article 24 discussed above. **7.94**

Article 28 deals with proof of a liquidator's appointment. This generally takes the form of a certified copy of the original appointment decision issued by the administrative or judicial authorities of the home Member State. This is in keeping with the general principle that the nature and scope of the administrator's or liquidator's powers will be governed by the *lex domus*. **7.95**

Article 29 allows for the possibility that the reorganization measure or decision to open winding-up proceedings can be registered in non-home Member State registers such as land and trade registers. **7.96**

Article 30 provides an exception to the primacy of the *lex domus* when it comes to considering so-called detrimental acts. Under this provision, the *lex domus* does not apply to the rules relating to the voidness, voidability, or unenforceability of legal acts detrimental to the creditors as a whole, where the beneficiary of these acts provides proof that the act **7.97** detrimental to the creditors as a whole is subject to the law of a Member State other than the home Member State, and that law does not allow any means of challenging that act in the case in point. See, for example, EFTA Court Case E-28/13 *re LBI hf v Merrill Lynch International Ltd (Landsbanki insolvency)*, 17 October 2014 holding that 'The expression "voidness, voidability or unenforceability of legal acts" in Article 30(1) of [the Winding-Up Directive] also refers to rescission in bankruptcy law on the basis of avoidance rules' [46] and that 'It must be assessed according to the rules of the home EEA State whether or not the beneficiary has proved that the law applicable to the act does not allow any means of challenge' [81].

7.98 Article 31 aims to protect third parties dealing with a credit institution after the adoption of measures or opening of winding-up proceedings in respect of assets such as ships, immovable assets, and, in short, financial instruments. This Article 31 provides that these transactions are governed by the law of the Member State within the territory of which the immovable asset is situated or under the authority of which the relevant register, account, or deposit system is kept. This is a clear derogation of the general application of the *lex domus*, albeit in line with Articles 20(c) (regarding immovable property, ships, and aircraft), 21 (regarding rights *in rem* prior to the reorganization measures and winding-up proceedings), and 24 (*lex rei sitae*, ie PRIMA, for financial instruments).

7.99 Article 32 provides that the effects of measures or winding-up proceedings in pending lawsuits are to be governed not by the *lex domus*, but solely by the law of the Member State in which the lawsuit is pending. The CJEU reaffirmed that Article 32 is an exception to the *lex domus* and that this exception must also apply under certain, specific circumstances if, pending the lawsuit, there is a second reorganization measure.[65]

7.100 Finally, Article 34 confirms that Member States were to bring the Directive into force by the appropriate laws, regulations, and administrative procedures by or on 5 May 2004.

E. Solvency II

Solvency II: scope

7.101 Article 267 caput and under (a) Solvency II has effect so that the insolvency regime of Solvency II Title IV apply to 'insurance undertakings'. Such an undertaking is in turn defined as one 'which has received official authorisation'.[66] The upshot of this is that an 'insurance undertaking' is one which is authorized to write direct insurance, both life as well as non-life insurance, as distinct from reinsurance business. Reinsurance companies are not authorized to write direct insurance as a normal rule.[67] On this basis such companies would therefore be governed by the Insolvency Regulation.[68]

---

[65] CJEU 29 April 2021, C-504/19, ECLI:EU:C:2021:335 (*Banco de Portugal, Fundo de Resolução, Novo Banco SA, Sucursal en España v VR*).
[66] Article 4 of Directive 2002/83/EC/Article 14 Solvency II.
[67] Whilst this is true on the continent, the UK practice is different, where insurance regulation covers both direct insurance and reinsurance and the same companies/Lloyds syndicates do both.
[68] It is submitted that this is possible by way of an approach: the term 'insurance undertaking' is not defined by the Insolvency Regulation (neither in OR nor RR).

7.102 Article 267 caput and under (b) Solvency II have effect so that the insolvency regime of, respectively, Solvency II Title IV also apply to 'branches' albeit within the EU but whose head offices are situated outside the EU. Article 268(b) Solvency II defines a branch as 'any permanent presence of an insurance undertaking in the territory of a Member State which carries out insurance business'.[69]

7.103 As in the Winding-Up Directive, Solvency II Title IV applies to 'reorganisation measures' and 'winding-up proceedings'. The first of these two expressions in turn embodies four elements, namely:

(a) intervention,
(b) by an administrative body or judicial authority,
(c) which is intended to preserve or restore the financial situation, and
(d) which has an effect upon the pre-existing rights of parties other than the insurance undertaking itself, such as the suspension of payments, the suspension of enforcement measures or the reduction of claims.

From the point of view of English law, the applicability of the first of these elements is not without difficulty. On the one hand statutory compositions for insolvency insurers have been viewed as outside the scope of such 'measures', even though a court order is required for sanction; on the other hand, it is not clear why an English company voluntary arrangement should also be excluded since it remains at all material times subject to potential judicial oversight.

7.104 It is perhaps easier to see why a solvent scheme under UK law should be excluded; here there could be said to be no 'intervention' but also that there would be an absence of any intention to preserve or restore financial stability. However, some solvent schemes do seek to preserve or restore financial stability.[70]

7.105 With regard to the term 'winding-up proceedings', the same appears to be a notion which involves six components. First, they must constitute collective proceedings; secondly, such proceedings should involve the realization and distribution of assets and their proceeds; thirdly, there must be 'intervention' by the appropriate administrative or judicial authority; fourthly, such intervention can involve termination by means of composition or by some other analogous measure; fifthly, such intervention and termination need not be founded on insolvency; and sixthly and finally, such intervention and/or termination can be voluntary.

Solvency II: selective commentary

7.106 The overall aim of Solvency II Title IV is perhaps best encapsulated in Recital (117) Solvency II which states:

> Since national legislation concerning reorganisation measures and winding-up proceedings is not harmonised, it is appropriate, in the framework of the internal market, to ensure

---

[69] It appears likely but not certain that if all branches are within the same Member State, each branch must be treated separately.

[70] For example, the Equitable Life scheme sought to stabilize the direct insurer. See also the Insurers (Reorganisation and Winding Up) Regulations 2004, specifically Art 5(5).

the mutual recognition of reorganisation measures and winding-up legislation of the Member States concerning insurance undertakings, as well as the necessary cooperation, taking into account the need for unity, universality, coordination and publicity for such measures and the equivalent treatment and protection of insurance creditors.

It might perhaps be conceded that to some extent the Solvency II does succeed in altering substantive national law in relation to the last item referred to in the quoted passage, namely the protection of insurance creditors.

7.107   On the definition of 'insurance undertakings', see above, paragraph 7.97.

7.108   In the United Kingdom, the term 'insurance' usually connotes and includes 'reinsurance'. Much the same approach is taken by a number of EU Member States, for example Finland, Denmark, and Luxembourg. However Solvency II had as its stated aim the creation of an EU-wide market based on the regime introduced by earlier Insurance Directives. Under Solvency II reinsurance across the Union is subject to a common system of authorization, prudential regulation, and solvency and, like direct insurers, reinsurers have a single home state authorization valid for the whole of the EU.

7.109   Whether a particular reinsurance company is within the scope of Solvency II Title IV will depend on whether it is in receipt of authorization to write direct business. If it in fact does write such business, there is no reason in principle why Solvency II Title IV should not apply to it. If despite the fact of authorization, in fact no direct business is conducted, the position is not clear. The practical solution is for such a company, when facing insolvency, to delimit its own powers so as to exclude the writing of direct business, if it wishes to place itself within the ambit and applicability of the Insolvency Regulation. Pending the institution of a full-blown regime with regard to insolvent reinsurers, such may be the best solution currently available.

7.110   As in the case of credit institutions, Solvency II Title IV covers EU undertakings authorized in a Member State as well as branches of a non-EU undertaking set up in one or more Member States. In the case of the latter type of undertaking, the home Member State is a state in which the branch has been granted authorization: if there are two or more branches, each branch will be treated separately.

7.111   As in the case of the Winding-Up Directive, Solvency II Title IV applies to 'reorganisation measures' as well as 'winding-up proceedings'. The former measures have already been considered above.[71] From what has already been said, identification of the element of 'intervention' by an administrative body or judicial authority is a key component in the equation. Hence in terms of English law at least, it is arguable that a company voluntary arrangement attracts a suitable degree of court scrutiny whilst a formal scheme of arrangement, albeit containing as it does formal court approval, nonetheless remains essentially a concordat between the company and its creditors.

7.112   With regard to winding-up proceedings, it is worth revisiting the observations made above that the Solvency II Title IV applies to all winding-up proceedings whether or not they are

---

[71] See above at paras 7.59–7.65.

founded on insolvency[72] and indeed whether they are voluntary or compulsory. It is equally important to note that Solvency II Title IV also provides that the adoption of reorganization measures in relation to an undertaking will not preclude the opening of winding-up proceedings.

7.113 Article 268 Solvency II sets out various important definitions. The word 'branch' is defined in Article 268 Solvency II as 'any permanent presence of an insurance undertaking in the territory of a Member State other than the home Member State which pursues insurance business'. There is an echo in that definition of the definition accorded to the term 'establishment' for the purposes of the RR. Other terms are more self-explanatory. The definition of 'Home Member State' is now to be found in Article 13(8) Solvency II and says, in pertinent part, that it means any of: (a) for non-life insurance, the Member State in which the head office of the insurance undertaking covering the risk is situated; and (b) for life insurance, the Member State in which the head office of the insurance undertaking covering the commitment is situated.

7.114 The position with regard to an undertaking with its head office outside the European Union but with branches in more than one Member State is similar to that in the case of credit institutions.[73] In such a case Article 296(1) Solvency II indicates that each such branch must be treated independently.

7.115 Other main terms employed, namely 'host Member State' (to be found in Article 13(9) Solvency II), 'competent authorities', 'administrator', and 'liquidator' (all to be found in Article 268(1) Solvency II) are again largely self-explanatory.

7.116 The term 'reorganisation measures' is not only defined as a separate term in Article 268(1)(c) Solvency II but is the subject of Articles 269–272 inclusive Solvency II. The definition is the same as that afforded to the same term in the Winding-Up Directive.[74] Article 269 Solvency II confirms that only the 'competent authorities' of the home Member State are entitled to decide on such measures with regard to an insurance undertaking and that such measures 'shall not preclude the opening of winding-up proceedings' by the same home Member State; Article 4(3). Article 269(4) Solvency II further confirms that the reorganization measures 'shall be fully effective' throughout the EU 'without any further formalities' including as against third parties in other Member States, even if the legislation of those other Member States does not provide for such measures or alternatively makes the implementation subject to conditions which are not fulfilled. Article 269(5) Solvency II reinforces this provision by establishing that the EU-wide effect of the reorganization measures will arise at the same time as they take effect under the relevant national law, that is the law of the home Member State.

7.117 Article 270 Solvency II confirms that the competent authorities in the home Member State must inform the same state's supervisory authorities regarding the former's decision. The latter authorities must then inform the supervisory authorities of all other Member States and not simply such of those states as reflect the particular commercial relationships of the undertaking in question.

---

[72] See Art 268(d) Solvency II.
[73] See above at para 7.23.
[74] See above at paras 7.49–7.51.

7.118 Article 270 Solvency II talks of informing other states of a decision on a reorganization measure taking place 'where possible before the adoption of such a measure and failing that immediately thereafter'. This suggests that it is necessary for only the notice of the measure to be communicated.

7.119 Article 271 Solvency II provides for the publication of the measures but only where an appeal is 'possible' in the home Member State, which refers to an appeal by parties other than the insurance undertaking itself. Furthermore such publication should be made only if the relevant national law requires it. Reference to an appeal seems wide enough to encompass an appeal to an administrative as well as to a judicial body. Article 271 Solvency II also contains a requirement to publish an extract from the document establishing the measures in the *Official Journal* of the EU. As far as Member States other than the home Member State are concerned, there exists a discretion to publish the decision.

7.120 Article 272 Solvency II reflects the terms of Article 7 of the Winding-Up Directive.[75]

7.121 Chapter III Solvency II deals with winding-up proceedings and covers Articles 8–18/273–284. As already pointed out,[76] such proceedings need not be founded on insolvency and can be voluntary or compulsory in nature. Article 273(1) Solvency II confirms that the entitlement to decide to open winding-up proceedings rests solely with the competent authorities within the home Member State. It also stresses that winding-up proceedings can take place whether or not prior reorganization measures have been adopted.

7.122 Article 273(2) Solvency II echoes Article 269 Solvency II and confirms that decisions to open winding-up proceedings are to be recognized without further formality in other Member States and are to be effective in such other states the moment they are effective in the home Member State.

7.123 Article 273 Solvency II deals with the provision of information regarding the relevant decision and mirrors Article 270 Solvency II.[77] First, the competent authorities of the home Member State must inform the supervisory authorities of the home Member State and then must inform the equivalent authorities in other Member States.

7.124 Article 274 Solvency II deals with the *lex domus* in terms which are similar to those contained in Article 10 of the Winding-Up Directive. It therefore deals not only with the question of jurisdiction but also with those conflict of law rules which replace the various national rules of private international law in so far as the latter apply to the winding-up of insurance undertakings.

7.125 The principal requirement in Article 274(1) Solvency II is that the law applicable is that of the home Member State or *lex domus*. That law is to apply to the decision which opens the proceedings, the proceedings themselves, and their effects unless the law of the home Member State of that insurance undertaking. For this reason, a clear understanding of the scope of 'winding-up proceedings' and when these must be understood to have commenced, is of great importance. In this context, the CJEU held that a decision of the competent authority to withdraw the authorization of the insurance undertaking concerned and to

---

[75] See above at paras 7.67 and 7.68.
[76] See above at paras 7.111 and 7.112.
[77] See above at para 7.117.

appoint a provisional liquidator cannot constitute a 'decision to open winding-up proceedings with regard to an insurance undertaking', unless the law of the home Member State of that insurance undertaking provides either that that provisional liquidator is empowered to realize the assets of that insurance undertaking and distribute the proceeds among its creditors or that the withdrawal of the authorization of that insurance undertaking has the effect of opening automatically the winding-up proceedings, without a separate authority being required to adopt a formal decision to that end.[78] Again, as in the case of the Winding-Up Directive, the overriding rule of *lex domus* is subject to a number of exceptions as set out in Articles 285–292 inclusive Solvency II which deal with such matters as third parties' rights in rem, reservation of title, and set-off.

7.126 The list of matters to which the *lex domus* applies contained in Article 274(2) Solvency II is, as in the case of Article 10 of the Winding-Up Directive, non-exhaustive.

7.127 Article 275 Solvency II is a key provision. It provides by Article 275(1) Solvency II that Member States shall ensure that insurance claims take precedence over other claims on the insurance undertaking by reference to one of two distinct approaches. First, the Member State can provide for insurance claims to be given absolute preference over all other claims with regard to assets which represent the technical provisions of the relevant undertaking (Article 275(1)(a) Solvency II). Alternatively the Member State can accord insurance claims priority over all other claims with respect to all of their assets except for claims by employees, public bodies in relation to taxes, claims by social security systems, and claims on assets subject to rights in rem (Article 275(1)(b) Solvency II).

7.128 Furthermore, Member States can provide that the whole or part of the expenses of a winding-up proceeding can take priority over insurance claims (Article 275(2) Solvency II).

7.129 The term 'insurance claim' is defined in Article 268(1)(g) Solvency II as meaning any amount which is owed by an insurance undertaking to insured persons, policy-holders, beneficiaries, or to any injured party having a direct right of action against the insurance undertaking and which arises out of an insurance contract in relation to direct insurance business, including amounts set aside for such persons when some elements of the debt are not yet known. The definition also includes premium refunds due from an insurer.

7.130 It appears to follow from Article 275 Solvency II that reinsurance creditors would fall to be dealt with after insurance claims, that is they would be treated as general creditors.

7.131 Article 275(3) Solvency II requires Member States who adopt the first of these two approaches in Article 10 to maintain a special register of the assets used to cover technical provisions.[79]

7.132 Article 277 Solvency II states that the home Member State may provide that where the rights of insurance creditors have been subrogated to a guarantee scheme established in that Member State, claims by the scheme shall not benefit from the provisions of Article 275(1)

---

[78] CJEU 12 November 2020, C-427/19, ECLI:EU:C:2020:914 (*Sofiyski rayonen sad—Bulgaria Bulstrad Vienna Insurance Group AD v Olympic Insurance Company Ltd*), C-427/19.
[79] Details of the contents of such a register and details of the manner in which it should be held are set out in the Annex to the Directive.

Solvency II. Although Article 277 clearly clothes the Member State with a discretion, it in effect reinforces the protection afforded to insurance creditors by Article 275 Solvency II.

7.133 Article 275(1)(b) Solvency II provides that insurance undertakings must indicate in their accounts at all times those claims recorded in the accounts which might take precedence over insurance claims.

7.134 Article 279 Solvency II deals with withdrawal of authorization in the event of the opening of winding-up proceedings. However, it allows a liquidator or other appointee of the competent authorities to pursue the business of the insurance undertaking if required for the purposes of the winding-up.

7.135 Article 280 Solvency II gives effect to the principle of publicity in similar terms to that which applies to reorganization measures in Article 271 Solvency II.[80] Here, however, publication would be required whether or not an appeal is possible. However, Article 280 Solvency II does not in terms provide that the winding-up proceedings will have effect regardless of whether the requirements for publicity set out in Article 280(1) and (2) Solvency II are satisfied. This is not to say that publicity is a precondition to the effectiveness of reorganization or winding-up provisions across the EU.[81]

7.136 Article 281 Solvency II reflects one of the prime motives of the Directive, namely that as much information as possible be given to creditors in relation to the opening of the reorganization measures or winding-up proceedings as well as with regard to the manner in which they unfold. The Article specifically requires the creditors of the particular undertaking in other Member States to be individually informed of the opening of the winding-up proceedings without delay. Article 271(2) Solvency II prescribes that the details which form the notification should include such matters as time limits, etc. However, it also provides that in the case of insurance claims as defined in Article 268(1)(g) Solvency II,[82] the notice must indicate the general effect of the winding-up proceedings on the insurance contracts, including the date on which the insurance contracts, etc will cease 'to produce effects'.

7.137 Article 282 Solvency II deals with the right to lodge claims. The basic aim is to ensure equality of treatment between creditors as between those in the home Member State and those in non-home Member States.[83] Although the entitlement under Solvency II Title IV to lodge claims extends only to creditors with a habitual residence, domicile, or head office within a Member State, the law governing the proceedings may well allow creditors from other states to lodge claims. Article 282(1) Solvency II specifically extends the right to lodge claims to public authorities which operate within a Member State. This last entitlement represents an exception to the general rule that foreign tax laws will not be enforced.

7.138 As in the case of the Winding-Up Directive,[84] although Article 282 Solvency II provides for a general right for EU-wide creditors to be able to lodge claims and proceedings regarding an insurance undertaking, it would certainly be the law applicable to the proceedings, that

---

[80] See above at para 7.119.
[81] This is on account of Art 273(2) Solvency II: see above at para 7.122.
[82] Art 268 Solvency II, see above at para 7.113.
[83] See Recital (21) of the Insurance Directive.
[84] See above at para 7.73.

is the *lex domus*, which in accordance with Article 274(2)(g) Solvency II will determine the rules governing the lodging, verification, and admission of claims.

Article 283 Solvency II deals with the question of which language is to be used in relation to the manner in which notification must be made to creditors and the manner in which claims are lodged.[85] The information in the notice to creditors need be only in the official language of the home Member State although the heading of the form which is used must be in all the official languages of the Union. However, in the case of insurance creditors, the notice must be provided in the official language of the Member State where the insurer has its habitual residence, domicile, or head office. **7.139**

As far as creditors are concerned, a creditor from a Member State other than the home Member State can lodge his claim in the official language of his own Member State. Again, however, the form used in order to lodge the claim must be headed in the official language of the home Member State. **7.140**

Article 284 Solvency II ends Chapter III by imposing a requirement that liquidators must keep all creditors in all other Member States informed as to the progress of the winding-up proceedings. **7.141**

Chapter IV of Title IV Solvency II sets out various provisions which are common to both reorganization measures and winding-up proceedings. Whilst Article 269 and 274 Solvency II provide for the general principle that the applicable law to reorganization measures and winding-up proceedings is the *lex domus*, there are, as in the case of the Winding-Up Directive, some important exceptions. **7.142**

The first principal exception is provided by Article 285 Solvency II. Employment contracts are governed in Solvency II: exclusively by the law of the Member State 'applicable' to such contracts. This law will generally be determined by reference to Article 8 Rome I Regulation.[86] It is important to note that the exception contained in Article 285(a) Solvency II means that the relevant national law will apply only to determine the effect of the opening of the reorganization measures or winding-up proceedings on the employment contract and any employment relationship. All other matters regarding the employment contract will remain governed by the law of the home Member State, for example the lodging, verification, and admission of claims, etc. **7.143**

Article 285(b) Solvency II addresses contracts conferring the right to use or acquire immovable property. Such contracts are to be governed solely by the law of the Member State in whose territory the immovable property is situated. The width of Article 285(b) Solvency II suggests that all forms of immovable-related contracts are included, for example leases and agreements for sale. **7.144**

Article 285(c) Solvency II deals with the publicly registered rights of an insurance undertaking in relation not only to immovable property but also to property, ships, and aircraft. The latter types of assets must be 'subject' to registration. If they are, the law of the home **7.145**

---

[85] There is a strong resemblance to Art 54 RR (equivalent to Arts 40 and 42(1) OR): see generally below at paras 8.729–8.735 (RR), 8.447–8.449, and 8.455–8.459 (OR), respectively.

[86] Regulation (EC) No 593/2008 of the European Parliament and of the Council of 17 June 2008 on the law applicable to contractual obligations (Rome I), OJ L177.

Member State should be incapable of affecting the systems for registration which exist or are in force in other Member States.

7.146 Article 286 Solvency II deals with third parties' rights in rem. Such rights insofar as they exist in respect of an insurance undertaking's assets situated within the territory of another Member State at the time of the opening of the relevant measures or proceedings, are not to be affected by such opening. In other words, secured creditors can exercise their security rights over an insurance undertaking's local assets in accordance with the local law irrespective of the effect of the *lex domus*.

7.147 No definition of a 'right in rem' appears anywhere in Solvency II Title IV. Article 286(1) Solvency II refers to 'specific assets' as well as to 'collections of indefinite assets as a whole which change from time to time'. The latter phrase appears to cover the case of a floating charge under English law.

7.148 Article 287 Solvency II deals with reservation of title. Its terms reflect the contents of Article 22 of the Winding-Up Directive.[87] This exception applies whenever a seller has rights based on a reservation of title claim regarding an asset which at the time of the opening of the reorganization measures or winding-up proceeding is located in the Member State other than the home Member State. In such a case the seller's rights are governed by the relevant national law. However, as with third parties' rights in rem, such reservation of title rights may still remain impeachable under the law of the home Member State as being void, voidable, or unenforceable. This will still leave a seller with the right to raise a defence to claims brought under the law of the home Member State if Article 290 Solvency II (dealing with detrimental acts) is relied upon.[88] That Article provides a defence to such a claim which would be brought under the law of the home Member State, by allowing the defendant to rely on the law of a Member State other than that of the home Member State if the latter governed the act in question. As will be pointed out in relation to Article 290 Solvency II such a defence in effect protects the legitimate expectations of creditors and third parties who acted in accordance with the law which governed that act and who therefore would not have expected that the law of the home Member State might invalidate or otherwise impeach that act.

7.149 Article 287(2) Solvency II resembles Article 10(2) RR.[89] It prevents an office-holder appointed in connection with the reorganization measure or winding-up proceeding from using the commencement of the measure or proceeding as a ground for rescinding a sale or transaction in a case where the relevant asset is at the time of the opening of the measure or proceeding situated in a Member State other than the home Member State. That clearly represents a substantive rule of law which would override not only any contractual provision to the contrary but also any national law which was also to such contrary effect.

7.150 Article 288 Solvency II deals with set-off. If set-off of a creditor's claim and an insurance undertaking's claim is allowed according to the law which governs the latter's claim, Article 288 Solvency II confirms that the opening of the measure or the proceedings is not to affect such right. For this purpose the law applicable to the creditor's claim is not

---

[87] See above at paras 7.77–7.78.
[88] See below at para 7.154.
[89] See generally below at paras 8.595 (RR) and 8.238–8.239 (OR).

relevant. Although Article 288 Solvency II provides that the conditions under which the set-off may be invoked remains a matter for the law of the home Member State, the latter law will apply to determine the availability of set-off regarding claims incurred following upon the opening of the relevant measure or the proceeding and also, more importantly, where set-off is disallowed under the law applicable to the claim of the insurance undertaking.

Article 289 Solvency II deals with regulated markets. It provides that the law of the home Member State will not apply in respect of the rights and obligations of parties to a regulated market. The term 'regulated market' is defined in Article 13(22) Solvency II. In general terms, a 'regulated market' is defined as either (in the case of a market situated in a Member State), a multilateral system operated and/or managed by a market operator, which brings together or facilitates the bringing together of multiple third-party buying and selling interests in financial instruments (as defined under Article 4(1)(21) MiFID II), or (in the case of a market situated in a third country) a financial market which is regarded by an undertaking's home Member State as a regulated market and the fact that the financial instruments dealt in on that market are of a quality comparable to that of the instruments dealt in on the regulated market or markets of the Home Member State. **7.151**

Unlike Solvency II Title IV, the Winding-Up Directive deals with an equivalent exception for netting agreements and repurchase agreements, whilst it also provides a conflict of laws rule for rights recorded in a 'register, account or centralised deposit system' (Articles 24, 25, and 26 of that Directive).[90] This no doubt reflects the reality that insurance undertakings are less likely than banks to be involved in the various forms of payments or settlement systems referred to. **7.152**

The exceptions set out in Article 289 Solvency II apply to the rights and obligations of parties in relation to a market. This is unlike the scope of the equivalent Article, namely Article 27, in the Winding-Up Directive[91] which applies only to contractual transactions carried out in the context of a regulated market. In consequence, Article 289 Solvency II appears to be broader and to cover all aspects relating to the relationship of an insurance undertaking to a market. **7.153**

Article 290 Solvency II deals with detrimental acts. The general rule is that the law of the home Member State governs the rules relating to the nullity, voidability, and unenforceability of legal acts detrimental to all creditors of an insurance undertaking.[92] There may be a challenge in the home Member State, for example to the creation of a security interest over assets in a non-home Member State. Article 290 Solvency II would provide a defence if the act in question was subject to non-home Member State law when that law did not permit such a challenge. **7.154**

Moreover such a defence must be raised by the parties seeking to rely on it. The defence only applies in relation to acts carried out prior to the opening of the relevant measures or **7.155**

---

[90] See above at paras 7.88–7.90.
[91] See above at para 7.91.
[92] See Art 9(2)(l), Art 274(2)(1) Solvency II.

proceedings. If the act in question is carried out after that time, the law of the home Member State will apply.[93]

7.156 Article 291 Solvency II revisits the protection afforded to immovable assets and publicly registered assets such as ships and aircraft, insofar as third party purchasers are concerned. It provides that if by an act concluded after adoption of the reorganization measures or the winding-up proceedings an insurance undertaking disposes of such an asset 'for a consideration', 'the validity of that act shall be governed by the law of the Member State within whose territory the immoveable asset is situated or under whose authority the register account or system is kept'.

7.157 It should be noted that Article 291 Solvency II does not state that the relevant national law is to apply 'solely'. In other words, both the law of the home Member State and the national law will apply.

7.158 The final exception to the applicability of the law of the home Member State is found in Article 292 Solvency II. This provides that the effect of reorganization measures or winding-up proceedings or a pending lawsuit concerning an asset or right of which the insurance undertaking has been divested shall be governed solely by the law of the Member State in which the lawsuit is pending.[94] Article 292 Solvency II does not extend to any enforcement proceeding arising out of a pending lawsuit. On the other hand, the CJEU clarified that the exception to the *lex domus* of Article 292 Solvency II does apply if the law of the Member State where the lawsuit is pending determines, first, that the opening of the winding-up proceedings suspends the proceedings pending, secondly, that those proceedings may not be resumed until the creditor has lodged his non-life insurance claim against the insurance undertaking and the bodies responsible for managing the winding-up proceedings have been summoned and, thirdly, that no order to pay compensation can be made but only its existence and amount can be established.[95]

7.159 Articles 293–295 Solvency II deal with predominantly formal matters. The first of these Articles states that an administrator's or liquidator's appointment shall be evidenced by a certified copy of the original decision of appointment or by any other certificate issued by the competent authorities of the home Member State. Article 27(2) and Article 293(2) and (3) Solvency II confirm that administrators and liquidators can exercise in all Member States all the powers that they can exercise in the home Member State but that with regard to acting in a non-home Member State, they shall comply with that law 'in particular with regard to procedures for the realisation of assets and the informing of employees'.

7.160 Article 294 Solvency II entitles an administrator, liquidator, or duly authorized person in the home Member State to require that the reorganization measure or decision to open winding-up proceedings be registered in a suitable public register such as a land or trade register, in the absence of a binding obligation to effect such a registration.

---

[93] On account of Art 279 Solvency II.
[94] See the commentary on Art 18 RR as well as *Mazur Media Ltd v Mazur Media GmbH* [2004] 1 WLR 2966.
[95] CJEU 13 January 2022, C-724/20, ECLI:EU:C:2022:9 (*Paget Approbois SAS/Depeyre entreprises SARL, Alpha Insurance A/S*).

Article 295 Solvency II preserves professional secrecy otherwise applicable to those persons or parties who have worked or otherwise been formally associated with insurance undertakings but note should be taken of the obligations of professional secrecy in Articles 64–69 Solvency II. The said Articles do allow the disclosure of information which does not concern third parties involved in attempts to rescue an undertaking where the undertaking is declared bankrupt or is otherwise the subject of a compulsory winding-up. **7.161**

Article 296 Solvency II deals with the position of an insurance undertaking in a non-Member State, ie where the head office is situated outside the EU, but which has branches in one or more Member States. In such a case the Member State or States in which the branch or branches of the undertaking is or are situated will be treated as the respective home Member State and the authorities of that state are to be treated as the competent authorities in relation to that undertaking. **7.162**

If there are branches in more than one Member State, then each such branch will be treated separately. Article 296 second and third sentences Solvency II provides that in such circumstances the competent authorities and the supervisory authorities in the home Member State should endeavour to co-ordinate their actions: equally any duly appointed administrators and liquidators should co-ordinate their actions accordingly. **7.163**

F. Bank Recovery and Resolution Directive

Title I: scope and definitions

As stated above[96] the EU harmonization of its bank resolution regime adopted in 2014 represented a major overhaul of the rules governing credit institutions and investment firms that experience financial difficulties.[97] It consists of a Bank Recovery and Resolution Directive (BRRD)[98] and a Single Resolution Mechanism (SRM). While BRRD applies to all EU Member States and had to be implemented into national laws, SRM has been adopted by means of the Single Resolution Mechanism Regulation (SRMR)[99] which may not be implemented but works directly. It applies only to the countries that use the euro as a currency **7.164**

---

[96] At para 7.07.
[97] This paragraph and the following ones have been based, in pertinent part, on M Haentjens et al, *New Bank Insolvency Law for China and Europe, Volume 2 (Europe)*—a project funded by the Royal Netherlands Academy of Arts and Sciences and the China Ministry for Education (2017) and G Moss, B Wessels, M Haentjens (eds), *EU Banking and Insurance Insolvency* (second edition, 2017), 177 et seq. See also generally M Haentjens and B Wessels (ed), *Crisis Management in the Banking Sector* (2015).
[98] Directive 2014/59/EU of the European Parliament and of the Council of 15 May 2014 establishing a framework for the recovery and resolution of credit institutions and investment firms and amending Council Directive 82/891/EEC, and Directives 2001/24/EC, 2002/47/EC, 2004/25/EC, 2005/56/EC, 2007/36/EC, 2011/35/EU, 2012/30/EU, and 2013/36/EU, and Regulations (EU) No 1093/2010 and (EU) No 648/2012, of the European Parliament and of the Council, OJ L173, as amended by Directive (EU) 2019/879 of the European Parliament and of the Council of 20 May 2019 amending Directive 2014/59/EU as regards the loss-absorbing and recapitalization capacity of credit institutions and investment firms and Directive 98/26/EC, OJ L150.
[99] Regulation (EU) No 806/2014 of the European Parliament and of the Council of 15 July 2014 establishing uniform rules and a uniform procedure for the resolution of credit institutions and certain investment firms in the framework of a Single Resolution Mechanism and a Single Resolution Fund and amending Regulation (EU) No 1093/2010, OJ L225, as amended by Regulation (EU) 2019/877 of the European Parliament and of the Council of 20 May 2019 amending Regulation (EU) No 806/2014 as regards the loss-absorbing and recapitalization capacity of credit institutions and investment firms, OJ L150.

or wish to accede to SRM. Moreover, where the BRRD directives provide for the harmonization of substantive rules of bank insolvency law in the broadest sense, SRMR specifically concerns the application of a unified resolution regime by the Single Resolution Board.[100]

7.165 BRRD and SRMR harmonized and unified substantive rules of EU bank resolution law, but BRRD also prescribed rules that apply in going concern and in the earliest stages of financial difficulties, as it involves three pillars: preparatory and preventive measures, early intervention measures, and resolution tools and powers. In contrast, SRMR concerns only resolution. Resolution here is understood as a process of orderly restructuring and if necessary the winding down of it as a whole or a part of it.

7.166 Although BRRD and SRMR harmonized, unified, and also modernized substantive rules of EU bank resolution law, it must also be concluded that BRRD and SRMR have so far been only partly successful in practice. On the one hand, their rules of mandatory bail-in, write-down, and conversion of capital instruments have made authorities reluctant to have the instruments apply to banks in distress. On the other hand, resolution authorities have interpreted the 'public interest test' (see also below, paragraph 7.198), one of the conditions for resolution, rather strictly, so that resolution has been rarely applied. See, also, for instance, the decisions of the Single Resolution Board re ABLV Bank of 23 February 2018.[101]

7.167 As a matter of principle, BRRD and SRMR harmonize and unify substantive law whilst the Winding-Up Directive focuses on co-ordination and conflict of law rules. BRRD and SRMR will therefore leave the principles set out above[102] intact. Yet for purposes of the Winding-Up Directive, 'reorganisation measures' now also include 'the application of the resolution tools and the exercise of resolution powers' provided for in BRRD, while the Winding-Up Directive's definition of 'winding-up proceedings' echoes what BRRD calls 'normal insolvency proceedings', viz 'collective insolvency proceedings which entail the partial or total divestment of a debtor and the appointment of a liquidator or an administrator normally applicable to institutions under national law and either specific to those institutions or generally applicable to any natural or legal person' (Article 2(1)(47) BRRD). In the regime accomplished by BRRD (and SRMR) these latter 'normal insolvency proceedings' will play only a secondary, if not marginal role as predominance is given to administrative intervention in the earliest stages so that collective proceedings are avoided. As one of the consequences thereof, for instance, BRRD nuances the principle of unity discussed above,[103] through the introduction of 'resolution colleges', of which not only the home state group-level resolution authority is a member, but also, *inter alia*, the resolution authorities of member states in which significant branches are located (Article 88(2)(d) BRRD). This college may eg have to reach an agreement on a resolution scheme for the entire group (Article 88(1)(f) BRRD).

7.168 Pursuant to Article 1(1)(a) and Article 2(1)(23) BRRD/Article 2 SRMR, this Directive and Regulation apply to credit institutions and investment firms. For the definition of

---

[100] The SRMR contains materially the same provisions as the BRRD. For that reason, and also because of SRMR's more limited remit, the following paragraphs will follow the BRRD's set-up and principally discuss the BRRD's provisions. Nonetheless, references to SRMR will be made where appropriate.
[101] Decisions of the SRB of 23 February 2018 SRB/EES/2018/09 and SRB/EES/2018/10.
[102] At paras 7.10–7.13.
[103] At para 7.11.

credit institution, Article 1(2)(2) BRRD refers to 'a credit institution as defined in point (1) of Article 4(1) of Regulation (EU) No 575/2013, not including the entities referred to in Article 2(5) of Directive 2013/36/EU'. Under Article 4(1)(1) of Regulation (EU) 575/2013, ie the CRR, a 'credit institution' is 'an undertaking the business of which is to take deposits or other repayable funds from the public and to grant credits for its own account'. In short, banks are the main subject of the regime the BRRD establishes. Article 2(5) of Directive 2013/36/EU, ie CRD IV, excludes certain institutions, principally central banks of the Member States and other financial institutions such as friendly societies and post office giro institutions from this definition.

Similarly to the 'definition' of credit institution, the term 'investment firm' is 'defined' in Article 1(2)(3) BRRD, as 'an investment firm as defined in point (2) of Article 4(1) of Regulation (EU) No 575/2013 that is subject to the initial capital requirement laid down in Article 28(2) of Directive 2013/36/EU'. Under Article 4(1)(2) CRR, an investment firm means 'a person as defined in point (1) of Article 4(1) of Directive 2004/39/EC, which is subject to the requirements imposed by that Directive, excluding the following: (a) credit institutions; (b) local firms; (c) firms which are not authorized to provide the ancillary service referred to in point (1) of Section B of Annex I to Directive 2004/39/EC, which provide only one or more of the investment services and activities listed in points 1, 2, 4 and 5 of Section A of Annex I to that Directive, and which are not permitted to hold money or securities belonging to their clients and which for that reason may not at any time place themselves in debt with those clients;'. Directive 2004/39/EC is the Markets in Financial Instruments Directive (MiFID),[104] which has been replaced by MiFID II[105] as of 2 January 2018. In short, BRRD and SRMR cover the larger investment firms. 7.169

Whilst European law generally does not treat groups of companies as a single entity either for the purposes of general corporate law or with regard to insolvency law, SRMR radically derogates from that approach as under this Regulation, the Single Resolution Board is empowered to take decisions in relation to certain categories of groups as a whole, as the Board is responsible for adopting all decisions relating to resolution for those groups pursuant to Article 7(2) SRMR. Under Article 1(1) BRRD, also 'financial institutions' that are a subsidiary of a credit institution, investment firm, or of, in short, a holding company of a financial group are covered. A financial institution is further defined (via Article 2(1)(4) BRRD/Article 3(1)(15) SRMR) in Article 4(1)(26) CRR, which says that a 'financial institution' means: 7.170

> an undertaking other than an institution [ie a credit institution or investment firm, MH], the principal activity of which is to acquire holdings or to pursue one or more of the activities listed in points 2 to 12 and point 15 of Annex I to Directive 2013/36/EU, including a financial holding company, a mixed financial holding company, a payment institution within the meaning of Directive 2007/64/EC of the European Parliament and of the Council of 13 November 2007 on payment services in the internal market,

---

[104] Directive 2004/39/EC of the European Parliament and of the Council of 21 April 2004 on markets in financial instruments amending Council Directives 85/611/EEC and 93/6/EEC and Directive 2000/12/EC of the European Parliament and of the Council and repealing Council Directive 93/22/EEC, OJ L145.

[105] Directive 2014/65/EU of the European Parliament and of the Council of 15 May 2014 on markets in financial instruments and amending Directive 2002/92/EC and Directive 2011/61/EU, OJ L173.

and an asset management company, but excluding insurance holding companies and mixed-activity insurance holding companies as defined in point (g) of Article 212(1) of Directive 2009/138/E.

7.171 A 'subsidiary' is defined (via Article 2(1)(5) BRRD/Article 3(1)(21) SRMR) as meaning:

(a) a subsidiary as defined in point (16) of Article 4(1) of Regulation (EU) No 575/2013, and for the purpose of applying Articles 7, 12, 17, 18, 45 to 45m, 59 to 62, 91 and 92 of this Directive to resolution groups referred to in point (b) of point (83b) of this paragraph, includes, where and as appropriate, credit institutions that are permanently affiliated to a central body, the central body itself, and their respective subsidiaries, taking into account the way in which such resolution groups comply with Article 45e(3) of this Directive;.

7.172 BRRD and SRMR also apply to, in short, a holding company of a financial group (Article 1(1)(c) and (d) BRRD/Article 2(b) SRMR).

7.173 Finally, Article 1(1)(e) BRRD has the BRRD also apply, under certain circumstances, to 'branches'. A 'branch' is defined (via Article 2 BRRD) as meaning 'a place of business which forms a legally dependent part of an institution and which carries out directly all or some of the transactions inherent in the business of institutions' (Article 4(1)(17) CRR). The European Banking Authority (EBA) has clarified in its Q&A published on 24 July 2015 that Article 1(1)(e) BRRD 'should be interpreted as meaning branches operated within the Union of Institutions established outside of the Union'. Thus, BRRD also applies to branches located in a Member State of institutions whose head office is established in a third country, including the UK.[106]

7.174 Article 2 BRRD and Article 3 SRMR contain too many definitions to be discussed here. Noteworthy is the definition of 'resolution' of Article 2(1)(1) BRRD, which reads: 'the application of a resolution tool or a tool referred to in Article 37(9) in order to achieve one or more of the resolution objectives referred to in Article 31(2)'. The resolution tools listed in Article 37(3) BRRD[107]/Article 22(2) SRMR form some of the central elements of the BRRD and SRMR and the regime these instruments create. Pursuant to Article 37(3) BRRD/Article 22(2) SRMR, the resolution tools are: the sale of business tool, the bridge institution tool, the asset separation tool, and the bail-in tool. 'Special management' as defined in Article 35 BRRD may be considered to represent an additional resolution tool. These 'resolution tools' will be discussed below.[108]

7.175 To apply the resolution tools just listed, resolution authorities need to be conferred 'resolution powers' which are listed in Articles 63–72 inclusive BRRD (Article 2(1)(20) BRRD).

---

[106] EBA, Single Rulebook Q&A. 2016_2578 available at <https://www.eba.europa.eu/single-rule-book-qa/-/qna/view/publicId/2016_2578>.
[107] The reference to Art 37(9) in the BRRD definition is probably erroneous, also considering the definition of 'resolution tool' in Art 2(1)(19) BRRD which redirects to Art 37(3) BRRD.
[108] At paras 7.191–7.208.

Title II: preparation

Article 3 provides that, in short, Member States must designate 'resolution authorities' to apply the resolution tools and exercise the resolution powers. **7.176**

Under Title II (Preparation) of the BRRD, institutions themselves must draw up 'recovery plans' whilst resolution authorities must have 'resolution plans' in place. Recovery plans must provide 'for measures to be taken by the institution to restore its financial position following a significant deterioration of its financial situation' (Article 5(1) BRRD). Not all institutions have to comply with the same level of preparation requirements. Certain institutions are subject to simplified obligations (Article 4(1) BRRD). The assessment of eligibility for simplified obligations should be made by each authority separately having regard to the impact that the failure of the institution could have on financial markets, on other institutions, on funding conditions, and on the wider economy, and taking account of the criteria set out in Article 4(1) BRRD. The criteria include, among others, the nature of the institution's business, shareholding structure, legal form, risk profile, size, legal status, and interconnectedness.[109] **7.177**

Resolution plans must provide 'for the resolution actions which the resolution authority may take where the institution meets the conditions for resolution' (Article 10(1) BRRD/ Article 8(6) SRMR). Recovery plans must be drawn up for groups by the 'Union parent undertaking' (Article 7(1) BRRD), that is a parent institution in a Member State which is not a subsidiary of another institution authorized in any Member State, or of a financial holding company or mixed financial holding company set up in any Member State (Article 4(1)(29) CRR via Article 2(1)(50) BRRD). Group resolution plans must be drafted by the 'group-level resolution authority' (Article 12(1) BRRD), that is the resolution authority in the Member State in which the consolidating supervisor is situated (Article 2(1)(44) BRRD). The 'consolidating supervisor' is defined as meaning a competent authority responsible for the exercise of supervision on a consolidated basis of EU parent institutions and of institutions controlled by EU parent financial holding companies or EU parent mixed financial holding companies (Article 4(1)(41) CRR via Article 2(1)(37) BRRD). The resolution plan must identify for each group the resolution entities and the resolution groups. It follows that the resolution plan must opt either for a so-called Multiple Point of Entry (MPE) strategy or for a Single Point of Entry (SPE) strategy, and, based on that choice, develop the possible resolution actions.[110] With regard to cross-border groups and significant entities and groups in the Member States participating in the SRM, the Single Resolution Board draws up the resolution plans just discussed (Article 7(2) SRMR). **7.178**

The Single Resolution Board and the (national) resolution authorities are required to assess constantly the extent to which a credit institution or a group of credit institutions is 'resolvable' by either liquidating it under normal insolvency proceedings or resolving it by applying the different resolution tools and powers, while avoiding significant adverse **7.179**

---

[109] See extensively on these criteria EBA/RTS/2017/11, 19 December 2017, Final Report, 'Draft regulatory technical standards on simplified obligations under Article 4(6) of Directive 2014/59/EU'.
[110] See Article 25 of the Commission Delegated Regulation (EU) 2016/1075 (DR) of 23 March 2016 and clarified by EBA in EBA, Final Q&A of 24 July 2015, available at <https://www.eba.europa.eu/single-rule-book-qa/-/qna/view/publicId/2015_2096>.

consequences for the financial systems and ensuring the continuity of the critical functions of the credit institution or the group entities (Article 15(1) and 16(1) BRRD/Article 10(1) SRMR).[111] The national resolution authorities and Single Resolution Board are empowered to demand measures necessary to reduce or remove impediments to the resolvability of the group or entity, such as the requirement to divest specific assets, to limit or cease specific activities, or to change legal or operational structures (Article 17(4) and (5) BRRD/Article 10(10)–(11) SRMR).[112] Also, pursuant to Article 15(4), on 18 July 2014, the EBA published final draft regulatory technical standards to specify the matters and criteria for the assessment of the resolvability of institutions or groups.[113]

7.180 Moreover, the national resolution authorities and Single Resolution Board have the authority to prohibit an entity from distributing monies, including paying out dividends on Common Equity Tier 1 and interest on Additional Tier 1 instruments, but also variable remuneration and pension benefits may be prohibited, when an entity fails to meet certain capital requirements. More precisely, the authorities may prohibit an entity from distributing more than what is called the 'Maximum Distributable Amount related to the minimum requirement for own funds and eligible liabilities (MREL)'[114] in situations where these entities fail to meet the combined buffer requirement as defined in CRD (Article 16a BRRD/Article 10a SRMR).

7.181 However, there are limits to the measures resolution authorities may take to remove substantive impediments to the resolvability of an entity. For instance, in its final Q&A published on 21 January 2022, EBA has clarified that there is no sufficient legal basis in the BRRD for resolution authorities to prohibit the concerned entity to enter into agreements governed by third country law that does not accept cross-border contractual recognition of bail-in (Article 17(5) BRRD).[115] See on the contractual recognition of bail in paragraph 7.255. Also, specific procedural requirements must be observed for groups, alongside with or in derogation from the general rules that govern the process of determining and removing impediments to resolvability (Article 18/Article 17 BRRD).[116]

7.182 Title II BRRD also contains a Chapter III under which, in short, parent institutions may enter into an agreement to provide financial support to group companies in financial difficulties. Where the BRRD refers to the term 'intra-group financial arrangements', it means a broad concept that includes 'agreements' (Article 19(2) BRRD).[117] On 9 July 2015 the EBA proved further clarification through its final draft Regulatory Technical Standards (RTS) and Guidelines, as well as final draft Implementing Technical Standards (ITS) on the provision of group financial support and their publication. These Technical Standards and Guidelines further specify the conditions under which one entity of a group can provide support to another group entity. The EBA considered that at the time, the regulatory

---

[111] Annex Section C BRRD sets out the matters that the resolution authority must examine when assessing the resolvability of an institution or a group.
[112] With regard to a group outside the scope of the SRM, the group-level resolution authority together with the resolution authority of the subsidiaries shall take reasonable steps to reach a joint decision on the application of measures to address or remove impediment to resolvability; Art 18 BRRD.
[113] These RTS have now been published in the OJ as Delegated Regulation (EU) 2016/1075 of 23 March 2016.
[114] See on MREL also Articles 45–45m BRRD/Article 12–12k SRMR.
[115] See <https://www.eba.europa.eu/single-rule-book-qa/-/qna/view/publicId/2015_2101>.
[116] See <https://www.eba.europa.eu/single-rule-book-qa/-/qna/view/publicId/2015_2100>.
[117] See clarified by EBA at <https://www.eba.europa.eu/single-rule-book-qa/-/qna/view/publicId/2016_2581>.

framework for intra-group financial support differed 'widely across the EU, in particular for those cases of subsidiaries supporting parent companies (upstream support), making it difficult for banking groups operating in more than one EU member States to allocate and manage liquidity optimally during periods of financial distress'.[118] In addition, the EBA clarified that Intra Group Financial Support (IGFS) does not include business-as-usual financial support agreements (such as guarantees, letters of comfort). Potential risks for financial stability caused by business-as-usual intragroup financial support are to be addressed through other instruments, such as the powers to remove impediments to resolvability (see eg Art 17(5)(a) BRRD).[119]

Title III: early intervention

In Title III of the BRRD (Early Intervention) supervisory authorities (rather than resolution authorities) are granted early intervention powers in order to intervene before the deterioration of the institution's financial and economic situation reaches a point at which authorities have no other alternative than resolution (Recital (40) BRRD).[120] The early intervention measures may be taken where the institution is in breach of, or is likely in the near future to be in breach of, certain prudential requirements (Article 27(1) BRRD).[121] The ECB and the national supervisory authorities have to inform the Single Resolution Board and the national resolution authorities about the early intervention in order for them to update the resolution plan and to prepare for a possible resolution (Article 27(2) BRRD/Article 13 SRMR). Under Article 27(4) the EBA has developed guidelines to promote consistent application of the triggers for use of the early intervention measures. These guidelines, which were published on 8 May 2015, are mostly based on the supervisory review and evaluation process (SREP). However, the Guidelines do not establish any quantitative thresholds for indicators that could be perceived as new capital or liquidity requirements.

7.183

The early intervention measures that may be taken by the supervisory authorities are (not exhaustively) (Article 27(1) BRRD): (a) require the management body of the institution to implement one or more of the arrangements or measures set out in the recovery plan or to update such a recovery plan and implement one or more of the arrangements or measures set out in the updated plan; (b) require the management body of the institution to examine the situation, identify measures to overcome any problems identified and draw up an action programme to overcome those problems and a timetable for its implementation; (c) require the management body of the institution to convene, or if the management body fails to comply with that requirement convene directly, a meeting of shareholders of the institution, and in both cases set the agenda and require certain decisions to be considered for adoption

7.184

---

[118] These ITS have been adopted as Commission Implementing Regulation (EU) 2016/911 of 9 June 2016 laying down implementing technical standards with regard to the form and the content of the description of group financial support agreements in accordance with Directive 2014/59/EU of the European Parliament and of the Council establishing a framework for the recovery and resolution of credit institutions and investment firms, C/2016/3440, OJ J153.
[119] See <https://www.eba.europa.eu/single-rule-book-qa/-/qna/view/publicId/2016_2579>.
[120] The early intervention powers supplement the measures already provided for in Section IV CRD IV.
[121] These are the prudential requirements of CRR and CRD IV. The EBA shall develop guidelines, adopted by the European Commission, to promote consistent application of the trigger for use of the early intervention measures (Art 27(4) BRRD).

by the shareholders; (d) require one or more members of the management body or senior management to be removed or replaced if those persons are found unfit to perform their duties; (e) require the management body of the institution to draw up a plan for negotiation on restructuring of debt with some or all of its creditors according to the recovery plan, where applicable; (f) require changes to the institution's business strategy; (g) require changes to the legal or operational structures of the institution; and (h) acquire, including through on-site inspections and provide to the resolution authority, all the information necessary in order to update the resolution plan and prepare for the possible resolution of the institution and for valuation of the assets and liabilities of the institution (Article 27(1) BRRD).[122] The EBA clarified that in fact, the BRRD does not require any early intervention measures to be taken before a precautionary recapitalization can take place or vice versa.[123]

7.185 If these arrangements and measures do not provide for a sufficient solution, the relevant supervisory authority may also remove and replace the management body or senior management (Article 28 BRRD).

7.186 Moreover, where the replacement of the management body or the senior management is deemed to be insufficient, the supervisory authorities may appoint a temporary administrator to replace the management of the institution or to work with this management (Article 29 BRRD). On 2 January 2019, for instance, the ECB appointed three temporary administrators and a three-member surveillance committee to take charge of Banca Carige and replace its Board of Directors.[124]

7.187 If, as regards groups, early intervention measures can be taken in relation to the Union parent undertaking, the consolidating supervisor must notify EBA and consult the other competent authorities within the 'supervisory college', ie the college in which the competent authorities of the home and host Member States co-operate[125] (Article 30(1) BRRD). The same applies for any subsidiary (Article 30(3) BRRD).

Title IV: resolution

7.188 Title IV of the BRRD concerns resolution. If 'conditions for resolution' are met, resolution authorities may place any entity covered by BRRD under resolution, apply the resolution tools and exercise the resolution powers as listed above.[126]

7.189 The application of resolution tools and the exercise of resolution powers must have regard to the five following 'resolution objectives' listed in Article 31(2) BRRD/Article 14(2) SRMR: to ensure the continuity of critical functions; to avoid a significant adverse effect on

---

[122] See EBA, Final report Guidelines on triggers for use of early intervention measures pursuant to Article 27(4) of Directive 2014/59/EU, EBA/GL/2015/03 8 May 2015 on the circumstances under which competent authorities should consider the application of early intervention measures to institutions, available at <https://www.eba.europa.eu/sites/default/documents/files/documents/10180/1067473/f6234078-a8cb-40a1-88f1-f22d446ca394/EBA-GL-2015-03%20Guidelines%20on%20Early%20Intervention%20Triggers.pdf?retry=1>.
[123] See on the relationship between precautionary recapitalization under Art 32(4)(d)(iii) BRRD and the early intervention measures under Art 27(1) BRRD, <https://www.eba.europa.eu/single-rule-book-qa/-/qna/view/publicId/2015_2516>.
[124] See <https://www.bankingsupervision.europa.eu/press/pr/date/2019/html/ssm.pr190102.en.html>.
[125] Art 2(1)(52) BRRD and Art 116 CRD IV.
[126] At paras 7.171–7.172.

the financial system, in particular by preventing contagion, including to market infrastructures, and by maintaining market discipline; to protect public funds by minimizing reliance on extraordinary public financial support; to protect depositors covered by Directive 2014/49/EU and investors covered by Directive 97/9/EC; and to protect client funds and client assets. These resolution objectives are of equal significance and must be balanced by the resolution authorities in each case (Article 31(3) BRRD/Article 14(3) SRMR).

Pursuant to Article 32(1) BRRD/Article 18(1) SRMR the conditions for resolution are: (1) that the institution is failing or likely to fail; (2) that there is no reasonable prospect that any alternative private sector measures or supervisory action would prevent the failure of the institution within a reasonable timeframe; and (3) that the resolution action is necessary in the public interest. In case of the resolution of a group, these conditions must be met, in principle, with regard to both the failing subsidiary and its parent company. Nonetheless, resolution action may also be taken with regard to a parent company that does not meet the resolution conditions, but one or more subsidiaries do, if the assets and liabilities of the relevant subsidiary are such that its failure threatens the institution or group as a whole or if the insolvency law of the Member State requires that the group be treated as a whole, and such resolution action is necessary (Article 33(4) BRRD). In its Q&A published on 24 July 2015 EBA clarified that there is no need for the third-country holding company to comply with Article 32 or Article 33 BRRD.[127] **7.190**

An institution is deemed to be failing or likely to fail if the institution infringes, or it will infringe in the near future, the requirements for continuing authorization in a way that would justify the withdrawal of the authorization by the ECB or national supervisory authority. Authorization can be withdrawn, for instance, if the institution has incurred or is likely to incur losses that will deplete all or a significant amount of its own funds.[128] An institution is also deemed failing or likely to fail if its assets are, or will be in the near future, less than its liabilities; if the institution is, or it will be in the near future, unable to pay its debts or other liabilities as they fall due; or if it requires extraordinary public financial support (Article 32(4) BRRD/Article 18(4) SRMR). **7.191**

A resolution action will be in the public interest if it achieves and is proportionate to one or more of the resolution objectives and winding-up of the institution under normal insolvency proceedings would not meet those resolution objectives to the same extent (Article 32(5) BRRD/Article 18(5) SRMR). As a consequence, prior to the application of the resolution tools, the winding-up of the failing institution through normal insolvency proceedings has to be considered by the authorities. In view of the resolution objectives,[129] it could be hypothesized that national insolvency proceedings would remain suitable only for the smaller credit institutions and investment firms.[130] On several occasions, however, **7.192**

---

[127] See EBA, Q&A, 2015_2072 at <https://www.eba.europa.eu/single-rule-book-qa/-/qna/view/publicId/2015_2072>.
[128] 'Own funds' means 'the sum of Tier 1 capital and Tier 2 capital' (Art 2(1)(38) BRRD and Art 4(1)(118) CRR).
[129] See para 7.188 above.
[130] Cf Recital (45) of the BRRD which says that '[a] failing institution should in principle be liquidated under normal insolvency proceedings. However, liquidation under normal insolvency proceedings might jeopardise financial stability, interrupt the provision of critical functions, and affect the protection of depositors. In such a case it is highly likely that there would be a public interest in placing the institution under resolution and applying resolution tools rather than resorting to normal insolvency proceedings.'

the Single Resolution Board decided that failing institutions of significant size also did not pass the 'public interest test'. See, for instance, the cases of Italian credit institutions Banco Popolare di Vicenza SpA and Veneto Banca SpA in 2017 (which banks then continued to be restructured under Italian law against a cost of EUR 17bn for the Italian taxpayer),[131] the case of Latvian bank ABLV Bank AS and its subsidiary ABLV Bank Luxembourg SA in 2018 and the case of AS PNB Banka in 2019. The Single Resolution Board found that the public interest test was met only with regard to Banco Popular Español SA in 2017 (which bank then continued to be resolved with use of the sale of business tool and was transferred to Banco Santander SA) and the subsidiaries of Austrian Sberbank Europe AG in 2022.[132]

7.193 Since the adoption of amendments to the BRRD in 2019 by means of Directive (EU) 2019/879, Article 32a(1) BRRD authorizes the relevant resolution authority to suspend 'any payment or delivery obligations' with regard to a failing institution. In essence, resolutions authorities thus now have the authority to impose a moratorium prior to resolution proper. Specifically, for such moratorium to be imposed, the following conditions must be met:

(a) a determination that the institution or entity is failing or are likely to fail has been made under point (a) of Article 32(1);
(b) there is no immediately available private sector measure referred to in point (b) of Article 32(1) that would prevent the failure of the institution or entity;
(c) the exercise of the power to suspend is deemed necessary to avoid the further deterioration of the financial conditions of the institution or entity; and
(d) the exercise of the power to suspend is either:
   (i) necessary to reach the determination provided for in point (c) of Article 32(1); or
   (ii) necessary to choose the appropriate resolution actions or to ensure the effective application of one or more resolution tools.

7.194 Under Article 34(1) BRRD/Article 15(1) SRMR, the resolution authorities must take appropriate measures to ensure that resolution actions are taken in accordance with the following general principles:

(a) the shareholders of the institution under resolution bear the first losses;
(b) the creditors bear the losses after the shareholders, in accordance with the order of priority provided in national insolvency law (as partly harmonised by the BRRD);[133]
(c) where appropriate, senior management of the institution under resolution is replaced;
(d) the management body and senior management provides all necessary assistance for the achievement of the resolution objectives;
(e) natural or legal persons are made liable under civil law or criminal law in the Member States for their responsibility for the failure of the institution;
(f) creditors of the same class are treated equitably;
(g) no creditor incurs greater losses than would have been incurred if the institution or entity would have been wound up under normal insolvency proceedings. This is the 'No Creditor Worse Off' (NCWO) principle. The shareholders and creditors who

---

[131] See <https://www.srb.europa.eu/en/content/banca-popolare-di-vicenza-veneto-banca>.
[132] See for a general overview of resolution actions, 'National Interests and Supranational Resolution in the European Banking Union', T H Troeger and A Kotovskaia (2022). SAFE Working Paper No 340, European Banking Institute Working Paper Series 2022—no 114.
[133] Especially Art 108 BRRD.

received less are compensated by the Single Resolution Fund in case the SRM applies or by the national financing arrangements;[134]

(h) deposits covered by the national deposit guarantee schemes[135] are fully protected; and
(i) the resolution action is taken in accordance with the safeguards of the SRMR and the BRRD. For example, in case of only a partial transfer of the assets, rights, or liabilities of the institution under resolution to another entity, the transactions under the same netting arrangements are protected against a separation.[136]

7.195 Chapter II of Title IV BRRD consists of a single provision (Article 35 BRRD/Article 23 SRMR) which concerns what may be considered an additional resolution tool: special management. The resolution authorities can appoint a 'special manager' for a maximum period of one year to replace the management body of the institution under resolution, which appointment has to be made public. In case of an insolvency of the institution and the relevant national insolvency law provides for a so-called 'insolvency management', this management may constitute the special management as established by the BRRD.[137] The BRRD specifies that the special manager is required to have the qualifications, ability, and knowledge to carry out his functions. He shall have the powers of the institution's shareholders and the management body, although the exercise of these powers is subject to the control of the resolution authority. The special manager has the duty to take the necessary measures to promote the BRRD's resolution objectives and to implement the resolution actions in accordance with the decisions of the resolution authority.

7.196 In line with the provisions on the temporary administrator in the stage of early intervention (see above, paragraph 7.185), the special manager can be removed by the resolution authority at any time and its actions can be made subject to the prior approval of or be limited by the resolution authority. Yet in contrast to the tasks and powers of the temporary administrator, the duty of the special manager in resolution may override any other duty of the management under the statute of the institution or under national law, in case they are not consistent. Possible measures include an increase of capital, reorganization of the ownership structure of the institution, or takeovers by institutions that are financially and organizationally sound, in accordance with the resolution tools provided for in the BRRD (Article 35(3) BRRD). With regard to entities operating in a group, the competent resolution authorities have to consider together whether it is appropriate to appoint the same special manager for all entities concerned (Article 35(7) BRRD/Article 23 SRMR).[138]

7.197 The application of resolution tools and the exercise of resolution powers requires an *ex-ante* valuation of the assets and liabilities of the failing institution. This valuation should provide a factual basis for several determinations with regard to the resolution process, such as whether the conditions for resolution are met, which resolution action is to be taken, and, in case of the application of the bail-in tool (to be discussed more extensively below), to what

---

[134] Art 73 BRRD.
[135] See Directive 2014/49/EU of the European Parliament and of the Council of 16 April 2014 on deposit guarantee schemes, OJ L173.
[136] See paras 7.227 and 7.228 below.
[137] Art 35(8) BRRD. Under Dutch law, for instance, this would be a 'curator', and under French law 'un administrateur en charge de la gestion de l'insolvabilité'.
[138] Under the SRM, the Single Resolution Board can appoint the same special manager for all entities in a group in case that is necessary to facilitate solution to redress the financial situation of those entities.

extent liabilities must be written down or converted. One of the purposes of the valuation is to ensure that any losses on the assets of the institution are fully recognized at the moment the resolution tools are applied (Article 36(4) BRRD/Article 20(5)(g) SRMR). Article 36(1) BRRD/Article 20(1) SRMR prescribes that such valuation is to be carried out by an independent third party. Another purpose of this valuation is to inform the decision on the appropriate resolution action to be taken.[139]

7.198 The EBA clarified that when a resolution authority decides to rely on more than one valuation, each of them should be considered as a conceptual section of the same overall valuation under Article 36 BRRD and should be judicially reviewable at the same conditions of a single valuation. In this respect, Article 36(13) BRRD excludes that an ex-ante valuation be subject to a separate right of appeal and can only be appealed in the context of the appeal against the resolution decision to apply a resolution tool or exercise write-down or conversion powers. It follows that, where two separate ex-ante valuations are prepared (eg, one for the purpose of determining whether the conditions for resolution are met and the other for informing the appropriate resolution action) each of them can be challenged when challenging the decision on resolution.[140]

7.199 Moreover, before any other resolution action is taken, capital instruments issued by the institution must fully absorb the losses of the institution by writing them down or converting them into equity, in accordance with the priority of claims under normal insolvency proceedings (Recital (81) and Articles 59 and 60 BRRD/Article 20 SRMR). This write-down or conversion of capital instruments (WDCI), however, is not only required prior to the application of any resolution tools and the exercise of resolution powers, but also at the point the relevant authority decides that the institution in question ceases to be viable without the exercise of this power, regardless of the application of any subsequent resolution action (Article 37(2) and 59(1) BRRD/Article 20(1) SRMR). Somewhat confusingly, in international publications the WDCI power is sometimes also called 'bail-in'. BRRD and SRMR, however, distinguish WDCI (which concerns capital instruments only) from the 'bail-in tool' (to be discussed below, and which concerns liabilities only). BRRD and SRMR thus envisage a two-step process in which WDCI always takes place first and which leads to a write down of the failing institution's capital, after which the bail-in tool may or may not be used as a resolution tool so as to write down (and convert) the institution's liabilities. See also below, paragraphs 7.209 et seq and 7.215.

7.200 Chapter IV of Title IV BRRD contains a substantiation of the resolution tools, viz the sale of business tool, the bridge institution tool, the asset separation tool, and the bail-in tool (as listed in Article 37(3) BRRD/Article 22(2) SRMR, see also above, paragraph 7.171), which will be commented on subsequently. Notably, resolution authorities may apply the asset separation tool only together with another resolution tool (Article 37(5) BRRD/Article 22(4) SRMR).

---

[139] See elaborately on the different purposes of valuation, the EBA final Q&A, published 21 January 2022 on Art 36(4)(a) BRRD, available at <https://www.eba.europa.eu/single-rule-book-qa/-/qna/view/publicId/2016_2583>.
[140] See the EBA final Q&A, published 21 January 2022 on Art 36(13) BRRD, available at <https://www.eba.europa.eu/single-rule-book-qa/-/qna/view/publicId/2016_2584>.

In order to maintain critical functions or viable parts of the institution in resolution, the resolution authorities are empowered by 'the sale of the business tool' to effect a sale of the institution or a part thereof to one or more private sector purchasers, by transferring shares or other instruments of ownership[141] issued by the institution under resolution or all or any of its assets, rights, or liabilities (Article 38(1) BRRD/Article 24 SRMR). Obtaining the consent of the shareholders or any third party other than the purchaser is not required for the transfer and any company or securities law procedural requirements may be suspended (Article 38(1) BRRD).[142] As mentioned already above, paragraph 7.191 the sale of business tool was used with regard to Banco Popular Español SA in 2017, after employment of WDCI (discussed above, paragraph 7.194). Specifically, as of 7 June 2017, all existing shareholders of Banco Popular Español SA were wiped out and subordinated debt qualifying as Tier 2 instruments were converted into shares. These new shares were subsequently transferred to Banco Santander SA for the price of 1 EUR.

7.201

Unless this would undermine the resolution objectives, the resolution authority is required to market the assets, rights, liabilities, and shares of the institution in a way that is transparent, is free from any conflict of interest, aims at maximizing the sale prices, and shall take into account the need for a fast resolution action (Article 39 BRRD).

7.202

For the transfer commercial terms are to be obtained, with any consideration going to the shareholders who have been deprived of their shares, or to the institution under resolution, in case of only a partial transfer of the business to the purchaser (Article 38(3)–(4) BRRD). In case of only a partial sale of the business of the institution, the residual institution from which the assets, rights, or liabilities have been transferred, is to be wound down under normal insolvency proceedings (Article 37(6) and Recital (50) BRRD/Article 22(5) SRMR). This is an example of instances where national (bank) insolvency laws continue to play a role in the context of resolution. Another example would be the instances where the NCWO principle is applied (see paragraphs 225 et seq).

7.203

In case no private buyer is quickly available or the failing institution is too big to merge with another institution, 'the bridge institution tool' enables the resolution authorities to transfer all or a part of the business of the institution under resolution to a temporary bridge institution, without consent of the shareholders or any third party other than the bridge institution itself (Article 40(1) and (2) BRRD/Article 25 SRMR).[143] This bridge institution is a legal entity wholly or partially owned by one or more public authorities, which may include the resolution authority, and is controlled by the resolution authority (Article 40(2) BRRD). It is created and must be operated with a view to maintaining access to critical functions and selling the business to a private sector purchaser when conditions are appropriate (Articles 40(2)(b) and 41(2) BRRD). The bridge institution may be considered as a continuation of the rights, functions, services, and activities of the institution under resolution, including

7.204

---

[141] Art 2(1)(61) BRRD defines 'instruments of ownership' as '[...] shares, other instruments that confer ownership, instruments that are convertible into or give the right to acquire shares or other instruments of ownership, and instruments representing interests in shares or other instruments of ownership.' This also includes pre-emptive rights to subscribe for shares. See EBA, Final Q&A, published on 21 January 2022, available at <https://www.eba.europa.eu/single-rule-book-qa/-/qna/view/publicId/2016_2717>.

[142] Art 38(8) and (9) BRRD detail how some securities law requirements may be suspended.

[143] S Madaus, 'Bank Failure and pre-emptive Planning' in M Haentjens and B Wessels (eds), *Bank Recovery and Resolution: A Conference Book* (2014) 61–62.

the right to operate in another Member State. It must have the necessary authorization to carry on these activities and services and must comply with prudential requirements (Articles 40(9), (10), and 41(1) BRRD).

7.205 The resolution authorities have the power to force a transfer of shares, rights, assets, or liabilities from the distressed institution to the bridge institution, but may in certain circumstances also transfer these shares, rights, assets, or liabilities back to the institution under resolution (Article 40(1) and (7) BRRD—as in the case of the sale of business tool: Article 38(6) BRRD). As with the sale of business tool, in case of only a partial transfer of the business of the institution to the bridge institution, the residual institution from which the assets, rights, or liabilities have been transferred, must be wound down under normal insolvency proceedings (Article 37(6) and Recital (50) BRRD/Article 22(5) SRMR). According to the EBA, the main difference between the sale of business and the bridge bank tool is that the former is composed of a single conceptual phase, while the latter necessarily entails more than one step.[144]

7.206 The bridge institution should maintain access of third parties to the critical functions provided by the institution under resolution (Article 41(2) BRRD).[145] In addition, the operations of the bridge institution are to be terminated when the bridge institution merges with another entity, it ceases to meet specific requirements, when all or substantially all its assets, rights, or liabilities are sold to a third party, or when the assets of the bridge institution are wound down and its liabilities are all discharged (Article 41(3) BRRD). If none of these outcomes occur within a reasonable period of time, ie in any event within two years, which may be extended with one or more additional one-year periods, the operations of the bridge institution shall be terminated as soon as possible and the business shall be wound down. Any proceeds as a result of the termination shall benefit the shareholders of the bridge institution (Article 41(3)(d) and 41(5)–(8) BRRD).

7.207 When the bridge institution is only partially publicly owned, the public authority must retain control.[146] If, further to the application of the bail-in tool, the bridge institution ceases to be at least partially publicly owned, depending on the circumstances, it may lose the status of bridge institution or it may remain under public control for a longer period.[147]

7.208 The asset separation tool is a resolution tool that authorizes the resolution authorities to transfer, without consent of the shareholders or any third party, certain assets, rights, and liabilities of the institution under resolution or a bridge institution to an asset management vehicle, a so-called 'bad bank' (Article 42(1) BRRD/Article 26 SRMR). As with the bridge institution tool, this is a legal entity wholly or partially owned by one or more public authorities, which may include the resolution authority, and is controlled by the resolution authority (Article 42(2)(a) BRRD). The tool may only be used if the liquidation of the transferred assets under normal insolvency proceedings would have an adverse effect on the

---

[144] See the EBA final Q&A, published 21 January 2022 on Art 36(13) BRRD, available at <https://www.eba.europa.eu/single-rule-book-qa/-/qna/view/publicId/2015_2360>.
[145] See the EBA final Q&A, published 21 January 2022 on Art 41(2) BRRD, available at <https://www.eba.europa.eu/single-rule-book-qa/-/qna/view/publicId/2015_2312>.
[146] As to the meaning of 'control', it should be understood as comprising at least the powers listed under Article 41(1)(a), (b), (c), (d), and (g) BRRD.
[147] See the EBA final Q&A, published 21 January 2022, available at <https://www.eba.europa.eu/single-rule-book-qa/-/qna/view/publicId/2015_2341>.

financial markets, the transfer of the assets, rights, or liabilities to the vehicle is necessary to ensure the proper functioning of the credit institutions under resolution or the bridge institution, or the transfer is necessary to maximize liquidation proceeds (Article 42(5) BRRD). Thus, an asset separation tool can serve to separate underperforming or toxic assets from the failing institution in order to cleanse that institution's balance sheet.[148] The asset management vehicle shall manage the assets transferred to the vehicle with the objective of maximizing their value through eventual sale or orderly wind-down (Article 42(3) BRRD). To prevent moral hazard (as the institution has been offloaded of its riskiest assets), the asset separation tool may only be applied together with another resolution tool (Article 37(5) BRRD).

Recital (67) BRRD states: **7.209**

> An effective resolution regime should minimise the costs of the resolution of a failing institution borne by the taxpayers. It should also ensure that systemic institutions can be resolved without jeopardising financial stability. The bail-in tool achieves that objective by ensuring that shareholders and creditors of the failing institution suffer appropriate losses and bear an appropriate part of those costs arising from the failure of the institution. The bail-in tool will therefore give shareholders and creditors of institutions a stronger incentive to monitor the health of an institution during normal circumstances [...]

Article 2(1)(57) BRRD/Article 3(1)(33) SRMR defines the 'bail-in tool' as '[...] the mechanism for effecting by a resolution authority of the write-down and conversion powers in relation to liabilities of an institution under resolution [...]' However, it only applies to the liabilities of an institution that are not so excluded in Articles 44(2) and (3) and 2(1) (71) BRRD, and therefore classify as 'eligible liabilities' (Article 27(3) SRMR). Article 45-45m BRRD and 12–12k SRMR define the amount of 'own funds' and eligible liabilities (also known as 'MREL' or minimum requirement of eligible liabilities) institutions must meet. The relevant resolution authorities determine on an individual basis the required minimum funds and eligible liabilities, expressed as a percentage of the total liabilities and own funds of the institution. Since the amendments of 2019, BRRD and SRMR now provide for highly technical rules specifying MREL, in order to preclude entities and investors from structuring the relevant entity's or group's capital in such a way that it would primarily consist of excluded liabilities so that WDCI and bail-in could not be effectively used.[149] **7.210**

The resolution authorities may use the bail-in tool only for two purposes: (i) to recapitalize an institution as a whole in order to restore its ability to comply with the conditions for authorization and to carry on its activities, and to sustain sufficient market confidence in the institution; or (ii) to guarantee financing a bridge institution, a sale of a business or an asset separation tool by converting to equity or reducing the principal amount of claims or debt instruments that are transferred (Article 43(2) BRRD/Article 27(1) SRMR).[150] In the first scenario the bail-in tool may only be applied if there is a reasonable prospect that the **7.211**

---

[148] M Schillig, 'Bank Resolution Regimes in Europe II–Resolution Tools and Powers' (2012) (available at: <http://papers.ssrn.com/sol3/papers.cfm?abstract_id=2136084>) 28.
[149] For a detailed analysis, see, eg, M Haentjens in: J Binder et al (eds), *Brussels Commentary on European Banking Union* (Beck Nomos Hart 2022).
[150] FJ Garcimartín, 'Resolution tools and derivatives' in M Haentjens and B Wessels (eds), *Bank Recovery and Resolution: A Conference Book* (2014) 182–83.

7.212 Article 44(2) BRRD/Article 27(3) SRMR excludes the following liabilities:

  (i) deposits covered by the national deposit guarantee schemes up to the coverage level;[151]
  (ii) liabilities which are secured by a charge, pledge, lien, or title transfer collateral, including covered bonds, up to the amount of the value of the collateral;[152]
  (iii) liabilities arising from the holding of client assets or client money or from the institution acting as a fiduciary in a fiduciary relationship, provided that the client or beneficiary is protected under applicable insolvency law or civil law;[153]
  (iv) liabilities to institutions (except entities in the same group) with an original maturity of less than seven days;
  (v) liabilities with a remaining maturity of less than seven days, owed to (operators of) systems designated according to the Settlement Finality Directive 1998 or to participants and arising from the participation in such a system;[154] and
  (vi) certain liabilities owed to an employee (for instance in relation to accrued salary), to a commercial or trade creditor (only if they arise from the provisions of goods and services that are critical to the daily functioning of the institution under resolution), to tax and social security authorities (if those liabilities are preferred under the applicable law) and to deposit guarantee schemes.

7.213 The above list however is subject to some flexibility, since the resolution authority in exceptional circumstances and under specific conditions may also exclude or partially exclude certain other liabilities from bail-in. The list of exclusions may for example be extended if it is not possible to bail in that liability within a reasonable time or if the exclusion is strictly necessary and is proportionate to achieve the continuity of critical functions and core business lines (Article 44(3) BRRD/Article 27(5) SRMR). Thus, the flexibility is provided to ensure the effective rescue and continuance of key functions of the institution under resolution and to avoid disturbances to financial markets.

7.214 As a matter of principle, derivatives are included within the eligible obligations. Yet the write-down and conversion powers with regard to liabilities that arise from derivatives are only to be exercised after a closing out of the derivatives. For that purpose, the resolution authorities are empowered to terminate and close out any derivative contract. With regard to derivatives transactions that are subject to the same master agreement, the value shall be calculated on a net basis (Article 49 BRRD).

7.215 Articles 48 and 60 BRRD determine the following sequence for exercising the write-down of and conversion powers, either in resolution (the bail-in tool) or at the point of non-viability (the WDCI powers, see also above, paragraph 7.194), respectively:

---

[151] Art 2(1)(94) BRRD. The current uniform coverage level is EUR 100,000.
[152] Art 2(1)(96) BRRD and Art 52(4) Directive 2009/65/EC.
[153] See Art 1(2) Directive 2009/65/EC ('UCITS IV') and Art 4(1) Directive 2011/61/EU ('AIFMD') for such protection.
[154] For a discussion of the Settlement Finality Directive see above, paras 7.24–7.27.

(1) Common Equity Tier 1 (eg the share capital) must be reduced first;
(2) then Additional Tier 1 instruments;
(3) then Tier 2 instruments (eg subordinated medium term bonds);
(4) then other subordinated debt, consistent with the normal insolvency sequence; and
(5) finally other eligible liabilities, consistent with the normal insolvency sequence (as harmonized by Article 108 BRRD).

When applying the write-down or conversion powers, the resolution authorities have to allocate the losses equally between the shares or other instruments of ownership and eligible liabilities of the same rank. Thus, provided that they have not been put on the list of exclusions, the principal amount of or outstanding amount payable in respect of those instruments or liabilities is reduced to the same extent pro rata to their value (Article 48(2) BRRD). **7.216**

Article 47 BRRD requires specific actions in respect of the institution's shareholders and holders of other instruments of ownership when the bail-in tool is applied.[155] The resolution authorities are required to either cancel the existing shares or other instruments of ownership or transfer them to the bailed-in creditors, or dilute those instruments of ownership as a result of the conversion of the capital instruments or eligible liabilities into instruments of ownership (ie WDCI). **7.217**

When the bail-in tool is applied, the management body or an administrator must draw up a business reorganization plan that sets out measures aimed at restoring the long-term viability of the institution or parts of its business within a reasonable timescale, such as the withdrawal from loss-making activities, changes to the operational systems and infrastructure within the institution, or the sale of assets or business lines (Article 52 BRRD/Article 27(16) SRMR). **7.218**

To enhance the effectiveness of the bail-in powers and to facilitate cross-border recognition, Article 55 BRRD requires a contractual recognition of bail-in. Institutions are required to include a contractual provision as regards eligible liabilities governed by the law of a third country, by which the creditors recognize that liability may be subject to the write-down and conversion powers, and agree to be bound by any reduction of the principal or outstanding amount due, any conversion or any cancellation as a consequence of the exercise of the powers. Institutions are required to comply with the obligation under Article 55(1) BRRD for every liability falling within its scope.[156] **7.219**

It is up to resolution authorities to assess compliance with Article 55 BRRD. More specifically, the resolution authorities will assess whether it is legally or otherwise impracticable to include in the contractual provisions governing a relevant liability the term required in accordance with Article 55(1) BRRD. Additionally, under Article 55(3) BRRD, resolution authorities are entitled to require from institutions a legal opinion on the legal enforceability **7.220**

---

[155] The EBA has classified Art 47 BRRD as *lex specialis* in relation to Art 60 BRRD and Art 21 SRMR. The reason EBA mentions is that Art 47 BRRD relates to treatment of shareholders in both bail-in and point of non-viability scenarios. See the EBA final Q&A, published 21 January 2022, available at <https://www.eba.europa.eu/single-rule-book-qa/-/qna/view/publicId/2015_3210>.

[156] This is without prejudice to the exemptions under the second and third subparagraphs of that provision and under Article 55(2) BRRD. See the EBA final Q&A, published 21 January 2022, available at <https://www.eba.europa.eu/single-rule-book-qa/-/qna/view/publicId/2015_2414>.

and effectiveness of the contractual term inserted in the contracts governed by third-country law.

7.221 Articles 56–58 BRRD preserve government 'financial stabilisation tools' by means of extraordinary public financial support through either public equity support or temporary public ownership. The government financial stabilization tools may only be used as a last resort (Article 56(3) BRRD). Public equity support means the provision of capital by the government to a failing institution in exchange for defined capital instruments (Article 57 BRRD). Temporary public ownership means, in short, nationalization (Article 58 BRRD).

7.222 Chapter V of Title IV BRRD confers to resolution authorities the powers to employ the WDCI instrument, ie to write down or convert (into Common Equity Tier 1 instruments) 'relevant capital instruments', that is Additional Tier 1 instruments and Tier 2 instruments. As already explained above, paragraph 7.194, this power has to be exercised, *inter alia*, at the point the conditions for resolution are met but before any resolution action is taken, if the institution ceases to be viable (as defined in Article 59(4) BRRD) unless the power would be exercised, or in case extraordinary public support would be required by the institution (Article 59(a), (b), and (e) BRRD, respectively/Article 21(1) SRMR). As a result, the relevant capital instruments fully absorb the losses of the issuing institution prior to or without subsequent application of any resolution tools and exercise of resolution powers (Recital (81) BRRD). In particular cases the issuing institution may be a viable subsidiary of a failing group. In those cases, the power of write-down or conversion of capital instruments can also be exercised. Also in that scenario, in relation to the instruments issued by that viable subsidiary belonging to the failing group, the conditions laid down in Article 59(3)(c) BRRD have to be met.[157]

7.223 In Chapter V of Title IV BRRD, resolution authorities are conferred the powers needed to apply the resolution tools discussed above. Article 63(1) lists the resolution powers, while Article 64(1) enumerates the so-called 'ancillary powers' which are granted to resolution authorities to exercise the resolution powers.

7.224 Article 66–67 BRRD requires Member States to ensure that the exercise of the transfer powers or write-down or conversion powers of the resolution authorities of another Member State has effect under their own laws, and that in case resolution actions are taken with regard to assets, shares, rights, and liabilities under the law of a third country, necessary steps are taken that the actions become effective under the law of that third country.

7.225 The European legislator has deemed the interests of market stability and effective resolution of a failing institution to be of greater value than the interests of counterparties to limit their risk by having their contracts (automatically) terminated. Hence, early termination rights can be subject either to (permanent) disapplication under Article 68 BRRD, or to a temporary stay under Article 71 BRRD (the latter to be ordered by the resolution authorities). Resolution authorities would be authorized to invoke a temporary stay on termination rights under Article 71, if, Article 68 notwithstanding, counterparties would continue to

---

[157] See the EBA final Q&A, published 21 January 2022, available at <https://www.eba.europa.eu/single-rule-book-qa/-/qna/view/publicId/2015 2957>.

remain entitled to employ early termination rights, for instance because these termination rights are not triggered by resolution measures per se.

7.226 More specifically, Article 68(3) BRRD provides, most notably, that contractual terms that allow for the termination, suspension, modification, netting, or set-off rights upon the occurrence of a 'crisis prevention measure',[158] 'crisis management measure',[159] or 'any event directly linked to the application of such a measure' (together: 'BRRD measures') cannot be exercised. Hence, this provision intends to permanently prevent that the very measures directed at a recovery or orderly resolution of a failing institution result in the collective termination of its contractual relationships, which obviously would have the opposite result. However, should the failing institution cease to perform its substantive contractual obligations, all rights of termination, set-off etc remain applicable as usual (Article 68(3)(caput) and (4) BRRD).

7.227 In addition, Article 68(1) precludes that a crisis prevention measure, crisis management measure, or any event directly linked to the application of such a measure, qualifies as an 'enforcement event' or as 'insolvency proceedings' in the context of the Financial Collateral Directive and the Settlement Finality Directive, respectively. Pursuant to the Collateral Directive, an 'enforcement event' means an event of default as agreed between parties. One of the consequences of the occurrence of such an event of default, is that close-out netting provisions become operable. In short, the occurrence of an enforcement event will prompt the operation of netting or set-off proceedings.[160] Consequently, the preclusion of a qualification of BRRD measures as an enforcement event under the Financial Collateral Directive prevents that termination rights are triggered.

7.228 Under the Settlement Finality Directive, 'insolvency proceedings' are defined as any legal collective measure intended to wind up or reorganise the institution.[161] By disapplying all provisions of the Settlement Finality Directive relating to insolvency proceedings as defined in that Directive, the BRRD indicates that, in short, contractual relationships with clearing and settlement systems may continue to function as usual, while stressing that BRRD measures are not to be regarded as proceedings involving 'the suspending of, or imposing limitations on, transfers or payments'.[162]

7.229 For the same reasons that early termination rights can be (permanently) disapplied, viz market stability and the orderly and effective resolution of a failing institution, the European legislator has empowered resolution authorities to impose a temporary stay on certain contractual certain rights and obligations. This temporary stay must be seen as complementary to the (pre-resolution) moratorium that may be imposed under Article 33a (see also above, paragraph 7.190). The (in-resolution) temporary stay powers consist of three separate but

---

[158] Pursuant to Art 1(1)(101) BRRD, ' "crisis prevention measure" means the exercise of powers to direct removal of deficiencies or impediments to recoverability under Article 6(6), the exercise of powers to address or remove impediments to resolvability under Article 17 or 18, the application of an early intervention measure under Article 27, the appointment of a temporary administrator under Article 29 or the exercise of the write down or conversion powers under Article 59.'
[159] Pursuant to Art 1(1)(102), ' "crisis management measure" means a resolution action or the appointment of a special manager under Article 35 or a person under Article 51(2) or under Article 72(1).'
[160] Arts 2(l) and 2(n), and 4(1) Collateral Directive.
[161] Art 2(j) Settlement Finality Directive.
[162] ibid.

related powers, each representing a power that the resolution authorities may employ at their discretion. First, Article 69 BRRD stipulates that authorities have the power to suspend certain obligations. Second, Article 70 BRRD defines the power to restrict the enforcement of security interests. Third, Article 71 BRRD codifies the power to temporarily suspend termination rights.

7.230 All three temporary stay powers have been restricted in several ways. First, they all are limited in temporal scope. The temporary stay starts as soon as the resolution authority has published a notice of the specific power employed.[163] The temporary stay lasts until midnight of the next business day. Midnight here, more specifically, means the midnight in the Member State of the resolution authority of the institution under resolution. A second means by which the resolution authorities' discretion to use the temporary stay powers is reined in (albeit not very strictly), is through the requirement of proportionality. For that reason, resolution authorities must have regard to the impact the exercise of this power has on 'the orderly functioning of financial markets'.[164] Third, to the exercise of all temporary stay powers, exceptions are made for important categories of contracts. In general, exceptions are always made for rights and obligations arising in the context of, in short, the failing institution's participation in market infrastructure systems. More specifically, market infrastructure systems are, in this context: systems of trading, clearing and settlement systems, central counterparties, and central banks. Consequently, where the Settlement Finality Directive derogates from normal insolvency laws with an aim to reduce the risk related to participating in payment and securities settlement systems,[165] these derogations are respected by the BRRD.[166]

7.231 In contrast to the continuation of market infrastructures' exceptional position, the derogations for collateralized finance transactions such as repurchase agreements and securities lending agreements, and derivatives have not been maintained. Thus, the temporary stay powers do not grant special status to these types of transactions, whilst the Collateral Directive had created specific rules for this category of transactions that oftentimes derogated from the normal insolvency laws in Member States.[167] The BRRD therefore rescinds these derogatory provisions insofar as they concern, in short, resolution measures (Article 118 BRRD).

7.232 Pursuant to Article 69(1) BRRD, authorities must have the power to suspend 'any payment or delivery obligations pursuant to any contract to which an institution under resolution is a party'. Article 69(2) BRRD explains that this means that if during the suspension period any of the failing institution's contractual payment or delivery obligations elapse, these payments or deliveries shall not be due until immediately upon expiry of the suspension period. Under Article 69(3) BRRD, the suspension power not only alters commitments on the part of the financial institution in resolution, but also works reciprocally. Counterparties

---

[163] Arts 69(1), 71(1), and 70(1) BRRD for the power to suspend certain obligations, termination rights, and enforcement of security interests, respectively.
[164] ibid Arts 69(5), 71(6), and 70(4) BRRD.
[165] Recital (2) Settlement Finality Directive.
[166] See above at paras 7.34 and 7.35.
[167] See above at para 7.40.

that have payment or delivery obligations towards the institution will see their obligations suspended for the same period of time.

A second power conferred upon the authorities charged with the orderly resolution of a failing institution is laid down in Article 70 BRRD, and this provision involves the power to temporarily restrict the enforcement of security interests. The authorities may invoke this power to prevent secured creditors of the institution under resolution from enforcing security interests in relation to any assets of that institution (Article 70(1) BRRD). **7.233**

Under the BRRD, resolution authorities have been conferred the powers to transfer assets and liabilities of a failing institution to a private purchaser or to a bridge institution. When that happens, the authorities need to be able to assess which contracts need to be transferred and determine the true value of the institution's assets and values.[168] Whilst Article 68 generally excludes (automatic) early termination rights in so far as they are triggered by resolution measures, early termination rights could also be triggered by other causes. In those situations, the value and scope of the balance sheet of the institution could change significantly and thus form an obstacle to the authorities' resolution strategy.[169] Consequently, Article 71 BRRD introduced the power of the resolution authorities to temporarily suspend a counterparty's right to terminate his contract(s) with an institution under resolution. Since Directive EU 2019/879 amended the BRRD, Article 71(a) now provides that counterparties must recognize that resolution authorities might terminate contracts or limit the scope of these contracts as just discussed. More specifically, Article 71(a) BRRD requires institutions to include in their financial contracts which they enter into and which are governed by third-country law, terms by which the parties recognize that the financial contract may be subject to the exercise of powers by the resolution authority to suspend or restrict rights and obligations under Articles 33a, 69, 70, and 71 and recognize that they are bound by the requirements of Article 68. **7.234**

When applying the resolution tools and exercising the resolution powers, the resolution authorities are not subject to requirements to notify any person or to obtain approval or consent of any person, including the shareholders and the creditors of the institution (Article 63(2) BRRD). However, the BRRD provides several safeguards to protect the interests of the persons affected, such as shareholders, creditors, and counterparties (Article 63(4) BRRD). **7.235**

As already mentioned above, paragraph 7.191, shareholders and creditors are protected by the NCWO or 'no creditor worse off'-principle (cf Article 34(1)(g) BBRD/Article 15(1)(g) SRMR). In practical terms, this means that where resolution authorities transfer only parts of the rights, assets, and liabilities of the institution under resolution, the shareholders and those creditors whose claims have not been transferred, receive in satisfaction of their claims at least as much as what they would have received if the institution under resolution had been wound up under normal insolvency proceedings. Also, where resolution authorities apply the bail-in tool, the shareholders and creditors whose claims have been written down or converted to equity may not incur greater losses than they would have incurred if **7.236**

---

[168] Recital (94) BRRD.
[169] See also FSB, Key Attributes 2014, I-Annex 5, para 1.1. and SN Grünewald, *Resolution Cross-Border Banking Crisis in the European Union* (2014) 96.

the institution under resolution had been wound up under normal insolvency proceedings (Article 73 BRRD).

7.237 To assess whether shareholders and creditors would have received better treatment if the institution under resolution had entered into normal insolvency proceedings, a valuation must be carried out by an independent person (Article 74(1) BRRD). Should the valuation find that shareholders and creditors would have received better treatment if the institution under resolution had entered into normal insolvency proceedings, they are entitled to the payment of the difference from the resolution financing arrangements (Article 75 BRRD).

7.238 Furthermore, in case of a partial transfer of assets, rights, and liabilities from the institution under resolution, the bridge institution or the asset management vehicle to another entity, Articles 76–80 BRRD seek to prevent the separation of transactions that are economically and functionally linked. These transactions include security arrangements, title transfer financial collateral arrangements, set-off and netting arrangements, covered bonds, and structured finance arrangements (including securitizations) (Article 76(1) BRRD).

7.239 Article 76 BRRD states as a general rule that the secured transactions discussed above should be awarded 'appropriate protection'. What such protection means is further clarified in the following Articles 77–80 BRRD, but these provisions all have in common that they prohibit partial transfers or the exercise of the contract modification power (see above, paragraph 7.237). Partial transfers may occur if the relevant resolution authorities would choose to transfer only some of the assets, rights, or liabilities of the institution they are resolving to another entity ('cherry-picking'). Also, they could choose to transfer just part of the assets, rights, or liabilities from a bridge institution or asset management vehicle to another person. Protection is also awarded against the exercise of the contract modification power, that is the power to 'cancel or modify the terms of a contract to which the institution under resolution is a party or substitute recipient as a party' (Articles 76(1)(a), (b) and 64(1)(f) BRRD). The safeguards of Articles 76–80 apply irrespective of the number of parties involved, how the secured transactions are created, and by which laws these transactions are governed (Article 76(3) BRRD).

7.240 Articles 77, 78, and 79 of the Directive provide specific rules for each of the three categories of secured transactions discussed above, viz title transfer financial collateral arrangements, set-off arrangements, and netting arrangements (Article 77), security arrangements (Article 78), and covered bonds and structured finance arrangements (Article 79). As stated above, all three provisions prohibit partial transfers or the exercise of the contract modification power, but all three contain an exception for covered deposits, ie for deposits guaranteed under a Deposit Guarantee Scheme. Thus, should an integral transfer of the secured transaction concerned result in there not being sufficient covered deposits left available, either with the transferor/bank under resolution or with the transferee, the resolution authorities are allowed to effectuate a partial transfer. As a result, the authorities may either transfer covered deposits without transferring 'other assets, rights or liabilities that are part of the same arrangement' or transfer 'those assets, rights or liabilities without transferring the covered deposits' (Articles 77(2), 78(2), and 79(2) BRRD). Also, under all three provisions, Member States are to ensure 'appropriate protection' whilst the Directive does not specify what this requirement exactly entails. In the absence of a specific description, an amount of flexibility is given to the Member States in order to properly adapt protective measures to the existing national regulation and legislation.[170]

Finally, trading, clearing, and settlement systems are also protected from partial transfers. More specifically, when applying a resolution tool the use of which requires a partial transfer, Member States are required to ensure that these market infrastructure systems can continue to operate unaffected as provided for in the Settlement Finality Directive (Article 80(2) BRRD). 7.241

Chapter VIII of Title IV BRRD prescribes several procedural obligations for both (the management body of) failing institutions, supervisory authorities, and resolution authorities. More specifically, it contains notification requirements (Articles 81 and 83 BRRD), requirements regarding the decision of the resolution authority whether the conditions for resolution have been met (Article 82 BRRD), and confidentiality requirements (Article 84 BRRD). Furthermore, a decision from the resolution authority must contain the reasons for that decision and include the determination that the institution meets or does not meet the conditions for resolution (Article 82(2)(a) BRRD). The EBA has clarified that, 'it is for the applicable national law to govern whether the determination under letters (a) Article 82(2) BRRD should be enshrined within the same formal decision or in two separate ones.'[171] 7.242

Title IV Chapter IX BRRD contains only two but important provisions. Article 85(1) BBRD recognizes the right for *ex-ante* judicial review at the national level and states that Member States may require that a decision to take a crisis prevention measure or a crisis management measure is subject to (*ex-ante*) judicial approval, provided that in respect of a decision to take a crisis management measure, according to national law, the procedure relating to the application for approval and the court's consideration are expeditious. BBRD Recital (92) substantiates that the court should give its decision within 24 hours and the relevant authority should take its decision immediately after the court has given its approval, without prejudice to the rights that interested parties might have in requesting the court to set aside the decision for a limited period after the resolution authority has taken the crisis management measure. 7.243

Under Article 85(2) and (3) BRRD, Member States' national law shall provide for a right of (*ex-post*) appeal against a decision to take a crisis prevention or a crisis management measure, respectively. The review shall be expeditious and national courts shall use, as a basis for their own assessment, the complex economic assessments of the facts undertaken by the resolution authority. 7.244

However, Article 85(4) BRRD provides that this right of appeal shall be subject to two limitations, given that it intends to address situations of extreme urgency, and the suspension of any decision of the resolution authorities might impede the continuity of critical functions.[172] First, the lodging of an appeal shall not automatically suspend the effects of the 7.245

---

[170] ISDA, Possible EU Framework for Bank Recovery and Resolution, Comment Letter to EC Directorate-General Internal Market and Services, 3 March 2011, 14. Under Dutch and English law, partial transfers are not void by law. Under the same jurisdictions, a partial transfer that has been effectuated contrary to the prohibition just discussed, would not result in setting aside any netting rights.

[171] EBA, Final Q&A, published 21 January 2022, available at <https://www.eba.europa.eu/single-rule-book-qa/-/qna/view/publicId/2015_2175>.

[172] Recital (90) BRRD.

challenged decision (Article 85(4)(a) BRRD). Second, the resolution authority's decision shall become immediately enforceable with a rebuttable presumption that a suspension of its enforcement would be against the public interest (Article 85(4)(b) BRRD).

7.246 In order to protect the interests of third parties acting in good faith who have acquired shares, other instruments of ownership, assets, rights, or liabilities of an institution under resolution, the annulment of a resolution authority's decision would not affect any subsequent administrative acts or transactions concluded by that resolution authority on the basis of the annulled decision. Compensation for the loss suffered by the applicant caused by the decision or act is the only type of remedy available for a wrongful decision or action by the resolution authorities (Article 85(4) BRRD).

7.247 Article 86 BRRD prescribes that, in short, normal insolvency proceedings may not be commenced except at the initiative of the resolution authority and that a decision placing an institution into normal insolvency proceedings shall be taken only with the consent of the resolution authority.

7.248 Article 85 SRMR provides for the establishment of an Appeal Panel with which any natural or legal person, including resolution authorities, may appeal the decisions of the Single Resolution Board as listed in Article 85(3) SRMR. Also these appeals have no suspensive effect (Article 85(6) SRMR). Against the decisions taken by the Appeal Panel or, where there is no right of appeal to the Appeal Panel, by the Board, proceedings may be brought before the CJEU (Article 86 SRMR).

Title V: cross-border group resolution

7.249 Title V BRRD concerns cross-border group resolution. For purposes of this Title V, a 'group' means a parent undertaking and its subsidiaries (Article 2(26) BRRD). A parent undertaking is further defined as a 'Union parent undertaking' meaning a Union parent institution, a Union parent financial holding company, or a Union parent mixed financial holding company, and a 'third-country parent undertaking' meaning a parent undertaking, a parent financial holding company, or a parent mixed financial holding company, established in a third country (ie outside the EU) (Articles 2(85) and 2(87) BRRD respectively). A 'subsidiary' is defined as 'Union subsidiary', which means an institution which is established in a Member State and which is a subsidiary of a third-country institution or a third-country parent undertaking (Article 2(84) BRRD). Similarly, a 'branch' means a 'Union branch', being a branch located in a Member State of a third-country institution (Article 2(89) BRRD). In addition, the BRRD uses the term 'group entity' meaning a legal person that is part of a group (Article 2(31) BRRD), while a 'group' is further specified a 'cross-border group'. This means a group 'having group entities established in more than one Member State' (Article 2(27) BRRD). 'Group resolution' means either of the following: (a) the taking of resolution action at the level of a parent undertaking or of an institution subject to consolidated supervision, or (b) the co-ordination of the application of resolution tools and the exercise of resolution powers by resolution authorities in relation to group entities that meet the conditions for resolution.[173]

---

[173] See Art 2(42) BRRD.

The central provision of Title V BRRD seems to be Article 88 BRRD, which provides that **7.250** group-level resolution authorities shall establish resolution colleges to carry out, in short, BRRD tasks and, where appropriate, to ensure co-operation and co-ordination with third-country resolution authorities. Resolution colleges shall in particular provide a framework for the group-level resolution authority, the other resolution authorities and, where appropriate, competent authorities and consolidating supervisors concerned.

Article 88(2) BRRD prescribes that resolution colleges should be populated by: the group-level resolution authority; the resolution authorities of each Member State in which a subsidiary covered by consolidated supervision is established; the resolution authorities of Member States where a parent undertaking of one or more institutions of the group is established; the resolution authorities of Member States in which significant branches are located; the consolidating supervisor and the competent authorities of the Member States where the resolution authority is a member of the resolution college; the competent ministries, where the resolution authorities which are members of the resolution college are not the competent ministries; the authority that is responsible for the deposit guarantee scheme of a Member State, where the resolution authority of that Member State is a member of a resolution college; and EBA (but which has no voting rights; Article 88(4) BRRD). **7.251**

The provisions concerning 'third-countries' have become of particular relevance since the United Kingdom has left the EU and therefore qualifies as such. Under Article 88(3) BRRD, resolution authorities of third countries where a parent undertaking or an institution established in the Union has a subsidiary institution or a branch that would be considered to be significant were it located in the Union may, at their request, be invited to participate in the resolution college as observers. The group-level resolution authority shall be the chair of the resolution college (Article 88(5) BRRD). **7.252**

Article 89(1) BRRD provides that where a third country institution or third country parent undertaking has Union subsidiaries established in two or more Member States, or two or more Union branches that are regarded as significant by two or more Member States, the resolution authorities of Member States where those Union subsidiaries are established or where those significant branches are located shall establish a 'European resolution college'. In such a case the European resolution college shall perform the functions and carry out the tasks specified in Article 88 with respect to the subsidiary institutions and, in so far as those tasks are relevant, to branches (Article 89(2) BRRD). However, the requirement to establish a European resolution college may be waived (Article 89(4) BRRD). **7.253**

Article 90(1) BRRD provides that subject to Article 84 ('Confidentiality') BRRD resolution authorities and competent authorities shall provide one another on request with all the information relevant for the exercise of the other authorities' tasks under the BRRD. It is for the group-level resolution authority to co-ordinate the flow of all relevant information between resolution authorities (Article 90(2) BRRD). **7.254**

When the group-level resolution authority receives a notification that an institution or any entity that is a subsidiary in a group, meets the conditions referred to in Article 32 ('Conditions for resolution') or Article 33 ('Conditions for resolution with regard to **7.255** financial institutions and holding companies') (see above, at paragraphs 7.184–7.186),[174] it will consult the other members of the relevant resolution college and must determine whether the resolution actions or other measures notified would make it likely that the conditions laid down in Article 32 or 33 BRRD would be satisfied in relation to a group entity in another Member State. If not, the resolution authority responsible for that institution or that entity may take the resolution actions or other measures notified. If so, the group-level resolution authority must, no later than 24 hours after receiving the notification propose a group resolution scheme and submit it to the resolution college (Article 91(2)–(5) BRRD).

7.256 Article 92 BRRD concerns group resolution and generally follows the structure Article 91 BRRD provides in relation to a subsidiary in a group. Where a group-level resolution authority decides that a Union parent undertaking for which it is responsible meets the conditions referred to in Article 32 or 33 BRRD, it must notify the consolidating supervisor, if different, and to the other members of the resolution college of the group in question. The group-level resolution authority may then decide to propose a group resolution scheme, on which a joint decision must be agreed between the group-level resolution authority and resolution authorities responsible for the relevant subsidiaries (Article 92(3) BRRD)—who may disagree, depart from the scheme, or take independent resolution actions or measures (Article 92(4) BRRD). Where the actions proposed by the group-level resolution authority under Article 92(1) BRRD do not include a group resolution scheme, the group-level resolution authority shall take its decision after consulting the members of the resolution college (Article 92(2) BRRD).

7.257 As stated above,[175] SRMR radically deviates from the above approach which reflects the traditional European view that generally does not treat groups of companies as a single entity, for under this Regulation, the Single Resolution Board is empowered to take decisions in relation to the groups covered by the Regulation as a whole. More specifically, and as a derogation of Title V of BRRD, Article 7(2) SRMR requires that the Single Resolution Board be responsible for adopting all decisions relating to the resolution for those groups.

Title VI: relations with third countries

7.258 Title VI of BRRD ('Relations with third countries') contains six provisions. Article 93(1) BRRD introduces the possibility of international agreements on co-operation between the resolution authorities and the relevant third country authorities. In the absence of such agreements Member States may enter into bilateral agreements with a third country until the entry into force of an agreement as just referred to (Article 93(4) BRRD).

7.259 Article 94 BRRD/Article 33 SRMR sets out rules for recognition and enforcement of third-country resolution proceedings in respect of third-country resolution proceedings unless and until an international agreement with the relevant third country enters into force, or following the entry into force of such an international agreement to the extent that recognition and enforcement of third-country resolution proceedings is not governed by that

---

[174] See paras 7.184–7.186 above.
[175] At para 7.167.

agreement. In essence, when there is a European resolution college, it must take a joint decision to recognize third-country resolution proceedings (Article 94(2) BRRD). If no joint decision has been reached or in the absence of a European resolution college each resolution college concerned makes its own decision on whether to recognize and enforce such proceedings (Article 94(3) BRRD).

On the grounds listed in Article 95 BRRD/Article 33(3) SRMR, a recognition or enforcement of third-country resolution proceedings may be refused. **7.260**

Article 96 BRRD provides that (EU) resolution authorities may exercise resolution powers in relation to a Union branch that is not subject to any third-country resolution proceedings or against whom recognition is refused. **7.261**

Article 97 BRRD introduces 'non-binding framework cooperation agreements', to be concluded by EBA with relevant third country authorities unless and until an international agreement with the relevant third country enters into force, or following the entry into force of such an international agreement to the extent that, in short, the framework co-operation agreement is not governed by that international agreement. The non-binding framework co-operation agreements are not to make provisions in relation to specific institutions, nor do they impose legal obligations upon Member States (Article 97(2) BRRD). Instead, they are intended to establish processes and arrangements between the participating authorities for sharing information and co-operation (Article 97(3) BRRD). Competent authorities or resolution authorities (including the Single Resolution Board, see Article 32(4) SRMR), where appropriate, shall conclude non-binding co-operation arrangements in line with the EBA framework arrangement with the relevant third-country authorities (Article 97(4) BRRD). An example of such a co-operation agreement can be found in the Framework Co-operation Arrangement the EBA has entered into with relevant US Authorities.[176] **7.262**

Finally, Article 98 BRRD sets rules for exchanging information with relevant third-country authorities. As a matter of principle, the provision prescribes that (EU) resolution authorities, competent authorities, and competent ministries may not exchange confidential information with third country authorities, unless certain listed conditions are met. **7.263**

Title VII: financing arrangements

Title VII of BRRD ('Financing Arrangements') concerns the financing of resolutions, for there are circumstances when the effectiveness of the resolution tools applied may depend on the availability of short-term funding for an institution or a bridge institution, the provision of guarantees to potential purchasers, or the provision of capital to the bridge institution (Recital (103) BRRD). Also, government financial stabilization tools, such as temporary public ownership may require short-term funding (Recital (8) BRRD). Title **7.264**

---

[176] See recital (5) of the Framework Co-operation Arrangement between the EBA and the Board of Governors of the Federal Reserve System, the Federal Deposit Insurance Corporation, the Office of the Comptroller of the Currency, the US Securities and Exchange Commission, and the New York State Department of Financial Services, available at <https://www.eba.europa.eu/sites/default/documents/files/documents/10180/1762986/e511be70-e5ca-485d-a37e-3809ac1ee532/Framework%20Agreement%20-%20EBA-US%20agencies%20-%20September%202017.pdf?retry=1>.

VII sets up a system for: (a) national financing arrangements; (b) the borrowing between national financing arrangements; and (c) the mutualization of national financing arrangements in the case of a group resolution (Article 99 BRRD).

7.265 Under Article 100 BRRD, all Member States must establish at least one financing arrangement for the purpose of ensuring the effective application by the resolution authority of the resolution tools and powers. Such an arrangement will be funded through: (a) *ex-ante* contributions with a view to reaching a target level of at least 1 per cent of the amount of covered deposits of all the institutions authorized in a certain territory; (b) *ex-post* extraordinary contributions as where the contributions specified in point (a) are insufficient; and (c) contract borrowings (Article 100(4) BRRD).

7.266 Article 101(1) BRRD lists exhaustively the purposes for which the financing arrangements may be used. Article 103 BRRD prescribes that Member States must raise contributions to the financing arrangement at least annually from the institutions authorized in their territory, and how those contributions should be calculated. This is a contribution system which is characterized as *ex-ante*.[177] Under Article 104 BRRD, extraordinary *ex-post* contributions may be raised from the institutions authorized in a certain territory, where the available financial means are not sufficient to cover the losses, costs, or other expenses incurred by the use of the financing arrangements.

7.267 Articles 105–107 BRRD elaborate on the borrowing between national financing arrangements (Article 106 BRRD) and the mutualization of national financing arrangements in the case of a group resolution (Article 107 BRRD). For purposes of such mutualization, the national financing arrangement of each institution that is part of a group contributes to the financing of the group resolution (Article 107(1) BRRD), and the group-level resolution authority, after consulting the resolution authorities of the institutions that are part of the group, shall propose a financing plan as part of the group resolution scheme provided for in Articles 91 and 92 (see above, paragraphs 7.244–7.245).[178] Under Article 109 BRRD, also the deposit guarantee scheme to which an institution is affiliated may be used for its resolution under certain circumstances.

7.268 As regards the SRM, the 'national financing arrangements' discussed above merge into a Single Resolution Fund, owned and managed by the Single Resolution Board (Articles 67–79 SRMR). The Single Resolution Fund thus is financed by contributions from the banking sector. Since 2022, the European Stability Mechanism can act as a 'backstop' should the Single Resolution Fund become depleted.[179]

7.269 Somewhat hidden but most importantly, Article 108 BRRD requires that Member States amend (if necessary) their national law governing normal insolvency proceedings so that: (i) that part of eligible deposits from natural persons and micro, small, and medium-sized enterprises which exceeds the coverage level provided for in Article 6 of Directive 2014/49/EU (now: EUR 100,000); and (ii) deposits that would be eligible deposits from

---

[177] See on the specifics of the ex-ante system the Delegated Regulation (EU) 2015/63—DR on ex ante contributions to resolution financing arrangements and also Autorité de contrôle prudentiel et de resolution on the subject matter at <https://www.eba.europa.eu/single-rule-book-qa/-/qna/view/publicId/2015_2507>.
[178] See paras 7.244–7.245 above.
[179] See, <www.esm.europa.eu>.

natural persons, micro, small, and medium-sized enterprises were they not made through branches located outside the Union of institutions established within the Union, rank higher than the ranking provided for the claims of ordinary unsecured, non-preferred creditors. Even higher ranking than the claims just referred to are covered deposits and deposit guarantee schemes subrogating to the rights and obligations of covered depositors in insolvency. On the other hand, lower than ordinary, unsecured claims (but still higher than contractually subordinated claims) rank those claims that result from debt instruments that meet the following conditions: (a) the original contractual maturity of the debt instruments is of at least one year; (b) the debt instruments contain no embedded derivatives and are not derivatives themselves; and (c) the relevant contractual documentation and, where applicable, the prospectus related to the issuance explicitly refer to this lower ranking under this paragraph. Thus, this Article 108 BRRD represents the EU harmonization of substantive national insolvency law, which is otherwise virtually absent in European law.

Title VIII: penalties

Articles 110–114 BRRD require that, in short, administrative penalties and other administrative measures be applied by resolution authorities or (where different) supervisory authorities where the national provisions transposing BRRD have not been complied with (Article 110(1) and (3) BRRD). Such administrative penalties must be published (Article 112 BRRD). **7.270**

Articles 38–41 SRMR contain substantive rules on the penalties the Single Resolution Board may impose, including their amounts, the aggravating or mitigating factors the Board must take into account, procedural safeguards, and disclosure and enforcement regulations. **7.271**

G. Central Counterparties Regulation

Since the adoption of Regulation (EU) 2021/23 of the European Parliament and of the Council of 16 December 2020 on a framework for the recovery and resolution of central counterparties (CCPRRR), Central counterparties (CCPs) are also covered by specific resolution legislation. As stated above, paragraph 7.08, CCPs are the legal persons that interpose themselves 'between the counterparties to the contracts traded on one or more financial markets, becoming the buyer to every seller and the seller to every buyer'.[180] The counterparties just referred to thus become counterparties to the CCP and are called 'clearing members'. Clients of clearing members may enter into derivatives through those clearing members. **7.272**

In paragraph 7.36, it was already noted that since the Global Financial Crisis of 2008, it was recognized that a CCP insolvency would have systemic consequences, but also that **7.273**

---

[180] Article 2(1) of Regulation (EU) No 648/2012 of the European Parliament and of the Council of 4 July 2012 on OTC derivatives, central counterparties, and trade repositories (EMIR).

CCPs should play a larger role in the clearing of, specifically, derivatives transactions.[181] Therefore, it was decided that significant categories of derivatives transactions should be required by law to be centrally cleared. In other words, for significant categories of derivatives transactions, a CCP must be interposed between the counterparties to those derivatives transactions, thus becoming the buyer to every seller and the seller to every buyer. In the EU, this central clearing requirement has been laid down in the EMIR, ie Regulation (EU) No 648/2012. As a consequence of EMIR and its mandatory central clearing requirements, CCPs have since assumed enormous amounts of risk, so that there was a clear policy reason for a specific CCP resolution regime. On 10 March 2022, the Financial Stability Board (FSB) asked attention to 'further strengthen the resilience and resolvability of CCPs in default and non-default loss scenarios'. More specifically the FSB addressed 'the need for, and develop as appropriate, international policy on the use, composition and amount of financial resources in recovery and resolution'.[182]

7.274 The CCPRRR has largely been based on the BRRD and SRMR and this Regulation is similarly structured. However, the CCPRRR takes into account the specificities of this category of financial institution. As the European legislator recognized that CCPs have different functions and business models, specific tools and powers are, according to the European legislator, needed for CCP failure scenarios that may be caused by the failure of the CCP's clearing members or as a result of non-default events.[183] In the remaining part of this chapter, some of the most noteworthy provisions of the CCPRRR will be discussed.

7.275 Similar to the BRRD, the CCPRRR includes a requirement for recovery plans and resolution plans (Articles 9–14 CCPRRR). Again, it is up to the resolution authorities together with the resolution colleges to assess the resolvability of the CCP in question. These entities must address and remove impediments to resolvability of the CCP (Article 15–17 CCPRRR). Additionally, early intervention measure under Title IV vary from, *inter alia*, the competent authority requiring the CCP to update recovery plans (Article 18 (1a/1b) CCPRRR) to the competent authority placing restrictions on remunerations of equity (Article 18m CCPRRR).

7.276 An example of an early intervention measure that is specific for CCPs is the provision of recompense to non-defaulting clearing members (Article 20 CCPRRR). This basically entails that the competent authority of the CCP may require the CCP to recompense the non-defaulting clearing members for their loss through cash payments or, where appropriate, may require the CCP to issue instruments recognizing a claim on the future profits of the CCP.

7.277 When considering the conditions for resolution, basically the same criteria (Article 22(1) CCPRRR) are used in the CCPRRR as in the BRRD (Article 32(1) BRRD).

---

[181] Recital (4) Regulation (EU) 2021/23 of the European Parliament and of the Council of 16 December 2020 on a framework for the recovery and resolution of central counterparties and amending Regulations (EU) No 1095/2010, (EU) No 648/2012, (EU) No 600/2014, (EU) No 806/2014, and (EU) 2015/2365 and Directives 2002/47/EC, 2004/25/EC, 2007/36/EC, 2014/59/EU, and (EU) 2017/1132 (CCPRRR), OJ L22/1.
[182] See FSB, 'Central Counterparty Financial Resources for Recovery and Resolution', published on 10 March 2022, p 1 available at <https://www.fsb.org/wp-content/uploads/P090322.pdf>.
[183] See Recital (10) of the CCP Regulation.

7.278 The CCPRRR provides four resolution tools (Article 27(1) CCPRRR). These tools are: a) the position and loss allocation tool; (b) the write-down and conversion tool; (c) the sale of business tool; and (d) the bridge CCP tool. The position and loss allocation tool is a tool that cannot, as such, be found in the BRRD. The position and loss allocation tool means that a resolution authority may terminate some or all of the following contracts of the CCP under resolution: (a) the contracts with the clearing member in default; (b) the contracts of the affected clearing service or asset class; and (c) the other contracts of the CCP under resolution (Article 29(1) CCPRRR). Resolution authorities may rely on this tool for various purposes. One of the purposes for using the position and loss allocation tool may be to restore the ability of the CCP to meet payment obligations as they fall due (Article 28 (3b)). Another purpose may be to support the transfer of the CCP's business by way of the sale of business tool to a solvent third party (Article 28(3d) CCPRRR). Significantly, the relevant resolution authority may reduce the amount of the CCP's payment obligations to non-defaulting clearing members where those obligations arise from gains due in accordance with the CCP's processes for paying variation margin or a payment that has the same economic effect (Article 30(1) CCPRRR).

7.279 The 'write down and conversion of instruments of ownership and debt instruments or other unsecured liabilities' tool (Articles 32–39 CCPRRR), in essence combines the 'write down and conversion of capital instruments' and the 'bail-in' tool as defined under the BRRD (see above, paragraphs 7.199 et seq). Also the sale of business and the bridge institution tools as defined in the BRRD can be found to a similar extent in CCPRRR (Articles 40–41 and Article 42 CCPRRR, respectively).

7.280 The resolution powers of the resolution authorities are laid down in Articles 48–59 CCPRRR, while the safeguards for different stakeholders, including shareholders, are listed in Articles 60–69 CCPRRR. In addition, CCPRRR contains several procedural obligations and legal protection mechanisms, including notification requirements (Article 70 CCPRRR) and *ex-ante* judicial approval (Article 74(1) CCPRRR).

7.281 The substantive part of the CCPRRR ends with Title VI containing provisions on the relation with third countries (Article 76–80 CCPRRR) and Title VII on administrative measures and penalties (Article 81–85 CCPRRR). Similar to BRRD, the Commission may enter into agreements with one or more third countries regarding the means of co-operation between the resolution authorities and the relevant third-country authorities in connection with recovery and resolution planning in relation to CCPs and third-country CCPs (Article 76(1) CCPRRR). Considering Brexit this may prove to be an important provision, because the most significant CCPs servicing the EU market are located in the UK.

8

COMMENTARY ON THE ORIGINAL INSOLVENCY PROCEEDINGS REGULATION AND THE RECAST INSOLVENCY PROCEEDINGS REGULATION

Commentary by Professor Christoph Paulus and Tom Smith KC

This commentary also incorporates additional commentary which was provided in the previous editions of this work by: Professor Michael Bogdan; Justice Timo Esko; Professor Ian Fletcher LLD QC (Hon); Professor Francisco Garcimartin; Stuart Isaacs KC; Professor Alberto Piergrossi; Professor Miguel Virgos; Professor Bob Wessels; and Alex Wood.

As with the previous edition of this text, this chapter first provides a commentary on the original Regulation ('OR')[1] on insolvency proceedings (1346/2000), which applies to proceedings opened before 26 June 2017, and then a commentary on the Recast Regulation ('RR'),[2] which applies to proceedings opened on or after 26 June 2017.[3] Despite the repeal of the OR, proceedings opened prior to 26 June 2017 will continue to be governed by the Original Regulation.[4]

The Recitals[5] to the OR and the RR are not reproduced here and can be found at Appendix 1 (OR) and Appendix 3 (RR).

The applicable principles of interpretation are dealt with in chapter 2 above. The principal tools of interpretation used here are the Recitals to the OR and RR, printed respectively in Appendices 1 and 3, and the Virgos-Schmit Report, referred to below and printed in Appendix 2. With regard to using the Recitals to OR and RR, care must be taken, since they are often copied or adapted from the Virgos-Schmit Report[6] and in such a case need to be considered in the context from which they are taken.[7]

The Virgos-Schmit Report was elaborated in relation to the OR in Virgos and Garcimartin, *The European Insolvency Regulation: Law and Practice* (Kluwer, 2004) ('VG').

---

[1] Council Regulation 1346/2000 of 29 May 2000, OJ L160 (30 June 200) p 1.
[2] Regulation (EU) 2015/848 of the European Parliament and of the Council of 20 May 2015 on insolvency proceedings, OJ L141, (5 June 2015) p 19.
[3] Article 84 RR.
[4] Article 84(2) RR. On a literal reading of Art 84 RR, there is a lacuna affecting insolvency proceedings opened on 26 June 2017 itself. To make sense of the provisions, Art 84(1) RR needs to be interpreted so as to make the RR applicable to proceedings opened *on or after* 26 June 2017: see the commentary on Art 84 RR below.
[5] 'Recitals' is the English legal expression for the numbered paragraphs which are preceded by 'Whereas'. The section with the Recitals can also be called the 'Preamble', *Josef Syska acting as the Administrator of Elektrim SA (In bankruptcy) v Vivendi Universal SA* (hereinafter referred to as *Elektrim v Vivendi*) [2008] EWHC 2155 (Comm), [2009] 1 All ER (Comm) 244.
[6] Set out in app 2 below; see also n 15 below.
[7] See eg in relation to Recital (13), which is taken from para 75 of the Virgos-Schmit Report, *Re Stojevic* [2007] BPIR 141, HCJ.

Council Regulation 1346/2000 on Insolvency Proceedings ('OR')

A. Chapter I: General Provisions	8.01
(OR) Article 1—Scope	8.01
General principles	8.01
Debtor	8.05
Defined insolvency proceedings	8.07
English insolvency proceedings	8.08
Excluded undertakings	8.09
Insurance undertakings	8.10
Credit institutions	8.13
Intra-Union effects	8.14
(OR) Article 2—Definitions	8.16
'Court'	8.17
'Judgment'	8.25
Time of the opening of proceedings	8.28
Member State in which assets are situated	8.33
'Establishment'	8.37
Place of operations	8.43
Human means	8.54
Goods	8.57
(OR) Article 3—International jurisdiction	8.60
The ideal: single proceedings with a universal effect	8.63
The reality: separate proceedings are permitted	8.64
The concept of 'opening'	8.65
The principle of effectiveness	8.79
Argument based on Article 38 OR	8.80
The 'relation back' theory	8.84
Main insolvency proceedings	8.85
Centre of main interests	8.85
The role of Recital (13)	8.88
Legal persons	8.92
Head office functions test	8.94
Groups of companies	8.102
The presumption under the UNCITRAL Model Law	8.107
Natural persons	8.108
Right to move COMI and 'forum shopping'	8.114
Terminated activities	8.122
Risk of conflicting decisions	8.123
The time at which COMI is assessed	8.132
Specifying type of proceeding requested	8.137
Potential conflict with non-EU jurisdictions	8.140
Evidence required by an English court	8.141
Statutory changes in England	8.145
Scope of insolvency proceedings	8.147
Insolvency proceedings limited to the territory of a Member State	8.166
'Establishment'	8.168
Terminated activities	8.169
Secondary Article 3(2) proceedings	8.172
Avoiding secondary proceedings	8.178
Pre-main Article 3(2) proceedings	8.181
(OR) Article 4—Law applicable	8.188
Article 4(2) OR	8.197
Article 4(2)(d) OR	8.198
Article 4(2)(e) OR	8.199
Article 4(2)(f) OR	8.202
Article 4(2)(h) OR	8.206
Article 4(2)(i) OR	8.208
Article 4(2)(j) OR	8.209
Article 4(2)(k) OR	8.210
Article 4(2)(m) OR	8.211
Exceptions to the general rule	8.215
(OR) Article 5—Third parties' rights in rem	8.217
(OR) Article 6—Set-off	8.232
(OR) Article 7—Reservation of title	8.241
(OR) Article 8—Contracts relating to immoveable property	8.245
(OR) Article 9—Payment systems and financial markets	8.247
(OR) Article 10—Contracts of employment	8.249
(OR) Article 11—Effects on rights subject to registration	8.253
(OR) Article 12—Community patents and trade marks	8.259
(OR) Article 13—Detrimental acts	8.260
(OR) Article 14—Protection of third-party purchasers	8.276
(OR) Article 15—Effects of insolvency proceedings on lawsuits pending	8.278
The effect of applying Article 15 OR	8.286
Article 15 OR is not limited to proprietary claims	8.292
Article 15 OR and arbitrations	8.294
B. Chapter II: Recognition of Insolvency Proceedings	8.296
(OR) Article 16—Principle	8.296
Extent of recognition	8.301
(OR) Article 17—Effects of recognition	8.305
(OR) Article 18—Powers of the liquidator	8.314
Main proceedings	8.314
Article 3(2) OR proceedings	8.327
(OR) Article 19—Proof of the liquidator's appointment	8.330
(OR) Article 20—Return and imputation	8.331
(OR) Article 21—Publication	8.336

(OR) Article 22—Registration in a public register	8.344	(OR) Article 34—Measures ending secondary insolvency proceedings	8.420
(OR) Article 23—Costs	8.349	(OR) Article 35—Assets remaining in the secondary proceedings	8.427
(OR) Article 24—Honouring of an obligation to a debtor	8.350	(OR) Article 36—Subsequent opening of the main proceedings	8.429
(OR) Article 25—Recognition and enforceability of other judgments	8.354	(OR) Article 37—Conversion of earlier proceedings	8.433
Recognition of insolvency judgments	8.354	(OR) Article 38—Preservation measures	8.437
Recognition of non-insolvency judgments	8.358	D. Chapter IV: Provision of Information for Creditors and Lodgement of their Claims	8.441
Mode of enforcement of insolvency judgments	8.359	(OR) Article 39—Right to lodge claims	8.441
Categorization of judgments	8.360	(OR) Article 40—Duty to inform creditors	8.446
Further points	8.362	(OR) Article 41—Content of the lodgement of a claim	8.449
(OR) Article 26—Public policy	8.365	'Alleges preference'	8.451
C. Chapter III: Secondary Insolvency Proceedings	8.375	'Security in rem'	8.452
(OR) Article 27—Opening of proceedings	8.377	'Guarantee'	8.453
(OR) Article 28—Applicable law	8.388	(OR) Article 42—Languages	8.455
(OR) Article 29—Right to request the opening of proceedings	8.389	E. Chapter V: Transitional and Final Provisions	8.460
(OR) Article 30—Advance payment of costs and expenses	8.394	(OR) Article 43—Applicability in time	8.460
(OR) Article 31—Duty to co-operate and communicate information	8.395	(OR) Article 44—Relationship to Conventions	8.463
(OR) Article 32—Exercise of creditors' rights	8.403	(OR) Article 45—Amendment of the Annexes	8.465
(OR) Article 33—Stay of liquidation	8.411	(OR) Article 46—Reports	8.468
		(OR) Article 47—Entry into force	8.469

A. Chapter I: General Provisions

(OR) Article 1—Scope

1. This Regulation shall apply to collective insolvency proceedings which entail the partial or total divestment of a debtor and the appointment of a liquidator.
2. This Regulation shall not apply to insolvency proceedings concerning insurance undertakings, credit institutions, investment undertakings which provide services involving the holding of funds or securities for third parties, or to collective investment undertakings.

General principles

8.01 Article 1 sets out the scope and subject-matter of the OR. This should be read in the light of the 'Recitals' to the OR which set out in some detail the rationale behind the OR. In particular, it is apparent that the OR is not only intended to deal with the fact that insolvencies increasingly have cross-border aspects but is also intended to be one element in the progress towards a complete and free internal market between all the Member States. This purpose should always be borne in mind given that national courts, taking their cue from the approach to legislation of the CJEU, are bound to adopt a purposive approach to the construction of the OR.[8]

---

[8] On the interpretation of the OR generally, see ch 2 above. In *Trustees of the Olympic Airlines SA Pension & Life Assurance Scheme v Olympic Airlines SA* [2015] 1 WLR 2399, counsel for the respondent submitted that the RR

The Recitals note that insolvencies and cross-border insolvency proceedings are factors **8.02** which can affect the proper functioning of the European internal market. Accordingly, it is desirable that cross-border insolvency proceedings should operate efficiently and effectively.[9] In order to achieve this there is a need for the co-ordination of the various measures which may be taken in relation to an insolvent debtor's assets across the European Union.[10] In addition it is said to be necessary for the proper functioning of the internal market that any incentives for parties to transfer assets or proceedings from one Member State to another (forum shopping) are avoided.[11] Furthermore, bankruptcy, proceedings relating to the winding-up of insolvent companies or other legal persons, judicial arrangements, compositions, and analogous proceedings[12] are excluded from the scope of the Convention on Jurisdiction and the Enforcement of Judgments in Civil and Commercial Matters signed in Brussels on 27 September 1968 (the Brussels Convention).[13]

It is therefore stated that the purpose of the OR is to be a Community law measure, binding[14] **8.03** and directly applicable in Member States, containing provisions relating to jurisdiction, recognition, and applicable law in respect of insolvency proceedings.[15] It is important to bear these statements of general principle in mind when considering the effect of the individual Articles. In general terms, the correct interpretation will be the one which promotes the general purpose of the OR.

Turning to the text of Article 1 itself, Article 1(1) states that the OR applies to collective **8.04** insolvency proceedings which entail the partial or total divestment of a debtor and the appointment of a liquidator. Article 1(1) thus encompasses four elements:

---

could be used as an aid to the interpretation of the OR. The Supreme Court did not address this submission in its judgment. It is considered that the RR should not be used as an aid to the interpretation of the OR, although the OR can plainly be used as an aid to the interpretation of the RR. Accordingly, there is minimal discussion of the RR in the commentary on the OR.

[9] Recitals (2), (3).
[10] Recital (3).
[11] Recital (4). Unfortunately, the Recital does not distinguish between 'good' forum shopping, ie seeking a forum which is likely to give the best outcome for creditors, from 'bad' forum shopping, where the debtor seeks to do the best for himself at the expense of his creditors. This is discussed further under *Right to move COMI and 'forum shopping'* at paras 8.113 et seq below. Emphasis was placed on the objective expressed in Recital (4) by the CJEU in its judgment in Case C-1/04 *Staubitz-Schreiber* [2006] ECR I-701, para 25, to support the court's purposive approach to its ruling on the capability of a debtor to move its COMI between the date when a request to open insolvency proceedings is lodged and the date when the court is able to deliver its judgment opening the proceedings. The thesis that it is the objective of the OR to counter 'opportunistic' and 'fraudulent' forum shopping, while accepting that it is appropriate 'on occasions' to encourage practices which have a beneficent purpose, was concisely stated by AG Colomer in his submissions to the CJEU in Case C-339/07 *Seagon v Deko Marty Belgium NV* [2009] ECR I-767 at para 60.
[12] The expression 'judicial arrangements, compositions and analogous proceedings' encompasses situations of actual or threatened insolvency: see the Jenard Report [1979] OJ C59/1 and the Schlosser Report [1979] OJ C59/71. The exception therefore applies to a restructuring plan under Part 26A of the English Companies Act 2006 given that in order to propose such a plan a company must have encountered or be likely to encounter financial difficulties: *Re Gategroup Guarantee Ltd* [2021] BCC 549 (a case in relation to the equivalent provision in the Lugano Convention).
[13] Recital (7). See Art 1(2) of the Brussels Convention. The Brussels Convention was replaced within the EU (except Denmark) by Regulation 44/2001 and then by Regulation 1215/2012 on jurisdiction and the recognition and enforcement of judgments in civil and commercial matters (referred to hereinafter as the Judgments Regulation). Art 1(2)(b) of the Judgments Regulation states that this Regulation does not apply to 'bankruptcy, proceedings relating to the winding-up of insolvent companies or other legal persons, judicial arrangements, compositions and analogous proceedings'.
[14] Being a Regulation, it has general application and is binding and directly applicable: Art 249 EC. See also ch 2 above and app 4 below in connection with Art 249 EC.
[15] Recital (8).

- Proceedings must be *collective*. The OR therefore does not apply to those proceedings which are commenced by one creditor only for his sole benefit. It follows that the OR does not apply to English administrative receiverships or to foreign equivalents.[16] Equally it does not include execution or debt collection proceedings commenced against a debtor by an individual creditor. On the other hand, winding-up petitions and administration applications by creditors, which may be driven by a subjective motivation of recovering a debt, are nevertheless regarded by English law as requests for administration or winding-up orders as class remedies.[17]
- The proceedings must be *insolvency* proceedings. It is said that this means that the proceedings must be based on the debtor's insolvency (as determined by national law) and not on any other grounds.[18] However, the question of whether or not a debtor is insolvent is a matter to be determined by national law; the OR is not aiming to create uniform legislation in this regard.[19] It follows that as a matter of English law the OR would not apply, for example, where a winding-up order is made on the grounds of public interest or on other 'non-insolvency' grounds.[20] However, a regulator's petition which is necessarily based on an allegation of insolvency will be covered.[21] Member States (such as the United Kingdom) which have proceedings which can be utilized either as insolvency proceedings or on grounds other than insolvency must ensure that their courts are aware of the requirement to make clear the grounds on which each of those proceedings has been commenced (ie based on insolvency or not) so that it can be easily determined whether or not the OR applies in each case. However, since the OR applies to rescue and reconstruction proceedings as well as traditional insolvency proceedings, even a threat or danger of insolvency will be sufficient to bring a proceeding within the OR. Thus, in *Bank Handlowy*,[22] the CJEU treated a French rescue procedure known as *sauveguarde* as an insolvency proceeding—even though *sauveguarde* is designed to prevent insolvency, and cannot be opened if the debtor has already become insolvent under French law. *Sauvegarde* is listed as an insolvency proceeding in Annex A of the OR, and the parties did not challenge its inclusion on the list.[23]

---

[16] And a fortiori, Law of Property Act receiverships are excluded from the scope of the OR.
[17] *Re Leigh Estates (UK) Ltd* [1994] BCC 292.
[18] The Virgos-Schmit Report, para 49(b). The Report deals with the OR when it was in the form of a proposed Convention. As described above, it did not prove possible to bring the Convention into force. However, the OR is modelled almost entirely on the terms of the Convention signed in November 1995 by 14 of the 15 states of the EU. The Virgos-Schmit Report has been cited in a number of national decisions, and also by AG Jacobs in his opinion in Case C-341/04 *Re Eurofood IFSC Ltd* [2006] ECR I-3813, and by AG Colomer in his Opinion in Case C-1/04 *Re Staubitz-Schreiber* [2006] ECR I-701. In *Trustees of the Olympic Airlines SA Pension & Life Assurance Scheme v Olympic Airlines SA* [2015] 1 WLR 2399, Lord Sumption described the Virgos-Schmit Report as an 'authoritative commentary' on the Convention (see [9] of the judgment), and held that it provided 'much the most useful source of guidance' on the interpretation of Art 2(h) (see [10] of the judgment).
[19] J-L Vallens, 'Procédures d'insolvabilité: présentation du règlement sur les procédures d'insolvabilité' Lamy Droit Commercial, No 125, August–September, 2. The laws of some Member States in this regard focus more on the strict accountancy test of whether assets exceed liabilities while others place greater emphasis on the failure to pay debts over a period of time.
[20] See *Re Marann Brooks CSV Ltd* [2003] BPIR 1159 where the court held that winding-up petitions presented on public interest grounds are not within the scope of the OR. The OR also does not apply to a resolution opening a members' voluntary winding-up proceeding ('MVL'), since an MVL is required to commence on the footing that the company is or will be solvent: Insolvency Act 1986, ss 89, 90. However, if insolvency ensues and the MVL is converted under s 96 to a creditors' voluntary liquidation ('CVL'), upon confirmation by the court the OR will apply.
[21] *FSA v Dobb White* [2004] BPIR 479 (regulator's petition for winding-up grounded on an allegation of insolvency required by the relevant statute).
[22] Case C-116/11 *Bank Handlowy w Warszawie SA v Christianapol sp z oo* [2013] Bus LR 956, ECLI: EU:C 2012:739.
[23] ibid at paras 31–35.

- The proceedings must entail the *total or partial divestment of the debtor*. 'Divestment' means the transfer to the liquidator of the power of administration and disposal over all or part of the debtor's assets or the limitation of those powers through the intervention and control of the debtor's actions.[24] It follows that it is sufficient that an insolvency proceeding involves a partial divestment of the debtor's assets for the OR to apply.[25]

The divestment may be partial with regard to the assets or with regard to the debtor's powers (he may, for example, retain certain authority to dispose of his assets subject to the supervision and approval by the liquidator).

- The proceedings must entail the *appointment of a liquidator*. For the purposes of the OR, a 'liquidator' is a broad concept and certainly goes much beyond the idea of a liquidator as understood in English insolvency law. Indeed, Article 2(b) of the OR states that a 'liquidator' is any person or body whose function is to administer or liquidate assets of which the debtor has been divested or to supervise the administration of his affairs. Those persons and bodies considered to be 'liquidators' for the purposes of the OR are set out in Annex C.[26] In relation to England and Wales ('England'): these are a liquidator, a supervisor of a voluntary arrangement, an administrator (including—as a result of a change to Annex C—administrators appointed out of court), the official receiver (acting as liquidator or trustee in bankruptcy), a trustee (in bankruptcy), and (as a result of a change to Annex C) a provisional liquidator.

Debtor

8.05 In addition to the four requirements above it is axiomatic that in all insolvency proceedings there must be a debtor. The reference to a 'debtor' in Article 1(1) is to any natural or legal person of that status and accordingly the OR applies to the insolvencies of individuals and companies and other legal entities.[27] Moreover, there is no distinction between the capacities in which individuals may have incurred liabilities.[28] However, the general rules defining jurisdiction only apply in respect of a debtor who has his 'centre of main interests' in one of the Member States.[29] Thus the OR does not apply at all where a debtor's centre of main interests is located outside the European Union or in Denmark.[30] For example, a company registered in England whose centre of main interests was in New York would be outside the OR.

---

[24] Virgos-Schmit Report, para 49(c).
[25] Accordingly the OR applies to cover voluntary arrangements since these typically involve divesting a debtor of at least some of his assets: see Annex A. But would the position be different in the case of an individual voluntary arrangement where all the contributions were provided by a third party? This may be a case where the fact that the proceeding is listed in Annex A takes precedence over strict compliance with the principles set out in Art 1(1): see also the discussion at para 8.07 below. The mechanism of *surrendement* in French law whereby a private individual may reach a settlement with his creditors is not included because of the absence of divestiture and also because of the amicable and contractual nature of the mechanism: see Vallens (n 19 above).
[26] See app 1 below.
[27] See Recital (9).
[28] Some Member States only apply insolvency proceedings to individuals when they are acting in the capacity of a trader. Under the OR each Member State in which proceedings are sought to be opened in respect of a debtor remains free to apply its own rules of national law to determine whether the proceedings should be opened.
[29] Art 3(1); Recital (14).
[30] See Recital (14). In *Re Arena Corp Ltd* [2004] BPIR 375, [2003] EWHC 3032 (Ch) the English court made a winding-up order in relation to a company which had its COMI in Denmark since Denmark had not opted into the OR (see Recital (33)) and therefore the OR did not apply so as to preclude the English court from making a winding-up order in respect of the company. Note: see the questions referred to the CJEU in Case C-148/08

8.06 It should be noted that there is no requirement that the insolvency proceedings result in the realization of the debtor's assets for the benefit of creditors. Thus the OR extends in principle to all forms of insolvency proceeding including both those which result in the winding-up of the debtor and those which result in the reorganization or restructuring of the debtor's affairs.

Defined insolvency proceedings

8.07 However, although these statements of general principle are important in understanding the OR, it will not generally be necessary for the courts to apply these principles and determine whether particular proceedings fall within the scope of the OR. The particular insolvency proceedings to which the OR applies are detailed in Annex A to the OR. In *Bank Handlowy*,[31] the CJEU considered the relationship between Annex A and Article 1(1), and established an important principle:

> [33] … Once proceedings are listed in Annex A to the Regulation, they must be regarded as coming within the scope of the Regulation. Inclusion in the list has the direct, binding effect attaching to the provisions of a Regulation.

The relevant proceedings in Annex A to the OR are set out in list form in order to provide for greater certainty in the application of the OR.[32] As such the principal practical importance of Article 1(1) is in determining whether such new insolvency proceedings as may be developed in the future should also be brought within the scope of the OR.[33]

English insolvency proceedings

8.08 As regards the jurisdiction of England, the OR applies to the following insolvency proceedings as listed in Annex A:

- Winding-up by the court.
- Creditors' voluntary winding-up (with confirmation by the court).[34]
- Administration, including appointments made by filing prescribed documents with the court.
- Voluntary arrangements under insolvency legislation.
- Bankruptcy.

Finn Mejnertsen v Betina Mandal Barsoe, reference by the Spanish Commercial Court concerning the position of Denmark. (The case was subsequently removed from the register: [2009] OJ C69/32.)

[31] Case C-116/11 *Bank Handlowy w Warszawie SA v Christianapol sp z oo* [2013] Bus LR 956, ECLI: EU:C 2012:739, at paras 31–35.

[32] J-L Vallens notes that whilst the draftsmen opted for this approach in the interests of certainty, it does heighten the risk that there may be certain proceedings which both fall outside the scope of the OR and are also excluded from the scope of the Regulation on Civil Jurisdiction and Judgments by Art 1(2)(b) of that Regulation: 'Le droit européen de la faillite: la Convention relative aux procédures d'insolvabilité' (1995) Actualité Legislative Dalloz 239.

[33] See Art 45 which sets out the procedure for the amendment of the annexes. Amendments were made to the annexes in 2004 upon the accession of the ten new Member States to the EU and further amendments were made between 2005 and 2014 pursuant to the procedure in Art 45: see Council Implementing Regulation (EU) 663/2014 of 5 June 2014. (Full references for all the amendments to the OR and to the three Annexes so far made under the Art 45 procedure are set out in ch 1 above at para 1.24: see at nn 45–51 and text thereto. See also ibid at nn 52–53, concerning additional amendments made on the occasions of enlargement of the membership of the EU.)

[34] The restriction of the application of the OR to only those creditors' voluntary liquidations which have been confirmed by the court reflects the fact that insolvency administrators in Europe are normally appointed by a court or other official body.

Excluded undertakings

8.09 Particular categories of undertaking have deliberately been left outside the scope of the OR. Article 1(2) states that the OR does not apply to insolvency proceedings in relation to insurance undertakings,[35] credit institutions (ie banks and similar entities),[36] investment undertakings which provide services involving the holding of funds or securities for third parties,[37] or to collective investment undertakings.[38] These entities were excluded from the scope of the OR because they are already subject to specific EU regulation and because it was envisaged that insolvencies of these undertakings which have cross-border elements will be co-ordinated by means of separate Directives.

Insurance undertakings

8.10 Council Directive (EC) 2001/17 on the reorganization and winding-up of insurance undertakings dealt with insolvency proceedings for insurers. This Directive was implemented into English law principally by the Insurers (Reorganisation and Winding up) Regulations 2004.[39] The provisions of the Directive have been subsumed into Directive 2009/138/EC ('Solvency II') under Title IV.

8.11 Although by its terms the OR does not apply to insolvency proceedings concerning insurance undertakings, there is no definition of 'insurance undertaking' in the OR. The scope of the exclusion has therefore to be worked out from the terms of the Directives.[40] Recital (2) to Directive 2001/17 points out that insurance undertakings are expressly excluded from the scope of the Regulation on insolvency proceedings. It seems, therefore, that what is excluded from the OR can be taken to be that which is *included* in the Directives. It is generally understood that the Directives are meant to plug a gap left by the OR. For the purposes of Solvency II, 'insurance undertaking' means a direct life or non-life insurance undertaking which has received official authorization under Article 14 of Solvency II: see Article 13(1). The reorganization and winding up provisions of the Directives thus do not apply to reinsurers as such.

8.12 The result in relation to reinsurance is not very clear. It may well be that those reinsurers who have been authorized to conduct direct insurance will be included in the insolvency

---

[35] See paras 8.10–8.13 below and see ch 7 above.

[36] A 'credit institution' is any entity covered by the definition in Council Directive (EEC) 77/780 [1977] OJ L322/30 (as amended by Council Directive (EC) 95/26): 'any undertaking whose activity is to receive deposits or other refundable funds and to grant loans for its own account'. See ch 7 above.

[37] An 'investment undertaking' is any entity covered by the definition in Council Directive (EC) 93/22 [1993] OJ L141/27 (as amended by Council Directive (EC) 95/26). See ch 7 above. In *Byers v Yacht Bull Corp* [2010] BCC 368, it was emphasized that an investment undertaking must provide services involving the 'holding of funds or securities for third parties' in order to fall within the Art 1(2) exception: other types of investment undertakings do not qualify (see [37] of the judgment).

[38] A 'collective investment undertaking' is any undertaking covered by the definition in Council Directive (EEC) 85/611 [1985] OJ L375/3 (as amended by Council Directive (EC) 95/26). See also ch 7 above. The exclusion refers to bodies which are authorized to carry on that type of business pursuant to the relevant directives and not to unauthorized collective investment undertakings: *FSA v Dobb White* [2004] BPIR 479.

[39] SI 2004/353. However, post-Brexit the 2004 Regulations have been amended by the Credit Institutions and Insurance Undertakings Reorganisation and Winding Up (Amendment) (EU Exit) Regulations 2019 (SI 2019/38). The Regulations address the fact that, unless otherwise agreed as part of UK withdrawal from the EU, the remaining EEA member states will no longer recognize the primacy of UK insolvency proceedings for credit institutions, insurance undertakings, investment firms and group companies whose home state is in the UK (UK institutions). Accordingly, the Regulations remove the prohibition on the UK courts making a winding-up or administration order against insolvent institutions whose home state is elsewhere in the EEA (EEA institutions).

[40] Directive 2001/17 is set out and discussed in detail by G Moss and T Smith in G Moss and B Wessels, *EU Banking and Insurance Insolvency* (2006).

aspects of the Directives and excluded from the OR but that any reinsurer who is *not* authorized to conduct direct insurance business is not included in the insolvency aspects of the Directives and therefore should be taken to be included in the OR. A further possibility is that a reinsurer who is authorized to write direct insurance is subject to the OR in respect of its reinsurance business and subject to the Directive in respect of its direct insurance business.

An argument against the latter possibility is the fact that it would be difficult to imagine insolvency proceedings regarding only some of the debtor's activities.

Credit institutions

8.13 Council Directive (EC) 2001/24 on the reorganization and winding up of credit institutions as amended deals with insolvency proceedings for banks and investment firms and with bank resolution proceedings.[41] This Directive was also implemented into English law by the Credit Institutions (Reorganisation and Winding Up) Regulations 2004.[42]

Intra-Union effects

8.14 It should be noted that the OR applies generally only to the intra-European Union *effects* of insolvency proceedings. It generally only creates effects as between Member States and not between Member States and non-Member States in relation to insolvency proceedings.[43]

8.15 It was also originally thought generally that the OR applied only to international jurisdiction and so did not regulate the domestic law position within a Member State.[44] However, the CJEU in *Schmid (as liquidator of the assets of Zimmermann) v Hertel* (Case C-328/12)[45] held that the German courts had jurisdiction under Article 3 to hear an avoidance action against a Swiss resident, even though there was no jurisdiction to do so under German domestic law.[46] It now seems to be the case that where a court has international jurisdiction to open insolvency proceedings within the OR and hear a case against a party outside the EU as part of such proceedings, it cannot refuse jurisdiction on the grounds of any limitation in domestic jurisdiction based on the residence of the defendant.

(OR) Article 2—Definitions

For the purposes of this Regulation:
(a) '**insolvency proceedings**' shall mean the collective proceedings referred to in Article 1(1). These proceedings are listed in Annex A;

---

[41] See ch 7 above.
[42] SI 2004/1045. Again, as now amended post-Brexit by the Credit Institutions and Insurance Undertakings Reorganisation and Winding Up (Amendment) (EU Exit) Regulations 2019.
[43] Member States for the purposes of the OR do not include Denmark, which was not bound by the OR: see Recital (33).
[44] Recital (15).
[45] [2014] 1 WLR 633, [2014] ILPr 11, [2014] BPIR 504.
[46] See the debate about the merits of this decision in C Paulus, 'The ECJ's Understanding of the Universality Principle' (2014) 27(5) Insolvency Intelligence 70 and G Moss, 'ECJ Takes Worldwide Jurisdiction' (2015) 28(1) Insolvency Intelligence 6. The CJEU justified its interpretation by reference to the principles of universalism, effectiveness, foreseeability, and legal certainty, as to which, see G Moss, 'Principles of EU Insolvency Law' (2015) 28(3) Insolvency Intelligence 40. See also Case C-295/13 *H v HK* (CJEU, Sixth Chamber) 4 December 2014, ECLI:EU:C:2014:2410.

(b) 'liquidator' shall mean any person or body whose function is to administer or liquidate assets of which the debtor has been divested or to supervise the administration of his affairs. Those persons and bodies are listed in Annex C;

(c) 'winding-up proceedings' shall mean insolvency proceedings within the meaning of point (a) involving realising the assets of the debtor, including where the proceedings have been closed by a composition or other measure terminating the insolvency, or closed by reason of the insufficiency of the assets. Those proceedings are listed in Annex B;

(d) 'court' shall mean the judicial body or any other competent body of a Member State empowered to open insolvency proceedings or to take decisions in the course of such proceedings;

(e) 'judgment' in relation to the opening of insolvency proceedings or the appointment of a liquidator shall include the decision of any court empowered to open such proceedings or to appoint a liquidator;

(f) 'the time of the opening of proceedings' shall mean the time at which the judgment opening proceedings becomes effective, whether it is a final judgment or not;

(g) 'the Member State in which assets are situated' shall mean, in the case of:
- tangible property, the Member State within the territory of which the property is situated,
- property and rights ownership of or entitlement to which must be entered in a public register, the Member State under the authority of which the register is kept,
- claims, the Member State within the territory of which the third party required to meet them has the centre of his main interests, as determined in Article 3(1);

(h) 'establishment' shall mean any place of operations where the debtor carries out a non-transitory economic activity with human means and goods.

Article 2 OR sets out the definitions which apply in interpreting and applying the OR. Articles 2(a), 2(b), and 2(c) OR defining the meanings of 'insolvency proceedings', 'liquidator',[47] and 'winding-up proceedings' respectively have already been discussed in relation to Article 1. **8.16**

'Court'
Article 2(d) OR sets out the definition of 'court' as the judicial body or any other competent body of a Member State empowered to open insolvency proceedings or to take decisions in the course of such proceedings. Since in certain Member States bodies other than the courts may commence insolvency proceedings and make decisions in the course of such proceedings, these bodies may, for these purposes, constitute courts.[48] **8.17**

In the case of a voluntary arrangement under the Insolvency Act 1986 in England, which is listed in Annex A to the OR, the question arises whether the meetings of members and creditors which are empowered to make the decision to place the company into a voluntary arrangement are to be regarded as a 'court' for the purposes of the OR. At first sight this **8.18**

---

[47] R 1.2 of the English Insolvency Rules 2016 provides that for the purposes of the Rules a person who falls within the definition of 'liquidator' as set out in Art 2(b) of the OR appointed in proceedings to which the OR applies in a member state other than the United Kingdom can be referred to as a 'member state liquidator'.
[48] See Virgos-Schmit Report, para 66, which also cross-refers to para 52 of that Report.

seems unlikely, since a meeting of creditors is not in any ordinary sense a competent body *of a Member State*. One would expect this phrase to refer to tribunals or other entities which are constituted and regulated by law or by the state.

8.19 However, a broader interpretation has been adopted with regard to the meaning of 'court' in Article 3(1) in order to make sense of the OR. In particular, since supervisors of voluntary arrangements come within the extended meaning of 'liquidator', if the voluntary arrangement is a main proceeding, in order to have his powers extend to other Member States as envisaged by Article 18, the supervisor will, under the terms of that Article, have to have been appointed by a 'court' having Article 3(1) jurisdiction. This can only refer to the meeting of creditors.

8.20 As was pointed out by Blackburne J in the *Salvage Association* case:[49]

> 21. The answer lies, in my view, in avoiding a too-literal approach to the application of the definition of 'court' in the Regulation and in understanding the reference in that definition to 'other competent body of a Member State' as applying not merely to some organ of the state but, more widely, to any body recognised as competent in that Member State to resolve upon (i.e. 'open') the insolvency proceedings in question. In this connection it is not without interest that para.66 of a Report by Miguel Virgos and Etienne Schmit published in July 1996 on the Convention on Insolvency Proceedings referred, in a commentary on the definition article of the Convention, in particular the Convention's definition of the expression 'court' (which, I understand, is word for word the same as in the Regulation), to the expression having 'a very broad sense' and as covering 'not only the judiciary or an authority which plays a similar role to that of a court or public authority ... but also a person or body empowered by national law to open proceedings or make decisions in the course of those proceedings ...

Thus in *Apperley Investments Ltd & others v Monsoon Accessorize Ltd*[50] the Irish High Court proceeded on the basis that the creditors' meeting was the relevant 'court' for the purposes of a company voluntary arrangement.

8.21 According to the Italian Council of State—the most prominent national jurisdictional authority for review of public agencies' acts—the Italian competent ministry or governmental department, in declaring the insolvency of a foreign company, must be considered as a '*court*' within the meaning of Article 2(d): see Council of State [Cons Stato], 6th Session, 25 January 2007, 267/2006, para 4.3 (published only in Italian in 21 *Diritto del commercio internazionale* 513 (2007)).

8.22 A more difficult question arises in relation to appointments of administrators in England by directors or secured creditors under paragraphs 14 and 22 of Schedule B1 to the Insolvency Act 1986 which are listed in Annex A. A person who makes such an appointment is obliged

---

[49] *Re The Salvage Association* [2003] BCC 504. The meeting of creditors will not, however, be a 'court' for the purposes of Art 234 EC (jurisdiction to seek preliminary rulings. See also Virgos-Schmit Report, para 52 (decisions by non-court entities not automatically to be treated as court rulings). However, in *Apperley Investments Ltd & others v Monsoon Accessorize Ltd* [2020] IEHC 523 (a case concerning a company voluntary arrangement) the Irish High Court treated the meeting of creditors as a 'court' for the purposes of Art 32 RR (recognition and enforcement of judgments).

[50] [2020] IEHC 523, at para 64 (a case in relation to the RR).

by paragraph 29 to file a notice of appointment with the court together with any other documents that may be required by the rules applying to such proceedings. However, as in the case of voluntary arrangements, the role of the court is only potential and is not necessary for the opening of the proceeding. In any case which may involve a non-UK element, it is best to avoid any out of court appointment of an administrator.[51]

If, after an initial appointment of an administrator has taken place out of court, a need arises to take action abroad in an EU Member State, a possible means of confirming or reinforcing the authority of the administrator in the eyes of courts or officials in other states unaccustomed to out of court procedures for opening insolvency may be by using paragraph 63 of Schedule B1 to the Insolvency Act 1986. The court's order giving directions to the effect that certain actions should be carried out abroad would simultaneously serve as proof of the administrator's status as an officer of the English court. It should also be noted that the wording of the UK entries in Annexes A and B were specially amended in 2005 to indicate that an administration is both an 'insolvency proceeding' and a 'winding-up proceeding' for the purposes of the OR, even where the initial appointment was made out of court. Although the efficacy of such an approach, using the 'directions application' facility in Schedule B1, may need to be tested before the courts in the first instance, it is submitted that it has the attraction of avoiding the initial expense involved in applying for an administration order in those cases where an out of court appointment is otherwise more convenient. **8.23**

In relation to English out of court administration appointments (by both the debtor or the holder of a qualifying floating charge), the appointor is simply required to identify if the OR applies and, if so, whether the proceeding is main or territorial[52] when completing the appointment documents to be filed with the court (following which, the appointment becomes effective). Under the out of court route, the English court does not make any determination concerning the location of the debtor's COMI or establishment, as the case may be. It is submitted that, irrespective of the existence of this self-certifying process or the absence of a formal 'judgment' from the court, the filing of the requisite documentation with the court constitutes a 'judgment opening insolvency proceedings' which requires recognition under Article 16. If a party wishes to dispute the jurisdictional basis on which the out of court appointment has been made, it must do so by recourse to the English court. Nevertheless, any risk of non-recognition of the appointment by another Member State or of an application to set aside or vary the appointment before the English court can be reduced by seeking the appointment of an administrator in court and ensuring that matters relating to jurisdiction are fully ventilated before the court. **8.24**

'Judgment'

Article 2(e) defines 'judgment' to *include* the decision of any court empowered to open insolvency proceedings or to appoint a 'liquidator'. This suggests that persons or bodies other **8.25**

---

[51] G Moss, 'On the Edge of Non-Recognition? Appointments of Administrators Under the Enterprise Act and the EC Regulation' (2004) 17 Insolvency Intelligence 13.
[52] Territorial proceedings include secondary proceedings, the latter being territorial proceedings opened under Art 3(2) subsequent to the opening of main proceedings and which, under Art 3(3), must be winding-up proceedings. An out of court administration appointment is possible as a secondary proceeding pursuant to Annex B.

than courts, even on the wide definition of the term 'court', may open insolvency proceedings or appoint liquidators within the OR.

8.26 The purpose of referring to decisions of courts in this context appears to be to mention the typical case, but also to make it clear that the reference is not exclusive.

8.27 If a proceeding within the OR is opened by a person or body other than a 'court', the recognition provisions in Articles 16–18 OR do not, at least on their literal terms, apply. 'Court' itself, however, has a very wide meaning; see paras 8.17–8.24 above.

Time of the opening of proceedings

8.28 Article 2(f) OR deals with the important question of the time at which insolvency proceedings are held to have been opened. This question is important because, as will be seen, many other aspects of the OR turn on the question of whether or not insolvency proceedings have been opened. Article 2(f) OR says that the time of opening of proceedings is the time at which the judgment opening the proceedings becomes effective, whether it is a final judgment or not.[53]

8.29 In *Shierson v Vlieland-Boddy*[54] the English Court of Appeal applied Article 2(f) and held that as a result the time at which the location of the COMI was to be determined for the purposes of Article 3 was the time at which at the judgment opening the proceedings would become effective. Thus before a court of a Member State can assume jurisdiction to open main insolvency proceedings, it must be satisfied that, at the time that it does so, the debtor's COMI is situated within the territory of that state.

8.30 However, that decision must now be read subject to the CJEU's subsequent decisions in *Staubitz-Schreiber*[55] and *Interedil*.[56] In the former case, the debtor had moved her COMI, which was in Germany at the time of her request to open proceedings, to Spain, after the request but prior to any opening. The CJEU held that this did not deprive the German courts of jurisdiction. It would have been contrary to the objectives of the OR to allow a debtor to move the COMI to another Member State, and thereby deprive the original court of its jurisdiction, after a request to open insolvency proceedings had been issued but prior to the determination of that request by the court. It would have encouraged debtors to move to more favourable jurisdictions and would have involved creditors in the time and expense of having to chase after debtors. *Staubitz-Schreiber* was cited by the CJEU in *Interedil* for the proposition that the correct time for judging the location of COMI was 'at the time when the request was lodged' to open insolvency proceedings (at para 55). In that case the debtor

---

[53] In relation to a CVL, a question arises as to whether the proceedings are opened when the meeting of members passes a resolution for the company to be wound up (at which point the company goes into liquidation under English law: s 247(2), Insolvency Act 1986) or when there is subsequent court confirmation of the liquidation (as required by Annex A of the OR). Since without court confirmation the CVL would not be a proceeding within the OR at all, the better view seems to be that for the purposes of the OR the proceedings will not be regarded as opened until there has been court confirmation of the CVL. Note, however, the contrary view set out at para 8.294 below.

[54] [2006] 2 BCLC 9.

[55] Case C-1/04 [2006] ECR I-701, [2006] BCC 639.

[56] Case C-396/09 *Interedil Srl, in liquidation v Fallimento Interedil Srl and Intesa Gestione Crediti SpA* [2011] ECR I-9915, [2012] BCC 851.

had been removed from the company register, but it was held that COMI should be judged as at the time the debtor was removed from the register (at para 58).[57]

In some Member States, the 'effects' of opening under domestic law are retrospective, but this does not mean that the 'time of opening' under the OR should be regarded as having taken place earlier. The Irish courts at first instance[58] and the Advocate General in *Eurofood*[59] appear to have regarded the time of opening as having taken place retrospectively in such a case but the point was left open by the CJEU[60] and it is suggested that a domestic law relation back of 'effects' cannot retrospectively alter the 'time of opening' under the OR for the purposes of the international allocation of jurisdiction between Member States.[61] **8.31**

In the *BenQ* case[62] there were two successive Dutch proceedings, both within the OR, where the 'effects' of the second related under Dutch law back to the start of the first. The Dutch court held that the opening of the second proceeding was to be regarded as having taken place when the first was opened, and thus ahead of a German opening which was regarded by the Dutch court as having taken place in between. In such a case it is a practical and sensible interpretation of the OR to treat the time of opening of the second proceeding as the time of opening of the first, even for the purposes of the allocation of international jurisdiction, since the transition from one proceeding to the other can be seen as a mere technicality and in substance there has only been one proceeding for the purposes of the OR. **8.32**

Member State in which assets are situated
Article 2(g) deals with the problem of identifying the Member State in which a debtor's assets are situated as follows: **8.33**

- In the case of tangible property, it is the Member State within the territory of which the property is situated.
- In the case of property and rights, ownership of or entitlement to which must be entered in a public register, it is the Member State under the authority of which the register is kept. This provision deals with the position of tangible property which is registered, such as aircraft and ships, and also of registered intangible property, such as patents and securities.[63]
- In the case of claims, it is the Member State within the territory of which the third party required to meet the claim has his centre of main interests (as determined under Article 3(1)). For example, in the *Stojevic* litigation in Austria, the debtor's claim against a Czech bank was held to be located in the Czech Republic and therefore fell within the main bankruptcy proceedings in the United Kingdom, which the Austrian

---

[57] See also *Re Melars Group Ltd* [2021] BCC 835, para 61: the question of the location of COMI is to be examined as at the date of the winding up petition (a case on the RR).
[58] *Re Eurofood IFSC Ltd* [2004] BCC 383, Irish High Court, Kelly J (left open and referred to the CJEU by the Irish Supreme Court at [2005] BCC 999).
[59] Case C-341/04 *Re Eurofood IFSC Ltd* [2006] ECR I-3813, [2005] BCC 1021.
[60] Case C-341/04 *Re Eurofood IFSC Ltd* [2006] BCC 397, [2006] ECR I-3813, CJEU (Grand Chamber).
[61] G Moss, 'When is a Proceeding Opened?' (2008) 21 Insolvency Intelligence 33, 37–39.
[62] *BenQ Mobile Holding BV* [2008] BCC 489, District Court of Amsterdam; G Moss, 'When is a Proceeding Opened?' (2008) 21 Insolvency Intelligence 33, 38–39; C Paulus, 'The Aftermath of Eurofood—BenQ Holding BV and the Deficiencies of the ECJ Decision' (2007) 20 Insolvency Intelligence 85; B Wessels, 'BenQ Mobile Holding BV Battlefield Leaves Important Questions Unresolved' (2007) 20 Insolvency Intelligence 103.
[63] A company will sometimes keep a subsidiary share register in a state other than the place of its own registration. In such a situation the relevant Member State may be the one under whose authority the main register is kept.

courts held they were obliged to recognize, and not in the subsequently opened Austrian bankruptcy, and therefore could not be assigned by the Austrian trustee back to the debtor.[64]

8.34 These criteria leave some areas of doubt, which are resolved by the RR: (i) are registered shares, which are registered in a private and not public register, to be treated as 'claims' for this purpose? (ii) Are bank accounts treated as 'claims' and those deemed located at the COMI of the bank, which may be in another Member State or outside the EU?

8.35 In the case of registered shares, VG at paragraph 313 suggests that they should be located where the company has its COMI and bearer shares should be treated like negotiable instruments. Where shares are held in the indirect holding system, they should be deemed located at the place where the account containing the shares is kept.

8.36 VG suggests at paragraph 312 that for the purposes of current and deposit bank accounts, each branch should be treated as if it were a separate entity and the claim should be deemed located at the branch serving the customer. Where there is a dispute as to whether assets are located in the main or the secondary proceedings, both the court of the main proceeding and that of the secondary proceeding have jurisdiction to decide the issue and where one court makes a decision, that must be respected by the other court.[65] In deciding the dispute, the criteria in Article 2(g) OR must be used and not the national law criteria of the court hearing the case,[66] even if the asset is said to be outside the EU.[67] This decision fails to give precedence to the main proceeding and potentially encourages a rush to court to obtain the first decision.

'Establishment'

8.37 Article 2(h) OR defines an 'establishment' as any place of operations where the debtor carries out a non-transitory economic activity with human means and goods. This definition is important because of the distinction in the OR between main and Article 3(2) insolvency proceedings: Article 3(2) proceedings[68] can only be commenced against a debtor if he has an establishment in the Member State concerned (see Article 3(2)).

8.38 Apparently, several states had wished to be able to commence territorial proceedings not only on the basis of the debtor having an establishment in the Member State but also if the debtor had assets in the Member State. In the negotiations surrounding the agreement of the OR, this ground for territorial proceedings was dropped and the mere presence of a debtor's assets within a Member State does not enable territorial proceedings to be commenced in that Member State where the OR applies. However, the concerns of those Member States

---

[64] (Austrian Supreme Court, 17 March 2005), 8 Ob 135/04t.
[65] Case 649/13 *Comité d'entreprise de Nortel Networks and Others* ECLI:EU:C:2015:384 (Judgment) and ECLI:EU:C:2015:44 (Opinion).
[66] ibid.
[67] ibid.
[68] The English legislation defines 'territorial proceedings' as proceedings opened in accordance with Arts 3(2) and 3(4) and which are listed in Annex A; and 'secondary proceeding' as proceedings opened in accordance with Arts 3(2) and 3(3) and listed in Annex B: Insolvency Rules 2016, r 1.2. To avoid the confusion that could arise from the possible ambiguity over the meaning of 'territorial proceedings', a term not defined in the OR itself, we have avoided the expression and used the term 'independent territorial proceedings' when referring to non-main proceedings opened before the opening of main proceedings and 'secondary proceedings' when referring to those opened after the opening of main proceedings. We use 'Article 3(2) proceedings' to cover both.

who desired there to be such a jurisdiction are meant to be reflected in the particularly broad definition of 'establishment' adopted.[69]

The approach taken by the UK Supreme Court is that the definition of 'establishment' must be read as a whole, because each element of the definition colours the other elements.[70] The debtor's activities must be 'economic', 'non-transitory', and carried on from a 'place of operations' using the debtor's assets and human agents. **8.39**

In *Interedil*,[71] the CJEU explained the concept of an establishment in the following terms: **8.40**

> 62. The fact that [the definition of 'establishment'] links the pursuit of an economic activity to the presence of human resources shows that a minimum level of organisation and a degree of stability are required. It follows that, conversely, the presence alone of goods in isolation or bank accounts does not, in principle, satisfy the requirements for classification as an 'establishment'.
>
> 63. Since, in accordance with Article 3(2) of the Regulation, the presence of an establishment in the territory of a Member State confers jurisdiction on the courts of that State to open secondary insolvency proceedings against the debtor, it must be concluded that, in order to ensure legal certainty and foreseeability concerning the determination of the courts with jurisdiction, the existence of an establishment must be determined, in the same way as the location of the centre of main interests, on the basis of objective factors which are ascertainable by third parties.

This approach was followed by the CJEU in the *Burgo* case.[72] The CJEU also held in that case that there is nothing in the OR to rule out the possibility that an 'establishment' can also be at the place of the registered office or in the same member State.[73] **8.41**

The objective nature of the test for the presence of an 'establishment' is also emphasized in paragraph 71 of the Virgos-Schmit Report, which states that a 'purely occasional place of operations cannot be classified as an "establishment" ... The decisive factor is how the activity appears externally, and not the intention of the debtor'. The foregoing passages from *Interedil* and the Virgos-Schmit Report were cited and applied by the UK Supreme Court in *Olympic Airlines*,[74] which is discussed below. **8.42**

Place of operations
In order for a debtor to have an 'establishment' in a Member State there must be a place of operations from which the debtor carries on economic activities. It follows that an office[75] or a shop from which the debtor carries on operations will be an establishment but the fact **8.43**

---

[69] See the Virgos-Schmit Report, para 70.
[70] See *Trustees of the Olympic Airlines SA Pension & Life Assurance Scheme v Olympic Airlines SA* [2015] 1 WLR 2399, para 13; and see also *Re Videology Ltd* [2019] BCC 195 (a case under the UNCITRAL Model Law and the Cross-Border Insolvency Regulations 2006).
[71] Case C-396/09 *Interedil Srl v Fallimento Interedil Srl and Intesa Gestione Crediti* SpA [2011] ECR I-9915, [2012] BCC 851.
[72] Case 327/13 *Burgo Group SpA v Illochroma SA (in liquidaton)*, para 31, citing Case C-396/09 *Interedil* EU:C:2011:671, para 62.
[73] Case 327/13 *Burgo Group SpA v Illochroma SA (in liquidaton)*, ruling 1.
[74] *Trustees of the Olympic Airlines SA Pension & Life Assurance Scheme v Olympic Airlines SA* [2015] 1 WLR 2399.
[75] Even an office with a secretary (one-man office) would do: *Re Stojevic* (Higher Regional Court (Court of Appeal) of Vienna, 9 November 2004), 28 R 225/04w (not reversed on this point by the Supreme Court).

that a debtor has assets in a Member State will not of itself be sufficient.[76] Accordingly, if a debtor has goods held in a warehouse operated by a third party this will not be an establishment and equally a holiday home operated by an individual debtor should not generally be considered an establishment since this is not usually a place where economic activity is carried on, at least not on a stable footing. A question might arise requiring judicial determination if the owner of a holiday home, in addition to maintaining it for personal and/or family use, adopts a practice of renting it out at other times to third parties on a commercial basis.

8.44 It is arguable that it would be different if the individual also had a non-temporary interest-earning bank account in the state in which he also had a holiday home since this might be argued to be an economic activity. However, the reference to economic activity being carried on with 'human means' is probably intended to distinguish between the situation where a debtor has a passive investment in a state from the situation where the debtor or a person or persons on his behalf are actively engaged in generating economic returns.

8.45 In addition, in order to qualify as an establishment a debtor's place of operations must have a certain level of organization and stability.[77] Accordingly, a purely occasional place of operations will not constitute an 'establishment'.

8.46 In England, the decision of the UK Supreme Court in *Olympic Airlines*[78] is the leading case on the concept of an 'establishment'. A main liquidation proceeding had been opened in Greece (the centre of main interests) in October 2009. Prior to October 2009, the company carried on business from a number of offices in the UK with the assistance of several dozen members of staff. However, after the winding-up of the company in Greece, the company's presence in the UK began to decline. In July 2010, the trustees of the company's pension scheme presented a petition against the company in England, with the intention of opening secondary proceedings. By that time, the company occupied only one office in the UK, where three members of staff on *ad hoc* contracts assisted the Greek liquidators to wind up the company's affairs.

8.47 The UK Supreme Court held that the presence of an establishment must be determined as at the date of the petition (being July 2010).[79] It stated that Article 2(h) does not simply require the debtor to be locatable or identifiable by a brass plate on a door. Rather, the debtor must carry on activities which, by their nature, involve business dealings with third parties.[80] Some activities which a company in liquidation might carry on may satisfy this requirement—for example, where a liquidator carries on business with a view to its disposal, or disposes of stock in trade on the market. However, where a company has no subsisting business, it is clearly not the case that the mere internal administration of its winding-up will qualify.[81] On this basis, it was held that the company did not have an establishment in the UK.

---

[76] See Case C-396/09 *Interedil Srl v Fallimento Interedil Srl and Intesa Gestione Crediti SpA* [2012] BCC 851, para 62 and *Re Stojevic* (Higher Regional Court (Court of Appeal) of Vienna, 9 November 2004), 28 R 225/04w (not reversed on this point by the Supreme Court).
[77] ibid.
[78] *Trustees of the Olympic Airlines SA Pension & Life Assurance Scheme v Olympic Airlines SA* [2015] 1 WLR 2399 (SC).
[79] ibid at para 5.
[80] ibid at para 13.
[81] ibid at para 14.

This conclusion is consistent with *Office Metro*,[82] which the UK Supreme Court cited with **8.48** apparent approval. In that case, the company's centre of main interests was in Luxembourg, where it had been placed into liquidation. The company had an English office, which the Luxembourg liquidators used to arrange the settlement of liabilities to associated companies, the forwarding of post and the taking of legal and accountancy advice. The court held that these facts were insufficient to constitute an establishment.

It has been said that the concept of 'establishment' adopted in the OR is intended to be **8.49** less restrictive than that which has been adopted by the CJEU in its interpretation of the expression 'branch, agency or any other establishment' in Article 5(5) of the Brussels Convention.[83]

In this context the CJEU has held that the concept of an establishment implies a place of **8.50** business which has the appearance of permanency so that third parties do not have to deal directly with the parent body.[84] However, one consequence of this definition has been that subsidiaries of a parent company could be considered to be establishments of the parent.[85] In this way the Article 5(5) definition is in fact too wide for the purposes of the OR since such a definition of establishment would interfere with the general jurisdictional rules which treat all companies as separate entities.[86] It is submitted that the definition of 'establishment' for the purposes of the OR will be similar to that developed for Article 5(5) save that separate subsidiary companies will not be considered to be establishments of the parent.[87]

In *Shierson v Vlieland-Boddy*[88] the English Court of Appeal held that the fact that a debtor **8.51** owned and controlled a property in England in the name of a letterbox BVI company nominee, which he let out to other parties, amounted to having an 'establishment' in England within the meaning of the OR. This conclusion is not easy to support.[89] As noted above, an 'establishment' is a place of operations with a degree of organization and stability from where the debtor carries on economic activities with human means and goods. The mere letting of a property does not constitute an 'establishment' in a case where the debtor does not have a 'place of operations' at the property which he lets out. It would be different if there were, for example, a block of flats or a complex of retail outlets and a letting office at the site. It is also not clear what the 'human means' were, unless that is a reference to letting agents used to rent the property. Even then, there is no suggestion that the agents had an office at the property. As far as the requirement of 'goods' is concerned, it is explained below

---

[82] *Re Office Metro Ltd* [2012] BCC 829.
[83] ibid. Art 5(5) provided that the courts of a contracting state have jurisdiction to determine disputes arising out of the operations of a branch, agency, or other establishment situated within that state. A similar provision is contained in the Judgments Regulation 1215/2012 as Art 7(5).
[84] Case 33/78 *Somafer SA v Saar-Ferngas AG* [1978] ECR 2183. In this regard entities such as exclusive distributorships have been held not be establishments for the purposes of Art 5(5): Case 14/76 *De Bloos SPRL v Bouyer SA* [1976] ECR 1497.
[85] See Case 218/86 *Schotte v Parfums Rothschild* [1987] ECR 4905. In this case it was, in fact, the parent company that was held to be an establishment of its own subsidiary.
[86] See Vallens (n 19 above).
[87] Vallens (n 19 above) supports the view that the notion of establishment in the OR is intended to be close to that in Art 5(5). See also *Telia AB v Hillcourt (Docklands) Ltd* [2002] EWHC 2377 (Ch), [2003] BCC 856 (see below).
[88] [2006] 2 BCLC 9.
[89] See G Moss, 'A Very Peculiar Establishment' (2006) 19 Insolvency Intelligence 20.

that this should be read as a reference to 'assets', and ownership of or an interest in land should be sufficient.

8.52 In the case of groups of companies, an establishment of a subsidiary company will not automatically also constitute an establishment of the parent company. In *Telia AB v Hilcourt (Docklands) Ltd*[90] the English High Court correctly held that the business premises in England of a Swedish debtor company's UK premises did not constitute an 'establishment' of the debtor.

8.53 In *Burgo Group*,[91] the CJEU held that the definition of 'establishment' in Article 2(h) does not rule out the possibility that an establishment could possess legal personality, or that an establishment could be situated in the Member State where the company has its registered office, provided it meets the criteria in Article 2(h).[92]

Human means

8.54 The 'human' means referred to in Article 2(h) must, it is submitted, be understood as referring to activities conducted by persons for whom the debtor is legally responsible, either as employer or as principal.[93]

8.55 In *Re Stojevic* (Higher Regional Court of Vienna, 9 November 2004), 28 R 225/04w the Austrian court rejected the idea that if a main proceeding had been opened previously in another Member State but the Austrian court thought that COMI was really in Austria, this would be sufficient, even in the absence of employees, to open a secondary proceeding in Austria as a 'countermeasure'. It further held that the activity of a human debtor himself was not enough to constitute 'human means' in this context, although an office with a secretary would suffice. Work done by an individual debtor for an Austrian corporation would also not suffice to constitute an establishment in Austria.

8.56 In the *BenQ* case in Germany,[94] where secondary proceedings were opened, it was held sufficient for the 'human means' requirement that work was done for the debtor by employees of another group company, ie it was not necessary for the 'human means' to be employees of the debtor itself.[95] In the *Office Metro* case in the UK,[96] it was held that the employees for this purpose could be employees of the debtor company, employees of a group company, or even independent contractors.

Goods

8.57 The use of the word 'goods' in Article 2(h) appears to be a mistranslation of '*biens*' in the French or '*Vermögenswerten*' in the German.[97] Those expressions would have been better rendered as 'assets',[98] since 'goods' are strictly speaking restricted to tangible movables. In

---

[90] [2003] BCC 856.
[91] Case 327/13 *Burgo Group SpA v Illochroma SA* [2015] 1 WLR 1046.
[92] ibid at para 32.
[93] Cited with approval in *Re Stojevic* (Higher Regional Court of Vienna, 9 November 2004) 28 R 225/04w.
[94] ZIP 10/2007 p 495 (District Court of Munich, 5 February 2007).
[95] See also Professor Paulus, 'The Aftermath of "Eurofood"—BenQ Holdings BV and the Deficiencies of the ECJ Decision' (2007) 20 Insolvency Intelligence 85, 85–86; Professor Wessels, 'BenQ Mobile Holding BV Battlefield leaves important questions unresolved' (2007) 20 Insolvency Intelligence 103, 105.
[96] *Re Office Metro Ltd, Trillium (Nelson) Properties Ltd v|Office Metro Ltd* [2011] EWHC 1191, [2012] BCC 829.
[97] See *Re Stojevic* (Higher Regional Court of Vienna, 9 November 2004) 28 R 225/04w.
[98] See the linguistic discussion in the English Court of Appeal case of *Newham v Khatun* [2005] 1 QB 37, paras 68–70, 78.

another EU legislative context, '*biens*' has been held to refer to movable and immovable property.[99] Since each language version of the OR is equally authoritative, UK courts should read the definition as referring to 'assets' and not 'goods'. The correctness of this analysis was confirmed in *Olympic Airlines*,[100] where Lord Sumption said that the word 'goods' is 'hardly a satisfactory English word to use in this context. It is apparent from the equivalent term in the other language versions that it means the same as "assets".[101]

8.58 The mistranslation was carried through to the English language version of the UNCITRAL Model Law, although there the words 'and services' have been added to broaden the concept of 'establishment'. However, in the enactment of the Model Law in Britain (England and Scotland) by the Cross-Border Insolvency Regulations 2006, the mistranslation has finally been corrected, on the recommendation of a Review Panel set up by the Insolvency Lawyers' Association, in Article 2(e) of Schedule 1, where 'establishment' is defined as 'any place of operations where the debtor carries out a non-transitory economic activity with human means and assets or services'.

8.59 In the case of *R AB*,[102] the Tallinn Court of Appeal in Estonia opened secondary proceedings in a case where the facts did not appear to disclose any 'goods' in the narrow sense of personal movables but there was land belonging to the debtor company which was contracted to be developed into a hunting lodge for tourists. The Tallinn Court of Appeal referred to a requirement to have 'assets' as part of the definition of 'establishment' (ie rather than 'goods').

(OR) Article 3—International jurisdiction

1. The courts of the Member State within the territory of which the centre of a debtor's main interests is situated shall have jurisdiction to open insolvency proceedings. In the case of a company or legal person, the place of the registered office shall be presumed to be the centre of its main interests in the absence of proof to the contrary.
2. Where the centre of a debtor's main interests is situated within the territory of a Member State, the courts of another Member State shall have jurisdiction to open insolvency proceedings against that debtor only if he possesses an establishment within the territory of that other Member State. The effects of those proceedings shall be restricted to the assets of the debtor situated in the territory of the latter Member State.
3. Where insolvency proceedings have been opened under paragraph 1, any proceedings opened subsequently under paragraph 2 shall be secondary proceedings. These latter proceedings must be winding-up proceedings.
4. Territorial insolvency proceedings referred to in paragraph 2 may be opened prior to the opening of main insolvency proceedings in accordance with paragraph 1 only:

---

[99] See *Newham v Khatun* above and Case 283/81 *CILFIT v Ministry of Health* [1982] ECR 3415.
[100] *Trustees of the Olympic Airlines SA Pension & Life Assurance Scheme v Olympic Airlines SA* [2015] 1 WLR 2399.
[101] ibid at para 3. See also *Re Office Metro Ltd, Trillium Nelson Properties Ltd v Office Metro Ltd* [2011] EWHC 1191, [2012] BCC 829. The mistake is corrected in the RR.
[102] 14 June 2006.

(a) where insolvency proceedings under paragraph 1 cannot be opened because of the conditions laid down by the law of the Member State within the territory of which the centre of the debtor's main interests is situated; or

(b) where the opening of territorial insolvency proceedings is requested by a creditor who has his domicile, habitual residence or registered office in the Member State within the territory of which the establishment is situated, or whose claim arises from the operation of that establishment.

8.60 Article 3 OR sets out the fundamental principles in relation to the allocation of international jurisdiction in respect of insolvency proceedings. It does not deal with the allocation of jurisdiction within a Member State.[103] It does not set out the criteria for exercising jurisdiction under domestic law:[104] see Article 4(2) OR. It does however override domestic law limitations on taking jurisdiction in cases affecting a non-Member State.[105]

8.61 Some Member States, such as the United Kingdom, are multi-jurisdictional states containing different law countries. In the United Kingdom, for the purposes of the OR, these are England (including Wales), Scotland, Northern Ireland, and Gibraltar. The allocation of jurisdiction to open proceedings as between those jurisdictions is a matter for the laws of the United Kingdom. The criteria for opening insolvency proceedings are governed by the domestic law of each law-country.

8.62 Article 3 OR also illustrates the tension which is at the heart of the OR: the reconciliation of the desire that in relation to each debtor there should just be a single set of insolvency proceedings which has universal effect with the pragmatic requirement to give effect to the demands of individual Member States to retain some control of proceedings commenced in respect of debtors who have interests within their jurisdiction.

The ideal: single proceedings with a universal effect

8.63 The main principle underlying the OR is that of the 'universality' of insolvency proceedings. This principle requires that when insolvency proceedings are commenced in relation to a debtor then those proceedings should comprise all of that debtor's assets wherever they might be located in the Member States and that furthermore no further separate insolvency proceedings should be permitted to be commenced.

The reality: separate proceedings are permitted

8.64 However, the general principle of universality was compromised in the OR and is limited by the possibility of the opening of one or more sets of insolvency proceedings, having territorial effect, in other Member States where the debtor has an 'establishment' (as defined in Article 2(h), and as interpreted by the CJEU in *Interedil*). These Article 3(2) proceedings are

---

[103] G Moss, 'Group Insolvency—Choice of Forum and Law: the European Experience under the Influence of English Pragmatism' (2007) 32 Brooklyn Journal of International Law 1005, 1007; G Moss, 'Group Insolvency—Forum—EC Regulation and Model Law Under The Influence of English Pragmatism Revisited' (2014) 9(1) Brooklyn Journal of Corporate, Financial & Commercial Law 250.

[104] *Re The Salvage Association* [2003] BCC 504, [2004] 1 WLR 174, para 13, Blackburne J. See also Case 327/13 *Burgo Group SpA v Illochroma SA* [2015] 1 WLR 1046, para 63.

[105] Case C-328/12 *Schmid v Hertel* [2014] 1 WLR 633, [2014] ILPr 11, [2014] BPIR 504. For contrasting commentaries on this case by C Paulus, 'The ECJ's Understanding of the Universality Principle' (2014) 27(5) Insolvency Intelligence 70; G Moss, 'ECJ Takes Worldwide Jurisdiction' (2015) 28(1) Insolvency Intelligence 1.

limited in effect to the particular Member State in which they are commenced[106] and are subject to rules of co-ordination with the main proceedings.[107] Nevertheless they represent a major incursion on the principle of universality.[108]

The concept of 'opening'

Although the concept of 'opening' is central to Article 3, the word is not defined in the OR.[109] Yet it is crucial for many purposes to know when an 'opening' has taken place. As noted above under Article 2(f) OR, the definition of 'the time of the opening of proceedings' only helps in a very limited way. **8.65**

An 'opening' will often follow a 'request' for an opening. The concept of 'request' is used in various places in the OR, such as Articles 3(4)(b), 25(1), and 38, and Recital (16) OR. It is, however, not defined. **8.66**

The main importance of being able to judge when there has been an 'opening' in the autonomous sense used in the OR is where a court in one Member State is asked to recognize the opening of a proceeding in another Member State. Although the use of 'open' in relation to insolvency proceedings may be familiar in Continental jurisdictions, it was unknown in the United Kingdom and Ireland prior to the OR and had no definite meaning. **8.67**

The automatic recognition provisions of Article 16 OR and following means that it is important to identify when proceedings are 'opened' for the purposes of the OR by the courts of a Member State. In the *Eurofood* case (*Re Eurofood IFSC Ltd*, Case C-341/04) the CJEU confirmed that the filing of a petition (request) seeking a winding-up order in Ireland on the grounds of insolvency, together with the appointment of a provisional liquidator (who displaced the directors) on an *ex parte* (without notice) application, without notice even to the company or its directors, represented the 'opening' of proceedings. In the *BenQ Mobile Holding BV* case[110] the opening of a *surséance van betaling* (temporary respite) proceeding in the Netherlands on an *ex parte* basis was held to be an opening for the purposes of the OR. In that case, BenQ Mobile Holding BV filed a request seeking *surséance van betaling* in Amsterdam on 27 December 2006 which the same day granted a temporary moratorium on payments. This was followed by a separate application made on 29 December to a Munich court for the opening of proceedings in Germany which ordered the opening of proceedings (*vorläufiges Insolvenzverfahren*) in Germany, which can be translated as 'preliminary', 'provisional', or 'temporary'. On 31 January 2007 the Amsterdam court opened final proceedings as main proceedings in the Netherlands. On 5 February 2007 the German court opened secondary proceedings in Germany recognizing that main proceedings had been opened in the Netherlands on 27 December 2006. **8.68**

---

[106] Art 3(2).
[107] See eg Arts 31, 33, and 37.
[108] In contrast, in relation to insolvent insurers and banks, the regimes under the relevant Directives make no provision for secondary proceedings but instead provide for true universality pursuant to which insolvency proceedings can be opened in, and only in, the home Member State of the insurer or bank: see ch 7 above and G Moss and B Wessels, *EU Banking and Insurance Insolvency* (2006).
[109] See generally G Moss, 'When is a Proceeding Opened?' (2008) 21 Insolvency Intelligence 33; Backner, 'The Battle over Jurisdiction in European Insolvency Law' (2006) 3 European Company & Financial Law Review 310. In relation to opening and the meaning of 'court', see under Art 2 OR above.
[110] *BenQ Mobile Holding BV* [2008] BCC 489, District Court of Amsterdam.

8.69 It is suggested that the rational interpretation of 'opening' would have accorded with its principal function of extending the 'effects' of the proceedings to other Member States pursuant to Article 16 OR and following, subject to the exceptions set out in the OR. On this basis, an 'opening' would take place, in accordance with the autonomous meaning used in the OR, when the general 'effects' of the proceeding applied, as opposed to partial or limited 'effects' which in some systems of law apply, usually as a safeguard for creditors, from either the date of the 'request' or from the date of the appointment of a provisional liquidator or temporary administrator etc. The stage at which the general effects apply is usually very easy to ascertain.

8.70 However, the CJEU in the *Eurofood* case[111] took a completely different view and held that the autonomous meaning of 'opening' in the OR meant either:

(a) 'a decision which is formally described as an opening decision by the legislation of the Member State of the court that handed it down' or
(b) a decision handed down following an application, based on the debtor's insolvency, seeking the opening of proceedings referred to in Annex A to the OR, where that decision involves divestment of the debtor and the appointment of a liquidator referred to in Annex C to the OR. Such divestment involves the debtor losing the powers of management which he has over his assets.'[112]

8.71 This approach brings considerable problems and uncertainties. With regard to 'opening' type (a) the domestic legislation of a state may not use the term 'opening'. In principle, no part of the autonomous concept of 'opening' should depend on any description supplied by domestic law.

8.72 With regard to opening type (b), the 'extended' meaning of the concept, this requires the coincidence of a number of factors:

(i) a decision;
(ii) following an application;
(iii) based on the debtor's insolvency;
(iv) seeking the opening of proceedings listed in Annex A;
(v) where that decision involves the divestment of the debtor in the sense of losing the powers of management which he has over his assets; and
(vi) the appointment of a liquidator listed in Annex C.

8.73 The main problems and anomalies connected with this approach stem from the uncertainties arising from requirements (v) and (vi), the lack of any requirement of finding that the debtor is insolvent (or likely to become insolvent without a rescue or reorganization), and the lack of any requirement of a proper *inter partes* hearing in which those affected (and in particular the debtor in a hostile or 'involuntary' case) can be heard by the court.

8.74 With regard to 'divestment', the appointment of a provisional liquidator in some Member States usually, but not necessarily, amounts to complete divestment (as in the United Kingdom and Ireland) but in others usually, but not always, amounts to only

---

[111] Case C-341/04 *Re Eurofood IFSC Ltd* [2006] ECR I-3813, [2006] BCC 397, CJEU (Grand Chamber).
[112] ibid, para 54.

partial divestment and complete divestment only occurs on 'opening' in the (a) sense (as in Germany). A court in another Member State would have to obtain a copy of the decision and have it translated, sometimes together with the relevant statute and/or case law to see what the effect is. Even then it is not clear whether total or partial divestment is required or something in between. Since this is an extended type of opening created by the CJEU, this question is not solved simply by referring to the fact that a proceeding within the OR may involve total or partial divestment under Article 1(1). The *BenQ* case[113] appears to suggest that partial divestment will suffice.

8.75 With regard to the requirement that the provisional liquidator be included in Annex C, at the time of the *Eurofood* decision there was no uniformity of practice: for example Ireland included him in Annex C but the United Kingdom did not.[114] Following *Eurofood* there was some catching up to ensure that advantage was taken of the *Eurofood* decision, for example by the United Kingdom.[115]

8.76 In the case of Germany, Annex C OR lists a provisional liquidator.[116] These can be 'weak' or 'strong' depending on the degree of control given over the debtor's assets. However, even the appointment of a 'weak' provisional liquidator has been held to be an opening of an insolvency proceeding.[117]

8.77 With regard to the lack of any need for a finding of insolvency or threatened insolvency, such a requirement is, as we have seen above in relation to Article 1, absolutely fundamental to the whole concept of insolvency proceedings. To allow 'insolvency' proceedings to be held to be opened within the meaning of the OR merely on the basis of an *allegation* of insolvency (as in the *Eurofood* case) is wrong in principle. For example, if a creditor requests the opening of a liquidation proceeding against a debtor company, alleging insolvency, and has a provisional liquidator appointed, this is counted by the CJEU as an opening (in the extended (b) sense) of an insolvency proceeding within the OR. However, if it later turns out that the debtor is and has throughout been solvent, the proceeding should never have been within the OR because it has never in reality been an insolvency proceeding. On the other hand, if the request was based on solvency and made as shareholder, and a provisional liquidator is appointed the extended meaning of opening invented by the CJEU does not apply, even if the debtor company turns out later to be and to have been at all times insolvent.

---

[113] *BenQ Mobile Holding BV* [2008] BCC 489, District Court of Amsterdam; See C Paulus, 'The Aftermath of Eurofood—BenQ Holding BV and the Deficiencies of the ECJ Decision' (2007) 20 Insolvency Intelligence 85; B Wessels, 'BenQ Mobile Holding BV Battlefield Leaves Important Questions Unresolved' (2007) 20 Insolvency Intelligence 103.

[114] Although, paradoxically, the positions of the UK and Ireland were exactly reversed in their respective lists included in Annex B to the Council of Europe Convention on Certain International Aspects of Bankruptcy (the Istanbul Convention 5 June 1990, *not yet in force*). The entry for the UK, listing the titles of those who are 'liquidators' for the purposes of Art 1(3) of that Convention, includes 'provisional liquidator'; the list for Ireland makes no mention of that office-holder. The reason for the omission of provisional liquidator from the UK list in the original Annex A to the EC Convention, and subsequently to Regulation 1346/2000 as first adopted, has never been officially disclosed. Cyprus included the office of provisional liquidator in its entry in Annex C from the time of joining the EU on 1 May 2004.

[115] The UK entry in Annex C was amended so as to include provisional liquidators by Council Regulation (EC) 694/2006 [2006] OJ L121/1 with effect from 7 May 2006.

[116] 'Vorläufiger Insolvenzverwalter'.

[117] *LG Patra*, Beschl.v.2.5.2007-316/06, ZIP 2007, 1875 (LS); *Westwood Shipping Lines Inc v Universal* [2012] EWHC 1394 (Comm).

8.78 With regard to the lack of any need for a proper *inter partes* hearing, this will give rise to potential problems which are dealt with under Article 26 OR below.

The principle of effectiveness

8.79 The CJEU's[118] concern in setting out their 'extended' type of 'opening' was to promote the 'effectiveness' of the proceedings.[119] It is impossible to see, however, why the principle of effectiveness should lead to this 'extended' form of opening. After the request for the opening of proceedings, any 'judgment'[120] by way of a preservation measure (ie pending the opening) given by a 'court' whose judgment has to be recognized in accordance with Article 16 (ie a judgment opening main proceedings) must automatically be recognized in other Member States pursuant to Article 25. This includes the appointment of a provisional liquidator, so it is completely unnecessary to hold that such an appointment constitutes an opening in order to make the OR effective.

Argument based on Article 38 OR

8.80 The CJEU considered the argument against its extended interpretation of opening based on Article 38 OR:

> 56. Both Mr Bondi and the Italian Government acknowledge that, in the main proceedings, the 'provisional liquidator' appointed by the High Court, by decision of January 27, 2004, appears amongst the liquidators mentioned in Annex C to the Regulation in relation to Ireland. They argue, however, that this is a case of a provisional liquidator, in respect of whom the Regulation contains a specific provision. They note that Art.38 of the Regulation [OR] empowers the provisional liquidator, defined in the 16th recital as the liquidator 'appointed prior to the opening of the main insolvency proceedings', to apply for preservation measures on the assets of the debtor situated in another Member State for the period between the request for the opening of insolvency proceedings and the judgment opening the proceedings. Mr Bondi and the Italian Government infer from that that the appointment of a provisional liquidator cannot open the main insolvency proceedings.
>
> 57. In that respect, it should be noted that Art.38 of the Regulation must be read in combination with Art.29, according to which the liquidator in the main proceedings is entitled to request the opening of secondary proceedings in another Member State. That Art.38 thus concerns the situation in which the competent court of a Member State has had main insolvency proceedings brought before it and has appointed a person or body to watch over the debtor's assets on a provisional basis, but has not yet ordered that that debtor be divested or appointed a liquidator referred to in Annex C to the Regulation. In that case, the person or body in question, though not empowered to initiate secondary insolvency proceedings in another Member State, may request that preservation measures be taken over the assets of the debtor situated in that Member State. That is, however, not the case in the main proceedings here, where the High Court has appointed a provisional liquidator referred to in Annex C to the Regulation and ordered that the debtor be divested.

---

[118] See also G Moss, 'Principles of EU Insolvency Law' (2015) 28(3) Insolvency Intelligence 40.
[119] Case C-341/04 *Eurofood IFSC Ltd* [2006] CJEU I-3813, [2006] BCC 397, CJEU (Grand Chamber), paras 52–54.
[120] See the wide interpretation given to this expression under Art 2(e) above.

With respect to the CJEU, its argument is mistaken. Article 29 refers to 'the liquidator in the main proceedings', in other words where a main proceeding has been opened. Article 38, as the CJEU says, deals with the earlier situation after the request but before the opening. However, it is clear that 'temporary administrator' in Article 38 OR has the same meaning as 'liquidator temporarily appointed *prior to the opening*' [emphasis added] in Recital (16),[121] which deals with the same subject matter. The appointment of such a liquidator *may or may not* divest the debtor—therefore 'divestment' cannot be the critical trigger for 'opening'. Also, such a liquidator may or may not be listed in Annex C OR,[122] so that cannot be the critical trigger either. **8.81**

The simpler and more satisfactory answer is that the autonomous meaning of 'opening' in the OR is the point at which the proceeding listed in Annex A has its general 'effects' which require to be recognized in other Member States under Article 16. However, unless and until the CJEU revises its view, we must struggle to apply the CJEU's normal and extended concepts of opening, with the resulting confusion and uncertainty. **8.82**

Note, however, that a perverse incentive could be created if the appointment of a provisional liquidator by a court were held not to mark the point in time from which the jurisdiction of that court is to be measured in any circumstances in which it becomes necessary to assess the competing claims of the courts of two Member States to be recognized as the 'first to open proceedings'. If a party who wishes to cause proceedings to be based in a different Member State, so as to be governed by its insolvency law, succeeds in persuading a court of that state that the debtor's COMI is located there, and that it should open insolvency proceedings with immediate effect, this could subvert the more orderly approach being undertaken in the court which has taken the initial step of appointing a provisional liquidator for purposes which may include the carrying out of an investigation into the full circumstances of the case before a decision is taken whether a winding-up order is appropriate. If it were to become legally possible for pre-emptive tactics undertaken in other Member States to circumvent the process in the state first engaged, those making the initial application might deem it more expedient to seek a winding-up order immediately, rather than to proceed via provisional liquidation in the first instance. This could give rise to less than satisfactory results in some circumstances, with potential wastage of costs. **8.83**

The 'relation back' theory
Although the CJEU itself did not deal with this, the Advocate General also expressed the view that because of the relation back of the winding-up order under Irish law to the filing of the petition, the date of filing was the date of 'opening' for the purposes of the OR.[123] With respect this is wrong for a number of reasons. Firstly, the Irish law relation back only provides that the proceedings are 'treated' (deemed) as if they began at the petition filing date, not that they actually did so, and the doctrine only exists for limited purposes such as the avoidance of dispositions by the debtor company between the filing and the opening. **8.84**

---

[121] Note that Recital (16) does not use the 'temporary administrator' wording used by Art 38 and paras 262, 263 of the Virgos-Schmit Report, so the deliberate use of 'liquidator temporarily appointed prior to the opening' as the equivalent concept is a very forceful and clear statement by the community legislator that that is what is meant by 'temporary administrator' in Art 38.
[122] Virgos-Schmit Report, para 263.
[123] [2005] BCC 1021, paras 89–95.

Secondly, the Advocate General has, in the *Eurofood* case itself, overlooked the effect under the OR of the intervening Italian opening of main proceedings. Ignoring the appointment of the provisional liquidator, the order of events was: (i) Irish petition filed, (ii) Italian opening, (iii) Irish winding-up order. Ignoring also the public policy argument for this purpose, the Advocate General has forgotten that when the matter returned to Ireland the Irish court was, under Article 16, bound to recognize the Italian opening and could not itself open a main proceeding. Any 'relation back' could only create the opening of a territorial proceeding. Thirdly and most fundamentally, it is a completely unacceptable notion that a domestic law relation back should be able to dictate the answer to a question of international jurisdiction.

Main insolvency proceedings

Centre of main interests

8.85 Article 3(1) provides that the courts of the Member State within the territory of which 'the centre of a debtor's main interests' (COMI) is situated have jurisdiction to open insolvency proceedings.[124] These are the *main proceedings* which in principle have universal scope and encompass all of the debtor's assets wherever located within the European Union (with the exception of Denmark).

8.86 The OR neither requires nor forbids the extension of the scope of Article 3(1) proceedings to assets located beyond the European Union, but such universalist ambition will usually be present pursuant to the national law of the Member State of the opening of the proceedings.

8.87 The concept of COMI is therefore an important one since it lies at the heart of the OR's principal jurisdictional rule. The concept is not, however, defined in the OR.

The role of Recital (13)

8.88 Recital (13) suggests COMI is the place where the debtor conducts the administration of his interests on a regular basis and is therefore ascertainable by third parties.

8.89 The wording of Recital (13) is taken from the first sub-paragraph of paragraph 75 of the Virgos-Schmit Report. That is a general statement about COMI (and not a definition), before the Report goes on to discuss the COMI of different types of debtors.

8.90 The CJEU in *Re Eurofood IFSC Ltd*[125] used the word 'definition' in relation to Recital (13) (paragraph 33), but in the context this is the equivalent of the phrase '[t]he scope of the concept is highlighted' in paragraph 32. In other words, Recital (13) provides clarification and not definition in any strict sense.

8.91 In *Re Stojevic*[126] the English court rejected an argument that Recital (13) was a definition of COMI:

> [31] In my judgment Recital (13) does not define the expression 'centre of main interests' and I do not understand the European Court of Justice to have said otherwise. The

---

[124] English Insolvency Rules 2016, r 1.2(2) provides that for the purposes of the Rules 'centre of main interests' has the same meaning as in the OR.
[125] [2006] ECR I-3813, [2006] Ch 508.
[126] [2007] BPIR 141, HCJ.

Regulation contains definitions of various expressions used in the Regulation, such as 'establishment', in Art 2, which is headed 'Definitions'. It is significant that the expression 'centre of main interests' does not appear amongst the expressions collected in that Article.

[32] I agree with Mr Moss and Mr Fuller, when they submitted that, in the context of the *Eurofood* case, the word 'definition' is used, in para [33] of the judgment, as the equivalent of the phrase '[t]he scope of that concept is highlighted', which is the language adopted in para [32] of the judgment, ie more in the nature of what we would call 'a description'. I reject Mr Robins' submission that Recital (13) contains a definition of the expression 'centre of main interests'.

[33] I also agree with Mr Moss and Mr Fuller, when they submitted that Recital (13) can only be properly understood by putting it back in its original context, namely para 75 of the Virgos-Schmit Report.

Legal persons

In the case of a company or 'legal person' the place of the registered office is presumed to be the COMI in the absence of proof to the contrary.[127] The circumstances in which the presumption will be rebutted were considered by the CJEU in *Re Eurofood IFSC Ltd*.[128] That case concerned Eurofood, an Irish incorporated subsidiary of Parmalat SpA which was itself incorporated in Italy. In this context, the CJEU considered the test for identifying the COMI of a subsidiary company where it and its parent have their registered offices in two different Member States. The CJEU referred to Recital (13) of the OR and stated that the Recital showed that the COMI had to be identified by reference to criteria that are both objective and ascertainable by third parties in order to ensure legal certainty and foreseeability concerning the determination of the court with jurisdiction to open main insolvency proceedings.[129] The CJEU held that it followed that, in determining the COMI of a debtor company, the presumption in favour of the registered office of that company could be rebutted only if factors which are both objective and ascertainable by third parties enable it to be established that an actual situation existed which was different from that which locating it at that registered office was deemed to reflect.[130] Importantly, the CJEU then went on specifically to comment that one of the situations where the presumption could be rebutted is in the case of (in the court's words) a '*letterbox*' company. **8.92**

The rationale for the presumption in the case of a legal person that a debtor's COMI will be found in the place of its registered office is that the registered office 'normally corresponds to the debtor's head office'.[131] It follows that any inquiry as to whether the COMI is in fact located in a Member State other than that in which the registered office is located, must centre on whether or not the head office functions of the debtor are carried out in that other state. The inquiry is more correctly focused on the question of the location of the place where **8.93**

---

[127] Art 3(1). See also B Wessels, 'The place of the registered office of a company: a cornerstone in the application of the EC Insolvency Regulation' (2006) 3 European Company Law, August 183–90.
[128] [2006] ECR I-3813, [2006] Ch 508.
[129] See also Case C-353/15 *Leonmobili et Leone*, ECLI:EU:C:2016:374.
[130] The CJEU approved and expanded upon this analysis in Case C-396/09 *Interedil Srl v Fallimento Interedil Srl and Intesa Gestione Crediti SpA* [2011] ECR I-9915, [2012] BCC 851, para 51. *Interedil* is discussed in greater detail below.
[131] Virgos-Schmit Report, para 75, last sub-paragraph.

head office functions are carried out than on the location of the head office since, in modern business conditions, the two are not necessarily in the same place. Furthermore, a company in a group of companies may not have its own head office, but its head office functions may be carried on at the group headquarters. It is where the head office functions are carried out that the company conducts the administration of its interests on a regular basis within the approach of Recital (13).

Head office functions test

8.94 In practice, therefore, in the case of legal persons, the place where a debtor administers his interests on a regular basis (and which is therefore ascertainable by third parties) has been equated with the place where the '*head office functions*' of the debtor are carried out.[132] The head office functions test has been adopted and followed in the case law. In particular, the head office functions test was adopted (at least implicitly) by the CJEU in *Interedil*:[133]

> 50. … where the bodies responsible for the management and supervision of a company are located in the same place as its registered office and the management decisions that the company are taken, in a manner that is ascertainable by third parties, in that place, the presumption … that the centre of the company's main interests is located in that place is wholly applicable.

This 'presumption' may be rebutted if 'from the viewpoint of third parties, the place in which a company's central administration is located is not the same as that of its registered office'.[134] The factors to be taken into account include the places where the debtor pursues economic activities and the places where the debtor's assets are situated, insofar as those places are ascertainable by third parties (although the matter must be determined in light of the individual circumstances of each case).[135] Ultimately, however, it is the 'company's actual centre of management and supervision and of the management of its interests' which is the crucial criterion.[136] It is suggested that this is simply a statement of the head office functions test.

8.95 In *Re Videology*[137] the English Court stated, having referred to the preceding paragraphs of the text in the previous edition of this work, that it did not consider that the decisions in *Eurofood* and *Interedil* focused attention narrowly on the question of the location of the place of the centre of management and supervision.[138] The Court further considered that a head office functions test involved functions beyond the functions of the directors and senior management in deciding policy for the company.[139] It is respectfully suggested that this is correct, and that the test is not confined to the place where the directors and senior

---

[132] Professor Wessels has criticized the head office functions approach and, instead, has advocated a 'contact with creditors' approach, as better reflecting the description of COMI given in Recital (13): see B Wessels, *International Insolvency Law* (2006) para 10597, and B Wessels, 'The place of the registered office of a company: a cornerstone in the application of the EC Insolvency Regulation' (2006) 3 European Company Law, August, 183–90.
[133] Case C-396/09 *Interedil Srl v Fallimento Interedil Srl and Intesa Gestione Crediti SpA* [2011] ECR I-9915, [2012] BCC 851.
[134] ibid at para 51.
[135] ibid at para 52.
[136] ibid at para 53.
[137] [2019] BCC 195. A case concerning the Cross-Border Insolvency Regulations 2006 and the UNCITRAL Model Law, but the Court held that the same principles applied to the question of COMI.
[138] ibid at para 42.
[139] ibid at para 47.

As to the earlier cases, in *Re BRAC Rent-A-Car International Inc*[140] the English High Court **8.96** held that it had jurisdiction to make an administration order in respect of a company incorporated in the United States on the grounds that its COMI was in England and Wales. In particular, the court found on the evidence that the COMI of the company was in England since, although its registered office was in the United States, it had never traded there and its operations were concluded almost entirely in the United Kingdom. The company traded from an address in England and had for a long time been registered under the Companies Acts as an oversea company. It had no employees in the United States, with virtually all its employees working in England, under contracts of employment governed by English law.[141]

Re Daisytek-ISA Ltd[142] concerned an English incorporated company which was a subsid- **8.97** iary of a United States company which had gone into Chapter 11 proceedings. The English company itself had subsidiaries incorporated in Germany and France. The English High Court made administration orders in respect of the European subsidiaries on the basis that their COMIs were in England, principally on the basis that their activities were coordinated from the head office in Bradford. The court also placed reliance on the fact that it appeared that a large majority of creditors knew (by virtue of the fact that the funding was supplied by the factoring agreement with the subsidiary of a United Kingdom bank and the fact that 70 per cent of purchase contracts were dealt with from Bradford) that Bradford was where many important functions of the German companies were carried out. Similar reasoning was applied in relation to the French company.

The head office functions test has been followed in various other cases both in England[143] **8.98** and in other EU states including France,[144] Germany,[145] and Hungary,[146] and was also endorsed by the Advocate General in *Eurofood*[147] in referring to the arguments put forward on behalf the Italian administrator and the Italian Government:

---

[140] [2003] 2 All ER 201, [2003] 1 WLR 1421.
[141] It should be noted that in one respect the reasoning in the *BRAC* decision was erroneous. The judge held that the OR itself had brought about an extension of the jurisdiction of the English court to make an administration order to any company whose COMI was in the UK. In fact, under the OR, the conditions for the opening of proceedings are left to the law of the relevant Member State (Art 4(2)(f) OR) and, accordingly, the provisions of the Insolvency Act 1986 had been amended to empower the English court to make an administration order over a company whose COMI is within the UK (see now Insolvency Act 1986, Sch B1, para 111(1A)). This analysis was adopted in *Re The Salvage Association* [2003] BCC 504.
[142] [2004] BPIR 30.
[143] *Re Energy Group Overseas BV and Energy Group Holdings BV* (20 November 2003), no judgment given; *Re Aim Underwriting Agencies (Ireland) Ltd* [2004] EWHC 2114 (Ch); *Re Ci4net.com Inc* [2005] BCC 277; *Re TXU German Finance BV* [2005] BPIR 209; *Re Collins & Aikman* [2006] BCC 606; *Re Damovo Group SA* (25 April 2007), no written judgment given but noted in European Cross-Border Insolvency at 4.46; *Re Lennox Holdings Plc* [2009] BCC 155.
[144] *Re MPOTEC GmbH* [2006] BCC 681, Tribunal de Commerce de Nanterre; *Re Energotech Sarl*, Tribunal de Grande Instance de Lure, 29 March 2006; *Re ISA Daisytek SAS* [2006] BCC 841, Cour de Cassation; *Re Eurotunnel Finance Ltd* (Paris Commercial Court, 2 August 2006) application to set aside dismissed on 15 January 2007 and appeal from refusal to set aside dismissed 29 November 2007.
[145] *Re Hettlage-Austria* (Amtsgericht, Munich, 4 May 2004). See <https://www.insol-europe.org/technical-content/european-insolvency-regulation>.
[146] *Re Parmalat Slovakia* (Municipal Court of Fejer/Székesfehérvár, 14 June 2004).
[147] Case C-341/04 *Eurofood IFSC Ltd* [2005] BCC 1021, paras 111–12. This passage was cited and applied in *Re Lennox Holdings Plc* [2009] BCC 155. See also Paulus, 'A Vision of the European Insolvency Law' (2008) 17 Norton Journal of Bankruptcy Law and Practice 607, 610.

111. Those two parties rely principally on the Virgós-Schmit Report, para.75, which states: 'Where companies and legal persons are concerned, the Convention presumes, unless proved to the contrary, that the debtor's centre of main interests is the place of his registered office. This place normally corresponds to the debtor's head office.' (Balz puts it in somewhat different terms: 'In the case of a mere mailbox registration, the headquarters will be treated as the centre of main interests' (p 504).)

Dr Bondi and the Italian Government submit that if it is to be demonstrated that the centre of main interests is somewhere other than the State where a company's registered office is located, it consequently needs to be shown that the 'head office' type of functions are performed elsewhere. The focus must be on the head office functions rather than simply on the location of the head office because a 'head office' can be just as nominal as a registered office if head office functions are not carried out there. In transnational business the registered office is often chosen for tax or regulatory reasons and has no real connection with the place where head office functions are actually carried out. That is particularly so in the case of groups of companies, where the head office functions for the subsidiary are often carried out at the place where the head office functions of the parent of the group are carried out.

112. I find those submissions sensible and convincing...

8.99 In *Re MPOTEC GmbH*[148] the Tribunal de Commerce of Nanterre noted that the courts of Member States had applied the concept of 'headquarters functions' in determining COMI and considered that, in the context of a group of companies, the concept of 'head-office functions' should be used to determine the location of the company's COMI.

8.100 In *Eurotunnel*[149] the Paris Tribunal de Commerce adopted a similar approach which focused on the fact that the strategic and operational management of the companies was run by a single committee based in Paris and that the financial management was also carried out there.

8.101 The CJEU has held that the mere fact that two companies use intermingled bank accounts (or transfer assets between each other without consideration) does not entail that the companies have the same COMI. Such facts may be difficult to ascertain by third parties, and have no direct relevance to the determination of COMI.[150]

Groups of companies

8.102 One of the notable aspects of the OR was that it did not deal with the position of groups consisting of a number of related companies.[151] Under the OR it would be possible to open

---

[148] *Re MPOTEC GmbH* [2006] BCC 681, Tribunal de Commerce de Nanterre.
[149] 2 August 2006.
[150] See Case C-191/10 *Rastelli Davide e C. Snc v Hidoux* [2011] ECR I-13209, [2013] 1 BCLC 329, paras 38–39. Under French law such confusion of assets can give the French court, which is conducting one set of insolvency proceedings over one debtor, jurisdiction to open insolvency proceedings in respect of another debtor. However, as this case decides, this domestic law French doctrine does not give the French court international jurisdiction within the OR to open the second proceedings if the COMI or an establishment is not located in France.
[151] See Virgos-Schmit Report, para 76. See generally G Moss, 'Group Insolvency—Choice of Forum and Law: the European Experience under the Influence of English Pragmatism' (2007) 32 Brooklyn Journal of International Law 1005; G Moss, 'Group Insolvency—Forum—EC Regulation and Model Law Under The Influence of English Pragmatism Revisited' (2014) 9(1) Brooklyn Journal of Corporate, Financial & Commercial Law 250.

main insolvency proceedings in relation to each individual company and there are no provisions in the OR which provide for any degree of co-operation between the different proceedings.¹⁵² Nor is there any express provision similar to the US concept of 'substantive consolidation', which sometimes enables separate corporate entities to be treated as one. Thus, in *Rastelli Davide*,¹⁵³ the CJEU considered a rule of French insolvency law, which enables two or more companies to be joined to a single insolvency proceeding where their assets have become 'intermixed'. The CJEU held that the COMI of each legal entity must be determined on an individual basis, notwithstanding any rule of domestic law which provides for consolidation in the event of insolvency.¹⁵⁴

8.103 The CJEU in *Eurofood* emphasized that in the case of groups of companies it is necessary to examine the location of each company's COMI individually and that there can be no automatic assumption that the location of a subsidiary's COMI will be the same as that of its parent. Nevertheless, it may well be the case that this inquiry leads to the conclusion that the location of each company's COMI is in fact in the same place, by virtue of the head office functions test in *Interedil*.¹⁵⁵ In many corporate structures, the head office functions for the entire group, consisting of the parent company and its subsidiaries, may be carried out from a single group head office. Applying *Interedil*, the COMI of each of the group companies may well be located at that head office. This was the conclusion reached by the English court in *Re Daisytek-ISA Ltd* (see above at para 8.97), *Re Crisscross Telecommunications Group*,¹⁵⁶ *Re Collins & Aikman*,¹⁵⁷ *Re MG Rover*,¹⁵⁸ and by the French courts in *Re MPOTEC GmbH*, *Re Energotech*, and *Eurotunnel* (the citations for each of which appear in note 144 above).

8.104 The practical advantage of such a conclusion is that, subject to the possibility of secondary proceedings, the insolvent group of companies may be subject to a de facto single set of insolvency proceedings with common office-holders in place. The benefits of this in terms of the efficient running of the proceedings and maximizing returns for creditors are obvious. Strictly, such considerations are not themselves factors relevant to the determination by the court of the location of the companies' COMIs, though there is suggestion in the French cases in particular that they have influenced the approach adopted.¹⁵⁹ In any event, it is suggested that the CJEU's implicit approval of the head office functions test in *Interedil* should be welcomed, and is likely to lead to sensible results for groups of companies.

8.105 It should, however, be noted that in a case 'where the estate of the debtor is too complex to administer as a unit or where differences in the legal systems concerned are so great that difficulties may arise from the extension of effects deriving from the law of the state of the opening to the other states where the assets are located', the liquidator in the main

---

¹⁵² In English law based jurisdictions co-operation is often ensured by having the same insolvency practitioners, or insolvency practitioners from the same major firm of accountants, appointed as liquidators in the separate insolvency proceedings for different companies in the same group.
¹⁵³ Case C-191/10 *Rastelli Davide e C. Snc v Hidoux* [2011] ECR I-13209, [2013] 1 BCLC 329.
¹⁵⁴ ibid at para 29.
¹⁵⁵ Case C-396/09 *Interedil Srl v Fallimento Interedil Srl and Intesa Gestione Crediti SpA* [2011] ECR I-9915, [2012] BCC 851.
¹⁵⁶ (20 May 2003), Rimer J.
¹⁵⁷ [2006] BCC 606.
¹⁵⁸ [2005] EWHC 874 (Ch).
¹⁵⁹ See in particular the *MPOTEC* and *Eurotunnel* decisions cited above, and subsequently, *Sobieski sp z oo* (a Polish registered company which is part of the French Belvedere SA group) (Tribunal de Commerce of Beaune, 16 July 2008).

proceedings may request the opening of secondary proceedings 'when the efficient administration of the estate so requires' (Recital (19)). This Recital may provide grounds to request the opening of secondary proceedings for, for example, a wholly owned subsidiary in another state, when the financial and commercial administration, the IT-platform, etc are shared with the debtor.

8.106 It is noteworthy that domestic courts often attempt to administer multinational enterprise failures by including in the same insolvency proceedings both the parent and the subsidiaries. Besides the above-mentioned *ISA-Daisytek* case, there are several other cases involving multinational enterprise failures, in which the insolvency process significantly involved the whole enterprise, regardless of the circumstance that the different subsidiaries' COMIs were located in different countries.[160] The presumption established by Article 3(2) was not plainly and regularly respected by domestic courts before the CJEU rendered the *Eurofood* decision. From this standpoint, as one scholar has recently argued 'the adjudication of transnational bankruptcy proceedings increasingly resembles a race against time in which creditors and debtors rush to choose the most favourable forum and courts compete to adjudicate the case'.[161] In fact, 'with billions of dollars at stake for bankruptcy professionals competing courts cannot be counted on to determine fairly and in good faith whether they are the home court of multinationals'.[162] This problem affects also the European context. In fact, '*Eurofood* indicated the actual status of the EC Regulation: that the lacunae of its regulatory framework run so deep that future insolvency proceedings in Europe would scarcely be efficient'.[163]

The presumption under the UNCITRAL Model Law

8.107 The presumption that COMI is located in the place of the registered office has also been adopted by the UNCITRAL Model Law on Cross-Border Insolvency, which has been enacted with different modifications in several countries. The presumption has been discussed in several decided cases in the United States, where the Model Law was enacted, with significant variations, as Chapter 15 of the US Bankruptcy Code. The US courts have given the presumption little weight and if there is *any* evidence before the court that the COMI may be elsewhere they will require proof that COMI is in the place of the registered office, even in an unopposed case.[164] The English Courts have however taken the approach that the meaning and approach to COMI under both the Model Law and the OR/RR should be the same.[165]

Natural persons

8.108 The use of the term 'interests' is intended to encompass a wide spread of activities extending beyond commercial, industrial, and professional activities to the general economic

---

[160] See in particular Tribunal of Rome, 26 November 2004, *Cirio Finance Luxembourg SA*, 2004 Foro it. 1567 (in Italian); Tribunal of Parma, 20 February 2004, *Eurofood IFSC Ltd*, ibid.
[161] M M Winkler, 'From Whipped Cream to Multibillion Euro Financial Collapse: The European Regulation on Translation Insolvency in Action' (2008) 26 Berkeley Journal of International Law 352, 369.
[162] L LoPucki, *Courting Failure: How Competition for Big Cases is Corrupting the Bankruptcy Courts* (2005) 209.
[163] Winkler (n 161 above) 369.
[164] *In Re Bear Stearns High-Grade Structured Credit Strategies Master Fund* 389 BR 325 (SDNY 2008) (US District Court of New York, 22 May 2008) (Chapter 15 case No 07-12383, Sweet DJ).
[165] *Re Videology* [2019] BCC 195.

activities of private individuals.¹⁶⁶ The concept of a debtor's COMI therefore applies equally to private individuals who do not carry on business as it does to corporate entities engaged in trade.

8.109 The COMI for natural persons will generally be their place of habitual residence.[167] In the case of 'professionals', however, it will be the place of their professional domicile.[168] This suggests that the centre of main interests is linked to the type of activity from which the insolvency or need for rescue/reconstruction arises. Thus, where an individual is carrying on business activities and it is the business that is at the root of the insolvency or need for rescue/restructuring, the centre of main interests may well be in the place of business rather than the place of habitual residence (if different).[169]

8.110 In a case where a natural person has their place of habitual residence and their sole immovable asset in different Member States, then the presumption that the COMI is in the place of habitual residence will not be rebutted solely because the only immovable property of that person is in a different Member State.[170]

8.111 Work done by a natural person on behalf of a legal person constitutes the carrying on of the business of the legal person and does not go towards establishing the place of COMI of the natural person.[171] Nor are the 'interests' of the legal person to be confused with the interests of the natural person, even if the natural person is a director or controller of the legal person.[172] 'Habitual residence' in this context must be distinguished from 'ordinary residence', as explained in *Re Stojevic*:[173]

> 59. The two concepts, habitual residence and ordinary residence, are very different and must not be confused. The difference is easier to ascertain, than it is to explain. Essentially, however, a man's habitual residence is his settled, permanent home, the place where he lives with his wife and family, until, in the case of the younger members of the family, they grow up and leave home, the place to which he returns from business trips elsewhere or abroad. A man's ordinary residence is a place where he lives, which is not his settled, permanent

---

[166] Virgos-Schmit Report, para 75.
[167] ibid para 75 fourth sub-paragraph; *Re Stojevic* [2007] BPIR 141, HCJ.
[168] Virgos-Schmit Report, para 75.
[169] Cited with approval in *Re Stojevic* [2007] BPIR 141, HCJ. This point is also the correct explanation of the decision of *Vennink v Fortis Bank* (Dutch Supreme Court, 9 January 2004): Vennink's centre of main interests was held to be located where he was carrying on business, which was the Netherlands, and not where he habitually resided, which was in Belgium. The English courts have also adopted the same, pragmatic analysis when deciding whether a debtor's COMI should be determined by reference to his personal domestic arrangements (principally linked to Spain) or his professional orientation as a self-proclaimed 'Swiss banker': *Skjevesland v Geveran Trading Co Ltd* [2003] BCC 391 (Jaques R), aff'd [2003] BCC 391 (Ch D, Judge Howarth) (holding that the debtor's COMI was in Switzerland).
[170] Case C-253/19 *MH and NI v OJ and Novo Banco*, a case concerning the RR. See further paragraph 8.562 below.
[171] *Re Stojevic* [2007] BPIR 141, HCJ. The point seems to have been overlooked in *Official Receiver v Eichler* [2007] BPIR 1636, HCJ (German doctor working for company in England. See however the subsequent re-hearing of this case, *Re Eichler (No 2)*, considered immediately above and also below at 8.116). See also *Re Stojevic* (Higher Regional Court, Vienna (Court of Appeal), 9 November 2004) 28 R 225/04w. A dictum to the contrary by Lewison J in *Cross Construction Sussex Ltd v Tseliki* [2006] BPIR 888, appears to have been given without the learned judge's attention being drawn to the Virgos-Schmit Report, in particular para 75. See also *Re Stojevic* (Higher Regional Court (Court of Appeal) of Vienna, 9 November 2004) 28 R 225/04w, making the same point in relation to 'establishment'.
[172] *Re Stojevic* [2007] BPIR 141, HCJ paras 56–57 (Croatian debtor with habitual residence in Austria controlled companies in the UK).
[173] [2007] BPIR 141, HCJ.

home, the place where he lives, when away from home on business or on holiday with his wife and family. Depending on the nature of his work, a man may well live away from his settled, permanent home for a greater number of days in any given year than he spends there with his wife and family.

8.112 Where a debtor resides in one Member State but is imprisoned in another, his COMI does not simply by reason of such imprisonment move to the second Member State.[174] In this case, the debtor had kept this residence in Luxembourg during the time he was kept in custody in Germany. Hence, there was not even a shadow of a doubt that the COMI of this individual was in Luxembourg and not in Germany. Consequently, this decision clarifies that the residence is a very strong criterion to define the COMI of an individual; that this criterion is very hard to overrule and, in particular, that it is not sufficient to be in custody to effectively establish a new residence and therefore, a new COMI.

8.113 The fact that the debtors' activities are illegal does not appear to affect the COMI.[175]

Right to move COMI and 'forum shopping'

8.114 It has been held by the Court of Appeal in England that a debtor has a right to move his COMI, even in a case where he is trying to remove himself from the Member State where he has incurred the debt and where his creditors are located.[176]

8.115 The courts in England have not, thus far, drawn a clear distinction between 'good' forum shopping (usually by a legal person) which occurs where a debtor moves COMI to benefit creditors and 'bad' forum shopping (usually by a natural person) where the debtor moves COMI to escape creditors. Advocate General Colomer has pointed out in his Opinions in *Staubitz-Schreiber*[177] and *Seagon v Deko Marty Belgium* (also known as *Frick Teppichboden*)[178] that EU law combats opportunistic and fraudulent choices of jurisdiction and not 'forum shopping' per se.

8.116 However, the English courts have also scrutinized bankruptcy (individual insolvency) petitions involving apparent COMI shopping with care. In *Re Eichler (No 2)*,[179] Chief Registrar Baister said:

> 190. This is one of a number of cases in which the courts have annulled bankruptcy orders made on petitions presented by German debtors where it has been established that the court had no jurisdiction to open the proceedings. The scope of the inquiries the court can make when faced with a debtor's bankruptcy petition and doubts about the truth of what a debtor says about where his centre of main interests is situated is limited, not least of all because there is an understandable reluctance to depart from the long established principle

---

[174] German Federal Court of Justice (Bundesgerichtshof), 8 November 2007, NZI 2008, 121.
[175] See *Re Tricontinental Exchange Ltd* 2006 WL 2671336, 349 BR 627 (Bankr ED Cal 2006) where the debtor was recognized under Chapter 15 of the US Bankruptcy Code (the US Enactment of the UNCITRAL Model Law) as having its COMI in St Vincent and the Grenadines, even though the insurance business run from there was unauthorized and illegal.
[176] *Shierson v Vlieland-Boddy* [2006] 2 BCLC 9, CA (UK debtor moved to Spain). See also *Official Receiver v Eichler* [2007] BPIR 1636, HCJ (German doctor with creditors in Germany moved to UK).
[177] C-1/04 [2006] ECR I-701, paras 7–77.
[178] C-339/07 [2009] ECR I-767, at para 49.
[179] [2011] BPIR 1293.

that evidence given on oath (or nowadays in a witness statement verified by a statement of truth) should not be disbelieved unless it is properly challenged or is inherently incredible.

191. In the light of persistent abuse of its jurisdiction, however, this court has now developed two practices when dealing with petitions where it has doubts about its jurisdiction. Before a bankruptcy order is made, a debtor may be required to file more detailed evidence than is required by rr 6.38 and 6.41 of the Insolvency Rules in order to establish that his centre of main interests really is in this country, exhibiting documentary evidence in support of his claim that it is situated here; and/or the court may adjourn the petition and require that notice of the hearing be given to the debtor's creditors so that they can appear and make representations at that stage in opposition to the making of the order instead of having to apply after the order has been made. It is hoped that in future those steps (and perhaps others which may develop in the future) will ensure that bankruptcy orders founded on sham claims as to jurisdiction or supported by a false statement of affairs are not made in the future.

8.117 A debtor may choose to move COMI in order to take advantage of more favourable restructuring laws which exist in a particular Member State.[180] Despite Recital (4) OR, which mentions the policy against 'forum shopping', there is nothing objectionable in principle with this if it is done with a view to benefiting creditors and not to prejudice them.[181] The ability to move COMI is also consistent with the principle of freedom of establishment within the EU.

8.118 To be successful, any movement of COMI must have sufficient substance to be credible and must also satisfy the requirements of Recital (13) that the COMI be the place where the debtor conducts the administration of his interests on a 'regular basis' and is therefore ascertainable by third parties. In *Official Receiver v Eichler*,[182] where a German doctor with German creditors had moved to the United Kingdom, it was said that while there was no minimum period of presence laid down in order to establish a move of COMI to another Member State, 'Common sense would seem to indicate that a few days (or even a few weeks) would be unlikely to suffice because that would be at odds with conducting the administration of one's interests in a place "on a regular basis…".'

8.119 Accordingly, the cases appear to emphasize that while COMI may be transferred, it nonetheless requires an 'element of permanence', as stated in *Re Ci4net.com Inc*.[183] In that case, the fact that the director of a company moved around frequently was not capable of moving the company's COMI. The court in *Shierson v Vlieland-Boddy*,[184] while recognizing the right of debtors to move their interests around the EU, applied the 'element of permanence' test to determine COMI and added that the court had a duty to scrutinize carefully situations where it appeared the move had been made with impending insolvency in mind.

---

[180] See A Marshall and C Pardiwala, 'Changing COMI Prior to Insolvency is Fair Game!' (2007) 4 International Corporate Rescue 318. This appears to have occurred in *PIN Group SA* (Amtsgericht Köln, 19 February) (73 IE 1-08), where there was a move of COMI to Germany from Luxembourg.
[181] This approach is accepted under the RR.
[182] [2007] BPIR 1636, HCJ.
[183] [2004] EWHC 1941, [2005] BCC 277.
[184] [2006] 2 BCLC 9, CA.

8.120 Where a debtor moves COMI, prior to any request for an opening in the original place of COMI, to another Member State, in order to avoid the original jurisdiction, the courts in England so far have failed to regard COMI as continuing in the original Member State and have accepted the move: *Shierson v Vlieland-Boddy*.[185] In the first edition of this work at paragraph 8.44 it was suggested that the OR could be interpreted in such a way as to treat a debtor who leaves his COMI to avoid his creditors as retaining the COMI, by analogy to the English law principle that a debtor who carries on business in England is treated as continuing that business until he has made arrangements to pay his debts.[186] In the case of a move of COMI within the EU, as in the *Shierson* case, this suggestion is complicated by the principle of freedom of establishment within the EU.

8.121 A similar issue arises where a debtor seeks to move its COMI outside the EU in order to avoid the commencement of insolvency proceedings in any Member State and to prejudice creditors in the EU. However, in such a case, there is no question of freedom of establishment within the EU and a more acute tension arises between the principle that COMI falls to be assessed as at the date of the opening of the proceedings with the need to prevent abuse of the OR by debtors. Where it can be shown that the steps to move COMI outside the EU are plainly abusive and for the purpose of avoiding insolvency proceedings under the OR, such steps should arguably be ignored.[187]

Terminated activities

8.122 What is the correct approach where the debtor has not moved COMI but has simply terminated its activities? Here again, it would seem to make sense to regard those activities as continuing for the purpose of assessing COMI.[188] This conclusion is consistent with the CJEU's analysis in *Interedil*,[189] in which the debtor company had ceased all economic activity (and, indeed, had been formally dissolved). The CJEU held that it was 'logical' to focus on the last COMI which the debtor had before being dissolved.[190]

Risk of conflicting decisions

8.123 Basing the jurisdiction to commence main proceedings on the concept of COMI is said to be beneficial to creditors since it is said to be easily ascertainable by them and therefore enables creditors to identify easily the Member State in which main proceedings would be commenced against a debtor.[191] It is possible that the courts of the various individual Member States might take different views on the application of the concept to the facts of a particular case. However, conflicting decisions in the same case should not occur because

---

[185] ibid.
[186] *Re A Debtor (No 784 of 1991)* [1992] Ch 554; *Re Theophile* [1950] AC 186, HL.
[187] Cf *Hans Brochier Holdings Ltd v Exner* [2006] EWHC 2594 (Ch), [2007] BCC 127, at para 8.372 below, and in ch 3 above at n 30. See also the discussion below under the heading 'Statutory Changes in England'.
[188] See Dr Andrea Csöke, *A Határon Átnyúló Fizetésképtelenségi Eljárások* (Cross-Frontier Insolvency Proceedings) (HVG-Orac, Budapest, 2008) 75.
[189] Case C-396/09 *Interedil Srl v Fallimento Interedil Srl and Intesa Gestione Crediti SpA* [2011] ECR I-9915, [2012] BCC 851.
[190] ibid at para 58. Every debtor has to have a COMI for the OR (or the RR) to be able to work and therefore a practical solution had to be found for cases of terminated activities or even terminated existence. Note however that this approach has not been applied to the concept of 'establishment' (see the commentary above to Art 2(h) OR, presumably because it is not *necessary* for any debtor to have an 'establishment' as defined by the OR: the OR (and RR) can work on the basis of there only being a main proceeding.
[191] Virgos-Schmit Report, para 75.

any finding by the court which deals with the matter first should be respected by any subsequent court.¹⁹² As the CJEU said in *Burgo Group*:¹⁹³

> 28. ... the decision taken by the court of a Member State to open main proceedings in respect of a debtor company, and the finding, at least by implication, that the centre of the debtor company's main interests is situated in that Member State, cannot, in principle, be called into question by the courts of the other Member States.

8.124 In particular, under Article 16 of the OR the judgment of the court opening proceedings is to be recognized and enforced in other Member States without further formality. This means that it is not possible for this decision to be reviewed in the courts of another Member State except in exceptional circumstances on grounds of public policy. This principle has been respected by the courts of the Member States, an approach which has been fundamental to the proper functioning of the OR. In *MG Probud*, the CJEU emphasized the importance of this principle, which is founded on the concept of mutual trust.¹⁹⁴

8.125 In *Re ISA-Daisytek SAS*¹⁹⁵ the French appellate courts held that they were not entitled to review the decision of the English court opening main insolvency proceedings in relation to a French company which the English court had found had its COMI in England. In *Daisytek* the German courts came to the same result.¹⁹⁶ The same conclusion was also reached by the French courts in *Re Rover France SAS*,¹⁹⁷ again concerning a French company which had been placed into administration in England. The French court held that it was obliged to recognize the decision of the English court opening proceedings and, in particular, that it was not open to the French court to refuse recognition on grounds of public policy under Article 26 of the OR. The Versailles Court of Appeal did point out that the judge in England had examined its jurisdiction by applying the relevant criterion, and stated that the English court had thus fulfilled the condition necessary for recognition. There may be a hint in the judgment that if the English court had not examined its jurisdiction or if it had not applied the relevant criterion, recognition may not have been forthcoming.

8.126 In *Eurofood* the CJEU held that on the proper interpretation of the first sentence of Article 16(1) OR, the main insolvency proceedings opened by a court of a Member State had to be recognized by the courts of the other Member States without those courts being able to review the jurisdiction of the court of the opening state. Both the Advocate General and the CJEU also referred to the narrow scope of the public policy exception in Article 26 OR. The CJEU held that, on the proper interpretation of Article 26, a Member State could refuse to recognize insolvency proceedings opened in another Member State where the decision to open the proceedings had been taken in flagrant breach of the fundamental right to be heard which a person concerned by such proceedings enjoyed. However, short of such a

---

¹⁹² Recital (22).
¹⁹³ Case 327/13 *Burgo Group SpA v Illochroma SA* [2015] 1 WLR 1046.
¹⁹⁴ Case C-444/07 *MG Probud Gdynia sp z oo* [2010] ECR I-417, [2010] BCC 453, paras 27–29. See also *Re Eurodis Electron plc* [2012] BCC 57, para 17 and Case 327/13 *Burgo Group SpA v Illochroma SA* [2015] 1 WLR 1046.
¹⁹⁵ [2003] BCC 984 (Court of Appeal of Versailles, 4 September 2003) and [2006] BCC 841 (Cour de Cassation, 27 June 2006).
¹⁹⁶ *Re ISA-Daisytek Deutschland GmbH* (Higher Regional Court of Dusseldorf, 9 July 2004).
¹⁹⁷ Commercial Court of Nanterre, 19 May 2005; Court of Appeal of Versailles, 15 December 2005.

manifest breach of the principles of natural justice, Article 26 will not be applicable and the decision of the court opening the proceedings will fall to be recognized.

8.127 Accordingly, the remedy for any person who is concerned that a court of a Member State may have mistakenly opened insolvency proceedings is to pursue the matter in accordance with the procedure for appeal and review under the law of that Member State with the ultimate possibility of a reference to the CJEU. Absent some serious irregularity which falls within the narrow scope of Article 26, the courts of other Member States will be bound to recognize the decision without review.

8.128 In the previous edition of this work, it was suggested by Professor Fletcher that it was unfortunate that the OR made no provision to enable conflicts between courts in different Member States regarding questions of jurisdictional competence to be resolved in an orderly and cost-efficient manner while proceedings are still at a relatively early stage, in contrast to the approach of the Brussels Convention (now Judgments Regulation 1215/2012) on jurisdiction and recognition of judgments,[198] where Articles 29–32 lay down a set of rules, some mandatory and others discretionary, which apply when proceedings involving the same cause of action, or related actions, are brought in the courts of different Member States. It was submitted that there was a strong case for amendment of the OR to be made, designed by analogy with Article 29 of Regulation 1215/2012, whereby a doctrine of *lis pendens* could be imposed to prevent any court other than 'the court first seised' from exercising jurisdiction to open insolvency proceedings until such time as the jurisdiction of the court first seised of an application for the opening of insolvency proceedings is established. For this purpose, the presentation of a petition for a winding-up by the court, combined with an application for the appointment of a provisional liquidator, could be regarded as a step whereby the court in question becomes 'seised' of the matter. It would be essential to include a provision requiring the court first seised to make the determination as to its own jurisdictional competence at the earliest possible time, and in fidelity to the principle of mutual trust mentioned in Recital (22), given the special factors of urgency that are attendant upon cases of insolvency. There is a powerful need for national courts to be scrupulous and conscientious in approaching their exercise of jurisdiction, mindful of the impact of their decisions in an EU-wide dimension. The principle of 'mutual trust', alluded to in Recital (22), is fundamental to ensuring that the OR operates in a way which is fair, and lacking in oppressive side-effects. The provision in Article 57 RR for cooperation between courts could furnish a platform for the resolution of conflicts of jurisdiction, provided that timely initiatives are taken by those concerned.

8.129 Paragraph 79 of the Virgos-Schmit Report discusses the problem where two Member States claim concurrent jurisdiction. Of interest, it is suggested that the courts will be able to take account of, among others, the general principles of procedural law which are valid in all Member States, including those derived from other Community Conventions, including the Brussels Convention (now Brussels Regulation). The CJEU in *Re Eurofood IFSC Ltd*[199] referred to *Erich Gasser v Misat Srl*[200] but did not take the opportunity to import the 'court first seised' doctrine.

---

[198] See also B Wessels, 'Mutual, Comity and Respect among States in International Insolvency Matters' in *Norton Annual Survey of Bankruptcy Law* (2005) 569–86.
[199] [2006] Ch 508.
[200] Case C-116/02 [2005] QB 1, [2003] ECR I-14693.

The intention of the OR was that the 'first court seised' doctrine should be imported **8.130**
into the OR,[201] as part of '... the general principles of procedural law which are valid in
all...'[202] Member States but the implications of para 79(3) of the Virgos-Schmit Report
were overlooked by the CJEU in *Eurofood*. If the foreign debtor was included in the insolvency proceedings already opened abroad, the domestic administrative authority
has no power to retain jurisdiction—unless the *ordre public* (public policy) exception
to recognition operates—and must therefore decline its jurisdiction in favour of the foreign judge, even if the latter was wrong in assessing the debtor's COMI.[203] This in turn
involves the already mentioned problem of courts competing to deal with large insolvency cases.

If the 'judgment opening proceedings' does not make clear that it constitutes main proceedings and does not deal with the basis on which the court has determined it has jurisdiction **8.131**
to open main proceedings (for example there is no judicial determination concerning the
location of the debtor's COMI), then query whether the court of another Member State
would be free to determine that the debtor's COMI is in its own jurisdiction and that it is
therefore free to open main proceedings (this might be possible if the first judgment could
be said to constitute the opening of territorial proceedings, such that opening of the subsequent proceedings as main proceedings does not infringe the obligation to recognize the
judgment of the first court under Article 16). Similarly, if the determination of the court's
jurisdiction has been made without a proper *inter partes* hearing (the location of the debtor's
COMI might be controversial), then query whether this would allow a court in another
Member State to rely on Article 26 OR to refuse to give recognition to that judgment and to
allow it to open its own main proceedings. This could be an issue in relation to English out
of court appointments, although the ability to apply to set aside the appointment before the
English court is likely to be a relevant factor against the availability of Article 26 OR in such
circumstances.

The time at which COMI is assessed

The terms of the OR contrast the 'opening' of insolvency proceedings with a 'request' for the **8.132**
opening of insolvency proceedings. Under Article 3(1), jurisdiction to open main proceedings is conferred on the courts of the Member State where the debtor's COMI is situated.
The location of COMI is however to be assessed as at the time of the request for the opening
of the proceedings.[204]

In *Staubitz-Schreiber*,[205] the debtor had moved her COMI, which was in Germany at the **8.133**
time of her request to open proceedings, to Spain, prior to any opening. The CJEU held

---

[201] See Virgos-Schmit Report at para 79(3) and VG at para 70 on p 52, where the point is explained in detail.
[202] Virgos-Schmit Report at para 79(3).
[203] Council of State (Cons Stato), 6th Session, 25 January 2007, No 267/2006, para 4.3 (published only in Italian in 21 Diritto del Commercio Internazionale 513 (2007) para 18, 18b).
[204] Case C-396/09 *Interedil Srl v Fallimento Interedil Srl and Intesa Gestione Crediti* SpA [2011] ECR-I 9915, [2012] BCC 851, para 55. (Case C-396/09) [2012] BCC 851, following Case C-1/04 *Staubitz-Schreiber* [2006] ECR I-701, [2006] BCC 639, para 29. In *Shierson v Vlieland-Boddy* the English Court of Appeal had held that the time at which the location of the COMI was to be determined was the time at which at the judgment opening the proceedings would become effective (see Art 2(f) OR). This case can no longer be relied on in respect of the relevant time for judging COMI.
[205] Case C-1/04 [2006] ECR I-701, [2006] BCC 639.

that this did not deprive the German courts of jurisdiction.[206] It would have been contrary to the objectives of the OR to allow a debtor to move jurisdiction after a request to open insolvency proceedings had been issued but prior to the determination of that request by the court. It would have encouraged debtors to move to more favourable jurisdictions and would have involved creditors in the time and expense of having to chase after debtors.

8.134 In principle, this means that it is open to a debtor to move its COMI and alter the place where there is jurisdiction to open main proceedings prior to the filing of the request for the opening of proceedings: see paragraphs 8.114 et seq above.

8.135 The ruling in *Staubitz-Schreiber* was applied by the Court of Appeal in Paris in *Tendance Edition Ltd v L'URSSAF de Paris*.[207] In that case the English registered company had its 'seat' in Paris and was enrolled in the commercial register in Paris at the time of the request to open proceedings made by the creditor. Prior to the opening, the debtor company moved its seat to England. It was held that the French courts retained jurisdiction.

8.136 In *Interedil*,[208] the CJEU confirmed the reasoning in *Staubitz-Schreiber*:

> 55. … The court has held that, where the centre of a debtor's main interests is transferred after the lodging of a request to open insolvency proceedings, but before the proceedings are opened, the courts of the member state within the territory of which the centre of main interests was situated at the time when the request was lodged retain jurisdiction to rule on those proceedings: In re Staubitz-Schreiber (Case C-1/04) [2006] ECR I-701, para 29. It must be inferred from this that, in principle, it is the location of the debtor's main centre of interests at the date on which the request to open insolvency proceedings was lodged that is relevant for the purpose of determining the court having jurisdiction.

Specifying type of proceeding requested

8.137 In England the request for opening and the judgment opening proceedings are required to specify whether main or territorial proceedings are sought to be opened but that is not the case at least in some other Member States. Where the judgment opening does not specify the type of proceeding being opened, it may be open to the courts of other Member States to recognize the proceedings as either main or territorial, depending on the evidence as to the place of COMI.

8.138 It seems that the OR leaves it to the law of the Member State of the forum to decide whether the applicant must specify whether he is applying for main proceedings pursuant to Article 3(1) or territorial proceedings pursuant to Article 3(2). A Swedish appellate court (RH[209] 2006:25) has held that a request for territorial proceedings, in a case where the COMI was in Sweden, had to be rejected. It could not result in the opening of main proceedings, as the court was not allowed to go beyond the applicant's request.

---

[206] This may be referred to as the principle of *perpetuatio fori*: see VG at para 68, p 50 and G Moss, 'Principles of EU Insolvency Law' (2015) 28(3) Insolvency Intelligence 40.
[207] 20 May 2008.
[208] Case C-396/09 *Interedil Srl v Fallimento Interedil Srl and Intesa Gestione Crediti* SpA [2011] ECR-I 9915, [2012] BCC 851, para 55.
[209] 'RH' is an abbreviation of 'Rättsfall från hovrätterna', meaning reports of decisions of Swedish courts of appeal (there are several appellate courts).

Although the OR does not expressly require a court opening insolvency proceedings under **8.139**
the OR to specify whether or not it is opening main or territorial proceedings, it must logically have been the intention of the OR that this should be specified, otherwise creditors and courts in other Member States will have no certainty as to the nature of the proceedings opened. VG is adamant that '... the court must *expressly record* whether it bases its jurisdiction on Articles 3.1 or 3.2.... i.e. it must disclose whether the proceedings in question are main proceedings or territorial proceedings (see Article 21.1) [footnote omitted].' Article 21.1 OR requires the liquidator, when he requests notice of the opening to be published in another Member State, to specify whether his proceedings are main or territorial.

Potential conflict with non-EU jurisdictions

In most non-EU jurisdictions, 'main' or potentially universal proceedings can be opened **8.140**
on the basis of the existence of a registered office, assets or business or, in the United States, even the placing of a relatively small sum in a special account for this purpose. In a case where COMI is held by an EU court to be in the European Union, the OR requires recognition of this proceeding and its liquidator on a mandatory basis. Accordingly, unless one of the exceptions in the OR applies, courts in other Member States must recognize the EU proceeding in preference to any non-EU proceeding.

Evidence required by an English court

One issue which arose concerned the nature and extent of the evidence which was required **8.141**
by an English court when opening insolvency proceedings in respect of a debtor in order to be satisfied that the debtor's centre of main interests is located in England and not in another Member State. Although not set out as an express requirement in the OR, the English court, like any other Member State court, had of its own motion (*ex officio*) to examine the question of its own jurisdiction.[210]

In the case of companies, given the presumption contained in Article 3(1), it was generally **8.142**
sufficient in the first instance to prove that the registered office of the company is in England and to confirm that there are no facts which would tend to rebut the presumption that the COMI is at the same place. In the case of bankruptcy, the onus of proving the location of the debtor's centre of main interests or establishment (as the case may be) was on the petitioning creditor.[211] However, in cases of suspicious forum shopping designed to disadvantage creditors, the English courts would require the debtor to present more detailed evidence than that which would ordinarily be required, and would, if appropriate, adjourn the petition to ensure that all interested creditors can make representations before the court.[212]

However, where a creditor was attempting to persuade an English court to open proceed- **8.143**
ings in respect of a company whose registered office is located outside England on the basis

---

[210] VG para 65.
[211] Cf the old law relating to proof of a debtor's domicile: the onus of proving the debtor's domicile is on the petitioning creditor but prima facie evidence can be adduced so as to throw the burden on the debtor: *Re Mitchell, ex p Cunningham* (1884) 13 QBD 418.
[212] *Re Eichler (No 2)* [2011] BPIR 1293, paras 190–91. This procedure was applied in *O'Donnell v Bank of Ireland* [2012] EWHC 3749 (Ch), a case of Irish bankruptcy tourism in England by Irish property developers, where the allegation of a successful COMI shift from Ireland to the UK was suspicious and was eventually rejected after notification to the principal creditors and a trial with cross-examination of the petitioners.

that the company's COMI is in England, it was obviously necessary to adduce evidence to rebut the presumption arising from the place of its registered office.

8.144 In principle, it was possible to use the out of court procedure to place a company into administration in England, even where the company is incorporated outside England, on grounds that the company's COMI is located in England. (It remains possible to rely on the location of COMI as basis for putting a company into administration.[213]) However, taking this route presents several risks.[214] In particular, since there will have been no judicial determination of the company's COMI, there is a risk that aggrieved creditors might seek to set aside the appointment. This obviously raises issues for the office-holder who cannot be sure that his appointment will be effective. It is suggested that where there is any doubt about the location of a company's COMI the better approach will nearly always be to make an application to the court making full disclosure of all the relevant facts.

Statutory changes in England

8.145 The concept of COMI potentially conflicted with the jurisdictional rules in the Insolvency Act 1986 and, in particular, in relation to individual debtors, with section 265 of the Act. For example, there could be cases where a debtor was domiciled in England in the English law sense, but had no 'establishment' in England and his centre of main interests was located in another Member State. Nevertheless, a literal application of section 265 would allow the English court to make a bankruptcy order against the debtor.[215] As a result, section 265 was amended to avoid any such conflict.[216]

8.146 There is no similar amendment in the case of corporate insolvency. In the case of winding-up by the court, section 221 of the Insolvency Act 1986 creates a general jurisdiction over foreign registered companies. The restrictions on jurisdiction are judge-made and the case law will now have to apply the OR. With regard to voluntary winding-up, section 221(4) contains a general bar on voluntary winding-up for foreign registered companies, but was amended to introduce an exception for cases covered by the OR.[217] In the case of corporate

---

[213] Insolvency Act 1986, Sch B1, para 111(1A).

[214] Cf the problems which arose in *Re Hans Brochier Holdings Ltd* [2006] EWHC 2594 (Ch) [2007] BCC 127. Although the company was incorporated in England, its operations were located in Germany and an attempt to place the company into administration in England by the out of court route was held to be invalid because its COMI was in Germany. In a further decision, the High Court held that the company did not even have an establishment in England. [Those seeking to make an out of court administration appointment should consider carefully whether the company's COMI or establishment is in the UK. If it is not, any appointment will be invalid and the purported appointor may be liable to the administrator under the court's discretion to impose a statutory indemnity for the invalid appointment. Note, also, that if the appointor is the debtor, the ability to commence administration as territorial proceedings prior to the opening of main proceedings elsewhere will be limited under Art 3(4). Therefore, seeking to rely on the existence of an establishment in the UK to justify the appointment at least in the UK may be of no use. It would, however, be possible for the debtor to open administration as *subsequent* territorial proceedings (such proceedings would then have to be secondary proceedings and be limited to winding-up proceedings), provided there was an establishment in the UK. (**AW**)]

[215] See *Henwood v Barlow Clowes International Ltd* [2008] EWCA Civ 577, [2008] All ER (D) 330. Note (by F Toube) in (2008) 21 Insolvency Intelligence 121.

[216] S 265(3) (now repealed post Brexit) was added by reg 14 of the Insolvency Act 1986 (Amendment) (No 2) Regulations 2002, SI 2002/1240: 'This section is subject to Article 3 of the EC Regulation. S.265 has since been further amended following Brexit by Insolvency (Amendment) (EU Exit) Regulations 2019, SI 2019/146. However, the location of the debtor's COMI in England and Wales remains a basis for jurisdiction to make a bankruptcy order post Brexit: see s 265(1)(a).

[217] Insolvency Act 1986 (Amendment) (No 2) Regulations 2002, reg 9. See *Re TXU German Finance BV* [2005] BPIR 209. This remains in place post Brexit.

voluntary arrangements and administration, the former ambiguity as to whether these proceedings were available to foreign registered companies was removed in relation to proceedings covered by the OR.[218]

Scope of insolvency proceedings

Although Article 3(1) provides a rule to determine which Member State is to have jurisdiction to open insolvency proceedings in relation to a debtor, it does not determine the *extent* of that jurisdiction. In particular, there is a question about the scope of insolvency proceedings: does the concept of insolvency proceedings extend to all ancillary actions commenced within the context of an insolvency or is it confined to the core proceeding itself? This question is important because it determines which regime is to provide the jurisdictional rules governing the action: the OR or the Recast Regulation on Civil Jurisdiction and Judgments 1215/2012 (the Judgments Regulation). 8.147

This issue is dealt with by applying the principle that the OR and the Judgments Regulation are complementary so that they do not overlap or leave gaps in their application. The CJEU has endorsed this principle in several cases, including *Nickel & Goeldner*,[219] *F-Tex*,[220] *Wiemer & Trachte*,[221] and *Riel*.[222] Thus, the scope of the OR can be identified by reference to the exceptions to the application of the Judgments Regulation. In this regard, Article 1(2)(b) of the Judgments Regulation provides that the Regulation does not apply to: 'bankruptcy, proceedings relating to the winding up of insolvent companies or other legal persons, judicial arrangements, compositions and analogous proceedings'. 8.148

The CJEU has held that proceedings relating to bankruptcy and winding-up will fall within the scope of this exception if they derive directly from the bankruptcy or winding-up and are closely connected with the insolvency proceedings.[223] 8.149

The CJEU has now dealt with numerous cases concerning the scope of what is now Article 1(2)(b) of the Judgments Regulation and, relatedly, the scope of Article 3(1) of the OR. This appears to be a fertile ground for satellite litigation. In *Seagon*,[224] the CJEU held that a German law avoidance action fell within the OR, and that the German court had jurisdiction over the Belgian corporate defendant against which the avoidance action had been brought. The key factors were (i) that the action was founded on German insolvency law, and (ii) that the German liquidator brought the action in the interests of the general body of creditors of the estate.[225] 8.150

---

[218] Insolvency Act 1986, s 1(4); Insolvency Act 1986, Sch B1, para 111(1A). Both these provisions have been further amended post Brexit.
[219] Case C-157/13 *Nickel & Goeldner Spedition GmbH v 'Kintra' UAB* [2015] QB 96, para 21.
[220] Case C-213/10 *F-Tex SIA v Lietuvos-Anglijos UAB* [2013] Bus LR 232, paras 21, 29, and 48.
[221] Case C-206/17 *Wiemer & Trachte GmbH v Tadzher*.
[222] Case C-47/18 *Skarb Pánstwa Rzeczpospolitej Polskiej—Generalny Dyrektor Dróg Krajowych i Autostrad v Stephan Riel* ECLI:EU:C:2019:754.
[223] Case 133/78 *Gourdain v Nadler* [1979] ECR 733. The CJEU has applied the same principle in a number of subsequent cases (cited below). In the English case law it had been held that claims by a liquidator to recover pre-liquidation debts are not sufficiently closely connected (*Re Hayward (Deceased)* [1997] Ch 45; *UBS AG v Omni Holding AG* [2001] 1 WLR 916, [2000] BCC 593; *Re Ultra Motorhomes International Ltd* [2006] BCC 57, 42–43). By contrast, proceedings to set aside a vulnerable transaction or in respect of wrongful or fraudulent trading would be sufficiently connected *Re Ultra Motorhomes International Ltd* [2006] BCC 57, 42.
[224] Case C-339/07 *Seagon v Deko Marty Belgium NV* [2009] ECR I-767, [2009] 1 WLR 2168.
[225] ibid at para 16.

8.151 In *SCT Industri*,[226] the CJEU held that an action before an Austrian court did not fall within the scope of what is now the Judgments Regulation, because it had a 'particularly close' link to Swedish insolvency proceedings.[227] The crucial factor was that the Austrian action related to the powers of a Swedish liquidator to dispose of certain assets belonging to the debtor, pursuant to provisions of Swedish insolvency law which derogated from the general rules of Swedish private law.[228] Accordingly, the exception in Article 1(2)(b) applied—notwithstanding that the Swedish insolvency proceedings had closed prior to the commencement of the Austrian action, and notwithstanding that the OR was not in force when the Swedish insolvency proceedings opened in 1993.[229]

8.152 In *German Graphics*,[230] the debtor company contracted to sell certain machines to a Dutch company. The contract contained a reservation of title clause. After the contract was made (but before the purchase price had been paid), a Dutch court placed the purchaser into compulsory liquidation. The vendor brought an action in Germany to recover the machines. The Dutch liquidator contended that the German action fell outside what is now the Judgments Regulation. However, the CJEU held that the exception in Article 1(2)(b) did not apply, because there was an insufficiently close link between the German action and the Dutch insolvency proceedings. The only issue before the German court related to the ownership of the machines. This issue of ownership can arise outside the context of insolvency, and does not depend on insolvency law (properly so-called).[231] The mere fact that the Dutch liquidator was a party to the proceedings was insufficient.[232] The CJEU held that the scope of the OR should be construed narrowly, whereas the scope of what is now the Judgments Regulation (and, in particular, the term 'civil and commercial matters') should be construed in a broad manner.[233]

8.153 In *F-Tex*,[234] the German liquidator asserted rights of action against a payee of the debtor's money, pursuant to claw-back provisions of the German insolvency code. Under German law, only the liquidator is entitled to bring such an action, unless the liquidator assigns his rights of action to a third party for the benefit of the general body of creditors. In this case, the liquidator assigned his rights of action to F-Tex (the sole creditor) in return for a share of the proceeds. F-Tex commenced proceedings in Lithuania, being the place of the payee's registered office. If the liquidator had brought the action himself, it would clearly have fallen within the Article 1(2)(b) exception. However, the CJEU held that the assignment to F-Tex severed the link between the claw-back action and the German insolvency proceedings, so that what is now the Judgments Regulation applied instead of the OR. The following factors were particularly significant: (i) unlike the liquidator, F-Tex was not required to act in the creditors' interests;[235] (ii) F-Tex could freely decide whether to bring the action;[236] and

---

[226] Case C-111/08 *SCT Industri AB v Alpenblume AB* [2009] ECR I-5655, [2010] Bus LR 559.
[227] ibid at para 26.
[228] ibid at paras 27–30.
[229] ibid at paras 18 and 30.
[230] Case C-292/08 *German Graphics Graphische Maschinen GmbH v Alice van der Schee* [2009] ECR I-8421, [2010] ILPr 1.
[231] ibid at para 32.
[232] ibid at para 33.
[233] ibid at paras 23–25. The reasoning in *German Graphics* was applied by the English High Court in *Byers v Yacht Bull* [2010] BCC 368, para 22ff. See also *Polymer Vision R&D Ltd v Van Dooren* [2012] ILPr 14, para 46ff.
[234] Case C-213/10 *F-Tex SIA v Lietuvos-Anglijos UAB* [2013] Bus LR 232.
[235] ibid at para 44.
[236] ibid at para 43.

(iii) the closure of the insolvency proceedings would have no effect on F-Tex's ability to bring the action.[237]

In *Nickel & Goeldner*,[238] the CJEU reiterated that, if an action is based on principles of insolvency law which derogate from the normal principles of private law, it falls within the Article 1(2)(b) exception.[239] The decisive criterion is not the procedural context of the action, but rather its legal basis.[240] Therefore, an action for the recovery of an ordinary debt brought by the liquidator of an company did not fall within the Article 1(2)(b) exception: the debt arose under a contract of carriage, and the action could have been brought by the company itself prior to the opening of insolvency proceedings. **8.154**

In *H v HK*,[241] the German liquidator of a company brought an action in Germany against its managing director under paragraph 64 of the Law on Limited Liability Companies, which provides as follows: 'the managing directors of a company are obliged to reimburse to the company payments made after the company is declared insolvent or after it has been established that its liabilities exceed its assets. That does not apply to payments, even those made after those events, that are compatible with the care to be expected of a prudent businessman'. The managing director was domiciled in Switzerland, and argued the action fell within what is now the Judgments Regulation. The liquidator contended that the action fell within the exception in Article 1(2)(b) (and, therefore, within Article 3(1) of the OR). The CJEU accepted the liquidator's argument, holding that it would be artificial to distinguish between claw-back actions (as in *Seagon* and *F-Tex*) and the action in the present case.[242] Paragraph 64 of the Law on Limited Liability Companies derogated from the ordinary rules of civil and commercial law, specifically because of the insolvency of the debtor company,[243] and therefore satisfied the test in *Nickel & Goeldner*. **8.155**

In *Valach*[244] the Slovak applicant sued an Austrian bank in Austria for damages resulting from defendant's participation as member of the creditors' committee in the Slovak insolvency proceeding. The Austrian courts' dismissal of the case for lack of international jurisdiction was upheld by the CJEU on the ground that the alleged infringement of duties as a member of the creditors' committee was directly based on an insolvency proceeding and was closely linked to it since the deciding court would have to clarify the extent of the duties owed as a member of a creditors' committee. Accordingly, the applicants were referred to their home courts. **8.156**

In *Tünkers*,[245] an unfair competition suit was at issue and the CJEU had to decide whether it fell under the Judgments Regulation or the OR. The insolvency administrator of a German insolvent company entered into a provisional transfer agreement with the German company Tünkers Maschinenbau GmbH (TM) and transferred the relevant assets to another **8.157**

---

[237] ibid at para 46. This may arguably be inconsistent with the CJEU's reasoning in Case C-111/08 *SCT Industri AB v Alpenblume AB* at para 30.
[238] Case C-157/13 *Nickel & Goeldner Spedition GmbH v 'Kintra' UAB* [2015] QB 96.
[239] ibid at para 24.
[240] ibid at para 27.
[241] Case C-295/13 *H v HK*.
[242] ibid at para 24.
[243] ibid at para 23.
[244] Case C-649/16 *Valach et al v Waldviertler Sparkasse Bank AG et al*.
[245] Case C-641/16 *Tünkers France et al v Expert France*, ECLI:EU:C:2017:847.

German company which was a subsidiary of TM. Thereupon, TM wrote letters to the French clients of the insolvent debtor inviting them to place their orders from now on with TM. The French affiliate of the debtor took the view that this invitation constituted an act of unfair competition and sued TM in Paris. TM argued that that Paris court lacked international jurisdiction pursuant to Article 3 OR. The Cour de Cassation referred the issue to the Luxembourg court which decided that the conduct of TM alone (and not also the insolvency administrator) was in dispute so that there was no direct basis of the insolvency proceeding and it lacked the necessary closeness of a link between the court action and the insolvency proceeding; since the rights acquired by TM could not retain a direct link with the debtor's insolvency.

8.158 In *Wiemer & Trachte*[246] the CJEU considered the scope of Article 3(1) in relation to the liquidation of a German company, with a Bulgarian branch. After the commencement of the liquidation, monies had been transferred from the company to the managing director of the Bulgarian branch. The German liquidator sought to recover these monies by claiming in the Bulgarian court that the transfers were invalid, having taken place after the commencement of the liquidation. The CJEU however held that the German court, as the court of the Member States in which the liquidation was commenced, had exclusive jurisdiction under Article 3(1) to hear the transaction avoidance claim, and thus that the Bulgarian court did not have jurisdiction. However, the judgment does not explain why the Bulgarian court could not entertain the liquidator's claim under Article 18(1) which allows a liquidator to exercise his powers in all other Member States. It is to be noted that the RR expressly permits the brining of transaction avoidance claims against a defendant in the state where he is domiciled in certain circumstances.

8.159 In *Riel*[247] the CJEU held that an action brought to establish the existence of claims against the debtor for the purposes of then lodging such claims in the insolvency proceeding of the debtor fell outside Article 1(2)(b) of the Judgments Regulation, and thus within Article 3(1) of the OR. It followed that Article 29 of the Judgments Regulation—which provides for a stay of proceedings where another court is first seised of proceedings involving the same cause of action and between the same parties—was of no application to the claim. Further, it was also held that Article 29 does not apply by analogy to proceedings under the OR.

8.160 In *UB v VA*[248] the issue concerned an action brought by an English trustee in bankruptcy seeking a declaration that transactions involving the sale of immovable property in France and the creation of a mortgage over the property were ineffective under English insolvency law on the basis that they were transactions for no consideration or at an undervalue. The CJEU held that English courts had exclusive jurisdiction to hear and determine the claim challenging the transactions under Article 3(1) OR since the claim derived directly from the bankruptcy and was closely connected with it. Moreover, since the jurisdiction in favour of the English court was exclusive, the French courts did not have jurisdiction to hear the claim. This was notwithstanding that the English court had authorized the trustee to bring the proceedings in France.

---

[246] Case C-206/17 *Wiemer & Trachte GmbH v Tadzher*.
[247] Case C-47/18 *Skarb Pánstwa Rzeczpospolitej Polskiej—Generalny Dyrektor Dróg Krajowych i Autostrad v Stephan Riel* ECLI:EU:C:2019:754.
[248] Case C-493/18 *UB v VA, Tiger SCI, WZ, Banque patrimoine et immobilier SA*.

On the other hand, in the *Feniks* case[249] the CJEU held that an *actio pauliana*, whereby a **8.161**
creditor with a debt arising under a contract with the debtor contended that the debtor had
transferred an asset away to a third party to the detriment of the creditor's rights, fell within
the scope of Article 7(1)(a) of the Judgements Regulation, and not within the OR.

In summary, when insolvency proceedings are commenced in a Member State, the juris- **8.162**
diction of that state to open those proceedings is governed by the OR. However, other proceedings arising within the insolvency proceedings will only be within the OR and outside the scope of what is now the Judgments Regulation by Article 1(2)(b) if they derive directly from the bankruptcy or winding-up and are closely connected with the insolvency proceedings. Thus actions by a liquidator to recover debts due to an insolvent company would not be excluded[250] and neither would claims against directors for breach of duty.[251] However, claims by a liquidator in respect of wrongful trading, preferences, or transactions at an undervalue will fall outside the scope of what is now the Judgments Regulation and therefore fall within the scope of insolvency proceedings governed by the OR.[252] Where the jurisdiction of the court to hear and determine an action does arise under Article 3(1) of the OR then it will be exclusive, to the exclusion of the jurisdiction of the courts of any other Member States.

The identification of the basis of jurisdiction for legal proceedings relating to an insolvency **8.163**
may be important since it will determine whether or not the rules and jurisprudence of the Judgments Regulation applies to those proceedings. For example, where, on analysis, proceedings before an English court fall within the insolvency exception, then the English court would be free to apply its discretionary powers to stay such proceedings, whereas the exercise of such powers is circumscribed where jurisdiction arises under the Judgments Regulation.[253]

It should be noted that the possession of Article 3(1) jurisdiction enables the court having **8.164**
such jurisdiction to order protective measures from the time of the request to open proceedings.[254] In the light of the decision in *Eurofood* a decision to appoint a provisional office holder such as a provisional liquidator will itself be a decision opening proceedings for the purposes of Article 3 if such provisional officeholder is a 'liquidator' for the purposes of the OR.[255]

---

[249] Case C-337/17 *Feniks sp z oo v Azteca Products & Services SL*.
[250] Case C-157/13 *Nickel & Goeldner Spedition GmbH v 'Kintra' UAB* [2015] QB 96.
[251] Case C-295/13 *H v HK* and see also *Grupo Torras SA v Sheikh Fahad Mohammed Al-Sabah* [1995] 1 Lloyd's Rep 374. Note also the judgment of the CJEU in Case C-267/97 *Coursier v Fortis Bank SA* [1999] ECR I-2543 that the question of the enforceability of a judgment obtained in foreign insolvency proceedings which was sought to be enforced pursuant to Art 36 of the Brussels Convention was to be determined by reference to the rules of private international law of the Member State in which enforcement was sought and not necessarily by the law governing the insolvency proceedings.
[252] Case 133/78 *Gourdain v Nadler* [1979] 1 ECR 733 and Case C-339/07 *Seagon v Deko Marty Belgium NV* [2009] ECR I-767, [2009] 1 WLR 2168. Likewise, an application for information and documents under section 236 of the Insolvency Act 1986 has been held to be outside the Judgments Regulation and would have been within the OR had the debtor's administration proceeding been subject to it: *Re MF Global UK Ltd (In Special Administration)* [2015] EWHC 2319, a special administration proceeding relating to an investment undertaking which was not a credit institution.
[253] Cf *Owusu v Jackson* [2005] QB 801.
[254] Virgos-Schmit Report, para 78. See also Art 38 of the OR.
[255] Annex C to the OR was amended to include a provisional liquidator as a 'liquidator' in the case of the UK.

8.165 Finally, it is important to bear in mind that Article 3(1) jurisdiction can be asserted against defendants residing outside of the EU. In *Schmid v Hertel*,[256] main proceedings had commenced in Germany. The liquidator brought a claw-back action in a German court against a defendant residing in Switzerland. The CJEU held that the German court had jurisdiction to hear and determine the action. Article 3(1) jurisdiction extends to all defendants, residing anywhere in the world. It is irrelevant whether the defendant resides in a Lugano State.[257]

Insolvency proceedings limited to the territory of a Member State

8.166 In addition to the main insolvency proceedings, Article 3(2) gives the courts of a Member State in which the debtor does not have his centre of main interests but has an 'establishment', jurisdiction to open insolvency proceedings in relation to that debtor. The critical point to note is that, in contrast to the main insolvency proceedings which have a universal effect, the effect of Article 3(2) insolvency proceedings is restricted to the assets of the debtor situated in the territory of the particular Member State.[258] Despite this, Article 3(2) proceedings represent an important exception to the general principle that the main insolvency proceedings are to have effect over all of the debtor's assets wherever situated (universal effect).[259]

8.167 Where both main and secondary proceedings are opened, the OR leaves unclear the consequences on the benefit of a current contract which is due to be performed in the Member State where secondary proceedings are opened. Article 4(2)(e) provides for the applicability of the *lex concursus* in such a case (save for the exceptions in Articles 5–15). However, under Article 3(2) the effects of the secondary proceedings are restricted to assets situated in that Member State. Article 2(g) provides that a claim is situated in the Member State where the third party required to meet the claim has his centre of main interests, and this could be the Member State in which main proceedings are opened.

'Establishment'

8.168 The definition of 'establishment' is set out in Article 2(h) (see paragraphs 8.37–8.59 above) which defines an 'establishment' as any place of operations where the debtor carries out a non-transitory economic activity with human means and goods. The effect of this is that it is insufficient for a debtor to have assets within a Member State; there must be a *place of operations* within the state in order for the courts of that state to have jurisdiction to open territorial proceedings.

Terminated activities

8.169 The question arises as to whether jurisdiction is retained to open secondary proceedings in a Member State where there has been an 'establishment' as defined by Article 2(h) but activities at the place of operations have ceased at the time of the request to open proceedings.[260]

---

[256] Case C-328/12 *Schmid v Hertel* [2014] 1 WLR 633. See also the commentary under Art 1 OR.
[257] Case C-295/13 *H v HK*, para 32.
[258] It should be noted that the effects of the secondary proceedings, based on that Member State's *lex fori* must be recognized in the other Member States.
[259] There are other specific exceptions to the principle of universal effect created by Arts 5, 6, and 7.
[260] See Dr Andrea Csöke, *A Határon Átnyúló Fizetésképtelenségi Eljárások* (Cross-Frontier Insolvency Proceedings) (HVG-Orac, Budapest, 2008) 75.

The answer to this question appears to be negative. In the UK Supreme Court case of *Olympic Airlines*,[261] the debtor had an establishment in England at the time when main proceedings opened in Greece. Over nine months later, the appellants presented a winding-up petition against the debtor in England. The UK Supreme Court held that the debtor had ceased to carry on any significant economic activities in England at the date of the petition. Accordingly, the debtor did not have an establishment in England at that date, and the English courts lacked jurisdiction to open secondary proceedings. It follows from *Olympic Airlines* that, if economic activities at the debtor's place of operations in a given Member State have ceased at the time of the request to open proceedings, the relevant Member State does not retain jurisdiction to open secondary proceedings against the debtor. (However, it is important to note that the new definition of 'establishment' in Article 2(10) RR has the effect of reversing the decision in *Olympic Airlines* in relation to similar facts. Under Article 2(10) RR, 'establishment' is defined as 'any place of operations where a debtor carries out or has carried out in the 3-month period prior to the request to open main insolvency proceedings a non-transitory economic activity with human means and assets'.)

8.170 There is in principle no limit on the number of Article 3(2) proceedings which may be commenced; if a debtor has a number of establishments in different Member States then a corresponding number of territorial insolvency proceedings can be commenced in each of those states.

8.171 There is a question here whether Article 3(2) jurisdiction can be taken even if the 'establishment' has been moved or disbanded in order to avoid jurisdiction. Similar points are considered in the commentary relating to main proceedings at paragraphs 8.114–8.121 above. The decision of the CJEU in *Staubitz-Schreiber*[262] in relation to COMI and the policy of the OR against forum shopping, indicates that a debtor will not be able to disband an establishment after a request to open insolvency proceedings has been made in order to avoid jurisdiction. However, prior to the making of a request to open proceedings, a debtor should be free to move or disband an establishment.[263] This is consistent with the principle of freedom of establishment and it will remain open to creditors to open main proceedings in the Member State where the debtor has its COMI.

Secondary Article 3(2) proceedings

8.172 Article 3(2) insolvency proceedings can be commenced even if main insolvency proceedings have previously been commenced in relation to the debtor. However, if main insolvency proceedings have already commenced, then Article 3(3) provides that the local insolvency proceedings can only be winding-up proceedings[264] (as opposed to reorganization proceedings) and are also in that case to be termed 'secondary proceedings'.

8.173 The restriction of secondary proceedings to winding-up proceedings can have unpleasant consequences. The example given prior to the amendment of Annex B was as follows.

---

[261] *Trustees of the Olympic Airlines SA Pension and Life Assurance Scheme v Olympic Airlines SA* [2015] 1 WLR 2399. See also n 189 above.

[262] Case C-1/04, *Staubitz-Schreiber* [2006] ECR I-701, [2006] BCC 639, CJEU.

[263] This is consistent with the approach of the UK Supreme Court in *Olympic Airlines SA Pensions & Life Assurance Scheme v Olympic Airlines SA* [2015] 1 WLR 2399 (SC).

[264] For those insolvency proceedings which are 'winding-up proceedings' for the purposes of the OR see Annex B of the OR. See app 1 below.

Suppose a corporate debtor's centre of main interests is in France, where the company's business is not viable, but there is an establishment and a separate, profitable business in England. It might well be desirable to place the company into administration in England. Prior to the amendment, unless the English jurisdiction opened proceedings first under Article 3(2), it was not possible to have administration proceedings in England. In the case of the United Kingdom, this has fortunately changed by the addition of administration to Annex B on the grounds that since the changes to domestic law under the Enterprise Act 2002 it is possible for administration to function as a liquidation proceeding. However, it may still be a problem in some of the other Member States.

8.174 The ability to open secondary proceedings in Member States where a debtor has an establishment, notwithstanding that main proceedings have already been opened in the Member State where the debtor has its COMI, may be problematic in practice. The initiation of secondary proceedings introduces multiple insolvency proceedings in relation to the debtor which will inevitably lead to increased costs and may also prejudice the successful achievement of the purposes of the main insolvency proceedings. Further, under the OR, a creditor does not need to satisfy any requirements in order to be able to open secondary proceedings;[265] the issue as to whether the requirements for the opening of secondary proceedings are satisfied is one for the relevant local law.

8.175 However, it is likely to generally be the case under the applicable local law that the question whether to open insolvency proceedings is ultimately one for the discretion of the court. Such court may well decline to exercise its discretion to open proceedings, notwithstanding that the formal requirements for the opening of proceedings were satisfied, if it could be shown that the opening of proceedings would prejudice the main proceedings and that the applicant creditor had no proper interest in the opening of secondary proceedings sufficient to override this consideration.

8.176 In *Burgo Group*,[266] the CJEU confirmed the propriety of this approach. The CJEU held that the OR does not create a 'right' to open secondary proceedings in any Member State where the debtor has an establishment. Rather, the courts of each Member State where the debtor has an establishment can exercise a discretion to refuse the opening of secondary proceedings, provided that the exercise of such a discretion is permitted by the domestic law of the relevant Member State.[267] Clearly, the risk of undermining main proceedings in another Member State is a factor which can be taken into account. However, Member States must not establish conditions for the opening of secondary proceedings which discriminate between creditors from different Member States, and national courts must take into account the purpose of secondary proceedings as described in the OR.[268]

---

[265] See the Virgos-Schmit Report, para 227 which notes that the right of creditors to commence secondary proceedings is not limited by the requirement of a specific interest and that the draft provision which envisaged that a creditor would only be able to open secondary proceedings if he could show that he would benefit from a more favourable legal status in those proceedings was deleted from the final text. See also Tschauner and Desch, 'Secondary Insolvency Proceedings in Germany over the Estate of a Dutch BV' (2007) 4 International Corporate Rescue 232.

[266] Case C-327/13 *Burgo Group SpA v Illochroma SA* [2015] 1 WLR 1046.

[267] ibid at para 63.

[268] ibid at paras 64–65 and 34.

In *Bank Handlowy*,²⁶⁹ the CJEU commented on the possibility of opening secondary proceedings where a detailed plan of reorganization was already being implemented under main proceedings in a different Member State. The CJEU observed that the opening of secondary proceedings in such a situation 'risks running counter to the purpose served by main proceedings, which are of a protective nature'.²⁷⁰ The CJEU referred to the principle of sincere co-operation, which requires a court with jurisdiction to open secondary proceedings to have regard to the objectives of the main proceedings and to take account of the scheme of the OR, which has the aim of ensuring efficient and effective cross-border insolvency proceedings through mandatory co-ordination of the main and secondary proceedings, guaranteeing the priority of the main proceedings.²⁷¹ **8.177**

Avoiding secondary proceedings
Secondary proceedings can disrupt the beneficial rescue or realization of a business.²⁷² Particularly in the case of a group which had traded prior to insolvency as one organization, it makes practical sense for the rescue, reconstruction, or insolvency proceedings to be run as a unity. In some situations, local creditors can be persuaded to abstain from starting secondary proceedings in the interests of a better realization by promising to respect local law priorities in the eventual distribution. **8.178**

In *Collins & Aikman*²⁷³ the administrators appointed by the English courts in main proceedings promised creditors in other Member States that if they did not cause secondary proceedings to be opened in their own states the administrators would respect local law priorities in making distributions. In most Member States the local creditors did not cause secondary proceedings to be opened and the English court agreed with the administrators that English domestic law allowed distributions to respect local law priorities in those cases. This resulted in a more beneficial realization of the businesses of the Collins & Aikman companies incorporated outside the United Kingdom and is a useful model in situations where the domestic law of a main proceeding is sufficiently flexible to follow the *Collins & Aikman* model.²⁷⁴ The *Collins & Aikman* model is now enshrined in Article 36 of the RR. **8.179**

In *Public Prosecutor v Segard (as Administrator for Rover SAS)* the Versailles Court of Appeal²⁷⁵ stated that in order to have secondary proceedings opened the applicant must show a valid purpose for such opening, such as improving the protection of local interests or the realization of assets.²⁷⁶ In that case the court refused to open secondary proceedings because the existence of single proceedings was beneficial to the sale of assets and **8.180**

---

[269] Case C-116/11 *Bank Handlowy w Warszawie SA v Christianapol sp z oo* [2013] Bus LR 956.
[270] ibid at para 59.
[271] ibid at para 62.
[272] See also G Moss, 'Group Insolvency—Choice of Forum and Law: the European Experience under the Influence of English Pragmatism' (2007) 32 Brooklyn Journal of International Law 1005, 1017–18; G Moss, 'Group Insolvency—Forum—EC Regulation and Model Law Under the Influence of English Pragmatism Revisited' (2014) 9(1) Brooklyn Journal of Corporate, Financial & Commercial Law 250.
[273] [2007] 1 BCLC 182, [2006] BCC 861, HCJ. See also *Re Nortel Networks SA* [2009] EWHC 206 (Ch), [2009] BCC 343.
[274] A Schroeder, 'Secondary Insolvency Proceedings' in Schultze and Braun, *Insolvency and Restructuring in Germany* (2008) 35, 37–38.
[275] 15 December 2005.
[276] At paras 44–47.

Pre-main Article 3(2) proceedings

8.181 If main insolvency proceedings have not yet been commenced in relation to the debtor, then Article 3(4) provides that Article 3(2) proceedings (in this commentary referred to as 'independent territorial proceedings') may only be commenced upon one of two conditions being satisfied.[278] Condition (a) of Article 3(4) provides for the situation where main insolvency proceedings cannot be commenced against a debtor.[279] In such circumstances there is no reason why there should be a restraint on the opening of territorial proceedings in other Member States.

8.182 Condition (b) is likely to be used more widely in practice. This condition permits a creditor who is domiciled or who has his habitual residence or registered office (as the case may be) in the Member State where an establishment of the debtor is situated to commence independent territorial insolvency proceedings against that debtor prior to main insolvency proceedings being commenced. In addition, a creditor whose claim arises from the operation of the establishment has a similar power to commence independent territorial proceedings.

8.183 It must be stressed that condition (b) merely restricts the right to *commence* independent territorial insolvency proceedings. After such proceedings have been opened, even other creditors are in principle permitted to participate by filing their claims etc.

8.184 It follows that where a debtor has its centre of main interests in another Member State, and no proceedings have been opened there, creditors will be restricted, even where under the ordinary national law the creditor would be able to open insolvency proceedings in relation to the debtor, by the need to fulfil one or other of the conditions.

8.185 The aim of this rule is to give effect to the fundamental principle of the OR that the main insolvency proceedings in relation to a debtor should be in the state where his 'centre of main interests' is situated whilst recognizing that local creditors may have a legitimate interest in pursuing insolvency proceedings against a debtor in their own Member State.[280] The conditions set by Article 3(4) are intended to achieve this aim.

8.186 One important advantage, already mentioned, of opening independent territorial proceedings before the opening of any main proceedings is the ability to have non-winding-up proceedings. Another important consequence is that a series of provisions in Articles 31–35 which regulate the relationship of main and secondary proceedings and ensure the primacy of the main proceedings, only apply to independent territorial proceedings in so far as the progress of the main and independent territorial proceedings permit: Article 36.

---

[277] ibid.

[278] However, in contrast to territorial proceedings commenced after the main proceedings, territorial proceedings commenced before main proceedings have been commenced can be either winding-up or reorganization proceedings.

[279] This might be the case where, eg, the law of the Member State in which the centre of the debtor's main interests is located requires a debtor to be a trader in order to be subject to insolvency proceedings and the debtor is not a trader.

[280] See Virgos-Schmit Report, para 84.

Article 37 provides for the possibility that the liquidator in the main proceedings may make **8.187** a request to convert the independent territorial proceeding into winding-up proceedings.

The ruling of the CJEU in *Zaza Retail*[281] is the leading case on independent territorial pro- **8.188** ceedings. In that case, the debtor had an establishment in Belgium, but had its COMI in the Netherlands. On the application of the Belgian prosecution service (which was acting in the public interest, and was not a creditor in the conventional sense), a Belgian court opened independent territorial proceedings against the debtor. On a preliminary reference to the CJEU, the Belgian prosecution service argued that Article 3(4)(a) conferred jurisdiction on the Belgian court to open independent territorial proceedings, because the Belgian prosecution service lacked *locus standi* to apply for the opening of insolvency proceedings in the Netherlands. The CJEU rejected this argument. From the mere fact that a specific person (in this case, the Belgian prosecution service) has no standing to apply for the opening of main insolvency proceedings, it does not follow that such proceedings 'cannot be opened'.[282] The impossibility of opening main proceedings must be determined objectively, and does not depend on the identity of the applicant.[283] Since other persons (such as ordinary creditors) had standing to apply for the opening of main proceedings in the Netherlands at all material times, Article 3(4)(a) had no application. The CJEU emphasized the importance of Recital (17), which states that independent territorial proceedings should be limited to what is 'absolutely necessary'.[284] Further, the CJEU held that the Belgian prosecution service could not be treated as a 'creditor' within Article 3(4)(b), because it had no right to lodge a claim against the debtor's estate,[285] and did not act as a representative of the creditors.[286] The concept of a 'creditor' should be construed strictly,[287] and does not include public authorities which act in the public interest rather than as creditors (or in the name or on behalf of creditors).[288]

(OR) Article 4—Law applicable

1. Save as otherwise provided in this Regulation, the law applicable to insolvency proceedings and their effects shall be that of the Member State within the territory of which such proceedings are opened, hereafter referred to as the 'State of the opening of proceedings'.
2. The law of the State of the opening of proceedings shall determine the conditions for the opening of those proceedings, their conduct and their closure. It shall determine in particular:
   (a) against which debtors insolvency proceedings may be brought on account of their capacity;

---

[281] Case C-112/10 *Procureur-generaal bij het hof van beroep te Antwerpen v Zaza Retail BV* [2011] ECR I-11525.
[282] ibid at para 24.
[283] ibid at para 21.
[284] ibid at para 22.
[285] ibid at para 31.
[286] ibid at para 32.
[287] ibid at para 29.
[288] ibid at para 34.

(b) the assets which form part of the estate and the treatment of assets acquired by or devolving on the debtor after the opening of the insolvency proceedings;
(c) the respective powers of the debtor and the liquidator;
(d) the conditions under which set-offs may be invoked;
(e) the effects of insolvency proceedings on current contracts to which the debtor is party;
(f) the effects of the insolvency proceedings on proceedings brought by individual creditors, with the exception of lawsuits pending;
(g) the claims which are to be lodged against the debtor's estate and the treatment of claims arising after the opening of insolvency proceedings;
(h) the rules governing the lodging, verification and admission of claims;
(i) the rules governing the distribution of proceeds from the realisation of assets, the ranking of claims and the rights of creditors who have obtained partial satisfaction after the opening of insolvency proceedings by virtue of a right in rem or through a set-off;
(j) the conditions for and the effects of closure of insolvency proceedings, in particular by composition;
(k) creditors' rights after the closure of insolvency proceedings;
(l) who is to bear the costs and expenses incurred in the insolvency proceedings;
(m) the rules relating to the voidness, voidability or unenforceability of legal acts detrimental to all the creditors.

8.189 In contrast to the Judgments Regulation[289] which deals with the questions of jurisdiction, recognition, and enforcement, the OR also contains conflict of laws rules which replace the various national rules of private international law in relation to insolvency proceedings. The reasons for this are explained in the Virgos-Schmit Report. In particular, it is said that insolvency proceedings are collective proceedings and in order for collective proceedings[290] to function effectively it is necessary for there to be clear legal positions. It follows that international insolvency proceedings can only be effectively conducted if the relevant states recognize not only the jurisdiction of the state in which the main proceedings were commenced but also the powers of the liquidators in those proceedings and the effect of any judgments given by the courts in those proceedings. This can only happen if there are harmonized rules on conflict of laws which provide a degree of certainty that, in the event of insolvency, rights created or granted in insolvency proceedings will be recognized throughout the Member States. In *German Graphics*,[291] the CJEU emphasized that the choice of law rules in Article 4 OR are conceptually independent from the jurisdiction rules in the Regulation on Civil Jurisdiction and Judgments, such that the former rules have 'no effect'[292] on the latter rules.

8.190 The general rule given effect to by Article 4(1) OR is that the law applicable to insolvency proceedings is that of the state where the proceedings are commenced ('the state of the

---

[289] Regulation (EU) 1215/2012 of the European Parliament and of the Council of 12 December 2012 on jurisdiction and the recognition and enforcement of judgments in civil and commercial matters.
[290] The collectivity of the proceedings does not mean that the law applicable to the proceedings will not apply to the rights of individual creditors who decline to participate in the proceedings, cf Case C-212/15—*ENEFI*, para 20.
[291] Case C-292/08 *German Graphics Graphische Maschinen GmbH v Alice van der Schee* [2010] ILPr 1.
[292] ibid at para 37.

opening of proceedings') (*lex concursus*). This general rule applies to both main insolvency proceedings and Article 3(2) OR insolvency proceedings (whether secondary proceedings or independent territorial proceedings).[293]

8.191 In relation to the general rule, it appears that the law of the state of the opening of proceedings applies to both matters of substantive law and matters of procedure which arise in the context of the insolvency proceedings.[294]

8.192 Since Article 4 is a conflict of laws provision,[295] it is probably meant to be a reference only to domestic insolvency law, excluding rules of private international law.[296]

8.193 The application of such domestic insolvency law under Article 4 OR can, however, in special cases, indirectly lead to the application of the law of another Member State. In *Collins & Aikman Europe SA*[297] the English court held that where the English court had opened main proceedings in respect of a number of companies incorporated in other Member States, the promises made by the administrators to local creditors to the effect that local law priorities would be respected if they did not cause secondary proceedings to be opened, led the English court to direct, as a matter of English law principles of justice, to apply, in the main proceedings, local law priorities to the claims of the creditors of each company.[298] This holds out the possibility of having a single main proceeding in relation to a debtor, without the need for secondary proceedings, whilst at the same time respecting the substantive rights which local creditors would have in secondary proceedings under the relevant local law.[299]

8.194 As noted above, under the jurisdictional rules contained in Article 3 of the OR, the court of a Member State may be empowered to make an order commencing insolvency proceedings in relation to a company incorporated in a different Member State but whose COMI is in the first state. Under Article 4, the law of the state where the proceedings are commenced will apply to the insolvency. However, because national insolvency law may be designed to apply to a company which is incorporated in that state or which has its operations there, this may give rise to difficulties when it is sought to apply this law to a company which is incorporated or has its operations elsewhere. Since in such a case, the application of the national law stems from Article 4, the national law ought to be interpreted purposively and in such a way as to give effect to the purpose of the OR.[300]

---

[293] Art 28 OR specifically deals with the position in relation to secondary proceedings. However, since Art 4(1) OR is stated as a general rule it must be taken as applying to independent territorial proceedings. See also the Virgos-Schmit Report, para 89.

[294] Virgos-Schmit Report, para 90. However, if a particular matter arises in the context of insolvency proceedings which falls outside the scope of the OR, then the Recast Brussels Regulation (EU) 1215/2012 will apply and accordingly the ordinary rules of private international law will be applicable.

[295] Virgos-Schmit Report, para 88.

[296] ibid para 87.

[297] [2007] 1 BCLC 182.

[298] The decision reflects the fact that the English Insolvency Act is not a mandatory code which requires the application of English substantive law in all circumstances.

[299] Amrei Schroeder, Secondary Insolvency Proceedings, in Schultze & Braun's *Insolvency and Restructuring Yearbook* (2008) 35, 37–38.

[300] eg s 233 of the English Insolvency Act 1986 deals with the disconnection of utility services to an insolvent company by UK utilities. On its face, this would not apply in relation to a foreign company which had its head office and COMI in England but its trading operations in a different Member State. In *Appell v Essent Netwerk BV* (District Court of Hertogenbosch, 31 October 2005), the Dutch Court held that s 233 would apply in relation to a Dutch company in administration in England so as to prohibit a Dutch utility from terminating supply.

8.195 Directors of a company incorporated under the law of one jurisdiction might find that they are exposed to the insolvency laws of other jurisdictions (ie the law(s) of the Member State(s) where the proceedings are opened). This important point will be relevant when advising directors of their duties in the twilight of insolvency. Further, such liability is not subject to the potential protection afforded by Article 13 OR (unless the source of the directors' liability relates to a matter falling within Article 4(2)(m)) OR.

8.196 The view has been expressed that the question of whether or not a director should be disqualified from acting as a director is outside the scope of Article 4 OR.[301]

Article 4(2) OR

8.197 Article 4(2) OR provides for a (non-exhaustive) list of specific matters in relation to the opening of proceedings, their conduct, and their closure to which the law of the state of the opening of proceedings applies. This list effectively represents examples of the application of the general rule in Article 4(1) OR and should not be taken as limiting the application of that rule in any way.

Article 4(2)(d) OR

8.198 In *CeDe Group*[302] the CJEU held that Article 4 did not apply to govern a set-off arising in the context of an action brought by a liquidator of a Polish company against a Swedish contractual counterparty in the Swedish courts for payment of a debt arising out of the supply of goods. The Swedish company asserted a set-off, exceeding the amount of the claimed debt, arising out of compensation said to be due for the failure to make deliveries and for defective supplies. Article 4 did not apply to govern the application of the set-off, since the action for payment of the debt did not fall within the exclusive powers of the liquidator and did not depend on the opening of insolvency proceedings, since it could have been brought independently of any insolvency proceedings.[303] The action for payment was not the 'direct and inseparable consequence' of the insolvency proceeding, and hence Article 4 was not applicable to govern the set-off.[304]

Article 4(2)(e) OR

8.199 Article 4(2)(e) provides that the law of the state of the opening of the proceedings determines the effect of the insolvency proceedings on current contracts to which the debtor is a party. This covers matters such as the termination of such contracts as a result of the opening of the proceedings and for these purposes the law which would otherwise be applicable to the contract may be displaced.[305] There are exceptions for contracts relating to immovable property and employment contracts (Articles 8 and 10).

8.200 The law of the state of the opening of the proceedings governs the effects on current contracts irrespective of whether such effects are invoked by the administrator (for example in order to escape some of the debtor's contractual obligations) or by the other party to the contract (for example a seller refusing to deliver goods because of anticipated non-payment).

---

[301] Professor Michael Bogdan at the European Academy of Law (ERA) in Trier on 18 September 2006.
[302] Case C-198/18 *CeDe Group AB v Kan sp z oo*.
[303] ibid at para 36.
[304] ibid at para 36.
[305] Virgos-Schmit Report, para 91(e).

The latter effect would be more appropriately governed by the law applicable to the contract in question, but that seems to be incompatible with the wording of Article 4(2)(e).

The term '*current contracts*' has been held by the English Commercial Court to include arbitration clauses.[306] It was also held that a pending arbitration claim falls within the exception to Article 4(2)(f) OR and into Article 15 OR (ie 'lawsuits pending') and that aspect was also confirmed by the Court of Appeal. The combined effect of the provisions is discussed further under Article 15 OR. **8.201**

Article 4(2)(f) OR

Article 4(2)(f) provides that the law of the state of the opening will determine the effects of the proceedings on 'proceedings brought by individual creditors'. All of the national laws of the Member States are believed to provide for an interruption or suspension of proceedings or at least executions or seizures of property by means of a stay of steps by individual creditors against the debtor or his assets upon insolvency (as opposed to reorganization) proceedings being opened in relation to that debtor and some also provide greater or lesser stays for reorganization proceedings. Where such a stay on actions against the debtor arises under the law of the state where main proceedings were opened, then such stay will have automatic effect across all Member States pursuant to Article 17 of the OR so as to preclude actions against the debtor otherwise than in accordance with the terms of that stay. **8.202**

Although put in very general terms, 'proceedings brought by individual creditors' in Article 4(2)(f) OR may be limited to 'individual enforcement actions',[307] that is against assets in the estate.[308] It must be remembered, however, that Article 4(2)(f) is simply part of a list of examples of the general rule in Article 4(2) that in accordance with Articles 4(1) and 4(2) the *lex concursus* governs the effects and conduct of the insolvency proceedings, including any stay of non-enforcement proceedings, subject to the exceptions such as Article 15 set out in the OR. **8.203**

The exception in Article 4(2)(f) for 'lawsuits pending' appears to contain an implied cross-reference to Article 15 and presumably covers the same ground as Article 15, in respect of which see the commentary under Article 15 below. As mentioned above under Article 4(2)(e) arbitration proceedings have been held to be covered by the expression 'lawsuits pending'. **8.204**

---

[306] *Elektrim v Vivendi* [2008] EWHC 2155 (Comm), aff'd (CA) sub nom *Syska v Vivendi Universal SA* [2009] EWCA Civ 677, [2010] BCC 348. [eg I Fletcher, 'Effect on Arbitration of the EU Regulation' (2009) 22 Insolvency Intelligence 60–62, and I Fletcher, 'The EU Insolvency Regulation and Pending Arbitration Proceedings: The Court of Appeal Ruling on Article 15' (2009) 22 Insolvency Intelligence 155–57. Notably, this sensible approach to the interpretation of Art 15 OR has been explicitly endorsed by the amended wording of Art 18 RR].

[307] Virgos-Schmit Report, para 142; Fletcher at para 4.42 of the first edition of this work; Virgos and Garcimartin, *The European Insolvency Regulation: Law and Practice* (2004) paras 253–55. Note that para 91(f) of the Report refers to 'executions brought by individual creditors', which appears to be based on the use of '*ejecuciones*' (executions) in the Spanish version. In English terminology, 'execution' refers only to a process *after* judgment (see *Re Overseas Aviation Engineering Ltd* [1963] 1 Ch 24, 39 (per Lord Denning MR)) whereas here processes before and after judgment are intended. In some EU jurisdictions it is possible to obtain a seizure of a debtor's property before or without judgment: see for example the attachment in France in Case C-85/12 *LBI hf v Kepler Capital Markets SA*.

[308] In the light of the words 'concerning an asset or right of which the debtor has been divested' in Art 15. See also commentary under Art 15 below. The request to open a secondary proceeding is an example of an individual enforcement action, cf Case C-212/15 *ENEFI*, para 32.

8.205 The application of Article 4(2)(f) OR is illustrated by the ruling of the CJEU in *MG Probud*.[309] In that case, a Polish court opened main proceedings against the eponymous debtor. Under Polish law, post-insolvency attachments are prohibited. Two days after the opening of main proceedings in Poland, administrative authorities in Germany made an attachment order against assets belonging to the debtor situated in Germany. The CJEU emphasized that the Polish main proceedings enjoyed universal effect, which could only be curtailed by the opening of secondary insolvency proceedings in Germany. No such secondary proceedings had been opened. Therefore, by virtue of Article 4(2)(f) (and also Article 4(2)(b)), the attachment order had been wrongly made.

Article 4(2)(h) OR

8.206 The rules relating to the lodging, verification, and admission of claims are governed by the law of the state of the opening of the proceedings. This covers matters such as the formal requirements for submitting a claim in the insolvency, the time limits for so doing[310] and the burden of proof. This is so even where the substantive law applicable to such claims is a different law.[311] However, the applicability of the law of the state of the opening of the proceedings subject to the rules relating to the lodgement of claims contained in the OR itself (see Articles 32 and 39–42 OR) will override national law to the contrary.

8.207 The Court of Appeal of Aix-en-Provence held in *Dawson International Trading Ltd v SARL Regimentals*[312] that whilst lodging, verification, and admission of claims are governed by the law of the proceeding (in this case, French law), the question of who is the proper authorized representative of a corporate creditor for the purposes of lodging a claim is determined by the national law of the company (in this case, Scots law).

Article 4(2)(i) OR

8.208 The law of the state of opening sets out 'the rules governing the distribution of proceeds from the realization of assets, the ranking of claims'. In special situations, however, the domestic law of the state of opening main proceedings may allow for distributions to respect local law priorities in another Member State. In *Collins & Aikman*[313] the administrators appointed by the English courts in main proceedings promised creditors in other Member States that if they did not cause secondary proceedings to be opened in their own states the administrators would respect local law priorities in making distributions. In most Member States the local creditors did not cause secondary proceedings to be opened and the English court agreed with the administrators that English domestic law allowed distributions to respect local law priorities in those cases. This resulted in a more beneficial realization of the businesses of the Collins & Aikman companies incorporated outside the United Kingdom and is a useful model in situations where the domestic law of a main proceeding is sufficiently flexible to follow the *Collins & Aikman* model.

---

[309] Case C-444/07 *MG Probud Gdynia sp z oo* [2010] ECR I-417, [2010] BCC 453.
[310] See Case C-212/15, *ENEFI Energiahatékonysági Nyrt v Direcția Generală Regională a Finanțelor Publice Brașov (DGRFP)*, ECLI:EU:C:2016:841 discussed in 8.209 below.
[311] So, the admissibility of a claim arising under a French law contract in an English administration is governed by English law not French law.
[312] 13 September 2007.
[313] [2006] BCC 861, HCJ.

Article 4(2)(j) OR

The rules relating to the conditions for and the effects of closure of insolvency proceedings **8.209**
are governed by the *lex concursus*. In *Bank Handlowy*,[314] the CJEU ruled that (by virtue
of Article 4(2)(j)) the concept of closure cannot be given an autonomous interpretation
under EU law. Rather, the concept of closure must be interpreted in accordance with the *lex
concursus*. In this respect, the concept of closure differs from the concept of opening, which
(by virtue of Article 16(1)) must be given an autonomous interpretation under EU law.[315]

Article 4(2)(k) OR

Article 4(2)(k) provides that the law of the state of the opening applies to creditor's rights **8.210**
after the closure of insolvency proceedings. Taken in conjunction with Articles 4(2)(g) and
(g), this means that such law would govern the position of a creditor which has failed to
lodge its claim in the proceeding in accordance with an applicable time limit and whose
claim has been forfeited. In *ENEFI*[316] the CJEU held that Article 4 applied in the context of
the failure by a Romanian tax authority to lodge a claim within the applicable time limit in
the insolvency proceeding of a Hungarian company. Time limits for the lodging of claims
are permissible and part of the *lex concursus*—subject, however, to the principles of equivalence and effectiveness.[317] It follows that the law of the state of the opening may have the
effect of extinguishing the creditor's right to bring enforcement proceedings or to open secondary proceedings in another Member State.

Article 4(2)(m) OR

With regard to Article 4(2)(m) OR, a literal reading of the phrase 'all the creditors' in the **8.211**
English version would lead to an absurd result. It is suggested that in the context it means
'creditors as a whole' or 'general body of creditors'. This approach may be supported by the
French and German versions which use the terms '*ensemble*' and '*Gesamtheit*' respectively.

A literal reading would be unworkable for a number of reasons. It would require proof that **8.212**
the act in question was detrimental to every single creditor. First, the act will almost certainly not be detrimental to the creditor who gets the relevant benefit. Even excluding that
creditor by necessary implication, there are a number of situations plainly intended to be
covered which do not involve every creditor other than the benefited creditor receiving a
detriment.

For example, if the debtor gives a creditor security in the nature of a right in rem which **8.213**
ranks in priority behind another secured creditor, this may well not be detrimental to the
prior security holder, but it is detrimental to creditors generally. Likewise, if there are sufficient assets to pay preferential creditors in full, a voidable payment or security given to one
creditor may not have a detrimental effect on preferential creditors but will again be detrimental to the general body of creditors.

---

[314] Case C-116/11 *Bank Handlowy w Warszawie SA and another v Christianapol sp z oo* [2013] Bus LR 956.
[315] ibid at paras 50–51.
[316] Case C-212/15, *ENEFI Energiahatékonysági Nyrt v Direcția Generală Regională a Finanțelor Publice Brașov (DGRFP)*, ECLI:EU:C:2016:841.
[317] ibid at para 30.

8.214 In *Kornhaas v Dithmar*[318] the CJEU held that an insolvency practitioner's claim against the managing director of the debtor company for reimbursement of payments made by that managing director before the opening of the insolvency proceedings but after the date on which the material insolvency of that company was established was subject to Article 4(2) OR even if those company was incorporated under the law of another member state.

Exceptions to the general rule

8.215 However, the general rule stated in Article 4(1) is subject to a considerable number of exceptions set out in Articles 5–15 of the OR:

(a) In certain cases the OR excludes some rights over assets located in another Member State, or the right of creditors to demand set-off accorded to them under the law of another state, from the effects of the main insolvency proceedings.[319] These rights are governed by the relevant national law and not by the law of the state of the opening of proceedings. See in this regard Article 5 (Third parties' rights in rem), Article 6 (Set-off) and Article 7 (Reservation of title).

(b) In other cases the OR specifically provides for the effects of insolvency proceedings to be governed not by the law of the state of the opening of proceedings but by the law of the particular state indicated by means of a specific connecting factor (which may or may not coincide with the state of the opening of proceedings).[320] See in this regard Article 8 OR (Contracts relating to immoveable property), Article 9 OR (Payment systems and financial markets), Article 10 OR (Contracts of employment), Article 11 OR (Effects on rights subject to registration), Article 14 OR (Protection of third-party purchasers) and Article 15 OR (Effects of insolvency proceedings in lawsuits pending). In this context, the law of the particular state concerned refers not to the general law but to the legal effects of the nearest equivalent insolvency procedure in that Member State.[321]

(c) In one case a specific asset may only be included in the main proceedings, see the EC intellectual property rights as mentioned in Article 12.

In this way the law of the insolvency proceedings is combined with different national laws which are applicable to particular matters which arise in the insolvency context.

8.216 Where one of the exceptions to Article 4 OR applies, presumably this covers proceedings required to enforce rights which fall under such exception.[322] For example, if a secured creditor has rights in rem excluded from Article 4 OR by Article 5 OR, the secured creditor must be able to take proceedings to enforce his rights. Moreover, such a right to take proceedings to enforce excluded rights must apply notwithstanding any stay of proceedings or *vis*

---

[318] Case C-594/14 *Simona Kornhaas v Thomas Dithman as liquidator of Kornhaas Montage und Diensteleistung Ltd*.

[319] Virgos-Schmit Report, para 92(1).

[320] ibid para 92(2).

[321] See ibid para 92(2) and the Austrian Supreme Court cases cited under Art 15 below. In England, in the case of *Mazur Media Ltd v Mazur Media GmbH* [2004] 1 WLR 2966 no reference was made to the Virgos-Schmit Report and the judgment mistakenly proceeds on the basis that the English court can only apply its general discretion: see further the commentary to Art 15 below.

[322] We are obliged to Stephen Robins, barrister of 3–4 South Square, Gray's Inn, London for drawing our attention to this issue.

attractiva concursus which might otherwise apply under the *lex concursus* by the application of Article 4(2)(f).[323]

(OR) Article 5—Third parties' rights in rem

1. The opening of insolvency proceedings shall not affect the rights in rem of creditors or third parties in respect of tangible or intangible, moveable or immoveable assets—both specific assets and collections of indefinite assets as a whole which change from time to time—belonging to the debtor which are situated within the territory of another Member State at the time of the opening of proceedings.
2. The rights referred to in paragraph 1 shall in particular mean:
   (a) the right to dispose of assets or have them disposed of and to obtain satisfaction from the proceeds of or income from those assets, in particular by virtue of a lien or a mortgage;
   (b) the exclusive right to have a claim met, in particular a right guaranteed by a lien in respect of the claim or by assignment of the claim by way of a guarantee;
   (c) the right to demand the assets from, and/or to require restitution by, anyone having possession or use of them contrary to the wishes of the party so entitled;
   (d) a right in rem to the beneficial use of assets.
3. The right, recorded in a public register and enforceable against third parties, under which a right in rem within the meaning of paragraph 1 may be obtained, shall be considered a right in rem.
4. Paragraph 1 shall not preclude actions for voidness, voidability or unenforceability as referred to in Article 4(2)(m).

8.217 As noted above, Article 5 OR creates an exception to the general rule stated in Article 4(1) OR that the law applicable to insolvency proceedings is that of the law of the state of the opening of proceedings. It also creates an exception to the general principle that the main insolvency proceedings are to have a universal scope (ie to have effect over all of the debtor's assets wherever situated). (The other exception to this principle is of course the fact that local assets may be subject to separate Article 3(2) OR proceedings.) This exception is part of a series of exceptions protecting legitimate expectations and certainty in relation to transactions in Member States other than the one in which proceedings are opened.[324]

8.218 There was felt to be a particular need for an exception in relation to rights in rem, since such rights 'are of considerable importance for the granting of credit'[325] and because the laws on security interests, and in particular on the creation, validity, and scope of security interests, differ widely across Member States.[326] Article 5 OR therefore provides, as an exception to the general rule under the Regulation that insolvency proceedings and their effects are governed by the law of the Member State in which they were opened,[327] that rights in rem shall

---

[323] See now Case C-327/13 *Burgo Group SpA v Illochroma SA* [2015] 1 WLR 1046.
[324] Recital (24).
[325] Recital (25).
[326] Recital (11).
[327] Art 4(1).

not be affected by the effects of the insolvency proceedings under this law. Article 5 OR can be understood as a *'negative conflict'* rule[328] in that it provides that rights in rem shall not be subject to the effects of the main proceedings arising under the law governing those proceedings.

8.219 The effect of Article 5(1) OR is to exclude third parties' rights in rem over local assets (ie situated in a state other than the state of the opening of proceedings) from the universal scope of the main insolvency proceedings. Equally, the general rule as to applicable law set out by Article 4(1) OR does not apply and matters relating to rights in rem are governed by their own applicable law.

8.220 The practical effect of Article 5(1) OR is that although the law of the state of the opening of main proceedings may claim local assets as part of the debtor's estate in those proceedings, the rights in rem of any third parties in relation to those assets are preserved in accordance with local law. This means, for example, that the holder of a security right can exercise that security over the debtor's local assets (in accordance with local law) regardless of whether or not the law governing the main insolvency proceedings permits this. However, because the local assets themselves (as opposed to the rights in rem over them) remain subject to the universal scope of the main proceedings, then any surplus remaining after the exercise of rights in rem will be subject to the law and scope of the main proceedings.

8.221 It should also be noted that Article 5(1) OR does not prevent secondary proceedings being commenced in respect of local assets which may prevent the enforcement of rights in rem over local assets (according to the local law applicable to the secondary proceedings). In addition, Article 5(1) OR applies only to rights in rem created before the commencement of the main proceedings; any such rights created afterwards are subject to law and the scope of the main insolvency proceedings.[329] The requirement in Article 5(1) OR that the assets be 'situated within the territory of another Member State at the time of the opening of proceedings' must be read in the light of the principle of effectiveness. In the *ERSTE Bank* case,[330] the security interest was over shares situated in Hungary, which was not a Member State at the time of the opening of the relevant main insolvency proceedings in Austria, but which was a Member State by the time declaratory relief was sought in Hungary. The CJEU held that the OR could only be made effective if the security over assets in Hungary qualified for protection under Article 5, even though Hungary was not a Member State when the main insolvency proceedings were opened and therefore the assets did not in a literal sense fall within Article 5 OR.

8.222 There is no general definition of a 'right in rem' in the Regulation and it appears that this is a matter to be determined by national law.[331] However, it must follow from the general scheme of the Regulation that an unreasonably wide definition of rights in rem should not be adopted since the effect of this would be to abrogate the fundamental principle behind the Regulation (that the main insolvency proceedings have universal scope) to an

---

[328] Per Virgos and Garcimartin (n 302 above) 163.
[329] Virgos-Schmit Report, para 96.
[330] Case C-527/10 *ERSTE Bank Hungary v Hungarian State* [2012] ILPr 38. See also G Moss, 'Principles of EU Insolvency Law' (2015) 28(3) Insolvency Intelligence 40.
[331] Virgos-Schmit Report, para 100. The national law in question is the law determined by the normal conflict of law rules of the forum, generally pointing to the *lex rei sitae* at the relevant time.

unacceptable extent. In these circumstances, it is probable that 'rights in rem' are to be construed narrowly as an exception to the general rule.

Furthermore, Article 5(2) OR does provide a list of rights which are to be regarded as being rights in rem within the meaning of Article 5(1). This list reflects the narrow definition which should be given to rights in rem. In particular, it is said that the list is based on the concept that a right in rem has two fundamental characteristics:[332] **8.223**

(a) a direct and immediate relationship between the right and the asset or assets it covers with the asset or assets being attached to the satisfaction of the right; and
(b) the absolute right of the holder of the right in rem to have the asset allocated to satisfaction of the right. This encompasses a requirement that the right be enforceable against third parties.

In line with these considerations, the CJEU has decided in the *Senior Home* case[333] that a charge which directly and immediately encumbered taxed real property and of which the owner of the real property had to accept enforcement by the tax authorities against the property constituted a right in rem for these purposes—irrespective of the fact that the existence of such statutory right in rem was not the result of a commercial transaction. **8.224**

It seems appropriate that when considering whether a right constitutes a 'right in rem' within the meaning of Article 5(1) OR, a court should consider whether the right has these two characteristics. It has been held by the CJEU that the right of a judgment creditor arising from attachment of a bank account by way of enforcement of a judgment will amount to a right in rem provided that under the national law concerned (usually the *lex situs* pursuant to Recital (25)), that right is exclusive in relation to the other creditors of the debtor company.[334] In relation to the position in Ireland (and previously also, in this context, England Scotland, Northern Ireland, and Gibraltar), it is noteworthy that the Virgos-Schmit Report at paragraph 104 expressly indicates that a floating charge is to be considered as a right in rem. This conclusion would in any event appear to follow from the fact that a floating charge satisfies the two fundamental characteristics of a right in rem set out above. **8.225**

The exception in favour of rights in rem should only apply as far as necessary to protect the holder of the rights in rem. If he has been satisfied in full from the asset or its proceeds, the balance should be available, in the absence of local Article OR 3(2) proceedings, to the 'liquidator' in main proceedings.[335] **8.226**

In certain jurisdictions the domestic insolvency legislation may provide the liquidator with the power to pay an equivalent amount representing the fair market value of the asset that is subject to the right in rem (for example in the Netherlands the liquidator has a *lossingsrecht*, a power to release). A literal reading of Article 5 OR allows the creditor to maximize his rights, but one could argue that the equivalent payment provision does not materially 'affect' the rights in rem of the holder. **8.227**

---

[332] ibid para 103.
[333] Case C-195/15 *SCI Senior Home v Gemeinde Wedemark, Hannoversche Volksbank eG*, ECLI:EU:C:2016:804.
[334] Case C-557/13 *Lutz v Bäuerle* [2015] ILPr 21.
[335] Recital (25).

8.228 The combined effect of Article 5(4) OR and Article 4(2)(m) OR should be noted. Article 4(2)(m) OR elaborates on the general rule in Article 4(1) and specifically provides that rules relating to the voidness, voidability, or unenforceability of legal acts detrimental to all creditors are to be governed by the law of the state of the opening of proceedings. Article 5(4) OR makes it clear that the specific exception to the general rule in Article 4(1) OR created by Article 5(1) OR does not operate so as to preclude any of the actions envisaged by Article 4(2)(m) (ie in relation to the voidness, voidability, or unenforceability of legal acts).

8.229 The Virgos-Schmit Report suggests that this means that the act by which a right in rem is created might be subject to challenge by an action which would be governed by the law of the state of the opening of the main proceedings (on the basis that the creation of a right in rem is detrimental to the unsecured creditors of a debtor).

8.230 These provisions must be considered with Article 13 OR (see below), which creates a kind of 'double actionability' test.

8.231 The combined effect of Articles 4(2)(m), 5, and 13 OR is illustrated by the *Lutz* case in the CJEU described in the commentary under Article 13 OR below.

(OR) Article 6—Set-off

1. **The opening of insolvency proceedings shall not affect the right of creditors to demand the set-off of their claims against the claims of the debtor, where such a set-off is permitted by the law applicable to the insolvent debtor's claim.**
2. **Paragraph 1 shall not preclude actions for voidness, voidability or unenforceability as referred to in Article 4(2)(m).**

8.232 Article 6 OR provides that the opening of insolvency proceedings does not affect a creditor's rights of set-off where they are permitted under the law applicable to the debtor's claim. Therefore such rights remain effective regardless of whether or not the law of the insolvency proceedings permits set-off in those proceedings. This is a very significant exception to the general rule set out in Article 4(2)(d) OR that the law governing the proceedings determines the conditions under which set-off may be invoked.

8.233 The combined effect of Article 4(2)(d) OR and Article 6 OR is that a creditor may be able to take advantage of rights of set-off either where this is permitted under the law of the *lex concursus* (pursuant to Article 4(2)(d)) OR or where this is permitted under the law applicable to the debtor's claim (pursuant to Article 6 OR).

8.234 The relationship between Article 6 and Article 4(2)(d) was considered by the CJEU in *CeDe Group*.[336] The CJEU held that Article 4 did not apply to govern a set-off arising in the context of an action brought by a liquidator of a Polish company against a Swedish contractual counterparty in the Swedish courts for payment of a debt arising out of the supply of goods. This was because the action for payment of the debt was not within the exclusive powers of the liquidator and did not depend on the opening of insolvency proceedings, since it could

---

[336] Case C-198/18 *CeDe Group AB v Kan sp z oo*.

have been brought independently of any insolvency proceedings.[337] The reference in Article 4(2)(d) to the conditions for invoking set-offs and to the effects of insolvency on current contracts does not mean that any claim relating to a contract where a party to that contract is subject to insolvency proceedings falls automatically within the concept of 'insolvency proceedings and their effects.[338] As such, the set-off was governed by Article 6.

8.235 It is important to note that the law which has to permit rights of set-off is the law applicable to the *debtor's* claim (and not to the creditor's claim). The wording of OR Article 6 does not require that the law in question be the law of a Member State, although it might be argued that such a requirement is implied: see the Virgos-Schmit Report at paragraph 93.[339]

8.236 It would appear that in determining the national law applicable to the debtor's claim the normal rules of private international law are to apply including, in particular, Regulation 593/2008 on the law applicable to contractual obligations ('Rome I') within the European Union.[340] A question may arise as to the courts in which the law applicable to a debtor's claim falls to be determined. On the face of it, the jurisdiction to adjudicate on a debtor's claim, including the determination of the law applicable to the claim, will fall to be decided in accordance with the Judgments Regulation,[341] since the debtor's claim is itself unlikely to be a matter relating to bankruptcy or the winding-up of companies or to fall within one of the other exceptions to the application of that Regulation. However, where the sole question to be determined by the court in relation to the debtor's claim is the applicable law for the purposes of Article 6 OR of the Insolvency Regulation then it seems likely that this will be considered as a matter relating to the insolvency proceedings so that the courts of the state of the opening of the proceedings will have jurisdiction to determine the issue.

8.237 One question which arises is whether the 'law' referred to in Article 6(1) is the general (civil or common) law of one Member State or whether it also encompasses that Member State's insolvency law. For example, under Dutch 'general civil law' a creditor is, according to the Civil Code of the Netherlands (Article 6:127), not able to set off a claim which has not yet matured, since maturity (payability) of the claim is a prerequisite. In Dutch insolvency law (Article 53, Bankruptcy Act), however, maturity is not a precondition. Authors defending the latter view hold the opinion that the creditor indeed can set-off. In other circumstances the former view would give the creditor a right to set-off, for example in general French law, that provides for relatively wide criteria to set-off. In the latter view—applying the 'double standard' of both civil law and insolvency law of France—the creditor cannot set off his claim, as French insolvency law applies quite narrow conditions. The example shows that with engineering of financial transactions, 'forum shopping' could raise the possibilities for set-off, although this seems to go against the rationale of the Regulation (see Recital (4)) indicating that for the proper functioning of the internal market it is necessary to avoid

---

[337] ibid at para 36.
[338] ibid at para 35.
[339] See however ch 4 above at paras 4.24–4.25 where it is argued that the omission of any limiting words from the drafting of Art 6 OR as finally enacted should be construed as an indication that this provision is intended to allow a wider spectrum of laws to be applicable, including those of third states, in order to respect parties' legitimate expectations as to the availability of set-off arising under their previously concluded, contractual agreements.
[340] Regulation (EC) 593/2008 of the European Parliament and of the Council of 17 June 2008 on the law applicable to contractual obligations (Rome I), OJ L177/6, 4 July 2008.
[341] Regulation (EU) 1215/2012.

'incentives for the parties to transfer assets or judicial proceedings from one member state to another, seeking to obtain a more favourable legal position (forum-shopping)'.

8.238 Article 6 OR makes it both possible and important for creditors who are likely to benefit from set-offs to try to ensure that the debtor's claim against them is governed by a law which permits the widest possible rights of set-off. For example, if an English lender lends money to a borrower who has his centre of main interests in France, in a French main insolvency proceeding there would be significantly narrower rights of set-off than in English law. The English lender can therefore try to insist that any dealing which may give rise to a claim against him by the debtor be governed by English law. If it is, the creditor can by reason of Article 6 OR rely on the wider rights of set-off permitted by English law.

8.239 It is considered that Article 6 OR covers only rights to set-off arising in respect of mutual claims incurred prior to the opening of the main insolvency proceedings. In respect of claims incurred after the opening of proceedings, the right to set-off should be determined in accordance with the law of the relevant insolvency proceedings pursuant to Article 4(2)(d) OR.

8.240 Article 9 OR provides for a specific case of set-off, between the parties to a payment or settlement system or to a financial market, to be governed solely by the law of the Member State applicable to the system or market concerned.

(OR) Article 7—Reservation of title

1. The opening of insolvency proceedings against the purchaser of an asset shall not affect the seller's rights based on a reservation of title where at the time of the opening of proceedings the asset is situated within the territory of a Member State other than the State of opening of proceedings.
2. The opening of insolvency proceedings against the seller of an asset, after delivery of the asset, shall not constitute grounds for rescinding or terminating the sale and shall not prevent the purchaser from acquiring title where at the time of the opening of proceedings the asset sold is situated within the territory of a Member State other than the State of the opening of proceedings.
3. Paragraphs 1 and 2 shall not preclude actions for voidness, voidability or unenforceability as referred to in Article 4(2)(m).

8.241 Article 7(1) OR excludes from the scope of the main insolvency proceedings a seller's rights based on a reservation of title where the asset is situated in a Member State other than the state of opening of the proceedings.[342] Although the seller's right will be rights in rem and therefore already covered by Article 5 OR, the separate reference in Article 7 OR settles any doubt which may otherwise arise under the law of any Member State.

---

[342] It will not apply where the asset is situated in the state of opening of the proceedings: Case C-292/08 *German Graphics Graphische Maschinen GmbH v van der Schee* [2009] ECR I-8421, [2010] ILPr 1.

Thus if there are main winding-up proceedings in England and the company had, prior **8.242** to the winding-up order, bought some goods from a supplier in France, and the goods are still in France, the French seller can enforce his reservation of title in respect of the goods, whether or not that reservation of title would be valid in England under English law.

Article 7(2) OR appears to be designed to prevent the 'liquidator' of a seller using the com- **8.243** mencement of insolvency proceedings as grounds for keeping or getting title back to goods which have been delivered to another Member State. It provides for a substantive rule of law to be applied in the Member States. It provides that after delivery of assets being sold, the commencement of insolvency proceedings against the seller are not to constitute grounds for rescission or termination of the sale and do not prevent the purchaser acquiring title, as long as the assets are, at the time of opening of the proceedings, in the territory of a member state other than the state of the opening of proceedings. This rule takes precedence over any contrary rules of national law. Presumably it overrides any contractual provision to the contrary.

As with Articles 5 and 6 OR, Article 4(2)(m) OR applies in relation to actions for voidness, **8.244** voidability, or unenforceability. Thus in the example given above, if the agreement to create reservation of title were voidable under English law as a result of the making of the winding-up order, the seller could not successfully rely on the reservation of title.

(OR) Article 8—Contracts relating to immoveable property

> The effects of insolvency proceedings on a contract conferring the right to acquire or make use of immoveable property shall be governed solely by the law of the Member State within the territory of which the immoveable property is situated.

The general principle of the Regulation is that the law of the Member State of the opening **8.245** of proceedings applies to govern those proceedings including determining the effects of the proceedings on any contracts to which the debtor is a party (see in particular Article 4(2)(e) OR). However, it was recognized that there is an equally important interest in permitting the relevant national law to apply to contracts concerning immovable property.[343] In particular, contracts relating to immovable property encompass a number of special factors, including of course the fact that the property is permanently located within a particular state, and the fact that contracts relating to immovable property are subject to special rules in many states, which make the application of relevant national law desirable.[344] Article 8 OR therefore gives effect to this by providing that effects of insolvency proceedings on a contract conferring the right to acquire or make use of immoveable property shall be governed solely by the law of the Member State within the territory of which the immoveable property is situated. The reference to the law of that Member State includes a reference to its insolvency law.[345]

---

[343] Virgos-Schmit Report, para 118.
[344] The mode of applying national law is described in the Virgos-Schmit Report at para 92(2). See also on this point the commentary under Art 15 below.
[345] Virgos-Schmit Report, para 118, third sub-paragraph.

8.246 Article 8 OR applies to contracts to 'acquire' or 'make use' of immovable property and it therefore applies to both contracts for the use of immovable property (such as leases) and contracts covering the sale and transfer of immovable property.[346]

(OR) Article 9—Payment systems and financial markets

1. Without prejudice to Article 5, the effects of insolvency proceedings on the rights and obligations of the parties to a payment or settlement system or to a financial market shall be governed solely by the law of the Member State applicable to that system or market.
2. Paragraph 1 shall not preclude any action for voidness, voidability or unenforceability which may be taken to set aside payments or transactions under the law applicable to the relevant payment system or financial market.

8.247 Article 9 OR provides for a further exception to the general conflict of laws rule stated in Article 4 OR. This time the law of the relevant Member State is to apply to govern the effects of insolvency proceedings on the rights and obligations of the parties to a payment or settlement system or to a financial market. Essentially the idea here is to prevent any confusion or lack of certainty which might result if the law of the state of the opening of proceedings was applied to financial market mechanisms such as the closing out of contracts, netting, and the realization of securities.[347] On the mode of applying national law, see paragraph 8.211 above.

8.248 The key terms 'payment or settlement system' and 'financial market' are not defined in the Regulation. The reference to payment and settlement systems is amplified in Recital (27) by a reference to Council Directive (EC) 98/26 on settlement finality in payment and securities systems. However, the term 'financial market' itself is potentially more ambiguous. In this regard, the Virgos-Schmit Report comments that a 'financial market' is understood to be a market where financial instruments, other financial assets or commodity futures and options are traded. Such a market is said to be characterized by regular trading and conditions of operation and access.[348]

(OR) Article 10—Contracts of employment

The effects of insolvency proceedings on employment contracts and relationships shall be governed solely by the law of the Member State applicable to the contract of employment.

8.249 Article 10 OR provides that the effects of insolvency proceedings on contracts of employment are to be governed solely by the national law applicable to the contract of employment. Again this provision recognizes that there is a legitimate interest in contracts of employment

---

[346] See also ibid para 119.
[347] See ibid para 120 and Recital (27) OR. See also ch 7 above.
[348] See the Virgos-Schmit Report, para 120.

and labour relations being governed only by the relevant national law. The mode of applying national law is described in paragraph 92(2) of the Virgos-Schmit Report. See also on this point the commentary under Article 15 OR below.

However, it is important to note the limits of this exception to the general rule. It applies only to the effects of the insolvency proceedings on contracts of employment. Thus other matters which may arise out of contracts of employment in the context of insolvency proceedings (such as the admission of claims and, importantly, the priority of any claims)[349] will be governed by the law of the state of the opening of proceedings. **8.250**

The question of which national law is applicable to a contract of employment will fall to be determined by the Rome I Regulation:[350] see in particular Articles 8 and 9 of the Rome I Regulation. **8.251**

It is possible that under certain circumstances employees working in one Member State and employed by a debtor who went insolvent in another Member State, will have less protection than the employees who are located in that other Member State, in which the *lex concursus* applies to the termination of employment contracts. If, for example, a German liquidator in main proceedings terminates the contracts of employees who fulfil their labour in the Netherlands, the German court must apply Dutch insolvency law (specific termination provisions in Article 40, Dutch Bankruptcy Act), given that Dutch law applies in these contracts. Article 68 of the Dutch Bankruptcy Act provides that a liquidator needs permission from the supervisory judge ('*rechter-commissaris*') to terminate contracts of employment. According to German law, no specific permission is required. As the nature of the act of the German liquidator is of German origin, the Dutch supervisory judge will probably refuse to take jurisdiction. This would result in a termination of employment contracts in the Netherlands without a previous, independent check. In practice this problem will in most cases be solved, as the Dutch employees will work in an 'establishment', and they for the protection of their rights may request a secondary proceeding, in which Dutch law will apply. **8.252**

(OR) Article 11—Effects on rights subject to registration

The effects of insolvency proceedings on the rights of the debtor in immoveable property, a ship or an aircraft subject to registration in a public register shall be determined by the law of the Member State under the authority of which the register is kept.

Article 11 OR recognizes an important legal and commercial reality: the fact that in many Member States rights in immovable property, ships, and aircraft are subject to schemes of registration. Such schemes of registration are themselves often the result of international arrangements. **8.253**

---

[349] See also Art 4(2)(h).
[350] See comments to Art 6 above, at 8.230, regarding the replacement of the Rome Convention by the Rome I Regulation.

8.254 Article 11 OR therefore provides that such rights are to be subject to the law of the state under whose authority the register is kept so as to uphold the integrity and effectiveness of such schemes of registration. There is clearly a justifiable interest in this since, as the Virgos-Schmit Report acknowledges, '[t]he systems for the registration of property play a significant role in protecting trade and legal certainty'.[351]

8.255 But there is a material difference between Article 11 OR and Articles 8, 9, and 10 OR. Those Articles state that the relevant matters are to be governed 'solely' by the law of the relevant Member State. Article 11 OR does not contain this word but instead states that the rights are to be determined by the law of relevant state (see also paragraph 8.23 and n 43 thereto above).

8.256 The effect of this deliberate change is explained in the Virgos-Schmit Report as being that the general applicability of the law of the state of the opening of proceedings is not displaced and that both this law and that of the relevant Member State apply cumulatively. In particular, it is said that the law of the state of registration will determine which, if any, aspects of the law of the state of the opening of proceedings are to apply.[352]

8.257 It has been suggested that Article 11 OR is designed to prevent rights which may be alien to the national registration system having to be registered.

8.258 It is important to note the limits of the Article 11 OR exception. For example, it does not extend to those rights over the assets of companies which are in England generally required to be registered at Companies House.[353] However, to the extent that such rights constitute rights in rem then they may fall under the Article 5 OR exception.

(OR) Article 12—Community patents and trade marks

> For the purposes of this Regulation, a Community patent, a Community trade mark or any other similar right established by Community law may be included only in the proceedings referred to in Article 3(1).

8.259 This Article is designed to replace certain rules contained in the Community Patent Convention[354] and the Council Regulation on Trademarks[355] relating to the insolvency proceedings in which Community-wide patent and trade mark rights could be included.[356] It was apparent that the inclusion of these Community-wide rights in different national insolvency proceedings in relation to the same debtor could give rise to difficulties. The rules in the Convention and the Regulation therefore provided that until such times as common rules for Member States in relation to insolvency proceedings were in force, the only Member State in which a Community patent or trade mark could be involved in

---

[351] Virgos-Schmit Report, para 130.
[352] ibid para 130. On the mode of applying national law, see 8.211 above.
[353] See the Companies Act 2006 (Amendment of Part 25) Regulations 2013.
[354] The European Patent Convention 1973, which was implemented into English law by the Patents Act 1977, did not create a Community-wide patent but rather enabled various national rights to be granted at the same time. Subsequent developments are dealt with under Art 15 RR below.
[355] Council Regulation (EC) 94/40 [1994] OJ L11/1.
[356] There is a further updating in Art 15 RR: see that provision and the commentary on it below.

insolvency proceedings was the state in which such proceedings were first brought.[357] These rules clearly lapsed upon the Insolvency Regulation coming into force and, accordingly, Article 12 OR introduces a new rule that Community intellectual property rights may only be included in the main insolvency proceedings commenced in relation to the debtor.[358]

(OR) Article 13—Detrimental acts

Article 4(2)(m) shall not apply where the person who benefited from an act detrimental to all the creditors provides proof that:
- the said act is subject to the law of a Member State other than that of the State of the opening of proceedings; and
- that law does not allow any means of challenging that act in the relevant case.

8.260 Article 13 OR relates back to Article 4(2)(m). As noted above, Article 4(2)(m) OR elaborates on the general rule in Article 4(1) OR that insolvency proceedings are to be governed by the law of the Member State of the opening of the proceedings. In this regard Article 4(2)(m) OR specifically provides that the law of the state of the opening of proceedings is to apply in determining the rules relating to the voidness, voidability, or unenforceability of legal acts detrimental to all creditors. Furthermore, Articles 5, 6, 7, and 9 OR which provide for specific exceptions to the general rule in Article 4(1) OR expressly provide that the effect of the exceptions is not to preclude any of the actions envisaged by Article 4(2)(m) OR. The probable effect of these provisions is explained above in relation to Article 5(4) OR.[359]

8.261 Article 13 OR provides that Article 4(2)(m) OR shall not in any event apply where the creditor satisfies the two conditions stated in Article 13. As to these conditions, the reference to 'any means' in the second condition is said to indicate that the act must not be capable of being challenged either under rules relating to insolvency or under the general law of the relevant Member State.[360] Furthermore, the act must actually be capable of being challenged in fact in the particular case and not just as a matter of principle; this is indicated by the reference in Article 13 to 'in the relevant case'.[361]

8.262 The CJEU has held in the *Lutz* case[362] that, in a German bankruptcy, where a detrimental act was governed by Austrian law, Article 13 applied to give the Austrian defendant a defence, because claw-back proceedings were brought outside the one-year limitation period mandated by Austrian law.[363] It did not matter that the bar was procedural[364] and that Austrian

---

[357] Art 41 of the Community Patent Convention; Art 21 of the Trade Marks Regulation.
[358] The new rule extends beyond patents and trade marks to other intellectual property rights established by Community law such as plant variety rights: Council Regulation (EC) 94/2100 [1994] OJ L227/1.
[359] See paras 8.223–8.226 above. The meaning of 'all the creditors' is discussed at paras 8.208–8.209 above.
[360] Virgos-Schmit Report, para 137; Lombardi Molinari, 'Avoidance of Transactions Under the E.U. Insolvency Regulation' (2008) Top Legal International I at V. See now *Nike v Sportland Oy* (Case C-310/14).
[361] ibid. See also *LBI hf v Merrill Lynch International*, EFTA Court, Case E 28/13 on Art 30 of Directive 2001/24 (the equivalent of Art 13 OR) at para 75. The onus of proof in relying on Art 13 is on the defendant: *Nike* (supra). Confirmed in Case C-54/16 (*Vinyls*), ECLI:EU:C:2017:433, paras 34–38.
[362] Case C-557/12 *Lutz v Bäuerle* [2015] ILPr 21.
[363] See also *LBI hf v Merrill Lynch International*, EFTA Court, Case E 28/13 on Art 30 of Directive 2001/24/EC, which is in similar terms to Art 13 OR, at para 77.
[364] ibid at para 74.

law did otherwise provide for claw-back proceedings in similar cases. The Regulation does not distinguish between substantive and procedural defences. Consequently, it is necessary not only that the *lex fori concursus* and the *lex causae* both have a means of challenging the relevant transaction, but that the relevant transaction could in fact be attacked under both systems of law, including compliance with any limitation periods.

8.263 A modification of the distinction between procedural and substantive defences was established in the *Vinyls* case.[365] The CJEU held that the existence of a procedural time bar specifying the time within which a defence against a claw-back claim had to be raised as well as other rules specifying the form in which the defence had to be raised were matters for the *lex fori*, ie they fall within the procedural law of the Member State in whose courts the dispute is pending—and that it is up to the local courts to determine whether or not these requirements are in line with the principles of equivalence and effectiveness. In this respect, the law must not be less favourable than the law governing similar domestic situations (principle of equivalence) and must not make it excessively difficult or impossible in practice to exercise the rights conferred by EU law (principle of effectiveness).

8.264 The CJEU in the *Lutz* case considered that the Article 13 OR defence did not in principle apply to acts which take place after the opening of insolvency proceedings. However, the CJEU considered that a right in rem was a special case, referring to Recital (25) OR, 'since these rights are of considerable importance for the granting of credit'. Article 5 OR enables a creditor to assert rights in rem *which had been acquired before the opening of insolvency proceedings*, even after the opening of insolvency proceedings. This was the only way to assert his right in rem effectively. Article 5 OR was thus a special case because it sought to protect acts taking place after the opening of insolvency proceedings. In order to ensure the effectiveness of Article 5(1) OR, the creditor is entitled to rely on Article 13 OR to protect the payment over of monies pursuant to the creation of a right in rem before such opening.

8.265 In the *Lutz* case, the creditor had attached monies of the debtor prior to the opening of insolvency proceedings and the monies were paid over to the creditor after the opening. That payment could not be recovered under German law because Article 13 OR gave the creditor a defence under Austrian law, which governed the creation of the security in Austria and the payment made under it.

8.266 With regard to the *lex causae* the CJEU decided in the *Vinyls* case[366] that a choice of law clause pursuant to the Rome I Regulation is to be respected also in the context of a dispute involving Articles 4(2)(m) and 13 OR even if both parties have their head offices in a single Member State on whose territory all the other elements relevant to the situation in question are located—unless the parties have chosen that law for abusive or fraudulent ends.

8.267 The potential challenge under the *lex causae* need not be under insolvency law:[367] Article 13 OR creates no such restriction.

---

[365] Case C-54/16 *Vinyls Italia SpA v Mediterranea di Navigazione SpA*, ECLI:EU:C:2017:433.
[366] Case C-4/16 *Vinyls Italia SpA v Mediterranea di Navigazione SpA*, ECLI:EU:C:2017:433 at 43-55.
[367] *LBI hf v Merrill Lynch International*, EFTA Court, Case E-28/13 on Art 30 of Directive, at para 74; see now *Nike v Sportland Oy* (Case C-310/14).

The standard of proof required and the question of whether the *lex causae* is treated as a **8.268**
matter of law or fact would seem to be a matter for the law of the Member State which
has opened the main proceedings and whose court is hearing an application to avoid a
transaction.[368]

Difficult situations may arise. For example under Finnish law the *actio Pauliana*[369] can **8.269**
be instituted within six months from a certain date. It is possible to have a three-month
extension of the time from the date the liquidator has become or should have become
aware of the relevant facts. Thus the question of whether an act is capable of being challenged 'in the relevant case' under Finnish law may depend on a judge's assessment of
the situation.

In considering the question of challengeability under insolvency law, it will be necessary to **8.270**
assume for the purposes of the domestic law, on the basis of the opening of the otherwise
applicable insolvency proceeding, some basic aspects of the criteria for challenging the act
in question, such as a finding of insolvency.[370]

Article 13 OR thus operates as an exception to the general applicability of the *lex fori* **8.271**
concursus and the onus is on the defendant to produce evidence which makes out the exception.[371] This will involve not only proving the relevant foreign law but also the relevant
facts.[372] This may be quite difficult in practice, since it may involve attempting to prove a
negative, such as lack of knowledge of wrongdoing by the debtor.[373]

The aim of the exception is to uphold the legitimate expectations of creditors or third par- **8.272**
ties with regard to the validity of the act in accordance with the normally applicable law.[374]

This aim played a central role in the *Oeltrans* case.[375] The liquidator of that German com- **8.273**
pany wanted to avoid a payment made to the defendant on behalf of a sister company. The
German Supreme Court referred to the CJEU the question whether the law applicable to the
relevant contract under the Rome I Regulation also governs the payment made by a third
party in performance of a contracting party's contractual payment obligation. The Court's
affirmative answer was based on the argument that (a) it is unforeseeable for a contracting
party whether or not a third party will pay the obligation and, if so, from which jurisdiction,
(b) that the alternative would be that all third-party payments would be governed by the *lex*
concursus pursuant to Article 4 OR which would run counter to the intention of Article 13
OR, and (c) that the purpose of the conflict of law-rules in the Rome I Regulation are intended to provide foreseeable results and legal certainty.

Article 13 OR applies only to acts carried out prior to the commencement of insolvency **8.274**
proceedings. Once insolvency proceedings are commenced the law of the state of those

---

[368] ibid at para 78; see now *Nike v Sportland Oy* (Case C-310/14).
[369] A common fraudulent transfer provision in Roman law based systems, analogous to Insolvency Act 1986, s 423 in England.
[370] Lombardi Molinari (n 349 above) VI.
[371] Virgos-Schmit Report, para 136; Lombardi Molinari (n 349 above) V.
[372] ibid V.
[373] ibid VII.
[374] Recital (24); Virgos-Schmit Report, para 138; Lombardi Molinari (n 349 above) V.
[375] Case C-73/20, *Oeltrans Gesellschaft v Frerichs*,

proceedings will apply and the assets of the debtor (wherever situated) will fall to be treated in accordance with that law. A creditor will not be able to rely on Article 13 to defeat this consequence.

8.275 Article 13 OR leads to the undesirable result that the parties to a contract detrimental to the general body of creditors may succeed in protecting it from being challenged by introducing into it a choice-of-law clause in favour of a legal system not permitting the challenge. The law thus chosen must be the law of a Member State but need not have any natural connection with the contract in question: no such connection is required by the Rome I Regulation.

(OR) Article 14—Protection of third-party purchasers

> Where, by an act concluded after the opening of insolvency proceedings, the debtor disposes, for consideration, of:
> - an immoveable asset, or
> - a ship or an aircraft subject to registration in a public register, or
> - securities whose existence presupposes registration in a register laid down by law,
>
> the validity of that act shall be governed by the law of the State within the territory of which the immoveable asset is situated or under the authority of which the register is kept.

8.276 Article 14 OR represents another exception to the general rule in Article 4(1) OR by providing that the law of the national state applies in relation to dispositions of certain property by a debtor to a third party after insolvency proceedings have been commenced. However, as is apparent from the terms of the Article, it applies only to dispositions of immoveable assets, ships, or aircraft which are registered and securities 'whose existence presupposes registration in a register laid down by law'. The mode of applying national law is described in paragraph 92(2) of the Virgos-Schmit Report. See also on this point the commentary under Article 15 OR below.

8.277 It appears that even the registration of immoveable assets and securities must be in a register that is public (see Article 2(g) OR). Similarly to Article 6 OR, Article 14 OR does not explicitly require that the applicable law be that of a Member State but such requirement seems to be implied (Virgos-Schmit Report, paragraph 93).[376] Together with Article 11 OR, Article 14 OR deviates from most of the Regulation's conflict rules by omitting the word 'solely'.

---

[376] The English, French, and German versions of the text refer to 'state' (*l'état, Staates*), whilst the Dutch text reads '*lidstaat*' (Member State). The scheme of the Regulation implies that Art 14 is limited to the law of the respective Member State. This may well be the correct approach in the context, although the Spanish and Portuguese ('*estado*') and Italian ('*stato*') versions also fail to specify 'Member' State.

(OR) Article 15—Effects of insolvency proceedings on lawsuits pending

The effects of insolvency proceedings on a lawsuit pending concerning an asset or a right of which the debtor has been divested shall be governed solely by the law of the Member State in which that lawsuit is pending.

Article 15 OR establishes the final exception to the general rule that insolvency proceedings are governed by the law of the state of the opening of the insolvency proceedings (*lex fori concursus*). This is that the relevant domestic law of the forum (*lex fori processus*) applies to determine the effect of insolvency proceedings on pending 'lawsuits' 'concerning an asset or a right of which the debtor has been divested'. **8.278**

As noted above, all of the national laws of the Member States are believed to provide for an interruption or suspension of proceedings or enforcement by means of a stay of steps by individual creditors against the debtor or his assets upon insolvency (as opposed to reorganization) proceedings being opened in relation to that debtor and some also provide stays for reorganization proceedings. Upon the opening of proceedings such a stay will operate automatically across the European Union by virtue of Articles 4(1), 4(2), and 17 OR. **8.279**

However, as noted under Article 4(2)(f) OR, Article 15 OR provides an exception to this[377] in the case of lawsuits which are already pending when the insolvency proceedings are opened which concern an asset or a right of which the debtor has been divested. Such pending lawsuits are to be dealt with solely under the law of the Member State in which the lawsuit is pending. One possible effect of this provision is to avoid the application of the rule of *vis attractiva concursus* which sometimes applies under the law of Member States pursuant to which pending proceedings may be removed from the civil or commercial court in which they are pursued into the exclusive control of the relevant bankruptcy court.[378] **8.280**

It is important to note that Article 15 OR applies only to 'lawsuits pending' at the time the insolvency proceedings are opened. Accordingly, it does not apply to lawsuits commenced after the opening of the insolvency proceedings (which will, therefore, be subject to any stay or *vis attractiva concursus* (see above) imposed under the law of the state of the opening of the proceedings). However, the text refers to 'lawsuits pending' not 'causes of action pending'. It follows that where a lawsuit is pending in, eg, Portugal in relation to a Luxembourg company which subsequently enters a bankruptcy process, the question whether the existing particulars of claim can be amended to allege a fresh cause of action is governed by Portuguese law as the law of the place where the lawsuit is pending **8.281**

In the earlier context of Article 4(2)(f) OR, the grammatical construction reads as if 'lawsuits pending' are intended to be a subset of 'proceedings brought by individual creditors'. This has not however been accepted as a correct interpretation of Article 15 OR by the CJEU. **8.282**

The alternative approach is to contrast individual enforcement actions (such as distress, execution, attachment, or sequestration) with 'lawsuits pending', the latter being directed **8.283**

---

[377] In principle, the exception in Art 15 is meant to be 'interpreted strictly': Case C-85/12 *LBI hf v Kepler Capital Markets SA* ECLI:EU:C:2013:697, a case on Art 32 of Directive 2001/24, which is in similar terms to Art 15 OR, at para 52.
[378] See para 4.43 above.

at obtaining a decision on the merits rather than enforcing against the debtor's assets.[379] Individual enforcement actions do not fall within Article 15 irrespective of whether or not they were pending at the time the insolvency proceedings were opened and are therefore governed by the *lex concursus*. On this approach, any pending actions can continue to judgment, for example to be used to make a claim to a distribution in the insolvency proceedings, but may not be used to seize or enforce judgment on any assets of the debtor if such recourse is barred by the *lex concursus*.[380]

8.284 This approach was adopted by the CJEU in *Kepler*,[381] where the CJEU made a distinction between 'lawsuits pending', which were held to cover 'only proceedings on the substance' (paragraph 54) and 'individual enforcement actions'[382] such as the pre-judgment attachments in that case. In *Kepler*, the creditor on 10 November 2008 obtained French law attachments in France against monies of the debtor, Landsbanki hf, (later LBI hf), held by a third party. On 5 December 2008, the Icelandic court granted Landsbanki a moratorium. On 22 November 2010 a winding-up order was made. Icelandic law retrospectively invalidated the attachments and effect had to be given to this invalidation in France. It is suggested that the same would have applied if the insolvency proceeding had been a main proceeding in one EU Member State (except Denmark) and the attachments had been made in another Member State, pursuant to Articles 4(2)(f) and 15 OR.

8.285 In *SAS Frontrange Solutions France v Van der Schee as liquidator of WOCL BV* the Court of Appeal in Paris[383] appears to have held that a French summary and provisional disclosure procedure designed to quantify a claim against the debtor was not within 'lawsuit pending' in Article 15 and the proceeding was dismissed on the basis that the claim should be lodged in the supervening Dutch liquidation.

In *Tarragó da Silveira v Massa Insolvente de Espírito Santo Financial Group SA*[384] the CJEU clarified based on language and policy considerations that the wording 'an asset or a right of which the debtor has been divested' includes an order against the insolvent debtor to pay a sum of money including monetary damages. Accordingly, Article 15 applied to a lawsuit pending before a court of a Member State (in that case Portugal) seeking an order that a debtor pay a sum of money due under a contract for the provision of services and pay monetary damages for failure to comply with that contractual obligation where the debtor had been placed into insolvency proceedings in Luxembourg.

The effect of applying Article 15 OR

8.286 Under Article 15 OR, the effect of a foreign insolvency on the proceedings concerning an asset or a right of which the debtor has been divested pending in a Member State is *'governed*

---

[379] Virgos-Schmit Report, para 142; Virgos & Garcimartin, paras 252–55; *Syska v Vivendi* [2010] 1 BCLC 467 (CA), para 16.

[380] See Case C-85/12 *LBI hf v Kepler Capital Markets SA* ECLI:EU:C:2013:697, discussed below. That was a case on Art 32 of Directive 2001/24, which is in similar terms to Art 15 OR.

[381] ibid.

[382] See also *Elektrim v Vivendi* [2008] EWHC 2155 (Comm), [2008] Lloyd's Rep 636, aff'd (CA) sub nom *Syska v Vivendi Universal SA* [2009] EWCA Civ 677, [2010] BCC 348. See notes by I Fletcher in (2009) 22 Insolvency Intelligence 60–62, and 155–57.

[383] 15 June 2007.

[384] Case C-250/17, ECLI:EU:C:2018:398.

solely' by the law of the Member State. As to this, the Virgos-Schmit Report states in a passage dealing generally with the exceptions contained in Articles 8–15:[385]

> ... the effects to be given to the proceedings opened in other [Member States] are the same effects attributed to a domestic proceedings of equivalent nature (liquidation, composition or reorganisation proceedings) by the law of the State concerned ...

8.287 This approach has been followed in three Austrian Supreme Court cases.[386] If that approach is correct, then in a case in which Article 15 OR applies, the court before which a 'lawsuit' is proceeding needs to consider what would be the equivalent *type* of proceeding (ie not necessarily an exactly equivalent proceeding) and to apply the effects of such proceeding under local law.

8.288 Unfortunately, however, the explanation in the Virgos-Schmit Report was overlooked in the English case of *Mazur Media Ltd v Mazur Media GmbH*,[387] which predated the Austrian Supreme Court decisions. In *Mazur Media* the defendant went into liquidation as a main proceeding in Germany but the general English law discretionary stay jurisdiction was held to apply instead of the statutory automatic stay which applies in English liquidation.

8.289 It is suggested that given the lack of any consideration of the Virgos-Schmit Report, that case cannot be taken to establish any real precedent. Moreover, the end result in that case may well have been the same in any event, even if the correct approach had been applied. It seems from the judgment that the judge would in the circumstances probably have given special permission, as he is entitled to do under the English statute, for the English action to proceed, despite the general automatic stay under English law.

8.290 In *Mazur Media* the relevant question was whether an action proceeding in England was automatically interrupted by the opening of liquidation proceedings against the defendant, a German company, in Germany. The judge held that the English liquidation law automatic stay did not apply. He held that he had, however, a general discretion to stay but should not use the discretion where the effect would have been to get round the normal rule of allocation of jurisdiction under the Judgments Regulation (44/2001). Had he been referred to paragraph 92(2) of the Virgos-Schmit Report he would, it is suggested, have held that the English law liquidation automatic stay did apply, but, since that stay is subject to a discretion vested in the court to allow the action to continue, on the special facts of that case he might have exercised his discretion to allow the proceedings to continue in England in any event.

8.291 Where the *lex concursus* imposes a stay but the *lex fori processus* does not, then where Article 15 applies, there is no stay. On the other hand if the *lex concursus* does not impose a stay but the *lex fori* does, a stay is imposed.[388]

---

[385] Virgos-Schmit Report, para 92(2).
[386] 24 January 2006, 10 Ob 80/05w; 23 February 2006 9 Ob 135/04z; 17 March 2005, 8 Ob 131/04d. In the second of these cases, which cites an article which in turn cites the Virgos-Schmit Report, the Austrian Supreme Court states that 'the Austrian court must operate the rules of the Austrian insolvency proceedings which are closest to the nature of the insolvency proceedings in the opening State and must suspend them or not on that basis'.
[387] [2004] 1 WLR 2966.
[388] Austrian Supreme Court, 23 February 2006, 9 Ob 135/04z.

Article 15 OR is not limited to proprietary claims

8.292 It is not clear from the literal wording in English whether the phrase 'concerning an asset or a right of which the debtor has been divested' means that the lawsuit, in order to fall within the Article 15 OR exception, has to concern some claim of proprietary right in or over an asset of the estate in order to be within Article 15 OR[389] or whether the claim can simply be one to a share in the estate. The English and some other language versions can be read as suggesting that Article 15 OR applies only to recovery of assets[390] whereas other language versions clearly refer to assets which are part of the debtor's 'estate'.[391] The English Commercial Court in the case of *Elektrim v Vivendi*[392] ruled in favour of the wider interpretation refusing to limit Article 15 to proprietary claims.

8.293 It is, however, clear that lawsuits concerning assets which are not part of the estate are not covered by Article 15 OR because they do not concern an asset of the estate.[393] Furthermore, the reference to an asset or right of which the debtor 'has been divested' refers to divestment by reason of the insolvency proceedings.[394]

Article 15 OR and arbitrations

8.294 It is not clear from a literal reading of Article 15 OR whether 'lawsuits' covers arbitration proceedings: in English and some other languages the expression suggests proceedings in court[395] but other language versions may be thought to be ambiguous on this point.[396] A policy distinction could be drawn between protecting court proceedings, which closely involve national sovereignty, and not protecting arbitration proceedings, which do not. On the other hand, it could be argued that extending the protection of Article 15 OR to arbitration would further the policy of protecting legitimate expectations, a policy goal set out in Recital (24) OR. This English Commercial Court in *Elektrim v Vivendi*[397] refused to draw a distinction between court and arbitral proceedings in this context and rejected this policy argument in favour of excluding arbitration from 'lawsuits pending'. Although there was no appeal against this finding, the Court of Appeal accepted the correctness of the proposition

---

[389] As held by Murphy J in the Irish High Court on 27 July 2005 in *Flightlease Ireland Ltd* [2005] IEHC 274, in relation to a proceeding in France which was merely a money claim. *Mazur Media Ltd v Mazur Media GmbH* [2004] 1 WLR 2966 was distinguished by Murphy J as a case where there was a proprietary claim. Note that the point does not appear to have been argued in the Austrian Supreme Court cases mentioned here under Art 15 OR, perhaps because the German version refers to '*Masse*' or 'estate' and not to divestment: see below.

[390] Eg the French '*concernant un bien ou un droit dont le debiteur est dessaisie*', or Italian '*relativo a un bene o a un diritto del quale il debitore e spossessato*'.

[391] Eg the versions which refer to the Continental concept of 'mass', ie 'estate', such as Spanish ('*masa*'), or German '*Masse*'. In the light of the Spanish version, the Virgos-Schmit Report unsurprisingly refers to 'estate' at para 142 (third sub-para). Note also the concept of 'divestment' in Art 1(1).

[392] [2008] EWHC 2155 (Comm) [2008] Lloyd's Rep 636, aff'd (CA) sub nom *Syska v Vivendi Universal SA* [2009] EWCA Civ 677, [2010] BCC 348, refusing to follow the Irish case of *Flightlease Ireland Ltd* [2005] IEHC 274.

[393] Austrian Supreme Court, 17 March 2005, 8 Ob 131/04d.

[394] *Syska v Vivendi* [2009] BPIR 163, para 38, *Rawlinson & Hunter Trustees SA v Kaupthing Bank* HF [2012] BCC 441, para 33.

[395] Eg the German '*Rechtstreit*' means 'lawsuit'.

[396] Eg the French '*instance*' can if suitably qualified refer to arbitral proceedings as in '*instance arbitral*'. On the other hand, in English one can refer to 'court of arbitration' but still be aware that a court is very different from an arbitral tribunal.

[397] [2008] EWHC 2155 (Comm), [2008] Lloyd's Rep 636, aff'd (CA) sub nom *Syska v Vivendi Universal SA* [2009] EWCA Civ 677, [2010] BCC 348, [2010] 1 BCLC 467. See notes by I Fletcher in (2009) 22 Insolvency Intelligence 60–62, and 155–57.

that an existing arbitration is a pending lawsuit within the meaning of Articles 15 and 4(2)(f) OR.[398]

It was also held at first instance in *Elektrim v Vivendi* that there was a conflict in that case **8.295** between the effect of Article 4(2)(e) OR on the one hand and Article 4(2)(f) OR (exception) and Article 15 OR on the other. This was because the effect of applying Polish law as the *lex concursus* under Article 4(2)(e) OR was to nullify the arbitration agreement as a 'current contract' and terminate the ongoing arbitration reference, whereas the effect of applying English law as the *lex fori processus* of the arbitration was to allow it to continue. On appeal, the Court of Appeal reached the same result as the Commercial Court, but rejected the notion that there was a conflict between Articles 4 and 15 OR, saying that each Article had its own sphere of operation.[399]

B. Chapter II: Recognition of Insolvency Proceedings

(OR) Article 16—Principle

1. Any judgment opening insolvency proceedings handed down by a court of a Member State which has jurisdiction pursuant to Article 3 shall be recognised in all the other Member States from the time that it becomes effective in the State of the opening of proceedings.
   This rule shall also apply where, on account of his capacity, insolvency proceedings cannot be brought against the debtor in other Member States.
2. Recognition of the proceedings referred to in Article 3(1) shall not preclude the opening of the proceedings referred to in Article 3(2) by a court in another Member State. The latter proceedings shall be secondary insolvency proceedings within the meaning of Chapter III.

Article 16 OR provides the basic principle of recognition for judgments[400] opening insol- **8.296** vency proceedings. Recognition takes place from the time that the 'judgment' (as defined) becomes effective in the state of the opening of proceedings.

Recognition must be provided without preconditions under local law.[401] The Regulation **8.297** therefore operates a system of automatic recognition: once insolvency proceedings have been commenced in one Member State then the opening of the insolvency proceedings and their effects are immediately recognized in all other Member States without any further steps having to be taken.

---

[398] Note that this rational conclusion has been adopted in the wording of the equivalent provision to Art 15 OR in the Recast Regulation. Art 18 RR bears the heading: 'Effects of insolvency proceedings on pending lawsuits or arbitral proceedings'.
[399] *Syska v Vivendi Universal SA* [2009] EWCA Civ 677, [2010] BCC 348, [2010] 1 BCLC 467.
[400] See commentary under Art 2 OR at paras 8.25–8.27 above.
[401] Eg there is no requirement that the decision to open the insolvency proceedings be published locally before the proceedings will be recognized; although publication can be required by any Member State where a debtor has an establishment (Art 21(2) OR), this is not a precondition of the proceedings being recognized. However, the liquidator appointed in the proceedings is required to procure a certificate evidencing his appointment so that he is then in a position to prove his position as liquidator: see Art 19 OR below.

8.298 Moreover, it is important to note that the OR imposes an obligation on a Member State to recognize proceedings opened in another Member State even when those proceedings could not have been commenced in the recognizing Member State.[402] For example, the laws of some states do not provide for insolvency proceedings to be brought against an individual who is not a trader; however, if such proceedings are opened in another Member State then those proceedings must be recognized regardless of the fact that it would not have been possible to have commenced those proceedings under domestic law. The recognizing state can, however, in certain limited circumstances invoke grounds of public policy to refuse recognition (see Article 26 OR).

8.299 The recognition of insolvency proceedings probably extends not only to judgments of 'courts' in the usual sense opening insolvency proceedings but also to the decisions of other bodies where the law of the state of the opening of proceedings empowers those bodies to commence insolvency proceedings.[403] A 'court' is defined in Article 2(d) OR as meaning 'the judicial body or any other competent body of a member state empowered to open insolvency proceedings or to take decisions in the course of such proceedings'.[404]

8.300 On this basis, a decision by meetings of a company's members and creditors to place the company into an insolvency proceeding would on this basis attract automatic recognition under the Regulation. Thus in *Apperley Investments Ltd & others v Monsoon Accessorize Ltd*[405] the Irish High Court proceeded on the basis that the creditors' meeting was the relevant 'court' for the purposes of an English company voluntary arrangement (CVA), although in the event it declined to recognize the CVA on public policy grounds. A CVA comes within the phrase 'Voluntary arrangements under insolvency legislation' in Annex A and there is no court judgment (in an English law sense) opening the proceedings.[406]

Extent of recognition

8.301 The principle of automatic recognition extends to both main and Article 3(2) OR insolvency proceedings which fall within the scope of the Regulation. Its principal effect is in relation to main proceedings, since Article 3(2) OR proceedings are in any event limited in effect to the territory of the Member State in which they are commenced, but note Article 18(2) OR authorizes the liquidator in Article 3(2) proceedings to act in other Member States in some situations.

8.302 The principle that main insolvency proceedings, once commenced, should be automatically recognized reflects the principle that these proceedings are to have universal effect over all

---

[402] Virgos-Schmit Report, para 148.
[403] ibid. See also Vallens, *European Insolvency Law: the Convention Relating to Insolvency Proceedings* (Actualité Legislative Dalloz, 1995).
[404] See Virgos-Schmit Report, para 52. See also the discussion of this question at paras 8.17–8.24 above.
[405] [2020] IEHC 523, para 64 (a case in relation to the RR).
[406] See discussion at paras 8.18–8.20 above. Note also that there is some court aspect in every case, since recourse is available for any interested party to challenge the propriety of CVA proceedings, whether at their inception or during their subsequent course of implementation, by application to the court under Insolvency Act 1986, s 6. Also, there is some court involvement in CVAs in every case in the sense that the chairman of the meetings of the company's members and creditors is obliged to report the results of the meetings to the court: Insolvency Act 1986, s 4(6).

of a debtor's assets wherever situated within the European Union (except Denmark).⁴⁰⁷ The general principle is however subject to important qualifications set out in the Regulation.⁴⁰⁸

8.303 Article 16(2) OR provides that the recognition by a Member State of main insolvency proceedings commenced in another Member State shall not preclude the opening of subsequent Article 3(2) OR proceedings (which would be 'secondary' proceedings⁴⁰⁹) in that Member State.⁴¹⁰ In all cases the question of whether or not secondary proceedings can be commenced after main proceedings have been commenced elsewhere falls to be determined by local law.⁴¹¹

8.304 There is no time limit for the opening of secondary proceedings. On one view, this is unfortunate, since the liquidator in the main proceedings runs the risk at all times that important assets may be taken over by secondary proceedings. In order to avoid this, the liquidator in the main proceedings may have to move, as soon as possible, all assets to his own country.

(OR) Article 17—Effects of recognition

1. The judgment opening the proceedings referred to in Article 3(1) shall, with no further formalities, produce the same effects in any other Member State as under this⁴¹² law of the State of the opening of proceedings, unless this Regulation provides otherwise and as long as no proceedings referred to in Article 3(2) are opened in that other Member State.
2. The effects of the proceedings referred to in Article 3(2) may not be challenged in other Member States. Any restriction of the creditors' rights, in particular a stay or discharge, shall produce effects vis-à-vis assets situated within the territory of another Member State only in the case of those creditors who have given their consent.

8.305 Article 17 OR spells out the effects of automatic recognition set out in Article 16 in relation to main insolvency proceedings and Article 3(2) OR proceedings. Under Article 17(1) OR the 'judgment'⁴¹³ opening the Article 3(1) OR proceedings is to have the same effects in

---

⁴⁰⁷ Although it seems clear that Denmark is not a 'Member State' for the purposes of Art 16, as the English courts have already held in relation to Art 3 (*Re Arena Corp. Ltd* [2004] BCC 375) and the German courts in relation to Art 25 ((District Court of Frankfurt, 24 January 2005), ZinsO (2005) 715), the Spanish Supreme Court referred this question to the CJEU in relation to Art 16 in Case C-148/08 *Finn Mejnersten v Betina Mandal Barsoe*. This reference was subsequently withdrawn.

⁴⁰⁸ It has also been held in England that the principle of automatic recognition prevents a court of one Member State from treating an order of a court in another Member State as a nullity even if it appears to have been made without jurisdiction. In *Re Eurodis Electron Plc* [2012] BCC 57, *main proceedings* had been opened in England but a Belgian court erroneously wound up and then dissolved the company. The time limit for setting aside the dissolution in Belgium having expired, the English administrators argued *inter alia* that the effect of Art 3, 16, and 17 OR was that the orders of the Belgian court winding up and dissolving the company should be ignored. Mann J rejected this argument.

⁴⁰⁹ Art 3(3) OR.
⁴¹⁰ See also the commentary to Art 3 OR above.
⁴¹¹ Art 4(2) OR, and see also Art 28 OR.
⁴¹² The original Art 17.1 of the Convention had 'the' instead of 'this': 'the' is clearly correct. The error has been corrected in Art 20(1) RR, which reinstates the word 'the'. The French and German versions use the equivalents of 'the'.
⁴¹³ The extended meaning of this term is dealt with in the commentary to Art 2(e) see paras 8.25 and 8.27 above.

all Member States as under the law of the state of the opening of proceedings.[414] This may mean that the judgment has more far-reaching effects in a Member State than would have been the case in relation to proceedings commenced in that State.

8.306 The 'effects' of a judgment opening proceedings would appear to include the divestment of the debtor, the appointment of a liquidator, the prohibition of individual executions, the inclusion of the debtor's assets in the estate, and the obligation on individual creditors to return what they have received after proceedings have been commenced.[415] The effects may be both procedural and substantive in nature.

8.307 However, in this regard, it should be noted that the applicability of the law of the state of the opening of proceedings is subject to the various exceptions stated in Articles 5–15 OR. Furthermore, the automatic recognition of the effects of a judgment commencing *main proceedings* is subject to two specific types of exceptions:

- where the Regulation provides otherwise (for example the exceptions relating to the rights in rem of third parties (Article 5 OR), the set-off of mutual debts (Article 6 OR), and to retention of title (Article 7 OR));[416]
- where Article 3(2) OR proceedings have been commenced in a Member State.

8.308 One weakness of the OR is that it does not oblige the court opening the proceedings to specify in its decision whether the proceedings are based on Article 3(1) or 3(2) OR, or are not covered by the Regulation at all (for example if the centre of the debtor's main interests is not situated within the European Union). This may cause confusion, in particular in other Member States. The Member States may, however, make such specifications obligatory by their national law.

8.309 In relation to Article 3(2) OR proceedings, it follows from the fact that these proceedings are intended to protect local interests, that the effects of main insolvency proceedings will not be recognized in relation to local assets. Once Article 3(2) OR proceedings are commenced, the local assets form part of those proceedings and are governed by local law. This enables local expectations with regard to such matters as local law priorities in respect of dividends and the validity of locally perfected security to be met. However, the primary position of main insolvency proceedings is reflected in the rules relating to co-ordination between main and Article 3(2) OR proceedings: see Articles 29–38 OR.

8.310 Article 17(2) OR provides for the recognition of Article 3(2) OR proceedings. Since these proceedings are limited in their effects to local assets, there is no need for their effects to be recognized over assets located in other Member States.[417] However, it is necessary for the

---

[414] The CJEU has decided that where a Member State has joined the EU after a judgment opening proceedings has been made in another Member State, that judgment produces effects in the new Member State, pursuant to Art 17(1) OR, from the date of its accession (Case C-527/10 *ERSTE Bank Hungary NYRT v Hungary* [2012] ILPr 38, para 36). The decision was based on the principle of effectiveness: see also G Moss, 'Principles of EU Insolvency Law' (2015) 28(3) Insolvency Intelligence 40.

[415] Virgos-Schmit Report, para 154.

[416] In addition, Art 26 OR might give rise to an exception where recognition of the insolvency proceeding is opposed by a Member State on the grounds of public policy.

[417] One might argue that recognition of an Art 3(2) OR proceeding need not be provided for in positive wording in Art 17(1) OR. However, a secondary proceeding may affect another proceeding, eg in a case where an asset, belonging to the debtor, has been transferred to the other proceeding, and there is an application of the equal treatment principle in Art 20 OR re sharing and returning certain dividends.

effect of the territorial proceedings over the local assets to be recognized in other Member States; thus Article 17(2) OR provides that these effects cannot be challenged in other Member States.

8.311 The second sentence of Article 17(2) OR deals primarily with two types of situations. The first is where the Article 3(2) OR proceedings have produced a stay of creditors' remedies. That stay cannot extend beyond the Member State where those proceedings have been opened save in respect of creditors outside who have consented.

8.312 The second specified situation is where Article 3(2) OR proceedings are concluded by creditors agreeing to discharge the debtor, for example by a compromise of their claims against the debtor.[418] Article 17(2) OR provides that, in the absence of specific consent from the creditor, the effect of any such discharge is limited to the debtor's assets situated in the Member State in which the territorial proceedings were commenced, leaving the creditor free to pursue the balance of his claim against the debtor's assets in other Member States.

8.313 It is not clear whether 'consent' in this context is restricted to individual consents or whether it would include legal mechanisms whereby a consent binding a minority can be given through a sufficient majority vote with the approval of a court.[419] It is suggested that there would have been little practical point in adding the consent exception unless a locally acceptable means of majority voting so as to bind a minority could supply the necessary consent. There is an analogous question arising from Article 34(2) OR which refers to a stay or discharge arising from a measure closing a secondary proceeding. The measure is not to have effect in respect of the debtor's assets not covered by the secondary proceedings without the consent of 'all'[420] the creditors having an interest. It may be intended that the consent of 'all' can, if need be, be acquired by the use of an appropriate legal mechanism, or the use of the word may suggest that such a process is ruled out.[421]

(OR) Article 18—Powers of the liquidator

1. The liquidator appointed by a court which has jurisdiction pursuant to Article 3(1) may exercise all the powers conferred on him by the law of the State of the opening of proceedings in another Member State, as long as no other insolvency proceedings have been opened there nor any preservation measure to the contrary has been taken there further to a request for the opening of insolvency proceedings in that State. He may in particular remove the debtor's assets from the territory of the Member State in which they are situated, subject to Articles 5 and 7.
2. The liquidator appointed by a court which has jurisdiction pursuant to Article 3(2) may in any other Member State claim through the courts or out of court that moveable property was removed from the territory of the State of the opening of proceedings to the territory of that other Member State after the opening of the insolvency

---

[418] See also Art 34(4) OR.
[419] As in the case of an English law 'scheme' (statutory compromise) under Part 26 of the Companies Act 2006.
[420] In the French version '*tous*' and in the German version '*alle*'.
[421] See also the commentary under that provision at para 8.425 below.

proceedings. He may also bring any action to set aside which is in the interests of the creditors.

3. In exercising his powers, the liquidator shall comply with the law of the Member State within the territory of which he intends to take action, in particular with regard to procedures for the realisation of assets. Those powers may not include coercive measures or the right to rule on legal proceedings or disputes.

Main proceedings

8.314 A key and very sensitive effect of recognition of the effects of main proceedings lies in the exercise of a liquidator's powers in other Member States.[422] This important area is set out expressly in Article 18 OR. For the meaning of 'court', see the commentary under Article 2 OR at paragraphs 8.17–8.24 above.

8.315 A 'liquidator' in a main proceeding cannot be required to obtain an *exequatur* before seeking to exercise his powers in the various Member States. Some civil law countries in the European Union would, apart from the Regulation, require such an *exequatur*, a formal judgment of the local court authorizing the execution of a foreign judgment after an exhaustive legal process amounting to a retrial.

8.316 The power of the liquidator that is specifically mentioned is the power to remove the debtor's assets from the territory of the Member State in which they are situated. This is perhaps the most common reason for attempting to exercise powers abroad and perhaps the most sensitive in terms of local interests.

8.317 The power is specifically made subject to the effects of Article 5 OR (Third parties' rights in rem) and Article 7 OR (Reservation of title). Parties with such rights rely on their title and to that extent stand outside the main insolvency proceedings. In addition to this, the powers of a liquidator may not be exercisable in another Member State in one of two sets of circumstances:

- when there are Article 3(2) OR proceedings in that Member State in relation to the debtor;
- when a preservation measure 'to the contrary' has been taken in relation to the assets of the debtor pursuant to a request to open Article 3(2) OR proceedings.

8.318 The first exception follows from the nature of Article 3(2) OR proceedings, which must be recognized as having effect in the relevant territory.[423] Once commenced, they take effect in relation to the local assets of the debtor and it follows that the powers of the liquidator in the main proceedings will not be effective as against those assets.[424]

8.319 The second exception is effectively an extension of the first and deals with the situation where a provisional protective measure has been taken pursuant to a request to open Article

---

[422] In all cases those powers must be exercised in accordance with the law of the Member State in which they are sought to be exercised: Art 18(3) OR (see paras 8.315 et seq below).
[423] Art 17(2).
[424] Though the co-ordination measures contained in the Regulation may apply (see Arts 31–37 OR).

3(2) OR proceedings (for example a request under Article 29 OR)[425] and such measure is inconsistent with the recognition of the powers of the liquidator in the main proceedings.

Two further important restrictions on the exercise by a liquidator in main proceedings of his powers in the other Member States are contained in Article 18(3) OR. **8.320**

The first is that in all cases a liquidator must exercise his powers in compliance with the law of the Member State within whose territory he seeks to take action. There are two different interpretations of this requirement. **8.321**

One analysis suggests that the restriction simply provides that the manner in which a liquidator is to exercise his powers is to be determined by local law but that the nature and extent of those powers will be determined by the law of the opening of proceedings (subject to the express prohibition on coercive measures and the power to rule on legal proceedings and disputes). The alternative view is that local law effectively determines the powers which a liquidator can exercise on the basis that if the exercise of a particular power is barred by local law then the liquidator will not be able to exercise that power in that state. **8.322**

The better view is that under Article 18(3) OR the nature, content, and extent of a liquidator's powers will be determined by reference to the law of the state of the opening of the proceedings but that the manner in which those powers are to be exercised must be in accordance with the relevant local law. In particular, this is consistent with the policy of the Regulation which provides that subject to specific exceptions, the law applicable to insolvency proceedings is that of the state of the opening of the proceedings. It probably also follows from the language of Article 18(3) OR which appears to draw a distinction between procedures (governed by local law) and substantive powers (governed by the law of the opening state subject to express bars on coercive measures and rights to rule on legal proceedings and disputes).[426] **8.323**

The exercise by a liquidator of his powers under the law of the opening state is not specifically referred to in the public policy exception in Article 26 OR. That Article seems to be referring to insolvency proceedings as a whole, but probably should be read as referring also to individual acts. Article 18 OR does not restrict the way in which a liquidator appointed in proceedings commenced in one state can exercise powers in another state by reference to any restriction on such powers had the liquidator been appointed pursuant to proceedings commenced in the latter state. **8.324**

As noted above, Article 18(3) OR contains complete bars on liquidators exercising certain powers at all in foreign Member States: **8.325**

- A liquidator is not able to take coercive 'measures' in another Member State. While it is not clear whether this restriction applies only to self-help measures or extends also to requests to a court to apply coercive measures, there appears to be no reason in principle why a liquidator should not be able to apply to a local court for such assistance if

---

[425] The liquidator in main proceedings can himself request the opening of territorial proceedings in a Member State where the debtor has an 'establishment': Art 29(a) OR.
[426] Leggatt J took an approach consistent with this view in *Aria Inc v Credit Agricole Corporate and Investment Bank* [2014] EWHC 872 (Comm), para 60 in relation to Greek insolvency proceedings, where he interpreted Art 18(3) as meaning that English law applied to procedural matters.

available under local law. Also, as a matter of principle, local law and courts should as far as possible make available to liquidators in main proceedings all the remedies available to local liquidators, so as to avoid discrimination against an EU citizen. This may sometimes necessitate the opening of secondary proceedings.
- Alternatively, it seems that a liquidator in a main proceeding can apply to his own court for an order applying coercive measures and then seek to have that order enforced in another Member State via Article 25 OR.[427]
- A liquidator is not able to rule on legal proceedings or disputes in a foreign Member State. Under the pre-Regulation law of some Member States, such as France, the same person can act both as insolvency administrator and as 'judge', ruling on disputes, subject to a right of appeal to a court. This is inimical to the legal policy of other Member States, including Germany, Ireland, and the United Kingdom, which take a strict attitude to any person being a judge in his own case.[428]

8.326 It seems that complaints alleging that a foreign liquidator has violated local rules (and thereby Article 18(3) OR) should be addressed to the supervising authorities in the Member State opening the proceedings rather than to the authorities in the Member State the rules of which have been violated.

Article 3(2) OR proceedings

8.327 Article 18(2) OR deals with the powers of 'liquidators'[429] in Article 3(2) OR proceedings. Clearly such liquidators have powers, as determined by the relevant national law, in relation to the local assets of the debtor. Generally speaking, such powers are limited to the Member State in which Article 3(2) OR proceedings are opened.[430] However, there are two areas where the powers of such a liquidator are extended to other Member States.

8.328 First, Article 18(2) OR provides that a liquidator appointed in Article 3(2) OR proceedings has the power to claim in any other Member State that movable property belonging to the debtor was removed from the state where the territorial proceedings were commenced after those proceedings had been commenced. This protects the integrity of the Article 3(2) OR proceedings. It also conforms to the policy against fraudulent or abusive forum shopping[431] which is embodied in the Regulation. Recital (4) OR states:

> It is necessary for the proper functioning of the internal market to avoid incentives for the parties to transfer assets or judicial proceedings from one Member State to another, seeking to obtain a more favourable legal position (forum shopping).

---

[427] In *Handelsveem BV v Hill* [2011] BPIR 1024, the Dutch Supreme Court held that an order by the English court, which had opened main proceedings, for the compulsory provision of information under s 366 of the Insolvency Act 1986 derived directly from insolvency proceedings for the purposes of Art 25(1) OR and was to be recognized. Consequently, the restriction on the use of coercive measures by a trustee in bankruptcy in Art 18(3) OR did not prohibit the English trustee in bankruptcy from seeking recognition and enforcement of the order of the English court in the Netherlands, if necessary with the application of coercive measures available under Dutch law.
[428] In English law this would be a breach of the principle of natural justice, '*nemo judex in sua causa*': see *Ex p Pinochet* [2000] AC 119 (HL).
[429] As defined in the Regulation: see the commentary to Art 1 OR at para 8.04 above.
[430] For a discussion of the point of time at which proceedings are 'opened' in the context of the Regulation, see the commentary to Art 2 OR at paras 8.28–8.32 above.
[431] See commentary in respect of Art 3 OR above.

Secondly, the liquidator in Article 3(2) OR proceedings may bring, in any Member State, **8.329** any action to set aside which is in the interests of the creditors.[432] The expression 'action to set aside' is said to encompass all actions for a declaration that an act or contract, entered into prior to the commencement of insolvency proceedings, is void or enforceable on the ground that the act or contract was for the benefit of one creditor and prejudiced the collective interests of the other creditors as a whole.[433]

(OR) Article 19—Proof of the liquidator's appointment

> The liquidator's appointment shall be evidenced by a certified copy of the original decision appointing him or by any other certificate issued by the court which has jurisdiction.
>
> A translation into the official language or one of the official languages of the Member State within the territory of which he intends to act may be required. No legalisation or other similar formality shall be required.

This Article provides for a simple, quick, and inexpensive mode of proof of appointment. **8.330** However, it should be noted that there is no corresponding rule relating to proof of the extent of powers of a liquidator. The Virgos-Schmit Report suggests that the scope of a liquidator's powers might be proved by way of a certificate issued by the court appointing him.[434] Such certificates may be a useful mode of providing at least prima facie evidence.

(OR) Article 20—Return and imputation

> 1. A creditor who, after the opening of the proceedings referred to in Article 3(1) obtains by any means, in particular through enforcement, total or partial satisfaction of his claim on the assets belonging to the debtor situated within the territory of another Member State, shall return what he has obtained to the liquidator, subject to Articles 5 and 7.
> 2. In order to ensure equal treatment of creditors a creditor who has, in the course of insolvency proceedings, obtained a dividend on his claim shall share in distributions made in other proceedings only where creditors of the same ranking or category have, in those other proceedings, obtained an equivalent dividend.

The aim of Article 20 OR is to ensure the equal treatment of non-preferential, unsecured **8.331** creditors throughout all states to which the Regulation applies. The policy of *pari passu* distribution for all creditors with the same ranking throughout the European Union (except Denmark) is one of the fundamental policies of the Regulation.

---

[432] The specific inclusion of this power in Art 18(2) does not mean that actions to set aside are otherwise excluded from the scope of Art 3(1), which does not expressly mention such actions (Case 339/07 *Seagon v Deko Marty Belgium NV* [2009] ECR I-767, [2009] 1 WLR 2168, paras 45–47).
[433] See Vallens (n 19 above) at n 144.
[434] Virgos-Schmit Report, para 170.

8.332 Article 20(1) OR establishes the opening of main proceedings as a base line after which an unsecured creditor cannot improve his position by going against the debtor's assets in another Member State. If he obtains satisfaction, he has to return what he has obtained to the liquidator in the main proceedings. The assumption appears to be that no such improvement is available under the law governing the main proceedings.

8.333 The obligation to return is subject to the proprietary rights safeguarded by Articles 5 and 7 OR.

8.334 In spite of the formulation 'by any means', Article 20(1) OR does not apply to dividends obtained in parallel insolvency proceedings. Such dividends are dealt with in Article 20(2).

8.335 Article 20(2) OR directly addresses the fact that separate sets of insolvency proceedings in respect of the same debtor are permitted under the Regulation and may lead to disparities between the returns to creditors. Article 20(2) OR does attempt to minimize the potential unfairness to creditors by restricting those creditors who receive a dividend in one set of proceedings from obtaining dividends in other proceedings until the creditors with the same ranking or in the same category in those other proceedings have received an equivalent dividend. In applying Article 20(2) OR, the Virgos-Schmit Report indicates that four rules are relevant:[435]

- No creditor may obtain more than 100 per cent of his claim.
- When a creditor is admitted for proof, the total amount of his claim is to be admitted (and not the amount as reduced by any dividend in other proceedings).
- A claim is not to be admitted for a distribution until such time as the creditors with the same ranking have obtained an equal percentage of satisfaction as that obtained by the creditor in the first set of proceedings. [Whether the ranking is the same depends on the law governing the second set of proceedings, ie the proceedings in which Article 20(2) OR is applied. (MB)]
- The ranking of each claim is determined for each of the proceedings by the law of the state of the opening of proceedings.[436]

(OR) Article 21—Publication

1. The liquidator may request that notice of the judgment opening insolvency proceedings and, where appropriate, the decision appointing him, be published in any other Member State in accordance with the publication procedures provided for in that State. Such publication shall also specify the liquidator appointed and whether the jurisdiction rule applied is that pursuant to Article 3(1) or Article 3(2).
2. However, any Member State within the territory of which the debtor has an establishment may require mandatory publication. In such cases, the liquidator or any authority empowered to that effect in the Member State where the proceedings

---

[435] Virgos-Schmit Report, para 175.
[436] Art 4(2)(i) OR.

referred to in Article 3(1) are opened shall take all necessary measures to ensure such publication.

Publication is not necessary for recognition of insolvency proceedings, of their effects, or of the appointment of a liquidator in other Member States. However, in the interests of openness and certainty, it was considered that provision should be made for publication of the commencement of insolvency proceedings.[437] **8.336**

Though it is very unfortunate that no central register of insolvency proceedings has been set up in the European Union, this omission has been addressed in the RR, which mandates the establishment of insolvency registers in Member States and provides for the implementation of a system to connect these registers.[438] **8.337**

Article 21 OR may give rise to more detailed domestic legislation in Member States for the possibility of publication (by whom, what, what languages, right to oppose by certain interested parties etc). **8.338**

Under Article 21(1) OR, it is up to the liquidator to decide whether or not to request that notice of the judgment commencing the insolvency proceedings and the decision appointing him be published in another Member State. However, Article 21(2) OR provides that any Member State in which the debtor has an establishment (a term defined in Article 2(h) OR) may itself require publication. **8.339**

In either case, Article 21 OR sets out the basic information which the publication must contain: **8.340**

- the identity of the liquidator appointed;
- whether the proceedings are Article 3(1) OR (main) proceedings or Article 3(2) OR proceedings.

There may be an important advantage in terms of Article 24(2) OR for the liquidator to publish the judgment opening proceedings in other Member States. After publication, a person honouring an obligation for the benefit of the debtor which should have been honoured for the benefit of the liquidator will be presumed, in the absence of proof to the contrary, to have been aware of the opening of proceedings and will therefore not have the protection of the deemed discharge of the obligation under Article 24(1) OR.[439] **8.341**

It may be desirable for Member States to require local publication so as to protect local creditors from having to return benefits under Article 20(1) OR that might be acquired in ignorance of the opening of main proceedings in another Member State. **8.342**

The absence of publication may in some Member States have as a consequence that a third party will be protected against a claim re ownership of property the third party has acquired. **8.343**

---

[437] See Virgos-Schmit Report, para 177.
[438] See the commentary to Art 24–27 RR in paras 8.625–8.636 below.
[439] See also the commentary under Art 24 OR in paras 8.349 and 8.350 below.

(OR) Article 22—Registration in a public register

1. The liquidator may request that the judgment opening the proceedings referred to in Article 3(1) be registered in the land register, the trade register and any other public register kept in the other Member States.
2. However, any Member State may require mandatory registration. In such cases, the liquidator or any authority empowered to that effect in the Member State where the proceedings referred to in Article 3(1) have been opened shall take all necessary measures to ensure such registration.

8.344 Article 22 OR is the corresponding provision to Article 21 OR, this time dealing with the registration of insolvency proceedings in a public register, but it deals only with the registration of *main* proceedings (not Article 3(2) OR proceedings) and only with the *judgment* opening main proceedings, not the appointment of the liquidator.

8.345 As with Article 21 OR, the Regulation provides that a liquidator may request registration of the judgment opening the proceedings, this time in the land register, trade register, and any other public register kept in Member States. The idea here is that registration of insolvency proceedings may protect the interests of third parties and help give full effect to insolvency proceedings.[440]

8.346 In addition, Article 22(2) OR provides that any Member State may require registration to take place.

8.347 Article 22 OR may give rise to more detailed domestic legislation in Member States for the possibility of registration (by whom, what, what languages, right to oppose by certain interested parties etc.) It should be noted that in some Member States for a specific type of registration several actual registers, in different locations, may be held. The Regulation does not provide a clear rule regarding in which register in a specific Member State the opening judgment may be registered. Domestic law may need to provide specific rules or need amending for that purpose.

8.348 The reason that Article 22 OR applies only to main insolvency proceedings (ie those commenced under Article 3(1) OR) and not to Article 3(2) OR proceedings seems to be that Article 3(2) OR proceedings do not affect assets located outside the relevant Member States.

(OR) Article 23—Costs

The costs of the publication and registration provided for in Articles 21 and 22 shall be regarded as costs and expenses incurred in the proceedings.

8.349 It can be inferred from this that the liquidator has to pay the cost of any publication and any applicable fee for any registration, whether voluntary or mandatory. He will normally have

---

[440] Virgos-Schmit Report, para 182.

an indemnity from the estate and be able to recover such expenditure from the assets of the estate.

(OR) Article 24—Honouring of an obligation to a debtor

1. Where an obligation has been honoured in a Member State for the benefit of a debtor who is subject to insolvency proceedings opened in another Member State, when it should have been honoured for the benefit of the liquidator in those proceedings, the person honouring the obligation shall be deemed to have discharged it if he was unaware of the opening of proceedings.
2. Where such an obligation is honoured before the publication provided for in Article 21 has been effected, the person honouring the obligation shall be presumed, in the absence of proof to the contrary, to have been unaware of the opening of insolvency proceedings; where the obligation is honoured after such publication has been effected, the person honouring the obligation shall be presumed, in the absence of proof to the contrary, to have been aware of the opening of proceedings.

8.350 Article 24 OR assumes that, under the insolvency law of the relevant proceedings, the honouring for the benefit of the debtor of an obligation which should have been honoured for the benefit of the liquidator will not normally discharge that obligation. The honouring would normally consist of the payment of a debt. Injustice could result where an obligation is honoured for the benefit of the debtor in another Member State in ignorance of the opening of insolvency proceedings. Accordingly, Article 24 OR provides that the person honouring the obligation in another Member State shall be deemed to have discharged it if he was unaware of the opening of proceedings.

8.351 In relation to awareness of proceedings, Article 24 OR sets up two presumptions based on the provisions as to publication set out in Article 21 OR. Article 24(2) OR states that if the obligation was honoured before the insolvency proceedings were published then there is a presumption that the person honouring the obligation was not aware of the insolvency proceedings. Conversely, if the obligation was honoured after the commencement of the insolvency proceedings had been published then it is presumed that the person was aware of those proceedings. In both cases the presumptions are rebuttable by producing proof to the contrary. The publication can reasonably have the above-mentioned effects only in relation to payments made in, or by persons residing in, the country where the publication took place.

8.352 The CJEU has held that Article 24 OR is not a conflict of laws rule, but a provision of substantive law that applies in each Member State independently of the law of the Member State in which insolvency proceedings were opened.[441] Interpreted in the light of Recital (30) OR, its purpose is to protect debtors of the insolvent debtor who have indirectly or directly honoured an obligation to the insolvent debtor in good faith.[442]

---

[441] Case 251/12 *Van Buggenhout v Banque Internationale à Luxembourg SA* [2014] ILPr 28, para 23.
[442] ibid at paras 26–31.

8.353 Where, however, an insolvent entity has requested that one of its debtors pay one of its creditors, such a payment is outside the scope of the protection provided by Article 24(1) OR; this is the case even where the paying debtor is a bank.[443] Were it otherwise, the assets of the insolvent entity could be transferred to specific creditors via unaware third parties and thus denude the assets available to the general body of creditors. This would be contrary to one of the principal objectives of the OR, as set out in Recital (4) OR, which is to prevent forum shopping.

(OR) Article 25—Recognition and enforceability of other judgments

1. Judgments handed down by a court whose judgment concerning the opening of proceedings is recognised in accordance with Article 16 and which concern the course and closure of insolvency proceedings, and compositions approved by that court shall also be recognised with no further formalities. Such judgments shall be enforced in accordance with Articles 31 to 51, with the exception of Article 34(2), of the Brussels Convention on Jurisdiction and the Enforcement of Judgments in Civil and Commercial Matters, as amended by the Conventions of Accession to this Convention.

   The first subparagraph shall also apply to judgments deriving directly from the insolvency proceedings and which are closely linked with them, even if they were handed down by another court.

   The first subparagraph shall also apply to judgments relating to preservation measures taken after the request for the opening of insolvency proceedings.

2. The recognition and enforcement of judgments other than those referred to in paragraph 1 shall be governed by the Convention referred to in paragraph 1, provided that that Convention is applicable.

3. The Member States shall not be obliged to recognise or enforce a judgment referred to in paragraph 1 which might result in a limitation of personal freedom or postal secrecy.

Recognition of insolvency judgments

8.354 The OR in earlier Articles provides for the automatic recognition of judgments[444] opening insolvency proceedings (Article 16 OR), of the effects of insolvency proceedings (Article 17 OR), and of the powers of a liquidator (Article 18 OR). Article 25 OR completes the picture by providing for the general recognition and enforcement of judgments relating to the conduct and closure of insolvency proceedings, where the judgment opening those

---

[443] ibid at paras 32–38. Although in this case the payment by the bank to a creditor of the insolvent entity at the latter's instigation fell outside the scope of Art 24, it did not necessarily follow that the bank had to reimburse the monies paid to the general body of creditors; the liability of the bank in this regard would be governed by the applicable national law.

[444] See generally B Wessels, 'Article 25 of the Insolvency Regulation; a hornet's nest' (2008) 21 Insolvency Intelligence 135.

proceedings has to be recognized under Article 16 OR. Two specific cases are mentioned, presumably for the avoidance of doubt:

(1) Judgments deriving directly from the insolvency proceedings and which are closely linked with them,[445] even if they were handed down by another court.[446] These are said to include actions to set aside voidable transactions, actions seeking the personal liability of directors under insolvency law, disputes about the admission or ranking of claims, and disputes as to whether property is part of the debtor's estate.[447]
(2) Judgments relating to preservation measures taken after a request for the opening of insolvency proceedings.[448]

Article 25(1) OR also specifically provides for the recognition of compositions approved by the court whose judgment opened the insolvency proceedings. Accordingly, pursuant to Article 25, a composition between the company and its creditors approved by the court in the main proceedings can, without further formality, have binding effect between the company and the creditors in all other Member States. A composition for these purposes may, for example, include a reorganization or restructuring plan. **8.355**

There is a question as to whether these effects are subject to the provisions contained in Chapter I of the OR and, in particular, Articles 5–15 OR which modify the general principle in Article 17 OR that the judgment opening proceedings shall produce the same effects in all Member States as it does in the Member State where the proceedings were opened. **8.356**

Of particular relevance in this context is Article 5 OR which provides that the opening of insolvency proceedings shall not affect the rights in rem of creditors or third parties. On its face, Article 5 OR applies only to the effects of the opening of insolvency proceedings and therefore, on a literal reading, would not apply to the effects of the recognition of a composition under Article 25 OR. However, it has been argued that Article 5 should be seen as **8.357**

---

[445] This reflects the decision of the CJEU in Case 133/78 *Gourdain v Nadler* [1979] ECR 733 (decided in relation to Art 1(2) of the Brussels Convention of 1968) that proceedings can be bankruptcy proceedings, if their nature properly indicates them to be such, even if not commenced in a bankruptcy court. The character of the judicial body which determines the action is not determinative of the nature of the action itself. See Virgos-Schmit Report, para 195. A similar conclusion was reached in relation to the OR in Case 339/07 *Seagon v Deko Marty Belgium NV* [2009] ECR I-767, [2009] 1 WLR 2168, in which the CJEU held that the courts of a Member State where insolvency proceedings have been opened have jurisdiction to decide an avoidance action against an entity whose registered office is in another Member State. Such actions fell within the scope of Art 3(1) of the Regulation.

[446] Wessels (n 444 above) 139 points out that the Dutch version uses words which mean 'other judge'. However, the French version has '*une autre juridiction*' and the German '*einem anderen Gericht*', which make it clear that a court is being referred to, in the sense that the judgment may be that of a court other than the court which opened the insolvency proceedings. In Case C-339/07 *Seagon v Deko Marty Belgium NV* [2009] ECR I-767, para 27 the CJEU confirmed that these words mean that it is for the Member State to determine the court with territorial and substantive jurisdiction and that this need not be the court which opened the insolvency proceedings.

[447] Virgos-Schmit Report, para 196. See also Case 157/13 *Nickel & Goeldner Spedition GmbH v 'Kintra' UAB* [2015] QB 96, in which the CJEU held that only actions which derive directly from and are closely connected to insolvency proceedings fall within the scope of the Regulation. They stated that the 'decisive criterion' was ' . . . not the procedural context of which that action is part, but the legal basis thereof . . . it must be determined whether the right or the obligation which respects the basis of the action finds its source in the common rules of civil and commercial law or in the derogating rules specific to insolvency proceedings.' (at para 27). In Case C-295/13 *H v HK* the CJEU held that an action brought by a liquidator under German law requiring directors to reimburse to the company payments made after the company was declared insolvent fell within the OR and outside Brussels 1, even though such an action can be brought even in the absence of insolvency proceedings. The fact that the action was being brought in the context of insolvency proceedings was regarded as critical.

[448] Such measures do not fall within the scope of the Brussels Convention/Brussels 1 Regulation/Brussels 1 Recast Regulation: Case 143/78 *De Cavel v De Cavel* [1979] ECR 1055.

protecting the rights of secured creditors generally[449] and, in the context of the recognition of compositions under Article 25, it has been suggested that the effects of such compositions will be subject to Article 5.[450] Balz has commented that secured creditors may not be impaired by a plan issued in connection with foreign insolvency proceedings.[451]

Recognition of non-insolvency judgments

8.358 Article 25(2) OR of the Insolvency Regulation expressly provides for the Brussels Convention to apply to the recognition and enforcement of these judgments which do not fall under Article 25(1). The purpose of this provision is to avoid any gaps between the Insolvency Regulation and the Convention in this regard.[452] The reference to the Brussels Convention should now be read as a reference to the equivalent provisions of the recast Brussels 1 Regulation, Regulation (EU) 1215/2012 of the European Parliament and the Council on jurisdiction and the recognition and enforcement of judgments in civil and commercial matters (recast).[453]

Mode of enforcement of insolvency judgments

8.359 Article 25(1) OR also provides that any judgments recognized pursuant to that provision are to be enforceable in accordance with Articles 31–51 of the Brussels Convention (except Article 34(2)). This should have been read after 1 March 2002 as referring to Articles 38–58 except for Article 45(2) of the original Judgments Regulation which came into effect on 1 March 2002 and subsequently to the equivalent articles in the Recast Judgments Regulation. This approach has the advantage of using the system of enforcement contained in the Judgments Regulation, derived from the system which was in place under the Brussels Convention, which has already been in practice for more than 50 years and is familiar to practitioners and to the courts.

Categorization of judgments

8.360 Before considering whether a judgment must be recognized and enforced under the OR via the Judgments Regulation, or under the Judgments Regulation alone, it is first necessary to determine whether the judgment falls outside the scope of the Judgments Regulation. This is indicated *inter alia* by the use of the words 'provided that that Convention is applicable' in Article 25(2) OR.[454]

8.361 The simple fact that a liquidator is party to proceedings is not enough to bring a judgment in those proceedings outside the scope of the Judgments Regulation, and thus allow its recognition and enforcement under Article 25 OR.[455] Conversely, where a liquidator exercises

---

[449] See Smart, 'Rights In Rem, Article 5 and the EC Insolvency Regulation: An English Perspective' (2006) International Insolvency Review 17, 23–4 and 33–4 and see the Virgos-Schmit Report, para 95.
[450] See Virgos and Garcimartin 384. But cf B Wessels, 'The Secured Creditor in Cross Border Finance Transactions Under the EU Insolvency Regulation' (2003) 18 JIBL & Reg 135, 140 who takes a different view arguing that the court in the main proceedings could hand down a judgment imposing a stay on the enforcement of rights in rem over assets in other Member States which could then be recognized and enforced under Art 25.
[451] M Balz, 'The European Convention on Insolvency Proceedings' (1996) 70 ABLJ 485, 509.
[452] Virgos-Schmit Report, para 197.
[453] OJ L351/1, 20 December 2012. The Recast Judgments Regulation was adopted on 12 December 2012 and commenced to apply from 10 January 2015.
[454] Case 292/08 *Graphische Maschinen GmbH v van der Schee* [2009] ECR I-8421, [2010] ILPr 1, para 20.
[455] ibid at para 33.

his powers in insolvency proceedings for the benefit of the creditors as a whole, such proceedings would fall outside the scope of the Judgments Regulation and, prima facie, Article 25 would apply.[456]

Further points

8.362 Article 25(1) OR expressly requires recognition without further formalities of judgments relating to preservation measures. This would seem to cover, for example, the appointment of an interim manager (in administration order proceedings) by the court.

8.363 Article 25(1) OR also expressly requires the recognition without further formalities of a composition approved by the court. It seems therefore, that if, for example in England, an administration order resulted in a scheme or plan sanctioned by the court under Parts 26 and 26A of the Companies Act 2006, that scheme or plan would be entitled to automatic recognition.

8.364 Courts often have power to make a confiscation order against a person who has been convicted of a criminal offence when it can be shown that his/her assets include the proceeds of crime. If that person also has ordinary unsecured debts when a problem arises as to whether the state—the beneficiary of the confiscation order—should have priority over the ordinary creditors. If the convicted person (or company) is already in some form of insolvency process, the state would seem not to have any priority at all and indeed it would not seem possible for a confiscation order to be made because the assets of the convicted person/company no longer belong beneficially to that person/company but are held for the creditors acting through the insolvency practitioner. This has subsequently been confirmed by the CJEU in Case 444/07 *MG Probud Gdynia sp z oo v Hauptzollamt Saarbrücken*,[457] a case in which concerned the lawfulness of an attachment of an entity's assets in Germany pursuant to an enforcement order after insolvency proceedings had been opened in Poland. The CJEU held that since main proceedings had been opened in Poland, Polish law was applicable to those proceedings and their effects. Polish law did not permit enforcement proceedings to be brought against a debtor's assets after the opening of insolvency proceedings and so such enforcement proceedings could not take place under the law of another Member State.

(OR) Article 26—Public policy

Any Member State may refuse to recognise insolvency proceedings opened in another Member State or to enforce a judgment handed down in the context of such proceedings where the effects of such recognition or enforcement would be manifestly contrary to that State's public policy, in particular its fundamental principles or the constitutional rights and liberties of the individual.

---

[456] Case 111/08 *SCT Industri AB v Alpenblume AB* [2009] ECR I-5655, [2010] Bus LR 559. In this case, the Regulation did not in fact apply because insolvency proceedings had been opened before its entry into force. See also the decision of the CJEU in Case C-444/07 *MG Probud Gdynia sp z oo* [2010] ECR I-417, [2010] BCC 453.
[457] [2010] ECR I-417, [2010] BCC 453.

8.365 Article 26 of the OR echoes what is now Article 45 of the Recast Judgments Regulation (which replaced Article 34(1) of the Judgments Regulation 44/2001, which in turn replaced Article 27 of the Brussels Convention of 1968) which permits a state to refuse to recognize a judgment given in another Member State where to do so would be manifestly contrary to the public policy of the recognizing state.

8.366 However, it should be noted that there are significant differences between the provisions of the Judgments Regulation and the Insolvency Regulation which affect the scope and effect of the 'public policy' exception to recognition. Thus, whereas Article 45(1)(a) of the former declares that a judgment *shall* not be recognized if to do so would be manifestly contrary to public policy (emphasis added), the drafting of Article 26 of the OR employs the word 'may', thus making it a matter of discretion whether to refuse recognition or enforcement on the public policy ground.[458] Moreover, the concluding words of Article 26 OR, not replicated anywhere in either iteration of the Judgments Regulation, focus upon two specific aspects of the public policy of the recognizing state, namely its fundamental principles or the constitutional rights and liberties of the individual. It may be further observed that the public policy exception, where invocable, need not result in the total rejection of the judgment emanating from the other Member State: it may be possible to refuse recognition or enforcement of the invidious portions of the judgment, while allowing other parts to enjoy effect.[459] The extent to which this may be possible will depend on the exact circumstances of the individual case.

8.367 In relation to the enforcement of judgments, many of the same principles which underpin the Judgments Regulation should apply. Thus:

- A recognizing state cannot review the merits of a judgment.[460]
- A recognizing state cannot review the jurisdiction of the court which gave judgment.[461] In this regard, it is for the judicial authorities of the state in which judgment was given to verify the jurisdiction of the courts which gave judgment.[462]

8.368 Furthermore, the 'public policy' exception is a narrow one and should be used in only exceptional circumstances. This is emphasized by the use of the word 'manifestly'.[463]

---

[458] Cited with approval in *Re Stojevic* (Vienna Higher Regional Court, 9 November 2004), 28 R 225/04w.
[459] See Virgos-Schmit Report, para 209.
[460] Cf Art 52 of the Recast Civil Jurisdiction Regulation 1215/2012 (which corresponds to Art 36 of the former version of the Regulation, 44/2001): 'Under no circumstances may a foreign judgment be reviewed as to its substance in the Member State addressed.' (So also Art 29 of the Brussels Convention of 1968). The same approach has been taken by the CJEU in relation to the Regulation: Case C-341/04 *Re Eurofood IFSC Ltd* [2006] ECR I-3813, [2006] Ch 508. See also *Public Prosecutor v Segard (as Administrator for Rover France SAS)* (Versailles Court of Appeal, 15 December 2005) para 37.
[461] Case C-341/04 *Re Eurofood IFSC Ltd* [2006] ECR I-3813, [2006] Ch 508; cf Art 45(3) of the Recast Civil Jurisdiction Regulation.
[462] See Virgos-Schmit Report, para 202(2).
[463] In matters in relation to the Judgments Regulation the CJEU is of the opinion that the public policy exception should be interpreted strictly and can only apply in exceptional cases: see Case C-7/98 *Krombach v Bamberski* [2000] ECR I-1935, and Case C-38/98 *Renault SA v Maxicar SpA* [2000] ECR I-2973. In *Krombach* the CJEU stated that there needed to be 'a manifest breach of a rule of law essential in the legal order of the state in which enforcement is sought, or of a right recognized as being fundamental within that legal order' for the exception to apply (para 37 of the judgment). In *Re Eurofood IFSC Ltd* the CJEU held that this case law applied to the interpretation of Art 26 OR: para 64 of the judgment.

In relation to 'public policy' itself, this is a national law concept and, accordingly, its **8.369** meaning may vary from state to state. However, given the need to uphold the purpose of the Regulation, 'public policy' should be interpreted strictly[464] and limited to those particularly important and fundamental principles of national law.[465] In this vein, the Virgos-Schmit Report refers to 'constitutionally protected rights and freedoms and fundamental policies of the requested state, including those of the Community'.[466]

In *Re Stojevic*,[467] the Austrian Supreme Court, upholding the Higher Regional of Vienna **8.370** (Court of Appeal), held that recognition could not be refused under Article 26 merely on the grounds that it was thought that the court opening prior main proceedings had taken jurisdiction without any proper basis. The point was sufficiently clear not to be referred to the CJEU for a preliminary ruling.

In *Re Eurofood IFSC Ltd*,[468] both the Advocate General and the CJEU itself referred to the **8.371** narrow scope of Article 26. The Advocate General stated:[469]

> In my view it is clear, first, and as Dr Bondi and the Italian Government stress, that the public policy exemption in Art 26 is intended to be of limited scope. That is borne out by the inclusion in that provision of the requirement that the effects of recognition should be 'manifestly' contrary to public policy, by the statement in recital 22 in the preamble to the Regulation that 'grounds for non-recognition should be reduced to the minimum necessary', and by the Virgos-Schmit Report, which states: 'The public policy exception ought to operate only in exceptional cases'. 33 (Point 204.)

The Court of Justice itself in the *Eurofood* case held that the Article 26 OR exception would apply where insolvency proceedings were opened in another Member State where the decision to open the proceedings '*was taken in flagrant breach of the fundamental right to be heard*'.[470] Importantly, however, the CJEU pointed out that the Irish court in that case could not hold that there was a breach of this fundamental right simply because there was no fair *oral* hearing, even though that might be fundamental to Irish notions of a fair hearing, if in all the circumstances (ie the ability to file written submissions) there was a fair hearing.[471]

Likewise, the special importance attached to employee protection by French insolvency law **8.372** does not afford the French courts a ground for non-recognition on the basis of public policy where English main proceedings offer much less protection.[472]

In the *Hans Brochier* case, administrators were appointed out of court in England in re- **8.373** spect of a German company on the basis of an assertion by the directors that COMI was in the United Kingdom. The German court[473] refused to recognize the opening in the United

---

[464] *Public Prosecutor v Segard (as Administrator for Rover France SAS)* (Versailles Court of Appeal, 15 December 2005) para 41, citing Recital (22) 'grounds for non-recognition should be reduced to the minimum necessary'.
[465] Case C-341/04 *Re Eurofood IFSC Ltd* [2006] ECR I-3813, [2006] Ch 508.
[466] Virgos-Schmit Report, para 205.
[467] (Austrian Supreme Court, 17 March 2005), 8 Ob 135/04t.
[468] C-341/04 [2006] ECR I-3813, [2006] Ch 508.
[469] Para 131.
[470] Para 67 of the judgment.
[471] Case C-341/04 *Re Eurofood IFSC Ltd* [2006] ECR I-3813, [2006] Ch 508, para 68.
[472] *Public Prosecutor v Segard (as Administrator for Rover France SAS)* Versailles Court of Appeal, 15 December 2005) paras 39–43.
[473] Amtsgericht Nürnberg, ZIP 2/2007 81.

Kingdom on the grounds that COMI was in Germany, the UK opening was fraudulent and that Article 26 OR applied. Subsequently, the UK administrators obtained a declaration from the English court that, in the light of further information from Germany, COMI was in Germany.[474] It followed that the opening of main proceedings had been invalid.

8.374 A key question may be to the extent to which creditors whose rights are affected by a proceedings, or a composition approved in the course of a proceeding, have had a sufficient right to participate in the proceedings. A right to a hearing is generally recognized as being a fundamental right and the public policy exception applies to procedural rights of participants in the insolvency proceedings. In *Apperley Investments Ltd & Ors v Monsoon Accessorize Ltd*[475] the Irish High Court declined to recognize an English CVA on public policy grounds on the basis that the creditors meeting which approved the CVA did not in practice allow for the making of representations by affected creditors or for the consideration of such representations.[476]

C. Chapter III: Secondary Insolvency Proceedings

8.375 Chapter III of the Regulation deals with 'secondary' insolvency proceedings.[477] Secondary proceedings are Article 3(2) OR proceedings which are opened in a Member State after main insolvency proceedings have already been commenced in another Member State (see Article 3(3) OR). These proceedings must be winding-up proceedings as listed in Annex B of the Regulation.

8.376 Although some of the provisions in Chapter III of the Regulation relate only to secondary proceedings, Articles 31–35 OR are also applied by Article 36 OR to independent territorial proceedings, ie those opened prior to the opening of main proceedings, 'in so far as the progress of those proceedings so permits'.

(OR) Article 27—Opening of proceedings

> The opening of the proceedings referred to in Article 3(1) by a court of a Member State and which is recognised in another Member State (main proceedings) shall permit the opening in that other Member State, a court of which has jurisdiction pursuant to Article 3(2), of secondary insolvency proceedings without the debtor's insolvency being examined in that other State. These latter proceedings must be among the proceedings listed in Annex B. Their effects shall be restricted to the assets of the debtor situated within the territory of that other Member State.

8.377 As a general principle, secondary proceedings once commenced are governed by the relevant national law (Article 4 OR). However, Article OR 27 modifies this principle to an

---

[474] *Hans Brochier Holdings Ltd v Exner* [2007] BCC 127.
[475] [2020] IEHC 523 (a case in relation to the RR).
[476] ibid at paras 109 and 117.
[477] See also the commentary to Art 3 OR at paras 8.59 et seq above.

extent by providing that where main proceedings have been commenced in relation to a debtor which is recognized in another Member State, then secondary proceedings can be commenced without the insolvency of the debtor having to be established. This exception to the application of national law reflects the fact that local secondary proceedings are to be regarded as being very much ancillary and subordinate to the main proceedings.

In such circumstances the principal role of the local court requested to open secondary proceedings is to examine whether main proceedings have been commenced in another Member State in relation to the relevant debtor, and whether those proceedings are insolvency proceedings within the meaning of Article 3(1) OR so that the Regulation applies. In this regard it is probably also open to the local court to examine whether or not the court opening the main proceedings based its judgment on a finding that the centre of the debtor's main interests was in that state. The local court will also have concurrent jurisdiction with the court of the main proceedings to determine what assets fall within the scope of any secondary proceedings that should be opened.[478] However, it should not be open to the local court to investigate whether or not a finding as to the centre of the debtor's main interests was correct; this is a matter which must be dealt with by the judicial authorities of the state concerned.[479] Recital (22) OR suggests that the decision of the first court which holds that it is opening main proceedings should be recognized in other Member States on the basis of 'the principle of mutual trust' between courts in different Member States. **8.378**

Most importantly, the public policy exception under Article 26 OR should not be invoked as a ground for refusing to recognize or enforce a judgment that has been based on a finding that the centre of main interests is in the Member State from which the judgment emanates.[480] Any party wishing to challenge the finding of the court of origin should utilize the available channels of appeal within the legal system of that state. **8.379**

If, however, the first 'court' as defined in the Regulation,[481] which may not be a court in any usual sense, does not make a finding that the debtor's centre of main interests was located in that state or that the proceedings are main proceedings (which would imply that the centre of main interests was in that state), it would seem to be open to courts in other Member States to make their own findings on the question until one 'court' makes such a finding in relation to its own proceeding. It is clearly desirable that 'courts' should always specify the type of proceeding they are opening. **8.380**

The ability to open secondary proceedings without proof of insolvency once main proceedings have been opened and are to be recognized, appears to assume that insolvency will have been established in the main proceedings. The direction in Article 27(1) OR that the opening of main insolvency proceedings in a Member State 'shall permit the opening' of secondary proceedings in another Member State within the territory of which the debtor has an establishment 'without the debtor's insolvency being examined in that other State' has however been interpreted by the CJEU to mean that the local court cannot examine the **8.381**

---

[478] Case C-649/13 *Comité d'entreprise de Nortel networks SA and others v Rogeau* (2015) ECLI:EU:C:2015:384.
[479] Virgos-Schmit Report, para 215 refers to 'the trust placed in judgments given by Community courts'.
[480] ibid para 202, where emphasis is placed upon the 'principle of Community trust and on the general legal presumption that the judgment handed down in another [member] state is valid'.
[481] See Art 2(d) OR and the commentary to Art 2 at OR paras 8.17–8.24 above.

insolvency of a debtor, even where the main proceedings do not require proof of insolvency under local law and have a protective purpose.[482]

8.382 The reference in Article 27 OR to recognition appears to import the notion that if recognition is not afforded to the Article 3(1) OR proceeding because it would be manifestly contrary to the other Member State's public policy pursuant to Article 26 OR, Article 27 OR will not apply. The local court must also be satisfied that it itself has jurisdiction to open Article 3(2) OR proceedings in relation to the debtor by reason of the debtor having an 'establishment' as defined in Article 2(h) OR in the Member State (see Article 3(2) OR).[483] The question of whether a debtor has an establishment in the local state is a question of fact to be determined by the local court.

8.383 The conditions for opening Article 3(2) OR proceedings in respect of a debtor are to be determined by the local court applying its national law, in accordance with Article 4(2) OR. Thus it is possible that in certain states it may not be possible to commence secondary proceedings against a debtor even though main proceedings have been commenced in another state, have to be recognized, and the debtor has an establishment in the state concerned. This may occur, for example, because the national law of that state prohibits insolvency proceedings being commenced against that debtor. For example, in certain states it is not possible to commence insolvency proceedings against public undertakings or against debtors who are not traders.[484]

8.384 The application of national law to govern the opening of secondary proceedings entails that the local court may exercise its discretion as to whether or not to open such proceedings, including consideration of whether it is appropriate to do so.[485] The framework of EU law however places constraints upon the exercise of any such discretion. For example, the principle of non-discrimination[486] precludes conditions for the opening of secondary proceedings which draw a distinction between creditors seeking the opening of such proceedings on the basis of their place of residence or registered office.[487] Correspondingly the local court must exercise its discretion with regard to the purpose of secondary proceedings,[488] as explained above, and also the objective of the main proceedings and the principle of sincere co-operation.[489] In principle then the local court may open secondary proceedings even if all the assets of the debtor are within that Member State and the purpose of the main proceedings is protective. In such a case the local court must however consider the purpose of the main proceedings and the effect of the opening of secondary proceedings on the achievement of that purpose.[490]

---

[482] Case C-116/11 *Bank Handlowy w Warszawie SA v Christianapol sp z oo* ECLI:EU:C:2012:739, [2013] BPIR 174, paras 64–74. In this case the *procédure de sauvegarde* under French law required only that the debtor 'demonstrate the existence of difficulties, which he is not able to overcome, such as to lead to the cessation of payments': see Arts L.620-2 of the French Commercial Code.
[483] See the commentary under those OR Arts at paras 8.37–8.59 and 8.163–8.176 above.
[484] See commentary to Art 1 OR ('General Principles') at para 8.05 above.
[485] Case C-327/13 *Burgo Group SpA v Illochroma SA* (in liquidation) (2014) ECLI:EU: 2158, paras 59–63 and 67.
[486] See Case C-109/09 *Deutsche Lufthansa* (2011) EU:C:2011:129, para 37 and the case law cited.
[487] Burgo group at n 485 above at para 64.
[488] ibid at para 65.
[489] ibid at para 66.
[490] Case C-116/11 *Bank Handlowy w Warszawie SA v Christianapol sp z oo* [2013] Bus LR 956, ECLI: EU:C 2012:739, paras 53–63.

Article 27 OR also repeats the principle set out in Article 3(2) OR that the effects of **8.385** secondary proceedings are limited to the assets of the debtor located in the Member State in which the secondary proceedings are commenced. However, Article 18(2) OR does provide that a liquidator in Article 3(2) proceedings has the power to act in any other Member State in order to recover any assets of the debtor which were moved out of the territory after the commencement of the Article 3(2) OR proceedings and, in addition, can bring any action to set aside a transaction which is in the interests of the creditors.

The jurisdiction to determine the Member State in which assets are situated, in accor- **8.386** dance with Article 2(g) OR, is concurrent as between the court of the main proceedings and that of the secondary proceedings. This follows from the construction of Articles 3(2) and 25(1) OR, as interpreted by the CJEU in the *Nortel* case.[491] A consequence of a concurrent jurisdiction is that, inevitably, there will be a race to judgment as between liquidators in certain instances. The principal justification for the construction in favour of a concurrent jurisdiction is that, on the one hand, the protection of local interests (which is the object of a secondary proceeding) would not be realized if, for example, a related action or other action integral to the secondary proceeding could not be adjudicated on by the local court;[492] and, on the other hand, that the utility of a main proceeding with capacity to decide all issues would be diminished, contrary to Article 3(1) OR and Article 4 OR, if that jurisdiction were exclusive and the court with control of the main proceedings did not also have jurisdiction.[493] This approach however fails to give effect to the superiority of the main proceedings.

In the *Nortel* case the Court of Justice explained that the situation of an asset within a given **8.387** Member State was a question not to be determined applying the law application under national choice of law rules. Article 2(g) OR provided an autonomous set of rules for the determination of an asset's *situs*, which rules displaced any which would otherwise be applicable under national rules of private international law.[494]

(OR) Article 28—Applicable law

Save as otherwise provided in this Regulation, the law applicable to secondary proceedings shall be that of the Member State within the territory of which the secondary proceedings are opened.

Article 28 OR is a specific instance of the general rule in Article 4 that the law applicable to **8.388** insolvency proceedings is the law of the state of the opening of the proceedings.

---

[491] C-649/13 *Comité d'entreprise de Nortel Networks SA and others v Rogeau* (2015) ECLI:EU: C:2015:384.
[492] ibid at paras 34–38.
[493] ibid at paras 40–42.
[494] ibid at paras 49–55.

(OR) Article 29—Right to request the opening of proceedings

The opening of secondary proceedings may be requested by:
(a) the liquidator in the main proceedings;
(b) any other person or authority empowered to request the opening of insolvency proceedings under the law of the Member State within the territory of which the opening of secondary proceedings is requested.

8.389 Article 29(a) OR establishes a right of the 'liquidator', as defined by Article 2(b) OR, in the main proceedings to request the opening of secondary proceedings whether or not the local law gives him that right. This may be a useful power for example where the liquidator needs to exercise powers, which cannot be exercised simply by reason of his appointment in the main proceedings, such as 'coercive measures'.[495]

8.390 A liquidator in main proceedings will be able to request the opening of secondary proceedings in other Member States simply by producing a certified copy of the original decision appointing him (see Article 19 OR), probably together with a translation into one of the official languages of the Member State in which he wishes to make the application.

8.391 The courts in the relevant Member State will not be able to dismiss the application on the grounds that the debtor is solvent, since it is expressly provided that there should be no examination of the debtor's solvency on a request to open secondary proceedings (Article 27 OR).

8.392 Article 29(b) OR provides a specific instance of the general rule in Article 4(2) that the conditions for opening proceedings are governed by the law of the state of the opening of the proceedings. In other words, the question as to which person or authority is empowered to seek the opening of secondary proceedings must be determined on the basis of the national law of the Member State within the territory of which the opening of such proceedings is sought.[496] In practice, this rule gives local creditors the ability to request the opening of local proceedings in order to protect local interests and prevent the removal of assets by the liquidator in the main proceedings. The right to seek the opening of secondary proceedings cannot, however, be restricted to creditors who have their domicile or registered office within the Member State in whose territory the relevant establishment is situated, or to creditors whose claims arise from the operation of that establishment.[497]

8.393 The Polish Supreme Court has held, on the basis of the Polish, German, and Lithuanian language versions of Article 29(b) OR that only persons who can request the opening of *secondary* proceedings under the relevant Member State law will fall within Article 29(b) OR.[498]

---

[495] Art 18(3).
[496] Case C-327/13 *Burgo Group SpA v Illochroma SA (in liquidation)* (2014) ECLI:EU: 2158, para 51.
[497] ibid.
[498] *Polmos Lancut SA* C III CZP 115/09, 20 January 2010; see Barlowski, 'Practical Problems in Applying Regulation 1346/2000' (2011) 8 Corporate Rescue 172.

(OR) Article 30—Advance payment of costs and expenses

Where the law of the Member State in which the opening of secondary proceedings is requested requires that the debtor's assets be sufficient to cover in whole or in part the costs and expenses of the proceedings, the court may, when it receives such a request, require the applicant to make an advance payment of costs or to provide appropriate security.

8.394 This provision provides for the fact that in certain jurisdictions insolvency proceedings cannot be commenced in relation to a debtor unless the debtor has sufficient assets to cover the costs and expenses of the proceedings. It is important to note that any such requirement must be part of the general law of the Member State concerned and cannot be introduced specifically for secondary proceedings commenced pursuant to the Regulation.[499]

(OR) Article 31—Duty to co-operate and communicate information

1. Subject to the rules restricting the communication of information, the liquidator in the main proceedings and the liquidators in the secondary proceedings shall be duty bound to communicate information to each other. They shall immediately communicate any information which may be relevant to the other proceedings, in particular the progress made in lodging and verifying claims and all measures aimed at terminating the proceedings.
2. Subject to the rules applicable to each of the proceedings, the liquidator in the main proceedings and the liquidators in the secondary proceedings shall be duty bound to cooperate with each other.
3. The liquidator in the secondary proceedings shall give the liquidator in the main proceedings an early opportunity of submitting proposals on the liquidation or use of the assets in the secondary proceedings.

8.395 Article 31 OR deals with a recurring problem in cross-border insolvencies relating to the same debtor, namely how to co-ordinate different proceedings in different jurisdictions. Prior to and outside the Regulation, solutions have to be developed between different insolvency administrators and their national courts.[500] Where the OR applies, there are mandatory provisions.

8.396 As the Virgos-Schmit Report states, co-operation between the various liquidators is necessary to ensure the smooth course of operations in the proceedings.[501] Article 31(1) OR therefore provides that as a general principle the liquidator in the main proceedings and the liquidators in any secondary proceedings should communicate information to each other (subject to any rules of national law restricting such communication) and in particular should immediately communicate any information which might be relevant to the other proceedings. The provision goes on to state that such information to be communicated includes information relating to the lodging and verification of claims and relating to

---
[499] See the Virgos-Schmit Report, para 228.
[500] See ch 5 above.
[501] Virgos-Schmit Report, para 229.

the termination of the proceedings. The duty to co-operate is however expressed as being '[s]ubject to the rules applicable to each of the proceedings'. Accordingly, the duty has not been construed as a freestanding obligation capable of overriding other mandatory features of the Regulation or the applicable law under the Regulation, for example the rules applicable to the distribution of assets.[502]

8.397 The Virgos-Schmit Report itself gives more detail about the type of information which it is envisaged is to be provided and exchanged.[503] This includes information relating to:

- the assets of the debtor;
- any actions planned or under way to recover assets or to obtain payment or to set aside transactions;
- the liquidation of assets;
- the lodging of claims;
- the verification of claims and any disputes arising;
- the ranking of creditors;
- planned reorganization measures;
- proposed compositions;
- allocation and payment of dividends;
- the progress of the proceedings.

The wording at the beginning of Article 31(1) 'Subject to the rules restricting the communication of information' appears to refer to domestic rules relating to privacy-sensitive data.

8.398 Article 31(2) OR adds to the duty to communicate information by introducing a general duty on liquidators in proceedings relating to the same debtor to co-operate with each other. It clearly makes sense that where 'liquidators'[504] are seeking to achieve a common goal (to maximize the return to the creditors of the debtor) then they should co-operate to try to achieve this aim. A use of Article 31(2) OR which was developed by the English court was to issue a letter of request to the courts of other Member States following the opening of main proceedings in order to secure a means by which the Member State liquidator is to be notified of any application to open secondary insolvency proceedings.[505] However, there will undoubtedly be circumstances where there is a tension between the aims of a liquidator in secondary proceedings and the aims of a liquidator in the main proceedings. For example, there may be a dispute as to whether or not a particular asset is a local asset (so falling under the secondary proceedings) or an asset in relation to which the main proceedings take effect.

8.399 Article 31(3) OR develops one particular aspect of the duty to co-operate by imposing a duty on the liquidator in secondary proceedings to permit the liquidator in the main proceedings an early opportunity to submit proposals on the secondary liquidation and the use of the debtor's assets in those proceedings. The Virgos-Schmit Report states that this mechanism might enable the liquidator in the main proceedings to prevent, for example,

---

[502] *Re Alitalia Linee Aeree Italiane SpA* [2011] 1 BCLC 606, paras 42–43.
[503] Virgo-Schmit Report, para 230.
[504] As defined in Art 2(b).
[505] *Re Nortel Networks SA* [2009] EWHC 206 (Ch), [2009] BCC 343, para 10. This is on the basis that courts as well as liquidators have a duty to co-operate: see 8.400 below.

the sale of assets in the secondary proceedings. However, there is no indication in Article 31(3) OR that the liquidator in the secondary proceedings is bound to comply with any proposals submitted to him by the main liquidator. Presumably the liquidator in the main proceedings could challenge any decision made by the liquidator in the secondary proceedings upon submitted proposals under the relevant national law.

8.400 The liquidator in the main proceedings may be able to lodge the claims of all those creditors who have lodged claims in the main proceedings in any secondary proceedings (see Article 32(2) OR) and will in any event be able to participate in the secondary proceedings 'on the same basis as a creditor' (Article 32(3) OR). This might itself give the liquidator in the main proceedings an influential role in the secondary proceedings.

8.401 Where a liquidator fails to comply with the duty to co-operate or to communicate information, the *lex concursus* of the Member State in which proceedings are opened and in which he is appointed, governs the question of his liability.

8.402 Article 31 OR does not expressly place a duty of co-operation on the courts of Member States, but such an obligation is to be implied.[506] The obligation on courts to co-operate is expressly spelt out in the UNCITRAL Model Law.[507]

(OR) Article 32—Exercise of creditors' rights

1. Any creditor may lodge his claim in the main proceedings and in any secondary proceedings.
2. The liquidators in the main and any secondary proceedings shall lodge in other proceedings claims which have already been lodged in the proceedings for which they were appointed, provided that the interests of creditors in the latter proceedings are served thereby, subject to the right of creditors to oppose that or to withdraw the lodgement of their claims where the law applicable so provides.
3. The liquidator in the main or secondary proceedings shall be empowered to participate in other proceedings on the same basis as a creditor, in particular by attending creditors' meetings.

8.403 Since Article 4(2)(h) OR provides that the law of the state of the opening of the proceedings governs the lodging of claims, Article 32(1) OR only applies to claims which are admissible under the law governing the proceedings in question (*lex concursus*).

8.404 It is necessary to allow creditors to claim in both main and secondary proceedings because the assets will be different and the priorities are likely to be different. These differences cannot completely be compensated for by the 'imputation' (hotchpot) provision in Article 20(2) OR.

---

[506] *Re Nortel Networks SA* [2009] BCC 343; *Re Collins & Aikman* (Higher Regional Court of Graz, 20 October 2005) 3 R 149/05 reported at NZI 2006 vol 11, p 660, *Re Stojevic* (Higher Regional Court, Vienna, 9 November 2004), 28 R 225/04w. See also the discussion of this question in Vallender, 'Judicial Co-operation within the EC Insolvency Regulation' (Winter 2007) 30 Eurofenix Insol Europe 8 et seq.
[507] UNCITRAL Model Law on Cross-Border Insolvency, Art 25.

8.405 It has been suggested that the ability to claim in both proceedings 'may engender considerable administrative complexity in cross-accounting and record keeping'.[508] If that proves to be the case in relation to a debtor, consideration should be given to simplifying the claims and distribution procedure by means of parallel compositions in the main and secondary proceedings.[509]

8.406 The creditors entitled to lodge claims in both proceedings pursuant to the Regulation are those creditors who have their habitual residence, domicile, or registered office in a Member State (Article 39 OR): of course the law governing the main or secondary proceedings may well allow creditors from other states to lodge claims. Creditors who are entitled to lodge claims include the tax and social security authorities of other Member States (Article 39 OR).

8.407 Article 32(2) OR avoids the need for individual creditors in main or secondary proceedings to come to grips with the linguistic and legal difficulties that may be found in trying to claim in the other type of proceeding.

8.408 Article 32(3) OR provides that a liquidator in each type of proceeding is entitled to participate[510] in the other type of proceeding on the same basis as a creditor, including participation by attending creditors' meetings. It might be thought from the wording of Article 32(3) OR that this would include a liquidator being entitled to exercise the voting rights attaching to the claims which he lodges in proceedings on behalf of creditors who have lodged claims in his proceedings. However, the Virgos-Schmit Report indicates that such a proposal was specifically rejected during the negotiations leading up to the agreement of the Regulation.[511]

8.409 The Regulation does not prevent the creditors in each of main and secondary proceedings themselves lodging claims in each proceeding. It is not clear in terms of the Regulation what is to happen if both the liquidator and one or more creditors in one proceeding lodge identical or overlapping claims in the other. Since *pari passu* treatment for creditors of equal standing is a fundamental principle of the Regulation, the claim (and each part of the claim) can only be counted once. The apparent ability for the same claim to be lodged by both creditors and liquidator suggests that if that happens the claims remain the creditors' claims and only the creditors can vote on them and receive dividends in respect of them.

8.410 It is not clear in what circumstances creditors would want to exercise their rights under Article 32(2) OR to oppose their claims being lodged in other proceedings by the liquidator or to exercise any right given by the applicable law to withdraw a claim previously lodged

---

[508] Fletcher (n 397 above) para 31-056.
[509] See also Art 34 OR. A technique used in one case was for the English court in charge of the main proceedings to authorize the liquidator to delegate to the foreign trustee in charge of the secondary insolvency proceedings in another Member State the distribution under the main proceeding, so that he could conduct a *de facto* joint distribution in both estates. This was possible because English law allows liquidators etc to delegate the performance of duties to an agent and because the creditor priorities in the two proceedings were the same. It was convenient because most creditors were in the secondary jurisdiction and claimed under the law of that jurisdiction.
[510] The English, French, and Dutch texts refer to 'participate'. The German text, however, has '*mitzuwirken*' (to co-operate). The latter wording suggests that the power vested in the liquidator by Art 32(3) OR only exists when he has lodged the creditor's claims pursuant to Art 32(2). This limitation does not make sense given the central principle of co-operation and communication.
[511] Virgos-Schmit Report, para 240.

in proceedings. One possible situation might be where a claim has been made by a creditor with a right in rem which the creditor has inadvertently omitted to disclose, and the omission might under the applicable law have the effect of waiving the right in rem. The lodging of a claim may also result in the creditor incurring certain costs.

(OR) Article 33—Stay of liquidation

1. The court, which opened the secondary proceedings, shall stay the process of liquidation in whole or in part on receipt of a request from the liquidator in the main proceedings, provided that in that event it may require the liquidator in the main proceedings to take any suitable measure to guarantee the interests of the creditors in the secondary proceedings and of individual classes of creditors. Such a request from the liquidator may be rejected only if it is manifestly of no interest to the creditors in the main proceedings. Such a stay of the process of liquidation may be ordered for up to three months. It may be continued or renewed for similar periods.
2. The court referred to in paragraph 1 shall terminate the stay of the process of liquidation:
   - at the request of the liquidator in the main proceedings,
   - of its own motion, at the request of a creditor or at the request of the liquidator in the secondary proceedings if that measure no longer appears justified, in particular, by the interests of creditors in the main proceedings or in the secondary proceedings.

There is an initial question as to whether Article 33 OR, in referring to the 'process of liquidation', is referring to the secondary proceedings or merely to the process of liquidation of assets within the secondary proceeding. In the series of cases involving the Collins & Aikman group of companies, the Austrian Higher Regional Court (Court of Appeal) in Graz[512] held that Article 33 only stays the process of liquidating assets and not the secondary proceedings as a whole. **8.411**

It is likely that the most common situation where a stay is requested is where the 'liquidator' in the main proceedings is seeking to rescue, reorganize, or sell the business or assets of the debtor as a whole (as in the *Collins & Aikman* case mentioned above) and therefore needs to avoid a liquidation of assets in the secondary proceedings. **8.412**

Although the powers of the local court in considering a request for a stay are limited, the court does have the power, as the price of the stay, to require the liquidator in the main proceedings to ensure that the interests of the creditors in the secondary proceedings (and individual classes of them) are properly looked after.[513] This may involve setting up a mechanism to ensure that the local creditors as a whole and each class of local creditors are better off than they would have been in a liquidation.[514] **8.413**

---

[512] (Oberlandesgericht, 20 October 2005), 3 R 149/05, NZI (Neue Zeitschrift für Insolvenz und Sanierung) 2006, vol 11, 660 on appeal from the Landesgericht Leoben, 31 August 2005, 17 p 56/05, NZI 2005, vol 11, 646.
[513] The limitations on the court's obligation to grant a stay have been described as 'unclear': Fletcher (n 397 above) para 31-053.
[514] The measures could be analogous to those used in *Re Collins & Aikman Europe SA* [2007] 1 BCLC 182, [2006] BCC 861; *Re MG Rover España SA* [2006] BCC 599, and *Re MG Rover Belux SA/NV* [2007] BCC 446.

8.414 The local court can only reject the request 'if it is manifestly of no interest to the creditors in the main proceedings'. The use of the word 'manifestly', as in the public policy exception in Article 26 OR, suggests that if a request is made it should only be rejected in a wholly exceptional case. The liquidator in the main proceedings should be allowed a margin of appreciation on his application as to whether a stay of the secondary proceedings is of any interest to the creditors in the main proceedings.

8.415 A stay may only be granted initially for a period of time up to three months, a period normally too short in practice for a rescue, reorganization, or sale as a going concern. However, there is no limit to the number of extensions of the stay for up to three months at a time. The effect of this seems to be to enable the local court to require reporting back to it by the liquidator in the main proceedings, through the mechanism of the extension applications, at intervals of no greater than three months at a time.

8.416 The Regulation is silent with regard to requests for reconsideration or an appeal against the (affirmative or negative) decision on a stay. Domestic law should fill in this gap.

8.417 The granting of a stay stops the liquidation of assets in the secondary proceedings, but it does not entitle the liquidator in the main proceedings to dispose of the same assets.

8.418 The local court is bound to terminate the stay on the application of the liquidator in the main proceedings: Article 33(2) OR. This refers to the stay granted under Article 33(1) OR; no doubt a different stay could then be granted under the local law governing the local proceedings if justified under it, for example if it were in the interests of local creditors: Article 4(2) OR.

8.419 The test under Article 33(2) OR on an application by a creditor or by the liquidator in the secondary proceedings for the termination of the stay is different from the approach to granting the stay. The stay has to be terminated if it is no longer justified in accordance with the interests of the creditors in the main proceedings and the interests of the creditors in the secondary proceedings. This test was held to be satisfied in the case of the Austrian proceedings relating to Collins & Aikman on the grounds that:

  (i) the creditors in the main and secondary proceedings were the same;
  (ii) the creditors would be paid in full by the proposed sale in the secondary proceeding; and
  (iii) the purchaser had good economic reasons for saying it could not keep its offer open until a later date and therefore any delay would threaten the ability to pay creditors of this company in full.[515]

(OR) Article 34—Measures ending secondary insolvency proceedings

1. Where the law applicable to secondary proceedings allows for such proceedings to be closed without liquidation by a rescue plan, a composition or a comparable measure, the liquidator in the main proceedings shall be empowered to propose such a measure

---

[515] (Leoben Landesgericht, 1 December 2005) 17 p 56/05 m, NZI 2006, vol 11, 663.

himself. Closure of the secondary proceedings by a measure referred to in the first subparagraph shall not become final without the consent of the liquidator in the main proceedings; failing his agreement, however, it may become final if the financial interests of the creditors in the main proceedings are not affected by the measure proposed.

2. Any restriction of creditors' rights arising from a measure referred to in paragraph 1 which is proposed in secondary proceedings, such as a stay of payment or discharge of debt, may not have effect in respect of the debtor's assets not covered by those proceedings without the consent of all the creditors having an interest.

3. During a stay of the process of liquidation ordered pursuant to Article 33, only the liquidator in the main proceedings or the debtor, with the former's consent, may propose measures laid down in paragraph 1 of this Article in the secondary proceedings; no other proposal for such a measure shall be put to the vote or approved.

8.420 A rescue plan or composition closing secondary proceedings is clearly a measure which may affect the main proceedings themselves. Article 34(1) OR recognizes the primacy of the main proceedings by giving special powers to the liquidator in the main proceedings in relation to the closure of secondary proceedings.

8.421 The liquidator in the main proceedings is himself empowered to propose a rescue plan, composition, or comparable measure available under the relevant national law to close secondary proceedings. This ensures that he has standing (*locus standi*) to make such an application, which he might otherwise not have under law governing the secondary proceedings.

8.422 Where any such measure is proposed by another person, then the liquidator in the main proceedings has a right of veto on the measure becoming final unless the financial interests of the creditors in the main proceedings are not affected by the proposed measure (Article 34(1) OR). This right of veto enables the liquidator in the main proceedings to assert the primacy of those proceedings. In relation to the question of whether or not the 'financial interests' of the creditors in the main proceedings are affected by the proposed composition, it appears that the reference to 'financial interests' means specifically whether or not the proposed measure will affect the dividend which the creditors in the main proceedings are likely to receive.[516]

8.423 Where the liquidator in the main proceedings has obtained a stay of the secondary proceedings in place pursuant to Article 33 OR, then Article 34(3) OR provides that only the liquidator in the main proceedings or the debtor with the liquidator's consent, may propose such a measure. This exclusivity provision gives the liquidator in the main proceedings an important degree of control over the secondary proceedings.

8.424 Just as all Article 3(2) OR proceedings cannot restrict creditors' rights in relation to assets in other Member States save in respect of 'those creditors who have given their consent' (Article 17(2) OR),[517] rescue/composition/comparable measures relating to a secondary proceeding cannot restrict creditors' rights in respect of assets not covered by the secondary

---

[516] Virgos-Schmit Report, para 249.
[517] See the commentary on this provision in paras 8.304–8.307 above.

proceedings without 'the consent of all the creditors having an interest' (Article 34(2) OR). It is not entirely clear why different language is used. It may be that in the case of Article 17(2) OR it is envisaged that there may be a mechanism for a majority to bind a minority so that all creditors or a class or group of creditors in one or more other Member States can become bound by the restriction, whereas the use of the word 'all' in Article 34(2) OR requires unanimity amongst creditors 'having an interest' in the foreign assets. It is not clear, however, that the use of the word 'all' is intended to have this effect. The phrase 'having an interest' is also different and presumably extends not only to interests in rem and rights to retention of title but also interests in a prospective dividend as an unsecured creditor. One suspects the translator did not appreciate that 'having an interest' in English law often refers to a proprietary interest and the phrase 'having an interest' should probably have read 'interested': compare the French version: '*les créanciers intéressés*'.[518]

8.425 In the case of English law, it is possible to 'close' secondary proceedings commenced in England (ie winding-up by the court, creditors' voluntary liquidation with confirmation by the court, and bankruptcy) by various means without liquidation. The phrase 'a rescue plan, a composition or a comparable measure' seems to fit a compromise or reorganization by means of a 'scheme' or 'restructuring plan' under Parts 26 and 26A of the Companies Act 2006. Such an exit would be recognized under Article 25 OR in other Member States as a composition approved by the court which opened the secondary proceedings.

8.426 Company voluntary arrangements ('CVAs') and individual voluntary arrangements ('IVAs') will also fit the phrase if their terms amount to a rescue or composition, which they normally would. However, these are proceedings covered by the Regulation as 'voluntary arrangements under insolvency legislation' in Annex A, and since they are not 'winding-up' proceedings listed in Annex B, they cannot be opened as secondary proceedings (ie Article 3(2) OR proceedings opened after the opening of main proceedings): Article 3(3) OR. If that were to stop CVAs and IVAs being used pursuant to Article 34 OR to end secondary proceedings it would be very unfortunate and contrary to the interests of creditors. The point of limiting secondary proceedings to winding-up proceedings is to maintain the primacy of the main proceedings; once the secondary proceedings start as winding-up proceedings, that primacy is maintained, in relation to rescues and compromises etc, by Article 34 OR. Therefore there is no reason to exclude CVAs and IVAs from the exit routes available, even if the result may look odd, in that it could lead to an exit via a procedure which could not be opened as a secondary proceeding in its own right and which would have to be recognized under Article 25 OR as a judgment concerning the 'closure' of the secondary proceeding. Pursuant to OR Article 36, Article 34 OR will also apply to Article 3(2) OR proceedings where main proceedings are opened subsequently. In such cases, schemes could undoubtedly be used to 'close' administration order proceedings. It is submitted that CVAs can also be so used, for the reasons suggested above.

---

[518] Note however that the text of Art 47(2) RR (the counterpart of Art 34(2) OR), employs the same form of words: '… without the consent of all the creditors having an interest.'

(OR) Article 35—Assets remaining in the secondary proceedings

If by the liquidation of assets in the secondary proceedings it is possible to meet all claims allowed under those proceedings, the liquidator appointed in those proceedings shall immediately transfer any assets remaining to the liquidator in the main proceedings.

Since the liquidator in the main proceedings will have had to lodge in the secondary proceedings the claims of creditors in the main proceedings, there may not often be a surplus in the secondary proceedings to be passed over to the main proceedings. However, the law governing the secondary proceedings may be more restrictive as to the types and amounts of claims admissible in those proceedings and that may lead to a surplus. **8.427**

It is consistent with the primacy of the main proceedings that the surplus in the secondary proceedings should go to pay claims admissible in the main proceedings rather than go to the debtor. By contrast, there is no provision for any surplus in the main proceedings to go to creditors in any secondary proceedings, reflecting the supremacy of the main proceedings. In certain cases this may cause injustice: for example, if the main proceedings exclude the claims of certain creditors or part of the quantum of such claims, and they can only claim in the secondary proceedings, the surplus in the main proceedings will go to the debtor and not to the creditors in the secondary proceedings. **8.428**

(OR) Article 36—Subsequent opening of the main proceedings

When the proceedings referred to in Article 3(1) are opened following the opening of the proceedings referred to in Article 3(2) in another Member State, Articles 31 to 35 shall apply to those opened first, in so far as the progress of those proceedings so permits.

Where Article 3(2) OR proceedings are commenced prior to the commencement of main proceedings (in accordance with Article 3(4) OR), they are not 'secondary' proceedings and may be referred to as 'independent territorial proceedings' or simply 'territorial' proceedings. **8.429**

Recital (17) OR states, however, that if main proceedings are opened 'the territorial proceedings become secondary'. The Virgos-Schmit Report similarly indicates that in such circumstances 'the proceedings opened at the place of the centre of main interests will be the main proceedings, while the proceedings previously opened at the place of the establishment *will have to be necessarily regarded as secondary proceedings*'[519] (emphasis added). This is a logical and realistic approach to the state of affairs resulting from the chronological sequence of opening of the relevant proceedings, but it can be observed that there is no formal provision within the body of the Regulation to the effect that the subsequent opening of main proceedings causes the previously-opened, Article 3(2) OR proceedings to be transformed into '*secondary proceedings*' as such. Article 36 thus provides a pragmatic solution to the problem of co-ordination between the two proceedings, while Article 37 OR enables the liquidator in the main proceedings to procure the conversion of territorial **8.430**

---

[519] Virgos-Schmit Report, para 254.

proceedings which do not qualify as 'winding-up' proceedings into one of the more limited range of proceedings listed in Annex B. In principle, however, rescue proceedings which have been commenced in the state where the debtor has an establishment, and which have been opened first in time, could continue on that basis in conjunction with rescue proceedings later opened at the debtor's centre of main interests, provided that the officeholder in the main proceedings does not choose to invoke the power available under Article 37 OR. A 'cross-border' rescue process could therefore be inaugurated, without the problems potentially engendered by the Regulation's somewhat inflexible rule that 'secondary proceedings must be winding-up proceedings'.[520] If time and circumstances so permit, it may be worthwhile in appropriate cases to arrange for the opening of concurrent, rescue-type proceedings to be co-ordinated in such a way that proceedings are first opened in those locations where the debtor has establishments, thereby enabling the 'lead' office-holder in the main proceedings to have the maximum flexibility in terms of the future conduct of the rescue process.

8.431 Independent territorial proceedings cannot simply be subject to Articles 31–35 OR in the same way as secondary proceedings, since their application may not be practical in the light of how far the independent territorial proceedings have progressed. Hence, Article 36 OR provides that Articles 31–35 OR are to apply to the territorial proceedings 'in so far as the progress of those proceedings so permits'.

8.432 The more limited application of Articles 31–35 OR in such cases illustrates another tactical advantage for local creditors in requesting, where there is an establishment in the Member State, the opening of Article 3(2) OR proceedings before main proceedings are opened.

(OR) Article 37—Conversion of earlier proceedings

The liquidator in the main proceedings may request that proceedings listed in Annex A previously opened in another Member State be converted into winding-up proceedings if this proves to be in the interests of the creditors in the main proceedings.

The court with jurisdiction under Article 3(2) shall order conversion into one of the proceedings listed in Annex B.

8.433 This Article, like Article 36 OR, applies to independent territorial proceedings, which can be reorganization proceedings, whereas 'secondary' proceedings can only be winding-up proceedings listed in Annex B of the Regulation.

8.434 As part of the primary role of main proceedings, Article 37 OR provides that the liquidator in the main proceedings can request the court with jurisdiction over the independent territorial proceedings to convert them into winding-up proceedings if that proves to be in the interests of the creditors in the main proceedings. This undoubtedly gives the liquidator standing to make such an application, even where he might not have had any under the local law.

---

[520] Art 3(3) OR and see also Art 27 OR.

Article 37 OR, in the English version, states in mandatory terms that the local court 'shall' **8.435**
order the conversion. This is a mistranslation, since the Virgos-Schmit Report at paragraph
258 makes it clear that conversion is not mandatory and, for example, neither the French
nor German versions have the equivalent of 'shall'.[521] The amendments to the English
Insolvency Rules have not treated conversion as being mandatory and in fact have given the
court an express discretion as to whether to order conversion or not.[522] If conversion is ordered,
it is mandatory that the proceedings be converted into a winding-up proceeding and
perhaps the word 'shall' in the English version can be understood in that sense.

There was plainly concern about this provision, because Portugal made a special declara- **8.436**
tion about Article 37 OR as follows:

> Article 37 of Council Regulation (EC) No 1346/2000 of 29 May 2000 on insolvency
> proceedings, which mentions the possibility of converting territorial proceedings opened
> prior to the main proceedings into winding up proceedings, should be interpreted as
> meaning that such conversion does not exclude judicial appreciation of the state of the
> local proceedings (as is the case in Article 36) or of the application of the interests of public
> policy as provided for in Article 26.[523]

Thus it seems that Portugal considers that the local court can take into account the state of
progress of the local proceedings in considering whether to convert them.

(OR) Article 38—Preservation measures

**Where the court of a Member State which has jurisdiction pursuant to Article 3(1)
appoints a temporary administrator in order to ensure the preservation of the debtor's
assets, that temporary administrator shall be empowered to request any measures to
secure and preserve any of the debtor's assets situated in another Member State, provided
for under the law of that State, for the period between the request for the opening of
insolvency proceedings and the judgment opening the proceedings.**

There is often a gap between the 'request' (application) to open insolvency proceedings and **8.437**
the actual 'opening'. In the meanwhile, it may well be necessary to take urgent steps both in
the state of proposed opening and elsewhere.[524] A 'temporary administrator' may well be
appointed in such a situation and empowered by the appointing court to take urgent steps
to safeguard assets. In the *Eurofood* case,[525] the CJEU stated:

> 57. In that respect, it should be noted that Art.38 of the Regulation must be read in combination
> with Art.29, according to which the liquidator in the main proceedings is entitled
> to request the opening of secondary proceedings in another Member State. That Art.38

---

[521] The French has '*ordonne*' (orders) and the German '*ordnet*' (orders). Notably, the English version of the equivalent provision of RR (Art 51(1)) states that '... the court ... *may* order the conversion of the secondary proceedings into another type of insolvency proceedings ...' (emphasis added).
[522] rr 1.33, 2.61, and 5.33.
[523] The Portuguese Declaration is published at [2000] OJ C183/1.
[524] See also the discussion at paras 8.65 et seq above.
[525] Case C-341/04 *Re Eurofood IFSC Ltd* [2006] ECR I-3813, [2006] Ch 508, CJEU (Grand Chamber).

thus concerns the situation in which the competent court of a Member State has had main insolvency proceedings brought before it and has appointed a person or body to watch over the debtor's assets on a provisional basis, but has not yet ordered that that debtor be divested or appointed a liquidator referred to in Annex C to the Regulation. In that case, the person or body in question, though not empowered to initiate secondary insolvency proceedings in another Member State, may request that preservation measures be taken over the assets of the debtor situated in that Member State.

8.438 They went on to hold that Article 38 OR did not apply to a situation where the court had appointed a provisional liquidator listed in Annex C OR and had divested the debtor of control of his business, since that opened the proceeding and gave rise to the application of Article 29 OR, which would enable the provisional liquidator to apply for the opening of proceedings in the other Member State. This ignores the fact that by the express terms of Recital (16) OR the concept of 'temporary administrator' in Article 38 OR is meant to be understood as 'a *liquidator* temporarily appointed *prior to the opening* of the main insolvency proceedings' (emphasis added).[526] A 'temporary administrator' within Article 38 OR need not in any event be within the definition of 'liquidator' in Article 2(b) OR or be listed in Annex C.[527]

8.439 Article 38 OR specifically gives a temporary administrator in main proceedings the power to apply in another Member State for measures to secure and preserve the debtor's assets in that state available under the local law until the opening of the main proceedings. This is an important step forward in that the temporary administrator now has standing (*locus standi*) to apply in the local court, regardless of whether he had it under the local law, and he is not hindered by the fact that his appointment is only interim.

8.440 The approach of the CJEU quoted above appears to confirm the view of the Virgos-Schmit Report that this power vested in a temporary administrator can only be exercised in relation to Member States where the debtor has an 'establishment', thereby corresponding with the jurisdictional requirement for the commencement of secondary proceedings.[528] There is no such limitation expressed in the language and it may be arguable that no such limitation should be implied. It would seem to be more practical for the powers of the temporary administrator to request preservation measures to be exercisable in all Member States where the debtor has assets. Assets of the debtor in Member States where there is no establishment are just as much or more in need of being secured and preserved than those in Member States where there is an establishment. It would make more practical sense if, contrary to the apparent view of the CJEU, Articles 38 and 29 OR were regarded as having independent operation, with Article 29 applying (as a result of its express reference to opening 'secondary proceedings') only to cases where there is an 'establishment' in the other Member State and Article 38 applying more generally.

---

[526] See also the commentary under Art 3, sub-heading 'The concept of Opening' at paras 8.80 et seq above.
[527] Virgos-Schmit Report, para 263.
[528] ibid para 262.

D. Chapter IV: Provision of Information for Creditors and Lodgement of their Claims

(OR) Article 39—Right to lodge claims

Any creditor who has his habitual residence, domicile or registered office in a Member State other than the State of the opening of proceedings, including the tax authorities and social security authorities of Member States, shall have the right to lodge claims in the insolvency proceedings in writing.

8.441 Article 32(1) OR read with Article 36 OR has already provided for the right of creditors to lodge claims in both the main and Article 3(2) OR proceedings. Article 39 OR identifies the type of non-domestic creditor who is entitled to lodge claims in the proceedings in question. The right to lodge claims is linked, not to nationality, but to residence and domicile. It prevents discrimination against creditors resident or domiciled or incorporated in other Member States.

8.442 There is a considerable advance in Article 39 OR in that the tax and social security authorities of other Member States are expressly entitled to lodge claims; therefore the principle, which can be found in the law of most states, that foreign tax laws will not be enforced does not apply to the lodging of claims by creditors in proceedings to which the Regulation applies.[529] The Regulation in this regard stands in contrast to the successive iterations of the Regulation on Civil Jurisdiction and Judgments which expressly exclude revenue and customs matters from its scope.[530] It is considered that as a result of the specific inclusion of tax and social security authorities of other Member States the Article 26 OR public policy exception cannot be used to block such claims.

8.443 On the other hand, Article 39 OR does not grant foreign tax claims the priority they may enjoy in their countries of origin (priority for domestic tax claims exists in, for example, Swedish law). This means that the tax authorities of such countries will probably request, whenever possible, the opening of secondary proceedings in order to preserve their priority rights at least in relation to the local assets.

8.444 Although the right to lodge claims is a substantive right under the Regulation, all procedural matters governing the process of lodging are governed by the relevant national law which applies to the proceedings in question (Article 4(2)(h) OR). Thus matters such as time limits for lodging claims and the conditions for admissibility of claims are to be dealt with under the law governing the proceedings (*lex concursus*).

The same applies to the form of lodging of claims: Article 39 OR speaks of lodging 'in writing', but this means merely that the written submission of a claim must be accepted as if done in proper form. The law governing the proceedings may accept a submission in another form.

---

[529] Relatedly, in Case C-212/15 *ENEFI*, para 40 the CJEU held that tax claims have no preferential status under the Regulation and thus may be barred as a result of a failure to comply with procedural rules concerning the lodging of claims. As to the rule against the enforcement of foreign revenue laws see Dicey, Morris, and Collins, *The Conflict of Laws* (14th edn, 2006) paras 5-020 et seq.

[530] Art 1(1) of the EU Regulation on Civil Jurisdiction and Judgments (recast) (1215/2012), which has applied since 10 January 2015, and which is identically worded to Art 1(1) of the original version of the Civil Jurisdiction and Judgments Regulation (44/2001).

8.445 It is important to note that Article 39 OR is concerned only with the rights of those creditors who have a habitual residence, domicile, or registered office in a Member State.[531] The rights of creditors situated outside the European Union and in Denmark are governed, like the rights of domestic creditors, solely by the law governing the proceedings.

(OR) Article 40—Duty to inform creditors

1. As soon as insolvency proceedings are opened in a Member State, the court of that State having jurisdiction or the liquidator appointed by it shall immediately inform known creditors who have their habitual residences, domiciles or registered offices in the other Member States.
2. That information, provided by an individual notice, shall in particular include time limits, the penalties laid down in regard to those time limits, the body or authority empowered to accept the lodgement of claims and the other measures laid down. Such notice shall also indicate whether creditors whose claims are preferential or secured in rem need lodge their claims.

8.446 Since there is as yet no EU register of insolvency proceedings,[532] it is particularly important that either the court opening the proceedings or the liquidator[533] appointed should be obliged to inform all known creditors situated in other Member States.

8.447 The law governing the proceedings may prescribe that creditors shall be given additional information, not listed in Article 40(2) OR, but it cannot dispense with any of the requirements listed there.

8.448 The sensitive question of the language of notification is dealt with in Article 42(1) OR.

(OR) Article 41—Content of the lodgement of a claim

A creditor shall send copies of supporting documents, if any, and shall indicate the nature of the claim, the date on which it arose and its amount, as well as whether he alleges preference, security in rem or a reservation of title in respect of the claim and what assets are covered by the guarantee he is invoking.

8.449 Article 41 OR constitutes an exception to the rule stated in Article 4(2)(h) OR that the lodging of claims is a matter governed by the national law applying to the proceedings in question (see also Article 39 OR and Article 42(2) OR). This provision is intended to

---

[531] In considering the domicile of companies and other legal persons it will probably be helpful to have regard to Art 63 of the recast Jurisdiction and Judgments Regulation 1215/2012 (Art 60 of the Regulation on Civil Jurisdiction and Judgments 44/2001). This provides that any such entity will be domiciled at the place where it has its (a) statutory seat or (b) central administration, or (c) principal place of business. Art 63(2) of Regulation 1215/2012 provides that in the case of Ireland, Cyprus, and the UK 'statutory seat' means the registered office (or if none, the place of incorporation). The expression 'registered office' used in Art 40 OR is probably equivalent to the expression 'statutory seat' used in Regulations 1215/2012 and 44/2001.

[532] Provisions are made for registers in the RR—see below.

[533] Without aligning domestic legislation it will be unclear whether the obligation to inform rests on the court or on the liquidator.

facilitate the exercise by creditors in Member States other than the state where the proceedings were commenced to exercise their right under Article 39 OR to lodge a claim in those proceedings.[534] Accordingly, Article 41 OR prevents the relevant national law from imposing restrictions, other than those stated in Article 41 OR itself, on the lodging of claims. However, Article 41 does require a creditor to submit all that information which is necessary for the liquidator to identify and deal with his claim.

The English text once again has linguistic problems and should not be read literally. **8.450**

'Alleges preference'
'Preference' in this context cannot have the usual English insolvency law meaning of better **8.451** treatment of one out of a class of creditors having the *same* ranking. In this context the phrase here must mean 'claim preferential ranking'.

'Security in rem'
Taken literally, this would be a tautology in English insolvency law terms, since a 'security' **8.452** within section 248(b)(i) of the Insolvency Act 1986 would be a right *in rem*, ie a proprietary right. In this context, 'security' must include non-proprietary rights, so that the entire phrase means 'security' in the English insolvency law sense.

'Guarantee'
In English law, this would normally refer to a contract of suretyship creating a secondary **8.453** personal liability.[535] In the present context it refers to the means of ensuring payment, whether by means of preferential ranking, proprietary security, or retention of title.[536]

In *Riel*[537] the CJEU held that Article 41 sets out the *maximum* requirements, relating to **8.454** the content of the lodgement of a claim, which may be imposed by national legislation on creditors who have their habitual residence, domicile or registered office in a Member State other than that in which the insolvency proceedings have been opened. Thus, where national legislation does not impose one of the requirements specified in Article 41, Article 41 does not have the effect of precluding the creditor's claim.

(OR) Article 42—Languages

1. The information provided for in Article 40 shall be provided in the official language or one of the official languages of the State of the opening of proceedings. For that purpose a form shall be used bearing the heading 'Invitation to lodge a claim. Time limits to be observed' in all the official languages of the institutions of the European Union.

---

[534] Virgos-Schmit Report, para 273.
[535] See Rowlatt, *Principal and Surety* (6th edn, 2011) ch 1.
[536] In the German version '*sicherheit*' ('security' in a wide sense) is used both for 'security' in the phrase corresponding to 'security in rem' and for 'guarantee'.
[537] Case C-47/18 *Skarb Pánstwa Rzeczpospolitej Polskiej—Generalny Dyrektor Dróg Krajowych i Autostrad v Stephan Riel* ECLI:EU:C:2019:754.

2. Any creditor who has his habitual residence, domicile or registered office in a Member State other than the State of the opening of proceedings may lodge his claim in the official language or one of the official languages of that other State. In that event, however, the lodgement of his claim shall bear the heading 'Lodgement of claim' in the official language or one of the official languages of the State of the opening of proceedings. In addition, he may be required to provide a translation into the official language or one of the official languages of the State of the opening of proceedings.

8.455 Article 42 provides for rules governing the language in which creditors are to be notified of proceedings and in which they can lodge their claims. Again the aim of this provision is to facilitate the exercise by creditors in all Member States of their rights in relation to all proceedings wherever commenced. The provision tries to balance the difficulties for the 'liquidator' on the one hand in dealing with foreign language documents against the difficulties faced by a creditor in trying to claim in foreign language proceedings.

8.456 Article 42(1) OR deals with the notices to be sent to creditors informing them of proceedings pursuant to Article 40 OR. Such notices are to be provided in the official language (or one of the official languages) of the state of the opening of proceedings. The liquidator cannot tell whether any particular creditor will be able to understand this language and the onus is on creditors to obtain translations where necessary. The creditor will, in any case, become aware of the nature of the notification, as it must be made on a form bearing the heading 'Invitation to lodge a claim. Time limits to be observed' in all the official languages of the European Union. The form will be produced by the Secretariat of the Council.

8.457 Article 42(2) OR deals with the lodging of claims by creditors. In relation to this, it is open to a creditor who is situated in a state other than the state of the relevant proceedings to submit his claim in an official language of the state in which he is situated. In this way the Regulation makes it easier for creditors in other Member States to exercise their rights in insolvency proceedings.

8.458 However, Article 42(2) OR also provides that any claim must be headed 'Lodgement of claim' in the official language of the state of the opening of proceedings. This means that even if the liquidator does not understand the language in which the claim is lodged he knows that the document is the lodging of a claim. He can then, under Article 42(2) OR, require a translation into an official language of the state of the opening of proceedings.

8.459 In *R Jung GmbH v SIFA SA*,[538] SIFA was in French administration proceedings and under French law claims had to be lodged by creditors within four months of the official date for the onset of insolvency, 5 December 2003. The German creditor Jung had lodged a claim document on 10 November 2003. The time for lodging the claim expired on 5 April 2004. On 12 May 2004 the creditors' representative informed Jung that he would be recommending rejection of the claim as not being valid under French law because of a failure to prove the authority of the person lodging the claim. On 24 May 2004 Jung's claim was

---

[538] [2006] BCC 678.

lodged again signed by an officer of Jung and in a subsequent letter it was explained that this officer was the managing director (*Geschäftsführer*) of Jung. Although Jung's claim was not contested on its merits, the Tribunal de Commerce[539] of Orleans rejected the claim. The Court of Appeal in Orleans reversed this decision and allowed the claim on the basis that there had been a failure to comply with Article 42: the invitation to make claims had only been in French and the heading 'Invitation to lodge a claim. Time limits to be observed' required by Article 42 had not been supplied in the official languages of the European Union and in particular had not been supplied in the language of the creditor, German. The Court of Appeal held that in these circumstances the only remedy which would give effect to Articles 40(1) and 42 OR was to extend the time allowed by French law for the lodging of the German creditor's claim. Jung's claim was thus accepted as being valid.

E. Chapter V: Transitional and Final Provisions

(OR) Article 43—Applicability in time

> The provisions of this Regulation shall apply only to insolvency proceedings opened after its entry into force. Acts done by a debtor before the entry into force of this Regulation shall continue to be governed by the law which was applicable to them at the time they were done.

8.460 The OR applies only to insolvency proceedings commenced after 31 May 2002 (for the commencement date see Article 47 OR). It has no retrospective application. Although repealed by the RR, the OR will continue to govern insolvency proceedings within the scope of the OR opened before 26 June 2017: Article 84(2) RR.

8.461 As the Regulation is based on a sophisticated interplay between main and secondary proceedings, it must be assumed that it applies only if both proceedings were commenced after the Regulation's entry into force. Even after the entry into force it is, therefore, impossible to open secondary proceedings governed by the Regulation, if there are no main proceedings opened after 31 May 2002.

8.462 In *Re Ultra Motorhomes International Ltd*[540] a CVA proceeding listed in Annex A was opened prior to the coming into force of the Regulation and a liquidation proceeding was opened in respect of the same debtor after the Regulation came into force. Under English law the two proceedings can in principle both continue, no automatic relation back to the start of the CVA takes place, and the Supervisor of the CVA (listed as a 'liquidator' in Annex C OR) can operate independently of the liquidation. It was held that proceedings by the Supervisor could not fall within the Regulation, even if they took place during the liquidation, which was a main proceeding under the Regulation.

---

[539] This type of court is not a 'commercial' court in the English sense, as the judges are part-time and not legally qualified.
[540] [2006] BCC 57.

(OR) Article 44—Relationship to Conventions

1. After its entry into force, this Regulation replaces, in respect of the matters referred to therein, in the relations between Member States, the Conventions concluded between two or more Member States, in particular:

    (a) the Convention between Belgium and France on Jurisdiction and the Validity and Enforcement of Judgments, Arbitration Awards and Authentic Instruments, signed at Paris on 8 July 1899;

    (b) the Convention between Belgium and Austria on Bankruptcy, Winding-up, Arrangements, Compositions and Suspension of Payments (with Additional Protocol of 13 June 1973), signed at Brussels on 16 July 1969;

    (c) the Convention between Belgium and the Netherlands on Territorial Jurisdiction, Bankruptcy and the Validity and Enforcement of Judgments, Arbitration Awards and Authentic Instruments, signed at Brussels on 28 March 1925;

    (d) the Treaty between Germany and Austria on Bankruptcy, Winding-up, Arrangements and Compositions, signed at Vienna on 25 May 1979;

    (e) the Convention between France and Austria on Jurisdiction, Recognition and Enforcement of Judgments on Bankruptcy, signed at Vienna on 27 February 1979;

    (f) the Convention between France and Italy on the Enforcement of Judgments in Civil and Commercial Matters, signed at Rome on 3 June 1930;

    (g) the Convention between Italy and Austria on Bankruptcy, Winding-up, Arrangements and Compositions, signed at Rome on 12 July 1977;

    (h) the Convention between the Kingdom of the Netherlands and the Federal Republic of Germany on the Mutual Recognition and Enforcement of Judgments and other Enforceable Instruments in Civil and Commercial Matters, signed at The Hague on 30 August 1962;

    (i) the Convention between the United Kingdom and the Kingdom of Belgium providing for the Reciprocal Enforcement of Judgments in Civil and Commercial Matters, with Protocol, signed at Brussels on 2 May 1934;

    (j) the Convention between Denmark, Finland, Norway, Sweden and Iceland on Bankruptcy, signed at Copenhagen on 7 November 1933;

    (k) the European Convention on Certain International Aspects of Bankruptcy, signed at Istanbul on 5 June 1990.

    (l) the Convention between the Federative People's Republic of Yugoslavia and the Kingdom of Greece on the Mutual Recognition and Enforcement of Judgments, signed at Athens on 18 June 1959;[541]

    (m) the Agreement between the Federative People's Republic of Yugoslavia and the Republic of Austria on the Mutual Recognition and Enforcement of Arbitral Awards and Arbitral Settlements in Commercial Matters, signed at Belgrade on 18 March 1960;

---

[541] S 18A of Annex 2 to the Act of Accession relating to the accession of Cyprus, the Czech Republic, Estonia, Hungary, Latvia, Lithuania, Malta, Poland, Slovakia, and Slovenia, under the heading 'Cooperation in the fields of justice and home affairs': [2003] OJ L236/711–13 added sub-paras (l)–(w) to Art 44(1).

(n) the Convention between the Federative People's Republic of Yugoslavia and the Republic of Italy on Mutual Judicial Cooperation in Civil and Administrative Matters, signed at Rome on 3 December1960;
(o) the Agreement between the Socialist Federative Republic of Yugoslavia and the Kingdom of Belgium on Judicial Cooperation in Civil and Commercial Matters, signed at Belgrade on 24 September1971;
(p) the Convention between the Governments of Yugoslavia and France on the Recognition and Enforcement of Judgments in Civil and Commercial Matters, signed at Paris on 18 May1971;
(q) the Agreement between the Czechoslovak Socialist Republic and the Hellenic Republic on Legal Aid in Civil and Criminal Matters, signed at Athens on 22 October 1980, still in force between the Czech Republic and Greece;
(r) the Agreement between the Czechoslovak Socialist Republic and the Republic of Cyprus on Legal Aid in Civil and Criminal Matters, signed at Nicosia on 23 April 1982, still in force between the Czech Republic and Cyprus;
(s) the Treaty between the Government of the Czechoslovak Socialist Republic and the Government of the Republic of France on Legal Aid and the Recognition and Enforcement of Judgments in Civil, Family and Commercial Matters, signed at Paris on 10 May1984, still in force between the Czech Republic and France;
(t) the Treaty between the Czechoslovak Socialist Republic and the Italian Republic on Legal Aid in Civil and Criminal Matters, signed at Prague on 6 December 1985, still in force between the Czech Republic and Italy;
(u) the Agreement between the Republic of Latvia, the Republic of Estonia and the Republic of Lithuania on Legal Assistance and Legal Relationships, signed at Tallinn on 11 November 1992;
(v) the Agreement between Estonia and Poland on Granting Legal Aid and Legal Relations on Civil, Labour and Criminal Matters, signed at Tallinn on 27 November 1998;
(w) the Agreement between the Republic of Lithuania and the Republic of Poland on Legal Assistance and Legal Relations in Civil, Family, Labour and Criminal Matters, signed in Warsaw on 26 January 1993;
(x) the Convention between Socialist Republic of Romania and the Hellenic Republic on legal assistance in civil and criminal matters and its Protocol, signed at Bucharest on 19 October 1972;
(y) the Convention between Socialist Republic of Romania and the French Republic on legal assistance in civil and commercial matters, signed at Paris on 5 November 1974;
(z) the Agreement between the People's Republic of Bulgaria and the Hellenic Republic on Legal Assistance in Civil and Criminal Matters, signed at Athens on 10 April 1976;
(aa) the Agreement between the People's Republic of Bulgaria and the Republic of Cyprus on Legal Assistance in Civil and Criminal Matters, signed at Nicosia on 29 April 1983;
(ab) the Agreement between the Government of the People's Republic of Bulgaria and the Government of the French Republic on Mutual Legal Assistance in Civil Matters, signed at Sofia on 18 January 1989;

(ac) the Treaty between Romania and the Czech Republic on judicial assistance in civil matters, signed at Bucharest on 11 July 1994;

(ad) the Treaty between Romania and Poland on legal assistance and legal relations in civil cases, signed at Bucharest on 15 May 1999.

2. The Conventions referred to in paragraph 1 shall continue to have effect with regard to proceedings opened before the entry into force of this Regulation.

3. This Regulation shall not apply:

(a) in any Member State, to the extent that it is irreconcilable with the obligations arising in relation to bankruptcy from a convention concluded by that State with one or more third countries before the entry into force of this Regulation;

(b) in the United Kingdom of Great Britain and Northern Ireland, to the extent that is irreconcilable with the obligations arising in relation to bankruptcy and the winding-up of insolvent companies from any arrangements with the Commonwealth existing at the time this Regulation enters into force.

8.463 Article 43(3)(b) OR, as far as England is concerned, appears to be a rather oblique reference to section 426 of the Insolvency Act 1986. Section 426 obliges the English courts to assist insolvency proceedings from countries specified by delegated legislation where a request has been made for assistance by the relevant foreign court. The English Court of Appeal has held that the giving of assistance under section 426 is not mandatory although the court should assist if it is properly able to do so.[542]

8.464 The designated countries are, except for the Republic of Ireland and (since the handover to China) Hong Kong, all members of the Commonwealth.[543] The effect of Article 43(3)(b) therefore appears to be that section 426 will take precedence over the provisions of the Regulation in relation to requests for assistance from the courts of Commonwealth countries or territories which were designated under section 426 on 31 May 2002. In relation to the Republic of Ireland and Hong Kong, it appears that the provisions of the Regulation will prevail, in the event of any conflict, over any request for assistance made in accordance with section 426 so that any assistance may only be granted to the extent consistent with the provisions of the Regulation.

(OR) Article 45—Amendment of the Annexes

The Council, acting by qualified majority on the initiative of one of its members or on a proposal from the Commission, may amend the Annexes.

---

[542] *Hughes v Hannover Ruckversicherungs AG* [1996] 1 BCLC 497. See also *Re Southern Equities Corp; England v Smith* [2000] 2 BCLC 21, CA, the reasoning of which is not easy to reconcile with *Hughes*. See also the discussion of s 426 in ch 5 above.

[543] The Co-operation of Insolvency Courts (Designation of Relevant Countries and Territories) Order 1986, SI 1986/2123 designated (1) the Republic of Ireland, (2) the 10 UK Overseas Territories (Anguilla, Bermuda, Cayman Islands, Falkland Islands, Gibraltar, Hong Kong, Montserrat, St Helena, Turks and Caicos Islands, and the Virgin Islands), and (3) 6 independent members of the Commonwealth (Australia, the Bahamas, Botswana, Canada, New Zealand, and Tuvalu). The Co-operation of Insolvency Courts (Designation of Relevant Countries) Order 1996, SI 1996/253 designated South Africa and Malaysia, and the Co-operation of Insolvency Courts (Designation of Relevant Countries) Order 1998, SI 1998/2766 designated Brunei Darussalam, all three countries being independent members of the Commonwealth. However, when Hong Kong rejoined the People's Republic of China as a Special Administrative Region, it ceased to be part of the Commonwealth.

The Annexes, which detail the various insolvency proceedings governed by the Regulation, can be amended from time to time. This covers the possibility that new insolvency procedures may be introduced in Member States which will then need to be regulated by the Regulation. **8.465**

The Annexes have in fact been amended by means of amending or implementing Regulations[544] several times and a consolidated version appears in Appendix 1. Additional changes have resulted from the accession of new Member States and changes to insolvency proceedings in Member States. **8.466**

It must be stressed that the Member State concerned does not have the right to amend the Annexes by itself, but must ask the Council to do so. In fact, the Annexes can be amended even against the will of the Member State in question. **8.467**

(OR) Article 46—Reports

No later than 1 June 2012, and every five years thereafter, the Commission shall present to the European Parliament, the Council and the Economic and Social Committee a report on the application of this Regulation. The report shall be accompanied if need be by a proposal for adaptation of this Regulation.

The relevant report was in fact submitted on 12 December 2012 (12/12/12). This system of review is being displaced by the new system in the RR—see below. **8.468**

(OR) Article 47—Entry into force

This Regulation shall enter into force on 31 May 2002.

See also Article 43 OR, which provides that the Regulation has no retrospective effect. **8.469**

The concluding sentence of the Regulation declares that it is binding in its entirety and directly applicable in the Member States in accordance with the Treaty establishing the European Community.[545] **8.470**

---

[544] Council Regulations (EC) 603/2005, 694/2006, 1791/2006, 681/2007, 788/2008, 210/2010, 663/2014, and 1792/2016. Full references to these amending Regulations are supplied in ch 1, Section E, above, in nn 45–51. See also n 53.

[545] See Art 249 EC reproduced at app 4 below.

Recast Regulation 2015/848 on Insolvency Proceedings ('RR')

A. **Chapter I: General Provisions** — 8.471
  (RR) Article 1—Scope — 8.471
    Proceedings must be public — 8.475
    Proceedings must be collective — 8.477
    Proceedings can be 'interim proceedings' — 8.482
    Proceedings must be 'based on laws relating to insolvency' — 8.484
    The purpose of proceedings must be rescue, adjustment of debt, reorganization, or liquidation — 8.486
    Proceedings must be one of three types — 8.488
    'Non-financial' difficulties — 8.499
    The Article 1(2) exclusions — 8.500
  (RR) Article 2—Definitions — 8.502
    Introduction — 8.502
    'Collective proceedings' — 8.503
    'Collective investment undertakings' — 8.507
    'Debtor in possession' — 8.511
    'Insolvency proceedings' — 8.513
    'Insolvency practitioner' — 8.516
    'Court' — 8.519
    'Judgment opening insolvency proceedings' — 8.522
    'The time of the opening of proceedings' — 8.526
    'The Member State in which assets are situated' — 8.527
    Registered shares — 8.534
    Book entry securities — 8.536
    Bank accounts — 8.538
    'Establishment' — 8.540
  (RR) Article 3—International jurisdiction — 8.549
    Introduction — 8.549
    Three presumptions — 8.553
    Territorial insolvency proceedings — 8.564
  (RR) Article 4—Examination as to jurisdiction — 8.572
  (RR) Article 5—Judicial review of the decision to open main insolvency proceedings — 8.576
  (RR) Article 6—Jurisdiction for actions deriving directly from insolvency proceedings and closely linked with them — 8.579
  (RR) Article 7—Applicable law — 8.584
  (RR) Article 8—Third parties' rights in rem — 8.587
  (RR) Article 9—Set-off — 8.588
  (RR) Article 10—Reservation of title — 8.589
  (RR) Article 11—Contracts relating to immoveable property — 8.590
  (RR) Article 12—Payment systems and financial markets — 8.592
  (RR) Article 13—Contracts of employment — 8.594
  (RR) Article 14—Effects on rights subject to registration — 8.596
  (RR) Article 15—European patents with unitary effect and Community trade marks — 8.597
  (RR) Article 16—Detrimental acts — 8.600
  (RR) Article 17—Protection of third-party purchasers — 8.602
  (RR) Article 18—Effects of insolvency proceedings on pending lawsuits or arbitral proceedings — 8.603

B. **Chapter II: Recognition of Insolvency Proceedings** — 8.610
  (RR) Article 19—Principle — 8.610
  (RR) Article 20—Effects of recognition — 8.611
  (RR) Article 21—Powers of the insolvency practitioner — 8.612
  (RR) Article 22—Proof of the insolvency practitioner's appointment — 8.617
  (RR) Article 23—Return and imputation — 8.618
  (RR) Article 24—Establishment of insolvency registers — 8.619
  (RR) Article 25—Interconnection of insolvency registers — 8.626
  (RR) Article 26—Costs of establishing and interconnecting insolvency registers — 8.628
  (RR) Article 27—Conditions of access to information via the system of interconnection — 8.629
  (RR) Article 28—Publication in another Member State — 8.631
  (RR) Article 29—Registration in public registers of another Member State — 8.635
  (RR) Article 30—Costs — 8.636
  (RR) Article 31—Honouring of an obligation to a debtor — 8.637
  (RR) Article 32—Recognition and enforceability of other judgments — 8.638
  (RR) Article 33—Public policy — 8.642

C. **Chapter III: Secondary Insolvency Proceedings** — 8.643
  (RR) Article 34—Opening of proceedings — 8.643

(RR) Article 35—Applicable law	8.646	
(RR) Article 36—Right to give an undertaking in order to avoid secondary insolvency proceedings	8.647	
(RR) Article 37—Right to request the opening of secondary insolvency proceedings	8.663	
(RR) Article 38—Decision to open secondary insolvency proceedings	8.667	
(RR) Article 39—Judicial review of the decision to open secondary insolvency proceedings	8.676	
(RR) Article 40—Advance payment of costs and expenses	8.678	
(RR) Article 41—Co-operation and communication between insolvency practitioners	8.679	
(RR) Article 42—Co-operation and communication between courts	8.684	
(RR) Article 43—Co-operation and communication between insolvency practitioners and courts	8.695	
(RR) Article 44—Costs of co-operation and communication	8.702	
(RR) Article 45—Exercise of creditors' rights	8.703	
(RR) Article 46—Stay of the process of realization of assets	8.704	
(RR) Article 47—Power of the insolvency practitioner to propose restructuring plans	8.705	
(RR) Article 48—Impact of closure of insolvency proceedings	8.709	
(RR) Article 49—Assets remaining in the secondary insolvency proceedings	8.711	
(RR) Article 50—Subsequent opening of the main insolvency proceedings	8.712	
(RR) Article 51—Conversion of secondary insolvency proceedings	8.713	
(RR) Article 52—Preservation measures	8.718	
D. Chapter IV: Provision of Information for Creditors and Lodgement of their Claims	**8.719**	
(RR) Article 53—Right to lodge claims	8.719	
(RR) Article 54—Duty to inform creditors	8.722	
(RR) Article 55—Procedure for lodging claims	8.728	
E. Chapter V: Groups of Companies	**8.737**	
Introduction	8.737	
Groups of companies	8.742	
Co-operation and communication	8.744	
(RR) Article 56—Co-operation and communication between insolvency practitioners	8.745	
(RR) Article 57—Co-operation and communication between courts	8.750	
(RR) Article 58—Co-operation and communication between insolvency practitioners and courts	8.754	
(RR) Article 59—Costs of co-operation and communication in proceedings concerning members of a group of companies	8.756	
(RR) Article 60—Powers of the insolvency practitioner in proceedings concerning members of a group of companies	8.757	
Co-ordination	8.761	
(RR) Article 61—Request to open group co-ordination proceedings	8.762	
(RR) Article 62—Priority rule	8.764	
(RR) Article 63—Notice by the court seised	8.767	
(RR) Article 64—Objections by insolvency practitioners	8.770	
(RR) Article 65—Consequences of objection to the inclusion in group co-ordination	8.772	
(RR) Article 66—Choice of court for group co-ordination proceedings	8.774	
(RR) Article 67—Consequences of objections to the proposed co-ordinator	8.776	
(RR) Article 68—Decision to open group co-ordination proceedings	8.777	
(RR) Article 69—Subsequent opt-in by insolvency practitioners	8.782	
(RR) Article 70—Recommendations and group co-ordination plan	8.784	
(RR) Article 71—The co-ordinator	8.786	
(RR) Article 72—Tasks and rights of the co-ordinator	8.787	
(RR) Article 73—Languages	8.791	
(RR) Article 74—Co-operation between insolvency practitioners and the co-ordinator	8.792	
(RR) Article 75—Revocation of the appointment of the co-ordinator	8.793	
(RR) Article 76—Debtor in possession	8.795	
(RR) Article 77—Costs and distribution	8.796	
F. Chapter VI: Data Protection	**8.798**	
(RR) Article 78—Data protection	8.798	
(RR) Article 79—Responsibilities of Member States regarding the processing of personal data in national insolvency registers	8.798	
(RR) Article 80—Responsibilities of the Commission in connection with the processing of personal data	8.798	
(RR) Article 81—Information obligations	8.798	
(RR) Article 82—Storage of personal data	8.798	
(RR) Article 83—Access to personal data via the European e-Justice Portal	8.798	
G. Chapter VII: Transitional and Final Provisions	**8.799**	
(RR) Article 84—Applicability in time	8.799	
(RR) Article 85—Relationship to Conventions	8.801	
(RR) Article 86—Information on national and Union insolvency law	8.803	
(RR) Article 87—Establishment of the interconnection of registers	8.804	

(RR) Article 88—Establishment and subsequent amendment of standard forms	8.805	(RR) Article 90—Review clause 8.807 (RR) Article 91—Repeal 8.812 (RR) Article 92—Entry into force 8.814
(RR) Article 89—Committee procedure	8.806	

A. Chapter I: General Provisions

(RR) Article 1—Scope

1. This Regulation shall apply to public collective proceedings, including interim proceedings, which are based on laws relating to insolvency and in which, for the purpose of rescue, adjustment of debt, reorganisation or liquidation:
   (a) a debtor is totally or partially divested of its assets and an insolvency practitioner is appointed;
   (b) the assets and affairs of a debtor are subject to control or supervision by a court; or
   (c) a temporary stay of individual enforcement proceedings is granted by a court or by operation of law, in order to allow for negotiations between the debtor and its creditors, provided that the proceedings in which the stay is granted provide for suitable measures to protect the general body of creditors, and, where no agreement is reached, are preliminary to one of the proceedings referred to in point (a) or (b).

Where the proceedings referred to in this paragraph may be commenced in situations where there is only a likelihood of insolvency, their purpose shall be to avoid the debtor's insolvency or the cessation of the debtor's business activities.

The proceedings referred to in this paragraph are listed in Annex A.

2. This Regulation shall not apply to proceedings referred to in paragraph 1 that concern:
   (a) insurance undertakings;
   (b) credit institutions
   (c) investment firms and other firms, institutions and undertakings to the extent that they are covered by Directive 2001/24/EC; or
   (d) collective investment undertakings.

8.471 Despite the original Article 1 confining the scope of the OR to 'insolvency proceedings', the list of such proceedings in Annex A OR was not, even at the start, limited to insolvency proceedings in any strict sense. For example, Annex A OR included UK administration proceedings, which do not require proof of actual insolvency but only that the corporate debtor was likely to become insolvent.

8.472 Despite the original definition in the original Article 1, even more clearly pre-insolvency proceedings such as the French *sauvegarde* proceeding were added by amendment to Annex A OR. *Sauvegarde* is in fact a proceeding for which the debtor must not be insolvent in the French law sense when the proceeding is opened.

8.473 The re-worded Article 1 brings the position up to date and covers both insolvency and pre-insolvency proceedings. It also clearly brings within the scope of the Recast Regulation (RR) proceedings which involve a debtor in possession.

Very importantly, the RR has kept the principle established by the *Bank Handlowy* case **8.474**
(C-116/11) of the CJEU to the effect that, in the case of a conflict between the definition in
Article 1 and Annex A, Annex A will prevail: see the definition of 'insolvency proceedings'
in Article 2(4) RR and Recital (9) RR which provides, in so far as material:

> Those insolvency proceedings are listed exhaustively in Annex A. In respect of the national
> procedures contained in Annex A, this Regulation should apply without any further
> examination by the courts of another Member State as to whether the conditions set out in
> this Regulation are met. National insolvency procedures not listed in Annex A should not
> be covered by this Regulation.

The conditions set out in the new Article 1 will however still be significant when questions
arise as to whether any further national insolvency or pre-insolvency proceeding should
be added to RR Annex A.[546] A test case for this assumption will come up when the newly
enacted legislation in, eg, the Netherlands and Germany on preventive restructuring frameworks provide two types of identical proceedings one of which is called 'public' (because
of notification) and the other 'private' (because there is no notification). The public proceedings will be added to Annex A so that the question arises under which set of rules their
private counterparts are to be recognized. Recital (7) RR states that the mere fact that a national procedure is not listed in Annex A should not imply that it falls automatically under
the Brussels Regulation.

Proceedings must be public
The first condition that must be fulfilled by proceedings to fall within the Regulation is that **8.475**
they must be public. The intention of the Council in proposing this was that proceedings
within the scope of the Regulation should be subject to publicity in order to identify the
claims and creditors and, by that means ensure the collective nature of the proceedings and
give creditors a possibility to challenge the jurisdiction of the court. This point is now made
by Recital (12) RR.

One aspect of the requirement that the proceedings should be public is the Council's wish to **8.476**
exclude insolvency proceedings which are confidential. Some proceedings under the laws
of some Member States, such as France, take the form of negotiations between the debtor
and certain creditors with a view to reaching an agreement on the debtor's refinancing or
reorganization. Such proceedings are notified to the court but are not made public. Several
other member states followed this example in the course of transposing the Directive EU
2019/1023 on Preventive Restructuring Frameworks. The Council considered that the confidential nature of such proceedings made it impossible for a creditor or a court in another
Member State to know that such proceedings were pending. In the light of this, it would be
difficult to provide for the recognition of their effects throughout the EU. This point is made
in Recital (13) RR.

---

[546] A Commission proposal to act as gatekeeper in relation to the addition of proceedings to Annex A was not
accepted and additions will have to be made by Amending Regulation(s). The original Regulation Art 45 procedure for amending annexes by qualified majority has not been retained by the RR.

Proceedings must be collective

8.477 This was an express requirement of the original text[547] and is therefore not a change. Proceedings such as receivership, when it takes the form of a secured creditor's remedy, in Ireland, remain outside the scope of the RR.

8.478 The term 'collective' was not defined in the OR but is now defined in Article 2(1) RR. As well as the obvious case of proceedings including all of the debtor's creditors, the definition covers proceedings which include 'a significant part' of a debtor's creditors, with the proviso that the proceedings do not affect the claims of creditors which are not involved in them. The wider definition is particularly significant for pre-insolvency restructuring proceedings, which may for example only affect financial creditors, but not trade creditors. That potential situation is expressly referred to in Recital (14) RR.

8.479 The term 'a significant part' is rather vague, but Recital (14) RR suggests that it refers to creditors to whom the debtor 'owes … a substantial proportion of the debtor's outstanding debts …'. Presumably, 'outstanding' does not imply that the debts have to be immediately due and payable, otherwise that would seriously restrict the ability of pre-insolvency proceedings to fall within the RR.

8.480 Recital (14) RR also suggests that proceedings which do not include all the creditors '… should be proceedings aimed at rescuing the debtor'. That is contrasted with proceedings which lead to the 'definitive' cessation of business or liquidation of assets, which ought to include all creditors.

8.481 Recital (14) RR further suggests that in the case of natural persons the proceedings will be regarded as collective even if certain types of claims, such as maintenance claims, are not discharged. In the systems of some Member States there are exceptions to the general discharge of debts in individual insolvency and Recital (14) RR ensures that these will still be regarded as collective proceedings.

Proceedings can be 'interim proceedings'

8.482 The Council proposed the express inclusion of 'interim proceedings', so as expressly to cover proceedings which, under the law of some Member States, could be opened and conducted for a certain period of time on an interim or provisional basis, before the court issues an order confirming the continuation of the proceedings on a non-interim basis. The Council however wished it to be clear that such interim proceedings need to comply with all the criteria set out in Article 1 RR, and that the only difference was that the proceedings would be conducted for a period of time on an interim or provisional basis. This point is now made in Recital (15) RR.

8.483 Presumably the concept of interim proceedings is meant to cover such things as the appointment of a provisional liquidator under Irish or German law. The appointment of a provisional liquidator under Irish law was held in the circumstances of the *Eurofood* case (C-341/04) to constitute the opening of a proceeding within the OR.[548]

---

[547] See the commentary above on the original text of the Regulation.
[548] See the commentary to Art 3 of the OR.

Proceedings must be 'based on laws relating to insolvency'

The RR requires proceedings covered by the RR to be 'based on laws relating to insolvency', but this does not prevent pre-insolvency proceedings being included, as long as they are provided by laws relating to insolvency. The Council's proposal here was to clarify the fact that proceedings not based on a law relating to insolvency but which are based on general company law not designed exclusively for insolvency situations should not be included in the Regulation. This point is now made in Recital (16) RR. Recital (16) RR also suggests the exclusion of specific types of proceedings in which the debts of an individual of very low income and low asset value are written off, as long as there is no provision for payment to creditors. **8.484**

The requirement that proceedings be based on laws relating to insolvency and the express exclusion in Recital (16) RR of proceedings based on general company law not designed exclusively for insolvency situations is potentially problematic, for example, insofar as the French droit de insolvabilité is (and has always been) codified in the Code de Commerce. This positioning is consequence of the traditional French understanding of insolvency law being part of business law. Accordingly, this requirement should be read flexibly; it appears primarily to have been intended to exclude the English scheme of arrangement from the Regulation's scope. **8.485**

The purpose of proceedings must be rescue, adjustment of debt, reorganization, or liquidation

The Council wished to have a Recital clarifying that the term 'adjustment of debt' should cover *inter alia* a reduction in the amount to be paid by the debtor or an extension of the payment period granted to the debtor. In the text of the OR, an adjustment of debt or composition was mentioned only as a mode of closing an insolvency proceeding: see the old Article 25(1). **8.486**

Recital (10) RR clarifies that the scope of the RR extends to rescue and restructuring proceedings, including those where the debtor remains in possession. The Recital also makes it clear that such proceedings include those for a debt discharge or a debt adjustment in relation to consumers and self-employed persons. **8.487**

Proceedings must be one of three types

As well as the requirement that the purpose of proceedings within the RR must be for 'rescue, adjustment of debt, reorganisation or liquidation', proceedings, to be within the RR, must be one of three kinds. **8.488**

Proceeding type (a) is one in which the debtor is totally or partially divested of its assets and an insolvency practitioner is appointed. The divesting requirement was present in the original Article 1(1). The reference in the old provision to a 'liquidator' being appointed has been replaced by the broader and more inclusive 'insolvency practitioner'. The definitive list of such persons was contained in the original Annex C and is now contained in Annex B RR. The term 'insolvency practitioner' is defined in Article 2(5) RR. When considering whether or not an 'insolvency practitioner' has been appointed in a particular proceeding in an EU Member State, a court in another Member State should only have to consult the new Annex B and should not be obliged to consider whether an 'insolvency practitioner' in **8.489** fact has any of the functions set out in Article 2(5)(i)–(v) RR. That is because the definition itself cross-refers to Annex B. A similar cross-reference in the OR led to the list in Annex A OR being regarded as conclusive by the CJEU: *Bank Handlowy* (C-116/11).

8.490 A type (b) proceeding is one in which the assets and affairs of the debtor are subject to 'control or supervision by a court'. Some proceedings which were listed in Annex A do not necessarily involve 'control or supervision' by a court, for example voluntary liquidation in the UK and voluntary arrangements in the UK. Recital (10) RR explains that proceedings can be within the RR on the basis that in this context 'control' includes situations where the court only intervenes on an 'appeal' by a creditor or other interested party. Here, the word 'appeal' must be a reference to an application. In some countries, such as France, the equivalent word to 'appeal' refers to or includes an application by a third party such as a creditor or other interested party. For Ireland (like for UK), the expression is unfortunate, because 'appeal' is only used to refer to applications to a higher court and not to the same court or a court of co-ordinate jurisdiction.

8.491 Nevertheless, Recital (10) RR makes it clear that proceedings such as the Dutch public proceeding or the German notified restructuring plan are correctly included in the RR, assuming other criteria are met.

8.492 The word 'court' is defined in Article 2(6) below RR.[549] Importantly, it includes both judicial and other competent bodies of a Member State empowered to either open proceedings, to confirm such an opening, or to take decisions in the course of such proceedings.

8.493 A type (c) proceeding involves a temporary stay of individual enforcement proceedings granted by a court or by operation of law, in order to allow for negotiations between the debtor and its creditors. There is a proviso that the proceedings in which the stay is granted must provide for suitable measures to protect the general body of creditors and, where no agreement is reached, the proceedings must be preliminary to a type (a) or (b) proceeding.

8.494 The Council proposal suggested that a Recital should clarify that the scope of the RR should extend to procedures where the court orders a temporary moratorium on enforcement actions brought by individual creditors where such actions may adversely affect negotiations and hamper the prospects of a restructuring of the debtor's business. This is now Recital (11) RR. That Recital also states that such procedures should not be detrimental to the general body of creditors and that, if no agreement on the restructuring plan can be reached, should be preliminary to other procedures covered by the RR.

8.495 Type (c) proceedings may often occur where there is no present insolvency in the sense of the law of the relevant Member State and only a 'likelihood of insolvency'. In such cases, the coda to Article 1(1) RR specifies that the purpose of the proceedings 'shall be to avoid the debtor's insolvency or the cessation of the debtor's business activities'. This should not be a difficult criterion to meet in most cases of this kind.

8.496 Recital (10) RR specifically refers to cases within the RR where there is only a 'likelihood of insolvency' and links it to cases where there may be a debtor in possession.

---

[549] See also Recital (20) RR.

Article 1(1)(c) RR refers to pre-insolvency proceedings where the debtor remains in full **8.497** control of his assets and affairs, ie without any court supervision, but restricts the creditors' individual rights with a temporary moratorium on enforcement actions to allow for negotiations between the debtor and his creditors to reach a refinancing or restructuring agreement. In this case, however, the RR lays down additional safeguards: (i) the proceedings must provide for suitable measures to protect the general body of creditors and (ii) they must be preliminary to one of the other two types of proceedings if no agreement is reached. Spanish pre-insolvency proceedings are a typical example of the proceedings envisaged by Article 1(1)(c). According to Article 5 bis (1) and (4) of the Spanish Insolvency Act,

> (T)he debtor may notify the Court which is competent to open insolvency proceedings that it has started negotiations with a view to reach a refinancing agreement […]. From the submission of the notification, no judicial or extrajudicial enforcement proceedings may be initiated on assets or rights that are necessary for the continuation of the debtor's professional or corporate activity until […] the formalization of the refinancing agreement.

If no agreement is reached within three months from such notification, the debtor must file for insolvency (Article 5 bis (5) of the Spanish Insolvency Act).

The jurisdiction to open these types of pre-insolvency proceedings is now governed by **8.498** Article 3 RR and their cross-border effects by Articles 19 and 32 RR. Thus, for example, if a Spanish company has entered into negotiations with its creditors to restructure its liabilities in accordance with Article 5 bis of the Spanish Insolvency Act (and included in Annex A), the affected creditors will be prevented from initiating individual enforcement proceedings not only in Spain but also in other Member States, and no main insolvency proceedings may be opened in other Member States. A judgment confirming a restructuring plan or a debt discharge will also be recognized and produce effects in the rest of the Member States under those provisions. However, a temporary moratorium: (i) may not affect the rights in rem of creditors or third parties over assets located in other Member States (see Article 8 RR); and (ii) it may only temporarily stay the opening of secondary proceedings in accordance with Article 38(3) RR for a maximum period of three months and provided that suitable measures to protect the interests of the local creditors are in place.

'Non-financial' difficulties

The Council proposal suggested that a Recital be added clarifying that the scope of the RR **8.499** may extend to cover proceedings which are triggered by situations in which the debtor faces what are referred to as 'non-financial' difficulties, provided that such difficulties give rise to a real and serious threat to the debtor's actual or future ability to pay his debts as they fall due. The time horizon for the determination of such a threat may extend to a period of several months or even longer. The example that is given is where the debtor has lost a contract which is of key importance to him. These points are now set out in Recital (17) RR.

The oddity from the point of view of English law is that what are described as non-financial difficulties, such as losing a key contract, would in England be categorized as falling within financial difficulties. The word 'financial' in this context appears in fact to refer to 'financing' difficulties, ie situations where it is the borrowing of money or taking on of credit that causes difficulties. By contrast, 'non-financial' appears to refer to difficulties which do not arise from the borrowing of money or the obtaining of credit.

The Article 1(2) exclusions

8.500 The exclusions remain generally similar to those set out in the OR and reference should be made to the commentary under the original Article 1(2) (8.09). There is, however, one important and radical change in that the Article 1(2) OR exclusion of 'investment undertakings which provide services involving the holding of funds or securities for third parties' is replaced by the exclusion in Article 1(2)(c) RR of 'investment firms and other firms, institutions and undertakings to the extent that they are covered by Directive 2001/24/EC …'. In other words, by limiting the exclusion to investment and other firms to those covered by the credit institutions reorganization and winding-up Directive, the RR is *including* previously excluded investment undertakings which are not covered by the Directive. For example, during the last major financial crisis in 2008/2009 it was found that certain major debtors which were thought to be 'banks' were not in fact credit institutions but investment firms, lacking any applicable Directive. However, it should be noted that the Directive was itself amended by Directive 2014/59/EU of the Parliament and the Council of 15 May 2015[550] (known as the 'BRRD', see chapter 7) so as to apply to 'investment firms as defined in point (2) of Article 4(1) of Regulation (EU) No 575/2013 of the European Parliament and of the Council [footnote omitted] and their branches located in Member States other than those in which they have their head offices.' In addition, there is an amendment which applies the Directive in 'the event of application of the resolution tools and exercise of the resolution powers provided for in Directive 2014/59/EU of the European Parliament and of the Council … to the financial institutions, firms and parent undertakings falling within the scope of Directive 2014/59/EU.' Thus the number of investment firms to which the Directive applies (and therefore the OR/RR does not), has been increased.

8.501 The rationale for the remaining exclusions in Recital (19) RR, which refers to 'special arrangements' and wide-ranging powers of intervention by national supervisory authorities does not provide a satisfactory reason for the exclusion of, and the failure to provide a Directive for, collective investment undertakings.

(RR) Article 2—Definitions

For the purposes of this Regulation:
1. 'collective proceedings' means proceedings which include all or a significant part of a debtor's creditors, provided that, in the latter case, the proceedings do not affect the claims of creditors which are not involved in them;
2. 'collective investment undertakings' means undertakings for collective investment in transferable securities (UCITS) as defined in Directive 2009/65/EC of the European Parliament and of the Council and alternative investment funds (AIFs) as defined in Directive 2011/61/EU of the European Parliament and of the Council;
3. 'debtor in possession' means a debtor in respect of which insolvency proceedings have been opened which do not necessarily involve the appointment of an insolvency practitioner or the complete transfer of the rights and duties to administer the debtor's

---

[550] OJ L173/190.

assets to an insolvency practitioner and where, therefore, the debtor remains totally or at least partially in control of its assets and affairs;
4. 'insolvency proceedings' means the proceedings listed in Annex A;
5. 'insolvency practitioner' means any person or body whose function, including on an interim basis, is to:
    (i) verify and admit claims submitted in insolvency proceedings;
    (ii) represent the collective interest of the creditors;
    (iii) administer, either in full or in part, assets of which the debtor has been divested;
    (iv) liquidate the assets referred to in point (iii); or
    (v) supervise the administration of the debtor's affairs.
    The persons and bodies referred to in the first subparagraph are listed in Annex B;
6. 'court' means:
    (i) in points (b) and (c) of Article 1(1), Article 4(2), Articles 5 and 6, Article 21(3), point (j) of Article 24(2), Articles 36 and 39, and Articles 61 to 77, the judicial body of a Member State;
    (ii) in all other articles, the judicial body or any other competent body of a Member State empowered to open insolvency proceedings, to confirm such opening or to take decisions in the course of such proceedings;
7. 'judgment opening insolvency proceedings' includes:
    (i) the decision of any court to open insolvency proceedings or to confirm the opening of such proceedings; and
    (ii) the decision of a court to appoint an insolvency practitioner;
8. 'the time of the opening of proceedings' means the time at which the judgment opening insolvency proceedings becomes effective, regardless of whether the judgment is final or not;
9. 'the Member State in which assets are situated' means, in the case of:
    (i) registered shares in companies other than those referred to in point (ii), the Member State within the territory of which the company having issued the shares has its registered office;
    (ii) financial instruments, the title to which is evidenced by entries in a register or account maintained by or on behalf of an intermediary ('book entry securities'), the Member State in which the register or account in which the entries are made is maintained;
    (iii) cash held in accounts with a credit institution, the Member State indicated in the account's IBAN, or, for cash held in accounts with a credit institution which does not have an IBAN, the Member State in which the credit institution holding the account has its central administration or, where the account is held with a branch, agency or other establishment, the Member State in which the branch, agency or other establishment is located;
    (iv) property and rights, ownership of or entitlement to which is entered in a public register other than those referred to in point (i), the Member State under the authority of which the register is kept;
    (v) European patents, the Member State for which the European patent is granted;
    (vi) copyright and related rights, the Member State within the territory of which the owner of such rights has its habitual residence or registered office;

(vii) tangible property, other than that referred to in points (i) to (iv), the Member State within the territory of which the property is situated;

(viii) claims against third parties, other than those relating to assets referred to in point (iii), the Member State within the territory of which the third party required to meet the claims has the centre of its main interests, as determined in accordance with Article 3(1);

10. 'establishment' means any place of operations where a debtor carries out or has carried out in the 3-month period prior to the request to open main insolvency proceedings a non-transitory economic activity with human means and assets;

11. 'local creditor' means a creditor whose claims against a debtor arose from or in connection with the operation of an establishment situated in a Member State other than the Member State in which the centre of the debtor's main interests is located;

12. 'foreign creditor' means a creditor which has its habitual residence, domicile or registered office in a Member State other than the State of the opening of proceedings, including the tax authorities and social security authorities of Member States;

13. 'group of companies' means a parent undertaking and all its subsidiary undertakings;

14. 'parent undertaking' means an undertaking which controls, either directly or indirectly, one or more subsidiary undertakings. An undertaking which prepares consolidated financial statements in accordance with Directive 2013/34/EU of the European Parliament and of the Council shall be deemed to be a parent undertaking.

Introduction

8.502 Many of the definitions in Article 2 RR were new additions. Among other changes, new definitions of 'collective proceedings', 'collective investment undertakings', 'debtor in possession', 'insolvency practitioner', 'court', 'the Member State in which assets are situated', 'establishment', and several other terms were included.

'Collective proceedings'

8.503 Article 1 OR stated that the OR applied to 'collective insolvency proceedings' without defining the term. Reference should be made to the commentary under Article 1 OR above.

8.504 The definition in Article 2 RR is in effect elaborated in Recital (14) RR. It makes the point that proceedings which involve only financial creditors should also be covered. This is an important practical point, since a number of viable, basically profitable companies can suffer from being overloaded with financial debt (eg resulting from a leveraged buy-out) and need to have the financial debt reorganized, without affecting the payment of trade creditors. The French *sauvegarde financière accélérée* is reserved exclusively to financial creditors; it is accordingly listed in Annex A.

8.505 The elaboration in Recital (14) RR also makes the point that proceedings which do not include all the creditors should be aimed at rescuing the debtor. Presumably, 'rescue' in this context includes similar concepts such as 'reorganization' and 'restructuring'. This is consistent with the further point made in Recital (14) RR that proceedings which lead to the 'definitive cessation of the debtor's activities or the liquidation of the debtor's assets should include all the debtor's creditors.' That appears to be the case contrasted with 'rescue' cases.

What if it is the *business* of the debtor that is rescued and not the debtor itself? On a literal **8.506**
reading of Recital (14) RR, such proceedings should include all the debtor's creditors; after
all, rescuing the business is usually done by selling it to a third party and is, thus, a form of
liquidation. In practice, this should not cause problems as the proceedings, in so far as they
affect the debtor, will normally include all the creditors from a legal point of view, even if
unsecured or junior creditors do not get a distribution.

'Collective investment undertakings'

The RR does not apply to collective investment undertakings: see Article 1(2)(d) RR. **8.507**
Collective investment undertakings were also excluded from the scope of the OR: see
Article 1(2) OR. The OR did not include a definition of 'collective investment undertakings'.
This omission has been remedied under the RR.

Article 2(2) RR provides that two types of entity qualify as collective investment undertak- **8.508**
ings: undertakings for collective investment in transferable securities (known as 'UCITS')
and alternative investment funds (known as 'AIFs'). The RR adopts the definition of UCITS
in the UCITS IV Directive,[551] and adopts the definition of AIF in the AIFM Directive.[552]

In brief (and with a degree of over-simplification), UCITS are retail mutual funds. More **8.509**
precisely, Article 1(2) of the UCITS IV Directive states that:

> ... UCITS means an undertaking:
> (a) with the sole object of collective investment in transferable securities or in other liquid
>   financial assets referred to in Article 50(1) of capital raised from the public and which
>   operate on the principle of risk-spreading; and
> (b) with units which are, at the request of holders, repurchased or redeemed, directly or in-
>   directly, out of those undertakings' assets. Action taken by a UCITS to ensure that the
>   stock exchange value of its units does not significantly vary from their net asset value
>   shall be regarded as equivalent to such repurchase or redemption.

All UCITS must be authorized in accordance with the UCITS IV Directive: see Article 5(1)
thereof.

In brief (and with a degree of over-simplification), AIFs comprise all collective investment **8.510**
undertakings which are not UCITS. More precisely, Article 4(1)(a) of the AIFM Directive
defines AIFs as:

> ... collective investment undertakings, including investment compartments thereof, which:
> (i) raise capital from a number of investors, with a view to investing it in accordance with
>   a defined investment policy for the benefit of those investors; and
> (ii) do not require authorisation pursuant to Article 5 of [the UCITS Directive].

Ultimately, the definition of 'collective investment undertakings' in Article 2(2) RR can
fairly be said to involve an element of circularity, since the very same term is used (but not
defined) in the provisions of the UCITS IV Directive and the AIFM Directive to which the

---

[551] Directive 2009/65/EC of the European Parliament and of the Council.
[552] Directive 2011/61/EU of the European Parliament and of the Council.

RR cross-refers. For further commentary on the definitions of UCITS and AIFs in the respective Directives, readers should refer to specialist commentaries.[553]

'Debtor in possession'

8.511 RR Article 2(3) introduces the concept of a debtor in possession, which means:

> ... a debtor in respect of which insolvency proceedings have been opened which do not necessarily involve the appointment of an insolvency practitioner or the complete transfer of the rights and duties to administer the debtor's assets to an insolvency practitioner and where, therefore, the debtor remains totally or at least partially in control of its assets and affairs.

The concept of a debtor in possession does not feature expressly in the OR. This is because in express terms the OR does not apply to insolvency proceedings unless such proceedings 'entail ... the appointment of a liquidator': see Article 1(1) OR. Thus, insolvency proceedings involving a debtor in possession will generally fall outside the scope of the OR. By contrast, debtor in possession proceedings are expressly included within the scope of the RR. As Recital (10) RR explains:

> The scope of this Regulation should extend to proceedings which promote the rescue of economically viable but distressed businesses and which give a second chance to entrepreneurs. It should, in particular, extend to proceedings which provide for restructuring of a debtor at a stage where there is only a likelihood of insolvency, and to proceedings which leave the debtor fully or partially in control of its assets and affairs. It should also extend to proceedings providing for a debt discharge or a debt adjustment in relation to consumers and self-employed persons, for example by reducing the amount to be paid by the debtor or by extending the payment period granted to the debtor. Since such proceedings do not necessarily entail the appointment of an insolvency practitioner, they should be covered by this Regulation if they take place under the control or supervision of a court. In this context, the term 'control' should include situations where the court only intervenes on appeal by a creditor or other interested parties.

Accordingly, Article 1(1) RR identifies three types of insolvency proceedings which fall within the scope of the RR: (a) proceedings in which a debtor is totally or partially divested of its assets; (b) proceedings in which the assets and affairs of a debtor are subject to control or supervision by a court; and (c) proceedings in which a temporary stay of individual enforcement proceedings is granted by a court or by operation of law, in order to allow for negotiations between the debtor and its creditors. Evidently, proceedings falling within categories (b) or (c) need not involve the appointment of an insolvency practitioner, and proceedings falling within category (a) can involve a debtor in 'partial' possession. This is an important change from the position which formerly prevailed under the OR.

8.512 There are a number of other new provisions in the RR dealing with the rights of debtors in possession. It would be wrong to suggest that the RR confers the same powers on debtors

---

[553] See eg G Walker and R Purves, *Financial Services Law* (4th edn, 2018).

in possession and insolvency practitioners: this is not so.[554] However, debtors in possession and insolvency practitioners share some of the same powers. For example, where a debtor in possession can bring avoidance proceedings under national law, Article 6(2) RR ensures that the jurisdictional scheme for such actions applies equally to insolvency practitioners and debtors in possession. By Articles 28 and 29 RR, a debtor in possession has the same rights and duties as an insolvency practitioner vis-à-vis publication and registration. Likewise, almost all of the provisions relating to prospective secondary proceedings in Article 38 RR apply to insolvency practitioners and debtors in possession alike.[555] In the same vein, Article 76 RR ensures that all the provisions of Chapter V apply both to insolvency practitioners and debtors in possession.

'Insolvency proceedings'

8.513 Article 2(4) RR defines insolvency proceedings as 'the proceedings listed in Annex A'. If a proceeding is included in Annex A RR, then it is within the scope of the RR even if it does not in fact meet the criteria laid down by the RR: Recital (9) RR. If it is not in RR Annex A, then it is not within the scope of the RR, even if it does meet those criteria: Recital (9) RR.

8.514 In contrast to the situation under the OR, changes of Annex A RR require a full-fledged legislative procedure. On 21 May 2021, the Commission has, thus, decided to initiate such a procedure because of the request of several member states (Netherlands, Germany, Italy, Cyprus, Poland, and Lithuania) to have Annex A (and B) amended. This is the result of the transposition of the Directive EU 2019/1023 of Preventive Restructuring Frameworks into the respective national legislation.

8.515 If there is a conflict between the definition in Article 1 RR and Annex A, Annex A prevails: the very fact that a proceeding appears in Annex A conclusively establishes that it constitutes an 'insolvency proceeding' to which the RR applies. The CJEU so held in the *Bank Handlowy* case[556] (decided under the OR), which remains good law under the RR. As Recital (9) explains:

> This Regulation should apply to insolvency proceedings which meet the conditions set out in it, irrespective of whether the debtor is a natural person or a legal person, a trader or an individual. Those insolvency proceedings are listed exhaustively in Annex A. In respect of the national procedures contained in Annex A, this Regulation should apply without any further examination by the courts of another Member State as to whether the conditions set out in this Regulation are met. National insolvency procedures not listed in Annex A should not be covered by this Regulation.

However, the conditions set out in Article 1 RR will be significant when questions arise as to whether an insolvency proceeding should be added to Annex A in the future.[557]

---

[554] See, among many other provisions, Art 21 RR (dealing with the powers of an insolvency practitioner), which does not apply to debtors in possession).
[555] Though see Art 38(4) RR, which only applies to insolvency practitioners.
[556] Case C-116/11 *Bank Handlowy w Warszawie SA v Christianapol sp z oo* [2013] Bus LR 956.
[557] A Commission proposal to act as 'gatekeeper' in relation to the addition of proceedings to Annex A was rejected, and additions will have to be made by amending the RR. The Art 45 OR procedure for amending annexes by qualified majority has not been retained by the RR.

'Insolvency practitioner'

8.516 The concept of a 'liquidator', which performed an essential function under the OR, has been replaced with the new concept of an 'insolvency practitioner' under the RR. Article 2(5) RR defines an insolvency practitioner as a person or body whose function (whether on a permanent or interim basis) is to (i) verify and admit claims submitted in insolvency proceedings; (ii) represent the collective interest of the creditors; (iii) administer, either in full or in part, assets of which the debtor has been divested; (iv) liquidate the assets referred to in point (iii); or (v) supervise the administration of the debtor's affairs. The language of Article 2(5) RR clearly indicates that it is sufficient if the relevant person performs one of the five identified functions.

8.517 Article 2(5) RR expressly provides for the possibility that an insolvency practitioner will perform his functions on an 'interim' basis only. This removes any doubt as to whether the RR applies to provisional liquidators (or other office-holders who act on an interim basis). As Recital (15) explains:

> This Regulation should also apply to proceedings that, under the law of some Member States, are opened and conducted for a certain period of time on an interim or provisional basis before a court issues an order confirming the continuation of the proceedings on a non-interim basis. Although labelled as 'interim', such proceedings should meet all other requirements of this Regulation.

Article 2(5) RR states that the categories of insolvency practitioners are 'listed in Annex B'.

8.518 Article 2(5) is supplemented by Recital (21), which states that:

> Insolvency practitioners are defined in this Regulation and listed in Annex B. Insolvency practitioners who are appointed without the involvement of a judicial body should, under national law, be appropriately regulated and authorized to act in insolvency proceedings. The national regulatory framework should provide for proper arrangements to deal with potential conflicts of interest.

By analogy to the approach to 'insolvency proceedings' in *Bank Handlowy*,[558] it seems that inclusion in Annex B RR is conclusive in favour of being within the definition and not being included in Annex B RR is conclusive as to exclusion from the concept. Complications have arisen under the OR and can continue to arise under the RR if for example an 'administrator' is listed in Annex A and a 'special administrator' is appointed in a specialist proceeding. If the relevant Member State court treats such a 'special administrator' as being within the concept of 'administrator', it would seem that that will also have to be accepted in the courts of other Member States, on the basis of mutual trust.

'Court'

8.519 There is a new definition of 'court' in Article 2(6) RR. The background to the new definition is explained in Recital (20):

---

[558] Case C-116/11 *Bank Handlowy w Warszawie SA v Christianapol sp z oo* [2013] Bus LR 956.

Insolvency proceedings do not necessarily involve the intervention of a judicial authority. Therefore, the term 'court' in this Regulation should, in certain provisions, be given a broad meaning and include a person or body empowered by national law to open insolvency proceedings. In order for this Regulation to apply, proceedings (comprising acts and formalities set down in law) should not only have to comply with the provisions of this Regulation, but they should also be officially recognised and legally effective in the Member State in which the insolvency proceedings are opened.

Article 2(6) RR distinguishes between two possible meanings of the term 'court'. The first meaning is 'the judicial body of a Member State': see Article 2(6)(i) RR. The second meaning is 'the judicial body or any other competent body of a Member State empowered to open insolvency proceedings, to confirm such opening or to take decisions in the course of such proceedings': see Article 2(6)(ii) RR.

8.520 In order to reduce potential ambiguity, Article 2(6)(i) RR lists the provisions of the RR in which 'court' should be construed in accordance with the first meaning. Those provisions are Articles 1(1)(b) and 1(1)(c) (dealing with the scope of the RR), Article 4(2) (dealing with determinations of jurisdiction by insolvency practitioners), Articles 5 and 6 (dealing with other jurisdictional matters), Article 21(3) (dealing with the powers of an insolvency practitioner), Article 24(2)(j) (dealing with the establishment of insolvency registers), Articles 36 and 39 (dealing with secondary proceedings), and Articles 61 to 77 (dealing with matters of co-ordination). In all other Articles of the RR, 'court' should be construed in accordance with the second meaning set out above: see Article 2(6)(ii) RR.

8.521 A creditors' meeting which approves a relevant procedure has been held to be a 'court or other competent body' within Article 2(d) OR and should therefore be recognized as a 'competent body of a Member State empowered to open insolvency proceedings' within Article 2(6) RR.[559] By parity of reasoning, the same must apply to a shareholders' meeting which places a company into a proceeding.

'Judgment opening insolvency proceedings'

8.522 The definition of 'judgment opening insolvency proceedings' is very similar to the definition of 'judgment' in the OR. Article 2(7) RR states that a 'judgment opening insolvency proceedings includes: (i) the decision of any court to open insolvency proceedings or to confirm the opening of such proceedings; and (ii) the decision of a court to appoint an insolvency practitioner'.

8.523 In Article 2(7) RR, 'court' means 'the judicial body or any other competent body of a Member State empowered to open insolvency proceedings, to confirm such opening or to take decisions in the course of such proceedings': see Article 2(6).

8.524 Article 19 RR provides that 'any judgment opening insolvency proceedings handed down by a court of a Member State which has jurisdiction pursuant to Article 3 shall be recognised in all other Member States from the moment that it becomes effective in the State of the opening of proceedings;' see also Articles 10(1) and 66(2).

---

[559] See *Re Salvage Association* [2003] EWHC 1028 (Ch); *Apperley Investments Ltd & Ors v Monsoon Accessorize Ltd* [2020] IEHC 523, para 64, and see commentary under Art 2(d) OR above.

8.525 The 'time of the opening of proceedings' is defined in Article 2(8) RR. The definition is much the same as to the definition of the same term in Article 2(f) OR and reference should be made to the commentary on Article 2(f) OR above.

'The time of the opening of proceedings'

8.526 This is in the same terms as the definition of the same words in Article 2(f) OR. Reference should be made to the commentary on Article 2(f) OR above.

'The Member State in which assets are situated'

8.527 Territorial proceedings only affect assets of the debtor which are situated in the Member State where the territorial proceedings were opened: see Article 3(2) RR. Article 2(9) RR contains a series of rules for determining the Member State in which the debtor's assets are located or treated as being located.[560] This will determine whether particular assets are within the main or territorial/secondary proceedings.

8.528 Article 2(g) OR is the predecessor of Article 2(9) RR. However, the latter provision is more complex than the former provision—but still not exhaustive. Under the OR, definition of 'the Member State where assets are situated' had only three limbs; under the RR, it has seven. Limbs (i), (ii), and (iii) of the OR definition are equivalent to limbs (vii), (iv) and (viii) of the RR definition (respectively). Limbs (i), (ii), (iii), (v), and (vi) of the RR definition are new.

8.529 The Article 2(g) OR trichotomy of (i) tangible property, (ii) rights which were required to be entered on a public register under the authority of a Member State, and (iii) 'claims' gave rise to uncertainty. Were the three categories intended to be exclusive, so that every asset had to be fitted into one of them? What was the position of registered shares? Did bank accounts fall under 'claims'? Where were intermediated securities located?

8.530 The RR does not clear up the question as to whether the definitions are exclusive in the sense of every asset having to be fitted into one category or another. However, new definitions deal with cases of uncertainty previously identified and therefore the risk of there being an asset not clearly included in one definition or another may be small—at least as long as digital assets (such as cryptocurrencies or the like) are not yet common.

8.531 In both Article 2(g) OR and the Article 2(9) RR the fact that the lists are preceded by the words 'in the case of:' suggests that the lists themselves are not intended to be exclusive in the sense that all types of asset must somehow be fitted into one or other of the cases listed, but rather that the lists simply provide rules to resolve questions of *situs* in respect of those classes of asset which are included in the lists.

8.532 Under the RR, the basic rules of the OR remain the same: tangible property is deemed to be situated in the Member State where the property is physically located; property rights which must be entered in a public register are deemed to be situated in the Member State which has 'authority' over the register; and claims against third parties (*choses in action*) other than money in bank accounts are deemed to be situated in the Member State where the obligor's centre of main interests is located.

---

[560] Strictly speaking, an intangible cannot have a location, but intangibles are treated as a matter of law as having a location determined by legal rules, a 'deemed' location.

However, these general principles are subject to a number of more specific rules, which seek to deal with the uncertainties created by the OR rules. **8.533**

Registered shares
Article 2(9)(i) RR deems registered shares in a company to be situated in the place of the company's registered office. **8.534**

The question arises whether a debtor who holds shares in an account with an equities broker owns 'registered shares' governed by Article 2(9)(i) RR or 'book entry securities' governed by Article 2(9)(ii) RR. Since (i) applies expressly to 'registered shares in companies other than those referred to in point (ii)', the implication is that registered shares can be 'book entry securities' within (ii) and that therefore an asset in the form of a right against an intermediary to shares held in an account will fall under (ii).[561] **8.535**

Book entry securities
Article 2(9)(ii) RR deems 'book entry securities' to be situated in the place where the register or account in which the entries are made is maintained. Book entry securities are 'financial instruments, the title to which is evidenced by entries in a register or account maintained by or on behalf of an intermediary'. In practice, most securities traded on the international capital markets are book entry securities. For example, where the debtor holds bonds through a clearing house (such as Euroclear or Clearstream), the debtor's interest in the bonds will constitute 'book entry securities' within the RR. **8.536**

This brings the RR into line with other EU financial services legislation. For example, Article 9 of the Financial Collateral Arrangements Directive[562] provides for proprietary issues relating to 'book entry securities collateral' to be governed by the 'law of the country in which the relevant account is maintained'. Article 9(2) of the Settlement Finality Directive[563] contains a similar provision. It is suggested that the *situs* of book entry securities should be determined in the same way under the RR, the Financial Collateral Arrangements Directive, and the Settlement Finality Directive. **8.537**

Bank accounts
Article 2(9)(iii) RR deems cash held in a bank account to be situated in the Member State indicated on the account's IBAN (international bank account number). The vast majority of bank accounts have an IBAN. Where an IBAN does not exist, Article 2(9)(iii) RR contains various fall-back rules. **8.538**

---

[561] In Ireland, the situation may be further complicated if the shares in the account are held by the intermediary (or its nominee) on trust for the debtor. Under company law the company would only recognize the registered holder as legal owner of the shares and the debtor would not have an asset as against the company unless and until it became the registered owner. The asset of the debtor pending any such registration would be its right against the intermediary as trustee and against any third party who acquired the shares with notice of the trust. See *Re LBIE* [2010] EWHC 2914 (Ch), para 226 and Moss, 'Intermediated Securities: Issues Arising From Insolvency', Ch 3 of Gullifer and Payne (ed), *Intermediated Securities: Legal Problems and Practical Issues* (Hart Publishing, 2010).
[562] Directive 2002/47/EC of the European Parliament and of the Council of 6 June 2002 on financial collateral arrangements.
[563] Directive 98/26/EC of the European Parliament and of the Council of 19 May 1998 on settlement finality in payment and securities settlement systems.

8.539 Finally, Article 2(9)(v) and 2(9)(vi) RR contain special provisions for determining the *situs* of intellectual property, including European patents and copyright. In cases of dispute about the *situs* of a particular asset the courts both of the member state of the main proceeding and those of the secondary proceeding have concurrent international jurisdiction.[564]

'Establishment'

8.540 Article 2(10) RR contains a revised definition of the term 'establishment', which builds on the OR definition in Article 2(h) OR.

8.541 As explained in the commentary on Article 3 RR (below), the concept of an establishment is essential to the allocation of territorial jurisdiction under the RR. If a debtor's centre of main interests is situated in one Member State, but the debtor has an establishment in another Member State, then the courts of the latter Member State have jurisdiction to open territorial proceedings against the debtor. Where territorial proceedings are opened after main proceedings have already opened in the debtor's centre of main interests, they are known as 'secondary insolvency proceedings'. Where territorial proceedings are opened before main proceedings have opened in the debtor's centre of main interests, they are known as 'independent territorial proceedings'.

8.542 The RR defines an establishment as a place of operations where either:

(1) the debtor currently carries out a non-transitory economic activity with human means and assets (the 'first limb'); or
(2) the debtor carried out a non-transitory economic activity with human means and assets within the three-month period prior to the request to open main proceedings (the 'second limb').

The first limb is derived from the definition of 'establishment' in Article 2(h) OR, and reference should be made to the commentary on Article 2(h) OR above. It does however confirm English case law to the effect that 'goods' in the OR version should be read as 'assets'.[565]

8.543 However, the second limb is new. The second limb was inserted at the request of the European Parliament, in a report prepared by Mr Klaus-Heiner Lehne (acting as rapporteur of the Committee on Legal Affairs) dated 20 December 2013. Most of the amendments proposed in the Lehne report are supported by a list of reasons. Unfortunately (and inexplicably), the Lehne report does not explain the reasons for inserting the second limb into the definition of 'establishment'. The likelihood is that the change is driven by a suspicion that the insolvency practitioner or debtor in possession in the main proceedings, or management prior to the opening of main proceedings, may close down the operations in the secondary jurisdiction in order to prevent the opening of a secondary proceeding and thus thwart the interests of local creditors.[566]

---

[564] Case 649/13 *Comité d'entreprise de Nortel Networks and Others* ECLI:EU:C:2015:384 (Judgment).
[565] The English case law, in particular *Re Olympic Airlines SA* [2015] 1 BCLC 589 (SC), para 3, is referred to in the commentary on Art 2(h) OR above.
[566] In *Re Olympic Airlines SA* [2015] 1 BCLC 589 (SC), the UK Supreme Court refused to open a secondary UK proceeding in the case of the Greek airline in main liquidation proceedings in Greece on the basis that the London branch was no longer carrying on any business activity at the London office at the time of the request to open secondary proceedings in England. While it was not suggested that in that case the operations were closed in order to thwart the opening, that was the effect. As explained below, if the same facts were to be repeated in a case arising

The second limb does not apply unless a request has been made to open main proceed- **8.544**
ings in the debtor's centre of main interests. Thus, under the second limb, the existence of
an establishment is dependent on (and relative to) the time of a particular request to open
main proceedings. Where a request has not been made to open main proceedings against
the debtor, the second limb of the definition does not apply. (This situation may arise where
a creditor makes a request to open independent territorial proceedings.) Further, it is suggested that the second limb does not apply unless main proceedings have actually been
opened against the debtor. If a request to open main proceedings is dismissed, the second
limb cannot apply: it would be absurd for the existence of an establishment to be determined by reference to the time of a failed request to open main proceedings. By parity of
reasoning, if a request to open main proceedings is pending (but has not been granted), it
should not be possible to prove that an establishment exists by relying on the second limb
of the definition: after all, the request to open main proceedings might be dismissed in due
course. More generally, it is suggested that 'the request to open main proceedings' in Article
2(10) RR means 'the successful request to open main proceedings'. That would also accord
with the rationale suggested for the new timing provision: if no main proceeding is actually
opened, it is unlikely that an establishment would be closed in order to prevent the opening
of territorial proceedings.

The second limb is one of several 'look-back periods' introduced by the RR. For example, **8.545**
Article 3(1) RR provides that if a debtor moves its registered office within three months
of a request to open insolvency proceedings, the presumption that the debtor's centre of
main interests is situated in the place of its registered office does not apply for the purposes of that request. (See the commentary below.) The essential function of the 'look-back
periods' in the RR is to prevent fraudulent or abusive forum shopping: see Recital (29) RR.
It is suggested that the second limb of the definition of 'establishment' also attempts to
combat fraudulent or abusive forum shopping. For example, if a professional person plans
or expects to become bankrupt in Ireland, the second limb ensures that he cannot prevent
his creditors from opening territorial proceedings merely by closing his establishments in
other Member States shortly before the presentation of a petition in Ireland. In short, the
second limb aims to prevent a debtor from impeding territorial proceedings by closing his
establishments within the three-month 'look-back period'.

The importance of the second limb can be illustrated by reference to the judgment of the UK **8.546**
Supreme Court in the *Olympic Airlines* case,[567] which was decided under the OR. Olympic
Airlines had been put into liquidation in Greece (being its centre of main interests) in
October 2009. Prior to October 2009, the company carried on business from a number of
offices in the UK with the assistance of several dozen members of staff. However, after the
winding-up of the company in Greece, the company's presence in the UK began to decline.
In July 2010, the trustees of the company's pension scheme presented a petition against the

---

under the RR, the winding down of operations at the company's English establishment following the opening of
main proceedings in Greece would not preclude the opening of secondary proceedings in England based on the
former existence of an active establishment there.

[567] *Trustees of the Olympic Airlines SA Pension and Life Assurance Scheme v Olympic Airlines SA* [2015] 1
WLR 2399.

company in England, with the intention of opening secondary proceedings. By that time, the company occupied only one office in the UK, where three members of staff on ad hoc contracts assisted the Greek liquidators to wind up the company's affairs. Lord Sumption, who gave the only judgment in the Supreme Court, held that the presence of an establishment must be determined at the date of the English petition (being July 2010). He held that the debtor had ceased to carry on any significant economic activities in England at that date. Accordingly, the debtor did not have an establishment in England within Article 2(h) OR.

8.547 The new second limb of the definition of 'establishment' in the RR had the effect of reversing the decision in *Olympic Airlines* for cases under the RR. The company clearly had an establishment in the UK within three months prior to the date when the request was made to open main proceedings in Greece. That is sufficient for the purposes of Article 2(10) RR.

8.548 The date for assessing whether an establishment exists in any given Member State has now changed from the original date of the opening of the secondary proceedings to two dates, namely the date on which the main insolvency proceedings were opened and three months before that date. This now makes it clear, therefore, that it will not be possible to 'change' a debtor's establishment after the opening of main proceedings. While this may prevent 'bad' forum shopping, it may also prevent 'good' forum shopping, eg by the debtor (likely to be acting through the office holder of the main insolvency proceedings) who might wish to move the establishment in order to allow a 'controlled' secondary proceeding for the benefit of the estate as a whole. Given that creditors remain free to seek to open a secondary proceeding at any time, the restriction on the prior ability to move the debtor's establishment in this way is questionable.

(RR) Article 3—International jurisdiction

1. The courts of the Member State within the territory of which the centre of the debtor's main interests is situated shall have jurisdiction to open insolvency proceedings ('main insolvency proceedings'). The centre of main interests shall be the place where the debtor conducts the administration of its interests on a regular basis and which is ascertainable by third parties.

   In the case of a company or legal person, the place of the registered office shall be presumed to be the centre of its main interests in the absence of proof to the contrary. That presumption shall only apply if the registered office has not been moved to another Member State within the 3-month period prior to the request for the opening of insolvency proceedings.

   In the case of an individual exercising an independent business or professional activity, the centre of main interests shall be presumed to be that individual's principal place of business in the absence of proof to the contrary. That presumption shall only apply if the individual's principal place of business has not been moved to another Member State within the 3-month period prior to the request for the opening of insolvency proceedings.

In the case of any other individual, the centre of main interests shall be presumed to be the place of the individual's habitual residence in the absence of proof to the contrary. This presumption shall only apply if the habitual residence has not been moved to another Member State within the 6-month period prior to the request for the opening of insolvency proceedings.

2. Where the centre of the debtor's main interests is situated within the territory of a Member State, the courts of another Member State shall have jurisdiction to open insolvency proceedings against that debtor only if it possesses an establishment within the territory of that other Member State. The effects of those proceedings shall be restricted to the assets of the debtor situated in the territory of the latter Member State.

3. Where insolvency proceedings have been opened in accordance with paragraph 1, any proceedings opened subsequently in accordance with paragraph 2 shall be secondary insolvency proceedings.

4. The territorial insolvency proceedings referred to in paragraph 2 may only be opened prior to the opening of main insolvency proceedings in accordance with paragraph 1 where
   (a) insolvency proceedings under paragraph 1 cannot be opened because of the conditions laid down by the law of the Member State within the territory of which the centre of the debtor's main interests is situated; or
   (b) the opening of territorial insolvency proceedings is requested by:
      (i) a creditor whose claim arises from or is in connection with the operation of an establishment situated within the territory of the Member State where the opening of territorial proceedings is requested; or
      (ii) a public authority which, under the law of the Member State within the territory of which the establishment is situated, has the right to request the opening of insolvency proceedings.

   When main insolvency proceedings are opened, the territorial insolvency proceedings shall become secondary insolvency proceedings.

Introduction

Article 3 RR contains the fundamental rules on the allocation of international jurisdiction **8.549** for insolvency proceedings. Article 3 RR is based on Article 3 OR, and the basic scheme is much the same. However, there are several significant differences between Article 3 RR and Article 3 OR, which are discussed in detail below.

Article 3(1) introduces the concept of a debtor's centre of main interests ('COMI'), **8.550** which is defined as 'the place where the debtor conducts the administration of its interests on a regular basis and which is ascertainable by third parties'. The latter phrase is derived from Recital (13) OR. It is doubtful that the draftsman's decision to transfer the phrase from the Recitals into the main body of Article 3(1) has any real significance. Indeed, subject to the specific modifications identified below, it is suggested that the concept of COMI should be construed in substantially the same manner under the RR and the OR. The commentary on Article 3 OR above deals with jurisprudence relating to the OR.

8.551 The basic scheme of Article 3 is relatively straightforward. In summary:

(1) If a debtor has its COMI within the EU (with the exception of Denmark), then the courts of the Member State where the debtor's COMI is situated have exclusive jurisdiction to open 'main insolvency proceedings': see Article 3(1) RR. Main proceedings enjoy universal effect across the EU: see Articles 19 and 20 RR. Indeed, as explained by the CJEU, the universal effect reaches even beyond the territory of the member states to confer jurisdiction on the court of the member state in which proceedings are opened to hear and determine avoidance action against third parties located outside the EU.[568]

(2) Where the debtor's COMI is situated in a Member State (MS1), but the debtor has an establishment in another Member State (MS2), the courts of MS2 have jurisdiction to open 'territorial insolvency proceedings': see Article 3(2) RR. Territorial proceedings are restricted to assets of the debtor which are situated in MS2.

(3) If the debtor does not have its COMI within the EU, or if the COMI is in Denmark, then the RR has no application, and the domestic rules of jurisdiction prevail.

8.552 Under the OR, it was possible (and wholly legitimate) for a debtor to shift its COMI in order to utilize the insolvency proceedings available in a different Member State, if the purpose was to benefit his creditors.[569] This is also the position under the RR. However, the debtor's COMI should always be readily identifiable by its creditors, especially where the debtor purports to move its COMI. This is reinforced by Recital (28), which is new:

> 'When determining whether the centre of the debtor's main interests is ascertainable by third parties, special consideration should be given to the creditors and to their perception as to where a debtor conducts the administration of its interests. This may require, in the event of a shift of centre of main interests, informing creditors of the new location from which the debtor is carrying out its activities in due course, for example by drawing attention to the change of address in commercial correspondence, or by making the new location public through other appropriate means.'[570]

The RR contains several provisions which are designed to make fraudulent or abusive COMI-shifting more difficult. These provisions are considered below.

Three presumptions

8.553 The second paragraph of Article 3(1) provides that, in the absence of proof to the contrary, the COMI of a company (or other legal person) is presumed to be the place of its registered office (the 'registered office presumption'). This is the same as the presumption under Article 3(1) OR. Recital (30) identifies the circumstances in which the registered office presumption can be rebutted:

> 'In the case of a company, it should be possible to rebut this presumption where the company's central administration is located in a Member State other than that of its

---

[568] Case C-328/12 *Schmid v Hertel*, ECLI:EU:C:2014:6 (a case relating to the OR).
[569] The approach here follows case-law under the OR—see for example Case C-396/09 *Interedil Srl v Fallimento Interedil Srl* [2011] ECR I-9915, [2012] BCC 851 and *Irish Bank Resolution Corp Ltd v Quinn* [2012] BCC 608.
[570] See the commentary under Art 3 OR.

registered office, and where a comprehensive assessment of all the relevant factors establishes, in a manner that is ascertainable by third parties, that the company's actual centre of management and supervision and of the management of its interests is located in that other Member State.'

This passage was included in the RR at the request of the European Commission,[571] and was designed as a restatement of the CJEU's reasoning in *Interedil*.[572]

8.554 The registered office presumption is expressly disapplied (by the second sentence of the second paragraph of Article 3(1)) if the company moved its registered office to another Member State within three months of the 'request for the opening of insolvency proceedings'. This is a novel addition to Article 3(1) RR, which is designed to prevent fraudulent or abusive forum shopping: see Recital (31) RR. Fraudulent and abusive forum shopping was a particular concern of the European Parliament, which had wanted an arbitrary time-limit restraint on moves of COMI. The disapplication of the presumption represents a compromise reached between the Parliament and the Council.

8.555 Thus, the registered office presumption is now dependent on (and relative to) the time of a particular request to open insolvency proceedings. If two requests are made at slightly different times to open insolvency proceedings against the same company, the registered office presumption may only apply in relation to one such request.

8.556 Importantly, the RR does not make it impossible for a company to move its COMI in less than three months. This was possible under the OR, and remains possible under the RR. Furthermore, the RR does not prevent a company from relying on a relocation of its registered office as evidence that its COMI has moved, even if the relocation occurred less than three months prior to the request to open insolvency proceedings. The RR merely prevents reliance on the registered office *presumption* if the company moved its registered office within three months of the request.

8.557 Irrespective of the new rules in Articles 56 et seq of the RR on group insolvencies, it is to be assumed that an intermingling of assets still does not permit the assumption of a (kind of) COMI shift. The *Rastelli* case[573] as well as those norms are to be understood as confirmation of the rule: one debtor, one insolvency, one case.

8.558 The OR did not contain any express presumptions concerning the COMI of a natural person. This gap was filled in by the RR. The second paragraph of Article 3(1) RR provides that, in the absence of proof to the contrary, the COMI of an individual exercising an independent business or professional activity is presumed to be his principal place of business. The professional activity presumption comes originally from paragraph 75 of the Virgos-Schmit Report, which states that 'in principle, the centre of main interests will in the case of professionals be the place

---

[571] See the Proposal of the European Commission dated 12 December 2012 (2012/0360 (COD)), at 3.1.2 of the Explanatory Memorandum.
[572] Case C-396/09 *Interedil Srl v Fallimento Interedil Srl and Intesa Gestione Crediti SpA* [2011] ECR I-9915, [2012] BCC 851. In some countries bankruptcy judges may not keep up to date with insolvency law decisions of the CJEU and it was thought preferable to put some basic points decided by case law in the text of the RR or in the Recitals to the RR.
[573] Case C-191/10 *Rastelli Davide e C. Snc v Jean-Charles Hidoux*.

of their professional domicile'. The expression 'independent business or professional activity' comes from VG at para 56(c).

8.559 The concept of an 'independent business or professional activity' is not completely clear. It seems to cover business or professional activities other than as an employee of an enterprise. VG at para 56(c) contrasts it with '*dependent* work'. It also excludes activities which are merely facets of the debtor's personal life (such as managing his own financial affairs). As in the case of companies and legal persons, the foregoing presumption is expressly disapplied if the relevant individual moved his principal place of business to a new Member State within three months of the request to open insolvency proceedings.

8.560 If an individual does not exercise an independent business or professional activity, his COMI is presumed (in the absence of proof to the contrary) to be the place of his habitual residence: see the third paragraph of Article 3(1) RR. This presumption also comes originally from paragraph 75 of the Virgos-Schmit Report, which states that 'for natural persons in general, the place of their habitual residence' should be treated as their COMI. VG refers to it at para 56(c).

8.561 The foregoing presumption is expressly disapplied if the individual moved his habitual residence to a new Member State within six months of the request for the opening of insolvency proceedings. The restriction on the normal presumption is once again the product of a compromise between the European Parliament (which wanted an arbitrary time limit) and the Council. The longer restriction on the presumption (being six months rather than three months) perhaps reflects the fact that a habitual residence is easier to move than a registered office or a principal place of business.

8.562 The concept of habitual residence features in numerous EU instruments, including (among others) the OR, the Brussels Regulation (Recast),[574] and legislation dealing with family law. Habitual residence must be given an autonomous interpretation under EU law.[575]

8.563 In *MH and NI v OJ and Novo Banco SA*[576] the CJEU considered a situation where the debtors were habitually resident and employed in the UK but had their only immovable asset in Portugal, which was also the place where the events which gave rise to their insolvency took place. The CJEU held that that the presumption that the debtors' COMI was in the place of their habitual residence was not rebutted by the fact that their sole immovable asset was in another member state.

Territorial insolvency proceedings

8.564 As noted above, where the debtor's COMI is situated in a Member State (MS1), but the debtor also has an establishment in another Member State (MS2), the courts of MS2 have jurisdiction to open territorial proceedings. Where territorial proceedings are opened after main proceedings have already opened, they are known as 'secondary insolvency proceedings': see Article 3(3) RR. All territorial proceedings must be secondary proceedings, unless the exceptions in Article 3(4) RR apply. There is no material change in this respect from the OR.

---

[574] Regulation (EU) No 1215/2012 of the European Parliament and of the Council of 12 December 2012 on jurisdiction and the recognition and enforcement of judgments in civil and commercial matters (recast), OJ L351/1, 20 December 2012.
[575] Case C-523/07 *Proceedings brought by A* [2009] ECR I-2805.
[576] Case C-253/19 *MH and NI v OJ and Novo Banco SA*.

An 'establishment' is defined as 'any place of operations where a debtor carries out or has **8.565** carried out in the 3-month period prior to the request to open main insolvency proceedings a non-transitory economic activity with human means and assets': see RR Article 2(10) RR. This is a new and important definition, the effect of which is discussed in the commentary on Article 2 above RR.

Under the OR, secondary proceedings were required to be winding-up proceedings (as de- **8.566** fined in Annex B OR, which excluded many restructuring, rescue or pre-insolvency proceedings). The idea was to reinforce the supremacy of the main proceeding.

However, this was an unfortunate and unpopular requirement, with potentially damaging consequences referred to in the commentary in respect of OR (above).

The RR however abolished the requirement for secondary proceedings to be winding- **8.567** up proceedings. Annex B OR, which contains a list of winding-up proceedings in each Member State, has been excised in its entirety from the RR.[577] It follows that the full array of insolvency proceedings listed in Annex A RR can (in principle) be used as secondary proceedings, provided that the necessary conditions under domestic law are satisfied. This ensures that 'the opening of secondary proceedings does not automatically thwart the rescue or restructuring of a debtor as a whole'.[578]

Where territorial proceedings are opened prior to the opening of main proceedings, they are **8.568** known as 'independent territorial proceedings'. Such proceedings 'are intended to be limited to what is absolutely necessary' (Recital (37) RR), and may be opened in three circumstances.

First, Article 3(4)(a) RR permits independent territorial proceedings to be opened if it is **8.569** impossible to open main proceedings because of the conditions laid down by the law of the Member State where the debtor's COMI is situated. For example, if the law of the COMI prevents non-traders from entering into insolvency proceedings, and the debtor is not a trader, then independent territorial proceedings can (at least in principle) be opened in any Member State where the debtor has an establishment. Article 3(4)(a) RR is identical to Article 3(4)(a) OR, and should be interpreted in the same manner. Reference should be made to the commentary on Article 3(4)(a) OR above.

Second, Article 3(4)(b)(i) RR permits independent territorial proceedings to be opened in **8.570** a particular Member State upon the request of a creditor whose claim arises from (or is in connection with) the operation of an establishment in that Member State. Under the equivalent provision of the OR, it was sufficient if the requesting creditor had his domicile, habitual residence, or registered office in the relevant Member State. This is no longer sufficient under the RR: it is necessary for the creditor's claim to arise from the operation of the relevant establishment, regardless of the creditor's domicile.

Third, Article 3(4)(b)(ii) RR permits independent territorial proceedings to be opened in **8.571** a particular Member State upon the request of a public authority which, under the law of that Member State, has the right to request the opening of insolvency proceedings. This is

---

[577] Annex B RR contains a list of insolvency practitioners, formerly listed in Annex C OR: see Art 2(5) RR.
[578] See the Proposal of the European Commission dated 12 December 2012 (2012/0360 (COD)), at 3.1.2 of the Explanatory Memorandum.

a novel provision, which appears to be designed as a response to the decision of the CJEU in *Zaza Retail*.[579] In that case, the debtor had its COMI in the Netherlands and an establishment in Belgium. Upon the application of the Belgian prosecution service (which was acting in the public interest, and was not a creditor in the conventional sense), a Belgian court opened independent territorial proceedings against the debtor. The CJEU ruled that the Belgian court had no jurisdiction to open such proceedings. In particular:

(1) The Belgian prosecution service argued that Article 3(4)(a) OR conferred jurisdiction on the Belgian court to open independent territorial proceedings, because the Belgian prosecution service lacked *locus standi* to apply for the opening of insolvency proceedings in the Netherlands. The CJEU rejected this argument. From the mere fact that a specific person (in this case, the Belgian prosecution service) has no standing to apply for the opening of main insolvency proceedings, it does not follow that such proceedings 'cannot be opened'. Other persons (namely, ordinary creditors) had standing to apply for the opening of main proceedings in the Netherlands at all material times, so Article 3(4)(a) OR had no application.

(2) Further, the CJEU held that the Belgian prosecution service could not be treated as a 'creditor' within Article 3(4)(b) OR, because it had no right to lodge a claim against the debtor's estate, and did not act as a representative of the creditors. The concept of a 'creditor' must be construed strictly, and does not include public authorities which act in the public interest rather than as creditors (or in the name or on behalf of creditors).

The foregoing principles remain good law. However, *Zaza Retail* would be decided differently under the RR. The Belgian prosecution service, being a public authority, would be entitled to rely on Article 3(4)(b)(ii) RR of the RR before the Belgian court. Although the Belgian prosecution is not a 'creditor' within Article 3(4)(b)(i) RR, this is irrelevant for the purposes of Article 3(4)(b)(ii) RR.

(RR) Article 4—Examination as to jurisdiction

1. A court seised of a request to open insolvency proceedings shall of its own motion examine whether it has jurisdiction pursuant to Article 3. The judgment opening insolvency proceedings shall specify the grounds on which the jurisdiction of the court is based, and, in particular, whether jurisdiction is based on Article 3(1) or (2).
2. Notwithstanding paragraph 1, where insolvency proceedings are opened in accordance with national law without a decision by a court, Member States may entrust the insolvency practitioner appointed in such proceedings to examine whether the Member State in which a request for the opening of proceedings is pending has jurisdiction pursuant to Article 3. Where this is the case, the insolvency practitioner shall specify in the decision opening the proceedings the grounds on which

---

[579] Case C-112/10 *Procureur-generaal bij het hof van beroep te Antwerpen v Zaza Retail BV* [2011] ECR I-11525.

jurisdiction is based and, in particular, whether jurisdiction is based on Article 3(1) or (2).

8.572 Article 4 RR was a new introduction in the RR, derived from the European Commission's original legislative proposal,[580] which included the following explanatory statement:[581]

> 'The proposal also improves the procedural framework for determining jurisdiction for the opening of proceedings. The proposal requires the court to examine its jurisdiction ex officio prior to opening insolvency proceedings and to specify in its decision on which grounds it based its jurisdiction … These changes aim at ensuring that proceedings are only opened if the Member State concerned actually has jurisdiction. It should therefore reduce the cases of forum shopping through abusive and non-genuine relocation of the COMI.'

The proposal reflects the suspicion in relation to cases under the OR that the courts of some Member States were not considering the question of international jurisdiction under the OR with sufficient care, thereby facilitating abusive or fraudulent forum shopping.

8.573 Article 4(1) RR reflects good practice under the OR. A question may however arise as to the degree of examination required. In a busy court list where the evidence suggests a purely national case, the examination may not have to be very detailed. In any case where there is a foreign element and suspicious circumstances suggesting eg 'bankruptcy tourism', the question of jurisdiction will need to be looked at much more carefully.

8.574 Article 4(2) RR enables Member States to empower insolvency practitioners (who have been appointed out of court) to determine whether the relevant Member State has jurisdiction pursuant to Article 3 RR. It is doubtful that this provision will have much of an impact. Where a problem of jurisdiction arises, the office-holder's only option usually is to apply to the court for directions.

8.575 Self-certified procedures (eg an out of court administration appointment) are however still possible. The Member State may entrust the office-holder to determine whether the Member State has jurisdiction following his purported appointment. It is assumed that the consequences of an invalid appointment will be sufficiently serious to encourage an office-holder to do this promptly after appointment where there is any uncertainty, but that may not be guaranteed in all jurisdictions. Of course, any creditor in any Member State (or even the debtor) now has the ability to challenge the opening of main proceedings on jurisdictional grounds and there is no time limit on a creditor being able to do so (a three-month time limit had been proposed but was not adopted). The absence of a time limit may of course leave the proceedings vulnerable to attack much later on although if there is doubt, the office-holder should make his determination (and seek court directions as necessary) promptly.

---

[580] See the Proposal of the European Commission dated 12 December 2012 (2012/0360 (COD)).
[581] ibid at 3.1.2 of the Explanatory Memorandum.

(RR) Article 5—Judicial review of the decision to open main insolvency proceedings

1. The debtor or any creditor may challenge before a court the decision opening main insolvency proceedings on grounds of international jurisdiction.
2. The decision opening main insolvency proceedings may be challenged by parties other than those referred to in paragraph 1 or on grounds other than a lack of international jurisdiction where national law so provides.

8.576 Article 5 RR was also a new provision. It is derived from the European Commission's original legislative proposal,[582] and is designed to ensure that all creditors (including foreign creditors) have *locus standi* to challenge a decision opening insolvency proceedings. Article 5 RR is one of those rules which have a harmonizing effect on the member states' insolvency law by creating a new remedy Union-wide.

8.577 Under the OR there was a concern that in some Member States an insolvency proceeding could be opened without notice to the debtor or without notice to creditors and there may not be recourse. Article 5 RR provides that regardless of national law rules, such recourse will be available.

8.578 Article 5(2) RR ensures that this right of challenge created by the RR is not interpreted as excluding a challenge under national law by a party or on a basis not provided for by the RR.

(RR) Article 6—Jurisdiction for actions deriving directly from insolvency proceedings and closely linked with them

1. The courts of the Member State within the territory of which insolvency proceedings have been opened in accordance with Article 3 shall have jurisdiction for any action which derives directly from the insolvency proceedings and is closely linked with them, such as avoidance actions.
2. Where an action referred to in paragraph 1 is related to an action in civil and commercial matters against the same defendant, the insolvency practitioner may bring both actions before the courts of the Member State within the territory of which the defendant is domiciled, or, where the action is brought against several defendants, before the courts of the Member State within the territory of which any of them is domiciled, provided that those courts have jurisdiction pursuant to Regulation (EU) No 1215/2012.
   The first subparagraph shall apply to the debtor in possession, provided that national law allows the debtor in possession to bring actions on behalf of the insolvency estate.
3. For the purpose of paragraph 2, actions are deemed to be related where they are so closely connected that it is expedient to hear and determine them together to avoid the risk of irreconcilable judgments resulting from separate proceedings.

---

[582] See the Proposal of the European Commission dated 12 December 2012 (2012/0360 (COD)) at 3.1.2 of the Explanatory Memorandum.

Article 6 RR was a new provision, which clarifies the relationship between the RR and the **8.579**
Brussels Regulation (Recast).[583] It is derived from the European Commission's original legislative proposal,[584] which includes the following explanatory statement:[585]

> ... the proposal clarifies that the courts opening insolvency proceedings also have jurisdiction for actions which derive directly from insolvency proceedings or are closely linked with them such as avoidance actions. This amendment codifies the case-law of the CJEU in the 'Deko Marty' decision.[586] Where such an action is related to another action against the same defendant which is based on general civil and commercial law, the proposal gives the liquidator the possibility to bring both actions in the courts of the defendant's domicile if these courts are competent pursuant to [the Judgments Regulation]. This rule would allow a liquidator to bring, for example, an action for directors' liability based on insolvency law together with an action against that director based on tort law or company law in the same court.

Thus, Article 6(1) RR was not designed to modify the law, but to codify the existing principles governing the relationship between the Judgments Regulation and the OR, as set out in the case law under the OR.

Recital (35) RR also explains the purpose of Article 6 RR: **8.580**

> The courts of the Member State within the territory of which insolvency proceedings have been opened should also have jurisdiction for actions which derive directly from the insolvency proceedings and are closely linked with them. Such actions should include avoidance actions against defendants in other Member States and actions concerning obligations that arise in the course of the insolvency proceedings, such as advance payment for costs of the proceedings. In contrast, actions for the performance of the obligations under a contract concluded by the debtor prior to the opening of proceedings do not derive directly from the proceedings. Where such an action is related to another action based on general civil and commercial law, the insolvency practitioner should be able to bring both actions in the courts of the defendant's domicile if he considers it more efficient to bring the action in that forum. This could, for example, be the case where the insolvency practitioner wishes to combine an action for director's liability on the basis of insolvency law with an action based on company law or general tort law.

Recital (7) RR states that: **8.581**

> Bankruptcy, proceedings relating to the winding-up of insolvent companies or other legal persons, judicial arrangements, compositions and analogous proceedings and actions related to such proceedings are excluded from the scope of [the Judgments Regulation]. Those proceedings should be covered by this Regulation. The interpretation of this Regulation should as much as possible avoid regulatory loopholes between the two instruments. However, the mere fact that a national procedure is not listed in Annex A to this Regulation should not imply that it is covered by [the Judgments Regulation].

---

[583] That is, Case C-339/07 *Seagon v Deko Marty Belgium NV* [2009] ECR I-767, [2009] 1 WLR 2168.
[584] That is, Regulation (EU) 1215/2012 of the European Parliament and of the Council of 12 December 2012 on jurisdiction and the recognition of judgments in civil and commercial matters (recast).
[585] See the Proposal of the European Commission dated 12 December 2012 (2012/0360 (COD)).
[586] ibid at 3.1.2 of the Explanatory Memorandum.

This confirms the well-established principle that the RR and the Judgments Regulation are intended to be complementary, so that they do not (at least in principle[587]) overlap or leave gaps in their application. The CJEU has endorsed this principle in several recent cases, including *Nickel & Goeldner*,[588] *F-Tex*,[589] and *Riel*.[590]

8.582 Although not expressly stated in the text, the CJEU has decided that the international jurisdiction granted to the courts is to be understood as being exclusive.[591] This might create problems when suing a party from a third state (ie outside of the member states) where recognition of the judgment is not guaranteed or when suing another member state's tax authorities for, eg, avoiding earlier tax payments; that tax authority may be able to rely on state immunity before foreign courts.

8.583 The principle that the RR and the Judgments Regulation are intended to be complementary must be construed subject to Article 6(2) RR, which is not a mere codification of the existing law. In summary: where an 'insolvency action' (A1) is related to a 'civil or commercial action' (A2) against the same defendant(s), the insolvency practitioner may bring both actions together in the Member State(s) where any of the defendants are domiciled, provided that such Member State(s) have jurisdiction in respect of A2 under the Judgments Regulation. The same rule applies to debtors in possession, provided that national law allows the debtor in possession to bring actions on behalf of the estate. The definition of 'related actions' in Article 6(3) RR is identical to the definition of the same term in Article 30(3) of the Brussels Regulation (Recast), and should be construed in the same manner.

(RR) Article 7—Applicable law

1. Save as otherwise provided in this Regulation, the law applicable to insolvency proceedings and their effects shall be that of the Member State within the territory of which such proceedings are opened (the 'State of the opening of proceedings').
2. The law of the State of the opening of proceedings shall determine the conditions for the opening of those proceedings, their conduct and their closure. In particular, it shall determine the following:
   (a) the debtors against which insolvency proceedings may be brought on account of their capacity;

---

[587] There are in fact some obvious gaps, even after allowing for the effect of Directive 2001/24/EC on the reorganization and winding up of credit institutions as amended and Solvency II: see 8.10–8.12 above. The gaps include insolvency proceedings for investment undertakings in the case of the OR, and collective investment undertakings in the case of both the OR and RR, all of which are excluded from both Judgments Regulation and the OR/RR as the case may be.

[588] Case C-157/13 *Nickel & Goeldner Spedition GmbH v 'Kintra' UAB* [2015] QB 96, para 21.

[589] Case C-213/10 *F-Tex SIA v Lietuvos-Anglijos UAB* [2013] Bus LR 232, paras 21, 29, and 48.

[590] Case C-47/18 *Skarb Państwa Rzeczpospolitej Polskiej—Generalny Dyrektor Dróg Krajowych i Autostrad v Stephan Riel* ECLI:EU:C:2019:754. Cf, additionally, Case C-535/17 *NK v Paribas Fortis NV* ECLI:EU:C:2019:96.

[591] Case C-493/18 *UB v VA, Tiger et al* ECLI:EU:C:2019:1046; Case C-296/17 *Wiemer & Trachte GmbH gegen Zhan Oved Tadzher* ECLI:EU:C:2018:902; Case C-649/16 *Peter Valach u a v Waldviertler Sparkasse Bank AG et al* ECLI:EU:C:2017:986; Case-641/16 *Tünkers France und Tünkers Maschinenbau GmbH gegen Expert France* ECLI:EU:C:2017:847.

(b) the assets which form part of the insolvency estate and the treatment of assets acquired by or devolving on the debtor after the opening of the insolvency proceedings;
(c) the respective powers of the debtor and the insolvency practitioner;
(d) the conditions under which set-offs may be invoked;
(e) the effects of insolvency proceedings on current contracts to which the debtor is party;
(f) the effects of the insolvency proceedings on proceedings brought by individual creditors, with the exception of pending lawsuits;
(g) the claims which are to be lodged against the debtor's insolvency estate and the treatment of claims arising after the opening of insolvency proceedings;
(h) the rules governing the lodging, verification and admission of claims;
(i) the rules governing the distribution of proceeds from the realisation of assets, the ranking of claims and the rights of creditors who have obtained partial satisfaction after the opening of insolvency proceedings by virtue of a right in rem or through a set-off;
(j) the conditions for, and the effects of closure of, insolvency proceedings, in particular by composition;
(k) creditors' rights after the closure of insolvency proceedings;
(l) who is to bear the costs and expenses incurred in the insolvency proceedings;
(m) the rules relating to the voidness, voidability or unenforceability of legal acts detrimental to the general body of creditors.

Article 7 RR is copied from Article 4 OR, and reference should be made to the commentary under Article 4 OR above. **8.584**

However, it should be noted that 'lawsuits pending' in Article 7(2)(f) RR in effect cross-refers to Article 18 RR, just as Article 4(2)(f) OR in effect cross-referred to Article 15 OR. The changes to Article 15 OR contained in Article 18 RR are commented on below under Article 18 RR. **8.585**

It should also be noted that just as Article 4(2)(m) OR was qualified by the 'double actionability' defence in Article 13 OR, Article 7(2)(m) RR is similarly qualified by Article 16 RR. **8.586**

(RR) Article 8—Third parties' rights in rem

1. The opening of insolvency proceedings shall not affect the rights in rem of creditors or third parties in respect of tangible or intangible, moveable or immoveable assets, both specific assets and collections of indefinite assets as a whole which change from time to time, belonging to the debtor which are situated within the territory of another Member State at the time of the opening of proceedings.
2. The rights referred to in paragraph 1 shall, in particular, mean:
    (a) the right to dispose of assets or have them disposed of and to obtain satisfaction from the proceeds of or income from those assets, in particular by virtue of a lien or a mortgage;

(b) the exclusive right to have a claim met, in particular a right guaranteed by a lien in respect of the claim or by assignment of the claim by way of a guarantee;
(c) the right to demand assets from, and/or to require restitution by, anyone having possession or use of them contrary to the wishes of the party so entitled;
(d) a right in rem to the beneficial use of assets.

3. The right, recorded in a public register and enforceable against third parties, based on which a right in rem within the meaning of paragraph 1 may be obtained shall be considered to be a right in rem.
4. Paragraph 1 shall not preclude actions for voidness, voidability or unenforceability as referred to in point (m) of Article 7(2).

8.587 This Article simply copies Article 5 OR without any material changes. There is a change to the cross-reference in Article 8(4) RR from a cross-reference to Article 4(2)(m) OR to a cross-reference to Article 7(2)(m) RR. Reference should be made to the commentary on Article 5 OR above.

(RR) Article 9—Set-off

1. The opening of insolvency proceedings shall not affect the right of creditors to demand the set-off of their claims against the claims of a debtor, where such a set-off is permitted by the law applicable to the insolvent debtor's claim.
2. Paragraph 1 shall not preclude actions for voidness, voidability or unenforceability as referred to in point (m) of Article 7(2).

8.588 Article 9 RR is copied from Article 6 OR without any material change. There is simply a change in Article 9(2) RR in changing the cross-reference from Article 4(2)(m) OR to Article 7(2)(m) RR. Reference should be made to the commentary on Article 6 OR above.

(RR) Article 10—Reservation of title

1. The opening of insolvency proceedings against the purchaser of an asset shall not affect sellers' rights that are based on a reservation of title where at the time of the opening of proceedings the asset is situated within the territory of a Member State other than the State of the opening of proceedings.
2. The opening of insolvency proceedings against the seller of an asset, after delivery of the asset, shall not constitute grounds for rescinding or terminating the sale and shall not prevent the purchaser from acquiring title where at the time of the opening of proceedings the asset sold is situated within the territory of a Member State other than the State of the opening of proceedings.
3. Paragraphs 1 and 2 shall not preclude actions for voidness, voidability or unenforceability as referred to in point (m) of Article 7(2).

8.589 Article 10 RR is copied from Article 7 OR without any material change. The only alteration is in the cross-reference in Article 10(3) RR from a cross-reference to Article 4(2)(m) OR to a cross-reference to Article 7(2)(m) RR. Reference should be made to the commentary on Article 7 OR above.

(RR) Article 11—Contracts relating to immoveable property

1. The effects of insolvency proceedings on a contract conferring the right to acquire or make use of immoveable property shall be governed solely by the law of the Member State within the territory of which the immoveable property is situated.
2. The court which opened main insolvency proceedings shall have jurisdiction to approve the termination or modification of the contracts referred to in this Article where:
   (a) the law of the Member State applicable to those contracts requires that such a contract may only be terminated or modified with the approval of the court opening insolvency proceedings; and
   (b) no insolvency proceedings have been opened in that Member State.

Article 11(1) RR is copied from Article 8 OR without any material change. Reference should be made to the commentary on Article 8 OR above. **8.590**

The change is contained in the additional paragraph Article 11(2) RR. Whereas Article 11(1) is a general exclusion from the effects of insolvency proceedings on a contract relating to immoveable property, causing the contract to be governed solely by the law of the Member State within the territory of which the immoveable property is situated, Article 11(2) RR creates an exception to that exception. It confers jurisdiction on the court which has opened main insolvency proceedings to approve the termination or modification of contracts relating to immoveable property in certain circumstances. The relevant circumstances are where the law of the Member State applicable to the contract requires that the contract may only be terminated or modified with the approval of the court opening insolvency proceedings and where no insolvency proceedings have been opened in that Member State. Without this conferral of jurisdiction, a serious problem may have arisen in such a case, if, for example, it were not possible to open secondary proceedings in the Member State within the territory of which the moveable property was situated. In any event, even where the opening of local territorial proceedings is possible in such a case, it would be an unnecessary expense and complication, which is avoided by this additional provision. **8.591**

(RR) Article 12—Payment systems and financial markets

1. Without prejudice to Article 8, the effects of insolvency proceedings on the rights and obligations of the parties to a payment or settlement system or to a financial market shall be governed solely by the law of the Member State applicable to that system or market.
2. Paragraph 1 shall not preclude any action for voidness, voidability or unenforceability which may be taken to set aside payments or transactions under the law applicable to the relevant payment system or financial market.

8.592 Article 12 RR is copied from Article 9 OR and contains no material change. The only change is the change in the cross-reference in Article 12(1) RR from a cross-reference to Article 5 OR to a cross-reference to Article 8 RR. Reference should be made to the commentary on Article 9 OR above.

8.593 The concept of payment or settlement systems in Article 12 is closely linked to the Directive 98/26/EC on settlement finality in payment and securities settlement systems ('Finality Directive'). However, a relatively widespread view is that the scope of Article 12 is broader than that of the Directive and also covers formal netting arrangements between three or more participants such as inter-company netting arrangements. The absence in the RR of an express rule on netting may help to explain this broad understanding of Article 12. Giving the economic importance of netting, the question of whether and to what extent netting arrangements are governed by Article 9 (set-off) and/or Article 12 (payment and settlement systems) could end up before the CJEU for clarification.

(RR) Article 13—Contracts of employment

1. The effects of insolvency proceedings on employment contracts and relationships shall be governed solely by the law of the Member State applicable to the contract of employment.
2. The courts of the Member State in which secondary insolvency proceedings may be opened shall retain jurisdiction to approve the termination or modification of the contracts referred to in this Article even if no insolvency proceedings have been opened in that Member State.
   The first subparagraph shall also apply to an authority competent under national law to approve the termination or modification of the contracts referred to in this Article.

8.594 Article 13(1) RR is copied from Article 10 OR and reference should be made to the commentary on Article 10 OR above.

8.595 The changes are contained in the new Article 13(2) RR. Under the OR, it was occasionally found necessary to apply for the opening of secondary proceedings simply in order to assist with the termination or modification of employment contracts.[592] The opening of secondary proceedings, which might be disruptive to the main proceedings and in any event would involve additional expense and potential delay, can now be avoided by the conferment of this power. The word 'retain' in this context should be read as 'have', since this type of jurisdiction usually arises in connection with local insolvency proceedings. The coda to Article 13(2) RR, which extends the same power to an authority competent under national

---

[592] For example, in *Re Nortel Networks SA* [2009] EWHC 1482 (Ch), [2010] BCC 21, where the English High Court gave the English administrators of the French registered debtor company permission to apply to the Versailles *tribunal de commerce* to open secondary proceedings to assist with redundancy of employees in France.

law to approve the termination or modification of employment contracts in the case of insolvency proceedings, deals with the situation where the approval of the termination or modification during local insolvency proceedings lies with an authority other than the court in charge of the insolvency proceedings.

(RR) Article 14—Effects on rights subject to registration

The effects of insolvency proceedings on the rights of a debtor in immoveable property, a ship or an aircraft subject to registration in a public register shall be determined by the law of the Member State under the authority of which the register is kept.

Article 14 RR is copied from Article 11 OR and the commentary on Article 11 OR above should be referred to. **8.596**

(RR) Article 15—European patents with unitary effect and Community trade marks

For the purposes of this Regulation, a European patent with unitary effect, a Community trade mark or any other similar right established by Union law may be included only in the proceedings referred to in Article 3(1).

Article 15 RR is based on the text of Article 11 OR, but the reference to 'a Community patent' has been replaced by 'a European patent with unitary effect' and the reference to 'Community Law' has been replaced by 'Union Law'.[593] **8.597**

The changes are in effect an updating to take account of developments in European patent law. For several decades the Member States of the European Union have been negotiating the creation of a European patent with unitary effect and a unified European patent court. In 2012, representatives of the EU Member States achieved a breakthrough agreement. The 'European Patent with Unitary Effect' is a European patent, granted by the European Patent Office (EPO) under the rules and procedures of the European Patent Convention, to which, upon request of the patent proprietor, unitary effect is given for the territory of the 25 Member States participating in the unitary patent scheme. The unitary patent will co-exist with national patents and with classical European patents. Patent proprietors will in future be able to choose between various combinations of classical European patents and unitary patents. The new patent regime is set out in Regulations 1257/2012 and 1260/2012. **8.598**

Some Member States (eg Spain and Italy) do not participate in Regulation 1257/2012 implementing enhanced co-operation in the area of the creation of unitary patent protection. However Article 15 is also applicable in these Member States in order to determine which assets belong to the estate of the main proceedings and which belong to the estate of the territorial proceedings. **8.599**

---

[593] See the Treaty on European Law (TEU) and the Treaty of the Functioning on the European Union (TFEU).

(RR) Article 16—Detrimental acts

Point (m) of Article 7(2) shall not apply where the person who benefited from an act detrimental to all the creditors provides proof that:
(a) the act is subject to the law of a Member State other than that of the State of the opening of proceedings; and
(b) the law of that Member State does not allow any means of challenging that act in the relevant case.

8.600 Article 16 RR is copied from Article 13 OR with no material change. The only change is a change in the cross-reference from a cross-reference to Article 4(2)(m) OR to Article 7(2)(m) RR. Reference should be made to the commentary on Article 13 OR above.

8.601 Article 16 can be invoked against the provisions of insolvency law on fraudulent or undervalued transfers. It is worth noting that Article 16 RR may also be applicable to rules of the *lex fori concursus* that fulfil an equivalent function to avoidance actions, but do not require the setting-aside of the challenged act. That is the case, for instance of rules that leave the transaction valid but give the insolvency practitioner the right to apply for a court order reversing its effects, or impose the subordination of the rights arisen out of the challenged act (eg the insolvency subordination of loans given by shareholders or insiders under some national laws).

(RR) Article 17—Protection of third-party purchasers

Where, by an act concluded after the opening of insolvency proceedings, a debtor disposes, for consideration, of:
(a) an immoveable asset;
(b) a ship or an aircraft subject to registration in a public register; or
(c) securities the existence of which requires registration in a register laid down by law;
the validity of that act shall be governed by the law of the State within the territory of which the immoveable asset is situated or under the authority of which the register is kept.

8.602 Article 17 RR is copied from Article 14 OR and reference should be made to the commentary on Article 14 OR above.

(RR) Article 18—Effects of insolvency proceedings on pending lawsuits or arbitral proceedings

The effects of insolvency proceedings on a pending lawsuit or pending arbitral proceedings concerning an asset or a right which forms part of a debtor's insolvency estate shall be governed solely by the law of the Member State in which that lawsuit is pending or in which the arbitral tribunal has its seat.

8.603 Article 18 RR is based on Article 15 OR but contains clarifications of its meaning and effect. The commentary on Article 15 OR above should be consulted for the background.

8.604 In Article 15 OR, the question arose whether 'lawsuit pending' included arbitration proceedings. Different language versions suggested different answers but the English Commercial Court in *Elektrim v Vivendi*[594] held that Article 15 OR included arbitration proceedings. This result is confirmed in the text of Article 18 RR.

8.605 The wording of Article 15 OR also gave rise to a question of whether Article 15 OR was (i) limited to proprietary claims and/or (ii) limited to claims that property belonged to the debtor: see the commentary relating to Article 15 OR above.

8.606 The English commercial court in the case of *Elektrim v Vivendi* (cited above) ruled that Article 15 OR was not limited to proprietary claims. The view was taken that Article 15 OR applied to any claim to a share in the estate.

8.607 The suggestion that Article 15 OR applied only to proprietary claims originated from the expression 'concerning an asset or a right of which the debtor has been divested'. This was actually a reference back to the formation of an estate by means of the 'divestment' of a debtor mentioned in Article 1(1) OR. Although the English text might have suggested, if read literally, that Article 15 OR only applied to the recovery of assets belonging, or formerly belonging, to the debtor, other language versions referred to assets which were part of the estate: see the commentary on Article 15 OR above.

8.608 By removing the reference to divesting, and making an express reference to the insolvency estate, Article 18 RR clarifies the fact that, as had been held in the English commercial court case of *Elektrim v Vivendi*, the provision is not restricted to proprietary claims. That, at least, appears to be the intention of the change in wording, although the reference is still to 'concerning an asset or a right which forms part of the debtor's insolvency estate',[595] which could be read as making a claim to ownership of some asset within the debtor's estate. It is suggested that the broader interpretation in *Elektrim v Vivendi*, namely that any claim which affects the insolvency estate by seeking a share of it, is the correct interpretation of the provision.

8.609 The reference in Article 18 to the law of the Member State where the dispute is pending does not extend to questions of international jurisdiction, which are subject to a uniform regime under the RR. The jurisdiction of the insolvency courts *only* extends to actions which are based on insolvency rules and are directly linked to the insolvency proceedings (see Article 6 RR). Conversely, actions based on general civil and commercial law (eg contract law) are subject to the Brussels I Regulation (see Recital 35 RR). This may have an indirect effect upon the validity and efficacy of arbitration agreements. Some national laws do not recognize the validity or efficacy of arbitration clauses in the case of insolvency in order to allow for the centralization of all disputes affecting the estate in the insolvency courts. However, this justification does not hold in the EU context, as with regard to actions based on general

---

[594] [2008] EWHC 2155 (Comm), [2008] 2 Lloyd's Rep 636, aff'd (CA) [2009] EWCA Civ 677, [2010] BCC 348.
[595] See also the same wording in Recital (73) RR.

civil and commercial law such centralization is not possible: if the validity of the arbitration agreement is nullified or its efficacy suspended by the insolvency proceedings, it would not mean that the dispute could be joined to the insolvency proceedings, but merely that the general rules on jurisdiction apply, in particular the Judgments Regulation. Therefore, if the main justification of the national rule invalidating or rendering inoperative the arbitration agreement is the concentration of disputes before the insolvency court, that justification does not hold when the RR governs the insolvency proceedings.

B. Chapter II: Recognition of Insolvency Proceedings

(RR) Article 19—Principle

1. Any judgment opening insolvency proceedings handed down by a court of a Member State which has jurisdiction pursuant to Article 3 shall be recognised in all other Member States from the moment that it becomes effective in the State of the opening of proceedings.
   The rule laid down in the first subparagraph shall also apply where, on account of a debtor's capacity, insolvency proceedings cannot be brought against that debtor in other Member States.
2. Recognition of the proceedings referred to in Article 3(1) shall not preclude the opening of the proceedings referred to in Article 3(2) by a court in another Member State. The latter proceedings shall be secondary insolvency proceedings within the meaning of Chapter III.

8.610 Article 19 RR is copied from Article 16 OR and reference should be made to the commentary on Article 16 OR above. Note however the RR provisions relating to the meaning of 'court' in Article 2(6) RR above.

(RR) Article 20—Effects of recognition

1. The judgment opening insolvency proceedings as referred to in Article 3(1) shall, with no further formalities, produce the same effects in any other Member State as under the law of the State of the opening of proceedings, unless this Regulation provides otherwise and as long as no proceedings referred to in Article 3(2) are opened in that other Member State.
2. The effects of the proceedings referred to in Article 3(2) may not be challenged in other Member States. Any restriction of creditors' rights, in particular a stay or discharge, shall produce effects vis-à-vis assets situated within the territory of another Member State only in the case of those creditors who have given their consent.

8.611 Article 20 RR is copied from Article 17 OR and reference should be made to the commentary under Article 17 OR above.

(RR) Article 21—Powers of the insolvency practitioner

1. The insolvency practitioner appointed by a court which has jurisdiction pursuant to Article 3(1) may exercise all the powers conferred on it, by the law of the State of the opening of proceedings, in another Member State, as long as no other insolvency proceedings have been opened there and no preservation measure to the contrary has been taken there further to a request for the opening of insolvency proceedings in that State. Subject to Articles 8 and 10, the insolvency practitioner may, in particular, remove the debtor's assets from the territory of the Member State in which they are situated.
2. The insolvency practitioner appointed by a court which has jurisdiction pursuant to Article 3(2) may in any other Member State claim through the courts or out of court that moveable property was removed from the territory of the State of the opening of proceedings to the territory of that other Member State after the opening of the insolvency proceedings. The insolvency practitioner may also bring any action to set aside which is in the interests of the creditors.
3. In exercising its powers, the insolvency practitioner shall comply with the law of the Member State within the territory of which it intends to take action, in particular with regard to procedures for the realization of assets. Those powers may not include coercive measures, unless ordered by a court of that Member State, or the right to rule on legal proceedings or disputes.

There is a change of terminology here, as there is throughout the RR, in that the expression 'liquidator' as defined in the OR has been replaced by 'insolvency practitioner' as defined in Article 2(5) RR and listed in Annex B. **8.612**

Otherwise Article 21(1) RR is copied in all material respects from Article 18(1) OR and the commentary to that Article should be referred to above. The cross-references in Article 18(1) OR to Articles 5 and 7 OR have been replaced by cross-references to Articles 8 and 10 RR. **8.613**

Article 21(2) RR, apart from exchanging 'liquidator' for 'insolvency practitioner' is identical to Article 18(2) OR and reference should be made to the commentary on Article 18 OR above. **8.614**

Article 21(3) RR is similar to Article 18(3) OR, but there is a significant change in the last sentence. The last sentence of both Article 18 OR and Article 21 RR state that the powers exercised by the insolvency administrator 'may not include coercive measures' or the right to rule on legal proceedings or disputes. With regard to the text of the OR, there is a question as to whether the prohibition on coercive measures applied to situations where (i) such measures were ordered by the court conducting the main insolvency proceedings and therefore in principle enforceable via Article 25 OR (see now Article 32 RR)[596] and/or (ii) the measures were ordered by a local court in another Member State. **8.615**

---

[596] In *Handelsveem BV v Hill* [2011] BPIR 1024 the Netherlands Supreme Court held that Art 18(3) OR did not apply to prevent a coercive measure ordered by the English court being recognized and enforced by the Netherlands courts via Art 25 OR.

8.616 Article 21(3) RR makes it clear that the liquidator in the main proceeding may exercise coercive measures in another Member State if they are ordered by a court of that Member State.[597] The change in the text has not however resolved whether the bar on coercive measures extends to orders of the court conducting the main insolvency proceedings which are required to be recognized under the RR equivalent of Article 25 OR, namely Article 32 RR. That issue remains to be decided by the CJEU.

(RR) Article 22—Proof of the insolvency practitioner's appointment

The insolvency practitioner's appointment shall be evidenced by a certified copy of the original decision appointing it or by any other certificate issued by the court which has jurisdiction.

A translation into the official language or one of the official languages of the Member State within the territory of which it intends to act may be required. No legalisation or other similar formality shall be required.

8.617 Article 22 RR is copied from Article 19 OR, save for the substitution of 'insolvency practitioner' for 'liquidator'. Reference should therefore be made to the commentary to Article 19 OR above.

(RR) Article 23—Return and imputation

1. A creditor which, after the opening of the proceedings referred to in Article 3(1), obtains by any means, in particular through enforcement, total or partial satisfaction of its claim on the assets belonging to a debtor situated within the territory of another Member State, shall return what it has obtained to the insolvency practitioner, subject to Articles 8 and 10.
2. In order to ensure the equal treatment of creditors, a creditor which has, in the course of insolvency proceedings, obtained a dividend on its claim shall share in distributions made in other proceedings only where creditors of the same ranking or category have, in those other proceedings, obtained an equivalent dividend.

8.618 Article 23 RR is copied from Article 20 OR and is identical to it, save for the substitution of 'insolvency practitioner' for 'liquidator' and for the alteration of the cross-references from Articles 5 and 7 OR to Articles 8 and 10 RR. Reference should be made to the commentary under Article 20 OR.

---

[597] Note that 'court' for this purpose is restricted to a 'judicial body': Art 2(6)(i) RR.

(RR) Article 24—Establishment of insolvency registers

1. Member States shall establish and maintain in their territory one or several registers in which information concerning insolvency proceedings is published ('insolvency registers'). That information shall be published as soon as possible after the opening of such proceedings.
2. The information referred to in paragraph 1 shall be made publicly available, subject to the conditions laid down in Article 27, and shall include the following ('mandatory information'):
   (a) the date of the opening of insolvency proceedings;
   (b) the court opening insolvency proceedings and the case reference number, if any;
   (c) the type of insolvency proceedings referred to in Annex A that were opened and, where applicable, any relevant subtype of such proceedings opened in accordance with national law;
   (d) whether jurisdiction for opening proceedings is based on Article 3(1), 3(2) or 3(4);
   (e) if the debtor is a company or a legal person, the debtor's name, registration number, registered office or, if different, postal address;
   (f) if the debtor is an individual whether or not exercising an independent business or professional activity, the debtor's name, registration number, if any, and postal address or, where the address is protected, the debtor's place and date of birth;
   (g) the name, postal address or e-mail address of the insolvency practitioner, if any, appointed in the proceedings;
   (h) the time limit for lodging claims, if any, or a reference to the criteria for calculating that time limit;
   (i) the date of closing main insolvency proceedings, if any;
   (j) the court before which and, where applicable, the time limit within which a challenge of the decision opening insolvency proceedings is to be lodged in accordance with Article 5, or a reference to the criteria for calculating that time limit.
3. Paragraph 2 shall not preclude Member States from including documents or additional information in their national insolvency registers, such as directors' disqualifications related to insolvency.
4. Member States shall not be obliged to include in the insolvency registers the information referred to in paragraph 1 of this Article in relation to individuals not exercising an independent business or professional activity, or to make such information publicly available through the system of interconnection of those registers, provided that known foreign creditors are informed, pursuant to Article 54, of the elements referred to under point (j) of paragraph 2 of this Article.
   Where a Member State makes use of the possibility referred to in the first subparagraph, the insolvency proceedings shall not affect the claims of foreign creditors who have not received the information referred to in the first subparagraph.
5. The publication of information in the registers under this Regulation shall not have any legal effects other than those set out in national law and in Article 55(6).

Article 24 RR is entirely new and stems from the proposal of the European Commission to establish national insolvency registers which will in time be interconnected.

8.620 Commentators have for a long period pointed out the difficulties that are caused by the lack of insolvency registers which can be searched electronically from other Member States and which preferably should be interconnected across the European Union.

8.621 One example of the difficulties created by the lack of searchable electronic registers is illustrated by the *Stojevic* case,[598] where shortly after the opening of main insolvency proceedings in the UK, a further, purportedly main, proceeding was opened in respect of the same debtor by the Austrian courts.

8.622 Article 24(1) RR lays down the obligation on Member States to establish and maintain one or more registers about insolvency proceedings. Although this is not spelt out, the implication from the following Articles is that the registers must be electronic and available on the internet.

8.623 Article 24(2) RR sets out in detail the information that should be contained in the register, although Member States are not precluded from including documents or additional information: Article 24(3) RR.

8.624 There is an exception to the detailed information required to be placed on the register in relation to what could be described as 'non-traders', ie 'individuals not exercising an independent business or professional activity'. In such a case, the bare bones information set out in Article 24(2)(j) RR is sufficient.

8.625 The date of publication in the register may have a significance under national law. As far as EU law is concerned, in accordance with Article 24(5) RR the time limit for lodging claims under Article 55(6) RR is required to be not less than 30 days following the publication of the opening of the insolvency proceedings in the register of the Member State of opening. There is an exception for cases within Article 24(4) RR, which allows for the publication of minimal information in relation to non-traders: the period for lodging claims is required to be not less than 30 days following the notice required to be given under Article 54 RR requiring the lodging of claims.

(RR) Article 25—Interconnection of insolvency registers

1. The Commission shall establish a decentralised system for the interconnection of insolvency registers by means of implementing acts. That system shall be composed of the insolvency registers and the European e-Justice Portal, which shall serve as a central public electronic access point to information in the system. The system shall provide a search service in all the official languages of the institutions of the Union in order to make available the mandatory information and any other documents or information included in the insolvency registers which the Member States choose to make available through the European e-Justice Portal.
2. By means of implementing acts in accordance with the procedure referred to in Article 87, the Commission shall adopt the following by 26 June 2019:

---

[598] Referred to at various points in the commentary on the OR—see the index of cases at the front of this work.

(a) the technical specification defining the methods of communication and information exchange by electronic means on the basis of the established interface specification for the system of interconnection of insolvency registers;
(b) the technical measures ensuring the minimum information technology security standards for communication and distribution of information within the system of interconnection of insolvency registers;
(c) minimum criteria for the search service provided by the European e-Justice Portal based on the information set out in Article 24;
(d) minimum criteria for the presentation of the results of such searches based on the information set out in Article 24;
(e) the means and the technical conditions of availability of services provided by the system of interconnection; and
(f) a glossary containing a basic explanation of the national insolvency proceedings listed in Annex A.

8.626 Article 25 RR requires the European Commission to establish a decentralized system for the interconnection of insolvency registers. The system will have to provide a search service in all the official languages of the institutions of the European Union in relation to the mandated information and any other documents for information included in the insolvency registers which the Member States choose to make available through the European e-Justice Portal.

8.627 Article 25(2) RR required the European Commission to adopt a number of steps by 26 June 2019. The interconnectivity of national registers is still some way away at the time of writing.[599]

(RR) Article 26—Costs of establishing and interconnecting insolvency registers

1. The establishment, maintenance and future development of the system of interconnection of insolvency registers shall be financed from the general budget of the Union.
2. Each Member State shall bear the costs of establishing and adjusting its national insolvency registers to make them interoperable with the European e-Justice Portal, as well as the costs of administering, operating and maintaining those registers. This shall be without prejudice to the possibility to apply for grants to support such activities under the Union's financial programmes.

8.628 One of the questions raised when interconnecting insolvency registers were suggested, was the source of finance. Article 26(1) RR provides that the establishment, maintenance, and future development of the system of interconnection of insolvency registers is to be financed from the general budget of the European Union. By contrast, Article 27(2) RR provides that each Member State shall bear the costs of establishing and adjusting its national insolvency registers to make them interoperable with the European e-Justice Portal and are

---

[599] See now Commission Implementing Regulation (EU) 2019/917 from 4 June 2019.

to bear their own costs of administering, operating, and maintaining the national registers. That responsibility is 'without prejudice' to the possibility of applying for grants to support such activities under the EU's financial programmes.

(RR) Article 27—Conditions of access to information via the system of interconnection

1. Member States shall ensure that the mandatory information referred to in points (a) to (j) of Article 24(2) is available free of charge via the system of interconnection of insolvency registers.
2. This Regulation shall not preclude Member States from charging a reasonable fee for access to the documents or additional information referred to in Article 24(3) via the system of interconnection of insolvency registers.
3. Member States may make access to mandatory information concerning individuals who are not exercising an independent business or professional activity, and concerning individuals exercising an independent business or professional activity when the insolvency proceedings are not related to that activity, subject to supplementary search criteria relating to the debtor in addition to the minimum criteria referred to in point (c) of Article 25(2).
4. Member States may require that access to the information referred to in paragraph 3 be made conditional upon a request to the competent authority. Member States may make access conditional upon the verification of the existence of a legitimate interest for accessing such information. The requesting person shall be able to submit the request for information electronically by means of a standard form via the European e-Justice Portal. Where a legitimate interest is required, it shall be permissible for the requesting person to justify his request by electronic copies of relevant documents. The requesting person shall be provided with an answer by the competent authority within 3 working days.

    The requesting person shall not be obliged to provide translations of the documents justifying his request, or to bear any costs of translation which the competent authority may incur.

8.629 Article 27(1) RR requires the information required to be registered by the RR to be available free of charge via the system of interconnected insolvency registers. By contrast, Member States which register non-mandatory documents or information may charge a 'reasonable fee' for access to those.

8.630 Article 27(3) and (4) RR make special provision where the individual debtors 'who are not exercising an independent business or professional activity' and where the insolvency proceedings are not related to an independent business or professional activity. In such cases searches can be restricted or access made conditional upon a request to the competent authority. Member States may make access conditional upon the verification of the existence of legitimate interests for accessing such information.

(RR) Article 28—Publication in another Member State

1. The insolvency practitioner or the debtor in possession shall request that notice of the judgment opening insolvency proceedings and, where appropriate, the decision appointing the insolvency practitioner be published in any other Member State where an establishment of the debtor is located in accordance with the publication procedures provided for in that Member State. Such publication shall specify, where appropriate, the insolvency practitioner appointed and whether the jurisdiction rule applied is that pursuant to Article 3(1) or (2).
2. The insolvency practitioner or the debtor in possession may request that the information referred to in paragraph 1 be published in any other Member State where the insolvency practitioner or the debtor in possession deems it necessary in accordance with the publication procedures provided for in that Member State.

8.631 Pending the establishment of interconnected EU-wide searchable registers in the future, the question of publication in other Member States of the opening of insolvency proceedings remains significant.

8.632 Article 28 RR is in some ways modelled on Article 21 OR, but there are significant changes.

8.633 Article 21 OR provided that the insolvency administrator 'may' request notice of the judgment of opening of proceedings and, where appropriate, the decision appointing him, be published in any other Member State, and allowed Member States in which the debtor had an establishment to require publication; Article 28(1) RR requires the insolvency practitioner or the debtor in possession to request publication in any other Member State where the debtor has an establishment. In addition, Article 28(2) RR allows the insolvency practitioner or the debtor in possession to request publication in any other Member State where they think it necessary.

8.634 Article 28(1) RR, second sentence, requires what is now the mandatory publication in any other Member State where the debtor has an establishment to specify, where appropriate, the insolvency practitioner appointed and whether the opening is a main proceeding under Article 3(1) RR or a territorial proceeding under Article 3(2) RR.

(RR) Article 29—Registration in public registers of another Member State

1. Where the law of a Member State in which an establishment of the debtor is located and this establishment has been entered into a public register of that Member State, or the law of a Member State in which immovable property belonging to the debtor is located, requires information on the opening of insolvency proceedings referred to in Article 28 to be published in the land register, company register or any other public register, the insolvency practitioner or the debtor in possession shall take all the necessary measures to ensure such a registration.
2. The insolvency practitioner or the debtor in possession may request such registration in any other Member State, provided that the law of the Member State where the register is kept allows such registration.

8.635 Article 29 RR is new. It requires registration of information in Article 28 RR regarding insolvency proceedings to be effected by the insolvency practitioner or debtor in possession where local law requires such registration in a public register. This may relate to a public register of establishments, immoveable property, company register, or any other public register.

(RR) Article 30—Costs

> The costs of the publication and registration provided for in Articles 28 and 29 shall be regarded as costs and expenses incurred in the proceedings.

8.636 Article 30 RR is copied from Article 23 OR, but the cross-references to Articles 21 and 22 OR have been updated to cross-references to Articles 28 and 29 RR. Reference should be made to the commentary on Article 23 OR above.

(RR) Article 31—Honouring of an obligation to a debtor

> 1. Where an obligation has been honoured in a Member State for the benefit of a debtor who is subject to insolvency proceedings opened in another Member State, when it should have been honoured for the benefit of the insolvency practitioner in those proceedings, the person honouring the obligation shall be deemed to have discharged it if he was unaware of the opening of the proceedings.
> 2. Where such an obligation is honoured before the publication provided for in Article 28 has been effected, the person honouring the obligation shall be presumed, in the absence of proof to the contrary, to have been unaware of the opening of insolvency proceedings. Where the obligation is honoured after such publication has been effected, the person honouring the obligation shall be presumed, in the absence of proof to the contrary, to have been aware of the opening of proceedings.

8.637 Article 31 RR is copied from Article 24 OR, save for the substitution of 'insolvency practitioner' for 'liquidator' in Article 31(1) RR and the cross-reference in Article 24(2) OR to Article 21 OR being changed to Article 28 RR in Article 31(2) RR. Reference should be made to the commentary on Article 24 OR above.

(RR) Article 32—Recognition and enforceability of other judgments

> 1. Judgments handed down by a court whose judgment concerning the opening of proceedings is recognised in accordance with Article 19 and which concern the course and closure of insolvency proceedings, and compositions approved by that court, shall also be recognised with no further formalities. Such judgments shall be enforced in accordance with Articles 39 to 44 and 47 to 57 of Regulation (EU) No 1215/2012.
> The first subparagraph shall also apply to judgments deriving directly from the insolvency proceedings and which are closely linked with them, even if they were handed down by another court.

The first subparagraph shall also apply to judgments relating to preservation measures taken after the request for the opening of insolvency proceedings or in connection with it.
2. The recognition and enforcement of judgments other than those referred to in paragraph 1 of this Article shall be governed by Regulation (EU) No 1215/2012 provided that that Regulation is applicable.

8.638 Article 32 RR essentially copies Article 25 OR, but updates it, apart from the changes mentioned below.

8.639 Article 32(1) RR is in essence a copy of Article 25(1) OR, save as follows. In Article 32(1) RR the cross-reference to Article 16 OR is replaced by cross-reference to Article 19 RR and the reference to the Brussels Convention on Jurisdiction and the Enforcement of Judgments in Civil and Commercial Matters as amended is replaced by a reference to the relevant Articles of the Recast Brussels Regulation (EU) 1215/2012.

8.640 Likewise in Article 32(2) RR the cross-reference to the Convention is replaced by cross-reference to the Regulation referred to in Article 32(1) RR.

8.641 Note that for the purpose of this provision the 'court' need not be a judicial body: Article 2(6) RR.

(RR) Article 33—Public policy

Any Member State may refuse to recognise insolvency proceedings opened in another Member State or to enforce a judgment handed down in the context of such proceedings where the effects of such recognition or enforcement would be manifestly contrary to that State's public policy, in particular its fundamental principles or the constitutional rights and liberties of the individual.

8.642 Article 33 RR is copied from Article 26 OR and the commentary on Article 26 OR should be referred to above.

C. Chapter III: Secondary Insolvency Proceedings

(RR) Article 34—Opening of proceedings

Where main insolvency proceedings have been opened by a court of a Member State and recognised in another Member State, a court of that other Member State which has jurisdiction pursuant to Article 3(2) may open secondary insolvency proceedings in accordance with the provisions set out in this Chapter. Where the main insolvency proceedings required that the debtor be insolvent, the debtor's insolvency shall not be re-examined in the Member State in which secondary insolvency proceedings may be opened. The effects of secondary insolvency proceedings shall be restricted to the assets of the debtor situated within the territory of the Member State in which those proceedings have been opened.

8.643 Article 34 RR is essentially similar in effect to Article 27 OR. It allows for the opening of secondary proceedings after main proceedings have been opened in another Member State.

8.644 In the *Bank Handlowy* case (C-116/11), the rather absurd conclusion had to be reached, as a matter of practicality, that even if the main proceedings were pre-insolvency proceedings, which could not take place if the debtor were insolvent, nevertheless Article 27 OR required courts in other Member States where there was an establishment to treat the debtor as insolvent for the purposes of opening secondary insolvency proceedings. This type of absurdity is now avoided, since the bar on re-examining the debtor's insolvency is now restricted to cases where the main proceedings require the debtor to be insolvent.

8.645 Article 27 OR had required any secondary proceeding to be a winding-up proceeding listed in Annex B OR. This requirement was widely criticized and appeared to be impractical. It was designed to emphasize the pre-eminence of the main proceedings, but opened up the danger of anomaly and injustice in cases where for example a rescue proceeding was needed in the secondary Member State. Article 34 RR does away with this restriction on the types of possible secondary proceedings. The list of winding-up proceedings in Annex B OR has disappeared and the list of insolvency practitioners formerly set out in Annex C OR has been moved to Annex B RR.

(RR) Article 35—Applicable law

Save as otherwise provided for in this Regulation, the law applicable to secondary insolvency proceedings shall be that of the Member State within the territory of which the secondary insolvency proceedings are opened.

8.646 Article 35 RR is copied from Article 28 OR and reference should be had to the commentary relating to Article 28 OR above.

(RR) Article 36—Right to give an undertaking in order to avoid secondary insolvency proceedings

1. In order to avoid the opening of secondary insolvency proceedings, the insolvency practitioner in the main insolvency proceedings may give a unilateral undertaking (the 'undertaking') in respect of the assets located in the Member State in which secondary insolvency proceedings could be opened, that when distributing those assets or the proceeds received as a result of their realisation, it will comply with the distribution and priority rights under national law that creditors would have if secondary insolvency proceedings were opened in that Member State. The undertaking shall specify the factual assumptions on which it is based, in particular in respect of the value of the assets located in the Member State concerned and the options available to realise such assets.
2. Where an undertaking has been given in accordance with this Article, the law applicable to the distribution of proceeds from the realisation of assets referred to in

paragraph 1, to the ranking of creditors' claims, and to the rights of creditors in relation to the assets referred to in paragraph 1 shall be the law of the Member State in which secondary insolvency proceedings could have been opened. The relevant point in time for determining the assets referred to in paragraph 1 shall be the moment at which the undertaking is given.

3. The undertaking shall be made in the official language or one of the official languages of the Member State where secondary insolvency proceedings could have been opened, or, where there are several official languages in that Member State, the official language or one of the official languages of the place in which secondary insolvency proceedings could have been opened.

4. The undertaking shall be made in writing. It shall be subject to any other requirements relating to form and approval requirements as to distributions, if any, of the State of the opening of the main insolvency proceedings.

5. The undertaking shall be approved by the known local creditors. The rules on qualified majority and voting that apply to the adoption of restructuring plans under the law of the Member State where secondary insolvency proceedings could have been opened shall also apply to the approval of the undertaking. Creditors shall be able to participate in the vote by distance means of communication, where national law so permits. The insolvency practitioner shall inform the known local creditors of the undertaking, of the rules and procedures for its approval, and of the approval or rejection of the undertaking.

6. An undertaking given and approved in accordance with this Article shall be binding on the estate. If secondary insolvency proceedings are opened in accordance with Articles 37 and 38, the insolvency practitioner in the main insolvency proceedings shall transfer any assets which it removed from the territory of that Member State after the undertaking was given or, where those assets have already been realised, their proceeds, to the insolvency practitioner in the secondary insolvency proceedings.

7. Where the insolvency practitioner has given an undertaking, it shall inform local creditors about the intended distributions prior to distributing the assets and proceeds referred to in paragraph 1. If that information does not comply with the terms of the undertaking or the applicable law, any local creditor may challenge such distribution before the courts of the Member State in which main insolvency proceedings have been opened in order to obtain a distribution in accordance with the terms of the undertaking and the applicable law. In such cases, no distribution shall take place until the court has taken a decision on the challenge.

8. Local creditors may apply to the courts of the Member State in which main insolvency proceedings have been opened, in order to require the insolvency practitioner in the main insolvency proceedings to take any suitable measures necessary to ensure compliance with the terms of the undertaking available under the law of the State of the opening of main insolvency proceedings.

9. Local creditors may also apply to the courts of the Member State in which secondary insolvency proceedings could have been opened in order to require the court to take provisional or protective measures to ensure compliance by the insolvency practitioner with the terms of the undertaking.

10. The insolvency practitioner shall be liable for any damage caused to local creditors as a result of its non-compliance with the obligations and requirements set out in this Article.
11. For the purpose of this Article, an authority which is established in the Member State where secondary insolvency proceedings could have been opened and which is obliged under Directive 2008/94/EC of the European Parliament and of the Council to guarantee the payment of employees' outstanding claims resulting from contracts of employment or employment relationships shall be considered to be a local creditor, where the national law so provides.

8.647 Article 36 RR is an entirely new provision and provides for what have been referred to as 'virtual secondaries'.

8.648 Where the main proceedings are pre-insolvency rescue restructuring or reorganization proceedings, with or without a composition, they can be badly disrupted by the opening of secondary proceedings in another Member State.

8.649 As a practical matter, it is often best to avoid secondary proceedings being opened. As it was pointed out in Moss, Fletcher & Isaacs: *The EC Regulation on Insolvency Proceedings* (2nd edn, 2009) at paragraph 8.151:

> 'Secondary proceedings can disrupt the beneficial rescue or realisation of the business. Particularly in the case of a group which had traded prior to insolvency as one organisation, it makes practical sense for the rescue, reconstruction or insolvency proceedings to be run as a unity. In some situations, local creditors can be persuaded to abstain from starting secondary proceedings in the interests of a better realisation by promising to respect local law priorities in the eventual distribution.'

There is then a citation of the *Collins & Aikman* Case,[600] which was subsequently followed by the *Nortel* Case.[601] In both those cases, a promise was made by the UK main administrator to respect local priorities in respect of distributions from assets which would have fallen into a secondary proceeding, *if* no request was made by local creditors to open a secondary proceeding. In *Collins & Aikman* the undertaking was given first and the court approved of this technique subsequently and held it to be legally effective. In *Nortel* the judge gave advanced permission and equally regarded the process as effective.

8.650 Subsequently in *Nortel* the judge agreed to reinforce the position by sending out letters of request to potential secondary jurisdictions to ask them to ensure that the main administrators were given notice of any request to open a secondary. An express provision requiring such notice to be given is now provided as Article 38(1) RR.

8.651 There was however a concern that the insolvency laws of some Member States were not flexible enough to overcome the apparent obstacle of the mandatory choice of law rules in Article 7 RR (previously Article 4 OR), which require distributions in the main proceeding to be carried out under the law of the main proceeding. English insolvency law is flexible enough to provide that in some cases, even applying English law pursuant to Article 7 RR

---

[600] [2007] 1 BCLC 182.
[601] [2009] BCC 343.

(previously Article 4 OR), the normal priorities can be departed from, including situations where an undertaking had been given to local creditors to respect their local priorities, in the interests of better realizations for creditors generally, provided that local creditors did not request the opening of local insolvency proceedings.

8.652 The European Council proposal, based on the original Commission proposal, included a new provision for the creation of such 'virtual secondaries', which is now contained in Article 36 RR. This creates a right on the part of the insolvency practitioner in the main proceeding to give an undertaking in order to avoid secondary proceedings. There are a series of detailed rules laid down and of course the provision has self-executing, mandatory effect throughout the EU (except Denmark). It thus overrides any provision of national law or practice whereby it is forbidden to depart from the national statutory scheme of distribution in any species of insolvency proceeding conducted under the laws of a given EU Member State. The transformation of the English rules' flexibility into strict elements of a codified law is not only a paradigm of the differences between Common Law and Continental Law; it might also turn out as having become impractical in this new form: to the best of our knowledge, no cases have not been reported of the new mechanism being used.

8.653 Article 36 RR empowers an insolvency practitioner to give a written 'unilateral' undertaking to comply with local law priorities that would apply in a secondary in relation to assets which are located in the local jurisdiction. The relevant time for looking at the assets is at the time the undertaking is given. Presumably, the word 'unilateral' is used to emphasize that the undertaking is not a matter of contract.

8.654 Article 36(2) RR then makes the local law applicable to the distribution of local assets, thereby avoiding any problem with what is now Article 7 RR.

8.655 Article 36(5) RR states that the undertaking 'shall be approved by the known local creditors'. This reads rather oddly in English, as if the known local creditors (as defined in Article 2(11) RR) were being ordered to approve the undertaking. However, there is then a statement about the voting rules that are to be applied, namely those applicable for the adoption of restructuring plans in the local jurisdiction. This seems to imply that the proposal is making the undertaking *subject* to approval by 'the known local creditors'. This accords with the text of Article 36(6) RR, which states that an undertaking given *and approved* under Article 36 'shall be binding on the estate'.

8.656 Enforcement of the undertaking is to take place, under the proposal, in the main proceedings (Article 36(8) RR), but provisional or protective measures can also be sought in the secondary jurisdiction (Article 36(9) RR). Rather worryingly for the insolvency practitioner in the main proceeding, he is to be made personally liable for not complying with the requirements of Article 36 (Article 36(10) RR).

8.657 There does not seem to be any scope for the insolvency practitioner to make his undertaking conditional upon the local creditors not requesting the opening of local proceedings. However, Article 38(2) RR requires a court facing such a request to turn it down if an undertaking 'in accordance with Article 36' has been given ' ... if it is satisfied that the undertaking adequately protects the general interests of local creditors.' Presumably the words 'in accordance with Article 36' import the need for local creditor approval under Article 36(5) RR, so that it is only undertakings given *and approved by local creditors* and therefore binding on the estate under RR Article 36(6) that can block the opening of a secondary proceeding.

8.658 Even if secondary proceedings are in fact opened, if an undertaking has been given and approved, it remains binding on the estate and the insolvency practitioner in the main proceeding is required to return to the secondary proceeding any assets (or their proceeds) which he has removed since the undertaking was given (Article 36(6) RR).

8.659 The requirement of approval by local creditors (Article 36(5) RR), may give rise to some paradoxical results. In some countries it may well be against the interests of the majority of local creditors for local priorities to apply, because of the priority awarded to governmental preferential creditors.[602] In such cases it would make sense for the local creditors to vote down the approval of the undertaking and rely on the priorities in the main proceeding, if that is likely to give them a better result.

8.660 The proposal expressly gives the insolvency practitioner in the main proceeding standing to apply to challenge a decision opening a secondary proceeding (Article 39 RR) on the grounds that the court did not comply with the conditions and requirements of Article 38 RR. This seems to cover for example a case where the local court opens a secondary despite the giving and acceptance by local creditors of an Article 36 RR undertaking which adequately protects the general interests of local creditors. Since Article 38(1) RR requires notice to be given of a request to open a secondary, the insolvency practitioner in the main proceeding should be able simply to oppose the opening rather than have to challenge it subsequently. However, if no notice has been given, that would seem to be an obvious case for a subsequent challenge.

8.661 The heading of Article 39 RR, giving standing as mentioned, reads rather oddly in English because it refers to 'judicial review' of the decision to open secondary proceedings. As a matter of legal English, 'judicial review' is only used for court challenges against administrative (or delegated legislative) decisions or regulations and not court decisions. Legal English would refer to an application to 'set aside' the opening, but the true meaning of 'judicial review' here appears to be clear from the context and the actual text of Article 39 RR, which refers to challenging the decision opening the proceedings before the courts of the Member State in which secondary proceedings have been opened.

8.662 Under Article 33 OR, the office-holder of the main proceedings was able to seek a stay of any secondary proceedings (in the court in which the secondary proceedings were opened). Such a stay was within the discretion of the court, the court having the power to require the office holder of the main proceeding to guarantee the interests of the local creditors. Now, the office-holder of the main proceedings has the 'right' to provide an undertaking and to put that to the local creditors in that secondary jurisdiction for approval. There are a number of issues with this change. First, this enfranchises local creditors and allows them to refuse the undertaking and to therefore strengthen their ability to seek secondary proceedings (including in circumstances where a local court might have exercised its discretion to stay under the previous Regulations). The undertaking has to be approved by reference to 'the rules on qualified majority and voting that apply for the adoption of restructuring

---

[602] This may for example occur in relation to Italy.

plans under the law of the Member State where secondary proceedings could have been opened' (Article 36(5) RR). It is not clear what those rules might be given that in certain jurisdictions, different voting regimes might apply. Also, given that the undertaking and 'local protection' might only need to cover a limited category of creditors (for example, those that have preferential status under that local law), it is not clear if this means that all creditors in that jurisdiction would have to vote on the undertaking, including those not affected by it or the opening of secondary proceedings. Third, the court seised of the request to open the secondary proceedings still retains the discretion to do so, although the court should take into account the fact that an undertaking has been approved. Article 33 OR remains (in a new Article 46 RR) albeit the stay is limited to staying 'the process of realisation of assets in whole or in part' as opposed to 'the process of liquidation in whole or in part' under old Article 33. It will be interesting to see whether new Article 36 is used in preference to the amended provisions of old Article 33.

(RR) Article 37—Right to request the opening of secondary insolvency proceedings

1. The opening of secondary insolvency proceedings may be requested by:
   (a) the insolvency practitioner in the main insolvency proceedings;
   (b) any other person or authority empowered to request the opening of insolvency proceedings under the law of the Member State within the territory of which the opening of secondary insolvency proceedings is requested.
2. Where an undertaking has become binding in accordance with Article 36, the request for opening secondary insolvency proceedings shall be lodged within 30 days of having received notice of the approval of the undertaking.

Article 37(1) RR is based on Article 29 OR. **8.663**

The reference in Article 29(a) OR to 'liquidator' has been replaced in Article 37(1)(a) RR by **8.664** 'insolvency practitioner'.

The text of Article 37(1)(b) RR is copied from the text of Article 29(b) OR. In relation to **8.665** this wording, a question arose as to whether the person who can request the opening of secondary proceedings under what is now Article 37(1)(b) RR has to be a person or authority who can request the opening of secondary proceedings under the relevant law of the Member State in question.[603] This question has not been resolved by the RR.

Article 37(2) RR is a new provision which ties in with the subject of 'virtual secondaries' **8.666** discussed under Article 36 RR. Article 37(2) RR provides that where an undertaking has become binding in accordance with Article 36, a request to open secondary proceedings must be lodged within 30 days of having received notice of the approval of the undertaking. This ability in effect to challenge the undertaking must be read subject to Article 38 RR below.

---

[603] In *Polmos Lancut SA*, the Polish Supreme Court on 20 January 2010 held on the basis of the Polish German and Lithuanian versions of Art 29(b) OR that only persons who can request the opening of secondary proceedings under the relevant Member State law fall within Art 29(b) OR. See 8.392 above.

(RR) Article 38—Decision to open secondary insolvency proceedings

1. A court seised of a request to open secondary insolvency proceedings shall immediately give notice to the insolvency practitioner or the debtor in possession in the main insolvency proceedings and give it an opportunity to be heard on the request.
2. Where the insolvency practitioner in the main insolvency proceedings has given an undertaking in accordance with Article 36, the court referred to in paragraph 1 of this Article shall, at the request of the insolvency practitioner, not open secondary insolvency proceedings if it is satisfied that the undertaking adequately protects the general interests of local creditors.
3. Where a temporary stay of individual enforcement proceedings has been granted in order to allow for negotiations between the debtor and its creditors, the court, at the request of the insolvency practitioner or the debtor in possession, may stay the opening of secondary insolvency proceedings for a period not exceeding 3 months, provided that suitable measures are in place to protect the interests of local creditors. The court referred to in paragraph 1 may order protective measures to protect the interests of local creditors by requiring the insolvency practitioner or the debtor in possession not to remove or dispose of any assets which are located in the Member State where its establishment is located unless this is done in the ordinary course of business. The court may also order other measures to protect the interest of local creditors during a stay, unless this is incompatible with the national rules on civil procedure.

    The stay of the opening of secondary insolvency proceedings shall be lifted by the court of its own motion or at the request of any creditor if, during the stay, an agreement in the negotiations referred to in the first subparagraph has been concluded.

    The stay may be lifted by the court of its own motion or at the request of any creditor if the continuation of the stay is detrimental to the creditor's rights, in particular if the negotiations have been disrupted or it has become evident that they are unlikely to be concluded, or if the insolvency practitioner or the debtor in possession has infringed the prohibition on disposal of its assets or on removal of them from the territory of the Member State where the establishment is located.
4. At the request of the insolvency practitioner in the main insolvency proceedings, the court referred to in paragraph 1 may open a type of insolvency proceedings as listed in Annex A other than the type initially requested, provided that the conditions for opening that type of proceedings under national law are fulfilled and that that type of proceedings is the most appropriate as regards the interests of the local creditors and coherence between the main and secondary insolvency proceedings. The second sentence of Article 34 shall apply.

8.667 Article 38 RR is an entirely new provision. Under the OR, there is a potential difficulty in avoiding the unnecessary opening of secondary proceedings in that, in some Member States, there was no requirement for notice to be given to a main liquidator of a request to open a secondary proceeding in that Member State. A partial remedy was used in England, in the case of *Re Nortel Networks SA*.[604] In this case, at the request of the administrators to

---

[604] [2009] BCC 343.

the main proceedings in England, the English High Court Judge sent letters of request to foreign courts where there might have been a request to open secondary proceedings asking them to ensure that notice was given to the main proceeding administrator before any secondary proceeding was opened.

8.668 Article 38(1) RR now requires the court, seised of a request to open a secondary proceeding, immediately to give notice to the insolvency practitioner or the debtor in possession in the main proceedings and give him an opportunity to be heard on the request.

8.669 Article 38(2) RR is linked to the topic of 'virtual secondaries' in Article 36 RR. Where the relevant undertaking in accordance with Article 36 RR has been given, the court seised of a request to open secondary proceedings shall, at the request of the insolvency practitioner, not open secondary proceedings if it is satisfied that the undertaking adequately protects the general interests of local creditors. Note that the same protection is not given to a main proceeding where there is a debtor in possession and no insolvency practitioner.

8.670 The introduction of an 'adequate protection' standard in Article 38 RR may give rise to some uncertainty. It is difficult to think what further may be needed, for there to be adequate protection of local creditors, than an undertaking to comply with local distribution and priority rights under the national law that the creditors would have if secondary proceedings were opened.

8.671 Article 38(3) RR is also a new provision. The first sub-paragraph deals with the type of pre-insolvency proceeding where there is a temporary stay of individual enforcement proceedings to allow for negotiations between the debtor and his creditors, being the type (c) proceedings referred to in Article 1 RR. In the case of such a type (c) proceeding, the court, at the request of the insolvency practitioner or the debtor in possession, has a discretion to stay the opening of secondary proceedings for not longer than three months, providing that suitable measures are in place to protect the interests of local creditors. In this case, the reference to the interests of local creditors presumably means the safeguarding of their potential rights in respect of the business and assets of the debtor.

8.672 Specifically, the second sub-paragraph provides for a discretion to order protective measures to protect the interests of local creditors by requiring the insolvency practitioner or the debtor in possession not to remove or dispose of any assets located in the Member State where his establishment is located, unless this is done in the ordinary course of business. This is intended to deal with the risk that the insolvency practitioner or debtor in possession running the main proceeding may, during the temporary stay of the opening of secondary proceedings, remove assets which would fall into such secondary proceedings.

8.673 The second sub-paragraph also gives the local court a discretion to order other measures to protect the interests of local creditors during a stay of the opening of secondary proceedings, unless this is incompatible with the national rules on civil procedure.

8.674 The third sub-paragraph provides a supplementary provision to the effect that the stay of the opening of secondary proceedings must be revoked by the court of its own motion or at the request of any creditor if, during the stay, an agreement in the negotiations has been concluded. Additionally, under the fourth sub-paragraph, the stay of the opening of secondary proceedings may be revoked in the court's discretion of its own motion or at the request of any creditor if the continuation of the stay is detrimental to the creditors' rights. Particular examples given are when negotiations have been disrupted or it has become evident that they are unlikely to be concluded or if the insolvency practitioner or debtor in possession has infringed the prohibition on disposal of assets or on removing them from the territory of the Member State where the establishment is located.

8.675 Article 38(4) RR is a new provision enabling the local court, at the request of the insolvency practitioner in the main proceedings to open a secondary proceeding of a different type from that initially requested as long as it is within the list of proceedings in Annex A. This can also only be done if the conditions for opening the other type of procedure under national law are fulfilled. Such a step should only be taken if the alternative procedure is the most appropriate taking account of the interests of the local creditors and/or of 'coherence' between the main and secondary proceedings. In such a case there is a cross-reference to Article 34 RR, second sentence, so that the debtor's insolvency is not to be re-examined, as long as the main proceedings require that the debtor be insolvent.

(RR) Article 39—Judicial review of the decision to open secondary insolvency proceedings

The insolvency practitioner in the main insolvency proceedings may challenge the decision to open secondary insolvency proceedings before the courts of the Member State in which secondary insolvency proceedings have been opened on the ground that the court did not comply with the conditions and requirements of Article 38.

8.676 This is a new provision, in respect of which see the commentary under Article 36 RR above.

8.677 'Judicial review' in the heading is once again a misnomer, since in English legal usage it refers to challenges to administrative action or delegated legislation, but the meaning is clear from the text.

(RR) Article 40—Advance payment of costs and expenses

Where the law of the Member State in which the opening of secondary insolvency proceedings is requested requires that the debtor's assets be sufficient to cover in whole or in part the costs and expenses of the proceedings, the court may, when it receives such a request, require the applicant to make an advance payment of costs or to provide appropriate security.

8.678 Article 40 RR is copied from Article 30 OR. Reference should be made to the commentary under Article 30 OR above.

(RR) Article 41—Co-operation and communication between insolvency practitioners

1. The insolvency practitioner in the main insolvency proceedings and the insolvency practitioner or practitioners in secondary insolvency proceedings concerning the same debtor shall cooperate with each other to the extent such cooperation is not incompatible with the rules applicable to the respective proceedings. Such cooperation may take any form, including the conclusion of agreements or protocols.
2. In implementing the cooperation set out in paragraph 1, the insolvency practitioners shall:
   (a) as soon as possible communicate to each other any information which may be relevant to the other proceedings, in particular any progress made in lodging and verifying claims and all measures aimed at rescuing or restructuring the debtor, or at terminating the proceedings, provided appropriate arrangements are made to protect confidential information;
   (b) explore the possibility of restructuring the debtor and, where such a possibility exists, coordinate the elaboration and implementation of a restructuring plan;
   (c) coordinate the administration of the realisation or use of the debtor's assets and affairs; the insolvency practitioner in the secondary insolvency proceedings shall give the insolvency practitioner in the main insolvency proceedings an early opportunity to submit proposals on the realisation or use of the assets in the secondary insolvency proceedings.
3. Paragraphs 1 and 2 shall apply mutatis mutandis to situations where, in the main or in the secondary insolvency proceedings or in any territorial insolvency proceedings concerning the same debtor and open at the same time, the debtor remains in possession of its assets.

Article 41 RR builds on and has essentially the same theme as Article 31 OR, with the differences explained below. **8.679**

First of all, the general change from 'liquidator' to 'insolvency practitioner' is made. Secondly, whereas Article 31 OR began with the duty to communicate information between insolvency administrators, and then set out a duty to co-operate, Article 41 RR begins with a general duty to co-operate and then goes on to mention communication as one branch of co-operation. The general duty of co-operation in Article 41 RR is only to the extent that such co-operation 'is not incompatible with the rules applicable to the respective proceedings'. **8.680**

Article 41(1) RR makes specific mention of protocols, which have been used as a tool of co-operation in a number of international groups, often between the UK and the United States and/or Canada. Specific mention is made of protocols in Article 41(1) RR, probably because Continental judges may be reluctant to approve protocols unless there is express mention of them under the heading of the duty to co-operate. **8.681**

Article 41(2) RR sets out three specific types of co-operation. Type (a) is the communication 'as soon as possible' of information relevant to the other proceedings. Type (b) requires the exploration of the possibility of restructuring the debtor and, where such restructuring **8.682** is possible, the co-ordination of 'the elaboration and implementation of a restructuring plan'. Type (c) requires the co-ordination of the administration of the realization or use of the debtor's assets and affairs. The insolvency practitioner in the secondary insolvency proceedings is required to give the insolvency practitioner in the main insolvency proceedings an early opportunity to submit proposals on the realization or use of the assets in the secondary insolvency proceedings.

8.683 Article 41(3) RR is an entirely new provision, designed to take account of the fact that under the RR there may not be an insolvency practitioner, but rather a debtor in possession. Article 41(3) RR provides that Article 41(1) and (2) are to apply *mutatis mutandis*.

(RR) Article 42—Co-operation and communication between courts

1. In order to facilitate the coordination of main, territorial and secondary insolvency proceedings concerning the same debtor, a court before which a request to open insolvency proceedings is pending, or which has opened such proceedings, shall cooperate with any other court before which a request to open insolvency proceedings is pending, or which has opened such proceedings, to the extent that such cooperation is not incompatible with the rules applicable to each of the proceedings. For that purpose, the courts may, where appropriate, appoint an independent person or body acting on its instructions, provided that it is not incompatible with the rules applicable to them.
2. In implementing the cooperation set out in paragraph 1, the courts, or any appointed person or body acting on their behalf, as referred to in paragraph 1, may communicate directly with, or request information or assistance directly from, each other provided that such communication respects the procedural rights of the parties to the proceedings and the confidentiality of information.
3. The cooperation referred to in paragraph 1 may be implemented by any means that the court considers appropriate. It may, in particular, concern:
   (a) coordination in the appointment of the insolvency practitioners;
   (b) communication of information by any means considered appropriate by the court;
   (c) coordination of the administration and supervision of the debtor's assets and affairs;
   (d) coordination of the conduct of hearings;
   (e) coordination in the approval of protocols, where necessary.

8.684 The OR text in Article 31 OR did not expressly require courts, as opposed to insolvency administrators, to co-operate in relation to main and secondary proceedings in respect of the same debtor. However, judicial interpretation in national courts[605] interpreted Article 31 OR as implying a duty of co-operation between courts. Absent any express duty in the text of OR, however, there was a doubt as to whether all national courts would adopt the

---

[605] *Re Nortel Networks SA* [2009] BCC 343; *Re Stojevic* 28 R 225/04w (Vienna Higher Regional Court, 9 November 2004).

same interpretation. Accordingly, Article 42 RR contains a new text expressly requiring co-operation and communication between courts.

Article 42(1) RR pushes the time at which co-operation is required back to the time that a court has before it a request to open insolvency proceedings. Once again the duty to co-operate is subject to the limitation that it must not be 'incompatible with the rules applicable to each of the proceedings'. **8.685**

In considering the question of co-operation and communication between national courts, various issues have been raised, including the question of whether the courts will have a common language. If the judges themselves do not have a common language, Article 42 RR provides a solution in that it gives an express power to 'appoint an independent person or body' acting on the instructions of the court, providing that that is not incompatible with the rules applicable to that court. The court can thus appoint a person or body which has a common language with either the judge or independent person appointed by the court in the other proceeding. **8.686**

Although there is a duty on the two or more courts to co-operate, there is no duty, but only a discretion to communicate directly with, or request information or assistance from, the other court. This discretion applies to any person or body appointed to act on behalf of either court. The communication, if any, is required to respect the procedural rights of the parties and the confidentiality of information. **8.687**

It is suggested that such procedural rights should be safeguarded by allowing the parties and their legal advisers to be present, either in person or by telephone or by video link in any communication between the two courts. Whereas as between the United States and Canada there have been communications between judges in the absence of parties, this would not seem to accord with European procedural rights and principles. **8.688**

Article 42(3) RR sets out five particular means of implementing the duty to co-operate, giving the courts a discretion as to which they use. **8.689**

Type (a) involves co-ordination in the appointment of insolvency practitioners. Where there is no problem of conflict, or any conflict issue can be resolved in some satisfactory way, it may often be cheaper and simpler to appoint partners of the same accountancy or law firm as insolvency practitioners in each proceeding. This is for example a common practice in the UK for insolvency practitioners in the case of different group companies. **8.690**

Type (b) is the communication of information 'by any means considered appropriate by the court'. In the limited number of communications that have so far taken place in relation to Europe, communication has been by telephone. However, with the advance of technology (and the experiences from the pandemic), courts should no doubt consider whether a video link could usefully be employed. **8.691**

Type (c) involves the co-ordination of the administration and supervision of the debtor's assets and affairs. In many cases, such administration will be simpler and cheaper if the assets which fall within both the main and the secondary proceedings can be treated *de facto* as a unity. **8.692**

Type (d) refers to the co-ordination of the conduct of hearings. It is important to note here that this is not a power to conduct joint hearings, which have sometimes taken place **8.693** between US and Canadian judges.⁶⁰⁶ Co-ordination would cover such matters as (i) the avoidance or clearing up of misunderstandings about procedure in each court, (ii) the co-ordination of proceedings so as to prevent one from undermining or pre-empting the other, (iii) agreement on which issues are suitable to be heard in each court, so as to avoid as far as possible any conflict in the decisions of each court.

8.694 Type (e) involves co-ordination in the approval of protocols, 'where necessary'. Such protocols will often be conditional on the approval of each court and it may be useful to co-ordinate approval so that it happens either simultaneously or very close together in time. Protocols have in the past been common between the courts of common law countries such as England, US, Canada, Bermuda, and Cayman.⁶⁰⁷ They have for example dealt with the division and co-ordination of the work of rescue or reconstruction or with the question of the payment of fees for insolvency practitioners.

(RR) Article 43—Co-operation and communication between insolvency practitioners and courts

1. In order to facilitate the co-ordination of main, territorial and secondary insolvency proceedings opened in respect of the same debtor:
   (a) an insolvency practitioner in main insolvency proceedings shall cooperate and communicate with any court before which a request to open secondary insolvency proceedings is pending or which has opened such proceedings;
   (b) an insolvency practitioner in territorial or secondary insolvency proceedings shall cooperate and communicate with the court before which a request to open main insolvency proceedings is pending or which has opened such proceedings; and
   (c) an insolvency practitioner in territorial or secondary insolvency proceedings shall cooperate and communicate with the court before which a request to open other territorial or secondary insolvency proceedings is pending or which has opened such proceedings;
   to the extent that such cooperation and communication are not incompatible with the rules applicable to each of the proceedings and do not entail any conflict of interest.
2. The cooperation referred to in paragraph 1 may be implemented by any appropriate means, such as those set out in Article 42(3).

8.695 Having laid down duties of co-operation (i) between insolvency practitioners and (ii) between courts, Article 43 RR sets out a duty of co-operation and communication between insolvency practitioners on the one hand and courts on the other. This again is completely new text.

---

⁶⁰⁶ Eg, in the US and Canadian proceedings concerning the Nortel group.
⁶⁰⁷ For a data base of protocols cf. <https://www.dropbox.com/sh/qp71ufpr0g4lpbr/AADm7SOBWoRmTm364iJKzl7Ua?dl=0>.

8.696 The duty of co-operation is created expressly in order to facilitate the co-ordination of main, independent territorial and secondary insolvency proceedings opened in respect of the same debtor. Three specific types of duty are set out.

8.697 Type (a) requires an insolvency practitioner in the main proceedings to co-operate and communicate with any court before which a request to open secondary proceedings is pending or which has opened such proceedings. Once again, the point at which the duty arises has been pushed back to the time when a request to open secondary proceedings has been made. A court presented with a request to open secondary proceedings may well have to consider whether such an opening is necessary or even beneficial in the interests of the general body of creditors. The court may well need information from the insolvency practitioner in the main proceedings in relation to this issue.

8.698 Type (b) is a requirement on an insolvency practitioner in territorial or secondary proceedings to co-operate and communicate with a court before which a request to open main proceedings is pending or which has opened such proceedings. Again the relevant point in time has been pushed back to the time a court is hearing a request to open main proceedings. In such a situation, there is likely to be less of a question whether main proceedings are necessary or useful, but it is conceivable that such situations will arise. If so, information from the insolvency practitioner in the territorial proceedings may be essential or at least useful. Once main proceedings have actually been opened, it may also be very important to receive information from the insolvency practitioner in any secondary insolvency proceedings in relation to business and assets in the territory of the secondary proceedings.

8.699 Type (c) is a duty on the insolvency practitioner in territorial or secondary insolvency proceedings to co-operate and communicate with a court before which there is a request to open yet another territorial or secondary proceeding or which has opened such a proceeding. The potential point of co-operation is again pushed back to the date of the request to open such other territorial or secondary proceedings. Once again it may be that the opening of the further territorial or secondary proceeding could damage the interests of creditors and once again the further court considering such a request may need or at least find useful information from the insolvency practitioner in other territorial or secondary proceedings.

8.700 Types (a)–(c) are each duties expressly subject to the relevant co-operation or communication not being incompatible with the rules applicable to each of the proceedings. They are also expressly subject to the question of any conflict of interest.

8.701 Article 43(2) RR makes applicable to the duty to co-operate in Article 43(1) RR the general ability to implement co-operation 'by any means that the court considers appropriate' provided in Article 42(3) RR, including the five particular means of co-operation set out in Article 42(3) RR.

(RR) Article 44—Costs of co-operation and communication

> The requirements laid down in Articles 42 and 43 shall not result in courts charging costs to each other for cooperation and communication.

8.702 The new provisions in Articles 42 and 43 RR spell out the express duty of co-operation between courts and between insolvency practitioners and courts also gives rise to a new question as to whether courts can charge costs to each other for co-operation and communication. Article 44 RR specifically states that they may not.

(RR) Article 45—Exercise of creditors' rights

1. Any creditor may lodge its claim in the main insolvency proceedings and in any secondary insolvency proceedings.
2. The insolvency practitioners in the main and any secondary insolvency proceedings shall lodge in other proceedings claims which have already been lodged in the proceedings for which they were appointed, provided that the interests of creditors in the latter proceedings are served by doing so, subject to the right of creditors to oppose such lodgement or to withdraw the lodgement of their claims where the law applicable so provides.
3. The insolvency practitioner in the main or secondary insolvency proceedings shall be entitled to participate in other proceedings on the same basis as a creditor, in particular by attending creditors' meetings.

8.703 Article 45 RR is copied from Article 32 OR, with the substitution of the new term 'insolvency practitioners' instead of 'liquidators'. Reference should be made to the commentary on Article 32 OR above.

(RR) Article 46—Stay of the process of realization of assets

1. The court which opened the secondary insolvency proceedings shall stay the process of realization of assets in whole or in part on receipt of a request from the insolvency practitioner in the main insolvency proceedings. In such a case, it may require the insolvency practitioner in the main insolvency proceedings to take any suitable measure to guarantee the interests of the creditors in the secondary insolvency proceedings and of individual classes of creditors. Such a request from the insolvency practitioner may be rejected only if it is manifestly of no interest to the creditors in the main insolvency proceedings. Such a stay of the process of realisation of assets may be ordered for up to 3 months. It may be continued or renewed for similar periods.
2. The court referred to in paragraph 1 shall terminate the stay of the process of realisation of assets:
   (a) at the request of the insolvency practitioner in the main insolvency proceedings;
   (b) of its own motion, at the request of a creditor or at the request of the insolvency practitioner in the secondary insolvency proceedings if that measure no longer appears justified, in particular, by the interests of creditors in the main insolvency proceedings or in the secondary insolvency proceedings.

8.704 The text of Article 46 RR is largely taken from the text of Article 33 OR and reference should be made to the commentary on Article 33 OR above. There is however one clarification. The

OR text referred to staying 'the process of liquidation'. This was held by a national court to refer only to a stay of the process of liquidation *of assets* and not the secondary proceedings as a whole.[608] This interpretation has now been adopted in the text of Article 46 RR, which now refers, not to a stay on the process of 'liquidation' but to a stay of the process of 'realization of assets'. Article 33 OR was headed 'Stay of Liquidation', reflecting the fact that the OR only permitted liquidation proceedings as secondary proceedings. Under RR, secondary proceedings need not be liquidation proceedings. It would therefore no longer be appropriate to refer to a stay of liquidation in any event. Otherwise the only change is the usual switch from 'liquidator' to 'insolvency practitioner'.

(RR) Article 47—Power of the insolvency practitioner to propose restructuring plans

1. Where the law of the Member State where secondary insolvency proceedings have been opened allows for such proceedings to be closed without liquidation by a restructuring plan, a composition or a comparable measure, the insolvency practitioner in the main insolvency proceedings shall be empowered to propose such a measure in accordance with the procedure of that Member State.
2. Any restriction of creditors' rights arising from a measure referred to in paragraph 1 which is proposed in secondary insolvency proceedings, such as a stay of payment or discharge of debt, shall have no effect in respect of assets of a debtor that are not covered by those proceedings, without the consent of all the creditors having an interest.

Article 47(1) and (2) RR are to a large extent taken from Article 34(1) and (2) OR, subject to the following changes. **8.705**

The first sentence of Article 47(1) RR is much the same as the first sentence of Article 34(1) OR, with the substitution of 'insolvency practitioner' for 'liquidator' and the qualification, added in Article 47 RR that the power of the main proceeding insolvency practitioner to propose a rescue plan, composition etc. must be 'in accordance with the procedure of that Member State'. However, Article 47(1) RR omits the second sentence of Article 34(1) OR. The former restriction on the closure of the secondary proceeding by a rescue plan composition or a comparable measure becoming final without the consent of the insolvency administrator in the main proceeding, subject to a further caveat, has been abolished. This change does represent a change in the balance of powers between the insolvency practitioners running the main and secondary proceedings respectively. The former restriction was part of a system which in several provisions placed emphasis on the supremacy of the main proceedings. **8.706**

Article 47(2) RR is copied from Article 34(2) OR. It is simply a corollary from the fact that the secondary proceedings are territorial and therefore have no effect on assets of a debtor not covered by the secondary proceedings. **8.707**

---

[608] See the *Collins & Aikman* case referred to in the commentary to Art 33 OR.

8.708 Article 47 RR now requires the office-holder of the main proceedings to comply with the procedure of the law of the Member State in which secondary proceedings have been opened in relation to any restructuring plan, composition, or comparable measure. This is a missed opportunity—allowing the office-holder to use a restructuring plan in accordance with the law of the Member State in which the main proceedings have been opened would have provided for significant cost and time savings.

(RR) Article 48—Impact of closure of insolvency proceedings

1. Without prejudice to Article 49, the closure of insolvency proceedings shall not prevent the continuation of other insolvency proceedings concerning the same debtor which are still open at that point in time.
2. Where insolvency proceedings concerning a legal person or a company in the Member State of that person's or company's registered office would entail the dissolution of the legal person or of the company, that legal person or company shall not cease to exist until any other insolvency proceedings concerning the same debtor have been closed, or the insolvency practitioner or practitioners in such proceedings have given consent to the dissolution.

8.709 This is a new provision. Article 48(1) RR states the obvious that the closure of insolvency proceedings does not prevent the continuation of other insolvency proceedings concerning the same debtor which is still open.

8.710 The real point comes in Article 48(2) RR, which makes provision for a problem which arose under the OR. Where a company registered in one Member State had its centre of main interests ('COMI') in another Member State and main proceedings were opened in the place of COMI, these could be undermined by the dissolution of the company, eg after the closure of a secondary proceeding, in the Member State of registration.[609] To avoid this kind of problem, Article 48(2) RR expressly provides that in such a case the relevant legal person or company 'shall not cease to exist' until any other insolvency proceeding concerning the same debtor has been closed or the insolvency practitioner or practitioners in such proceedings have given their consent to the dissolution. Such consent might be forthcoming if for example, a company is in liquidation and that liquidation is deemed to continue even if the company is dissolved and ceases to exist.

(RR) Article 49—Assets remaining in the secondary insolvency proceedings

If, by the liquidation of assets in the secondary insolvency proceedings, it is possible to meet all claims allowed under those proceedings, the insolvency practitioner appointed in those proceedings shall immediately transfer any assets remaining to the insolvency practitioner in the main insolvency proceedings.

---

[609] *Re Eurodis Electron Plc* [2012] BCC 57.

Article 49 RR is in effect a copy of Article 35 OR, apart from the usual change from 'liquida- **8.711** tor' to 'insolvency practitioner'. In view of the fact that secondary proceedings no longer have to be liquidation proceedings, it might have been more appropriate to change 'liquidation' to realization, and that had been done in a previous draft, but 'liquidation' has reappeared for a reason we are not aware of. In other respects, reference may be made to the commentary to Article 35 OR above.

(RR) Article 50—Subsequent opening of the main insolvency proceedings

Where the proceedings referred to in Article 3(1) are opened following the opening of the proceedings referred to in Article 3(2) in another Member State, Articles 41, 45, 46, 47 and 49 shall apply to those opened first, in so far as the progress of those proceedings so permits.

Article 50 RR is copied from Article 36 OR, except that the previous cross-references to **8.712** Articles 31 to 35 OR are replaced by cross-references to Articles 41, 45 to 47, and 49 RR.

(RR) Article 51—Conversion of secondary insolvency proceedings

1. **At the request of the insolvency practitioner in the main insolvency proceedings, the court of the Member State in which secondary insolvency proceedings have been opened may order the conversion of the secondary insolvency proceedings into another type of insolvency proceedings listed in Annex A, provided that the conditions for opening that type of proceedings under national law are fulfilled and that that type of proceedings is the most appropriate as regards the interests of the local creditors and coherence between the main and secondary insolvency proceedings.**
2. **When considering the request referred to in paragraph 1, the court may seek information from the insolvency practitioners involved in both proceedings.**

This is a new conversion provision, replacing the old one in Article 37 OR. **8.713**

Whereas Article 37 OR was concerned with the conversion of territorial proceedings **8.714** into winding-up proceedings, since secondary proceedings are no longer required to be winding-up proceedings, this form of conversion has become redundant.

The new provision is a general power to convert secondary proceedings into another type of **8.715** insolvency proceeding listed in Annex A and therefore within the scope of the RR. The proviso is the obvious one that—parallel to Article 38(4) RR—the conditions for opening the new type of procedure under national law are fulfilled and that the other type of procedure is the 'most appropriate for taking account of the interests of the local creditors and of coherence between the main and secondary insolvency proceeding'.

8.716 This is a useful power. For example where rescue type proceedings have been opened in the main jurisdiction and liquidation proceedings in the secondary jurisdiction, it may be convenient for there to be parallel rescue proceedings in both Member States.

8.717 Article 51(2) RR contains a new discretion to seek information from the insolvency practitioners in both proceedings. This again is very useful, in order to make sure that the court considering the request from the insolvency practitioner in the main proceedings for conversion is fully informed.

(RR) Article 52—Preservation measures

> Where the court of a Member State which has jurisdiction pursuant to Article 3(1) appoints a temporary administrator in order to ensure the preservation of a debtor's assets, that temporary administrator shall be empowered to request any measures to secure and preserve any of the debtor's assets situated in another Member State, provided for under the law of that Member State, for the period between the request for the opening of insolvency proceedings and the judgment opening the proceedings.

8.718 Article 52 RR is identical to Article 38 OR and reference should be made to the commentary under Article 38 OR.

D. Chapter IV: Provision of Information for Creditors and Lodgement of their Claims

(RR) Article 53—Right to lodge claims

> Any foreign creditor may lodge claims in insolvency proceedings by any means of communication, which are accepted by the law of the State of the opening of proceedings. Representation by a lawyer or another legal professional shall not be mandatory for the sole purpose of lodging of claims.

8.719 Article 53 RR is an updated version of Article 39 OR and reference should be made to the commentary on Article 39 OR above.

8.720 The updating concerns the method of lodging claims. In the second edition of this work at paragraph 8.405 Professor Michael Bogdan suggested that, despite the reference to claims being lodged 'in writing' the law governing the proceedings might accept a submission in another form. This is now put into an express statutory form in Article 53 RR. The text now states that the creditors within Article 53 RR may lodge claims 'by any means of communication, which are accepted by the law of the State of opening'.

8.721 In addition, there is a new and useful express provision which makes it clear that representation by a lawyer or other legal professional is not to be required for the purpose of lodging claims. That avoids the further expense and complication of hiring a legal professional where that is otherwise required by local law.

D. CHAPTER IV: PROVISION OF INFORMATION FOR CREDITORS

(RR) Article 54—Duty to inform creditors

1. As soon as insolvency proceedings are opened in a Member State, the court of that State having jurisdiction or the insolvency practitioner appointed by that court shall immediately inform the known foreign creditors.
2. The information referred to in paragraph 1, provided by an individual notice, shall in particular include time limits, the penalties laid down with regard to those time limits, the body or authority empowered to accept the lodgement of claims and any other measures laid down. Such notice shall also indicate whether creditors whose claims are preferential or secured in rem need to lodge their claims. The notice shall also include a copy of the standard form for lodging of claims referred to in Article 55 or information on where that form is available.
3. The information referred to in paragraphs 1 and 2 of this Article shall be provided using the standard notice form to be established in accordance with Article 88. The form shall be published in the European e-Justice Portal and shall bear the heading 'Notice of insolvency proceedings' in all the official languages of the institutions of the Union. It shall be transmitted in the official language of the State of the opening of proceedings or, if there are several official languages in that Member State, in the official language or one of the official languages of the place where insolvency proceedings have been opened, or in another language which that State has indicated it can accept, in accordance with Article 55(5), if it can be assumed that that language is easier to understand for the foreign creditors.
4. In insolvency proceedings relating to an individual not exercising a business or professional activity, the use of the standard form referred to in this Article shall not be obligatory if creditors are not required to lodge their claims in order to have their claims taken into account in the proceedings.

8.722 Article 54 RR begins by essentially copying Article 40(1) and (2) OR into Article 54(1) and (2) RR, with usual substitution of 'insolvency practitioner' for 'liquidator'. There are however certain additions.

8.723 Firstly, the notice required to be sent to creditors in other Member States is required to include a copy of the new standard form for lodging of claims referred to in Article 55 RR, or information on where that form is available.

8.724 Furthermore, Article 54(3) RR requires the information required to be given under Article 54 to be provided using the standard notice form to be established in accordance with Article 88 RR. This form is to be published in the European e-Justice Portal and is to bear the heading 'Notice of Insolvency Proceedings' in all the official languages of the institutions of the Union.

8.725 Article 54(3) RR also provides that the notice must be transmitted in the official language of the State of the opening or, if there are several official languages in the official language or one of the official languages of the place where insolvency proceedings are being opened, or in another language which that State has indicated it can accept in accordance with Article 55(5) RR if it can be assumed that that language is easier to understand for the foreign creditors.

8.726 In cases where the relevant official language is little understood outside the Member State, the Member State can under Article 55(5) RR indicate that it accepts any official language of the institutions of the Union other than its own. Thus for example a notice by a Dutch, Finnish, Latvian, Estonian, or Hungarian insolvency practitioner might be able to use English if that has been accepted by their relevant Member State under Article 55(5) RR. It could certainly be assumed that English (as a modern *lingua franca*) would be easier to understand for the foreign creditors.

8.727 There is a special exception in Article 54(4) RR with regard to insolvency proceedings relating to an individual not exercising a business or professional activity. In such a case the use of the standard form is not obligatory, provided that creditors are not required to lodge their claims in order to have their debts taken into account in the proceedings.

(RR) Article 55—Procedure for lodging claims

1. Any foreign creditor may lodge its claim using the standard claims form to be established in accordance with Article 88. The form shall bear the heading 'Lodgement of claims' in all the official languages of the institutions of the Union.
2. The standard claims form referred to in paragraph 1 shall include the following information:
   (a) the name, postal address, e-mail address, if any, personal identification number, if any, and bank details of the foreign creditor referred to in paragraph 1;
   (b) the amount of the claim, specifying the principal and, where applicable, interest and the date on which it arose and the date on which it became due, if different;
   (c) if interest is claimed, the interest rate, whether the interest is of a legal or contractual nature, the period of time for which the interest is claimed and the capitalised amount of interest;
   (d) if costs incurred in asserting the claim prior to the opening of proceedings are claimed, the amount and the details of those costs;
   (e) the nature of the claim;
   (f) whether any preferential creditor status is claimed and the basis of such a claim;
   (g) whether security in rem or a reservation of title is alleged in respect of the claim and if so, what assets are covered by the security interest being invoked, the date on which the security was granted and, where the security has been registered, the registration number; and
   (h) whether any set-off is claimed and, if so, the amounts of the mutual claims existing on the date when insolvency proceedings were opened, the date on which they arose and the amount net of set-off claimed.

   The standard claims form shall be accompanied by copies of any supporting documents.
3. The standard claims form shall indicate that the provision of information concerning the bank details and the personal identification number of the creditor referred to in point (a) of paragraph 2 is not compulsory.

4. When a creditor lodges its claim by means other than the standard form referred to in paragraph 1, the claim shall contain the information referred to in paragraph 2.
5. Claims may be lodged in any official language of the institutions of the Union. The court, the insolvency practitioner or the debtor in possession may require the creditor to provide a translation in the official language of the State of the opening of proceedings or, if there are several official languages in that Member State, in the official language or one of the official languages of the place where insolvency proceedings have been opened, or in another language which that Member State has indicated it can accept. Each Member State shall indicate whether it accepts any official language of the institutions of the Union other than its own for the purpose of the lodging of claims.
6. Claims shall be lodged within the period stipulated by the law of the State of the opening of proceedings. In the case of a foreign creditor, that period shall not be less than 30 days following the publication of the opening of insolvency proceedings in the insolvency register of the State of the opening of proceedings. Where a Member State relies on Article 24(4), that period shall not be less than 30 days following a creditor having been informed pursuant to Article 54.
7. Where the court, the insolvency practitioner or the debtor in possession has doubts in relation to a claim lodged in accordance with this Article, it shall give the creditor the opportunity to provide additional evidence on the existence and the amount of the claim.

This is a new provision replacing the much simpler and shorter provision contained in Article 41 OR. **8.728**

There was a concern under the OR that foreign creditors might be put to considerable expense and trouble in lodging claims. Article 55(1) RR provides that any foreign creditor may lodge his claim using the standard claims form to be established in accordance with Article 88. **8.729**

Two points are then taken over from OR Article 42(2) RR. First of all, Article 55(5) RR provides, as did Article 42(2) OR, that claims may be lodged in any official language of the Union. As before, the insolvency practitioner, and now also, the debtor in possession, may however require the creditor to provide a translation into the official language of the Member State of the opening of proceedings or, if there are several official languages in that Member State, the official language or one of the official languages of the place where insolvency proceedings have been opened or any other language which the Member State has indicated it can accept. **8.730**

Under Article 42(2) OR it was only where a creditor lodged a claim in his own Member State language that the claim had to bear the heading 'Lodgement of Claim' in the official language or one of the official languages of the State of the opening of proceedings. Under Article 55(1) RR the new standard form is to have the heading 'Lodgement of Claims' in all the official languages of the institutions of the Union. **8.731**

Article 55(2) RR provides for eight headings of information to be provided in the standard claim form, being much more extensive than the basic points formerly required under Article 41 OR. **8.732**

8.733 Article 55 RR requires claims forms to be accompanied by copies of supporting documents, if any, as did Article 41 OR. Article 55(1) RR uses the word 'may' in respect of a foreign creditor lodging his claim using the standard claim form. This, together with Article 55(4) RR, which expressly refers to a creditor lodging his claim by 'other means than the standard form' show that the use of the standard form is optional and not mandatory.

8.734 There was a concern under the OR that time limits in some member States were very short and also inflexible. Article 55 RR has an entirely new provision setting down a minimum period of 30 days during which a foreign creditor can lodge a claim after the publication of the opening of insolvency proceedings in the insolvency register of the Member State of opening.

8.735 In cases where a Member State is making use of the exception in Article 24(4) RR which permits a Member State to avoid making certain information publicly available through a system of interconnection of insolvency registers, in the case of individuals not exercising an independent business or professional activity, Article 55(6) RR requires a minimum period of 30 days from the foreign creditor being informed pursuant to the insolvency practitioner's duty to inform known creditors with habitual residences, domiciles or registered offices in other Member States pursuant to Article 54 RR.

8.736 Article 55(7) RR lays down a minimum standard of conduct for an insolvency practitioner in relation to claims. Where he has 'doubts' in relation to a claim lodged pursuant to Article 55 RR, then the insolvency practitioner is obliged to give the creditor an opportunity to provide additional evidence of the existence and the amount of the claim.

E. Chapter V: Groups of Companies

Introduction

8.737 One of the key changes made in the RR was to introduce a new Chapter V dealing specifically with insolvency proceedings involving a group of companies. In practice, many corporate insolvencies will involve a group of companies often located across different jurisdictions, rather than a single corporate entity, and one of the perceived deficiencies of the OR as originally enacted was a lack of any provision to deal specifically with the insolvency of a group of companies. In the case of a group insolvency, it is likely to be inefficient and destructive of value for there to be separate unco-ordinated insolvency proceedings in respect of each of the individual corporate entities which comprise the group, as opposed to a single group-wide process.

8.738 In practice, in a number of cases such as *Collins & Aikman* and *Nortel*,[610] the issue had been dealt with by the Court concluding that the COMI of each of the companies within the group was located in a single jurisdiction. The effect of this conclusion was that co-ordinated insolvency processes in a single jurisdiction and involving the same insolvency office-holders could then be put in place. In both *Collins & Aikman* and *Nortel*, the Court

---

[610] *Collins & Aikman* [2007] 1 BCLC 182; *Re Nortel Networks SA* [2009] BCC 343.

found that the COMIs of each of the companies within the European groups was located in England so that English administration proceedings were opened in relation to each of the European companies as main proceedings with the same insolvency office-holders appointed. This meant that the insolvency proceedings in respect of the group could be closely co-ordinated and managed. In both cases, this approach worked successfully. Other member states adopted the same or similar approach after an initial period of concern and irritation about the English approach.

8.739 However, this approach is obviously dependent on the COMI of each of the companies within the group being in a single jurisdiction. Depending on the corporate organization of the group of companies in question, this may or may not be the case. Moreover, the approach adopted in *Collins & Aikman* and *Nortel* does not preclude the possibility of secondary proceedings being opened in other jurisdictions.

8.740 One of the possible techniques in dealing with the insolvencies of groups of companies is to substantively consolidate the insolvency proceedings in respect of the individual corporate entities into a single insolvency proceeding. This is a technique which may be adopted in Chapter 11 bankruptcy cases in the United States and which is permitted in France in cases of intermingling of assets (cf Case C-191/10 *Rastelli*[611]). The revisions to the RR dealing with groups do not, however, go as far as allowing for substantive consolidation of the insolvencies of individual corporate entities. Rather two approaches have been adopted:

1. a general requirement for co-operation and communication where there are insolvency proceedings which relate to two or more members of a group of companies; and
2. a new concept of 'group co-ordination proceedings' which is intended to provide for the co-ordination of insolvency proceedings in respect of members of a group of companies—but which has proven so far to be impracticable.

It is important to note, however, that the new provisions do not preclude the possibility previously adopted in cases like *Collins & Aikman* and *Nortel* of finding that the COMIs of all of the group companies are in the same Member State and appointing the same insolvency office-holder in the proceedings relating to each company. Recital (50) to the RR makes clear that this possibility remains open, and it may still be the most effective approach in many cases provided that it is justified on the facts.

8.741 Any office-holder appointed over any entity in a group insolvency will be able to request group co-ordination proceedings. The Regulations adopt a principle of 'court first seised' in relation to an application to open such proceedings. The Regulations eschew a principle which might otherwise require the jurisdiction of the 'most important' insolvency proceeding in the group to be identified (eg based on where a group's most crucial functions are performed). While this militates in favour of simplicity, it may result in more minor office-holders rushing to their courts to seek to open group co-ordination proceedings. This risk is mitigated by the ability of at least two-thirds of the insolvency office-holders appointed over the group companies to pre-agree that one particular jurisdiction is the most appropriate, in which case that jurisdiction will have exclusive jurisdiction.

---

[611] Case C-191/10 *Rastelli Davide e C. v Jean-Charles Hidoux*.

Furthermore, the court first seised must notify other office-holders (who are to be affected by the group plan) and be satisfied that (i) it is appropriate to open group co-ordination proceedings and (ii) that no creditor of any group member anticipated to participate in the proceeding is likely to be financially disadvantaged by the inclusion of such member in the proceedings. How one will be able to demonstrate that (ii) has or has not been satisfied (depending on whether one is seeking or opposing the application) is far from clear in evidentiary terms. Ultimately, participation in the group proceeding is voluntary (and non-participation means that that group member will not have to bear any costs), see Article 65 RR. This may significantly undermine the utility of the procedure and even allow an element of bargaining by office-holders for their preferred jurisdiction on account of a threat not to participate. Further, even if a local proceeding is included in the group proceedings, the local office-holder of such proceeding is not obliged to follow in whole or in part the co-ordinator's recommendation or the group co-ordination plan (although it must then give reasons to the persons it is required to report to under local law and the co-ordinator), see Article 70 RR. Again, this may significantly undermine the utility of the group procedure.

Groups of companies

8.742 Chapter V applies to groups of companies, and it is therefore important to understand the meaning and scope of this. This term is defined in Article 2(11) RR as meaning 'a parent undertaking and its subsidiary undertakings'. In turn:

- 'Parent undertaking' is defined as meaning 'an undertaking which controls, either directly or indirectly, one or more subsidiary undertakings'.
- An undertaking which prepares consolidated financial statements pursuant to Directive 2013/34/EU of 26 June 2013 is deemed to be a parent undertaking.
- The term 'subsidiary undertaking' is not defined in the Regulation. However, it appears to follow from the definition of 'parent undertaking' that an entity which is controlled (directly or indirectly) by a second entity will be a subsidiary undertaking vis-à-vis that second entity (and that the second entity will be a parent undertaking).

It follows from these definitions that the concept of a 'group of companies' is based on the concept of control (direct and indirect). Accordingly, where one company controls (directly or indirectly) another company there will be a 'group of companies' for the purposes of Chapter V of the RR. Further guidance as to the meaning of 'control' in this context can also be derived from Directive 2013/34/EU on annual financial statements (which, as noted above, is referenced in the definition of 'parent undertaking'). Recital (31) of that Directive provides that:

'Consolidated financial statements should present the activities of a parent undertaking and its subsidiaries as a single economic entity (a group). Undertakings controlled by the parent undertaking should be considered as subsidiary undertakings. Control should be based on holding a majority of voting rights, but control may also exist where there are agreements with fellow shareholders or members. In certain circumstances control may be effectively exercised where the parent holds a minority or none of the shares in the subsidiary.'

In other words, 'control' is likely to exist where one company controls a majority of voting rights in another company. However, 'control' may also arise in other circumstances where the relevant company does not hold a majority of the shares but there are other agreements in place conferring control. In practice, this means that the question of whether there is a 'group of companies' is likely to be fact-sensitive and will depend on evidence of the existence of control between the relevant entities.

Finally, the rules in Chapter V relating to groups of companies only apply to the extent **8.743** that proceedings relating to different members of the same group of companies have been opened in more than one Member State (Recital (58) RR). In other words, they have no application to insolvency proceedings taking place in respect of members of the same group of companies within the same Member State.

Co-operation and communication

Section 1 of Chapter V (Articles 56 to 60 RR) deals with co-operation and communication **8.744** where there are insolvencies of the members of a group of companies. The basic structure of the legislation is to impose duties to co-operate and communicate: (1) duties on insolvency office-holders appointed in respect of group companies to co-operate and communicate with each other (Article 56 RR), (2) duties on courts seised of insolvency proceedings in respect of group companies to co-operate and communicate with each other (Article 57 RR), and (3) duties on insolvency office-holders appointed in respect of group companies to co-operate and communicate with courts seised of insolvency proceedings in respect of other group members (Article 58 RR). In addition, insolvency office-holders are given rights and powers in relation to the insolvency proceedings of other group companies (Article 60 RR).

(RR) Article 56—Co-operation and communication between insolvency practitioners

1. Where insolvency proceedings relate to two or more members of a group of companies, an insolvency practitioner appointed in proceedings concerning a member of the group shall cooperate with any insolvency practitioner appointed in proceedings concerning another member of the same group to the extent that such cooperation is appropriate to facilitate the effective administration of those proceedings, is not incompatible with the rules applicable to such proceedings and does not entail any conflict of interest. That cooperation may take any form, including the conclusion of agreements or protocols.
2. In implementing the cooperation set out in paragraph 1, insolvency practitioners shall:
   (a) as soon as possible communicate to each other any information which may be relevant to the other proceedings, provided appropriate arrangements are made to protect confidential information;
   (b) consider whether possibilities exist for coordinating the administration and supervision of the affairs of the group members which are subject to insolvency proceedings, and if so, coordinate such administration and supervision;

(c) consider whether possibilities exist for restructuring group members which are subject to insolvency proceedings and, if so, coordinate with regard to the proposal and negotiation of a coordinated restructuring plan.

For the purposes of points (b) and (c), all or some of the insolvency practitioners referred to in paragraph 1 may agree to grant additional powers to an insolvency practitioner appointed in one of the proceedings where such an agreement is permitted by the rules applicable to each of the proceedings. They may also agree on the allocation of certain tasks amongst them, where such allocation of tasks is permitted by the rules applicable to each of the proceedings.

8.745 Article 56 RR contains the core obligation for insolvency officeholders to co-operate where there are insolvency proceedings in relation to members of the same group of companies. It is important to note that the obligation to co-operate is mandatory ('shall'). However, the obligation is qualified in three important respects:

1. the obligation to co-operate is limited to the extent appropriate 'to facilitate the effective administration of the proceedings'—in other words, on its face, the focus is on the efficient administration of the insolvency proceedings, rather than on a broader obligation to co-operate to (for example) enhance returns to creditors;
2. the obligation to co-operate is subject to the rules applicable to the relevant insolvency proceeding;
3. the obligation to cooperate is also subject to the principle that it should not entail any conflict of interest—this presumably reflects the point that where (for example) there is a disputed claim between the two estates then the obligation of the insolvency officeholders to co-operate will need to be circumscribed accordingly.

In relation to the content of the obligation to co-operate, as noted above, it is on its face primarily focused on furthering the effective administration of the insolvencies. This would no doubt encompass matters such as the sharing of information and co-operation in relation to claims made by the estates and incoming claims into the estates.

8.746 This is consistent with Article 56(2)(a) RR which imposes a mandatory obligation on insolvency office-holders to communicate to each other, as soon as possible, any information which may be relevant to the other proceedings (provided appropriate arrangements are made to protect confidential information). It is to be noted that this obligation is again mandatory ('shall') and cast in very broad terms ('any' information which 'may' be relevant to the other proceedings). The intention appears to be that, in practice, there should be a free flow of information between the different insolvency proceedings.[612] A key issue for office-holders appointed in relation to companies within a group of companies would be to consider how best to facilitate this exchange of information.

8.747 The first of the other aspects of co-operation which are specifically mentioned in Article 56(2) RR is to consider whether it is possible to co-ordinate the administration and supervision of the affairs of group companies which are subject to insolvency proceedings. This is consistent with the obligation in Article 56(1) RR to facilitate the 'effective administration' of

---

[612] Art 56(2) RR does not say anything about the language in which information is to be provided or how the costs of translations are to be borne. Contrast this with Arts 73 and 77.

the proceedings. The question is the scope of the concepts of 'administration' and 'supervision' for these purposes. They would appear to encompass the management of the business of the group where it is continuing to trade, but they may arguably also extend to encompass the realization of assets where a group is being wound down. In practice, a co-ordinated approach to the realization of assets may be the area where co-operation between the different insolvency office-holders of group companies is most required, given that many groups are organized on the basis of business lines or divisions rather than on the basis of legal entities. In order to obtain full value of the sale of assets which span different legal entities, a co-operative approach is likely to be essential. The recitals to the RR note the importance of a co-ordinated approach to asset realization where there are main and secondary proceedings in relation to a single debtor (see Recital (45) RR); the same considerations will often apply in relation to groups of companies.

8.748 The final specific area of co-operation set out in Article 56(2) RR is an obligation on office-holders to consider whether possibilities exist for restructuring group members and, if so, to co-ordinate with respect to the proposal and negotiation of a co-ordinated restructuring plan. This obligation is complemented by Article 60(1)(b) RR which allows an office-holder to apply for a stay of the realization of assets in a foreign proceeding in order to allow a restructuring plan to be implemented.

8.749 Article 56 RR suggests that the cooperation may take the form of agreements or protocols. Recital (46) RR provides further guidance as to the type of agreements and protocols envisaged ranging from simple generic agreements to more detailed and specific agreements which establish a framework of principles to govern multiple insolvency proceedings.

(RR) Article 57—Co-operation and communication between courts

1. Where insolvency proceedings relate to two or more members of a group of companies, a court which has opened such proceedings shall cooperate with any other court before which a request to open proceedings concerning another member of the same group is pending or which has opened such proceedings to the extent that such cooperation is appropriate to facilitate the effective administration of the proceedings, is not incompatible with the rules applicable to them and does not entail any conflict of interest. For that purpose, the courts may, where appropriate, appoint an independent person or body to act on its instructions, provided that this is not incompatible with the rules applicable to them.
2. In implementing the cooperation set out in paragraph 1, courts, or any appointed person or body acting on their behalf, as referred to in paragraph 1, may communicate directly with each other, or request information or assistance directly from each other, provided that such communication respects the procedural rights of the parties to the proceedings and the confidentiality of information.
3. The cooperation referred to in paragraph 1 may be implemented by any means that the court considers appropriate. It may, in particular, concern:
   (a) coordination in the appointment of insolvency practitioners;
   (b) communication of information by any means considered appropriate by the court;

(c) coordination of the administration and supervision of the assets and affairs of the members of the group;
(d) coordination of the conduct of hearings;
(e) coordination in the approval of protocols where necessary.

8.750 Whereas Article 56 RR provides for co-operation between insolvency office-holders, RR Article 57 provides for co-operation between courts. As with Article 56 RR, the mandatory obligation imposed by Article 57(1) RR to co-operate is cast in broad and general terms, although subject to the same qualifications as those contained in Article 56(1) RR which qualify the obligations on insolvency office-holders to co-operate with each other. Although Article 57(1) RR imposes a general duty on courts to co-operate, in practice the duty is only likely to be invoked when an application is made by a party (for example, an office-holder in insolvency proceedings relating to another group company) for relief.

8.751 The scope of the obligation to cooperate is likely to depend on what is understood by facilitating 'the effective administration of the proceedings' and the qualification relieving the Court from the obligation to co-operate where this is 'incompatible with the rules applicable' to the insolvency proceeding. These provisions both suggest that co-operation cannot affect the substantive rights of creditors in the relevant insolvency proceeding; as noted in relation to Article 56 RR, the concept of co-operation appears to be primarily focused on matters such as information sharing, rather than on matters which go to substantive rights.

8.752 As to the methods of implementing co-operation, Article 57(2) RR empowers the court to communicate directly with the other court or to request information or assistance directly, subject to the procedural rights of the parties and the confidentiality of information. In practice, this appears to be similar to the 'letter of request' procedure, which is a feature of cross-border insolvency in common law jurisdictions, under which the courts of one country where an insolvency is taking place may request assistance from the courts of another state.

8.753 In addition, Article 57(3) RR identifies a number of specific methods through which co-operation can be achieved. Notably, this includes co-ordination in the appointment of insolvency practitioners. The recitals to the RR envisage the possibility that the courts in different Member States may co-operate by appointing the same office-holders in insolvency proceedings in respect of different companies in the same group (Recital (47)), although this is expressly subject to local rules concerning the qualification and licensing of insolvency practitioners.

(RR) Article 58—Co-operation and communication between insolvency practitioners and courts

An insolvency practitioner appointed in insolvency proceedings concerning a member of a group of companies:
(a) shall cooperate and communicate with any court before which a request for the opening of proceedings in respect of another member of the same group of companies is pending or which has opened such proceedings; and

(b) may request information from that court concerning the proceedings regarding the other member of the group or request assistance concerning the proceedings in which he has been appointed;

to the extent that such cooperation and communication are appropriate to facilitate the effective administration of the proceedings, do not entail any conflict of interest and are not incompatible with the rules applicable to them.

8.754 RR Article 58 is the final of the three provisions in Chapter V requiring co-operation and communication; it requires co-operation and communication between an insolvency office-holder appointed in an insolvency proceeding in respect of a group member and the courts in other states where insolvency proceedings in respect of other group members are taking place. The obligation to co-operate is again mandatory but subject to the same qualifications as contained in Articles 56 and 57 RR.

8.755 Article 58(b) RR additionally enables the office-holder appointed in the insolvency proceeding of one group company to apply directly to a foreign court seised of the insolvency proceeding in respect of another group company without having first to apply to the court for a letter of request addressed to the foreign court. The office-holder may request either information or assistance. This may mean that, in practice, the more efficient route for an insolvency office-holder seeking assistance from a foreign court seised of an insolvency proceeding in respect of another group company is to approach that court directly, rather than applying to his own court for a request to be made to the foreign court for assistance pursuant to Article 57 RR.

(RR) Article 59—Costs of co-operation and communication in proceedings concerning members of a group of companies

The costs of the cooperation and communication provided for in Articles 56 to 60 incurred by an insolvency practitioner or a court shall be regarded as costs and expenses incurred in the respective proceedings.

8.756 Article 59 RR provides that the costs of co-operation and communication which are incurred are to be a cost and expense of the relevant insolvency proceeding. To this extent, Article 59 RR may have the effect of enlarging the categories of expense allowed for under the relevant domestic legislation.

(RR) Article 60—Powers of the insolvency practitioner in proceedings concerning members of a group of companies

1. An insolvency practitioner appointed in insolvency proceedings opened in respect of a member of a group of companies may, to the extent appropriate to facilitate the effective administration of the proceedings:
   (a) be heard in any of the proceedings opened in respect of any other member of the same group;

(b) request a stay of any measure related to the realisation of the assets in the proceedings opened with respect to any other member of the same group, provided that:
  (i) a restructuring plan for all or some members of the group for which insolvency proceedings have been opened has been proposed under point (c) of Article 56(2) and presents a reasonable chance of success;
  (ii) such a stay is necessary in order to ensure the proper implementation of the restructuring plan;
  (iii) the restructuring plan would be to the benefit of the creditors in the proceedings for which the stay is requested; and
  (iv) neither the insolvency proceedings in which the insolvency practitioner referred to in paragraph 1 of this Article has been appointed nor the proceedings in respect of which the stay is requested are subject to coordination under Section 2 of this Chapter;
(c) apply for the opening of group coordination proceedings in accordance with Article 61.

2. The court having opened proceedings referred to in point (b) of paragraph 1 shall stay any measure related to the realisation of the assets in the proceedings in whole or in part if it is satisfied that the conditions referred to in point (b) of paragraph 1 are fulfilled.

Before ordering the stay, the court shall hear the insolvency practitioner appointed in the proceedings for which the stay is requested. Such a stay may be ordered for any period, not exceeding 3 months, which the court considers appropriate and which is compatible with the rules applicable to the proceedings.

The court ordering the stay may require the insolvency practitioner referred to in paragraph 1 to take any suitable measure available under national law to guarantee the interests of the creditors in the proceedings.

The court may extend the duration of the stay by such further period or periods as it considers appropriate and which are compatible with the rules applicable to the proceedings, provided that the conditions referred to in points (b)(ii) to (iv) of paragraph 1 continue to be fulfilled and that the total duration of the stay (the initial period together with any such extensions) does not exceed 6 months.

8.757 To complete the provisions dealing with co-operation and communication in relation to insolvency proceedings in respect of group companies, Article 60 RR confers powers and rights on an office-holder appointed in an insolvency of a group company. These rights comprise:

- A right to be heard in insolvency proceedings relating to other members of the same group of companies
- A right to request a stay of the realization of assets in insolvency proceedings relating to any other member of the same group of companies.
- A right to apply for the opening of group co-ordinating proceedings.

8.758 The right to request a stay of realization of assets ties in with the concept of a co-ordinated restructuring plan provided for by Article 56(2)(c) RR. Pursuant to that Article, insolvency office-holders in insolvency proceedings relating to group companies are obliged to consider whether group companies can be restructured through a co-ordinated restructuring plan. Article 60(1)(b) RR then provides that, where such a plan has been proposed and stands a reasonable prospect of success, a stay of the realization of assets may be imposed in order to allow the proper implementation of the plan.

8.759 The imposition of such a stay is subject to the four conditions mentioned in Article 60(1)(b)(i)–(iv) RR. However, where these conditions are satisfied, then the court is obliged to grant the stay that is not discretionary. The stay is to be for any period, not exceeding three months, which the court considers to be appropriate. The stay may then be extended provided that the total duration of the stay does not exceed six months.

8.760 An office-holder appointed over any group member may be heard in any proceeding concerning another member within the same group. Crucially, such office-holder can also request a stay, up to a maximum of six months, of any measure taken by another office-holder to realize assets in the proceedings of another group company, subject to certain conditions. Again, this may represent an incursion on one office-holder's powers to administer the estate in favour of allowing another office-holder to seek a stay in order to impose a degree of co-ordination. Again, it is clear that one can foresee differences of opinion between office-holders as to the most appropriate strategy with further recourse to the courts to resolve such matters.

Co-ordination

8.761 The second technique adopted in the RR for dealing with groups of companies is the new concept of 'group coordination proceedings' which is intended to provide for the co-ordination of insolvency proceedings in respect of members of a group of companies. In essence, these proceedings involve the appointment of a 'group coordinator' to oversee the insolvency proceedings or restructuring of a group of companies and to facilitate a 'group coordination plan'. His position is best seen as a mediator who tries to get the affected insolvency practitioners to act in concert. However, there are a number of detailed procedural rules which govern participation in group co-ordination proceedings and which make it so overly complex that it has, to the best of our knowledge, not yet been utilized.

(RR) Article 61—Request to open group co-ordination proceedings

1. Group coordination proceedings may be requested before any court having jurisdiction over the insolvency proceedings of a member of the group, by an insolvency practitioner appointed in insolvency proceedings opened in relation to a member of the group.
2. The request referred to in paragraph 1 shall be made in accordance with the conditions provided for by the law applicable to the proceedings in which the insolvency practitioner has been appointed.
3. The request referred to in paragraph 1 shall be accompanied by:
   (a) a proposal as to the person to be nominated as the group coordinator ('the coordinator'), details of his or her eligibility pursuant to Article 71, details of his or her qualifications and his or her written agreement to act as coordinator;

(b) an outline of the proposed group coordination, and in particular the reasons why the conditions set out in Article 63(1) are fulfilled;

(c) a list of the insolvency practitioners appointed in relation to the members of the group and, where relevant, the courts and competent authorities involved in the insolvency proceedings of the members of the group;

(d) an outline of the estimated costs of the proposed group coordination and the estimation of the share of those costs to be paid by each member of the group.

8.762 Article 61 RR confers jurisdiction on the courts of Member States to consider requests for the opening of group co-ordination proceedings. Any court having jurisdiction over the insolvency proceeding in respect of a member of the relevant group of companies may consider such a request. The request may be made by an office-holder appointed in any insolvency proceeding in respect of a member of the group. However, a creditor does not itself have standing to make a request for the opening of group co-ordination proceedings. Article 61(2) RR also envisages that the law under which an insolvency office-holder has been appointed may impose conditions regulating the ability of that office-holder to apply to open group co-ordination proceedings.[613]

8.763 Article 61(3) RR sets out the material which is required to accompany such an application. As envisaged by Article 61(2) RR, it is likely that requests for the opening of group co-ordination proceedings will also be subject to procedural rules laid down under the relevant national laws.

(RR) Article 62—Priority rule

Without prejudice to Article 66, where the opening of group coordination proceedings is requested before courts of different Member States, any court other than the court first seised shall decline jurisdiction in favour of that court.

8.764 Article 62 RR introduces the 'first seised' rule, a central part of the Judgments Regulation dealing with jurisdiction in civil proceedings, into the RR. It provides that where the opening of group co-ordination proceedings is requested in the courts of different Member States, then only the court first seised will have jurisdiction in relation to that request. Although this rule has the benefit of simplicity and clarity—at least once the interconnected register of Articles 24 et seq unfolds its complete functionality—it does mean that in practice there may well be a rush to file requests for group co-ordination proceedings in order to render a particular court first seised. The question of when the court is 'seised' for these purposes is likely to be determined in the same way as under the Judgments Regulation that is when the application is issued rather than served.

8.765 Article 62 RR is subject to the effect of Article 66 RR which, as noted below, allows the requisite majority of insolvency office-holders appointed in insolvencies of members of a group of companies to agree that the courts of a single Member State should have exclusive jurisdiction to deal with group co-ordination proceedings.

---

[613] See also Recital (52) RR: 'where the law applicable to the insolvency so requires, this insolvency practitioner should obtain the necessary authorisation before making such a request.'

The potential hazards resulting from the inclusion into the RR of the 'court first seised' prin- **8.766** ciple which has long been a feature of the EU Judgments Regulation (and its predecessor, the Brussels Convention) should not be underestimated. It is likely that, when matters of interpretation of this expression in the context of the RR come to be considered by the CJEU, it will replicate the commercially obtuse interpretation developed in that Court's own previous case decisions interpreting the Brussels Convention of 1968 and the Judgments Regulation. In the most notorious of these decisions, the *Erich Gasser* case, the CJEU adamantly refused to accept the long-established proposition that a valid agreement on jurisdiction should prevail over a party's recourse to tactics designed to defeat or delay the proper course of justice by launching illegitimate proceedings in the courts of some other country whose judicial processes could be expected to occupy a great deal of time before reaching the conclusion that the terms of the jurisdiction clause must be respected.[614] While it is of course the case that Article 62 is expressed to operate 'subject to Article 66' (which is dealt with below), there may be a period of delay due to the practical difficulty in co-ordinating the views of the various insolvency practitioners appointed in the respective insolvency proceedings of the members of the group so as to arrive at an agreement whereby at least two-thirds of them concur in the designation of the most appropriate court for the opening of group co-ordination proceedings. This could result in value-destructive uncertainty while the 'court first seised' awaits the outcome of efforts aimed at over-reaching the priority rule of Article 62 RR via the exception created by Article 66 RR.

(RR) Article 63—Notice by the court seised

1. The court seised of a request to open group coordination proceedings shall give notice as soon as possible of the request for the opening of group coordination proceedings and of the proposed coordinator to the insolvency practitioners appointed in relation to the members of the group as indicated in the request referred to in point (c) of Article 61(3), if it is satisfied that:
   (a) the opening of such proceedings is appropriate to facilitate the effective administration of the insolvency proceedings relating to the different group members;
   (b) no creditor of any group member expected to participate in the proceedings is likely to be financially disadvantaged by the inclusion of that member in such proceedings; and
   (c) the proposed coordinator fulfils the requirements laid down in Article 71.
2. The notice referred to in paragraph 1 of this Article shall list the elements referred to in points (a) to (d) of Article 61(3).
3. The notice referred to in paragraph 1 shall be sent by registered letter, attested by an acknowledgment of receipt.
4. The court seised shall give the insolvency practitioners involved the opportunity to be heard.

---

[614] Case C-116/02 *Erich Gasser GmbH v MISAT srl* [2003] ECR I-14693, [2005] QB 1. These procedural tactics are sometimes called 'torpedo-suits'.

8.767 Article 63 RR deals with the procedure for the opening of group co-ordination proceedings. This provides for a two-stage process. The first stage is an initial consideration of the request made by the relevant insolvency office-holder for the opening of group co-ordination proceedings. At this stage, the court to whom the request has been addressed must consider whether the request satisfies requirements (a) to (c) in Article 63(1) RR.

8.768 The requirements in (a) to (c) of Article 63(1) RR focus on the central questions of (1) whether group co-ordination proceedings will assist with the effective administration of the different insolvency proceedings, (2) whether any creditor will be financially disadvantaged by group co-ordination proceedings, and (3) whether the proposed coordinator satisfies the relevant requirements. The second requirement, in particular, appears to be focussed on the question of whether group co-ordination proceedings will be likely to have a net positive benefit for creditors after allowing for the costs of those proceedings. As stated in Recital (54) RR, group co-ordination proceedings should 'have a generally positive impact on the creditors'. Recital (55) RR also makes clear that 'the advantages of group coordination proceedings should never be outweighed by the costs of these proceedings'.

8.769 If the court is satisfied that these requirements are met, then the request will move to the second stage of the process. For these purposes, the court will require notice to be given of the request to all the insolvency practitioners appointed in insolvency proceedings of members of the group of companies. The notice must contain the information prescribed in Article 61(3)(a)–(d) RR and must be sent by registered letter. Following the giving of such notice, a further hearing will take place, at which the various insolvency office-holders will have opportunity to the heard, and at which the court will decide whether or not to open group co-ordination proceedings.

(RR) Article 64—Objections by insolvency practitioners

1. An insolvency practitioner appointed in respect of any group member may object to:
   (a) the inclusion within group coordination proceedings of the insolvency proceedings in respect of which it has been appointed; or
   (b) the person proposed as a coordinator.
2. Objections pursuant to paragraph 1 of this Article shall be lodged with the court referred to in Article 63 within 30 days of receipt of notice of the request for the opening of group coordination proceedings by the insolvency practitioner referred to in paragraph 1 of this Article.

   The objection may be made by means of the standard form established in accordance with Article 88.
3. Prior to taking the decision to participate or not to participate in the coordination in accordance with point (a) of paragraph 1, an insolvency practitioner shall obtain any approval which may be required under the law of the State of the opening of proceedings for which it has been appointed.

8.770 Following receipt of a notice sent following the first stage of the process established under Article 63 RR, any insolvency office-holder appointed in the insolvency of a group member may lodge an objection to (a) the inclusion of that group member in the group co-ordination proceedings and/or (b) to the choice of the co-ordinator. The objection must be sent within 30 days of receipt of the notice and may be made on the standard form established by the Commission pursuant to Article 88 RR.

8.771 As explained by Article 65 RR, the consequences of an objection to the inclusion of the insolvency group member in coordination proceedings is that the co-ordination proceedings will necessarily not apply to that group member. Accordingly, before lodging any such objection, the relevant insolvency office-holder must first obtain any authorization which is required under the law applicable to that insolvency. On the other hand, an objection to the choice of co-ordinator does not have any automatic effect; rather, it is for the court to whom the request to open co-ordination proceedings has been addressed to decide on the appointment of the co-ordinator in light of any such objections (see further Article 67 RR below).

(RR) Article 65—Consequences of objection to the inclusion in group co-ordination

1. Where an insolvency practitioner has objected to the inclusion of the proceedings in respect of which it has been appointed in group coordination proceedings, those proceedings shall not be included in the group coordination proceedings.
2. The powers of the court referred to in Article 68 or of the coordinator arising from those proceedings shall have no effect as regards that member, and shall entail no costs for that member.

8.772 Article 65 RR provides that where the relevant insolvency office-holder has objected to the inclusion of the insolvency proceedings of group member in respect of which he has been appointed in co-ordination proceedings, then the co-ordination proceedings shall not apply to such insolvency proceedings. This is an automatic rule, and does not involve any element of discretion or judgment by the court to whom the request for the opening of co-ordination proceedings has been made. According to Recital (53) RR, the right to object reflects the essentially 'voluntary nature' of group co-ordination proceedings.

8.773 As noted below, Article 69 RR provides for a subsequent right to request 'opt in' where an insolvency office-holder has originally objected to inclusion of insolvency proceedings within co-ordination proceedings.

(RR) Article 66—Choice of court for group co-ordination proceedings

1. Where at least two-thirds of all insolvency practitioners appointed in insolvency proceedings of the members of the group have agreed that a court of another Member State having jurisdiction is the most appropriate court for the opening of group co-ordination proceedings, that court shall have exclusive jurisdiction.

2. The choice of court shall be made by joint agreement in writing or evidenced in writing. It may be made until such time as group coordination proceedings have been opened in accordance with Article 68.
3. Any court other than the court seised under paragraph 1 shall decline jurisdiction in favour of that court.
4. The request for the opening of group coordination proceedings shall be submitted to the court agreed in accordance with Article 61.

8.774 Article 66 RR qualifies the 'first seised' rule provided for in Article 62 RR. It allows the requisite majority of office-holders appointed in insolvencies of members of a group of companies to agree that the courts of a single Member State should have exclusive jurisdiction to deal with group co-ordination proceedings. For these purposes, the requisite majority is two-thirds of the relevant insolvency office-holders. It is to be noted that the relevant majority is based on a simple poll of the relevant insolvency office-holders and is not, for example, weighted to take account of the different value of claims or assets in the different insolvency proceedings of group members.

8.775 Pursuant to Article 66(2) RR, such an agreement may be made at any time until group co-ordination proceedings have actually been opened. In other words, the agreement may be made after a request for the opening of group co-ordination proceedings has been lodged until such time as the court actually adjudicates in favour of the request.

(RR) Article 67—Consequences of objections to the proposed co-ordinator

Where objections to the person proposed as coordinator have been received from an insolvency practitioner which does not also object to the inclusion in the group coordination proceedings of the member in respect of which it has been appointed, the court may refrain from appointing that person and invite the objecting insolvency practitioner to submit a new request in accordance with Article 61(3).

8.776 Article 67 RR deals with the situation where an insolvency office-holder has not objected to the inclusion of the insolvency of the group member in respect of which he has been appointed in the co-ordination proceedings, but has objected to the proposed co-ordinator. As noted above, such an objection does not have the automatic effect of disqualifying the proposed co-ordinator from appointment; rather it is for the Court to whom the request for co-ordination proceedings has been addressed to consider whether the person has been appointed. No doubt, the court would consider the grounds for the objection, as well as assessing whether the proposed co-ordinator satisfies the requirements of Article 71 RR. Given the voluntary nature of co-ordination proceedings and the purpose of co-ordination proceedings as facilitating the more efficient administration of the insolvencies of the group members, it is obviously important that a co-ordinator commands the confidence of the insolvency office-holders appointed in the insolvencies of the group members.

(RR) Article 68—Decision to open group co-ordination proceedings

1. After the period referred to in Article 64(2) has elapsed, the court may open group coordination proceedings where it is satisfied that the conditions of Article 63(1) are met. In such a case, the court shall:
   (a) appoint a coordinator;
   (b) decide on the outline of the coordination; and
   (c) decide on the estimation of costs and the share to be paid by the group members.
2. The decision opening group coordination proceedings shall be brought to the notice of the participating insolvency practitioners and of the coordinator.

8.777 Article 68 RR deals with the second stage of the process for the commencement of co-ordination proceedings. As noted above, pursuant to Article 63 RR, if the court is satisfied that the requirements in Article 63(1)(a)–(c) RR are satisfied, then a notice is to be sent to all of the relevant insolvency office-holders. Following the expiration of 30 days following the receipt of such notices by the insolvency office-holders, the court will then hold a further hearing to decide whether to open co-ordination proceedings. At this hearing, the insolvency office-holders will have a right to be represented and heard.

8.778 The court will no doubt consider whether its initial views as to the satisfaction of the requirements in Article 63(1)(a)–(c) RR remain justified in light of any representations made by the insolvency office-holders and in light of any further information. A relevant factor may well be the extent to which objections have been lodged pursuant to Article 64(1)(a) RR with the effect that insolvency proceedings in respect of individual group members will not be included within any co-ordination proceedings.

8.779 If the court decides to open co-ordination proceedings then, pursuant to Article 68(1)(a)–(c) RR, it must appoint a co-ordinator, decide on the outline of the co-ordination and decide on the estimated costs and the share to be paid by the various group members. These requirements reflect the matters required to be contained in the application for the commencement of co-ordination proceedings pursuant to Article 61(3) RR.

8.780 The language in Article 68(1)(c) RR which requires the court to 'decide on the estimation of costs' is somewhat vague but appears to encompass the idea that the court should, when opening the co-ordination proceedings, approve an estimate of the costs of those proceedings. The Recitals to the RR and the provisions of the RR envisage that if it becomes apparent subsequently that the estimated costs will be exceeded by more than 10 per cent the co-ordinator should inform the insolvency office-holders of the participating group companies and should return to the court for prior approval of the additional costs to be incurred above the original estimate (Recital (55) RR and Article 72(6) RR).

8.781 The RR does not provide any guidance as to the manner in which costs should be shared as between the estates of the group members participating in the co-ordination proceedings. An obvious yardstick would be by reference to the relative gross assets in the relevant estates. Such an approach would appear to be fairer to the relevant creditors than simply splitting the costs between the relevant insolvency estates pro rata. However, given the predominantly voluntary nature of this proceeding, the participating insolvency practitioners should clarify this question, too, beforehand.

(RR) Article 69—Subsequent opt-in by insolvency practitioners

1. In accordance with its national law, any insolvency practitioner may request, after the court decision referred to in Article 68, the inclusion of the proceedings in respect of which it has been appointed, where:
   (a) there has been an objection to the inclusion of the insolvency proceedings within the group coordination proceedings; or
   (b) insolvency proceedings with respect to a member of the group have been opened after the court has opened group coordination proceedings.
2. Without prejudice to paragraph 4, the coordinator may accede to such a request, after consulting the insolvency practitioners involved, where
   (a) he or she is satisfied that, taking into account the stage that the group coordination proceedings has reached at the time of the request, the criteria set out in points (a) and (b) of Article 63(1) are met; or
   (b) all insolvency practitioners involved agree, subject to the conditions in their national law.
3. The coordinator shall inform the court and the participating insolvency practitioners of his or her decision pursuant to paragraph 2 and of the reasons on which it is based.
4. Any participating insolvency practitioner or any insolvency practitioner whose request for inclusion in the group coordination proceedings has been rejected may challenge the decision referred to in paragraph 2 in accordance with the procedure set out under the law of the Member State in which the group coordination proceedings have been opened.

8.782 Article 69 RR provides for a right to request 'opt in' to co-ordination proceedings in two circumstances. The first is whether there was originally an objection to inclusion of a particular insolvency proceeding within the co-ordination proceeding. As noted above, the automatic effect of such an objection pursuant to Article 65 RR is that the relevant insolvency proceeding will not be included in the group co-ordination proceedings. The second circumstance is whether insolvency proceedings in respect of a group member were opened after the commencement of co-ordination proceedings.

8.783 In either of these circumstances, the relevant insolvency office-holder may request the inclusion of the relevant insolvency proceedings in the co-ordination proceedings. The co-ordinator must consult with all the insolvency office-holders in the insolvency proceedings currently comprised in the co-ordination proceedings. The co-ordinator may then accede to such a request provided either that:

- the criteria in Article 63(1)(a) and (b) RR are satisfied (ie whether group co-ordination proceedings will assist with the effective administration of the different insolvency proceedings and whether any creditor will be financially disadvantaged by group co-ordination proceedings) bearing in mind the stage of the co-ordination proceedings; or
- all the insolvency office-holders in the insolvency proceedings currently comprised in the co-ordination proceedings agree.

Any request for inclusion in co-ordination proceedings which is refused may be subject to challenge in accordance with the law of the Member State where the group co-ordination proceedings were opened.

(RR) Article 70—Recommendations and group co-ordination plan

1. When conducting their insolvency proceedings, insolvency practitioners shall consider the recommendations of the coordinator and the content of the group coordination plan referred to in Article 72(1).
2. An insolvency practitioner shall not be obliged to follow in whole or in part the coordinator's recommendations or the group coordination plan.

    If it does not follow the coordinator's recommendations or the group coordination plan, it shall give reasons for not doing so to the persons or bodies that it is to report to under its national law, and to the coordinator.

8.784 Article 70 RR deals with the impact of co-ordination proceedings on the insolvency proceedings in respect of the participating group members. Pursuant to Article 70(1) RR, the relevant insolvency office-holders are required to 'consider' the recommendations made by the co-ordinator and the group co-ordination plan. There is, however, no obligation to abide by and follow such recommendations and plan. Indeed, Article 70(2) RR makes expressly clear that there is no such obligation.

8.785 That said, in circumstances where the insolvency proceedings of a group member are subject to co-ordination proceedings (because there has been no objection made pursuant to Article 65 RR), then the expectation would be that in the ordinary course the insolvency office-holder would follow the recommendations of the co-ordinator and the contents of the co-ordination plan. Article 70(2) RR recognizes this since it provides that, if an insolvency office-holder does not follow the recommendations or the plan, then he must give his reasons for not doing so. These are to be provided to the relevant bodies specified in national law and to the co-ordinator himself.

(RR) Article 71—The co-ordinator

1. The coordinator shall be a person eligible under the law of a Member State to act as an insolvency practitioner.
2. The coordinator shall not be one of the insolvency practitioners appointed to act in respect of any of the group members, and shall have no conflict of interest in respect of the group members, their creditors and the insolvency practitioners appointed in respect of any of the group members.

8.786 Article 71 RR sets out the requirements which need to be satisfied for a person to be appointed as co-ordinator. First of all, the relevant person must be authorized under the law of a Member State (seemingly not necessarily one of the affected member states where proceedings have been opened over group members) to act as an insolvency practitioner.

Secondly, no person who is already an insolvency office-holder in respect of any group member can be appointed as co-ordinator; this contrasts with the possibilities given under Article 56(2), last sentence RR. Thirdly, the person must not have any conflict of interest in respect of any of (a) any group members, (b) any creditors of group members, or (c) the insolvency office-holders appointed in respect of any group members.

(RR) Article 72—Tasks and rights of the co-ordinator

1. The coordinator shall:
   (a) identify and outline recommendations for the coordinated conduct of the insolvency proceedings;
   (b) propose a group coordination plan that identifies, describes and recommends a comprehensive set of measures appropriate to an integrated approach to the resolution of the group members' insolvencies. In particular, the plan may contain proposals for:
      (i) the measures to be taken in order to re-establish the economic performance and the financial soundness of the group or any part of it;
      (ii) the settlement of intra-group disputes as regards intra-group transactions and avoidance actions;
      (iii) agreements between the insolvency practitioners of the insolvent group members.
2. The coordinator may also:
   (a) be heard and participate, in particular by attending creditors' meetings, in any of the proceedings opened in respect of any member of the group;
   (b) mediate any dispute arising between two or more insolvency practitioners of group members;
   (c) present and explain his or her group coordination plan to the persons or bodies that he or she is to report to under his or her national law;
   (d) request information from any insolvency practitioner in respect of any member of the group where that information is or might be of use when identifying and outlining strategies and measures in order to coordinate the proceedings; and
   (e) request a stay for a period of up to 6 months of the proceedings opened in respect of any member of the group, provided that such a stay is necessary in order to ensure the proper implementation of the plan and would be to the benefit of the creditors in the proceedings for which the stay is requested; or request the lifting of any existing stay. Such a request shall be made to the court that opened the proceedings for which a stay is requested.
3. The plan referred to in point (b) of paragraph 1 shall not include recommendations as to any consolidation of proceedings or insolvency estates.
4. The coordinator's tasks and rights as defined under this Article shall not extend to any member of the group not participating in group coordination proceedings.
5. The coordinator shall perform his or her duties impartially and with due care.
6. Where the coordinator considers that the fulfilment of his or her tasks requires a significant increase in the costs compared to the cost estimate referred to in point (d) of Article 61(3), and in any case, where the costs exceed 10% of the estimated costs, the coordinator shall:

(a) **inform without delay the participating insolvency practitioners; and**
(b) **seek the prior approval of the court opening group coordination proceedings.**

Article 72 RR is an important provision which sets out the tasks which the co-ordinator **8.787** is required to undertake and the rights conferred on him to enable him to perform those tasks. The co-ordinator's tasks fall into two broad categories:

- first, to produce recommendations for the co-ordinated conduct of the various insolvency proceedings;
- secondly to produce a group co-ordination plan.

The group co-ordination plan is likely to be the centrepiece of any co-ordination proceedings. In the case of insolvency proceedings which are directed at rehabilitating and restructuring the relevant group companies and/or their businesses, the plan may include measures applicable across the relevant companies for restructuring liabilities and operations. In the case of insolvency proceedings which are directed at realizing assets for distribution to creditors, the plan may include co-ordinated measures for realizing assets and dealing with inter-group liabilities and claims.

However, it is important to note that the RR makes expressly clear that a plan may not in- **8.788** volve the consolidation of proceedings or estates (Article 72(3) RR). This reflects the general approach of the RR in rejecting substantive consolidation as an approach for dealing with the insolvencies of groups of companies.

As a counterpoint to Article 72(1) RR, Article 72(2) RR confers various rights and powers **8.789** on the co-ordinator. These include:

1. A right to participate at both hearings and creditors' meetings in the insolvency proceedings of any group member, providing such group member is participating in the co-ordination proceedings: Article 72(4) RR.
2. A power to mediate any dispute between the insolvency office-holders of group members, providing such group members are participating in the co-ordination proceedings: Article 72(4) RR. This raises the question of whether, where there is a dispute between two such insolvency office-holders, it is a prerequisite to seek to mediate the dispute through the co-ordinator (where one has been appointed) before commencing court proceedings. The better view is probably that it is not, on the footing that Article 72(2)(b) RR confers a power on the co-ordinator to mediate disputes rather than making such mediation compulsory.
3. A power to present the co-ordination plan to relevant persons as required under the national law applicable to the co-ordinator.
4. A right to request information from any insolvency office-holder in respect of any group members participating in group co-ordination proceedings: Article 72(4) RR. The condition is that the relevant information is or might be of use when identifying and outlining strategies and measures in order to co-ordinate the proceedings. Given the terms of Article 72(2)(d) RR (it is sufficient that the information 'might' be of use), this represents a broad information gathering power.
5. A right to request a stay (for up to six months) of any insolvency proceeding of a group member participating in group co-ordination proceedings: Article 72(4) RR. This is the counterpart of the power conferred on individual office-holders under Article 60(1) RR to request a stay in order to implement a restructuring plan, although, unlike

the power under Article 60(1) RR, the power conferred by Article 72(2)(e) RR is not limited to a stay of the realization of assets but extends to a stay of the relevant insolvency proceedings generally.

Article 72(5) RR expresses the general duty imposed on co-ordinators to perform his or her duties impartially and with due care. The Article does not identify whether the duty is owed to the company or to the creditors (or both), or whether it could be subject to an action brought by one or more creditors.

8.790 The group co-ordinator's substantial powers (including the power to stay proceedings in respect of any group member, albeit subject to conditions) could interfere with the other office-holders' ability to administer their respective proceedings. Disputes on this will invariably increase costs to the estate. This aspect of the co-ordinator's power and its potential impact on creditors will need to be monitored. It is clear that one can foresee differences in opinion between local office-holders and a co-ordinator as to what may be in the best interests of the local office-holders' creditors and what may be in the best interests of the group as a whole. This may also increase the risk that office-holders will opt out of such proceedings until the plan is clear and acceptable to them and opt in under Article 69 at a later stage. See also Article 72(4) RR which makes it clear that the co-ordinator's tasks and rights do not extend to any member of the group not participating in group co-ordination proceedings. In terms of role, the co-ordinator must be a person who could act as an insolvency practitioner under the laws of any Member State (the regulation of such persons may vary widely from state to state). The co-ordinator's tasks and rights are set out in Article 72 RR and the grounds for the revocation of his appointment in Article 75 RR. However, it is clear that the co-ordinator is a pure creature of the Regulation—while the co-ordinator is required to perform his duties impartially and with due care, it is not clear to whom his duties are owed (the office-holders, the debtor, the creditors?) and what the avenues of recourse against him or her might be.

(RR) Article 73—Languages

1. The coordinator shall communicate with the insolvency practitioner of a participating group member in the language agreed with the insolvency practitioner or, in the absence of an agreement, in the official language or one of the official languages of the institutions of the Union, and of the court which opened the proceedings in respect of that group member.
2. The coordinator shall communicate with a court in the official language applicable to that court.

8.791 Article 73 RR deals with the issue of the language of communications in co-ordination proceedings—which is surprising, given the more or less voluntary nature of the co-ordination proceeding from which one might derive that the relevant persons have already found a common understanding. It provides for two options. Either communications take place in the language agreed between the co-ordinator and the relevant insolvency office-holder. Alternatively, absent agreement, communications are to be in the language which is one of the official languages of the Union and of the court which opened the relevant insolvency proceedings in which the insolvency office-holder is appointed. In practice, it would no doubt be most efficient for the co-ordinator and all of the relevant insolvency office-holders to agree that all communications should take place in a single language. Absent agreement, Article 73 RR imposes a potentially expensive burden on co-ordinators to translate all communications into the home languages of each of the relevant insolvency office-holders.

(RR) Article 74—Co-operation between insolvency practitioners and the co-ordinator

1. **Insolvency practitioners appointed in relation to members of a group and the co-ordinator shall cooperate with each other to the extent that such cooperation is not incompatible with the rules applicable to the respective proceedings.**
2. **In particular, insolvency practitioners shall communicate any information that is relevant for the coordinator to perform his or her tasks.**

Article 74 RR imposes an obligation on the relevant insolvency office-holders and the co-ordinator himself to co-operate with each other. The notion of co-operation is inherent in co-ordination proceedings, and it is therefore unsurprising to find such an obligation imposed. Article 74(2) RR amplifies the co-operation obligation as extending to a requirement to communicate 'any' information that is relevant to the performance by the co-ordinator of his tasks. **8.792**

(RR) Article 75—Revocation of the appointment of the co-ordinator

The court shall revoke the appointment of the coordinator of its own motion or at the request of the insolvency practitioner of a participating group member where:
(a) **the coordinator acts to the detriment of the creditors of a participating group member; or**
(b) **the coordinator fails to comply with his or her obligations under this Chapter.**

Article 75 RR imposes on the Court which opened the co-ordination proceedings an obligation to revoke the appointment of a co-ordinator either of its own motion or on the request of an insolvency office-holder of a group participating in the proceeding. The conditions for such a removal are either that the co-ordinator has acted to the detriment of the creditors of a participating group member or has failed to comply with his obligations under Chapter V of the RR. **8.793**

There is, however, no ability for a creditor of a participating group company to request the removal of a co-ordinator. **8.794**

(RR) Article 76—Debtor in possession

The provisions applicable, under this Chapter, to the insolvency practitioner shall also apply, where appropriate, to the debtor in possession.

8.795 Article 76 makes clear that the provisions in relation to co-ordination proceedings also apply to a group member which is the subject of debtor in possession proceeding within the scope of the RR.

(RR) Article 77—Costs and distribution

1. The remuneration for the coordinator shall be adequate, proportionate to the tasks fulfilled and reflect reasonable expenses.
2. On having completed his or her tasks, the coordinator shall establish the final statement of costs and the share to be paid by each member, and submit this statement to each participating insolvency practitioner and to the court opening coordination proceedings.
3. In the absence of objections by the insolvency practitioners within 30 days of receipt of the statement referred to in paragraph 2, the costs and the share to be paid by each member shall be deemed to be agreed. The statement shall be submitted to the court opening coordination proceedings for confirmation.
4. In the event of an objection, the court that opened the group coordination proceedings shall, upon the application of the coordinator or any participating insolvency practitioner, decide on the costs and the share to be paid by each member in accordance with the criteria set out in paragraph 1 of this Article, and taking into account the estimation of costs referred to in Article 68(1) and, where applicable, Article 72(6).
5. Any participating insolvency practitioner may challenge the decision referred to in paragraph 4 in accordance with the procedure set out under the law of the Member State where group coordination proceedings have been opened.

8.796 Article 77 RR deals with the costs of co-ordination proceedings. As noted above, one of the key criteria for determining whether co-ordination proceedings are appropriate is whether the benefits of the co-ordination proceedings outweigh the costs. Where the court opens co-ordination proceedings, it must approve an estimate of costs for those proceedings and determine the shares to be paid by the relevant group companies participating in the co-ordination proceedings.

8.797 Article 77(1) RR establishes the general principle that the co-ordinator should receive adequate and proportionate remuneration for his work and be entitled to recover reasonable expenses. In terms of procedure, following the completion of the co-ordination work, the co-ordinator is to produce a final statement of costs detailing the share to be paid by each participating group member. The statement is deemed to be agreed absent an objection being received from the relevant insolvency office-holder within 30 days of its receipt. In the event of any objection, the court which opened the co-ordination proceedings will determine the matter pursuant to Article 77(4) RR.

F. Chapter VI: Data Protection

(RR) Article 78—Data protection

1. National rules implementing Directive 95/46/EC shall apply to the processing of personal data carried out in the Member States pursuant to this Regulation, provided that processing operations referred to in Article 3(2) of Directive 95/46/EC are not concerned.
2. Regulation (EC) No 45/2001 shall apply to the processing of personal data carried out by the Commission pursuant to this Regulation.

(RR) Article 79—Responsibilities of Member States regarding the processing of personal data in national insolvency registers

1. Each Member State shall communicate to the Commission the name of the natural or legal person, public authority, agency or any other body designated by national law to exercise the functions of controller in accordance with point (d) of Article 2 of Directive 95/46/EC, with a view to its publication on the European e-Justice Portal.
2. Member States shall ensure that the technical measures for ensuring the security of personal data processed in their national insolvency registers referred to in Article 24 are implemented.
3. Member States shall be responsible for verifying that the controller, designated by national law in accordance with point (d) of Article 2 of Directive 95/46/EC, ensures compliance with the principles of data quality, in particular the accuracy and the updating of data stored in national insolvency registers.
4. Member States shall be responsible, in accordance with Directive 95/46/EC, for the collection and storage of data in national databases and for decisions taken to make such data available in the interconnected register that can be consulted via the European e-Justice Portal.
5. As part of the information that should be provided to data subjects to enable them to exercise their rights, and in particular the right to the erasure of data, Member States shall inform data subjects of the accessibility period set for personal data stored in insolvency registers.

(RR) Article 80—Responsibilities of the Commission in connection with the processing of personal data

1. The Commission shall exercise the responsibilities of controller pursuant to Article 2(d) of Regulation (EC) No 45/2001 in accordance with its respective responsibilities defined in this Article.
2. The Commission shall define the necessary policies and apply the necessary technical solutions to fulfil its responsibilities within the scope of the function of controller.

3. The Commission shall implement the technical measures required to ensure the security of personal data while in transit, in particular the confidentiality and integrity of any transmission to and from the European e-Justice Portal.
4. The obligations of the Commission shall not affect the responsibilities of the Member States and other bodies for the content and operation of the interconnected national databases run by them.

(RR) Article 81—Information obligations

Without prejudice to the information to be given to data subjects in accordance with Articles 11 and 12 of Regulation (EC) No 45/2001, the Commission shall inform data subjects, by means of publication through the European e-Justice Portal, about its role in the processing of data and the purposes for which those data will be processed.

(RR) Article 82—Storage of personal data

As regards information from interconnected national databases, no personal data relating to data subjects shall be stored in the European e-Justice Portal. All such data shall be stored in the national databases operated by the Member States or other bodies.

(RR) Article 83—Access to personal data via the European e-Justice Portal

Personal data stored in the national insolvency registers referred to in Article 24 shall be accessible via the European e-Justice Portal for as long as they remain accessible under national law.

8.798 These provisions are entirely new and deal with data protection. This is a subject beyond the scope of this work and a specialist source on data protection should be consulted.

G. Chapter VII: Transitional and Final Provisions

(RR) Article 84—Applicability in time

1. The provisions of this Regulation shall apply only to insolvency proceedings opened after 26 June 2017. Acts committed by a debtor before that date shall continue to be governed by the law which was applicable to them at the time they were committed.
2. Notwithstanding Article 91 of this Regulation, Regulation (EC) No 1346/2000 shall continue to apply to insolvency proceedings which fall within the scope of that Regulation and which have been opened before 26 June 2017.

8.799 Article 84(1) RR provides that the RR will only apply to insolvency proceedings opened 'after' 26 June 2017. Article 84(2) RR provides that OR will continue to apply to insolvency proceedings within the scope of the OR and which were opened before 26 June 2017. This leaves the rather odd position that nothing on the face of this Article seems to be provided for any insolvency proceeding opened on 26 June 2017. However, it seems clear from Article 92 (which is dealt with below) that 'after' needs to be read as 'on or after', so that a proceeding opened on 26 June 2017 will be governed by the RR.

Article 84 RR provides that acts 'committed' by a debtor before 26 June 2017 will continue to be governed by the law which was applicable to them at the time they were committed. This appears to be in accord with the general principle of non-retroactivity. Again, the wording is odd, because it is not clear what law would apply to an act done by a debtor on 26 June 2017. However, the words 'after 26 June 2017' should in the light of Article 92 (which is dealt with below) be interpreted as 'on or after 26 June 2017'. **8.800**

(RR) Article 85—Relationship to Conventions

1. This Regulation replaces, in respect of the matters referred to therein, and as regards relations between Member States, the Conventions concluded between two or more Member States, in particular:
   (a) the Convention between Belgium and France on Jurisdiction and the Validity and Enforcement of Judgments, Arbitration Awards and Authentic Instruments, signed at Paris on 8 July 1899;
   (b) the Convention between Belgium and Austria on Bankruptcy, Winding-up, Arrangements, Compositions and Suspension of Payments (with Additional Protocol of 13 June 1973), signed at Brussels on 16 July 1969;
   (c) the Convention between Belgium and the Netherlands on Territorial Jurisdiction, Bankruptcy and the Validity and Enforcement of Judgments, Arbitration Awards and Authentic Instruments, signed at Brussels on 28 March 1925;
   (d) the Treaty between Germany and Austria on Bankruptcy, Winding-up, Arrangements and Compositions, signed at Vienna on 25 May 1979;
   (e) the Convention between France and Austria on Jurisdiction, Recognition and Enforcement of Judgments on Bankruptcy, signed at Vienna on 27 February 1979;
   (f) the Convention between France and Italy on the Enforcement of Judgments in Civil and Commercial Matters, signed at Rome on 3 June 1930;
   (g) the Convention between Italy and Austria on Bankruptcy, Winding-up, Arrangements and Compositions, signed at Rome on 12 July 1977;
   (h) the Convention between the Kingdom of the Netherlands and the Federal Republic of Germany on the Mutual Recognition and Enforcement of Judgments and other Enforceable Instruments in Civil and Commercial Matters, signed at The Hague on 30 August 1962;
   (i) the Convention between the United Kingdom and the Kingdom of Belgium providing for the Reciprocal Enforcement of Judgments in Civil and Commercial Matters, with Protocol, signed at Brussels on 2 May 1934;
   (j) the Convention between Denmark, Finland, Norway, Sweden and Iceland on Bankruptcy, signed at Copenhagen on 7 November 1933;

(k) the European Convention on Certain International Aspects of Bankruptcy, signed at Istanbul on 5 June 1990;

(l) the Convention between the Federative People's Republic of Yugoslavia and the Kingdom of Greece on the Mutual Recognition and Enforcement of Judgments, signed at Athens on 18 June 1959;

(m) the Agreement between the Federative People's Republic of Yugoslavia and the Republic of Austria on the Mutual Recognition and Enforcement of Arbitral Awards and Arbitral Settlements in Commercial Matters, signed at Belgrade on 18 March 1960;

(n) the Convention between the Federative People's Republic of Yugoslavia and the Italian Republic on Mutual Judicial Cooperation in Civil and Administrative Matters, signed at Rome on 3 December 1960;

(o) the Agreement between the Socialist Federative Republic of Yugoslavia and the Kingdom of Belgium on Judicial Cooperation in Civil and Commercial Matters, signed at Belgrade on 24 September 1971;

(p) the Convention between the Governments of Yugoslavia and France on the Recognition and Enforcement of Judgments in Civil and Commercial Matters, signed at Paris on 18 May 1971;

(q) the Agreement between the Czechoslovak Socialist Republic and the Hellenic Republic on Legal Aid in Civil and Criminal Matters, signed at Athens on 22 October 1980, still in force between the Czech Republic and Greece;

(r) the Agreement between the Czechoslovak Socialist Republic and the Republic of Cyprus on Legal Aid in Civil and Criminal Matters, signed at Nicosia on 23 April 1982, still in force between the Czech Republic and Cyprus;

(s) the Treaty between the Government of the Czechoslovak Socialist Republic and the Government of the Republic of France on Legal Aid and the Recognition and Enforcement of Judgments in Civil, Family and Commercial Matters, signed at Paris on 10 May 1984, still in force between the Czech Republic and France;

(t) the Treaty between the Czechoslovak Socialist Republic and the Italian Republic on Legal Aid in Civil and Criminal Matters, signed at Prague on 6 December 1985, still in force between the Czech Republic and Italy;

(u) the Agreement between the Republic of Latvia, the Republic of Estonia and the Republic of Lithuania on Legal Assistance and Legal Relationships, signed at Tallinn on 11 November 1992;

(v) the Agreement between Estonia and Poland on Granting Legal Aid and Legal Relations on Civil, Labour and Criminal Matters, signed at Tallinn on 27 November 1998;

(w) the Agreement between the Republic of Lithuania and the Republic of Poland on Legal Assistance and Legal Relations in Civil, Family, Labour and Criminal Matters, signed at Warsaw on 26 January 1993;

(x) the Convention between the Socialist Republic of Romania and the Hellenic Republic on legal assistance in civil and criminal matters and its Protocol, signed at Bucharest on 19 October 1972;

(y) the Convention between the Socialist Republic of Romania and the French Republic on legal assistance in civil and commercial matters, signed at Paris on 5 November 1974;

(z) the Agreement between the People's Republic of Bulgaria and the Hellenic Republic on Legal Assistance in Civil and Criminal Matters, signed at Athens on 10 April 1976;

(aa) the Agreement between the People's Republic of Bulgaria and the Republic of Cyprus on Legal Assistance in Civil and Criminal Matters, signed at Nicosia on 29 April 1983;

(ab) the Agreement between the Government of the People's Republic of Bulgaria and the Government of the French Republic on Mutual Legal Assistance in Civil Matters, signed at Sofia on 18 January 1989;

(ac) the Treaty between Romania and the Czech Republic on judicial assistance in civil matters, signed at Bucharest on 11 July 1994;

(ad) the Treaty between Romania and the Republic of Poland on legal assistance and legal relations in civil cases, signed at Bucharest on 15 May 1999

2. The Conventions referred to in paragraph 1 shall continue to have effect with regard to proceedings opened before the entry into force of Regulation (EC) No 1346/2000.

3. This Regulation shall not apply:

(a) in any Member State, to the extent that it is irreconcilable with the obligations arising in relation to bankruptcy from a convention concluded by that Member State with one or more third countries before the entry into force of Regulation (EC) No 1346/2000;

(b) in the United Kingdom of Great Britain and Northern Ireland, to the extent that is irreconcilable with the obligations arising in relation to bankruptcy and the winding-up of insolvent companies from any arrangements with the Commonwealth existing at the time Regulation (EC) No 1346/2000 entered into force.

The text of Article 85 is, apart from small adjustments referred to below, copied from Article 44 OR (as amended from time to time when new countries acceded) and should generally be made to the commentary on Article 44 OR above. **8.801**

There are slight adjustments in Article 85(2) and (3) RR as a result of the transition from the OR to the RR, but they do not alter the original effect of the OR. **8.802**

(RR) Article 86—Information on national and Union insolvency law

1. The Member States shall provide, within the framework of the European Judicial Network in civil and commercial matters established by Council Decision 2001/470/EC [footnote omitted]), and with a view to making the information available to the public, a short description of their national legislation and procedures relating to insolvency, in particular relating to the matters listed in Article 7(2).
2. The Member States shall update the information referred to in paragraph 1 regularly.
3. The Commission shall make information concerning this Regulation available to the public.

This is an entirely new provision requiring Member States to provide a short description of their national legislation and procedures relating to insolvency and in particular relating **8.803** to the matters listed in Article 7(2) RR, which refers in detail to the conditions for opening and closing insolvency proceedings and their conduct. Member States are required to update the information regularly. The provision of such information is with a view to making the information available to the public. Article 86(3) RR places the duty on the European Commission to make information concerning RR itself available to the public.

(RR) Article 87—Establishment of the interconnection of registers

> The Commission shall adopt implementing acts establishing the interconnection of insolvency registers as referred to in Article 25. Those implementing acts shall be adopted in accordance with the examination procedure referred to in Article 89(3).

8.804 This is a new provision requiring the European Commission to adopt implementing Acts establishing the interconnection of the national insolvency registers. Those implementing Acts are to be adopted in accordance with the 'examination' procedure referred to in Article 89(3) RR, which is dealt with below.

(RR) Article 88—Establishment and subsequent amendment of standard forms

> The Commission shall adopt implementing acts establishing and, where necessary, amending the forms referred to in Article 27(4), Articles 54 and 55 and Article 64(2). Those implementing acts shall be adopted in accordance with the advisory procedure referred to in Article 89(2).

8.805 This is a new provision requiring the European Commission to adopt implementing Acts establishing and, where necessary, amending the standard forms referred to in Articles 27(4), 54, 55, and 64(2) RR. These implementing Acts are to be adopted in accordance with the advisory procedure referred to in Article 89(2) RR, which is dealt with below.

(RR) Article 89—Committee procedure

> 1. The Commission shall be assisted by a committee. That committee shall be a committee within the meaning of Regulation (EU) No 182/2011.
> 2. Where reference is made to this paragraph, Article 4 of Regulation (EU) No 182/2011 shall apply.
> 3. Where reference is made to this paragraph, Article 5 of Regulation (EU) No 182/2011 shall apply.

8.806 Article 89 RR provides that the European Commission is to be assisted by a committee within the meaning of Regulation (EU) Number 182/2011 laying down rules and general principles concerning mechanisms for control by Member States of the Commission's exercise of implementing powers.

(RR) Article 90—Review clause

1. No later than 27 June 2027, and every 5 years thereafter, the Commission shall present to the European Parliament, the Council and the European Economic and Social Committee a report on the application of this Regulation. The report shall be accompanied where necessary by a proposal for adaptation of this Regulation.
2. No later than 27 June 2022, the Commission shall present to the European Parliament, the Council and the European Economic and Social Committee a report on the application of the group coordination proceedings. The report shall be accompanied where necessary by a proposal for adaptation of this Regulation.
3. No later than 1 January 2016, the Commission shall submit to the European Parliament, the Council and the European Economic and Social Committee a study on the cross-border issues in the area of directors' liability and disqualifications.
4. No later than 27 June 2020, the Commission shall submit to the European Parliament, the Council and the European Economic and Social Committee a study on the issue of abusive forum shopping.

Article 46 OR provided for reports to be prepared by the Commission on the application of the OR with any proposals for 'adaptation' of the OR. In the case of Article 90 RR, Article 90(1) RR provides that no later than 27 June 2027 and every five years thereafter the European Commission is to present a report on the application of the RR. It is to be accompanied where necessary by a proposal for 'adaptation' of the RR. **8.807**

In the case of group co-ordination proceedings in particular, a new type of procedure brought in by the RR, the European Commission is required to present a report no later than 27 June 2022. **8.808**

Article 90(3) RR requires that as soon as 1 January 2016 the European Commission is to submit a study on the cross-border issues in the area of directors' liability and disqualifications. **8.809**

Article 90(4) RR deals with a particular concern of the European Parliament, namely abusive forum shopping. A study on this subject is required to be presented by the European Commission no later than 27 June 2020. **8.810**

All the reports referred to are required to be presented to the European Parliament, the Council, and the European Economic and Social Committee. **8.811**

(RR) Article 91—Repeal

Regulation (EC) No 1346/2000 is repealed.

References to the repealed Regulation shall be construed as references to this Regulation and shall be read in accordance with the correlation table set out in Annex D to this Regulation.

This is necessarily a new provision, since it provides for the repeal of the OR. It has to be borne in mind however that pursuant to Article 84(2) RR the repealed OR is to continue to **8.812** apply to insolvency proceedings within the scope of the OR which had been opened before 26 June 2017.

8.813 There is a further helpful interpretational provision to the effect that references to the OR are to be construed as references to the RR and are to be read in accordance with the correlation table set out in Annex D to the RR. This is significant because it means that references in other legislation or in contracts are to be read as references to the equivalent provisions in the RR. Although this is not clearly spelt out, presumably this interpretational provision will not take effect until the RR itself takes effect, ie on 26 June 2017: see the commentary to Article 84 RR above.

(RR) Article 92—Entry into force

> This Regulation shall enter into force on the twentieth day following that of its publication in the Official Journal of the European Union.
>
> It shall apply from 26 June 2017, with the exception of:
> (a) Article 86, which shall apply from 26 June 2016;
> (b) Article 24(1), which shall apply from 26 June 2018; and
> (c) Article 25, which shall apply from 26 June 2019.

8.814 Article 92 RR provides that the RR is to enter into force on the 20th day following that of its publication in the Official Journal of the European Union. That publication took place on 5 June 2015.

8.815 Article 92 RR further provides that generally RR provisions will apply 'from 26 June 2017' with certain exceptions. The provision that it will apply 'from' 26 June 2017 suggests that the reading of Article 84(1) as if it read 'on or after 26 June 2017' is correct.

8.816 There are three exceptions to the application of the RR from 26 June 2017. Exception (a) is that Article 86 RR, which requires Member States to provide information by way of a short description of their national legislation and procedures relating to insolvency takes effect 'from 26 June 2016'. Exception (b) relates to Article 24(1) RR, which relates to the establishment of national insolvency registers by Member States and that provision is to apply 'from 26 June 2018'. Exception (c) relates to Article 25 RR, which relates to the Commission's obligation to establish a system for the interconnection of national insolvency registers and that provision is to apply 'from 26 June 2019'.

9

THE ONGOING POTENTIAL APPLICATION OF THE RR IN THE UK

A.	Introduction	9.01	D. Recognition of Foreign (EU) Proceedings in the UK—Recourse to the UNCITRAL Model Law on Cross-Border Insolvency	9.17
B.	The Continued Relevance of Tests from the RR as the Basis for Opening UK Insolvency Proceedings	9.07		
C.	The Continued Relevance of the RR for UK Insolvency Proceedings Opened Before the End of the Brexit Implementation Period	9.15	E. Reliance on Section 426 of the Insolvency Act 1986 and the Common Law	9.33

A. Introduction

With Brexit, the UK ended its membership of the EU. The process led to a formal UK/EU withdrawal agreement[1] and the enactment in the UK of the European Union (Withdrawal Agreement) Act 2020. The UK's membership of the EU formally came to an end on 31 January 2020. There followed a Brexit transition period (the 'Transition Period'), which ended at 11pm GMT on 31 December 2020. This was followed by the coming into force of a Trade and Co-operation Agreement between the UK and EU on 1 January 2021.[2] The Trade and Co-operation Agreement is largely bereft of provisions on judicial co-operation in civil matters and, in particular, in relation to insolvency proceedings. **9.01**

Under the Insolvency (Amendment) (EU Exit) Regulations 2019 (SI 2019/46), which came into force on 31 December 2020, as amended by the Insolvency (Amendment) (EU Exit) (No 2) Regulations 2019 (SI 2019/1459), and the Insolvency (Amendment) (EU Exit) Regulations 2020 (SI 2020/647), the RR (renamed the Retained Recast Regulation (the 'Retained RR')) continues to be applicable to insolvency proceedings opened prior to the end of the Transition Period; and, after the end of the Transition Period, UK law has retained as a basis for its jurisdiction the elements of the RR which provide for a debtor to **9.02**

---

[1] Agreement on the withdrawal of the United Kingdom of Great Britain and Northern Ireland from the European Union and the European Atomic Energy Community. The text of the withdrawal agreement is at <https://www.gov.uk/government/publications/new-withdrawal-agreement-and-political-declaration>.
[2] See <https://ec.europa.eu/info/relations-united-kingdom/eu-uk-trade-and-cooperation-agreement_en>.

be put into insolvency proceedings if it has its COMI in the UK or its COMI is in an EU Member State and there is an establishment in the UK.[3]

9.03 The post-Brexit application of the RR in the UK as set out above was referred to in *Re Investin Quay House Ltd*.[4] In that case, the fact that the winding up petition was presented prior to the end of the Transition Period following the UK's withdrawal from the EU did not mean that the pre-Brexit regime under the RR applied.[5] This was because the issue of the petition does not constitute 'the time of the opening of proceedings' under Article 2(8) of the RR (which is in the same terms as Article 2(f) of the OR). Under Article 2(8), the time of the opening of the proceedings means 'the time at which the judgment opening insolvency proceedings becomes effective, regardless of whether the judgment is final or not'.

9.04 Before Brexit, the UK had three main statutory vehicles for international/cross-border cooperation in insolvency matters: (1) the RR (supplemented by sector-specific instruments); (2) the UNCITRAL Model Law on Cross-Border Insolvency (the 'Model Law'), implemented in the UK by the Cross-Border Insolvency Regulations[6] (the 'CBIR'); and (3) section 426 of the Insolvency Act 1986. Additionally, there was the common law, to the extent that it had not been superseded in relation to particular matters.

9.05 The logic of Brexit suggested that the RR should altogether cease to have any application or relevance as far as the UK was concerned and that the UK would then prima facie have to rely upon the Model Law/CBIR regime, possibly supplemented by the common law, to govern its relations with EU Member States in respect of insolvency matters. However, the RR is a much more comprehensive legal instrument than the Model Law/CBIR[7] and the UK has adopted a more nuanced approach in which aspects of the RR have been retained.[8]

9.06 This chapter will consider the new jurisdictional tests from the RR preserved in UK law as the basis for opening insolvency proceedings in the UK. It will then consider the RR's continued relevance where main insolvency proceedings had already been opened before Brexit. After that, it considers the recognition of EU proceedings in the UK under the Model Law and common law rules.

---

[3] Article 67(3)(c) of the EU/UK Withdrawal Agreement: 'Regulation (EU) 2015/848 of the European Parliament and of the Council shall apply to insolvency proceedings, and actions referred to in Article 6(1) of that Regulation, provided that the main proceedings were opened before the end of the transition period'.
[4] [2021] EWHC 2371 (Ch), paras 28–30.
[5] See *Re Merdeco (Cardiff) Ltd* [2021] EWHC 386 (Ch), paras 50–69.
[6] SI 2006/1030.
[7] Currently, only Greece, Poland, Romania, and Slovenia of the remaining members of the EU are on the list maintained by UNCITRAL of countries that have adopted the Model Law—see <http://www.uncitral.org/uncitral/en/uncitral_texts/insolvency/1997Model_status.html>.
[8] One possible option would have been for the UK, post-Brexit, to maintain the provisions of the RR in force insofar as they apply to the UK. However, that would have meant the UK automatically recognizing insolvency proceedings opened in EU Member States and judgments handed down in the course of insolvency proceedings, whereas EU Member States would not necessarily recognize similar proceedings and judgments emanating from the UK.

B. The Continued Relevance of Tests from the RR as the Basis for Opening UK Insolvency Proceedings

The principal relevance of the RR is that, in relation to proceedings opened since 1 January 2021, if a debtor's COMI is in England or Wales, it provides a basis for the court's jurisdiction. UK insolvency proceedings may now be opened where the proceedings are opened for the purposes of rescue, adjustment of debt, reorganization, or liquidation and the centre of the debtor's main interests (COMI) is either in the UK; or in an EU Member State other than Denmark[9] and there is an establishment in the UK. These grounds derive from the Retained RR and are in addition to any grounds for jurisdiction to open insolvency proceedings which apply in the laws of any part of the UK. **9.07**

This new rule applies to the following proceedings: winding up by or subject to the supervision of the court; creditors' voluntary winding up with confirmation by the court; administration, including appointments made by filing prescribed documents with the court; and voluntary arrangements under insolvency legislation. **9.08**

It does not, however, apply to insolvency proceedings that concern insurance undertakings, credit institutions, investment firms and other firms, institutions and undertakings to the extent that they are covered by the Credit Institutions (Reorganisation and Winding up) Regulations 2004 or collective investment undertakings. **9.09**

For the purpose of the new rule, references to the COMI have the same meaning as in Article 3 of the Retained RR and 'establishment' has the same meaning as in Article 2(10) of the Retained RR. **9.10**

The new rule to a large extent duplicates the existing UK jurisdictional grounds. If a company registered in an EU Member State has its COMI or an establishment in the UK, then especially if some other factors exist, the company is likely to be deemed to be sufficiently connected with the UK to warrant the opening of UK insolvency proceedings as an unregistered company under section 221 or 225 of the Insolvency Act 1986. If the assertion of UK jurisdiction is founded specifically on 'centre of main interests' or 'establishment' factors, this may facilitate however, more straightforward recognition and enforcement of UK proceedings in EU Member States, since the latter are more familiar with these factors as grounds for jurisdiction in cross-border cases; hence the legislative amendments specifically enunciating these jurisdictional heads in a post-Brexit scenario.[10] The same extension or duplication of jurisdiction also applies in the case of individual bankruptcy. **9.11**

Before Brexit, the jurisdiction of the English courts to open bankruptcy and other individual insolvency proceedings in respect of a debtor was substantially amended and curtailed by the RR. These limitations have now been removed. The jurisdiction of the English courts is now unfettered in this respect but the proceedings must still consider 'benefit' to the debtor and creditors and other relevant factors. **9.12**

---

[9] Denmark is not bound by or subject to the application of the RR—see recital 88. Accordingly, there was the exclusion of Denmark in the Insolvency (Amendment) (EU Exit Regulations) 2019, SI 2019/146, which retains and modifies some elements of the RR in UK law.

[10] See also Insolvency Rules 2016 (as amended) r 1.7 and for examples in various types of insolvency proceedings see r 2.31, 2.14(2A), 3.3(2)(h), 7.51(n), 8.3(q), and 10.49(2)(f).

9.13 For the purposes of the Retained RR, there are special definitions of the expressions COMI and 'establishment'. Sections 265(4) and (5) of the amended Insolvency Act 1986 now reference these definitions. In applying the jurisdictional tests based on COMI or 'establishment', the UK courts will no doubt be influenced by the decisions of national courts in the EU and the CJEU but such decisions are not binding on the UK courts.

9.14 Moreover, in exercising their jurisdiction, UK courts are not subject to the express territorial and geographical bounds of the RR. They could make a bankruptcy order on either COMI or 'establishment' grounds and irrespective of whether the order is likely to be recognized across the EU. However, it is likely that the need and likelihood of cross-border recognition may be particular factors in determining whether, and to what extent, this jurisdictional freedom is exercised by the English courts.

C. The Continued Relevance of the RR for UK Insolvency Proceedings Opened Before the End of the Brexit Implementation Period

9.15 As already observed, unless there was some replacement treaty or other bilateral arrangements, the logic of Brexit suggests that the RR should altogether have ceased to apply or be relevant in the UK. The UK would then rely on the Model Law/CBIR regime, possibly supplemented by the common law, to govern its relations with EU Member States in respect of insolvency matters. In a statement in the UK Government technical guidance on 'Handling civil cases that involve EU countries if there's no Brexit deal', the UK government explained that:

> If the UK continued to apply the [EU] rules unilaterally after exit, the UK's status as a third country would mean that EU countries would not consider the UK to be covered by these rules. As a result, UK citizens, businesses and families would not benefit from these rules. Because of this loss of reciprocity, in the event of a no deal scenario, we would repeal most of the existing civil judicial cooperation rules and instead use the domestic rules which each UK legal system currently applies in relation to non-EU countries. In some specific areas ... we would retain elements of the current EU rules, where they either do not rely on reciprocity to operate or where they currently form the basis for our existing domestic or international rules.[11]

9.16 The Insolvency (Amendment) (EU Exit) Regulations 2019[12] largely deprived the RR of continued force and effect in the UK. The UK government however placed great store in safeguarding legitimate expectations and the security of transactions. Therefore, the RR continues to apply where main insolvency proceedings have been opened before the end of the Transition Period. In other words, the existing EU rules will still apply to establishment of jurisdiction, and recognition and enforcement of any resulting judicial decision whether

---

[11] See <https://www.parliament.uk/globalassets/documents/lords-committees/eu-justice-subcommittee/justiceforfamilies/attachment-2--cjc--insolvency---published.pdf> (March 2019) at p 2.

[12] See also, SI 2019/146. Post-Brexit, the territorial limits on the court's winding up jurisdiction under section 117(7) Insolvency Act 1986 are removed. Moreover, there is now explicit authority in the UK to wind up a company that has either its COMI, or an establishment, in the UK.

or not the decision has been handed down before, or after, the expiry of this period. This exception for pending proceedings means that the RR will have a long tail since insolvency proceedings can of course continue for an extended period.

D. Recognition of Foreign (EU) Proceedings in the UK— Recourse to the UNCITRAL Model Law on Cross-Border Insolvency

Post-Brexit,[13] insolvency practitioners in the remaining EU Member States may apply for recognition of the foreign insolvency proceeding in question in the UK courts under the Model Law,[14] which the UK implemented through the CBIR. The process of obtaining recognition is generally relatively straightforward once the not very onerous procedural requirements have been observed. However, the fact that it is necessary to apply to the court as distinct from automatic recognition under the RR adds to the delay and expense. **9.17**

Substantively, the RR is a much more comprehensive legal instrument than the Model Law. The fact that the Model Law did not go as far as the Insolvency Proceedings Regulation is understandable.[15] The Insolvency Proceedings Regulation is an EU legal instrument and the EU Member States have agreed to pool their sovereignty and to work towards an ever closer Union.[16] In contrast, UNCITRAL is a United Nations organ in which the link between member states is much more diffuse. The differences between the Insolvency Proceedings Regulation and the Model Law regime should be highlighted. **9.18**

The Model Law gives foreign insolvency practitioners access to local courts; provides for the recognition of foreign insolvency proceedings; deals with some of the consequences of recognition and provides for the co-ordination of insolvency proceedings opened in different States. It does not, however, directly allocate jurisdiction to open insolvency proceedings; nor does it deal with choice of law issues: it does not purport to say which law should govern insolvency proceedings that are opened in a particular State. Moreover, while recognition of insolvency proceedings opened in another EU Member State is automatic under the Insolvency Regulation, under the Model Law it is dependent on an application to the court. By virtue of the Insolvency Proceedings Regulation, insolvency proceedings have the same effect in other EU Member States as they have in the law of the insolvency forum,[17] whereas under the Model Law the consequences of recognition depend on the law of the recognizing State. **9.19**

The Model Law does deploy the same concepts of COMI and establishment that underpin the Insolvency Proceedings Regulation. In *Re Stanford International Bank Ltd*,[18] the EU **9.20**

---

[13] See para 5.82 et seq above.
[14] <https://uncitral.un.org/en/texts/insolvency/modellaw/cross-border_insolvency>. For a list of countries that have adopted the Model Law, see <https://uncitral.un.org/en/texts/insolvency/modellaw/cross-border_insolvency/status>.
[15] For comparisons between the Model Law and the Insolvency Proceedings Regulation, see Reinhard Bork, 'The European Insolvency Regulation and the UNCITRAL Model Law on Cross-Border Insolvency' (2017) 26 International Insolvency Review 246.
[16] See Art 1 of the Treaty on European Union, which refers to the Treaty marking 'a new stage in the process of creating an ever closer union among the peoples of Europe'.
[17] Articles 19, 20, and 32.
[18] [2010] EWCA Civ 137, [2011] Ch 33, para 54.

case law on the meaning of COMI was used in England in a Model Law context. Also, in *Re Videology Ltd*, Snowden J said that 'for so long as the UK remains a party to the Recast EIR, I can see no obvious basis upon which I should adopt any different approach in relation to the concept of COMI under the CBIR/Model Law and the Recast EIR'.[19] However, there are differences of detail between the two instruments on the definition of an 'establishment'.[20]

9.21 The effect of recognition under the Model Law is also more limited than that under the Insolvency Proceedings Regulation. The basic rule under the Insolvency Proceedings Regulation is that insolvency proceedings have the same effect throughout the EU as they have in the Member State of opening whereas this is not the case under the Model Law regime. If foreign proceedings are recognized as 'main' proceedings under the Model Law, then certain consequences follow. First, on recognition there is a stay on proceedings against the debtor's assets but legal proceedings may still be instituted to prevent an action from becoming statute-barred[21] and the stay is subject to the other exceptions found in domestic insolvency law. The right of a qualified party to request the opening of domestic insolvency proceedings is also preserved though the effect of such proceedings is confined to assets located in the recognizing State. Second, there is a stay on executions against the debtor's assets. Third, any right of the debtor to transfer, encumber, or otherwise dispose of any assets is suspended.

9.22 Article 20(2) CBIR provides that the stay is to have 'the same in scope and effect' as if the debtor had been the subject of a winding-up order under the Insolvency Act 1986. It is specifically stated, however, that the stay does not affect rights to enforce security, rights to repossess goods under hire-purchase and retention of title agreements, rights of set-off, and rights pertaining to financial market transactions to the extent that all these rights would be exercisable in a UK context. Where however, the foreign proceedings are rescue or reorganization proceedings rather than liquidation proceedings, the foreign representative at the time of applying for recognition of the foreign proceedings can apply for the effects of the stay to be modified and more appropriate relief to be granted under Article 21. This Article gives the court discretion on what relief to grant when foreign non-main proceedings are recognized; here there are no prima facie consequences following from recognition. Article 21 also confers discretion to grant additional relief when foreign proceedings are recognized as main proceedings.[22] The Article 21 discretion has been exercised in many UK Model Law recognition cases, including in *Re Pan Oceanic Maritime Inc*[23] where the more extensive stay associated with UK administration proceedings that bars the enforcement of security was granted rather than the limited liquidation stay.

9.23 The discretionary relief available under Article 21 can take the form amongst other things of: (1) providing for the examination of witnesses, the taking of evidence or the delivery

---

[19] [2018] EWHC 2186 (Ch), para 28.
[20] Contrast Art 2(c) Sch 1 CBIR with Art 2(10) RR. In the CBIR context 'establishment' is defined as meaning 'any place of operations where the debtor carries out a non-transitory economic activity with human means and assets or services'. In the Insolvency Regulation context it is defined as meaning 'any place of operations where a debtor carries out or has carried out in the 3-month period prior to the request to open main insolvency proceedings a non-transitory economic activity with human means and assets'. In other words, there is a 'lock back' period under the Insolvency Regulation and the absence of any specific reference to 'services'.
[21] Article 20(3) of the Model Law and Cross Border Insolvency Regulations, Sch 1, Art 20(4).
[22] Articles 20(6) and 21, SI 2006/1030, Sch 1, Cross-Border Insolvency Regulations 2006.
[23] [2010] EWHC 1734 (Ch).

of information concerning the debtor's assets, affairs, rights, obligations, or liabilities; (2) entrusting the administration or realization of all or part of the debtor's assets to the foreign representative or another person designated by the court; (3) extending interim relief; and (4) granting any further relief that might be available to an insolvency office holder in domestic proceedings.

However, Article 21[24] does not explicitly allow a UK court to apply foreign insolvency law when granting recognition. The application of foreign insolvency law was held also not to be impliedly permitted in *Re Pan Ocean Co Ltd*[25] and *Bakhshiyeva v Sberbank of Russia*,[26] in which *Re Pan Ocean* was applied.

9.24

In *Re Pan Ocean*, Morgan J rejected the argument for a broad interpretation of the expression 'any appropriate relief' in Article 21 of the Model Law that would permit the application of foreign insolvency law. He considered the preliminary materials leading to the elaboration of the Model Law and said it was not intended that 'any appropriate relief' should allow a recognizing court to grant relief that it could not grant in relation to a domestic insolvency. The court declined to follow the US decision in *Re Condor Insurance Co Ltd*[27] that permitted the application of foreign insolvency law by a recognizing court in certain circumstances. It suggested that the legislative context and legislative history were different in the US and the US court may have misinterpreted the background negotiations that led to the Model Law. Reference was also made to the decision of the UK Supreme Court in *Rubin v Eurofinance SA* where Lord Collins said that the Model Law provided 'the type of relief that would be available in the case of a domestic insolvency'.[28] *Rubin* supported the view that while Art 21 should be given a wide interpretation, the relief available was essentially of a procedural nature.[29]

9.25

In *Pan Ocean*, the court refused to give effect to provisions of Korean insolvency law that allowed contractual termination clauses under an English law governed contract to be overridden. Morgan J said:[30]

9.26

> In some cases, it can be argued that anyone who does business with a foreign company which might thereafter enter a process of insolvency, governed by the insolvency law of its country of registration, should expect that the insolvency will be governed by that law ... However, in the present case, the parties had deliberately chosen English law as the law of the contract. Whereas the parties might have expected that a Korean court would

---

[24] The UK Insolvency Service has consulted on whether the discretionary relief available under Article 21 should be expressly amended to include reference to the implementation of an insolvency related judgment – see 'Implementation of two UNCITRAL Model Laws on Insolvency Consultation' (7 July 2022) and available at <https://www.gov.uk/government/consultations/implementation-of-two-uncitral-model-laws-on-insolvency/implementation-of-two-uncitral-model-laws-on-insolvency-consultation>.
[25] [2014] EWHC 2124 (Ch), [2014] Bus LR 1041.
[26] [2018] EWCA Civ 2802, [2019] 1 BCLC 1. The case is also known *as Re OJSC International Bank of Azerbaijan*.
[27] (2010) 601 F 3d 319.
[28] [2012] UKSC 46, [2013] 1 AC 236, para 143.
[29] For criticism see Jay Lawrence Westbrook, 'Ian Fletcher and the Internationalist Principle' (2015) 3 Nottingham Insolvency and Business Law E-Journal 565: 'Despite our high and continuing respect for the British courts, many of us on the west side of the Atlantic have been distressed by In re Rubin and its progeny'. See also Jay Lawrence Westbrook, 'Interpretation Internationale' (2015) 87 Temple Law Review 739.
[30] [2014] EWHC 2124 (Ch), [2014] Bus LR 1041, para 112. Under the Corporate Insolvency and Governance Act 2020 the provisions of UK insolvency law have now been brought more into line with the relevant provisions of Korean insolvency law on contractual termination clauses that were considered in *Pan Ocean*.

apply Korean insolvency law to the insolvency of the company, they might have been very surprised to find that an English court would apply Korean insolvency law to the substantive rights of the parties under a contract which they had agreed should be governed by English law.

9.27 That analysis, which it is submitted is correct, was carried a stage further in *Bakhshiyeva v Sberbank of Russia*[31] where it was held that the Model Law could not be used to undermine the long-established principle that the discharge of a debt under foreign bankruptcy or restructuring law will not be given effect in the UK if the contract creating the debt is governed by English law.[32] This is the so-called rule in *Gibbs v La Société Industrielle et Commerciale des Métaux*.[33] In that case, it was held that the foreign bankruptcy law was irrelevant because it was 'not a law of the country to which the contract belongs, or one by which the contracting parties can be taken to have agreed to be bound; it is the law of another country by which they have not agreed to be bound'.[34] The principle has been acknowledged by the Privy Council in *New Zealand Loan and Mercantile Agency Company v Morrison*;[35] by the House of Lords in *National Bank of Greece and Athens v Metliss*[36] and most recently by the UK Supreme Court in *Goldman Sachs International v Novo Banco SA*.[37] In the latter case, Lord Sumption said:[38]

> The rescue of failing financial institutions commonly involves measures affecting the rights of their creditors and other third parties. Depending on the law under which the rescue is being carried out, these measures may include the suspension of payments, the writing down of liabilities, moratoria on their enforcement, and transfers of assets and liabilities to other institutions. At common law measures of this kind taken under a foreign law have only limited effect on contractual liabilities governed by English law. This is because the discharge or modification of a contractual liability is treated in English law as being governed only by its proper law, so that measures taken under another law, such as that of a contracting party's domicile, are normally disregarded....

---

[31] [2018] EWCA Civ 2802, [2019] 1 BCLC 1.
[32] [2018] EWCA Civ 2802, para 95. The court also drew a distinction between liquidation and restructuring proceedings. See however, the more recent comments of the Privy Council in *UBS AG New York v Fairfield Sentry Ltd* [2019] UKPC 20 which arguably point in a different direction. The court said at para 14: 'In any event, it is by no means clear that incorporation of the UNCITRAL Model Law would disincline, let alone forbid, a court from applying a foreign insolvency law. 'It appears to the Board that the United States Courts have interpreted the relevant statutory provisions as permitting the application of foreign insolvency law in both their now-superseded section 304 of the US Bankruptcy Code (*In re Metzeler* 78 BR 674, 677 (Bkrtcy SDNY 1987) and chapter 15 of the US Bankruptcy Code, which is based on the Model Law ... *In re Atlas Shipping A/S* 404 BR 726, (April 27 2009, SDNY), *In re Condor Insurance Ltd* 601 F 3d 319 (March 17 2010, 5th Cir), and *In re Hellas Telecommunications II* 535 BR 543, 566–67 (Bkrtcy SDNY 2015)).' In *Re Agrokor dd* 591 BR 163 (Bankr SDNY 2018), the US Bankruptcy Court for the Southern District of New York, having previously entered an order recognizing a Croatian company's restructuring proceeding under chapter 15 of the US Bankruptcy Code, recognized and enforced a settlement agreement that restructured English-law debt, even though enforcement of the settlement agreement would represent a refusal to extend comity to the rule in *Gibbs*. The rule in *Gibbs* has also been departed from in Singapore, see *Re Pacific Andes Resources Development Ltd* [2016] SGHC 210, in particular at paras 46–52.
[33] (1890) 25 QBD 399.
[34] (1890) 25 QBD 399 at 406.
[35] [1898] AC 349.
[36] [1958] AC 509. See also the approval of the *Gibbs* principle by Lord Hope in Joint *Administrators of Heritable Bank plc v Winding up Board of Landsbanki Islands HF* [2013] UKSC 13, [2013] 1 WLR 725, para 44. Note also the statement by Lord Hoffmann in *Wight v Eckhardt Marine GmbH* [2003] UKPC 37, [2004] 1 AC 147, para 11 that the question whether an obligation has been extinguished is governed by its proper law.
[37] [2018] UKSC 34, [2018] 1 WLR 3683.
[38] Paragraph 12.

D. RECOGNITION OF FOREIGN (EU) PROCEEDINGS IN THE UK

The *Gibbs* rule survived an attack in *Global Distressed Alpha Fund v PT Bakrie*,[39] where it was held that the movement towards 'universalism' in insolvency proceedings did not allow a first instance judge to disregard the established doctrine. In *Bakrie*,[40] the court considered whether the discharge of an English law governed debt under Indonesian bankruptcy and restructuring law would be given effect in the UK on the basis of the principle of universality since the debtor was an Indonesian company with its business operations based in Indonesia. While the court rejected this argument, it did refer to various criticisms of the *Gibbs* principle, in particular that while a debt governed by English law will not be discharged by a foreign bankruptcy, the debtor's movable assets situated in England are taken to have vested in the foreign trustee in bankruptcy. The debtor remains liable to pay its debts but has been deprived of the means that enable this to be done. Furthermore, it was likely that the debtor's creditors would have foreseen the possibility that the restructuring of the Indonesian debts might take place in Indonesia. This hypothesis suggests that recognition of the Indonesian bankruptcy discharge would not be unjust. **9.28**

In *Bakhshiyeva*,[41] the court rejected an attempt to sidestep the *Gibbs* principle through the grant of a permanent stay under the discretionary relief provisions in Article 21 of the Model Law. It was held that, when recognizing foreign insolvency proceedings, the court did not have the power to grant a permanent stay or moratorium that prevented creditors from exercising their rights under a contract that was governed by English law. The *Gibbs* rule still applied. It was held that to make such an order would amount to varying or discharging substantive rights by the expedient of granting procedural relief. This course of action had no legislative authorization. If foreign insolvency or restructuring law purported to modify the English law governed rights and obligations of creditors without their consent or participation in the proceedings, then the English courts would not grant a permanent stay under the CBIR that would have the effect of giving effect to the foreign proceedings and restraining enforcement of the rights still enjoyed under English law. **9.29**

The position is, however, different under the Insolvency Proceedings Regulation. What is now Article 7(2) of the RR states that the law of the State of the opening of proceedings shall determine the conditions for the opening of those proceedings, their conduct and their closure. The provision then sets out a non-exhaustive list of matters that are specifically referred to the law governing the opening of the proceedings. **9.30**

These matters are both substantive and procedural in nature. They include: **9.31**

'(g) the claims which are to be lodged against the debtor's estate and the treatment of claims arising after the opening of insolvency proceedings;
(h) the rules governing the lodging, verification and admission of claims;
(i) the rules governing the distribution of proceeds from the realisation of assets, the ranking of claims and the rights of creditors who have obtained partial satisfaction after the opening of insolvency proceedings by virtue of a right in rem or through a set-off;
(j) the conditions for and the effects of closure of insolvency proceedings, in particular by composition;
(k) creditors' rights after the closure of insolvency proceedings.'

---

[39] [2011] EWHC 256 (Comm), [2011] 1 WLR 2038.
[40] *Global Distressed Alpha Fund v PT Bakrie Investindo* [2011] EWHC 256 (Comm), [2011] 1 WLR 2038.
[41] [2018] EWCA Civ 2802, [2019] 1 BCLC 1 affirming [2018] EWHC 59 (Ch).

9.32 The ECJ decision in Case C-594/14 *Kornhaas v Dithmar*[42] gives an expansive interpretation to Article 7 but there is no need for an expansive interpretation.[43] On a reasonable construction of the words used in the provision, in particular the language quoted above, the modification of English law governed obligations under insolvency proceedings opened in EU Member States would be automatically recognized and implemented throughout the EU (including the UK pre-Brexit) pursuant to the Insolvency Proceedings Regulation. This conclusion was reached in the UK in *Bank of Baroda v Maniar*.[44] The court took the view that the effect of the Insolvency Proceedings Regulation was to trump the *Gibbs* rule. It cited a leading text[45] to the effect that where main insolvency proceedings in another EU Member State are closed and the closure has, under the law of that State, the effect of discharging the debtor, that discharge must be recognized in the UK even if it is not an effective discharge under the law applicable to the contract which in this case, was English law.[46]

E. Reliance on Section 426 of the Insolvency Act 1986 and the Common Law

9.33 Notwithstanding the legislative implementation of the Model law, section 426 Insolvency Act 1986 remains on the UK statute books. It enables courts to respond favourably to requests for assistance from courts exercising insolvency jurisdiction in certain designated foreign States and territories. The list of designated countries is, however, quite circumscribed and does not include, for instance, the US although it does include Australia.[47] It is presently confined to certain common law countries—certain ex-colonies and dependencies—and the Republic of Ireland, which is the only EU Member State designated.

9.34 The request may seek the application of either UK or the relevant foreign insolvency law.[48] The UK courts are generally guided by the terms of the request but are not obliged to give assistance whenever it is requested. While the statute appears to lay down an obligation to lend assistance to the requesting foreign court, the Court of Appeal has confirmed in *Hughes v Hannover Ruckversicherungs AG*[49] that the court enjoys a continued discretion

---

[42] CJEU, 10 December 2015, C-594/14, ECLI:EU:C:2015:806.
[43] See also the comments of AG Bobek, 9 June 2016, *ENEFI v DGRFP*, C-212/15, ECLI:EU:C:2016:427, on the width of what is now Art 7.
[44] [2019] EWHC 2463 (Comm).
[45] *Dicey, Morris and Collins on the Conflict of Laws* (15th edn, 2012) at para 31–114.
[46] The court declined to follow the more restricted approach suggested by Knowles J in *Edgeworth Capital Luxembourg Sarl v Maud* [2015] EWHC 3464 (Comm). While he did not find it necessary to reach a definitive conclusion on the issue, Knowles J seemed sympathetic to the notion that a debt arising under a contract governed by English law was not capable of being discharged by insolvency proceedings in a foreign jurisdiction that were commenced under the Insolvency Regulation.
[47] For the designated list see Co-operation of Insolvency Courts (Designation of Relevant Countries and Territories) Order 1986, SI 1986/2123, as amended by SI 1996/253 and SI 1998/2766.
[48] See also *UBS AG New York v Fairfield Sentry Ltd* [2019] UKPC 20 where Lord Hodge observed at para 15 that it was 'not uncommon for the courts in one country to apply the insolvency laws of another when giving assistance to the latter country'.
[49] [1997] BCC 921. It was said at 938: 'The obligation to assist is imposed on a court, not some executive agency. It would in my view require very clear words to justify a conclusion that the court in England was not intended by Parliament to perform its normal function of seeking to do justice in accordance with the law. There is no such indication.'

E. RELIANCE ON SECTION 426 INSOLVENCY ACT 1986 AND THE COMMON LAW

and may reject the request for assistance although '[t]he particular assistance requested should be given unless there is some good reason for not doing so'.[50] In *Hughes* itself, the request was actually turned down because the circumstances had changed materially since the date of the request.

9.35 An English court under section 426 may provide any form of assistance comparable with that given in English insolvency proceedings, whether the assistance takes the form of an order under the Insolvency Act 1986 or pursuant to the court's general equitable jurisdiction. The available forms of assistance include an order for examination of a company officer pursuant to section 236 Insolvency Act 1986; an injunction to restrain the institution or continuation of proceedings against the debtor company; a declaration recognizing the right and title of a foreign representative to assets; and the appointment of a receiver over the company's assets within the jurisdiction. In *Centaur Litigation SPC v Terrill*,[51] the assistance granted to the Cayman court took the form of a worldwide freezing order in respect of the assets of a director of the debtor company who may have been implicated in wrongdoing.

9.36 The concept of common law judicial assistance in respect of cross-border insolvency proceedings has been developed in recent years by the UK Supreme Court[52] and the Privy Council.[53] A principle of 'modified universalism' has been enunciated under which insolvency proceedings opened in a debtor's 'home' jurisdiction should be recognized and given effect in other countries throughout the world. Insofar as possible, the courts should try to implement a single scheme of distribution applicable to all the debtor's assets. The universality or otherwise of insolvency proceedings was discussed by the Privy Council in *Cambridge Gas Transport Corporation v Official Committee of Unsecured Creditors (of Navigator Holdings Plc)*[54] where Lord Hoffmann said:[55]

> The English common law has traditionally taken the view that fairness between creditors requires that, ideally, bankruptcy proceedings should have universal application. There should be a single bankruptcy in which all creditors are entitled and required to prove. No one should have an advantage because he happens to live in a jurisdiction where more of the assets or fewer of the creditors are situated.

9.37 However, more recent decisions however, have acknowledged the boundaries of judicial creativity and common law judicial assistance stating that any assistance given is subject to local law and public policy and cannot be used to undermine or usurp local

---

[50] The court, however, in *Hughes* did stress that the request could not be conclusive as to the manner in which the discretion of the court should be exercised.
[51] [2015] EWHC 3420 (Ch). Norris J said at para 28 that s 426(5) undoubtedly confers a discretion on the court whose assistance is requested but in this case the discretion was exercised in favour of giving assistance.
[52] *Re HIH Casualty and General Insurance Ltd* [2008] UKHL 21, [2008] 1 WLR 852.
[53] *Cambridge Gas Transport Corporation v Official Committee of Unsecured Creditors (of Navigator Holdings Plc)* [2006] UKPC 26, [2007] 1 AC 508. The Judicial Committee of the Privy Council has appellate jurisdiction in relation to certain UK overseas territories and ex-colonies and dependencies, principally in the Caribbean; see <www.jcpc.org>.
[54] [2006] UKPC 26, [2007] 1 AC 508. See also Lord Hoffmann in *Re HIH Casualty and General Insurance Ltd* [2008] UKHL 21, [2008] 1 WLR 852 at para 7 referring to the principle of modified universalism as the 'golden thread' running through English cross-border insolvency law since the eighteenth century and in the *Cambridge Gas* case referring to it as an 'aspiration' at para 17.
[55] At para 16 of the judgment.

law-making.[56] The leading decision is that of the Privy Council in *Singularis Holdings v Pricewaterhouse Coopers*.[57] It was held that while under the principle of 'modified universalism', the court had a common law power to assist foreign insolvency proceedings, the exercise of the power was subject to the constraints of local law and local policy norms. The fact that local law might permit local liquidators to do certain things in the case of a domestic insolvency did not necessarily mean that a foreign liquidator could do the same, or equivalent things, in the absence of statutory authorization.

9.38 In *Rubin*[58] the UK Supreme Court by a four to one majority overturned an English Court of Appeal decision that a monetary default judgment given in US bankruptcy proceedings could be enforced in England. This was the case even though it could not have been enforced if it had been given in the ordinary US courts of law because the defendant was not considered to be 'present' in the US nor had it submitted to the jurisdiction of the US courts.

9.39 The Court of Appeal had accepted as a general principle of private international law that insolvency law, whether applying to individuals or to corporate entities, should be unitary and universal. In its view, therefore, there should be unitary insolvency proceedings in a court of the insolvent's domicile that should receive worldwide recognition and also apply to all the insolvent's assets. It held that the concept of insolvency proceedings as a *sui generis* category of private international law included transactional avoidance mechanisms. Avoidance proceedings were said to be central to the collective enforcement regime in insolvency and were governed by the special insolvency rules.

9.40 However, the UK Supreme Court held the Court of Appeal decision was wrong because, in the Supreme Court's view, it was not an incremental development of existing principles but rather a radical departure from substantially settled law. It said that a change in the settled law governing the recognition and enforcement of judgments had all the hallmarks of legislation, and was a matter for legislative decision rather than judicial innovation. According to Lord Collins:[59]

> the introduction of judge-made law extending the recognition and enforcement of foreign judgments would be only to the detriment of United Kingdom businesses without any corresponding benefit ... a person in England who might have connections with a foreign territory which were only arguably 'sufficient' would have to actively defend foreign proceedings which could result in an in personam judgment against him, only because the proceedings are incidental to bankruptcy proceedings in the courts of that territory ... [I]t might suggest that foreigners who have bona fide dealings with the United States might have to face the dilemma of the expense of defending enormous claims in the United States or not defending them and being at risk of having a default judgment enforced abroad.

---

[56] See *Rubin v Eurofinance SA* [2012] UKSC 46, [2013] 1 AC 236 and *Singularis Holdings v PricewaterhouseCoopers* [2014] UKPC 36, [2015] 1 AC 1675.
[57] [2014] UKPC 36, where Lord Neuberger referred at para 157 to the 'extreme version' of the principle of universality propounded by Lord Hoffmann in *Cambridge Gas*.
[58] *Rubin v Eurofinance SA* [2012] UKSC 46, [2013] 1 AC 236.
[59] [2013] 1 AC 236, para 130.

E. RELIANCE ON SECTION 426 INSOLVENCY ACT 1986 AND THE COMMON LAW

Critics of the Supreme Court's decision argue that it makes it more difficult for liquidators **9.41** and insolvency administrators to recover assets on behalf of the insolvency estate that have been illicitly transferred abroad. Lord Collins anticipated and countered this criticism by suggesting that direct remedies might be available to recover assets for the benefit of creditors. He pointed out that avoidance claims by a liquidator of an Australian company may be the subject of a request by the Australian court pursuant to section 426(4) of the Insolvency Act 1986, applying Australian law under s 426(5).[60]

---

[60] In addition, Art 23 of the Model Law allows for the possibility of avoidance claims to be brought by foreign representatives under the Insolvency Act 1986.

APPENDIX 1

European Union: Council Regulation (EC) No. 1346/2000 of 29 May 2000 on Insolvency Proceedings

The Council of the European Union,
Having regard to the Treaty establishing the European Community, and in particular Article 61(c) and 67(1) thereof,
Having regard to the initiative of the Federal Republic of Germany and the Republic of Finland,
Having regard to the opinion of the European Parliament,[1]
Having regard to the opinion of the Economic and Social Committee,[2]
Whereas:

(1) The European Union has set out the aim of establishing an area of freedom, security and justice.
(2) The proper functioning of the internal market requires that cross-border insolvency proceedings should operate efficiently and effectively and this Regulation needs to be adopted in order to achieve this objective which comes within the scope of judicial cooperation in civil matters within the meaning of Article 65 of the Treaty.
(3) The activities of undertakings have more and more cross-border effects and are therefore increasingly being regulated by Community law. While the insolvency of such undertakings also affects the proper functioning of the internal market, there is a need for a Community act requiring coordination of the measures to be taken regarding an insolvent debtor's assets.
(4) It is necessary for the proper functioning of the internal market to avoid incentives for the parties to transfer assets or judicial proceedings from one Member State to another, seeking to obtain a more favourable legal position (forum shopping).
(5) These objectives cannot be achieved to a sufficient degree at national level and action at Community level is therefore justified.
(6) In accordance with the principle of proportionality this Regulation should be confined to provisions governing jurisdiction for opening insolvency proceedings and judgments which are delivered directly on the basis of the insolvency proceedings and are closely connected with such proceedings. In addition, this Regulation should contain provisions regarding the recognition of those judgments and the applicable law which also satisfy that principle.
(7) Insolvency proceedings relating to the winding-up of insolvent companies or other legal persons, judicial arrangements, compositions and analogous proceedings are excluded from the scope of the 1968 Brussels Convention on Jurisdiction and the Enforcement of Judgments in Civil and Commercial Matters,[3] as amended by the Conventions on Accession to this Convention.[4]
(8) In order to achieve the aim of improving the efficiency and effectiveness of insolvency proceedings having cross-border effects, it is necessary, and appropriate, that the provisions on jurisdiction, recognition and applicable law in this area should be contained in a Community law measure which is binding and directly applicable in Member States.

---

[1] Opinion delivered on 2 March 2000 (not yet published in the Official Journal).
[2] Opinion delivered on 26 January 2000 (not yet published in the Official Journal).
[3] [1972] OJ L299, p 32.
[4] [1975] OJ L204, p 28; [1978] OJ L304, p 1; [1982] OJ L388, p 1; [1989] OJ L285, p 1; [1997] OJ C15, p 1.

(9) This Regulation should apply to insolvency proceedings, whether the debtor is a natural person or a legal person, a trader or an individual. The insolvency proceedings to which this Regulation applies are listed in the Annexes. Insolvency proceedings concerning insurance undertakings, credit institutions, investment undertakings holding funds or securities for third parties and collective investment undertakings should be excluded from the scope of this Regulation. Such undertakings should not be covered by this Regulation since they are subject to special arrangements and, to some extent, the national supervisory authorities have extremely wide-ranging powers of intervention.

(10) Insolvency proceedings do not necessarily involve the intervention of a judicial authority; the expression 'court' in this Regulation should be given a broad meaning and include a person or body empowered by national law to open insolvency proceedings. In order for this Regulation to apply, proceedings (comprising acts and formalities set down in law) should not only have to comply with the provisions of this Regulation, but they should also be officially recognized and legally effective in the Member State in which the insolvency proceedings are opened and should be collective insolvency proceedings which entail the partial or total divestment of the debtor and the appointment of a liquidator.

(11) This Regulation acknowledges the fact that as a result of widely differing substantive laws it is not practical to introduce insolvency proceedings with universal scope in the entire Community. The application without exception of the law of the State of opening of proceedings would, against this background, frequently lead to difficulties. This applies, for example, to the widely differing laws on security interests to be found in the Community. Furthermore, the preferential rights enjoyed by some creditors in the insolvency proceedings are, in some cases, completely different. This Regulation should take account of this in two different ways. On the one hand, provision should be made for special rules on applicable law in the case of particularly significant rights and legal relationships (e.g. rights in rem and contracts of employment). On the other hand, national proceedings covering only assets situated in the State of opening should also be allowed alongside main insolvency proceedings with universal scope.

(12) This Regulation enables the main insolvency proceedings to be opened in the Member State where the debtor has the centre of his main interests. These proceedings have universal scope and aim at encompassing all the debtor's assets. To protect the diversity of interests, this Regulation permits secondary proceedings to be opened to run in parallel with the main proceedings. Secondary proceedings may be opened in the Member State where the debtor has an establishment. The effects of secondary proceedings are limited to the assets located in that State. Mandatory rules of coordination with the main proceedings satisfy the need for unity in the Community.

(13) The 'centre of main interests' should correspond to the place where the debtor conducts the administration of his interests on a regular basis and is therefore ascertainable by third parties.

(14) This Regulation applies only to proceedings where the centre of the debtor's main interests is located in the Community.

(15) The rules of jurisdiction set out in this Regulation establish only international jurisdiction, that is to say, they designate the Member State the courts of which may open insolvency proceedings. Territorial jurisdiction within that Member State must be established by the national law of the Member State concerned.

(16) The court having jurisdiction to open the main insolvency proceedings should be enabled to order provisional and protective measures from the time of the request to open proceedings. Preservation measures both prior to and after the commencement of the insolvency proceedings are very important to guarantee the effectiveness of the insolvency proceedings. In that connection this Regulation should afford different possibilities. On the one hand, the court competent for the main insolvency proceedings should be able also to order provisional protective measures covering assets situated in the territory of other Member States. On the other hand, a liquidator temporarily appointed prior to the opening of the main insolvency proceedings should be able, in the Member States in which an establishment belonging to the

debtor is to be found, to apply for the preservation measures which are possible under the law of those States.
(17) Prior to the opening of the main insolvency proceedings, the right to request the opening of insolvency proceedings in the Member State where the debtor has an establishment should be limited to local creditors and creditors of the local establishment or to cases where main proceedings cannot be opened under the law of the Member State where the debtor has the centre of his main interest. The reason for this restriction is that cases where territorial insolvency proceedings are requested before the main insolvency proceedings are intended to be limited to what is absolutely necessary. If the main insolvency proceedings are opened, the territorial proceedings become secondary.
(18) Following the opening of the main insolvency proceedings, the right to request the opening of insolvency proceedings in a Member State where the debtor has an establishment is not restricted by this Regulation. The liquidator in the main proceedings or any other person empowered under the national law of that Member State may request the opening of secondary insolvency proceedings.
(19) Secondary insolvency proceedings may serve different purposes, besides the protection of local interests. Cases may arise where the estate of the debtor is too complex to administer as a unit or where differences in the legal systems concerned are so great that difficulties may arise from the extension of effects deriving from the law of the State of the opening to the other States where the assets are located. For this reason the liquidator in the main proceedings may request the opening of secondary proceedings when the efficient administration of the estate so requires.
(20) Main insolvency proceedings and secondary proceedings can, however, contribute to the effective realisation of the total assets only if all the concurrent proceedings pending are coordinated. The main condition here is that the various liquidators must cooperate closely, in particular by exchanging a sufficient amount of information. In order to ensure the dominant role of the main insolvency proceedings, the liquidator in such proceedings should be given several possibilities for intervening in secondary insolvency proceedings which are pending at the same time. For example, he should be able to propose a restructuring plan or composition or apply for realisation of the assets in the secondary insolvency proceedings to be suspended.
(21) Every creditor, who has his habitual residence, domicile or registered office in the Community, should have the right to lodge his claims in each of the insolvency proceedings pending in the Community relating to the debtor's assets. This should also apply to tax authorities and social insurance institutions. However, in order to ensure equal treatment of creditors, the distribution of proceeds must be coordinated. Every creditor should be able to keep what he has received in the course of insolvency proceedings but should be entitled only to participate in the distribution of total assets in other proceedings if creditors with the same standing have obtained the same proportion of their claims.
(22) This Regulation should provide for immediate recognition of judgments concerning the opening, conduct and closure of insolvency proceedings which come within its scope and of judgments handed down in direct connection with such insolvency proceedings. Automatic recognition should therefore mean that the effects attributed to the proceedings by the law of the State in which the proceedings were opened extend to all other Member States. Recognition of judgments delivered by the courts of the Member States should be based on the principle of mutual trust. To that end, grounds for non-recognition should be reduced to the minimum necessary. This is also the basis on which any dispute should be resolved where the courts of two Member States both claim competence to open the main insolvency proceedings. The decision of the first court to open proceedings should be recognized in the other Member States without those Member States having the power to scrutinize the court's decision.
(23) This Regulation should set out, for the matters covered by it, uniform rules on conflict of laws which replace, within their scope of application, national rules of private international law. Unless otherwise stated, the law of the Member State of the opening of the proceedings

should be applicable (lex concursus). This rule on conflict of laws should be valid both for the main proceedings and for local proceedings; the lex concursus determines all the effects of the insolvency proceedings, both procedural and substantive, on the persons and legal relations concerned. It governs all the conditions for the opening, conduct and closure of the insolvency proceedings.

(24) Automatic recognition of insolvency proceedings to which the law of the opening State normally applies may interfere with the rules under which transactions are carried out in other Member States. To protect legitimate expectations and the certainty of transactions in Member States other than that in which proceedings are opened, provisions should be made for a number of exceptions to the general rule.

(25) There is a particular need for a special reference diverging from the law of the opening State in the case of rights in rem, since these are of considerable importance for the granting of credit. The basis, validity and extent of such a right in rem should therefore normally be determined according to the lex situs and not be affected by the opening of insolvency proceedings. The proprietor of the right in rem should therefore be able to continue to assert his right to segregation or separate settlement of the collateral security. Where assets are subject to rights in rem under the lex situs in one Member State but the main proceedings are being carried out in another Member State, the liquidator in the main proceedings should be able to request the opening of secondary proceedings in the jurisdiction where the rights in rem arise if the debtor has an establishment there. If a secondary proceeding is not opened, the surplus on sale of the asset covered by rights in rem must be paid to the liquidator in the main proceedings.

(26) If a set-off is not permitted under the law of the opening State, a creditor should nevertheless be entitled to the set-off if it is possible under the law applicable to the claim of the insolvent debtor. In this way, set-off will acquire a kind of guarantee function based on legal provisions on which the creditor concerned can rely at the time when the claim arises.

(27) There is also a need for special protection in the case of payment systems and financial markets. This applies for example to the position-closing agreements and netting agreements to be found in such systems as well as to the sale of securities and to the guarantees provided for such transactions as governed in particular by Directive 98/26/EC of the European Parliament and of the Council of 19 May 1998 on settlement finality in payment and securities settlement systems.[5] For such transactions, the only law which is material should thus be that applicable to the system or market concerned. This provision is intended to prevent the possibility of mechanisms for the payment and settlement of transactions provided for in the payment and set-off systems or on the regulated financial markets of the Member States being altered in the case of insolvency of a business partner. Directive 98/26/EC contains special provisions which should take precedence over the general rules in this Regulation.

(28) In order to protect employees and jobs, the effects of insolvency proceedings on the continuation or termination of employment and on the rights and obligations of all parties to such employment must be determined by the law applicable to the agreement in accordance with the general rules on conflict of law. Any other insolvency-law questions, such as whether the employees' claims are protected by preferential rights and what status such preferential rights may have, should be determined by the law of the opening State.

(29) For business considerations, the main content of the decision opening the proceedings should be published in the other Member States at the request of the liquidator. If there is an establishment in the Member State concerned, there may be a requirement that publication is compulsory. In neither case, however, should publication be a prior condition for recognition of the foreign proceedings.

(30) It may be the case that some of the persons concerned are not in fact aware that proceedings have been opened and act in good faith in a way that conflicts with the new situation. In order to protect such persons who make a payment to the debtor because they are unaware that

---

[5] [1988] OJ L166, p 45.

foreign proceedings have been opened when they should in fact have made the payment to the foreign liquidator, it should be provided that such a payment is to have a debt-discharging effect.
(31) This Regulation should include Annexes relating to the organisation of insolvency proceedings. As these Annexes relate exclusively to the legislation of Member States, there are specific and substantiated reasons for the Council to reserve the right to amend these Annexes in order to take account of any amendments to the domestic law of the Member States.
(32) The United Kingdom and Ireland, in accordance with Article 3 of the Protocol on the position of the United Kingdom and Ireland annexed to the Treaty on European Union and the Treaty establishing the European Community, have given notice of their wish to take part in the adoption and application of this Regulation.
(33) Denmark, in accordance with Articles 1 and 2 of the Protocol on the position of Denmark annexed to the Treaty on European Union and the Treaty establishing the European Community, is not participating in the adoption of this Regulation, and is therefore not bound by it nor subject to its application.

HAS ADOPTED THIS REGULATION:

CHAPTER I: GENERAL PROVISIONS

Article 1

Scope

1. This Regulation shall apply to collective insolvency proceedings which entail the partial or total divestment of a debtor and the appointment of a liquidator.
2. This Regulation shall not apply to insolvency proceedings concerning insurance undertakings, credit institutions, investment undertakings which provide services involving the holding of funds or securities for third parties, or to collective investment undertakings.

Article 2

Definitions

For the purposes of this Regulation:

(a) 'insolvency proceedings' shall mean the collective proceedings referred to in Article 1(1). These proceedings are listed in Annex A;
(b) 'liquidator' shall mean any person or body whose function is to administer or liquidate assets of which the debtor has been divested or to supervise the administration of his affairs. Those persons and bodies are listed in Annex C;
(c) 'winding-up proceedings' shall mean insolvency proceedings within the meaning of point (a) involving realising the assets of the debtor, including where the proceedings have been closed by a composition or other measure terminating the insolvency, or closed by reason of the insufficiency of the assets. Those proceedings are listed in Annex B;
(d) 'court' shall mean the judicial body or any other competent body of a Member State empowered to open insolvency proceedings or to take decisions in the course of such proceedings;
(e) 'judgment' in relation to the opening of insolvency proceedings or the appointment of a liquidator shall include the decision of any court empowered to open such proceedings or to appoint a liquidator;
(f) 'the time of the opening of proceedings' shall mean the time at which the judgment opening proceedings becomes effective, whether it is a final judgment or not;
(g) 'the Member State in which assets are situated' shall mean, in the case of:
— tangible property, the Member State within the territory of which the property is situated,

- property and rights ownership of or entitlement to which must be entered in a public register, the Member State under the authority of which the register is kept,
- claims, the Member State within the territory of which the third party required to meet them has the centre of his main interests, as determined in Article 3(1);

(h) 'establishment' shall mean any place of operations where the debtor carries out a non-transitory economic activity with human means and goods.

Article 3

International jurisdiction

1. The courts of the Member State within the territory of which the centre of a debtor's main interests is situated shall have jurisdiction to open insolvency proceedings. In the case of a company or legal person, the place of the registered office shall be presumed to be the centre of its main interests in the absence of proof to the contrary.
2. Where the centre of a debtor's main interests is situated within the territory of a Member State, the courts of another Member State shall have jurisdiction to open insolvency proceedings against that debtor only if he possesses an establishment within the territory of that other Member State. The effects of those proceedings shall be restricted to the assets of the debtor situated in the territory of the latter Member State.
3. Where insolvency proceedings have been opened under paragraph 1, any proceedings opened subsequently under paragraph 2 shall be secondary proceedings. These latter proceedings must be winding-up proceedings.
4. Territorial insolvency proceedings referred to in paragraph 2 may be opened prior to the opening of main insolvency proceedings in accordance with paragraph 1 only:
   (a) where insolvency proceedings under paragraph 1 cannot be opened because of the conditions laid down by the law of the Member State within the territory of which the centre of the debtor's main interests is situated; or
   (b) where the opening of territorial insolvency proceedings is requested by a creditor who has his domicile, habitual residence or registered office in the Member State within the territory of which the establishment is situated, or whose claim arises from the operation of that establishment.

Article 4

Law applicable

1. Save as otherwise provided in this Regulation, the law applicable to insolvency proceedings and their effects shall be that of the Member State within the territory of which such proceedings are opened, hereafter referred to as the 'State of the opening of proceedings'.
2. The law of the State of the opening of proceedings shall determine the conditions for the opening of those proceedings, their conduct and their closure. It shall determine in particular:
   (a) against which debtors insolvency proceedings may be brought on account of their capacity;
   (b) the assets which form part of the estate and the treatment of assets acquired by or devolving on the debtor after the opening of the insolvency proceedings;
   (c) the respective powers of the debtor and the liquidator;
   (d) the conditions under which set-offs may be invoked;
   (e) the effects of insolvency proceedings on current contracts to which the debtor is party;
   (f) the effects of the insolvency proceedings on proceedings brought by individual creditors, with the exception of lawsuits pending;
   (g) the claims which are to be lodged against the debtor's estate and the treatment of claims arising after the opening of insolvency proceedings;

(h) the rules governing the lodging, verification and admission of claims;
(i) the rules governing the distribution of proceeds from the realisation of assets, the ranking of claims and the rights of creditors who have obtained partial satisfaction after the opening of insolvency proceedings by virtue of a right in rem or through a set-off;
(j) the conditions for and the effects of closure of insolvency proceedings, in particular by composition;
(k) creditors' rights after the closure of insolvency proceedings;
(l) who is to bear the costs and expenses incurred in the insolvency proceedings;
(m) the rules relating to the voidness, voidability or unenforceability of legal acts detrimental to all the creditors.

Article 5

Third parties' rights in rem

1. The opening of insolvency proceedings shall not affect the rights in rem of creditors or third parties in respect of tangible or intangible, moveable or immoveable assets—both specific assets and collections of indefinite assets as a whole which change from time to time—belonging to the debtor which are situated within the territory of another Member State at the time of the opening of proceedings.
2. The rights referred to in paragraph 1 shall in particular mean:
    (a) the right to dispose of assets or have them disposed of and to obtain satisfaction from the proceeds of or income from those assets, in particular by virtue of a lien or a mortgage;
    (b) the exclusive right to have a claim met, in particular a right guaranteed by a lien in respect of the claim or by assignment of the claim by way of a guarantee;
    (c) the right to demand the assets from, and/or to require restitution by, anyone having possession or use of them contrary to the wishes of the party so entitled;
    (d) a right in rem to the beneficial use of assets.
3. The right, recorded in a public register and enforceable against third parties, under which a right in rem within the meaning of paragraph 1 may be obtained, shall be considered a right in rem.
4. Paragraph 1 shall not preclude actions for voidness, voidability or unenforceability as referred to in Article 4(2)(m).

Article 6

Set-off

1. The opening of insolvency proceedings shall not affect the right of creditors to demand the setoff of their claims against the claims of the debtor, where such a set-off is permitted by the law applicable to the insolvent debtor's claim.
2. Paragraph 1 shall not preclude actions for voidness, voidability or unenforceability as referred to in Article 4(2)(m).

Article 7

Reservation of title

1. The opening of insolvency proceedings against the purchaser of an asset shall not affect the seller's rights based on a reservation of title where at the time of the opening of proceedings

the asset is situated within the territory of a Member State other than the State of opening of proceedings.
2. The opening of insolvency proceedings against the seller of an asset, after delivery of the asset, shall not constitute grounds for rescinding or terminating the sale and shall not prevent the purchaser from acquiring title where at the time of the opening of proceedings the asset sold is situated within the territory of a Member State other than the State of the opening of proceedings.
3. Paragraphs 1 and 2 shall not preclude actions for voidness, voidability or unenforceability as referred to in Article 4(2)(m).

Article 8

Contracts relating to immoveable property

The effects of insolvency proceedings on a contract conferring the right to acquire or make use of immoveable property shall be governed solely by the law of the Member State within the territory of which the immoveable property is situated.

Article 9

Payment systems and financial markets

1. Without prejudice to Article 5, the effects of insolvency proceedings on the rights and obligations of the parties to a payment or settlement system or to a financial market shall be governed solely by the law of the Member State applicable to that system or market.
2. Paragraph 1 shall not preclude any action for voidness, voidability or unenforceability which may be taken to set aside payments or transactions under the law applicable to the relevant payment system or financial market.

Article 10

Contracts of employment

The effects of insolvency proceedings on employment contracts and relationships shall be governed solely by the law of the Member State applicable to the contract of employment.

Article 11

Effects on rights subject to registration

The effects of insolvency proceedings on the rights of the debtor in immoveable property, a ship or an aircraft subject to registration in a public register shall be determined by the law of the Member State under the authority of which the register is kept.

Article 12

Community patents and trade marks

For the purposes of this Regulation, a Community patent, a Community trade mark or any other similar right established by Community law may be included only in the proceedings referred to in Article 3(1).

Article 13

Detrimental acts

Article 4(2)(m) shall not apply where the person who benefited from an act detrimental to all the creditors provides proof that:

— he said act is subject to the law of a Member State other than that of the State of the opening of proceedings, and
— that law does not allow any means of challenging that act in the relevant case.

Article 14

Protection of third-party purchasers

Where, by an act concluded after the opening of insolvency proceedings, the debtor disposes, for consideration, of:

— an immoveable asset, or
— a ship or an aircraft subject to registration in a public register, or
— securities whose existence presupposes registration in a register laid down by law, the validity of that act shall be governed by the law of the State within the territory of which the immoveable asset is situated or under the authority of which the register is kept.

Article 15

Effects of insolvency proceedings on lawsuits pending

The effects of insolvency proceedings on a lawsuit pending concerning an asset or a right of which the debtor has been divested shall be governed solely by the law of the Member State in which that lawsuit is pending.

CHAPTER II: RECOGNITION OF INSOLVENCY PROCEEDINGS

Article 16

Principle
1. Any judgment opening insolvency proceedings handed down by a court of a Member State which has jurisdiction pursuant to Article 3 shall be recognized in all the other Member States from the time that it becomes effective in the State of the opening of proceedings.
   This rule shall also apply where, on account of his capacity, insolvency proceedings cannot be brought against the debtor in other Member States.
2. Recognition of the proceedings referred to in Article 3(1) shall not preclude the opening of the proceedings referred to in Article 3(2) by a court in another Member State. The latter proceedings shall be secondary insolvency proceedings within the meaning of Chapter III.

Article 17

Effects of recognition
1. The judgment opening the proceedings referred to in Article 3(1) shall, with no further formalities, produce the same effects in any other Member State as under this law of the State of the

opening of proceedings, unless this Regulation provides otherwise and as long as no proceedings referred to in Article 3(2) are opened in that other Member State.
2. The effects of the proceedings referred to in Article 3(2) may not be challenged in other Member States. Any restriction of the creditors' rights, in particular a stay or discharge, shall produce effects vis-à-vis assets situated within the territory of another Member State only in the case of those creditors who have given their consent.

Article 18

Powers of the liquidator

1. The liquidator appointed by a court which has jurisdiction pursuant to Article 3(1) may exercise all the powers conferred on him by the law of the State of the opening of proceedings in another Member State, as long as no other insolvency proceedings have been opened there nor any preservation measure to the contrary has been taken there further to a request for the opening of insolvency proceedings in that State. He may in particular remove the debtor's assets from the territory of the Member State in which they are situated, subject to Articles 5 and 7.
2. The liquidator appointed by a court which has jurisdiction pursuant to Article 3(2) may in any other Member State claim through the courts or out of court that moveable property was removed from the territory of the State of the opening of proceedings to the territory of that other Member State after the opening of the insolvency proceedings. He may also bring any action to set aside which is in the interests of the creditors.
3. In exercising his powers, the liquidator shall comply with the law of the Member State within the territory of which he intends to take action, in particular with regard to procedures for the realisation of assets. Those powers may not include coercive measures or the right to rule on legal proceedings or disputes.

Article 19

Proof of the liquidator's appointment

The liquidator's appointment shall be evidenced by a certified copy of the original decision appointing him or by any other certificate issued by the court which has jurisdiction.
A translation into the official language or one of the official languages of the Member State within the territory of which he intends to act may be required. No legalisation or other similar formality shall be required.

Article 20

Return and imputation

1. A creditor who, after the opening of the proceedings referred to in Article 3(1) obtains by any means, in particular through enforcement, total or partial satisfaction of his claim on the assets belonging to the debtor situated within the territory of another Member State, shall return what he has obtained to the liquidator, subject to Articles 5 and 7.
2. In order to ensure equal treatment of creditors a creditor who has, in the course of insolvency proceedings, obtained a dividend on his claim shall share in distributions made in other proceedings only where creditors of the same ranking or category have, in those other proceedings, obtained an equivalent dividend.

Article 21

Publication

1. The liquidator may request that notice of the judgment opening insolvency proceedings and, where appropriate, the decision appointing him, be published in any other Member State in accordance with the publication procedures provided for in that State. Such publication shall also specify the liquidator appointed and whether the jurisdiction rule applied is that pursuant to Article 3(1) or Article 3(2).
2. However, any Member State within the territory of which the debtor has an establishment may require mandatory publication. In such cases, the liquidator or any authority empowered to that effect in the Member State where the proceedings referred to in Article 3(1) are opened shall take all necessary measures to ensure such publication.

Article 22

Registration in a public register

1. The liquidator may request that the judgment opening the proceedings referred to in Article 3(1) be registered in the land register, the trade register and any other public register kept in the other Member States.
2. However, any Member State may require mandatory registration. In such cases, the liquidator or any authority empowered to that effect in the Member State where the proceedings referred to in Article 3(1) have been opened shall take all necessary measures to ensure such registration.

Article 23

Costs

The costs of the publication and registration provided for in Articles 21 and 22 shall be regarded as costs and expenses incurred in the proceedings.

Article 24

Honouring of an obligation to a debtor

1. Where an obligation has been honoured in a Member State for the benefit of a debtor who is subject to insolvency proceedings opened in another Member State, when it should have been honoured for the benefit of the liquidator in those proceedings, the person honouring the obligation shall be deemed to have discharged it if he was unaware of the opening of proceedings.
2. Where such an obligation is honoured before the publication provided for in Article 21 has been effected, the person honouring the obligation shall be presumed, in the absence of proof to the contrary, to have been unaware of the opening of insolvency proceedings; where the obligation is honoured after such publication has been effected, the person honouring the obligation shall be presumed, in the absence of proof to the contrary, to have been aware of the opening of proceedings.

Article 25

Recognition and enforceability of other judgments

1. Judgments handed down by a court whose judgment concerning the opening of proceedings is recognized in accordance with Article 16 and which concern the course and closure of insolvency proceedings, and compositions approved by that court shall also be recognized with no further formalities. Such judgments shall be enforced in accordance with Articles 31 to 51, with the exception of Article 34(2), of the Brussels Convention on Jurisdiction and the Enforcement of Judgments in Civil and Commercial Matters, as amended by the Conventions of Accession to this Convention.

    The first subparagraph shall also apply to judgments deriving directly from the insolvency proceedings and which are closely linked with them, even if they were handed down by another court.

    The first subparagraph shall also apply to judgments relating to preservation measures taken after the request for the opening of insolvency proceedings.

2. The recognition and enforcement of judgments other than those referred to in paragraph 1 shall be governed by the Convention referred to in paragraph 1, provided that that Convention is applicable.

3. The Member States shall not be obliged to recognize or enforce a judgment referred to in paragraph 1 which might result in a limitation of personal freedom or postal secrecy.

Article 26[6]

Public policy

Any Member State may refuse to recognize insolvency proceedings opened in another Member State or to enforce a judgment handed down in the context of such proceedings where the effects of such recognition or enforcement would be manifestly contrary to that State's public policy, in particular its fundamental principles or the constitutional rights and liberties of the individual.

CHAPTER III: SECONDARY INSOLVENCY PROCEEDINGS

Article 27

Opening of proceedings

The opening of the proceedings referred to in Article 3(1) by a court of a Member State and which is recognized in another Member State (main proceedings) shall permit the opening in that other Member State, a court of which has jurisdiction pursuant to Article 3(2), of secondary insolvency proceedings without the debtor's insolvency being examined in that other State. These latter proceedings must be among the proceedings listed in Annex B. Their effects shall be restricted to the assets of the debtor situated within the territory of that other Member State.

---

[6] Note the Declaration by Portugal concerning the application of Arts 26 and 37 [2000] OJ C183, p 1. [2007] OJ C183, p1.

Article 28

Applicable law

Save as otherwise provided in this Regulation, the law applicable to secondary proceedings shall be that of the Member State within the territory of which the secondary proceedings are opened.

Article 29

Right to request the opening of proceedings

The opening of secondary proceedings may be requested by:

(a) the liquidator in the main proceedings;
(b) any other person or authority empowered to request the opening of insolvency proceedings under the law of the Member State within the territory of which the opening of secondary proceedings is requested.

Article 30

Advance payment of costs and expenses

Where the law of the Member State in which the opening of secondary proceedings is requested requires that the debtor's assets be sufficient to cover in whole or in part the costs and expenses of the proceedings, the court may, when it receives such a request, require the applicant to make an advance payment of costs or to provide appropriate security.

Article 31

Duty to cooperate and communicate information

1. Subject to the rules restricting the communication of information, the liquidator in the main proceedings and the liquidators in the secondary proceedings shall be duty bound to communicate information to each other. They shall immediately communicate any information which may be relevant to the other proceedings, in particular the progress made in lodging and verifying claims and all measures aimed at terminating the proceedings.
2. Subject to the rules applicable to each of the proceedings, the liquidator in the main proceedings and the liquidators in the secondary proceedings shall be duty bound to cooperate with each other.
3. The liquidator in the secondary proceedings shall give the liquidator in the main proceedings an early opportunity of submitting proposals on the liquidation or use of the assets in the secondary proceedings.

Article 32

Exercise of creditors' rights

1. Any creditor may lodge his claim in the main proceedings and in any secondary proceedings.
2. The liquidators in the main and any secondary proceedings shall lodge in other proceedings claims which have already been lodged in the proceedings for which they were appointed, provided that the interests of creditors in the latter proceedings are served thereby, subject to the right of creditors to oppose that or to withdraw the lodgement of their claims where the law applicable so provides.
3. The liquidator in the main or secondary proceedings shall be empowered to participate in other proceedings on the same basis as a creditor, in particular by attending creditors' meetings.

Article 33

Stay of liquidation

1. The court, which opened the secondary proceedings, shall stay the process of liquidation in whole or in part on receipt of a request from the liquidator in the main proceedings, provided that in that event it may require the liquidator in the main proceedings to take any suitable measure to guarantee the interests of the creditors in the secondary proceedings and of individual classes of creditors. Such a request from the liquidator may be rejected only if it is manifestly of no interest to the creditors in the main proceedings. Such a stay of the process of liquidation may be ordered for up to three months. It may be continued or renewed for similar periods.
2. The court referred to in paragraph 1 shall terminate the stay of the process of liquidation:
    — at the request of the liquidator in the main proceedings,
    — of its own motion, at the request of a creditor or at the request of the liquidator in the secondary proceedings if that measure no longer appears justified, in particular, by the interests of creditors in the main proceedings or in the secondary proceedings.

Article 34

Measures ending secondary insolvency proceedings

1. Where the law applicable to secondary proceedings allows for such proceedings to be closed without liquidation by a rescue plan, a composition or a comparable measure, the liquidator in the main proceedings shall be empowered to propose such a measure himself.

    Closure of the secondary proceedings by a measure referred to in the first subparagraph shall not become final without the consent of the liquidator in the main proceedings; failing his agreement, however, it may become final if the financial interests of the creditors in the main proceedings are not affected by the measure proposed.
2. Any restriction of creditors' rights arising from a measure referred to in paragraph 1 which is proposed in secondary proceedings, such as a stay of payment or discharge of debt, may not have effect in respect of the debtor's assets not covered by those proceedings without the consent of all the creditors having an interest.
3. During a stay of the process of liquidation ordered pursuant to Article 33, only the liquidator in the main proceedings or the debtor, with the former's consent, may propose measures laid down in paragraph 1 of this Article in the secondary proceedings; no other proposal for such a measure shall be put to the vote or approved.

Article 35

Assets remaining in the secondary proceedings

If by the liquidation of assets in the secondary proceedings it is possible to meet all claims allowed under those proceedings, the liquidator appointed in those proceedings shall immediately transfer any assets remaining to the liquidator in the main proceedings.

Article 36

Subsequent opening of the main proceedings

Where the proceedings referred to in Article 3(1) are opened following the opening of the proceedings referred to in Article 3(2) in another Member State, Articles 31 to 35 shall apply to those opened first, in so far as the progress of those proceedings so permits.

Article 37[7]

Conversion of earlier proceedings

The liquidator in the main proceedings may request that proceedings listed in Annex A previously opened in another Member State be converted into winding-up proceedings if this proves to be in the interests of the creditors in the main proceedings.

The court with jurisdiction under Article 3(2) shall order conversion into one of the proceedings listed in Annex B.

Article 38

Preservation measures

Where the court of a Member State which has jurisdiction pursuant to Article 3(1) appoints a temporary administrator in order to ensure the preservation of the debtor's assets, that temporary administrator shall be empowered to request any measures to secure and preserve any of the debtor's assets situated in another Member State, provided for under the law of that State, for the period between the request for the opening of insolvency proceedings and the judgment opening the proceedings.

CHAPTER IV: PROVISION OF INFORMATION FOR CREDITORS AND LODGEMENT OF THEIR CLAIMS

Article 39

Right to lodge claims

Any creditor who has his habitual residence, domicile or registered office in a Member State other than the State of the opening of proceedings, including the tax authorities and social security authorities of Member States, shall have the right to lodge claims in the insolvency proceedings in writing.

Article 40

Duty to inform creditors

1. As soon as insolvency proceedings are opened in a Member State, the court of that State having jurisdiction or the liquidator appointed by it shall immediately inform known creditors who have their habitual residences, domiciles or registered offices in the other Member States.
2. That information, provided by an individual notice, shall in particular include time limits, the penalties laid down in regard to those time limits, the body or authority empowered to accept the lodgement of claims and the other measures laid down. Such notice shall also indicate whether creditors whose claims are preferential or secured in rem need lodge their claims.

Article 41

Content of the lodgement of a claim

A creditor shall send copies of supporting documents, if any, and shall indicate the nature of the claim, the date on which it arose and its amount, as well as whether he alleges preference, security in rem or a reservation of title in respect of the claim and what assets are covered by the guarantee he is invoking.

---

[7] Note the Declaration by Portugal concerning the application of Arts 26 and 37 ([2000]OJ C183, p 1).

Article 42

Languages

1. The information provided for in Article 40 shall be provided in the official language or one of the official languages of the State of the opening of proceedings.
   For that purpose a form shall be used bearing the heading 'Invitation to lodge a claim. Time limits to be observed' in all the official languages of the institutions of the European Union.
2. Any creditor who has his habitual residence, domicile or registered office in a Member State other than the State of the opening of proceedings may lodge his claim in the official language or one of the official languages of that other State. In that event, however, the lodgement of his claim shall bear the heading 'Lodgement of claim' in the official language or one of the official languages of the State of the opening of proceedings. In addition, he may be required to provide a translation into the official language or one of the official languages of the State of the opening of proceedings.

CHAPTER V: TRANSITIONAL AND FINAL PROVISIONS

Article 43

Applicability in time

The provisions of this Regulation shall apply only to insolvency proceedings opened after its entry into force. Acts done by a debtor before the entry into force of this Regulation shall continue to be governed by the law which was applicable to them at the time they were done.

Article 44

Relationship to Conventions

1. After its entry into force, this Regulation replaces, in respect of the matters referred to therein, in the relations between Member States, the Conventions concluded between two or more Member States, in particular:
   (a) the Convention between Belgium and France on Jurisdiction and the Validity and Enforcement of Judgments, Arbitration Awards and Authentic Instruments, signed at Paris on 8 July 1899;
   (b) the Convention between Belgium and Austria on Bankruptcy, Winding-up, Arrangements, Compositions and Suspension of Payments (with Additional Protocol of 13 June 1973), signed at Brussels on 16 July 1969;
   (c) the Convention between Belgium and the Netherlands on Territorial Jurisdiction, Bankruptcy and the Validity and Enforcement of Judgments, Arbitration Awards and Authentic Instruments, signed at Brussels on 28 March 1925;
   (d) the Treaty between Germany and Austria on Bankruptcy, Winding-up, Arrangements and Compositions, signed at Vienna on 25 May 1979;
   (e) the Convention between France and Austria on Jurisdiction, Recognition and Enforcement of Judgments on Bankruptcy, signed at Vienna on 27 February 1979;
   (f) the Convention between France and Italy on the Enforcement of Judgments in Civil and Commercial Matters, signed at Rome on 3 June 1930;
   (g) the Convention between Italy and Austria on Bankruptcy, Winding-up, Arrangements and Compositions, signed at Rome on 12 July 1977;
   (h) the Convention between the Kingdom of the Netherlands and the Federal Republic of Germany on the Mutual Recognition and Enforcement of Judgments and other Enforceable Instruments in Civil and Commercial Matters, signed at The Hague on 30 August 1962;

(i) the Convention between the United Kingdom and the Kingdom of Belgium providing for the Reciprocal Enforcement of Judgments in Civil and Commercial Matters, with Protocol, signed at Brussels on 2 May 1934;

(j) the Convention between Denmark, Finland, Norway, Sweden and Iceland on Bankruptcy, signed at Copenhagen on 7 November 1933;

(k) the European Convention on Certain International Aspects of Bankruptcy, signed at Istanbul on 5 June 1990;

(l) The Convention between the Federative People's Republic of Yugoslavia and the Kingdom of Greece on the Mutual recognition and Enforcement of Judgments, signed at Athens on 18 June 1959;

(m) the Agreement between the Federative People's Republic of Yugoslavia and the Republic of Austria on the Mutual Recognition and Enforcement of Arbitral Awards and Arbitral Settlements in Commercial Matters, signed at Belgrade on 18 March 1960;

(n) the Convention between the Federative People's Republic of Yugoslavia and the Republic of Italy on Mutual Judicial Cooperation in Civil and Administrative Matters, signed at Rome on 3 December 1960;

(o) the Agreement between the Socialist Federative Republic of Yugoslavia and the Kingdom of Belgium on Judicial Cooperation in Civil and Commercial Matters, signed at Belgrade on 24 September 1971;

(p) the Convention between the Governments of Yugoslavia and France on the Recognition and Enforcement of Judgments in Civil and Commercial Matters, signed at Paris on 18 May 1971;

(q) the Agreement between the Czechoslovak Socialist Republic and the Hellenic Republic on Legal Aid in Civil and Criminal Matters, signed at Athens on 22 October 1980, still in force between the Czech Republic and Greece.

(r) the Agreement between the Czechoslovak Socialist Republic and the Republic of Cyprus on Legal Aid in Civil and Criminal Matters, signed at Nicosia on 23 April 1982, still in force between the Czech Republic and Cyprus;

(s) the Treaty between the Government of the Czechoslovak Socialist Republic and the Government of the Republic of France on Legal Aid and the Recognition and Enforcement of Judgments in Civil, Family and Commercial Matters, signed at Paris on 10 May 1984, still in force between the Czech Republic and France;

(t) the Treaty between the Czechoslovak Socialist Republic and the Italian Republic on Legal Aid in Civil and Criminal Matters, signed at Prague on 6 December 1985, still in force between the Czech Republic and Italy;

(u) the Agreement between the Republic of Latvia, the Republic of Estonia and the Republic of Lithuania on Legal Assistance and Legal Relationships, signed at Tallinn on 11 November 1992;

(v) the Agreement between Estonia and Poland on Granting Legal Aid and Legal Relations on Civil, Labour and Criminal Matters, signed at Tallinn on 27 November 1998;

(w) the Agreement between the Republic of Lithuania and the Republic of Poland on Legal Assistance and Legal Relations in Civil, Family, Labour and Criminal Matters, signed in Warsaw on 26 January 1993;

(x) the Convention between Socialist Republic of Romania and the Hellenic Republic on legal assistance in civil and criminal matters and its Protocol, signed at Bucharest on 19 October 1972;

(y) the Convention between Socialist Republic of Romania and the French Republic on legal assistance in civil and commercial matters, signed at Paris on 5 November 1974;

(z) the Agreement between the People's Republic of Bulgaria and the Hellenic Republic on Legal Assistance in Civil and Criminal Matters, signed at Athens on 10 April 1976;

(aa) the Agreement between the People's Republic of Bulgaria and the Republic of Cyprus on Legal Assistance in Civil and Criminal Matters, signed at Nicosia on 29 April 1983;

(ab) the Agreement between the Government of the People's Republic of Bulgaria and the Government of the French Republic on Mutual Legal Assistance in Civil Matters, signed at Sofia on 18 January 1989;

(ac) the Treaty between Romania and the Czech Republic on judicial assistance in civil matters, signed at Bucharest on 11 July 1994;

(ad) the Treaty between Romania and Poland on legal assistance and legal relations in civil cases, signed at Bucharest on 15 May 1999.

2. The Conventions referred to in paragraph 1 shall continue to have effect with regard to proceedings opened before the entry into force of this Regulation.

3. This Regulation shall not apply:

(a) in any Member State, to the extent that it is irreconcilable with the obligations arising in relation to bankruptcy from a convention concluded by that State with one or more third countries before the entry into force of this Regulation;

(b) in the United Kingdom of Great Britain and Northern Ireland, to the extent that is irreconcilable with the obligations arising in relation to bankruptcy and the winding-up of insolvent companies from any arrangements with the Commonwealth existing at the time this Regulation enters into force.

Article 45

Amendment of the Annexes

The Council, acting by qualified majority on the initiative of one of its members or on a proposal from the Commission, may amend the Annexes.

Article 46

Reports

No later than 1 June 2012, and every five years thereafter, the Commission shall present to the European Parliament, the Council and the Economic and Social Committee a report on the application of this Regulation. The report shall be accompanied if need be by a proposal for adaptation of this Regulation.

Article 47

Entry into force

This Regulation shall enter into force on 31 May 2002.

This Regulation shall be binding in its entirety and directly applicable in the Member States in accordance with the Treaty establishing the European Community.

The Annexes are reproduced below as amended by Council Implementing Regulation (EU) No 663/2014 of 5 June 2014.

The Annexes are reproduced below as amended by Council Implementing Regulation (EU) No 663/2014 of 5 June 2014.

ANNEX A

Insolvency proceedings referred to in Article 2(a)

Belgique/België

— Het faillissement/La faillite,
— De gerechtelijke reorganisatie door een collectief akkoord/La réorganisation judiciaire par accord collectif,
— De gerechtelijke reorganisatie door overdracht onder gerechtelijk gezag/La réorganisation judiciaire par transfert sous autorité de justice,
— De collectieve schuldenregeling/Le règlement collectif de dettes,
— De vrijwillige vereffening/La liquidation volontaire,
— De gerechtelijke vereffening/La liquidation judiciaire,
— De voorlopige ontneming van beheer, bepaald in artikel 8 van de faillissementswet/Le dessaisissement provisoire, visé à l'article 8 de la loi sur les faillites,

БЪЛГАРИЯ

— Производство по несъстоятелност,

Česká Republika

— Konkurs,
— Reorganizace,
— Oddlužení,

Deutschland

— Das Konkursverfahren,
— Das gerichtliche Vergleichsverfahren,
— Das Gesamtvollstreckungsverfahren,
— Das Insolvenzverfahren,

Eesti

— Pankrotimenetlus,

Éire/Ireland

— Compulsory winding-up by the court,
— Bankruptcy,
— The administration in bankruptcy of the estate of persons dying insolvent,
— Winding-up in bankruptcy of partnerships,
— Creditors' voluntary winding-up (with confirmation of a court),
— Arrangements under the control of the court which involve the vesting of all or part of the property of the debtor in the Official Assignee for realisation and distribution,
— Company examinership,
— Debt Relief Notice,
— Debt Settlement Arrangement,
— Personal Insolvency Arrangement,

ΕΛΛΑΔΑ

— Η πτώχευση,
— Η ειδική εκκαθάριση εν λειτουργία,
— Σχέδιο αναδιοργάνωσης,
— Απλοποιημένη διαδικασία επί πτωχεύσεων μικρού αντικειμένου,

España

— Concurso,

France

— Sauvegarde,
— Redressement judiciaire,
— Liquidation judiciaire,

Hrvatska

— Stečajni postupak,

Italia

— Fallimento,
— Concordato preventivo,
— Liquidazione coatta amministrativa,
— Amministrazione straordinaria,

ΚΥΠΡΟΣ

— Υποχρεωτική εκκαθάριση από το Δικαστήριο,
— Εκούσια εκκαθάριση από μέλη,
— Εκούσια εκκαθάριση από πιστωτές,
— Εκκαθάριση με την εποπτεία του Δικαστηρίου,
— Διάταγμα Παραλαβής και πτώχευσης κατόπιν Δικαστικού Διατάγματος,
— Διαχείριση της περιουσίας προσώπων που απεβίωσαν αφερέγγυα,

Latvija

— Tiesiskās aizsardzības process,
— Juridiskās personas maksātnespējas process,
— Fiziskās personas maksātnespējas process,

Lietuva

— Įmonės restruktūrizavimo byla,
— Įmonės bankroto byla,

— Įmonės bankroto procesas ne teismo tvarka,
— Fizinio asmens bankroto byla,

Luxembourg

— Faillite,
— Gestion contrôlée,
— Concordat préventif de faillite (par abandon d'actif),
— Régime spécial de liquidation du notariat,
— Procédure de règlement collectif des dettes dans le cadre du surendettement,

Magyarország

— Csődeljárás,
— Felszámolási eljárás,

Malta

— Xoljiment,
— Amministrazzjoni,
— Stralċ volontarju mill-membri jew mill-kredituri,
— Stralċ mill-Qorti,
— Falliment f'każ ta' negozjant,

Nederland

— Het faillissement,
— De surséance van betaling,
— De schuldsaneringsregeling natuurlijke personen,

Österreich

— Das Konkursverfahren (Insolvenzverfahren),
— Das Sanierungsverfahren ohne Eigenverwaltung (Insolvenzverfahren),
— Das Sanierungsverfahren mit Eigenverwaltung (Insolvenzverfahren),
— Das Schuldenregulierungsverfahren,
— Das Abschöpfungsverfahren,
— Das Ausgleichsverfahren,

Polska

— Postępowanie naprawcze,
— Upadłość obejmująca likwidację,
— Upadłość z możliwością zawarcia układu,

Portugal

— Processo de insolvência,
— Processo especial de revitalização,

România

— Procedura insolvenței,
— Reorganizarea judiciară,
— Procedura falimentului,

Slovenija

— Stečajni postopek,
— Skrajšani stečajni postopek,
— Postopek prisilne poravnave,
— Prisilna poravnava v stečaju,

Slovensko

— Konkurzné konanie,
— Reštrukturalizačné konanie,

Suomi/Finland

— Konkurssi/konkurs,
— Yrityssaneeraus/företagssanering,

Sverige

— Konkurs,
— Företagsrekonstruktion,

United Kingdom

— Winding-up by or subject to the supervision of the court,
— Creditors' voluntary winding-up (with confirmation by the court),
— Administration, including appointments made by filing prescribed documents with the court,
— Voluntary arrangements under insolvency legislation,
— Bankruptcy or sequestration.

ANNEX B

Winding-up proceedings referred to in Article 2(c)

Belgique/België

— Het faillissement/La faillite,
— De vrijwillige vereffening/La liquidation volontaire,
— De gerechtelijke vereffening/La liquidation judiciaire,
— De gerechtelijke reorganisatie door overdracht onder gerechtelijk gezag/La réorganisation judiciaire par transfert sous autorité de justice,

БЪЛГАРИЯ

— Производство по несъстоятелност,

Česká Republika

— Konkurs,

Deutschland

— Das Konkursverfahren,
— Das Gesamtvollstreckungsverfahren,
— Das Insolvenzverfahren,

Eesti

— Pankrotimenetlus,

Éire/Ireland

— Compulsory winding-up,
— Bankruptcy,
— The administration in bankruptcy of the estate of persons dying insolvent,
— Winding-up in bankruptcy of partnerships,
— Creditors' voluntary winding-up (with confirmation of a court),
— Arrangements under the control of the court which involve the vesting of all or part of the property of the debtor in the Official Assignee for realisation and distribution,

ΕΛΛΑΔΑ

— Η πτώχευση,
— Η ειδική εκκαθάριση,
— Απλοποιημένη διαδικασία επί πτωχεύσεων μικρού αντικειμένου,

España

— Concurso,

France

— Liquidation judiciaire,

Hrvatska

— Stečajni postupak,

Italia

— Fallimento,
— Concordato preventivo,
— Liquidazione coatta amministrativa,
— Amministrazione straordinaria,

ΚΥΠΡΟΣ

— Υποχρεωτική εκκαθάριση από το Δικαστήριο,
— Εκκαθάριση με την εποπτεία του Δικαστηρίου,
— Εκούσια εκκαθάριση από πιστωτές, με επιβεβαίωση του Δικαστηρίου,
— Πτώχευση,
— Διαχείριση της περιουσίας προσώπων που απεβίωσαν αφερέγγυα,

Latvija

— Juridiskās personas maksātnespējas process,
— Fiziskās personas maksātnespējas process,

Lietuva

— Įmonės bankroto byla,
— Įmonės bankroto procesas ne teismo tvarka,

Luxembourg

— Faillite,
— Régime spécial de liquidation du notariat,
— Liquidation judiciaire dans le cadre du surendettement,

Magyarország

— Felszámolási eljárás,

Malta

— Stralċ volontarju,
— Stralċ mill-Qorti,
— Falliment inkluż il-ħruġ ta' mandat ta' qbid mill-Kuratur f'każ ta' negozjant fallut,

Nederland

— Het faillissement,
— De schuldsaneringsregeling natuurlijke personen,

Österreich

— Das Konkursverfahren (Insolvenzverfahren),

Polska

— Upadłość obejmująca likwidację,

Portugal

— Processo de insolvência,

România

— Procedura falimentului,

Slovenija

— Stečajni postopek,
— Skrajšani stečajni postopek,

Slovensko

— Konkurzné konanie,

Suomi/Finland

— Konkurssi/konkurs,

Sverige

— Konkurs,

United Kingdom

— Winding-up by or subject to the supervision of the court,
— Winding-up through administration, including appointments made by filing prescribed documents with the court,
— Creditors' voluntary winding-up (with confirmation by the court),
— Bankruptcy or sequestration.

ANNEX C LIQUIDATORS REFERRED TO IN ARTICLE 2(B)

Belgique/België

— De curator/Le curateur,
— De gedelegeerd rechter/Le juge-délégué,
— De gerechtsmandataris/Le mandataire de justice,
— De schuldbemiddelaar/Le médiateur de dettes,
— De vereffenaar/Le liquidateur,
— De voorlopige bewindvoerder/L'administrateur provisoire,

БЪЛГАРИЯ

— Назначен предварително временен синдик,
— Временен синдик,
— Постоянен) синдик,
— Служебен синдик,

Česká Republika

— Insolvenční správce,
— Předběžný insolvenční správce,
— Oddělený insolvenční správce,
— Zvláštní insolvenční správce,
— Zástupce insolvenčního správce,

Deutschland

— Konkursverwalter,
— Vergleichsverwalter,
— Sachwalter (nach der Vergleichsordnung),
— Verwalter,
— Insolvenzverwalter,
— Sachwalter (nach der Insolvenzordnung),
— Treuhänder,
— Vorläufiger Insolvenzverwalter,

Eesti

— Pankrotihaldur,
— Ajutine pankrotihaldur,
— Usaldusisik,

Éire/Ireland

— Liquidator,
— Official Assignee,
— Trustee in bankruptcy,
— Provisional Liquidator,

— Examiner,
— Personal Insolvency Practitioner,
— Insolvency Service,

ΕΛΛΑΔΑ

— Ο σύνδικος,
— Ο εισηγητής,
— Η επιτροπή των πιστωτών,
— Ο ειδικός εκκαθαριστής,

España

— Administradores concursales,

France

— Mandataire judiciaire,
— Liquidateur,
— Administrateur judiciaire,
— Commissaire à l'exécution du plan,

Hrvatska

— Stečajni upravitelj,
— Privremeni stečajni upravitelj,
— Stečajni povjerenik,
— Povjerenik,

Italia

— Curatore,
— Commissario giudiziale,
— Commissario straordinario,
— Commissario liquidatore,
— Liquidatore giudiziale,

ΚΥΠΡΟΣ

— Εκκαθαριστής και Προσωρινός Εκκαθαριστής,
— Επίσημος Παραλήπτης,
— Διαχειριστής της Πτώχευσης,

Latvija

— Maksātnespējas procesa administrators,

Lietuva

— Bankroto administratorius,
— Restruktūrizavimo administratorius,

Luxembourg

— Le curateur,
— Le commissaire,
— Le liquidateur,
— Le conseil de gérance de la section d'assainissement du notariat,
— Le liquidateur dans le cadre du surendettement,

Magyarország

— Vagyonfelügyelő,
— Felszámoló,

Malta

— Amministratur Proviżorju,
— Riċevitur Uffiċjali,
— Stralċjarju,
— Manager Speċjali,
— Kuraturi f'każ ta' proċeduri ta' falliment,

Nederland

— De curator in het faillissement,
— De bewindvoerder in de surséance van betaling,
— De bewindvoerder in de schuldsaneringsregeling natuurlijke personen,

Österreich

— Masseverwalter,
— Sanierungsverwalter,
— Ausgleichsverwalter,
— Besonderer Verwalter,
— Einstweiliger Verwalter,
— Sachwalter,
— Treuhänder,
— Insolvenzgericht,
— Konkursgericht,

Polska

— Syndyk,
— Nadzorca sądowy,
— Zarządca,

Portugal

— Administrador de insolvência,
— Administrador judicial provisório,

România

— Practician în insolvență,
— Administrator judiciar,
— Lichidator,

Slovenija

— Upravitelj prisilne poravnave,
— Stečajni upravitelj,
— Sodišče, pristojno za postopek prisilne poravnave,
— Sodišče, pristojno za stečajni postopek,

Slovensko

— Predbežný správca,
— Správca,

Suomi/Finland

— Pesänhoitaja/boförvaltare,
— Selvittäjä/utredare,

Sverige

— Förvaltare,
— Rekonstruktör,

United Kingdom

— Liquidator,
— Supervisor of a voluntary arrangement,
— Administrator,
— Official Receiver,
— Trustee,
— Provisional Liquidator,
— Judicial factor.

APPENDIX 2

Virgos-Schmit Report on the Convention on Insolvency Proceedings

Explanatory note
This Report was produced during the concluding phase of the negotiations for a Convention on Insolvency Proceedings under the auspices of the Council of the European Union. The text was circulated in draft form among the Member States between November 1995 and May 1996, and was revised in the light of resulting comments. A finalized text was produced by the Legal Linguistic Experts' working party and was allocated the EU Council reference 6500/1/96, REV1, DRS 8 (CFC). It was never formally adopted or officially published by the EU Council, however, as the projected Convention lapsed after 23 May 1996, having failed to receive the required signature by all 15 Member States within the time allowed. Because of the close identity of substance between the provisions of the EC Regulation 1346/2000 and those of the Convention, the Virgos-Schmit Report remains an important aid to interpretation of the Regulation. It is reproduced here in the final revision, dated 8 July 1996, which has kindly been made available by its joint author, Professor Miguel Virgos.

EUROPEAN UNION   Brussels, 8 July 1996
THE COUNCIL

6500/1/96
REV 1
LIMITE
DRS 8 (CFC)
NOTE

Subject: Report on the Convention of [sic] Insolvency Proceedings
Delegations will find attached the above text, as finalized by the Legal Linguistic experts' working party.

Report on the Convention on Insolvency Proceedings[1]
By
MIGUEL VIRGOS
Professor, Universidad Autonoma of Madrid
(who contributed the background and general introduction and the comments on Articles 1 to 26, 43 to 46, territorial application and Article 48)
and
ETIENNE SCHMIT
Magistrate, Deputy Public Prosecutor, Luxembourg
(who contributed the comments on Article 3(2) to 3(4) and Articles 27 to 42, 47, and 49 to 55)

---

[1] The text of the Convention on Insolvency Proceedings was published in Official Journal No L00000 [sic]. The Convention, open for signature in Brussels on 23 November 1995, was signed on that day by the Plenipotentiaries of the following 12 Member States: Belgium, Denmark, Germany, Greece, Spain, France, Italy, Luxembourg, Austria, Portugal, Finland, and Sweden.

CONTENTS

I. Background to the Convention 561
II. General Introduction to the Convention 562
   A. Scheme of the Convention 562
   B. Reasons for the Convention 562
   C. Scope 563
   D. The main and secondary model of insolvency proceedings 564
   E. The main insolvency proceedings 564
   F. Protection of local interest within the main proceedings 565
   G. Local insolvency proceedings: 'independent' and 'secondary' territorial proceedings 565
   H. Functions of the local proceedings 566
   I. Coordination of local insolvency proceedings 567
III. Analysis of the Provisions 568
   A. Preamble 568
   B. Chapter 1: General Provisions 570
   Article 1: Scope 570
   Article 2: Definitions 573
   Article 3: International jurisdiction 576
   Article 4: Law applicable 579
   Article 5: Third parties' rights in rem 581
   Article 6: Set-off 583
   Article 7: Reservation of title 584
   Article 8: Contracts relating to immovable property 585
   Article 9: Payment systems and financial markets 585
   Article 10: Contracts of employment 586
   Article 11: Effects on rights subject to registration 586
   Article 12: Community patents and trademarks 587
   Article 13: Detrimental acts 588
   Article 14: Protection of third-party purchases 588
   Article 15: Effects of insolvency Procedure on lawsuits pending 589
   C. Chapter II: Recognition of Insolvency Proceedings 589
   Article 16: Principle 589
   Article 17: Effects of recognition 590
   Article 18: Powers of the liquidator 592
   Article 19: Proof of the liquidator's appointment 593
   Article 20: Return and imputation 594
   Article 21: Publication 595
   Article 22: Registration in a public register 596
   Article 23: Costs 597
   Article 24: Honouring of an obligation to a debtor 597
   Article 25: Recognition and enforceability of other judgments 597
   Article 26: Public Policy 600
   D. Chapter III: Secondary Insolvency Proceedings 602
   Article 27: Opening of insolvency proceedings 602
   Article 28: Applicable law 604
   Article 29: Right to request the opening of proceedings 604
   Article 30: Advance payment of costs and expenses 604
   Article 31: Duty to cooperate and communicate information 605
   Article 32: Exercise of creditors' rights 605
   Article 33: Stay of liquidation 607
   Article 34: Measures ending secondary insolvency proceedings 608
   Article 35: Assets remaining in the secondary proceedings 609

Article 36: Subsequent opening of the main proceedings 609
Article 37: Conversion of earlier proceedings 609
Article 38: Preservation measures 610
E. Chapter IV: Provision of information for creditors and lodgement of their claims 611
Article 39: Right to lodge claims 611
Article 40: Duty to inform creditors 611
Article 41: Content of the lodgement of a claim 612
Article 42: Languages 612
F. Chapter V: Interpretation by the Court of Justice of the European Communities 613
Article 43: Jurisdiction of the Court of Justice 613
Article 44: Preliminary ruling proceedings 613
Article 45: Proceedings brought by a competent authority 614
Article 46: Reservations 615
G. Chapter VI: Transitional and Final Provisions Territorial Application 615
Article 47: Applicability in time 615
Article 48: Relationship to other Conventions 616
Article 49: Signature, ratification and entry into force 617
Article 50: Accession to the Convention 617
Article 51: Notification by the depositary 617
Article 52: Duration of the Convention 617
Article 53: Revision or evaluation of the Convention 617
Article 54: Amendment of the Annexes 618
Article 55: Deposit of the Convention 618

I. BACKGROUND TO THE CONVENTION

1. The absence of a Convention on in solvency proceedings within the framework of the Community is viewed as a shortcoming in the completion of the internal market. It seems hard to accept that undertakings' activities are increasingly being regulated by Community law while national law alone continues to apply in the event of the failure of an undertaking. This consideration prompted Community Ministers for Justice, meeting informally in San Sebastian from 25 to 27 May 1989, to express the wish that a solution be found and to relaunch the negotiations on a Convention on this matter between the Member States and to give instructions to that effect to an ad hoc Working Party on the Bankruptcy Convention set up within the Council of the European Communities, as it then was.

   A number of national experts (...) was therefore designated. The ad hoc Working Party met from 1991 until the conclusion of the definitive text of the Convention in 1995. Dr Manfred Balz (from Germany) was nominated chairman of the committee of experts. He was also the main author of the various drafts discussed during the negotiations.

2. A limited number of bilateral conventions do indeed exist between some Member States (see Article 48 of the Convention); however, Member States should be linked by a multilateral convention which, through mutual recognition of proceedings opened in each of the Member States, would permit coordination of the measures to be taken regarding an insolvent debtor's assets. To date, attempts to draw up a suitable instrument have been unsuccessful.

3. Bankruptcy, proceedings relating to the winding-up of insolvent companies or other legal persons, judicial arrangements, compositions and analogous proceedings were excluded from the scope of the Convention on Jurisdiction and the Enforcement of Judgments in Civil and Commercial Matters, signed in Brussels on 27 September 1968 and revised for the accession of new Community Member States in 1978, 1982 and 1989 (see OJCE No C 189 of 28 July 1990) hereafter referred to as the '1968 Brussels Convention'. Regarding those proceedings, a committee of experts met, under the auspices of the Commission of the European Communities, between 1963 and 1980 to draw up a first, and subsequently (following the Community's enlargement as from 1973) a second, draft Convention (see Bulletin of the European Communities,

Supplement 2/82, containing both the Draft Convention and the explanatory report). The latter Convention was studied by an EC Council Working Party from 1982 until 1985, when work was suspended for lack of sufficient consensus.

That draft Convention provided for single proceedings (with exclusive competence to decree bankruptcy conferred on the Courts of [sc. the] State in which the debtor's centre of administration was located) which would be recognized in the other Contracting States, and parallel local proceedings were not permitted in those other States. The principles of 'unity' (a single proceeding for the whole territory of the Community) and 'universality' (the proceedings comprise all debtor's assets, wherever located) which governed the proceedings were therefore scrupulously followed in this text.

4. In the meantime, negotiations had been initiated within the Council of Europe which culminated in the adoption of a 'European Convention on Certain International Aspects of Bankruptcy', opened for signing in Istanbul on 5 June 1990 hereafter referred to as the '1990 Istanbul Convention' (see the Convention and its explanatory report in Council of Europe, International aspects of bankruptcy, Strasbourg 1990).

    It must be pointed out, however, that it is not certain that any Member State will ratify the 1990 lstanbul Convention. Moreover, Article 40 thereof allows scope for reservations on either Chapter 11 (Exercise of certain powers of the liquidator) or Chapter III (Secondary insolvency proceedings), which involves a serious risk of disparity as between Contracting States.

    Notwithstanding, the text of the 1990 Istanbul Convention remains important since it introduced more flexibility into the underlying principles of unity and universality.

5. The earlier Community draft ran into a number of obstacles. The principles of unity of the bankruptcy proceedings, on which it was based, led in particular to some complex provisions needed to take account of safeguards and privileges existing only in one or other Member State. Those provisions included the possibility of forming national 'sub-estates' with regard to security interests, privileges and priority claims. Overall, the system proved to be too complicated and ambitious.

For that reason, the new Community Convention on insolvency proceedings offers solutions which are as simple and flexible as possible. Above all, it is based on the principle of the universality of the proceedings limited, however, by the possible opening of one or more sets of secondary proceedings the effects of which are confined to the Member State or Member States in which they were opened.

The parallelism between the main proceedings (recognized elsewhere) and the secondary proceedings (enabling creditors in another Contracting State to invoke a local instrument in order to safeguard their interests) has made it possible to avoid over-rigid centralization, which hitherto appeared to be unacceptable to some Member States. Mandatory rules of coordination with the main proceedings guarantee the needs of unity in the Community.

II. GENERAL INTRODUCTION TO THE CONVENTION

A. Scheme of the Convention

6. The Convention is divided into six Chapters with a total of 55 Articles. A Preamble, which contains important information about the scope and character of the Convention, and three Annexes, which form an integral part of it, complement its provisions.

    Chapter I (Articles 1–15) defines the scope of application of the Convention (Articles 1–2), lays down the rules of direct international jurisdiction (Article 3), and determines the national law applicable through uniform conflict of laws rules (Articles 4–15).

    Chapter II (Articles 16–26) addresses the recognition and enforcement of insolvency proceedings opened in other Contracting States and the recognition of the liquidator's powers.

    Chapter III (Articles 27–38) contains the rules on secondary proceedings and on their coordination with the main proceedings and with other secondary proceedings.

Chapter IV (Articles 39–42) introduces several uniform rules on the right to lodge claims, the duty to provide information and the language to be used.

Chapter V (Articles 43–46) confers jurisdiction to interpret the Convention on the Court of Justice of the European Communities.

Chapter VI (Articles 47–55) contains the transitional and final provisions, including those regarding the applicability in time of the Convention (Article 47), its relationship to other Conventions (Article 48) and the procedures to amend the Annexes (Article 54), which list the insolvency proceedings to which the Convention applies and the persons who or organs which may be recognized as liquidator under the Convention.

B. Reasons for the Convention

7. To date, from a Private International Law perspective, the situation in the Community in the field of insolvency has been far from encouraging. There was a conflict of laws at both the internal level, with divergent national substantive rules, and the international level, with different Private International Law solutions.

   Unlike contracts, insolvencies do not form an area of the law where private spontaneous cooperation can compensate for the lack of a common legal framework at the international level. Institutional cooperation is needed to provide a certain legal order to avoid incentives for the parties to transfer disputes or goods from one State to another, seeking to obtain a more favourable legal position ('forum shopping'), or to realize their individual claims independently of the costs which this may entail for the creditors as a whole or to the going-concern value of the debtor's firm.

   Only a multilateral Convention among all the Member States may discourage the opportunistic conduct of debtors or creditors from taking place and allow for the efficient administration of the financial crisis of firms and individuals within the Community. The Convention on insolvency proceedings provides such a mandatory legal framework of intra-Community cooperation.

   The Convention implements Article 220 of the Treaty establishing the European Community (hereafter referred to as the 'EC Treaty') and complements the 1968 Brussels Convention. It also confers on the Court of Justice of the European Communities jurisdiction to rule on the interpretation of its provisions. But, unlike the 1968 Brussels Convention, it also contains conflict of law rules. There are important grounds which justify this difference.

8. Insolvency proceedings are collective proceedings. Collective action needs clearly determined legal positions to provide for an adequate bargaining environment. This is true not only once the insolvency proceedings have been opened, but also before they have been opened (when the debtor is already in economic difficulties), as the rights 'in bankruptcy' will influence negotiations for a possible 'pre-bankruptcy' reorganization.

   Furthermore, international insolvency proceedings can be effectively conducted only if the States concerned recognize the jurisdiction of the courts of the State of the opening of the proceedings, the powers of their liquidators and the effects of their judgments. They may accept it only if the rules on conflict of laws are also harmonized, because harmonized conflict of law rules prove [sic] a degree of certainty that, in the event of insolvency, rights created or granted in their jurisdictions will be recognized throughout the Contracting States.

C. Scope

9. The Convention applies to collective insolvency proceedings which entail the partial or total divestment of a debtor and the appointment of a liquidator. Two Annexes to the Convention determine the national proceedings covered by the Convention. These Annexes form an integral part of the Convention.

10. Insurance undertakings, credit institutions, investment undertakings holding funds or securities for third parties and collective investment undertakings are all excluded from the scope of the Convention. Community discussions are under way regarding reorganization and winding-up proceedings for these entities.
11. The Convention deals only with the intra-Community effects of insolvency proceedings. It applies only when the centre of the debtor's main interests lies within the territory of a Contracting State (i.e. the Community, see point 300). Even then, the Convention does not regulate the effect of the proceedings vis-à-vis third States. In relation to third States, the Convention does not impair the freedom of the Contracting States to adopt the appropriate rules.

D. The main and secondary model of insolvency proceedings

12. The Convention tries to provide a 'neutral mechanism' for international cooperation, honouring the basic expectations of the parties, independently of the Contracting State in which they are situated. For this purpose, it follows a combined model of the existing principles of regulation of international bankruptcies (universality or territoriality of effects and unity or plurality of proceedings).

    The idea of a single exclusive universal form of insolvency proceedings for the whole of the Community is difficult to implement without modifying, by the application of the law of the State of the opening of proceedings, pre-existing rights created before insolvency under the different national laws of other Contracting States. The reason for this lies in the absence of a uniform system of security rights in Europe, and in the great diversity of national insolvency laws as regards criteria for the priority to be given to the different classes of creditors.
13. In this legal context, the Convention seeks to reconcile the advantages of the principle of universality and the necessary protection of local interests. This explains why a combined model has been adopted which permits local proceedings to coexist with the main universal proceedings.
14. Insolvency proceedings may be opened in the Contracting State where the debtor has the centre of his main interests. Insolvency proceedings opened in that State will be main proceedings of universal character; 'main', because if local proceedings are opened, they will be subject to mandatory rules of coordination and subordination to it, and 'universal', because, unless local proceedings are opened, all assets of the debtor will be encompassed therein, wherever located.

    Single main proceedings are always possible within the Community but the Convention does not exclude the opening of local proceedings, controlled and governed by the national law concerned, to protect those local interests. Local proceedings have only territorial scope, limited to the assets located in the State concerned. To open such local proceedings it is necessary that the debtor possesses an establishment in the territory of the State of the opening of proceedings (hereafter referred to as the 'State of the opening'). In relation to the main proceedings, local insolvency proceedings can only be 'secondary proceedings', since the latter are to be coordinated with and subordinated to the main proceedings.

E. The main insolvency proceedings

15. The 'main insolvency proceedings' can be opened only in the Contracting State where the debtor has established the 'centre of his main interests' (hereinafter 'F1 State'). Normally it will be the place of the registered office in the case of legal persons. There can be only one main set of insolvency proceedings.
16. The main insolvency proceedings may be winding-up or reorganization proceedings, as listed in Annexe A to the Convention.
17. The law of the State of the opening (lex concursus) is generally applicable to the insolvency proceedings. It governs the opening of the proceedings, their conduct and their closure.
18. Some aspects are regulated directly by the Convention, which provides a uniform system of individual notification, lodgement of claims and use of language:

(a) Creditors abroad must be duly informed of the opening of the proceedings. An individual notice must be sent to all known creditors domiciled in other Contracting States;

Where necessary, a notice of the opening of the proceedings shall be published in other Contracting States in accordance with their national publication procedures (F2 laws). Contracting States within the territory of which the debtor has an establishment may demand mandatory publication.

(b) Creditors who have their habitual residence, domicile or registered office in a Contracting State may participate in the main proceedings, whatever the nature (public or private) of their claims.

19. Main proceedings are always universal. This has a number of important legal consequences:
    (a) Assets located outside the State of opening are also included in the proceedings and sequestrated as from the opening of proceedings on a world-wide basis;
    (b) All creditors are encompassed;
    (c) Proceedings opened in one Member State will produce effects throughout the whole territory of the Contracting States (ie the Community). The recognition of the effects of the proceedings in other Contracting States is automatic, by force of law, without the need for an exequatur, and is independent of publication;

    However, enforcement of judgments will require prior limited control by the national courts, through an exequatur. If the conditions set out by the Convention are satisfied, the national Courts are obliged to grant it.

    The Convention follows the model of 'extension' to the other States (to F2, F3, etc.) of the effects laid down by the national law of the State where the main proceedings have been opened (F1).

    (d) The liquidator appointed in the main proceedings has authority to act in all the other Contracting States, without the need for an exequatur. He may remove assets from the State in which they are located. In exercising these powers (granted by F1 laws), the liquidator must comply with the laws of the State concerned (F2). This is particularly the case if coercion is necessary to gain control of the assets (he must then request the assistance of the local authorities);
    (e) Individual execution is not possible against the assets of a debtor located in any Contracting State;
    (f) There is a legal duty to surrender to the insolvency proceedings the proceeds recovered by individual execution or obtained from the debtor's voluntary payment out of assets located abroad.

20. Local insolvency proceedings opened in accordance with the Convention limit the universal scope of the main proceedings. Assets located in the Contracting State where a court opens local insolvency proceedings are subject only to the local proceedings. However, the universal character of the main proceedings reveals itself through the mandatory rules of coordination of the local proceedings with the main proceedings, which include some specific powers of intervention given by the Convention to the liquidator of the main proceedings (see points 36(3) and 38) and the transfer of any surplus in the local proceedings to the main proceedings.

F. Protection of local interest within the main proceedings

21. The application by the State of the opening of proceedings of its law and the automatic extension of the effects of those proceedings to all Community Member States may interfere with the rules under which local market transactions are carried out in other States. For this reason, in the provisions governing the main proceedings, the Convention gives due attention to important local interests: protection of legitimate expectations and security of transactions.

22. To this end, the Convention excludes certain rights over assets located in another Contracting State from the effects of the main proceedings or declares that those effects must be decided by the insolvency laws of the States concerned, and not by the law of the State of the opening of the proceedings.

23. 1. Exclusion from the effects of the main proceedings:
   (a) The opening of insolvency proceedings will not affect pre-existing rights in rem of creditors or other third parties over assets situated in a different Contracting State at the time of the opening of the proceedings. The same rule is also applicable to reservations of title. Firms may obtain credit under conditions which could not be offered without this kind of guarantee.

   If the law of the State in which the security is located permits these rights to be affected, the liquidator (or any authorized creditor) has to request the opening of local insolvency proceedings to achieve this result. The position of the secured creditors will then be the same as in a purely domestic bankruptcy. Only security rights which are in the legal form of a 'right in rem' qualify for this benefit.
   (b) Set-off rights governed by the law of a Contracting State other than the State of the opening receive a solution parallel to that of rights in rem.
2. In other cases, the Convention amends the rule that the law of the State of opening (F1) is applicable and provides that the law of the State concerned (F2) shall govern certain specific effects of the insolvency. In this way, the effects in a given State of insolvency proceedings opened in another Contracting State will be the same as in a domestic case.
   (a) To protect the local systems of registration of property rights, the admissible effects of the insolvency proceedings on rights of the debtor in respect of immovable assets, ships or aircraft subject to registration are determined by the insolvency laws of the State of registration.
   (b) Furthermore, in order to protect bona-fide third-party purchasers the Convention provides that the law of the Contracting State in which the assets are situated applies in the case where the debtor disposes for consideration of immovable assets after the opening of insolvency proceedings in another Contracting State. In the case of aircraft, ships or securities subject to registration, the law of the State of registration applies.
   (c) To avoid disruptions in payment systems and financial markets, which may be protected by national law against the normal rules of insolvency law, the effects of the insolvency proceedings are determined by the law of the State the law of which governs the payment system or financial market.
   (d) The effects of the insolvency proceedings on contracts conferring rights to make use of or acquire immovable property, and on employment contracts and relationships are governed respectively by the laws of the State in which they are situated and by the law applicable to the contract.

G. Local insolvency proceedings: 'independent' and 'secondary' territorial proceedings

24. Local insolvency proceedings may be opened in the Contracting State where the debtor has an establishment. The effects of local proceedings are limited to the assets located in that State. Local insolvency proceedings are always 'territorial'.
25. The Convention permits the opening of local proceedings both before and after main proceedings have been opened in the Contracting State where the debtor has his centre of main interests. Local insolvency proceedings are considered as 'independent' territorial insolvency proceedings in the first case (since there are as yet no main proceedings to which they are subordinated) and as 'secondary' territorial insolvency proceedings in the latter case.

    Independent proceedings become secondary proceedings once main proceedings have been opened, subject to some special rules (see points 31, 37 and 38).

26. Both types of proceedings are subject to rules of coordination with the main proceedings (in the case of independent territorial proceedings, after the opening of the main proceedings) and with other local proceedings.
27. The law of the State of the opening of the local proceedings is applicable to the local insolvency proceedings (see point 17).

    The right to participate in local insolvency proceedings is not limited to local creditors. Once local proceedings have been opened, all creditors (whether local or not) may participate directly or through the liquidator in the main proceedings. This openness guarantees respect for the principle of equal treatment of creditors throughout the Community. As the Community forms an internal market, there can be no restrictions on participation in local proceedings based on the place of origin of the creditor's claim, or on the place of residence of the creditor.
28. The Convention does not restrict the right of any creditor to demand the opening of secondary territorial insolvency proceedings.
29. Secondary territorial insolvency proceedings may only be winding-up proceedings (see also point 31).
30. The right to request the opening of independent territorial proceedings is limited to local creditors and creditors of the local establishment or to cases where main proceedings cannot be opened under the applicable law. The purpose of these restrictions is to avoid the existence of parallel local proceedings which are not coordinated in the framework of the main Community proceedings.

    Such limitations would not impair the individual rights of the creditors to recover debts: if no collective insolvency proceedings are opened, they may resort to individual enforcement measures.
31. Independent territorial proceedings may be winding-up or reorganization proceedings as listed in Annexe A or Annexe B to the Convention.

    In the case of reorganization proceedings, the subsequent opening of the main proceedings makes them subject to the possibility of conversion into winding-up proceedings, if the liquidator in the main proceedings so requests. It such a conversion is not requested, the local proceedings may continue as reorganization proceedings.

H. Functions of the local proceedings

32. The first function of local proceedings is the 'protection of local interests'. Creditors may request the opening of local territorial proceedings to protect themselves against the effects of the law of another Contracting State. They can thus be certain that, even if the debtor's centre of interests is located in another Contracting State, their legal position will be the same as in domestic proceedings. This possibility makes sense for creditors who cannot rely on the recognition of their rights (or their preferential rank) in proceedings in another Contracting State. Further, it also makes sense for creditors who cannot count on the application of the law of another Contracting State (for instance, small creditors who participated only in domestic transactions with the local establishment of an undertaking of another Contracting State, etc).
33. The second function of local proceedings is to serve as 'auxiliary proceedings' to the main proceedings.

    The liquidator in the main proceedings may request the opening of secondary proceedings when the efficient administration of the estate so requires. This may be, for instance, the case where the estate of the debtor is too complex to administer as a unit, where differences in the legal systems concerned are so great that difficulties may arise from the extension of effects deriving from the law of the State of the opening to the other States where the assets are located. It will be always the case where the liquidator in the main proceedings seeks to affect the rights in rem of creditors or other third parties in respect of assets situated in another State at the time of the opening.

I. Coordination of local insolvency proceedings

34. Parallel main and local insolvency proceedings represent an intermediate stage between the individual actions undertaken by the creditors and the 'collective action' in the full sense of the term, represented by single universal proceedings. Cooperation is made easier, since the liquidators' role of intermediary limits the number of parties, reducing the overall complexity.

    However, the method of coordination established between the local proceedings is as important as their existence. In order to encourage cooperation, the Convention permits all creditors, irrespective of the State of origin of their claims, to participate in the local proceedings (local proceedings are not reserved for local creditors).

35. Secondary insolvency proceedings are subject to coordination with the main proceedings in a number of ways to ensure that due attention is given to the interests of the main insolvency without encroaching on the specific functions of the secondary proceedings. Some of these rules of coordination apply also to secondary proceedings inter se (see points 36(1), (2) and (5)).

36. 1. The Convention imposes a duty of reciprocal cooperation and exchange of information on all liquidators in both the main and secondary proceedings.
    2. All liquidators are empowered to:
        (a) lodge in other proceedings the claims already lodged in the proceedings for which they have responsibility; this power is very important for small creditors, whose claims may thus be lodged in proceedings in another Contracting State without great expense, and also for the liquidator in the main proceedings, since it can reinforce his powers to influence the secondary proceedings;
        (b) participate in those proceedings.
    3. The liquidator in the main proceedings is, as such, empowered to:
        (a) request the opening of secondary insolvency proceedings;
        (b) make proposals with a view to the winding-up or other use of the assets in the secondary proceedings;
        (c) propose any rescue plan, composition or comparable measure in the secondary proceedings or require such arrangements to be subject to conditions, his consent being in principle required to that effect;
        (d) request a stay on the liquidation of the assets in the secondary proceedings. Such request may be rejected by the local court only if it is manifestly of no interest to the creditors in the main proceedings. The reason behind this is a desire to provide time for a reorganization or composition to be concluded in the main proceedings, or for the sale of the whole undertaking or establishment.
    4. Any assets remaining after winding-up and distribution in local proceedings pass to the main proceedings.
    5. Any creditor may keep what he has obtained in secondary proceedings but may not participate in the distribution of the estate in the main insolvency proceedings until the other creditors with the same ranking (according to the law of the main proceedings) have obtained, in percentage, an equivalent dividend. The same rule is applicable when the creditor seeks to participate in other secondary proceedings. A consolidated account of dividends must be drawn up for all of the Contracting States (ie the Community.)

37. Independent territorial insolvency proceedings also become 'subordinated' proceedings as soon as main proceedings are opened within the Community. In this case, the same coordination rules to which secondary proceedings are subject apply to the extent that the progress of the independent proceedings so permits. After the opening of main proceedings, local insolvency proceedings may therefore continue not as independent proceedings but as secondary proceedings.

38. In addition, the liquidator in the main proceedings has the specific right to request the conversion of the previously opened independent territorial proceedings of a reorganizational nature (see points 31, 86 and 210) into winding-up proceedings (with a view to easier coordination with the main insolvency proceedings).

39. The Convention does not address the exceptional situation of two parallel independent territorial proceedings taking place at the same time in the Community, without main proceedings having been opened in the Contracting State where the debtor has his centre of main interests. It should be possible to apply, by analogy, the same conventional rules which serve to coordinate secondary insolvency proceedings inter se (see points 36(1),(2) and (5)).

III. ANALYSIS OF THE PROVISIONS

A. Preamble

40. The preamble to the Convention contains several important items of information regarding the role of the Convention within the Community system.
41. The first concerns the legal basis of the Convention. The preamble cites Article 220 of the EC Treaty as that basis.
    Consequently, the characteristics of the Convention on insolvency proceedings are as follows:
    — all Member States must ratify the Convention,
    — powers to give rulings on interpretation are conferred on the Court of Justice of the European Communities. Unlike the 1968 Brussels Convention and the Rome Convention of 19 June 1980 on the Law applicable to Contractual Obligations, hereafter referred to as the '1980 Rome Convention', these powers are granted in the text of the Convention itself and not in additional protocols,
    — there can be no reservations, except as regards the conferral of powers on the Court of Justice of the European Communities (see Article 46) (see points 57 et seq).
42. The Convention on insolvency proceedings complements the system of international jurisdiction and recognition and enforcement of judgments set up in the 1968 Brussels Convention, which is also based on Article 220 of the EC Treaty.

    However, the Convention on insolvency proceedings goes beyond the scope of the 1968 Brussels Convention, since it not only governs international jurisdiction and the recognition of judgments but also contains rules on conflicts regarding the law applicable to the proceedings and effects thereof. A Convention on the mutual recognition of insolvency proceedings would not be possible without the guarantee of respect for acquired rights offered by a uniform system of rules on conflict of laws. Harmonized conflict of law rules guarantee acquired rights so that, in the event of insolvency, rights created in each state will be recognized in other Contracting States.
43. The Convention on insolvency proceedings does not contain any explicit provision regarding its interpretation. In the same way as in the 1968 Brussels Convention and the 1980 Rome Convention, two principles should be followed when interpreting its provisions: the principle of respect for the international character of the rule, and the principle of uniformity.

    The Convention is a self-contained legal structure, and its concepts cannot be placed in the same category as concepts belonging to national law. The Convention must retain the same meaning within different national systems. Its concepts may not therefore be interpreted simply as referring to the national law of one or other of the States concerned.

    When the substance of a problem is directly governed by the Convention, the international character of the Convention requires an autonomous interpretation of its concepts. An autonomous interpretation implies that the meaning of its concepts should be determined by reference to the objectives and system of the Convention, taking into account the specific function of those concepts within this system and the general principles which can be inferred from all the national laws of the Contracting States.

    However, the Convention itself may require the meaning of a concept to be found in the applicable national law, when it does not wish to interfere with the national laws or when the function of a specific provision of the Convention so requires. This is the case, for example, with the concept of insolvency in Article 1 or the concept of rights in rem as laid down in Article 5 of the Convention.

Uniformity of interpretation is required in order to ensure equality in the rights and obligations derived from the Convention for the Contracting States and for the persons concerned irrespective of the Contracting State in which they are located. To this end, the Convention confers powers of interpretation on the Court of Justice of the European Communities.

44. The second important piece of information concerns the territorial framework of the Convention, which covers only the 'intra-Community effects' of insolvency proceedings. The Convention governs only internal conflicts of the Community, with two further limitations:

   (a) the [sic] Convention does not govern all intra-Community conflicts. It covers only cases where the centre of the debtor's main interests is located in a Contracting State. When the centre of the debtor's main interests is outside the territory of a Contracting State, the Convention does not apply. In such a case, it is up to the private international law of Member States to decide whether insolvency proceedings may be opened against the debtor and on the rules and conditions to be applied;

   This holds true regardless of whether the debtor has assets or creditors in other Contracting States and whether the question of the effects of such proceedings in other Contracting States is raised (see point 82);

   (b) Even when the centre of a debtor's main interests is in a Contracting State and the Convention is applicable, its provisions are restricted to relations with other Contracting States. Where non-Member States are concerned, it is the responsibility of each Member State to define the appropriate conflict rules.

   Hence, for example, Article 8 governs the effects of insolvency proceedings on contracts relating to the immovable property of the debtor, as an exception to the general applicability of the law of the State of the opening (ex Article 4), but is applicable only when the immovable property is located in a Contracting State. If the asset in question is situated in a non-Contracting State, the Convention does not govern the case. It is for the State opening the proceedings to decide whether or not an exception to the general applicability of its law is advisable, and under what terms.

45. As the Convention provides only partial (intra-Community) rules, it needs to be supplemented by the private international law provisions of the State in which the insolvency proceedings were opened.

   When incorporating the Convention into their legislations, the Contracting States will therefore have to examine whether their current rules can appropriately implement the rules of the Convention or whether they should establish new rules to that end. In this respect, nothing prevents Contracting States from extending all or some of the solutions of the Convention unilaterally on an extra-Community basis, as part of their national law.

46. The third important item of information relates to the relations between this Convention and Community secondary legislation. The Convention represents the general framework of intra-Community cooperation in the area of insolvency proceedings. However, as in the 1968 Brussels Convention (Article 57(3)) and the 1980 Rome Convention (Article 20), the principle of the primacy of secondary Community law is explicitly enshrined in it. For this reason, the preamble stresses that the Convention does not affect the possible application of the provisions of Community law, or of national law harmonized in accordance with those provisions, which govern insolvency proceedings in particular areas.

   This principle does not prevent certain rules of the Convention from directly amending the solutions contained in previous Community acts (see Article 12).

47. The fourth item of information concerns the binding nature of the Convention, the provisions of which, including the rules on conflicts of law, should be applied by the court of its own motion even if they are not invoked by the parties concerned.

   Although there is no specific mention of this point in the Convention, this was the solution adopted in the 1968 Brussels Convention. Substantial grounds for the binding nature do exist in the Convention on insolvency proceedings, since it deals with collective proceedings which by their very nature are likely to affect multiple interests and individuals. This binding nature is necessary to strengthen the legal protection of individuals established in the Community, since the Convention represents the basic guarantee of their rights vis-à-vis insolvency proceedings opened in other Contracting States.

However, it is for the national law to determine whether the judge is himself bound to establish the facts or whether it is for the interested parties to establish them (see Schlosser Report on the 1968 Brussels Convention, point 22).

B. Chapter I: General Provisions

Article 1

Scope

48. Article 1(1) defines the scope of the Convention by means of the concept of 'collective insolvency proceedings'. Given that it has to encompass widely differing national proceedings, Article 1 restricts itself to providing a very broad framework. Paragraph 1 defines this framework, requiring four cumulative conditions, which will be described below.

    It should be pointed out here that, for the Convention to be applied, it is not sufficient that the proceedings in question meet these conditions in a generic way. Under Article 2(a) and (c), for insolvency proceedings to be covered by the Convention the proceedings concerned must also have been expressly entered by the State concerned in the lists of proceedings in the Annexes, which form an integral part of this Convention. Only those proceedings expressly entered in the list will be considered 'insolvency proceedings' as covered by the Convention and will be able to benefit from its provisions. In an area where national laws differ considerably, the lists are aimed at providing legal certainty regarding the proceedings to which the Convention may be applied.

    In short, Article 1(1) lays down the conditions which enable proceedings to be added to the lists in the Convention by Contracting States, and only when the proceedings are included in the appropriate list will the Convention be applicable (see Article 2 (a) and (c)).

49. Article 1(1) defines the proceedings to which the Convention applies on the basis of four fundamental conditions:

    (a) proceedings must be 'collective', ie all the creditors concerned may seek satisfaction only through the insolvency proceedings, as individual action will be precluded;

    (b) the proceedings must be based on the debtor's 'insolvency' and not on any other grounds.

    The Convention is based on the idea of financial crisis, but does not provide its own definition of insolvency. It takes this from the national law of the country in which proceedings are opened.

    There is no test of insolvency other than that demanded by the national legislation of the State in which proceedings are opened. Thus, if a national law is based on the occurrence of an act of bankruptcy listed in the bankruptcy law or on the evidence that the debtor has ceased to pay his debts, it is sufficient for one of these facts to be established in order that insolvency proceedings be opened and the Convention applied.

    By way of exception, it may happen that one of the forms of proceedings listed in Annexe A or Annexe B to the Convention is not confined to bankruptcy law but serves several purposes. Such a proceeding falls within the scope of the Convention only if it is based on the debtor's insolvency (where appropriate the 1968 Brussels Convention will be applied). This is the case with winding-up proceedings under British and Irish law (see points 55 et seq of the Schlosser Report to the 1968 Brussels Convention).

    Thus, States which list proceedings which can be used for purposes other than insolvency, must provide sufficient means of identification of the proceedings to facilitate the application of the Convention. For instance, requiring their courts or competent bodies to specify clearly the grounds on which the decision to open proceedings is based, so that these can then be used as an identification 'label';

(c) the proceedings must entail the total or partial divestment of the debtor, that is to say the transfer to another person, the liquidator, of the powers of administration and of disposal over all or part of his assets, or the limitation of these powers through the intervention and control of his actions. It should be remembered that partial divestment, whether of his assets or his power of administration, is sufficient. The legal nature that such divestment may take, depending on the national legislation applicable, has no bearing on the application of the Convention to the proceedings in question;

(d) the proceedings should entail the appointment of a liquidator. This requirement is directly linked to the previous condition. The concept of liquidator used by the Convention is, once again, a very broad concept. Under Article 2(b) it includes any person or body whose function is to administer or realize the assets or supervise the management of the debtor's business. The court itself may fulfil this role. The persons or bodies considered to be liquidators by the Convention are set out in the list in Annexe C to the Convention.

50. All the proceedings listed in Annexe A have two ultimate consequences: the total or partial divestment of the debtor and the appointment of a liquidator. However, distortions would arise if the Convention were to apply only from the time when these consequences occur. The initial stages of insolvency proceedings could be excluded from the Convention's system of international cooperation. These consequences are necessary for proceedings to appear in the lists in Annexe A. However, once the proceedings have been included, it is sufficient to open proceedings in order that the Convention should apply from the outset.

51. Article 1(1) of the Convention does not include in its final version the condition that the proceedings may entail the realization of the debtor's assets.

Limiting the application of the Convention to winding-up proceedings would have had the advantage of simplifying the resulting rules. The disadvantage would have been that it would have excluded from European cooperation very important proceedings in bankruptcy practice in certain Contracting States, such as the 'suspensión de pagos' in Spain or the 'surséance van betaling' in the Netherlands.

Economic analysis shows that retaining the option between two possibilities in insolvency law (winding-up or reorganization) is in itself a sound decision. The same should hold true in the international arena. There is no economic reason to justify the exclusion of reorganization proceedings from international cooperation. The Convention also contains sufficient mechanisms to protect creditors' interests (eg the possibility of opening territorial insolvency proceedings in accordance with national law). For some Contracting States the exclusion of reorganization proceedings would therefore be unjustified.

The outcome of the negotiations was a compromise to extend the Convention system to insolvency proceedings the main aim of which was not winding-up but reorganization.

As part of this compromise, however, local territorial proceedings opened after the main proceedings may only be winding-up proceedings (see points 83 and 86). If opened before, local territorial proceedings may be reorganization proceedings as listed in Annexe A, but are subject to conversion into winding-up proceedings if the liquidator of the main proceedings so requests. The complications of compatibility and coordination between secondary reorganization proceedings (of which there could be several, if the debtor was based in several different Contracting States) and the main proceedings have led to this restriction.

52. The Convention is drawn up on the basis of insolvency proceedings conducted by the courts. This will be the general rule.

However, Article 1 does not require the proceedings necessarily to involve the intervention of a judicial authority (or of an authority with an equivalent role). They must be proceedings (comprising a minimum number of acts and formalities as set down in law) which are officially recognized and legally effective in the State in which the proceedings are opened and which fulfil the four conditions set out in Article 1(1).

The requirement of intervention by a judicial authority was deliberately excluded to allow the Convention to be applied to ordinary non-judicial collective proceedings in countries such as the United Kingdom and Ireland (especially the creditor's [sic] voluntary winding-up). These proceedings offer sufficient guarantees (including access to the courts, for the legality of the proceedings to be supervised and for any questions which may arise to be settled) in order that they be brought under the Convention. Their practical significance justifies this: they represent an important percentage of all corporate insolvency cases. Once again, the Convention has enough mechanisms to defend the positions of the creditors (the possibility of secondary proceedings, public order exceptions, safeguard of acquired rights, etc) to enable these proceedings to benefit from the Convention system.

The fact that non-judicial proceedings are covered in the Convention does not mean that they are dealt with as if they were judicial proceedings or that the decisions adopted in the course of these proceedings are regarded as having the effect of a court ruling. It simply means the rules of the Convention must be applied with flexibility taking into account that they were drawn up on the basis of proceedings conducted by a court.

From this point of view, the Convention guarantees a positive answer to two essential questions:

1. these proceedings have to be recognized as collective insolvency proceedings pursuant to Article 1. Once proceedings have been opened in a Contracting State in accordance with Article 3, the creditors must seek payment of their debts through these collective proceedings, even if they are not conducted by the courts. Any question relating to the conduct of the proceedings or the decisions taken in the course of those proceedings, should be referred to the courts of that State;
2. the appointment of the liquidator and the powers conferred on him by the law of the State where proceedings were opened must be recognized in other Contracting States. However if the liquidator wishes to exercise his powers in another Contracting State, it is necessary for the Contracting States having proceedings of this type (the United Kingdom and Ireland) to introduce into their national legislation a system of confirmation by the courts of the nature of the proceedings and the appointment of the liquidator. This condition is shown in the list in Annexe A which contains the proceedings designated by each country. In both cases these are termed proceedings 'with confirmation of or by a court'.

53. Finally, Article 1(1) does not require that a debtor have a particular status. The Convention applies equally to all proceedings, whether these involve a natural person or a legal person, a trader or an individual (see comments on Article 4).
54. Article 1(2): The Convention does not cover insolvency proceedings concerning insurance undertakings, credit institutions, investment undertakings which provide services involving the holding of funds or securities for third parties, or collective investment undertakings.

Contracting States subject these entities to prudential supervision through national regulatory authorities in order to minimize the risk to the relevant industries and to the financial system as a whole. All these entities are subject to specific Community regulations in the exercise of freedom of establishment and freedom to provide services, which are founded on the principle of control by the authorities of the State of origin of the entity in question. Negotiations are under way for Directives on reorganization measures and winding-up proceedings for credit institutions and insurance undertakings and Directives concerning insolvency proceedings relating to other entities described in this point are expected to follow. It has been agreed, therefore, that insolvency proceedings relating to the aforementioned entities should be excluded from the scope of this Convention.

55. The exclusion of credit institutions and insurance undertakings was agreed to by all Member States only after a statement by the Council and the Commission regarding the need to step up work on insolvency proceedings involving institutions and undertakings referred to in Article 1(2).
56. The excluded entities and undertakings are defined not in the Convention but by other instruments of Community law. The provisions currently applicable are mentioned in points 57 to 60.

The entities and undertakings which fall under the definitions given by the relevant Community Regulations and Directives are excluded from the Convention. Once an entity or an undertaking falls under the said definitions, the fact that the specific rules laid down by those Community Regulations or Directives are not, for any other reason, applicable to them does not alter this rule.

57. An 'insurance undertaking' is any entity covered by the First Council Directive 73/239/EEC of 24 July 1973 on the coordination of laws, regulations and administrative provisions relating to the taking up and pursuit of the business of direct insurance other than life assurance as last amended by Directive 95/26/EC and by the First Council Directive 79/267/EEC of 5 March 1979 on the coordination of laws, regulations and administrative provisions relating to the taking up and pursuit of the business of direct life assurance, as last amended by Directive 95/26/EC.
58. A 'credit institution' is any entity covered by the definition in the First Council Directive 77/780/EEC of 12 December 1977 on the coordination of the laws, regulations and administrative provisions relating to the taking up and pursuit of the business of credit institutions as last amended by Directive 95/26/EC, which is an enterprise whose activity consists of receiving deposits or other reimbursable funds from the public and granting loans on its own account.
59. An 'investment undertaking' is any entity covered by the definition in Council Directive 93/22/EEC of 10 May 1993 on investment services in the securities field as amended by Directive 95/26/ EC (Article 1); in other words, any enterprise which regularly carries out a professional activity consisting of supplying third parties with an investment service concerning securities (and money-market instruments). Examples of an investment service are: the receiving, transfer and buying or selling of securities on behalf of another person, dealing in these securities on one's own behalf, management on a discretionary and individualized basis of investment portfolios of securities in accordance with a mandate given by the investors.
60. A 'collective investment undertaking' is any undertaking covered by the definition set out in Council Directive 85/611/EEC of 20 December 1985 on the coordination of laws, regulations and administrative provisions relating to undertakings for collective investment in transferable securities (UCITS) as last amended by Directive 95/26/EC; in other words, any body whose sole aim is the joint investment of securities from capital collected from the public, whose operations are subject to the principles of risk sharing, and the shares of which are, on the bearer's request, bought or paid back, directly or indirectly, from the assets of those bodies.

Article 2

Definitions

61. Article 2 provides definitions of a series of concepts which appear throughout the Convention.
62. Article 2(a) indicates that, for the purposes of the Convention, 'insolvency proceedings' refer to proceedings which meet the conditions in Article 1(1) and are included in Annexe A to the Convention which forms an integral part thereof. Hence only the proceedings included in the Annexe may benefit from the system of recognition in the Convention.

    Contracting States may amend the list of their proceedings by using the revision mechanism laid down in Article 54.
63. Article 2(b): the concept of 'liquidator' is understood in a broad sense, to encompass any person or body who or which is appointed to administer or realize the bankrupt's assets, or to supervise the management of the debtor's affairs (the full or partial divestment of the debtor being one of the pre-conditions if the proceedings are to fall under the Convention).

    The identification of those persons or bodies of national law who or which may be characterized as 'liquidator' for the purposes of the Convention is established by means of their inclusion in the list of Annexe C of the Convention.

    When the court itself performs, according to the national law, functions of administration of the debtor's assets, it may qualify as 'liquidator' within the meaning of the Convention. It is, however, necessary that the State in question states in Annexe C of the Convention that its courts may act as liquidator.
64. Article 2(c): the concept of 'winding-up proceedings' aims to define the type of proceedings acceptable as secondary proceedings.

For the reasons given in point 51, only insolvency proceedings within the meaning of Article 1 which, in addition, may entail the realization of the debtor's assets can be secondary proceedings after the main proceedings have been opened.

The fact that winding-up proceedings may be brought to a close through agreement with the creditors, or in some other way, thus putting an end to the debtor's insolvency, does not alter this qualification if the essential aim of the proceedings is to proceed with winding-up.

The Contracting States must enter in the list in Annexe B those proceedings which serve as secondary proceedings. If a State fails to include specific proceedings in the list in Annexe B, these proceedings may not then benefit from the provisions of the Convention. All Contracting States must include at least one type of proceedings in the list in Annexe B.

65. The Convention does not restrict the types of proceedings which can serve as independent territorial proceedings opened before the main proceedings in accordance with Article 3(4).

    These proceedings may be those included in Annexe A (including reorganization proceedings) or Annexe B (only winding-up proceedings). However, once the main proceedings are opened, the liquidator in the main proceedings is empowered to request the conversion of any local insolvency proceedings opened in accordance with Article 3(4) into winding-up proceedings listed in Annexe B.

66. Article 2(d): the expression 'court' is taken in a very broad sense. It covers not only the judiciary or an authority which plays a role similar to that of a court or public authority (as was the case with earlier draft versions of the Convention), but also a person or body empowered by national law to open proceedings or make decisions in the course of those proceedings (see point 52).

    This wording brings this Convention close to the concept of 'competent authority' in Article 4 of the 1990 Istanbul Convention, where the explanatory report (in point 23) states that the term 'competent authority' for the opening of proceedings may include the competent body of a legal person which decides on its own winding-up for reasons of insolvency as is the case in Ireland and the United Kingdom.

67. Article 2(e): 'judgment' must be taken in a broad sense to mean 'decision', consistent with what is said in point 66.

68. Article 2(f): 'the time of the opening of proceedings' is very important, since many questions are settled by reference to it. The time of the opening of proceedings is deemed to be the time when the decision begins to be effective under the law of the State of the opening of the proceedings.

    The Convention does not require the decision to open insolvency proceedings to be final. It is sufficient for it to have effect in the State of opening and for its effects not to have been stayed.

    In the case of non-judicial proceedings of the 'creditors' voluntary winding-up' type, the working party discussed whether, in order to fix the time of opening, the same rule should be used or whether the date of confirmation by the court of the nature of the proceedings and the appointment of the liquidator should be taken as the reference point. Only in order to allow the liquidator to exercise his powers on the territory of another Contracting State would it be necessary to take the date of confirmation by the court as the reference (see point 52). For all other matters, the general rule given above in this point stands.

69. Article 2(g): 'the Contracting State in which assets are situated'. This definition is important in so far as the main proceedings do not affect certain rights on assets located abroad (see Articles 5 and 7) and territorial proceedings can only affect the assets located in the State in which proceedings are opened. To this extent the Convention must help to determine what criteria regarding location are to be followed. In reality, the Convention does no more than stress traditional solutions of private international law which are well known in all the Contracting States.

    Thus, tangible property is considered to be located in the place in which it is physically situated.

    Property and rights ownership of or entitlement to which must be entered in a public register in order to establish rights in rem over them are considered to be located in the State under the authority of which the register is kept. This provision is applicable, for example, in the case of ship and aircraft registers, and also extends to intangible property, such as patents or securities. The

State under whose authority the register is kept is not necessarily the State in which the register is physically situated (eg it may be a consular register or centralized international register).

'Public register' does not mean a register kept by a public authority, but rather a register for public access, an entry in which produces effects vis-à-vis third parties. It also includes private registers with these characteristics, recognized by the national legal system concerned.

In the case of Community patents, trademarks and other similar rights of Community origin, Article 12 states that these can only be included in main proceedings based on Article 3(1) (see point 133).

Finally, claims are deemed to be situated in the State where the debtor required to meet the claim in question (and not the insolvent debtor) has his centre of main interests. The concept of 'centre of main interests' is the same as that specified in Article 3(1) (see point 75).

70. Article 2(h): The concept of 'establishment' is linked to the basis of international jurisdiction to open territorial proceedings. In this regard, it should be mentioned that Article 3(2), in which the jurisdiction to open such territorial proceedings is dealt with, was one of the most debated provisions throughout the negotiations.

Several Contracting States wished to have the possibility of basing territorial proceedings not only on the presence of an establishment, but also on the mere presence of assets of the debtor (assigned to an economic activity) without the debtor having an establishment.

For the sake of an overall consensus on the Convention, those States agreed to abandon the presence of assets as a basis for international competence provided that the concept of establishment is interpreted in a broad manner but consistently with the text of the Convention. This explains the very open definition given in Article 2(h).

In the Convention, the mere presence of assets (eg the existence of a bank account) does not enable local territorial proceedings to be opened. The presence of an establishment of the debtor within the jurisdiction concerned is necessary.

Though defended by one State, the possibility of adopting the same concept of establishment in the Convention as that given by the Court of Justice of the European Communities in its interpretation of Article 5(5) of the 1968 Brussels Convention was ruled out. The majority of States preferred an independent concept to be developed.

Indeed, the Court of Justice of the European Communities emphasized that the special powers laid down in Article 5 of the 1968 Brussels Convention must be strictly interpreted vis-à-vis the general forum of the place of domicile of the defendant. Under these conditions, to import a concept from the 1968 Brussels Convention involved the risk of conveying a possibly restrictive interpretation of the concept of establishment to the Convention on insolvency proceedings, which was precisely the opposite of what most of the working party intended. For this reason, they opted to give the Convention its own definition, which is contained in Article 2.

71. For the Convention on insolvency proceedings, 'establishment' is understood to mean a place of operations through which the debtor carries out an economic activity on a non-transitory basis, and where he uses human resources and goods.

Place of operations means a place from which economic activities are exercised on the market (ie externally), whether the said activities are commercial, industrial or professional.

The emphasis on an economic activity having to be carried out using human resources shows the need for a minimum level of organization. A purely occasional place of operations cannot be classified as an 'establishment'. A certain stability is required. The negative formula ('non-transitory') aims to avoid minimum time requirements. The decisive factor is how the activity appears externally, and not the intention of the debtor.

The rationale behind the rule is that foreign economic operators conducting their economic activities through a local establishment should be subject to the same rules as national economic operators as long as they are both operating in the same market. In this way, potential creditors concluding a contract with a local establishment will not have to worry about whether the company is a national or foreign one. Their information costs and legal risks in the event of insolvency of the debtor will be the same whether they conclude a contract with a national undertaking or a foreign undertaking with a local presence on that market.

Naturally, the possibility of opening local territorial insolvency proceedings makes sense only if the debtor possesses sufficient assets within the jurisdiction. Whether or not these assets are linked to the economic activities of the establishment is of no relevance.

Article 3

International jurisdiction

72. The rules of jurisdiction set out in the Convention establish only international jurisdiction, that is to say, they designate the Contracting State the courts of which may open insolvency proceedings. Territorial jurisdiction within that Contracting State must be established by the national law of the State concerned.
73. Main insolvency proceedings

    Article 3(1) enables main insolvency universal proceedings to be opened in the Contracting State where the debtor has his centre of main interests. Main insolvency proceedings have universal scope. They aim at encompassing all the debtor's assets on a world-wide basis and at affecting all creditors, wherever located.

    Only one set of main proceedings may be opened in the territory covered by the Convention.
74. Which persons or legal entities may be subject to insolvency proceedings is determined by national law. Where the international jurisdiction rule mentions the debtor, this means the natural persons or legal entity (whether a legal person or not) concerned.
75. The concept of 'centre of main interests' must be interpreted as the place where the debtor conducts the administration of his interests on a regular basis and is therefore ascertainable by third parties.

    The rationale of this rule is not difficult to explain. Insolvency is a foreseeable risk. It is therefore important that international jurisdiction (which, as we will see, entails the application of the insolvency laws of that Contracting State) be based on a place known to the debtor's potential creditors. This enables the legal risks which would have to be assumed in the case of insolvency to be calculated.

    By using the term 'interests', the intention was to encompass not only commercial, industrial or professional activities, but also general economic activities, so as to include the activities of private individuals (eg consumers). The expression 'main' serves as a criterion for the cases where these interests include activities of different types which are run from different centres.

    In principle, the centre of main interests will in the case of professionals be the place of their professional domicile and for natural persons in general, the place of their habitual residence.

    Where companies and legal persons are concerned, the Convention presumes, unless proved to the contrary, that the debtor's centre of main interests is the place of his registered office. This place normally corresponds to the debtor's head office.
76. The Convention offers no rule for groups of affiliated companies (parent-subsidiary schemes).

    The general rule to open or to consolidate insolvency proceedings against any of the related companies as a principal or jointly liable debtor is that jurisdiction must exist according to the Convention for each of the concerned debtors with a separate legal entity.

    Naturally, the drawing up of a European norm on associated companies may affect this answer.
77. Article 3(1) gives the courts in the State of the opening of proceedings jurisdiction in relation to insolvency proceedings. However, the Convention contains no rule defining the limits of this jurisdiction.

    This is a fundamental question since it raises the issue of the relationship between the Convention on insolvency proceedings and the 1968 Brussels Convention and their respective scope.

    Certain Contracting States recognize a 'vis attractiva concursus' in their national law, by virtue of which the Court which opens the insolvency proceedings has within its jurisdiction not only the actual insolvency proceedings but also all the actions arising from the insolvency.

    Although the projection of this principle in the international domain is controversial, the 1982 Community Draft Convention contained a provision in Article 15 which, according to the

Lemontey Report, was inspired by the 'vis attractiva' theory. This Article conferred on the courts of the State of the opening of insolvency proceedings jurisdiction over a wide series of actions resulting from the insolvency.

Neither this precept nor this philosophy has been adopted in this Convention. There is no provision in Article 3 of the Convention addressing this problem. However, the Convention's silence on the matter is only partial. Article 25 thereof contains the delimitation criterion between both the 1968 Brussels Convention and this Convention.

This criterion is directly taken from the Court of Justice of the European Communities. It was outlined by the Court of Justice in the interpretation of Article 1(2) of the 1968 Brussels Convention in its Judgment of 22 February 1979 (Case 133/78, *Gourdain v Nadler* [1979] ECR 733).

Article 1(2) of the 1968 Brussels Convention excludes 'bankruptcy, proceedings relating to the winding-up of insolvent companies or other legal persons, judicial arrangements, compositions and analogous proceedings' from its scope. In that Judgment the Court of Justice of the European Communities used the nature of the action taken as the criterion for determining whether or not the jurisdiction rules of the 1968 Brussels Convention applied. According to this criterion, actions directly derived from insolvency and in close connection with the insolvency proceedings are excluded from the 1968 Brussels Convention. Logically, to avoid unjustifiable loopholes between the two Conventions, these actions are now subject to the Convention on insolvency proceedings and to its rules of jurisdiction.

78. The rule on international jurisdiction in Article 3(1) enables the court having jurisdiction to open main insolvency proceedings to order provisional and protective measures from the time of the request to open proceedings.

Preservation measures both prior to and after the commencement of the insolvency proceedings are very important to guarantee the effectiveness of the insolvency proceedings. They may be ordered by the court having jurisdiction according to Article 3(1) irrespective of the Contracting State where the assets or persons concerned (either debtor or a creditor) are located. Such measures may adopt a wide-range of forms, according to the national law of the court ordering them (eg interlocutory orders to do or not to do, appointment of a temporary administrator, attachment of assets).

These preservation measures shall be recognized and enforced in other Contracting States, according to the conditions set out in Article 25 of the Convention (see point 198).

Article 3(1) does not prevent the liquidator, or any other empowered person, from going to the place where the preservation is to be carried out (eg the State in which the assets are located) and asking the local courts to adopt provisional measures available under the national law. This possibility presupposes that the courts of that State enjoy jurisdiction to adopt such measures under their national law (as should usually be the case), and the fulfilment of the subject-matter requirements of that law (evidence of a good prima facie case, sufficient urgency, security to cover damages which may be caused, etc).

These preservation measures are ancillary to the main proceedings. Logically, they remain subordinated to the decisions taken in the course of the main proceedings by the court having jurisdiction under Article 3(1) and which benefit from the system of recognition and enforcement of the Convention. Hence, under Articles 16 and 25, such a court may even stipulate that those preservation measure are to be lifted, modified or continued (see point 198).

The possibility of going to the court of the place where the measures are to take effect is referred to again in Article 38, although with a different purpose. Article 38 empowers the temporary administrator appointed after the request for the opening of main insolvency proceedings, but before such opening, to call directly on the authorities of any other Contracting State to adopt preservation measures provided under the insolvency law of this State for winding-up proceedings on the debtor's assets situated in its territory, as a pre-opening stage of secondary proceedings (see point 262).

79. The Convention does not provide any express rule to resolve cases where the courts of two Contracting States concurrently claim jurisdiction in accordance with Article 3(1). Such

conflicts of jurisdiction must be an exception, given the necessarily uniform nature of the criteria of jurisdiction used.

Where disputes do arise, to solve them, the courts will be able to take account of:
1. the Convention's system according to which:
   (a) each court is obliged to verify its own international jurisdiction in accordance with the Convention;
   (b) the principle of Community trust, according to which once the first court of a Contracting State has adopted a decision, the other States are required to recognize it (see points 202 and 220).
2. the possibility of a request for a preliminary ruling to the Court of Justice of the European Communities, guaranteeing the uniformity of the contents of the criteria for international jurisdiction and its appropriate interpretation in the given case;
3. the general principles of procedural law which are valid in all Contracting States; these principles include those derived from other Community Conventions such as the 1968 Brussels Convention.

80. Local insolvency proceedings

Article 3(2) enables territorial proceedings to be opened in the State in which the debtor has an establishment, as defined in Article 2(h), under the following conditions.

In cases where the debtor's centre of main interests is located in a Contracting State, the courts of other Contracting States have no power to open main insolvency proceedings.

However, any of these Contracting States may open territorial proceedings, the effectiveness of which is restricted to the assets situated in that State, if the debtor has an establishment in the territory of that State. The mere presence of assets is not sufficient to open territorial proceedings.

Depending on whether or not main proceedings have been opened, the proceedings shall be secondary or independent territorial proceedings.

81. Article 3(2) does not grant jurisdiction to open territorial proceedings to the courts of a State where the debtor does not have an establishment. The assets located in that State cannot, therefore, be included in territorial proceedings, but revert to the main proceedings, if such have been opened.

82. Should the debtor's centre of main interests be located outside the territory of the Contracting States, it is not within the jurisdiction of any Contracting State to open insolvency proceedings within the scope of the Convention. Article 3(1) and (2) assumes [sic] that the centre of main interests is in a Contracting State.

When the centre of main interest does not lie in a Contracting State, national law determines the international jurisdiction of its courts. The effects of such proceedings are not governed by this Convention (see point 44).

83. Secondary territorial insolvency proceedings

Article 3(3) requires that after main proceedings have been opened by the competent court within the meaning of Article 3(1), the subsequent proceedings opened by the court of the State where the establishment is located, in accordance with Article 3(2), are secondary proceedings, subject to Chapter III.

In the event of there being a number of establishments located in different Contracting States, several sets of secondary proceedings may be opened.

The secondary proceedings under Article 3(3) may not be reorganization proceedings, rather they must be winding-up proceedings as mentioned in Annexe B. This rule is reaffirmed in Article 27 (see comments re Article 27 (points 211 et seq)).

84. Independent territorial insolvency proceedings

Article 3(4) deals with situations which exist prior to the opening of main proceedings. This is the result of efforts to reconcile two essentially conflicting approaches.

In line with the philosophy expressed most particularly in Articles 3(1) and (2) and Article 27, the court of the debtor's centre of main interests is the only one having jurisdiction to open main proceedings. These proceedings should naturally encompass all the debtor's assets regardless of the State in which the property is located.

Under the first approach, it is only as an exception to the universal proceedings that territorial proceedings may be opened in advance, in order to satisfy 'local' creditors as to the assets present in that State. Indeed, it is difficult to imagine that 'local' creditors who hold a favourable ranking in the State where the property is located would want to transfer all the assets to another State where their ranking would be less favourable. It is likewise difficult for States without any creditors holding a preferential ranking to accept the transfer of all the assets abroad.

The other approach involves seeking to protect local creditors by allowing national rules on the opening of proceedings to follow their normal course, even in a State where an establishment is located, and even at all times, prior to and regardless of the opening of proceedings in the State of the centre of main interests. This approach takes into account the insolvency of an establishment and the creditors' interest in territorial proceedings or the general interest in territorial proceedings to reorganize an establishment of social and economic importance within that State, and grants less consideration to the principle of the universality of insolvency proceedings.

85. Article 3(4) adopts the following rule:

    The courts of a Contracting State having jurisdiction under Article 3(2) may open, prior to the main proceedings, territorial insolvency proceedings called for this reason independent territorial proceedings, in only two cases:

    1. The conditions for opening the insolvency proceedings, as set out by the law of the State where the centre of main interests is located, do not allow main proceedings to be opened.

       That will be the case if, for example, the debtor cannot be subject to insolvency proceedings, eg where the applicable law requires the debtor to be a trader, and this is not the case, or where the debtor is a public company which the law of the State of the centre of main interests does not allow to be declared insolvent.

    2. A local creditor or a creditor of the local establishment, within the meaning of Article 3(4)(b), requests territorial proceedings be opened.

       The protected creditor to whom this right to request the opening of territorial proceedings is granted is one:

       (a) whose habitual residence, domicile and registered office is in the State where the establishment is located,

       (b) or whose claim arises from the operation of that establishment (eg an employee working for that establishment; a person who entered through the establishment into an undertaking which must be performed in that State; the tax authorities and social security bodies).

    Outside these two possible cases, the court having jurisdiction to open the territorial proceedings cannot open proceedings prior to the opening of proceedings in the centre of main interests.

86. The territorial proceedings mentioned in Article 3(4) may be winding-up proceedings or reorganization proceedings mentioned in Annexe A or Annexe B.

    In the event of the subsequent opening of the main proceedings, independent territorial proceedings become secondary proceedings, in accordance with the special rules of Articles 36 and 37 of the Convention.

    Furthermore, reorganization proceedings as mentioned in Annexe A will, at the request of the liquidator in the main proceedings, be converted into secondary winding-up proceedings, in accordance with Articles 36 and 37 (see points 210, 254 to 261). If the liquidator in the main proceedings does not request this conversion, the territorial proceedings may continue as organization proceedings.

Article 4

Law applicable

87. The Convention sets out, for the matters covered by it, uniform rules on conflict of laws which replace national rules of private international law.

When these rules on conflict of laws talk of the 'applicable law', they refer to the internal law of the Contracting State designated by the rule, excluding its rules of private international law.

88. General rule on conflict of laws

Article 4 lays down the basic rule on conflict of laws of the Convention. This Article determines the law applicable to the insolvency proceedings, the conduct thereof and their effects: unless otherwise stated by this Convention, the law of the Contracting State of the opening of the proceedings is applicable (lex concursus).

89. This rule on conflict of laws is valid both for the main proceedings and for local proceedings (secondary or independent territorial proceedings).

To avoid any doubts, Article 28 reiterates this solution for the secondary proceedings. Although Article 28 only considers the secondary proceedings, it is clear that the application of the law of the State of the opening of the proceedings operates as the general conflict of laws rule of the Convention and is also valid for independent territorial proceedings.

90. The law of the State of the opening of proceedings determines all the effects of the insolvency proceedings, both procedural and substantive, on the persons and legal relations concerned.

This law governs all the conditions for the opening, conduct and closure of the insolvency proceedings. It stipulates, inter alia, who may be subject to insolvency proceedings, the requirements to open them and who may present the petition; it determines the nature and the extent of the debtor's divestment and the assets covered by it; it outlines the organization of the administration of the estate and regulates the designation of the liquidator and his powers; it decides the admissibility of claims and the rules on distribution and preferences; it governs the closure of the proceedings and its consequences, etc.

The substantive effects referred to the competence of the law of the State of the opening by Article 4, are those typical of insolvency law, ie effects which are necessary for the insolvency proceedings to fulfil its aims. To this extent, the law of the State of the opening may displace (unless the Convention provides otherwise), the law normally applicable, under the common pre-insolvency rules on conflict of laws, to the act concerned. This happens for instance when Article 4 makes applicable the law of the State of opening of proceedings to invalidate any act (eg a contract) detrimental to all the creditors, even if that act is governed under the general rules on conflict of laws (if a contract, those of the 1980 Rome Convention), by the law of a different State.

91. To facilitate its interpretation, Article 4(2) contains a non-exhaustive list of questions that are governed by the law of the State of the opening.

(a) whether a particular debtor by virtue of his status (eg trader/non-trader, public law company) may be subject to insolvency proceedings (Article 4(2)(a)). This rule is valid for both the main proceedings and for secondary proceedings, where the solution to the case may be different. This paragraph is linked to Article 3(4)(a) and Article 16(2) (see points 85 and 148);

(b) which assets form part of the estate and the treatment of assets acquired by the debtor after the opening of proceedings;

(c) the respective powers of the debtor and the liquidator. This paragraph is linked to Article 14 (see point 141);

(d) the conditions under which set-offs may be invoked. This paragraph is linked to Articles 6 and 9 (see points 107 to 111 and 120 et seq);

(e) the effects of the proceedings on current contracts to which the debtor is party (paragraph (e)). To the extent necessary, the law of the State of the opening displaces the law of the contract determined in accordance with the 1980 Rome Convention. This paragraph is linked to Articles 8 and 10 (see points 116 to 119; 125 et seq);

(f) the effects of the insolvency proceedings on executions brought by individual creditors, their suspension or prohibition after the opening of collective insolvency proceedings. However, the effects of the proceedings on lawsuits pending remain subject to the law of the Contracting State where the lawsuit is pending, ex Article 15 (see point 142);

(g) the claims which are to be lodged against the debtor's estate and the treatment of claims arising after the opening of insolvency proceedings (ie claims arising in the administration and management of the assets which in many systems benefit from preferential payment);

(h) the rules governing the lodging, verification and admission of claims. It must be borne in mind that Chapter IV of the Convention sets out a number of uniform rules on this subject. As regards claims that are admissible, Article 39 acknowledges 'iure conventionis' that Contracting States' public law claims can be lodged in insolvency proceedings opened in other Contracting States. This precept expressly stipulates the right of the tax and social security authorities of any Contracting State to submit their claims in insolvency proceedings opened pursuant to the Convention;

(i) the ranking (privileges, preferences, etc) and the rules on distribution of the assets realized. As in all main or secondary proceedings the national law of the State of the opening is applicable, the ranking of a claim may vary for each of the proceedings in which it is lodged;

(j) the conditions and effects of the closure of proceedings, including closure by composition or equivalent measure;

(k) the rights of the creditors subsequent to the closure of the proceedings, including any possible discharge of the debtor;

(l) the costs and expenses of the proceedings;

(m) the voidness, voidability or unenforceability of legal acts that may be detrimental to all the creditors. The applicable national law determines whether action must be taken to obtain their invalidation or whether the decision to open proceedings automatically entails invalidation. To the extent necessary, the law of the State of the opening displaces the law normally applicable to the act in question. This paragraph is to be taken in conjunction with Article 13 (see point 135).

In the case of secondary proceedings, the local rules on invalidation of a detrimental act shall be applicable only in so far as damage has been caused to the debtor's assets which are in this State (eg to the estate of the secondary proceedings). For instance, the act in question (sale, establishment of a right in rem) involves an asset which was located in this State at the relevant time.

92. Exceptions to the general rule on conflicts of law of Article 4

The application, by the courts in the State of the opening of proceedings, of their national insolvency law and the automatic extension of its effects to all the Contracting States (see Articles 16 and 25) may interfere with the rules under which transactions are carried out in these States.

To protect legitimate expectations and the certainty of transactions in States other than that in which proceedings are opened (for in the latter State all the operators have to count on the application of its laws) the Convention provides for a number of exceptions to the general rule:

1. In certain cases, the Convention excludes some rights over assets located abroad from the effects of the insolvency proceedings (as in Articles 5, 6 and 7).

2. In other cases, it ensures that certain effects of the insolvency proceedings are governed not by the law of the State of the opening (F1), but by the law of the State concerned (see Articles 8, 9, 10, 11, 14 and 15). In such cases, the effects to be given to the proceedings opened in other Contracting States are the same effects attributed to a domestic proceedings of equivalent nature (liquidation, composition, or reorganization proceedings) by the law of the State concerned (F2).

93. The exceptions to the application of the law of the State of the opening (Article 4) are referred to in Articles 5 to 15 of the Convention. Apart from Articles 6 and 14, which by systemic arguments must be interpreted in the same way, the exception is made in favour of the law of a 'Contracting State'.

This does not mean that, by a contrario interpretation, the law of the State of the opening of proceedings is applicable where the State concerned is not a Contracting State. The need to protect legitimate expectations and the certainty of transactions is equally valid in relations with non-Contracting States. The group's intention was simply to regulate these cases in line with the general restriction of the Convention to the intra-Community effect of insolvency proceedings (see point 44). Contracting States are, therefore, free to decide which rules they deem most appropriate in other cases (the same ones as in Articles 5 to 15 of the Convention, or others).

Article 5

Third parties' rights in rem

94. This provision excludes from the effects of the proceedings rights in rem of third parties and creditors in respect of assets belonging to the debtor which, at the time of the opening of proceedings, are situated within the territory of another Contracting State.

    If the assets are situated in a non-Contracting State, Article 5 does not govern the issue (see points 44 and 93).

95. In order to understand the functioning of Article 5, account should be taken of the fact that main insolvency proceedings based on Article 3(1) have a universal scope. All the assets of the debtor shall be subject to the main proceedings irrespective of the State where they are situated unless territorial proceedings are opened. The law of the State of the opening of the main proceedings shall determine which of those assets shall be regarded as forming a part of the estate in the main proceedings and which shall be excluded (see Article 4(2)(b)).

    A part of those assets may be subject to third parties' rights in rem. The Convention does not make it obligatory for these assets to be included in or excluded from the estate in the main proceedings. The Convention imposes only an obligation to respect third parties' rights in rem over assets located within the territory of a Contracting State different from the State of the opening of proceedings.

    The creation, validity and scope of these rights in rem are governed by their own applicable law (in general, the 'lex rei sitae' at the relevant time) and cannot be affected by the opening of insolvency proceedings.

    This means that although the law of the State of the opening stipulates that all assets are part of the estate, the holder of the right in rem retains all his rights in respect of the assets in question. For instance, the holder of the right in rem may exercise the right to separate the security from the estate and, where necessary, to realize the asset individually to satisfy the claim. On the other hand, the liquidator, even if he is in possession of the asset, cannot take any decision on that asset which might affect the right in rem created on it, without the consent of its holder (see also point 161).

96. Article 5 only applies to the rights in rem created before the opening of proceedings. If they are created after the opening, Article 4 shall apply without exception (without prejudice to Article 14).

97. The fundamental policy pursued is to protect the trade in the State where the assets are situated and legal certainty of the rights over them. Rights in rem have a very important function with regard to credit and the mobilization of wealth. They insulate their holders against the risk of insolvency of the debtor and the interference of third parties. They allow credit to be obtained under conditions that would not be possible without this type of guarantee.

    Rights in rem can only properly fulfil their function in so far as they are not more affected by the opening of insolvency proceedings in other Contracting States than they would be by the opening of national insolvency proceedings. This aim could be achieved through alternative solutions which were in fact discussed in the working party. However, to facilitate the administration of the estate the simplicity of the formula laid down in the current Article 5 was preferred by the majority: insolvency proceedings do not affect rights in rem on assets located in other Contracting States.

98. The rule does not 'immunize' rights in rem against the debtor's insolvency. If the law of the State where the assets are located allows these rights in rem to be affected in some way, the liquidator (or any other person empowered to do so) may request secondary insolvency proceedings be opened in that State if the debtor has an establishment there. The secondary proceedings are conducted according to national law and allow the liquidator to affect these rights under the same conditions as in purely domestic proceedings.

99. Article 5 states that the proceedings shall not affect rights in rem in respect of assets located in other Contracting States and not that the proceedings shall not affect assets located in another State. As main proceedings are universal (ex Article 3(1)) they encompass all the debtor's assets.

This is important if the value of the security is greater than the value of the claim guaranteed by the right in rem. The creditor will be then obliged to surrender to the estate any surplus of the proceeds of sale.

Without affecting the economic value of the right or its immediate realizability, it also gives the liquidator the power to decide on the immediate payment of the claim guaranteed, and thus avoid the loss in value that certain assets could suffer when they are realized separately.

100. Article 5 refers to 'rights in rem' but does not define what these are. The Convention does not intend to impose its own definition of a right in rem, running the risk of describing as rights in rem legal positions which the law of the State where the assets are located does not consider to be rights in rem, or of not encompassing rights in rem which do not fulfil the conditions of that definition.

The Convention acknowledges the interest of each State in protecting its market's trade, in the form of respect of rights in rem acquired over assets of the debtor located in that country under the law that is applicable before the opening of the insolvency proceedings.

For this reason, the characterization of a right as a right in rem must be sought in the national law which, according to the normal pre-insolvency conflict of law rules, governs rights in rem (in general, the lex rei sitae at the relevant time). In this sense, the Convention adopts a 'lege causae' characterization.

101. The only departure from the above statement is found in Article 5(3), which for the purposes of Article 5, directly and independently of national law, considers as a right in rem any right entered in a public register and enforceable against third parties, allowing a right in rem to be obtained.

102. However, the rationale of Article 5 imposes certain limits to the national qualification of a right in rem. It must be borne in mind that Article 5 represents an important exception as regards the application of the law of the State of the opening and the universal effect of the main proceedings. It must equally be remembered that secondary proceedings are only possible if the debtor has an establishment in that Contracting State. The mere presence of assets is not enough in order to open such proceedings.

An unreasonably wide interpretation of the national concept of a right in rem to include, for instance, rights simply reinforced by a right to claim preferential payment, as is the case for a certain number of privileges, would make the Convention meaningless, and such a wide interpretation is not to be attributed to Article 5.

103. In order to facilitate the application of the Convention and avoid doubts Article 5(2) provides a list of types of rights that are normally considered by national laws as rights in rem.

This list is inspired in two main considerations. The first, that a right which exists only after insolvency proceedings have been opened, but not before, is not a right in rem for the purposes of Article 5 (which protect pre-existing rights).

The second, that a right in rem basically has two characteristics (see also the concept of rights in rem in the Member States in point 166 of the Schlosser Report on the 1968 Brussels Convention):

(a) its direct and immediate relationship with the asset it covers, which remains linked to its satisfaction, without depending on the asset belonging to a person's estate or on the relationship between the holder of the right in rem and another person;

(b) the absolute nature of the allocation of the right to the holder. This means that the person who holds a right in rem can enforce it against anyone who breaches or harms his right without his assent (eg such rights are typically protected by actions to recover); that the right can resist the alienation of the asset to a third party (it can be claimed erga omnes, with the restrictions characteristic of the protection of the bona fide purchaser); and that the right can thus resist individual enforcement by third parties and in collective insolvency proceedings (by its separation or individual satisfaction).

104. A right in rem may not only be established with regard to specific assets but also with regard to assets as a whole. Security rights such as the 'floating charge' recognized in United Kingdom and Irish law can, therefore, be characterized as a right in rem for the purposes of the Convention. Likewise, rights characterized under national law as rights in rem over intangible assets or over rights are also included (see Article 5(1)).
105. This provision is based on non-fraudulent location of the assets.
106. The establishment of a right in rem in favour of a particular creditor or third party could be an act detrimental to all the creditors. In this case, the general rules of the Convention governing actions for voidness, voidability or unenforceability of legal acts are applicable (see Article 4(2)(m), and Article 13).

Article 6

Set-off

107. This Article deals with set-off in the same way as Article 5 dealt with rights in rem. When under the normally applicable rules on conflict of laws the right to demand the set-off stems from a national law other than the 'lex concursus', Article 6 allows the creditor to retain this possibility as an acquired right against the insolvency proceedings: the right to set-off is not affected by the opening of proceedings.
108. Set-off is a part of the law of obligations governed by the relevant rules of private international law regarding the law applicable to obligations. By including two claims which offset each other, the question arises whether the right to set-off stems from:
    (a) the cumulative application of laws applicable to the two claims or
    (b) the law applicable to the claim of the debtor ('passive' claim in the set-off) against which the creditor intends to set off his counter-claim against the debtor ('active' claim in the set-off).
    The Convention opts for this second interpretation when it derives the right to set-off from the 'law applicable to the insolvent debtor's claim' (ie from the law applicable to the claim where the insolvent debtor is the creditor in relation to the other party).
109. The laws of some Contracting States altogether restrict or prohibit set-off in insolvency. Article 4 subjects insolvency set-off to the competence of the law of the State of the opening of the insolvency proceedings.
    If insolvency proceedings are opened, it falls therefore to the 'lex concursus' to govern admissibility and the conditions under which set-off can be exercised against a claim of the debtor.
    If the 'lex concursus' allows for set-off, no problem will arise and Article 4 should be applied in order to claim the set-off as provided for by the law. On the other hand, if the 'lex concursus' does not allow for set-off (eg since it requires both claims to be liquidated, matured and payable prior to a certain date), then Article 6 constitutes an exception to the general application of that law in this respect, by permitting the set-off according to the conditions established for insolvency set-off by the law applicable to the insolvent debtor's claim ('passive' claim).
    In this way, set-off becomes, in substance, a sort of guarantee governed by a law on which the creditor concerned can rely at the moment of contracting or incurring the claim.
110. Article 6 covers only rights to set-off arising in respect of mutual claims incurred prior to the opening of the insolvency proceedings. After this time, Article 4 is applied without exception to decide whether or not the set-off is admissible. Contractual set-off implies an agreement subject to its own applicable law according to the 1980 Rome Convention. The same rationale on which Article 5 is based explains that in the event of a contractual set-off agreement covering different claims between two parties, the law of the Contracting State applicable to that agreement will continue to govern the set-off of claims covered by the agreement and incurred prior to the opening of the insolvency proceedings.
111. As in the case of Article 5, any actions detrimental to all the creditors may be corrected by bringing actions for voidness, voidability or unenforceability as set out in Article 4(2)(m).

Article 7

Reservation of title

112. In the same way as Article 5, this provision seeks to protect trade by excluding from the scope of insolvency proceedings the reservation of title on property which, at the time the proceedings were opened, was located in a Contracting State other than the State of the opening.

    The remarks made with regard to Article 5 apply here mutatis mutandis. The biggest difference between Article 5 and Article 7 concerns Article 7(2) which contains a uniform substantive rule.

113. The first paragraph governs the insolvency of the purchaser of an asset, by allowing the seller to preserve his rights based on the reservation of title. For this to occur, the asset must be located at the time when the insolvency proceedings are opened in a Contracting State other than the one where the proceedings are opened. If its location changes after the opening of the proceedings, this does not affect the application of the provision.

114. The second paragraph covers the insolvency of the seller of an asset after delivery of the asset, allowing the sale to remain valid. If the purchaser continues to make payments, he shall acquire title at the end of the period set out in the contract. For this rule to be applied, it is also a requirement that at the time the insolvency proceedings are opened the asset is located within a State other than the State of the opening of proceedings.

115. Of course, actions for voidness, voidability or unenforceability, as provided for in Article 4(2)(m) can also be brought against these reservations of title.

Article 8

Contracts relating to immovable property

116. Insolvency law may have an impact on current contracts. Thus, for instance, in the case of mutual obligations pending fulfilment, the liquidator may be empowered to decide either on the performance or termination of the contract. The aim of rules of this kind is to protect the estate from the obligation to perform contracts which may be disadvantageous in these new circumstances.

117. The general rule on conflicts of law is that it falls to the law of the Contracting State of the opening of proceedings to regulate the effects of the proceedings on current contracts to which the debtor is a party (Article 4(2)(e)).

    To this extent, the applicable national insolvency law interferes with and displaces the rules applicable to contracts, which derive from the law applicable under the 1980 Rome Convention.

118. This rule, which overall is positive for the general interests of the creditors may be detrimental to other interests. In all the Contracting States, contracts covering immovable property are subject to special rules, both of conflict of laws as well as of international jurisdiction, in order to take into account several interests: those of the parties to the contract (eg tenants) and the general interests protected by the State in which the immoveable property is to be found.

    Protection of these specific interests justify [sic] an exception to the application of the law of the State of the opening of proceedings. Hence Article 8 makes the effects of the insolvency proceedings exclusively subject to the law of the Contracting State where the immovable property is located.

    Solely means that only the law of the Contracting State of location of the immovable [property] (including its insolvency law), and not the 'lex concursus' under Article 4, is applicable to establish these effects.

119. Article 8 not only covers contracts for the use of immovable property (rental, leasing) but also includes contracts covering the transfer of the immovable property (sale).

Article 9

Payment systems and financial markets

120. The intention of Article 9 is for any effects on transactions subject to a payment or settlement system or to a financial market of insolvency proceedings opened in another Contracting State to be the same as those in proceedings under national law. By making the effects of insolvency exclusively subject to the law applicable to the payment system and the financial market, general confidence in these mechanisms is protected.

    The aim of this provision is to avoid any modification of the mechanisms for regulating and settling transactions provided for in payment or settlement systems or on the organized financial markets operating in Contracting States, in the event of insolvency of a party to a transaction which would otherwise result if the 'lex concursus' applied. The relevant mechanisms include closing out contracts and netting, and in so far as the security is situated in that Contracting State, the realization of securities.

    Payment systems and markets involve large-scale transactions and as a consequence have been found to require special rules to guarantee their smooth operation and security. That is why the law governing the particular system or market concerned remains applicable.

    A financial market is not defined but is understood to be a market in a Contracting State where financial instruments, other financial assets or commodity futures and options are traded. It is characterized by regular trading and conditions of operation and access and it is subject to the law of the relevant Contracting State, including appropriate supervision, if any, by the regulatory authorities of that Contracting State.

121. Article 9 means that only the law governing the system or market in question can be applied to the relevant transactions affected by an insolvency and not the 'lex concursus' as provided by Article 4.Thus, the complex problems of potential conflicts of the two laws are avoided and the certainty of transactions is preserved.

122. For the same reason, any possible voidness, voidability or unenforceability of a payment or transaction carried out under this system or market and which may be detrimental to all the creditors, remains subject to the same solution: the law applicable to the payment system or financial market governs these cases.

123. To determine the law applicable to European payment systems account must be taken of the work in progress in the Community on those systems.

124. The reference to Article 5 means that protection of rights in rem of any kind of creditors or third parties over assets belonging to the debtor is always carried out in the same way under the Convention: by reference to the location of the assets, regardless of the type of creditor or institution which may benefit from its function as a guarantee. Rights in rem affect third parties and uniform treatment of them is essential in order to protect trade.

Article 10

Contracts of employment

125. Article 10 derogates from the general application of the law of the State of the opening of proceedings (Article 4) and makes the effects of the proceedings on employment contracts and on labour relations subject to the law of the Contracting State applicable to the contract of employment, including its law on insolvency.

    This Article aims to protect employees and labour relations from the application of a foreign law, different from that which governs the contractual relations between employer and employees. For this reason, effects of the insolvency proceedings on the continuation or termination of the employment relationship and on the rights and obligations of each party under such relationship are to be determined by the law applicable to the contract under the general conflict of laws rules.

126. The 1980 Rome Convention will determine the law applicable to employment contracts (see, in particular, its Articles 6 and 7).
127. The word 'solely' emphasizes that only the law applicable to the employment contract is applied in order to establish these effects and not the 'lex concursus' as provided by Article 4. Any problem regarding possible conflicts between the two laws is therefore avoided.
128. Insolvency questions other than those relating to the impact of the opening of proceedings on contract and employment relationships remain subject to the general competence of the law of the State of the opening, ex Article 4. Thus, for instance, the following would be covered, the question of whether or not workers' claims arising out of their employment shall be protected by a privilege, the prescribed amount protected and the rank of the privilege if any, etc. In the same way as lodgement, verification and admission of claims, all these questions are subject to the law of the State of the opening (Article 4(2)(h)).

    Guaranteed payments of workers' claims in cases of insolvency of the employer, ensured by a national institution under a wage guarantee scheme in the event of insolvency governed by the national law of a Contracting State, are subject to the law of that State.

Article 11

Effects on rights subject to registration

129. The application of the law of the State of the opening (F1) to determine the effects of the insolvency proceedings also on the assets of debtors located in another Contracting State may come into conflict with national registration systems, when this law provides for effects or consequences different from or unknown to the system of the State of registration (eg a statutory lien of the general body of creditors over the debtor's property).
130. The Convention does not try to modify the systems either of registration or of rights in rem of the Contracting States. The systems for the registration of property play a significant role in protecting trade and legal certainty. General confidence in its contents and consequences should be protected under the same conditions, whether the insolvency proceedings are opened in the State of registration or in another Contracting State.

    To preserve these systems, Article 11 establishes an exception to the application of the law of the State of the opening. This exception is, however, more limited than the exceptions contained in Articles 8, 9 and 10 of the Convention. Contrary to these provisions, Article 11 does not submit the effects of the insolvency proceedings 'solely' to the law of the Contracting State under the authority of which the register is kept. This means that the general applicability of the law of the State of the opening in accordance with Article 4 is not displaced. Hence, a sort of cumulative application of both laws is necessary.

    Under Article 11, the law of the Contracting State of registration will therefore determine the modifications which, required by the law of the State of the opening, may be prompted by the insolvency proceedings and affect the rights of the debtor over immovable property, ships and aircraft subject to registration, the requisite entries in the register and the consequences thereof. In consequence, the law of the Contracting State of registration decides which effects of the insolvency proceedings are admissible and affect the rights of the debtor subject to registration in that State.

    However, this rule does have certain disadvantages. While it makes access to different national registers easier, it means that the effects may be different for each Contracting State. The administration of the insolvency proceedings by a liquidator thus becomes more complex, although it increases in certainty. With that in mind, this rule is limited to registers on immovable property, ships and aircraft.
131. Article 11 does not refer to assets but to rights subject to registration in public registers, the purpose of which is to determine who is the holder or which are the rights in rem over the assets. It also includes systems of registration of deeds relating to immovable property to effect priorities such as the Registry of Deeds which exists in Ireland.

Article 11 refers only to the effects on the rights of the debtor over immovable property, ships or aircraft. For rights in rem, whether registered or not, of creditors or third parties acquired before the opening of the insolvency proceedings, see Article 5.
132. For the concept of 'public register', see comments on Article 2.

Article 12

Community patents and trademarks

133. The Agreement relating to Community patents (1989 Luxembourg Agreement), Council Regulation (EC) No 40/94 of 20 December 1993 on the Community trademark and Council Regulation (EC) No 2100/94 of 27 July 1994 on Community plant variety rights all create rights which cover the whole territory of the Community,

    This Convention opens up the possibility of insolvency proceedings with universal effect (thus encompassing the whole Community territory) if the debtor's centre of main interests is located in a Contracting State.

    However, the Patent Convention contained in the 1989 Luxembourg Agreement (Article 41), the 1993 Regulation on the Community trademark (Article 21), and the 1994 Regulation on Community plant variety rights (Article 25), contain a rule to the effect that a Community right derived therefrom may be included only in the first proceedings (regardless of whether these are main or territorial proceedings) opened in a Contracting State. This rule was logical in so far as common regulations on international insolvency proceedings were lacking. With this Convention it is logical to allocate those Community rights to the main proceedings. Article 12 of the Convention seeks to modify the rule established by the Patent Convention, the Regulation on the Community trademark and the Regulation on Community plant variety rights and to replace it with Article 12.

134. As may be concluded from Article 3(1), Article 12 is operative only when the debtor has his centre of main interests in a Contracting State. In all other cases, ie when this centre is located outside the Community, the provisions of the Patent Convention (Article 41), the Regulation on the Community trademark (Article 21) and the Regulation on Community plant variety rights (Article 25) shall be applied.

Article 13

Detrimental acts

135. This provision must be taken in conjunction with Article 4(2)(m). The basic rule of the Convention is that the law of the State of the opening governs, under Article 4, any possible voidness, voidability or unenforceability of acts which may be detrimental to all the creditors' interests. This same law determines the conditions to be met, the manner in which the nullity and voidability function (automatically, by allocating retrospective effects to the proceedings or pursuant to an action taken by the liquidator, etc) and the legal consequences of nullity and voidability.

136. Article 13 represents a defence against the application of the law of the State of the opening, which must be pursued by the interested party, who must claim it.

    It acts as a 'veto' against the invalidity of the act decreed by the law of the State of the opening. This mechanism is easier to apply than other possible solutions based on the cumulative application of the two laws. It is now clear that all the conditions, content and the consequences of the voidability are borrowed from the law of the State of the opening. The only purpose of Article 13 and the law governing the act concerned is to reject the application of that law in a given case.

137. In this respect, Article 13 provides that the rules of the law of the State of the opening shall not apply when the person who has benefited from the contested act provides proof that:
    1. the act in question (eg a contract) is subject to the law of a Contracting State other than the State of the opening of the proceedings;

2. the law of that other State does not allow for this act to be challenged by any means. By 'any means' it is understood that the act must not be capable of being challenged using either rules on insolvency or general rules of the national law applicable to the act (eg to the contract referred to in paragraph (1)).

'In the relevant case' means that the act should not be capable of being challenged in fact ie after taking into account all the concrete circumstances of the case. It is not sufficient to determine whether it can be challenged in the abstract.

138. The aim of Article 13 is to uphold legitimate expectations of creditors or third parties of the validity of the act in accordance to the normally applicable national law, against interference from a different 'lex concursus'.

From the perspective of the protection of legitimate expectations, the operation of Article 13 is justified with regard to acts carried out prior to the opening of the insolvency proceedings, and threatened by either the retroactive nature of the insolvency proceedings opened in another country or actions to set aside previous acts of the debtor brought by the liquidator in those proceedings.

After the proceedings have been opened in a Contracting State, the creditor's reliance on the validity of the transaction under the national law applicable in non-insolvency situations is no longer justified. Thenceforth, all unauthorized disposals by the debtor are in principle ineffective by virtue of the divestment of his powers to dispose of the assets and such effect is recognized in all Contracting States. Article 13 does not protect against such an effect of the insolvency proceedings and it is not applicable to disposals occurring after the opening of the insolvency proceedings.

139. This rule covers both the main proceedings and the secondary proceedings (in each case with regard to the law of the State of the opening of the respective proceedings).

Article 14

Protection of third-party purchasers

140. This provision was initially based on the desire to protect the confidence of third parties in the content of property registers when the debtor, after the insolvency proceedings have been opened, disposes for consideration of an asset from the estate, and the opening of proceedings or the restrictions on the debtor have not yet been entered or referred to in the register in question. The final drafting of this Article goes further and covers all acts of disposal concerning immovable assets which take place after the opening of the insolvency proceedings.

To be protected by Article 14, it is necessary that the debtor dispose of the asset for consideration (eg not gratuitously).

141. In principle, any act of disposal by the debtor after the proceedings have been opened shall be ineffective in accordance with the law of the State of the opening (as this law deprives the debtor of his powers of disposal).

However, in order to protect trade and reliance on systems of publication of rights in rem, the protection of bona fide third parties should be no different in respect of proceedings in another Contracting State as compared to domestic proceedings.

If the proceedings opened in another Contracting State do not appear in the local register, the only way adequately to protect confidence in the system of publication regarding rights in rem over assets, without any loopholes, is to make the effects of disposal subject to the law of the Contracting State under the authority of which the register is kept or, in the case of immovable property, to the law of the Contracting State where the immovable property is located.

Property covered by this Article means an immovable asset, ships or aircraft subject to registration in a public register and securities the existence of which presupposes registration (dematerialized securities, see point 69).

An act of disposal must be understood to include not only transfers of ownership but also the constitution of a right in rem relating to such property.

Article 15

Effects of the insolvency procedure on lawsuits pending

142. The Convention distinguishes between the effects of insolvency on individual enforcement proceedings and those on lawsuits pending.

    The effects on individual enforcement actions are governed by the law of the State of the opening (see Article 4(2)(f)) so that the collective insolvency proceedings may stay or prevent any individual enforcement action brought by creditors against the debtor's assets.

    Effects of the insolvency proceedings on other legal proceedings concerning the assets or rights of the estate are governed (ex Article 15) by the law of the Contracting State where these proceedings are under way. The procedural law of this State shall decide whether or not the proceedings are to be suspended, how they are to be continued and whether any appropriate procedural modifications are needed in order to reflect the loss or the restriction of the powers of disposal and administration of the debtor and the intervention of the liquidator in his place.

C. Chapter II: Recognition of Insolvency Proceedings

Article 16

Principle

143. To recognize foreign judgments is to admit for the territory of the recognizing State the authority which they enjoy in the State where they were handed down.

    The Convention accords immediate recognition of judgments concerning the opening, course and closure of insolvency proceedings which come within its scope and of judgments handed down in direct connection with such insolvency proceedings.

    Recognition is automatic within the system of the Convention. It requires no preliminary decision by a court of the requested State.

144. Article 16 establishes the general principle of recognition, in the territory of the Contracting States (eg the Community), of a judgment opening insolvency proceedings adopted by the competent authorities of a Contracting State under Article 3 of the Convention.

145. Only insolvency proceedings within the scope of the Convention benefit from the system of recognition of the Convention. To fall within such scope, the proceedings must be listed in the Annexes to the Convention.

    Proceedings not listed in those Annexes shall not be eligible for recognition under the Convention nor shall they prevent the recognition of proceedings provided for in the Convention even though they were opened earlier.

146. The general principle of recognition is valid for all proceedings opened in a Contracting State under Article 3, ie for both main proceedings and territorial, either secondary or independent. Obviously, in the second case recognition will be limited to the territorial effects of the proceedings.

147. A judgment opening proceedings need not necessarily be a final judgment (not subject to ordinary appeal) in order to enjoy recognition. Such judgment whether final or provisional shall have effect in the whole territory covered by the Convention as long as it is effective in the State of the opening of proceedings.

    The Convention is based on the principle of Community trust and on the 'favor recognitionis', so that national borders are no obstacle to the efficient administration of international insolvency proceedings throughout the Community.

148. The Convention imposes an obligation to recognize insolvency proceedings opened in another Contracting State, even when such proceedings cannot be brought against the debtor in that

State, due to his professional capacity or to his public or private nature, as in the case of non-traders in certain States.

Main insolvency proceedings may be opened in a State (F1) in accordance with its own law, although in another Contracting State (F2) insolvency proceedings cannot be brought against the debtor by virtue of his professional capacity (ie a non-trader). The second State (F2) in such a case is obliged to recognize and, where appropriate, enforce the foreign judgment. The State requested (F2) cannot invoke public policy in its territory to oppose recognition on those grounds (under Article 26).

Since the main proceedings can be opened only if the debtor has his centre of main interests in the State of the opening, it seems logical that the decision of the law of that State to allow collective insolvency proceedings against that debtor should be respected by the other Contracting States, whose connection with the debtor is restricted to the existence of an establishment or assets.

However, these other States (ie F2) will not be obliged to open local secondary proceedings against that debtor, since the conditions laid down by their insolvency law, which is applicable pursuant to Article 28, have not been fulfilled.

The opposite hypothesis, ie the impossibility of opening main proceedings because the law of the Contracting State competent under Article 3(1) does not allow it, presents no difficulties. The Convention expressly recognizes the possibility of opening territorial proceedings. Where the law of a State which has jurisdiction under Article 3(2) allows insolvency proceedings against that kind of debtor, it will be possible to open independent territorial proceedings (see Article 3(4)).

Naturally, the territorial proceedings have effects only in the State of the opening of proceedings and do not extend them to the territory of other States (see point 156); they do not therefore affect the situation of the debtor in other States. Only the main proceedings have that effect (see point 212)

149. The relationship between the recognition of main proceedings under Article 3(1) and the possibility of opening territorial proceedings under Article 3(2) is referred to in Article 16(2). The recognition of main proceedings does not preclude the subsequent opening of secondary territorial proceedings (see point 212).

Article 17

Effects of recognition

150. Whereas Article 16 establishes the general principle of the recognition of a judgment opening insolvency proceedings, Article 17 distinguishes between the recognition of main proceedings and that of territorial proceedings.
151. Recognition of the main proceedings

    The universality of main proceedings opened under Article 3(1), embracing all the debtor's assets and creditors, implies recognition of the proceedings and their effects in the States in which those assets or creditors are situated. The Convention guarantees this universality through the setting up of a system of mandatory automatic recognition in all Contracting States. The Convention reinforces this by making the consequence of recognition the 'extension' to all other Contracting States of the effects attributed to those proceedings by the law of the State of the opening of proceedings.
152. 'Automatic recognition' means immediate recognition by virtue of the Convention (ipso iure recognition) without any need to resort to preliminary proceedings to declare it effective. Since recognition is not subject to prior proceedings, the authorities of the requested State which may be confronted with the judgment opening proceedings may determine incidentally whether it is a judgment under the Convention and whether grounds for refusal under Article 26 exist.

153. Article 17 lays down a model of recognition based on the extension of the effects of the judgment in a Contracting State to the whole territory covered by the Convention. Proceedings opened in another Contracting State will not, as regards their effects, be equated with national proceedings but will be recognized in other Contracting States with the same effects attributed to them by the law of the State of the opening (= 'extension model').

   The law of the State of the opening (and not the law of the requested State) shall be applicable to determine those effects. This shall apply to all the effects of the proceedings in another Contracting State, both procedural and substantive (see point 90). The substantive effects are included by virtue of the general applicability which the Convention attributes to the law of the State of the opening (see Article 4) and they are therefore subject to the same exceptions as are provided for by the Convention in respect of that law (see Articles 5 et seq).

154. The system of automatic recognition and the extension model reinforce the universality of the main proceedings. From the time fixed by the law of the State of the opening, the judgment opening proceedings produces its effects with equal force in all Contracting States. The divestment of the debtor, the appointment of the liquidator, the prohibition on individual executions, the inclusion of the debtor's assets in the estate regardless of the State in which they are situated, the obligation to return what has been obtained by individual creditors after opening, etc, are all effects laid down by the law of the State of the opening which are simultaneously applicable in all Contracting States.

155. The recognition of main proceedings under Article 3(1) shall be limited by the opening of territorial proceedings in accordance with Article 3(2).

   The main proceedings cannot produce its effects in respect of the assets and legal situations which come within the jurisdiction of territorial proceedings opened. The territorial proceedings protect local interests and for this purpose the national law applies. However, the main proceedings may influence the conduct of territorial proceedings as a result of coordination and subordination rules which derive from the Convention and to which territorial proceedings are subject.

156. Recognition of territorial proceedings

   Territorial proceedings can affect only the assets situated in the State of the opening. Recognition cannot imply, therefore, the extension of the effects of those proceedings to property situated in other Contracting States. Recognition of territorial proceedings means admitting the validity of the opening of the local proceedings and of the effects which they produce over the assets located in the territory of the State of the opening, which cannot be challenged in other Contracting States.

   This is the case, for example, where the liquidator in those proceedings has to demand the return of assets belonging to the estate in the secondary proceedings which were transferred abroad without authorization after the opening of proceedings.

   Moreover the opening of the territorial proceedings limits the extra-territorial effects of the main proceedings which may no longer include the assets situated in the State where those territorial proceedings were opened, except for the surplus assets in the secondary proceedings under Article 35. The main proceedings must observe that limitation.

157. Article 17(2), second sentence, covers the case of territorial proceedings, either secondary or independent, which may conclude by authorizing the debtor to postpone payment or even by discharging the remaining debt.

   It may be clearly seen that, in the case of proceedings under Article 3(2), this reduction of creditors' rights can apply only to the debtor's estate situated in the State of the opening of the territorial proceedings. The creditors concerned will, therefore, be able to seek unlimited satisfaction of all their debts from the assets situated in other Contracting States. Naturally, nothing prevents the creditors from voluntarily agreeing to a further reduction of their rights affecting assets situated outside the State of opening of territorial proceedings. However, that supplementary restriction can be relied on only against creditors who have accepted it personally and not by a majority vote. This principle should be seen in conjunction with Article 34(2).

Article 18

Powers of the liquidator

158. The main effect of the recognition of insolvency proceedings opened in a Contracting State is the recognition of the appointment of the liquidator and of his powers in all other Contracting States. The term 'liquidator' must be understood in the wide sense of the definition given in Article 2 of the Convention.
159. By virtue of that recognition, the liquidator appointed in proceedings in a Contracting State will be able, in other Contracting States, to exercise the powers conferred on him by the law of the State of the opening.

    The liquidator's powers, their nature and their scope will be determined by the law of the State of the opening of the proceedings in respect of which he was appointed. That law also establishes the liquidator's obligations.
160. As the Convention provides for a system of automatic recognition of insolvency proceedings, the appointment of the liquidator and the exercise of his powers are covered by that same automatic effect. Neither the exequatur nor the publication provided for in Article 21 is necessary for the liquidator to be able to exercise his powers in other Contracting States.
161. Within the limits laid down in the Convention, the liquidator in the main proceedings may exercise all his powers in the other Contracting States (ie in the whole of the territory of the Community).

    In order to remove any doubts, Article 18 expressly stipulates that the liquidator may even transfer assets out of the State in which they are situated. In doing so, the liquidator must respect Articles 5 and 7 of the Convention, since the proceedings cannot affect rights in rem of creditors or third parties over assets situated, at the time of the opening, in a Contracting State other than the State of the opening of proceedings. To the extent that it is required by the right in rem, the removal of those assets to another State may be subject to the consent of the holder of the right in rem.

    The creditors can prevent such transfer by requesting the opening of secondary proceedings concerning those assets (provided that the conditions laid down in Article 3(2) and (3) are fulfilled).
162. The powers of the liquidator in the main proceedings are subject to two general restrictions.
163. The first derives from the possible opening of territorial insolvency proceedings in another Contracting State (under Article 3(2)).

    This restriction is logical, since the assets cannot be subject to the powers of two different liquidators. Once territorial proceedings have been opened, the direct powers of the liquidator in the main proceedings no longer apply to assets situated in the State of the opening of the territorial proceedings. The liquidator in the territorial proceedings has exclusive powers over those assets. This does not imply that the main liquidator loses all influence over the debtor's estate situated in the other Contracting State, but that that influence must be exercised through the powers conferred on that liquidator by the Convention to coordinate the territorial proceedings and the main proceedings (see Articles 31 to 37).

    Article 18 extends this first restriction to cases where provisional protective measures incompatible with the exercise of those powers have been already adopted as a consequence of the request to open territorial proceedings.

    The liquidator in the main proceedings is entitled under the Convention to request secondary proceedings (Article 29).
164. The second restriction provided for in Article 18(3) derives from the liquidator's obligation, when exercising his powers, to comply with the law of the State within the territory of which he intends to take action.

    (a) The general principle of prohibiting the exercise of coercive power in another State also applies to a foreign liquidator. The latter can take action in other States only if he complies with that principle. Hence Article 18 expressly prohibits direct recourse to coercive measures. Any use of force or coercive action is excluded.

If persons affected by a liquidator's acts do not voluntarily agree to their performance and if coercive measures are required with regard to assets or persons, the liquidator must apply to the authorities of the State where the assets or persons are located to have them adopted and implemented. The Convention allows a foreign liquidator from another Contracting State, on the basis of the automatic recognition of his appointment and his powers, to petition those authorities to adopt distraint measures against such assets or persons in accordance with national law.

(b) The liquidator shall exercise his powers without infringing the laws of the State in which he takes action.

For example, the liquidator may transfer the assets belonging to the estate to another Contracting State. This power may be subject to rules limiting the free movement of goods. Thus, if an asset is part of the historical and cultural heritage of a Contracting State, it may be subject to an export ban protected under Article 36 of the EC Treaty. This prohibition naturally also applies to the liquidator. With regard to this type of asset, he may not exercise his general power to transfer assets.

(c) With regards to procedures for the realization of assets, the liquidator shall comply with the law of the State where the assets are located. The law of the State of the opening shall establish the extent of the powers of the liquidator and the manners in which they may be exercised. Only that law can determine, for example, whether the sale of immovable property can be private (person-to-person) or if sale by public auction is necessary. However, once the form of sale has been decided according to that law, the procedures by which the assets are realized must be in accordance with the provisions of national law. In our example, if the law of the State of the opening requires a sale by public auction, the procedure of carrying out the sale in the State where the immovable property is situated shall be determined by the law of the latter State.

165. The liquidator in territorial proceedings is subject to a supplementary restriction. His powers of administration and disposal have the same scope as the proceedings from which they derive, ie they are territorial. However, assets subject to these proceedings may have been removed to other Contracting States after the opening of proceedings.

In this case, Article 18(2) clearly states that the liquidator may apply to these other Contracting States and request from their courts the return of the asset or may insist on such transfer for any other purpose useful to the local proceedings. He may also bring any action to set aside which is in the interest of the creditors (see point 224).

166. The Convention contains no rule regarding opposition to the exercise of powers by the liquidator. General rules shall therefore be applicable.

Consequently, the authorities of the State in which the powers are intended to be exercised shall have jurisdiction to take a decision if the grounds for opposition lie in the non-recognition, in accordance with the Convention, of the proceedings opened in another Contracting State or of the judgment appointing the liquidator. This is also the case where the grounds for opposition are a breach by the liquidator of the provisions of the Convention which govern the exercise of his powers in other States, for instance, Article 18(1) or Article 3(3).

If the opposition concerns the substance of the exercise of those powers, ie the justification for a measure which the liquidator intends to take, jurisdiction lies with the judicial authorities of the State of the opening of proceedings.

Article 19

Proof of the liquidator's appointment

167. This provision derives from Article 2 of the 1990 Istanbul Convention. In contrast to the draft Community Convention of 1982, it was not thought necessary to establish a uniform model for the certificate attesting the appointment of the liquidator.

168. The proof of the liquidator's appointment may be established by a duly certified copy of the original decision, issued by a person authorized by the State in which the decision originated or by any other certificate issued by the competent court attesting the appointment.

169. The certified copy of the decision or the official certificate of the appointment shall require no legalization or other similar formality, such as the certificate ('apostille') provided for by the 1961 Hague Convention abolishing the requirement of legalization for foreign public documents.

 A translation into the official language or languages of the Contracting State in which the liquidator intends to act may be required. This translation shall take into account the requirements established in this State regarding translations of official documents. For example, if we accept the parallel with the provisions of Article 48, second subparagraph, of the 1968 Brussels Convention the translation is certified by a person authorized for that purpose by one of the Contracting States, whether that of the opening of proceedings or that in which the liquidator intends to exercise his powers.

170. The Convention contains no rules regarding the means of proving the scope of the powers of the liquidator.

 It seems reasonable that, in the case of doubt or opposition, these powers, based on the law of another Contracting State, are established by the person who invokes them. Proof may be by means of a certificate issued by the Court appointing the liquidator, which shall define his powers, or by any other means of evidence admitted by the law of the State where the liquidator intends to exercise his powers.

Article 20

Return and imputation

171. The Convention considers its geographical scope (the Community) to be a single economic area. The main proceedings shall therefore produce effects within the whole of the territory of the Contracting States. Also for this reason, where the Convention allows for the opening of secondary proceedings, the whole area should be taken as a reference for the distribution of dividends, making it compulsory to take into account the sum obtained in each set of proceedings by means of a sort of consolidated account of the dividends obtained on a European scale. The aim of this Article is to guarantee the equal treatment of all the creditors of a single debtor.

172. Rule regarding return (Article 20(1))

 The rule on return is the consequence of the universality of the main proceedings, which encompass all the debtor's assets, wherever they are situated, and affect all the creditors. As a result of this principle of universality, it is evident that a creditor who, after the opening of proceedings, obtains total or partial satisfaction of his claim individually (by means of payment by the debtor or execution of assets situated in other States) breaches the principle of collective satisfaction on which the insolvency proceedings are based. Hence, the obligation to return 'what has been obtained'. The liquidator may demand either the return of the assets received or the equivalent in money.

173. The previous rule operates within the limits of Articles 5 and 7, which exclude from the scope of the main proceedings rights in rem of creditors and third parties in respect of the debtor's assets situated outside the State of the opening of proceedings at that time. As long as these Articles apply, a creditor who obtains satisfaction of claims guaranteed by rights in rem by realization of the security does not enrich himself to the detriment of the estate and does not breach the principle of collective satisfaction (see comment on Article 5).

174. Rule regarding imputation (Article 20(2))

 The Convention allows for the opening of parallel insolvency proceedings (see Article 3). Thus, when a creditor obtains satisfaction in insolvency proceedings opened in another Contracting State, he does not breach a law, but simply exercises a right (see Article 32(1)).

 For this reason, Article 20(2) allows a creditor to keep what he has obtained in the first proceedings in which distribution took place. Nevertheless, in order to guarantee the equality of all creditors on a Community level, they may not, once this payment has been received, participate in other distributions until all creditors of the same ranking have obtained equal satisfaction.

175. The method of calculation is relatively simple. It comprises four rules:
   1. Nobody may obtain more than 100% of his claims.
   2. The total original amount of the claim (100% of its initial value) shall be taken into account, and not the remaining amount (satisfaction obtained in other proceedings is not deducted).

      If claims were not taken into account in each of the proceedings at 100% of their amount (without deducting the part satisfied in other proceedings), it would not be possible to guarantee the equal treatment of creditors participating in several proceedings.

      The only exception to the second rule is that of claims secured by rights in rem or through a set-off, the secured parts of which are not affected by insolvency proceedings (see Articles 5, 6 and 7). The Convention lays down no rule on whether the amount of the original claim or the remaining claim shall be taken into account; this question is left to the rules of the law of the State of the opening (see Article 4(2)(i)).
   3. A claim is not taken into account in the distribution until such time as the creditors with the same ranking have obtained an equal percentage of satisfaction in these proceedings as that obtained by its holder in the first proceedings.

      For example, if creditor X in proceedings opened in a Contracting State F1 has obtained 5% on an ordinary unsecured claim with an amount of 75, he cannot take part in the distribution in the proceedings opened in another Contracting State F2 (where he has also lodged his claim) until the ordinary unsecured creditors have obtained 5%. If in F2 the percentage of satisfaction attains 8% for ordinary unsecured creditors, creditor X may participate in it only with regard to the difference, ie up to 3% (8% minus 5% already obtained in F1 = 3%). This 3% shall apply to the whole claim (to the 100% of its initial amount of 75), in accordance with the second rule mentioned above.

      Conversely, if the first proceedings are in F2 where the creditors obtain a percentage of satisfaction of 8%, despite also having lodged their claims in the proceedings opened in F1, they shall not participate in the distribution in F1, since the ordinary unsecured creditors there obtain only 5%, whereas they have already obtained 8% in F2.

      Thus, regardless of which proceedings take place first, the creditors of both F1 and F2 who have lodged their claims in both proceedings shall obtain an equal final dividend (8% of the total claim).
   4. The ranking or category of each claim is determined for each of the proceedings by the law of the State of the opening (Article 4(2)(i)). Since different insolvency laws apply to the different proceedings (each is governed by its own national law), the ranking of the same claim lodged in two different proceedings may not be the same in both. The only ranking or category which is taken into account in order to apply Article 20(2) is that given to the claim by the law governing proceedings in which distribution is to be effected.

      Hence, for the calculation of the dividend, only the percentage of satisfaction obtained in other proceedings, and not the rank or category which the claim enjoyed in those other proceedings, is taken into account. Thus in our example, if the claim of creditor X is an ordinary unsecured claim in F1 but it benefits from a preference in F2, it follows that it has already obtained 5% in F1, no matter what the ranking was; this percentage is, for the purposes of calculation, compared to the dividend which the rules in force in F2 apply to preferential claims. If these claims obtain a dividend of 25% in F2, creditor X shall benefit from a dividend of 20% in F2 (25% minus 5% already obtained in F1 = 20%).

176. In practice, if a number of claims have been lodged both in the insolvency proceedings opened in F1 and F2, the liquidator in the F2 proceedings may calculate the distribution in F2 by stages, for each rank. In our example, up to 5% (dividend obtained in F1) he will not take into account the claims already satisfied in F1. Once the claims lodged only in F2 have attained 5%, if there are remaining assets to be distributed he will make a further calculation introducing also the claims already satisfied in F1 together with the claims lodged only in F2, in order to determine the new dividend.

Article 21

Publication

177. The publication of the opening of insolvency proceedings in another Contracting State is not a precondition for the recognition of those proceedings or for the recognition and exercise of the powers of the liquidator appointed in such proceedings.

    The principal aim of publication is to contribute to the security of trade in the States where the debtor has assets or where he conducts business, by drawing his creditors' and future contracting parties' attention to the legal situation of the debtor.

178. Although recognition is not dependent on publication of the opening of the proceedings, publication may produce significant legal effects in relation to the evaluation of the behaviour of the persons concerned, within the framework of either the Convention (for example Article 24) or the national law to be applied.

179. The initiative to publish in other States is vested in the liquidator. For this purpose, he will have to evaluate all the circumstances (eg individual creditors cannot be identified) and the need for trade security (eg an establishment remains in operation in another State where future creditors should be informed).

    This rule shall not prevent the courts of the State of the opening from ordering publication if its national insolvency law provides for this.

180. Any Contracting State in which the debtor has an establishment may provide for mandatory publication of the opening of insolvency proceedings. In no cases may this mandatory publication constitute a precondition for recognition (this would breach the rules of the Convention).

    Article 21(2) explicitly states that in the case of mandatory publication, the latter must be arranged by the liquidator or the authority designated by the State of the opening of proceedings. Where necessary, the national law of the State which provides for such mandatory publication will determine the liquidator's liability when the latter has not taken the necessary measures to arrange publication.

181. The Convention establishes no uniform mechanism for publication but stipulates that it should be in accordance with the arrangements laid down by the law of the State in which it is to take place. On the other hand, the Convention does determine what information is to be published: the basic content of the judgment opening proceedings and, where necessary (for example, if there are a number of appointments), the basic content of the decision appointing the liquidator. In both cases, it should always indicate the identity of the liquidator appointed and specify the jurisdiction rule applied (Article 3(1) or Article 3(2)). This does not exclude other items of information which may be of interest to third parties or creditors (deadlines for lodging claims, etc).

    In the case of publication as referred to in Article 21(2), the compulsory information required may not go beyond the information mentioned in paragraph 1 of that Article.

Article 22

Registration in a public register

182. Registration in a public register is not a precondition for recognition of insolvency proceedings opened in another Contracting State or for recognition of the powers conferred on the liquidator appointed thereunder. Nevertheless, the registers play a significant role for the trade security. The trust of third parties acting in good faith on the basis of information contained in these registers is protected in all Member States. For this reason, but also to guarantee the full effectiveness of the insolvency proceedings, the Convention empowers the liquidator to request the registration of the judgment opening insolvency proceedings in another Contracting State.

    This rule shall not prevent the courts of the State of the opening from ordering the liquidator to register in other States, if its national insolvency law so provides.

The form and content of the registration shall be subject to the law of the Contracting State under the authority of which the register is kept. Such Contracting State should allow registration of proceedings in another Contracting State under conditions similar to those applied for the registration of national proceedings.

183. The Contracting States cannot demand an exequatur as a precondition for access to the registration of a judgment handed down in another Contracting State. Recognition shall be automatic.

Each State may, however, decide if the authority responsible for the register at the time of registration should, incidentally, check whether the decision is recognizable under the Convention.

184. The registration requirement relates to the main proceedings, since by definition the territorial proceedings cannot affect assets situated outside the State of the opening of proceedings.

185. The Contracting States may request mandatory registration in their registers (when the debtor is a holder of registered assets, for example). In no case may such mandatory publication be a precondition for recognition.

Where necessary, the national law of the State of registration will determine the liquidator's liability when the latter has not taken the necessary measures to ensure such registration.

Article 23

Costs

186. The Convention considers the expenditure arising from the publication and registration measures laid down in Articles 21 and 22 as costs incurred in the proceedings. The proposal by some delegations to limit this definition to the expenditure arising from action by the liquidator (Article 21(1) and Article 22(1)) and not to that arising from the mandatory publication or registration requested by a State different from the State of the opening and conduct of proceedings was not approved.

Article 24

Honouring of an obligation to a debtor

187. The automatic recognition of insolvency proceedings opened in another Contracting State, and the lack of any general system of prior publication, guarantee the immediate effectiveness of the judgment opening proceedings in all the Contracting States.

Nevertheless, in some cases, a number of those persons may be unaware of the opening of proceedings and may act in good faith in contradiction with these new circumstances. In this connection, Article 24 provides for a solution to the problem where an obligation is honoured in good faith for the benefit of a debtor, when it should have been honoured for the benefit of the liquidator in the proceedings in another Contracting State. This Article establishes that the person honouring the obligation shall be deemed to have discharged it if he was unaware of the opening of proceedings.

Article 24 is therefore based on a double presumption. If the obligation is honoured before the publication provided for in Article 21 has occurred in the State concerned (eg the State in which the person honouring the obligation is established or the State in which the obligation is honoured, as the case may be), there shall be a presumption of ignorance. If the obligation is honoured after publication has taken place, there shall be a presumption of awareness. These two presumptions are rebuttable, but under each of them the burden of proof shifts from one party to the other. So, for instance, once publication has taken place, it shall be for the debtor honouring the obligation in question to provide evidence rebutting the presumptions.

188. In Article 24(1) the place where an obligation is honoured means the place where the obligation has been performed in fact by the debtor of the obligation.

Article 25

Recognition and enforceability of other judgments

189. Introduction

The Convention refers firstly to the recognition of the opening of insolvency proceedings (Article 16) and to its effects (Articles 17 to 24).

The recognition of judgments relating to the conduct and closure of the insolvency proceedings and of judgments adopted in the framework of those proceedings is dealt with generally in Article 25.This provision also regulates the enforcement of all judgments, including, where necessary, the judgment opening proceedings, as regards all its consequences except the opening itself (see point 143).

190. To enforce is to put into execution. Enforcement implies the exercise of the State's coercive power to ensure compliance.

The principle of exclusive territorial sovereignty precludes the direct exercise of a State's power within the territory of other States. By virtue of this principle, direct application of coercive powers is limited to the authorities of the State where the assets or persons to which this action relates are situated. The Convention has not altered this state of affairs.

As a consequence, the enforcement of judgments of other Contracting States shall depend on prior authorization by the authorities of the State in which it must be carried out. This authorization is obtained by means of a special procedure: the procedure called exequatur.

The exequatur does not deal with the enforcement itself, but with the prior authorization needed for enforcement. Enforcement in the strict sense shall be carried out by the competent national authorities by means of the procedures established by the national law for the enforcement of equivalent domestic judgments. The Convention on insolvency proceedings, like the 1968 Brussels Convention, deals only with the first aspect (prior authorization and its conditions).

If the conditions laid down by the Convention are fulfilled, the authorities of the requested State shall be obliged to grant this authorization, pursuant to the Convention. National law thereafter determines the methods by which the judgment of another Contracting State is enforced by the national authorities. The usual methods of coercive enforcement of the national law will be used, adapted, where necessary, to guarantee the 'effet utile' of the Convention, ie to render effective in other States the specific decision taken by the foreign court.

191. Judgments relating to insolvency proceedings (Article 25(1), first subparagraph)

Judgments relating to the conduct and closure of insolvency proceedings present no specific problem of characterization.

The recognition of these judgments operates in the same way and with the same effects as the judgment opening proceedings which we have already mentioned (see Articles 16 and 17).

The Convention subjects any composition approved by the competent court of the State of the opening to the same system of recognition.

192. As regards the enforcement of all these judgments and, where necessary, of the composition, various possibilities were examined at the negotiations. The idea finally adopted was to use the same system as for the enforcement of judgments in civil and commercial matters provided for by the 1968 Brussels Convention. This explains the reference in Article 25(1) to the rules on enforcement in the 1968 Brussels Convention.

Thus, the simplified system of exequatur provided for in that Convention will be used for the enforcement of judgments adopted in the framework of insolvency proceedings (see Articles 31 to 51 of the 1968 Brussels Convention; for a thorough analysis of that system see also the reports on that Convention).

As under the 1968 Brussels Convention (see Article 31 thereof), in order for enforcement to take effect in the State requested, the judgment should be already enforceable in the State in which it was given (State of origin) and that effect should not have been suspended there. A judgment cannot produce more effects in other States than in the State of origin.

However, grounds for rejection of the exequatur are taken not from the 1968 Brussels Convention (Article 34(2) of the 1968 Brussels Convention is expressly excluded), but from the Convention on insolvency proceedings (see Article 26).

193. It is important to stress that Article 25(3) excludes from the obligation to recognize and enforce those judgments handed down in another Contracting State which might result in a limitation of the personal freedom or postal secrecy of the insolvent debtor or of any other person who may be affected by the limitations derived from the insolvency proceedings.

    This is an area which relates directly to fundamental rights and the Contracting States preferred to retain their freedom as to the recognition and enforcement of such decisions, regardless of the Convention on insolvency proceedings. Each State will decide autonomously on the treatment of such decisions when they originate in another Contracting State.

194. Judgments arising from insolvency proceedings (Article 25(1), second subparagraph)

    The Convention also governs the recognition and enforcement of judgments arising from insolvency proceedings. These are judgments directly deriving from bankruptcy law which have a direct link to the insolvency proceedings but do not relate to the opening, conduct and closure of insolvency proceedings.

    Recognition and enforcement of such judgments are always governed by the Convention whether they are adopted by the bankruptcy court or by an ordinary court, as could be the case under national law.

195. The raison d'être of this provision derives from the Judgment of the Court of Justice of 22 February 1979 (Case 133/78 *Gourdain v Nadler* [1979] ECR 733). Called upon to interpret Article 1(2) of the 1968 Brussels Convention (which excludes the field of bankruptcy, winding-up of insolvent companies, compositions and analogous proceedings from its scope), the Court of Justice adopted a criterion to define bankruptcy based on the nature of the action undertaken. According to this criterion, actions the direct legal basis of which is the insolvency law and which are closely linked with the insolvency proceedings are not covered by the 1968 Brussels Convention. The character of the judicial body which decides on this action is of no importance.

    In accordance with this decision of the Court of Justice, such actions should be subject to the Convention on insolvency proceedings or, otherwise, in the overall Convention rules there might be unjustifiable gaps between the general Convention and the specific Convention. For this reason, Article 25(1), second subparagraph, of the Convention on insolvency proceedings expressly adopts the same criterion of delimitation.

196. In order for the Convention on insolvency proceedings to apply it is necessary that the action undertaken directly derives from insolvency law and be closely connected with the insolvency proceedings.

    Such is the case of actions which are based on (and not only affected by) insolvency law and are only possible during the insolvency proceedings or in direct relation with them. It includes actions to set aside acts detrimental to the general body of creditors (see Article 13); actions on the personal liability of directors based upon insolvency law, ie the 'action en combement pour insuffisance d'actif' vis-à-vis the managers of the company provided by the French Law, which the Court of Justice of the European Communities considered as a bankruptcy action in its Judgment of 22 February 1979, Case 133/78; actions relating to the admission or the ranking of a claim; disputes between the liquidator and the debtor on whether an asset belongs to the bankrupt's estate, etc.

    However, actions deriving from law other than that relating to insolvency should not be included, even though they may be affected by the opening of proceedings (actively or passively). Such is the case of actions on the existence or the validity under general law of a claim (eg a contract) or relating to its amount; actions to recover another's property the holder of which is the debtor; and, in general, actions that the debtor could have undertaken even without the opening of insolvency proceedings.

197. The purpose of Article 25(2) is to avoid gaps between the Convention on insolvency proceedings and the 1968 Brussels Convention. The exclusion of insolvency proceedings as provided for in Article 1(2) of the 1968 Brussels Convention should be interpreted in accordance with the

definition of insolvency proceedings given by the Convention on insolvency proceedings and the criteria incorporated in Article 25 thereof.

198. Preservation measures (Article 25(1), third subparagraph)

The same system of recognition and enforcement shall apply to preservation measures ordered by a court having jurisdiction under Article 3(1) after the request for the opening of insolvency proceedings.

Article 25 covers preservation measures adopted both before and after the opening of insolvency proceedings, Article 25(1) third subparagraph ensures that from the moment of the request of the opening of insolvency proceedings covered by the Convention, all preservation measures necessary to protect the future effectiveness of those proceedings fall under the system of this Convention.

199. The reason for this rule lies in the case law of the Court of Justice of the European Communities. According to the judgment of 27 March 1979 (Case 143/78 *De Cavel v De Cavel* [1979] ECR 1055), provisional orders and protective measures shall be included in the scope of the 1968 Brussels Convention, not by virtue of 'their own nature' but of 'the nature of the rights which they serve to protect'. Since insolvency proceedings are expressly excluded from the scope of the 1968 Brussels Convention (Article 1 subparagraph 2), that Convention cannot apply to measures adopted prior to the opening of insolvency proceedings to guarantee its future effectiveness. In view of the practical significance of preservation measures in insolvency matters it seemed logical to establish a rule expressly including those measures in the scope of the Convention.

200. The resulting system for preservation measures is similar to the one laid down by the 1968 Brussels Convention for preservation measures in civil and commercial matters (see, however, point 207). This solution is of immediate practical importance. There are many examples of preservation measures that should have extraterritorial scope and cover the whole Community (eg after the request for the opening of proceedings and with sufficient grounds, attempted fraudulent concealment of assets, the judge who has jurisdiction under Article 3(1) issues a provisional injunction prohibiting the disposal of assets by the debtor).

201. To understand the recognition and enforcement system for preservation measures, it must be taken into account that this Convention (as well as the 1968 Brussels Convention) governs both jurisdiction for adopting binding judgments (which is attributed to the courts of the State where the centre of the debtor's main interests is situated (F1)) and the recognition and enforcement of such judgments in other Contracting States.

The court having jurisdiction under Article 3(1) also has jurisdiction to decide, for example, the seizure of the debtor's assets, even though they are situated abroad, or any other preservation measure (see point 78). This decision shall be entitled, according to Article 25, to its recognition and enforcement in the Contracting State where the assets concerned are situated (F2).

Recognition and enforcement of that decision always fall under the exclusive authority of the courts of the State where the measure is to be carried out (F2).

The courts in F2 will only verify that it is a decision covered by the Convention, that it emanates from the judge who claims jurisdiction under Article 3(1) and that the said measure does not breach public policy. It is not necessary, nor may it be requested, that the requirements laid down by the national law of F2 for the direct adoption of equivalent preservation measures be fulfilled.

Once the exequatur has been granted according to the Convention, the enforcement itself shall be done using the mechanisms of enforcement available under the domestic law of F2 (see point 190).

Article 26

Public policy

202. Defences against recognition and enforcement—Introduction

The Convention is based on the principle of Community trust and on the general legal presumption that the judgment handed down in another Contracting State is valid. For this

reason it establishes that the only ground for opposing recognition is that the judgment handed down in another Contracting State is contrary to the public policy of the requested State. As a consequence:
1. The foreign judgment cannot be the subject of review as regards its substance (révision au fond). All questions regarding the substance must be discussed before the courts of the State of the opening of proceedings. In the State where recognition or enforcement is requested, the court may only decide whether the foreign judgment will have effects contrary to its public policy.
2. The Convention contains no provisions as to the verification of the international jurisdiction of the court of the State of origin (the court in the State of the opening of proceedings which has jurisdiction under Article 3 of the Convention). The courts of the requested States may not review the jurisdiction of the court of the State of origin, but only verify that the judgment emanates from a court of a Contracting State which claims jurisdiction under Article 3 of the Convention.

It is for the judicial authorities of the State in which the judgment originated (F1) to verify and control its international jurisdiction under the Convention. Any interested party seeking to challenge the jurisdiction of a national court must go to the State of the opening of proceedings to appeal against the decision asserting jurisdiction. The court may refer the interpretation of Article 3 (international jurisdiction) to the Court of Justice of the European Communities for a preliminary ruling (see Article 44).

203. Public Policy

The exception in Article 26 is the traditional exception that a judgment of a foreign court need not be recognized or enforced if such recognition or enforcement is contrary to the public policy in the Contracting State in which recognition or enforcement is sought.

204. The public policy exception ought to operate only in exceptional cases. For this reason Article 26 requires recognition or enforcement of the foreign judgment to be 'manifestly' contrary to public policy.

Furthermore, Article 26 does not require the compatibility with public policy of the rule or principle applied by the foreign court to be ascertained in the abstract, but that the result of recognition or enforcement of the judgment offends against public policy. Verification of conformity with public policy is directed towards the result of the recognition or enforcement, which means that all the circumstances peculiar to the case, including the connection with the requested State, are relevant.

205. Public policy derives from national law, and therefore the concept does not necessarily have a uniform content throughout the Community. Public policy is based on the fundamental principles of the law of the requested State. It involves, in particular, constitutionally protected rights and freedoms, and fundamental policies of the requested State, including those of the Community.

However, public policy cannot be used by Contracting States to unilaterally challenge the system of the Convention. Unreasonably wide interpretations of public policy are not covered by Article 26.(See also point 208.)

206. Public policy operates as a general clause as regards recognition and enforcement, covering fundamental principles of both substance and procedure.

Public policy may thus protect participants or persons concerned by the proceedings against failures to observe due process. Public policy does not involve a general control of the correctness of the procedure followed in another Contracting State, but rather of essential procedural guarantees such as the adequate opportunity to be heard and the rights of participation in the proceedings. Rights of participation and non-discrimination play a special role in the case of plans to reorganize businesses or compositions, in relation to creditors whose participation is hindered or who are the subject of unfounded discrimination.

The 1968 Brussels Convention deals separately, in Article 27, with the conditions concerning the serving of documents and the time necessary to prepare the defence, which form part of (but do not exhaust) the guarantees of the right of defence. However, in view of the special nature of insolvency proceedings, which are collective proceedings with special rules of individual notice

(Article 40) and publicity (Article 21), and taking into account that the most important criterion of international jurisdiction is the State of the debtor's centre of main interests, which in principle will normally be that of the domicile or seat of the debtor, the group preferred to leave these conditions to case law.

However, if within the context of insolvency proceedings individual decisions are taken vis-à-vis a specific creditor, it seems reasonable to provide guarantees equivalent to those laid down in Article 27 of the 1968 Brussels Convention.

207. All the Contracting States provide for the possibility of taking, under certain urgent circumstances, ex parte preservation measures without an ex ante hearing of the party concerned. Naturally, for these measures to be constitutional, in most States they are subject to special requirements guaranteeing respect of due process (eg cumulatively, evidence of a good prima facie case, serious urgency, lodging of a guarantee by the applicant, immediate notification of the person concerned and the real possibility of challenging the adoption of the measures).

The Convention does not rule out the possibility of such measures being recognized 'by virtue of their nature'. Whether they are recognized (and, where appropriate, enforced) or not depends on whether or not they are compatible with the public policy of the requested State in which the judgment is to take effect (F2).

208. For the reasons explained in point 193, the Convention excludes judgments affecting personal freedom or postal secrecy from the obligation of recognition and enforcement, so that the States will not be obliged to resort to this exemption clause (Article 25(3)).

Conversely, as stated in point 148, in order to prevent the use of public policy to paralyse such recognition or enforcement, the Convention does not allow the use of the status of the debtor (eg trader/non-trader) to prevent recognition of a judgment handed down in another Contracting State (second subparagraph of Article 16(1)).

209. Public policy may result in total or partial rejection of the judgments handed down in another Contracting State.

210. The Portuguese Republic indicated in a unilateral statement made at the meeting of the Council of the European Union on 25 September 1995 that, under the conditions set out in Article 26, Portuguese public policy might be invoked to defend important local interests against the application of Article 37, which concerns the conversion of territorial proceedings opened before the main proceedings, where those interests are not sufficiently taken into account in such conversion.

D. Chapter III: Secondary Insolvency Proceedings

Article 27

Opening of insolvency proceedings

211. The Convention permits the opening of local proceedings by the courts of the State where the debtor has an establishment (Article 3(2)).

After main proceedings have been opened in a Contracting State, those local proceedings can only be 'secondary' proceedings.

Secondary proceedings are governed by national law. The Convention, however, modifies the conditions established by the national law for the opening of insolvency proceedings in two aspects:
1. The national law requirement of insolvency of the debtor need not be met, in so far as the judgment opening main insolvency proceedings in another Contracting State is recognized.
2. The right to request the opening of insolvency proceedings is directly given by the Convention to the liquidator of the main proceedings.

The remaining conditions are those of the national law (see Articles 28 and 29(b)) without modifications, ie if local insolvency proceedings can be opened on account of the status of the debtor, persons empowered to request the opening, etc.

212. Let us explain those conditions: the judgment opening insolvency proceedings by the court of the State in which the centre of the debtor's main interests is situated has the specific effect of allowing territorial proceedings to be opened in the State where the debtor has an establishment, without the court of the State in which the establishment is situated having to examine the insolvency of the debtor.

213. The court where the opening of secondary proceedings is requested examines whether the proceedings opened in another Contracting State and by virtue of which the opening of territorial proceedings is requested are covered by Article 16: ie the judgment opens a set of insolvency proceedings as listed in Annexe A, it is delivered by a court which has declared that it has jurisdiction within the meaning of Article 3(1) and it is effective.

Moreover, the court examines its international jurisdiction for opening territorial proceedings, as well as its domestic jurisdiction, and, concerning those aspects not covered by the Convention, the conditions for opening proceedings provided for by national legislation.

214. The proceedings by virtue of which the opening of secondary proceedings is requested must be proceedings included in Annexe A to the Convention.

They must be proceedings based on the debtor's insolvency (see point 49(b), fourth and fifth subparagraphs for the problem posed by winding-up proceedings in Ireland and the United Kingdom).

215. The proceedings by virtue of which the opening of secondary proceedings is requested must be opened by a court of a Contracting State which has jurisdiction, as provided for in Article 3(1): such a court has verified that the centre of the debtor's main interests is situated in that State and it bases its jurisdiction on those grounds to open proceedings which may claim to be the main proceedings.

The court which is required to open secondary proceedings cannot verify the correctness of the appraisal of the first court, whose judgment benefits from the trust placed in judgments delivered by Community courts.

216. The court where the opening of secondary proceedings is requested also examines whether the foreign judgment is effective.

217. If the judgment opens an insolvency proceeding mentioned in Annexe A, acknowledges that it constitutes the opening of main proceedings and has begun to be effective, that judgment is recognized within the meaning of Article 16.

The requirement for opening secondary proceedings laid down by the Convention is thus met.

218. In consequence, the court where the opening of secondary proceedings is requested does not have to examine the debtor's insolvency.

219. Furthermore, the court requested to open secondary proceedings examines its jurisdiction within the meaning of Article 3(2).

The debtor must have an establishment as defined in Article 2(h) on the territory in question. If there is no establishment, no secondary proceedings will be opened.

In the latter case, the main proceedings will produce their full effects on the territory where the debtor does not have an establishment, but does have assets. Chapter II of the Convention comes into play and the liquidator in the main proceedings may exercise all his powers on that territory. Thus, for instance, as the mere existence of a credit balance in a bank account does not constitute an establishment, the liquidator in the main proceedings may, subject in particular to the rights in rem of third parties referred to in Article 5, order the transfer of such money to the State of the opening in order to distribute it amongst the creditors involved in the main proceedings.

220. In examining its international jurisdiction within the meaning of Article 3(2), the court appraises the facts to determine whether the debtor has an establishment in that territory. In fact, the court may be led to consider that the debtor's activities in that territory constitute more than a simple establishment and could have been considered as the centre of the debtor's main interests.

The principle of trust attached to decisions of courts within the Community does not allow those courts to call into question the appraisal of the court that has declared itself competent in accordance with Article 3(1) (see point 215).

A court which establishes that the judgment opening the main proceedings has the quality of a recognized judgment and that the debtor has a place of activity in its territory that can be considered to be an establishment will be led to open territorial secondary proceedings.

221. In accordance with Article 3(3), secondary insolvency proceedings opened after the main proceedings must be winding-up proceedings within the meaning of Article 2(c). Their purpose is to realize the debtor's assets. The proceedings are mentioned in Annexe B to the Convention.

The court cannot open insolvency proceedings the purpose of which is the reorganization of the debtor's business or of his financial situation.

The discussions on the Convention have finally resulted in the inclusion of both winding-up proceedings and reorganization proceedings in the main insolvency proceedings.

In the case of proven insolvency at the centre of the debtor's main interests, it is difficult to conceive, under certain legal systems in the Community, of an establishment dependent on the insolvent person being separately the subject of reorganization. Furthermore, coordination between the main proceedings and the secondary reorganization proceedings was regarded by most Contracting States as so complex technically as to be difficult to carry out.

In order to confer the widest possible scope on the Convention by recognizing not only winding-up proceedings—accepted from the beginning of discussion as proceedings to be recognized—but also reorganization proceedings, it was decided to allow only secondary winding-up proceedings.

This solution shows the dependency of the secondary proceedings vis-à-vis the main proceedings of a universal nature.

222. National legislation determines more specifically the court which has territorial jurisdiction.

It should be noted that the Convention deals with international jurisdiction but does not specify which court has jurisdiction among the courts of the Contracting State in which an establishment is situated.

States shall ensure that their legislation designates the court which has territorial jurisdiction to open secondary proceedings.

223. The court also applies its national law regarding the conditions for opening proceedings which are not the subject of a rule of the Convention (Article 4(2)).

National law determines the persons against whom insolvency proceedings may be brought (Article 4(2)(a)). Where, for example, national legislation does not permit insolvency proceedings against a person who does not have the capacity of a trader, or against a public undertaking, the possibility of secondary proceedings is excluded.

224. In accordance with Article 3(2), secondary proceedings only produce effects with regard to the debtor's assets situated in the territory of the Contracting State where the establishment is situated.

The secondary liquidator has, however, the right to act outside his territory in order to recover an asset moved out of that State after the opening of the secondary proceedings or in fraud against the creditors of those proceedings (Article 18(2)). He is also allowed to bring actions in other States for the voidness, voidability or unenforceability of detrimental legal acts (Article 4(2)(m) and Article 13). The purpose of these actions outside the territory is, in fact, the return of assets which were legally situated in the territory of the proceedings at the time of the opening or which, without fraud, would have been situated in the territory of the proceedings at the time of the opening.

The action of the secondary liquidator in the matter of the return of assets which are actually situated abroad but which should normally be included in the secondary proceedings is to be assessed on the basis of the law of the secondary proceedings, pursuant in particular to Article 4(2)(m), subject to Article 13 (see points 91(l) and 135 to 139).

Article 28

Applicable law

225. This Article expressly stipulates that, save as otherwise provided by the Convention, the law of the State in which secondary proceedings are opened shall apply to those proceedings.

    In fact, this reiterates Article 4, which is interpreted as meaning that the law applicable to the main proceedings is the law of the State where the main proceedings are opened, and the law applicable to the secondary proceedings is the law of the State of the opening of the secondary proceedings.

Article 29

Right to request the opening of proceedings

226. The Convention authorizes the liquidator in the main proceedings to request the opening of secondary proceedings. The temporary administrator who, according to national law, may be appointed after the request of the opening of the main insolvency proceedings but before the opening itself, is not covered by Article 29(a) (see point 262).

    The liquidator in secondary proceedings has, however, no right derived from the Convention to request the opening of other secondary proceedings.

    This rule states the relationship of dependence of the secondary proceedings upon the main proceedings.

227. Furthermore, the persons and authorities empowered by national law to request the opening of the insolvency proceedings referred to in Annexe B are also entitled to request the opening of secondary proceedings.

    The right of these persons and therefore the right of the creditors to bring about proceedings is not limited by the requirement of a specific interest.

    The provision envisaged in the discussions, whereby only the creditors who would benefit from a more favourable legal status in the secondary proceedings than in the main proceedings (for example, a more favourable ranking) could request the opening of secondary proceedings, has been deleted.

    On the other hand, Article 29(b) confers the right to have proceedings opened on any person, without distinction.

    It should be noted that the right to request the opening of territorial proceedings before the opening of the main proceedings is limited to those proceedings referred to in Article 3(4)(b) (see point 85).

Article 30

Advance payment of costs and expenses

228. Various legislations rule out the possibility of insolvency proceedings where the debtor's assets are insufficient to cover in whole or in part the costs and expenses of the proceedings.

    The Convention takes these legislations into account.

    The provision in Article 30 is understood to mean that where national law does not require sufficient assets in order to open insolvency proceedings, it cannot introduce such a requirement for secondary proceedings only.

    Should national law rule out insolvency proceedings where assets are insufficient, the Convention upholds this law and allows the court to require from the applicant, including the liquidator, an advance payment of costs, or an appropriate security. The terms 'may require' do not confer a power on the court but mean that national legislation continues to apply.

Article 31

Duty to cooperate and communicate information

229. The main proceedings and the secondary proceedings are interdependent proceedings which concern a debtor with several centres of activity and assets spread over several territories.

    The debtor's creditors participate, or may have an interest in participating, in several proceedings. Cooperation and information between the liquidators is thus necessary to ensure the smooth course of operations in the various proceedings.

230. The exchange of information between the liquidators concerns in particular:
    - the assets,
    - the actions planned or under way in order to recover assets: actions to obtain payment or actions for set aside,
    - possibilities for liquidating assets,
    - claims lodged,
    - verification of claims and disputes concerning them,
    - the ranking of creditors,
    - planned reorganization measures,
    - proposed compositions,
    - plans for the allocation of dividends,
    - the progress of operations in the proceedings.

231. The duty to communicate information may be limited by national legislation on data exchange, eg by legislation relating to the protection of computerized personal data.

232. The duty of the liquidators to exchange information is complemented by the obligation to cooperate with each other. The liquidators have a duty to act in concert with a view to the development of proceedings and their coordination, and to facilitate their respective work.

233. Article 31(3) expressly mentions a specific obligation of information and cooperation that affects the liquidator in the secondary proceedings, on the grounds of primacy of the main proceedings over the secondary proceedings. The liquidator in the secondary proceedings must give the liquidator in the main proceedings the opportunity to submit proposals on the realization or use of the assets in the secondary proceedings. The secondary liquidator must therefore inform the main liquidator of any use or realization of these assets.

    This obligation may enable the main liquidator, for example, to prevent the sale of assets involved in the secondary proceedings, the preservation of which may be deemed advisable from the viewpoint of the reorganization of the business at the centre of main interests and to request a stay of the liquidation through the application of Article 33.

    The obligation considered in Article 31(3) refers to important assets or decisions (such as continuation or cessation of the activities of the establishment) in the secondary proceedings. It should not be interpreted in such a broad way as in practice to paralyse the work of the liquidator in the secondary proceedings.

234. Where appropriate, the applicable national law will determine the liquidator's liability when the latter has not respected the duties arising from Article 31.

Article 32

Exercise of creditors' rights

235. Pursuant to Article 4(2)(h), the law of the State of the opening of the proceedings determines the rules governing the lodging of claims.

    However, national law concerning the creditors entitled to lodge claims is replaced by the provision in Article 32(1), which entitles any creditor to lodge his claim in the main proceedings and in any secondary proceedings.

    The creditor is entitled to lodge claims in the proceedings of his choice, even in several proceedings.

The right to lodge claims of creditors with their domicile, habitual residence, or registered office in a Contracting State other than the State of the opening of the proceedings is restated in Article 39. For comments on the scope of that Article, see points 265–270.

236. Article 32(2) establishes the liquidator's right to lodge in other proceedings claims which have already been lodged in his proceedings. The Convention modifies national legislation concerning the lodging of claims, simply by adding a right for the liquidator to lodge claims (see point 237).

Both the liquidator in the main proceedings and each liquidator in secondary proceedings may lodge claims in the other proceedings.

The aim of this provision is to facilitate the exercise of the rights of those creditors who lodge claims in certain proceedings permitting their claims to be also lodged by the liquidator in other proceedings, and finally, to permit the liquidators to reinforce their influence in other proceedings.

237. The rights of the creditors are preserved in so far as they may oppose the lodging of their claims in other proceedings by the liquidator or withdraw any previous lodgement in other proceedings.

The Convention allows creditors the right to oppose a claim lodged in other proceedings by the liquidator.

On the other hand, the right to withdraw a claim lodged by the liquidator is governed by the law applicable to the proceedings in which the claim has been presented: creditors' rights are subject to the law of the State in which the proceedings are opened and it is a question of determining the rights of creditors in the proceedings in which the claim has been presented.

In so far as the liquidator's claim is lodged on behalf of the creditor, the issue of withdrawal is not a new one, and national laws establish the creditor's right to withdraw the claim lodged.

238. The lodging of a claim by the liquidator has the same effects as the lodging of a claim by the creditor: the liquidator acts on behalf of the creditor and in his stead. The Convention mentions this right of the liquidator to lodge claims.

However, national rules concerning the period for lodging, the consequences of delayed lodging, the admissibility and well-foundedness of the lodging and the expenses linked to the verification of the claims remain unchanged (see point 267).

239. Under Article 32(2), liquidators should lodge in other proceedings claims which have already been lodged in their own proceedings. The obligation to lodge such claims exists only in so far as it is in the general interests of all the creditors or of a class of creditors.

It is effective subject to the individual creditor's right to oppose the lodging of the claim.

The creditor may have various reasons for opposing the lodging of his claim in proceedings other than those he has selected. For example, as the liquidator's claim is lodged on his behalf, and as national law determines the rules for the lodging and verification of claims, including the costs, the creditor may run the risk in the other proceedings of incurring costs which he is not willing to bear.

Appraisal of the specific interest in lodging claims rests with the creditor, who must defend his interests himself. In a way, he has already made a choice when lodging his claim in a certain State.

Specific appraisal of the interest involves an examination in accordance with the law applicable to the claim and, as regards the status of the claim, in accordance with the legislation of the State in which the lodging is envisaged (Article 4(2)(h)).

This specific appraisal for each claim would involve a difficult task for the liquidator, and would be a costly and lengthy procedure.

However, the aim of the Article is different. Under Article 32(2) the liquidator's task to lodge exists only when it is clearly in the general interest of all creditors in his proceedings or of a class of them.

For example, if the liquidator finds that the assets to be distributed in other proceedings are so significant that even the ordinary unsecured creditors in his proceedings may receive a dividend, in competition with the ordinary unsecured creditors lodging claims in the other proceedings, the lodging of the claim may be useful and will take place.

Moreover, he will also lodge a claim where a creditor, rather than lodging a claim himself, has informed the liquidator of the interest of the lodging of his claim.

He will obviously not lodge a claim if the lodgement would be irrevocably delayed and therefore not appropriate.

The liquidator's task, thus delimited, may improve the situation of the creditors, without complicating the proceedings to the detriment of creditors.

240. Article 32(3) empowers any liquidator to participate in other proceedings. The aim of the provision is to better ensure the presence of creditors and the expression of their interests through the liquidator.

In order to resolve the frequent absence of creditors, the Convention allows the liquidator to attend creditors' meetings.

The text stipulates that the liquidator shall participate in other proceedings 'on the same basis as a creditor'. Obviously, the liquidator has the right to express his opinion in the course of the proceedings, and more specifically at the meeting of creditors involved in the other proceedings. However, the Convention does not establish the specific content of the liquidator's right to participate and does not determine how the liquidator shall exercise the rights of the creditors in his proceedings.

It should be noted that the provisions permitting the liquidator who lodges claims already lodged in the other proceedings to exercise the voting right deriving from a claim lodged, and the provisions concerning the simultaneous exercise by several liquidators of the voting right arising from a claim, were rejected in the course of negotiations.

Participation by the liquidator may be regulated by national law.

Article 33

Stay of liquidation

241. At the request of the liquidator in the main proceedings, the process of liquidation in the secondary proceedings may be stayed in whole or in part.

    This provision establishes the primacy of the main proceedings, but it equally takes into account the interests of the creditors in the secondary proceedings.

242. The liquidator in the main proceedings submits a request for the stay of liquidation in the secondary proceedings.

    The court may not refuse the stay except if it is manifestly not in the interests of the creditors in the main proceedings.

    The grounds for request of a stay may be appraised only in relation to the interests of the creditors in the main proceedings.

243. The interests of the creditors in the main proceedings in the stay of liquidation that the court takes into consideration can assume different aspects. For example, the preservation of the estate situated in the State of the secondary proceedings may be useful with a view to selling the main business or the secondary establishment to a purchaser or with a view to a composition. The safeguarding of some of the elements of the assets, useful within a reorganization, or with a view to a sale 'en masse' together with some of the assets involved in the main proceedings may justify a partial stay on the liquidation.

244. The court may take into account the interests of all the creditors in the secondary proceedings, as well as those of certain groups of creditors, imposing on the liquidator in the main proceedings a guarantee which it determines as appropriate, before ordering the stay.

245. The stay is limited to a maximum of three months. Once this period is over, it may be extended for another three months maximum each time. The number of successive extensions is not limited.

    The liquidation process which is restarted after a stay can be stayed again, and the stay can be renewed. The number of new stays is not limited.

246. The decision on a stay does not terminate the liquidation process. The effects brought about by the opening of proceedings pursuant to the law of the State of the opening of proceedings, eg as

regards the exercise of individual actions, come into play. The liquidation process simply does not continue.
247. Where the stay no longer appears to be justified, the court terminates it. A stay may be terminated at any moment. The court may act:
   - at the request of the liquidator in the main proceedings, or
   - of its own motion, or
   - at the request of the liquidator in the secondary proceedings, or
   - at the request of a creditor.

   If, in particular, the interests of the creditors in the main proceedings, or those of the creditors in the secondary proceedings no longer appear to justify the stay, it is to be terminated.

   Consideration of the interests of the creditors in the secondary proceedings may lead by themselves to an end to the stay.

Article 34

Measures ending secondary insolvency proceedings

248. If the law of the State in which the secondary proceedings are opened allows insolvency proceedings to be closed by means of a rescue plan, a composition, or a comparable measure, all those stipulated by that law, may propose such a measure. In addition, the Convention empowers the liquidator in the main proceedings to propose it himself.
249. Under rescue plans, compositions or comparable measures, the creditors may accept a rescheduling of debts or waive some of their rights and the debtor may undertake to meet certain conditions. All of which may affect the interests in the main proceedings. For this reason, the Convention requires that, to become final, such a measure must obtain the consent of the liquidator in the main proceedings.

   In adopting his decision, the liquidator may take into consideration all the interests of the creditors in the main proceedings, including the interests in reorganizing and continuing the main business.

   Should, however, the liquidator in the main proceedings oppose the rescue plan, the composition or a comparable measure in the secondary proceedings, the Convention permits his agreement to be waived, and the secondary proceedings may be closed if the financial interests of the creditors in the main proceedings are not affected by the measure proposed.

   The concept of financial interests is more restrictive than that of the interest of the creditors in the main proceedings, which may, for instance, justify a stay on secondary proceedings and which is examined in point 243.

   The financial interests are estimated by evaluating the effects which the rescue plan or the composition has on the dividend to be paid to the creditors in the main proceedings. If those creditors could not reasonably have expected to receive more, after the transfer of any surplus of the assets remaining in the secondary proceedings (ex Article 35), in the absence of a rescue plan or a composition, their financial interests are not thereby affected.
250. The effects of secondary proceedings are confined to assets situated within the territory of the State in which they have been opened.

   Consequently, a rescue plan or a composition restricting creditors' rights may apply only to the assets covered by the secondary proceedings and not to the debtor's other assets situated outside that State.

   A composition confined in its effects to the assets involved in the proceedings shall be arrived at under the conditions laid down by the applicable law and, where appropriate, by a majority decision of the creditors. The rights of all the creditors, including the minority creditors who disagree with the measure, would be affected as regards the assets relevant to those proceedings.

   A composition restricting creditors' rights may be reached in the secondary proceedings with effects on assets not covered by those proceedings, provided that it is agreed to by every creditor concerned by that measure, ie having an interest affected by the measure.

251. In the event of a stay of the process of liquidation in the secondary proceedings only a measure for a composition proposed by the liquidator in the main proceedings, or by the debtor with that liquidator's agreement, may be put to the vote or approved.

The stay is ordered at the request of the liquidator in the main proceedings on account of the interests of the creditors in those proceedings. During this period, the course of the main proceedings must not be disrupted by measures not agreed to by the liquidator.

Efforts to bring about the reorganization of the main business may have led to a stay. Article 34(3), prohibiting for the duration of the stay any composition not proposed by the liquidator in the main proceedings or by the debtor with his agreement, enables the interests of the creditors who brought about the stay to be taken into consideration (see point 243).

Article 35

Assets remaining in the secondary proceedings

252. If the assets in the secondary proceedings are sufficient to meet all claims allowed in them, any assets not distributed are to be transferred to the main proceedings.

    The liquidator shall transfer the remaining assets to the liquidator in the main proceedings.

    The transfer of any remaining assets to the main proceedings reflects the primary nature of those proceedings.

253. Assets will be distributed amongst all creditors whose claims are allowed in the secondary proceedings. The Convention allows creditors to lodge claims in any proceedings, so that even creditors with preferential claims in the main proceedings who might be ordinary unsecured creditors in the secondary proceedings will have an incentive to lodge claims in order, at least, to have their claims met in the same way and at the same time as other ordinary unsecured creditors.

    The scale of the assets to be distributed will attract creditors. If the assets were such that any surplus remains after distribution amongst all creditors whose claims were admitted to these proceedings, only those claims not lodged or not admitted will remain unsatisfied and may be affected by the transfer of the remaining assets to the main proceedings.

Article 36

Subsequent opening of the main proceedings

254. Should a court in the State in which the centre of the debtor's main interests is located, open insolvency proceedings in accordance with Article 3(1), after independent territorial proceedings have been opened by a court in a State in which there is an establishment, pursuant to Article 3(2), the proceedings opened at the place of the centre of main interests will be the main proceedings, while the proceedings previously opened at the place of the establishment will have to be necessarily regarded as secondary proceedings.

255. In so far as the progress of the independent territorial proceedings, opened first, so permits, the rules for coordination between the main proceedings and the secondary proceedings as laid down in Articles 31 to 35 are to be followed.

Article 37

Conversion of earlier proceedings

256. Pursuant to Articles 3(3) and 27, secondary proceedings opened at the place in which an establishment is situated after the main proceedings, are to be winding-up proceedings within the meaning of Article 2(c), as listed in Annexe B.

    Where, prior to the opening of main proceedings, independent territorial insolvency proceedings listed in Annexe A but not in Annexe B are opened, these latter proceedings may be converted into winding-up proceedings listed in Annexe B in the event of main proceedings being opened.

257. Under the Convention, the liquidator in the main proceedings shall be entitled to request that independent territorial reorganization proceedings, as mentioned in Annexe A, be converted into secondary winding-up proceedings.

    The Convention does not prohibit the law of a Contracting State competent under Article 3(4) from allowing the liquidator in the main proceedings simply to request the closure of independent territorial reorganization proceedings under the conditions laid down by that law.

258. The court is not obliged to order conversion of the proceedings at the liquidator's request. It is necessary that the conversion proves to be in the interests of the creditors in the main proceedings.

    This provision reflects the primary nature of the main proceedings. (See also point 210.)

259. If conversion is not requested by the liquidator or ordered by the court, territorial proceedings may continue as reorganization proceedings.

260. As a result of conversion, the proceedings will be conducted as secondary winding-up insolvency proceedings in accordance with Article 36.

261. Should any territorial proceedings opened prior to main proceedings in a Contracting State where an establishment is situated not be proceedings listed in Annexe A, they will not be covered by the Convention.

    Main proceedings that are opened after the territorial proceedings have all the effects laid down in the Convention; the liquidator in the main proceedings is allowed to exercise his powers in other Contracting States and to request the opening of secondary proceedings. Consequently, these territorial proceedings may not continue. The national law must adopt the appropriate solution that would conform with the provisions of the Convention: that could for example be the closing of the territorial proceedings.

Article 38

Preservation measures

262. In order to avoid any change in the debtor's estate to the detriment of creditors from the date on which the opening of insolvency proceedings is requested to the date on which the judgment opening them is handed down, certain laws provide for the appointment of a temporary administrator.

    Article 29 authorizes the liquidator in the main proceedings, but not such temporary administrator, to request the opening of secondary proceedings in any other Contracting State where the debtor has an establishment.

    However, as a pre-opening stage of secondary insolvency proceedings, Article 38 allows the temporary administrator designated by a court competent to open main proceedings to request measures to secure and preserve the debtor's assets situated in any other Contracting State, provided for under the law of this State for the period between the request for the opening of insolvency proceedings and the opening itself. As a pre-opening stage of secondary proceedings, Article 38 presupposes the existence of an establishment of the debtor in that Contracting State (see Article 3(2)). For the same reason, the preservation measures available will be those which, under the national insolvency law of that State, correspond to winding-up proceedings.

    Once appointed, the liquidator in the main proceedings will decide whether or not to request the opening of secondary proceedings.

    If the request is made, the national courts of the State of the opening of secondary proceedings will decide on the continuation or modification of such measures. Until that moment or, also, if the opening of secondary proceedings is not finally requested, the preservation measures taken over the assets of the debtor situated in that State will be subordinated to the decisions taken by the court competent under Article 3(1), which benefit from the system of recognition and enforcement of the Convention, in similar terms as those already explained in point 78 of this report.

263. The position of a temporary administrator appointed after the request, but before the opening, of the main insolvency proceedings has to be seen in relation to the provisional task of preserving the assets which is entrusted to him. Such temporary administrator, whose task is more limited, does not correspond exactly with the definition in Article 2(b) of a liquidator in insolvency proceedings and is not necessarily listed in Annexe C.

Article 38 allows the temporary administrator to request in the State where the debtor has an establishment preservation measures of a more general character than those contemplated in point 78, fourth paragraph, of this report.

E. Chapter IV: Provision of Information for Creditors and Lodgement of their Claims

264. Chapter IV specifies the information which the court or the liquidator is required to provide to creditors and the rules for lodging claims.

These provisions are applicable both to main proceedings and to territorial (independent or secondary) insolvency proceedings.

Article 39

Right to lodge claims

265. Article 39 establishes a rule of substantive law, laying down the right of foreign creditors, ie of any creditor who has his habitual residence, domicile or registered office in another Contracting State, to lodge claims in writing in insolvency proceedings. This provision derogates, in the way specified below, from the application of national law, pursuant to Article 4(2)(h).

To clear up any doubts, it is specified that the right of any foreign creditor to lodge claims includes the tax authorities and social security authorities of other Contracting States.

It should be noted that Article 32, allows all creditors to participate in the main or secondary proceedings, as they choose, and even in several proceedings (see point 235).

266. Establishing the right of foreign creditors to lodge claims means that lodgement of their claims cannot be disallowed on the grounds that the creditor is situated in another Contracting State or that the claim is governed by the public law of another Contracting State.

267. However, under Article 4(2)(h), the national law of the State of the opening will govern the time limit for lodging claims, the effect of a late lodgement, and the admissibility and well-foundedness of the lodgement.

268. In addition, the national law of each proceedings determines the costs, to the charge of a creditor, attached to the claim and to the verification of the debts.

The prudent creditor will take into account the rules relevant to the costs, and will appreciate the interest that a claim presents. He will examine the ranking that the law of the proceedings accords to his claim and the importance of the assets that will be distributed.

269. The right to lodge claims for creditors situated in the State in which proceedings are opened is governed by national law.

Moreover, the Convention does not concern itself with the rights of creditors situated outside the Contracting States. The right of creditors from outside the Community to lodge claims is governed by national law.

270. The Convention gives creditors the right to lodge claims in writing, but it does not prevent national law from permitting claims to be lodged in any other more favourable form for creditors.

Article 40

Duty to inform creditors

271. The court having jurisdiction or the liquidator must, without delay, inform known creditors who have their habitual residence, domicile or registered office in the other Contracting States of the opening of insolvency proceedings and of the need to lodge their claims.

    The Convention aims to improve the situation of intra-Community creditors situated outside the State in which proceedings are opened.

    The liquidator's duty to inform creditors situated in the State in which proceedings are opened is governed by national law.

    The Convention does not take into consideration creditors from outside the Community to whom the national law of the State in which the proceedings are opened applies.

272. Article 40(2) lays down the form and the content to be taken by the information provided for creditors.

    The liquidator is required to send a notice to each creditor. This notice has to state the time limits for lodging claims, the legal consequences laid down for failing to meet those time limits and the person or body with whom claims must be lodged. It must specify whether creditors with preferential claims or claims secured in rem are required to lodge them.

    The compulsory contents of the notice as laid down in the Convention are designed to protect foreign creditors; national laws may not reduce the contents of the notice. A national law may stipulate additional information in the interests of creditors.

Article 41

Content of the lodgement of a claim

273. Under Article 4(2)(h) the lodging of claims is subject to the law of the State of the opening of proceedings.

    Article 41 constitutes, together with Articles 39 and 42(2), an exception to that rule in so far as it stipulates the content of claims lodged by creditors situated in another Contracting State.

    The requirements set out in Article 41 are intended to identify the claim which is sought to be lodged. As this provision is meant to facilitate the exercise of intra-Community creditors' rights, national legislation may impose no additional conditions on the content of the lodgement of claims by foreign creditors protected by the Convention.

    According to the Convention, a creditor may lodge his claim in writing (Article 39), supplying copies of supporting documents, if any, stating:
    - the nature of the claim,
    - the date on which it arose,
    - its amount.

    It must also specify any preference, security right or reservation of title alleged, as well as the assets covered by the guarantee invoked.

274. Under Article 4(2)(h), however, national law governs the verification and admission of claims and determines the procedure by which a creditor must establish his claim in order to have it admitted to the proceedings.

Article 42

Languages

275. The information for creditors regarding the opening of proceedings for their debtor's insolvency and the lodging of claims is to be given in an official language of the State of the opening of proceedings.

In order to help those creditors who do not understand the language of the State in which proceedings are opened, the information notice has to be headed 'Invitation to lodge a claim. Time limits to be observed'. This heading is to be given in all the official languages of the Community.

The heading, drawn up by the Secretariat of the Council of the European Union, will be published together with the Convention and the report.

276. Creditors from other Contracting States are allowed to lodge claims in an official language of the State in which they have their habitual residence, domicile or registered office.

However, their written statement must be headed 'Lodgement of claim' in a language of the State in which proceedings are opened.

In order to avoid delay in lodging claims and unnecessary lodgement costs, claims may be lodged in the creditor's language or, to be more exact, in the language of the State in which he lives or carries on his business.

277. Bearing in mind the scale of intra-Community trade and interpretation of economies, especially in border regions, as well as the understanding of one another's languages, a systematic requirement that claims be lodged in an official language of the State of the proceedings may run counter to the interests of creditors without being really necessary.

Use of the creditor's language is therefore the rule; a translation into the official language may be required in the course of the proceedings if this proves necessary.

F. Chapter V: Interpretation by the Court of Justice of the European Communities

278. The conferral of jurisdiction on the Court of Justice to give rulings on interpretation is not an innovation of the Convention on insolvency proceedings. The system of conferral follows the system established by Article 177 of the EC Treaty and adopted by the Protocols of 3 June 1971 concerning the interpretation by the Court of Justice of the 1968 Brussels Convention, and the Protocols of 19 December 1988 concerning the interpretation of the 1980 Rome Convention. Both Protocols were examined in the reports by Mr P. Jenard and Mr A. Tizziano (see OJ No C 189 of 28 July 1990 and No C 219 of 3 September 1990). We refer to those reports for further details.

Article 43

Jurisdiction of the Court of Justice

279. By virtue of this rule new powers of interpretation are conferred on the Court of Justice of the European Communities, supplementing its existing powers. In addition to this Convention and its Annexes, this jurisdiction also applies to future Conventions on accession by States which become Members of the European Union. Article 50 requires the new Members to follow the system of the Convention on insolvency proceedings and to make such adjustments and amendments as may be necessary. This explains the reference to future Conventions.

This jurisdiction covers the actual rules for the conferral of powers, so that it is for the Court of Justice to interpret the rules determining the scope of its jurisdiction or the procedures by which it may be exercised.

280. Jurisdiction in matters of interpretation means that the Court of Justice rules only on the interpretation of the text of the Convention and it is for the national court to apply the rules according to this interpretation and to give a judgment on the substance of the matter.

281. In contrast to the 1968 Brussels Convention and the 1980 Rome Convention, the conferral of jurisdiction to interpret is to be found in the text of the Convention and not in a separate Protocol. This emphasizes the close relationship between this Convention and the Community legal system and the significance of the uniform interpretation of those rules.

282. Both the Protocol on the Statute of the Court of Justice and the Rules of Procedure of the Court of Justice shall apply.

283. The Convention provides for two procedural channels through which the Court of Justice can resolve any problem of interpretation. The first involves preliminary ruling proceedings, as laid down by Article 44 of the Convention following the model of Article 177 of the EC Treaty. The second, included in Article 45 of the Convention, could be termed 'proceedings in the interests of the law'.

Article 44

Preliminary ruling proceedings

284. These are proceedings whereby a national court before which a case is brought requests the Court of Justice of the European Communities to give a preliminary ruling on the interpretation of a provision of the Convention or its Annexes, the application of which in the case in point has raised questions which must be resolved in order for a decision to be given on the substance of the matter.
285. The Convention determines the national courts which make such a request to the Court of Justice. Only the expressly designated courts are duly empowered, ie the higher law courts (such as the Tribunal Supremo in Spain, the Cour de Cassation in France, etc) which are listed in Article 44(a), and other courts when acting as courts of appeal. In the second case it is not necessary for the court to be officially entitled a 'Court of Appeal'. However, it must be involved in hearing appeals against judgments of a lower court. The power to request a preliminary ruling on interpretation is not granted to the courts of first instance.
286. The question must be one raised in a case pending before the court which submits the request for interpretation. The Court of Justice therefore resolves the questions of interpretation concerning cases pending before a national court.
287. It must be a question on which the national court considers a decision on interpretation to be 'necessary' for the judgment, ie it must be a problem of interpretation on which the solution to the case depends. If the different possibilities of interpretation lead to the same result, this requirement would not be fulfilled. The national court must assess in each individual case whether or not this need exists.
288. National courts have the power to submit questions of interpretation of their own motion to the Court of Justice. A request by a party is not necessary. If such a request is made the national court is not obliged to refer to the Court of Justice.
289. This Convention does not oblige national courts to submit questions of interpretation to the Court of Justice but it simply allows them to make such requests if all the abovementioned requirements are fulfilled.

    The need for speed in the conduct of insolvency proceedings explains the choice of a flexible formula which allows the national courts to decide on whether a preliminary ruling is appropriate. The Convention does not impose any criteria.

    The national court may take into account the estimated time needed for a ruling by the Court of Justice, the general significance of the question for the proceedings, the formal request of the parties directly affected (as we know, this does not bind the national court), etc.
290. The Convention does not mention a possible suspensive effect of the preliminary ruling on the insolvency proceedings until such time as the Court of Justice settles the problem of interpretation.

    The question of the average time for obtaining preliminary rulings is a serious problem in the area of insolvency proceedings.
291. In order to solve the question of suspensive effect, several facts [sic] should be taken into account:
    1. The jurisdiction of the Court of Justice derives directly from the powers conferred on it by the Convention on insolvency proceedings and its scope is defined by the latter.
    2. This conferral of jurisdiction is aimed at better fulfilling the specific objectives of the Convention on insolvency proceedings. The advantages of uniformity of interpretation must be counterbalanced by the need for efficiency in insolvency proceedings.

3. Time is a crucial factor in insolvency proceedings. They are opened as a consequence of a financial crisis. Promptness of action is imperative in order to avoid a depreciation of existing assets. The suspension of the insolvency proceedings may even preclude the possibility of reorganization. For this reason, many national legislations exclude the suspensive effect of appeals to higher courts in the case of insolvency proceedings. In addition, the collective nature of insolvency proceedings implies that a partial problem should not necessarily alter the main course of the proceedings.

292. In this context, the Convention leaves it to the national law of the State of the opening of proceedings to determine whether preliminary ruling proceedings before the Court of Justice should have suspensive effect. As there is no formal obligation to submit the question of interpretation to the Court of Justice, the most appropriate solution seems to be to confer on the national court the power to decide on whether or not it is necessary to interrupt the insolvency proceedings.

Article 45

Proceedings brought by a competent authority

293. These proceedings can be described as proceedings brought 'in the interests of the law', since the solution to proceedings under way does not depend on the ruling; it is designed to guarantee uniformity of interpretation in the future, when the national courts of different Contracting States have handed down contradictory interpretations of the rules of the Convention.
294. The request to the Court of Justice shall be brought by the Procurators-General of the Supreme Courts of Appeal of the Contracting States or any other authority designated by a Contracting State.
295. In order that this national authority may make a request to the Court of Justice, it is necessary for a national court of the same State to have given a final judgment which contradicts the interpretation given by the Court of Justice or by the courts of other Contracting States mentioned in Article 44 (the higher courts or those acting as appeal courts).
296. The ruling on the interpretation given by the Court of Justice does not affect the judgments which gave rise to it. Its aim is merely to clarify the interpretation for the future, without creating definitive binding precedent.
297. Article 45 incorporates proceedings established by the 1971 Protocols on the 1968 Brussels Convention and by the 1988 Protocols on the 1980 Rome Convention. Further comments may be found in the respective reports (see point 278).

Article 46

Reservations

298. The possibility of entering a reservation is not at the discretion of the State, but depends on the existence of an impediment for constitutional reasons relating to the conferral of jurisdiction to the Court of Justice.
299. The rationale of this reservation is to allow one Member State to minimize the risk of constitutional difficulties at the ratification stage of the Convention, which it felt might arise through the conferral of jurisdiction on the Court of Justice of the European Communities. The difficulties would arise in the event of the Convention being deemed to go beyond the limits of the objectives defined by Article 220 of the EC Treaty.

On the other hand, it was felt by other Contracting States that conferral of jurisdiction for interpretation on the Court of Justice is fundamental to the proper functioning of the system set up by the Convention on insolvency proceedings. A uniform interpretation by this Court is necessary to ensure that the rights and obligations deriving from the Convention are the same for all persons, irrespective of the Contracting State in which the party or person concerned is located. Hence, to mitigate as far as possible such risk, it was agreed that the scope of the Convention should be strictly limited to the intra-Community effects of the insolvency proceedings covered by the Convention. Thus, the perfect adaptation of the Convention to the scope of Article 220 of the EC Treaty would counterbalance the extension of its content to the rules on conflict of laws, without which the system of recognition of insolvency proceedings would distort legal certainty within the Community (see point 42).

G. Chapter VI: Transitional and Final Provisions Territorial Application

300. The Convention has no provisions governing territorial application. Consequently, the general rules of public international law, ie Article 29 of the 1969 Vienna Convention on the Law of Treaties are applicable.
301. This means that, in principle, the Convention on insolvency proceedings applies to the whole territory of the Contracting States. This includes non-European territories which are an integral part of the territory of these States. However, the autonomy of these territories can vary widely. Consequently, the Contracting States may exclude or reserve the application of the Convention to these territories by means of a declaration to that effect. This is the case, for example, with the Netherlands in relation to the Netherlands Antilles and Aruba.
302. For the same reason, the Convention does not apply to those territories whose international relations are assumed by any of the Contracting States, but which are not an integral part of their territory, being a separate entity. In principle, the Convention does not apply to them, no matter whether they are European or non-European territories. Should a Contracting State with such responsibility wish to extend the scope of the Convention to those territories, extension would only take effect if no other Contracting State opposed it.

Article 47

Applicability in time

303. Article 47 establishes two rules concerning the time of the application of the Convention. The Convention is applicable only to insolvency proceedings opened after the entry into force of the Convention. Acts done by the debtor before the entry into force of the Convention shall continue to be governed by the law which was applicable to them at the time they were done.

    These two rules were prompted by the concern not to alter existing situations and relations which were governed by specific legal rules at the time of the introduction of the new rules of the Convention into the legal systems of the Contracting States.
304. The Convention applies to insolvency proceedings opened after the entry into force of the Convention; it does not apply to proceedings opened beforehand.

    The Convention allows the opening of several sets of proceedings some of which may be opened before and some after entry into force.

    If proceedings are opened on the basis of the debtor's centre of main interests after the entry into force of the Convention, it could have been thought that, in view of the primacy of the main proceedings in the operation of the Convention, the latter would apply even if proceedings had previously been opened away from the centre of main interests. This solution was not adopted, because it might disturb the course of proceedings opened in accordance with the law applicable at the time of opening. Reorganization proceedings opened in a State where the debtor's centre of main interests is not situated would have to be converted. Rules on conflict of laws would where appropriate have to be modified in the course of proceedings by the application of those in the Convention. Proceedings of a universal nature opened in accordance with the criteria of international jurisdiction laid down in the national law applicable would, where appropriate, be classified as territorial proceedings if, within the meaning of the Convention, the centre of main interests was not situated in the State of the opening of the earlier proceedings.

If earlier proceedings were opened in the State considered by the Convention as being the State where the debtor's centre of main interests is located, those proceedings will not be covered by the Convention. Before the entry into force of the Convention these proceedings may produce effects outside the State of the opening pursuant to the rules applicable under the different national laws. In the case of the earlier opening of proceedings in the State of the centre of main interests, proceedings opened after entry into force in the State where the debtor has an establishment are not subject to the Convention.

The rule in Article 47 has an absolute character: if insolvency proceedings are opened against a given debtor prior to the entry into force of the Convention in a Contracting State, any proceedings opened after the entry into force are not subject to the Convention, irrespective of whether such later proceedings are main or secondary proceedings within the meaning of the Convention.

305. In order to determine whether proceedings are opened before or after the entry into force of the Convention, the concept of the time of opening of proceedings, as established by the Convention, applies (see also point 68). Insolvency proceedings opened in advance do not come within the scope of the Convention if the judgment opening proceedings produced effects before the entry into force of the Convention.

306. The law applicable to the acts done by the debtor before the entry into force of the Convention continues to govern these acts.

    This rule is prompted by the concern to avoid making the acts of the debtor subject to new rules and is aimed at keeping the relations to which the debtor is party subject to the law which governed his acts.

    As regards the purpose of the rule, the determination of the acts done by the debtor and the time at which they are done are governed by the applicable law.

Article 48

Relationship to other Conventions

307. Article 48 establishes the relationship between the new Convention on insolvency proceedings and other international instruments which govern the Private International Law questions of international insolvencies, ie jurisdiction to open insolvency proceedings, law applicable to the proceedings and their effects, and the recognition and enforcement in other States of such proceedings. Article 48 deals with:
    1. the relationship between the Convention and Treaties already concluded between certain Contracting States, in Article 48(1);
    2. the relationship between the Convention and Treaties already concluded with third States, in Article 48(3).

308. Article 48(1) contains a list of the Conventions which will be superseded after the entry into force of the Convention on Insolvency Proceedings as between the States which are party to it. Such replacement will be subject to:
    1. the provisions of Article 48(1) itself, pursuant to which these Conventions will continue to take effect in matters to which this Convention does not apply;
    2. the provisions of Article 48(2) relating to insolvency proceedings opened before the entry into force of this Convention, which shall continue to be governed by the Conventions referred to in the list of Article 48(1), where applicable (see also Article 47).

309. The list of previous Conventions superseded, as between the Contracting States, by this Convention includes the 1990 Istanbul Convention, and the Convention between Denmark, Finland, Norway, Sweden and Iceland on Bankruptcy, signed at Copenhagen on 7 November 1933.

310. Article 48(3) concerns the problem of the compatibility of the Convention on Insolvency Proceedings with Treaties already concluded between a Contracting State and a third State.

    To the extent that the application of this Convention would be irreconcilable with obligations arising out of Conventions or other international Agreements already concluded with a third

State, the Convention on Insolvency Proceedings will not apply. To determine if the application of this Convention is or is not irreconcilable with the obligations arising out of another existing Convention, it should be examined whether they entail legal consequences which are mutually exclusive.

The Convention on Insolvency Proceedings is only applicable when the debtor's centre of main interests is in the territory of a Contracting State. Furthermore, its provisions are restricted to relations with other Contracting States (see point 44). Hence, conflicts with other Conventions will seldom arise.

Article 49

Signature, ratification and entry into force

311. The Convention shall be deposited with the Secretary-General of the Council of the European Union.
312. The decision-making process allowing a State to bind itself by the Convention shall be governed by the national law of each State. The Convention shall be subject to ratification, acceptance or approval by the signatory States.
313. The Convention shall enter into force on the first day of the sixth month following that of the last deposit of the instrument of ratification, acceptance or approval.

Article 50

Accession to the Convention

314. The future Member States of the European Union shall be required to accept this Convention as a basis for the negotiations necessary to ensure the implementation of Article 220 of the EC Treaty.

    A special Convention may be concluded between the Contracting States and the future Member State for the purpose of introducing the necessary adjustments.

Article 51

Notification by the depositary

315. The Secretary-General of the Council of the European Union shall notify the signatory States of the deposit of each instrument of ratification, acceptance or approval of the Convention, the date of entry into force, and any other act, notification or communication relating to this Convention.

Article 52

Duration of the Convention

316. The Convention shall remain in force for an unlimited duration.

    It does not contain any particular provision governing withdrawal of a State from the Convention. Any withdrawal is subject to the general law of international treaties.

Article 53

Revision or evaluation of the Convention

317. The Convention shall be the subject of a conference for the revision or evaluation of this Convention if any Contracting State so requests.

In the case of such request from a State the President of the Council of the European Union must convene the conference.
318. If no evaluation conference is held at the request of a Contracting State in the ten years that follow entry into force, the President of the Council of the European Union shall convene such a conference.

Article 54

Amendment of the Annexes

319. Each Contracting State may amend Annexes A, B and C which list the insolvency proceedings that may be the subject of main proceedings (list A: reorganization proceedings and winding-up proceedings) or of secondary proceedings (list B: winding-up proceedings), as well as the persons or organs which can assume the functions of a liquidator (list C).
   The right of the States to amend the lists is subject to two restrictions.
   The new proceedings included in lists A or B must correspond to the definitions of the proceedings given in Article 1(1) and Article 2(a) (list A, see points 48 and 62) and Article 2(c) (list B, see point 64).
320. Each Contracting State may amend the Annexes at any time.
   The State shall address to the Secretary-General of the Council of the European Union, the depositary of the Convention under Article 49(1), a declaration containing the amendment which it wishes to make to an Annexe.
321. The depositary of the Convention will notify the signatory States and the Contracting States of the content of any such declaration.
322. The amendment that a State wishes to make to an Annexe must be subject to the acceptance by the Contracting or signatory States. It is not necessary for the States to communicate their acceptance expressly: if any State has not objected to the amendment within three months from the date of notification of the amending declaration, the amendment of the Annexe shall be deemed to be accepted.
   Even if the Convention does not expressly stipulate this, the objection of a State should be notified to the depositary of the Convention who received the amending declaration. The depositary shall notify the communicated objection to the Contracting States (see Article 51(c)). Where an objection is communicated by a State, the amendment will not come into force. A solution to a divergence between two States could be sought by convening of [sic] a conference for revision.
323. The declaration for the amendment of an Annexe which was not objected to shall come into force on the first day of the month after the three-month period following the notification of the amending declaration to the Contracting and signatory States by the depositary.

Article 55

Deposit of the Convention

324. The Convention shall be drawn up in twelve languages; all texts shall be equally authentic.
   The Convention shall be deposited with the Secretary-General of the Council of the European Union.

APPENDIX 3

This text is meant purely as a documentation tool and has no legal effect. The Union's institutions do not assume any liability for its contents. The authentic versions of the relevant acts, including their preambles, are those published in the Official Journal of the European Union and available in EUR-Lex. Those official texts are directly accessible through the links embedded in this document

▶B REGULATION (EU) 2015/848 OF THE EUROPEAN PARLIAMENT AND OF THE COUNCIL

of 20 May 2015

on insolvency proceedings

(recast)

(OJ L 141, 5.6.2015, p. 19)

Amended by:

		Official Journal		
		No	page	date
▶M1	Regulation (EU) 2017/353 of the European Parliament and of the Council of 15 February 2017	L57	19	3.3.2017
▶M2	Regulation (EU) 2018/946 of the European Parliament and of the Council of 4 July 2018	L171	1	6.7.2018
▶M3	Regulation (EU) 2021/2260 of the European Parliament and of the Council of 15 December 2021	L455	4	20.12.2021

Corrected by:

▶C1 Corrigendum, OJ L 349, 21.12.2016, p. 9 (2015/848)

►REGULATION (EU) 2015/848 OF THE EUROPEAN PARLIAMENT AND OF THE COUNCIL

of 20 May 2015

on insolvency proceedings

(recast)

THE EUROPEAN PARLIAMENT AND THE COUNCIL OF THE EUROPEAN UNION,

Having regard to the Treaty on the Functioning of the European Union, and in particular Article 81 thereof,

Having regard to the proposal from the European Commission,

After transmission of the draft legislative act to the national parliaments,

Having regard to the opinion of the European Economic and Social Committee [1],

Acting in accordance with the ordinary legislative procedure [2],

Whereas:

(1) On 12 December 2012, the Commission adopted a report on the application of Council Regulation (EC) No 1346/2000 [3]. The report concluded that the Regulation is functioning well in general but that it would be desirable to improve the application of certain of its provisions in order to enhance the effective administration of cross-border insolvency proceedings. Since that Regulation has been amended several times and further amendments are to be made, it should be recast in the interest of clarity.

(2) The Union has set the objective of establishing an area of freedom, security and justice.

(3) The proper functioning of the internal market requires that cross-border insolvency proceedings should operate efficiently and effectively. This Regulation needs to be adopted in order to achieve that objective, which falls within the scope of judicial cooperation in civil matters within the meaning of Article 81 of the Treaty.

(4) The activities of undertakings have more and more cross-border effects and are therefore increasingly being regulated by Union law. The insolvency of such undertakings also affects the proper functioning of the internal market, and there is a need for a Union act requiring coordination of the measures to be taken regarding an insolvent debtor's assets.

(5) It is necessary for the proper functioning of the internal market to avoid incentives for parties to transfer assets or judicial proceedings from one Member State to another, seeking to obtain a more favourable legal position to the detriment of the general body of creditors (forum shopping).

---

[1] OJ C 271, 19.9.2013, p. 55.
[2] Position of the European Parliament of 5 February 2014 (not yet published in the Official Journal) and position of the Council at first reading of 12 March 2015 (not yet published in the Official Journal). Position of the European Parliament of 20 May 2015 (not yet published in the Official Journal).
[3] Council Regulation (EC) No 1346/2000 of 29 May 2000 on insolvency proceedings (OJ L 160, 30.6.2000, p. 1).

(6) This Regulation should include provisions governing jurisdiction for opening insolvency proceedings and actions which are directly derived from insolvency proceedings and are closely linked with them. This Regulation should also contain provisions regarding the recognition and enforcement of judgments issued in such proceedings, and provisions regarding the law applicable to insolvency proceedings. In addition, this Regulation should lay down rules on the coordination of insolvency proceedings which relate to the same debtor or to several members of the same group of companies.

(7) Bankruptcy, proceedings relating to the winding-up of insolvent companies or other legal persons, judicial arrangements, compositions and analogous proceedings and actions related to such proceedings are excluded from the scope of Regulation (EU) No 1215/2012 of the European Parliament and of the Council ([4]). Those proceedings should be covered by this Regulation. The interpretation of this Regulation should as much as possible avoid regulatory loopholes between the two instruments. However, the mere fact that a national procedure is not listed in Annex A to this Regulation should not imply that it is covered by Regulation (EU) No 1215/2012.

(8) In order to achieve the aim of improving the efficiency and effectiveness of insolvency proceedings having cross-border effects, it is necessary, and appropriate, that the provisions on jurisdiction, recognition and applicable law in this area should be contained in a Union measure which is binding and directly applicable in Member States.

(9) This Regulation should apply to insolvency proceedings which meet the conditions set out in it, irrespective of whether the debtor is a natural person or a legal person, a trader or an individual. Those insolvency proceedings are listed exhaustively in Annex A. In respect of the national procedures contained in Annex A, this Regulation should apply without any further examination by the courts of another Member State as to whether the conditions set out in this Regulation are met. National insolvency procedures not listed in Annex A should not be covered by this Regulation.

(10) The scope of this Regulation should extend to proceedings which promote the rescue of economically viable but distressed businesses and which give a second chance to entrepreneurs. It should, in particular, extend to proceedings which provide for restructuring of a debtor at a stage where there is only a likelihood of insolvency, and to proceedings which leave the debtor fully or partially in control of its assets and affairs. It should also extend to proceedings providing for a debt discharge or a debt adjustment in relation to consumers and self-employed persons, for example by reducing the amount to be paid by the debtor or by extending the payment period granted to the debtor. Since such proceedings do not necessarily entail the appointment of an insolvency practitioner, they should be covered by this Regulation if they take place under the control or supervision of a court. In this context, the term 'control' should include situations where the court only intervenes on appeal by a creditor or other interested parties.

(11) This Regulation should also apply to procedures which grant a temporary stay on enforcement actions brought by individual creditors where such actions could adversely affect negotiations and hamper the prospects of a restructuring of the debtor's business. Such procedures should not be detrimental to the general body of creditors and, if no agreement on a restructuring plan can be reached, should be preliminary to other procedures covered by this Regulation.

(12) This Regulation should apply to proceedings the opening of which is subject to publicity in order to allow creditors to become aware of the proceedings and to lodge their claims, thereby ensuring the collective nature of the proceedings, and in order to give creditors the opportunity to challenge the jurisdiction of the court which has opened the proceedings.

(13) Accordingly, insolvency proceedings which are confidential should be excluded from the scope of this Regulation. While such proceedings may play an important role in some Member States,

---

[4] Regulation (EU) No 1215/2012 of the European Parliament and of the Council of 12 December 2012 on jurisdiction and the recognition and enforcement of judgments in civil and commercial matters (OJ L 351, 20.12.2012, p. 1).

their confidential nature makes it impossible for a creditor or a court located in another Member State to know that such proceedings have been opened, thereby making it difficult to provide for the recognition of their effects throughout the Union.

(14) The collective proceedings which are covered by this Regulation should include all or a significant part of the creditors to whom a debtor owes all or a substantial proportion of the debtor's outstanding debts provided that the claims of those creditors who are not involved in such proceedings remain unaffected. Proceedings which involve only the financial creditors of a debtor should also be covered. Proceedings which do not include all the creditors of a debtor should be proceedings aimed at rescuing the debtor. Proceedings that lead to a definitive cessation of the debtor's activities or the liquidation of the debtor's assets should include all the debtor's creditors. Moreover, the fact that some insolvency proceedings for natural persons exclude specific categories of claims, such as maintenance claims, from the possibility of a debt-discharge should not mean that such proceedings are not collective.

(15) This Regulation should also apply to proceedings that, under the law of some Member States, are opened and conducted for a certain period of time on an interim or provisional basis before a court issues an order confirming the continuation of the proceedings on a non-interim basis. Although labelled as 'interim', such proceedings should meet all other requirements of this Regulation.

(16) This Regulation should apply to proceedings which are based on laws relating to insolvency. However, proceedings that are based on general company law not designed exclusively for insolvency situations should not be considered to be based on laws relating to insolvency. Similarly, the purpose of adjustment of debt should not include specific proceedings in which debts of a natural person of very low income and very low asset value are written off, provided that this type of proceedings never makes provision for payment to creditors.

(17) This Regulation's scope should extend to proceedings which are triggered by situations in which the debtor faces non-financial difficulties, provided that such difficulties give rise to a real and serious threat to the debtor's actual or future ability to pay its debts as they fall due. The time frame relevant for the determination of such threat may extend to a period of several months or even longer in order to account for cases in which the debtor is faced with non-financial difficulties threatening the status of its business as a going concern and, in the medium term, its liquidity. This may be the case, for example, where the debtor has lost a contract which is of key importance to it.

(18) This Regulation should be without prejudice to the rules on the recovery of State aid from insolvent companies as interpreted by the case-law of the Court of Justice of the European Union.

(19) Insolvency proceedings concerning insurance undertakings, credit institutions, investment firms and other firms, institutions or undertakings covered by Directive 2001/24/EC of the European Parliament and of the Council ([5]) and collective investment undertakings should be excluded from the scope of this Regulation, as they are all subject to special arrangements and the national supervisory authorities have wide-ranging powers of intervention.

(20) Insolvency proceedings do not necessarily involve the intervention of a judicial authority. Therefore, the term 'court' in this Regulation should, in certain provisions, be given a broad meaning and include a person or body empowered by national law to open insolvency proceedings. In order for this Regulation to apply, proceedings (comprising acts and formalities set down in law) should not only have to comply with the provisions of this Regulation, but they should also be officially recognised and legally effective in the Member State in which the insolvency proceedings are opened.

(21) Insolvency practitioners are defined in this Regulation and listed in Annex B. Insolvency practitioners who are appointed without the involvement of a judicial body should, under national law, be appropriately regulated and authorised to act in insolvency proceedings. The national

---

[5] Directive 2001/24/EC of the European Parliament and of the Council of 4 April 2001 on the reorganisation and winding-up of credit institutions (OJ L 125, 5.5.2001, p. 15).

regulatory framework should provide for proper arrangements to deal with potential conflicts of interest.
(22) This Regulation acknowledges the fact that as a result of widely differing substantive laws it is not practical to introduce insolvency proceedings with universal scope throughout the Union. The application without exception of the law of the State of the opening of proceedings would, against this background, frequently lead to difficulties. This applies, for example, to the widely differing national laws on security interests to be found in the Member States. Furthermore, the preferential rights enjoyed by some creditors in insolvency proceedings are, in some cases, completely different. At the next review of this Regulation, it will be necessary to identify further measures in order to improve the preferential rights of employees at European level. This Regulation should take account of such differing national laws in two different ways. On the one hand, provision should be made for special rules on the applicable law in the case of particularly significant rights and legal relationships (e.g. rights *in rem* and contracts of employment). On the other hand, national proceedings covering only assets situated in the State of the opening of proceedings should also be allowed alongside main insolvency proceedings with universal scope.
(23) This Regulation enables the main insolvency proceedings to be opened in the Member State where the debtor has the centre of its main interests. Those proceedings have universal scope and are aimed at encompassing all the debtor's assets. To protect the diversity of interests, this Regulation permits secondary insolvency proceedings to be opened to run in parallel with the main insolvency proceedings. Secondary insolvency proceedings may be opened in the Member State where the debtor has an establishment. The effects of secondary insolvency proceedings are limited to the assets located in that State. Mandatory rules of coordination with the main insolvency proceedings satisfy the need for unity in the Union.
(24) Where main insolvency proceedings concerning a legal person or company have been opened in a Member State other than that of its registered office, it should be possible to open secondary insolvency proceedings in the Member State of the registered office, provided that the debtor is carrying out an economic activity with human means and assets in that State, in accordance with the case-law of the Court of Justice of the European Union.
(25) This Regulation applies only to proceedings in respect of a debtor whose centre of main interests is located in the Union.
(26) The rules of jurisdiction set out in this Regulation establish only international jurisdiction, that is to say, they designate the Member State the courts of which may open insolvency proceedings. Territorial jurisdiction within that Member State should be established by the national law of the Member State concerned.
(27) Before opening insolvency proceedings, the competent court should examine of its own motion whether the centre of the debtor's main interests or the debtor's establishment is actually located within its jurisdiction.
(28) When determining whether the centre of the debtor's main interests is ascertainable by third parties, special consideration should be given to the creditors and to their perception as to where a debtor conducts the administration of its interests. This may require, in the event of a shift of centre of main interests, informing creditors of the new location from which the debtor is carrying out its activities in due course, for example by drawing attention to the change of address in commercial correspondence, or by making the new location public through other appropriate means.
(29) This Regulation should contain a number of safeguards aimed at preventing fraudulent or abusive forum shopping.
(30) Accordingly, the presumptions that the registered office, the principal place of business and the habitual residence are the centre of main interests should be rebuttable, and the relevant court of a Member State should carefully assess whether the centre of the debtor's main interests is genuinely located in that Member State. In the case of a company, it should be possible to rebut this presumption where the company's central administration is located in a Member State other than that of its registered office, and where a comprehensive assessment of all the relevant factors establishes, in a manner that is ascertainable by third parties, that

the company's actual centre of management and supervision and of the management of its interests is located in that other Member State. In the case of an individual not exercising an independent business or professional activity, it should be possible to rebut this presumption, for example where the major part of the debtor's assets is located outside the Member State of the debtor's habitual residence, or where it can be established that the principal reason for moving was to file for insolvency proceedings in the new jurisdiction and where such filing would materially impair the interests of creditors whose dealings with the debtor took place prior to the relocation.

(31) With the same objective of preventing fraudulent or abusive forum shopping, the presumption that the centre of main interests is at the place of the registered office, at the individual's principal place of business or at the individual's habitual residence should not apply where, respectively, in the case of a company, legal person or individual exercising an independent business or professional activity, the debtor has relocated its registered office or principal place of business to another Member State within the 3-month period prior to the request for opening insolvency proceedings, or, in the case of an individual not exercising an independent business or professional activity, the debtor has relocated his habitual residence to another Member State within the 6-month period prior to the request for opening insolvency proceedings.

(32) In all cases, where the circumstances of the matter give rise to doubts about the court's jurisdiction, the court should require the debtor to submit additional evidence to support its assertions and, where the law applicable to the insolvency proceedings so allows, give the debtor's creditors the opportunity to present their views on the question of jurisdiction.

(33) In the event that the court seised of the request to open insolvency proceedings finds that the centre of main interests is not located on its territory, it should not open main insolvency proceedings.

(34) In addition, any creditor of the debtor should have an effective remedy against the decision to open insolvency proceedings. The consequences of any challenge to the decision to open insolvency proceedings should be governed by national law.

(35) The courts of the Member State within the territory of which insolvency proceedings have been opened should also have jurisdiction for actions which derive directly from the insolvency proceedings and are closely linked with them. Such actions should include avoidance actions against defendants in other Member States and actions concerning obligations that arise in the course of the insolvency proceedings, such as advance payment for costs of the proceedings. In contrast, actions for the performance of the obligations under a contract concluded by the debtor prior to the opening of proceedings do not derive directly from the proceedings. Where such an action is related to another action based on general civil and commercial law, the insolvency practitioner should be able to bring both actions in the courts of the defendant's domicile if he considers it more efficient to bring the action in that forum. This could, for example, be the case where the insolvency practitioner wishes to combine an action for director's liability on the basis of insolvency law with an action based on company law or general tort law.

(36) The court having jurisdiction to open the main insolvency proceedings should be able to order provisional and protective measures as from the time of the request to open proceedings. Preservation measures both prior to and after the commencement of the insolvency proceedings are important to guarantee the effectiveness of the insolvency proceedings. In that connection, this Regulation should provide for various possibilities. On the one hand, the court competent for the main insolvency proceedings should also be able to order provisional and protective measures covering assets situated in the territory of other Member States. On the other hand, an insolvency practitioner temporarily appointed prior to the opening of the main insolvency proceedings should be able, in the Member States in which an establishment belonging to the debtor is to be found, to apply for the preservation measures which are possible under the law of those Member States.

(37) Prior to the opening of the main insolvency proceedings, the right to request the opening of insolvency proceedings in the Member State where the debtor has an establishment should be

limited to local creditors and public authorities, or to cases in which main insolvency proceedings cannot be opened under the law of the Member State where the debtor has the centre of its main interests. The reason for this restriction is that cases in which territorial insolvency proceedings are requested before the main insolvency proceedings are intended to be limited to what is absolutely necessary.

(38) Following the opening of the main insolvency proceedings, this Regulation does not restrict the right to request the opening of insolvency proceedings in a Member State where the debtor has an establishment. The insolvency practitioner in the main insolvency proceedings or any other person empowered under the national law of that Member State may request the opening of secondary insolvency proceedings.

(39) This Regulation should provide for rules to determine the location of the debtor's assets, which should apply when determining which assets belong to the main or secondary insolvency proceedings, or to situations involving third parties' rights *in rem*. In particular, this Regulation should provide that European patents with unitary effect, a Community trade mark or any other similar rights, such as Community plant variety rights or Community designs, should only be included in the main insolvency proceedings.

(40) Secondary insolvency proceedings can serve different purposes, besides the protection of local interests. Cases may arise in which the insolvency estate of the debtor is too complex to administer as a unit, or the differences in the legal systems concerned are so great that difficulties may arise from the extension of effects deriving from the law of the State of the opening of proceedings to the other Member States where the assets are located. For that reason, the insolvency practitioner in the main insolvency proceedings may request the opening of secondary insolvency proceedings where the efficient administration of the insolvency estate so requires.

(41) Secondary insolvency proceedings may also hamper the efficient administration of the insolvency estate. Therefore, this Regulation sets out two specific situations in which the court seised of a request to open secondary insolvency proceedings should be able, at the request of the insolvency practitioner in the main insolvency proceedings, to postpone or refuse the opening of such proceedings.

(42) First, this Regulation confers on the insolvency practitioner in main insolvency proceedings the possibility of giving an undertaking to local creditors that they will be treated as if secondary insolvency proceedings had been opened. That undertaking has to meet a number of conditions set out in this Regulation, in particular that it be approved by a qualified majority of local creditors. Where such an undertaking has been given, the court seised of a request to open secondary insolvency proceedings should be able to refuse that request if it is satisfied that the undertaking adequately protects the general interests of local creditors. When assessing those interests, the court should take into account the fact that the undertaking has been approved by a qualified majority of local creditors.

(43) For the purposes of giving an undertaking to local creditors, the assets and rights located in the Member State where the debtor has an establishment should form a sub-category of the insolvency estate, and, when distributing them or the proceeds resulting from their realisation, the insolvency practitioner in the main insolvency proceedings should respect the priority rights that creditors would have had if secondary insolvency proceedings had been opened in that Member State.

(44) National law should be applicable, as appropriate, in relation to the approval of an undertaking. In particular, where under national law the voting rules for adopting a restructuring plan require the prior approval of creditors' claims, those claims should be deemed to be approved for the purpose of voting on the undertaking. Where there are different procedures for the adoption of restructuring plans under national law, Member States should designate the specific procedure which should be relevant in this context.

(45) Second, this Regulation should provide for the possibility that the court temporarily stays the opening of secondary insolvency proceedings, when a temporary stay of individual enforcement proceedings has been granted in the main insolvency proceedings, in order to preserve the efficiency of the stay granted in the main insolvency proceedings. The court should be able

to grant the temporary stay if it is satisfied that suitable measures are in place to protect the general interest of local creditors. In such a case, all creditors that could be affected by the outcome of the negotiations on a restructuring plan should be informed of the negotiations and be allowed to participate in them.

(46) In order to ensure effective protection of local interests, the insolvency practitioner in the main insolvency proceedings should not be able to realise or re-locate, in an abusive manner, assets situated in the Member State where an establishment is located, in particular, with the purpose of frustrating the possibility that such interests can be effectively satisfied if secondary insolvency proceedings are opened subsequently.

(47) This Regulation should not prevent the courts of a Member State in which secondary insolvency proceedings have been opened from sanctioning a debtor's directors for violation of their duties, provided that those courts have jurisdiction to address such disputes under their national law.

(48) Main insolvency proceedings and secondary insolvency proceedings can contribute to the efficient administration of the debtor's insolvency estate or to the effective realisation of the total assets if there is proper cooperation between the actors involved in all the concurrent proceedings. Proper cooperation implies the various insolvency practitioners and the courts involved cooperating closely, in particular by exchanging a sufficient amount of information. In order to ensure the dominant role of the main insolvency proceedings, the insolvency practitioner in such proceedings should be given several possibilities for intervening in secondary insolvency proceedings which are pending at the same time. In particular, the insolvency practitioner should be able to propose a restructuring plan or composition or apply for a suspension of the realisation of the assets in the secondary insolvency proceedings. When cooperating, insolvency practitioners and courts should take into account best practices for cooperation in cross-border insolvency cases, as set out in principles and guidelines on communication and cooperation adopted by European and international organisations active in the area of insolvency law, and in particular the relevant guidelines prepared by the United Nations Commission on International Trade Law (Uncitral).

(49) In light of such cooperation, insolvency practitioners and courts should be able to enter into agreements and protocols for the purpose of facilitating cross-border cooperation of multiple insolvency proceedings in different Member States concerning the same debtor or members of the same group of companies, where this is compatible with the rules applicable to each of the proceedings. Such agreements and protocols may vary in form, in that they may be written or oral, and in scope, in that they may range from generic to specific, and may be entered into by different parties. Simple generic agreements may emphasise the need for close cooperation between the parties, without addressing specific issues, while more detailed, specific agreements may establish a framework of principles to govern multiple insolvency proceedings and may be approved by the courts involved, where the national law so requires. They may reflect an agreement between the parties to take, or to refrain from taking, certain steps or actions.

(50) Similarly, the courts of different Member States may cooperate by coordinating the appointment of insolvency practitioners. In that context, they may appoint a single insolvency practitioner for several insolvency proceedings concerning the same debtor or for different members of a group of companies, provided that this is compatible with the rules applicable to each of the proceedings, in particular with any requirements concerning the qualification and licensing of the insolvency practitioner.

(51) This Regulation should ensure the efficient administration of insolvency proceedings relating to different companies forming part of a group of companies.

(52) Where insolvency proceedings have been opened for several companies of the same group, there should be proper cooperation between the actors involved in those proceedings. The various insolvency practitioners and the courts involved should therefore be under a similar obligation to cooperate and communicate with each other as those involved in main and secondary insolvency proceedings relating to the same debtor. Cooperation between the insolvency practitioners should not run counter to the interests of the creditors in each of the proceedings, and

such cooperation should be aimed at finding a solution that would leverage synergies across the group.

(53) The introduction of rules on the insolvency proceedings of groups of companies should not limit the possibility for a court to open insolvency proceedings for several companies belonging to the same group in a single jurisdiction if the court finds that the centre of main interests of those companies is located in a single Member State. In such cases, the court should also be able to appoint, if appropriate, the same insolvency practitioner in all proceedings concerned, provided that this is not incompatible with the rules applicable to them.

(54) With a view to further improving the coordination of the insolvency proceedings of members of a group of companies, and to allow for a coordinated restructuring of the group, this Regulation should introduce procedural rules on the coordination of the insolvency proceedings of members of a group of companies. Such coordination should strive to ensure the efficiency of the coordination, whilst at the same time respecting each group member's separate legal personality.

(55) An insolvency practitioner appointed in insolvency proceedings opened in relation to a member of a group of companies should be able to request the opening of group coordination proceedings. However, where the law applicable to the insolvency so requires, that insolvency practitioner should obtain the necessary authorisation before making such a request. The request should specify the essential elements of the coordination, in particular an outline of the coordination plan, a proposal as to whom should be appointed as coordinator and an outline of the estimated costs of the coordination.

(56) In order to ensure the voluntary nature of group coordination proceedings, the insolvency practitioners involved should be able to object to their participation in the proceedings within a specified time period. In order to allow the insolvency practitioners involved to take an informed decision on participation in the group coordination proceedings, they should be informed at an early stage of the essential elements of the coordination. However, any insolvency practitioner who initially objects to inclusion in the group coordination proceedings should be able to subsequently request to participate in them. In such a case, the coordinator should take a decision on the admissibility of the request. All insolvency practitioners, including the requesting insolvency practitioner, should be informed of the coordinator's decision and should have the opportunity of challenging that decision before the court which has opened the group coordination proceedings.

(57) Group coordination proceedings should always strive to facilitate the effective administration of the insolvency proceedings of the group members, and to have a generally positive impact for the creditors. This Regulation should therefore ensure that the court with which a request for group coordination proceedings has been filed makes an assessment of those criteria prior to opening group coordination proceedings.

(58) The advantages of group coordination proceedings should not be outweighed by the costs of those proceedings. Therefore, it is necessary to ensure that the costs of the coordination, and the share of those costs that each group member will bear, are adequate, proportionate and reasonable, and are determined in accordance with the national law of the Member State in which group coordination proceedings have been opened. The insolvency practitioners involved should also have the possibility of controlling those costs from an early stage of the proceedings. Where the national law so requires, controlling costs from an early stage of proceedings could involve the insolvency practitioner seeking the approval of a court or creditors' committee.

(59) Where the coordinator considers that the fulfilment of his or her tasks requires a significant increase in costs compared to the initially estimated costs and, in any case, where the costs exceed 10 % of the estimated costs, the coordinator should be authorised by the court which has opened the group coordination proceedings to exceed such costs. Before taking its decision, the court which has opened the group coordination proceedings should give the possibility to the participating insolvency practitioners to be heard before it in order to allow them to communicate their observations on the appropriateness of the coordinator's request.

(60) For members of a group of companies which are not participating in group coordination proceedings, this Regulation should also provide for an alternative mechanism to achieve a

coordinated restructuring of the group. An insolvency practitioner appointed in proceedings relating to a member of a group of companies should have standing to request a stay of any measure related to the realisation of the assets in the proceedings opened with respect to other members of the group which are not subject to group coordination proceedings. It should only be possible to request such a stay if a restructuring plan is presented for the members of the group concerned, if the plan is to the benefit of the creditors in the proceedings in respect of which the stay is requested, and if the stay is necessary to ensure that the plan can be properly implemented.

(61) This Regulation should not prevent Member States from establishing national rules which would supplement the rules on cooperation, communication and coordination with regard to the insolvency of members of groups of companies set out in this Regulation, provided that the scope of application of those national rules is limited to the national jurisdiction and that their application would not impair the efficiency of the rules laid down by this Regulation.

(62) The rules on cooperation, communication and coordination in the framework of the insolvency of members of a group of companies provided for in this Regulation should only apply to the extent that proceedings relating to different members of the same group of companies have been opened in more than one Member State.

(63) Any creditor which has its habitual residence, domicile or registered office in the Union should have the right to lodge its claims in each of the insolvency proceedings pending in the Union relating to the debtor's assets. This should also apply to tax authorities and social insurance institutions. This Regulation should not prevent the insolvency practitioner from lodging claims on behalf of certain groups of creditors, for example employees, where the national law so provides. However, in order to ensure the equal treatment of creditors, the distribution of proceeds should be coordinated. Every creditor should be able to keep what it has received in the course of insolvency proceedings, but should be entitled only to participate in the distribution of total assets in other proceedings if creditors with the same standing have obtained the same proportion of their claims.

(64) It is essential that creditors which have their habitual residence, domicile or registered office in the Union be informed about the opening of insolvency proceedings relating to their debtor's assets. In order to ensure a swift transmission of information to creditors, Regulation (EC) No 1393/2007 of the European Parliament and of the Council ([6]) should not apply where this Regulation refers to the obligation to inform creditors. The use of standard forms available in all official languages of the institutions of the Union should facilitate the task of creditors when lodging claims in proceedings opened in another Member State. The consequences of the incomplete filing of the standard forms should be a matter for national law.

(65) This Regulation should provide for the immediate recognition of judgments concerning the opening, conduct and closure of insolvency proceedings which fall within its scope, and of judgments handed down in direct connection with such insolvency proceedings. Automatic recognition should therefore mean that the effects attributed to the proceedings by the law of the Member State in which the proceedings were opened extend to all other Member States. The recognition of judgments delivered by the courts of the Member States should be based on the principle of mutual trust. To that end, grounds for non-recognition should be reduced to the minimum necessary. This is also the basis on which any dispute should be resolved where the courts of two Member States both claim competence to open the main insolvency proceedings. The decision of the first court to open proceedings should be recognised in the other Member States without those Member States having the power to scrutinise that court's decision.

---

[6] Regulation (EC) No 1393/2007 of the European Parliament and of the Council of 13 November 2007 on the service in the Member States of judicial and extrajudicial documents in civil and commercial matters (service of documents), and repealing Council Regulation (EC) No 1348/2000 (OJ L 324, 10.12.2007, p. 79).

(66) This Regulation should set out, for the matters covered by it, uniform rules on conflict of laws which replace, within their scope of application, national rules of private international law. Unless otherwise stated, the law of the Member State of the opening of proceedings should be applicable (*lex concursus*). This rule on conflict of laws should be valid both for the main insolvency proceedings and for local proceedings. The *lex concursus* determines all the effects of the insolvency proceedings, both procedural and substantive, on the persons and legal relations concerned. It governs all the conditions for the opening, conduct and closure of the insolvency proceedings.

(67) Automatic recognition of insolvency proceedings to which the law of the State of the opening of proceedings normally applies may interfere with the rules under which transactions are carried out in other Member States. To protect legitimate expectations and the certainty of transactions in Member States other than that in which proceedings are opened, provision should be made for a number of exceptions to the general rule.

(68) There is a particular need for a special reference diverging from the law of the opening State in the case of rights *in rem*, since such rights are of considerable importance for the granting of credit. The basis, validity and extent of rights *in rem* should therefore normally be determined according to the *lex situs* and not be affected by the opening of insolvency proceedings. The proprietor of a right *in rem* should therefore be able to continue to assert its right to segregation or separate settlement of the collateral security. Where assets are subject to rights *in rem* under the *lex situs* in one Member State but the main insolvency proceedings are being carried out in another Member State, the insolvency practitioner in the main insolvency proceedings should be able to request the opening of secondary insolvency proceedings in the jurisdiction where the rights *in rem* arise if the debtor has an establishment there. If secondary insolvency proceedings are not opened, any surplus on the sale of an asset covered by rights *in rem* should be paid to the insolvency practitioner in the main insolvency proceedings.

(69) This Regulation lays down several provisions for a court to order a stay of opening proceedings or a stay of enforcement proceedings. Any such stay should not affect the rights *in rem* of creditors or third parties.

(70) If a set-off of claims is not permitted under the law of the State of the opening of proceedings, a creditor should nevertheless be entitled to the set-off if it is possible under the law applicable to the claim of the insolvent debtor. In this way, set-off would acquire a kind of guarantee function based on legal provisions on which the creditor concerned can rely at the time when the claim arises.

(71) There is also a need for special protection in the case of payment systems and financial markets, for example in relation to the position-closing agreements and netting agreements to be found in such systems, as well as the sale of securities and the guarantees provided for such transactions as governed in particular by Directive 98/26/EC of the European Parliament and of the Council ([7]). For such transactions, the only law which is relevant should be that applicable to the system or market concerned. That law is intended to prevent the possibility of mechanisms for the payment and settlement of transactions, and provided for in payment and set-off systems or on the regulated financial markets of the Member States, being altered in the case of insolvency of a business partner. Directive 98/26/EC contains special provisions which should take precedence over the general rules laid down in this Regulation.

(72) In order to protect employees and jobs, the effects of insolvency proceedings on the continuation or termination of employment and on the rights and obligations of all parties to such employment should be determined by the law applicable to the relevant employment agreement, in accordance with the general rules on conflict of laws. Moreover, in cases where the termination of employment contracts requires approval by a court or administrative authority, the Member State in which an establishment of the debtor is located should retain jurisdiction to grant such approval even if no insolvency proceedings have been opened in that Member State. Any other

---

[7] Directive 98/26/EC of the European Parliament and of the Council of 19 May 1998 on settlement finality in payment and securities settlement systems (OJ L 166, 11.6.1998, p. 45).

questions relating to the law of insolvency, such as whether the employees' claims are protected by preferential rights and the status such preferential rights may have, should be determined by the law of the Member State in which the insolvency proceedings (main or secondary) have been opened, except in cases where an undertaking to avoid secondary insolvency proceedings has been given in accordance with this Regulation.

(73) The law applicable to the effects of insolvency proceedings on any pending lawsuit or pending arbitral proceedings concerning an asset or right which forms part of the debtor's insolvency estate should be the law of the Member State where the lawsuit is pending or where the arbitration has its seat. However, this rule should not affect national rules on recognition and enforcement of arbitral awards.

(74) In order to take account of the specific procedural rules of court systems in certain Member States flexibility should be provided with regard to certain rules of this Regulation. Accordingly, references in this Regulation to notice being given by a judicial body of a Member State should include, where a Member State's procedural rules so require, an order by that judicial body directing that notice be given.

(75) For business considerations, the main content of the decision opening the proceedings should be published, at the request of the insolvency practitioner, in a Member State other than that of the court which delivered that decision. If there is an establishment in the Member State concerned, such publication should be mandatory. In neither case, however, should publication be a prior condition for recognition of the foreign proceedings.

(76) In order to improve the provision of information to relevant creditors and courts and to prevent the opening of parallel insolvency proceedings, Member States should be required to publish relevant information in cross-border insolvency cases in a publicly accessible electronic register. In order to facilitate access to that information for creditors and courts domiciled or located in other Member States, this Regulation should provide for the interconnection of such insolvency registers via the European e-Justice Portal. Member States should be free to publish relevant information in several registers and it should be possible to interconnect more than one register per Member State.

(77) This Regulation should determine the minimum amount of information to be published in the insolvency registers. Member States should not be precluded from including additional information. Where the debtor is an individual, the insolvency registers should only have to indicate a registration number if the debtor is exercising an independent business or professional activity. That registration number should be understood to be the unique registration number of the debtor's independent business or professional activity published in the trade register, if any.

(78) Information on certain aspects of insolvency proceedings is essential for creditors, such as time limits for lodging claims or for challenging decisions. This Regulation should, however, not require Member States to calculate those time-limits on a case-by-case basis. Member States should be able to fulfil their obligations by adding hyperlinks to the European e-Justice Portal, where self-explanatory information on the criteria for calculating those time-limits is to be provided.

(79) In order to grant sufficient protection to information relating to individuals not exercising an independent business or professional activity, Member States should be able to make access to that information subject to supplementary search criteria such as the debtor's personal identification number, address, date of birth or the district of the competent court, or to make access conditional upon a request to a competent authority or upon the verification of a legitimate interest.

(80) Member States should also be able not to include in their insolvency registers information on individuals not exercising an independent business or professional activity. In such cases, Member States should ensure that the relevant information is given to the creditors by individual notice, and that claims of creditors who have not received the information are not affected by the proceedings.

(81) It may be the case that some of the persons concerned are not aware that insolvency proceedings have been opened, and act in good faith in a way that conflicts with the new circumstances. In order to protect such persons who, unaware that foreign proceedings have been opened, make a payment to the debtor instead of to the foreign insolvency practitioner, provision should be made for such a payment to have a debt-discharging effect.

(82) In order to ensure uniform conditions for the implementation of this Regulation, implementing powers should be conferred on the Commission. Those powers should be exercised in accordance with Regulation (EU) No 182/2011 of the European Parliament and of the Council ([8]).

(83) This Regulation respects the fundamental rights and observes the principles recognised in the Charter of Fundamental Rights of the European Union. In particular, this Regulation seeks to promote the application of Articles 8, 17 and 47 concerning, respectively, the protection of personal data, the right to property and the right to an effective remedy and to a fair trial.

(84) Directive 95/46/EC of the European Parliament and of the Council ([9]) and Regulation (EC) No 45/2001 of the European Parliament and of the Council ([10]) apply to the processing of personal data within the framework of this Regulation.

(85) This Regulation is without prejudice to Regulation (EEC, Euratom) No 1182/71 of the Council ([11]).

(86) Since the objective of this Regulation cannot be sufficiently achieved by the Member States but can rather, by reason of the creation of a legal framework for the proper administration of cross-border insolvency proceedings, be better achieved at Union level, the Union may adopt measures in accordance with the principle of subsidiarity as set out in Article 5 of the Treaty on European Union. In accordance with the principle of proportionality, as set out in that Article, this Regulation does not go beyond what is necessary in order to achieve that objective.

(87) In accordance with Article 3 and Article 4a(1) of Protocol No 21 on the position of the United Kingdom and Ireland in respect of the area of freedom, security and justice, annexed to the Treaty on European Union and the Treaty on the Functioning of the European Union, the United Kingdom and Ireland have notified their wish to take part in the adoption and application of this Regulation.

(88) In accordance with Articles 1 and 2 of Protocol No 22 on the position of Denmark annexed to the Treaty on European Union and the Treaty on the Functioning of the European Union, Denmark is not taking part in the adoption of this Regulation and is not bound by it or subject to its application.

(89) The European Data Protection Supervisor was consulted and delivered an opinion on 27 March 2013 ([12]),

HAVE ADOPTED THIS REGULATION:

---

[8] Regulation (EU) No 182/2011 of the European Parliament and of the Council of 16 February 2011 laying down the rules and general principles concerning mechanisms for control by the Member States of the Commission's exercise of implementing powers (OJ L 55, 28.2.2011, p. 13).

[9] Directive 95/46/EC of the European Parliament and of the Council of 24 October 1995 on the protection of individuals with regard to the processing of personal data and on the free movement of such data (OJ L 281, 23.11.1995, p. 31).

[10] Regulation (EC) No 45/2001 of the European Parliament and of the Council of 18 December 2000 on the protection of individuals with regard to the processing of personal data by the Community institutions and bodies and on the free movement of such data (OJ L 8, 12.1.2001, p. 1).

[11] Regulation (EEC, Euratom) No 1182/71 of the Council of 3 June 1971 determining the rules applicable to periods, dates and time limits (OJ L 124, 8.6.1971, p. 1).

[12] OJ C 358, 7.12.2013, p. 15.

CHAPTER I

GENERAL PROVISIONS

Article 1

Scope

1. This Regulation shall apply to public collective proceedings, including interim proceedings, which are based on laws relating to insolvency and in which, for the purpose of rescue, adjustment of debt, reorganisation or liquidation:
    (a) a debtor is totally or partially divested of its assets and an insolvency practitioner is appointed;
    (b) the assets and affairs of a debtor are subject to control or supervision by a court; or
    (c) a temporary stay of individual enforcement proceedings is granted by a court or by operation of law, in order to allow for negotiations between the debtor and its creditors, provided that the proceedings in which the stay is granted provide for suitable measures to protect the general body of creditors, and, where no agreement is reached, are preliminary to one of the proceedings referred to in point (a) or (b).

    Where the proceedings referred to in this paragraph may be commenced in situations where there is only a likelihood of insolvency, their purpose shall be to avoid the debtor's insolvency or the cessation of the debtor's business activities.

    The proceedings referred to in this paragraph are listed in Annex A.

2. This Regulation shall not apply to proceedings referred to in paragraph 1 that concern:
    (a) insurance undertakings;
    (b) credit institutions;
    (c) investment firms and other firms, institutions and undertakings to the extent that they are covered by Directive 2001/24/EC; or
    (d) collective investment undertakings.

Article 2

Definitions

For the purposes of this Regulation:

(1) 'collective proceedings' means proceedings which include all or a significant part of a debtor's creditors, provided that, in the latter case, the proceedings do not affect the claims of creditors which are not involved in them;
(2) 'collective investment undertakings' means undertakings for collective investment in transferable securities (UCITS) as defined in Directive 2009/65/EC of the European Parliament and of the Council ([1]) and alternative investment funds (AIFs) as defined in Directive 2011/61/EU of the European Parliament and of the Council ([2]);
(3) 'debtor in possession' means a debtor in respect of which insolvency proceedings have been opened which do not necessarily involve the appointment of an insolvency practitioner or the complete transfer of the rights and duties to administer the debtor's assets to an insolvency practitioner and where, therefore, the debtor remains totally or at least partially in control of its assets and affairs;

---

[1] Directive 2009/65/EC of the European Parliament and of the Council of 13 July 2009 on the coordination of laws, regulations and administrative provisions relating to undertakings for collective investment in transferable securities (UCITS) (OJ L 302, 17.11.2009, p. 32).

[2] Directive 2011/61/EU of the European Parliament and of the Council of 8 June 2011 on Alternative Investment Fund Managers and amending Directives 2003/41/EC and 2009/65/EC and Regulations (EC) No 1060/2009 and (EU) No 1095/2010 (OJ L 174, 1.7.2011, p. 1).

(4) 'insolvency proceedings' means the proceedings listed in Annex A;
(5) 'insolvency practitioner' means any person or body whose function, including on an interim basis, is to:
   (i) verify and admit claims submitted in insolvency proceedings;
   (ii) represent the collective interest of the creditors;
   (iii) administer, either in full or in part, assets of which the debtor has been divested;
   (iv) liquidate the assets referred to in point (iii); or
   (v) supervise the administration of the debtor's affairs.
   The persons and bodies referred to in the first subparagraph are listed in Annex B;
(6) 'court' means:
   (i) in points (b) and (c) of Article 1(1), Article 4(2), Articles 5 and 6, Article 21(3), point (j) of Article 24(2), Articles 36 and 39, and Articles 61 to 77, the judicial body of a Member State;
   (ii) in all other articles, the judicial body or any other competent body of a Member State empowered to open insolvency proceedings, to confirm such opening or to take decisions in the course of such proceedings;
(7) 'judgment opening insolvency proceedings' includes:
   (i) the decision of any court to open insolvency proceedings or to confirm the opening of such proceedings; and
   (ii) the decision of a court to appoint an insolvency practitioner;
(8) 'the time of the opening of proceedings' means the time at which the judgment opening insolvency proceedings becomes effective, regardless of whether the judgment is final or not;
(9) 'the Member State in which assets are situated' means, in the case of:
   (i) registered shares in companies other than those referred to in point (ii), the Member State within the territory of which the company having issued the shares has its registered office;
   (ii) financial instruments, the title to which is evidenced by entries in a register or account maintaine d by or on behalf of an intermediary ('book entry securities'), the Member State in which the register or account in which the entries are made is maintained;
   (iii) cash held in accounts with a credit institution, the Member State indicated in the account's IBAN, or, for cash held in accounts with a credit institution which does not have an IBAN, the Member State in which the credit institution holding the account has its central administration or, where the account is held with a branch, agency or other establishment, the Member State in which the branch, agency or other establishment is located;
   (iv) property and rights, ownership of or entitlement to which is entered in a public register other than those referred to in point (i), the Member State under the authority of which the register is kept;
   (v) European patents, the Member State for which the European patent is granted;
   (vi) copyright and related rights, the Member State within the territory of which the owner of such rights has its habitual residence or registered office;
   (vii) tangible property, other than that referred to in points (i) to (iv), the Member State within the territory of which the property is situated;
   (viii) claims against third parties, other than those relating to assets referred to in point (iii), the Member State within the territory of which the third party required to meet the claims has the centre of its main interests, as determined in accordance with Article 3(1);
(10) 'establishment' means any place of operations where a debtor carries out or has carried out in the 3-month period prior to the request to open main insolvency proceedings a non-transitory economic activity with human means and assets;
(11) 'local creditor' means a creditor whose claims against a debtor arose from or in connection with the operation of an establishment situated in a Member State other than the Member State in which the centre of the debtor's main interests is located;
(12) 'foreign creditor' means a creditor which has its habitual residence, domicile or registered office in a Member State other than the State of the opening of proceedings, including the tax authorities and social security authorities of Member States;
(13) 'group of companies' means a parent undertaking and all its subsidiary undertakings;

(14) 'parent undertaking' means an undertaking which controls, either directly or indirectly, one or more subsidiary undertakings. An undertaking which prepares consolidated financial statements in accordance with Directive 2013/34/EU of the European Parliament and of the Council ([3]) shall be deemed to be a parent undertaking.

Article 3
International jurisdiction

1. The courts of the Member State within the territory of which the centre of the debtor's main interests is situated shall have jurisdiction to open insolvency proceedings ('main insolvency proceedings'). The centre of main interests shall be the place where the debtor conducts the administration of its interests on a regular basis and which is ascertainable by third parties.

   In the case of a company or legal person, the place of the registered office shall be presumed to be the centre of its main interests in the absence of proof to the contrary. That presumption shall only apply if the registered office has not been moved to another Member State within the 3-month period prior to the request for the opening of insolvency proceedings.

   In the case of an individual exercising an independent business or professional activity, the centre of main interests shall be presumed to be that individual's principal place of business in the absence of proof to the contrary. That presumption shall only apply if the individual's principal place of business has not been moved to another Member State within the 3-month period prior to the request for the opening of insolvency proceedings.

   In the case of any other individual, the centre of main interests shall be presumed to be the place of the individual's habitual residence in the absence of proof to the contrary. This presumption shall only apply if the habitual residence has not been moved to another Member State within the 6-month period prior to the request for the opening of insolvency proceedings.

2. Where the centre of the debtor's main interests is situated within the territory of a Member State, the courts of another Member State shall have jurisdiction to open insolvency proceedings against that debtor only if it possesses an establishment within the territory of that other Member State. The effects of those proceedings shall be restricted to the assets of the debtor situated in the territory of the latter Member State.

3. Where insolvency proceedings have been opened in accordance with paragraph 1, any proceedings opened subsequently in accordance with paragraph 2 shall be secondary insolvency proceedings.

4. The territorial insolvency proceedings referred to in paragraph 2 may only be opened prior to the opening of main insolvency proceedings in accordance with paragraph 1 where
   (a) insolvency proceedings under paragraph 1 cannot be opened because of the conditions laid down by the law of the Member State within the territory of which the centre of the debtor's main interests is situated; or
   (b) the opening of territorial insolvency proceedings is requested by:
      (i) a creditor whose claim arises from or is in connection with the operation of an establishment situated within the territory of the Member State where the opening of territorial proceedings is requested; or
      (ii) a public authority which, under the law of the Member State within the territory of which the establishment is situated, has the right to request the opening of insolvency proceedings.

   When main insolvency proceedings are opened, the territorial insolvency proceedings shall become secondary insolvency proceedings.

---

[3] Directive 2013/34/EU of the European Parliament and of the Council of 26 June 2013 on the annual financial statements, consolidated financial statements and related reports of certain types of undertaking, amending Directive 2006/43/EC of the European Parliament and of the Council and repealing Council Directives 78/660/EEC and 83/349/EEC (OJ L 182, 29.6.2013, p. 19).

Article 4

Examination as to jurisdiction

1. A court seised of a request to open insolvency proceedings shall of its own motion examine whether it has jurisdiction pursuant to Article 3. The judgment opening insolvency proceedings shall specify the grounds on which the jurisdiction of the court is based, and, in particular, whether jurisdiction is based on Article 3(1) or (2).
2. Notwithstanding paragraph 1, where insolvency proceedings are opened in accordance with national law without a decision by a court, Member States may entrust the insolvency practitioner appointed in such proceedings to examine whether the Member State in which a request for the opening of proceedings is pending has jurisdiction pursuant to Article 3. Where this is the case, the insolvency practitioner shall specify in the decision opening the proceedings the grounds on which jurisdiction is based and, in particular, whether jurisdiction is based on Article 3(1) or (2).

Article 5

Judicial review of the decision to open main insolvency proceedings

1. The debtor or any creditor may challenge before a court the decision opening main insolvency proceedings on grounds of international jurisdiction.
2. The decision opening main insolvency proceedings may be challenged by parties other than those referred to in paragraph 1 or on grounds other than a lack of international jurisdiction where national law so provides.

Article 6

Jurisdiction for actions deriving directly from insolvency proceedings and closely linked with them

1. The courts of the Member State within the territory of which insolvency proceedings have been opened in accordance with Article 3 shall have jurisdiction for any action which derives directly from the insolvency proceedings and is closely linked with them, such as avoidance actions.
2. Where an action referred to in paragraph 1 is related to an action in civil and commercial matters against the same defendant, the insolvency practitioner may bring both actions before the courts of the Member State within the territory of which the defendant is domiciled, or, where the action is brought against several defendants, before the courts of the Member State within the territory of which any of them is domiciled, provided that those courts have jurisdiction pursuant to Regulation (EU) No 1215/2012.

    The first subparagraph shall apply to the debtor in possession, provided that national law allows the debtor in possession to bring actions on behalf of the insolvency estate.
3. For the purpose of paragraph 2, actions are deemed to be related where they are so closely connected that it is expedient to hear and determine them together to avoid the risk of irreconcilable judgments resulting from separate proceedings.

Article 7

Applicable law

1. Save as otherwise provided in this Regulation, the law applicable to insolvency proceedings and their effects shall be that of the Member State within the territory of which such proceedings are opened (the 'State of the opening of proceedings').

2. The law of the State of the opening of proceedings shall determine the conditions for the opening of those proceedings, their conduct and their closure. In particular, it shall determine the following:
    (a) the debtors against which insolvency proceedings may be brought on account of their capacity;
    (b) the assets which form part of the insolvency estate and the treatment of assets acquired by or devolving on the debtor after the opening of the insolvency proceedings;
    (c) the respective powers of the debtor and the insolvency practitioner;
    (d) the conditions under which set-offs may be invoked;
    (e) the effects of insolvency proceedings on current contracts to which the debtor is party;
    (f) the effects of the insolvency proceedings on proceedings brought by individual creditors, with the exception of pending lawsuits;
    (g) the claims which are to be lodged against the debtor's insolvency estate and the treatment of claims arising after the opening of insolvency proceedings;
    (h) the rules governing the lodging, verification and admission of claims;
    (i) the rules governing the distribution of proceeds from the realisation of assets, the ranking of claims and the rights of creditors who have obtained partial satisfaction after the opening of insolvency proceedings by virtue of a right *in rem* or through a set-off;
    (j) the conditions for, and the effects of closure of, insolvency proceedings, in particular by composition;
    (k) creditors' rights after the closure of insolvency proceedings;
    (l) who is to bear the costs and expenses incurred in the insolvency proceedings;
    (m) the rules relating to the voidness, voidability or unenforceability of legal acts detrimental to the general body of creditors.

Article 8

Third parties' rights in rem

1. The opening of insolvency proceedings shall not affect the rights *in rem* of creditors or third parties in respect of tangible or intangible, moveable or immoveable assets, both specific assets and collections of indefinite assets as a whole which change from time to time, belonging to the debtor which are situated within the territory of another Member State at the time of the opening of proceedings.
2. The rights referred to in paragraph 1 shall, in particular, mean:
    (a) the right to dispose of assets or have them disposed of and to obtain satisfaction from the proceeds of or income from those assets, in particular by virtue of a lien or a mortgage;
    (b) the exclusive right to have a claim met, in particular a right guaranteed by a lien in respect of the claim or by assignment of the claim by way of a guarantee;
    (c) the right to demand assets from, and/or to require restitution by, anyone having possession or use of them contrary to the wishes of the party so entitled;
    (d) a right *in rem* to the beneficial use of assets.
3. The right, recorded in a public register and enforceable against third parties, based on which a right *in rem* within the meaning of paragraph 1 may be obtained shall be considered to be a right *in rem*.
4. Paragraph 1 shall not preclude actions for voidness, voidability or unenforceability as referred to in point (m) of Article 7(2).

Article 9

Set-off

1. The opening of insolvency proceedings shall not affect the right of creditors to demand the set-off of their claims against the claims of a debtor, where such a set-off is permitted by the law applicable to the insolvent debtor's claim.

2. Paragraph 1 shall not preclude actions for voidness, voidability or unenforceability as referred to in point (m) of Article 7(2).

Article 10

Reservation of title

1. The opening of insolvency proceedings against the purchaser of an asset shall not affect sellers' rights that are based on a reservation of title where at the time of the opening of proceedings the asset is situated within the territory of a Member State other than the State of the opening of proceedings.
2. The opening of insolvency proceedings against the seller of an asset, after delivery of the asset, shall not constitute grounds for rescinding or terminating the sale and shall not prevent the purchaser from acquiring title where at the time of the opening of proceedings the asset sold is situated within the territory of a Member State other than the State of the opening of proceedings.
3. Paragraphs 1 and 2 shall not preclude actions for voidness, voidability or unenforceability as referred to in point (m) of Article 7(2).

Article 11

Contracts relating to immoveable property

1. The effects of insolvency proceedings on a contract conferring the right to acquire or make use of immoveable property shall be governed solely by the law of the Member State within the territory of which the immoveable property is situated.
2. The court which opened main insolvency proceedings shall have jurisdiction to approve the termination or modification of the contracts referred to in this Article where:
   (a) the law of the Member State applicable to those contracts requires that such a contract may only be terminated or modified with the approval of the court opening insolvency proceedings; and
   (b) no insolvency proceedings have been opened in that Member State.

Article 12

Payment systems and financial markets

1. Without prejudice to Article 8, the effects of insolvency proceedings on the rights and obligations of the parties to a payment or settlement system or to a financial market shall be governed solely by the law of the Member State applicable to that system or market.
2. Paragraph 1 shall not preclude any action for voidness, voidability or unenforceability which may be taken to set aside payments or transactions under the law applicable to the relevant payment system or financial market.

Article 13

Contracts of employment

1. The effects of insolvency proceedings on employment contracts and relationships shall be governed solely by the law of the Member State applicable to the contract of employment.
2. The courts of the Member State in which secondary insolvency proceedings may be opened shall retain jurisdiction to approve the termination or modification of the contracts referred to in this Article even if no insolvency proceedings have been opened in that Member State.

The first subparagraph shall also apply to an authority competent under national law to approve the termination or modification of the contracts referred to in this Article.

Article 14

Effects on rights subject to registration
The effects of insolvency proceedings on the rights of a debtor in immoveable property, a ship or an aircraft subject to registration in a public register shall be determined by the law of the Member State under the authority of which the register is kept.

Article 15

European patents with unitary effect and Community trade marks
For the purposes of this Regulation, a European patent with unitary effect, a Community trade mark or any other similar right established by Union law may be included only in the proceedings referred to in Article 3(1).

Article 16

Detrimental acts
Point (m) of Article 7(2) shall not apply where the person who benefited from an act detrimental to all the creditors provides proof that:

(a) the act is subject to the law of a Member State other than that of the State of the opening of proceedings; and
(b) the law of that Member State does not allow any means of challenging that act in the relevant case.

Article 17

Protection of third-party purchasers
Where, by an act concluded after the opening of insolvency proceedings, a debtor disposes, for consideration, of:

(a) an immoveable asset;
(b) a ship or an aircraft subject to registration in a public register; or
(c) securities the existence of which requires registration in a register laid down by law;

the validity of that act shall be governed by the law of the State within the territory of which the immoveable asset is situated or under the authority of which the register is kept.

Article 18

Effects of insolvency proceedings on pending lawsuits or arbitral proceedings
The effects of insolvency proceedings on a pending lawsuit or pending arbitral proceedings concerning an asset or a right which forms part of a debtor's insolvency estate shall be governed solely by the law of the Member State in which that lawsuit is pending or in which the arbitral tribunal has its seat.

CHAPTER II

RECOGNITION OF INSOLVENCY PROCEEDINGS

Article 19

Principle

1. Any judgment opening insolvency proceedings handed down by a court of a Member State which has jurisdiction pursuant to Article 3 shall be recognised in all other Member States from the moment that it becomes effective in the State of the opening of proceedings.
   The rule laid down in the first subparagraph shall also apply where, on account of a debtor's capacity, insolvency proceedings cannot be brought against that debtor in other Member States.
2. Recognition of the proceedings referred to in Article 3(1) shall not preclude the opening of the proceedings referred to in Article 3(2) by a court in another Member State. The latter proceedings shall be secondary insolvency proceedings within the meaning of Chapter III.

Article 20

Effects of recognition

1. The judgment opening insolvency proceedings as referred to in Article 3(1) shall, with no further formalities, produce the same effects in any other Member State as under the law of the State of the opening of proceedings, unless this Regulation provides otherwise and as long as no proceedings referred to in Article 3(2) are opened in that other Member State.
2. The effects of the proceedings referred to in Article 3(2) may not be challenged in other Member States. Any restriction of creditors' rights, in particular a stay or discharge, shall produce effects vis-à-vis assets situated within the territory of another Member State only in the case of those creditors who have given their consent.

Article 21

Powers of the insolvency practitioner

1. The insolvency practitioner appointed by a court which has jurisdiction pursuant to Article 3(1) may exercise all the powers conferred on it, by the law of the State of the opening of proceedings, in another Member State, as long as no other insolvency proceedings have been opened there and no preservation measure to the contrary has been taken there further to a request for the opening of insolvency proceedings in that State. Subject to Articles 8 and 10, the insolvency practitioner may, in particular, remove the debtor's assets from the territory of the Member State in which they are situated.
2. The insolvency practitioner appointed by a court which has jurisdiction pursuant to Article 3(2) may in any other Member State claim through the courts or out of court that moveable property was removed from the territory of the State of the opening of proceedings to the territory of that other Member State after the opening of the insolvency proceedings. The insolvency practitioner may also bring any action to set aside which is in the interests of the creditors.
3. In exercising its powers, the insolvency practitioner shall comply with the law of the Member State within the territory of which it intends to take action, in particular with regard to procedures for the realisation of assets. Those powers may not include coercive measures, unless ordered by a court of that Member State, or the right to rule on legal proceedings or disputes.

Article 22

Proof of the insolvency practitioner's appointment

The insolvency practitioner's appointment shall be evidenced by a certified copy of the original decision appointing it or by any other certificate issued by the court which has jurisdiction.

A translation into the official language or one of the official languages of the Member State within the territory of which it intends to act may be required. No legalisation or other similar formality shall be required.

Article 23

Return and imputation

1. A creditor which, after the opening of the proceedings referred to in Article 3(1), obtains by any means, in particular through enforcement, total or partial satisfaction of its claim on the assets belonging to a debtor situated within the territory of another Member State, shall return what it has obtained to the insolvency practitioner, subject to Articles 8 and 10.
2. In order to ensure the equal treatment of creditors, a creditor which has, in the course of insolvency proceedings, obtained a dividend on its claim shall share in distributions made in other proceedings only where creditors of the same ranking or category have, in those other proceedings, obtained an equivalent dividend.

Article 24

Establishment of insolvency registers

1. Member States shall establish and maintain in their territory one or several registers in which information concerning insolvency proceedings is published ('insolvency registers'). That information shall be published as soon as possible after the opening of such proceedings.
2. The information referred to in paragraph 1 shall be made publicly available, subject to the conditions laid down in Article 27, and shall include the following ('mandatory information'):
   (a) the date of the opening of insolvency proceedings;
   (b) the court opening insolvency proceedings and the case reference number, if any;
   (c) the type of insolvency proceedings referred to in Annex A that were opened and, where applicable, any relevant subtype of such proceedings opened in accordance with national law;
   (d) whether jurisdiction for opening proceedings is based on Article 3(1), 3(2) or 3(4);
   (e) if the debtor is a company or a legal person, the debtor's name, registration number, registered office or, if different, postal address;
   (f) if the debtor is an individual whether or not exercising an independent business or professional activity, the debtor's name, registration number, if any, and postal address or, where the address is protected, the debtor's place and date of birth;
   (g) the name, postal address or e-mail address of the insolvency practitioner, if any, appointed in the proceedings;
   (h) the time limit for lodging claims, if any, or a reference to the criteria for calculating that time limit;
   (i) the date of closing main insolvency proceedings, if any;
   (j) the court before which and, where applicable, the time limit within which a challenge of the decision opening insolvency proceedings is to be lodged in accordance with Article 5, or a reference to the criteria for calculating that time limit.
3. Paragraph 2 shall not preclude Member States from including documents or additional information in their national insolvency registers, such as directors' disqualifications related to insolvency.

4. Member States shall not be obliged to include in the insolvency registers the information referred to in paragraph 1 of this Article in relation to individuals not exercising an independent business or professional activity, or to make such information publicly available through the system of interconnection of those registers, provided that known foreign creditors are informed, pursuant to Article 54, of the elements referred to under point (j) of paragraph 2 of this Article.

   Where a Member State makes use of the possibility referred to in the first subparagraph, the insolvency proceedings shall not affect the claims of foreign creditors who have not received the information referred to in the first subparagraph.
5. The publication of information in the registers under this Regulation shall not have any legal effects other than those set out in national law and in Article 55(6).

Article 25

Interconnection of insolvency registers

1. The Commission shall establish a decentralised system for the interconnection of insolvency registers by means of implementing acts. That system shall be composed of the insolvency registers and the European e-Justice Portal, which shall serve as a central public electronic access point to information in the system. The system shall provide a search service in all the official languages of the institutions of the Union in order to make available the mandatory information and any other documents or information included in the insolvency registers which the Member States choose to make available through the European e-Justice Portal.
2. By means of implementing acts in accordance with the procedure referred to in Article 87, the Commission shall adopt the following by 26 June 2019:
   (a) the technical specification defining the methods of communication and information exchange by electronic means on the basis of the established interface specification for the system of interconnection of insolvency registers;
   (b) the technical measures ensuring the minimum information technology security standards for communication and distribution of information within the system of interconnection of insolvency registers;
   (c) minimum criteria for the search service provided by the European e-Justice Portal based on the information set out in Article 24;
   (d) minimum criteria for the presentation of the results of such searches based on the information set out in Article 24;
   (e) the means and the technical conditions of availability of services provided by the system of interconnection; and
   (f) a glossary containing a basic explanation of the national insolvency proceedings listed in Annex A.

Article 26

Costs of establishing and interconnecting insolvency registers

1. The establishment, maintenance and future development of the system of interconnection of insolvency registers shall be financed from the general budget of the Union.
2. Each Member State shall bear the costs of establishing and adjusting its national insolvency registers to make them interoperable with the European e-Justice Portal, as well as the costs of administering, operating and maintaining those registers. This shall be without prejudice to the possibility to apply for grants to support such activities under the Union's financial programmes.

Article 27

Conditions of access to information via the system of interconnection

1. Member States shall ensure that the mandatory information referred to in points (a) to (j) of Article 24(2) is available free of charge via the system of interconnection of insolvency registers.
2. This Regulation shall not preclude Member States from charging a reasonable fee for access to the documents or additional information referred to in Article 24(3) via the system of interconnection of insolvency registers.
3. Member States may make access to mandatory information concerning individuals who are not exercising an independent business or professional activity, and concerning individuals exercising an independent business or professional activity when the insolvency proceedings are not related to that activity, subject to supplementary search criteria relating to the debtor in addition to the minimum criteria referred to in point (c) of Article 25(2).
4. Member States may require that access to the information referred to in paragraph 3 be made conditional upon a request to the competent authority. Member States may make access conditional upon the verification of the existence of a legitimate interest for accessing such information. The requesting person shall be able to submit the request for information electronically by means of a standard form via the European e-Justice Portal. Where a legitimate interest is required, it shall be permissible for the requesting person to justify his request by electronic copies of relevant documents. The requesting person shall be provided with an answer by the competent authority within 3 working days.

The requesting person shall not be obliged to provide translations of the documents justifying his request, or to bear any costs of translation which the competent authority may incur.

Article 28

Publication in another Member State

1. The insolvency practitioner or the debtor in possession shall request that notice of the judgment opening insolvency proceedings and, where appropriate, the decision appointing the insolvency practitioner be published in any other Member State where an establishment of the debtor is located in accordance with the publication procedures provided for in that Member State. Such publication shall specify, where appropriate, the insolvency practitioner appointed and whether the jurisdiction rule applied is that pursuant to Article 3(1) or (2).
2. The insolvency practitioner or the debtor in possession may request that the information referred to in paragraph 1 be published in any other Member State where the insolvency practitioner or the debtor in possession deems it necessary in accordance with the publication procedures provided for in that Member State.

Article 29

Registration in public registers of another Member State

1. Where the law of a Member State in which an establishment of the debtor is located and this establishment has been entered into a public register of that Member State, or the law of a Member State in which immovable property belonging to the debtor is located, requires information on the opening of insolvency proceedings referred to in Article 28 to be published in the land register, company register or any other public register, the insolvency practitioner or the debtor in possession shall take all the necessary measures to ensure such a registration.

2. The insolvency practitioner or the debtor in possession may request such registration in any other Member State, provided that the law of the Member State where the register is kept allows such registration.

Article 30

Costs

The costs of the publication and registration provided for in Articles 28 and 29 shall be regarded as costs and expenses incurred in the proceedings.

Article 31

Honouring of an obligation to a debtor

1. Where an obligation has been honoured in a Member State for the benefit of a debtor who is subject to insolvency proceedings opened in another Member State, when it should have been honoured for the benefit of the insolvency practitioner in those proceedings, the person honouring the obligation shall be deemed to have discharged it if he was unaware of the opening of the proceedings.
2. Where such an obligation is honoured before the publication provided for in Article 28 has been effected, the person honouring the obligation shall be presumed, in the absence of proof to the contrary, to have been unaware of the opening of insolvency proceedings. Where the obligation is honoured after such publication has been effected, the person honouring the obligation shall be presumed, in the absence of proof to the contrary, to have been aware of the opening of proceedings.

Article 32

Recognition and enforceability of other judgments

1. Judgments handed down by a court whose judgment concerning the opening of proceedings is recognised in accordance with Article 19 and which concern the course and closure of insolvency proceedings, and compositions approved by that court, shall also be recognised with no further formalities. Such judgments shall be enforced in accordance with Articles 39 to 44 and 47 to 57 of Regulation (EU) No 1215/2012.

   The first subparagraph shall also apply to judgments deriving directly from the insolvency proceedings and which are closely linked with them, even if they were handed down by another court.

   The first subparagraph shall also apply to judgments relating to preservation measures taken after the request for the opening of insolvency proceedings or in connection with it.
2. The recognition and enforcement of judgments other than those referred to in paragraph 1 of this Article shall be governed by Regulation (EU) No 1215/2012 provided that that Regulation is applicable.

Article 33

Public policy

Any Member State may refuse to recognise insolvency proceedings opened in another Member State or to enforce a judgment handed down in the context of such proceedings where the effects of such recognition or enforcement would be manifestly contrary to that State's public policy, in particular its fundamental principles or the constitutional rights and liberties of the individual.

CHAPTER III

SECONDARY INSOLVENCY PROCEEDINGS

Article 34

Opening of proceedings

Where main insolvency proceedings have been opened by a court of a Member State and recognised in another Member State, a court of that other Member State which has jurisdiction pursuant to Article 3(2) may open secondary insolvency proceedings in accordance with the provisions set out in this Chapter. Where the main insolvency proceedings required that the debtor be insolvent, the debtor's insolvency shall not be re-examined in the Member State in which secondary insolvency proceedings may be opened. The effects of secondary insolvency proceedings shall be restricted to the assets of the debtor situated within the territory of the Member State in which those proceedings have been opened.

Article 35

Applicable law

Save as otherwise provided for in this Regulation, the law applicable to secondary insolvency proceedings shall be that of the Member State within the territory of which the secondary insolvency proceedings are opened.

Article 36

Right to give an undertaking in order to avoid secondary insolvency proceedings

1. In order to avoid the opening of secondary insolvency proceedings, the insolvency practitioner in the main insolvency proceedings may give a unilateral undertaking (the 'undertaking') in respect of the assets located in the Member State in which secondary insolvency proceedings could be opened, that when distributing those assets or the proceeds received as a result of their realisation, it will comply with the distribution and priority rights under national law that creditors would have if secondary insolvency proceedings were opened in that Member State. The undertaking shall specify the factual assumptions on which it is based, in particular in respect of the value of the assets located in the Member State concerned and the options available to realise such assets.
2. Where an undertaking has been given in accordance with this Article, the law applicable to the distribution of proceeds from the realisation of assets referred to in paragraph 1, to the ranking of creditors' claims, and to the rights of creditors in relation to the assets referred to in paragraph 1 shall be the law of the Member State in which secondary insolvency proceedings could have been opened. The relevant point in time for determining the assets referred to in paragraph 1 shall be the moment at which the undertaking is given.
3. The undertaking shall be made in the official language or one of the official languages of the Member State where secondary insolvency proceedings could have been opened, or, where there are several official languages in that Member State, the official language or one of the official languages of the place in which secondary insolvency proceedings could have been opened.
4. The undertaking shall be made in writing. It shall be subject to any other requirements relating to form and approval requirements as to distributions, if any, of the State of the opening of the main insolvency proceedings.
5. The undertaking shall be approved by the known local creditors. The rules on qualified majority and voting that apply to the adoption of restructuring plans under the law of the Member State where secondary insolvency proceedings could have been opened shall also apply to the approval of the undertaking. Creditors shall be able to participate in the vote by distance means of communication, where national law so permits. The insolvency practitioner shall inform the known local creditors of the undertaking, of the rules and procedures for its approval, and of the approval or rejection of the undertaking.

6. An undertaking given and approved in accordance with this Article shall be binding on the estate. If secondary insolvency proceedings are opened in accordance with Articles 37 and 38, the insolvency practitioner in the main insolvency proceedings shall transfer any assets which it removed from the territory of that Member State after the undertaking was given or, where those assets have already been realised, their proceeds, to the insolvency practitioner in the secondary insolvency proceedings.
7. Where the insolvency practitioner has given an undertaking, it shall inform local creditors about the intended distributions prior to distributing the assets and proceeds referred to in paragraph 1. If that information does not comply with the terms of the undertaking or the applicable law, any local creditor may challenge such distribution before the courts of the Member State in which main insolvency proceedings have been opened in order to obtain a distribution in accordance with the terms of the undertaking and the applicable law. In such cases, no distribution shall take place until the court has taken a decision on the challenge.
8. Local creditors may apply to the courts of the Member State in which main insolvency proceedings have been opened, in order to require the insolvency practitioner in the main insolvency proceedings to take any suitable measures necessary to ensure compliance with the terms of the undertaking available under the law of the State of the opening of main insolvency proceedings.
9. Local creditors may also apply to the courts of the Member State in which secondary insolvency proceedings could have been opened in order to require the court to take provisional or protective measures to ensure compliance by the insolvency practitioner with the terms of the undertaking.
10. The insolvency practitioner shall be liable for any damage caused to local creditors as a result of its non-compliance with the obligations and requirements set out in this Article.
11. For the purpose of this Article, an authority which is established in the Member State where secondary insolvency proceedings could have been opened and which is obliged under Directive 2008/94/EC of the European Parliament and of the Council ([4]) to guarantee the payment of employees' outstanding claims resulting from contracts of employment or employment relationships shall be considered to be a local creditor, where the national law so provides.

Article 37

Right to request the opening of secondary insolvency proceedings

1. The opening of secondary insolvency proceedings may be requested by:
    (a) the insolvency practitioner in the main insolvency proceedings;
    (b) any other person or authority empowered to request the opening of insolvency proceedings under the law of the Member State within the territory of which the opening of secondary insolvency proceedings is requested.
2. Where an undertaking has become binding in accordance with Article 36, the request for opening secondary insolvency proceedings shall be lodged within 30 days of having received notice of the approval of the undertaking.

Article 38

Decision to open secondary insolvency proceedings

1. A court seised of a request to open secondary insolvency proceedings shall immediately give notice to the insolvency practitioner or the debtor in possession in the main insolvency proceedings and give it an opportunity to be heard on the request.

---

[4] Directive 2008/94/EC of the European Parliament and of the Council of 22 October 2008 on the protection of employees in the event of the insolvency of their employer (OJ L 283, 28.10.2008, p. 36).

2. Where the insolvency practitioner in the main insolvency proceedings has given an undertaking in accordance with Article 36, the court referred to in paragraph 1 of this Article shall, at the request of the insolvency practitioner, not open secondary insolvency proceedings if it is satisfied that the undertaking adequately protects the general interests of local creditors.
3. Where a temporary stay of individual enforcement proceedings has been granted in order to allow for negotiations between the debtor and its creditors, the court, at the request of the insolvency practitioner or the debtor in possession, may stay the opening of secondary insolvency proceedings for a period not exceeding 3 months, provided that suitable measures are in place to protect the interests of local creditors.

    The court referred to in paragraph 1 may order protective measures to protect the interests of local creditors by requiring the insolvency practitioner or the debtor in possession not to remove or dispose of any assets which are located in the Member State where its establishment is located unless this is done in the ordinary course of business. The court may also order other measures to protect the interest of local creditors during a stay, unless this is incompatible with the national rules on civil procedure.

    The stay of the opening of secondary insolvency proceedings shall be lifted by the court of its own motion or at the request of any creditor if, during the stay, an agreement in the negotiations referred to in the first subparagraph has been concluded.

    The stay may be lifted by the court of its own motion or at the request of any creditor if the continuation of the stay is detrimental to the creditor's rights, in particular if the negotiations have been disrupted or it has become evident that they are unlikely to be concluded, or if the insolvency practitioner or the debtor in possession has infringed the prohibition on disposal of its assets or on removal of them from the territory of the Member State where the establishment is located.
4. At the request of the insolvency practitioner in the main insolvency proceedings, the court referred to in paragraph 1 may open a type of insolvency proceedings as listed in Annex A other than the type initially requested, provided that the conditions for opening that type of proceedings under national law are fulfilled and that that type of proceedings is the most appropriate as regards the interests of the local creditors and coherence between the main and secondary insolvency proceedings. The second sentence of Article 34 shall apply.

Article 39

Judicial review of the decision to open secondary insolvency proceedings

The insolvency practitioner in the main insolvency proceedings may challenge the decision to open secondary insolvency proceedings before the courts of the Member State in which secondary insolvency proceedings have been opened on the ground that the court did not comply with the conditions and requirements of Article 38.

Article 40

Advance payment of costs and expenses

Where the law of the Member State in which the opening of secondary insolvency proceedings is requested requires that the debtor's assets be sufficient to cover in whole or in part the costs and expenses of the proceedings, the court may, when it receives such a request, require the applicant to make an advance payment of costs or to provide appropriate security.

Article 41

Cooperation and communication between insolvency practitioners

1. The insolvency practitioner in the main insolvency proceedings and the insolvency practitioner or practitioners in secondary insolvency proceedings concerning the same debtor shall cooperate with each other to the extent such cooperation is not incompatible with the rules applicable to the

respective proceedings. Such cooperation may take any form, including the conclusion of agreements or protocols.
2. In implementing the cooperation set out in paragraph 1, the insolvency practitioners shall:
   (a) as soon as possible communicate to each other any information which may be relevant to the other proceedings, in particular any progress made in lodging and verifying claims and all measures aimed at rescuing or restructuring the debtor, or at terminating the proceedings, provided appropriate arrangements are made to protect confidential information;
   (b) explore the possibility of restructuring the debtor and, where such a possibility exists, coordinate the elaboration and implementation of a restructuring plan;
   (c) coordinate the administration of the realisation or use of the debtor's assets and affairs; the insolvency practitioner in the secondary insolvency proceedings shall give the insolvency practitioner in the main insolvency proceedings an early opportunity to submit proposals on the realisation or use of the assets in the secondary insolvency proceedings.
3. Paragraphs 1 and 2 shall apply mutatis mutandis to situations where, in the main or in the secondary insolvency proceedings or in any territorial insolvency proceedings concerning the same debtor and open at the same time, the debtor remains in possession of its assets.

Article 42

Cooperation and communication between courts

1. In order to facilitate the coordination of main, territorial and secondary insolvency proceedings concerning the same debtor, a court before which a request to open insolvency proceedings is pending, or which has opened such proceedings, shall cooperate with any other court before which a request to open insolvency proceedings is pending, or which has opened such proceedings, to the extent that such cooperation is not incompatible with the rules applicable to each of the proceedings. For that purpose, the courts may, where appropriate, appoint an independent person or body acting on its instructions, provided that it is not incompatible with the rules applicable to them.
2. In implementing the cooperation set out in paragraph 1, the courts, or any appointed person or body acting on their behalf, as referred to in paragraph 1, may communicate directly with, or request information or assistance directly from, each other provided that such communication respects the procedural rights of the parties to the proceedings and the confidentiality of information.
3. The cooperation referred to in paragraph 1 may be implemented by any means that the court considers appropriate. It may, in particular, concern:
   (a) coordination in the appointment of the insolvency practitioners;
   (b) communication of information by any means considered appropriate by the court;
   (c) coordination of the administration and supervision of the debtor's assets and affairs;
   (d) coordination of the conduct of hearings;
   (e) coordination in the approval of protocols, where necessary.

Article 43

Cooperation and communication between insolvency practitioners and courts

1. In order to facilitate the coordination of main, territorial and secondary insolvency proceedings opened in respect of the same debtor:
   (a) an insolvency practitioner in main insolvency proceedings shall cooperate and communicate with any court before which a request to open secondary insolvency proceedings is pending or which has opened such proceedings;
   (b) an insolvency practitioner in territorial or secondary insolvency proceedings shall cooperate and communicate with the court before which a request to open main insolvency proceedings is pending or which has opened such proceedings; and
   (c) an insolvency practitioner in territorial or secondary insolvency proceedings shall cooperate and communicate with the court before which a request to open other territorial or secondary

insolvency proceedings is pending or which has opened such proceedings; to the extent that such cooperation and communication are not incompatible with the rules applicable to each of the proceedings and do not entail any conflict of interest.
2. The cooperation referred to in paragraph 1 may be implemented by any appropriate means, such as those set out in Article 42(3).

Article 44

Costs of cooperation and communication

The requirements laid down in Articles 42 and 43 shall not result in courts charging costs to each other for cooperation and communication.

Article 45

Exercise of creditors' rights

1. Any creditor may lodge its claim in the main insolvency proceedings and in any secondary insolvency proceedings.
2. The insolvency practitioners in the main and any secondary insolvency proceedings shall lodge in other proceedings claims which have already been lodged in the proceedings for which they were appointed, provided that the interests of creditors in the latter proceedings are served by doing so, subject to the right of creditors to oppose such lodgement or to withdraw the lodgement of their claims where the law applicable so provides.
3. The insolvency practitioner in the main or secondary insolvency proceedings shall be entitled to participate in other proceedings on the same basis as a creditor, in particular by attending creditors' meetings.

Article 46

Stay of the process of realisation of assets

1. The court which opened the secondary insolvency proceedings shall stay the process of realisation of assets in whole or in part on receipt of a request from the insolvency practitioner in the main insolvency proceedings. In such a case, it may require the insolvency practitioner in the main insolvency proceedings to take any suitable measure to guarantee the interests of the creditors in the secondary insolvency proceedings and of individual classes of creditors. Such a request from the insolvency practitioner may be rejected only if it is manifestly of no interest to the creditors in the main insolvency proceedings. Such a stay of the process of realisation of assets may be ordered for up to 3 months. It may be continued or renewed for similar periods.
2. The court referred to in paragraph 1 shall terminate the stay of the process of realisation of assets:
    (a) at the request of the insolvency practitioner in the main insolvency proceedings;
    (b) of its own motion, at the request of a creditor or at the request of the insolvency practitioner in the secondary insolvency proceedings if that measure no longer appears justified, in particular, by the interests of creditors in the main insolvency proceedings or in the secondary insolvency proceedings.

Article 47

Power of the insolvency practitioner to propose restructuring plans

1. Where the law of the Member State where secondary insolvency proceedings have been opened allows for such proceedings to be closed without liquidation by a restructuring plan, a composition or a comparable measure, the insolvency practitioner in the main insolvency proceedings shall be empowered to propose such a measure in accordance with the procedure of that Member State.

2. Any restriction of creditors' rights arising from a measure referred to in paragraph 1 which is proposed in secondary insolvency proceedings, such as a stay of payment or discharge of debt, shall have no effect in respect of assets of a debtor that are not covered by those proceedings, without the consent of all the creditors having an interest.

Article 48

Impact of closure of insolvency proceedings

1. Without prejudice to Article 49, the closure of insolvency proceedings shall not prevent the continuation of other insolvency proceedings concerning the same debtor which are still open at that point in time.
2. Where insolvency proceedings concerning a legal person or a company in the Member State of that person's or company's registered office would entail the dissolution of the legal person or of the company, that legal person or company shall not cease to exist until any other insolvency proceedings concerning the same debtor have been closed, or the insolvency practitioner or practitioners in such proceedings have given consent to the dissolution.

Article 49

Assets remaining in the secondary insolvency proceedings

If, by the liquidation of assets in the secondary insolvency proceedings, it is possible to meet all claims allowed under those proceedings, the insolvency practitioner appointed in those proceedings shall immediately transfer any assets remaining to the insolvency practitioner in the main insolvency proceedings.

Article 50

Subsequent opening of the main insolvency proceedings

Where the proceedings referred to in Article 3(1) are opened following the opening of the proceedings referred to in Article 3(2) in another Member State, Articles 41, 45, 46, 47 and 49 shall apply to those opened first, in so far as the progress of those proceedings so permits.

Article 51

Conversion of secondary insolvency proceedings

1. At the request of the insolvency practitioner in the main insolvency proceedings, the court of the Member State in which secondary insolvency proceedings have been opened may order the conversion of the secondary insolvency proceedings into another type of insolvency proceedings listed in Annex A, provided that the conditions for opening that type of proceedings under national law are fulfilled and that that type of proceedings is the most appropriate as regards the interests of the local creditors and coherence between the main and secondary insolvency proceedings.
2. When considering the request referred to in paragraph 1, the court may seek information from the insolvency practitioners involved in both proceedings.

Article 52

Preservation measures

Where the court of a Member State which has jurisdiction pursuant to Article 3(1) appoints a temporary administrator in order to ensure the preservation of a debtor's assets, that temporary administrator shall be empowered to request any measures to secure and preserve any of the debtor's assets situated in another Member State, provided for under the law of that Member State, for the period between the request for the opening of insolvency proceedings and the judgment opening the proceedings.

CHAPTER IV

PROVISION OF INFORMATION FOR CREDITORS AND LODGEMENT OF THEIR CLAIMS

Article 53

Right to lodge claims

Any foreign creditor may lodge claims in insolvency proceedings by any means of communication, which are accepted by the law of the State of the opening of proceedings. Representation by a lawyer or another legal professional shall not be mandatory for the sole purpose of lodging of claims.

Article 54

Duty to inform creditors

1. As soon as insolvency proceedings are opened in a Member State, the court of that State having jurisdiction or the insolvency practitioner appointed by that court shall immediately inform the known foreign creditors.
2. The information referred to in paragraph 1, provided by an individual notice, shall in particular include time limits, the penalties laid down with regard to those time limits, the body or authority empowered to accept the lodgement of claims and any other measures laid down. Such notice shall also indicate whether creditors whose claims are preferential or secured *in rem* need to lodge their claims. The notice shall also include a copy of the standard form for lodging of claims referred to in Article 55 or information on where that form is available.
3. The information referred to in paragraphs 1 and 2 of this Article shall be provided using the standard notice form to be established in accordance with Article 88. The form shall be published in the European e-Justice Portal and shall bear the heading 'Notice of insolvency proceedings' in all the official languages of the institutions of the Union. It shall be transmitted in the official language of the State of the opening of proceedings or, if there are several official languages in that Member State, in the official language or one of the official languages of the place where insolvency proceedings have been opened, or in another language which that State has indicated it can accept, in accordance with Article 55(5), if it can be assumed that that language is easier to understand for the foreign creditors.
4. In insolvency proceedings relating to an individual not exercising a business or professional activity, the use of the standard form referred to in this Article shall not be obligatory if creditors are not required to lodge their claims in order to have their claims taken into account in the proceedings.

Article 55

Procedure for lodging claims

1. Any foreign creditor may lodge its claim using the standard claims form to be established in accordance with Article 88. The form shall bear the heading 'Lodgement of claims' in all the official languages of the institutions of the Union.
2. The standard claims form referred to in paragraph 1 shall include the following information:
    (a) the name, postal address, e-mail address, if any, personal identification number, if any, and bank details of the foreign creditor referred to in paragraph 1;

(b) the amount of the claim, specifying the principal and, where applicable, interest and the date on which it arose and the date on which it became due, if different;
(c) if interest is claimed, the interest rate, whether the interest is of a legal or contractual nature, the period of time for which the interest is claimed and the capitalised amount of interest;
(d) if costs incurred in asserting the claim prior to the opening of proceedings are claimed, the amount and the details of those costs;
(e) the nature of the claim;
(f) whether any preferential creditor status is claimed and the basis of such a claim;
(g) whether security *in rem* or a reservation of title is alleged in respect of the claim and if so, what assets are covered by the security interest being invoked, the date on which the security was granted and, where the security has been registered, the registration number; and
(h) whether any set-off is claimed and, if so, the amounts of the mutual claims existing on the date when insolvency proceedings were opened, the date on which they arose and the amount net of set-off claimed.

The standard claims form shall be accompanied by copies of any supporting documents.

3. The standard claims form shall indicate that the provision of information concerning the bank details and the personal identification number of the creditor referred to in point (a) of paragraph 2 is not compulsory.
4. When a creditor lodges its claim by means other than the standard form referred to in paragraph 1, the claim shall contain the information referred to in paragraph 2.
5. Claims may be lodged in any official language of the institutions of the Union. The court, the insolvency practitioner or the debtor in possession may require the creditor to provide a translation in the official language of the State of the opening of proceedings or, if there are several official languages in that Member State, in the official language or one of the official languages of the place where insolvency proceedings have been opened, or in another language which that Member State has indicated it can accept. Each Member State shall indicate whether it accepts any official language of the institutions of the Union other than its own for the purpose of the lodging of claims.
6. Claims shall be lodged within the period stipulated by the law of the State of the opening of proceedings. In the case of a foreign creditor, that period shall not be less than 30 days following the publication of the opening of insolvency proceedings in the insolvency register of the State of the opening of proceedings. Where a Member State relies on Article 24(4), that period shall not be less than 30 days following a creditor having been informed pursuant to Article 54.
7. Where the court, the insolvency practitioner or the debtor in possession has doubts in relation to a claim lodged in accordance with this Article, it shall give the creditor the opportunity to provide additional evidence on the existence and the amount of the claim.

CHAPTER V

INSOLVENCY PROCEEDINGS OF MEMBERS OF A GROUP OF COMPANIES

SECTION 1

Cooperation and communication

Article 56

Cooperation and communication between insolvency practitioners

1. Where insolvency proceedings relate to two or more members of a group of companies, an insolvency practitioner appointed in proceedings concerning a member of the group shall cooperate with any insolvency practitioner appointed in proceedings concerning another member of the same group to the extent that such cooperation is appropriate to facilitate the effective administration

of those proceedings, is not incompatible with the rules applicable to such proceedings and does not entail any conflict of interest. That cooperation may take any form, including the conclusion of agreements or protocols.
2. In implementing the cooperation set out in paragraph 1, insolvency practitioners shall:
   (a) as soon as possible communicate to each other any information which may be relevant to the other proceedings, provided appropriate arrangements are made to protect confidential information;
   (b) consider whether possibilities exist for coordinating the administration and supervision of the affairs of the group members which are subject to insolvency proceedings, and if so, coordinate such administration and supervision;
   (c) consider whether possibilities exist for restructuring group members which are subject to insolvency proceedings and, if so, coordinate with regard to the proposal and negotiation of a coordinated restructuring plan.

For the purposes of points (b) and (c), all or some of the insolvency practitioners referred to in paragraph 1 may agree to grant additional powers to an insolvency practitioner appointed in one of the proceedings where such an agreement is permitted by the rules applicable to each of the proceedings. They may also agree on the allocation of certain tasks amongst them, where such allocation of tasks is permitted by the rules applicable to each of the proceedings.

Article 57

Cooperation and communication between courts

1. Where insolvency proceedings relate to two or more members of a group of companies, a court which has opened such proceedings shall cooperate with any other court before which a request to open proceedings concerning another member of the same group is pending or which has opened such proceedings to the extent that such cooperation is appropriate to facilitate the effective administration of the proceedings, is not incompatible with the rules applicable to them and does not entail any conflict of interest. For that purpose, the courts may, where appropriate, appoint an independent person or body to act on its instructions, provided that this is not incompatible with the rules applicable to them.
2. In implementing the cooperation set out in paragraph 1, courts, or any appointed person or body acting on their behalf, as referred to in paragraph 1, may communicate directly with each other, or request information or assistance directly from each other, provided that such communication respects the procedural rights of the parties to the proceedings and the confidentiality of information.
3. The cooperation referred to in paragraph 1 may be implemented by any means that the court considers appropriate. It may, in particular, concern:
   (a) coordination in the appointment of insolvency practitioners;
   (b) communication of information by any means considered appropriate by the court;
   (c) coordination of the administration and supervision of the assets and affairs of the members of the group;
   (d) coordination of the conduct of hearings;
   (e) coordination in the approval of protocols where necessary.

Article 58

Cooperation and communication between insolvency practitioners and courts

An insolvency practitioner appointed in insolvency proceedings concerning a member of a group of companies:

(a) shall cooperate and communicate with any court before which a request for the opening of proceedings in respect of another member of the same group of companies is pending or which has opened such proceedings; and

(b) may request information from that court concerning the proceedings regarding the other member of the group or request assistance concerning the proceedings in which he has been appointed;

to the extent that such cooperation and communication are appropriate to facilitate the effective administration of the proceedings, do not entail any conflict of interest and are not incompatible with the rules applicable to them.

Article 59

Costs of cooperation and communication in proceedings concerning members of a group of companies

The costs of the cooperation and communication provided for in Articles 56 to 60 incurred by an insolvency practitioner or a court shall be regarded as costs and expenses incurred in the respective proceedings.

Article 60

Powers of the insolvency practitioner in proceedings concerning members of a group of companies

1. An insolvency practitioner appointed in insolvency proceedings opened in respect of a member of a group of companies may, to the extent appropriate to facilitate the effective administration of the proceedings:
   (a) be heard in any of the proceedings opened in respect of any other member of the same group;
   (b) request a stay of any measure related to the realisation of the assets in the proceedings opened with respect to any other member of the same group, provided that:
      (i) a restructuring plan for all or some members of the group for which insolvency proceedings have been opened has been proposed under point (c) of Article 56(2) and presents a reasonable chance of success;
      (ii) such a stay is necessary in order to ensure the proper implementation of the restructuring plan;
      (iii) the restructuring plan would be to the benefit of the creditors in the proceedings for which the stay is requested; and
      (iv) neither the insolvency proceedings in which the insolvency practitioner referred to in paragraph 1 of this Article has been appointed nor the proceedings in respect of which the stay is requested are subject to coordination under Section 2 of this Chapter;
   (c) apply for the opening of group coordination proceedings in accordance with Article 61.
2. The court having opened proceedings referred to in point (b) of paragraph 1 shall stay any measure related to the realisation of the assets in the proceedings in whole or in part if it is satisfied that the conditions referred to in point (b) of paragraph 1 are fulfilled.

Before ordering the stay, the court shall hear the insolvency practitioner appointed in the proceedings for which the stay is requested. Such a stay may be ordered for any period, not exceeding 3 months, which the court considers appropriate and which is compatible with the rules applicable to the proceedings.

The court ordering the stay may require the insolvency practitioner referred to in paragraph 1 to take any suitable measure available under national law to guarantee the interests of the creditors in the proceedings.

The court may extend the duration of the stay by such further period or periods as it considers appropriate and which are compatible with the rules applicable to the proceedings, provided that the conditions referred to in points (b)(ii) to (iv) of paragraph 1 continue to be fulfilled and that the total duration of the stay (the initial period together with any such extensions) does not exceed 6 months.

SECTION 2

Coordination

Subsection 1

Procedure

Article 61

Request to open group coordination proceedings

1. Group coordination proceedings may be requested before any court having jurisdiction over the insolvency proceedings of a member of the group, by an insolvency practitioner appointed in insolvency proceedings opened in relation to a member of the group.
2. The request referred to in paragraph 1 shall be made in accordance with the conditions provided for by the law applicable to the proceedings in which the insolvency practitioner has been appointed.
3. The request referred to in paragraph 1 shall be accompanied by:
   (a) a proposal as to the person to be nominated as the group coordinator ('the coordinator'), details of his or her eligibility pursuant to Article 71, details of his or her qualifications and his or her written agreement to act as coordinator;
   (b) an outline of the proposed group coordination, and in particular the reasons why the conditions set out in Article 63(1) are fulfilled;
   (c) a list of the insolvency practitioners appointed in relation to the members of the group and, where relevant, the courts and competent authorities involved in the insolvency proceedings of the members of the group;
   (d) an outline of the estimated costs of the proposed group coordination and the estimation of the share of those costs to be paid by each member of the group.

Article 62

Priority rule

Without prejudice to Article 66, where the opening of group coordination proceedings is requested before courts of different Member States, any court other than the court first seised shall decline jurisdiction in favour of that court.

Article 63

Notice by the court seised

1. The court seised of a request to open group coordination proceedings shall give notice as soon as possible of the request for the opening of group coordination proceedings and of the proposed coordinator to the insolvency practitioners appointed in relation to the members of the group as indicated in the request referred to in point (c) of Article 61(3), if it is satisfied that:
   (a the opening of such proceedings is appropriate to facilitate the effective administration of the insolvency proceedings relating to the different group members;
   (b) no creditor of any group member expected to participate in the proceedings is likely to be financially disadvantaged by the inclusion of that member in such proceedings; and
   (c) the proposed coordinator fulfils the requirements laid down in Article 71.
2. The notice referred to in paragraph 1 of this Article shall list the elements referred to in points (a) to (d) of Article 61(3).
3. The notice referred to in paragraph 1 shall be sent by registered letter, attested by an acknowledgment of receipt.
4. The court seised shall give the insolvency practitioners involved the opportunity to be heard.

Article 64

Objections by insolvency practitioners

1. An insolvency practitioner appointed in respect of any group member may object to:
   (a) the inclusion within group coordination proceedings of the insolvency proceedings in respect of which it has been appointed; or
   (b) the person proposed as a coordinator.
2. Objections pursuant to paragraph 1 of this Article shall be lodged with the court referred to in Article 63 within 30 days of receipt of notice of the request for the opening of group coordination proceedings by the insolvency practitioner referred to in paragraph 1 of this Article.
   The objection may be made by means of the standard form established in accordance with Article 88.
3. Prior to taking the decision to participate or not to participate in the coordination in accordance with point (a) of paragraph 1, an insolvency practitioner shall obtain any approval which may be required under the law of the State of the opening of proceedings for which it has been appointed.

Article 65

Consequences of objection to the inclusion in group coordination

1. Where an insolvency practitioner has objected to the inclusion of the proceedings in respect of which it has been appointed in group coordination proceedings, those proceedings shall not be included in the group coordination proceedings.
2. The powers of the court referred to in Article 68 or of the coordinator arising from those proceedings shall have no effect as regards that member, and shall entail no costs for that member.

Article 66

Choice of court for group coordination proceedings

1. Where at least two-thirds of all insolvency practitioners appointed in insolvency proceedings of the members of the group have agreed that a court of another Member State having jurisdiction is the most appropriate court for the opening of group coordination proceedings, that court shall have exclusive jurisdiction.
2. The choice of court shall be made by joint agreement in writing or evidenced in writing. It may be made until such time as group coordination proceedings have been opened in accordance with Article 68.
3. Any court other than the court seised under paragraph 1 shall decline jurisdiction in favour of that court.
4. The request for the opening of group coordination proceedings shall be submitted to the court agreed in accordance with Article 61.

Article 67

Consequences of objections to the proposed coordinator

Where objections to the person proposed as coordinator have been received from an insolvency practitioner which does not also object to the inclusion in the group coordination proceedings of the member in respect of which it has been appointed, the court may refrain from appointing that person and invite the objecting insolvency practitioner to submit a new request in accordance with Article 61(3).

Article 68

Decision to open group coordination proceedings

1. After the period referred to in Article 64(2) has elapsed, the court may open group coordination proceedings where it is satisfied that the conditions of Article 63(1) are met. In such a case, the court shall:
   (a) appoint a coordinator;
   (b) decide on the outline of the coordination; and
   (c) decide on the estimation of costs and the share to be paid by the group members.
2. The decision opening group coordination proceedings shall be brought to the notice of the participating insolvency practitioners and of the coordinator.

Article 69

Subsequent opt-in by insolvency practitioners

1. In accordance with its national law, any insolvency practitioner may request, after the court decision referred to in Article 68, the inclusion of the proceedings in respect of which it has been appointed, where:
   (a) there has been an objection to the inclusion of the insolvency proceedings within the group coordination proceedings; or
   (b) insolvency proceedings with respect to a member of the group have been opened after the court has opened group coordination proceedings.
2. Without prejudice to paragraph 4, the coordinator may accede to such a request, after consulting the insolvency practitioners involved, where
   (a) he or she is satisfied that, taking into account the stage that the group coordination proceedings has reached at the time of the request, the criteria set out in points (a) and (b) of Article 63(1) are met; or
   (b) all insolvency practitioners involved agree, subject to the conditions in their national law.
3. The coordinator shall inform the court and the participating insolvency practitioners of his or her decision pursuant to paragraph 2 and of the reasons on which it is based.
4. Any participating insolvency practitioner or any insolvency practitioner whose request for inclusion in the group coordination proceedings has been rejected may challenge the decision referred to in paragraph 2 in accordance with the procedure set out under the law of the Member State in which the group coordination proceedings have been opened.

Article 70

Recommendations and group coordination plan

1. When conducting their insolvency proceedings, insolvency practitioners shall consider the recommendations of the coordinator and the content of the group coordination plan referred to in Article 72(1).
2. An insolvency practitioner shall not be obliged to follow in whole or in part the coordinator's recommendations or the group coordination plan.

If it does not follow the coordinator's recommendations or the group coordination plan, it shall give reasons for not doing so to the persons or bodies that it is to report to under its national law, and to the coordinator.

Subsection 2

General provisions

Article 71

The coordinator

1. The coordinator shall be a person eligible under the law of a Member State to act as an insolvency practitioner.
2. The coordinator shall not be one of the insolvency practitioners appointed to act in respect of any of the group members, and shall have no conflict of interest in respect of the group members, their creditors and the insolvency practitioners appointed in respect of any of the group members.

Article 72

Tasks and rights of the coordinator

1. The coordinator shall:
   (a) identify and outline recommendations for the coordinated conduct of the insolvency proceedings;
   (b) propose a group coordination plan that identifies, describes and recommends a comprehensive set of measures appropriate to an integrated approach to the resolution of the group members' insolvencies. In particular, the plan may contain proposals for:
      (i) the measures to be taken in order to re-establish the economic performance and the financial soundness of the group or any part of it;
      (ii) the settlement of intra-group disputes as regards intra-group transactions and avoidance actions;
      (iii) agreements between the insolvency practitioners of the insolvent group members.
2. The coordinator may also:
   (a) be heard and participate, in particular by attending creditors' meetings, in any of the proceedings opened in respect of any member of the group;
   (b) mediate any dispute arising between two or more insolvency practitioners of group members;
   (c) present and explain his or her group coordination plan to the persons or bodies that he or she is to report to under his or her national law;
   (d) request information from any insolvency practitioner in respect of any member of the group where that information is or might be of use when identifying and outlining strategies and measures in order to coordinate the proceedings; and
   (e) request a stay for a period of up to 6 months of the proceedings opened in respect of any member of the group, provided that such a stay is necessary in order to ensure the proper implementation of the plan and would be to the benefit of the creditors in the proceedings for which the stay is requested; or request the lifting of any existing stay. Such a request shall be made to the court that opened the proceedings for which a stay is requested.
3. The plan referred to in point (b) of paragraph 1 shall not include recommendations as to any consolidation of proceedings or insolvency estates.
4. The coordinator's tasks and rights as defined under this Article shall not extend to any member of the group not participating in group coordination proceedings.
5. The coordinator shall perform his or her duties impartially and with due care.
6. Where the coordinator considers that the fulfilment of his or her tasks requires a significant increase in the costs compared to the cost estimate referred to in point (d) of Article 61(3), and in any case, where the costs exceed 10 % of the estimated costs, the coordinator shall:
   (a) inform without delay the participating insolvency practitioners; and
   (b) seek the prior approval of the court opening group coordination proceedings.

Article 73

Languages

1. The coordinator shall communicate with the insolvency practitioner of a participating group member in the language agreed with the insolvency practitioner or, in the absence of an agreement, in the official language or one of the official languages of the institutions of the Union, and of the court which opened the proceedings in respect of that group member.
2. The coordinator shall communicate with a court in the official language applicable to that court.

Article 74

Cooperation between insolvency practitioners and the coordinator

1. Insolvency practitioners appointed in relation to members of a group and the coordinator shall cooperate with each other to the extent that such cooperation is not incompatible with the rules applicable to the respective proceedings.
2. In particular, insolvency practitioners shall communicate any information that is relevant for the coordinator to perform his or her tasks.

Article 75

Revocation of the appointment of the coordinator

The court shall revoke the appointment of the coordinator of its own motion or at the request of the insolvency practitioner of a participating group member where:

(a) the coordinator acts to the detriment of the creditors of a participating group member; or
(b) the coordinator fails to comply with his or her obligations under this Chapter.

Article 76

Debtor in possession

The provisions applicable, under this Chapter, to the insolvency practitioner shall also apply, where appropriate, to the debtor in possession.

Article 77

Costs and distribution

1. The remuneration for the coordinator shall be adequate, proportionate to the tasks fulfilled and reflect reasonable expenses.
2. On having completed his or her tasks, the coordinator shall establish the final statement of costs and the share to be paid by each member, and submit this statement to each participating insolvency practitioner and to the court opening coordination proceedings.
3. In the absence of objections by the insolvency practitioners within 30 days of receipt of the statement referred to in paragraph 2, the costs and the share to be paid by each member shall be deemed to be agreed. The statement shall be submitted to the court opening coordination proceedings for confirmation.
4. In the event of an objection, the court that opened the group coordination proceedings shall, upon the application of the coordinator or any participating insolvency practitioner, decide on the costs and the share to be paid by each member in accordance with the criteria set out in paragraph 1 of this Article, and taking into account the estimation of costs referred to in Article 68(1) and, where applicable, Article 72(6).
5. Any participating insolvency practitioner may challenge the decision referred to in paragraph 4 in accordance with the procedure set out under the law of the Member State where group coordination proceedings have been opened.

CHAPTER VI

DATA PROTECTION

Article 78

Data protection

1. National rules implementing Directive 95/46/EC shall apply to the processing of personal data carried out in the Member States pursuant to this Regulation, provided that processing operations referred to in Article 3(2) of Directive 95/46/EC are not concerned.
2. Regulation (EC) No 45/2001 shall apply to the processing of personal data carried out by the Commission pursuant to this Regulation.

Article 79

Responsibilities of Member States regarding the processing of personal data in national insolvency registers

1. Each Member State shall communicate to the Commission the name of the natural or legal person, public authority, agency or any other body designated by national law to exercise the functions of controller in accordance with point (d) of Article 2 of Directive 95/46/EC, with a view to its publication on the European e-Justice Portal.
2. Member States shall ensure that the technical measures for ensuring the security of personal data processed in their national insolvency registers referred to in Article 24 are implemented.
3. Member States shall be responsible for verifying that the controller, designated by national law in accordance with point (d) of Article 2 of Directive 95/46/EC, ensures compliance with the principles of data quality, in particular the accuracy and the updating of data stored in national insolvency registers.
4. Member States shall be responsible, in accordance with Directive 95/46/EC, for the collection and storage of data in national databases and for decisions taken to make such data available in the interconnected register that can be consulted via the European e-Justice Portal.
5. As part of the information that should be provided to data subjects to enable them to exercise their rights, and in particular the right to the erasure of data, Member States shall inform data subjects of the accessibility period set for personal data stored in insolvency registers.

Article 80

Responsibilities of the Commission in connection with the processing of personal data

1. The Commission shall exercise the responsibilities of controller pursuant to Article 2(d) of Regulation (EC) No 45/2001 in accordance with its respective responsibilities defined in this Article.
2. The Commission shall define the necessary policies and apply the necessary technical solutions to fulfil its responsibilities within the scope of the function of controller.
3. The Commission shall implement the technical measures required to ensure the security of personal data while in transit, in particular the confidentiality and integrity of any transmission to and from the European e-Justice Portal.
4. The obligations of the Commission shall not affect the responsibilities of the Member States and other bodies for the content and operation of the interconnected national databases run by them.

Article 81

Information obligations

Without prejudice to the information to be given to data subjects in accordance with Articles 11 and 12 of Regulation (EC) No 45/2001, the Commission shall inform data subjects, by means of publication through the European e-Justice Portal, about its role in the processing of data and the purposes for which those data will be processed.

Article 82

Storage of personal data

As regards information from interconnected national databases, no personal data relating to data subjects shall be stored in the European e-Justice Portal. All such data shall be stored in the national databases operated by the Member States or other bodies.

Article 83

Access to personal data via the European e-Justice Portal

Personal data stored in the national insolvency registers referred to in Article 24 shall be accessible via the European e-Justice Portal for as long as they remain accessible under national law.

CHAPTER VII

TRANSITIONAL AND FINAL PROVISIONS

Article 84

Applicability in time

- C1 1. The provisions of this Regulation shall apply only to insolvency proceedings opened from 26 June 2017. Acts committed by a debtor before that date shall continue to be governed by the law which was applicable to them at the time they were committed.
- B 2. Notwithstanding Article 91 of this Regulation, Regulation (EC) No 1346/2000 shall continue to apply to insolvency proceedings which fall within the scope of that Regulation and which have been opened before 26 June 2017.

Article 85

Relationship to Conventions

1. This Regulation replaces, in respect of the matters referred to therein, and as regards relations between Member States, the Conventions concluded between two or more Member States, in particular:
   (a) the Convention between Belgium and France on Jurisdiction and the Validity and Enforcement of Judgments, Arbitration Awards and Authentic Instruments, signed at Paris on 8 July 1899;
   (b) the Convention between Belgium and Austria on Bankruptcy, Winding-up, Arrangements, Compositions and Suspension of Payments (with Additional Protocol of 13 June 1973), signed at Brussels on 16 July 1969;
   (c) the Convention between Belgium and the Netherlands on Territorial Jurisdiction, Bankruptcy and the Validity and Enforcement of Judgments, Arbitration Awards and Authentic Instruments, signed at Brussels on 28 March 1925;
   (d) the Treaty between Germany and Austria on Bankruptcy, Winding-up, Arrangements and Compositions, signed at Vienna on 25 May 1979;

(e) the Convention between France and Austria on Jurisdiction, Recognition and Enforcement of Judgments on Bankruptcy, signed at Vienna on 27 February 1979;
(f) the Convention between France and Italy on the Enforcement of Judgments in Civil and Commercial Matters, signed at Rome on 3 June 1930;
(g) the Convention between Italy and Austria on Bankruptcy, Winding-up, Arrangements and Compositions, signed at Rome on 12 July 1977;
(h) the Convention between the Kingdom of the Netherlands and the Federal Republic of Germany on the Mutual Recognition and Enforcement of Judgments and other Enforceable Instruments in Civil and Commercial Matters, signed at The Hague on 30 August 1962;
(i) the Convention between the United Kingdom and the Kingdom of Belgium providing for the Reciprocal Enforcement of Judgments in Civil and Commercial Matters, with Protocol, signed at Brussels on 2 May 1934;
(j) the Convention between Denmark, Finland, Norway, Sweden and Iceland on Bankruptcy, signed at Copenhagen on 7 November 1933;
(k) the European Convention on Certain International Aspects of Bankruptcy, signed at Istanbul on 5 June 1990;
(l) the Convention between the Federative People's Republic of Yugoslavia and the Kingdom of Greece on the Mutual Recognition and Enforcement of Judgments, signed at Athens on 18 June 1959;
(m) the Agreement between the Federative People's Republic of Yugoslavia and the Republic of Austria on the Mutual Recognition and Enforcement of Arbitral Awards and Arbitral Settlements in Commercial Matters, signed at Belgrade on 18 March 1960;
(n) the Convention between the Federative People's Republic of Yugoslavia and the Italian Republic on Mutual Judicial Cooperation in Civil and Administrative Matters, signed at Rome on 3 December 1960;
(o) the Agreement between the Socialist Federative Republic of Yugoslavia and the Kingdom of Belgium on Judicial Cooperation in Civil and Commercial Matters, signed at Belgrade on 24 September 1971;
(p) the Convention between the Governments of Yugoslavia and France on the Recognition and Enforcement of Judgments in Civil and Commercial Matters, signed at Paris on 18 May 1971;
(q) the Agreement between the Czechoslovak Socialist Republic and the Hellenic Republic on Legal Aid in Civil and Criminal Matters, signed at Athens on 22 October 1980, still in force between the Czech Republic and Greece;
(r) the Agreement between the Czechoslovak Socialist Republic and the Republic of Cyprus on Legal Aid in Civil and Criminal Matters, signed at Nicosia on 23 April 1982, still in force between the Czech Republic and Cyprus;
(s) the Treaty between the Government of the Czechoslovak Socialist Republic and the Government of the Republic of France on Legal Aid and the Recognition and Enforcement of Judgments in Civil, Family and Commercial Matters, signed at Paris on 10 May 1984, still in force between the Czech Republic and France;
(t) the Treaty between the Czechoslovak Socialist Republic and the Italian Republic on Legal Aid in Civil and Criminal Matters, signed at Prague on 6 December 1985, still in force between the Czech Republic and Italy;
(u) the Agreement between the Republic of Latvia, the Republic of Estonia and the Republic of Lithuania on Legal Assistance and Legal Relationships, signed at Tallinn on 11 November 1992;
(v) the Agreement between Estonia and Poland on Granting Legal Aid and Legal Relations on Civil, Labour and Criminal Matters, signed at Tallinn on 27 November 1998;
(w) the Agreement between the Republic of Lithuania and the Republic of Poland on Legal Assistance and Legal Relations in Civil, Family, Labour and Criminal Matters, signed at Warsaw on 26 January 1993;
(x) the Convention between the Socialist Republic of Romania and the Hellenic Republic on legal assistance in civil and criminal matters and its Protocol, signed at Bucharest on 19 October 1972;
(y) the Convention between the Socialist Republic of Romania and the French Republic on legal assistance in civil and commercial matters, signed at Paris on 5 November 1974;

(z) the Agreement between the People's Republic of Bulgaria and the Hellenic Republic on Legal Assistance in Civil and Criminal Matters, signed at Athens on 10 April 1976;
   (aa) the Agreement between the People's Republic of Bulgaria and the Republic of Cyprus on Legal Assistance in Civil and Criminal Matters, signed at Nicosia on 29 April 1983;
   (ab) the Agreement between the Government of the People's Republic of Bulgaria and the Government of the French Republic on Mutual Legal Assistance in Civil Matters, signed at Sofia on 18 January 1989;
   (ac) the Treaty between Romania and the Czech Republic on judicial assistance in civil matters, signed at Bucharest on 11 July 1994;
   (ad) the Treaty between Romania and the Republic of Poland on legal assistance and legal relations in civil cases, signed at Bucharest on 15 May 1999.
2. The Conventions referred to in paragraph 1 shall continue to have effect with regard to proceedings opened before the entry into force of Regulation (EC) No 1346/2000.
3. This Regulation shall not apply:
   (a) in any Member State, to the extent that it is irreconcilable with the obligations arising in relation to bankruptcy from a convention concluded by that Member State with one or more third countries before the entry into force of Regulation (EC) No 1346/2000;
   (b) in the United Kingdom of Great Britain and Northern Ireland, to the extent that is irreconcilable with the obligations arising in relation to bankruptcy and the winding-up of insolvent companies from any arrangements with the Commonwealth existing at the time Regulation (EC) No 1346/2000 entered into force.

Article 86

Information on national and Union insolvency law

1. The Member States shall provide, within the framework of the European Judicial Network in civil and commercial matters established by Council Decision 2001/470/EC ([5]), and with a view to making the information available to the public, a short description of their national legislation and procedures relating to insolvency, in particular relating to the matters listed in Article 7(2).
2. The Member States shall update the information referred to in paragraph 1 regularly.
3. The Commission shall make information concerning this Regulation available to the public.

Article 87

Establishment of the interconnection of registers

The Commission shall adopt implementing acts establishing the interconnection of insolvency registers as referred to in Article 25. Those implementing acts shall be adopted in accordance with the examination procedure referred to in Article 89(3).

Article 88

Establishment and subsequent amendment of standard forms

The Commission shall adopt implementing acts establishing and, where necessary, amending the forms referred to in Article 27(4), Articles 54 and 55 and Article 64(2). Those implementing acts shall be adopted in accordance with the advisory procedure referred to in Article 89(2).

---

[5] Council Decision 2001/470/EC of 28 May 2001 establishing a European Judicial Network in civil and commercial matters (OJ L 174, 27.6.2001, p. 25).

Article 89

Committee procedure

1. The Commission shall be assisted by a committee. That committee shall be a committee within the meaning of Regulation (EU) No 182/2011.
2. Where reference is made to this paragraph, Article 4 of Regulation (EU) No 182/2011 shall apply.
3. Where reference is made to this paragraph, Article 5 of Regulation (EU) No 182/2011 shall apply.

Article 90

Review clause

1. No later than 27 June 2027, and every 5 years thereafter, the Commission shall present to the European Parliament, the Council and the European Economic and Social Committee a report on the application of this Regulation. The report shall be accompanied where necessary by a proposal for adaptation of this Regulation.
2. No later than 27 June 2022, the Commission shall present to the European Parliament, the Council and the European Economic and Social Committee a report on the application of the group coordination proceedings. The report shall be accompanied where necessary by a proposal for adaptation of this Regulation.
3. No later than 1 January 2016, the Commission shall submit to the European Parliament, the Council and the European Economic and Social Committee a study on the cross-border issues in the area of directors' liability and disqualifications.
4. No later than 27 June 2020, the Commission shall submit to the European Parliament, the Council and the European Economic and Social Committee a study on the issue of abusive forum shopping.

Article 91

Repeal

Regulation (EC) No 1346/2000 is repealed.
References to the repealed Regulation shall be construed as references to this Regulation and shall be read in accordance with the correlation table set out in Annex D to this Regulation.

Article 92

Entry into force

This Regulation shall enter into force on the twentieth day following that of its publication in the *Official Journal of the European Union*.
It shall apply from 26 June 2017, with the exception of:

(a) Article 86, which shall apply from 26 June 2016;
(b) Article 24(1), which shall apply from 26 June 2018; and
(c) Article 25, which shall apply from 26 June 2019.

This Regulation shall be binding in its entirety and directly applicable in the Member States in accordance with the Treaties.

ANNEX A

INSOLVENCY PROCEEDINGS REFERRED TO IN ARTICLE 2, POINT (4)

BELGIQUE/BELGIË

— Het faillissement/La faillite,
— De gerechtelijke reorganisatie door een collectief akkoord/La réorganisation judiciaire par accord collectif,
— De gerechtelijke reorganisatie door een minnelijk akkoord/La réorganisation judiciaire par accord amiable,
— De gerechtelijke reorganisatie door overdracht onder gerechtelijk gezag/La réorganisation judiciaire par transfert sous autorité de justice,
— De collectieve schuldenregeling/Le règlement collectif de dettes,
— De vrijwillige vereffening/La liquidation volontaire,
— De gerechtelijke vereffening/La liquidation judiciaire,
— De voorlopige ontneming van het beheer, als bedoeld in artikel XX.32 van het Wetboek van economisch recht/Le dessaisissement provisoire de la gestion, visé à l'article XX.32 du Code de droit économique,

БЪЛГАРИЯ

— Производство по несъстоятелност,
— Производство по стабилизация на търговеца,

ČESKÁ REPUBLIKA

— Konkurs,
— Reorganizace,
— Oddlužení,

DEUTSCHLAND

— Das Konkursverfahren,
— Das gerichtliche Vergleichsverfahren,
— Das Gesamtvollstreckungsverfahren,
— Das Insolvenzverfahren,
— Die öffentliche Restrukturierungssache,

EESTI

— Pankrotimenetlus,
— Võlgade ümberkujundamise menetlus,

ÉIRE/IRELAND

— Compulsory winding-up by the court,
— Bankruptcy,
— The administration in bankruptcy of the estate of persons dying insolvent,
— Winding-up in bankruptcy of partnerships,
— Creditors' voluntary winding-up (with confirmation of a court),
— Arrangements under the control of the court which involve the vesting of all or part of the property of the debtor in the Official Assignee for realisation and distribution,
— Examinership,
— Debt Relief Notice,
— Debt Settlement Arrangement,
— Personal Insolvency Arrangement,

ΕΛΛΑΔΑ

— Η πτώχευση,
— Η ειδική εκκαθάριση εν λειτουργία,
— Σχέδιο αναδιοργάνωσης,
— Απλοποιημένη διαδικασία επί πτωχεύσεων μικρού αντικειμένου,
— Διαδικασία εξυγίανσης,

ESPAÑA

— Concurso,
— Procedimiento de homologación de acuerdos de refinanciación,
— Procedimiento de acuerdos extrajudiciales de pago,
— Procedimiento de negociación pública para la consecución de acuerdos de refinanciación colectivos, acuerdos de refinanciación homologados y propuestas anticipadas de convenio,

FRANCE

— Sauvegarde,
— Sauvegarde accélérée,
— Sauvegarde financière accélérée,
— Redressement judiciaire,
— Liquidation judiciaire,

HRVATSKA

— Stečajni postupak,
— Predstečajni postupak,
— Postupak stečaja potrošača,
— Postupak izvanredne uprave u trgovačkim društvima od sistemskog značaja za Republiku Hrvatsku,

ITALIA

— Fallimento
— [until 15 May 2022],
— Liquidazione giudiziale
— [from 16 May 2022],
— Concordato preventivo,
— Liquidazione coatta amministrativa,
— Amministrazione straordinaria,
— Accordi di ristrutturazione,
— Procedure di composizione della crisi da sovraindebitamento del consumatore (accordo o piano)

[until 15 May 2022],
— Liquidazione dei beni

[until 15 May 2022],
— Ristrutturazione dei debiti del consumatore

[from 16 May 2022],
— Concordato minore

[from 16 May 2022],
— Liquidazione controllata del sovraindebitato

[from 16 May 2022],
ΚΥΠΡΟΣ

— Υποχρεωτική εκκαθάριση από το Δικαστήριο,
— Εκούσια εκκαθάριση από μέλη,

- Εκούσια εκκαθάριση από πιστωτές,
- Εκκαθάριση με την εποπτεία του Δικαστηρίου,
- Διάταγμα παραλαβής και πτώχευσης κατόπιν Δικαστικού Διατάγματος,
- Διαχείριση της περιουσίας προσώπων που απεβίωσαν αφερέγγυα,
- Διορισμός Εξεταστή,
- Προσωπικά Σχέδια Αποπληρωμής,

LATVIJA

- Tiesiskās aizsardzības process,
- Juridiskās personas maksātnespējas process,
- Fiziskās personas maksātnespējas process,

LIETUVA

- Juridinio asmens restruktūrizavimo byla,
- Juridinio asmens bankroto byla,
- Juridinio asmens bankroto procesas ne teismo tvarka,
- Fizinio asmens bankroto procesas,

LUXEMBOURG

- Faillite,
- Gestion contrôlée,
- Concordat préventif de faillite (par abandon d'actif),
- Régime spécial de liquidation du notariat,
- Procédure de règlement collectif des dettes dans le cadre du surendettement,

MAGYARORSZÁG

- Csődeljárás,
- Felszámolási eljárás,
- Nyilvános szerkezetátalakítási eljárás

[from 1 July 2022],

MALTA

- Xoljiment,
- Amministrazzjoni,
- Stralċ volontarju mill-membri jew mill-kredituri,
- Stralċ mill-Qorti,
- Falliment f'każ ta' kummerċjant,
- Proċedura biex kumpanija tirkupra,

NEDERLAND

- Het faillissement,
- De surseance van betaling,
- De schuldsaneringsregeling natuurlijke personen,
- De openbare akkoordprocedure buiten faillissement,

ÖSTERREICH

- Das Konkursverfahren (Insolvenzverfahren),
- Das Sanierungsverfahren ohne Eigenverwaltung (Insolvenzverfahren),
- Das Sanierungsverfahren mit Eigenverwaltung (Insolvenzverfahren),
- Das Schuldenregulierungsverfahren,
- Das Abschöpfungsverfahren,
- Das Europäische Restrukturierungsverfahren,

POLSKA

— Upadłość,
— Postępowanie o zatwierdzenie układu,
— Postępowanie o zatwierdzenie układu na zgromadzeniu wierzycieli przez osobę fizyczną nieprowadzącą działalności gospodarczej,
— Przyspieszone postępowanie układowe,
— Postępowanie układowe,
— Postępowanie sanacyjne,

PORTUGAL

— Processo de insolvência,
— Processo especial de revitalização,
— Processo especial para acordo de pagamento,

ROMÂNIA

— Procedura insolvenței,
— Reorganizarea judiciară,
— Procedura falimentului,
— Concordatul preventiv,

SLOVENIJA

— Postopek preventivnega prestrukturiranja,
— Postopek prisilne poravnave,
— Postopek poenostavljene prisilne poravnave,
— Stečajni postopek: stečajni postopek nad pravno osebo, postopek osebnega stečaja in postopek stečaja zapuščine,

SLOVENSKO

— Konkurzné konanie,
— Reštrukturalizačné konanie,
— Oddlženie,

SUOMI/FINLAND

— Konkurssi/konkurs,
— Yrityssaneeraus/företagssanering,
— Yksityishenkilön velkajärjestely/skuldsanering för privatpersoner,

SVERIGE

— Konkurs,
— Företagsrekonstruktion,
— Skuldsanering.

ANNEX B

INSOLVENCY PRACTITIONERS REFERRED TO IN ARTICLE 2, POINT (5)

BELGIQUE/BELGIË

— De curator/Le curateur,
— De gerechtsmandataris/Le mandataire de justice,
— De schuldbemiddelaar/Le médiateur de dettes,

— De vereffenaar/Le liquidateur,
— De voorlopige bewindvoerder/L'administrateur provisoire,

БЪЛГАРИЯ

— Назначен предварително временен синдик,
— Временен синдик,
— (Постоянен) синдик,
— Служебен синдик,
— Доверено лице,

ČESKÁ REPUBLIKA

— Insolvenční správce,
— Předběžný insolvenční správce,
— Oddělený insolvenční správce,
— Zvláštní insolvenční správce,
— Zástupce insolvenčního správce,

DEUTSCHLAND

— Konkursverwalter,
— Vergleichsverwalter,
— Sachwalter (nach der Vergleichsordnung),
— Verwalter,
— Insolvenzverwalter,
— Sachwalter (nach der Insolvenzordnung),
— Treuhänder,
— Vorläufiger Insolvenzverwalter,
— Vorläufiger Sachwalter,
— Restrukturierungsbeauftragter,

EESTI

— Pankrotihaldur,
— Ajutine pankrotihaldur,
— Usaldusisik,

ÉIRE/IRELAND

— Liquidator,
— Official Assignee,
— Trustee in bankruptcy,
— Provisional Liquidator,
— Examiner,
— Personal Insolvency Practitioner,
— Insolvency Service,

ΕΛΛΑΔΑ

— Ο σύνδικος,
— Ο εισηγητής,
— Η επιτροπή των πιστωτών,
— Ο ειδικός εκκαθαριστής,

ESPAÑA

— Administrador concursal,
— Mediador concursal,

FRANCE

— Mandataire judiciaire,
— Liquidateur,
— Administrateur judiciaire,
— Commissaire à l'exécution du plan,

HRVATSKA

— Stečajni upravitelj,
— Privremeni stečajni upravitelj,
— Stečajni povjerenik,
— Povjerenik,
— Izvanredni povjerenik,

ITALIA

— Curatore,
— Commissario giudiziale,
— Commissario straordinario,
— Commissario liquidatore,
— Liquidatore giudiziale,
— Professionista nominato dal Tribunale,
— Organismo di composizione della crisi nella procedura di composizione della crisi da sovraindebitamento del consumatore

[until 15 May 2022],
— Organismo di composizione della crisi da sovraindebitamento

[from 16 May 2022],
— Liquidatore,

ΚΥΠΡΟΣ

— Εκκαθαριστής και Προσωρινός Εκκαθαριστής,
— Επίσημος Παραλήπτης,
— Διαχειριστής της Πτώχευσης,
— Εξεταστής,
— Σύμβουλος Αφερεγγυότητας,

LATVIJA

— Maksātnespējas procesa administrators,
— Tiesiskās aizsardzības procesa uzraugošā persona,

LIETUVA
— Nemokumo administratorius,

LUXEMBOURG

— Le curateur,
— Le commissaire,
— Le liquidateur,
— Le conseil de gérance de la section d'assainissement du notariat,
— Le liquidateur dans le cadre du surendettement,

MAGYARORSZÁG

— Vagyonfelügyelő,
— Felszámoló,
— Szerkezetátalakítási szakértő

[from 1 July 2022],
MALTA

- Amministratur Proviżorju,
- Riċevitur Uffiċjali,
- Stralċjarju,
- Manager Speċjali,
- Kuraturi f'każ ta' proċeduri ta' falliment,
- Kontrolur Speċjali,

NEDERLAND

- De curator in het faillissement,
- De bewindvoerder in de surseance van betaling,
- De bewindvoerder in de schuldsaneringsregeling natuurlijke personen,
- De herstructureringsdeskundige in de openbare akkoordprocedure buiten faillissement,
- De observator in de openbare akkoordprocedure buiten faillissement,

ÖSTERREICH

- Masseverwalter,
- Sanierungsverwalter,
- Restrukturierungsbeauftragter,
- Besonderer Verwalter,
- Einstweiliger Verwalter,
- Sachwalter,
- Treuhänder,
- Insolvenzgericht,
- Konkursgericht,

POLSKA

- Syndyk,
- Nadzorca sądowy,
- Zarządca,
- Nadzorca układu,
- Tymczasowy nadzorca sądowy,
- Tymczasowy zarządca,
- Zarządca przymusowy,

PORTUGAL

- Administrador da insolvência,
- Administrador judicial provisório,

ROMÂNIA

- Practician în insolvență,
- Administrator concordatar,
- Administrator judiciar,
- Lichidator judiciar,

SLOVENIJA
- Upravitelj,

SLOVENSKO

- Predbežný správca,
- Správca,

SUOMI/FINLAND

— Pesänhoitaja/boförvaltare,
— Selvittäjä/utredare,

SVERIGE

— Förvaltare,
— Rekonstruktör.

ANNEX C

Repealed Regulation with list of the successive amendments thereto

Council Regulation (EC) No 1346/2000
(OJ L 160, 30.6.2000, p. 1)
Council Regulation (EC) No 603/2005
(OJ L 100, 20.4.2005, p. 1)
Council Regulation (EC) No 694/2006
(OJ L 121, 6.5.2006, p. 1)
Council Regulation (EC) No 1791/2006
(OJ L 363, 20.12.2006, p. 1)
Council Regulation (EC) No 681/2007
(OJ L 159, 20.6.2007, p. 1)
Council Regulation (EC) No 788/2008
(OJ L 213, 8.8.2008, p. 1)
Implementing Regulation of the Council (EU) No 210/2010
(OJ L 65, 13.3.2010, p. 1)
Council Implementing Regulation (EU) No 583/2011
(OJ L 160, 18.6.2011, p. 52)
Council Regulation (EU) No 517/2013
(OJ L 158, 10.6.2013, p. 1)
Council Implementing Regulation (EU) No 663/2014
(OJ L 179, 19.6.2014, p. 4)
Act concerning the conditions of accession of the Czech Republic, the Republic of Estonia, the Republic of Cyprus, the Republic of Latvia, the Republic of Lithuania, the Republic of Hungary, the Republic of Malta, the Republic of Poland, the Republic of Slovenia and the Slovak Republic and the adjustments to the Treaties on which the European Union is founded
(OJ L 236, 23.9.2003, p. 33)

ANNEX D

Correlation table

Regulation (EC) No 1346/2000	This Regulation
Article 1	Article 1
Article 2, introductory words	Article 2, introductory words
Article 2, point (a)	Article 2, point (4)
Article 2, point (b)	Article 2, point (5)

Regulation (EC) No 1346/2000	This Regulation
Article 2, point (c)	—
Article 2, point (d)	Article 2, point (6)
Article 2, point (e)	Article 2, point (7)
Article 2, point (f)	Article 2, point (8)
Article 2, point (g), introductory words	Article 2, point (9), introductory words
Article 2, point (g), first indent	Article 2, point (9)(vii)
Article 2, point (g), second indent	Article 2, point (9)(iv)
Article 2, point (g), third indent	Article 2, point (9)(viii)
Article 2, point (h)	Article 2, point 10
—	Article 2, points (1) to (3) and (11) to (13)
—	Article 2, point (9)(i) to (iii), (v), (vi)
Article 3	Article 3
—	Article 4
—	Article 5
—	Article 6
Article 4	Article 7
Article 5	Article 8
Article 6	Article 9
Article 7	Article 10
Article 8	Article 11(1)
—	Article 11(2)
Article 9	Article 12
Article 10	Article 13(1)
—	Article 13(2)
Article 11	Article 14
Article 12	Article 15
Article 13, first indent	Article 16, point (a)
Article 13, second indent	Article 16, point (b)
Article 14, first indent	Article 17, point (a)
Article 14, second indent	Article 17, point (b)
Article 14, third indent	Article 17, point (c)
Article 15	Article 18
Article 16	Article 19
Article 17	Article 20
Article 18	Article 21
Article 19	Article 22
Article 20	Article 23
—	Article 24
—	Article 25
—	Article 26
—	Article 27
Article 21(1)	Article 28(2)
Article 21(2)	Article 28(1)
Article 22	Article 29
Article 23	Article 30
Article 24	Article 31
Article 25	Article 32
Article 26	Article 33
Article 27	Article 34
Article 28	Article 35

Regulation (EC) No 1346/2000	This Regulation
—	Article 36
Article 29	Article 37(1)
—	Article 37(2)
—	Article 38
—	Article 39
Article 30	Article 40
Article 31	Article 41
—	Article 42
—	Article 43
—	Article 44
Article 32	Article 45
Article 33	Article 46
Article 34(1)	Article 47(1)
Article 34(2)	Article 47(2)
Article 34(3)	—
—	Article 48
Article 35	Article 49
Article 36	Article 50
Article 37	Article 51
Article 38	Article 52
Article 39	Article 53
Article 40	Article 54
Article 41	Article 55
Article 42	—
—	Article 56
—	Article 57
—	Article 58
—	Article 59
—	Article 60
—	Article 61
—	Article 62
—	Article 63
—	Article 64
—	Article 65
—	Article 66
—	Article 67
—	Article 68
—	Article 69
—	Article 70
—	Article 71
—	Article 72
—	Article 73
—	Article 74
—	Article 75
—	Article 76
—	Article 77
—	Article 78
—	Article 79
—	Article 80
—	Article 81

Regulation (EC) No 1346/2000	This Regulation
—	Article 82
—	Article 83
Article 43	Article 84(1)
—	Article 84(2)
Article 44	Article 85
—	Article 86
Article 45	—
—	Article 87
—	Article 88
—	Article 89
Article 46	Article 90(1)
—	Article 90(2) to (4)
—	Article 91
Article 47	Article 92
Annex A	Annex A
Annex B	—
Annex C	Annex B
—	Annex C
—	Annex D

Index

The terms lex concursus, lex fori and lex concourses are used interchangeably in different chapters depending on the authors' preference

acquis communautaire 1.25
administration orders 5.137, 6.100, 8.10, 8.23, 8.96, 8.362–8.363, 8.426
administrative or judicial authorities 7.50, 7.54–7.65, 7.95
administrators
  appointed by a court or official body 8.08
  appointed out of court 8.04, 8.373
  asset recovery 9.41
  communication between 8.680, 8.684
  English appointments 5.19, 8.22, 8.179, 8.193, 8.208, 8.302, 8.373, 8.667
  home Member States 7.159
  Jersey 5.77
  Korean 5.104
  Original Regulation (OR) 8.395
  secondary insolvency proceedings 8.650
  Solvency II 7.159, 7.163
  temporary 5.229, 7.186, 7.196, 7.226, 8.69, 8.81, 8.437–8.440
Advocates General 2.31, 8.31, 8.84, 8.98, 8.115, 8.126, 8.371
aircraft 4.46–4.47, 4.54, 7.83, 7.98, 7.145, 7.156, 8.33, 8.253, 8.276, 8.596, 8.602
alternative investment funds (AIFs) 7.26, 7.28, 8.508
Amsterdam Treaty 2.32
ancillary proceedings
  judicial assistance 5.55–5.72
  jurisdiction to conduct 3.55–3.60
applicable law
  Original Regulation (Art 4) 8.189–8.216
    Art 4(2) OR 8.197
    Art 4(2)(d) OR 8.198
    Art 4(2)(e) OR 8.199–8.201
    Art 4(2)(f) OR 8.202–8.205
    Art 4(2)(h) OR 8.206–8.207
    Art 4(2)(i) OR 8.208
    Art 4(2)(j) OR 8.209
    Art 4(2)(k) OR 8.210
    Art 4(2)(m) OR 8.211–8.216
    Art 28 OR 8.388
    exceptions to the general rule 8.215–8.216
  Recast Regulation (RR):
    Art 6 RR, impact of 4.68
    Art 7 RR 8.584–8.586
    Art 35 RR 8.646
applicability in time
  Original Regulation (OR) 8.460–8.462
  Recast Regulation (RR) 8.799–8.800
arbitral proceedings 8.603–8.609
arbitration clauses 8.201, 8.609

assets
  English insolvency proceedings 6.114
  EU security rights 6.110–6.143, 6.154–6.158, 6.164–6.170
  Germany 6.113, 6.128–6.130, 6.143
  indefinite 6.46–6.47
  Ireland 6.112, 6.138–6.142
  Italy 6.153
  Luxembourg 6.176
  Member State in which assets are situated 8.33–8.36
    definitions 8.527–8.533
  Original Regulation (OR) 8.427–8.428
  ownership of 4.16
  Recast Regulation (RR) 8.711
  recovery of 8.292, 8.397, 8.607, 9.41
  registered 6.61
  remission of 5.33, 5.110
  right to dispose of 6.48–6.49
  rights in rem 6.85–6.86
  secondary insolvency proceedings 8.427–8.428
    assets remaining 8.427–8.428, 8.711
    staying the realization of assets 5.220–5.222
  Spain 6.111, 6.115, 6.137
  specific 6.46–6.47
  stay of the process of realization of 8.704
  surplus 5.226, 6.112, 8.427–8.428
  tangible 6.64
  United Kingdom 6.82–6.84
  United States (New York) 6.150–6.152
  'which form part of the estate' 6.18–6.21
  see also fixed charges; flawed assets; floating charges; secured assets
automatic relief 5.96–5.98
automatic stay
  cross-border regulations 6.104
  English liquidation law 6.106, 8.288–8.290
  forcible interruption of proceedings 4.56
  lex concursus 4.26
  practical examples 6.147, 6.151–6.152
  recognition, effects of 5.96
automatic stay and suspension 5.97–5.98

Balz committee 1.04, 1.19, 8.98, 8.357
bank accounts
  English 6.181–6.190
  German 6.171–6.174
  location of secured assets 6.60–6.61
  Recast Regulation (RR) 8.538–8.539
Bank Recovery and Resolution Directive (BRRD) 7.164–7.271
  cross-border group resolution (Title V) 7.249–7.257

Bank Recovery and Resolution Directive
    (BRRD) (*cont.*)
  definitions (Title I) 7.164–7.175
  early intervention (Title III) 7.183–7.187
  financing arrangements (Title VII) 7.264–7.269
  penalties (Title VIII) 7.270–7.271
  preparation (Title II) 7.176–7.182
  resolution (Title IV) 7.188–7.248
  scope (Title I) 7.164–7.175
  third countries, relations with (Title
    VI) 7.258–7.263
Banking Directive 7.04, 7.44
Banking Union 7.06–7.07
Bankruptcy Code (US) 2.28, 5.28, 5.86, 5.88, 5.103,
    6.146–6.147, 6.150–6.152, 8.107, 8.113, 9.27
Bankruptcy Convention 1.04, 1.10–1.13, 1.19, 5.116,
    5.170
banks
  common insolvency principles 7.10–7.18
  Germany 6.171–6.174
book entry securities
  location of secured assets 6.59
  Recast Regulation (RR) 8.536–8.537
branch(es): definition 7.23–7.24, 7.44, 7.48, 7.113,
    7.173, 7.249
Brexit
  Central Counterparties Regulation 7.281
  common law 5.08, 9.04
  effect of 5.117–5.123
  English assets 6.114
  English insolvency proceedings, impact of 6.134
  English scheme of arrangement 3.10, 5.164
  Exit Regulations (2019) 5.89, 5.118–5.119, 5.138,
    5.228
    bankruptcy orders 8.145
    credit institutions 8.13
    duty of cooperation 5.203
    entry into force 9.02, 9.16
    Explanatory Memorandum 5.121
    impact of 5.122
    insurance undertakings 8.10
  foreign insolvency proceedings 9.17
  implementation period 9.15–9.16
  Insolvency Proceedings Regulation, effect on 5.02,
    9.32
  legislative effect of 5.03, 8.146, 9.11
  lex causae 4.52
  Model Law/ CBIR regime 9.05–9.06, 9.15
  'no deal' Brexit 9.15
  pre-Brexit context 5.06
    duty of cooperation 5.203
    group coordination proceedings 5.216
    judgment opening insolvency proceedings 5.127
    jurisdiction of English courts 9.12–9.14
    main proceedings, opening of 5.137
    Member State liquidator's duty to inform
      creditors 5.154
    personal liability 5.194
    schemes of arrangement 5.164

  secured assets 6.91
  statutory vehicles 9.04
  time of the opening of proceedings 9.03
  'property', definition of 5.140
  Recast Regulation (RR):
    applicability 5.117
    current UK application 5.117–5.123, 9.01–9.41
    reciprocal application, changes to 5.123
    recognition and enforcement, effect on 5.123
    relevance of tests 9.07–9.14
    Retained Regulation 5.119, 6.91, 9.13
  Rome I Regulation, application of 4.33
  statutory instruments (SIs) 6.88
  third states 4.23
  transaction avoidance 4.52
  transition period 9.01–9.02, 9.16
  UNCITRAL Model Law 5.02, 5.82
  Withdrawal Agreement 5.117, 9.01
  see also **United Kingdom**
Brussels I 2.22–2.23, 2.25, 2.37, 3.09, 3.28, 3.56, 3.58–
    3.59, 4.02, 4.43, 4.60, 8.609
Brussels Convention 1.10–1.12, 1.14, 2.22, 2.23, 2.25,
    2.37, 3.56, 4.43, 5.146, 8.02, 8.49, 8.128–8.129,
    8.162, 8.354, 8.358–8.359, 8.365, 8.367, 8.639, 8.766

Central Counterparties Regulation 7.272–7.281
  settlement finality 7.35–7.37
centre of administration 1.14–1.15
Centre of main interests (COMI)
  main insolvency proceedings 8.85–8.87
  time of assessment 8.132–8.136
  right to move 8.114–8.121
choice of law rules 4.01–4.68
  exceptions 4.19–4.58
    community trademarks 4.48
    contracts of employment 4.43–4.45
    contracts relating to immovable
      property 4.40–4.41
    detrimental acts protected from
      avoidance 4.49–4.52
    effects on pending lawsuits 4.56–4.58
    European patents with unitary effect 4.48
    payment systems and financial markets 4.42
    protection of third-party purchasers 4.53–4.55
    reservation of title 4.36–4.39
    rights subject to registration 4.46–4.47
    set-off 4.31–4.35
    third parties' rights in rem 4.20–4.30
  lex concursus 4.05–4.18, 4.62
    action for performance of a contract 4.17
    asset ownership 4.16
    delineation of the scope of the RR and other fields
      of law 4.13
    guarantees, binding nature of 4.15
    time limitation 4.14
    tort cases against a third party 4.18
  material scope of 4.59–4.61
  Original Regulation (OR)
    general principles 4.02–4.03

preliminary rules 4.01–4.04, 4.59–4.61
principal amendments 4.61–4.68
renvoi 4.04
Recast Regulation (RR) 4.01–4.58
exceptions 4.63–4.67
impact on the applicable law 4.68
lex concursus 4.62
principal amendments 4.61–4.68
claims lodgement
content of lodgements 8.449–8.454
alleges preference 8.451
guarantee 8.453–8.454
security *in rem* 8.452
duty to inform creditors 8.446–8.448, 8.722–8.727
languages 8.455–8.459
Original Regulation (OR) 8.441–8.459
'*alleges preference*' 8.451
content 8.449–8.454
duty to inform creditors 8.446–8.448
'guarantee' 8.453–8.454
languages 8.455–8.459
right to lodge claims 8.441–8.445
'security in rem' 8.452
procedure for 8.728–8.736
provision of information for creditors 8.441–8.459, 8.719–8.736
right to lodge claims 8.441–8.445, 8.719–8.721
claw-back claims
judicial assistance 5.50–5.54
security over shares in EU subsidiaries 6.175–6.180
closure of insolvency proceedings
effects of closure, by composition 6.28
enforcement of insolvency practitioners' rights and powers 5.223–5.226
impact of 8.709–8.710
coercive measures 5.188–5.189, 8.322–8.325, 8.389, 8.615–8.616
common law torts
Brexit, effect of 9.33–9.41
recognition and enforcement 5.07–5.72
UK legal framework 6.94–6.98
Collateral Directive 7.38–7.40
collateral security 6.13, 6.74, 7.34
collective investment undertakings
definitions (Art 2 RR) 8.507–8.510
financial institutions excluded from RR 7.26–7.29
collective proceedings 3.06, 7.42, 7.54–7.55, 7.105, 7.167, 8.189, 8.481, 8.502–8.506
communication *see* co-operation and communication
Community legal instruments 2.01–2.42
Community legal order
interpretation 2.20–2.23
multilingualism 2.24–2.29
Community patents and trade marks
Art 12 OR 8.259
choice of law rules 4.48
location of secured assets 6.62
unitary effect 4.48, 8.597–8.599

companies *see* groups of companies
company shareholders 3.34, 4.59, 6.26, 7.184, 7.194–7.195, 7.201–7.204, 7.206–7.209, 7.217, 7.235–7.237, 7.280, 8.77, 8.521, 8.601, 8.742
company voluntary arrangements (CVAs) 2.11, 2.14, 2.26, 7.103, 7.111, 8.20, 8.146, 8.300, 8.426
competent authorities 7.61, 7.65, 7.115–7.117, 7.121, 7.123, 7.125, 7.134, 7.159, 7.162–7.163, 7.178, 7.187, 7.250–7.251, 7.254, 7.262–7.263, 7.275–7.276, 8.630, 8.761
compromise plans 6.28
confidentiality
information 5.205, 5.214, 7.263, 8.683, 8.687, 8.746, 8.752
proceedings 3.07, 6.138, 8.476
requirements 7.242, 7.254
conflict of laws *see* choice of law rules; *lex concursus*
contracts of employment *see* employment contracts
conversion
of earlier proceedings 8.432–8.436
of secondary insolvency proceedings 8.713–8.717
recognition and enforcement 5.227–5.228
co-ordination *see* co-ordinators; co-operation and communication; groups of companies
co-ordinators 8.786
appointment, revocation of 8.793–8.794
insolvency practitioners, co-operation with 8.792
objections to proposed 8.776
rights of 8.787–8.790
tasks of 8.787–8.790
co-operation and communication 8.744
costs of 8.702, 8.756
courts 5.212–5.216, 8.684–8.694, 8.750–8.753
courts and office-holders 5.113–5.114
insolvency practitioners 8.679–8.683, 8.745–8.749
co-ordinators and 8.792
courts and 8.695–8.701, 8.754–8.755
costs and expenses
advance payment of 8.394, 8.678
co-operation and communication 8.702
proceedings concerning members of a group of companies 8.756
distribution 8.796–8.797
insolvency registers 8.628
recognition of insolvency proceedings 8.349, 8.636
court(s)
co-operation and communication between 5.212–5.216, 8.684–8.694, 8.750–8.753
insolvency practitioners, co-operation with 8.695–8.701, 8.754–8.755
office-holders, co-operation with 5.113–5.114
Covid-19 pandemic 8.691
credit institutions
general provisions 8.13
Recast Regulation (RR), exclusion from 7.23–7.24
Credit Institutions Directive 5.138
creditors
duty to inform 8.446–8.448, 8.722–8.727
equal treatment of 5.196–5.201

654　INDEX

creditors (*cont.*)
　legal acts detrimental to 6.29–6.33
　provision of information for 8.441–8.459,
　　8.719–8.736
　rights, exercise of 5.217–5.219, 8.403–8.410, 8.703
　secured 6.16–6.41
　voluntary winding-up 2.11, 2.26, 6.127, 8.08, 9.08
　see also claims lodgement
cross-border security *see* security rights
current contracts 4.06, 4.10, 4.40, 6.16, 8.167, 8.199–
　8.201, 8.234, 8.295

data protection 8.797
　access to personal data 8.797
　Commission, responsibilities of the 8.797
　European e-Justice Portal 8.797
　information obligations 8.797
　Member States, responsibilities of 8.797
　national insolvency registers 8.797
　personal data storage 8.797
debt
　adjustment of 8.486–8.487
　proof of 6.23–6.24
debtor(s)
　general provisions 8.05–8.06
　honouring obligations to 8.350–8.353, 8.637
　in possession 8.511–8.512, 8.795
deemed discharge 8.341
defined insolvency proceedings 8.07
Denmark 1.02, 1.22, 2.21, 3.19, 3.22, 3.44, 4.26, 4.33,
　4.52, 5.115, 5.120, 6.15, 7.108, 8.05, 8.85, 8.284,
　8.302, 8.331, 8.445, 8.551, 8.652, 9.07
deposit guarantee schemes 7.06, 7.15, 7.194, 7.212,
　7.240, 7.251, 7.267, 7.269
detrimental acts
　Art 13 OR 8.260–8.275
　creditors 6.29–6.33
　protected from avoidance (Art 16 RR) 4.49–4.52,
　　8.600–8.601
direct applicability 2.10–2.16
direct business 7.109
direct effect 2.17–2.18
disclosure of confidential information *see*
　confidential information
distribution of proceeds 6.25–6.27
　see also remission of assets
divestment 1.24, 2.25, 3.05, 5.136, 7.167, 8.04, 8.70,
　8.72, 8.74, 8.81, 8.293, 8.306, 8.607
doctrine of supremacy 2.01
double actionability test 8.230, 8.586
Draft Convention (1960–1980) 1.08–1.18

EC Regulation on Insolvency Proceedings *see* Original
　Regulation (OR); Recast Regulation (RR)
employees 4.43–4.45, 4.64, 6.49, 7.127, 7.159, 8.55–
　8.56, 8.96, 8.252
employment contracts
　Art 10 OR 8.249–8.252
　Art 13 RR 4.43–4.45, 8.594–8.595

enforcement of insolvency judgments 8.359
English insolvency proceedings 8.08
　assets 6.114
　bank accounts 6.181–6.190
　case law 5.180–5.183
　evidence required by English courts 8.141–8.144
　impact of 6.134
　see also United Kingdom
enlargement of the European Union 1.25
equality of treatment
　creditors 5.196–5.201
establishment
　amendment of standard forms 8.805
　definitions 8.37–8.42, 8.168, 8.540–8.548
　insolvency registers 8.619–8.625
　interconnection of registers 8.804
European Central Bank (ECB) 7.06, 7.34
European Court of Justice (ECJ) 2.30–2.42
　criteria for references 2.34–2.40
　jurisdiction 2.32–2.33
　procedure 2.41–2.42
European e-Justice Portal 8.797
European integration 1.09, 1.12
European Union insolvency framework 7.01–7.09
European Union membership enlargement 1.25
excluded undertakings 8.09
exclusions from the regulation 7.19–7.29,
　8.500–8.501
　collective investment undertakings 7.26–7.29
　credit institutions 7.23–7.24
　insurance undertakings 7.20–7.22
　investment firms 7.25
expenses *see* costs and expenses

financial collateral 7.30–7.40
Financial Collateral Directive 7.38–7.40
financial institutions 7.01–7.281
　common principles 7.10–7.18
　EU framework for insolvencies 7.01–7.09
　general framework 7.01–7.18
　see also Bank Recovery and Resolution Directive
　　(BRRD); banks; Central Counterparties
　　Regulation; Collateral Directive; credit
　　institutions; Credit Institutions Directive;
　　exclusions from the regulation; Insurance
　　Directive/Solvency II; Settlement Finality
　　Directive; Winding-Up Directive; winding-
　　up proceedings
financial markets *see* payment systems and financial
　markets
financial services
　legislation 8.537
　markets 7.02
Finland 1.02, 1.04, 1.06, 2.02, 2.06, 2.28, 7.108
fixed charges 1.22
　assets 6.46
　holders 6.27
flawed assets 6.42
floating charges 1.22, 6.27, 6.49, 7.147, 8.24, 8.225

INDEX   655

assets 6.44, 6.46
security 4.29–4.30
floating charge security 4.29–4.30
foreign creditors 5.31, 5.154–5.155, 5.162, 6.24,
    6.122, 8.576, 8.725–8.726, 8.729, 8.733–8.735
definition 5.115, 5.148, 8.501
foreign insolvency practitioners 5.17, 5.149, 5.151,
    9.19
foreign insolvency proceedings 5.89–5.91
recognition of 9.17–9.32
foreign office-holders 5.12–5.20
foreign orders against third parties 5.21–5.31
forum concursus 1.18, 4.38
see also *lex concursus*
forum shopping
main insolvency proceedings 8.114–8.121
jurisdiction to conduct 3.30–3.39
see also **Centre of main interests (COMI)**
France 5.185, 6.53, 8.97–8.98, 8.125, 8.160, 8.173,
    8.237–8.238, 8.242, 8.284–8.285, 8.325, 8.476,
    8.490, 8.740

Germany 1.02, 2.02, 2.28, 4.61, 6.51, 6.53, 6.110,
    6.135–6.136, 6.171, 6.173, 8.30, 8.56, 8.68, 8.74,
    8.76, 8.97–8.98, 8.112, 8.133, 8.152, 8.155,
    8.165, 8.205, 8.288, 8.290, 8.325, 8.364, 8.373,
    8.474, 8.514
assets 6.113, 6.128–6.130, 6.143
banks 6.171–6.174
German borrowers 6.159–6.163, 6.171–6.174
good faith 4.54, 5.95, 7.71, 7.246, 8.106, 8.352
goods 8.57–8.59
groups of companies 8.737–8.797
choice of court for group co-ordination
    proceedings 8.774–8.775
co-operation and communication 8.744–8.756,
    8.792
between courts 8.750–8.753
between insolvency practitioners 8.745–8.749
between insolvency practitioners and
    co-ordinators 8.792
between insolvency practitioners and
    courts 8.754–8.755
proceedings concerning members of groups of
    companies 8.756
co-ordination 8.761
co-ordinators 8.786, 8.787–8.794
appointment, revocation of 8.793–8.794
cooperation with insolvency practitioners 8.792
tasks and rights of 8.787–8.790
consequences of objection to the inclusion in group
    co-ordination 8.772–8.773
consequences of objections to the proposed
    co-ordinator 8.776
context 8.737–8.742
costs and distribution 8.796–8.797
debtor in possession 8.795
decision to open group co-ordination
    proceedings 8.777–8.781

group co-ordination plan 8.784–8.785
group co-ordination proceedings, request to
    open 8.762–8.763
groups of companies 8.742–7.743
insolvency practitioners, powers of 8.757–8.760
languages 8.791
main insolvency proceedings 8.102–8.106
notice by the court seised 8.767–8.769
objections by insolvency practitioners 8.770–8.771
priority rule 8.764–8.766
Recast Regulation 8.737–8.797
recommendations 8.784–8.785
subsequent opt-in by insolvency
    practitioners 8.782–8.783
see also **co-ordinators**

harmonization 1.12, 1.16, 1.20, 4.36, 7.164, 7.269
head office functions test 8.94–8.101
historical outline
adoption of the EC Regulation on
    Insolvency 1.01–1.02
European Community becomes European
    Union 1.05
from Convention to Regulation 1.22–1.23
Insolvency Convention project evolution of the
    text 1.03–1.07
    Phase I Draft Convention (1960–1980) 1.08–1.18
    Phase II Convention on Insolvency Proceedings
        (1995) 1.19–1.23
Maastricht Treaty 1.05, 2.31
Original Insolvency Proceedings Regulation
    (OR) 1.19–1.23
in force 1.24–1.25
post-2002 developments 1.24–1.25
revision of the Regulation (2012–2015) 1.26–1.27
Recast Insolvency Regulation 2015 (RR) 1.28
Home Member State 3.17–3.18, 7.03, 7.48, 7.56,
    7.59–7.64, 7.67–7.68, 7.72–7.73, 7.80, 7.85,
    7.95–7.97, 7.110, 7.113, 7.116–7.163
host Member State 7.48, 7.61–7.65, 7.71, 7.85, 7.115,
    7.187
hotchpot rule 4.27, 5.114, 5.196–5.201, 8.404
human means 8.54–8.56

immovable property
contracts relating to:
    Art 8 OR 8.245–8.246
    Art 11 RR 4.40–4.41, 8.590–8.591
imputation see **return and imputation**
individual voluntary arrangements (IVAs) 2.11,
    5.228, 8.04, 8.426
information see **creditors; data protection;
    interconnection; judicial assistance; provision
    of information**
Insolvency Act 1986
common law 9.33–9.41
recognition and enforcement 5.73–5.81
UK legal framework 6.99–6.102
Insolvency Convention project 1.03, 1.07, 2.23, 4.29

insolvency practitioner(s)
  appointment 8.612–8.617
    proof of 5.149–5.150
  co-operation 8.679–8.683, 8.745–8.749
    between insolvency practitioners 5.202–5.211
    with co-ordinators 8.792
    with courts 5.212–5.216, 8.695–8.701, 8.754–8.755
    with groups of companies 8.745–8.749
  definitions 8.516–8.518
  enforcement of rights and powers of 5.184–5.232
    closure of insolvency proceedings 5.223–5.226
    conversion of secondary insolvency proceedings 5.227–5.228
    duty of cooperation 5.202–5.216
    equal treatment of creditors (hotchpot rule) 5.196–5.201
    exercise of creditors' rights 5.217–5.219
    preservation measures 5.229–5.232
    staying the realization of assets in secondary proceedings 5.220–5.222
  foreign 5.17, 5.149, 5.151, 9.19
  objections by 8.770–8.771
  rights and powers 8.757–8.760
    enforcement of 5.184–5.232
    powers 5.184–5.195
    to propose restructuring plans 8.705–8.708
  subsequent opt-in by 8.782–8.783
Insolvency Proceedings Regulation
  background 2.01–2.05
  definition 2.19–2.29
  as an EU legal instrument 2.01–2.42
  interpretative issues 2.30–2.42
    CJEU 2.30–2.42
    criteria for references 2.34–2.40
    EU legal order 2.20–2.23
    jurisdiction 2.32–2.33
    multilingual legal order 2.24–2.29
    procedure 2.41–2.42
  legal attributes 2.06–2.18
    direct applicability 2.10–2.16
    direct effect 2.17–2.18
insolvency registers
  establishment of 8.619–8.625
    costs 8.628
  interconnection of 8.626–8.627
    costs 8.628
  personal data, processing of 8.797
Insolvency Regulation *see* Original Regulation (OR); Recast Regulation (RR)
Insurance Directive/Solvency II 7.04–7.05, 7.21, 7.101–7.163
  scope 7.101–7.105
  selective commentary 7.106–7.163
insurance undertakings
  exclusion from RR 7.20–7.22
  general provisions 8.10–8.12
  see also financial institutions
intellectual property rights 4.23, 4.48, 8.215, 8.259, 8.539

interconnection
  conditions of access 8.629–8.630
  of insolvency registers 8.626–8.627
    costs 8.628
  establishment 8.804
intercreditor agreements 6.164–6.170
international jurisdiction
  Original Regulation (OR) 8.60–8.188
    avoiding secondary proceedings 8.178–8.180
    'establishment' 8.168
    insolvency proceedings limited to the territory of a Member State 8.166–8.188
    'opening', concept of 8.65–8.84
    pre-main Art 3(2) proceedings 8.181–8.188
    secondary Art 3(2) proceedings 8.172–8.177
    separate proceedings are permitted 8.64
    single proceedings with a universal effect 8.63
    terminated activities 8.169–8.171
  Recast Regulation (RR) 8.549–8.571
    context 8.549–8.552
    presumptions 8.553–8.563
    territorial insolvency proceedings 8.564–8.571
  scope and jurisdiction 3.23–3.69
    forum shopping 3.30–3.39
    further conditions to opening territorial proceedings 3.43–3.48
    grounds of jurisdiction 3.24–3.29, 3.40–3.42
    jurisdiction to conduct ancillary proceedings 3.55–3.60
    jurisdiction to conduct group co-ordination proceedings 3.66–3.69
    jurisdiction to conduct main insolvency proceedings 3.24–3.39
    jurisdiction to conduct territorial insolvency proceedings 3.40–3.54
    jurisdiction to order protective and preservation measures 3.61–3.65
    scope of territorial proceedings 3.49–3.54
interpretation
  Court of Justice of the EU 2.30–2.42
    criteria for references 2.34–2.40
    jurisdiction 2.32–2.33
  EU legal order 2.20–2.23
  multilingual legal order 2.24–2.29
investment firms 7.25
investment funds 7.26–7.28, 8.508
'investment services and activities' 7.25, 7.43, 7.169
investment undertakings 3.17, 8.09, 8.162, 8.500, 8.581
  see also collective investment undertakings
Ireland, Republic of 1.06, 2.04, 3.22, 4.29, 4.31, 5.73, 6.99–6.100, 6.170, 6.190, 8.67–8.68, 8.74–8.75, 8.80, 8.84, 8.225, 8.325, 8.464, 8.477, 8.490, 8.545, 9.33
  assets in 6.112, 6.138–6.142, 6.164–6.165, 6.168–6.169
  establishments 6.110–6.143, 6.181–6.190
  German bank branches 6.171–6.174
  no territorial or secondary proceedings 6.118–6.125, 6.138–6.141

INDEX 657

territorial or secondary proceedings 6.126–6.127, 6.142
Istanbul Convention 1.04, 1.19, 5.149
Italy 6.148–6.149, 6.159, 6.161, 6.163, 8.92, 8.514, 8.599
  assets 6.153

'judgment': definitions 8.25–8.27
judgments
  categorization of 8.360–8.361
  mode of enforcement of insolvency judgments 8.359
  opening insolvency proceedings 8.522–8.525
  recognition and enforceability of other judgments 8.637–8.641
  recognition of 5.163–5.167
    'dovetailing' principle 5.169–5.183
    CJEU case law 5.177–5.179
    English case law 5.180–5.183
    insolvency judgments 8.354–8.357
    non-insolvency judgments 8.358
    Recast Judgments Regulation 5.168
    under the RR 5.163–5.183
judicial assistance
  ancillary insolvency proceedings 5.55–5.72
  claw-back claims 5.50–5.54
  general principles 5.32–5.39
  obtaining information 5.45–5.49
  stay of proceedings and related relief 5.40–5.44
judicial review
  of the decision to open main insolvency proceedings 8.576–8.578
  of the decision to open secondary insolvency proceedings 8.676–8.677
junior lenders 6.164, 6.169, 6.170
jurisdictional provisions 1.14, 2.14, 5.03
  see also international jurisdiction

'known creditors' 6.24, 7.63, 7.68, 8.446, 8.735

land and trade registers 7.96
languages 8.455–8.459, 8.791
lawsuits pending see pending lawsuits
legal attributes 2.06–2.18
  direct applicability 2.10–2.16
  direct effect 2.17–2.18
letterbox companies 5.13, 8.51, 8.92
lex causae 4.10–4.11, 4.14, 4.17, 4.28, 4.50, 4.52, 6.31–6.33, 6.48, 6.76, 8.262, 8.266–8.268
lex concursus 4.05–4.18, 4.62
  action for performance of a contract 4.17
  asset ownership 4.16
  delineation of the scope of the RR and other fields of law 4.13
  guarantees, binding nature of 4.15
  time limitation 4.14
  tort cases against a third party 4.18
lex domus 7.67, 7.69, 7.73–7.74, 7.79–7.81, 7.89, 7.92, 7.95, 7.97–7.99, 7.124–7.126, 7.138, 7.142, 7.146, 7.158

lex fori 3.33–3.35, 3.39, 3.52, 4.05, 4.14, 6.32, 8.166, 8.263, 8.291
lex fori concursus 3.12, 3.14, 3.30, 3.38, 3.47, 3.48, 3.59, 3.61, 4.49, 6.13, 6.32, 6.38, 6.48, 6.68, 6.75, 6.82, 6.85, 6.119, 6.153, 8.262, 8.271, 8.278, 8.601
lex fori processus 8.278, 8.291, 8.295
lex rei sitae 6.39, 6.49, 6.74, 6.82, 6.83, 6.140–6.141, 7.85, 7.98, 8.222
lex situs 2.27, 4.21–4.22, 4.27, 4.30, 4.37, 4.40, 4.54, 6.13, 6.68, 8.225
life insurance 7.21–7.22, 7.101, 7.113, 7.158, 8.11
Life Insurance Directive 7.21
liquidation 8.486–8.487
  stay of 8.410–8.419
liquidators(s)
  appointment, proof of 8.330
  powers 8.314–8.329
    Art 3(2) OR proceedings 8.327–8.329
    main proceedings 8.314–8.326
local creditors 1.16, 3.47, 3.64–3.65, 5.12, 5.39, 5.44, 5.115, 5.219, 5.221, 5.227, 8.178–8.179, 8.185, 8.193, 8.208, 8.342, 8.392, 8.413, 8.418, 8.432, 8.498, 8.543, 8.649, 8.651, 8.655, 8.657, 8.659–8.660, 8.662, 8.669–8.675, 8.715
local practices 1.17
lodgement of claims see claims lodgement
Lugano Convention 2.23, 5.164, 8.02, 8.165
Luxembourg 4.29, 5.62–5.63, 6.58, 6.175, 6.177–6.178, 6.180, 7.108, 7.192, 8.48, 8.112, 8.157, 8.281, 8.285
  assets 6.176
  borrowers 6.181–6.190

Maastricht Treaty 1.02, 1.05, 4.33
main insolvency proceedings
  jurisdiction to conduct 3.24–3.39
    forum shopping 3.30–3.39
    grounds of jurisdiction 3.24–3.29
  Original Regulation (OR) 8.85–8.165
    centre of main interests (COMI) 8.85–8.87
    conflicting decisions, risk of 8.123–8.131
    evidence required by an English court 8.141–8.144
    forum shopping 8.114–8.121
    groups of companies 8.102–8.106
    head office functions test 8.94–8.101
    legal persons 8.92–8.93
    natural persons 8.108–8.113
    potential conflict with non-EU jurisdictions 8.140
    presumption under the UNCITRAL Model Law 8.107
    Recital (13), role of 8.88–8.91
    right to move COMI 8.114–8.121
    scope of insolvency proceedings 8.147–8.165
    specifying type of proceeding requested 8.137–8.139
    statutory changes in England 8.145–8.146

main insolvency proceedings (cont.)
  terminated activities 8.122
  time at which COMI is assessed 8.132–8.136
  Recast Regulation (RR):
    judicial review of the decision to
      open 8.576–8.578
    subsequent opening of 8.712
Member States of the European Union
  insolvency proceedings limited to the territory of a
      Member State 8.166–8.188
    avoiding secondary proceedings 8.178–8.180
    'establishment' 8.168
    pre-main Art 3(2) proceedings 8.181–8.188
    secondary Art 3(2) proceedings 8.172–8.177
    terminated activities 8.169–8.171
  Member State in which assets are situated 8.33–8.36
  publication in another Member State 8.631–8.634
  registration in public registers of another Member
      State 8.635
  responsibilities for personal data in national
      insolvency registers 8.797
members' voluntary winding-up 8.04
multilingual legal order 2.24–2.29

national courts 1.23, 2.17, 2.24, 2.31–2.32, 2.34, 2.38,
    2.40–2.42, 3.14, 3.26, 3.29, 5.176, 6.08, 6.32, 7.244,
    8.01, 8.128, 8.176, 8.395, 8.684, 8.686, 8.704, 9.13
natural persons 8.108–8.113
negative conflict rule 8.218
Netherlands 1.06, 4.31, 6.58, 6.154, 6.156, 8.68, 8.188,
    8.227, 8.237, 8.252, 8.474, 8.514, 8.571
netting arrangements 4.42, 7.16, 7.33, 7.39, 7.85, 7.89,
    7.92–7.93, 7.152, 7.194, 7.226–7.227, 7.238,
    7.240, 7.247, 8.593
non-financial difficulties 8.499
non-insolvency judgments 8.358
non-proprietary rights 8.452
notice by the court seised 8.767–8.769

'opening', concept of 8.65–8.84
  argument based on Art 38 OR 8.80–8.83
  effectiveness, principle of 8.79
  'relation back' theory 8.84
opening of insolvency proceedings
  Brexit, impact of 9.31
  choice of law rules 4.06, 4.11, 4.22, 4.25, 4.27–4.28,
      4.36, 4.38, 4.49, 4.53–4.54
  financial institutions 7.33, 7.71
  Original Regulation (OR) 8.80, 8.128, 8.132, 8.154,
      8.188, 8.198, 8.232, 8.234, 8.264–8.265, 8.350,
      8.354, 8.357, 8.364, 8.554, 8.561, 8.571, 8.631,
      8.734
  recognition and enforcement 5.119, 5.133, 5.152,
      5.159, 5.164, 5.187, 5.190–5.191, 5.193, 5.195,
      5.199, 5.229
  scope and jurisdiction 3.44, 3.62–3.63
  security rights 6.10, 6.13, 6.16, 6.20, 6.24, 6.35–
      6.36, 6.49, 6.54, 6.74, 6.76, 6.81, 6.124, 6.149,
      6.177, 6.184

see also main insolvency proceedings; secondary
    insolvency proceedings
Original Regulation (OR) 8.01–8.470
  arbitrations 8.294–8.295
  claims lodgement Original Regulation
      (OR) 8.441–8.459
    'alleges preference' 8.451
    content 8.449–8.454
    duty to inform creditors 8.446–8.448
    'guarantee' 8.453–8.454
    languages 8.455–8.459
    right to lodge claims 8.441–8.445
    'security in rem' 8.452
  community patents and trade marks 8.259
  contracts of employment 8.249–8.252
  contracts relating to immoveable
      property 8.245–8.246
  definitions 8.16–8.59
    'court' 8.17–8.24
    'establishment' 8.37–8.42
    goods 8.57–8.59
    human means 8.54–8.56
    'judgment' 8.25–8.27
    Member State in which assets are
        situated 8.33–8.36
    place of operations 8.43–8.53
    time of the opening of proceedings 8.28–8.32
  detrimental acts 8.260–8.275
  effect of applying Art 15 OR 8.286–8.291
  effects of insolvency proceedings on lawsuits
      pending 8.278–8.295
  effects on rights subject to registration 8.253–8.258
  general provisions 8.01–8.15
    credit institutions 8.13
    debtor 8.05–8.06
    defined insolvency proceedings 8.07
    English insolvency proceedings 8.08
    excluded undertakings 8.09
    general principles 8.01–8.04
    insurance undertakings 8.10–8.12
    intra-Union effects 8.14–8.15
  international jurisdiction 8.60–8.188
    avoiding secondary proceedings 8.178–8.180
    'establishment' 8.168
    insolvency proceedings limited to the territory of
        a Member State 8.166–8.188
    'opening', concept of 8.65–8.84
    pre-main Art 3(2) proceedings 8.181–8.188
    secondary Art 3(2) proceedings 8.172–8.177
    separate proceedings are permitted 8.64
    single proceedings with a universal effect 8.63
    terminated activities 8.169–8.171
  law applicable 8.189–8.216
    Art 4(2) OR 8.197
    Art 4(2)(d) OR 8.198
    Art 4(2)(e) OR 8.199–8.201
    Art 4(2)(f) OR 8.202–8.205
    Art 4(2)(h) OR 8.206–8.207
    Art 4(2)(i) OR 8.208

INDEX 659

Art 4(2)(j) OR 8.209
Art 4(2)(k) OR 8.210
Art 4(2)(m) OR 8.211–8.216
 exceptions to the general rule 8.215–8.216
main insolvency proceedings 8.85–8.165
 centre of main interests (COMI) 8.85–8.87
 conflicting decisions, risk of 8.123–8.131
 evidence required by an English court 8.141–8.144
 forum shopping 8.114–8.121
 groups of companies 8.102–8.106
 head office functions test 8.94–8.101
 legal persons 8.92–8.93
 natural persons 8.108–8.113
 potential conflict with non-EU jurisdictions 8.140
 presumption under the UNCITRAL Model Law 8.107
 Recital (13), role of 8.88–8.91
 right to move COMI 8.114–8.121
 scope of insolvency proceedings 8.147–8.165
 specifying type of proceeding requested 8.137–8.139
 statutory changes in England 8.145–8.146
 terminated activities 8.122
 time at which COMI is assessed 8.132–8.136
'opening', concept of 8.65–8.84
 argument based on Art 38 OR 8.80–8.83
 effectiveness, principle of 8.79
 'relation back' theory 8.84
payment systems and financial markets 8.247–8.248
proprietary claims 8.292–8.293
recognition of insolvency proceedings 8.296–8.374
 Art 3(2) OR proceedings 8.327–8.329
 categorization of judgments 8.360–8.361
 costs 8.349
 effects 8.305–8.313
 enforceability of other judgments 8.354–8.364
 extent 8.301–8.304
 honouring of an obligation to a debtor 8.350–8.353
 insolvency judgments 8.354–8.357
 key points 8.362–8.364
 liquidators, powers of 8.314–8.329
 main proceedings 8.314–8.326
 mode of enforcement 8.359
 non-insolvency judgments 8.358
 principle 8.296–8.304
 proof of liquidator's appointment (Art 19) 8.330
 public policy 8.365–8.374
 public registers 8.344–8.348
 publication 8.336–8.343
 recognition 8.354–8.364
 return and imputation 8.331–8.335
reservation of title 8.241–8.244
secondary insolvency proceedings 8.375–8.440
 advance payment of costs and expenses 8.394
 applicable law 8.388
 assets remaining in 8.427–8.428
 conversion of earlier proceedings 8.432–8.436
 duty to cooperate and communicate information 8.395–8.402
 exercise of creditors' rights 8.403–8.410
 measures ending 8.420–8.426
 opening of proceedings 8.377–8.387
 preservation measures 8.437–8.440
 right to request the opening of proceedings 8.389–8.393
 stay of liquidation 8.410–8.419
 subsequent opening of main proceedings 8.429–8.432
 set-off 8.232–8.240
 third parties' rights in rem 8.217–8.231
 third-party purchasers, protection of 8.276–8.277
 transitional and final provisions 8.460–8.470
  amendment of the annexes 8.465–8.467
  applicability in time 8.460–8.462
  entry into force 8.469–8.470
  relationship to Conventions 8.463–8.464
  reports 8.468
 see also Recast Regulation (RR); recognition of insolvency proceedings; secondary insolvency proceedings

pandemic *see* Covid-19 pandemic
parent undertaking 5.115, 7.43, 7.178, 7.187, 7.249, 7.251–7.253, 7.256, 8.500, 8.742
patents
 community patents and trade marks 8.259, 8.597–8.599
 European patents 6.62
 with unitary effect 4.48, 8.597–8.599
payment systems and financial markets
 Art 9 OR 8.247–8.248
 Art 12 RR 8.592–8.593
 choice of law rule 4.42
pending lawsuits
 effects on 4.56–4.58
 Art 15 OR 8.278–8.295
 Art 18 RR 8.603–8.609
personal data *see* data protection
place of operations 8.43–8.53
preferential claims 5.81, 6.27
preferential creditors 1.16, 6.27, 6.124, 8.213, 8.659
Preliminary Draft Convention (1970) 1.03, 1.08
preservation measures
 Art 38 OR 8.437–8.440
 Art 52 RR 5.229–5.232, 8.718
 jurisdiction to order 3.61–3.65
principle of single entity 7.13, 7.47, 7.59, 7.170, 7.257
principle of unity 1.16–1.18, 3.17–3.18, 3.53–3.54, 3.60, 7.11, 7.59, 7.106, 7.167, 8.178, 8.649, 8.692
principle of universality 1.16–1.18, 3.17–3.18, 3.26, 3.30, 3.53–3.54, 3.60, 7.12, 7.59, 7.107, 8.63–8.64, 9.28, 9.36–9.37
priority of claims *see* distribution of proceeds; preferential creditors; security rights; unsecured creditors

priority rule 8.764–8.766
professional secrecy 7.161
proof of debt 6.23–6.24
proprietary claims 8.292–8.293
proprietary rights 5.191, 7.85, 7.92–7.93, 8.292, 8.333, 8.452
provision of information *see* claims lodgement; creditors
provisional liquidators 1.24, 5.19, 5.147, 5.232, 7.125, 8.04, 8.68–8.69, 8.74–8.80, 8.83–8.84, 8.128, 8.164, 8.438, 8.483, 8.517
public policy
   Art 26 OR 8.365–8.374
   Art 33 RR 8.642
     exception to recognition 5.142–5.148
public proceedings 8.475–8.476
public registers 8.344–8.348
   another Member State 8.635
publication of proceedings
   another Member State 8.631–8.634
   Art 21 OR 8.336–8.343
   recognition under the RR (Arts 24–29) 5.151–5.162
publicity principle 1.04, 3.07, 7.106, 7.135, 8.475
purposive interpretation 1.23, 2.05, 4.67, 5.103, 8.02
purposive statutory construction 2.26, 8.01

Recast Regulation (RR) 8.472–8.816
   claims lodgement 8.719–8.736
     right to lodge claims 8.719–8.721
     duty to inform creditors 8.722–8.727
     procedure 8.728–8.736
   data protection 8.797
     access to personal data 8.797
     Commission, responsibilities of the 8.797
     European e-Justice Portal 8.797
     information obligations 8.797
     Member States, responsibilities of 8.797
     national insolvency registers 8.797
     personal data storage 8.797
   definitions 8.502–8.548
     bank accounts 8.538–8.539
     book entry securities 8.536–8.537
     collective investment undertakings 8.507–8.510
     collective proceedings 8.503–8.506
     'court' 8.519–8.521
     debtor in possession 8.511–8.512
     'establishment' 8.540–8.548
     insolvency practitioners 8.516–8.518
     insolvency proceedings 8.513–8.515
     judgment opening insolvency proceedings 8.522–8.525
     Member State in which assets are situated 8.527–8.533
     registered shares 8.534–8.535
     time of the opening of proceedings 8.526
   examination as to jurisdiction 8.572–8.575
     good practice 8.573–8.575
   general provisions 8.471–8.609
     applicable law 8.584–8.586
     arbitral proceedings 8.603–8.609
     Community trade marks 8.597–8.599
     detrimental acts 8.600–8.601
     effects on rights subject to registration 8.596
     employment contracts 8.594–8.595
     European patents with unitary effect 8.597–8.599
     immoveable property, contracts relating to 8.590–8.591
     judicial review of decision to open main insolvency proceedings 8.576–8.578
     jurisdiction for actions deriving directly from insolvency proceedings 8.579–8.583
     payment systems and financial markets 8.592–8.593
     pending lawsuits 8.603–8.609
     reservation of title 8.589
     set-off 8.588
     third parties' rights in rem 8.587
     third-party purchasers, protection of 8.602
   groups of companies 8.737–8.797
     co-operation and communication 8.744–8.756, 8.792
     co-ordination 8.761
     co-ordinators 8.786, 8.787–8.794
     choice of court for group co-ordination proceedings 8.774–8.775
     consequences of objection to the inclusion in group co-ordination 8.772–8.773
     consequences of objections to the proposed co-ordinator 8.776
     context 8.737–8.742
     costs and distribution 8.796–8.797
     debtor in possession 8.795
     decision to open group co-ordination proceedings 8.777–8.781
     group co-ordination plan 8.784–8.785
     group co-ordination proceedings, request to open 8.762–8.763
     groups of companies 8.742–7.743
     insolvency practitioners, powers of 8.757–8.760
     languages 8.791
     main insolvency proceedings 8.102–8.106
     notice by the court seised 8.767–8.769
     objections by insolvency practitioners 8.770–8.771
     priority rule 8.764–8.766
     Recast Regulation 8.737–8.797
     recommendations 8.784–8.785
     subsequent opt-in by insolvency practitioners 8.782–8.783
   international jurisdiction 8.549–8.571
     context 8.549–8.552
     presumptions 8.553–8.563
     territorial insolvency proceedings 8.564–8.571
   scope 8.471–8.501
     adjustment of debt 8.486–8.487
     'based on laws relating to insolvency' 8.484–8.485

INDEX 661

collective proceedings 8.477–8.481
exclusions 8.500–8.501
interim proceedings 8.482–8.483
liquidation 8.486–8.487
non-financial difficulties 8.499
public proceedings 8.475–8.476
reorganization 8.486–8.487
tripartite nature of proceedings 8.488–8.498
secondary insolvency proceedings 8.643–8.718
advance payment of costs and expenses 8.678
applicable law 8.646
assets remaining 8.711
conversion 8.713–8.717
co-operation and communication 8.679–8.701
costs of co-operation and communication 8.702
decision to open 8.667–8.675
exercise of creditors' rights 8.703
impact of closure of insolvency proceedings 8.709–8.710
judicial review of the decision to open 8.676–8.677
opening of proceedings 8.643–8.645
power of insolvency practitioners to propose restructuring plans 8.705–8.708
preservation measures 8.718
right to give an undertaking in order to avoid 8.647–8.662
right to request the opening of 8.663–8.666
stay of the process of realization of assets 8.704
subsequent opening of main insolvency proceedings 8.712
transitional and final provisions 8.799–8.816
applicability in time 8.799–8.800
committee procedure 8.806
entry into force 8.814–8.816
information on national and Union insolvency law 8.803
interconnection of registers, establishment of 8.804
relationship to Conventions 8.801–8.802
repeal 8.812–8.813
review clause 8.807–8.811
standard forms, establishment and amendment of 8.805
see also data protection; co-operation and communication; groups of companies; Original Regulation (OR); recognition of insolvency proceedings; secondary insolvency proceedings
receivership 8.04, 8.477
Recitals to the OR and RR 1.23, 1.28, 2.27–2.28, 3.26, 3.32–3.33, 3.35, 5.204, 5.208, 6.11–6.12, 6.54, 8.01–8.02, 8.550, 8.747, 8.753, 8.780
recognition of insolvency proceedings 5.01–5.232
context 5.01–5.05
insolvency practitioners, enforcement of rights and powers of 5.184–5.232
closure of insolvency proceedings 5.223–5.226
conversion of secondary insolvency proceedings 5.227–5.228
cooperation and communication between courts 5.212–5.216
cooperation and communication between insolvency practitioners 5.202–5.211
duty of cooperation 5.202–5.216
equal treatment of creditors (hotchpot rule) 5.196–5.201
exercise of creditors' rights 5.217–5.219
powers of the insolvency practitioner 5.184–5.195
preservation measures 5.229–5.232
staying the realization of assets in secondary proceedings 5.220–5.222
Original Regulation (OR) 8.296–8.374
Art 3(2) OR proceedings 8.327–8.329
categorization of judgments 8.360–8.361
costs 8.349
effects 8.305–8.313
enforceability of other judgments 8.354–8.364
extent 8.301–8.304
honouring of an obligation to a debtor 8.350–8.353
insolvency judgments 8.354–8.357
key points 8.362–8.364
liquidators, powers of 8.314–8.329
main proceedings 8.314–8.326
mode of enforcement 8.359
non-insolvency judgments 8.358
principle 8.296–8.304
proof of liquidator's appointment (Art 19) 8.330
public policy 8.365–8.374
public registers 8.344–8.348
publication 8.336–8.343
recognition 8.354–8.364
return and imputation 8.331–8.335
outside the regulation 5.06–5.114
ancillary insolvency proceedings 5.55–5.72
claw-back claims 5.50–5.54
common law 5.07–5.72
general principles 5.32–5.39
Insolvency Act (1986) 5.73–5.81
obtaining information 5.45–5.49
recognizing the authority of a foreign office-holder 5.12–5.20
recognizing foreign orders against third parties 5.21–5.31
stay of proceedings and related relief 5.40–5.44
Recast Regulation (RR) 5.115–5.183, 8.610–8.642
Brexit, effect of 5.117–5.123
CJEU case law 5.177–5.179
costs 8.636
'dovetailing' principle 5.169–5.183
effects of recognition 5.133–5.141, 8.611
enforcement 5.168
English case law 5.180–5.183
general principle of recognition 5.214–5.132
honouring of an obligation to a debtor 8.637

recognition of insolvency proceedings (*cont.*)
  insolvency practitioners, appointment and
    powers of 8.612–8.617
  insolvency registers 8.619–8.628
  interaction with the Recast Judgments
    Regulation 5.168
  interconnection, system of 8.629–8.630
  judgments outside the Regulation 5.169–5.183
  principle 8.610
  proof of insolvency practitioner's
    appointment 5.149–5.150
  public policy 8.642
  public policy exception to
    recognition 5.142–5.148
  publication in another Member
    State 8.631–8.634
  publication and registration 5.151–5.162
  recognition and enforceability of other
    judgments 8.637–8.641
  recognition of judgments 5.163–5.167
  registration in public registers of another
    Member State 8.635
  return and imputation 8.618
  terminology, use of 5.115–5.116
  UK application 5.117–5.123
  UNCITRAL Model Law 5.82–5.114
    automatic relief 5.96–5.98
    conditions for recognition 5.92–5.95
    cooperation between courts and
      office-holders 5.113–5.114
    discretionary relief 5.99–5.110
    effects of recognition 5.96–5.110
    foreign main proceeding 5.89–5.91
    non-main proceeding 5.89–5.91
    origins and enactment 5.82–5.85
    rights of direct access and
      intervention 5.111–5.112
    scope 5.86–5.88
registered assets 6.61
registered shares
  definitions 8.534–8.535
  location of secured assets 6.58
registers *see* insolvency registers; interconnection;
  public registers
registration of proceedings
  public registers 8.344–8.348
    another Member State 8.635
  publication and 5.151–5.162
  rights subject to 4.46–4.47
  effects on 8.253–8.258, 8.596
regulated markets 7.85, 7.94, 7.151, 7.153
reinsurance 5.65, 7.22, 7.101, 7.108–7.109, 7.130, 8.12
Reinsurance Directive *see* Insurance Directive/
  Solvency II
'relation back' theory 6.71, 8.84
remission of assets 5.33, 5.110
  see also distribution of proceeds
renvoi 4.04
reorganization measures 7.59–7.65
repeal 8.812–8.813
reports 8.468

repos 7.92–7.93
repurchase agreements 6.42, 7.85, 7.89, 7.91–7.92,
  7.152, 7.231
rescue 8.486–8.487
reservation of title
  Art 7 OR 8.241–8.244
  Art 10 RR 8.589
return and imputation
  Art 20 OR 8.331–8.335
  Art 23 RR 8.618
review clause 8.807–8.811
right to lodge claims
  Art 39 OR 8.441–8.445
  Art 53 RR 8.719–8.721
rights in rem
  assets located in the EU 6.85–6.86
  definition of 4.28, 6.42–6.55
    CJEU case law 6.51–6.55
    other rights 6.50
    right to dispose of assets and to obtain
      satisfaction from the proceeds 6.48–6.49
    specific assets and collections of indefinite
      assets 6.46–6.47
  security in rem 8.452
  third parties 4.20–4.30
    Art 5 OR 8.217–8.231
    Art 8 RR 8.587
    floating charge security 4.29–4.30
    situs of property 4.24
    time factor 4.25–4.27
rights subject to registration
  choice of law rule 4.46–4.47
  effects on 8.253–8.258, 8.596
Rome Convention 4.04, 4.33, 8.251

schemes of arrangement 5.34, 5.56, 5.86, 5.126, 5.164,
  7.111, 8.485, 8.551
scope and jurisdiction 3.01–3.69
  forum shopping 3.30–3.39
  grounds of jurisdiction 3.24–3.29, 3.40–3.42
  international jurisdiction 3.23–3.69
  jurisdiction to conduct:
    ancillary proceedings 3.55–3.60
    co-ordination proceedings 3.66–3.69
    main insolvency proceedings 3.24–3.39
    territorial insolvency proceedings 3.40–3.54
  jurisdiction to order protective and preservation
    measures 3.61–3.65
  scope of the RR 3.01–3.22
    material scope 3.03–3.14
    personal scope 3.15–3.18
    preliminary rules 3.01–3.02
    territorial scope 3.19–3.22
  territorial proceedings:
    further conditions to opening 3.43–3.48
    jurisdiction to conduct 3.40–3.54
    scope of 3.49–3.54
  see also Original Regulation (OR); Recast
    Regulation (RR)
secondary insolvency proceedings
  Original Regulation (OR) 8.375–8.440

advance payment of costs and expenses 8.394
applicable law 8.388
assets remaining in 8.427–8.428
conversion of earlier proceedings 8.432–8.436
duty to cooperate and communicate information 8.395–8.402
exercise of creditors' rights 8.403–8.410
measures ending 8.420–8.426
opening of proceedings 8.377–8.387
preservation measures 8.437–8.440
right to request the opening of proceedings 8.389–8.393
stay of liquidation 8.410–8.419
subsequent opening of main proceedings 8.429–8.432
Recast Regulation (RR) 8.643–8.718
advance payment of costs and expenses 8.678
applicable law 8.646
assets remaining 8.711
conversion 8.713–8.717
co-operation and communication 8.679–8.701
costs of co-operation and communication 8.702
decision to open 8.667–8.675
exercise of creditors' rights 8.703
impact of closure of insolvency proceedings 8.709–8.710
judicial review of the decision to open 8.676–8.677
opening of proceedings 8.643–8.645
power of insolvency practitioners to propose restructuring plans 8.705–8.708
preservation measures 8.718
right to give an undertaking in order to avoid 8.647–8.662
right to request the opening of 8.663–8.666
stay of the process of realization of assets 8.704
subsequent opening of main insolvency proceedings 8.712
secured assets
location of 6.56–6.68
bank accounts 6.60–6.61
book entry securities 6.59
claims 6.65–6.68
copyrights 6.63
European patents 6.62
registered assets 6.61
registered shares 6.58
tangible assets 6.64
outside the RR 6.92–6.93
secured creditors
articles of relevance to 6.16–6.41, 6.50
assets which form part of the estate 6.18–6.21
distribution of proceeds (questions of priority) 6.25–6.27
effects of closure on insolvency proceedings 6.28
other matters not expressly covered by Article 7(2) 6.34
proof of debt 6.23–6.24
stay of enforcement proceedings 6.22
unenforceability of legal acts 6.29–6.33
voidness and voidability 6.29–6.33

security agreements 6.10, 6.134, 6.139, 6.143, 6.171
security rights 6.01–6.190
bank accounts 6.60–6.61
book entry securities 6.59
claims 6.65–6.68
claw-back claims 6.175–6.180
context 6.01–6.10
copyrights 6.63
European patents 6.62
European Union:
assets 6.110–6.143, 6.154–6.158, 6.164–6.170
establishments outside 6.144–6.153
law 6.144–6.153
legal framework 6.11–6.86
Germany:
assets 6.113, 6.128–6.130, 6.143
banks 6.171–6.174
German borrowers 6.159–6.163, 6.171–6.174
intercreditor agreement 6.164–6.170
Ireland:
assets 6.112, 6.138–6.142
establishments 6.110–6.143, 6.181–6.190
German bank branches 6.171–6.174
no territorial or secondary proceedings 6.118–6.125, 6.138–6.141
territorial or secondary proceedings 6.126–6.127, 6.142
Italy:
assets 6.153
local law security 6.110–6.134
location of secured assets 6.56–6.68
Luxembourg:
assets 6.176
borrowers 6.181–6.190
non-EU law 6.144–6.153
practical examples 6.110–6.190
Recast Regulation (RR):
Articles 8 and 16, relationship between 6.80–6.81
insolvency proceedings to which the RR applies 6.14–6.15
purposes 6.11–6.13
recognition of EU insolvency proceedings outside 6.92–6.93
UK status 6.87–6.91
rights in rem, definition of 6.42–6.55
CJEU case law 6.51–6.55
collections of indefinite assets 6.46–6.47
other rights 6.50
right to dispose of assets and to obtain satisfaction from the proceeds 6.48–6.49
specific assets 6.46–6.47
registered assets 6.61
registered shares 6.58
secured creditors *see* **secured creditors**
secured indebtedness 6.154–6.158
security over shares in an EU subsidiary 6.175–6.180
set-off rights 6.181–6.190
'shall not affect', definition of 6.74–6.79
Spain:
assets 6.111, 6.115, 6.137

security rights (*cont.*)
  borrowers 6.110–6.158, 6.164–6.170, 6.175–6.180
  establishments 6.159–6.163
  insolvency or preventive restructuring proceedings 6.117
  law security 6.135–6.143
  no main proceedings 6.116
  proceedings, recognition of 6.131–6.133
  restructuring proceedings 6.159–6.163
  tangible assets 6.64
  'time of the opening of proceedings', definition of 6.69–6.73
  United Kingdom:
    assets in England 6.114
    assets located in 6.82–6.84
    common law 6.94–6.98
    Cross-Border Regulations 6.103–6.109
    effects on rights in rem over assets located in the EU 6.85–6.86
    English bank accounts 6.181–6.190
    English insolvency proceedings 6.134
    Insolvency Act (1986)(s 426) 6.99–6.102
    legal framework 6.87–6.109
    Recast Regulation, status of 6.87–6.91
  United States:
    assets in New York 6.150–6.152
seller's rights 4.37, 7.148, 8.241
senior lenders 6.164, 6.167–6.170
set-off
  Article 6 OR 8.232–8.240
  Article 9 RR 4.31–4.35, 8.588
  bank accounts 6.181–6.190
  choice of law rule 4.31–4.35
settlement finality 7.30–7.40
Settlement Finality Directive 7.30–7.34
settlement systems 2.23, 4.42, 7.31–7.38, 7.152, 7.228, 7.230, 7.241, 8.240, 8.247–8.248, 8.593
ships/shipping 4.46–4.47, 4.54, 5.57, 6.64, 6.66, 7.83, 7.98, 7.145, 7.156, 8.33, 8.253, 8.276
single entity principle 7.13, 7.47, 7.59, 7.170, 7.257
single proceedings with universal effect 8.63
Single Resolution Mechanism (SRM) 7.164
Single Resolution Mechanism Regulation (SRMR) 7.07, 7.164
Single Supervisory Mechanism (SSM) 7.06
situs of property 4.24
  see also *lex situs*
Spain 6.86, 6.110, 6.112, 6.118–6.120, 6.130, 6.146, 6.149–6.151, 6.154–6.155, 6.175, 6.177, 8.30, 8.133, 8.498, 8.599
  assets 6.111, 6.115, 6.137
  borrowers 6.110–6.158, 6.164–6.170, 6.175–6.180
  establishments 6.159–6.163
  insolvency or preventive restructuring proceedings 6.117
  law security 6.135–6.143
  no main proceedings 6.116
  proceedings, recognition of 6.131–6.133
  restructuring proceedings 6.159–6.163
standard forms 8.805

stay of liquidation 8.410–8.419
stay of proceedings and related relief 5.40–5.44, 6.22
stay of the process of realization of assets 8.704
supremacy
  Community-wide 1.15
  doctrine of supremacy of EU law 2.01, 6.88
  of main proceedings 8.248, 8.566, 8.706
surplus assets 5.226, 6.112, 8.427–8.428
surplus proceeds of sale 6.79, 6.112, 6.125, 6.130

teleological statutory construction 2.26, 6.68
temporary administrators 5.229, 7.186, 7.196, 7.226, 8.69, 8.81, 8.437–8.440
territorial proceedings
  Article 3 RR 8.564–8.571
  further conditions to opening 3.43–3.48
  Ireland 6.142
  no territorial proceedings 6.118–6.125, 6.126–6.127, 6.138–6.141
  jurisdiction to conduct 3.40–3.54
  scope of 3.19–3.22, 3.49–3.54
third-party purchaser protection
  choice of law rule 4.53–4.55
  Original Regulation (OR) 8.276–8.277
  Recast Regulation (RR) 4.53–4.55, 8.602
third-party rights in rem 4.20–4.30
  floating charge security 4.29–4.30
  Original Regulation (OR) 8.217–8.231
  Recast Regulation (RR) 4.20–4.30, 8.587
  rights in rem, meaning of 4.28
  situs of property 4.24
  time factor 4.25–4.27
time of opening of proceedings 6.69–6.73, 8.28–8.32, 8.526
torts 4.18
trade marks *see* Community patents and trade marks
transaction avoidance 4.11, 4.50–4.52, 5.103, 5.166, 6.176, 8.158
transactions at undervalue 6.29
transferable securities 7.26–7.27, 8.508–8.509
trespass 5.16

UNCITRAL Model Law on Cross-Border Insolvency
  Brexit, effect of 9.17–9.32
  presumption under 8.107
  recognition and enforcement 5.82–5.114
    automatic relief 5.96–5.98
    conditions for recognition 5.92–5.95
    cooperation between courts and office-holders 5.113–5.114
    discretionary relief 5.99–5.110
    effects of recognition 5.96–5.110
    foreign main proceeding 5.89–5.91
    non-main proceeding 5.89–5.91
    origins and enactment 5.82–5.85
    rights of direct access and intervention 5.111–5.112
    scope 5.86–5.88

UCITS (Undertakings for Collective Investment in Transferable Securities) 7.26–7.29, 8.508–8.510
unenforceability 6.29–6.33
United Kingdom (UK) 1.02, 1.06, 2.04, 8.325, 8.373
 administration proceedings 8.173
 assets located in 6.82–6.84
  Member State in which assets are situated 8.33
 common law 5.24, 6.94–6.98, 9.33–9.41
 companies incorporated outside 8.179, 8.208
 Cross-Border Regulations 6.103–6.109
 divestment 8.74
 effects of insolvency proceedings opened in 6.85–6.86
 Eurofood decision 8.75
 foreign insolvency proceedings 9.40
 German creditors 8.118
 Insolvency Act (1986) 5.74, 6.99–6.102
  reliance on 9.33–9.41
 insolvency proceedings 8.04
 insurance 7.108
 legal framework 4.42, 6.87–6.109
 markets 4.42
 opening insolvency proceedings, criteria for 8.61, 8.67
 Recast Regulation, status of 6.15, 6.87–6.91
  continued relevance of tests as basis for opening proceedings 9.07–9.14
  continued relevance for UK insolvency proceedings 9.15–9.16
  ongoing potential application 9.01–9.41
  recognition of EU insolvency proceedings 5.117–5.123, 6.92–6.93
 recognition of foreign (EU) proceedings 9.17–9.32
 Rome I Regulation 4.33
 secured assets 6.92–6.93
 set-off 4.31
 third-countries, provisions for 7.252
 UNCITRAL Model Law 5.82, 9.17–9.32
 United States:
  corporations and UK law 8.96–8.97
  enforcement of bankruptcy proceedings 9.38
  relations 9.33
 Winding-Up Directive 7.46
 see also Brexit; English insolvency proceedings
United States (US)
 assets in New York 6.150–6.152
 Bankruptcy Code 2.28, 5.28, 5.86, 5.88, 5.103, 6.146–6.147, 6.150–6.152, 8.107, 8.113, 9.27
 Bankruptcy Court 5.26, 5.28, 5.43, 5.105
 bankruptcy law 6.149
 Chapter 11 proceedings 5.43, 5.89, 6.106–6.107
 communications between judges in the absence of parties 8.688
 company incorporation 8.96–8.97
 cooperation agreements 7.262
 corporate insolvency proceedings 8.740
 corporations 5.44, 5.212
 'establishment' 5.89

federal bankruptcy law 3.30, 6.150
foreign insolvency proceedings 5.88, 9.40
judges 8.693
opening of insolvency proceedings 6.149, 8.140
protocols, use of 8.681, 8.694
Securities and Exchange Commission 7.262
substantive consolidation, concept of 8.102
UK relations 9.33
 enforcement of bankruptcy proceedings 9.38
UNCITRAL Model Law 5.88, 5.103, 8.107, 9.25
unity principle 1.16–1.18, 3.17–3.18, 3.53–3.54, 3.60, 7.11, 7.59, 7.106, 7.167, 8.178, 8.649, 8.692
universality principle 1.16–1.18, 3.17–3.18, 3.26, 3.30, 3.53–3.54, 3.60, 7.12, 7.59, 7.107, 8.63–8.64, 9.28, 9.36–9.37

Virgos-Schmit Report on the Convention on Insolvency Proceedings
 choice of law rules 4.03, 4.28, 4.40, 4.45, 4.47, 4.54–4.55
 Insolvency Proceedings Regulation 2.28
 Original Regulation (OR) 8.42, 8.89, 8.91, 8.98, 8.129–8.130, 8.189, 8.225, 8.229, 8.235, 8.248–8.249, 8.254, 8.256, 8.276–8.277, 8.286–8.290, 8.330, 8.369, 8.371, 8.396–8.397, 8.399, 8.408, 8.430, 8.435, 8.440, 8.558, 8.560
 recognition and enforcement 5.116, 5.136, 5.143, 5.201
 relevant rules 8.335
 security rights 6.13, 6.36, 6.38, 6.43–6.44, 6.48, 6.54, 6.77, 6.79, 6.179
vis attractiva concursus 4.56, 8.280–8.281
voidability 6.29–6.33
voidness 6.29–6.33
voluntary arrangements 2.11, 8.04, 8.18–8.19, 8.22
 under insolvency legislation 8.08, 8.300, 8.426, 9.08
 United Kingdom 8.490
 see also Company Voluntary Arrangements (CVAs); individual voluntary arrangements (IVAs)
voluntary winding-up
 creditors 2.11, 2.26, 6.127, 8.08, 9.08
 foreign registered companies 8.146
 members 8.04

Winding-up Directive 7.41–7.100
 common provisions 7.73–7.100
 definitions 7.41–7.58
 reorganization measures 7.59–7.65
 scope 7.41–7.58
winding-up proceedings 7.66–7.72
 see also voluntary winding-up
'with no further formalities' 5.134–5.135, 5.164
wrongdoing 9.35
 by debtors 8.271
wrongful acts 4.18, 7.246
wrongful interference 5.194
wrongful removal 5.194
wrongful trading 8.149, 8.162